April 16–20, 2013
Dallas, Texas, USA

I0047357

**Association for
Computing Machinery**

Advancing Computing as a Science & Profession

ICMR'13

Proceedings of the Third ACM
International Conference on Multimedia Retrieval

Sponsored by:

SIGMM

Supported by:

University of Texas at Dallas, The University of Tennessee at Chattanooga, and University of California at Irvine

**Association for
Computing Machinery**

Advancing Computing as a Science & Profession

The Association for Computing Machinery
2 Penn Plaza, Suite 701
New York, New York 10121-0701

Notice to Past Authors of ACM-Published Articles
ACM intends to create a complete electronic archive of all articles and/or other material previously published by ACM. If you have written a work that has been previously published by ACM in any journal or conference proceedings prior to 1978, or any SIG Newsletter at any time, and you do NOT want this work to appear in the ACM Digital Library, please inform permissions@acm.org, stating the title of the work, the author(s), and where and when published.

ISBN: 978-1-4503-2033-7 (Digital)
ISBN: 978-1-4503-2275-1 (Print)

Additional copies may be ordered prepaid from:

ACM Order Department
PO Box 30777
New York, NY 10087-0777, USA

Phone: 1-800-342-6626 (USA and Canada)
+1-212-626-0500 (Global)
Fax: +1-212-944-1318
E-mail: acmhelp@acm.org
Hours of Operation: 8:30 am – 4:30 pm ET

Printed in the USA

Message from the General Chairs

We are delighted to welcome you, on behalf of the entire organizing committee, to the 3rd ACM International Conference on Multimedia Retrieval (ICMR 2013), held between April 16–19, 2013, in Dallas, Texas, USA.

ACM ICMR is the premier scientific conference for multimedia retrieval held worldwide, with the stated mission "to illuminate the state of the art in multimedia retrieval by bringing together researchers and practitioners in the field of multimedia retrieval". The conference aims to promote intellectual exchanges and interactions among scientists, engineers, students, multimedia researchers in academia as well as industry through various events, including keynote talk, oral, special, and poster sessions focused on research challenges and solutions, technical and industrial demonstrations of prototypes, tutorials, research and industrial panel.

In terms of numbers, we had around 96 valid submissions for the regular research papers of which 17 were accepted for oral presentation (17.7% acceptance rate) and 15 were accepted for poster presentation (giving an overall acceptance of 33 papers with 33.3% acceptance rate). We also have 5 research papers that were accepted as oral presentation papers for the special session on *Social Events in Web Multimedia*. We then have 15 technical demonstrations of systems showcasing key research contributions. Last, but not the least, the conference also has 2 state-of-the-art tutorials on advances in machine learning and similarity indexing for multimedia data.

One key new aspect of this 3rd ICMR is that we added a new event on doctoral symposium where we will have six research students presenting their dissertation research problems and get advice from leading multimedia retrieval researchers from all over the world. We believe this event would help us mentor future multimedia retrieval research leaders.

We would like to acknowledge those who have contributed to the success of ICMR 2013. First of all, we would like to thank all authors who submitted papers to the technical program, demonstrations, and the doctoral symposium. We also thank the authors of the accepted papers who will present their work in ICMR 2013, and the panelists, the tutorial speakers, and the keynote speaker who have accepted to participate in the conference to discuss current and future challenges in the field of multimedia retrieval and to propose innovative solutions. We are grateful to the members of the technical program committee, the TPC Chairs, Marcel Worring, John Smith, and Tat-Seng Chua, as well as the external reviewers who have helped put together a high-quality program. We would also acknowledge other members of the ICMR 2013 organizing committees who have put together other valuable parts of ICMR 2013 such as the tutorials, technical demonstrations, panel, industry & practitioners' session, and the doctoral symposium. We also thank the many student volunteers for their invaluable help at every step of the process. We would like to thank the staff of ACM and Sheridan Communications for their continuous support.

Finally, we would like to thank our sponsors SIGMM and the supporters, the University of Texas at Dallas, the University of California, Irvine, and the University of Tennessee at Chattanooga, who have extended their generous support to ICMR 2013.

We are sure that you will enjoy the ACM ICMR 2013 conference.

Ramesh Jain
ACM ICMR 2013 General Chair
University of California, Irvine, USA

Balakrishnan (Praba) Prabhakaran
ACM ICMR 2013 General Chair
University of Texas, Dallas, USA

Table of Contents

Session A: Best Paper Session

Session B: Media Retrieval

Session C: Media Classification and Search

Session D: Summarization, Recommendation & Geo-Tagging

Session E: Applications of Face and Object Recognition

Session F: Object Analysis and Retrieval

Special Session: Social Events in Web Multimedia

Poster Session

Demo Session

Doctoral Session

Author Index

ICMR 2013 Program Committee

Program Committee: Marcel Worring *(University of Amsterdam)*

Tat-Seng Chua *(National University of Singapore)*

John Smith *(IBM T.J. Watson Research Center)*

Prabha Balakrishnan *(The University of Texas at Dallas)*

Ramesh Jain *(University of California, Irvine)*

Laurent Amsaleg *(CNRS-IRISA)*

Benoit Huet *(Eurecom)*

Ajay Divakaran *(Sarnoff Corporation)*

Dong Liu

John Kender *(Columbia University)*

Pinaki Sinha *(University of California, Irvine)*

Martha Larson *(Delft University of Technology)*

Dick Bulterman *(CWI)*

Georges Quénot *(Laboratoire d'Informatique de Grenoble, CNRS)*

Gerald Friedland *(International Computer Science Institute)*

Yun Fu *(University at Buffalo (SUNY))*

Guo-Jun Qi *(University of Illinois at Urbana-Champaign)*

Tan Hung Khoon *(University Tunku Abdul Rahman)*

Heng Tao Shen *(University of Queensland)*

Ralph Ewerth *(Jena University of Applied Sciences, Germany)*

Peng Cui *(Tsinghua University)*

Wei-Ta Chu *(National Chung Cheng University)*

K. Selcuk Candan *(Arizona State University)*

Mingyan Gao

Naoko Nitta *(Osaka University)*

Jianping Fan *(UNCC)*

Richang Hong

Shuicheng Yan *(National University of Singapore)*

Yu-Gang Jiang *(Fudan University)*

Jun Wang

Meng Wang *(AKiiRA Media Systems Inc.)*

Chong-Wah Ngo *(City University of Hong Kong)*

Lingyu Duan *(Peking University)*

Changsheng Xu *(Chinese Academy of Sciences)*

Wen-Huang Cheng *(Academia Sinica)*

Ichiro Ide *(Nagoya University)*

Keiji Yanai *(University of Electro-Communications)*

Alex Hauptmann *(Carnegie Mellon University)*

Zheng-Jun Zha *(NUS)*

Xiangdong Zhou *(Fudan University)*

Xiaobai Liu

Steven C.H. Hoi *(Nanyang Technological University)*

ICMR 2013 Conference Organization

General Chairs: Ramesh Jain *(University of California, Irvine, USA)*
Balakrisknan Prabhakaran *(University of Texas at Dallas, USA)*

Program Chairs: Marcel Worring *(University of Amsterdam, The Netherlands)*
John Smith *(IBM Research, New York, USA)*
Tat-Seng Chua *(National University of Singapore)*

Special Sessions Chairs: Shih-Fu Chang *(Columbia University, USA)*
Qi Tian *(University of Texas at San Antonio, USA)*

Panels Chairs: Alan Smeaton *(Dublin City University, Ireland)*
Nicu Sebe *(University of Trento, Italy)*

Industry and Practitioner Chairs: Shin'ichi Satoh *(National Institute of Informatics, Japan)*
Alex Hauptman *(Carnegie Mellon University, USA)*

Tutorials Chairs: Svetha Venkatesh *(Curtin University, Australia)*
Dinh Phung *(Deakin University, Australia)*

Publicity Chairs: Alberto del Bimbo *(University of Firenze, Italy)*
Jiebo Luo *(University of Rochester, USA)*
Xirong Li *(Renmin University of China)*

Demonstrations and Retrieval Challenges Competition Chairs: Cees Snoek *(University of Amsterdam, The Netherlands)*
Rahul Sukthankar *(Google Research & CMU, USA)*
Carlos Busso *(University of Texas at Dallas, USA)*
Yansong(Jennifer) Ren *(Alcatel-Lucent, Plano, Texas)*

Proceeding & Registration Chair: Ming Li *(California State University, Fresno)*

Web Chair: Yu Cao *(The University of Tennessee at Chattanooga, USA)*

Local Arrangement Chairs: Xiaohu Guo *(University of Texas at Dallas, USA)*
Vibhav Gogate *(University of Texas at Dallas, USA)*

ICMR 2013 Sponsor & Supporters

Sponsor:

Supporters:

THE UNIVERSITY of
TENNESSEE **Ur**
CHATTANOOGA

UCIrvine
University of California, Irvine

Retrieving Geo-Location of Videos with a Divide & Conquer Hierarchical Multimodal Approach

Michele Trevisiol [1*]
trevi@yahoo-inc.com

Hervé Jégou [2]
herve.jegou@inria.fr

Jonathan Delhumeau [2]
jonathan.delhumeau@inria.fr

Guillaume Gravier [3]
guillaume.gravier@irisa.fr

[1]Web Research Group
Universitat Pompeu Fabra
Barcelona, Spain

[1]Yahoo! Research
Barcelona, Spain

[2]INRIA
Rennes, France

[3]CNRS/IRISA
Rennes, France

ABSTRACT

This paper presents a strategy to identify the geographic location of videos. First, it relies on a multi-modal cascade pipeline that exploits the available sources of information, namely the user's upload history, his social network and a visual-based matching technique. Second, we present a novel divide & conquer strategy to better exploit the tags associated with the input video. It pre-selects one or several geographic area of interest of higher expected relevance and performs a deeper analysis inside the selected area(s) to return the coordinates most likely to be related to the input tags. The experiments were conducted as part of the MediaEval 2012 Placing Task. Our approach, which differs significantly from the other submitted techniques, achieves the best results on this benchmark when considering the same amount of external information, *i.e.* when not using any gazetteers nor any other kind of external information.

Categories and Subject Descriptors

H.3.1 [**Information Storage and Retrieval**]: Content Analysis and Indexing; H.3.3 [**Information Storage and Retrieval**]: Information Search and Retrieval

Keywords

Geotags, Location, Placing Task, Video Annotation, Flickr

1. INTRODUCTION

Geotagging is the process of automatically adding geographical identification metadata to media objects, in particular to images and videos. This geo-information is called *geotag(s)*, and usually consists of the latitude and longitude world-map coordinates. Determining the place where the content has been captured dramatically extends the knowledge around the media object, especially when combined

---

* Work done while visiting PhD student at INRIA Rennes

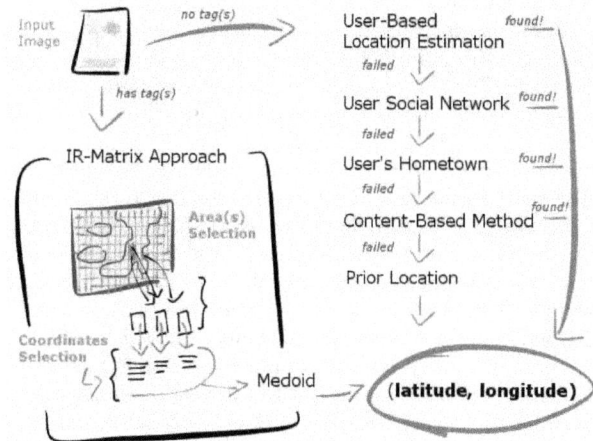

Figure 1: Approach Model Sketch.

with time information. Linking time- and geographical-related content offers a new and practical way of automatically searching, organizing or visualizing personal and professional media databases. It also enables the retrieval of various relevant content such as web pages, hence providing users with a wide variety of location-specific information.

In recent years, we have witnessed a dramatic increase in the number of such geotagged media data. Due to the massive spreading of GPS-enabled cameras and mobile phones, geographic coordinates are captured and attached to the content generated by these devices. However, most of the media available remain deprived of this information. For this reason, the problem of automatically assigning geotags to media content (and conversely) is a challenge that increasingly interests the Multimedia community, as reflected by the success of the Mediaeval benchmark's placing task [16]. This paper presents an efficient and effective geotagging system to address this problem, which is illustrated in Figure 1. A multimodal strategy hierarchically processes the sources of information by decreasing order of expected informativeness: Tags, user's upload history and social graph, user's personal information (home town) and visual content. When the most reliable information is missing, the system solely relies on the most informative amongst the remaining sources, with the prior most likely location as a final backup. We do not assume any prior knowledge about the city or country the video was taken in.

Beyond this strategy, a key contribution is the tag analysis technique introduced to extract clues about the location.

Our motivation is to identify the tags that are likely to convey some geographical information and to discard the ones that are deemed irrelevant. Indeed, by classifying 54% of the tags from Flickr images using WordNet[1], Sigurbjörnsson and van Zwol [19] observed that 28% of these tags were classified as locations, which suggests that tags have various degree of interest with respect to geotagging.

After filtering out noisy tags in a pre-processing step, we propose two different tag processing techniques, both scalable and not limited to tags that are location names. The first technique implements a text matching rule and serves as a (strong) baseline. The second approach is a radically different tag analysis technique. Based on a divide & conquer strategy, the relationship between tags and coordinates is analyzed to better reflect the informativeness of tags with respect to location.

Our multimodal framework and this new joint tag/location method are the main contributions of this paper. As secondary contributions, we show the interest of different strategies borrowed from other contexts. In particular, we show that the Okapi BM25 weighting scheme [20] is of interest in our context of video localization. Similarly, we have imported some techniques first proposed for image retrieval.

Experiments are carried out on the MediaEval 2012 placing task. Our method is compared with the best participating teams using the official evaluation protocol, and is shown to outperform the state of the art in the same setup, i.e., when using the same official input provided by the organizers. The specific interest of our tag-analysis technique is demonstrated by comparing it to a strong baseline, which by itself already achieves state-of-the-art performance.

The paper is organized as follows. Section 2 describes the background on geotagging, including related work and solutions adopted by Mediaeval participants that we compare with. An overview of our multimodal processing pipeline and its components are presented in Section 3. The new joint tag/location method which is detailed separately in Section 4. The experimental setup and results are shown in Section 5. Section 6 concludes the paper.

2. BACKGROUND

This section makes a brief overview of key approaches and trends for geotagging of images and videos. As this topic has received growing attention in the multimedia, computer vision and social networks communities, we refer to the recent survey by Luo et al. [11] for a wider overview of the techniques. We also present the placing task of the MediaEval 2012 benchmark and detail some approaches designed by some participants. They will serve as a comparison benchmark in the experiments.

2.1 Related work

The location of a video or image is typically extracted from two main sources of information, namely the textual information (i.e., tags, title, description) and the visual characteristics (i.e., global/local features). This specific information might be combined with some prior statistics on possible locations. In some situations, the media data is not associated with any textual information, therefore determining the location relies on the only available information, i.e., the image or video itself. In contrast to the

techniques exploiting metadata such as tags or EXIF information, these approaches are usually referred to as content-based approaches. In this line of research, Hays and Efros [3] proposed a purely visual approach[2] that estimates the image location as a probability distribution over the Earth's surface. Penatti et al. [14] proposed an approach called bag-of-scenes. First, they create a dictionary of scenes from places of interest, where each of them can be represented by a certain type of low-level features. Then, each video frame is compared with the dictionary and the most similar scene is selected. This allows associating a scene with each frame in order to save more semantic information.

However, the content-based approach alone is not reliable enough to be considered effective. Multimodal solutions exploit more sources of information, in particular textual information. The words extracted from the available text (i.e., title, description and tags) are often associated to geographic coordinates to determine the most common words for each possible location. An example of such an approach is the work of Serdyukov et al. [17], which constructs a $m \times n$ grid based on latitude and longitude, where each cell represents a location. Images whose locations are known are associated with their corresponding grid cells. Finally, a language model is estimated from the tags associated with a particular location, taking into account neighbors' influence and leveraging spatial ambiguity. Sergieh et al. [18] worked on the reciprocal problem, proposing a statistical model for automatic image annotation. Given an image with coordinates, they infer some relevant tags based on textual information from images in the database that are physically located nearby and which have similar visual content. Crandall et al. [2] used both image content and textual metadata to predict the location of an image at two levels of granularity: city level (about 100km), and at the individual landmark level (about 100m). However they limited their experiments to a specific set of landmarks in a fixed set of cities. In contrast, the problem considered in this paper makes no assumptions on the data set and on the level of granularity in the detection step. O'Hare and Murdock [13] proposed a statistical language modeling approach, also dividing the Earth into grid cells. Their approach is based on the Word-Document paradigm, and they investigate several ways to estimate the models, based on the term frequency and the user frequency.

2.2 MediaEval 2012

MediaEval is an international evaluation campaign in which the Placing Task [16] is dedicated to the geo-localization problem addressed in this paper. The goal is to determine as accurately as possible the location, in terms of latitude and longitude, of a set of Flickr videos. The task covers several cases, called runs, each of them being restricted by some constraints on the type of information used. To ensure that the training data is the same for all techniques so as to provide a fair comparison, we focus on techniques that only used the information provided by MediaEval. Hence, extra resources, such as gazetteers (e.g., GeoNames, WordNet) or any kind of external information (e.g., Wikipedia, Google Maps), are excluded from all the experiments so as to focus on the data processing techniques proposed.

---

[1]http://wordnet.princeton.edu/

[2]Note that the dataset they consider only includes images associated with a geotag such as a country, a city or as a touristic site (e.g., "Pisa", "Nikko", "Orlando").

	no tags	single tag	size
Train Set	454,338 (14.2%)	27,488 (0.9%)	3,200,757
Test Set	1,902 (45.5%)	139 (3.3%)	4,182

Table 1: Number of media objects without tags.

2.2.1 Dataset description

The MediaEval 2012 Placing task dataset gathers content from Flickr in Creative Common license and is divided into a train set with both images ($\approx 3.2M$) and videos ($\approx 15K$) and a test set with 4,182 videos, from more than $71K$ users. Metadata is associated with each media object and consists of various information such as ownership (Flickr user id and nickname), timestamps (upload and shot time), textual data (tags/keywords, title and description), social network (owner's contact user ids), comments and favorites (contents and users that made them) and, of course, the latitude and longitude within a certain level of accuracy. Note that in Flickr there are 16 levels of accuracy, from the most general (i.e., country name) to the most specific (i.e., street address). Table 1 summarizes the number of objects with tag(s) associated for each dataset. Clearly, the test set includes a large proportion of videos with no tags. Moreover, as tags are arbitrarily added by users without any constraint or rule, a large proportion of the tags is meaningless. Overall, many annotated objects are not associated with a single useful tag. This makes this benchmark both challenging and realistic.

2.2.2 Evaluation protocol

Our evaluation strictly follows the rules of the MediaEval 2012 placing task. The accuracy of the estimated location is measured by *great circle* distances between the predicted and the actual geo-coordinates encoded in the video. The Haversine distance is used to measure the discrepancy between the estimated location and the real one. The ground-truth is supplied by Flickr users at upload time.

2.2.3 Description of submitted geotagging techniques

Various approaches were taken by MediaEval's participants to address the problem. This section presents some representative methods, including the most successful ones, which are included in the comparison of Section 5. **Choi et al. [1] gave priority to the textual information,** using title and tags/keywords, but discarding the description. They computed a geographic spread for each word (in tags and title), similar to what we do. In addition, they exploited the GeoNames database to have a toponym resolution in order to filter out irrelevant words. They also included part-of-speech retrieved to perform more precise filtering using Augmented-WordNet[3]. In case of no candidate coordinates, they used the user's home location, or as last resort, the prior location (i.e., fixed location computed *a priori*). **Li et al. [10] extended the successful bag-of-scenes technique** [14], including the histogram of motion patterns. They aggregated with a fusion module both a textual (based on tags, title and description) and a visual approach. Interesting results are presented for the content-based (visual) task, but they are not the main focus of this paper. **Popescu and Ballas [15]** tackled the problem by splitting the Earth surface in small cells of size 0.01 of latitude and longitude degree, characterized by a set of tags and their probability of occurrence in that cell. They

selected only pairs of tags with a high probability of occurrence within a smaller radius in order to extract a set of unambiguous pairs of potential toponyms. Then they matched the tags for each test video with the cells of the unambiguous pair (if it is found), or with the whole set of cells, considering as top ranked the selected cells and their neighbors. **Van Laere et al. [9]** applied a divide & conquer approach splitting the problem in two phases. Given the test video, in the first step they find the most likely cluster to contain the location with a Naive Bayes classifier. Then with a similarity search, they find the training items whose tags are the closest to the ones of the test video. If the test video has no tags, they use user's hometown, title and description as if they were regular tags. As a last resort, they also used a prior static location. **Kelm et al. [8] presented a hierarchical framework** that combines textual and visual features for different granularity. First they divide up the Earth in regions using meridians and parallels, then they generated textual and visual prototypes for each of them. For the textual part, they translated in English tags, title and description, then they extracted words using a NLP approach, and finally they applied a stemmer and a stop-word elimination. Given the test video, they select the region and the images/videos with highest probability to contain the extracted words (using a bag-of-words approach). Then, given a list of ranked candidates, with a visual search they select the most similar.

3. MULTI-MODAL CASCADE

This section describes our multimodal and hierarchical processing pipeline. It starts with a tag comparison technique based on frequency matching, followed by a description of how the remaining sources of information are processed. As shown in Table 1, many videos in the test set are not described by tags. To handle these cases, we exploit additional information in a pipeline: If one source of information is absent or fail to provide a reliable prediction, the next is considered. The pipeline operates in the following order which was chosen according to the amount of information conveyed by each source, as discussed later in the experimental section: a) tags b) user's upload history, social information, c) user's home town, d) content-based matching, e) prior-location. This process is illustrated in Fig. 1.

3.1 Tag processing: IR-frequency

The frequency tag processing technique proposed hereafter is the first way we propose to exploit the tags. This technique, which is referred to as *IR-frequency* in the following, mainly serves as a baseline. A better novel technique will be presented in the dedicated Section 4.

3.1.1 Pre-processing

Flickr normalizes the set of raw tags by lower-casing them, removing white space and stop-words, and replacing commas with white space. For example, the set of tags "Trip 2010, Sagrada Familia, Barcelona" becomes "trip2010 sagradafamilia barcelona". Remember that tags are arbitrarily chosen by a user to describe the image. Hence, they might be inconsistent with the image content or location. We further normalized tags so as to defined a set of clean tags, Tc_{train} derived from T_{train}, the entire set of tags in the training data. We removed the accents, discarded numeric tags (almost never relevant for the location), and removed numeric

[3]http://ai.stanford.edu/~rion/swn

characters from the alphanumeric tags. A stop-list containing common words (*e.g.*, travel, birthday, cat, geotag, camera) and product or brand names (*e.g.*, iPhone, Canon) was used to filter out non informative tags. So called machine tags[4] (or *mtags*), *i.e.*, one or more tags that Flickr recognized as a location (usually a country name or sometimes a city name), are kept unchanged and will be processed independently of the other tags as they are highly accurate and relevant. Note that after pre-processing, only 39.9 % of the videos contain tags.

3.1.2 *Geo-relevance filtering*

For a baseline method based on direct tag matching, selecting tags relevant to the geo-location is a crucial step. Apart from machine tags which are deemed relevant, we implemented a geo-relevance filtering based on the geographic spread of a tag in the training data. Figure 2 illustrate this idea by showing how some tags are spread across the globe: Tags specific to a location (bottom row) are mostly concentrated in a small area while others (top row) exhibit a high dispersion.

To select relevant tags in Tc_{train}, we compute for each tag t_i its frequency of occurence f_{t_i} in the training data and the average Haversine distance d_{t_i} between the coordinates of the data which contain t_i. Tags that do not match the following condition

$$\forall t_i \in T_{\text{train}}, \quad t_i \in Tc_{\text{train}} \iff \begin{cases} f_{t_i} \le 50, \\ d_{t_i} \ge 200. \end{cases}$$

are removed from Tc_{train} where the thresholds were experimentally defined.

3.1.3 *Frequency matching*

Given the set of tags retained, one can group coordinates associated to the same set of tags. The idea is first, to preselect some set of tags that have at least one mtag in common (if available otherwise a normal tag), and finally to rank each of them by the occurrences of the common (m)tags.

We consider each training document, image or video, as a geo-annotated document described by a set of tags. For each set of tags, including machine tags, we collect all the coordinates from documents described by the same set of tags, along with the number of such documents. For example, for the set of tags "france", "pompidou" and "paris", we collect the following coordinates (48.8611, 2.3521):12, (48.6172, 2.213):3.

Given a test video, if it contains mtags we retrieve all the documents where there is at least one common mtag, otherwise we do the same with tags. Those documents are further ranked according to the number of tags they share with the test video. The top ranked document (or documents in case of equality) is selected and the medoid of all the locations attached to the corresponding set of tags, weighted by the number of occurences of the coordinates, is taken as the test material's geo-coordinate.

3.2 User data processing

When no tags are left after filtering or if no documents in the training data is found with at least one tag in common with the test video, we rely on the user data provided to predict a location.

---

[4] http://www.flickr.com/groups/api/discuss/72157594497877875/

3.2.1 *User upload history*

For each user with images or videos in the training set, we picked a pre-computed *user location* based on the most frequent location for his content. We found that 35.6 % of the users in the test set appear in the training data. Assuming that users tend to visit the same places more than once, we seek to exploit the documents previously uploaded. For each user in the training set, we compute the medoid of the geo-coordinates of all its training data. The obtained location is used as geo-coordinate when tag-based geotagging fails. We observed that using the user prior location significantly improved the results.

3.2.2 *Social network extension*

For users not present in the training data, we make use of their social connections to infer a potential location. The idea is to find the user locations of all the contacts and use the medoid as the most likely location for the test video. This general idea is refined based on the groups which are used in Flickr user connections, namely *family*, *friends*, and *contacts*. We assume that *family* is closer to *friends* which in turn is closer to *contacts* and process the groups in that specific order. If the user has enough connections in one group, then the video location is obtained from the contacts in the group. Else, we move on to the next group.

Using both user upload history and social network extension, 79% of the test videos are covered.

3.2.3 *User hometown*

In case neither upload history nor social connections are available, the hometown of the user, as given by its Flickr profile is used. When available, the hometown is given as a place name, *e.g.*, "San Francisco, California, United States", rather than as coordinates. We process the hometown information as if they were tags describing the test video, applying the same process as described in Section 3.1.3 to determine geo-coordinates. Note however that the user hometown is not always well specified (*i.e.*, only the state or the country is specified) and is not always precise (*e.g.*, with very large cities like New York, the estimated coordinates can be very far from the real ones).

3.3 Content-based processing

Content-based geo-tagging exploiting image matching is finally used. However, the input video set is not large enough with respect to the total number of locations, and include many indoor scenes. Therefore the visual approach, which requires the same views of a given location, is less important than other sources of information. Anyway, for this purpose each keyframe or image is described based on SIFT local descriptors computed over a dense grid. A power law of 0.5 is applied before L2 normalization [7]. PCA and whitening are applied before aggregating vectors into a global high-dimensionality VLAD descriptor [7] which is reduced to dimension 1,024 by PCA, whitened and normalized. An index is built from those descriptors using product quantization [6] which enables fast approximate nearest neighbor search on all of the test keyframes. For each query, we get the coordinates of the best candidate keyframes and return their medoid.

3.4 When all elses fail...

As a last chance, if all elses fail, we assign a default prior

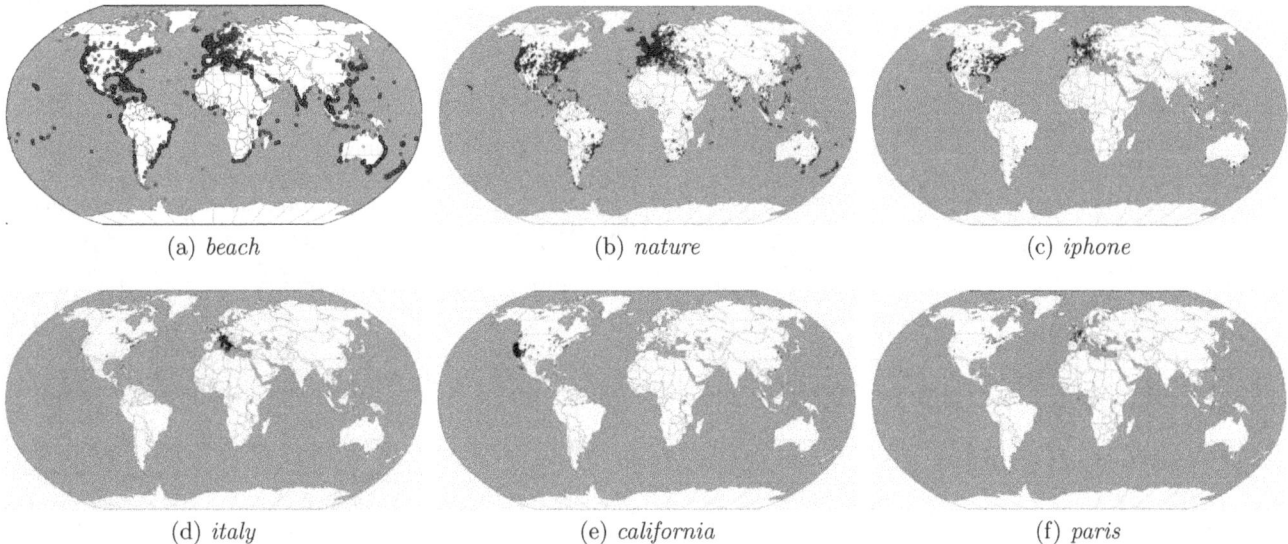

(a) *beach*   (b) *nature*   (c) *iphone*

(d) *italy*   (e) *california*   (f) *paris*

Figure 2: Coordinates of six tags plotted on the world map. The first row shows the spreading of three tags that are not locations. The second one shows respectively a country, a state, and a city.

location regardless of the content. We experimented two strategies for the default location: The medoid of all locations in the training data—which falls near Tokyo—or the medoid of all locations from the training data with no tags—which falls in London.

4. HIERARCHICAL METHOD

The tag processing described in the previous section remains limited and we seek to develop a new approach better exploiting the information conveyed by the tags. In the following, we propose a hierarchical approach based on the vector-space model, using the divide & conquer paradigm, to infer the relationship between tags and locations. This method will be referred to as *IR-matrix* in the following, by analogy to the word-document matrix analysis performed in some information retrieval techniques.

The tags of a given test video are considered as a *query vector*. The idea is to first determine the approximate geographic area in which the video is likely to belong, and to find in turn the most probable coordinates from the known locations in that area. The geographic areas are arbitrarily defined by quantifying the coordinates on a grid, where each cell of the grid is described by a vector of tag weights according to the tag relevances to the area considered. Each geographic area is further defined by a set of geo-coordinates also described with a specific tag vector. The test document is represented as a weighted vector of tags from which the most likely areas and the most likely coordinates are determined.

The steps described in this section replaces the tag filtering and frequency matching in the pipeline described in the previous section. The other steps are left unchanged.

4.1 Tag weighting

Describing a geographic area or a specific coordinate as a set of tags with weights require a weighting scheme that reflects the relationship between tags and coordinates. Similar quantities as those used for tag filtering in section 3.1.2, namely frequency and average distance, are used to mea-

sure the relevance of a tag. Rather than eliminating non relevant tags as before, a low weight is given. The following heuristics was used to identifying how *geo-descriptive* a tag is: $\forall t_i \in Tc_{\text{train}}$

$$w_{t_i} = \begin{cases} -1 & \text{if } f_{t_i} > 100K \text{ or } d_{t_i} < 0.2 \\ 10 & \text{if } f_{t_i} \geq 200 \text{ and } 10 \leq d_{t_i} \leq 50 \\ 5 & \text{if } f_{t_i} \geq 150 \text{ and } d_{t_i} \leq 70 \\ 1 & \text{otherwise} \end{cases}$$

This weighting was designed to assign higher weights to tags representing geographic information, *i.e.*, not only places but also references to locations such as monuments. Figure 3 shows an example of tags with the highest weight ($w_{t_i} = 10$) sorted by f_{t_i} as opposed to tags sorted by frequency only. All tags with high weights clearly designate locations. Figure 6 shows some examples of weighted query tags.

4.2 Finding the areas

Given a set of tags from a test video, we first want to identify the most likely geographic area(s).

Areas were defined by quantifying the coordinates on a cell grid of 0.1°, *i.e.* a coordinates with latitude 41.12 and longitude −1.23 belongs to the area identified as (41.1, −1.2). Though not the most compact representation, quantization on a cells grid is computationally not expensive. Each cell j in the grid is described by a vector where each bin corresponds to a tag with the corresponding weight defined as:

$$w'_{t_i,j} = f_{t_i,j} w_{t_i,j} \qquad (1)$$

where $f_{t_i,j}$ is the number of occurences of t_i in the area j, and $w_{t_i,j}$ is defined from $f_{t_i,j}$ as in section 4.1.

The set of areas is thus represented by a matrix whose rows correspond to tags and whose columns correspond to the geographic areas. The Okapi weighting scheme is applied to all entries in the area matrix—see section 4.4 for details—before smoothing using signed SQRT and L2 normalization, generalizing to text features results from image processing [5]. The area that best fits a test image represented as a vector of tag weights is obtained by multiplying

5

Tag	Frequency	Average Distance
geotagged	81948	183.600974549
water	36645	394.109273724
beach	35799	189.702712644
nature	35791	330.458447429
2009	35411	158.518797983
2008	34788	163.01576923
california	34756	17.3347855177
2007	33791	163.774148222
sky	32268	500.652309767
travel	29636	227.985879656
usa	27933	112.840988813
italy	26432	28.2242237023
sea	25435	264.814684265
france	25128	30.1802960837
sunset	24839	530.829445257
landscape	24291	399.483239901
snow	24251	252.464879232
europe	24173	121.315134058
blue	23187	554.374093842
2006	22802	188.297981051
australia	22746	48.9602486282
night	22745	439.445587846
germany	22060	30.3288003332
winter	21605	264.227771688
tree	21335	626.460930315
canada	20611	44.1591343262
spain	20583	33.9538296347
bw	20475	504.583508417
architecture	20155	331.577365854
japan	19859	33.8409323297
green	19822	585.402442074
uk	19675	33.246712809
clouds	19597	617.251967179
flower	19563	631.402098385
england	19477	25.9678916173
park	19245	289.55492473
vacation	18870	220.652637728

Tag	Frequency	Average Distance
california	34756	17.3347855177
italy	26432	28.2242237023
france	25128	30.1802960837
australia	22746	48.9602486282
germany	22060	30.3288003332
canada	20611	44.1591343262
spain	20583	33.9538296347
japan	19859	33.8409323297
uk	19675	33.246712809
england	19477	25.9678916173
espana	14740	36.3307740002
scotland	14418	20.0878818974
italia	14266	29.7714336536
deutschland	12469	26.6710348635
mexico	11248	44.1710727199
washington	10528	29.2185701167
texas	9811	26.8342797456
florida	9773	19.2311687716
newyork	9550	26.7850834626
portugal	9005	36.4910584785
switzerland	8842	19.0660337254
sweden	8825	43.4298253824
taiwan	8614	8.58611101877
ireland	8277	27.8336567598
newzealand	7804	34.7207757884
greece	7734	28.8041197511
ontario	7684	13.5533928009
oregon	7501	21.9655577751
unitedkingdom	7469	45.7784858581
netherlands	7258	23.4561091895
austria	6670	17.0680578585
colorado	6659	29.0537398392
thailand	6508	23.5652696046
nsw	6231	28.5942670687
arizona	6041	26.381253062
sanfrancisco	6021	41.1354079352
nyc	5917	32.7179331764

Figure 3: On the left side of the line, there are listed tags before the weighting scheme is applied. On the right side instead, there are shown the tags with highest score ($w_{t_i} = 10$). Both of lists are sorted by term frequency (tf_{t_i}).

the query vector by the area matrix, thus providing a ranked list of areas. The area with the highest matching score is selected, several areas being selected in case of equality.

4.3 Finding the coordinates

Given a selected area, we proceed to find the most likely coordinates for the tags of the test video, following the same principle as before. Similarly to what is done for areas, a tag/coordinate matrix is used to represent coordinates within each area, where each row corresponds to a tag and each column corresponds to a coordinate in the area cell. The weights in the matrix are obtained following the same procedure as for the area matrix, with tag frequencies computed for each coordinate. Okapi weighting, smoothing and L2 normalization are also applied. Given a test query obtained from the tags of the test videos, a ranked list of coordinates is obtained within each of the areas selected in the previous step. The best ranked coordinates are selected from each of the ranked lists and the medoid is used as the geo-coordinates for the test video.

4.4 Tuning Okapi BM25

While tf-idf is commonly employed as a weighting scheme for text representation in the vector-space model, the Okapi BM25 weighting scheme was experimentally found to perform better in our case, confirming previous results [20]. The Okapi weighs are defined as

$$W_{BM}(j, t_i) = \sum IDF(t_i) \times \frac{w'_{t_i,j} \times (k+1)}{w'_{t_i,j} + k \times (1 - b + b \times \frac{|D|}{avg_{dl}})}$$

where $w'_{t_i,j}$ is defined by Eq. 1, avg_{dl} is the average number of tags per training sample, k and b are free parameters usually chosen as $k \in [1.2, 2.0]$ and $b = 0.75$ [12]. The IDF

radius(km)	0.001	0.01	0.1	1.2	10	20
1	**756**	749	752	720	714	713
10	1626	**1641**	1627	1601	1587	1582
100	2071	2086	**2095**	2085	2071	2068
1000	2737	2739	2751	**2760**	2763	2760
10000	3885	3884	3890	**3892**	3889	3891

Table 2: Estimating values of k_1 for the step of selection of the area, comparing different values of k_1 from 0.001 to 20. For each radius (in km) the correctly detected coordinates for the test videos are counted.

radius(km)	$k_{1,1}=0.001$ / $k_{1,2}=0.001$	$k_{1,1}=0.001$ / $k_{1,2}=1.2$	$k_{1,1}=0.1$ / $k_{1,2}=0.1$	$k_{1,1}=1.2$ / $k_{1,2}=1.2$
1	**786**	756	752	720
10	**1635**	1626	1628	1601
100	2071	2065	**2091**	2079
1000	2759	2753	2769	**2774**
10000	3962	3959	**3964**	**3964**

Table 3: Estimating values of k_1 for first ($k_{1,1}$, selection of the area) and for second step ($k_{1,2}$, selection of coordinates). Where for each radius (in km) the correctly detected coordinates for the test videos are counted.

part instead is given by

$$IDF(q_i) = \log \frac{N - N_{t_i} + 0.5}{N_{t_i} + 0.5}$$

where N is the total number of training samples, and N_{t_i} is the number of samples containing tag t_i.

We experimented different values of k, both for area selection and coordinates selection. Contrary to the conclusions of Whissell *et al.* [20], where large values of k ($k \geq 20$) improve the results, we found that small values of k performed better in our case. Table 2 shows some results in terms of coordinates correctly identified for various values of k. While large values decrease performance, small values of k tend to increase the accuracy at a small radius (*i.e.*, 1 km). Various combination of k, for the coarse grain area selection and the fine grain coordinate selection where tested, results being reported in table 3. Combining small values of k improves for both the 1 km and 10 km radii.

5. EXPERIMENTS

We evaluate our approaches with the dataset from MediaEval's 2012 Placing Task described in Section 2.2. Our system was trained using the 3.2M geotagged images and videos released by the organizers. As shown as an outcome of the 2011's campaign, the tag information is the most reliable one. However, in many situations, a large proportion of the videos have no tag after our filtering steps, for instance about 60% on the Mediaeval benchmark. That is why this section first discusses the respective interests of the other sources of information, which led us to determine the order of priority in our cascade multi-modal approach. We then present how our system performs on the Placing Task of MediaEval 2012, and shows the large improvement brought the IR-Matrix method of Section 4 compared to the baseline tag method and to the submitted techniques.

5.1 Sources of information

Section 3 introduced the secondary sources of information that we exploit when the test video is not associated with any tag after the filtering step. In our cascade architecture, an important choice is the order in which the corresponding

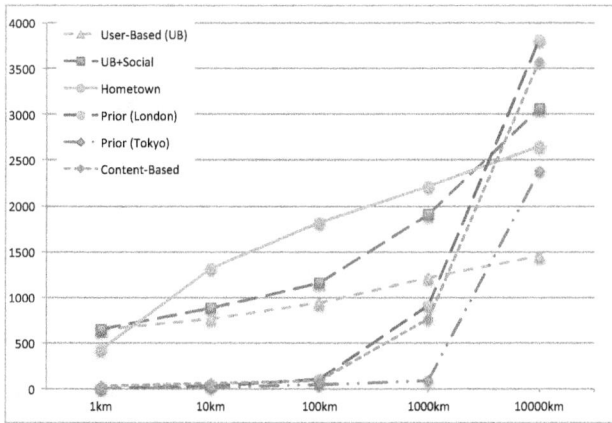

Figure 4: Cumulative values of correctly detected locations for pipeline methods: number of video founds (y-axis) in a radius of x km (x-axis).

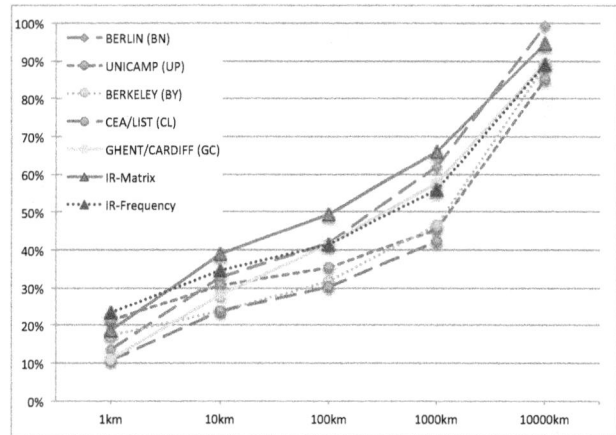

Figure 5: Cumulative correctly detected locations: rate of video founds (y-axis) in a radius of x km (x-axis).

methods appear in the pipeline, as this order impacts the final quality of the system. For this purpose, we have evaluated the respective geo-tagging accuracy provided by each component of our system[5]. Figure 4 shows the number of correctly identified locations for varying radius and for the different sources, except for the visual search, which provides inferior results. For example, in the 1 km radius, the user-based estimation identifies more than 600 video locations, while the estimation with Hometown finds less than 500 of them. However, for radius higher than 1 km, the interest of the Hometown improves and gives the best results among the secondary sources of information. Another observation is the social connections are useful and significantly improve an estimation based only on the other metadata related to the user. The content-based approach is performing poorly due to the types of test videos that contain mainly indoor scenes. However for the smaller radii (1km and 10km) it is slightly better than the prior location, and for this reason in our pipeline approach it is used before. The prior location does not use any information about the query and, as to be expected, leads to a very imprecise estimation which only impacts the 1000 and 10000 km precision measures. Interestingly, London and Tokyo give very different performances. However, in our opinion, this prior information is not really interesting for a real application, as it is not related to a particular video. The fact that the Hometown gives the best results for radius higher than $1km$ suggests that it should be used as the primary alternative to the tag-based method. However, when combining the different sources in cascade, our preliminary experiments showed that it is worth exploiting user-based and social information first.

To conclude this discussion, our final framework uses the UB+Social as a primary alternative to the tag-based method (See Section 3). If this fails to output a location, we use the Hometown estimation instead if provided, else the visual search engine. The prior location is used as a final backup.

5.2 IR-MATRIX Evaluation

This Section compares the results of our approach to the ones shown by the participants at MediaEval 2012 Placing Task. In addition, we separately show the interest of the

IR-Matrix technique introduced in Section 4 over the IR-frequency baseline (See Section 3). These two tag-based approaches are evaluated using the same pipeline, *i.e.*, in the same multi-modal cascade. Therefore, the results of these methods are directly comparable[6]. Figure 5 shows that, overall, our IR-Matrix technique performs the best except in two cases: The last radius, 10000 km, mainly depends on the Prior location and has arguably no practical interest. As mentioned in footnote, the 1 km measurement is not reliable because it is impacted by the artifacts of the train/test duplicates.

Discussion. Among the various methods submitted to Mediaeval'2012, different textual filters have been used. BY [1] computes a geographic spreading based on the spatial variance distribution filtering tags with high variance. BN [8] performs a more complex procedure, translating everything (also title and description) in English, applying a stemming and stop-word filtering, and finally extracting words with a NLP approach. CL [15] works only with tags that have been used by at least two users, and considers only pairs of unambiguous pre-computed toponyms.

Our IR-Matrix technique is less restrictive than these technique because it does not discard any tag, except the ones filtered by a common stop-word list. Instead, it automatically assigns different weights to each of them, which is less radical than the techniques mentioned above and leads to exploit more tags, thereby reducing the information loss. In addition, by considering each cell of the Earth grid as a separate "document", our Word-Document matrix-based approach better identifies the relationship between tags and localization, which in turn provides a useful measure of geo-informativeness to tags.

Concerning the secondary methods, only CL exploited the user's previous uploads in the case where no tags is associated to the test video, and nobody used the social information in order to expand this knowledge. This gives a slight improvement which is exploited in both our IR-matrix and IR-frequency methods.

---

[5]Note that this evaluation of the respective interest of information sources was first done on the 2011's Mediaeval campaign, without knowing the 2012's test data.

[6]There is a bias for the 1 km radius measure, as some test images were also included in the training set. This basically favors the baseline approach for this measure (and other systems) because one could match some test videos perfectly based on irrelevant tags. We have not exploited this knowledge in our system.

piazzabra **verona italy** veneto
northernitaly worldheritagesite unesco
unescoworldheritagesite fountain
waterfeature ~~video~~ videoclip

provence southoffrance **france**
bouchesdurhone
provencealpescotedazur
aixenprovence coursmirabeau fountain
~~video~~ videoclip hotspring

**norfolk england unitedkingdom
greatbritain** westnorfolk hunstanton
beach sea thewash northsea
cliff cliffs ~~video~~ videoclip chalk redchalk
carstone whitechalk
eastanglia

Figure 6: Query examples with tags. Lightness and size indicate initial weights ($w_{t_i} = \mathbf{10}$, 5 or), ignored tags are striked-through (~~stop-words~~ or).

6. CONCLUSIONS

This paper introduces a novel system for geo-tagging videos which significantly outperforms techniques of the state of the art, as demonstrated by our experiments performed on the last Mediaeval benchmark.

A key contribution is the novel IR-Matrix location/tag technique based on the Divide & Conquer paradigm, which is simply and efficiently implemented by (query)vector-matrices multiplications. It first provides an estimation of the area of interest, which is then used to determine more precise coordinates that best match the input set of tags. It significantly outperforms a more conventional tag-vector matching technique, such as our IR-Frequency baseline which first detects all the images and videos that contain the specific tag(s), and then selects the one with the highest number of matches. As a complementary technique, we show the interest of the Okapi weighting scheme in this context.

When no reliable tag is available, our processing cascade allows our system to make a prediction based on other sources of information, such as user-related metadata or visual content. To our knowledge, our system is also the first to exploit the social connections for this geo-tagging task.

Although we only considered the meta-data provided in the Mediaeval benchmark, i.e., the Flickr data associated with the videos, we believe that integrating external sources of information, such as a gazetteer, should further improve the overall localization performance, as demonstrated by other works in the field.

7. ACKNOWLEDGMENTS

This work was partially funded by OSEO, French state agency for innovation, in the framework of the Quaero project and by Grant TIN2009-14560-C03-01 of the Ministry of Science and Innovation of Spain. Furthermore, we would like to thank Vincent Claveau for his helpful suggestions.

8. REFERENCES

[1] J. Choi, G. Friedland, V. Ekambaram, and K. Ramchandran. The 2012 ICSI/Berkeley Video Location Estimation System. In *MediaEval*, 2012.

[2] D. Crandall, L. Backstrom, D. Huttenlocher, and J. Kleinberg. Mapping the World's Photos. In *WWW*, 2009.

[3] J. Hays and A. A. Efros. IM 2 GPS : estimating geographic information from a single image. In *CVPR*, 2008.

[4] M. Jain, R. Benmokhtar, P. Gros, and H. Jégou. Hamming Embedding Similarity-based Image Classification. In *ICMR*, Jun. 2012.

[5] H. Jégou and O. Chum. Negative evidences and co-occurrences in image retrieval: the benefit of PCA and whitening. In *ECCV*, Oct. 2012.

[6] H. Jégou, M. Douze, and C. Schmid. Product quantization for nearest neighbor search. *PAMI*, 33(1), Jan. 2011.

[7] H. Jégou, F. Perronnin, M. Douze, J. Sánchez, P. Pérez, and C. Schmid. Aggregating local image descriptors into compact codes. *PAMI*, Sep. 2012.

[8] P. Kelm, S. Schmiedeke, and T. Sikora. How Spatial Segmentation improves the Multimodal. In *MediaEval*, 2012.

[9] O. V. Laere, S. Schockaert, and J. Quinn. Ghent and Cardiff University at the 2012 Placing Task. In *MediaEval*, 2012.

[10] L. Li, J. Almeida, and D. Pedronette. A Multimodal Approach for Video Geocoding. In *MediaEval*, 2012.

[11] J. Luo, D. Joshi, J. Yu, and A. Gallagher. Geotagging in multimedia and computer vision–a survey. *Multimedia Tools Appl.*, 51(1), Jan. 2011.

[12] C. D. Manning, P. Raghavan, and H. Schütze. *Introduction to Information Retrieval*. Cambridge University Press, 2008.

[13] N. O'Hare and V. Murdock. Modeling locations with social media. *Information Retrieval*, Apr. 2012.

[14] O. A. B. Penatti, L. T. Li, J. Almeida, and R. da S. Torres. A Visual Approach for Video Geocoding using Bag-of-Scenes. In *ICMR*, 2012.

[15] A. Popescu and N. Ballas. CEA LIST's Participation at MediaEval 2012 Placing Task. In *MediaEval*, 2012.

[16] A. Rae and P. Kelm. Working Notes for the Placing Task at MediaEval 2012. In *MediaEval*, 2012.

[17] P. Serdyukov, V. Murdock, and R. van Zwol. Placing flickr photos on a map. In *SIGIR*, May 2009.

[18] H. M. Sergieh, G. Gianini, M. Döller, H. Kosch, E. Egyed-Zsigmond, and J.-M. Pinon. Geo-based Automatic Image Annotation. In *ICMR*, 2012.

[19] B. Sigurbjörnsson and R. van Zwol. Flickr tag recommendation based on collective knowledge. In *WWW*, 2008.

[20] J. Whissell and C. Clarke. Improving document clustering using Okapi BM25 feature weighting. *Information Retrieval*, 14, 2011.

A Unified Framework for Context Assisted Face Clustering

Liyan Zhang   Dmitri V. Kalashnikov   Sharad Mehrotra

Department of Computer Science
University of California, Irvine

ABSTRACT

Automatic face clustering, which aims to group faces referring to the same people together, is a key component for face tagging and image management. Standard face clustering approaches that are based on analyzing facial features can already achieve high-precision results. However, they often suffer from low recall due to the large variation of faces in pose, expression, illumination, occlusion, etc. To improve the clustering recall without reducing the high precision, we leverage the heterogeneous context information to iteratively merge the clusters referring to same entities. We first investigate the appropriate methods to utilize the context information at the cluster level, including using of "common scene", people co-occurrence, human attributes, and clothing. We then propose a unified framework that employs bootstrapping to automatically learn adaptive rules to integrate this heterogeneous contextual information, along with facial features, together. Experimental results on two personal photo collections and one real-world surveillance dataset demonstrate the effectiveness of the proposed approach in improving recall while maintaining very high precision of face clustering.

Categories and Subject Descriptors

H.3.3 [**Information Systems**]: Information Search and Retrieval—*Clustering*

Keywords

Face Clustering, Context Information, Bootstrapping

1. INTRODUCTION

With the explosion of massive media data, the problem of image organization, management and retrieval has become an important issue [11] [21]. Naturally, the focus in many image collections is people. To better understand and

This work was supported in part by NSF grants CNS-1118114, CNS-1059436, CNS-1063596. It is part of NSF supported project *Sherlock @ UCI* (http://sherlock.ics.uci.edu): a UC Irvine project on Data Quality and Entity Resolution [1].

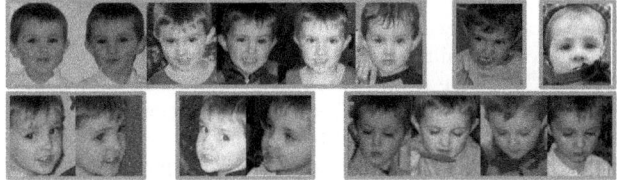

Figure 1: Example of Face Clusters by Picasa

manage the human-centered photos, face tagging that aims to help users associate people names with faces becomes an essential task. The fundamental problem towards face tagging and management is face clustering, which aims to group faces that refer to the same people together.

Clustering faces based on facial appearance features is the most conventional approach. It has been extensively studied and significant progress has been achieved in the last two decades [2] [6] [7]. These standard techniques have already been employed in several commercial systems such as Google Picasa, Apple iPhoto, and Microsoft EasyAlbum. These systems usually produce face clusters that have high precision (faces in each cluster refer to the same person), but low recall (faces of a single person fall into different clusters). In addition, a large number of small/singleton face clusters are often returned, which bring heavy burden on the users to label all the faces in the album. Fig. 1 illustrates the example of face clustering result, where faces of a single person fall into six different (pure) clusters, instead of one. One reason for low recall is due to the large variation of faces in pose, expression, illumination, occlusion, etc. That makes it challenging to group faces correctly by using the standard techniques that focus primarily on facial features and largely ignore the context. Another reason is that when systems like Picasa ask for manual feedback from the user, users most often prefer to merge pure (high-precision) clusters rather than manually clean contaminated (low-recall) ones. Consequently, such systems are often tuned to strongly prefer the precision over recall. The goal of our work is to leverage heterogeneous context information to improve the recall of cluster results without reducing the high precision.

Prior research efforts have extensively explored using contextual features to improve the quality of face clustering [16] [17] [19] [20]. In general, in contrast to our work, such techniques often aim at exploring just one (or a few) contextual feature types, with the merging decision often made at the image level only. We, however, develop a unified framework that integrates heterogeneous context information together to improve the performance of face clustering. The framework learns the roles and importance of different feature types from data. It can take into account time decay of features and makes the merging decision at both image and cluster levels. Examples of types of contextual cues that have been used in the past include geo-location and image capture time [21], people co-occurrence [14] [16] [17], social norm and conventional positioning observed [10], human attributes [13], text or other linked information [4] [18], clothing [9] [20], etc. For instance, [13] proposes to employ human attributes as an additional features. However, the authors do not explore the different roles that each attribute type plays in identifying different people. Social context, such as people co-occurrence, has been investigated in [14] [16] [17]. But these approaches do not deal with cluster-level co-occurrence information. Clothing information has been used extensively in face clustering [9] [20]. However, these techniques do not employ the important time decay factor in leveraging clothing information.

The overall unified framework is illustrated in Figure 2. We start with the initial set of clusters generated by the standard approach for the given photo collection. The initial clusters have high precision but low recall. We iteratively merge the clusters that are likely to refer to the same entities to get higher recall. We use contextual and facial features in two regards: for computing similarities (how similar are two clusters) and for defining constraints (which clusters cannot refer to the same person). The framework then uses bootstrapping to learn the importance of different heterogeneous feature types directly from data. To achieve higher quality, this learning is done adaptively per cluster in a photo collection, because the importance of different features can change from person to person and in different photo collections. For example, clothing is a good distinguishing feature in a photo album where people's clothes are distinct, but a weak feature in a photo collection where people are wearing uniform. We employ the ideas of bootstrapping to partially label any given dataset in automated fashion without any human input. These labels then allow us to learn the importance of various features directly from the given photo collection. Clusters are then merged iteratively, based on the importance of the learned features and computed similarity, to produce a higher quality clustering.

The rest of this paper is organized as follows. We start by formally defining the problem in Section 2. In Section 3, we describe how to leverage the context information at the cluster level, including common scene, people co-occurrence, human attributes, and clothing. In Section 4, we propose the unified framework which automatically learns rules to integrate heterogeneous context information together to iteratively merge clusters. The proposed approach is empirically evaluated in Section 5. Finally, we conclude in Section 6 by highlighting key points of our work.

2. PROBLEM DEFINITION

Suppose that a human-centered photo album P_h contains K images $\{I_1, I_2, \ldots, I_K\}$, see Figure 2. Assume that n faces are detected in P_h, with each face denoted as f_i for $i = 1, 2, \ldots, n$, or $f_i^{I_k}$ (that is, f_i is extracted from image I_k). Suppose that by applying the standard algorithm which is based on facial features, we obtain N clusters $\{C_1, C_2, \ldots, C_N\}$, where each cluster is assumed to be pure, but multiple clusters could refer to the same entity. Our goal is to leverage heterogeneous context information to merge clusters such that we still get very high precision clusters but also improve the recall.

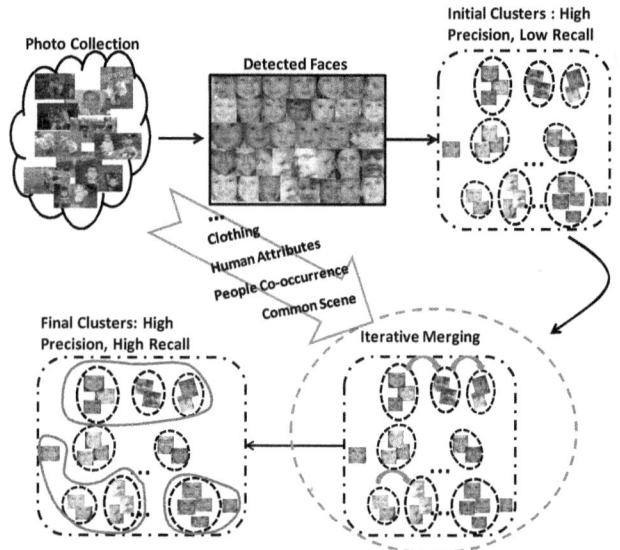

Figure 2: The General Framework

There have been many studies that analyze behaviors of different metrics for measuring quality of clustering. A recent prominent study by Artiles et al. suggests that B-cubed precision, recall and F-measure is one of the best combination of metrics to use according to many criteria [3]. Let $C(f_i)$ be the cluster that f_i is put into by a clustering algorithm. Let $L(f_i)$ be to the real category/label (person) f_i refers to in the ground truth. Given two faces f_i and f_j, the correctness $Correct(f_i, f_j)$ is defined as:

$$Correct(f_i, f_j) = \begin{cases} 1 & \text{if } L(f_i) = L(f_j) \wedge C(f_i) = C(f_j) \\ 0 & \text{otherwise} \end{cases}$$

B-cubed precision of an item f_i is computed as the proportion of correctly related items in its cluster (including itself): $Pre(f_i) = \frac{\sum_{f_j : C(f_i) = C(f_j)} Correct(f_i, f_j)}{\|\{f_j | C(f_i) = C(f_j)\}\|}$. The overall B-cubed precision is the averaged precision of all items: $Pre = \frac{1}{n} \sum_{i=1}^{n} Pre(f_i)$. Similarly, B-cubed recall of f_i is the proportion of correctly related items in its category: $Rec(f_i) = \frac{\sum_{f_j : L(f_i) = L(f_j)} Correct(f_i, f_j)}{\|\{f_j | L(f_i) = L(f_j)\}\|}$. The overall recall is then: $Rec = \frac{1}{n} \sum_{i=1}^{n} Rec(f_i)$. The F-measure is then defined as the harmonic mean of the precision and recall.

3. CONTEXT FEATURE EXTRACTION

Most prior research effort focus on leveraging context features directly at the face level [9] [13] [14]. That is, the similarity is computed between two faces and not two clusters. In this section, we will describe how to utilize context features at the cluster level. Context features are not only able to provide additional contextual *similarity* information to link clusters that co-refer (refer to the same entity), but also generate *constraints* that identify clusters that cannot co-refer (cannot refer to the same entity).

3.1 Context Similarities

3.1.1 Common Scene

It is common for a photographer to take multiple photos of the same "scene" in a relatively short period of time. This phenomenon happens for example when the photographer wants to ensure that at least some of the pictures taken will be of acceptable quality, or when people pose for photos

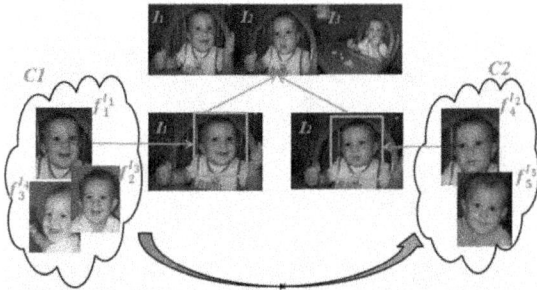

Figure 3: Example of Common Scene

and change their poses somewhat in the sequence of common scene photos. Common scene photos are often taken within small intervals of time from each other and they contain almost the same background and almost the same group of people in each photo. Surprisingly, we are not aware of much existing work that would use common scene detection to improve face-clustering performance. However common scene detection can provide additional evidence to link clusters describing the same entity, since images in a common scene often contain the same people.

To divide images into common scene clusters, some EXIF information (such as image captured time, geo-location, camera model, etc.), and image visual features (color, texture, shape) and image file name can be leveraged. Suppose that in a photo album P_h containing K images $\{I_1, I_2, ..., I_K\}$, the algorithm finds M common scene clusters. Let $CS(I_k)$ denotes the common scene of image I_k. Based on the assumption that two images forming the common scene might describe the same entities, two entities even with dissimilar facial appearances might be linked by the common scene.

For example, as shown in Figure 3, C_1 and C_2 are two initial face clusters based on face appearance. Face $f_1^{I_1}$, extracted from image I_1, belongs to cluster C_1, and face $f_4^{I_2}$ extracted from image I_2 is put into C_2. Since images I_1 and I_2 share the common scene $CS(I_1) = CS(I_2)$, it is possible they describe the same entities. Thus faces $f_1^{I_1}$ and $f_4^{I_2}$ have some possibility to be the same, and the two face clusters C_1 and C_2 are linked to each other via the common scene.

Thus the context similarity $S^{cs}(C_m, C_n)$ of two face clusters C_m and C_n based on common scene is defined as the number of distinct common scenes between the pairs of images from each cluster:

$$\mu_{mn}^{cs} = \{CS(I_k)|CS(I_k) = CS(I_l)) \wedge (f_i^{I_k} \in C_m) \wedge (f_j^{I_l} \in C_n)\} \quad (1)$$

$$S^{cs}(C_m, C_n) = \| \mu_{mn}^{cs} \| \quad (2)$$

Thus μ_{mn}^{cs} is the set of common scenes across two face clusters C_m and C_n. $S^{cs}(C_m, C_n)$ is the cardinality of set μ_{mn}^{cs}. The larger value $S^{cs}(C_m, C_n)$ is, the higher the likelihood that C_m and C_n refer to the same entity.

3.1.2 People Co-occurrence

The surrounding faces can provide vital evidence in recognizing the identity of a given face in an image. Suppose that "Rose" and "John" are good friends and often take photos together, then the identity of one person will probably imply the other. In [17], Wu et al. investigated people co-occurrence feature and proposed a social context similarity measurement by counting the common co-occurred single clusters between two clusters. However, this measurement could be greatly improved because single cluster linkage alone is not strong evidence. In this section, we propose a

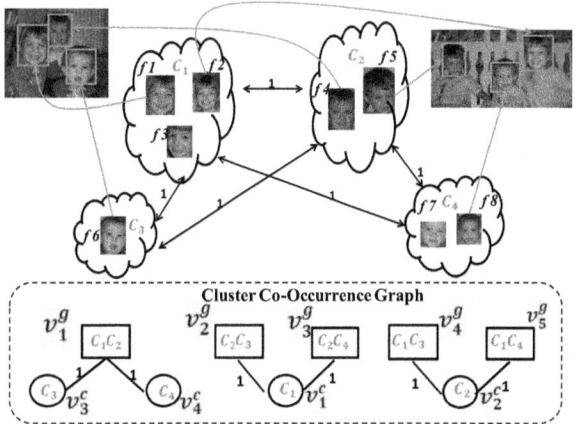

Figure 4: Example of People Co-occurrence

new social context similarity measurement, which use the common cluster-group as evidence to link clusters. Experiments reveal that the linkage of cluster-groups is more reliable than the linkage of single cluster.

Cluster co-occurrence. First, let us define the co-occurrence relationship between two clusters. We will say that clusters C_m and C_n co-occur in/via image I_k, if I_k contains at least two faces such that one is from C_m and the other one is from C_n. In general, the co-occurrence measure $Co(C_m, C_n)$ returns the number of distinct images in which C_m and C_n co-occur:

$$Co(C_m, C_n) = \| \{I_k | \exists f_i^{I_k}, f_j^{I_k} \text{ s.t. } (f_i^{I_k} \in C_m) \wedge (f_j^{I_k} \in C_n)\} \|$$

The co-occurrence relationship between three and more face clusters has a similar definition. Consider the faces in Figure 4 as an example. There, C_1, C_2, C_3, C_4 are four initial face clusters. Since there exists an image I_1 that contain three faces f_1, f_4 and f_6 such that $f_1 \in C_1$, $f_4 \in C_2$, $f_6 \in C_3$, thus $Co(C_1, C_2, C_3) = 1$. Similarly, for the clusters C_1, C_2, C_4 it holds $Co(C_1, C_2, C_4) = 1$. Based on common sense, we know that a person cannot co-occur with himself in an image unless the image is doctored or contains a reflection, e.g., in a mirror. Consequently, clusters connected via a non-zero co-occurrence relationship should refer to different entities. This property will be used later on by the framework to generate context *constraints*.

Co-occurrence graph. The co-occurrence of two face clusters reveals the social relationship between them and between the people they correspond to. We now will describe how to construct cluster co-occurrence graph. Observe that if two face clusters have similar co-occurrence relationships, then the two face clusters might refer to the same entity. This is since people tend to appear with the same group of people in photos, e.g., the same friends. In the example in Figure 4, both C_3 and C_4 co-occur with C_1 and C_2. Such co-occurrence can serve as extra evidence that C_3 and C_4 possibly refer to the same entity. Notice, to demonstrate this graphically, we can represent C_3 and C_4 as nodes in a graph both of which are linked together via a different node that corresponds to C_1 and C_2 as a single cluster-group.

To analyze the various co-occurrences among clusters, we construct the cluster co-occurrence graph $G = (V, E)$. G is a labeled undirectional graph. The set of nodes V in the graph consists of two types of nodes: $V = V^c \cap V^g$. Node $v_i^c \in V^c$ corresponds to each single face cluster C_i. Node $v_j^g \in V^g$ corresponds to each face cluster-group found in an image. The group nodes are constructed as follows. For each image

I_k that contains at least two faces, let Φ^{I_k} denote the set of all the clusters that contain faces present in I_k. We construct $\parallel \Phi^{I_k} \parallel$ cluster-groups, where each group is a set of clusters $\Phi^{I_k} \setminus \{C_j\}$ for each $C_j \in \Phi^{I_k}$. For example, if image I_1 has faces for three clusters $\Phi^{I_1} = \{C_1, C_2, C_3\}$, then the groups are going to be $\{C_1, C_2\}$, $\{C_1, C_3\}$, and $\{C_2, C_3\}$. A node v_j^g is created once per each distinct group. Edge $e_{ij} \in E$ is created between nodes v_i^c and v_j^g only when v_i^c occurs in the context of group v_j^g at least once, that is when exists at least one image I_k such that $v_i^c \cap v_j^g = \Phi^{I_k}$. Edge e_{ij} is labeled with the number of such images, i.e., edge weight $w_{ij} = \parallel \{I_k | v_i^c \cap v_j^g = \Phi^{I_k}\} \parallel$.

Consider Figure 4 as an example. For images I_1 and I_2 we have $\Phi^{I_1} = \{C_1, C_2, C_3\}$, $\Phi^{I_2} = \{C_1, C_2, C_4\}$. Thus we construct four V^c nodes for C_1, C_2, C_3, C_4, and five V^g nodes for $\{C_1, C_2\}$, $\{C_1, C_3\}$, $\{C_2, C_3\}$, $\{C_1, C_4\}$, $\{C_2, C_4\}$. Edges are created accordingly.

From the cluster co-occurrence graph, we observe that if two V^c nodes v_m^c and v_n^c connects to the same V^g node v_k^g, then v_m^c and v_n^c possibly refer to the same entity. For instance, in Figure 4, both C_3 and C_4 connects with $\{C_1, C_2\}$, so C_3 and C_4 are possibly the same. The context similarity from cluster co-occurrence $S^{co}(C_m, C_n)$ for C_m and C_n can be then defined as the flow between these two clusters,

$$S^{co}(C_m, C_n) = \sum_{V^g_k \leftrightarrow V^c_m, V^g_k \leftrightarrow V^c_n} \min(w_{mk}, w_{kn}) \quad (3)$$

In general, the co-occurrence similarity between two clusters can be measured as the sum of weights of paths which link them through V^g nodes. The larger the number/weight of paths that link C_m and C_n, the higher the likelihood that C_m and C_n refer to the same entity.

3.1.3 Human Attributes

Human attributes, such as gender, age, ethnicity, facial traits, etc., are important evidence to identify a person. By considering attributes, many uncertainties and errors for face clustering can be avoided, such as confusing "men" with "women", "adults" with "children", etc. To get attribute values for a given face, we use the attribute system [13]. It returns values for the 73 types of attributes, such as "black hair", "big nose", or "wearing eyeglasses". Thus, with each face f_i we associate a 73-D attribute vector denoted as A^{f_i}.

In [13], Kumar et al. suggests that attributes can be used to help face verification by choosing some measurement (e.g., cosine similarity) to compute attribute similarities. However, the importance of each type of attribute usually differs when identifying different entities. For example, in a photo album containing just one baby, age is an important factor for identifying this baby; while if several babies exist in an album, then age is not a strongly discriminative feature. Thus, it is essential to determine the importance of attributes for identifying a given entity in the photo collections.

To achieve this, we learn the importance of attributes from the face cluster itself, by leveraging *bootstrapping*. Here, bootstrapping refers to the process of being able to automatically label part of the data, without any human input, and then use these labels to train a classifier. The learned classifier is then used to label the remaining data. One of

---

Notice, in general, there could be different models for assigning weights to paths in addition to the flow model considered in the paper. For example, paths that go through larger group nodes could be assigned higher weight since larger groups of people tend to be better context than smaller ones.

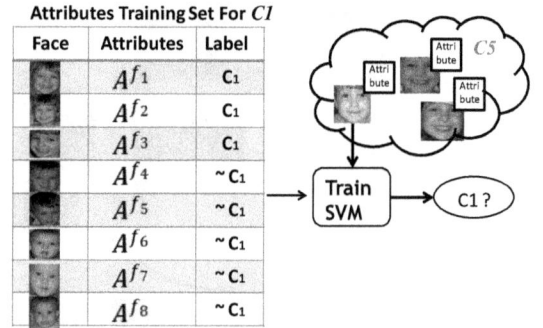

Figure 5: Example of Human Attributes

the main challenges in applying bootstrapping is to be able to provide these partial labels. The general idea of our solution is that faces that belong to one face cluster are very likely to refer to the same entity due to the purity of the initial clusters, hence they can form the positive samples. In turn, faces from two clusters that co-occur in the same image most likely refer to the different people (since a person cannot co-occur with himself in a photo), which can be used to construct the negative samples.

Based on the above discussion, the training dataset can be constructed for each cluster. Figure 5 illustrates the attribute training dataset for identifying C_1 from the example in Figure 4. Three faces f_1, f_2, f_3 fall into C_1, so the attributes of these three faces $A^{f_1}, A^{f_2}, A^{f_3}$ are labeled as C_1. Since the other three clusters C_2, C_3, C_4 have the co-occurrence relationship with C_1, they are considered to describe different entities. Thus the attributes of faces from the other three clusters can be treated as the negative samples. In this way, the attribute training dataset can be constructed automatically for each cluster.

After the attribute training dataset is constructed, a classifier, such as SVM, can be learned for each cluster C_m. Given a 73-D attribute feature A^{f_i} for any face f_i, the task of the classifier is to output whether this face f_i belongs to C_m. In addition to outputting a binary yes/no decision, modern classifiers can also output the probability that f_i belongs to C_m, denoted as $P^A(f_i \in C_m)$. Thus, by applying classifier learned for C_m to each face in an unknown face cluster C_n, we can compute the average probability that C_n belongs to C_m, denoted as $S^A(C_n \leadsto C_m)$:

$$S^A(C_n \leadsto C_m) = \frac{1}{\parallel C_n \parallel} \sum_{f_i \in C_n} P^A(f_i \in C_m) \quad (4)$$

Attribute similarity between C_m and C_n is defined as,

$$S^{attr}(C_m, C_n) = \frac{S^A(C_n \leadsto C_m) + S^A(C_m \leadsto C_n)}{2} \quad (5)$$

That is, the attribute based similarity $S^{attr}(C_m, C_n)$ between two clusters is the average of the average probability of one cluster to belong to the other.

3.1.4 Clothing Information

Clothing information could be a strong feature for determining the identity of a person. However, clothing is a time-sensitive feature since people can change their clothes. Clothing has been considered in the previous work for face clustering, e.g. in [20], but not as a time-sensitive feature described next.

In this section, we introduce time decay factor to control the effect of clothing in identifying people. We propose that the similarity between f_i and f_j should be a function of time:

$$S^c(f_i, f_j) = sim(ch_{f_i}, ch_{f_j}) \times e^{-\triangle t/2s^2} \qquad (6)$$

In the above formula, $sim(ch_{f_i}, ch_{f_j})$ refers to the clothing similarity computed only on visual features. Notation $\triangle t$ refers to the capture time difference between 2 faces. By construction, the above time-decay function incorporates the relationship between $\triangle t$ and the effectiveness of clothing features. The smaller $\triangle t$ is, the more effective clothing feature is. With the time difference value $\triangle t$ growing, the effectiveness of clothing feature is decreasing. When the time difference $\triangle t$ is much larger than the time slot threshold s, the clothing feature becomes ineffective.

To compute the clothing similarity, the first step is to detect the location of clothing for the given face, which can be implemented by leveraging the techniques from [9] or simply using a bounding box below detected faces. After that, some low level image features (color, texture) can be extracted to represent the clothing information, and then similarities can be computed.

To obtain the cluster similarity from clothing information, we can compute the clothing similarity between each pair of faces and then choose the maximum value:

$$S^{cloth}(C_m, C_n) = \max_{f_i \in C_m, f_j \in C_n} S^c(f_i, f_j) \qquad (7)$$

Thus the clothing similarity between C_m and C_n is computed by selecting the maximum clothing similarity between each pair of faces respectively falling in the 2 face clusters.

3.2 Context Constraints

In the previous section we have explained how context features can be used as extra positive evidence for computing similarity between clusters. Context features, such as people co-occurrence and human attributes, can also provide *constraints* or negative evidence, which can be used to identify clusters that should refer to different entities.

From cluster co-occurrence relationship, we can derive that two face clusters with $Co(C_m, C_n) > 0$ should refer to definitely different entities, because a person cannot co-occur with himself (in normal cases). Thus we can define that if $Co(C_m, C_n) > 0$, the context dissimilarity from co-occurrence feature is 1, denoted as $D^{co}(C_m, C_n) = 1$.

From human attributes, we can derive that two clusters with vastly different attributes values, such as age, gender, ethnicity information should refer to different entities. Thus we can define that if two clusters C_m and C_n have distinct age, gender, ethnicity attribute values, then context dissimilarity from human attributes feature is 1, referred as $D^{attr}(C_m, C_n) = 1$. Then we can define the context dissimilarity measurement between two clusters as follows:

$$D(C_m, C_n) = \begin{cases} 1 & \text{if } D^{co}(C_m, C_n) = 1 \text{ or } D^{attr}(C_m, C_n) = 1 \\ 0 & \text{otherwise} \end{cases}$$

Thus $D(C_m, C_n) = 1$ means C_m and C_n are most likely different, $D(C_m, C_n) = 0$ means that the dissimilarity measure between C_m and C_n cannot tell if they are different or not. The context constraints will be leveraged to implement the bootstrapping ideas explained in the following section.

4. THE UNIFIED FRAMEWORK

In the previous section we have discussed how to leverage the context information from two aspects: computing context similarities (S^{cs}, S^{co}, S^{attr}, S^{cloth}) and context constraints (D^{co}, D^{attr}). In this section, we will develop an ap-

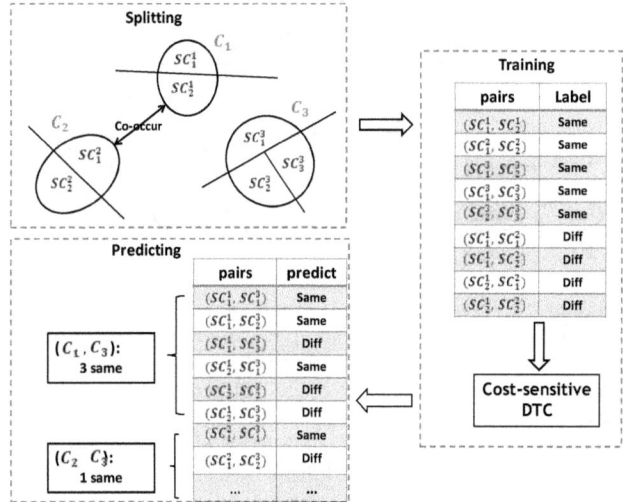

Figure 6: Example of Bootstrapping Process

proach for integrating these heterogeneous context features together to facilitate face clustering.

One possible solution for aggregating these context features is to compute the overall similarity as weighted linear sum of the context similarities. The overall similarity can then be used to merge clusters that do not violate the context constraints. However, this basic solution has several limitations: it is too coarse-grained and it could be difficult to set the weights that would work best for all possible photo collections. Alternatively, the other option is to automatically learn some rules to combine these context features together to make a merging decision. If the rules are satisfied, the two face clusters can be merged. For example, a rule could be if $S^{cs}(C_m, C_n) > 3$ and $S^{co}(C_m, C_n) > 4$, then merge C_m and C_n. The experiments reveal that if the rules are defined appropriately, significantly better merging results can be achieved compared to the basic solution.

Nevertheless, it is hard to define and fix rules that would work well for all possible photo albums. Instead, rules that are automatically tuned to each photo collection would naturally perform better. This is since the importance of each type of context feature usually varies due to the diversity of image datasets. For example, clothing might be important evidence in a photo album where people's clothing is distinct, but it will lose the effect in a photo collection where people wearing uniform. Thus, inspired by [5] [12] [15], we propose a unified framework that can automatically learn and adapt the rules to get high quality of face clustering.

4.1 Construction of Training Dataset

To automatically learn the rules, training dataset is often required. However, since we are trying to automatically learn and tune the rules per each photo collection, it is unlikely that training data will be available, as it will not accompany each given collection. Nevertheless, such rules could be learned by leveraging bootstrapping and semi-supervised learning techniques. To apply those techniques, we need to automatically partially label the dataset. The constructed training dataset should contain positive samples (same face cluster pairs) and negative samples (different face cluster pairs). The key challenge is to be able to automatically, without any human input, label the positive and negative samples for part of the data.

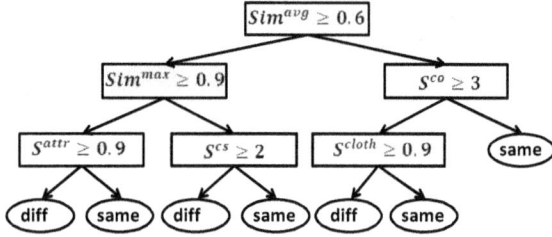

Figure 7: Example of Decision Tree Classifier

In the above section, we discuss that the context information can provide constraints to distinguish clusters referring to different entities. For example, two face clusters with co-occurrence relationship, or distinct attribute values (age, gender, ethnicity), are most likely different. Based on this observation, the negative samples can be constructed.

Then the next issue becomes how to obtain the positive pairs. Due to the purity of initial face clusters, faces that are part of one face cluster refer to the same entity. If we split an initial face cluster into smaller clusters, then these split smaller clusters should refer to the same entity. Thus the split smaller clusters will form the positive sample pairs.

4.1.1 Strategy for Splitting Clusters

Many splitting strategies can be adopted for splitting existing pure clusters into subclusters. For example, one equi-part strategy is to split each initial face cluster into two (or other fixed number of) roughly equally-sized subclusters. An alternative equi-size strategy is to predefine the subcluster size (e.g., $sz = 10$ faces) and then split each cluster into subclusters of that size. The equi-size strategy has demonstrated a consistent advantage over other tested options since some of the context features similarities depend on cluster sizes. For example, the context similarity between two large clusters is usually stronger than the similarity between two small clusters. Thus, by considering split clusters of roughly the same size, the effect of cluster size is reduced.

Consider N initial pure face clusters $C_1, C_2, \ldots, C_N$, and the predefined subcluster size is sz. Then each cluster C_m with $\| C_m \| > sz$, can be randomly divided into $\left\lceil \frac{\|C_m\|}{sz} \right\rceil$ subclusters, denoted as $\{SC_1^m, SC_2^m, \ldots\}$. Figure 6 illustrates an example of splitting clusters.

4.1.2 Automatic Labeling

After splitting clusters into subclusters, the next task is to automatically label the positive and negative training samples. Due to the purity of the initial face clusters, if two subclusters come from the same initial cluster, they form the positive sample, labeled as the "same" pair. If two subclusters come from two different clusters that have co-occurrence relation or distinct attribute values, then the two subclusters form the negative sample, labeled as "diff" pair. Thus, given two subclusters SC_i^m and SC_j^n, the label $La(SC_i^m, SC_j^n)$ can be generated as follows:

$$La(SC_i^m, SC_j^n) = \begin{cases} same & \text{if } m = n, \\ diff & \text{if } D(C_m, C_n) = 1, \\ unknown & \text{otherwise.} \end{cases}$$

Figure 6 illustrates how to construct the training dataset. As shown in Figure 6, subcluster pairs coming from the same initial cluster are labeled as "same" pairs, e.g., (SC_1^1, SC_2^1), (SC_1^2, SC_2^2), etc. Since C_1 and C_2 have the co-occurrence relationship, each subcluster pair respectively deriving from C_1 and C_2 will compose the "diff" pairs, e.g., (SC_1^1, SC_1^2), (SC_1^1, SC_2^2), etc.

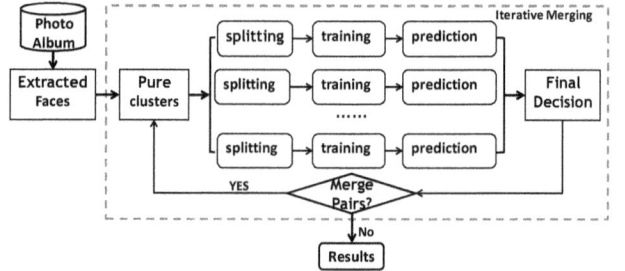

Figure 8: Iterative Merging Framework

4.1.3 Feature Construction

After splitting clusters into subclusters, the algorithm will try to determine which subclusters refer to the same entity. To do that, it first needs to associate a feature vector with each subcluster pair. After that, it will use a classifier to predict whether or not the pair co-refers.

Specifically, for each pair of subclusters SC_i^m and SC_j^n the algorithm associates four features that correspond to the cluster level context similarities $S^{cs}, S^{co}, S^{attr}, S^{cloth}$, as described in Section 3. In addition, the face appearance similarities between two subclusters are also important, which are measured in three ways: (1) the maximum similarity between face pairs, denoted as Sim^{max}; (2) the minimum similarity between face pairs Sim^{min}; (3) the average similarity of face pairs, referred as Sim^{avg}. Therefore, the algorithm associates 4 types of context features and 3 types of face-based features with each subcluster pairs. Other types of features can also be integrated to this unified framework.

4.2 Classifier Training and Predicting

After the automatic construction of the partially labeled training dataset, the next goal is to learn the merging rules from this training data. Then the learned rules can be applied to predict "same/different" labels for the pairs of subclusters that have been labeled "unknown" before. In this scenario, we choose to use *cost-sensitive* variant of the Decision Tree Classifier (DTC) as the classifier to learn the rules, though other classifiers might also be applied. The reason for using cost-sensitive and not regular DTC is that a single incorrect merge decision can very negatively affect the precision of clusters. That would defeat the purpose of our goal of improving the recall while maintaining the same high precision of the initial clustering. The cost-sensitive version of DTC allows to set the cost of false-positive errors to be much higher than that of false-negative errors. Therefore, we train a very conservative classifier which will try to avoid the false-positive errors thus ensuring high precision of the resulting clusters. To avoid over-fitting problem, we prune the over-fitted branches from the DTC. Figure 7 illustrated an example of the learned DTC.

As shown in Figure 6, the learned DTC can be applied to relabel previously "unknown" pairs by assigning "same" or "diff" labels. For example, in Figure 6, pair (SC_1^1, SC_1^3) is predicted to be "same", and pair (SC_1^1, SC_3^3) to be "diff".

To make the overall merging decision for the face clusters, we need to combine the decisions of the corresponding subclusters. For example, in Figure 6, analyzing the predictions for face cluster pair (C_1, C_3), we discover that 3 subcluster pairs are labeled "same", and 3 pairs are labeled "diff". Similarly, for cluster pair (C_2, C_3), 1 subcluster pair is labeled "same", and 5 pairs are labeled "diff". Hence the issue is how to make the final merging decision.

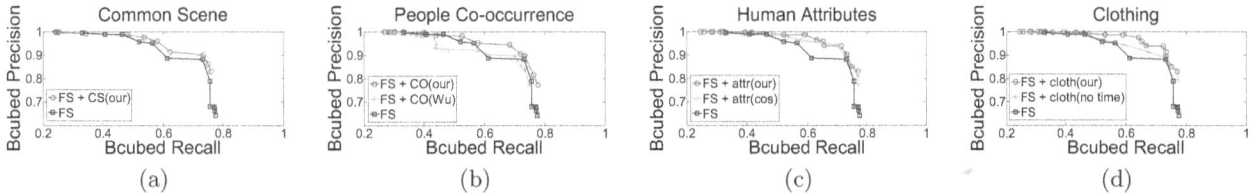

Figure 9: Effectiveness of Extracted Context Features

4.3 Final Merging Decision

Due to the randomness of the splitting strategy, the prediction results might differ with differently split clusters. To reduce the uncertainty introduced by the random splitting strategy, we propose to repeat the "splitting-training-predicting" process multiple times. If two face clusters are predicted to be "same" every time, then the face cluster pair should have higher probability to refer to the same entity.

4.3.1 Multiple Splitting-Training-Predicting

Based on the above discussion, the algorithm repeats the "splitting-training-predicting" process multiple times. Each time, the algorithm splits the initial face clusters into subclusters randomly, constructs the training dataset, trains the classifiers, predicts the "unknown" pairs, and then map the subcluster pairs predictions into the merge decisions. Let $T^{same}(C_m, C_n)$ be the number of times that face cluster pair C_m and C_n are predicted to be "same". Similarly, let $T^{diff}(C_m, C_n)$ be the number of times they are predicted to be different. Naturally, the larger T^{same} is, the higher the probability is that this cluster pair refer to the same entity.

4.3.2 Final Decision

After perform the "splitting-training-predicting" process t times (e.g., $t = 5$), we can compute T^{same} and T^{diff} values for each pair of clusters, based on which the final merging decision can be made. For example, merge a pair when its $\frac{T^{same}+1}{T^{diff}+1}$ ratio exceed a certain threshold. To avoid early propagation of the incorrect merges, a higher threshold can be selected in the first several iterations, which can be decreased gradually in the subsequent iterations.

4.4 Iterative Merging Strategy

Figure 8 demonstrates the overall iterative merging framework. As shown in Figure 8, after the faces are extracted from the photo album, facial visual features are used to group the faces into initial clusters, which are very pure (high precision, low recall). Then our goal is to merge the pure cluster pairs in order to improve the recall without reducing the high precision. Leveraging multiple context information, and applying bootstrapping ideas, we perform the "splitting-training-predicting" process several times, and then make the combined merging decision. Based on the final decision, some face cluster pairs will be merged and updated, and then the next iteration will be repeated until no merging pairs are obtained. Then the final clustering results are achieved.

5. EXPERIMENTS AND RESULTS

In this section, we evaluate our algorithm on three human-centered data collections: Gallagher, Wedding, and Surveillance. The characteristics of these datasets are listed in Table 1. Gallagher [9] is a public family album containing photos of three children, other family members and their friends. The wedding dataset has been downloaded from Web Picasa. It captures people in a wedding ceremony, in-

Dataset	#Images	#Faces	#People	Image Pixels
Gallagher	591	1064	37	2576×1716
Wedding	643	1433	31	400×267
Surveillance	1030	70	45	704×480

Table 1: Experimental Dataset

cluding the bride, the groom, their relatives and friends. The surveillance dataset contains images that capture the daily life of faculty and students in the 2nd floor of a computer science building. To evaluate the performance of the proposed approach, we use B-cubed precision and recall defined in Eqs. (1) and (2) as the evaluation metrics.

5.1 Experimental Results

First, we run some experiments to demonstrate the importance of using different context feature types. Then we compare our clustering results with those obtained by Picasa and affinity propagation [8] algorithms, to illustrate the overall effectiveness of our unified framework.

5.1.1 Context Feature Comparison

As shown in Figure9, a series of experiments are performed on the Gallagher dataset to test the effectiveness of the proposed 4 types of context similarities. Each plot in Figure 9 corresponds to one type of context similarity. Each plot compares the baseline algorithm that uses only face similarity (denoted as FS) with our framework which is allowed to use just one given context feature type instead of all 4 types.

Figure 9(a) illustrates that the clustering performance can be improved by combining common scene (CS) feature with facial similarities (FS). The improvement is not very significant because only 50 cluster pairs are linked by common sense feature in Gallagher dataset. Figure 9(b) shows the comparison between our approach (CO(our)) and Wu's approach (CO(Wu)) [17] in leveraging people co-occurrence feature. The performance of our approach is much better than Wu's approach because we use the cluster groups as evidence to link two clusters, which is more reliable than the linkage of single cluster. Figure 9(c) demonstrates that our approach (attr(our)) outperforms the cosine similarity measurements (attr(cos)) in using human attributes feature. The advantage of our approach is because we automatically learn the relative importance of various attribute types in identifying different people. Figure 9(d) shows the advantage of our approach (cloth(our)) compared with the approach without considering time factor (cloth(no time)) in utilizing clothing information. This demonstrates the advantage of adding time decay factor to clothing information.

5.1.2 Clustering Results Comparison

To evaluate the performance of the proposed unified framework, we compare our clustering results with affinity propagation (AP) [8] and Picasa's face clustering toolkit, as shown in Figure 10. Four types of context information and facial visual similarities are integrated into our framework. B-cubed precision and recall are computed as the evaluation metric-

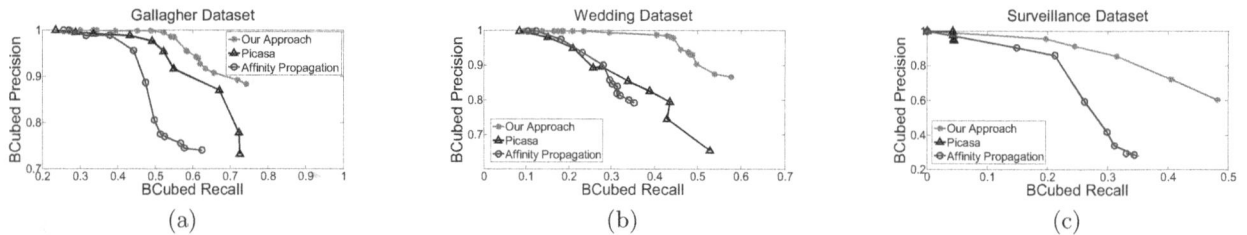

Figure 10: Comparison of Clustering Performance with Affinity Propagation and Picasa on Three Datasets.

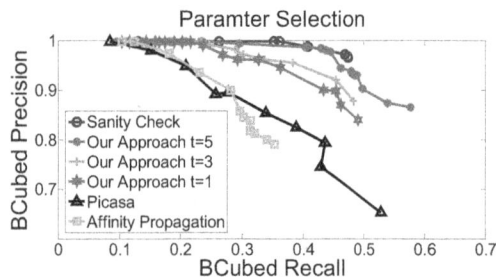

Figure 11: Comparison of Different Parameters

s. In our clustering framework, several parameters need to be selected, the split cluster size (sz), and number of times to perform "splitting-training-predicting" process t. In this experiment we set $sz = 10$ and $t = 5$.

When performing affinity propagation, we combine the 4 types of context features with equal weight, and then aggregate context features and facial feature with equal weight to construct the overall similarity. By adjusting the preference parameter p in AP, we are able to control the precision vs. recall tradeoff for AP. Picasa allows users to specify the cluster threshold (from 50 to 95) to control the precision vs. recall tradeoff. With the increasing of threshold, the recall reduces and the precision increases.

As demonstrated in Figure 10, our unified framework outperforms Affinity Propagation (AP) and Picasa in all the three datasets. The gained advantage is due to leveraging the bootstrapping idea to automatically learn and tune the merging rules per each dataset, and due to using the conservative merging strategy that guarantees the high precision. In addition, our framework is more reliable for data with lower quality images because the context features are less sensitive to image resolution. This is not the case for Picasa, as its performance drops dramatically with the decreasing of image quality. The experiments illustrate that our unified framework reaches high quality and at the same time is more reliable than the other two techniques.

5.1.3 Effectiveness and Efficiency

Figure 11 shows the comparison of clustering results when choosing different values for parameter t (the number of times to perform "splitting-training-predicting" process). The larger t can provide more reliable clustering results because it can reduce the uncertainties introduced by random splitting. However, The larger t will reduce the efficiency of the algorithm. The experiments illustrate that when $t = 5$, our performance is approaching the "sanity check" results (merging rules learned from ground truth). And when $t = 1$, our results are still better than affinity propagation and Picasa. Thus our approach is able to achieve a good result without sacrificing efficiency.

6. CONCLUSION

In this paper we have proposed a unified framework for in-

tegrating heterogeneous context information (including common scene, people co-occurrence, human attributes and clothing) to improve the quality/recall of face clustering. The context information has been used for both: computing context similarities to link clusters that co-refer as well as for generating context constraints to differentiate clusters that do not co-refer. The proposed unified framework leverages bootstrapping to automatically learn the adaptive rules to integrate heterogeneous context information together to iteratively merge clusters, in order to improve the recall of clustering results. Our experiments on the real-world datasets demonstrated the effectiveness of the extracted context features and of the overall unified framework.

7. REFERENCES

[1] Project sherlock @ uci. http://sherlock.ics.uci.edu.
[2] T. Ahonen, A. Hadid, and et al. Face description with local binary patterns: Application to face recognition. In *IEEE Trans. Pattern Anal*, 2006.
[3] E. Amigo and et al. A comparison of extrinsic clustering evaluation metrics based on formal constraints. In *Technical Report*, 2008.
[4] T. L. Berg, A. C. Berg, and et al. Names and faces in the news. In *IEEE ICPR*, 2004.
[5] Z. Chen, D. V. Kalashnikov, and S. Mehrotra. Adaptive graphical approach to entity resolution. In *JCDL*, 2007.
[6] N. Dalal and B. Triggs. Histograms of oriented gradients for human detection. In *CVPR*, 2005.
[7] K. Etemad and R. Chellappa. Discriminant analysis for recognition of human face images. In *AVBPA*, 1997.
[8] B. J. Frey and D. Dueck. Clustering by passing messages between data points. In *Science*, 2007.
[9] A. Gallagher and T. Chen. Clothing cosegmentation for recognizing people. In *IEEE CVPR*, 2008.
[10] A. Gallagher and T. Chen. Understanding images of groups of people. In *IEEE CVPR*, 2009.
[11] J.Tang, S. Yan, R. Hong, G. Qi, and T. Chua. Inferring semantic concepts from community-contributed images and noisy tags. In *ACM Multimedia*, 2009.
[12] D. V. Kalashnikov, Z. Chen, S. Mehrotra, and R. Nuray-Turan. Web people search via connection analysis. In *TKDE*, 2011.
[13] N. Kumar and et al. Describable visual attributes for face verification and image search. In *IEEE TPAMI*, 2011.
[14] Y. J. Lee and K. Grauman. Face discovery with social context. In *BMVC*, 2011.
[15] R. Nuray-Turan, D. V. Kalashnikov, and S. Mehrotra. Exploiting web querying for web people search. In *ACM TODS*, 2012.
[16] K. Shimizu, N. Nitta, and et al. Classification based group photo retrieval with bag of people features. In *ICMR*, 2012.
[17] P. Wu and F. Tang. Improving face clustering using social context. In *ACM Multimedia*, 2010.
[18] J. Yagnik and A. Islam. Learning people annotation from the web via consistency learning. In *MIR*, 2007.
[19] L. Zhang, R. Vaisenberg, S. Mehrotra, and D. V. Kalashnikov. Video entity resolution: Applying er techniques for smart video surveillance. In *PerCom Workshops*, 2011.
[20] W. Zhang and et al. Beyond face: Improving person clustering in consumer photos by exploring contextual information. In *ICME*, 2010.
[21] M. Zhao, Y. Teo, and et al. Automatic person annotation of family photo album. In *CIVR*, 2006.

Indexing and Searching 100M Images with Map-Reduce

Diana Moise
INRIA Rennes
Diana.Moise@inria.fr

Gylfi Gudmundsson
INRIA Rennes
Gylfi.Gudmundsson@inria.fr

Denis Shestakov
INRIA Rennes
Denis.Shestakov@inria.fr

Laurent Amsaleg
IRISA-CNRS
Laurent.Amsaleg@irisa.fr

ABSTRACT

Most researchers working on high-dimensional indexing agree on the following three trends: (i) the size of the multimedia collections to index are now reaching millions if not billions of items, (ii) the computers we use every day now come with multiple cores and (iii) hardware becomes more available, thanks to easier access to Grids and/or Clouds. This paper shows how the Map-Reduce paradigm can be applied to indexing algorithms and demonstrates that great scalability can be achieved using Hadoop, a popular Map-Reduce-based framework. Dramatic performance improvements are not however guaranteed a priori: such frameworks are rigid, they severely constrain the possible access patterns to data and scares resource RAM has to be shared. Furthermore, algorithms require major redesign, and may have to settle for sub-optimal behavior. The benefits, however, are many: simplicity for programmers, automatic distribution, fault tolerance, failure detection and automatic re-runs and, last but not least, scalability. We share our experience of adapting a clustering-based high-dimensional indexing algorithm to the Map-Reduce model, and of testing it at large scale with Hadoop as we index 30 billion SIFT descriptors. We foresee that lessons drawn from our work could minimize time, effort and energy invested by other researchers and practitioners working in similar directions.

Categories and Subject Descriptors

H.3.4 [**Systems and Software**]: Distributed systems

Keywords

High-Dimensional Indexing, Map-Reduce, Hadoop.

1. INTRODUCTION

Multimedia collections now reach sizes that were unthinkable a few years back. Many papers published lately in multimedia research venues have experimental sections where the collections used for evaluations contain millions of images or billions of descriptors [9, 17, 12]. The quest for improving speed, scale and performance is still there, however.

The processing power of each computer has also grown, as well as the size of grids and now clouds. Architectures are now all 64bits, allowing for huge on-board RAM capacities, tens of gigabytes are not uncommon, and hundreds possible. All computers now come multi-cored and thus writing parallel programs is no longer reserved to some elite, equipped with exceptional machines.

Such architectures are appealing when processing massive collections of multimedia material, especially when *creating* high-dimensional indices. Taking a raw collection of high-dimensional descriptors and creating for it an index to allow subsequent ultra-fast searches is still a long, complex, costly, and resource-consuming task. When the raw descriptor collection is on the order of terabytes, as is the case when indexing tens of millions of real world image using SIFT [18], then indexing may take days or even weeks. Parallel and distributed architectures are also needed when *searching* indices in order to exhibit a very high query throughput.

This paper describes a complete Map-Reduce based high-dimensional indexing approach running on top of the Hadoop distributed framework. It builds on a very simple yet very effective and efficient state-of-the-art centralized indexing algorithm that is prototypical of the major trends we can observe in the indexing literature [8]. It uses *clustering* as an unstructured vectorial quantizer to create clusters grouping descriptors. At search time, one or few clusters are fetched and the descriptors they contain compared to the query vector. From this starting point, the three contributions described in this paper are:

1. **Index creation with Map-Reduce.** We propose a Map-Reduce based high-dimensional index creation scheme enabling the fast indexing of billions of descriptors, terabytes of data. This index creation technique scales very well with growth of the data collection and/or available hardware resources. Its principles are very simple and can be applied to other indexing schemes as long as they can be turned into a divide-and-conquer process.

2. **Index search with Map-Reduce.** For some applications, throughput is way more important than is the response time of individual queries. We propose a index search scheme that is geared toward throughput as it processes very efficiently large batches of queries. We show this search technique is essentially bounded

by the performance of I/Os, which leaves a lot of room for possible improvements.

3. **Very large scale experiments.** We evaluate index creation and search using an image collection containing roughly 100 million images, this is about 30 billion SIFT descriptors or about 4 terabytes of data. The extensive experiments ran on this very large-scale dataset provide a basis for a discussion on the problems raised when managing so much data with Hadoop and a grid. We thus draw several lessons we want to share.

The paper is structured as follows. Section 2 gives the necessary background to understand the remainder of this paper. Section 3 presents the high-dimensional indexing scheme we start from and that we extend to fit with the Map-Reduce paradigm. These extensions are described in details in the Section 4. Section 5 presents the context of the experiments and implementation details. Then, Section 6 gives the performance results. Section 7 concludes.

2. BACKGROUND

This section briefly describes the recent evolutions in hardware making possible the use of Map-Reduce as well as distributed and parallel frameworks dedicated to grid and cloud computations such as Hadoop. We also briefly mention the state-of-art in high dimensional indexing techniques.

2.1 Hardware

Multi-core CPUs have been around for a long time in specialized systems. But around 2005, multi-core architectures hit the mass market and everyone could have a machine with multiple cores, by default. Today, a standard desktop has 2–4 cores, and a server has 1–4 CPUs, each with 2–24 cores.

The performance of the applications depends of course on the number of cores they use for their computations, on the nature of the computation, as well as on their access pattern to data. High-performance computing typically has complicated iterative/recursive computations using the same data, or just-created data, from one iteration to the other. Once the calculation starts from the data in memory, it proceeds and runs instructions on the data that is cached very close to the processor, requiring to access RAM only every once in a while and, when the calculation is over, to save the final result. In this case, the CPUs are kept busy while the underlying hardware is not stressed.

This is not at all the case for high-dimensional indexing and retrieval applications for which consuming data is central. All the work is data-driven, not calculus-driven. Data is fetched from disks, then installed in memory and then transfered to the processor where it does not stays that long before being moved back elsewhere. Once processed, data has to follow the inverse route at index creation time, as each data item is then typically assigned to a group of similar elements stored on disks and later used during retrieval. Data locality and the underlying hardware are therefore key for the performance of such *big data* applications.

2.2 Map-Reduce

The Map-Reduce framework is originally by Google [4] and it is a programming model for processing extremely large datasets. It exploits data independence to do automatic distributed parallelism. The developer is tasked with implementing the *Map* and the *Reduce* functions. The input data is distributed in blocks to the participating machines using the distributed Google file system GFS [6].

When a job is launched, the system automatically spawns as many Map functions as there are data blocks to process. Each mapper reads the data iteratively as a key/value pair record, processes it and, if necessary, outputs key/value pair bound for a Reduce function. All records with the same key go to the same Reduce task. The framework thus includes a copy-merge-sort data shuffle step, where data from several mappers gets directed to specific reducers depending on their key. Once enough data is locally available to reducers, they process the records and produce the final output.

The Map-Reduce run-time environment transparently handles the partitioning of the input data, schedules the execution of tasks across the machines and manages the communications between processing nodes when sending/receiving the records to process. The run-time environment also deals with node failures and restarts aborted tasks on nodes, possibly on replicated data in case of unavailability. The framework uses as little network bandwidth as possible by processing data where it resides or at the nearest available node, paying attention to the network topology and minimizing reading over machine-rack boundaries.

2.3 Hadoop and HDFS

The Map-Reduce programming model has been implemented by the open-source community through the Hadoop project.Maintained by the Apache Foundation and supported by Yahoo!, Hadoop has rapidly gained popularity in the area of distributed data-intensive computing. The core of Hadoop consists of the Map-Reduce implementation and the Hadoop Distributed File System (HDFS). Hadoop is now the de-facto reference Map-Reduce implementation.

The architecture of Hadoop consists of a single master *jobtracker* and multiple slave *tasktrackers*. The jobtracker's main role is to act as the task *scheduler* of the system, by assigning work to the tasktrackers. Each tasktracker has of a number of available *slots* for running tasks. Every active map or reduce task takes up one slot, thus a tasktracker usually executes several tasks simultaneously.

When dispatching map tasks to tasktrackers, the jobtracker strives at keeping the computation as close to the data as possible. This technique is enabled by the data-layout information previously acquired by the jobtracker. If the work cannot be hosted on the actual node where the data resides, priority is given to nodes closer to the data (belonging to the same network rack). The jobtracker first schedules map tasks, as the reducers must wait for the map execution to generate the intermediate data. The jobtracker is also in charge of monitoring tasks and dealing with failures.

HDFS [22] was built with the purpose of providing storage for *huge files* with *streaming data access patterns*, while running on clusters of *commodity hardware*. HDFS implements concepts commonly used by distributed file systems: data is organized into files and directories, a file is split into fixed-size blocks that are distributed across the cluster nodes. The blocks are called *chunks* and are usually of 64 MB in size (this parameter specifying the chunk size is configurable).

The architecture of HDFS consists of several *datanodes* storing the data chunks and a centralized *namenode* responsible for keeping the file metadata and the chunk location. HDFS handles failures through chunk-level replication (default 3 replicas). When distributing the replicas to the datanodes, HDFS employs a rack-aware policy: the first replica is stored on a datanode in the same rack, and the second replica is shipped to a datanode belonging to a different rack (randomly chosen).

In addition to being used in cluster computing, Hadoop is becoming a de-facto standard for cloud computing. The generic nature of clouds allows resources to be purchased on-demand, especially to augment local resources for specific large or time-critical tasks. Several organizations offer cloud compute cycles that can be accessed via Hadoop. Amazon's Elastic Compute Cloud contains tens of thousands of virtual machines, and supports Hadoop with minimal effort.

2.4 Image retrieval

Content-based image retrieval systems can now manage collections having sizes that could not even be envisioned years back. Most systems can handle several million images [16, 12], billions of descriptors [17, 13], or address web-scale problems [5, 1]. The ImageTerrier platform [9] uses Hadoop. The scale of their system is smaller since they index about 10 million images with a bag of feature approach.

Overall, most high-dimensional indexing schemes use some form of partitioning where the data is split into little groups at indexing time, and one or few such groups are loaded and analysed at retrieval time. All indexing schemes differ by the technique they use to create groups. They typically rely on scalar quantization (such as LSH [7, 3]) or on vectorial quantization (this is VideoGoogle [23] and all its derivatives, including [9]). The algorithm we use in this paper belongs to this second category, as it is presented next.

3. EXTENDED CLUSTER PRUNING AS A STARTING POINT

We decided to build on top of the extended Cluster Pruning (eCP) algorithm [8] for several reasons we highlight at the end of this section. eCP is a centralized high-dimensional indexing strategy. eCP is very related to the well-known k-means approach. As k-means, eCP adopts an unstructured quantization scheme to create clusters containing similar descriptors. eCP is designed to be I/O friendly as it assumes the data collection is too large to fit in memory and must reside on secondary storage.

3.1 Indexing and Searching with eCP

eCP randomly picks C points from the collection that are used as the representatives of the C clusters the algorithm will eventually build. C is determined from having set the average number of data points each cluster should contain. This number is called the TargetSize, ts, and $C = N/ts$ where N is the number of points in the collection. eCP then organizes the C representatives in a multi-level hierarchy composed of L levels. The points from the data collection that remain are read one after the other, traverse the tree of representatives and are eventually assigned to the closest cluster representative at the bottom of the tree. The multi-level hierarchy allows to assign points with a logarithmic complexity. Once all the data collection has been processed, then eCP has created C clusters as well as a tree of representatives, all this being stored on disk. Note the tree of representative is rather small and can fit in main memory.

Searching with eCP requires to navigate down the tree of representatives by following the path indicated at each level

by the representative that is the closest to the query point. Then, the corresponding bottom cluster is fetched, and the distances between the query point and all the points in that cluster are computed to get the k-nearest neighbors.

eCP compensates its somewhat brutal clustering by adopting ideas from various state-of-art indexing schemes. It uses a form of soft-assignment [2, 21] while building the tree of representatives. With soft-assignment, each representative is not solely assigned to its closest parent representative, but it is assigned to its a closest representatives. Note a applies only to the tree of representatives, not to the data stored in the clusters. It also uses a form of multi-probe approach at search time as more than one cluster can be searched, as it has been proposed for LSH [19, 15]. eCP can probe the b clusters that are the closest to the query point.

3.2 Motivation for eCP

We port eCP to Map-Reduce and not another state-of-the-art indexing solutions for the following reasons:

- eCP is quite representative of the core principles underpinning many of the unstructured quantization-based high-dimensional indexing algorithms that perform very well [23, 11].

- eCP is not iterative by nature while traditional indexing schemes based on k-means are. At every iteration of a k-means process, and in order to eventually converge, new representatives must be computed based on the previous round. Distributing k-means or any other algorithm that needs rounds to converge is costly as a global state must be reconstructed and propagated to all participants. Having no such rounds with eCP was a strong motivation for using this algorithm, as distributing and parallelising it were greatly simplified.

- eCP pre-calculates a representative hierarchy that is used to significantly speed-up the assignment of points to clusters. This is key for performance when data collections are terabytes sized in order to have a indexing approach usable *in practice*.

- eCP proved to return good quality result despite the crude process it uses to create clusters. This is shown in the experimental section of this paper.

- Due to the extreme simplicity of its search procedure, eCP indeed covers a large spectrum of existing indexing approaches. A behavior very similar to the one of VideoGoogle [23] can be obtained if instead of computing the distances to all the points in the fetched cluster(s) eCP simply returns the cluster identifier, as each cluster is indeed a visual word. It can also behave quite similarly to the vectorial variant of LSH when it processes the contents of the clusters [20]. eCP is also compatible with the best indexing solutions that are known today and that rely on some form of smart descriptor aggregation [12].

4. MAP-REDUCING eCP

In this section we present how can eCP be adapted to fit with the Map-Reduce paradigm. We first describe the index creation and then move to describing the search process.

4.1 Index Creation with Map-Reduce

The index creation process of eCP can be split into two main phases. During Phase #1, the creation of the index tree, cluster representatives are picked from the collection and organized in a in-memory tree. During Phase #2, vectors are assigned to clusters.

Obviously, Phase #2 is the prime candidate for parallelization and distribution. It is clear that chopping the entire data collection into independent parts assigned to physically distinct nodes is going to speed up the whole process.

In contrast, Phase #1 is computationally cheap and requires no distribution. Therefore, picking C random points and building the in-memory hierarchy is done on a single machine once ts, a and L have been set. The resulting hierarchy of representatives is then sent to the various nodes involved in the construction of the index. Each node will use this hierarchy to assign its subset of the data collection to clusters. Results will be consistent across nodes as the hierarchy is identically replicated everywhere.

Map tasks do the assignments. Each mapper loads the representative hierarchy and clusters the data by reading-assigning-emitting every descriptor in it's block of data. The key emitted is the identifier of the cluster the descriptor is assigned to.

Reduce tasks receive records grouped and sorted on their cluster identifier from the shuffle. All reducers do is to propagate to disk the data they receive to form the bottom level of the index, i.e., the clusters themselves. Note some bookeeping is needed to keep track of cardinalities, etc.

4.2 Search with Map-Reduce

The Map-Reduce abstraction is geared towards efficiently streaming multi-megabyte blocks of data to map tasks. Such behaviour is quite opposite to the one of an indexing system that rapidly returns the points from the collection that are the most similar to the query point. In this case, a very small percentage of the indexed data is read from disks, one or few clusters at most. This, in turn, optimizes the response times of each query. Other applications need throughput, where sacrificing individual query response time is acceptable so that multiple queries can be run simultaneously. Copyright infringement applications typically need throughput.

Being a batch processing framework, Map-Reduce is not designed for answering individual queries, but is well suited for processing massive batches of queries. A batch is typically in the range of 10^4–10^7 query descriptors extracted from the associated images. It is easy to reorder query descriptors in a batch according to the cluster identifiers into which each query points falls, clusters being subsequently used for searching for the k-nearest neighbors. Such scheme minimizes the disk I/Os: one cluster fetched in memory is read only once and used to answer all the query descriptors in the batch that match with this cluster.[1]

All mappers receive the whole query batch with query descriptors ordered by cluster identifiers, and start to process their blocks of data. All blocks are read, but their contents is processed only if points they contain belong to the clusters needed by at least one query descriptor from the batch. Batching consumes RAM at each mapper since they have to maintain several k-nn tables for all the query points con-

cerned with the current cluster under analysis. Tables can be deallocated when map tasks cross cluster boundaries, and a series of records are emitted. Special care must be taken when a single cluster spans more than one data block.

Overall, the cost for processing a batch is either entirely dominated by the cost of reading all data blocks, or dominated by the CPU for distance computations if the batch is really large or if there are very many points in each cluster.

5. CONTEXT OF THE EXPERIMENTS

The experiments were carried out on the Grid'5000 [14] testbed. The Grid'5000 project is a widely-distributed infrastructure devoted to providing an experimental platform for the research community. The platform is spread over ten geographical sites located through the French territory and one in Luxembourg. We could get access to the machines belonging to the Rennes site only.

5.1 Datasets, Queries and Ground-Truth

The dataset we used in our experiments has been created for the Quaero project.[2] One of the Quaero partners, Exalead, collected roughly 100 million images by harvesting the Web. To limit the size of data and to facilitate sharing among the partners in the Quaero project, images have been resized to only 150pixels on their largest side. SIFT descriptors were then extracted from these images, resulting in about 30 billion descriptors, i.e. 300 SIFT descriptors per image on average. To best of our knowledge, this image collection is one of the largest collections encountered in the content-based retrieval literature.

To evaluate the quality of indexing, we used that data collection as a distracting dataset into which we have drown the well studied INRIA Copydays evaluation set [10]. We resize Copydays images to the same size as our distractors and then use a copyright violation detection scenario, where we include 127 original images in our indexed database and use the associated 3055 generated variants (crop+scale, scale change+jpeg compression and manually generated strong distortions such as print-crumple-scan) as the queries. We then simply count how frequently the original images are returned as the top result. Many query images are visually such that only a very small number of SIFT descriptors can be extracted from their contents, e.g., 1% of the images have less than 8 descriptors. Finding the original images from their modified versions is therefore sometimes very challenging. Getting 100% accuracy is impossible as some image variants have zero SIFT descriptors (too dark e.g.).

5.2 Implementation Details

Several implementation details must be clarified to know how eCP works with Map-Reduce and Hadoop.

Preparing the dataset. The descriptors extracted from the image set are stored as binary files comprising records of 132 bytes; each record defines a descriptor and consists of a 4-byte integer for the image identifier followed by the 128 bytes of the actual descriptor. Overall, the 30 billion descriptors occupy just below 4 TeraBytes on disks. We first implemented a conversion mechanism creating *SequenceFiles* from binary data. A SequenceFile is a Hadoop-specific data

---

[1]Hadoop *reads only once all the data blocks*, so grouping query descriptors per cluster is compulsory in this work.

[2]Quaero is a research and innovation program adressing automatic processing of multimedia and multilingual content.

file employed for dealing with binary data. It consists of a header and one or multiple records. The header contains metadata that HDFS uses to parse the records. The records in a SequenceFile are fixed-sized and are defined as a single key-value pair. Several features (such as support for block compression and *sync markers* allowing to seek to the boundary of a record) make SequenceFiles an optimal choice for processing binary data with Hadoop. The descriptor conversion to SequenceFiles in HDFS creates records with the image identifier as the key, and the descriptor as the value.

Building the tree of representatives. We developed a Java implementation of the creation of the index tree containing cluster representatives. This tree of representatives is built outside Hadoop and serialized to a file subsequently used for clustering the data collection.

Creating the index: clustering. The clustering process assigning points to cluster representatives uses the index tree to efficiently discover the cluster each point belongs to. The Hadoop application consists of a map function that loads the tree of representatives and then reads the block of data it has to process. Each point from this block traverses the index tree until its closest cluster representative is known. Then the map task emits a *(cluster-id, point)* and loops. The reduce function simply outputs in SequenceFiles the records received from the mappers. It is key to realize the index tree is loaded by each map task at startup time. The tree will thus be loaded as many times as there are map tasks needed to complete an entire Hadoop job execution.

Searching batches of queries. A batch contains a very large number of query descriptors. Before being used to search the index, the query descriptors are reordered according to the identifier of the cluster each query points falls into. To do this, each query descriptor traverse the tree of representatives until it hits the bottom level, at which point the cluster identifier is known. To keep track of these identifiers for every query descriptor we build a lookup table. This table is created outside Hadoop and sent to every map task when a batch search is fired.

When spawned, mappers start by loading the lookup table.[3] A mapper then receives its block of data. It then finds in its block the records having any of the cluster identifiers existing in the lookup table. Only those records are subsequently used for distance calculation. It is possible that not all records of a block are used because (i) it is unlikely all query points of one batch will fall into distinct clusters, (ii) there are typically much more clusters than query points in a batch, (iii) a block typically contains several clusters. Mappers emit k-nn results.

6. PERFORMANCE RESULTS

After having presented the experimental setup, this section gives the performance results for running the index creation process on Hadoop. We then move to the performance of the batch search.

6.1 Experimental setup

We could have access to 129 nodes belonging to our local grid infrastructure. The nodes form three clusters, each composed of identical machines, as it is reported in Table 1.

---

[3]When a batch is very large, then this table consumes a lot of memory. Partial loading of the table is work in progress.

Cluster id	#Nodes	#CPU@Freq	#Cores /CPU	RAM	Local Disk
Cl_1	64	2 Intel@2.50GHz	4	32GB	138GB
Cl_2	25	2 Intel@2.93GHz	4	24GB	433GB
Cl_3	40	2 AMD@1.70GHz	12	48GB	232GB

Table 1: Cluster Configurations.

%age	#Imgs.	#Desc.	Data Size	C	L	Index Size
10%	10M	3.3×10^9	0.5TB	652K	4	193MB
20%	20M	7.8×10^9	1.0TB	1.5M	4	461MB
100%	100M	30.2×10^9	4TB	6M	5	1.8GB

Table 2: Index Configurations.

While each cluster has a highly connective internal network, inter-cluster bandwidth is limited. In practice, some of 129 nodes may be down at any given point of time. The Hadoop framework was deployed as follows: the namenode, jobtracker and the job client are each on a dedicated machine, while the other nodes serve as both datanodes and tasktrackers.

At the level of HDFS, we use the default replication factor of 3 for the input data. In addition to facilitating the tolerance of faults, data replication favors local execution of mappers and minimizes the number of remote map executions, this being key for performance. We however typically set the output replication factor to 1 only. A larger value adds a substantial overhead to the running time because one replica goes to a remote rack. That cost becomes significant given the size of our data set.

To facilitate the experiments as well as to get a better understanding of the scalability issues, we indexed images subsets containing roughly 10% and 20% of the entire collection in addition to indexing the full 100M images. Details on the resulting configurations are reported in the Table 2. In all cases, $a = 3$ when soft-assigning the representatives in the index tree; this does not apply to data in clusters, see Section 3.1. The value of ts is also the same when indexing each (sub-)set, it is set $ts = 5,000$. This gives clusters containing 5,000 points, occupying 645KB, on average. On the one hand this creates quite a lot of clusters, on the other hand, each is quick to analyze at searching time. ts and the number of descriptors in each set to index give C, and L is set such that the cost of traversing the tree of representatives stays roughly the same across the configurations.

6.2 Index Creation

This section reports the performance results for running the index creation process on Hadoop, while increasing the data set from 10M to 100M images. For these experiments, the chunk size at the level of HDFS was set to 128 MB, as recommended by Hadoop, when dealing with large data.

6.2.1 Exp. #1: 10M images, 3.3B Descs., 0.5TB

The first experiment indexes 10% of the image collection, i.e., about 10 million images, 3.3 billion descriptors, 0.5 Tera-Bytes of data. This corresponds to the first line of Table 2. With this setting, 3,478 map tasks are to run—this is determined by Hadoop from the number of data blocks needed to store the raw descriptor collection. For this experiment, we configured Hadoop such that each node run simultaneously up to 8 mappers and 2 reducers. We used 20 to 50 processing nodes belonging to the Cl_1 cluster.

For all execution rounds, we checked the logs created during runs and observed that most of the map tasks were executed locally (only 20-40 out of 3,478 map tasks read remote blocks of data); this is a consequence of having set the replication factor to 3 for the input data, enabling Hadoop to favor most of the time local task execution. Replication is important for performance. We observed a 10% increase of the response time when setting the replication factor to 1 for the input data.

We now turn to the time it takes to complete the creation of the index. The measurements are reported in Table 3. The second column of this table gives the average time it takes to create the index when varying the number of nodes. Of course, the more nodes, the faster each terminates. The third column shows the total work where the times for all nodes are summed up. Several comments are in order. First, having no increase is a sign of having a global system that scales. Second, it is rather surprising to observe the work decreases as the number of nodes increases. This is a direct consequence of some of the Hadoop architectural design decisions colliding with the specific characteristics of our application: (i) the total number of map tasks to run is determined from the data collection size divided by the size of a block (128MB here, resulting in running 3,478 map tasks); (ii) the total number of map tasks is totally independent from the number of nodes used to run the entire job; (iii) a new map task is spawned every time a new block of data is to process; (iv) at spawning time, a map task has to load whatever auxiliary information it needs to correctly process the data in its block (in our case, the tree of representatives, 193MB to load every 128MB of data to index!).

It thus results that every map task has to load the tree of representatives. Spawning a mapper thus includes a fixed overhead for reading the tree of representatives. This tree is loaded again and again, even by mappers running on the same node. Overall, a large fraction of the differences in running time can be explained by considering the number of loads of this tree that can happen in parallel. With 50 nodes, more parallelism is possible, thus the overhead is less prevalent and the work diminishes compared to 20 nodes. It is also likely this data gets better cached when used that frequently with 50 nodes.

Lesson #1. Performance are hurt when two conditions are met: (i) the data collection occupies *many* blocks, hence many map tasks have to be run, and (ii) each map task need to load *a lot of auxiliary information* at startup time. It is key to reduce as much as possible the overhead payed by each map task at spawning time. One possible option is to increase the size of the blocks of data to a value that is significantly larger than the ones recommended by Hadoop, typically 64MB or 128MB. Setting this to 512MB or few GB in turn reduces the number of map tasks to spawn and thus reduces in proportion the time wasted when each map task starts. Note, however, that big data blocks may cause some nodes to run out of disk space as the temp area buffering the data produced by mappers and consumed by reducers fills up faster when blocks are big. We kept using 128MB blocks for this reason. It is also useful to compress as much as possible that auxiliary information to reduce its load time and to generously replicate it across the system to avoid disks/network hot-spots.

#Nodes	Time(min)	Work(min)
20	149.3	2,986
30	95.7	2,871
40	61.8	2,472
50	45.2	2,260

Table 3: Indexing 10%, varying number of nodes.

6.2.2 *Exp. #2: 20M images, 7.8B Descs., 1.0TB*

The second experiment indexes 20% of the full set, that is 1TB of data, about 20 million images and 7.8 billion descriptors. This gives 8,178 map tasks to run. We extended the deployment setup and used 57 nodes from Cl_1, 15 from Cl_2 and 36 from Cl_3, for a total of 108 nodes. Here again, 3 nodes are dedicated to managing the system, leaving 105 tasktrackers nodes. The system is again set to using, per machine, at most 8 slots for mapping and 2 for reducing.

Aside the obvious differences in the hardware and the size of the data set used here, we must highlight a key difference this experiment has with respect to the previous one indexing 10% of the dataset. Here, the tree of representatives used to guide and do the assignment of points is much larger. It uses about 1.5M representatives. Not only this occupies a lot more RAM (461MB), but it takes longer for each mapper to load from disks that tree in memory and to create the data structure for subsequent assignments. It also means more distance calculations are needed to assign a descriptor as there are more representatives eventually guiding to a larger number of clusters. For these reasons, the overall work for clustering this dataset is significantly larger than it is in the case of the previous experiment.

Here, with 108 nodes, it takes 71 minutes to complete the indexing and the total work amounts to 7,455 minutes. This increased amount of work is also in part caused by the uneven distribution of the representatives in the tree, from one level to the other. Therefore, a large fraction of the data traverses rather dense branches of the tree of representatives, which, in turn, requires to do more distance calculations to find the closest representative guiding to the next lower level.

6.2.3 *Exp. #3: 100M images, 30.2B Descs., 4TB*

The third experiment indexes the full dataset using 108 nodes. With this configuration, the tree of representative is large as it uses more than 6 million data points to accommodate with the 30.2 billion descriptors to cluster. The tree occupies roughly 1.8GB in RAM.[4] This forced us to reduce the number of map tasks per machine to 4 only as otherwise not enough RAM was available for each mapper.

With this setting, it took about 10 hours to cluster the entire data set. A careful analysis of the logs shows that 99% of the reduce tasks where completed after 520 minutes, and the remaining 1% reduce tasks completed after 80 additional minutes. The reason behind this behavior is in part the uneven distribution of points to clusters.

But there is another explanation to this response time. Finely analyzing the data collection, we discovered that it contains hundred thousands of *identical* distracting images that turn out to come from a small set of explicit web sites having different URLs redirecting to a unique point. This

---

[4]Note 1.8GB of auxiliary info have to be loaded every 128MB of data to cluster! This encourages using significantly larger block sizes, see Lesson #1 above.

is unfortunate, but it is a good example of what happens in the real world when indexing images. It would have been possible to filter these images but this would have required a specific ad hoc process we will integrate in the future. The direct impact of so much duplicates is that there is a small set of clusters into which the descriptors of these images accumulate, creating very large, unbreakable clusters, and writing them to disks takes a lot of time.

Lesson #2. Hadoop's map tasks are completely independent and each require to load the tree of representatives. When this auxiliary information is large, then each map task consumes a significant portion of the RAM available on a node. In turn, it means map tasks are unable to run inside every available core in a node, because there is not enough RAM. It is unfortunate to waste some of the processing power leaving cores idle because there is no way to share data, even *read-only data* (as is the tree of representatives) between map tasks running on the same node. This observation suggests for application programmers to implement multi-threaded map tasks. This is way more complicated to program but it is one option for using all the processing power of nodes while circumventing Hadoop's inflexible architecture. With multi-threaded map tasks, a single task would load the auxiliary data only once and then would process its block of data faster thanks to its multiple threads running on multiple cores. In the case of this experiment with the full data set, one single map task could then use up to 6 threads processing data in parallel on Cl_3, overall keeping the 24 cores constantly busy, instead of using only 4 cores now.

6.3 Batch searching

This section reports the performance results obtained when searching the full data collection with batches of query images. The images in the batch are the 3,055 variants from the Copydays evaluation set. The results are expressed both in terms of response time and search quality. Response time wise, we record the time it takes to complete the query batch using the 110 nodes, almost as in Exp. #2 and #3. Quality wise, we search for the 20 nearest neighbors of each query point computed from the query images. There are just below 1M query points in the batch. Each nearest neighbor votes for the image from the indexed collection it belongs to, and the votes are aggregated to eventually return the identifiers of the most similar images. We have a rather strict success criterion for searching: the search succeeds if and only if the original image identified from its query quasi copy has rank 1; the search fails otherwise. The percentages given when discussing quality thus correspond to counting the number of times original images are ranked first.

The lookup table built from the descriptors in a batch (see Section 5.2) is stored as an HDFS file read by all search mappers when they are spawned. It takes about 3 minutes to build this lookup table on a single core outside Hadoop. The lookup table file is replicated three times to reduce contention when mappers access it. The block size for the indexed data is 128MB, with hence 33,483 mappers to run. To avoid remote reads, we replicated the indexed data in HDFS using a replication factor set to two.

6.3.1 Exp. #4: Time and Quality, 100M images

Searching the entire batch took 1,623 sec. on average, or just over 27 minutes. This gives an average processing

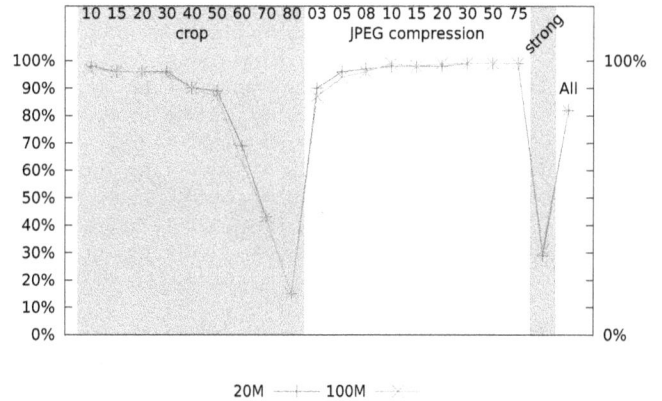

Figure 1: Search Quality, Copydays evaluation set

time per image of under 530ms. Figure 1 shows the quality results of the search. This figure plots for every family of variants the percentage of original images found at rank 1. It also plot the average percentage across all variants at the far right end of the Figure. Note for comparison we also measured the quality when indexing 20% of the data collection (see Exp.#2). From the Figure, it is clear that eCP returns high quality results, except for some severely attacked images such as when 80% of the image is cropped and then it is rescaled to its original size, or when strong manual variants are applied. Note, we count as search failures the cases when no descriptor can be computed on the query images (this happens for 6 variants). It is interesting to observe search quality does not significantly degrades when the size of the distracting dataset increases. Overall, 82.68% of Copydays variants are found when drowning them in 20M images, and we find 82.16% of them when drown in 100M images. This is a clear assessment that eCP is a very viable indexing technique.

6.3.2 Discussion

Aside the experiment described above, we have done many other performance evaluations varying several parameters. We briefly report the key results we found.

Lesson #3. Most of the mappers read the data locally, only about 1% of remote reads were observed. This is again the case for setting the replication factor to a value above 1. We have not seen any major performance improvement for any value > 2. In contrast, maintaining a single copy of the indexed data causes roughly 8 to 10% remote reads, hurting performance. Rack awareness and replication are good for performance, and not only for coping with failures. Note, we experienced several nodes failures and happily observed that Hadoop re-ran tasks, eventually completing the runs.

Lesson #4. We have re-blocked the indexed data before running the search to see the impact of using larger blocks, as suggested earlier. When setting the block size to 512MB, we observed a dramatic response time improvement when using batches containing roughly 12,000 images (roughly 3.7M descriptors). Times decrease down to roughly 1,500 seconds (instead of 3,500 when blocks are 128MB), simply because there are only 8,808 mappers loading the lookup table (its size is roughly 1GB) instead of more than 33,000. This is really making a case for using larger blocks.

Lesson #5. Hadoop is architectured such that all the blocks of data are read. Therefore, search runs are totally dominated by I/Os until the batch has enough points to keep the CPU extremely busy doing distance calculations. Using the 20% index configuration and 512MB blocks, we have ran batches containing only one query image (312 query descriptors), and this takes 323 seconds while the Copydays batch (1M query descriptors)runs in 388 seconds. The difference is quite small (15%), especially because it includes an I/O bounded step (loading the batch) in addition to the extra CPU work, likely almost entirely hidden by the I/Os.

Observation #6. We also used this index configuration to check the impact of using a varying number of nodes on the time it takes to run the Copydays batch. With 30 nodes, it takes about 1,048 seconds, 744 seconds for 40 nodes and 388 seconds with the 100 nodes. The total work is stable when using 30 and 40 nodes (respectively 31,440s and 29,760s) but jumps to 38,800s when using all the nodes. Part of the extra cost comes from the fix time it takes to launch Hadoop, it is always about 20 to 40 seconds, which becomes a significant part of a running time that is around 400 seconds.

7. CONCLUSIONS

This paper presents a Map-Reduced based implementation of an high-dimensional indexing algorithm that uses clustering to build small groups of data, subsequently searched. The performance of this algorithm have been demonstrated in terms of speed gains when using more hardware. It has also been demonstrated in terms of quality as we show it correctly identifies about 82% of the images from a state-of-the-art evaluation set drown in 100M distracting images. Several lessons can be drawn from this work such as the case for using data blocks of a size larger than the one Hadoop is recommending, or the case for implementing multi-threaded map tasks to fully use the processing power of cores while avoiding RAM issues.

Overall, Hadoop is helpful for achieving scalability. Properly setting its parameters is not trivial, however, as described in the paper. We observed that very often, running an experiment that creates and/or searches an index is not what consumes the largest amount of time. It is rather copying the data to HDFS before being ready to launch experiments, or getting out the indexed data from the grid for being used elsewhere. Feeding a grid/cloud with all the required data through limited bandwidth is a very practical problem.

This work was partly achieved as part of the Quaero Project, funded by OSEO, French State agency for innovation.

8. REFERENCES

[1] M. Batko, F. Falchi, C. Lucchese, D. Novak, R. Perego, F. Rabitti, J. Sedmidubský, and P. Zezula. Building a web-scale image similarity search system. *Multimedia Tools Appl.*, 47(3), 2010.

[2] F. Chierichetti, A. Panconesi, P. Raghavan, M. Sozio, A. Tiberi, and E. Upfal. Finding near neighbors through cluster pruning. In *PODS*, 2007.

[3] M. Datar, N. Immorlica, P. Indyk, and V. S. Mirrokni. Locality-sensitive hashing scheme based on p-stable distributions. In *SCG*, 2004.

[4] J. Dean and S. Ghemawat. Mapreduce: simplified data processing on large clusters. *Commun. ACM*, 51(1), 2008.

[5] M. Douze, H. Jégou, H. Singh, L. Amsaleg, and C. Schmid. Evaluation of gist descriptors for web-scale image search. In *CIVR*, 2009.

[6] S. Ghemawat, H. Gobioff, and S.-T. Leung. The google file system. In *SOSP*, 2003.

[7] A. Gionis, P. Indyk, and R. Motwani. Similarity search in high dimensions via hashing. In *VLDB*, 1999.

[8] G. Gudmundsson, B. T. Jónsson, and L. Amsaleg. A large-scale performance study of cluster-based high-dimensional indexing. In *VLS-MCMR Workshop with ACM MM*, 2010.

[9] J. S. Hare, S. Samangooei, D. P. Dupplaw, and P. H. Lewis. Imageterrier: an extensible platform for scalable high-performance image retrieval. In *ICMR*, 2012.

[10] H. Jégou, M. Douze, and C. Schmid. Hamming embedding and weak geometric consistency for large scale image search. In *ECCV*, 2008.

[11] H. Jégou, M. Douze, and C. Schmid. Product quantization for nearest neighbor search. *IEEE Trans. on PAMI*, 2011.

[12] H. Jégou, F. Perronnin, M. Douze, J. Sánchez, P. Pérez, and C. Schmid. Aggregating local image descriptors into compact codes. *IEEE Trans. on PAMI*, 2011.

[13] H. Jégou, R. Tavenard, M. Douze, and L. Amsaleg. Searching in one billion vectors: Re-rank with source coding. In *ICASSP*, 2011.

[14] Y. Jégou, S. Lantéri, J. Leduc, and all. Grid'5000: a large scale and highly reconfigurable experimental Grid testbed. *Intl. Journal of HPC Applications*, 20(4), 2006.

[15] A. Joly and O. Buisson. A posteriori multi-probe locality sensitive hashing. In *MM*, 2008.

[16] H. Lejsek, F. H. Amundsson, B. T. Jónsson, and L. Amsaleg. NV-Tree: An efficient disk-based index for approximate search in very large high-dimensional collections. *IEEE Trans. on PAMI*, 2009.

[17] H. Lejsek, B. T. Jónsson, and L. Amsaleg. NV-Tree: nearest neighbors at the billion scale. In *ICMR*, 2011.

[18] D. Lowe. Distinctive image features from scale invariant keypoints. *IJCV*, 60(2), 2004.

[19] Q. Lv, W. Josephson, Z. Wang, M. Charikar, and K. Li. Multi-probe lsh: efficient indexing for high-dimensional similarity search. In *VLDB*, 2007.

[20] L. Paulevé, H. Jégou, and L. Amsaleg. Locality sensitive hashing: A comparison of hash function types and querying mechanisms. *Pattern Recognition Letters*, 2010.

[21] J. Philbin, O. Chum, M. Isard, J. Sivic, and A. Zisserman. Lost in quantization: Improving particular object retrieval in large scale image databases. In *CVPR*, 2008.

[22] K. Shvachko, H. Kuang, S. Radia, and R. Chansler. The hadoop distributed file system. In *MSST*, 2010.

[23] J. Sivic and A. Zisserman. Video google: A text retrieval approach to object matching in videos. In *ICCV*, 2003.

Feature Propagation on Image Webs for Enhanced Image Retrieval

Eric Brachmann
TU Dresden
01062 Dresden, Germany
eric.brachmann@tu-dresden.de

Marcel Spehr
TU Dresden
01062 Dresden, Germany
marcel.spehr@tu-dresden.de

Stefan Gumhold
TU Dresden
01062 Dresden, Germany
stefan.gumhold@tu-dresden.de

ABSTRACT

The bag-of-features model is often deployed in content-based image retrieval to measure image similarity. In cases where the visual appearance of semantically similar images differs largely, feature histograms mismatch and the model fails. We increase the robustness of feature histograms by automatically augmenting them with features of related images. We establish image relations by image web construction and adapt a label propagation scheme from the domain of semi-supervised learning for feature augmentation. While the benefit of feature augmentation has been shown before, our approach refrains from the use of semantic labels. Instead we show how to increase the performance of the bag-of-features model substantially on a completely unlabeled image corpus.

Categories and Subject Descriptors

H.3.1 [**Information Storage and Retrieval**]: Content Analysis and Indexing; I.4.6 [**Image Processing and Computer Vision**]: Segmentation

Keywords

content-based image retrieval; bag-of-features; image similarity; image webs; co-segmentation

1. INTRODUCTION

Measuring similarity between images is an essential part in many image processing applications. I.e. CBIR usually aims for retrieving images semantically similar to a specific query image. If no textual information is supplied one has to compute a visual similarity based on global or local image features.

This work focuses on the improvement of local image features. They are created by finding characteristic local patterns in images and describing them with (usually high-dimensional) feature vectors. The popular *bag-of-features* (BOF) [13] approach quantizes those vectors using a set of prototypical local patterns (also called *visual words*) and counting them in histograms. Two images are compared by measuring the intersection of their histograms. The more similar features they have in common, the more similar they are.

A common issue in feature based approaches for measuring image similarity are changes in acquisition conditions. The feature sets of images depicting identical objects vary under viewpoint changes until they stop to overlap. As the perspective shifts, features disappear and new features emerge. The robustness of common interest point descriptors can only partially compensate for this effect. The BOF similarity decreases until the model eventually fails even though the depicted object remains the same. Figure 1 illustrates the effect schematically.

We propose to overcome this issue by propagating features over a network of images. The method described in [4] can be used to construct image graphs of large, unstructured image collections. The construction itself is solely based on visual characteristics. No semantic knowledge is involved. Edges between images are established using *affine co-segmentation*. This web is used to propagate visual words among connected images using an adapted version of the method specified in [1].

Our results reveal that the transitive exchange of visual characteristics reduces the visual gap, caused by changing acquisition conditions. We benchmark our method on standard data sets, and show that through the additional robustness of BOF image signatures, retrieval performance in image search applications is substantially increased.

2. RELATED WORK

Sivic and Zisserman [13] introduced the bag-of-features image search in analogy to the bag-of-words search for text documents. Dictionaries of visual words are found by clustering feature descriptors of large, generic image collections. Thereupon, feature descriptors of arbitrary images can be assigned to the pre-calculated clusters which become visual words. Each image is represented by a histogram of visual words, a so called BOF. Feature locations and geometries are completely discarded. Entries of a visual word histogram $\mathbf{x}$ are weighted according to the *tf-idf* schema. Visual words that appear often in an image but are rare throughout the image collection receive a large weight. Similarity of two images is measured by the dot product $\mathbf{x_1} \cdot \mathbf{x_2}$ of their weighted visual word histograms. An inverted file structure facilitates fast image retrieval in very large image collections.

Since its initial proposal, many extensions of BOF search

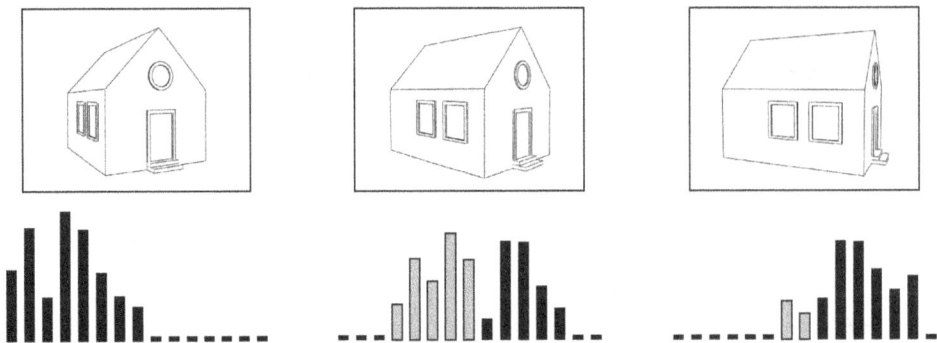

Figure 1: Illustration of BOF failure. Three images of the same object are depicted along with their visual word histograms. The viewpoint changes increasingly from left to right. The first and second histogram still overlap to large extents, marked in gray. However, the appearance of the object has changed too much in the third image. The overlap is minimal, and the similarity measure fails. Transitive feature exchange can prevent the failure.

systems have been published. With the resulting performance boost, BOF search systems still produce state of the art results on many image retrieval data sets[5]. Query expansion [3] takes the top retrieval results for an image, and re-runs the search by treating them as new queries. The approach is motivated by the observation that the top results are often relevant to the search query. The expanded query set is regarded as an enriched query representation. The retrieval results of all queries are combined, and ranked by similarity. By performing multiple searches for each query, query expansion multiplies retrieval times.

Spatial re-ranking[12] adds a verification step to BOF retrieval. It checks whether locations of matching features between the query and each top retrieval result are consistent by searching affine transformations between feature sets. Due to its computational cost, spatial re-ranking can only be applied to a small set of top retrieval results. Even so, it impairs the online response time of a retrieval system. We use the same approach of spatial verification to establish reliable image connections during image web construction. But in our case, it is done in a pre-processing step, that does not influence online query times.

Jegou et al.[5] present a complete state of the art BOF retrieval configuration. They augment BOF image signatures with binary strings that prevent wrong visual word matches even with coarse visual dictionaries. Instead of expensive spatial re-ranking after retrieval, they exploit weak geometric consistency (WGC). Simplified geometric information is embedded directly into the inverted file. It penalizes images during retrieval where matching features are inconsistent in terms of characteristic scale and dominant orientation compared to the query. A multiple assignment strategy prevents missing valid matches of similar features due to assignment to different visual words. The modifications of Jegou et al. require an adapted version of the inverted file structure with increased memory demand. Although cheaper than full spatial re-ranking, WGC constrains slow down retrieval. We adopt WGC constraints but instead of penalizing inconsistent images during retrieval, we use WGC checks during image web construction to further increase correctness probability when establishing image relations. The result of our approach is a set of enriched image signatures that may be used in any classical BOF retrieval system. The structure

of the inverted file itself is not altered. In our experiments, we show that the size of the inverted file can be reduced by feature propagation. If desired, all above-mentioned modifications to BOF searches can be deployed along with our proposal.

Our approach is inspired by recent findings in [6]. The authors create visual and textual clusters of an image collection. The visual clustering is based on BOF similarity. The textual clustering is based on text labels. The text clusters thus represent (noisy) semantic information. The authors form extended visual clusters by combining the visual clusters with the textual clusters. Then, they distribute visual words in this extended visual cluster. This way, visual characteristics are exchanged between images that are semantically related. This benefits the retrieval performance.

We adopt the idea of [6], but go without any text labels or other semantic information. We deploy highly structured image relations in the form of image webs. In the following, we first describe our approach, state our experimental setup, and finally report the results we obtained after feature propagation.

3. IMAGE WEBS

Before we propagate features within an image collection, we discover its inherent image relations. A relation exists when two images display a common object. We largely follow the approach of Heath et al.[4] to construct highly interconnected image graphs that they coined image webs. Edge additions proceed in an order that leads to a fast rise in algebraic connectivity. This measure corresponds to the ability of a graph to distribute information. Hence, image webs are well suited for our purpose. Below, we summarize the image web construction briefly.

Heath et al. use affine co-segmentation to decide whether an edge exists between two images. Affine-invariant feature detectors locate salient image regions. Features are matched via their SIFT descriptors and reliable matches are selected using Lowe's ratio criterion[7]. A RANSAC-based, iterative process extracts subsets of matches that are related by an affine transformation between images. The union of feature subsets per image serves as a segmentation of the co-occurring image area. Heath et al. used these areas for visualization. We, however, are only interested in the fact whether at least one co-occurring area was found or not, and insert edges accordingly.

We extended the affine co-segmentation process in two aspects. Heath et al. used Harris affine[9], Hessian affine[9] and MSER[8] detectors to locate salient regions. We additionally included the ASIFT[14] detector for its robustness to viewpoint change. More affine co-segmentations succeed when it is included. ASIFTs large computation time and space requirements may pose a problem. We dealt with this issue by reducing image resolution for this detector.

Our second modification is an additional verification step for sets of co-segmented features. During our experiments, we observed a significant amount of wrong image associations, especially when the images showed repetitive patterns like nets, fences or texts. With such images, descriptor matches become arbitrary and chances are that some random subset adheres to an affine transformation. We accommodated for this by adapting the concept of weak geometric consistency (WGC)[5] constrains. For each matching feature pair found by affine co-segmentation we calculate the difference in characteristic scale and dominant orientation, respectively. Because these feature characteristics are computed in normalized local image frames the differences should be similar for corresponding sets of feature pairs, and diverse otherwise. WGC constraints were used by Jegou et al.[5] to re-rank retrieval results in BOF image searches. We deploy WGC to verify the validity of co-segmented feature pairs. We compute the variances of scale and orientation differences, $\sigma^2_{\Delta s}$ and $\sigma^2_{\Delta \alpha}$, of each co-segmented region. If the variances are larger than pre-determined thresholds, we deem the region inconsistent, and discard it.

This validation approach does not work with ASIFT features. Instead of affine normalization, it deploys affine simulations and calculates features in transformed image space. When sets of feature matches bridge different affine simulations, scale and orientation differences are inconsistent, even if the match is correct. Instead of excluding ASIFT from the WGC checks we calculate $\sigma^2_{\Delta s}$ and $\sigma^2_{\Delta \alpha}$ over the union of all detectors. Although ASIFT adds some distortion to these values, we are still able to define reliable thresholds to tell consistent and inconsistent feature match sets apart.

With these adaptions to the affine co-segmentation process we proceed with image web construction in two phases as Heath et al.[4] suggest: sparse web construction and densification. In the first phase, clusters of connected images are determined. A truncated BOF similarity ranking of image pairs of the corpus is formed. Affine co-segmentations are attempted in that order and edges are inserted where they succeed. No affine co-segmentation is performed for image pairs that already belong to the same connected component. This leads to a fast growth of sparsely connected image clusters. The first phase ends when the rate of successful co-segmentations drops below a threshold.

In the second phase, each cluster is augmented with edges that lead to a large increase in algebraic connectivity. Therefore, all remaining edges are ranked according to the absolute difference in the entries of the Fiedler vector associated with those images the edge would connect. The Fiedler vector is the Eigenvector corresponding to the second smallest Eigenvalue of a graphs Laplacian matrix. This Eigenvalue equals the algebraic connectivity. Affine co-segmentations proceed in the order of the new ranking until the algebraic

connectivity of the current cluster converges. The image web construction is complete when all clusters were densified.

4. FEATURE PROPAGATION

We base our approach on *label propagation on similarity graphs* as presented in [1]. The authors discuss typical scenarios of semi-supervised learning where one has labeled and unlabeled data points. The goal is to spread known labels within a graph that covers the complete data set. This way, unlabeled samples receive existing labels from other samples.

The problem is broken down to one of class assignment. There are two classes: 1 and -1. The class affiliation is known for some samples, and unknown for others. In the latter case, the samples receive a class value of 0. This information is subsumed in a label vector $\hat{Y}$, that contains the initial class value for every node in the similarity graph. The similarity graph itself is represented by an affinity matrix W. The entries $W_{ij} \geq 0$ state whether the nodes i and j are related. The simplest variant is to set $W_{ij} = 1$ between connected nodes, and $W_{ij} = 0$ otherwise.

Once $\hat{Y}$ and W have been constructed, an iterative algorithm starts. In essence, the positive and negative class values of labeled samples influence the class values of unlabeled samples dependent on the local neighbourhood in the similarity graph. The procedure stops when the label vector $\hat{Y}$ converges. Finally, all samples whose entries in the label vector are negative receive class -1, and all samples whose entries are positive receive class 1. The authors of [1] describe two different algorithms: One where the classes of the labeled samples are fixed (they are reset after each iteration), and one where the classes of labeled samples may change during the procedure.

We regard every image cluster of an image web separately. In the following, we refer to these image clusters as image graphs. Every node in the graph is an image, the edges were established by affine co-segmentation. We construct the affinity matrix W dependent on a parameter k. The entry W_{ij} is 1 if the nodes i and j are connected by a path of length $k + 1$ in the image graph, i.e. for $k = 0$, only direct neighbours are related in the affinity matrix W. I.e. k regulates the size of the local neighbourhood of an image. The diagonal entries $W_{ii} = 0$.

We regard each visual word as a separate label. The assignment of class values $\in \{-1, 0, 1\}$ is problematic. We only have the information whether a visual word appears in an image, or not. We cannot distinguish between labeled and unlabeled samples. If a visual word does not appear, we do not know whether it must not appear (class -1), or whether its appearance is unknown (class 0).

However, it is unreasonable to assign class values of 1 for visual word appearance, and class values of 0 for visual word absence. In that case, features would be distributed throughout the image graph until they reach all nodes. Negative class values are essential. Therefore, we set the class value to the appearance count $c \geq 1$ if a visual word appears in an image, and -1 otherwise. This way, we construct the label vector $\hat{Y}$ for all images of the image graph. We use the appearance count c instead of the class value 1 to increase the weight of visual words that appear multiple times in an image. Note that this variant does not involve unlabeled samples (class 0). Because of that, we cannot deploy the algorithm of [1] where the class assignments of labeled samples (classes -1 and 1) are fixed. Nothing would happen in our case. We use the variant, that allows initial classes to change.

Input for feature propagation are the affinity matrix W, the initial label vector $\hat{Y}^{(0)}$ depending on the current visual word, and a parameter $\alpha \in (0,1)$ that determines tendency of an image to keep its original signature. The smaller α the more difficult it is for the original signatures to change. Following [1], we construct a diagonal degree matrix D with

$$D_{ii} = \sum_j W_{ij}, \qquad (1)$$

the sum of the rows of W. We also construct a diagonal matrix A,

$$A = \frac{\alpha}{1-\alpha}\left(D + \epsilon I\right) + I, \qquad (2)$$

where I is the identity matrix and ϵ is a small term for numerical stability. Note that our equation for A is slightly simplified compared to the definition in [1] because all our samples are labeled. We proceed with the propagation as follows:

$$\hat{Y}^{(t+1)} = A^{-1}\left(\frac{\alpha}{1-\alpha}\,W\hat{Y}^{(t)} + \hat{Y}^{(0)}\right). \qquad (3)$$

After the iteration converged, we assign the current visual word to all images i, where $\hat{Y}_i > 0$ with the appearance count $c = \lceil \hat{Y}_i \rceil$.

We repeat the whole process for every visual word in the dictionary. The set of new features for an image arises from all features with appearance counts $c > 0$ after propagation. Note, that originally existing features might disappear from an image if negative weights prevail in its local graph neighbourhood. As a result, it is possible that images end up without any features after propagation. We treat them like singular images outside the image web, and use their original signatures during retrieval.

We tested two different variants of incorporating the propagation results:

1. In the *default* variant, we substitute the original feature set of an image with the feature set after propagation.

2. In the *augmented* variant, we use the original feature set per image, and augment it with those features that were added during the propagation. I.e. the new signature is formed by the union of the original feature set with the feature set after propagation.

In an additional variant, we collected all visual words that disappeared from the image web during propagation. We speculated that these visual words, due to their irregular appearance, might be associated with clutter, and, therefore, harm retrieval. We erased them from the visual word dictionary and performed image search with the resulting filtered dictionary. The retrieval performance was clearly inferior to the baseline. Rigid exclusion of these visual words was harmful. We will not consider this approach any further.

5. EVALUATION

5.1 Datasets

We tested our approach on two data sets: INRIA holidays[5] and Oxford buildings[12].

Oxford buildings contains 5063 photos of several prominent buildings of Oxford along with some clutter images. Since certain objects are covered by many photos and some photos depict multiple objects, this data set is especially suited for image web construction. Because of its size, it represents a realistic application scenario. For each image, the authors provide pre-calculated features and pre-assigned visual words. Groundtruth consists of 55 queries with associated relevant images. The relevant images are divided into two groups, "good" and "ok", depending on how much of the query object is visible. We do not differentiate between these two groups. An additional group "junk" consists of images that we ignore during evaluation as suggested in [12]. The data set refines queries with regions of interest which we do not use.

INRIA holidays contains 1491 personal holiday photos covering diverse natural scenes and man made environments. The structure of this data set differs considerably from Oxford buildings. It includes much more diverse, discontiguous scenes. Since only very few images belong together, it is much less suited for image web construction. Groundtruth is given in the form of 500 disjoint groups of related images. Each group contains only a small number of images, 3 on average. The first image of each group serves as query, and the remaining images are relevant retrieval results. Similar to the Oxford data set, the authors provide pre-calculated features for each image, but no pre-assigned visual words. Instead, they provide generic visual dictionaries ranging from 100 to $200k$ visual words. We assign visual words using FLANN[11] and the $200k$ dictionary. Furthermore, pre-calculated features of 1M random Flickr images are available on the INRIA holidays website. We use them to assemble distractor image signatures to test the robustness of our BOF implementation.

5.2 BOF Baseline

We implemented a basic BOF image search following the description of Sivic and Zisserman[13]. As has been suggested before[5], we deploy an adjusted *tf-idf* weighting. The original *term frequency* (*tf*) weight corresponds to a L_1 normalization of feature histograms. In our experiments, we achieved slightly better results with the L_2 norm. Similar to many retrieval scenarios we assess performance in terms of mean average precision (*mAP*). For computation of mAP, we adapted code published together with Oxford buildings. We use our implementation of the basic BOF image search to calculate baseline performance values on both data sets.

5.3 Web Construction

We used affine co-segmentation with the following parameters: We deploy the software of Mikolajczyk[10] to extract Hessian-Affine, Harris-Affine and MSER features. The ASIFT demo code[14] adds ASIFT features. In the case of ASIFT, we rescaled images by a factor of 0.4 to decrease the computational load. We perform feature matching with FLANN[11] and use Lowe's ratio criterion[7] with $r = 0.7$ for match filtering. The RANSAC implementation of OpenCV[2] determines feature sets related by affine trans-

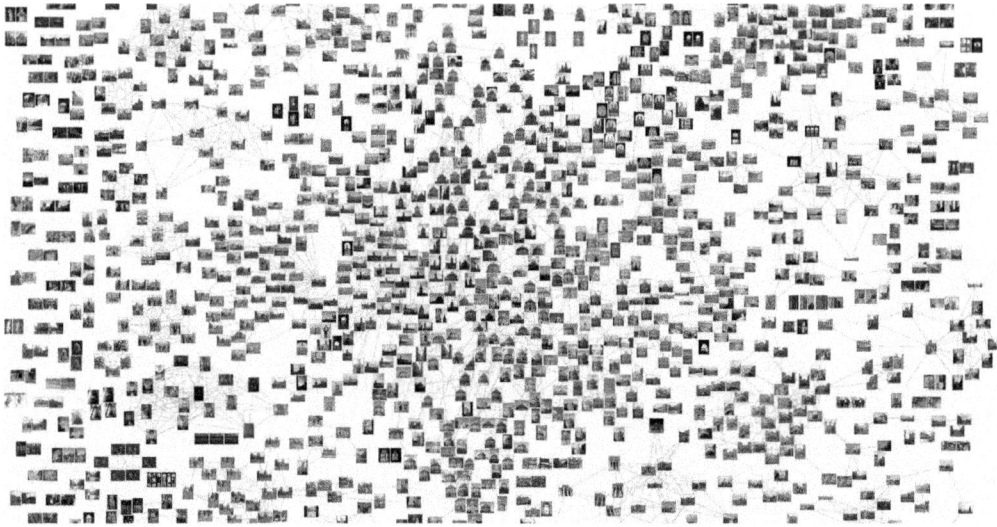

Figure 2: Part of the dense Oxford buildings image web. The largest cluster is clearly visible at the center. Smaller clusters are located towards the left and right margins.

formations with a reprojection error of 5 pixels. We accept feature sets if they consist of at least 20 features in both images.

For WGC checks after affine co-segmentation we allowed a maximal variance $\sigma^2_{\Delta_\alpha}$ of 1.0 for orientation differences, and a maximal variance $\sigma^2_{\Delta_s}$ of 0.1 for scale differences. We defined these thresholds after manually examining cases where affine co-segmentation yielded wrong results. We found that the variance of orientation differences is much more expressive than the variance of scale differences.

We tested our configuration of affine co-segmentation by manually validating its outcome on approximately 1300 image pairs of Oxford buildings. Only 13 of them were flawed.

Based on affine co-segmentation we constructed dense image webs of Oxford buildings and INRIA holidays. We stopped the initial sparse web construction when less than 20 co-segmentations were successful per 1000 image pairs processed. We stopped densification when the algebraic connectivity improved less than 5% of its initial rise. We found that a reasonable stopping criterion for densification is imperative. If all possible image connections are established, local image neighbourhoods become too big and generic for feature propagation. This results in decreased retrieval performance.

The Oxford buildings web consists of 363 distinct image clusters dominated by one large cluster with 547 images. The second largest cluster counts 100 images, and most of the cluster consist of 5 images or less. Altogether, ca 40% of the images appear in the image web. For all other images co-segmentation found no reliable partner. Reasons include the depiction of singular object, large changes in acquisition conditions, or image clutter. Figure 2 shows a part of the Oxford buildings web. The INRIA holidays web consists of 328 clusters with ca 50% of all images. All clusters are small with 2 to 10 images. Figure 3 shows one cluster of the INRIA holidays web in detail.

5.4 Propagation

Based on the image webs, we propagate features according to Section 4. Propagation depends on two parameters:

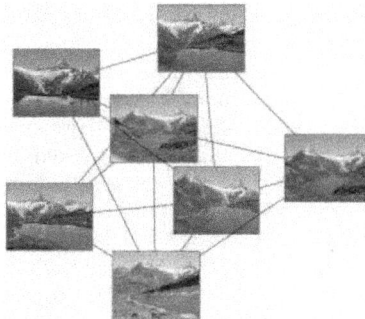

Figure 3: One image cluster of the INRIA holidays image web.

α that determines the weight of the initial image signature. With a large α images tend to attract more features from their neighbourhood. The parameter k determines the size of the local image neighbourhood. During our preliminary experiments, we observed a value of $k = 1$ to be advantageous and fixed it for the experiments reported below. I.e., the local neighbourhood of an image consists of all images connected with a path of length 2. For α, we used values of 0.1, 0.5 and 0.9 to test strong, moderate and weak influence of the initial image signature.

For images that do not appear in the image web, we keep the original signature. This also applies to images that end up without any features after *default* propagation. We compare mAP after propagation with the baseline values of the basic BOF search implementation. For the queries, we always use the original, unaltered image signatures when calculating the mAP.

We do not use distractor images during image web construction and feature propagation. We add distractor signatures afterwards to test the robustness of the feature propagation impact on retrieval performance.

5.5 Results

Table 1 subsumes our evaluation results on INRIA holidays used in conjunction with a dictionary of 200k visual words. With a basic BOF implementation we achieve a baseline mAP of 0.554 without distractor images. This is comparable to the baseline value reported in [5]. The results clearly show the benefit of feature propagation. *Default* feature propagation with $\alpha = 0.5$ results in a mAP of 0.594, i.e. an improvement of 7.1% over the baseline value. No propagation variant harms retrieval. We observe the benefit of a large α although there is no further improvement beyond $\alpha = 0.5$.

The impact of distractor images is straight forward. With more distractors added to the image collection, chances increase that they are confused with relevant images. MAPs are dropping for the baseline BOF search as well as for all propagation variants. However, the performance decrease is much smaller after feature propagation, see Figure 4. With 100,000 distractors the relative improvement over the basic BOF search rises to 30%. Image signatures clearly became more robust. Note that we used unaltered query signatures. Hence, mutual adaptions of queries and database images through feature propagation are ruled out.

For the most part, we can reproduce our observations for Oxford buildings. The baseline mAP is much smaller with 0.320. The data set contains more images of homogeneous objects, so there is more room for confusion. Furthermore, the homogeneous images exploit the expressiveness of the generic INRIA 200k dictionary only to some extent. Although performance is lower for Oxford buildings on absolute terms, the relative improvement through feature propagation is higher than for INRIA holidays. The best results are again achieved with *default* propagation and $\alpha = 0.5$. Without distractors, we boost the mAP to 0.409, an improvement of 27.7%. The improvment is stable in regard to distractors, see Figure 5. With 100,000 distractor images our best result is a mAP of 0.360 compared to the baseline of 0.223, a significant improvement of 60%.

We also performed feature propagation on the pre-assigned visual words of Oxford buildings. They are based on a much larger dictionary of 1M words that was furthermore learned on Oxford buildings itself. Naturally, it is much more expressive for this data set. We observe a high baseline mAP of 0.545. Here, we noticed dropping retrieval performance through feature propagation, see Table 3. With *default* propagation mAP drops by 9.3% for $\alpha = 0.5$, and by 3.3% for $\alpha = 0.9$. We attribute this to the sparseness of visual words with the 1M dictionary. Sparse visual words are more likely to vanish through *default* propagation. This can happen to an extent where the expressiveness of image signatures suffers. *Augmented* propagation prevents such effects. Indeed, with $\alpha = 0.5$ we achieve a mAP of 0.571, an improvement of 4.8%. We were not able to test the robustness with distractor signatures here, because the 1M word dictionary was not published.

5.6 Performance

The construction time of the web is dominated by the feature matching during affine co-segmentation. It took a few seconds each time on a single core (2.20 GHz). The sparse web construction has a complexity of $O(n)$ where n is the number of image pairs considered. We stopped after the rate of successful co-segmentations dropped below

a threshold. Densification time depends on cluster size. In the worst case, all possible edges considered between images of an cluster are valid edges. Then, one potential edge is removed per iteration and all remaining potential edges have to be re-ranked. This results in a complexity of $O(p^2)$ for one cluster, where the number of potential edges $p = n \times k$ with n being the number of images in the cluster, and k being the number of most similar images considered to form image pairings. We used $k = 25$. For the larger Oxford buildings data set, image web construction took about a day on a single workstation.

The complexity of one propagation iteration is $O(n^2)$ in the number of images within the graph. The number of iterations depends on the convergence behavior of the label vectors, i.e. on the structure of the data set. The size of the dictionary determines the number of propagations that need to be performed. In our experiments, propagation times ranged from several minutes for INRIA holidays to several hours for Oxford buildings, again on a single workstation.

Our implementation does not exploit the various possibilities for parallelization at the later stages of feature propagation on image webs. Densification is independent for each cluster. Same goes for propagation for each visual word. Both processes can run in parallel, respectively. This does not apply for sparse web construction, and densification within one cluster because each co-segmentation does affect the list of subsequent co-segmentations.

Feature propagation has an effect on the amount of data a CBIR system has to manage. With *default* propagation, features from neighbouring images may be added to signatures, other features may vanish. In our experiments, the latter was the case far more often, and inverted files tended to become smaller. This is not possible in the *augmented* variant, where features can only be added to the initial image signatures. Thus, inverted files enlarge. In both variants, parameter α regulates the severity of the effect. A large α leads to a high decrease or increase of an inverted file, respectively. *Default propagation* decreases the inverted file size by 8% to 17% for INRIA holidays, and by 17% to 29% for Oxford buildings. *Augmentation* increases the inverted file size by up to 8% for INRIA holidays but only up to 3% for Oxford buildings.

Feature propagation is a one-time pre-processing step. It does not involve post-processing of retrieval results with additional operations, nor does it change the nature of image signatures. Thus, it does not influence query response times of CBIR systems compared to basic BOF retrieval. In theory, changing signature sizes could alter the accumulation time of similarity scores in the inverted file structure. However, we did not observe such an effect. Query times were stable.

6. CONCLUSION

Using affine co-segmentation, we constructed image webs of two data sets with several thousand images. We incorporated weak geometric consistency constraints in a novel way to estimate the reliability of a set of feature matches. This way, we detect and prevent wrong association between image pairs. As a result, we increase the correctness of the emerging image web considerably.

We used the image web to propagate visual words along image connections. To our knowledge, visual word propagation on completely unlabeled data is a new approach. We

Table 1: Evaluation of feature propagation on INRIA holidays in conjunction with a generic 200k word dictionary. The best performance per row is marked in bold face.

distractors	mAP baseline	mAP propagation *default*			mAP propagation *augmented*		
		$\alpha = 0.1$	$\alpha = 0.5$	$\alpha = 0.9$	$\alpha = 0.1$	$\alpha = 0.5$	$\alpha = 0.9$
0	0.554	0.566	**0.594**	0.592	0.570	0.576	0.575
1,000	0.530	0.546	**0.576**	0.574	0.548	0.562	0.563
10,000	0.463	0.487	**0.533**	0.532	0.486	0.526	0.529
100,000	0.382	0.423	**0.498**	0.498	0.422	0.489	0.495

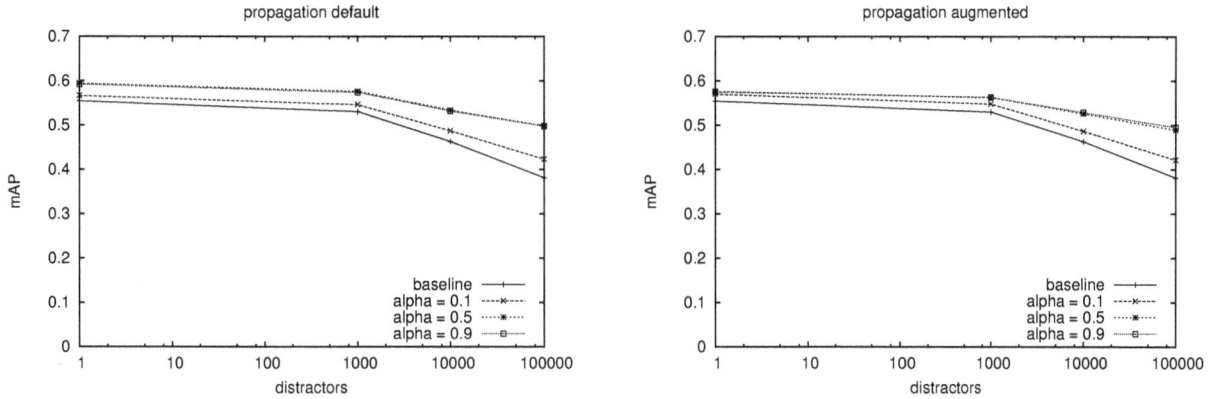

Figure 4: Impact of the number of distractor images on retrieval performance for INRIA holidays.

Table 2: Evaluation of feature propagation on Oxford buildings in conjunction with a generic 200k word dictionary. The best performance per row is marked in bold face.

distractors	mAP baseline	mAP propagation *default*			mAP propagation *augmented*		
		$\alpha = 0.1$	$\alpha = 0.5$	$\alpha = 0.9$	$\alpha = 0.1$	$\alpha = 0.5$	$\alpha = 0.9$
0	0.320	0.370	**0.409**	0.338	0.334	0.365	0.368
1,000	0.315	0.366	**0.407**	0.338	0.327	0.359	0.363
10,000	0.294	0.345	**0.400**	0.333	0.306	0.340	0.344
100,000	0.223	0.284	**0.360**	0.309	0.235	0.271	0.284

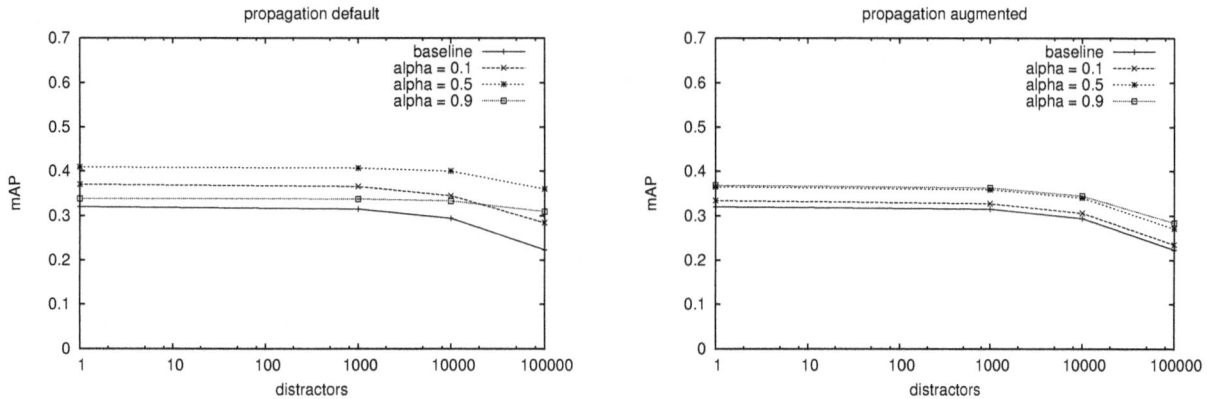

Figure 5: Impact of the number of distractor images on retrieval performance for Oxford buildings.

Table 3: Evaluation of feature propagation on Oxford buildings in conjunction with a data-set-specific 1M word dictionary. The best performance is marked in bold face.

mAP baseline	mAP propagation *default*			mAP propagation *augmented*		
	$\alpha = 0.1$	$\alpha = 0.5$	$\alpha = 0.9$	$\alpha = 0.1$	$\alpha = 0.5$	$\alpha = 0.9$
0.545	0.553	0.494	0.527	0.553	**0.571**	0.564

showed, how techniques of semi-supervised learning can be adapted and deployed in this setup. We observed an increase in retrieval performance by up to 28%. This benefit is even more distinctive when distractor images are involved. Image signatures become considerably more robust. We also demonstrated that feature propagation is suited to reduce the amount of data necessary to describe an image collection. This is because sparsely distributed features are filtered out through propagation. This effect can cause problems for very large dictionaries that naturally entail sparsity. If too many features disappear retrieval performance suffers. This can be prevented when the original signatures stay fixed, and are only augmented through propagation.

The results of feature propagation can be easily incorporated into existing BOF search infrastructures. Feature propagation optimizes an inverted file without changing its composition. This separates it from approaches like Hamming embedding[5] or WGC constraints[5] that require a modified inverted file structure. Also, the propagation process runs in an offline stage, and does not impair the online query times of a system. The approach is complementary to other optimization strategies, like re-ranking based on spatial consistency[12], or query expansion[3]. It can thus boost the performance of state of the art BOF image searches even further.

Our feature propagation framework leaves many possibilities for variations. Image web connections can be weighted according to path length, image similarity or co-segmented area size. Feature exchange can be limited to features within co-segmented areas. This way, only sub-signatures of co-occurring objects would be enriched. Other methods than affine co-segmentation can be deployed, e.g. co-segmentation based on fitting homographies or fundamental matrices. Image relations could even be established based on full stereo reconstructions which yield further possibilities of verification. Fast web densification and feature propagation can be enforced by restricting the maximal cluster size during sparse web construction. A dissimilarity ranking could ensure sufficient heterogeneity for these small clusters. We leave these possibilities as future work.

7. ACKNOWLEDGMENTS

This work has partially been supported by the European Social Fund and the Federal State of Saxony within project VICCI (#100098171). This work was also supported by the DFG Priority Program 1335: Scalable Visual Analytics.

8. REFERENCES

[1] Y. Bengio, O. Delalleau, and N. Le Roux. Label Propagation and Quadratic Criterion. In O. Chapelle, B. Schölkopf, and A. Zien, editors, *Semi-Supervised Learning*, pages 193–216. MIT Press, 2006.

[2] G. Bradski. The OpenCV Library. *Dr. Dobb's Journal of Software Tools*, 2000.

[3] O. Chum, J. Philbin, J. Sivic, M. Isard, and A. Zisserman. Total recall: Automatic query expansion with a generative feature model for object retrieval. In *IEEE International Conference on Computer Vision*, 2007.

[4] K. Heath, N. Gelfand, M. Ovsjanikov, M. Aanjaneya, and L. Guibas. Image webs: Computing and exploiting connectivity in image collections. In *Computer Vision and Pattern Recognition (CVPR), 2010 IEEE Conference on*, pages 3432 –3439, june 2010.

[5] H. Jegou, M. Douze, and C. Schmid. Hamming embedding and weak geometric consistency for large scale image search. In *Proceedings of the 10th European Conference on Computer Vision: Part I*, ECCV '08, pages 304–317, Berlin, Heidelberg, 2008. Springer-Verlag.

[6] Y.-h. Kuo, H.-t. Lin, W.-h. Cheng, Y.-h. Yang, and W. H. Hsu. Unsupervised auxiliary visual words discovery for large-scale image object retrieval. *Discovery*, 1(c):1–8, 2011.

[7] D. G. Lowe. Distinctive image features from scale-invariant keypoints. *Int. J. Comput. Vision*, 60(2):91–110, Nov. 2004.

[8] J. Matas, O. Chum, U. Martin, and T. Pajdla. Robust wide baseline stereo from maximally stable extremal regions. In *Proceedings of British Machine Vision Conference*, volume 1, pages 384–393, London, 2002.

[9] K. Mikolajczyk and C. Schmid. Scale & affine invariant interest point detectors. *Int. J. Comput. Vision*, 60(1):63–86, Oct. 2004.

[10] K. Mikolajczyk, T. Tuytelaars, C. Schmid, A. Zisserman, J. Matas, F. Schaffalitzky, T. Kadir, and L. V. Gool. A comparison of affine region detectors. *International Journal of Computer Vision*, 65(1/2):43–72, 2005.

[11] M. Muja and D. G. Lowe. Fast approximate nearest neighbors with automatic algorithm configuration. In *International Conference on Computer Vision Theory and Application VISSAPP'09)*, pages 331–340. INSTICC Press, 2009.

[12] J. Philbin, O. Chum, M. Isard, J. Sivic, and A. Zisserman. Object retrieval with large vocabularies and fast spatial matching. In *Proceedings of the IEEE Conference on Computer Vision and Pattern Recognition*, 2007.

[13] J. Sivic and A. Zisserman. Video Google: A text retrieval approach to object matching in videos. In *Proceedings of the International Conference on Computer Vision*, volume 2, pages 1470–1477, Oct. 2003.

[14] G. Yu and J.-M. Morel. ASIFT: An Algorithm for Fully Affine Invariant Comparison. *Image Processing On Line*, 2011, 2011.

Learning Attribute-aware Dictionary for Image Classification and Search

Junjie Cai[†], Zheng-Jun Zha[‡], Huanbo Luan[‡], Shiliang Zhang[†] and Qi Tian[†]
[†]Department of Computer Science, University of Texas at San Antonio
[‡]School of Computing, National University of Singapore
{caijunjieustc,junzzustc,luanhuanbo,slzhang.jdl}@gmail.com, qitian@cs.utsa.edu

ABSTRACT

Bag-of-visual words (BoW) model has recently been well advocated for image classification and search. However, one critical limitation of existing BoW model is the lack of semantic information. To alleviate the impact of this issue, it is imperative to construct semantic-aware visual dictionary. In this paper, we propose a novel approach for learning visual word dictionary embedding intermediate-level semantics. Specifically, we first introduce an Attribute-aware Dictionary Learning(AttrDL) scheme to learn multiple sub-dictionaries with specific semantic meanings. We divide training images into different sets and each represents a specific attribute. For each image set, an attribute-aware sub-vocabulary is learned. Hence, these resulting sub-vocabularies are more discriminative for semantics than the traditional vocabularies. Second, to get semantic-aware and discriminative BoW representation with the learned sub-vocabularies, we adopt the idea of ℓ_{21}-norm regularized sparse coding and recode the resulting sparse representation of each image. Experimental results show that the proposed scheme outperforms the state-of-the-art algorithms in both image classification and search tasks.

Categories and Subject Descriptors

H.3.3 [**Information Retrieval**]: Information Retrieval and Indexing

General Terms

Algorithm, Measurement, Experimentation

Keywords

bag-of-visual words, image classification and search

1. INTRODUCTION

Bag-of-visual words(BoW) model has been widely used in various vision tasks, including image categorization[5], search[1, 37] and object recognition[12]. BoW model is commonly acquired with three steps: (i) image local feature extraction; (ii) dictionary generation; (iii) feature coding and pooling. A lot of approaches have been proposed for visual dictionary learning and sparse coding [8][9][10][32]. Generally, a over-complete dictionary is learned from low-level local features. The ℓ_0 or ℓ_1 norm are then used to pursuit sparse representation based on the dictionary. Example works include the Method of Optimal Directions(MOD) with ℓ_0 sparsity penalty proposed by Engan et al.[9], the greedy K-SVD algorithm by Aharon et al.[8], and an efficient formulation with ℓ_1 sparsity measure by Lee et al. [10], etc. Recently, Krause et al.[13] propose a submodular dictionary selection method for sparse BoW representation and prove that the dictionary (which is selected greedily) is close to the global optimum solution if the original data set satisfies the submodular condition. Unfortunately, the fact that most of the real-world image sets may not satisfy the submodular condition degrades the application scope of submodular dictionary selection. More importantly, dictionary or visual words learned by above approaches mainly focus on decreasing the reconstruction error in BoW model and do not convey semantic meanings, thus show limited discriminative power for high-level semantics. In this paper, we endeavor to alleviate the negative influence of lacking semantic meanings by learning attribute-aware dictionaries.

Attributes can be regarded as a set of mid-level semantic preserving concepts[35]. Different from low-level visual features, each attribute has an explicit semantic meaning, e.g., "eye". Due to the advantages of being semantic-aware, attribute has been studied recently and is revealing its power in various applications[1][14][15][20]. Several attempts have been made to embed semantic attribute into conventional image classification scenario. By using attribute classifiers, Su et al.[20] propose to alleviate the semantic gap between visual words and high level concept, focusing on polysemy phenomenon of particular visual words. By randomly splitting the training data, Farhadi et al.[24] exhaustively train thousands of classifiers and then chose some of the discriminative ones as attributes(e.g., attributes that "cat" and "dog" have but "sheep" and "horse" do not). Kumar et al.[14] define a set of binary attributes called *similes* for face verifications. Each attribute detector in similes is exclusively trained for one specific category, e.g., "the Angelina Jolie's mouth". Recently, Parikh and Grauman [25] propose a new strategy to compare the relative strength of attributes, *e.g.*, "while A and B are both *shiny*, A is *shinier* than B". Instead of being trained by binary classifiers, relative attributes are learned by ranking functions(*e.g.*, the ranking SVM). The output of a ranking function indicates the relative presence of the corresponding attribute.

In this paper, we propose a novel approach for learning visual word dictionary with intermediate-level semantic attributes, leading to semantic-aware visual representation. We introduce an Attribute-aware Dictionary Learning(AttrDL) scheme to learn multiple sub-dictionaries with specific semantic meanings. Training images are divided into different sets, each of which represents a specific attribute. An attribute-aware sub-vocabulary is learned based on each set. Figure 1 illustrates the proposed framework, which contains an off-line training part and an online-testing part. Offline, we first learn a set of binary classifiers, each of which predicts the presence of an attribute in an image. Then, for each attribute, we select a set of images which contain this attribute. We extract low-level local features from these images and learn a sub visual dictionary corresponding to the pre-defined attribute. Because each sub-dictionary is specialized for a certain attribute, we reasonably assume that it effectively preserves specific semantic meanings. After learning all the individual sub-dictionaries, we concatenate them to get the final visual dictionary, namely *attribute-aware dictionary*. In the on-line part, for each test image, we encode its features with the attribute-aware dictionary using a regularized sparse coding algorithm. The codes of descriptors are then aggregated together and refined with pooling strategy to get the final BoW image representation, which is then adopted as image feature for image classification and retrieval.

The main contributions of this paper can be summarized as follows:

- Attribute-aware dictionary conveys explicit semantics, thus is more discriminative to image semantics than traditional visual dictionaries.

- We investigate the sparsity of image representation over the learned dictionary and exploit ℓ_{21}-norm as the constraints to encode the visual features. The resulting BoW representation shows strong discriminative power in image classification and retrieval tasks.

The rest of this paper is organized as follows. Section 2 reviews the related works. Section 3 describes the formulation of our proposed method, including dictionary learning and regularized sparse coding. Experimental results on several publicly available data sets are reported in Section 4, followed by the conclusions in Section 5.

2. RELATED WORK

Recent years have witnessed an increasing number of research works on image classification [22, 33] and search [17, 38]. This work focuses on improving image classification and search by incorporating visual vocabulary with more semantics, which is closely related to image local feature extraction[6], visual codebook generation[20], learning semantic attributes from object recognition[12], and classifier learning[5]. Nevertheless, detailed survey of either direction is beyond the scope of this paper. Thus, we focus on two

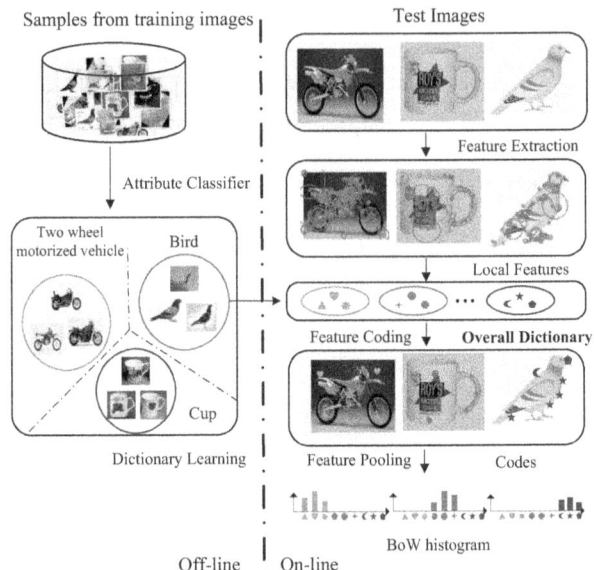

Figure 1: Flowchart of the proposed Attribute-aware Dictionary Learning(AttrDL) framework for image classification and search.

most relevant topic: dictionary learning and sparse coding approach.

Current approaches to dictionary learning can be loosely categorized into two categories: *unsupervised* dictionary learning and *supervised* dictionary learning.

Unsupervised dictionary learning learns a dictionary guided by reconstruction optimization which minimizes the residual errors of reconstructing the original signals. For instance, the MOD algorithm[9] iteratively updates the codebook and the centroids from nearest neighbor clustering are regarded as codewords. Aharon *et al.*[8] generalize the k-means clustering process and propose the K-SVD algorithm to learn an overcomplete dictionary from image patches. It follows the same pattern of MOD by updating the bases iteratively but the new basis is generated directly from the SVD calculation result. Lee *et al.*[10] treat dictionary learning as a least square problem after the sparse coefficients are fixed and efficiently solve it using its Lagrange dual. The dictionaries learned via unsupervised learning commonly show poor discriminative power as they are optimal for reconstruction but not for classification.

Recently, several supervised dictionary learning methods have been proposed to enhance discriminative power by combining sub-dictionaries from various categories [1][4][11]. Zhou *et al.*[12] propose a joint dictionary learning(JDL) algorithm to leverage inter-object visual correlation for dictionary learning. Then JDL learns C sub-dictionaries for C classes (each one corresponds to a specific class) and a common shared dictionary for a group of visually correlated object classes. However, limited number of category-based sub-dictionaries (*e.g.* $C = 5$)could be negative for classification performance, as most of test images will be unclear represented with high-level concept. Hence, the approach is ineffective web image classification.

Additionally, several sparse coding strategies have been advocated to boost final classification performance. Yang *et al.* [4] propose an extension of SPM by using Sparse Coding (ScSPM), and show state-of-the-art performance in image classification. By replacing k-means with sparse coding, their method jointly learns the optimal codebook and searches for the optimal weights to be assigned to the visual words for each local feature. In this way, both the discriminative power of codebook and the accuracy of the reconstruction are improved. Gao *et al.*[5] propose a Laplacian sparse coding method which preserves the consistency in sparse representations of similar local features. Cao *et al.*[1] introduce a weakly supervised sparse coding to exploit the Classemes-based attribute labeling to refine the descriptor coding procedure. All the aforementioned coding schemes are applied on local features independently. One limitation of these schemes is that they disregard semantic correlation that transmitted from overall dictionaries. To the best of our knowledge, our work presents the first attempt towards exploring the ℓ_{21}-norm based regularizer in the coding step of the BoW approach.

Meanwhile, a wealth of works have been devoted to visual words aggregation [3, 29], which focuses on the pooling step in the BoW representation pipeline. Instead, our work focuses on the attribute-aware dictionary learning step and can be combined with any pooling method.

3. FORMULATION

In this section, we propose an attribute-aware dictionary learning scheme to endow semantic meaning to multiple sub-dictionaries. Each sub-dictionary is learned from a set of images, which corresponds to a semantic attribute. Then a new ℓ_{21}-norm sparse coding method is proposed based on the overall dictionaries which is acquired by concatenating the sub-dictionaries together. Finally, we present average pooling approach required to generate the final BoW representation.

3.1 Dictionary Learning

Let us consider a codebook denoted by $D \in \Re^{d*K}$, with K the size of the codebook and d the dimensionality of a visual word. The codebook is constructed on a subset of local descriptors $\{x_i; x_i \in \Re^d; i = 1, ..., N\}$ extracted from the training dataset. The classical dictionary learning model could be represented by:

$$(D, Z) = \arg \min_{D,Z} \|X - DZ\|_{\ell_1}^2 + \lambda \|Z\|_{\ell_1} \\ s.t. \|d_k\|_{\ell_2}^2 = 1, for \quad \forall k = 1, ..., K, \tag{1}$$

If $K > d$, then D is called an overcomplete dictionary.

For each attribute a_i, we select image set $\mathcal{I}_i$ which shares common attribute a_i and their corresponding SIFT feature set is X_i. We could learn a dictionary D_i with respect to a specific attribute a_i.

$$(D_i, Z_i) = \arg \min_{D_i, Z_i} \sum_{i=1}^{C} \left\{ \|X_i - D_i Z_i\|_{\ell_2}^2 + \lambda \|Z_i\|_{\ell_1} \right\} \\ + \beta \Psi(Z_1, ..., Z_C) \tag{2}$$

where $Z_i = [z_{i1}, z_{i2}, ..., z_{iN}]$ are the codes for descriptor-set X_i, and λ is denoted as the sparsity of codes. $\Psi(Z_1, ..., Z_C)$ is a discrimination term. Here we give the definition of $\Psi(Z_i)$ as $tr(S_W) - tr(S_B)$. S_W evaluates between-attibutes scatter matrix and S_B represents within-attribute scatter matrix.

Specifically, S_W and S_B are defined as

$$S_W = \sum_{j=1}^{C} \sum_{z_i \in Z_j} (z_i - \mu_j)(z_i - \mu_j)^T \\ S_B = \sum_{j=1}^{C} n_i (\mu_j - \mu)(\mu_j - \mu)^T \tag{3}$$

where μ_j and μ are the mean vector of Z_j and Z respectively, and n_i is the number of selected features in image set $\mathcal{I}_i$. Suppose there are C attributes $\{a_1, a_2, ..., a_C\}$ and $X = [X_1, X_2, ..., X_C] \in \Re^{d*N}$ is the dataset, wherein $X_i \in \Re^{d*N_i}$ ($N = \sum_{i=1}^{C} N_i$) represent the images corresponding to the ith attribute. Denote the overall dictionary as $D = [D_1, D_2, ..., D_C] \in \Re^{d*K}$ in which $K = \sum_{i=1}^{C} K_i$, $D_i \in \Re^{d*K_i}$ stands for the ith attribute. We could easily learn overall dictionary D by iteratively optimizing with respect to $\{D_i\}_{i=1}^{C}$ and $\{Z_i\}_{i=1}^{C}$. The optimization problem in Equation 2 is not convex with respect to D_i and Z_i simultaneously, but it is convex once the other fixed.

Therefore, the optimization is achieved iteratively through two sub-procedures: (1) computing the sparse codes Z_i by fixing the dictionaries. (2) updating the dictionaries D_i by fixing the codes. In consideration of relationship with respect to various attributes in terms of S_B and S_W, we also need to update Z_i by fixing Z_j, $j \neq i$ and the objective function is given as

$$\|X_i - D_i Z_i\|_{\ell_2}^2 + \lambda \|Z_i\|_{\ell_1} + \beta \psi(Z_i) \tag{4}$$

where $\psi(Z_i)$ is the discrimination term when the other attribute image sets are all fixed, given as

$$\psi(Z_i) = \|Z_i - M_i\|_{\ell_2}^2 - \sum_{j=1}^{C} \|M_j - M\|_{\ell_2}^2 \tag{5}$$

where $M_i \in \Re^{K_i*N_i}$ consists of N_i copies of the mean vector μ_i as its columns, $M_j \in \Re^{K_j*N_j}$ and $M \in \Re^{K_j*N_j}$ are produced by stacking N_j copies of μ_j and μ as their column vectors, respectively. Previous works[8][12] show that ℓ_2-norm terms above are differentiable and we employ feature-sign search algorithm[10] to iteratively solve the ℓ_1-norm penalty term, which guarantees to converge to a local minimum.

3.2 Revisit on Sparse Coding

After the step of dictionary learning, we transform local features to the corresponding global pooling feature. In the original BoW method [26], coding local descriptors is performed with hard assignment. Each local descriptor is assigned with the nearest visual word, *i.e.*,

$$\arg \min_Z \sum_{i=1}^{N} \|x_i - Dz_i\|_{\ell_2}^2 \\ s.t. \|z_i\|_{\ell^0} = 1, \|z_i\|_{\ell^1} = 1, z_i \geq 0, \forall i \tag{6}$$

The cardinality constraint error means that there will be only one non-zero element in each code z_i. However, such coding uses one code word to coarsely denote the original local feature, resulting in huge quantization loss. Using sparse coding [4] as an alternative could effectively depress such quantization errors. Therefore, coding is performed by solving the ℓ_1-norm regularized approximate problem:

$$\arg \min_Z \sum_{i=1}^{N} \|x_i - Dz_i\|_{\ell_2}^2 + \lambda \|z_i\|_{\ell_1}, \lambda \in \Re \tag{7}$$

Nevertheless, this optimization problem is computationally expensive and leads to non-consistent encoding of similar descriptors. Indeed, it might select different bases for similar descriptors due to the over-completeness of the codebook, which results in large deviations in representing similar local features. Therefore, Yang *et al.* [2] further propose more efficient and consistent coding methods relying on the locality property introduced by [28]. The generalized formulation of the Locality Constrained Coding(LCC) problem is as follows:

$$\arg\min \sum_{i=1}^{N} \|x_i - Dz_i\|_{\ell_2}^2 + \lambda \|v_i \odot z_i\|_{\ell_2}^2, \quad (8)$$
$$s.t. \ 1^T z_i = 1$$

where v_i represents the Euclidean distance between x_i and the basis vectors.

An alternative to improve the consistency of sparse coding is proposed by [5]. It adds the Laplacian matrix to the objective function in Equation 7 to perform codebook learning as well as local feature coding, *i.e.*,

$$\arg\min_{D,Z} \|X - DZ\|_{\ell_2}^2 + \lambda \sum_{i=1}^{N} \|z_i\|_{\ell_1} + \beta tr(ZLZ^T), \quad (9)$$
$$s.t. \ \|d_j\|^2 \leq 1$$

Due to the large number of local descriptors in a dataset, *e.g.*, each image with 400×300 resolution commonly contains more than 500 SIFT features. Constructing the Laplacian matrix and learning sparse codes simultaneously is computationally infeasible.

3.3 Regularized Sparse Coding

All the aforementioned coding schemes are applied on local features independently, disregarding semantic correlation that transmitted from overall dictionaries. We aim to learn a semantic-aware BoW histogram over ℓ_{21}-norm based coding regularizer, such that the sparse codes can preserve an attribute-level image similarity. Just like the use of ℓ_1-norm for sparse recovery, the ℓ_{21}-norm has recently been well known to facilitate group sparsity[23]. Bengio *et al.*[23] point out that there are hidden groups contained in the sparse codes. Each visual feature could be reconstructed using a sparse linear combination of both common and group-specific sub-dictionaries. In our paper, assuming C attributes, each group of sparse codes corresponds to an attribute-aware sub-dictionary. To the best of our knowledge, our work presents the first attempt towards exploring the ℓ_{21}-norm based regularizer in the coding step of the BoW approach.

For a specific image, we represent its descriptor set as X_k and the corresponding sparse representation as Z_k. Each image has the sparsity with the respect to the pre-defined attribute.

$$\hat{Z}_k = \min_{Z_k} \|X_k - DZ_k\|_{\ell_2}^2 + \lambda \|Z_k\|_{\ell_{21}} \quad (10)$$

For the codes set of image descriptors $Z_k \in \Re^{p*n_k}$,its ℓ_{21}-norm is defined as

$$\|Z\|_{\ell_{21}} = \sum_{i=1}^{p} \sqrt{\sum_{j=1}^{n_k} Z_{ij}^2} \quad (11)$$

This regularized term is the combination of both ℓ_1 and ℓ_2 norms. The codes are projected from several groups of

Algorithm 1 Attribute-aware Dictionary Learning(AttrDL)

Input: Low-level visual feature set $\{X_i\}_{i=1}^{C}$, $i = \{1, \ldots, C\}$,
Output: The Attribute-aware Dictionary $D = [D_1, \ldots, D_C]$.
1: Initialize $\{D_i\}_i^C$ and $\{Z_i\}_i^C$ independently.
2: **repeat**
3:     For each attribute a_i, update Z_i by solving
    $\min_{Z_i} \|X_i - D_i Z_i\|_{\ell_2}^2 + \lambda \|Z_i\|_{\ell_1} + \psi(Z_i)$
4:     For each attribute a_i, update D_i by solving
    $\min_{D_i} \|X_i - D_i Z_i\|_{\ell_2}^2$ using its Lagrange dual.
5: **until** convergence on certain rounds
6: Stack column-wisely to form overall dictionary $D = [D_1, \ldots, D_C]$.
7: **repeat**
8:     For each image in the dataset, encode all the features of the image by using Equation 10
9: **until**

visual words and each group corresponds to one attribute-aware dictionary D_i. The designed ℓ_{21}-norm term enjoys several attractive properties. First, each visual word is restricted to be evenly related to multiple features as imposed by the ℓ_2 norm regularization. Second, the ℓ_1 norm is used to sum the codes across groups and imposed to encourage the codes $\hat{Z}_k$ to be sparse[10]. As there are limited number of attributes distributed on each image, each feature is also sparsely represented by groups of attribute-aware visual words. Utilizing the group structure of ℓ_1 norm ensures more robust and accurate coding.

Finally, Algorithm 1 outlines the proposed dictionary learning procedure. After that, the codes of the descriptors are aggregated together to get the corresponding pooled feature. We use function $f(\hat{Z}_k)$ to denote the feature pooling which summarizes the joint distribution of local descriptors in the image.

$$\gamma_k = f(\hat{Z}_k) \quad (12)$$

Specifically two pooling methods have been widely used,

- max pooling: $f(\hat{Z}_k) = \left\|\hat{Z}_k\right\|_\infty = \max_{n_k} \hat{z}_k$

- average pooling: $f(\hat{Z}_k) = \frac{1}{n_k}\left\|\hat{Z}_k\right\|_{\ell_1} = \frac{1}{n_k}\sum_{n=1}^{n_k} \hat{z}_k$

We define the image level feature over the sparse representation matrix $\hat{Z}$ by average pooling over n_k features and adopt Spatial Pyramid Matching(SPM)[4] which preserves the spatial information to get the final BoW image representation.

4. EXPERIMENTS

We conduct extensive experiments to evaluate our AttrDL in web image classification and search, and also compare with several state-of-the-art approaches, including Sparse spatial Pyramid Matching(ScSPM), Locality-constrained Linear Coding(LLC) and Laplacian Sparse Coding(LScSPM), respectively. The evaluation is conducted on several publically available datasets.

4.1 Experimental Configurations

We adopt the Classemes[6] based attribute detector to convert each image to a Classemes vector, whose definition comes from the concept of the Large Scale Concept Ontology for Multimedia(LSCOM) including 2,659 attribute categories. Among the highly weighted Classemes in [6], we select 100 attributes considering two aspects: (a) the attributes that appear most frequently in the images of dataset. (b) we also list the images which do not cover specific attribute. Then we sort average prediction score by ascending order and select top 100 attributes[1].

We use dense ℓ_2-normalized SIFT[26]as image local feature due to its reasonably good performance in image recognition[3]. previous works show that smaller step size in dense SIFT extraction gets better performance. However, smaller step size also results in more SIFT descriptors and increases the computational cost. Referring to previous work[3][5], we fix the step size and patch size to 8 and 16 respectively. We also resize the maximum side of each image to 300 pixels. We randomly select $(1.0 \sim 1.2) \times 10^5$ features to generate codebook for each data set. For SPM, we use the top 3 layers and set same weight for each layer[7]. In our implementation, the sub-dictionary of each attribute contains 500 visual word, and the total number of visual word is 50K. The most important two parameters of the formulation are the sparsity of the sparse codes and coefficient β in discrimination term. We follow the same setting as LScSPM[5]. Specifically, λ and β are set to 0.3 and 0.1 respectively in the experiments.

For image classification, we use one-versus-all linear SVM[2] as the classifier because it is efficient to train and shows reasonably good performance in average feature pooling based image classification. We repeat the experimental process by randomly selecting the training and testing images to obtain reliable results. Classification of new sample is done by a winner-takes-all strategy, in which the image is recognized as the category with the highest classification score. In SVM, the choice of kernel function is quite important to the classification performance. We here adopt histogram intersection kernel, which has been proven to be effective and efficient for classification over histogram like features, such as bag-of-visual words[36]. For feature vectors $(x, z) \in \Re_+^n$, the intersection kernel is

$$k(x, z) : \sum_{k=1}^{n} min(x(i), z(i)) \qquad (13)$$

For search task, bag-of-visual words image representation can be effectively indexed with *inverted file*[34]. An inverted file is composed of many lists of images, each corresponds to a visual word. We build a table that points from the word number to the indices of the images in which that visual word occurs. By scanning the image lists in inverted file with the visual words contained in query, database images sharing common visual words with the query could be efficiently retrieved. The similarities between images are computed based on *tf-idf*[34] weighting strategy.

Table 1: Classification accuracy (%) comparison on Caltech-101

Algorithms	5 training	15 training	30 training
ScSPM[4]	-	67.00	73.20
LLC[2]	51.15	65.43	73.44
LScSPM[5]	52.25	66.38	73.54
AttrDL	**55.82**	**68.76**	**78.28**

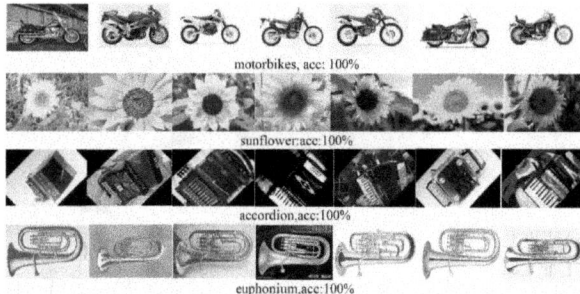

Figure 2: Example images from classes with highest classification accuracy from the Caltech-101 dataset.

4.2 Evaluation on Image Classification Task

4.2.1 Caltech101

The Caltech-101 dataset [19] contains 9144 images from 102 categories, including 101 object categories and 1 additional background category. The number of images per category ranges from 31 to 800. Following the setting in [2], we randomly select 5, 15 and 30 images respectively for training and report the classification accuracies over the 102 categories. In our evaluation, overall 10 classes achieve 100% classification accuracy with 30 training images per class. Figure 2 illustrates some example images from those classes.

Table 1 summarizes the detailed performance comparison between the proposed method and several other methods[2][4][5] on the Caltech-101 dataset. As shown, our method achieves the best performance and outperforms ScSPM by 2.6% for 15 training images and 7.2% for 30 training images.

Table 2: Classification accuracy (%) comparison on 15 scenes dataset

Algorithms	Average Classification Rate
ScSPM[4]	80.28
LLC[2]	79.24
LScSPM[5]	89.75
AttrDL	**93.83**

4.2.2 Scene15

Scene-15 dataset is composed of 15 scene classes. Each class contains 200 to 400 images and there are 4485 images in total. This dataset contains various scene images, *e.g.*, out-door street, in-door kitchen, living room, etc. As in [4], we randomly select 100 images from each class as training samples, and then use the rest images for testing. We list the performances based on different methods in Table 2. Moreover, the confusion matrix based on our algorithm is shown in Figure 3. Obviously from Table 2, the proposed method outperforms the ScSPM by about 13% which demonstrates the effectiveness of our method. Since we use attribute-aware sparse coding instead of sparse coding along

---

[1]Due to limited pages, we list selected attributes with respect to Scene15 datasets in Table 3.

[2]http://www.csie.ntu.edu.tw/cjlin/libsvm/

	suburb	coast	forest	highway	insidecity	mountain	opencountry	street	tallbuilding	PARoffice	bedroom	industrial	kitchen	livingroom	store
suburb	97.6	0	0	0	0	0	0	0	0	0	0	2.4	0	0	0
coast	0	92.8	0	3.8	0	0.3	0	0.1	0.3	0	0.1	1	1.6	0	0
forest	0.8	0	96	0	0	0.2	0	0	0	0	0	3	0	0	0
highway	0	0	2	92	0	3	0	0	0	0.6	0.5	0.3	1.6	0	0
insidecity	0.5	0	0	0	92.3	0	0.8	1.8	0.9	1.5	0.2	0	0	0.5	1.5
mountain	0	0.1	0.15	2.5	0	95.6	0.7	0.25	0.2	0	0.1	0	0	0.2	0
opencountry	0.4	0.2	0	0.2	0	2.3	95.4	0.1	0	0.6	0.2	0.1	0	0.5	0
street	0	0	0	0.3	0	0	0	98.4	0.2	0	0	1.1	0	0	0
tallbuilding	0	0	2.3	0.1	0	0	0.1	0	96.8	0.2	0	0	0.5	0	0
PARoffice	0	2	0	0	0.2	0	0	0	0	95.3	0	0	0	0	2.5
bedroom	0	0	0	0.2	0	0.5	3.6	1	0	1	92.6	0	1.1	0	0
industrial	0	0.5	0	0	0.1	0	0	3	0	0	1	94.3	1	0	0.1
kitchen	0	0	0	2	1.3	3	0	0	0	0	0	0	86.5	2.2	5
livingroom	0.1	0	0	1.6	0	0	1.1	0	0	0	3	0	3	91.2	0
store	0.3	0	0.8	0.5	0	0	0.5	0	0	0.2	0	0.2	0	5	92.5

Figure 3: Confusion Matrix on Scene-15 Data Set(%). In confusion matrix, the entry in the i-th row and j-th column is the percentage of images from class i that are misidentified as class j. Average classification rates for individual classes are listed along the diagonal.

with spatial pyramid matching and max pooling, we are able to preserve more information and reduce the quantization loss. Besides, by incorporating the attribute information, we are able to learn semantic-aware visual dictionary instead of traditional dictionary only conveying visual clues. This makes the final image representation more discriminative hence improves the image classification performance. Nevertheless, we notice that our algorithm is not effective in distinguishing the class "living room" from "kitchen", and this may result from that they share a wealth of common semantic attributes.

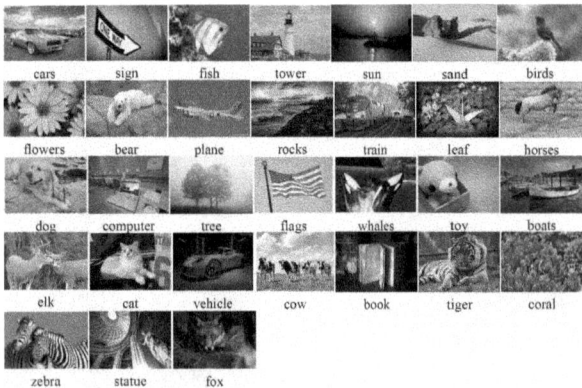

Figure 4: Example images from NUS-WIDE-OBJECT dataset.

4.2.3 NUS-WIDE-OBJECT

NUS-WIDE-OBJECT dataset contains 30,000 manually labeled images belong to 31 object classes. All of these images are collected from Flickr[3] web site. The entire dataset is separated into two subsets: 17,927 images as training sub-

[3]http://www.flickr.com/

set and the remaining 12,073 images as testing subset. Some sample images are illustrated in Figure 4.

Figure 5 provides the performance comparison of different approaches in terms of average accuracy. In particular, Figure 5(a) shows the comparison among Classemes descriptor[6], Visual Attribute Feature(VAF)[20] descriptor and our method with respect to different number of training samples. We can see that our scheme outperforms either the pure Classemes attribute based descriptor or VAF. Figure 5(b) shows that comparison with respect to various dictionary sizes. With the increase of codebook size, our approach demonstrates remarkable superiority over conventional approach.

The above results demonstrate the effectiveness of our proposed method on web image classification. The main reason behind this are two folds. First, we incorporate semantic attribute into BoW pipeline instead of purely relying on attribute vector or visual descriptor. We embed specific semantic meaning into individual sub-dictionary and concatenate the sub-dictionaries together for more fine-grained and discriminative dictionary. Second, we involve more useful semantic attributes within the dictionary as we increase the codebook size. Therefore, the corresponding encoded features could be semantic-aware and thus contribute more to classification performance.

Figure 6 presents the detailed results over all the categories on the NUS-WIDE-OBJECT dataset. We can see that our approach outperforms the other methods on most of the categories. While the traditional BoW methods purely based on low-level visual features may suffer from the large quantization loss especially on the Web image dataset, the proposed method exploits intermediate-level semantic attributes and thus more suitable for bag-of-visual words image representation and more effective for Web image classification.

4.3 Evaluation on Image Search Task

4.3.1 Holidays+Flickr1M

To further test the effectiveness of our model, we validate our performance on the Holidays + Flickr1M benchmark [31], which is the combination of Holidays near-duplicate image search with 1 million Flickr images. Flickr1M are distractor images for large scale image search. Compared to Holidays, the Flickr datasets are slightly biased, because they include low-resolution images and more photos of humans. The performance is measured the official performance metric AP which corresponds to the area under a non-interpolated recall/precision curve. We average the APs over all the queries to create mean Average Precision(mAP) to evaluate the accuracy performance of overall evaluation result:

$$mAP = \frac{1}{Q} \sum_{q=1}^{Q} \frac{\sum_{r=1}^{N_{relevent}^q} P(r)}{N_{relevant}^q} \quad (14)$$

where $q = 1$ to Q is the total queries for evaluation. $N_{relevant}^q$ is the number of relevant documents to the qth query; r is the rth relevant document; $P(r)$ is the precision at the cutoff rank of document r.

Figure 7 shows the performance comparison of our AttrDL approach with Vocabulary Tree[7] and Weak Geometric Consistency(WGC)[31] on the large scale dataset. We combined the Holidays dataset with a varying number of

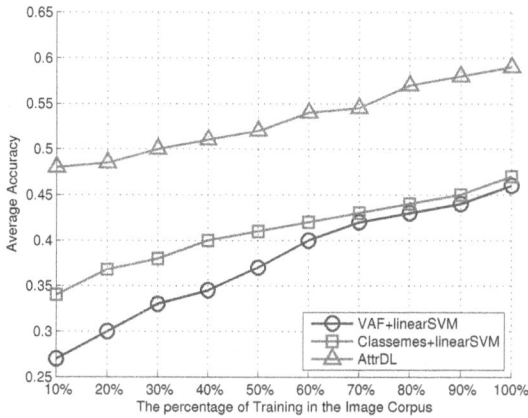

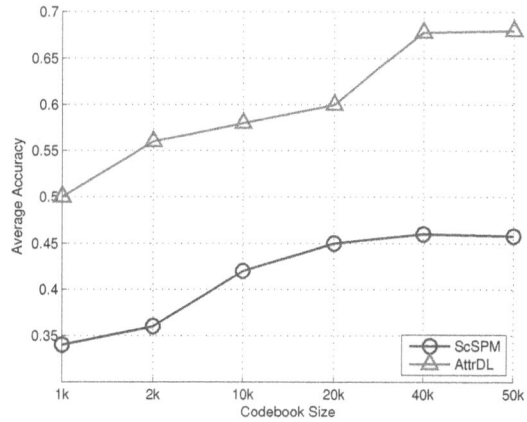

(a)	(b)

Figure 5: Evaluation of our proposed Attribute-aware Dictionary Learning(AttrDL) approach on NUS-WIDE-OBJECT dataset. (a) the tuning of training example volume; (b) the tuning of codebook sizes.

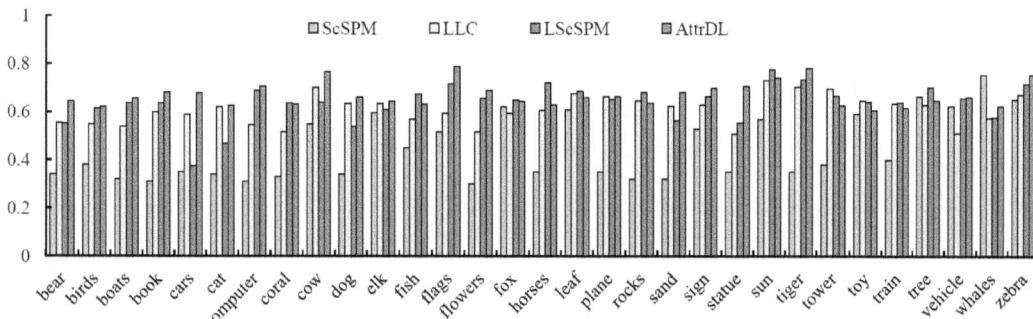

Figure 6: Detailed classification performance over the 31 categories on the NUS-WIDE-OBJECT dataset.

images from the 1M Flickr dataset. Our method achieves competitive performance on this dataset. This result validates the effectiveness of combining semantic attribute into the flowchart of image search tasks.

5. CONCLUSION

In this paper, we introduced a novel approach for learning semantic-aware visual representation. We first embedded semantic information into visual dictionary with semantic attributes. A ℓ_{21} norm regularzed sparse coding algorithm was then used to generate sparse representation based on the semantic-aware visual dictionary. Experimental results on several public datasets have demonstrated the effectiveness of the proposed approach.

6. ACKNOWLEDGMENTS

This work was supported in part to Dr. Qi Tian by ARO grant W911BF-12-1-0057, NSF IIS 1052851, Faculty Research Awards by Google, FXPAL, and NEC Laboratories of America, respectively. This work was supported in part by NSFC 61128007.

7. REFERENCES

[1] L. Cao, R. Ji, Y. Gao, Y, Yang and Q. Tian. Weakly supervised sparse coding with geometric consistency pooling. In *CVPR*, 2012.

[2] J. Wang, J. Yang, K. Yu, F. Lv, T. Huang and Y. Gong. Locality-constrained linear coding for image classification. In *CVPR*, 2010.

[3] J. Feng, B. Ni, Q. Tian and S. Yan. Geometric ℓ_p-norm feature pooling for image classification. In *CVPR*, 2011.

[4] J. Yang, K. Yu, Y. Gong and T. Huang. Linear spatial pyramid matching using sparse conding for image classification. In *CVPR*, 2009.

[5] S. Gao, I. Tsang, L.-T.Chia, and P. Zhao. Local features are not lonely - Laplacian sparse coding for image classification. In *CVPR*, 2011.

[6] L. Torresani, M. Szummer, and A. Fitzgibbon. Efficient object category recognition using Classemes. In *ECCV*, 2010.

[7] S. Lazebnik, C. Schmid and J. Ponce. Beyond bags of features: Spatial pyramid matching for recognizing natural scene categories. In *CVPR*, 2006.

[8] M. Aharon, M. Elad, and A. Bruckstein. K-svd: an alogrithm for designing overcomplete dictionaries for sparse representation. Transaction on Image Processing, 2006.

[9] K. Engan, S. O. Aase, and J. H. Husoy. Method of optimal directions for frame design. In *ICASSP*, 1999.

[10] H. Lee, A. Battle, R. Raina and A. Y. Ng. Efficient sparse coding algorithms. In *NIPS*, 2007.

[11] J. Mairal, F. Bach, J. Ponce, G. Saprio and A. Zisserman. Supervised dictionary learning. In *NIPS*, 2008.

[12] N. Zhou, Y. Shen, J. Peng and J. Fan. Learning inter-related visual dictionary for object recognition. In *CVPR*, 2012.

[13] A. Krause and D. Dueck. Submodular dictionary leanring for sparse representation. In *ICML*, 2011.

[14] N. Kumar, A. C. Berg, P. N. Belhumeur and S. K. Nayar. Attribute and simile classifers for face verification. In *ICCV*, 2009.

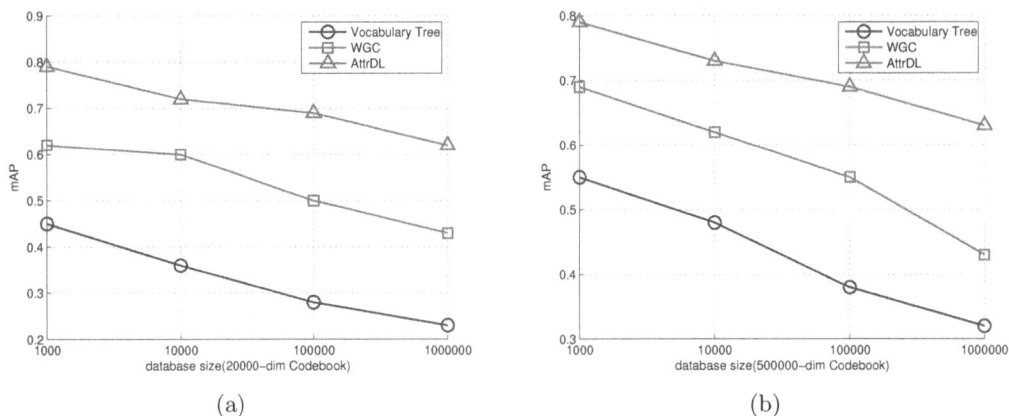

Figure 7: Performance comparisons on Holidays + Flickr1M.

bay	lumberyard	space in ahoc	factory building	transportation event	modern shelter construction
dam	backpacker	farm building	foundry building	bamboo covered region	outdoors exposed to weather
bank	rainy area	frontage road	information store	sewage infrastructure	train transportation device
at sea	small town	grain elevator	military building	yard building grounds	cruise missile air launched
landing	sunny area	business route	state route major	body of water generic	surface transportation event
barrier	urban park	current source	transporter crash	adverse social action	three lanes or wider roadway
tannery	conveyance	portal covering	construction site	construction artifact	ethnic group of east indians
tornado	cul de sac	public property	control structure	multi individual agent	nuclear reactor cooling tower
daytime	foggy area	cannery factory	convent residence	heavy industry facility	completely cloud covered area
waterway	legal agent	helping an agent	anti armor grenade	chemical plant facility	ballistic missile medium range
elevated	sanatoriums	national parkway	open space content	building security system	food or drink preparation device
gas field	cloudy area	physical barrier	upper middle class	air transportation event	astronomical observatory building
land body	environment	roadway junction	vacationer tourist	customary system of links	shadows (localized spatial things)
oil field	municipality	storage facility	conscious activity	eastern hemisphere person	ballistic missile intermediate range
bathhouse	grassy region	vegetable matter	facility construct	information transfer event	ballistic missile submarine launched
	island region	wooden buildings	state route primary	two lanes or wider roadway	cfo managing director media manager etc
	live bodypart	contact location	commercial building	coarse grained soil region	entertainment or recreation organization

Table 3: 100 attributes selected from Classemes in the dataset of Scene15

[15] C. Lampert, H. Nickisch and S. Harmeling. Learning to detect unseen object classes by between-class attribute transfer. In *CVPR*, 2009.

[16] G. Griffin, A. Holub and P. Perona. Caltech-256 object category dataset. Technical report, California Institute of Technology, 2007.

[17] Z.-J. Zha, L. Yang, T. Mei, M. Wang and Z. Wang. Visual Query Suggestion. In *MM*, 2009.

[18] S. Lazebnik, C. Schmid and J. Ponce. Beyond bags of features: Spatial pyramid matching for recognizing natural scene categories. In *CVPR*, 2006.

[19] F. Li, R. Fergus and P. Perona. Learning generative visual models from few traning examples: an incremental bayesian approach tested on 101 object categories. In *CVPR workshop*, 2004.

[20] Y. Su and F. Jurie. Improving image classification using semantic attributes. International Journal of Computer Vision, 2012.

[21] J. Liu, Y. Yang and M. Shah. Learning semantic visual vocabularies using diffusion distance. In *CVPR*, 2009.

[22] Z.-J. Zha, X.-S. Hua, T. Mei, J.Wang, G.-J. Qi and Z. Wang. Joint Multi-Label Multi-Instance Learning for image classification. In *CVPR*, 2009.

[23] S. Bengio, F. Pereira, Y. Singer and D. Strelow. Group sparse coding. In *NIPS*, 2009.

[24] A. Farhadi, I. Endres, D. Hoiem and D. Forsyth. Describing objects by their attributes. In *CVPR*, 2009.

[25] D. Parikh and K. Grauman. Relative attributes. In *ICCV*,2011.

[26] D. G. Lowe. Distinctive image features from scale-invariant keypoints. International Journal of Computer Vision, 2007.

[27] G. Patterson and J. Hays. SUN Attribute Database: Discovering, Annotating, and Recognizing Scene Attributes In *CVPR*, 2012.

[28] K. Yu, T. Zhang and Y. Gong. Nonlinear learning using local coordinate coding. In *NIPS*, 2009.

[29] J. Carreira, R. Caeoiro, J. Batista and C. Sminchisescu. Semantic segmentation with second-order pooling. In *ECCV*, 2012.

[30] J. Deng, A. Berg, K. Li and L. Feifei. What does classifying more than 10,000 image categories tell us? In *ECCV*, 2010.

[31] H. Jegou, M. Douze and C. Schmid. Hamming embedding and weak geometric consistency for large scale image search. In *ECCV*, 2008.

[32] A. Shabou and H. L. Borgne. Locality-constrained and spatially regularized coding for scene categorization. In *CVPR*, 2012.

[33] Z.-J. Zha, T. Mei, J.Wang, Z. Wang and X.-S. Hua. Graph-based Semi-Supervised Learning with Multiple Lables. In *JVCIR*, 2009.

[34] P. Raghavan, C. D. Manning and H. Schtze. An introduction to information retrieval. Cambridge University Press, 2008.

[35] J. Cai, Z. Zha, W. Zhou and Q. Tian. Attribute-assisted Reranking for Web Image Retrieval. In *MM*, 2012.

[36] J. Cai, Z. Zha, Y. Zhao and Z. Wang. Evaluation Of Histogram Based Interest Point Detector In Web Image Classification And Search. In *ICME*, 2010.

[37] S. Zhang, Q. Tian, G. Hua, Q. Huang and S. Li. Discriptive visual words and visual phrases for image applications. In *MM*, 2009.

[38] Z.-J. Zha, L. Yang, T. Mei, M. Wang and Z. Wang. Visual Query Suggestion: Towards capturing user intent in internet image search. In *TOMCCAP*, 2010.

Signature Matching Distance
for Content-based Image Retrieval

Christian Beecks
RWTH Aachen University
beecks@cs.rwth-aachen.de

Steffen Kirchhoff
Harvard University
kirchhoff@fas.harvard.edu

Thomas Seidl
RWTH Aachen University
seidl@cs.rwth-aachen.de

ABSTRACT

We propose a simple yet effective approach to content-based image retrieval: the *signature matching distance*. While recent approaches to content-based image retrieval utilize the bag-of-visual-words model, where image descriptors are matched through a common visual vocabulary, signature-based approaches use a distance between signatures, i.e. between image-specific bags of locally aggregated descriptors, in order to quantify image dissimilarity. In this paper, we focus on the signature-based approach to content-based image retrieval and propose a novel distance function, the signature matching distance. This distance matches coincident visual properties of images based on their signatures. In particular, by investigating different descriptor matching strategies and their suitability to match signatures, we show that our approach is able to outperform other signature-based approaches to content-based image retrieval. Moreover, in combination with a simple color and texture-based image descriptor, our approach is able to compete with the majority of bag-of-visual-words approaches.

Categories and Subject Descriptors

H.3.3 [**Information Search and Retrieval**]: Retrieval models, Search process; I.4.10 [**Image Processing and Computer Vision**]: Image representation

General Terms

Algorithms, Experimentation, Performance

Keywords

content-based image retrieval, distance function, feature signature, signature matching distance

1. INTRODUCTION

Content-based image retrieval [5, 20] denotes the process of retrieving images from an image database that share similar contents with respect to a given query image or query sketch. The probably most frequently employed approach to perform this task is the *bag-of-visual-words* (BoVW) model

[19], which has been further investigated in recent years in order to maximize the retrieval performance. Jégou et al. [8] introduced *Hamming embedding*, which has been enhanced by Jain et al. [7] through an asymmetric version. Other approaches are the *vectors of locally aggregated descriptors* [11] and the *compressed Fisher vectors* [16], which are particularly designed for large-scale image retrieval. In general, these approaches outperform the conventional BoVW model by improving the visual vocabulary through a more descriptive quantization of the underlying feature space. This comes along with a computational extensive preprocessing phase. Besides the extraction of local feature descriptors, such as SIFT [12], a large and descriptive visual vocabulary is learned in order to model image similarity more precisely.

An alternative approach to content-based image retrieval is the *signature-based* model. Instead of describing all images by means of the same visual vocabulary, signature-based approaches represent each image individually through an image-specific visual vocabulary, which can be adapted to specific image properties dynamically, even at runtime. The resulting image representations, namely the signatures, can then be compared by distance-based dissimilarity measures [1, 17] such as the *earth mover's distance* [18] or the *signature quadratic form distance* [2].

If one is willing to model image similarity in a content-based way, either by the BoVW model or the signature-based model, one of the major challenges lies in the definition of a suitable similarity model that concentrates on the characteristic features of the images and facilitates an efficient image retrieval process. According to the latest findings [7, 11], comparing visual features of images by matching their corresponding image descriptors along a visual vocabulary has shown to achieve the highest retrieval performance in terms of efficiency and accuracy.

In this paper, we take advantage of this matching-based similarity definition and incorporate it into the signature-based model. We introduce the *signature matching distance* (SMD) as a novel approach to content-based image retrieval. The SMD adaptively defines the dissimilarity between two images based on a matching between their signatures and thus without the necessity of a common visual vocabulary. As a result, the proposed SMD is able to outperform other signature-based approaches to content-based image retrieval in terms of efficiency and accuracy. Moreover, by using a simplistic color and texture-based image descriptor, our performance evaluation on the Holidays [8] and UKBench [14] benchmark image databases reveals that the SMD is able to compete with the majority of BoVW approaches.

2. APPROACHES TO CONTENT-BASED IMAGE RETRIEVAL

In order to carry out the process of content-based image retrieval, images are modeled mathematically. This is done by first describing characteristic image properties through local feature descriptors, such as SIFT [12], and then by quantizing these descriptors in order to derive a compact and indexable image representation. While *bag-of-visual-words approaches* (BoVW) use the same quantization for all images of a database, *signature-based approaches* use a specific quantization for each image individually.

2.1 BoVW Approaches

Sivic and Zisserman [19] came up with the idea of modeling image similarity with the bag-of-visual-words model. The idea of this model is to define a similarity value between images by means of their visual word occurrences with respect to a *visual vocabulary*. Thus, an image $\mathcal{I}$ with descriptors $f(\mathcal{I}) = \{x_i\}_{i=1}^n \subset \mathbb{R}^d$ is described by assigning each descriptor x_i to its nearest visual word $q(x_i)$. The occurrences of the visual words are then counted and additionally weighted by a *tf-idf* weighting scheme such that an image $\mathcal{I}$ is finally described by the BoVW-vector $v_{\mathcal{I}} = (\text{tf-idf}(s_1), \ldots, \text{tf-idf}(s_k))^T \in \mathbb{R}^k$, where $s_j = |q^{-1}(j) \cap f(\mathcal{I})|$ denotes the number of image descriptors that are assigned to visual word j for $1 \leq j \leq k$. Typically, the similarity between two images $\mathcal{I}$ and $\mathcal{J}$ is then modeled by the normalized dot product $\text{BoVW}(v_{\mathcal{I}}, v_{\mathcal{J}}) = \frac{v_{\mathcal{I}}^T \cdot v_{\mathcal{J}}}{|v_{\mathcal{I}}| \cdot |v_{\mathcal{J}}|}$.

Jégou et al. [8] enhanced the conventional BoVW model by the *Hamming embedding*. The basic idea of this approach is to increase the descriptiveness of the visual vocabulary by additionally taking into account the descriptor distributions along the visual words. For this purpose, each descriptor x_i of an image $\mathcal{I}$ is not only assigned to a visual word $q(x_i)$ but also to a binary signature $b(x_i) \in \{0,1\}^{d_b}$ that approximates the location of the descriptor within the Voronoi cell of $q(x_i)$. Thus, an image $\mathcal{I}$ with descriptors $f(\mathcal{I}) = \{x_i\}_{i=1}^n$ is quantized by the set of tuples $x = \{(q(x_i), b(x_i))\}_{i=1}^n$. The similarity between two images $\mathcal{I}$ and $\mathcal{J}$ with descriptor quantizations $x = \{(q(x_i), b(x_i))\}_{i=1}^n$ and $y = \{(q(y_j), b(y_j))\}_{j=1}^m$ is then defined by $\text{HE}(x,y) = \frac{1}{\sqrt{m}} \sum_{i=1}^n \sum_{j=1}^m f_{\text{HE}}(x_i, y_j)$ with the Hamming embedding matching function $f_{\text{HE}}(x_i, y_j) = \text{tf-idf}(q(x_i))^2$ if and only if $q(x_i) = q(y_j) \wedge \text{H}(b(x_i), b(y_j)) \leq h_t$ and zero otherwise. Here, H denotes the Hamming distance and $h_t \in \mathbb{R}$ a fixed Hamming threshold with $0 \leq h_t \leq d_b$.

Jain et al. [7] introduced the idea of an *asymmetric Hamming embedding* by replacing the Hamming distance $\text{H}(b(x_i), b(y_j))$ between the binary signatures $b(x_i)$ and $b(y_j)$ of two descriptors x_i and y_j that are assigned to the same visual word $q(x_i) = q(y_j)$ with a sum of asymmetric distances that reflect the proximity of the descriptors more precisely.

Perronnin et al. [16] exploited the *Fisher kernel framework* [6] in order to describe each image by its gradients of the log-likelihood function given a common generative model. In this way, the generative model is used as a visual vocabulary. By using a *Gaussian mixture model* $p(x) = \sum_{i=1}^k \pi_i \cdot \mathcal{N}_{\mu_i, \Sigma_i}(x)$ with diagonal covariance matrices Σ_i, each image $\mathcal{I}$ with descriptors $f(\mathcal{I}) \subset \mathbb{R}^d$ is then represented by its *Fisher vector* $\mathcal{G}_{\mathcal{I}} = (G_1, \ldots, G_k)^T \in \mathbb{R}^{k \cdot d}$ with components $G_i = \frac{1}{\sqrt{\pi_i}} \sum_{x \in f(\mathcal{I})} \text{P}(i|x) \cdot \Sigma^{-1} \cdot (x - \mu_i) \in \mathbb{R}^d$, where $\text{P}(i|x) = \frac{\pi_i \cdot \mathcal{N}_{\mu_i, \Sigma_i}(x)}{\sum_{j=1}^k \pi_j \cdot \mathcal{N}_{\mu_j, \Sigma_j}(x)}$ denotes the soft assign-

ment of descriptor x to visual word i, which is modeled by the Gaussian density $\mathcal{N}_{\mu_i, \Sigma_i}$ for $1 \leq i \leq k$. The similarity between two images $\mathcal{I}$ and $\mathcal{J}$ is then defined by the dot product $\text{FV}(\mathcal{G}^{\mathcal{I}}, \mathcal{G}^{\mathcal{J}}) = \mathcal{G}_{\mathcal{I}}^T \cdot \mathcal{G}_{\mathcal{J}}$. The authors further propose to binarize/normalize these vectors by using *power normalization*, *locality sensitive hashing* [4], or *spectral hashing* [23].

Jégou et al. [11] introduced the *vector of locally aggregated descriptors* (VLAD) as a simplified non-probabilistic version of the Fisher vector. By assuming equal probabilities $\pi_i = \frac{1}{k}$ and *isotropic* covariance matrices Σ_i, the Fisher vector of each image $\mathcal{I}$ with descriptors $f(\mathcal{I}) \subset \mathbb{R}^d$ becomes the VLAD-descriptor $\mathcal{V}_{\mathcal{I}} = (V_1, \ldots, V_k)^T \in \mathbb{R}^{k \cdot d}$ with components $V_i = \sum_{x \in f(\mathcal{I}) \wedge q(x) = i} (x - \mu_i) \in \mathbb{R}^d$, where each mean $\mu_i \in \mathbb{R}^d$ is the visual word representing $q(x) = i$ for $1 \leq i \leq k$. Given two images $\mathcal{I}$ and $\mathcal{J}$, their distance is defined by $\text{VLAD}(\mathcal{V}_{\mathcal{I}}, \mathcal{V}_{\mathcal{J}}) = \text{L}_2(\mathcal{V}_{\mathcal{I}}, \mathcal{V}_{\mathcal{J}})$. Further, normalizations of the VLAD-descriptors have been proposed [11].

2.2 Signature-based Approaches

Signature-based approaches quantize the descriptors of each image individually by means of an image-specific visual vocabulary, namely the *signature* [18]. Given a descriptor space $\mathbb{R}^d$, a signature X is defined by a finite set of representatives $\text{R}_X \subset \mathbb{R}^d$, where each representative is additionally assigned to a non-negative weight by a weighting function $w_X : \text{R}_X \rightarrow \mathbb{R}^{\geq 0}$. Thus, a signature X can be defined mathematically as the graph of its weighting function w_X, i.e. $X = \{(x, w_X(x)) | x \in \text{R}_X\}$. Given an image $\mathcal{I}$, its signature can be computed by clustering the set of extracted descriptors $f(\mathcal{I})$ and defining the representatives of the signature by the cluster centroids. The weighting function can be defined by the corresponding cluster sizes. In this way, the representatives and weights correspond to the visual words and their frequencies of an image-specific visual vocabulary. Since these visual words differ, signature-based approaches apply a so-called *ground distance* $\delta : \mathbb{R}^d \times \mathbb{R}^d \rightarrow \mathbb{R}$ between all representatives in order to define a *signature distance*.

The *earth mover's distance* (EMD) [18] is a *transformation-based* approach measuring the cost of transforming one signature into another. The earth mover's distance EMD_δ between two signatures X and Y is defined as a minimum cost flow over all possible flows $[f_{xy}] = F \in \mathbb{R}^{|\text{R}_X| \times |\text{R}_Y|}$ between the elements $x, y \in \text{R}_X \cup \text{R}_Y$, i.e. $\text{EMD}_\delta(X,Y) = \min_F \left\{ \frac{\sum_{x \in \text{R}_X} \sum_{y \in \text{R}_Y} f_{xy} \cdot \delta(x,y)}{\min\{\sum_{x \in \text{R}_X} w_X(x), \sum_{y \in \text{R}_Y} w_Y(y)\}} \right\}$, subject to the constraints $\forall x, y : f_{xy} \geq 0$, $\forall x \in \text{R}_X : \sum_{y \in \text{R}_Y} f_{xy} \leq w_X(x)$, $\forall y \in \text{R}_Y : \sum_{x \in \text{R}_X} f_{xy} \leq w_Y(y)$, and $\sum_{x \in \text{R}_X} \sum_{y \in \text{R}_Y} f_{xy} = \min\{\sum_{x \in \text{R}_X} w_X(x), \sum_{y \in \text{R}_Y} w_Y(y)\}$.

The *perceptually modified Hausdorff distance* (PMHD) [15] is a *matching-based* approach. A *matching* between two signatures X, Y can be defined as $\text{m}_{X \rightarrow Y} = \{(x, \pi_{X \rightarrow Y}(x)) | \forall x \in \text{R}_X\}$, where the *matching function* $\pi_{X \rightarrow Y} : \text{R}_X \rightarrow \text{R}_Y$ maps each representative $x \in \text{R}_X$ to one representative $y \in \text{R}_Y$. Additionally, a cost function $\text{c} : 2^{\text{R}_X \times \text{R}_Y} \rightarrow \mathbb{R}$ defines the cost of a matching. The perceptually modified Hausdorff distance is then defined as $\text{PMHD}_\delta(X, Y) = \max\{\text{c}(\text{m}_{X \rightarrow Y}), \text{c}(\text{m}_{Y \rightarrow X})\}$. The matching $\text{m}_{X \rightarrow Y}$ is defined by the graph of the matching function $\pi_{X \rightarrow Y}(x) = \text{argmin}_{y \in \text{R}_Y} \left\{ \frac{\delta(x,y)}{\min\{w_X(x), w_Y(y)\}} \right\}$, and the cost c of the matching is defined as $\text{c}(\text{m}_{X \rightarrow Y}) = \sum_{(x,y) \in \text{m}_{X \rightarrow Y}} \frac{w_X(x)}{\sum_{(x,y) \in \text{m}_{X \rightarrow Y}} w_X(x)} \cdot \frac{\delta(x,y)}{\min\{w_X(x), w_Y(y)\}}$. The matching $\text{m}_{Y \rightarrow X}$ is defined analogously.

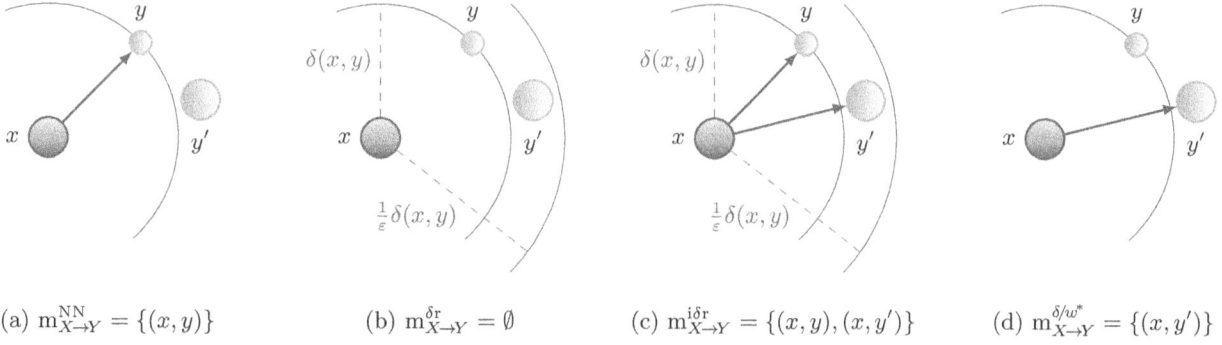

(a) $m_{X \to Y}^{NN} = \{(x, y)\}$ (b) $m_{X \to Y}^{\delta r} = \emptyset$ (c) $m_{X \to Y}^{i\delta r} = \{(x, y), (x, y')\}$ (d) $m_{X \to Y}^{\delta / w^*} = \{(x, y')\}$

Figure 1: Illustration of the different matching strategies between two signatures $X = \{(x, w_X(x))\}$ **and** $Y = \{(y, w_Y(y)), (y', w_Y(y'))\}$**: (a) nearest neighbor matching, (b) distance ratio matching, (c) inverse distance ratio matching, and (d) distance weight ratio matching.**

The *signature quadratic form distance* (SQFD) [2] is a *correlation-based* approach that uses a *similarity function* s : $\mathbb{R}^d \times \mathbb{R}^d \to \mathbb{R}$ to quantify similarities among representatives of the signatures. Based on a similarity function s, we define the *weighted similarity correlation* between two signatures X and Y as $X \cdot_s Y = \sum_{x \in R_X} \sum_{y \in R_Y} w_X(x) \cdot w_Y(y) \cdot s(x, y)$. The signature quadratic form distance $SQFD_s$ is then defined as follows: $SQFD_s(X, Y) = \sqrt{X \cdot_s X - X \cdot_s Y - Y \cdot_s X + Y \cdot_s Y}$.

To sum up, BoVW approaches utilize a common visual vocabulary in order to match image descriptors to predetermined visual words. In contrast, signature-based approaches utilize image-specific visual vocabularies in order to adapt the distance computation to individual descriptor distributions. Depending on the intended notion of similarity, different types of distances can thus be used. For instance for the purpose of content-based image retrieval where image similarity is frequently assessed by the amount of properties the images share, it is meaningful to attribute the distance computation to the most similar parts of the signatures. This is done by a *matching*, as investigated in the next section.

3. SIGNATURE MATCHING STRATEGIES

In this section, we present different matching strategies and discuss their suitability for modeling similarity between signatures. Given two signatures X and Y with their representatives R_X and R_Y, a *matching* $m_{X \to Y}$ between X and Y is defined as a subset of the Cartesian product of their representatives, i.e. $m_{X \to Y} \subseteq R_X \times R_Y$. This definition includes the assignment of multiple representatives from R_X to R_Y and vice versa. The most intuitive way to match representatives between signatures is by means of the concept of the nearest neighbor, which is defined for an element $x \in \mathbb{R}^d$, a ground distance δ, and a set $R \subset \mathbb{R}^d$ as $NN_{\delta,R}(x) = \{y \mid y = \operatorname{argmin}_{y' \in R} \delta(x, y')\}$. This leads to the following definition of the *nearest neighbor matching* [13].

DEFINITION 1. *Nearest Neighbor Matching*
Given two signatures X, Y *and a ground distance* δ, *the* nearest neighbor matching $m_{X \to Y}^{NN} \subseteq R_X \times R_Y$ *from* X *to* Y *is defined as:*

$$m_{X \to Y}^{NN} = \{(x, y) \mid y \in NN_{\delta, R_Y}(x)\}.$$

The nearest neighbor matching $m_{X \to Y}^{NN}$ satisfies both *left totality* and *right uniqueness*, i.e. $\forall x \in R_X \exists y \in R_Y : (x, y) \in m_{X \to Y}^{NN}$ and $\forall x \in R_X, \forall y, z \in R_Y : (x, y) \in m_{X \to Y}^{NN} \land (x, z) \in m_{X \to Y}^{NN} \Rightarrow y = z$. Each representative $x \in R_X$ is matched to

the representative $y \in R_Y$ that minimizes $\delta(x, y)$. Thus, the nearest neighbor matching $m_{X \to Y}^{NN}$ is of size $|m_{X \to Y}^{NN}| = |R_X|$. Figure 1(a) provides an example of $m_{X \to Y}^{NN}$ where $x \in R_X$ is matched to $y \in R_Y$. As can be seen in this example, the distance $\delta(x, y)$ and $\delta(x, y')$ differs only marginally. Thus, the nearest neighbor matching becomes ambiguous, since both representatives y and y' serve as good matching candidates.

A well-known strategy to overcome the issue of ambiguity of the nearest neighbor matching is given by the *distance ratio matching* [13]. Intuitively, it is defined by matching only those parts of the signatures that are unique with respect to the ratio of the nearest and second nearest neighbor.

DEFINITION 2. *Distance Ratio Matching*
Given two signatures X, Y *and a ground distance* δ, *the distance ratio matching* $m_{X \to Y}^{\delta r} \subseteq R_X \times R_Y$ *from* X *to* Y *is defined by a parameter* $\varepsilon \in [0, 1]$ *as:*

$$m_{X \to Y}^{\delta r} =$$
$$\{(x, y) \mid y \in NN_{\delta, R_Y}(x) \land y' \in NN_{\delta, R_Y \setminus \{y\}}(x) \land \frac{\delta(x, y)}{\delta(x, y')} < \varepsilon\}.$$

The distance ratio matching $m_{X \to Y}^{\delta r}$ does not satisfy left totality but it satisfies right uniqueness, i.e. every $x \in R_X$ is matched to at most one $y \in R_Y$. Thus, the size of this matching is $|m_{X \to Y}^{\delta r}| \leq |R_X|$. In the extreme case, the matching could even be empty, i.e. $m_{X \to Y}^{\delta r} = \emptyset$, as illustrated in Figure 1(b). In fact, the matching $m_{X \to Y}^{\delta r}$ epitomizes a defensive matching strategy. It completely rejects those pairs that result in an ambiguous matching. Since we empirically found that this behavior jeopardizes the retrieval performance, see Section 5, we propose a more offensive strategy that works the other way around. Instead of excluding those pairs (x, y) and (x, y') from $m_{X \to Y}^{NN}$ that cause ambiguity, we propose to include them, as formalized in the definition below.

DEFINITION 3. *Inverse Distance Ratio Matching*
Given two signatures X, Y *and a ground distance* δ, *the inverse distance ratio matching* $m_{X \to Y}^{i\delta r} \subseteq R_X \times R_Y$ *from* X *to* Y *is defined by a parameter* $\varepsilon \in [0, 1]$ *as:*

$$m_{X \to Y}^{i\delta r} = m_{X \to Y}^{NN} \cup$$
$$\{(x, y') \mid y \in NN_{\delta, R_Y}(x) \land y' \in NN_{\delta, R_Y \setminus \{y\}}(x) \land \frac{\delta(x, y)}{\delta(x, y')} > \varepsilon\}.$$

In contrast to the distance ratio matching, the inverse variant $m_{X \to Y}^{i\delta r}$ satisfies left totality but not right uniqueness. As can be seen in Figure 1(c), each $x \in R_X$ is assigned to

43

at most two representatives from signature Y. This leads to a matching size of $|m_{X\to Y}^{i\delta r}| \leq 2 \cdot |R_X|$. In general, it can be shown that the inverse distance ratio matching is a generalization of the nearest neighbor matching, while the distance ratio matching is a specialization, i.e. it holds that $m_{X\to Y}^{\delta r} \subseteq m_{X\to Y}^{NN} \subseteq m_{X\to Y}^{i\delta r}$ with equality for $\varepsilon = 1$.

The aforementioned matchings consider only the spatial distance δ between two representatives $x \in R_X$ and $y \in R_Y$ in a descriptor space $\mathbb{R}^d$, not their weights $w_X(x)$ and $w_Y(y)$. These weights may nonetheless significantly contribute to the similarity definition. Thus, we propose the *distance weight ratio matching*, which is defined in a self-adjusting manner for two representatives $x \in R_X$ and $y \in R_Y$ by means of their *distance weight ratio* $\delta/w^*(x,y) = \delta(x,y)/\min\{w_X(x), w_Y(y)\}$. By utilizing this ratio δ/w^*, we define the distance weight ratio matching free of any predefined threshold as it is used for the calculation of the PMHD.

DEFINITION 4. *Distance Weight Ratio Matching*
Given two signatures X, Y and a ground distance δ, the distance weight ratio matching $m_{X\to Y}^{\delta/w^*} \subseteq R_X \times R_Y$ from X to Y is defined as:

$$m_{X\to Y}^{\delta/w^*} = \{(x,y) \mid y = \operatorname{argmin}_{y' \in R_Y} \delta/w^*(x,y')\}.$$

The distance weight ratio matching $m_{X\to Y}^{\delta/w^*}$ satisfies both left totality and right uniqueness. Thus, this matching is of size $|m_{X\to Y}^{\delta/w^*}| = |R_X|$. In addition to only minimizing the distance between representatives, this matching also considers the weights of the representatives. By dividing the ground distance δ between two representatives x and y by their minimal weight, this matching penalizes those representatives y that have a smaller weight than representative x. This is illustrated in Figure 1(d). Although representative y is located slightly closer to x than representative y', x is not matched to y since the fact that $w_Y(y) < w_X(x)$ increases the distance weight ratio such that $\delta/w^*(x,y') < \delta/w^*(x,y)$. As a consequence, the distance weight ratio matching suppresses the contribution of noisy representatives of the signatures.

We have presented four different matching strategies that allow to match coincident visual properties of signatures. Based on these matchings, we introduce the *signature matching distance* in the following section.

4. SIGNATURE MATCHING DISTANCE

In this section, we introduce our novel signature-based approach to content-based image retrieval, the *signature matching distance* (SMD). This will be complemented by an analysis of its properties and suitable cost functions that provide a theoretical means of assessing the quality of a matching.

4.1 Definition

The fundamental idea of the SMD is to model the distance between two signatures by means of the cost of the symmetric difference of the matching elements of the signatures. In general, the *symmetric difference* $A \triangle B$ of two sets A and B is the set of elements which are contained in either A or B but not in their intersection $A \cap B$, i.e. $A \triangle B = A \cup B \setminus A \cap B$. By adapting this concept to matchings between signatures X and Y, the set A becomes the matching $m_{X\to Y}$ from signature X to Y, and the set B becomes the matching $m_{Y\to X}$ from signature Y to X. The symmetric difference $m_{X\to Y} \triangle m_{Y\to X} = \{(x,y) \mid (x,y) \in m_{X\to Y} \oplus (y,x) \in m_{Y\to X}\}$

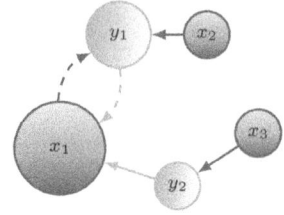

Figure 2: Matching-based principle of the SMD between two signatures $X = \{(x_i, w_X(x_i))\}_{i=1}^{3}$ and $Y = \{(y_i, w_Y(y_i))\}_{i=1}^{2}$. While the symmetric difference $m_{X\to Y} \triangle m_{Y\to X}$ completely neglects the matching between x_1 and y_1, the SMD includes this bidirectional matching dependent on parameter λ.

can then be evaluated by a cost function in order to model a distance between the corresponding signatures X and Y.

An example of the symmetric difference $m_{X\to Y} \triangle m_{Y\to X}$ between two signatures $X = \{(x_i, w_X(x_i))\}_{i=1}^{3}$ and $Y = \{(y_i, w_Y(y_i))\}_{i=1}^{2}$ is depicted in Figure 2, where the representatives of X and Y are shown by blue and orange circles, and the corresponding weights are indicated by the respective diameters. In this example, the distance weight ratio matching defines the matchings $m_{X\to Y}^{\delta/w^*} = \{(x_1, y_1), (x_2, y_1), (x_3, y_2)\}$ and $m_{Y\to X}^{\delta/w^*} = \{(y_1, x_1), (y_2, x_1)\}$, which are depicted by blue and orange arrows between the corresponding representatives of the signatures. As can be seen in the figure, the symmetric difference $m_{X\to Y} \triangle m_{Y\to X} = \{(x_2, y_1), (x_3, y_2), (x_1, y_2)\}$ completely neglects bidirectional matches that are depicted by the dashed arrows, i.e. it neglects those pairs of representatives $x \in R_X$ and $y \in R_Y$ for which holds that $(x,y) \in m_{X\to Y} \wedge (y,x) \in m_{Y\to X}$.

On the one hand, excluding these bidirectional matches corresponds to the idea of measuring dissimilarity by those elements of the signatures that are less similar, on the other hand the exclusion of bidirectional matches reduces the discriminability of similar signatures whose matchings mainly comprise bidirectional matches. In order to balance this trade-off, we generalize the symmetric difference and define the SMD with an additional real-valued parameter $\lambda \in [0,1]$ that models the *exclusion of bidirectional matchings* from the distance computation.

DEFINITION 5. *Signature Matching Distance*
Given two signatures X and Y, a matching strategy m, and a cost function c, the signature matching distance SMD between X and Y with respect to parameter $\lambda \in [0,1]$ is defined as follows:

$$\text{SMD}_\lambda(X, Y) = c(m_{X\to Y}) + c(m_{Y\to X}) - 2\lambda \cdot c(m_{X\leftrightarrow Y}).$$

The computation of the SMD between two signatures X and Y is carried out by adding the costs $c(m_{X\to Y})$ and $c(m_{Y\to X})$ of matching representatives from X to Y and from Y to X, and subtracting the cost $c(m_{X\leftrightarrow Y})$ of the corresponding bidirectional matching $m_{X\leftrightarrow Y} = \{(x,y) \mid (x,y) \in m_{X\to Y} \wedge (y,x) \in m_{Y\to X}\}$. The cost $c(m_{X\leftrightarrow Y})$ are multiplied by parameter $\lambda \in [0,1]$ and doubled, since bidirectional matches occur in both matchings $m_{X\to Y}$ and $m_{Y\to X}$. As mentioned above, the parameter λ models the exclusion of bidirectional matchings. In particular, a value of $\lambda = 0$ includes the cost of bidirectional matchings in the distance computation, while a value of $\lambda = 1$ excludes the cost of bidirectional matchings in the distance computation. In case $\lambda = 1$ the SMD between two signatures X and Y becomes

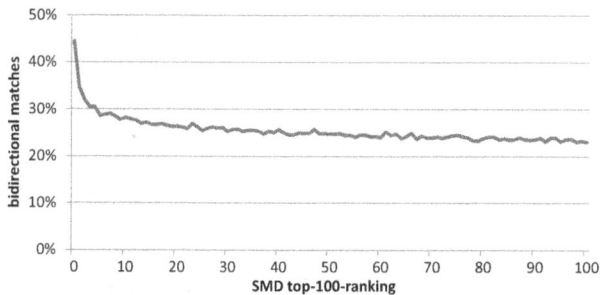

Figure 3: Percentage of bidirectional matches for the distance weight ratio matching m^{δ/w^*} on the Holidays database for the 100 most similar images.

the cost of the symmetric difference of the corresponding matchings, i.e. $\mathrm{SMD}_{\lambda=1}(X, Y) = \mathrm{c}(\mathrm{m}_{X \to Y} \,\Delta\, \mathrm{m}_{Y \to X})$.

But which particular role play bidirectional matches for the purpose of content-based image retrieval? We briefly discuss their impact on the dissimilarity definition before we continue with describing one prominent way of assessing the cost of a matching by means of a ground distance.

4.2 Bidirectional Matches

Intuitively, bidirectional matches describe a more stable relationship between two representatives of the corresponding signatures than unidirectional matches. Consequently, the number of bidirectional matches between two signatures should increase with increasing similarity of the corresponding images. We could observe this intuition empirically on the Holidays image database by measuring the percentage of bidirectional matches on basis of the distance weight ratio matching m^{δ/w^*}. As can be seen in Figure 3, the average percentage of bidirectional matches for the 100 most similar images regarding multiple queries decreases with increasing rank of the images. While the matching between the query and its nearest neighbor on average comprises 44% bidirectional matches, this number diminishes to 23% for the images at ranking position 100. Further, the least similar images contain only 10% bidirectional matches.

As a consequence, adjusting the parameter λ to a value of smaller than 1 in order to include the cost of bidirectional matches seems to be appropriate for most similarity definitions. We will investigate the choice and stability of the parameter λ in Section 5.

4.3 Cost Functions

The calculation of the SMD between two signatures follows a two-step approach. First, a matching between the representatives of the signatures is determined. Second, this matching is evaluated according to a cost function. A naive way of assessing the cost of a matching consists in counting the number of matches. This would, however, only roughly reflect the similarity relationship between two signatures, because the cardinality of a matching does not take into account the coincident characteristics of the matching elements. An alternative that considers the differences of the matching elements are ground distance-based cost functions.

DEFINITION 6. *Ground Distance-based Cost Functions* *Given a matching* $\mathrm{m}_{X \to Y}$ *between two signatures* X *and* Y *and a ground distance* δ*, we define the following* ground

distance-based cost functions $\mathrm{c} : 2^{\mathrm{R}_X \times \mathrm{R}_Y} \to \mathbb{R}^{\geq 0}$:

$$\mathrm{c}_\delta(\mathrm{m}_{X \to Y}) = \sum_{(x,y) \in \mathrm{m}_{X \to Y}} w_X(x) \cdot w_Y(y) \cdot \delta(x, y),$$

$$\mathrm{c}_{\delta/w^*}(\mathrm{m}_{X \to Y}) = \sum_{(x,y) \in \mathrm{m}_{X \to Y}} w_X(x) \cdot w_Y(y) \cdot \delta/w^*(x, y).$$

The idea of both ground distance-based cost functions is to evaluate a matching $\mathrm{m}_{X \to Y}$ by its weighted ground distances δ or its weighted distance weight ratios δ/w^* between the matching representatives x and y of the signatures X and Y. The more similar the matching representatives, the smaller the values of δ and δ/w^*, thus the lower the cost of the respective matching. Intuitively, provided that the weights of the signatures are normalized, i.e. $\sum_{x \in \mathrm{R}_X} w_X(x) = \sum_{y \in \mathrm{R}_Y} w_Y(y) = 1$, these cost functions are equivalent to the expected ground distance and to the expected distance weight ratio constrained to the matching $\mathrm{m}_{X \to Y}$, i.e. $\mathrm{c}_\delta(\mathrm{m}_{X \to Y}) = \mathrm{E}[\delta | \mathrm{m}_{X \to Y}]$ and $\mathrm{c}_{\delta/w^*}(\mathrm{m}_{X \to Y}) = \mathrm{E}[\delta/w^* | \mathrm{m}_{X \to Y}]$, respectively. The normalization of the signature weights is necessary in order to not favor smaller matchings over larger matchings.

To sum up, the SMD is a matching-based distance function designed for signatures. Provided that the computation time complexity of the underlying matching $\mathrm{m}_{X \to Y}$ lies in $\mathcal{O}(|\mathrm{R}_X| \cdot |\mathrm{R}_Y|)$ and that the cost function can be computed in linear time complexity with respect to the matching size, i.e. for a given matching $\mathrm{m}_{X \to Y}$ between two signatures X and Y its time complexity lies in $\mathcal{O}(|\mathrm{m}_{X \to Y}|)$, the SMD has a quadratic computation time complexity of $\mathcal{O}(|\mathrm{R}_X| \cdot |\mathrm{R}_Y|)$.

5. PERFORMANCE EVALUATION

In this section, we study the performance of the SMD and compare it to that of state-of-the-art content-based image retrieval approaches. For this purpose, we used the Holidays [8] and UKBench [14] image databases, both providing a solid ground truth for benchmarking image retrieval approaches. The Holidays database comprises 1,491 holiday photos corresponding to a large variety of scene types. It was designed to test the robustness, for instance, to rotation, viewpoint, and illumination changes and provides 500 selected queries. The UKBench database consists of 10,200 images showing 2,550 different objects or scenes that are photographed from four different viewpoints. The first image of each object or scene serves as query object.

Based on these databases, we generated signatures by extracting local feature descriptors and by clustering them with the k-means algorithm. We extracted three different descriptors: a low-dimensional descriptor denoted by PCT [1], which is based on position, color, and texture, as well as the SIFT [12] and CSIFT [3] descriptors. The PCT descriptor describes the relative spatial information of a pixel, its CIELAB color value, and its first and second Tamura texture features [21], which are coarseness and contrast. We utilized a random sampling of 40,000 pixels to extract the PCT descriptors and the Harris-Laplace detector to extract the SIFT and CSIFT descriptors. The color descriptor software provided by van de Sande et al. [22] was used to extract the SIFT and CSIFT descriptors. After having extracted the local feature descriptors, we applied the k-means clustering algorithm to generate multiple signatures per image by varying the signature size between 10 and 100.

Table 1: Retrieval performance of the SMD on the Holidays and UKBench databases by using different combinations of matching strategies and descriptors. The ground distance is set to $\delta = L_1$, the cost function is set to c_{δ/w^*}, and bidirectional matches are not excluded, i.e. $\lambda = 0$. The parameter $\varepsilon \in [0,1]$ defines the threshold of the matchings $m^{\delta r}$ and $m^{i\delta r}$.

| | | Holidays | | | UKBench | | | |
		MAP	ε	size	MAP	score	ε	size
m^{NN}	PCT	0.810	–	100	0.845	3.20	–	60
	SIFT	0.653	–	40	0.463	1.75	–	20
	CSIFT	0.735	–	20	0.531	2.00	–	20
$m^{\delta r}$	PCT	0.810	1.0	100	0.845	3.20	1.0	60
	SIFT	0.653	1.0	40	0.463	1.75	1.0	20
	CSIFT	0.735	1.0	20	0.531	2.00	1.0	20
$m^{i\delta r}$	PCT	**0.822**	0.8	70	**0.860**	3.27	0.7	60
	SIFT	0.663	0.6	40	0.517	1.98	0.8	90
	CSIFT	0.755	0.8	30	0.591	2.23	0.8	20
m^{δ/w^*}	PCT	0.819	–	90	0.855	3.24	–	100
	SIFT	0.656	–	40	0.463	1.74	–	20
	CSIFT	0.725	–	20	0.529	2.00	–	20

Table 2: Retrieval performance of the signature-based approaches on the Holidays and UKBench databases.

| | | Holidays | | UKBench | | |
		MAP	size	MAP	score	size
EMD	PCT	0.720	90	0.741	2.78	50
	SIFT	0.678	70	0.536	2.05	90
	CSIFT	0.749	40	0.605	2.31	30
PMHD	PCT	0.804	80	**0.866**	3.30	90
	SIFT	0.673	70	0.531	2.03	90
	CSIFT	0.755	40	0.594	2.27	30
SQFD	PCT	0.761	40	0.766	2.86	60
	SIFT	0.690	80	0.585	2.23	100
	CSIFT	0.756	20	0.494	2.25	20
SMD	PCT	**0.810**	100	0.845	3.20	60
	SIFT	0.653	40	0.463	1.75	20
	CSIFT	0.735	20	0.531	2.00	20

5.1 Performance Analysis of the SMD

The retrieval performance of the SMD is summarized in Table 1, where we report the *mean average precision* (MAP) values for the Holidays and UKBench databases and the *score* [14] for the latter. The score denotes the average number of relevant images ranked within the four nearest neighbors of a query. The retrieval performance is based on all queries defined by the ground truth of the corresponding databases. We additionally include the optimal values of parameter $\varepsilon \in [0,1]$, which defines the threshold of the matchings $m^{\delta r}$ and $m^{i\delta r}$. The reported values were obtained by using the distance weight ratio cost function c_{δ/w^*} with the Manhattan ground distance L_1 since we empirically found that this combination outperforms the other variants.

As can be seen in Table 1, both databases reveal the same tendencies. First, the SMD on PCT-based signatures outperforms that on SIFT-based and CSIFT-based signatures by reaching the highest MAP values of 0.822 and 0.860 on the Holidays and UKBench databases with signatures of sizes 70 and 60, respectively. Second, the distance ratio matching $m^{\delta r}$ provides acceptable retrieval performance only when setting its inherent threshold ε to a value of 1, thus turning this matching into the nearest neighbor matching, i.e. $m^{NN} = m^{\delta r}$. Third, the retrieval performance of the aforementioned matchings and of the distance weight ratio matching m^{δ/w^*} is slightly below that of our proposed inverse distance ratio matching $m^{i\delta r}$, which mitigates the issue of matching ambiguity.

We continue with investigating the stability of the SMD with respect to the parameters $\varepsilon \in [0,1]$ and $\lambda \in [0,1]$ that model the matching threshold and the influence of bidirectional matches. Figures 4 and 5 depict the retrieval performance for the Holidays and UKBench databases by utilizing the matching $m^{i\delta r}$ in combination with PCT-based signatures, since this combination has shown the highest retrieval performance. As can be seen in Figure 4(a) and Figure 5(a), the threshold ε of the matching $m^{i\delta r}$ is less sensitive to changes the larger the signature size, and vice versa. By setting the matching threshold ε to an approximate value of 0.7, which corresponds to the empirical observation of Mikolajczyk and Schmid [13], and using PCT-based signa-

tures of size greater than 30, the retrieval performance of the SMD stays above a MAP value of 0.8 for both databases. In general, the retrieval performance of the SMD is further improved by excluding the costs of bidirectional matches, as shown in Figure 4(b) and Figure 5(b). By increasing the parameter λ to the values of 0.85 and 0.90, the SMD achieves the MAP values of 0.834 and 0.876 on the Holidays and UKBench databases, respectively.

5.2 Comparison to Signature-based Approaches

Let us now compare the SMD to the other signature-based approaches. In particular, we compare it to the earth mover's distance (EMD), the perceptually modified Hausdorff distance (PMHD), and the signature quadratic form distance (SQFD). The results are summarized in Table 2, where we report the highest MAP values that we have achieved for the other signature-based approaches and, in order to preserve comparability, the MAP values for the SMD with default parameter $\lambda = 0$ and the nearest neighbor matching strategy m^{NN}. In general, the reported values reveal the same tendency as those shown in Table 1. The highest retrieval performance is achieved when using PCT-based signatures, except the EMD on the Holidays database, where the CSIFT descriptor performs best. The default SMD outperforms the other signature-based approaches on the Holidays database, while it is outperformed by the PMHD on the UKBench database. However, as has been shown in the previous section, the SMD is able to improve the retrieval performance when adapting the parameters appropriately.

We finally analyze the efficiency of the SMD in comparison to the other signature-based approaches. For this purpose, we measured the computation times needed to perform 1 million distance computations on a single-core 3.4 GHz machine. We implemented all signature-based approaches in Java 1.6. On average, the SMD is approximately three times faster than the PMHD, 15 times faster than the SQFD, and 84 times faster than the EMD. By using PCT-based signatures of size 10, the SMD performs 1 million distance computations in 1.4s. This value increases to 82.8s when using PCT-based signatures of size 100. We thus conclude that the SMD is able to outperform other signature-based approaches to content-based image retrieval in terms of efficiency and accuracy.

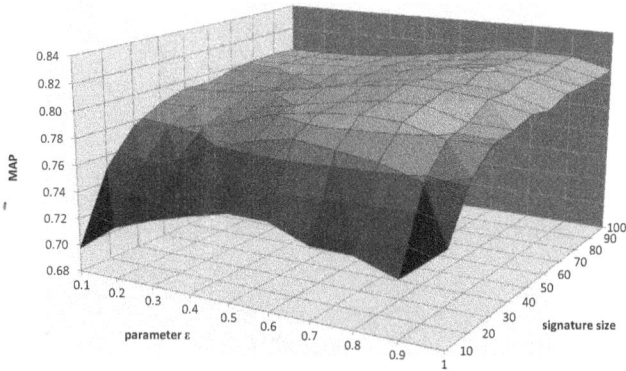 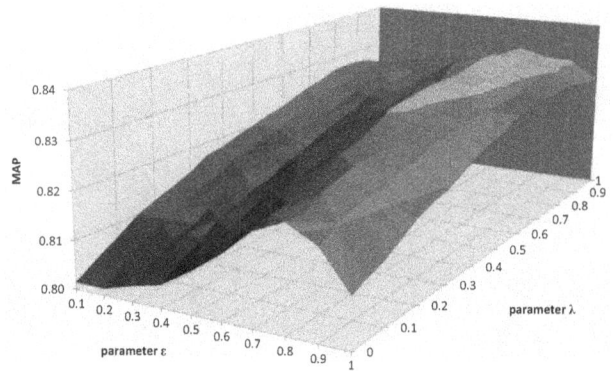

(a)   (b)

Figure 4: Mean average precision values of the SMD on the Holidays database by using the inverse distance ratio matching $m^{i\delta r}$. (a): MAP values as a function of the parameter ε and the signature size (parameter $\lambda = 0$), (b): maximum MAP values over all signature sizes as a function of the parameters ε and λ.

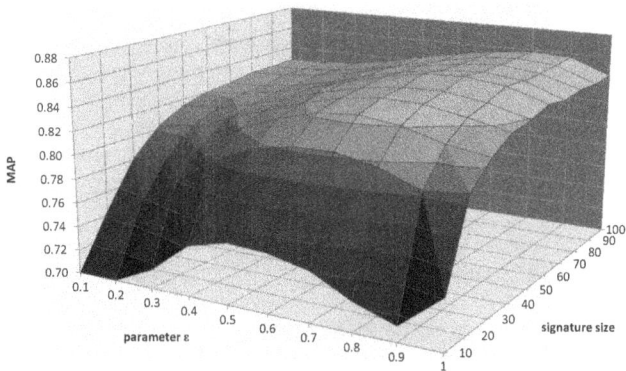 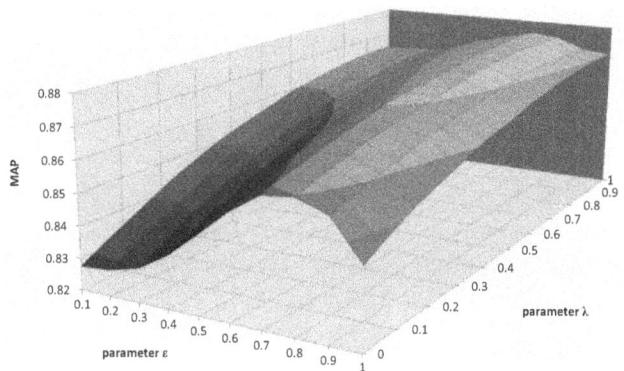

(a)   (b)

Figure 5: Mean average precision values of the SMD on the UKBench database by using the inverse distance ratio matching $m^{i\delta r}$. (a): MAP values as a function of the parameter ε and the signature size (parameter $\lambda = 0$), (b): maximum MAP values over all signature sizes as a function of the parameters ε and λ.

5.3 Comparison to BoVW Approaches

We compare the performance of our proposed approach to those of the conventional bag-of-visual-words approaches (BoVW) as well as to recent extensions, namely Hamming embedding (HE), compressed Fisher vectors (FV), vector of locally aggregated descriptors (VLAD), and asymmetric Hamming embedding (AHE). Since our focus lies on investigating the maximum achievable retrieval performance in the context of content-based image retrieval, we report the MAP values of the BoVW approaches obtained by optimizing their parameters and refer to the corresponding research articles for details concerning the parameter selection and optimization of the particular methods.

The retrieval performance results are summarized in Table 3. As can be seen in the table, the classic BoVW approach with a vocabulary size of 20k and 200k visual words is generally outperformed by the extensions of the BoVW model and our signature-based approach. Among the BoVW extensions, the AHE and the FV approaches reach the highest retrieval performance on the Holidays and UKBench databases, respectively. The proposed SMD is able to compete with these approaches. It shows the highest and the

second highest retrieval performance on the Holidays and UKBench databases.

Regarding the computation times of recent BoVW approaches, Jain et al. [7] report a value of 1.7s for HE and 2.9s for AHE while Perronnin et al. [16] report a value of 0.4s for FV when searching 1 million images. Jégou et al. [10] report a value of 7.2s for VLAD on a 10 million image dataset which approximately corresponds to 0.72s for 1 million images. All computation times are measured on a single-core CPU. However, since the implementation details are not apparent in the respective research articles, it is infeasible to directly compare the runtimes of the different approaches. We nonetheless report these values in order to give a rough idea on the magnitude of runtime and the applicability for content-based image retrieval tasks.

Summarizing, the performance evaluation shows that the SMD competes with the state-of-the-art approaches to content-based image retrieval by using a simplistic color and texture-based image descriptor. In fact, it outperforms the AHE approach that shows the best results so far [7] on the Holidays database.

Table 3: Retrieval performance of the signature-based approaches and the bag-of-visual-words approaches on the Holidays and UKBench databases.

	Holidays	UKBench	
	MAP	MAP	score
BoVW (20k) (from [9])	0.469	0.752	–
BoVW (200k) (from [9])	0.572	0.771	–
HE (from [9])	0.813	**0.878**	3.42
FV (from [16])	0.735	–	**3.50**
VLAD (from [11])	0.621	–	3.35
AHE (from [7])	0.819	–	–
Our approach	**0.834**	0.876	3.34

6. CONCLUSIONS AND FUTURE WORK

In this paper, we have addressed the problem of content-based image retrieval by means of the signature-based model. To this end, we have outlined two complementary approaches to content-based image retrieval, namely the bag-of-visual-words model and the signature-based model. We investigated different matching strategies and analyzed their suitability to match coincident visual properties between images based on their signatures. We proposed a novel matching strategy, the inverse distance ratio matching, and a novel distance function, the signature matching distance (SMD). Besides the theoretical definition of this distance, we investigated its properties and studied its performance in comparison to both the bag-of-visual-words approaches and the other signature-based approaches on different benchmark image databases.

Our performance evaluation reveals that the SMD is able to outperform other signature-based approaches to content-based image retrieval in terms of efficiency and accuracy. Moreover, the SMD shows a higher performance than the majority of bag-of-visual-words approaches by using a simple color and texture-based image descriptor. We thus conclude, that the SMD is a simple yet effective signature-based approach that is able to compete with the state of the art in content-based image retrieval.

As future work, we plan to investigate signature-based indexing methods in order to apply the SMD to large-scale image retrieval.

Acknowledgments

This work is partially funded by the Excellence Initiative of the German federal and state governments and by DFG grant SE 1039/7-1.

7. REFERENCES

[1] C. Beecks, M. S. Uysal, and T. Seidl. A comparative study of similarity measures for content-based multimedia retrieval. In *ICME*, pages 1552–1557, 2010.

[2] C. Beecks, M. S. Uysal, and T. Seidl. Signature Quadratic Form Distance. In *CIVR*, pages 438–445, 2010.

[3] G. J. Burghouts and J.-M. Geusebroek. Performance evaluation of local colour invariants. *CVIU*, 113(1):48–62, 2009.

[4] M. Charikar. Similarity estimation techniques from rounding algorithms. In *STOC*, pages 380–388, 2002.

[5] R. Datta, D. Joshi, J. Li, and J. Z. Wang. Image retrieval: Ideas, influences, and trends of the new age. *ACM Comput. Surv.*, 40(2), 2008.

[6] T. Jaakkola and D. Haussler. Exploiting generative models in discriminative classifiers. In *NIPS*, pages 487–493, 1998.

[7] M. Jain, H. Jégou, and P. Gros. Asymmetric hamming embedding: taking the best of our bits for large scale image search. In *ACM Multimedia*, pages 1441–1444, 2011.

[8] H. Jégou, M. Douze, and C. Schmid. Hamming Embedding and Weak Geometric Consistency for Large Scale Image Search. In *ECCV (1)*, pages 304–317, 2008.

[9] H. Jégou, M. Douze, and C. Schmid. Improving Bag-of-Features for Large Scale Image Search. *IJCV*, 87:316–336, 2010.

[10] H. Jégou, M. Douze, C. Schmid, and P. Pérez. Aggregating local descriptors into a compact image representation. In *CVPR*, pages 3304–3311, 2010.

[11] H. Jégou, F. Perronnin, M. Douze, J. Sánchez, P. Pérez, and C. Schmid. Aggregating local image descriptors into compact codes. *IEEE TPAMI*, 2011.

[12] D. G. Lowe. Distinctive Image Features from Scale-Invariant Keypoints. *IJCV*, 60(2):91–110, 2004.

[13] K. Mikolajczyk and C. Schmid. A performance evaluation of local descriptors. *IEEE TPAMI*, 27(10):1615–1630, 2005.

[14] D. Nistér and H. Stewénius. Scalable recognition with a vocabulary tree. In *CVPR (2)*, pages 2161–2168, 2006.

[15] B. G. Park, K. M. Lee, and S. U. Lee. A New Similarity Measure for Random Signatures: Perceptually Modified Hausdorff Distance. In *ACIVS*, pages 990–1001, 2006.

[16] F. Perronnin, Y. Liu, J. Sánchez, and H. Poirier. Large-scale image retrieval with compressed Fisher vectors. In *CVPR*, pages 3384–3391, 2010.

[17] Y. Rubner, J. Puzicha, C. Tomasi, and J. M. Buhmann. Empirical Evaluation of Dissimilarity Measures for Color and Texture. *CVIU*, 84(1):25 – 43, 2001.

[18] Y. Rubner, C. Tomasi, and L. J. Guibas. The Earth Mover's Distance as a Metric for Image Retrieval. *IJCV*, 40(2):99–121, 2000.

[19] J. Sivic and A. Zisserman. Video Google: A Text Retrieval Approach to Object Matching in Videos. In *ICCV*, pages 1470–1477, 2003.

[20] A. W. M. Smeulders, M. Worring, S. Santini, A. Gupta, and R. Jain. Content-Based Image Retrieval at the End of the Early Years. *IEEE TPAMI*, 22(12):1349–1380, 2000.

[21] H. Tamura. Texture features corresponding to visual perception. *IEEE Trans. on Systems, Man, and Cybernetics*, 8(6):460–473, 1978.

[22] K. E. A. van de Sande, T. Gevers, and C. G. M. Snoek. Evaluating color descriptors for object and scene recognition. *IEEE TPAMI*, 32(9):1582–1596, 2010.

[23] Y. Weiss, A. Torralba, and R. Fergus. Spectral hashing. In *NIPS*, pages 1753–1760, 2008.

Tag Completion based on Belief Theory and Neighbor Voting

Amel Znaidia
CEA, LIST,
Vision & Content Engineering
Laboratory
Gif-sur-Yvettes, France
amel.znaidia@cea.fr

Hervé le Borgne
CEA, LIST,
Vision & Content Engineering
Laboratory
Gif-sur-Yvettes, France
herve.le-borgne@cea.fr

Céline Hudelot
Ecole Centrale Paris
Applied Mathematics &
Systems Laboratory
Antony, France
celine.hudelot@ecp.fr

ABSTRACT

We address the problem of tag completion for automatic image annotation. Our method consists in two main steps: creating a list of "candidate tags" from the visual neighbors of the untagged image then using them as pieces of evidence to be combined to provide the final list of predicted tags. Both steps introduce a scheme to tackle with imprecision and uncertainty. First, a bag-of-words (BOW) signature is generated for each neighbor using local soft coding. Second, a sum-pooling operation across the BOW of the k nearest neighbors provides the list of "candidate tags". Finally, we use neighbors as pieces of evidence to be combined according to the Dempster's rule to predict the more relevant tags. The method is evaluated in the context of image classification and that of tag suggestion. The database used for visual neighbors search contains 1.2 million images extracted from Flickr. Classification is evaluated on the well known Pascal VOC 2007 and MIR Flickr datasets, on which we obtain similar or better results than the state-of-the-art. For tag suggestion, we manually annotated 241 queries. As well, we obtain competitive results on this task.

Categories and Subject Descriptors

H.3.1 [**Content Analysis and Indexing**]: Indexing methods; H.2.4 [**Database Management**]: Systems-Multimedia databases

General Terms

Algorithms, Experimentation

Keywords

Tag completion, tag suggestion, local soft coding, belief theory, bag of words, image annotation, classification

Tags :
Dog, corgie,50mm, captain, Seattle, SonyA200, Minolta.

No Tag

Figure 1: Example of images from Flickr Website with its associated tags.

1. INTRODUCTION

Online social media services, such as Flickr[1], allow users to share their photos with other people for social interaction. An important feature of these services is that users can annotate their photos with their own tags, in order to facilitate future search and sharing. The main purpose of the users being to make their picture popular to the public, it conflicts with an objective description of the images [1]. Consequently, tags generated by users on Flickr are usually imperfect and only 50% are actually related to the content of the image [12]. These "imperfections" recovers different problems. Above the ones related to the objectivity of users, the human-generated tags (folksonomy) are prone to errors. On the left image of figure 1, only "dog" actually describe the visual content of the image. Other tags are related to shooting conditions ("SonyA200", "Minolta", "50mm") or to subjective context ("captain","Seattle"). One could suggest other relevant tags for this image, such as "animal" or "canine". Other images are simply not annotated at all (figure 1 right), making them almost unusable for research and automatic sharing.

In this paper, we address the problem of tag completion for automatic image annotation. Last trends to generating tags for images without any annotation rely on the idea that if many distinct users use the same tags to label visually similar images, then these tags are likely to reflect the visual contents of the annotated images. Starting from this intuition, classic neighbor voting algorithm use information from the k-nearest neighbors (kNNs) to predict tags [22]. Unfortunately, in the context of social tagging, the tags are

[1]http://www.flickr.com/

freely assigned by users, with various motivations and different judgments on the relevance between a tag and an image. Consequently, tags in social tagging setting are much more uncertain compared to labels in traditional classification problems. In the original voting kNN algorithm, the image is assigned to the majority class according to its k-nearest neighbors, independently of the relevance of each neighbor. Moreover, the classical kNN methods does not deal with ambiguity and imprecise information because of the limitation of the probabilistic framework.

We propose a method to tackle these problems of robustness and effectiveness. First, we start by searching the k nearest neighbors using some visual information. For each neighbor, we compute a bag-of-words (BOW) based signature using locality constraint. Contrary to a classic BoW signature, tags are coded according to several of their closer codewords from a learned codebook. Such a coding has already been proven to be efficient, both for classification from the visual information only [15] and a multimedia context as well [27]. Second, a sum-pooling operation across the BOW of the k nearest neighbors provides the list of "candidate tags". Finally, basic belief masses are obtained for each nearest neighbor using the distances between this pattern and its neighbors. Their fusion leads to the list of final predicted tags. This last step is derivated from the Evidential kNN [4] that apply the Dempster's rule of combination to a nearest neighbors classifier.

As explained in section 2, our approach differs from existing techniques on two main points. The first novelty is that we use tag corpus knowledge to enrich nearest neighbors description from existing tags. Second and most important difference, we explicitly use a formalism, Belief theory (see section 2.3), which is able to handle neighbors conflict and deal with tag imperfections.

Our work is evaluated in the context of image classification and that of tag suggestion. Classification is evaluated on the well known Pascal VOC 2007 [6] and MIR Flickr [10] datasets, containing 10k to 20k images and 20 to 99 concepts. We evaluated both our method alone as well as lately fused with image-only descriptor for multimodal classification. For tag suggestion, a third database is derived from the one used in [20, 14] for which we created a new ground truth[2], by manually annotating 241 queries. The database used for visual neighbors search contains 1.2 million images extracted from Flickr.

The remainder of this paper is structured as follows. In Section 2 we describe previous works related to image annotation. A section is specially dedicated to Belief theory and the contextual similarity [18] that is used later to express the similarity between two tags. In Section 3, we introduce our method to tackle with tag completion. Experiments that prove the performance of our approach, in terms of accuracy and robustness, are reported and discussed in Section 4 and 5.

2. RELATED WORK

In this section, we review works closely related to our motivation for tag completion for automatic image annotation. First, we describe previous works related to image annotation. Second, we present the contextual similarity that is

---

[2] http://elm.eeng.dcu.ie/~hlborgne/tagcompletion.html

used later to express the similarity between two tags. Finally, we introduce some basic notions of Belief theory.

2.1 Image annotation

Several approaches have been proposed for annotating images by mining the web images with surrounding descriptions. These methods can be classified into two categories: model-based methods and search-based methods.

Model-based methods cast the problem of tag prediction as a binary classification problem where a classifier is learned for each tag. Therefore, almost all classification methods can be applied. One approach is to treat the annotation problem as a translation/projection from images to tags. It is usually performed using the image-tag co-occurrence information [5]. This approach is extended by [17] to latent space using latent semantic analysis techniques. In [13], authors proposed a real-time system based on 2D Multiresolution Hidden Markov Model (MHMM). Images in every category focus on a semantic theme and are described collectively by several words. A category of images is consequently referred to as a semantic concept. Tang et al. [21] proposed a kNN-sparse graph-based semi-supervised learning approach for label propagation over noisily-tagged web images.

Unlike model-based approaches, the search-based methods do not need to be constrained in a fixed vocabulary or model. It assumes that images with similar visual content are annotated by similar tags. Recently, nearest neighbor models have been investigated in the annotation community with promising results. Notably, Torralba et al. [22], collected about 80 million tiny images, each of which is labeled with one of the 75, 062 abstract nouns from WordNet. By fully leveraging on the redundancy of information on the Web, they claimed that with sufficient number of samples, the simple nearest neighbor classifier can achieves reasonable performance for several object/scene detection tasks, when compared with the more sophisticated state-of-the-art techniques. In the same direction, Li et al. [14] proposed an algorithm that learns tag relevancy by accumulating votes from visually similar neighbors. In fact, given a user-tagged image, they first perform a kNN search to find its visual neighbors. The tag relevance is determined as the probability that this tag being used to annotate the neighborhood images minus the probability of the tag being used in the entire collection. Wang et al. [24] proposed to build a normalized histogram of tags and group names counts from the k-nearest neighbor images. Text classifiers is then trained on the text features. A separate visual classifier is also learned and the final prediction is obtained from a third classifier trained on the confidence values returned by both the textual and the visual classifiers. Guillaumin et al. [7] have proposed the tag propagation (TagProp) method to annotate a input image by propagating the tags of the weighted nearest neighbors of that input image. The weighted nearest neighbors were identified by optimally integrating several image similarity metrics. Makadia et al. [16] recently have developed the joint equal contribution (JEC) technique, where they used a combination of multiple features and distance metrics to find the nearest neighbors of the input image and a greedy algorithm for transferring tags from visually similar images. Recently, Wu et al. [25] proposed a framework for tag completion. They represent the image-tag relation by a tag matrix, and search for the optimal tag matrix consistent with both the observed tags and the pairwise visual similarity between images. This optimization problem is solved using a sub-gradient descent based approach.

Compared with our approach, most existing techniques does not make use of tag corpus knowledge to enrich nearest neighbors description from existing tags. Moreover, there is no explicit use of a formalism which is able to handle neighbors conflict and to deal with tag imperfections.

2.2 Contextual similarity

In this section, we introduce the contextual similarity used later to aggregate image tags into a bag-of-words signature using local soft coding.

In [18], an adaptation of the TF-IDF model to the social space is proposed in order to compute the social relatedness of two tags. Let $\mathbf{S}$ be the matrix of size $N \times K$ defined by:

$$\mathbf{S}(i,j) = \text{users}(\mathbf{t}_i, \mathbf{t}_j) \times \log(\frac{\text{users}_{\text{collection}}}{\text{users}_{\text{collection}(\mathbf{t}_j)}}), \quad (1)$$

where $\mathbf{t}_i$ is the target tag, $\mathbf{t}_j$ is an element of the codebook, $\text{users}(\mathbf{t}_i, \mathbf{t}_j)$ is the number of distinct users who associate the tag $\mathbf{t}_i$ to the tag $\mathbf{t}_j$ among the top results returned by the Flickr API for $\mathbf{t}_i$; $\text{users}_{\text{collection}(\mathbf{t}_j)}$ is the number of distinct users from a pre-fetched subset of Flickr users that have tagged photos with tag $\mathbf{t}_j$, and N is the number of unique tags associated to photos of the dataset and K is the size of the codebook. Note that some of the tags can have entries on both dimensions of matrix S. In the current work, we consider a fixed set of tags, that is a tag-codebook.

Relying on this matrix, a Flickr model for a given tag $\mathbf{t}_i$ is proposed in [18] as the following vector of weights:

$$\mathbf{w}_i = [w_{i,1}, w_{i,2}, ..., w_{i,K}]^T, \quad (2)$$

with $w_{i,j}$ the normalized social weight defined by:

$$w_{i,j} = \frac{\mathbf{S}(i,j)}{max\{\mathbf{S}(i,k), k = 1, ..., K\}}. \quad (3)$$

Thereby, given two tag-Flickr models $\mathbf{w}_i$ and $\mathbf{w}_j$, we compute the contextual similarities between their related tags $\mathbf{t}_i$ and $\mathbf{t}_j$ using the cosine similarity:

$$\text{sim}_{\text{contextual}}(\mathbf{t}_i, \mathbf{t}_j) = \frac{\mathbf{w}_i^T \mathbf{w}_j}{||\mathbf{w}_i||||\mathbf{w}_j||}. \quad (4)$$

2.3 Belief Theory

The belief theory, also called evidence theory or Dempster-Shafer (DS) theory [19] is more and more employed in order to take into account the uncertainties and imprecisions in pattern recognition. The evidence theory is based on the use of functions defined on a *frame of discernment* Ω, represented as the set of all hypothesis in a certain domain. A basic belief assignment (BBA) is a function m that defines the mapping from the power set of Ω to the interval $[0,1]$ and verifies:

$$m : 2^\Omega \rightarrow [0,1] \quad (5)$$

$$\sum_{A \in 2^\Omega} m(A) = 1 \quad (6)$$

The quantity $m(A)$ can be interpreted as a measure of the belief that is committed exactly to A, given the available evidence. A subset $A \in 2^\Omega$ with $m(A) > 0$ is called a *focal element* of m.

In DS theory, two functions of evidence can be deduced from m and its associated focal elements, belief function Bel and plausibility function Pl. $Bel(A)$ is the measure of the total belief committed to a set A. The belief function is defined as a mapping $Bel : 2^\Omega \rightarrow [0,1]$ that satisfies $Bel(\emptyset) = 0, Bel(\Omega) = 1$ and for each focal element A, we have:

$$Bel(A) = \sum_{\emptyset \neq B \subseteq A} m(B) \quad (7)$$

The *plausibility* of A, $Pl(A)$, represents the amounts of belief that could potentially placed in A and defined as:

$$Pl(A) = \sum_{A \cap B \neq \emptyset} m(B) \quad (8)$$

When several pieces of evidence are available through their BBA, they can be combined with the Dempster's rule of combination:

$$m_1 \oplus m_2 = \begin{cases} \frac{\sum_{B \cap C = A} m_1(B) m_2(C)}{1 - \sum_{B \cap C = \emptyset} m_1(B) m_2(C)}, & \forall \ A \subseteq \Omega, \ A \neq \emptyset \\ 0 & if \ A = \emptyset \end{cases} \quad (9)$$

3. PROPOSED METHOD

The proposed method for tag suggestion using visually similar images is given in figure 2. It consists in two main steps: creating a list of "candidate tags" from the visual neighbors of the untagged image then using them as pieces of evidence to be combined to provide the final list of predicted tags.

Given an untagged image I, we start by searching the k nearest neighbors using visual information (color, texture). First, we compute a BOW signature for each neighbor based on local soft coding. Second, a sum-pooling operation across the BOW of the k nearest neighbors is performed to obtain the list of "candidate tags" (the most frequent). Finally, basic belief masses are obtained for each nearest neighbor using the distances between this pattern and its neighbors. Their fusion leads to the list of final predicted tags.

3.1 Finding candidate tags

Tag-based features bring a complementary description to enrich the semantic description of a given image and we address two issues associated to textual features here. In order to build robust BoW based tag-signatures toward quantization errors, we rely on the locality-constrained coding method that has proved to be effective for visual features when paired with max-pooling [15, 27].

Let I be an untagged image and $\mathcal{N} = \{I^1, \dots I^k\}$ the set of its nearest neighbors according to a given measure, within an image database. These resources (image database, visual features and similarity function) are not precised at this point but their importance will be discussed later (section 6). Each image I^r has a set of tags $T^r = \{t_1^r \dots t_{n_r}^r\}$. Let consider as well a textual codebook $\mathcal{B} = \{b_1 \dots b_B\}$ that has been built previously (detailed in section 4). Each tag $\mathbf{t}_p^r \in T^r$ is then coded according to its M nearest neighbors of the codebook:

$$z_{p,q} = \begin{cases} \text{sim}_{\text{contextual}}(\mathbf{t}_p^r, \mathbf{b}_q) & \text{if } \mathbf{b}_q \in \mathcal{N}_M(\mathbf{t}_p^r), \\ 0 & \text{otherwise}, \end{cases} \quad (10)$$

where $\mathcal{N}_M(\mathbf{t}_p^r)$ denotes the M-nearest neighbors of $\mathbf{t}_p^r$, under the contextual similarity detailed in section 2.2. Another

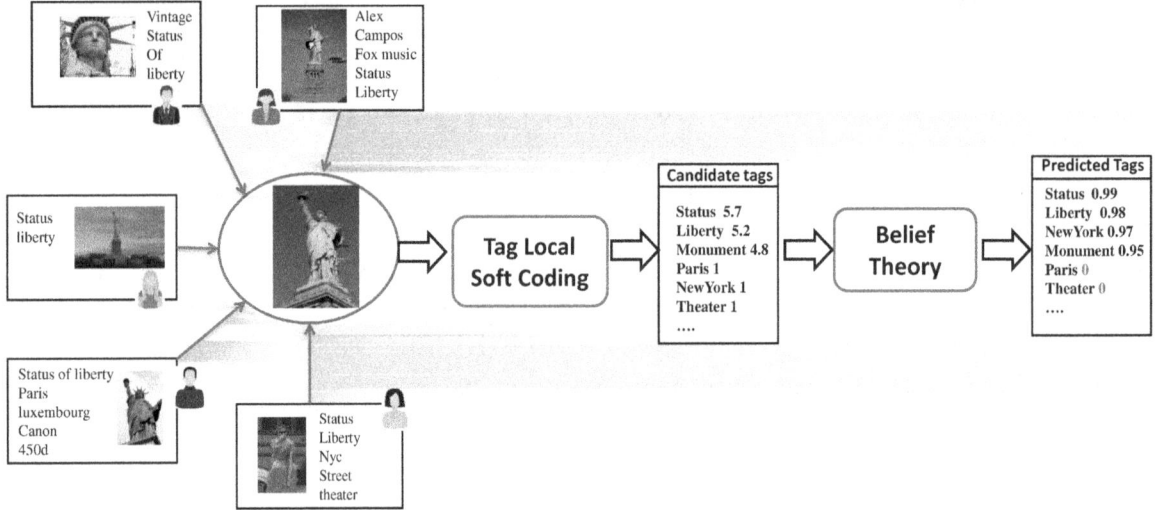

Figure 2: The flowchart of our tag completion approach based on local soft coding and belief theory. First, we compute a bag-of-words (BOW) signature for each neighbor based on local soft coding. Second, a sum-pooling operation across the BOW of the k nearest neighbors is performed to obtain the list of the most frequent tags. Finally, pieces of evidence from neighbors are combined using Dempster's rule to obtain the set of predicted tags.

similarity between tags and codewords may be used here. The locality assumption in the tag-space induces sparse codes while reducing the reconstruction errors, mainly in terms of semantic reconstruction. The final tag-signature vector results from an aggregation by the maximal values of the coded tags:

$$c_q^r = max_{p=1}^{Card(T^r)}(z_{p,q}) \qquad (11)$$

$\mathbf{c^r} = [c_1^r \ldots c_B^r]$ is then the tag-signature vector for the rth neighbor. To obtain the list of "candidate tags", a sum-pooling operation is performed across the k nearest neighbors tag-signature, as follows:

$$C_q = \sum_{r=1}^{k}(c_q^r) \qquad (12)$$

The entries of $\mathbf{C} = [C_1 \ldots C_B]$ with the largest values constitutes the list of "candidate tags". The number of "candidate tags" kept is arbitrarily set to 10 in our experiments.

3.2 Predicting the final tags

In the following, we denote $\Omega = \{t_1, ..., t_n\}$ the set of "candidate tags". Each pair (I^i, t_j), where $(I^i \in \mathcal{N}, t_j \in \Omega)$, constitutes a distinct item of evidence regarding the relevance of the tag t_j to describe the visual content of the untagged image I. If I is "close" to I^i according to the relevant metric d, then one will be inclined to believe that both images can be tagged with the same tag. On the contrary, if $d(I, I^i)$ is very large, then the consideration of I^i will leave us in a situation of almost complete ignorance concerning the tag t_j. Consequently, this item of evidence may be postulated to induce a Basic Belief Assignment (BBA) $m(.|I^i)$, over the k nearest neighbors, defined by:

$$m(\{t_j\}|I^i) = \alpha\phi_j(d^i) \qquad (13)$$

$$m(\Omega|I^i) = 1 - \alpha\phi_j(d^i) \qquad (14)$$

where $d^i = d(I, I^i)$ is the distance between the untagged image I and a neighbor I^i, α is a parameter such that $0 < \alpha < 1$ and ϕ_j is a decreasing function verifying $\phi_j(0) = 1$ and $lim_{d\to\infty}\phi_j(d) = 0$. One choice for the function ϕ_j can be :

$$\phi_j(d) = exp(-\gamma_j d^2) \qquad (15)$$

In [4], it was proposed to set $\alpha = 0.95$ and γ_j to the inverse of the mean distance between images tagged with the tag t_j. This heuristic yields good results on average. These parameters can be determined also by optimizing a performance criterion as shown in [4]. For simplicity, we choose the first alternative. As a result of considering k nearest neighbors we obtain k BBA for each tag that can be combined using Dempster's rule of combination to form a final BBA for each tag contained in this neighborhood as follows:

$$m = m(.|I^1) \oplus ... \oplus m(.|I^k) \qquad (16)$$

Adapting this definition, m can be shown to have the following expression:

$$m(\{t_j\}) = \frac{1}{K}(1 - \prod_{i \in \mathcal{N}_j}(1 - \alpha\phi_j(d^i)))\prod_{l \neq j}\prod_{i \in \mathcal{N}_l}(1 - \alpha\phi_l(d^i)) \qquad (17)$$

$$m(\Omega) = \frac{1}{K}\prod_{l=1}^{n}\prod_{i \in \mathcal{N}_l}(1 - \alpha\phi_l(d^i)) \qquad (18)$$

where $\mathcal{N}_j$ is the subset of neighbors from $\mathcal{N}$ tagged with the tag t_j and K is a normalization factor. Hence the focal elements of m are singletons and the whole frame Ω. Consequently, the credibility and the plausibility can be defined as follows:

$$bel(\{t_j\}) = m(\{t_j\}) \qquad (19)$$

$$pl(\{t_j\}) = m(\{t_j\}) + m(\Omega) \qquad (20)$$

These two functions can be used to decide if the tag is relevant to describe the image content. In our case, for fair comparison with the state-of-the-art, we choose to sort the list of "candidate tags" by decreasing credibility values and keep only the p tags with highest values.

4. EXPERIMENTS

The proposed method is evaluated in the context of two applications: image classification and tag suggestion.

4.1 Dataset

For image classification, we report results based on two widely used datasets: MIR Flickr [10] and Pascal VOC 2007 [6]. Both image sets were collected from Flickr but they differ significantly. For instance, MIR Flickr contains a wider variety of concepts whereas Pascal VOC 2007 classes are better balanced.

- **PASCAL VOC 2007** dataset [6] consists of 9,963 images (5011 for training) annotated according to 20 classes. The dataset is one of the most challenging because of the large variation on view size, illumination, scale, deformation and clutter, as well as complex backgrounds. About 38% images are not tagged at all (Table 1).

- **MIR Flickr** dataset [10] consists of 8,000 images for training and 10,000 for testing belonging to 99 highly diversified concepts. These concepts describe the scene ("indoor, outdoor , landscape, etc.", depicted objects "car, animal, person etc."), the type of image content ("portrait, graffiti, art, etc."), events ("travel, work, etc."), quality issues ("overexposed, underexposed, blurry, etc.") and emotions ("funny, cute, nice, scary, etc. "). About 10% images are not tagged at all (Table 1).

- **Flickr 1.2 million** consists of 1.2 million images downloaded from Flickr having no overlap with the untagged images used for test. This collection is used for visual neighbors searching.

For tag suggestion task, we want to evaluate our method on the dataset used in [20, 14]. It consists of 331 images downloaded from Flickr. This dataset is created by manually assessing the relevance of user's tags with respect to images. An example of images, given in figure 3, shows that the proposed ground truth do not reflect perfectly the images visual content and thus former evaluation of some systems leaded to quite poor results (*e.g* [14] obtained below 0.15

Table 1: Number and proportion of untagged images in training and test sets, for Pascal VOC 2007 and MIR Flickr datasets.

Dataset	# untagged Train	# untagged Test
Pascal VOC 2007 (prop. total)	1917 (38.3%)	1847 (37.3%)
MIR Flickr (prop. total)	812 (10.1%)	930 (9.3%)

Initial ground truth	2005, february	2006 , costume october	2006, Asia, chinese, City travel	2006
Our ground truth	Music, concert Live, Show, Lights, night	People, portrait Makeup, Girl	Baby, sleeping, Bicycle, man Market, Asia	Girl, music Party, Food

Figure 3: Example of images from the dataset of [20]. First row represents ground truth proposed by [20] and the second row represents our manually annotations used as ground truth for tag suggestion evaluation.

MAP and 0.1 Precision@5). We thus decided to manually re-annotate the dataset to better reflect the image visual content. For this, we followed a protocol inspired from the collaborative annotation tool of TrecVid [2] showing that annotating a small fraction of carefully chosen samples of a collection is enough to achieve similar performance (or even better) compared to those obtained with the entire collection. We thus downloaded all the images available on Flickr among the 331, resulting into a collection of 241 images. We run our method as well as two recent ones [24, 14] on these queries to collect potential tags. Then, we manually annotated the queries by keeping the tags that reflect the image visual content[3].

4.2 Experimental protocol

We compared our method with two approaches: the Tag Frequency [24] and the Tag Relevancy [14].

- Tag Frequency [24]: for a query image, we find its k nearest neighbor images from the auxiliary dataset using visual features. Tags and group name associated with these nearest neighbors are treated as an individual item in the text representation. The text feature is a normalized histogram of tag and group name counts from the k nearest neighbor images.

- Tag Relevancy [14]: is calculated by accumulating votes from visually similar neighbors. In fact, given a user-tagged image, they first perform a kNN search to find its visual neighbors. The tag relevance is determined as the probability that this tag being used to annotate the neighborhood images minus the probability of the tag being used in the entire collection.

For the sake of fair comparison, the same processing chain is considered, following literature settings to ensure consistency.

---

[3]this collection is available at: http://elm.eeng.dcu.ie/~hlborgne/tagcompletion.html

Searching Visual Neighbors: The visual similarity between two images are measured by the similarity between their corresponding visual features. Though numerous works have been done for visual feature representation, it is still a challenging problem for content-based image retrieval [22]. For fair comparison, the set of k nearest neighbors used as a starting point of our method is determined according to the visual similarity computed between the same visual feature as [14]. It consists in a combined 64-dimensional global feature for its empirically success in searching millions of web images [23]. It is composed of a 44-dimensional color correlgoram in the 44-bin HSV color space [9], 14-dimensional color texture moments [26], and 6-dimensional RGB color moments. The three features are normalized to unit length and concatenated into the final $64D$ feature. The dissimilarity between images are measured using the Euclidean distance between features. To search for visual neighbors, we adopt K-means clustering based indexing methods. First for indexing, the whole dataset is divided into smaller blocks by K-means clustering. Then for a query, we find neighbors within fewer blocks closest to the query. The search space is thus reduced. For both visual feature extraction and neighbors searching, we use the implementation of [14]. We fixed the number of visual neighbors to 100 for both applications (this number is discussed in section 5.1).

BoW-signature: For the PascalVOC textual codebook, we kept the tags that appear at least 8 times, leading to a dictionary of size 804. In the case of MIR Flickr, we kept the tags used by at least 3 different users, resulting into a textual codebook of 2500 tags. For local soft coding, the neighborhood in the tag feature space was set to 50.

Tag suggestion experiment: for each method, we select the top 5 tags as final suggestion for each untagged image. For tag suggestion, we evaluate directly the performance on these tags.

Image classification experiment: we build a BOW based signature as explained above. A one-versus-all linear kernel based Support Vector Machine (SVM) classifier is learned for each method and we compare their performances in terms of Mean Average Precision (MAP). A separate visual classifier is also learned and fused with the textual classifier learned from each method for a multimodal classification. This visual classifier is totally independent from the one used to search for visual neighbors for untagged images. For the visual classifier, SIFT descriptors are extracted and coded using local soft coding. The patch-size is fixed to 16×16 pixels and the step size for dense sampling to 6 pixels. For the local soft coding, we consider a neighborhood of size 5 and the softness parameter β is set to 10. We use a visual codebook of size $4,000$ created using the K-means clustering method on a randomly selected subset of SIFTs from the training dataset ($\approx 10^5$ SIFTs). To aggregate the obtained codes, we perform a max-pooling operation. As well, a spatial pyramid decomposition into 3 levels ($1 \times 1, 2 \times 2, 3 \times 3$) is adopted. Textual and visual classifiers are combined by averaging their corresponding predictions.

5. RESULTS

Before presenting results to both targeted applications (image classification and tag suggestion), we present one experiment to study how results may vary according to the number of visual neighbors considered.

5.1 Impact of visual neighborhood size

The number of nearest neighbors is an important parameter in tag suggestion methods based on nearest neighbors. To analyze the impact of neighborhood size, we tried various values of $k \in \{50, 100, 200, 500\}$ on the Pascal VOC 2007. As shown in figure 4, our method outperforms the

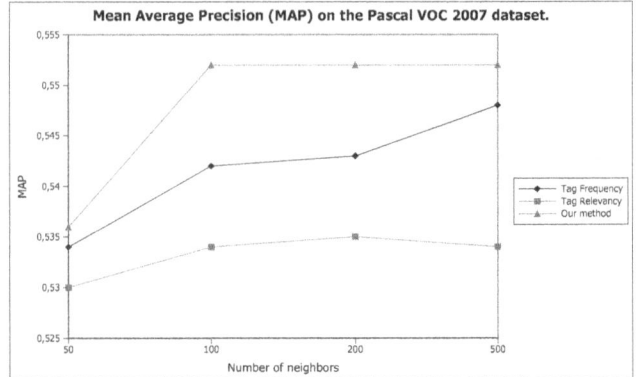

Figure 4: Performance on the Pascal VOC 2007 dataset in terms of Mean Average Precision with respect to the number of nearest neighbors.

two baseline methods for all neighborhood size. Both baseline methods tend to suggest tags occurring frequently in the neighborhood and treat all neighbors equally while the distances between the image and its neighbors are ignored. By contrast, our method starts by predicting new tags by the local soft coding step to enrich the neighbors description and uses the distances to promote the most closed neighbors. In fact, our method reaches the best score (0.552 MAP) with only 100 neighbors and remains stable while varying the neighborhood size. Hence, our method is more effective and stable.

5.2 Tag Suggestion

In Table 2, we report the precision at rank 5 (P@5) on the manually annotated 241 queries. Precision at rank k is defined as the proportion of suggested tags that is relevant, averaged over all photos. As well, we obtain competitive results in tag suggestion task. The tag frequency [24] results are surprisingly better than those of tag relevancy [14] on average. It can be explained by the accuracy of visual search which is query-dependent.

Table 2: Comparison of our system to the state-of-the art methods on the tag suggestion task.

Method	Average Precision@5
Tag Relevancy [14]	0,349
Tag Frequency [24]	0,387
Our method	**0,413**

An example of images with suggested tags by the three methods is illustrated in figure 5. As we can see, original tags are imperfect and most of them are subjective. Let's note that these tags are not used in the three methods. Obviously, we can observe that tags predicted by our method are more relevant than those predicted by the two baseline methods. Our approach is more likely to rank relevant tags ahead of irrelevant ones (shown in bold in figure 5) which is not the case for both tag relevancy and tag frequency.

Original tags	*Cape cod Bass river lighthouse*	*plants nature cornwall stonehenge 2005.05.03 xato Vwhiz philip anderson*	*Iceland Reykjavík 2000.09.03*
Tag Relevancy	architecture house **tower** **flag** building	**food** flower **salad** strawberry red	boat blue **city** travel boats
Tag Frequency	architecture **water** house street **car**	**food** flower red nature **salad**	blue **street** **city** **canon** sky
Our Method	architecture house houses blue sky	flowers flower nature red **food**	blue boat sky Cloud **street**

Figure 5: Examples of tag suggestion by different methods. The bold font indicates irrelevant suggested tags. Original tags are not used.

5.3 Image classification

In Table 3, we compare the results of the textual classifier based on suggested tags for the three methods on the Pascal VOC 2007 dataset. Results on the MIR Flickr dataset are shown in Table 4. By comparing results on both datasets, we can see that the proposed method based on local soft coding and belief theory gives better results than the baseline methods based on only tag frequency. Our method leads to scores that are three (resp. one) points above the baseline methods on MIR Flickr (resp. Pascal VOC 2007) dataset.

Table 3: Classification performances on PASCAL VOC 07 in terms of Mean Average Precision (MAP), for different methods: 1)based on textual classifier only, 2) based on the combination of textual and visual classifiers

Method	Textual	Multimodal
Tag Relevancy [14]	0.534	0.668
Tag Frequency [24]	0.542	0.676
Our method	**0.552**	**0.684**

To demonstrate the effectiveness of suggested tags in multimodal image classification, a separate visual classifier is also learned and fused with the textual classifier learned from each method as detailed in section 4.2. From results shown in Table 3 and Table 4, we can conclude that our method is more effective than the baseline methods. Furthermore, with a simple combination of linear SVM based output classifiers, we obtain similar or better results than the state-of-the-art on multi-modal image classification on both datasets [8, 3, 27]. These results demonstrate the usefulness of the evidence

formalism to handle neighbors conflict and to deal with tag imperfections. Over the two datasets, our method clearly dominates the remaining methods.

Table 4: Classification performances on MIR Flickr in terms of Mean Average Precision (MAP), for different methods based on: 1) textual classifier only, 2) the combination of textual and visual classifiers.

Method	Textual	Multimodal
Tag Relevancy [14]	0.337	0.412
Tag Frequency [24]	0.343	0.417
Our method	**0.37**	**0.440**

In fact, in the baseline methods, the image is assigned to the tag with the majority votes according to its nearest neighbors, independently of the relevance of each neighbor. When nearest neighbors have been tagged subjectively by users, noisy tags will be inevitably assigned to the untagged image due to conflicts or lack of knowledge. First, in the local soft coding step, our method gives a degree of confidence about each tag. Second by exploiting the distance between the untagged image and its nearest neighbors based on belief theory, we are able to reduce the risk of assigning wrongly some tags to an image when the degrees of confidence are not high. That explains the good performances of our method.

6. CONCLUDING REMARKS

We introduced a novel approach for tag suggestion based on local soft coding and belief theory. First, a list of "candidate tags" is created from the visual neighbors of the untagged image, using both local soft coding and two consecutive pooling steps. Then, these tag-signatures are used as pieces of evidence to be combined to provide the final list of predicted tags. This fusion is based on the Dempster's rule of combination, in accordance with the Evidential kNN framework. Hence, both steps support a scheme to tackle with imprecision and uncertainty that are inherent to this type of information in a social media context. The experiments that we carried out for image classification on two publicly available datasets show that we obtain comparable or better results than the state-of-the-art methods: on Pascal VOC 2007 results are improved of one point both for multimedia and textual-only descriptions; on MIR Flickr, our method leads to scores that are two points above recent state-of-the art methods. For tag suggestion, we manually annotated 241 queries to propose a new benchmark to the community. For that application as well, we obtained competitive results, with a score two points better than the best recent state-of-the-art method.

Visual neighbors were obtained from an image database containing 1.2 million images extracted from Flickr. This resource is crucial to obtain good raw results for the application considered. Even if our method obtain better results than other recent ones, all of them would benefit from an improved resource. A first direction to improve it is to use a potentially better visual signature to get the neighbors. However, we must keep a certain efficiency in practice to avoid prohibitive time responses to find neighbors. For this, we may search them into a compressed domain that allows to fit large databases into memory [11]. A more difficult direction of research will be the improvement of the annotation of the resource itself. As we explained, lots of the current annotations are far from being perfect (it is one of the reason we re-annotated the queries to evaluate the work). Hence, this work can naturally be continued into the process of cleaning large multimedia resources.

7. ACKNOWLEDGMENTS

This work is supported by grants from DIGITEO and Région Ile-de-France. We acknowledge support from the French ANR (Agence Nationale de la Recherche) via the PERIPLUS (ANR-10-CORD-026) project, and the Caisse des Dépôts via the EGONOMY project (O12709-67155). We thank Börkur Sigurbjörnsson and Xirong Li for helping us to get the 1.2 million images ressour-ce as well as the 331 query identifiers. We are grateful to Xirong Li for the public implementation of their Tag relevance learning algorithm[4].

8. REFERENCES

[1] M. Ames and M. Naaman. Why we tag: motivations for annotation in mobile and online media. In *Proceedings of the SIGCHI*, pages 971–980, New York, NY, USA, 2007. ACM.

[2] S. Ayache and G. Quénot. Evaluation of active learning strategies for video indexing. *Journal of Image Communication*, 22(7-8):692–704, Aug. 2007.

[3] A. Binder, W. Samek, M. Kloft, C. Müller, K.-R. Müller, and M. Kawanabe. The Joint Submission of the TU Berlin and Fraunhofer FIRST (TUBFI) to the ImageCLEF2011 Photo Annotation Task. In *CLEF (Notebook Papers/Labs/Workshop)*, 2011.

[4] T. Denoeux. A k-nearest neighbor classification rule based on dempster-shafer theory. *IEEE Transaction on systems, man and cybernetics*, 25:804–813, 1995.

[5] P. Duygulu, K. Barnard, J. F. G. d. Freitas, and D. A. Forsyth. Object recognition as machine translation: Learning a lexicon for a fixed image vocabulary. ECCV '02, pages 97–112, London, UK, UK, 2002. Springer-Verlag.

[6] M. Everingham, L. Van Gool, C. K. I. Williams, J. Winn, and A. Zisserman. The PASCAL Visual Object Classes Challenge 2007 (VOC2007) Results.

[7] M. Guillaumin, T. Mensink, J. Verbeek, and C. Schmid. TagProp: discriminative metric learning in nearest neighbor models for image auto-annotation. ICCV'09, pages 309 – 316, Kyoto, Japon, Sept. 2009. IEEE Computer society.

[8] M. Guillaumin, J. Verbeek, and C. Schmid. Multimodal semi-supervised learning for image classification. CVPR '10, pages 902 – 909, 2010.

[9] J. Huang, S. R. Kumar, M. Mitra, W.-J. Zhu, and R. Zabih. Image indexing using color correlograms. CVPR '97, Washington, DC, USA, 1997. IEEE Computer Society.

[10] M. J. Huiskes and M. S. Lew. The MIR flickr retrieval evaluation. In *ACM international conference on Multimedia information retrieval (ICMR)*, pages 39–43, 2008.

[11] H. Jégou, F. Perronnin, M. Douze, J. Sánchez, P. Pérez, and C. Schmid. Aggregating local image descriptors into compact codes. *IEEE Transactions on Pattern Analysis and Machine Intelligence*, Sept. 2012.

[12] L. S. Kennedy, S. fu Chang, and I. V. Kozintsev. To search or to label?: predicting the performance of search-based automatic image classifiers. MIR '06, pages 249–258, 2006.

[13] J. Li and J. Z. Wang. Real-time computerized annotation of pictures. *IEEE Trans. Pattern Anal. Mach. Intell.*, 30(6):985–1002, June 2008.

[14] X. Li, C. G. M. Snoek, and M. Worring. Learning social tag relevance by neighbor voting. *IEEE Transactions on Multimedia*, 11(7):1310–1322, November 2009.

[15] L. Liu, L. Wang, and X. Liu. In Defense of Soft-assignment Coding. ICCV '11, 2011.

[16] A. Makadia, V. Pavlovic, and S. Kumar. Baselines for image annotation. *International Journal of Computer Vision*, 90(1):88–105, 2010.

[17] F. Monay and D. Gatica-Perez. On image auto-annotation with latent space models. Proceedings of the eleventh ACM international conference on Multimedia, pages 275–278, New York, NY, USA, 2003. ACM.

[18] A. Popescu and G. Grefenstette. Social media driven image retrieval. In *ACM International Conference on Multimedia Retrieval (ICMR)*, pages 33:1–33:8, 2011.

[19] G. Shafer. *A Mathematical Theory of Evidence*. Princeton University Press, Princeton, 1976.

[20] B. Sigurbjörnsson and R. van Zwol. Flickr tag recommendation based on collective knowledge. WWW '08, pages 327–336, New York, NY, USA, 2008. ACM.

[21] J. Tang, R. Hong, S. Yan, T.-S. Chua, G.-J. Qi, and R. Jain. Image annotation by knn-sparse graph-based label propagation over noisily tagged web images. *ACM Transactions on Intelligent Systems and Technology (TIST)*, 2(2):14, 2011.

[22] A. Torralba, R. Fergus, and W. T. Freeman. 80 million tiny images: A large data set for nonparametric object and scene recognition. *IEEE Trans. Pattern Anal. Mach. Intell.*, 30(11):1958–1970, Nov. 2008.

[23] C. Wang, F. Jing, L. Zhang, and H.-J. Zhang. Scalable search-based image annotation. *Multimedia Syst.*, 14(4):205–220, 2008.

[24] G. Wang, D. Hoiem, and D. A. Forsyth. Building text features for object image classification. In *CVPR*, pages 1367–1374, 2009.

[25] L. Wu, R. Jin, and A. K. Jain. Tag completion for image retrieval. *IEEE Transactions on Pattern Analysis and Machine Intelligence*, 99(PrePrints), 2012.

[26] H. Yu, M. Li, H.-J. Zhang, and J. Feng. Color texture moments for content-based image retrieval. ICIP '10, pages 24–28, 2003.

[27] A. Znaidia, A. Shabou, A. Popescu, H. Le Borgne, and C. Hudelot. Multimodal feature generation framework for semantic image classification. In *ICMR*, International Conference on Multimedia Retrieval, ICMR '12, Hong Kong, China, June 5-8, 2012, page 38, 2012.

---

[4]http://staff.science.uva.nl/ xirong/software/tagrel/index.html

Searching Visual Instances with Topology Checking and Context Modeling

Wei Zhang, Chong-Wah Ngo
Department of Computer Science, City University of Hong Kong, Kowloon, Hong Kong
wzhang34@student.cityu.edu.hk, cscwngo@cityu.edu.hk

ABSTRACT

Instance Search (INS) is a realistic problem initiated by TRECVID, which is to retrieve all occurrences of the querying object, location, or person from a large video collection. It is a fundamental problem with many applications, and also a challenging problem different from the traditional concept or near-duplicate (ND) search, since the relevancy is defined at instance level. True responses could exhibit various visual variations, such as being small on the image with different background, or showing a non-homography spatial configuration. Based on the Bag-of-Words model, we propose two techniques tailored for Instance Search. Specifically, we explore the use of (1) an elastic spatial topology checking technique based on Delaunay Triangulation (DT), and (2) a practical background context modeling method by simulating the "stare" behavior of human eyes. With DT, we improve the quality of visual matching by accumulating evidence from local topology-preserving patches, significantly boosting the ranks of topology consistent results. On the other hand, we increase the information quantity for visual matching with the "stare" model, such that instances appearing in both similar and different background can be highly ranked as results. The proposed techniques are evaluated on the INS datasets of TRECVID, achieving large performance gain with small computation overhead, compared with several existing methods.

Categories and Subject Descriptors

H.3.3 [**Information Search and Retrieval**]: Retrieval models

General Terms

Algorithms, Performance, Experimentation

Keywords

Instance Search; TRECVID; Spatial Topology Checking; Context Modeling

1. INTRODUCTION

This paper addresses a practical problem in real life: given several visual examples of an instance topic, retrieve all video clips that contain the instance from a video dataset. With the increasing number of videos generated every day, searching for a certain topic (e.g., an object, a location, or a person) in large video collections [17] is a feature highly demanded by many applications, such as archive video search, personal video organization/browsing, law enforcement, protection of brand/logo. As shown in Figure 1, the problem of retrieving instances is challenging, considering the large visual variations introduced by totally different background (1st row), different viewpoints of 3D objects (2nd row), scale changes (3rd row), and small objects (1st and 4th rows).

The formal definition of Instance Search (INS) is initiated by TRECVID [17]: given several visual examples of a search topic with the corresponding binary masks indicating the locations of the instance, find all video segments that contain one or more occurrences of the query instance. Though similar, the problem of INS is different from its close relatives: concept-based search and Near-Duplicate (ND) search [4, 19]. For concept-based search, the relevancy is defined at the semantic level, and any results with the same semantic meaning meet the searching criteria. For example, searching "plane" should return planes with any types, colors, and sizes, while INS should only return the same plane as specified in the query. It also differs from ND search, where certain image operations (e.g., scaling, rotation, cropping, noises, and text overlay) are applied on the source image to produce NDs. For INS, the instance could appear in a totally different background context with different viewpoints, as long as the video segments contain the same instance. In general, ND search is more useful for whole image search, since both the instance and background can be exploited for visual matching. On the other hand, INS has less information to leverage, since the background is not necessarily useful in this case.

Although INS can be formulated as a traditional image retrieval problem, it has its own peculiarities in several ways:

1. Different from ND search, instances often occupy a small area on the image, and the background context is often different among images with the same instance.

2. A manually labeled ROI (Region-of-Interest) is often available for the query, so that we can distinguish the instance under query and background context. The labeling of ROI can be easily done with the help of touch screens.

Considering the characteristics of INS, a potential diffi-

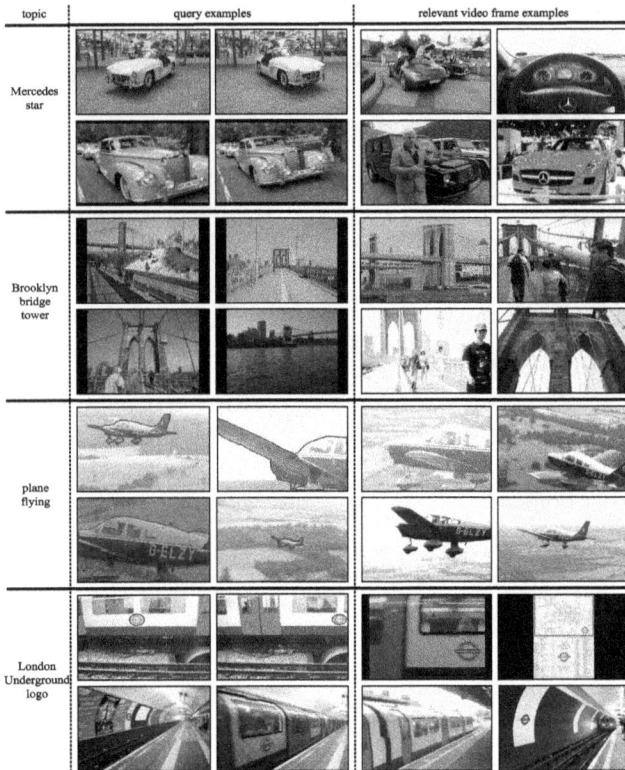

Figure 1: Examples of query topics in TRECVID datasets. Columns from left to right: topic name, image examples for the topic, and examples for relevant video keyframes. Contours of the ROI/mask are outlined with blue curves on each query image.

culty is that there is much less visual information to be exploited, especially when the size of query instance is small, as shown in Figure 1. Querying with such less information is error-prone, since the limited information is often not discriminative enough to retrieve instances out of a large video collection. As a result, lacking of quality and quantity information for visual matching becomes the major difficulty for INS. To tackle this problem, we propose two methods from different perspectives. The first one is by taking better use of the available information by modeling the spatial topology consistency. In other words, the lack of quantitative information is compensated by quality matching via topology checking. With an elastic topology model for spatial checking, we attempt to boost the ranking of relevant instances by making better use of the spatial information. Different from previous methods that impose a linear transformation over the absolute matching locations, we sketch and match the spatial topology based on Delaunay Triangulation. The second strategy seeks a way to increase the amount of query information by carefully considering the information from background context. Generally, we trust the information from the ROI, and it is risky to consider the areas outside. However, the information outside the ROI may enrich the limited information and provide more cues about the instance. The key is when to consider the context and how to weight the contribution from each parts. Inspired by the way of visual perception for human eyes, we enrich

the instance under query by introducing a "stare" model to improve the discriminative power of instances.

The main contributions of this paper can be summarized as follows:

• We apply a triangulation based spatial consistency checking method originally proposed for image search [21]. The method emphasizes the topological consistency for quality matching. Rather than imposing a strict transformation for geometric consistency checking, a graph is constructed to encode the topology information for matched points. This gives better tolerance to true responses in INS by accumulating evidence from local regularities of the instance.

• Background context is modeled into the query by using the "stare" model that simulates the visual perception behavior of human eyes. Both NDs, which share common background with the query, and instances with novel background can be retrieved.

The remaining paper is organized as follows. Section 2 describes related work. Sections 3 presents the topology checking method with Delaunay Triangulation to improve the quality on visual matching, while Section 4 proposes the "stare" model for context modeling to increase the quantity of matchings. Section 5 presents our experimental results on the datasets of TV11 and TV12, and finally Section 6 concludes this paper.

2. RELATED WORK

The proposed method is rooted in the Bag-of-Words (BoW) retrieval model, which was initially used in text retrieval. Since introduced in [16], it has been widely used in multimedia retrieval community for its good tradeoff between performance and scalability. Standard BoW technique consists of several key components: image description, visual vocabulary, feature quantization, and inverted file. Images are first scanned for stable and representative regions [12, 11] and the local features [11] are extracted afterwards. The offline trained visual vocabulary defines a quantization function of the feature space, such that features quantized to the same visual word are considered to be similar. At the time of online retrieval, only a small subset of features is traversed with the help of inverted file.

Various modifications have been proposed to improve the original BoW method. Studies on fast vocabulary training [14] and the hierarchical structure [13] enable the million scale vocabulary with fine quantization [24]. Hamming Embedding [8], product quantization [10], and soft/multiple assignments [15, 8] further reduce the quantization error by better partitioning the feature space or smoothing the error. Query expansion [5] improves the recall significantly by formulating a refined query in each iteration.

Among all the variants of BoW, spatial consistency checking has always been a big branch, since the original BoW model makes no guarantee on the spatial regularity of visually matched patches. Filtering isolated matching points [16], bundling spatially-clustered features [20] impose a weak spatial constraint on visually matched feature points. However, these constraints are often too loose to reject the large number of false positives, especially for a large dataset. On the other hand, most of the strong spatial checking techniques are rooted in the planar homography [7] that requires the scene under view to be planar or the camera centers being at a fixed location. In practice, it is often approximated as the affine model [14], which works well for small areas, buildings with planar facades, or small viewpoint changes. Latest techniques rooted in the homography model include WGC [8], E-WGC [23], and GVP [22], which have gained great success in the past few years in terms of retrieval performance. However, the homography model works best on ND [19] or near identical [4] dataset. For 3D objects taken from different viewpoints, the exact spatial configuration is the epipolar geometry [7] with the fundamental matrix projecting a point to its epipolar line. Only a few works [2, 3] explore this model, which successfully retrieve some of the missed matching points for 3D structures. However, unlike the one-to-one mapping for homography, the fundamental matrix can only project a point on one image to a line on the other image, which is also considered to be a weak constraint. However, spatial checking for INS, which consists not only non-planar/3D structures (violating the planar homography), but also non-rigid instances (violating even the epipolar geometry), is seldomly addressed before.

The use of background context is trivial for traditional ND search, and most existing works just uses or discards the context completely. For example, since the background is also part of the query for ND search, it is fully included for retrieving ND images in [19, 4, 23]. For mobile search, where a ROI comes in handy, such as Google Goggles [1] and Snaptell[2], the background context is often ignored. However, for the problem of INS, the context information should be modeled to enrich the limited query information, in order to retrieve novel instances in different background as well as NDs when available.

3. SPATIAL TOPOLOGY CHECKING

While suitable for the visual similarity measurement, BoW does not guarantee the spatial regularity of matched features. However, spatial information is crucial for visual recognition, and is even important for instance retrieval, considering the limited number of features on the query target. Different from ND search, there exists lots of non-planar structures and 3D objects (Figure 1) that do not follow the planar homography transformation. Moreover, there are even non-rigid instances (e.g., person) that do not follow the epipolar geometry. Most of the existing works impose a linear transformation, which works best for planar and rigid instances. For general instance types including non-rigid and non-planar objects, we elastically model the spatial topology with Delaunay Triangulation based visual words matching [21]. In this section, we first summarize the essential spatial configurations [7] of corresponding points for INS, and then propose our spatial topology checking method.

3.1 Spatial Configurations for INS

Let x_1 and x_2 be the homogeneous coordinates of corresponding points on the query and reference image, respectively. Spatial locations for planar scenes can be related by a planar homography matrix $\mathbf{H}$: $x_1 = \mathbf{H}x_2$, which defines a point-to-point mapping between correspondences of a planar plane or two views taken with fixed camera centers, which suits well for ND search. When it comes to 3D objects, the intrinsic projective geometry between two views becomes the epipolar geometry encapsulated by the

[1]http://www.google.com/mobile/goggles/
[2]http://snaptell.com/

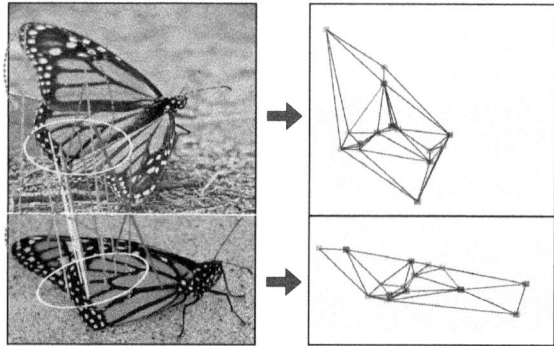

Figure 2: Illustration of the spatial topology checking method based on Delaunay Triangulation (DT). Left: two images with their matched features lined up. Note the matched words are indicated with the same color. Right: the triangulation graphs sketching the topology of matching points on the left.

fundamental matrix $\mathbf{F}$: $\mathbf{x_1^T F x_2} = \mathbf{0}$, which only defines a weak point-to-line mapping. Things are more complicated for INS, which includes plenty of 3D structures and even non-rigid instances (such as persons, animals). Neither planar homography nor epipolar geometry fits in this case. For example, previous spatial checking techniques fail on the the butterfly example in Figure 2, since the spatial variation is caused by a non-planar instance with a non-rigid motion. This section partially addresses this problem by proposing an elastic model that emphasizes the spatial topology regularity.

3.2 Topology Checking via Triangulation

Delaunay Triangulation: This is a technique widely used in Computer Graphics for building meshes out of a set of points. A Delaunay Triangulation [6] for a set of points $\mathbf{P}$ on a 2D plane is a triangulation $\mathrm{DT}(\mathbf{P})$, so no point in $\mathbf{P}$ is inside the circumcircle of any triangle in $\mathrm{DT}(\mathbf{P})$. DT maximizes the sum of the minimum angles of all triangles after triangulation, such that regular/balanced triangles, rather than skinny ones, are preferred. Compared to other triangulation of the points, the smallest angle in Delaunay Triangulation is at least as large as the smallest angle in any other triangulations [1].

Motivation: Since there is no uniform transformation for the non-planar/non-rigid objects that occurs in INS, we seek for solutions from another perspective, i.e., topology. Our motivation is that the spatial topology tends to be stable for (1) different views of 3D objects for small/moderate viewpoint changes, and (2) locally rigid/planar parts of a non-rigid/non-planar instance. For example, among different views of the "plane flying" and "Brooklyn bridge tower" in Figure 1, relative positions of feature points stays the same for local near planar surfaces as well as for non-severe viewpoint changes; the butterfly in Figure 2 has non-rigid motion, but most of the local rigid sub-structures (e.g., the wing) still keeps their spatial layout consistent. We apply an elastic spatial consistency checking strategy to be able to accumulate evidence from these locally consistent patches in 3D view changes and non-rigid transformations.

Our model should be neither too weak to reject inconsistent spatial layouts nor too strong to rule out true spatial configurations. Specifically, the model should be able to (1) accumulate evidence from locally consistent patches and tolerant small motions/viewpoint changes for non-planar/non-rigid instances; (2) work reasonably for NDs; and (3) effectively filter inconsistent spatial configurations. Instead of modeling the transformation for absolute spatial locations, we use a "sketch-match" process to model the topology of spatial layouts of matched feature points. Since our method is based on Delaunay Triangulation, we name our spatial checking as DT in short.

Sketch: For instance search, given the matched words between a query instance Q and a reference image R, DT sketches the spatial structures of Q and R respectively based on the matching locations. Figure 2 shows an example of the triangulation constructed on matched points of Q and R.

For DT, it is a deterministic algorithm and the resulting triangles tend to be "regular", such that spatially neighbored points are coupled as edges and triangles, which are stable against small spatial perturbations as long as the topology holds. Note that the topology information is sketched into the graph after triangulation. For example, each edge (triangle) depicts the spatial nearness of two (three) points, and the full set of edges (triangles) gives a rather detailed "sketch" for the relative positioning of matched features. In this way, the absolute locations of the matched features are discarded and only the topology remains. Note this representation is invariant to scale, rotation changes.

For constructing meshes, the one-to-one mapping constraint needs to be enforced to ensure the number of nodes in each graph is identical. This is done by enforcing a point from Q to match only one point on R with the smallest Hamming distance. The enforcement effectively prevents an excessive number of redundant matches, an effect known as the "burstiness" [9].

Match: After triangulation, the spatial consistency is measured by graph matching. We have compared several strategies by considering different local structures (such as edges, triangles), and different weighting functions in terms of performance and efficiency, resulting in a computational efficient approach for matching graphs. With ΔQ denoting the mesh of Q, the geometric consistency of R and Q is measured as:

$$\mathrm{BF}(Q, R) = \|\mathbf{E}_{\Delta Q} \cap \mathbf{E}_{\Delta R}\|, \tag{1}$$

where $\mathbf{E}_{\Delta Q}$ denotes the edge set of ΔQ, and BF indicates the number of common edges[3] between Q and R. The retrieval score of R is then weighted by $\mathrm{BF}(Q, R)$. This measurement works well in practice, because the features are coupled together while matching, resulting much lower false positive rate.

3.3 Discussion

After triangulation, the mesh can be regarded as an "abstract", or the approximation for the original shape. In computer graphics, this mesh is usually used to approximate the original shape. While in our case, the edge is encoded with the information of spatial topology for matched feature points. By viewing this mesh as a graph, the process of *sketch* discards the absolute spatial locations and leaves only the relative spatial nearness of a set of points distributed on a plane. Then the *match* process measures the topological

---
[3]Two edges are regarded as common if their vertices share the same visual words.

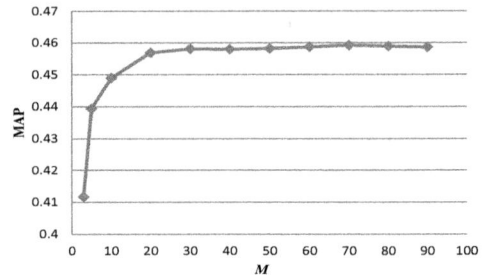

Figure 3: Sensitivity test of M on TV11, by applying DT on different number of max matching points.

layout consistency as graph similarity. Figure 2 gives an example on how DT works. Due to the non-rigid motion of the flipping wings, there are no linear transformations that could transform the matching locations from one to the other. If RANSAC is used with a linear model (either homography or epipolar), only a fraction of the "good" matches could survive, because the dominant linear transformation (e.g., defined by the matches in the yellow solid ellipse) will rule out many other good matches (e.g., matches on the wing in red dashed ellipse). For example, E-WGC is only able to locate five true matches for similarity ranking. DT, on the contrary, can accumulate evidences from both wings (yellow and red ellipses) and obtain a much higher confidence in topological similarity, since only relative positioning is sketched. Besides the locally consistent patches, non-rigid or non-planar regions of an object can also be partially tolerated as long as the motion of 3D structure is not severe. Interestingly, this assumption often holds for real life objects in practice. For example, when people are walking, spatial locations of each body parts only move in a small range, which would result in a graph different from that for irrelevant objects. In Figure 2, the high similarity score is also partially contributed by the this kind of topological consistency between wings.

While simple, DT has the following merits: (1) the relative spatial position of words is considered, (2) no assumption of any transformation model is made, (3) a certain degree of freedom for variations of word positions is allowed. Compared to weak spatial checking techniques, criterion (1) considers the topology of words, and thereby is more effective in measuring geometric consistency. Compared with strict spatial checking [23, 22], criterion (2) does not impose any prior knowledge on types of instances and transformations, and thus the checking of geometric coherency is looser. However, by allowing variations of local changes as stated by criterion (3), DT is a flexible model, which is more adaptable to INS. A fundamental difference between DT and other spatial checking techniques is that no pruning of false matches or model estimation is involved. Instead, DT enumerates the potential true matches with the local topology consistency based on criteria (1) and (3), while tolerating good matches by not imposing any prior constraints based on criterion (2).

3.4 Complexity

Time: The two major steps of DT are the triangulation and the counting of common edges. The first step can be efficiently conducted by divide-and-conquer in $O(n \log n)$ time, where n is the number of matched words between Q and R. The second step can be done by a simple linear scan of edges with $O(|e|)$, where $|e| = O(n)$ is the number of edges. So the computation is dominated by $O(n \log n)$. In our experiments, since a large vocabulary is used, n is quite small a number in most cases. Whenever n is larger than some value M, random sampling is performed to limit maximal M matching points, such that only a small random subset of matches is evaluated by Eq. (1). Figure 3 shows the sensitivity test on TV11 dataset. As shown, larger M gives more detailed sketch and better performance. When M is large enough, the performance tends to be stable. In our experiments, we set $M = 30$ to balance the efficiency and performance. In practice, DT runs fast, since it is only applied on images that have common visual words with the query image.

Space: For DT, we need to keep track of the matched points locations $[(q_x, q_y), (r_x, r_y)]$ between the query q and each reference image r. For a dataset with N images, $4 \times M \times N$ short integers are needed, which is approximate 288 MB, if $M = 30$ and $N = 10^6$ for a million scale dataset.

4. CONTEXT MODELING WITH "STARE"

Another problem for INS is how to use the background context. The ROI region alone gives clean and precise description for the target but less information, while the whole image carries more cues with more noises. The region inside ROI is definitely important, since it indicates the searching focus. However, we know little about the relevancy between the instance and the background context. Whether to use context information is by no means easy to tell, without the knowledge of the reference dataset beforehand.

Inspired by the perception behavior of human eyes, we weight features in different regions with a "stare" model to simulate human eye-sighting. At the time of starring at something, human eyes always have a *focus* (f), where things can be captured clear and nice, and scenes away from the *focus* "blurs" accordingly. In our "stare" model, the *focus* is a virtual point defined as the center of ROI, and the surrounding regions are down-weighted by a Gaussian function. The complete weighting function $k(x)$ for a feature x is given as:

$$k(x) = \begin{cases} 1, & \text{if } x \in \textbf{ROI}, \\ \exp(-\frac{\|x-f\|^2}{2\delta^2}), & \text{otherwise}, \end{cases} \text{ with } \delta^2 = -\frac{diag^2}{8 \ln 0.1}, \tag{2}$$

where $diag$ is the length of diagonal axis of the query image. Figure 4 (left) is an illustration with a circular ROI located at the center of a square picture. With the assumption of uniformly distributed feature points on the image plane, integrating the weights on ROI and background according to Eq. 2 gives the contribution ratio $f(r, N)$ of features inside the ROI while retrieving:

$$f(r, N) = \frac{\int_{x \in ROI} 1 \mathrm{d}x}{\int_{x \in \overline{ROI}} \exp(-\frac{\|x-f\|^2}{2\delta^2}) \, \mathrm{d}x + \int_{x \in ROI} 1 \mathrm{d}x} \tag{3}$$

Figure 4 (right) plots the simulation result of this ratio of contribution $f(r, N)$ with respect to the ratio of sizes ($2r/diag$). With the "stare" model, we adjust the weights on object and context adaptively for different sizes of instances. We tend to lay more emphasis on context for smaller instances, and vice verse. Note the curve in Figure 4 (right) is not completely sigmoid-like, since part of the ROI is out of the image when the ratio $\frac{2r}{diag} \in (\frac{\sqrt{2}}{2}, 1]$.

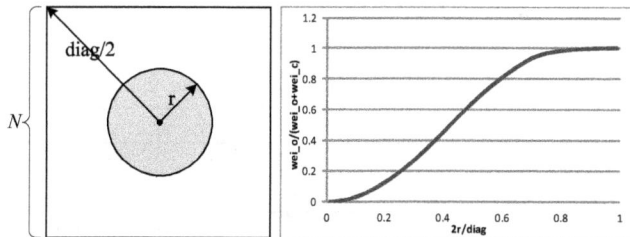

Figure 4: Left: illustration of the "stare" model with a circular ROI (with radius r) on a square image (resolution: $N \times N$). Right: the proportion of accumulated weights from ROI (the object), with respect to the ratio of sizes "$2r/diag$".

Table 1: Statistics for TV11 & TV12.

	# topic	# query	# video	# frame	# feature
TV11	25	95	21k	574k	484m
TV12	21	102	75k	822k	1,323m

5. EXPERIMENT

This section evaluates the proposed methods for spatial checking (DT) and context modeling ("stare"). We start by introducing the TRECVID INS datasets, and then evaluate the performance of each method by comparing with other state-of-the-art techniques.

5.1 Dataset and Retrieval Model

Dataset: We use the TRECVID [17] INS datasets in years 2011 and 2012, named as TV11 and TV12, for experiments. The datasets contain video clips/shots cut from BBC Rushes and Flickr videos respectively for TV11 and TV12. The queries are topics on person, object, and location entities, which are delimited with several image examples together with the masks indicating the instances. The task [17] is to locate for each query topic up to the 1000 clips most likely to contain a recognizable instance of the entity. Figure 1 shows some query topics together with their corresponding ground truth video frames in the datasets. Table 1 summarizes the statistics of the datasets, and Table 2 lists the query topics in TRECVID datasets. Although there are only 25 (21) topics in TV11 (TV12), they cover a wide range of real life instances including objects, locations, and person. On average, each topic has 3.8 (4.9) image examples for TV11 (TV12), and a binary mask is also provided for each image example. Mean inferred AP (denoted as MAP for short) is used for evaluation.

Retrieval Model: Unless otherwise mentioned, the following BoW-based retrieval model is adopted for all the experiments. For offline processing, keyframes are extracted at the rate of one frame per second from raw videos, and Hessian-affine detector [12] and SIFT [11] descriptor are used for feature extraction. A hierarchical vocabulary [13] with 250k leaf nodes is constructed using K-Means in a top-down manner. Then, the features are indexed with an inverted file for fast retrieval. Auxiliary information, including Hamming signature [8] and spatial locations, are also indexed for word filtering and geometric checking. During online retrieval, a similar procedure is carried out for each query example. To reduce quantization error, a descriptor is assigned to multiple visual words by soft-weighting [15]. By

Table 2: Topic lists for TV11 & TV12 datasets.

TV11		TV12	
ID	Topic Name	ID	Topic Name
9023	setting sun	9048	Mercedes star
9024	upstairs, inside windmill	9049	Brooklyn bridge tower
9025	fork	9050	Eiffel tower
9026	trailer	9051	Golden Gate Bridge
9027	SUV	9052	London Underground logo
9028	plane flying	9053	Coca-cola logo - letters
9029	downstairs, inside windmill	9054	Stonehenge
9030	yellow dome with clock	9055	Sears/Willis Tower
9031	the Parthenon	9056	Pantheon interior
9032	spiral staircase	9057	Leshan Giant Buddha
9033	newsprint balloon	9058	US Capitol exterior
9034	tall, cylindrical building	9059	baldachin-St.Peter's Basilica
9035	tortoise	9060	Stephen Colbert
9036	all yellow balloon	9061	Pepsi logo - circle
9037	windmill seen from outside	9062	One WTO building
9038	female presenter X	9063	Prague Castle
9039	Carol Smilie	9064	Empire State Building
9040	Linda Robson	9065	Hagia Sophia interior
9041	monkey	9066	Hoover Dam exterior
9042	male presenter Y	9067	MacDonald's arches
9043	Tony Clark's wife	9068	PUMA logo animal
9044	American flag		
9045	lantern		
9046	grey-haired lady		
9047	airplane-shaped balloon		

Figure 6: Examples on the ranks of retrieved images. For each example, the query is shown on left, and the corresponding retrieved images are on the right. The ranks of the retrieved image given by different spatial verification techniques are indicated by the numbers on the right hand side, ordered by DT, BoW, WGC, E-WGC, and GVP from top to bottom.

traversing the index with HE filtering, images sharing common visual words are rapidly retrieved from the reference dataset. Since the final relevancy is evaluated at video level, the score for each video clip is obtained by accumulating scores from its keyframes, and the evidence of each query example is linearly combined by average fusion for the final ranking list.

5.2 Performance Comparison

We compare the following approaches: WGC (Weak Geometric Consistency) [8], E-WGC (Enhanced WGC) [23], GVP (Geometric-preserving Visual Phrases) [22], and our proposed approach DT. All the approaches are built on top of the BoW model described in Section 5.1. GVP is a voting approach that uses offset (or translation) information for rapid geometric checking. WGC, in contrast, votes the dominant scale and orientation for fast but weak geometric checking. E-WGC incorporates the advantages of GVP and WGC by voting the translation after scale and orientation compensation. We also test variants of DT by applying it on the whole query image (denoted as DT), instance only (denoted as DT_O), and context modeling using "stare" (denoted as DT_C).

5.2.1 Spatial Checking

Generally, in the set of matched points between two images using BoW method, there are many mismatches and outliers due to photometric and geometric variations. Applying a geometric consistency checking is important to remove false positives and improve the performance. Figure 5 contrasts the performances of different spatial checking techniques, and Figure 6 shows several search examples with the ranking information attached on the right side. The baseline method of BoW does not use any spatial checking techniques and ranks results purely based on visual similarity. WGC, E-WGC, GVP and DT, which impose a spatial consistency constraint on the matching points, show similar or better performances as BoW. In particular, WGC filters false matches by voting the dominant scale and orientation between two images, but makes no guarantee on consistent spatial layouts for the matching points. E-WGC considers the scale, orientation, and translation jointly into an affine model, and votes the dominant translation offsets after compensating the difference of scale and orientation.

It works well for ND search, since scaling, rotating, and translating the image are common operations to generate NDs. However, both WGC and E-WGC suffer from imprecise scale/orientation estimation during feature extraction, especially for images with heavy noises, non-rigid objects, or 3D scenes captured from different viewpoints. GVP can be regarded as a special case of E-WGC, when two images are with identical scale and orientation. In other words, GVP votes the translation without compensating scale and orientation. Thus, it gets rid of the potential variations in scale/orientation estimation by assuming features from two images share the same scale and orientation, but also becomes more sensitive to scale/orientation changes even for ND pairs. Note that the spatial consistency model used in WGC, E-WGC, and GVP are all rooted in planar homography. Although they are able to rank some true responses (mainly near duplicates) higher, the final performance is downgraded because of the large number of falsely pruned true matches. This observation coincides with that in [18], where only a few topics benefits from the homography model and others does not. In our case, eight (seven) topics in TV11 (TV12) are improved by imposing the homography-based techniques, while other topics show similar or worse performance. Note for topics that totally violate the homography, the stronger the model it uses, the worse the performance is. For example, the topics 9026 (trailer) and 9057 (Leshan Giant Buddha) are with 3D objects viewed from different viewpoints, so they suffer less on WGC, which is a weak constraint, than on E-WGC and GVP, which are strong point-to-point transformations.

DT, instead of using a homography-based transformation, models the topology layout of matching points into a graph. It has several benefits. First, it is born to be invariant to scale/orientation changes. Since only the connectivity of nodes matters for a graph, scaling and rotating the image result in exactly the same graph. For example, the query and reference images shown in the last row of Figure 6 give

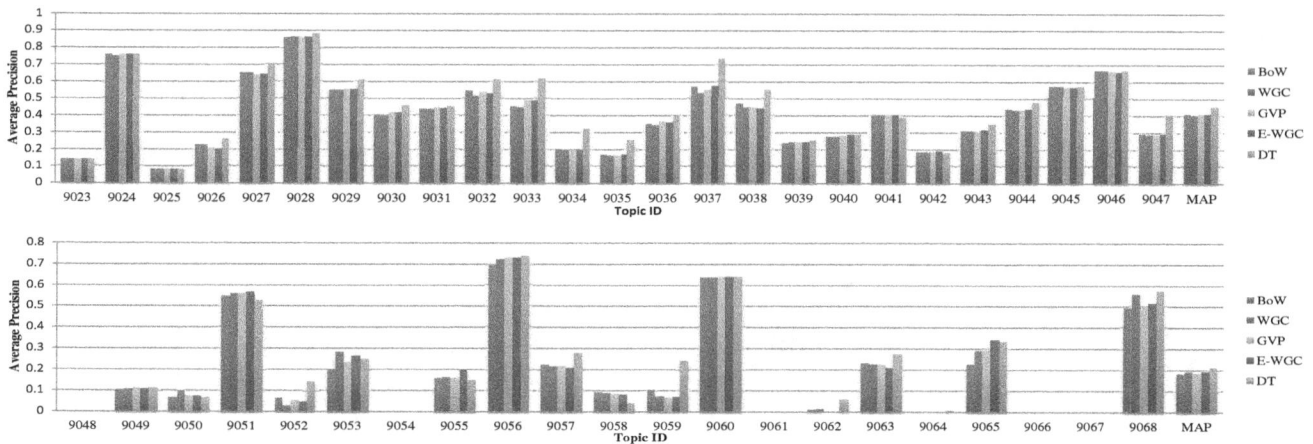

Figure 5: Performance comparison for different spatial checking techniques. Top: TV11. Bottom: TV12.

Figure 8: Effect of context modeling. The query and retrieved images are shown on the left and right sides, respectively. The ranking of different strategies on the retrieved images are indicated on the right hand side, ordered by the ranks given by applying context modeling with "stare" model (DT_C), whole image (DT), and instance only (DT_O).

the same graph, as long as the corresponding features can be matched. While for WGC and E-WGC, the requirement for small noises in the scale/orientation estimation makes them less robust in result ranking. Second, for non-homography spatial configurations introduced by different views of non-planar objects (first two rows of Figure 6) and non-rigid motions (3rd row), DT still get some evidence from the local topology-preserving regions. Third, for small number of the matching points caused by scale changes (left example in last row) or blur/noise/compression (right example in last row), DT actively boosts the ranking of the results according to Eq. 1, as long as the matched points are topologically consistent. While for other methods based on voting-and-pruning, the true responses with small number of matching point can only be boosted when the higher ranked false positives are downgraded by pruning of false positive matches. In other words, by (1) being invariant to scale/orientation changes, (2) allowing to get evidence from local topology-consistent sub-regions, and (3) act actively on boosting topology consistent results, true responses in INS have better chances to be boosted in the ranking list for DT than other homography-based methods.

5.2.2 Context Modeling

For TRECVID INS datasets, some instances in the reference videos appear in the same background context, while others in totally different context. Retrieving using either the whole image or the region inside ROI could miss some instances in the top list. Context modeling is designed to tradeoff between this situation and aims to bring both types of instances to top positions in the ranking list. Figure 7 shows the performance of different strategies of using context, including our context modeling with "stare", retrieving with the object inside ROI and whole image. We test these strategies on both methods without (BoW) and with (DT) spatial checking. By comparing the overall performances, the context does contain some useful information, since the method with BoW_O/DT_O gives worse result than BoW_C/DT_C on most topics. Our context modeling performs best among all variants for both BoW and DT, showing its effectiveness in retrieving instances with different background, without hurting too much on the ND results with the same background. Figure 8 further lists some examples, showing the tradeoff between exploring instances with different background and retrieving NDs with the same background. As shown in the 1st row, the ranks of ND results are only slightly downgraded by context modeling with "stare", since NDs usually cover the whole image and it still remains easy to retrieve with even down-weighted context information. While for instances appearing in different background as the query image (2nd row of Figure 8), the process of down-weighting of background context becomes essential to boost the rankings for results in different background context. The "stare" model shows the best performance for both BoW and DT, almost on every topics, except those with dense and discriminative features already, such as (2nd row of Figure 8) landmarks (9050: Eiffel tower, 9058: US Capitol exterior) and logos (9053: Coca-cola logo, 9068: PUMA logo). In such cases, adding more context confuses the targets that are already strong and clear. However, the ranks are not significantly downgraded and still remains top in the list, since the weighting in Eq. 2 still lay a lot of emphasis on instances with plenty of features.

5.3 Speed Efficiency

The experiments are conducted on a 8-core 2.67GHz computers with 30GB RAM. Only one core is used for online retrieval. Table 3 details the average running time for searching one query image from each dataset. As shown, BoW runs fastest among all the methods. WGC, GVP, and E-

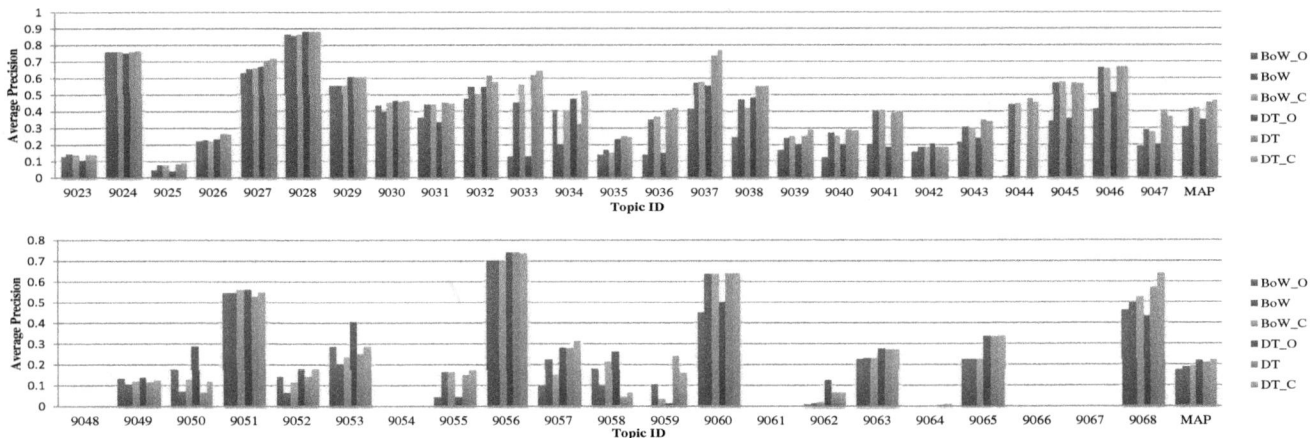

Figure 7: Performance comparison for different strategies of using context. Top: TV11. Bottom: TV12.

Table 3: The average running time (in milliseconds) for each method. The time includes feature quantization and online retrieval, but not feature extraction.

	BoW	WGC	GVP	E-WGC	DT	DT_C
TV11	173	232	227	292	217	219
TV12	625	885	851	989	875	880

WGC have a voting step to calculate the dominant transformation parameters, making them slower than BoW. DT and DT_C are also slower than BoW by introducing an extra step for triangulation and graph matching. Note the computation overhead for context modeling is negligible in practice. However, the extra time for DT is compensated by large performance gain. Note it takes much longer time for TV12 than TV11 in our experiments, since the number of features in TV12 is much more than that in TV11.

6. CONCLUSIONS

We have presented our approaches for searching instances from video collection, in the scenario of limited number of features for the query target and general spatial configurations. For INS, making better use of the limited information, including spatial and context cues, is critical for better performance. Specifically, DT, which improves the quality of visual matching by emphasizing the topology layouts of the matching points, boosts true results by accumulating evidence from local topology-preserving regions. To increase the amount of information for matching, context modeling via "stare" shows good tradeoff between exploration on instances with different background and exploitation on NDs with similar background. Our experimental result shows the effectiveness and efficiency of our methods for the problem of Instance Search.

7. ACKNOWLEDGMENTS

The work described in this paper was fully supported by a grant from the Research Grants Council of the Hong Kong Special Administrative Region, China (CityU 118812).

8. REFERENCES

[1] http://en.wikipedia.org/wiki/Delaunay_triangulation.
[2] R. Arandjelovic and A. Zisserman. Efficient image retrieval for 3d structures. In *BMVC*, 2010.
[3] O. Chum and J. Matas. Large-scale discovery of spatially related images. *PAMI*, 32:371–377, 2010.
[4] O. Chum, J. Philbin, M. Isard, and A. Zisserman. Scalable near identical image and shot detection. In *CIVR*, 2007.
[5] O. Chum, J. Philbin, J. Sivic, M. Isard, and A. Zisserman. Total Recall: Automatic Query Expansion with a Generative Feature Model for Object Retrieval. In *ICCV*, pages 1–8, 2007.
[6] B. N. Delaunay. Sur la sphère vide. *Bulletin of Academy of Sciences of the USSR*, (6):793–800, 1934.
[7] R. I. Hartley and A. Zisserman. *Multiple View Geometry in Computer Vision*. Cambridge University Press, 2004.
[8] H. Jégou, M. Douze, and C. Schmid. Hamming embedding and weak geometric consistency for large scale image search. In *ECCV*, 2008.
[9] H. Jégou, M. Douze, and C. Schmid. On the burstiness of visual elements. In *CVPR*, 2009.
[10] H. Jégou, M. Douze, and C. Schmid. Product quantization for nearest neighbor search. *PAMI*, 33(1):117–128, 2011.
[11] D. Lowe. Distinctive image features from scale-invariant keypoints. *IJCV*, 60(2):91–110, 2004.
[12] K. Mikolajczyk and C. Schmid. Scale & affine invariant interest point detectors. *IJCV*, 60:63–86, October 2004.
[13] D. Nister and H. Stewenius. Scalable recognition with a vocabulary tree. In *CVPR*, pages 2161–2168, 2006.
[14] J. Philbin, O. Chum, M. Isard, J. Sivic, and A. Zisserman. Object retrieval with large vocabularies and fast spatial matching. In *CVPR*, 2007.
[15] J. Philbin, M. Isard, J. Sivic, and A. Zisserman. Lost in quantization: Improving particular object retrieval in large scale image databases. In *CVPR*, 2008.
[16] J. Sivic and A. Zisserman. Video Google: A text retrieval approach to object matching in videos. In *ICCV*, 2003.
[17] A. F. Smeaton, P. Over, and W. Kraaij. Evaluation campaigns and trecvid. In *MIR*, 2006.
[18] C. G. M. Snoek, K. van de Sande, A. Habibian, S. Kordumova, Z. Li, M. Mazloom, S. Pintea, R. Tao, D. Koelma, and A. W. M. Smeulders. The mediamill trecvid 2012 semantic video search engine. In *TRECVID*, 2012.
[19] X. Wu, A. G. Hauptmann, and C.-W. Ngo. Practical elimination of near-duplicates from web video search. In *ACMMM*, pages 218–227, 2007.
[20] Z. Wu, Q. Ke, M. Isard, and J. Sun. Bundling features for large scale partial-duplicate web image search. In *CVPR*, pages 25–32, Aug. 2009.
[21] W. Zhang, L. Pang, and C. W. Ngo. Snap-and-ask: Answering multimodal question by naming visual instance. In *ACMMM*.
[22] Y. Zhang, Z. Jia, and T. Chen. Image retrieval with geometry preserving visual phrases. In *CVPR*, 2011.
[23] W. Zhao, X. Wu, and C. W. Ngo. On the annotation of web videos by efficient near-duplicate search. *TMM*, 2010.
[24] C. Zhu and S. Satoh. Large vocabulary quantization for searching instances from videos. In *ICMR*, 2012.

Fisher Kernel based Relevance Feedback for Multimodal Video Retrieval

Ionuţ Mironică
LAPI, University Politehnica of
Bucharest, Romania
imironica@imag.pub.ro

Bogdan Ionescu
LAPI, University Politehnica of
Bucharest, Romania
bionescu@imag.pub.ro

Jasper Uijlings
DISI, University of Trento, Italy
jrr@disi.unitn.it

Nicu Sebe
DISI, University of Trento, Italy
sebe@disi.unitn.it

ABSTRACT

This paper proposes a novel approach to relevance feedback based on the Fisher Kernel representation in the context of multimodal video retrieval. The Fisher Kernel representation describes a set of features as the derivative with respect to the log-likelihood of the generative probability distribution that models the feature distribution. In the context of relevance feedback, instead of learning the generative probability distribution over all features of the data, we learn it only over the top retrieved results. Hence during relevance feedback we create a new Fisher Kernel representation based on the most relevant examples. In addition, we propose to use the Fisher Kernel to capture temporal information by cutting up a video in smaller segments, extract a feature vector from each segment, and represent the resulting feature set using the Fisher Kernel representation. We evaluate our method on the MediaEval 2012 Video Genre Tagging Task, a large dataset, which contains 26 categories in 15.000 videos totalling up to 2.000 hours of footage. Results show that our method significantly improves results over existing state-of-the-art relevance feedback techniques. Furthermore, we show significant improvements by using the Fisher Kernel to capture temporal information, and we demonstrate that Fisher kernels are well suited for this task.

Categories and Subject Descriptors

H.3.1 [**Content Analysis and Indexing**]: [Indexing methods]; H.3.3 [**Information Search and Retrieval**]: [Retrieval models, query formulation, relevance feedback]

General Terms

Algorithms, Performance, Experimentation

Keywords

Relevance feedback, Fisher kernels, multimodal video retrieval

1. INTRODUCTION

The actual challenge of the existing information retrieval systems is in their capability of identifying and selecting only relevant information, according to some user specifications. This issue became more critical due to increase of technology, e.g. portable multimedia terminals, wireless transmission protocols, imaging devices which basically makes the information accessibile from everywhere. In order to improve performance, existing systems are turning towards multimodal approaches attempting to exploit the benefits of fusing various modalities such as text, visual and audio. Despite the high variability of automatical content descriptors used and of the classification techniques, Content Based Video Retrieval Systems (CBVR) are inherently limited by the gap between the real world and its representation through computer vision techniques [1].

An effective way to narrow the semantic gap is to use the user's feedback in the retrieval process, which is known as Relevance Feedback (RF). A general RF scenario can be formulated as follow: for a certain retrieval query, the user marks what results are relevant and non-relevant. Then, the system automatically computes a better representation of the information and/or retrains the classifier to better refine results. Relevance feedback can go through one or more iterations of this sort. This basically improves the system's response based on query related ground-truth.

In this paper, we propose a new RF approach for video genre retrieval, using a combination of Fisher Kernels with SVM Classifiers. Fisher Kernels (FK) are a powerful framework which combines the advantages of a generative algorithm with the strengths of discriminative approaches [2]. The main idea of FK is to describe a signal with a gradient vector derived from a generative probability model (Gaussian Mixture Model - GMM) and then to train this representation with a discriminative classifier (in most of the cases SVM). The Fisher Kernels have been successfully applied to many fields from image categorization [3], to audio indexing [5] and handwritten word-spotting [4], but, to our knowledge, the FK have never been used in Relevance Feedback, or in video classification.

In order to describe a document, most of the RF strategies

use a single feature vector. However, video documents can be considered as a sequence of scenes, and the features from each scene can be used to model and retrieve the video content. Because we use the Fisher Kernel framework, we can retain some form of temporal relations of the video scenes in our relevance feedback approach.

Experimental tests conducted on the large video database MediaEval Genre Tagging task 2012 [6] and using current state-of-the-art multimodal video descriptors, prove that the proposed RF increases retrieval performance and outperforms other classic approaches. In addition, the proposed approach allows a fast implementation similar to a classical SVM RF strategy, but with a higher increase of performance. We also propose several modifications to the original framework that can boost the accuracy of the RF algorithm.

2. RELATED WORK

The idea of relevance feedback is to take advantage of the user's input on the initially returned results for a given query and to use this information to refine and improve the quality of the results. Relevance feedback has proven to increase retrieval accuracy, and to give more personalized results for the user [10] [11] [12] [13] [15]. Recently, a relevance feedback track was organized by TREC to evaluate and compare different relevance feedback algorithms for text descriptors [7]. However, relevance feedback was successfully used not only for text retrieval, but also for image features [11] [12] [13] [15] and multimodal video features [10] [21].

Most of the relevance feedback algorithms can be divided in two main classes: those that change the feature's representation, and, those that use a re-learning strategy with a classifier.

One of the earliest and most successful RF algorithms is the Rocchio algorithm [9] [10]. Using the set of R relevant and N non-relevant documents selected from the current user relevance feedback window, the Rocchio algorithm modifies the feature of the initial query by adding the features of positive examples and subtracting the features of negative examples to the original feature.

The Relevance Feature Estimation (RFE) algorithm [11] assumes that for a given query, according to the user's subjective judgment, some specific features may be more important than other features. The idea of the re-weighting strategy is to analyze the relevant objects in order to understand which dimensions are more important than others. Every feature has an importance weight computed as $w_i = 1/\sigma$ where σ denotes the variance of relevant documents. Therefore, features with higher variance with respect to the relevant queries become less important than elements with a reduced variation.

More recently, machine learning techniques found their application with relevance feedback approaches. In these approaches, the relevance feedback problem can be formulated as a two class classification of the negative and positive samples. After a training step, all the documents are ranked according to the classifiers's confidence level. Some of the most successful techniques use Support Vector Machines [12], Nearest Neighbor [13], classification trees, e.g. Random Forest [15], or boosting techniques, e.g. AdaBoost [14].

However, all these techniques have problems when there is only a limited number or an asymmetric number of positive and negative feedback samples provided by the user.

There have been several attempts to overcome this. More recent approaches to relevance feedback include Biased Discriminant Euclidean Embedding [17] and Active Reranking for Web Image Search [18]. However, all of these approaces have only been applied to image datasets.

In video retrieval, most of relevance feedback approaches have focused on pseudo-relevance feedback. In general, pseudo-relevance feedback algorithms assume that a substantial number of video shots in the top of the ranking are relevant [19]. The information associated with these top-ranked pseudo-relevant shots is then used to update the initial retrieval results.

In this paper, we propose a new method, denoted Fisher Kernels Relevance Feedback (FKRF). We will show that we can improve the performance of classical RF retrieval systems by using the Fisher kernel method. Furthermore, the use of the Fisher kernel representation enables us to represent a complete video while retaining a form of temporal information.

3. PROPOSED FISHER KERNEL RELEVANCE FEEDBACK

3.1 Fisher Kernel Theory

The Fisher kernels were designed as a framework to combine the benefits of generative and discriminative approaches. The general idea is to represent a signal as the gradient of the probability density function that is a learned generative model of that signal. Intuitively, such Fisher vector representation measures how to modify the parameters of the probability density function in order to best fit the signal, similar to the measurements in a gradient descent algorithm for fitting a generative model. The Fisher vector is subsequently used in a discriminative classifier. In this paper we follow [2] and use a Gaussian Mixture Model (GMM) followed by a linear SVM.

Let $X = \{x_1, x_2, ..., x_T\}$ be a set of T multimodal video descriptors. Now X can be represented by its gradient vector with respect to a Gaussian Mixture Model u_λ with parameters λ:

$$G(X)_\lambda = \frac{1}{T} \nabla_\lambda \log(u_\lambda(X)) \tag{1}$$

The gradient vector is, by definition, the concatenation of the partial derivatives with respect to the model parameters. Let μ_i and σ_i be the mean and the standard deviation of i's Gaussian centroid, $\gamma(i)$ be the soft assignment of descriptor x_t to Gaussian i, and let D denote the dimensionality of the descriptors x_t. $G_{\mu,i}^x$ is the D-dimensional gradient with respect to the mean μ_i and standard deviation σ_i of Gaussian i. Mathematical derivations lead to [3]:

$$G_{\mu,i}^x = \frac{1}{T\sqrt{\omega_i}} \sum_{t=1}^{T} \gamma(i) \frac{x_t - \mu_i}{\sigma_i} \tag{2}$$

$$G_{\sigma,i}^x = \frac{1}{T\sqrt{2\omega_i}} \sum_{t=1}^{T} \gamma(i) \left[\frac{(x_t - \mu_i)^2}{\sigma_i^2} - 1 \right] \tag{3}$$

where the division between vectors is a term-by-term operation. The final gradient vector G^x is the concatenation of the $G_{\mu,i}^x$ and $G_{\sigma,i}^x$ vectors, for $i = 1...K$.

3.2 Proposed Fisher Kernel RF Algorithm

Our relevance feedback method works as follows. Using a single video as query, we rank all videos using a nearest-neighbor strategy. Then, the user selects from the top n videos which ones are relevant or which ones are not, where n is typically small (20 in our experiments). We learn a generative Gaussian Mixture model from the first n retrieved documents. Then we re-represent the top k videos using a Fisher Kernel representation with respect to this GMM, where k is typically large (2000 in our experiments). We only consider the top k as it is unlikely that relevant videos are ranked lower in the initial ranking. Afterwards, we train an SVM on the Fisher vectors of the top n user labeled results. We apply this SVM on the top k videos to obtain a final ranking.

The algorithm is given in Algorithm 1. We now briefly describe the details for re-representing the features after relevance feedback using the Fisher Kernel and the subsequent learning procedure.

Altering features after user's feedback. After the initial query using nearest-neighbor search, we train a Gaussian Mixture model on the features of the top n videos, regardless of their true relevance. In a practical application this allows the training of the Gaussian Mixture model in the background during the time that the user is giving feedback. For optimization reasons we initialize the centroids with a kmeans output. An important choice for the Fisher Kernel representation is the number of clusters c. As for each cluster the dimensionality of the representation doubles, for a practical system the number of clusters has to be low. We experiment with a value of c between 1 and 5 in Section 5.2.

The size of the Fisher Kernel representation is twice the size of the original feature times the number of clusters c. To make the Fisher Kernel computationally feasible, we first apply PCA on the original feature vectors of the documents. We compute PCA individually on each feature type and reduce the dimensions by 10%. After having obtained the mixture model, we convert the original features of the top k videos into the Fisher Kernel representation using Equations 2 and 3. For both the GMM clustering and the Fisher projection we use the software obtained from [3].

Finally, we perform normalization on the Fisher vectors as [2] has found this to significantly increase performance. In our method we experiment with the following normalization strategies: L1 and L2 normalizations, power normalization $(f(x) = sign(x)\sqrt{\alpha|x|})$, logarithmic normalization $(f(x) = sign(x)log(1 + \alpha|x|))$ and combinations of them.

Training - reranking step. We use the Fisher representations of the top n videos, along with the labels obtained using feedback from the user, to train a two-class SVM classifier. SVMs are appropriate for relevance feedback as they are relatively robust to the situation in which only few training examples are available. Indeed, SVMs have been successfully used in several RF approaches [12]. In our experiments, we test two types of SVM kernels: a fast linear kernel and the RBF nonlinear kernel. While linear SVMs are very fast in both training and testing, SVMs with an RBF kernel are more accurate in many classification tasks.

3.3 Frame Aggregation with Fisher kernel

Most of content based systems involve two main steps: feature extraction and document ranking. The first step

---

Algorithm 1: The Fisher Kernels Relevance Feedback Algorithm

Initial parameters:

Labeled Sample set: X_i and labels Y_i;
Unlabeled Sample set: X_r;
SVM Classifier parameters (C, γ);
n: the window size;

Start:

do 10% PCA reduction for all multimodal features;

Altering features step:

Compute GMM centroids for X_i;
for $x \subset Xi$ **do**
$\quad$ *compute $FK(x) = FK(x, GMM)$;*
$\quad$ *normalize $FK(x)$;*

Training - reranking step:

train $SVM(C, \gamma)$ using FK features;

for $x \subset Xr$ **do**
$\quad$ *compute $FK(x) = FK(x, GMM)$;*
$\quad$ *normalize $FK(x)$;*
$\quad$ *compute $h(x) = SvmConfidenceLevel(FK(x))$;*
sort $h(x)$ values;
show new ranked list according to $h(x)$ values;

---

mainly consists of computing one feature per document that needs to capture as many relevant characteristic for that document category as possible. For video documents, most of the approaches compute a feature for each frame, and then aggregate all the features in one descriptor by computing the mean, variance or other statistics over all the frames. But, by aggregating these statistics in these ways, the notion of time is lost. Alternatively, we can represent a video by multiple vectors and compute the distance between two sets of points using, for example, the Earth Mover distance [24]. However, using such a metric involves a huge computational cost for large databases.

By using the Fisher kernel representation, we obtain a natural solution to the problem above. The Fisher Kernel was originally designed to map multiple vectors into a fixed length representation, and this approach is exactly what we need for this problem. It takes advantage of the expressive power of generative models to map sequences of features of variable length, such as video sequences, into a fixed length representation.

For cutting up the video into temporal fragments, one approach is to divide the video document into frames and to compute a visual descriptor for each video frame. However, for large multimedia databases the number of frames is huge (25 frames per second and thousands of hours of video footage) and this approach can create computational problems. In order to efficiently browse through the significant video content, summarization is required [27]. So, we extract a small collection of salient images (keyframes) that best represent the underlying content [27].

We train the Gaussian Mixture model on the features of the top n videos. Once the generative model is trained, for every training sequence of feature vectors $X_i = \{x_1; x_2; ..; x_T\}$, composed of T feature vectors we transform it into a vector of fixed dimension. The only difference between the previous

art: Art Forum Berlin | autos: Joe's 2009 Geneva | comedy: Sassy Kids | food: Cumin salad

gaming: Arkham Asylum | literature: Aaron Lansky | music: JON HAMMOND Band | web: Ruby for Newbies

videoblogging: Christian | religion: The Boyle Lecture | travel: Indie Travel | politics: Oil Spill Laws

BronxTalk | Oct. 10, 2011 | Lawrence Lessig | Student Elections Turn Violent | Governor Tomblin Whio?

Figure 1: Image examples for several video genres. The bottom images correspond to videos from the same genre category, i.e. "politics" (source blip.tv).

approach and this one regards on what data the GMM has learned. Instead of using one global aggregated video feature, we will use more features per document. The resulting Fisher kernel representation will have the same number of dimensions. Experiments from Section 5.5 will show the performance of temporal Fisher Kernels on the Relevance feedback problem.

4. EXPERIMENTAL SETUP

4.1 Dataset

The validation of the proposed content descriptors is carried out in the context of the MediaEval 2012 Benchmarking Initiative for Multimedia Evaluation, the Video Genre Tagging Task [6]. This task addresses the automatic categorization of web media genres used with the blip.tv platform (see http://blip.tv/). For testing, we use the MediaEval 2012 Video Genre Tagging dataset consisting of 15000 sequences (up to 2000 hours of video footage), labeled according to 26 video genre categories, namely: art, autos and vehicles, business, citizen journalism, comedy, conferences and other events, documentary, educational, food and drink, gaming, health, literature, movies and television, music and entertainment, personal of auto-biographical, politics, religion,school and education, sports, technology, environment, mainstream media, travel, videoblogging, web development and "default" category (accounts for movies which cannot be assigned to neither one of the previous categories).

The main challenge of this task is the diversity of videos that contain high level concepts for videos genres, each genre category has a high variety of video materials. Figure 1 illustrates image examples from the dataset.

4.2 Evaluation

In our experiments we consider the scenario that user feedback is automatically simulated from the known class membership of each video document (ground truth is provided with the databases). This approach allows a fast and extensive simulation which is necessary to evaluate different methods and parameter settings. Such simulations are common practice for RF [11] [12] [14].

To assess the retrieval performance, we use several measures. First, we compute the classical precision and recall. Precision is the fraction of retrieved documents that are relevant to the search (measure of false positives) and recall is the fraction of the documents that are relevant to the query and successfully retrieved (measure of false negatives). The system retrieval response is assessed with the precision-recall curves, which plots the precision for all the recall rates that can be obtained according to the current document class population. Second, to provide a global measure of performance we determine the overall Mean Average Precision - MAP as the area under the uninterpolated precision-recall curve.

In our evaluation we systematically consider each document from the database as a query document and retrieve the remainder of the database accordingly. Precision, recall and MAP are averaged over all retrieval experiments. Experiments were conducted for various browsing top n, ranging from 10 to 30 documents. For space and brevity reasons, in the following we shall present only the results using the top 20 videos per window. The general observations in this paper hold for all values of n.

4.3 Content descriptors

For video descriptors we have used a broad range of descriptors including: visual, audio and text. Competitive results have been obtained using these descriptors on MediaEval Genre Tagging task 2012 [6].

Audio features

Block-based audio features (11,242 values) [28] capture the temporal properties of the audio signal. We choose a set of audio descriptors that are computed from overlapping audio blocks. On each block, we compute the Spectral Pattern which characterizes the soundtrack's timbre, delta Spectral Pattern which captures the strength of onsets, variance delta Spectral Pattern which represents the variation of the onset strength over time, Logarithmic Fluctuation Pattern which captures the rhythmic aspects, Spectral Contrast Pattern, Correlation Pattern which compute the temporal relation of loudness changes and timbral features: Local Single Gaussian Model and Mel-Frequency Cepstral Coefficients. Sequence aggregation is achieved by taking the mean, variance and median over all blocks.

Standard audio features (196 values) [29] [30] - we used a set of general-purpose audio descriptors: Linear Predictive Coefficients (LPCs), Line Spectral Pairs (LSPs), MFCCs, Zero-Crossing Rate (ZCR), spectral centroid, flux, rolloff and kurtosis, augmented with the variance of each feature over a certain window (we used the common setup for capturing enough local context that is equal to 1.28s). For a clip, we take the mean and standard deviation over all frames.

Visual descriptors

MPEG-7 related descriptors(1,009 values) [31] - we adopted standard color and texture-based descriptors such as: Local Binary Pattern (LBP), autocorrelogram, Color Coherence Vector (CCV), Color Layout Pattern (CLD), Edge Histogram (EHD), Scalable Color Descriptor (SCD), classic color histogram (hist) and color moments. For each sequence, we aggregate the features by taking the mean, dispersion, skew-

Table 1: Comparison between feature accuracy (MAP) using different metrics without RF.

Feature	Manhatan	Euclidian	Mahalanobis	Cosinus	Bray Curtis	Chi Square	Canberra
Hog Features	17.02%	**17.18%**	17.07%	17.00%	17.10%	17.07%	16.67%
Structural Features	10.87%	10.55%	11.14%	2.18%	10.92%	11.58%	**14.82%**
MPEG 7 related	12.37%	10.85%	21.14%	08.69%	13.34%	13.34%	**25.97%**
Standard Audio Features	7.76%	7.78%	**29.26%**	15.28%	7.78%	8.04%	1.58%
Block-based audio	19.33%	19.58%	20.21%	**21.23%**	19.71%	19.99%	20.37%
Text Features	8.32%	7.15%	5.39%	17.64%	**20.40%**	9.83%	9.68%

ness, kurtosis, median and root mean square statistics over all frames.

Global HoG (81 values) [32] - from this category, we compute global Histogram of oriented Gradients (HoG) over all frames.

Structural descriptors (1,430 values) - the structural description [33] is based on a characterization of geometric attributes for each individual contour, e.g. degree of curvature, angularity, circularity, symmetry and "wiggliness", as proposed in [33]. These descriptors were reported to be successfully employed in tasks such as the annotation of photos and object categorization [34].

In this work, we decided not to use Bag of Words strategies. In preliminary experiments we found that in order to get results as good or better than the other visual features, we need large dictionaries that create computational problems for the large dataset we use.

Text descriptors

TF-IDF (extracted with automatical speech recognition algorithms ASR, with 3,466 values, provided by the MediaEval organizers [35]) - we use the standard Term Frequency-Inverse Document Frequency approach. First, we filter the input text by removing the terms with a document frequency less than 5%-percentile of the frequency distribution. We reduce further the term space by keeping only those terms that discriminate best between genres according to the 2-test. We generate a global list by retaining for each genre class, the m terms (e.g. m = 150 for ASR) with the highest 2 values that occur more frequently than in complement classes. This results in a vector representation for each document that is subsequently cosine normalized to remove the influence of the length of transcripts.

We used in our framework eight combinations of multimodal video descriptors: Visual (1 - MPEG-7 related descriptors, 2 - Hog Features, 3 - Structural descriptors, 4 - Combination of All Visual descriptors), Audio (5 - Standard audio features, 6 - Block-based audio descriptor), Text descriptors (7 -TF-IDF - ASR-based), and 8 - combination of all of them. All the visual and audio descriptors are normalized to L_∞ norm, and text descriptors to cosine normalization.

5. RESULTS

In the following subsections, we present our experiments. The first experiment (Section 5.1) motivates the choice of the best metric that provides the best accuracy for each feature. In the second experiment (Section 5.2), we study the influence of Fisher Kernel parameters on system's accuracy, and in Section 5.3 we compare our work with state-of-the-art techniques. In Section 5.4 we compare our method with a Fisher Kernel representation by learning a GMM on *all*

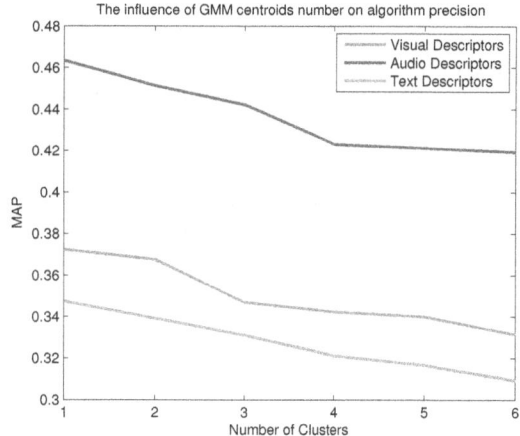

Figure 2: The influence of GMM centroids number on system performance for T=1.

the data and in Section 5.5 we illustrate the advantage of Fisher Kernels approach on video RF using more than one descriptor per video document.

5.1 Evaluating feature metrics

Some distance measures are better adapted to the structure of the descriptor than others [22]. In this work we have tested the performance of several metrics. We made the assumption that a better initial performance will generate a better relevance feedback algorithm performance [22].

We tested a broad variety of metrics [23]: Euclidean (L2), Manhattan (L1) (particular cases of the Minkovski distance), probabilistic divergence measures: Canberra [26]; intersection family: Cosine Distance, Chi-Square distance used in machine learning and data clustering and Mahalanobis [25]. The performance of metrics is presented in Table 1. These experiments were performed on the entire MediaEval 2012 dataset.

We conclude that each feature has its own preferred metric. In the rest of our experiments we use for each feature its best metric as indicated in Table 1 (bolded results).

5.2 RF using Fisher Kernels

In this experiment we study the influence of Fisher Kernel parameters on the system's performance.

We first analyze the influence of the number of Gaussian centroids. Figure 2 presents the variation of MAP using a different number of Gaussian centroids. It can be observed that the best results are obtained using only a single Gaussian centroid. In this case the size of Fisher Kernel descriptors will be 2 times bigger than the document descriptor.

Table 2: The influence of different normalization algorithms on system's performance (mean average precision values).

Features / Normalization	Visual	Audio	Text
Without normalization	37.25%	38.68%	31.13%
L1	36.82%	37.97%	29.83%
L2	39.22%	41.94%	30.51%
Log Norm	38.61%	42.01%	**35.07%**
PN	38.51%	41.37%	34.93%
PN + L2 Norm	39.20%	42.98%	30.12%
PN + L1 Norm	**39.46%**	**43.23%**	31.71%

Secondly, we presents the influence of Fisher normalization strategies on system performance. In [3], it was demonstrated that some normalization strategies can improve the performance of Fisher Kernels. The results are presented in Table 2.

It can be observed that using the combination of L1 normalization - alpha normalization we obtained the best results for visual and audio features, while the highest performance for text features is obtained with logarithmic normalization. Another observation is that using the L1 normalization alone, the results are lower than in the case when L1 is used in combination with other normalizations.

In order to compare our algorithm with other relevance feedback approaches, we have selected the settings that provide the greatest improvement in performance: one GMM centroid, L1 normalization with alpha normalization for audio and visual descriptors and logarithmic normalization for text descriptors. We also used 2 SVM kernels: a linear SVM classifier and a nonlinear RBF kernel.

5.3 Comparison to state-of-the-art techniques

In the following, we compare our approach against other validated algorithms from the literature, namely: the Rocchio algorithm [9], Relevance Feature Estimation (RFE) [11], Support Vector Machines (SVM) [12], AdaBoost (BOOST) [14], Random Forests (RF) [15] and Nearest Neighbor [13].

Figure 3 presents the precision-recall curves after relevance feedback for different descriptor categories. Generally, all RF strategies provide significant improvement in retrieval performance compared to the retrieval without RF (see the dashed black and blue lines in Figure 3). Better performance is obtained with audio descriptors, while text and visual descriptors have similar performance.

The highest performance is obtained using standard audio descriptors, with an increase of MAP from 29.35% (without RF) to 46.34% and with all combined features from 30.29% to 46.80%.

We present in Table 3 the MAP values for different features combinations. The FKRF approach has the highest values for most of the cases, except for the combination of all visual descriptors, where the random trees RF achieve the highest performance values. The highest increase in system performance is obtained using MPEG 7 descriptors, increase of 4 MAP percents (from 40.80% using FKRF RBF to 36.85% with random forests) and block based audio (from 43.96% using FKRF Linear to 39.87% using Boost RF). At the other end, the smallest increase in performance is obtained for text features (from 45.80% using FKRF RBF to 45.31 using random forests).

In most of the cases, RFE and random forests provide good results, but our approach is better. We conclude that

Table 4: Comparison between FKRF RBF on all data (T=1) and RFRF RBF (T=1) (MAP values).

Feature	FKRF for all data	FKRF RBF
Visual Features	34.02%	**38.23%**
Standard Audio	38.25%	**46.34%**
Text	32.37%	**35.14%**

the proposed approach improves the retrieval performance, outperforming some other existing approaches, e.g. Rocchio, RFE, SVM, Random Trees, etc.

5.4 Fisher Kernel representation on all data

We could also generate a Fisher Kernel representation by learning a GMM on *all* the data. A valid question is therefore: do we obtain good results because the Fisher Kernel representation is in general more powerful than our initial features, or are our performance improvements caused by altering the features with respect to the top n results? In the former case, we can just alter the features once offline, which would speed up computation. Yet if this is the case we would just prove that the Fisher kernel representation is more powerful than our initial features, independent of our relevance feedback settings.

To test this, we train a GMM on all the feature vectors of the whole dataset, and represent all videos as Fisher vectors with respect to this global mixture model. We use these features in the SVM RF framework and compare this with our proposed Fisher Kernel RF framework. Notice that the only differences between these two systems are on what data the GMM is learned and when the features are changed to the Fisher kernel representation.

GMM on *all* data drastically reduce the system performance. The results are presented in Table 4. It can be observed that the performance drops with 4 percents for visual features and with more than 8 percents for audio features.

We conclude that altering the data based on the top n videos is crucial for obtaining good performance. This validates our claim that the Fisher Kernel is particularly suited for use in a Relevance Feedback application.

5.5 Frame Aggregation with Fisher kernel

In the following, we will show the improvements using FK approach on RF, when we use more then one feature per video document. Because these are preliminary experiments, we used in this work only two types of visual descriptors: HoG descriptors and MPEG 7 related descriptors, that are more representative for the visual information.

For this experiment, we extract a small collection of salient frames using [27], and compute a visual feature for each frame. Because, we now have more data, we can learn more complex GMM. Therefore, we estimate that the optimal number of centroids used by the Fisher Vectors is higher than one. Indeed, Figure 4 presents the variation of MAP using a different number of Gaussian centroids. It can be observed that the best results are obtained using 6 to 10 number of centroids.

In the end, we present in Table 5 a comparison between the MAP values of previous global FKRF approach and the frame aggregation FKRF approach. The frame aggregation Fisher kernel representation for RF tends to provide better retrieval performance in all cases with more than 4 percents increase of performance (from 29.59% to 32.87% for HoG

Table 3: Comparison with state of the art algorithms (mean average precision values).

Feature	Without RF	Rocchio	NB	BOOST	SVM	RF	RFE	FK Linear	FK RBF
HoG	17.18%	25.57%	24.18%	26.72%	26.49%	26.89%	27.5%	29.46%	**29.59%**
Structural	14.82%	21.96%	23.73%	23.63%	24.62%	24.69%	23.91%	**26.28%**	23.96%
MPEG 7	25.97%	30.88%	34.09%	32.55%	32.90%	36.85%	31.93%	40.50%	**40.80%**
All Visual	26.18%	32.98%	34.25%	35.99%	36.08%	**42.28%**	32.43%	41.33%	42.23 %
Standard Audio	29.26%	32.71%	34.88%	32.88%	38.58%	40.46%	44.32%	44.80%	**46.34%**
Block Based Audio	21.23%	35.39%	35.22%	39.87%	31.46%	33.41%	31.96%	**43.96%**	43.69%
Text	20.40%	32.55%	26.91%	26.93%	34.70%	34.70%	25.82%	34.84%	**35.14%**
All Features	30.29%	37.91%	39.88%	38.88%	40.93%	45.31%	44.93%	46.43%	**46.80%**

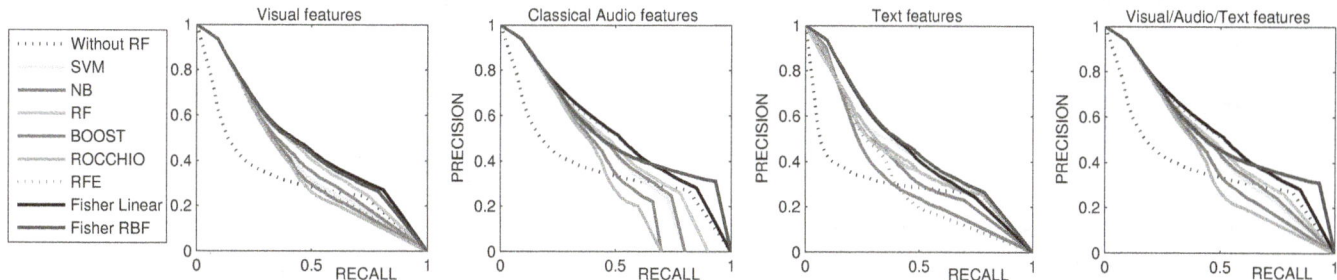

Figure 3: Precision-recall curves for different content descriptors and combinations 1 - Combination of All Visual descriptors), 2 - Standard audio features, 3 - Text descriptors and 4 - combination of all features.

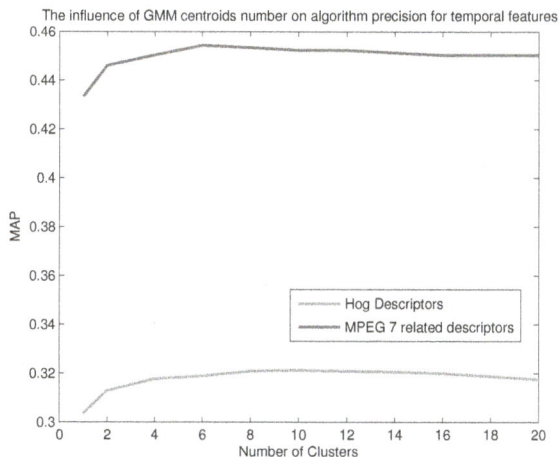

Figure 4: The influence of GMM centroids number on system performance using frame aggregation FKRF approach.

Table 5: Comparison between global FKRF and frame aggregation FKRF (MAP values).

Feature	FKRF Linear (T=1)	FKRF RBF (T=1)	Frame aggregation FKRF Linear	Frame aggregation FKRF RBF
HoG	29.46%	29.59%	32.12%	**32.87%**
MPEG 7	40.50%	40.80%	44.69%	**45.43%**

features and from 40.80% to 45.43% from MPEG 7 related descriptors). Another interesting result is that using MPEG 7 related descriptors alone, with temporal information, we achieve similar performance to audio features.

We conclude that frame aggregation Fisher Kernels approach improves the video retrieval performance and surpasses the global Fisher Kernel approach.

5.6 Computational Efficiency

All the experiments were done on a single core of a 3.00 Ghz Intel Core Duo E8400 processor. Using Fisher Kernel in combination with Linear SVM and global video features, we generate a RF iteration in less than half of second. By aggregating all the frames with Fisher kernels, the execution time of a RF iteration is near to 2 seconds.

We conclude that this represents a reasonable waiting time for users in a real system scenario.

6. CONCLUSIONS

In this paper we have proposed a new method of relevance feedback using the Fisher Kernels. We addressed relevance feedback techniques in the context of video retrieval and discussed a new approach that combines the generative models with discriminative classifiers (SVM's) for relevance feedback problem, using Fisher Kernels theory.

Tested on a large scale video database (MediaEval 2012) and using several descriptors, our FKRF approach improves the retrieval performance, outperforming other existing Relevance Feedback approaches, such as: Rocchio, Nearest Neighbors RF, Boost RF, SVM RF, Random Forest RF and RFE.

Additionally, we present a novel method to capture temporal information by using the Fisher Kernel to use more than one feature per video. The experiments with visual descriptors showed that using more features vectors to describe a video document, instead of only one, the performance is drastically improved, from 40.80 to 45.83 for MPEG 7 related descriptors and from 29.59% to 32.87% for HoG features. We showed that we do not need large number of clusters to train the FK framework as we achieve the best performance with only 5-10 clusters. This makes the proposed approach implementable for a real time RF approach.

In future work we will adapt the method to address a higher diversity of video categories (use of the Internet). Futhermore, we want to extend the Fisher kernel to other modalities, namely text and audio, and to use elaborated spatio-temporal features.

Acknowledgments

This work was supported by the Romanian Sectoral Operational Programme Human Resources Development 2007-2013 through the Financial Agreement $POSDRU/89/1.5/S/62557$. We also acknowledge the 2012 Genre Tagging Task of the MediaEval Multimedia Benchmark [6] for providing the test data set.

7. REFERENCES

[1] A. W. Smeulders, M. Worring, S. Santini, A. Gupta, R. Jain: "Content-based Image Retrieval at the End of the Early years", IEEE Trans. PAMI, 2000.

[2] T. Jaakkola, D. Haussler: "Exploiting generative models in discriminative classifiers", In Advances in Neural Information Processing Systems 1999.

[3] F. Perronnin, J. Sanchez, T. Mensink: "Improving the Fisher Kernel for Large-Scale Image Classification", ECCV, 2010.

[4] F. Perronnin, J.A. Rodriguez-Serrano, "Fisher Kernels for Handwritten Word-spotting", 10th International Conference on Document Analysis and Recognition Pages 106-110, 2009.

[5] P. Moreno and R. Rifkin. "Using the Fisher kernel method for web audio classification", International Conference on Acoustics, Speech, and Signal Processing, pages 2417-2420, 2000.

[6] http://www.multimediaeval.org/mediaeval2012/

[7] A. F. Smeaton, P. Over, W. Kraaij: "High-Level Feature Detection from Video in TRECVid: a 5-Year Retrospective of Achievements", Springer Series on Multimedia Content Analysis Theory and Applications, pp. 151-174, 2009.

[8] http://trec.nist.gov

[9] J. Rocchio: "Relevance Feedback in Information Retrieval", The Smart Retrieval System Experiments in Automatic Document Processing, G. Salton (Ed.), Prentice Hall, Englewood Cliffs NJ, pp. 313-323, 1971.

[10] N. V. Nguyen, J.-M. Ogier, S. Tabbone, A. Boucher: "Text Retrieval Relevance Feedback Techniques for Bag-of-Words Model in CBIR", ICMLPR, 2009.

[11] Y. Rui, T. S. Huang, M. Ortega, M. Mehrotra, S. Beckman: "Relevance feedback: a power tool for interactive content-based image retrieval", IEEE Transactions on Circuits and Video Technology, 1998.

[12] S. Liang, Z. Sun: "Sketch retrieval and relevance feedback with biased SVM classification", Pattern Recognition Letters, 29, pp. 1733-1741, 2008.

[13] G. Giacinto: "A Nearest-Neighbor Approach to Relevance Feedback in Content-Based Image Retrieval", ACM Confenference on Image and Video Retrieval, 2007.

[14] J. Yu, Y. Lu, Y. Xu, N. Sebe, Q. Tian: "Integrating Relevance Feedback in Boosting for Content-Based Image Retrieval", ASSP, 2007.

[15] Y. Wu, A. Zhang: "Interactive pattern analysis for relevance feedback in multimedia information retrieval", Multimedia Systems, 10(1), pp. 41-55, 2004.

[16] L. Yuanhua Lv, C. Zhai: "Adaptive Relevance Feedback in Information Retrieval", Information and Knowledge Management Conference, 2009.

[17] W. Bian, D. Tao: "Biased discriminant euclidean embedding for content-based image retrieval", IEEE Trans. Image Process., 545-554, 2010.

[18] D. Tao, X. Li, S. Maybank: "Negative samples analysis in relevance feedback" IEEE Trans. Knowl. Data Eng., 568-580, 2010.

[19] A. G. Hauptmann, M. G. Christel, and R. Yan: "Video retrieval based on semantic concepts", Proceedings of the IEEE, vol. 96, pp. 602-622, 2008.

[20] T. Mei, B. Yang, X. Hua, S. Li: "Contextual Video Recommendation by Multimodal Relevance and User Feedback", Information Systems (TOIS), 2011.

[21] B. Ionescu, K. Seyerlehner, I. Mironica, C. Vertan, P. Lambert: "An Audio-Visual Approach to Web Video Categorization", MTAP, 2012.

[22] I. Mironica, B. Ionescu, C. Vertan: "The influence of the similarity measure to relevance feedback", in Proceedings of the European Signal Processing Conference, Eusipco 2012.

[23] S.H. Cha: "Comprehensive Survey on Distance/Similarity Measures Between Probability Density Functions", Int. Journal of Mathematical Models and Methods in Applied Sciences, 2007.

[24] Y. Rubner, C. Tomasi, L. J. Guibas: "A Metric for Distributions with Applications to Image Databases", European Conference on Computer Vision, 1998.

[25] E. Deza, M.M. Deza: "Dictionary of Distances", Elsevier Science, 1st edition, 2006.

[26] M. Hatzigiorgaki, A. N. Skodras: "Compressed Domain Image Retrieval: A Comparative Study of Similarity Metrics", SPIE Visual Communications and Image Processing, vol. 5150, 2003.

[27] P. Kelm, S. Schmiedeke, T. Sikora, "Feature-based video key frame extraction for low quality video sequences", WIAMIS, 2009.

[28] K. Seyerlehner, M. Schedl, T. Pohle, P. Knees: "Using Block Level Features for Genre Classification, Tag Classification and Music Similarity Estimation", Music Information Retrieval Evaluation eXchange, 2010.

[29] C. Liu, L. Xie, H. Meng: "Classification of music and speech in mandarin news broadcasts", Conf. on Machine Speech Communication 2007.

[30] Yaafe core features, http://yaafe.sourceforge.net/

[31] T. Sikora: "The MPEG-7 Visual Standard for Content Description - An Overview", IEEE Transactions on Circuits and Systems for Video Technology, 2001.

[32] O. Ludwig, D. Delgado, V. Goncalves, U. Nunes: "Trainable Classifier-Fusion Schemes: An Application To Pedestrian Detection", IEEE Int. Conference On Intelligent Transportation Systems, 1, pp. 432-437, 2009.

[33] C. Rasche: "An Approach to the Parameterization of Structure for Fast Categorization", Int. Journal of Computer Vision, 87(3), pp. 337-356, 2010.

[34] S. Nowak, M. Huiskes: "New strategies for image annotation: Overview of the photo annotation task at ImageClef 2010", In the Working Notes of CLEF 2010.

[35] L. Lamel, J.-L. Gauvain: "Speech Processing for Audio Indexing", Int. Conf. on Natural Language Processing, LNCS, 5221, pp. 4-15, Springer Verlag, 2008.

A Cross-media Evolutionary Timeline Generation Framework Based on Iterative Recommendation

Shize Xu
xsz@pku.edu.cn

Liang Kong
klangelfox@gmail.com

Yan Zhang*
zhy@cis.pku.edu.cn

Department of Machine Intelligence, Peking University, Beijing, China
Key Laboratory on Machine Perception, Ministry of Education, Beijing, China

ABSTRACT

Summarization methods such as timelines have greatly helped people to understand all kinds of news events within limited time. However, there are few studies probing into cross-media summarization, for example, generating timelines which contain both texts and images that can reinforce each other.

In this paper, we tackle this important and challenging problem by proposing a novel solution. Specifically, we first reveal three requisite characteristics of an ideal image-text timeline. With the idea of recommendation, all these requisites will be modeled respectively, and fused compactly in a unified cross-media framework. Finally, we put all sentences and images into either the schema of referrer or the schema of recommended candidate, and the former recommends the latter. After changing their roles iteratively, we can achieve the optimal timelines which will significantly improve user experience and satisfaction. Experiments on real-world datasets show that the timelines generated by our framework outperform several competitive baselines.

Categories and Subject Descriptors

H.4 [**Information Systems Applications**]: Miscellaneous

General Terms

Algorithms, Experimentation

Keywords

Summarization; Cross-media; Timeline

1. INTRODUCTION

In the era of Web2.0, we often face the enormous news reports from different websites. Traditionally, the text contents compose of the reports but nowadays, various modalities of tremendous information flourish, i.e. news photos. To help news consumers quickly grasp the main idea of the

---

*Corresponding author

news, a more concise and convenient system over multimedia information should be provided. Especially for a complex event with a large collection of texts and images, users can easily get lost without an effective representation.

Generally, almost all existing multi-document summarization researches focus on either texts [4, 8] or images [20, 22] in isolation. Admittedly text information is more precise and exquisite compared with images. On the other hand, the information that an image brings to people is always plentiful and vivid. In order to help to see the overall picture of an event, we need to summarize both texts and images. Fortunately, there are already some cross-media summarization methods [6, 25] as well as systems like *NewsBlaster*[7] provide summaries that give a representative gist of a cluster. However, such methods just focus on providing the latent knowledge of images but don't extend to the problem of evolutionary summarization. Thus the exploration and analysis of cross-media evolutionary summarization is academically novel and challenging.

Among various layouts of news summarizations, timeline is an attractive method as it can capture how a news topic evolves over time. A timeline usually consists of several component summaries, which have different timestamps. The news websites usually spend a lot of human efforts on providing image-text timelines. Figure 1 is a manual example from *Wikipedia*. After investigation we can draw three requisites for an image-text timeline. *First,* from *intra-media* and *intra-date* views, both texts and images should present the most valuable information within one day (for day-based timeline). *Second,* from *inter-date* view, each component summary should keep contextual relevance and temporal coherence between the consecutive days. *Third,* from *inter-media* view, texts and images should appear concordantly and enrich each other. How to make use of these three requisites decides the quality of the generated timelines.

In order to solve this problem, we propose a novel solution borrowing the idea of recommendation. All sentences and images are the candidates for making up the final timeline. A principle derived from the three requisites is that when we are judging a candidate, we should take into consideration the "opinions" from other candidates, despite the constraints of same media type and same timestamp. Figure 2 shows the sketch of this idea, which will be formally described in Section 3.1. In our work, each candidate can recommend the others with a certain degree and in turn can be recommended. Intuitively, the more positive recommendations a candidate gets, the more authority it will gain. Furthermore, a more authoritative candidate will make more com-

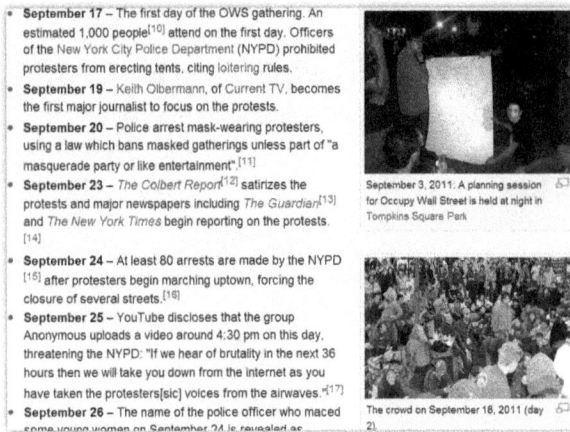

Figure 1: A part of manually generated timeline about Occupy Wall Street from Wikipedia

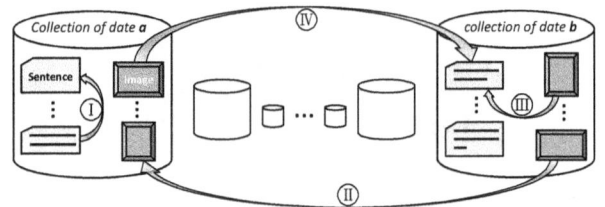

Figure 2: We model four types of recommendations (the arrows). I: intra-media and intra-date; II: intra-media and inter-date; III: inter-media and intra-date; IV: inter-media and inter-date.

pelling recommendations. Besides authority, the temporal gap as well as the difference of media type also influence the recommendation. Thus the semantic analysis between different media is required. These factors will be discussed in Section 3.2. Finally the unified framework is brought out in Section 3.3 to offer a platform and let candidates recommend each other iteratively. We also conduct our approach on the real-world datasets and verify the effectiveness when comparing with other related systems.

The rest of this paper is organized as follows. Section 2 investigates some related researches. We introduce our methodology in Section 3. Experimental results in Section 4 verify the effectiveness of our approach. Finally, we conclude this paper and present our future work in Section 5.

2. RELATED WORK

Generally speaking, multi-document summarization can be either extractive or abstractive. We mainly focus on the former which extracts the information deemed most important to the summary. Various techniques have been used for this type of MDS, exploiting similarity measures between pairs of sentences. Graph-based text summarization techniques have been widely used in recent years. TextRank [16] and LexPageRank [18] use algorithms similar to PageRank and HITS to compute sentence importance. Previous work shows that the use of visual materials not only enables retention of information but also promotes comprehension [17]. Thus the cross-media fusion is necessary. Wu et al. propose a framework of multimodal information fusion for multimedia data analysis by learning the optimal combination of multimodal information with the superkernel fusion of the constructed independent modalities [23].

Multimedia summarization involves the research on multimedia retrieval. Taking image for instance, there have been many accesses to obtaining its semantic knowledge from *annotated* data on various levels. Some researchers suggest that visual materials should be given as much attention as text and not merely viewed as supporting the text [11].

Since textual and visual information are quite different from each other, how to make a good transformations to mine latent knowledge from *unannotated* images is of great concern. Feng et al. use visual words to describe visual fea-

tures and then propose a probabilistic model based on the assumption that images and their co-occurring textual data are generated by mixtures of latent topics [9]. A multilabel propagation scheme is represented with hashing-accelerated graph construction and KL-divergence oriented loss function by Chen et al. [5]. They reveal the inter-label relationship and finally returns robust and useful probabilistic label vectors for images. Further, recent researches have focused on user-centered services. To personalize image annotation models, Li et al. propose a linear fusion framework which jointly exploits a user's tagging history as well as content-based image annotation [12]. Even based on the video media, Hong et al. research by mining and threading key shots, and then summarize a large set of diverse videos to provide an overview of queried news events for users.

Many researches manage to understand images and make effort to join them with texts, however, few of them are able to integrate images and texts into a unified framework, make them understand and reinforce each other. To the best of our knowledge, our work is one innovative research in the cross-media timeline summarization field.

3. METHODOLOGY

The original form of a dataset are a collection of news documents, divided into a set of sentences and images with different timestamps. Each item in the dataset is a candidate for selection to compose the final timeline. We denote whole collection as C, and $C = C_S \cup C_I$, where C_S is the subset with textual media bias and C_I with visual media bias. We can imagine the "recommendation" as vividly as that a person named c_1 says "if you are selecting me to make up the final timeline, could you please pick c_2 too? Because he/she matches me well and makes us look so great." In this way the candidate c_2 receives a "recommendation" from c_1. Intuitively, the more recommendations a candidate receives, the more salient it will be.

To provide a more unified vision, we restructure each candidate $c \in C$ as a set of attribute values conforming to the candidate schema: $c = \langle c.auth, c.date, c.tv, c.vv \rangle$. $c.auth$ denotes the authority of c, and $c.date$ is c's timestamp, which in this paper is day-based. For each $c \in C$, we extract its semantic features and represent as $c.tv$ in textual vector space. extract its visual features and represent them as $c.vv$ in visual vector space. Visual features are also extracted for image and represented as $c.vv$ in visual vector space. The semantically learning will be shown later with more details. In the following elaboration of our framework, dateset C is the important knowledge base.

3.1 Formalizing the Problem

We model the recommending action as a triple $\langle C^\dagger, C^\ddagger, R \rangle$, representing the referrer set, the recommended candidate set and the mapping function that decides the recommending confidence degree. $\dagger$ is used as the symbol of referrer nd $\ddagger$ is the symbol of recommended candidate. Then we will give some definitions to formalize the problem.

Given the research object set C, we would like to technically study on their interaction. Since we propose to let them recommend each other, the action set A that contain all positive recommendation is what we are interested in. $A := \{a_1, a_2, \ldots\}$, where each element $a \in A$ denotes an recommending action.

Definition 1. **Recommending Action.** *A recommending action a is a triple $\langle c_i^\dagger, c_j^\ddagger, r \rangle$, where $c_i^\dagger, c_j^\ddagger \in C$ and $c_i^\dagger \neq c_j^\ddagger$. Action a represents that candidate $c_i^\dagger$ recommends $c_j^\ddagger$ with a confidence degree r.*

All positive recommendations compose the action set A, which is the major object of our study. Next we can define two kinds of subsets as characteristics for each candidate.

Definition 2. **Referrer-action Subset.** *The referrer action subset $A_{c_i}^\dagger \subseteq A, c_i \in C$, and $A_{c_i}^\dagger := \{a \in A \mid \exists c_j^\ddagger \in C, a = \langle c_i^\dagger, c_j^\ddagger, r \rangle\}$. $A_{c_i}^\dagger$ denotes the set of actions that c_i is the referrer and recommends others.*

Definition 3. **Recommended-action Subset.** *The recommended action subset $A_{c_i}^\ddagger \subseteq A, c_i \in C$, and $A_{c_i}^\ddagger := \{a \in A \mid \exists c_j^\dagger \in C, a = \langle c_j^\dagger, c_i^\ddagger, r \rangle\}$. $A_{c_i}^\ddagger$ denotes the set of actions that c_i is the recommended candidate and is recommended by others.*

The original intention of the recommending idea is to gather other candidates' opinions and estimate the importance of each, defined as *authority*, which is the key indicator for us to select and generate our summaries. Generally, a candidate that receive many authoritative recommendations is also authoritative, and vice versa. The following estimation of candidate c_i's authority is derived from this intuition.

$$c_i.auth = \sum_{a \in A_{c_i}^\ddagger} \{ \frac{r}{|A_{c_j}^\dagger|} \mid \exists c_j^\dagger \in C, a = \langle c_j^\dagger, c_i^\ddagger, r \rangle \} \quad (1)$$

The main idea of this estimation is to merge all the received recommendations together to measure its authority. Note that $|A_{c_j}^\dagger|$ is used to normalize the influence of $c_j^\dagger$, and in this way, we can significantly reduce kinds of noises, i.e., $c_j^\dagger$ recommends all the others. At the last step of our solution, for each day we select the top images/sentences with timestamp restricted from a priority queue, which maintains the candidates by their authority.

To finish the authority estimation of every candidate, the most important things is to decide confidence degree r for every action. Recall from Figure 2, we can find that there are different types of recommending actions between different candidates, and thus different confidence degrees are required. We first define the confidence degree mapping as $R : C \times C \times F \to \texttt{float}$, where F is the recommending functions set. Given a referrer and a recommended candidate, we pick the appropriate function from F then can decide the confidence degree r. Therefore the mapping model becomes the main focus in the following discussion.

3.2 Modeling Confidence Degree

The mapping model R measures the confidence degree of a recommending action. Given the referrer $c_i^\dagger$ and the recommended candidate $c_j^\ddagger$, we can think of several factors that influence the degree but three of them are the most essential. They are the authority of referrer $c_i^\dagger$, the temporal gap between $c_i^\dagger$ and $c_j^\ddagger$, and most important and challenging, the mutual semantic understanding between them.

As we analyzed before, the more authority a candidate has, the more seriously others take its recommendation. Thus we should take the referrer's authority into account when modeling the confidence degree. Moreover, it is suggested that if a candidate gains a high authority, it is not only individually important, but also globally coherent. That's why this factor becomes the key indicator for sentence/image selection to keep high quality of timeline. Besides authority, we will further model the other two factors in detail.

3.2.1 Temporal Gap

Recall from the three requisites mentioned before, it's a challenge to model the *inter-date* view, and keep temporal coherence and global relevance for a timeline. Figure 2 indicates that a *intra-date* recommendation makes different impact from a *inter-date* recommendation. We need a measure to quantified the impact decay reasonably. Inspired by [2], we employ *Gaussian* kernel to define the decay function $\Gamma(c_i^\dagger, c_j^\ddagger)$, where there exsits a recommending action $a = \langle c_i^\dagger, c_j^\ddagger, r \rangle \in A$.

$$\Gamma(c_i^\dagger, c_j^\ddagger) = \exp[\frac{- \mid c_i^\dagger.date - c_j^\ddagger.date \mid}{2\sigma^2}]$$

Parameter σ, which controls the spread of kernel curves, will be tuned in later experiments. It's worth noting that the optimal setting of σ may vary according to the news dataset. Sentences and images with wider semantic scope will require a higher value of σ, and vice versa. By modeling temporal gap for recommending action, we can guarantee the individuality of each component summary and the contextual coherence of the whole timeline.

3.2.2 Semantic Understanding

The essential requirement of a positive recommendation is that the referrer has to know the candidate well. It makes sense to follow the assumption that if a candidate is relevant to the referrer, the referrer will understands it well and is more likely to recommend it. So measuring the relevance between each candidate is a primary task. Though there are several ways to estimate the relevance on different levels, a appropriate method should be on more semantical level to tackle our cross-media problem. Two situations can be also derived from Figure 2, which are intra-media relevance and inter-media relevance. Since candidates in different media have different attributes, we first take a close look for these attributes.

Considering $c \in C_S$, the extraction of $c.tv$ can be the most simple. We do statistics on the words for all sentences in C_S then obtain a dictionary. After the preprocessing such as stemming and stop words removal, we can define a textual vector space, each dimension of which corresponds to a text word. To reduce the noises of common words, the classical weighting pair of *TF-IDF* is employed to weight each dimension of $c.tv$. Note that our work is on sentence-level, so we analogously substitute *inverse-sentence-frequency (ISF)* for *IDF*. And $c.vv$ is set to be *null*.

On the other hand, if $c \in C_I$, the feature extraction differs a lot. We manage to learn both content- and context-based knowledge of each image by following Jiang et al.'s approach [10]. Feature vector $c.vv$ of an image are extracted based on its *Gabor* visual features, and semantic textual feature $c.tv$ is extracted based on its context texts. We utilize the *Scale Invariant Feature Transform (SIFT)* algorithm [14] instead of Gabor, since it is detectable even under changes in image scale, noise and illumination. Besides, finding the access to its context texts is also challenging. Fortunately, the segmentation tool *VIPS* [3] can help us to segment web original documents, and then the rendering tool *WebKit* [1] is used to determine text blocks whose coordinates are neighboring to each specified image. In this way we successfully get images and their text contexts.

We confront two issues. One is the dimension size of textual and visual vector space both are high-dimensional, the other is each feature vector may be really sparse. To overcome these two troubles, we continue following Jiang's work which presents an effective approach by employing a multilingual retrieval model via the vague transformation [15]. Specifically, a mid layer with domain knowledge is added to reduce the dimension, and moreover, provide semantic-level methods of measuring three kinds of vector similarity $sim(tv, tv)$, $sim(vv, vv)$ and $sim(vv, tv)$.

Next, we manage to achieve the final relevance functions. Given any two candidates and their feature vectors, a specific relevance function is chosen to measure their relevance. The definitions varies from two different situations. The first function $rel_\alpha(c_i^\dagger, c_j^\ddagger)$ is designed for the *intra-media* situation that $M(c_i^\dagger) = M(c_j^\ddagger)$, where $M(c) \in \{sentence, image\}$ denotes the media type of c. The second function $rel_\beta(c_i^\dagger, c_j^\ddagger)$ is for the *intra-media* situation that $M(c_i^\dagger) \neq M(c_j^\ddagger)$. rel_α is simply defined as the linear combination of feature vectors' similarities. Supposing that $c_i^\dagger, c_j^\ddagger \in C_I$, we have

$$
\begin{aligned}
\mathrm{rel}_\alpha(c_i^\dagger, c_j^\ddagger) =\ & \mathrm{rel}_\alpha(\langle c_i^\dagger.tv, c_i^\dagger.vv \rangle, \langle c_j^\ddagger.tv, c_j^\ddagger.vv \rangle) \\
=\ & \lambda_1 \cdot \mathrm{sim}(c_i^\dagger.tv, c_j^\ddagger.tv) \\
& + (1 - \lambda_1) \cdot \mathrm{sim}(c_i^\dagger.vv, c_j^\ddagger.vv)
\end{aligned}
$$

Similarly, for the situation of *inter-media*, supposing that $c_i^\dagger \in C_I$ and $c_j^\ddagger \in C_S$, we define rel_β as follows:

$$
\begin{aligned}
\mathrm{rel}_\beta(c_i^\dagger, c_j^\ddagger) =\ & \mathrm{rel}_\beta(\langle c_i^\dagger.tv, c_i^\dagger.vv \rangle, \langle c_j^\ddagger.tv, null \rangle) \\
=\ & \lambda_2 \cdot \mathrm{sim}(c_i^\dagger.tv, c_j^\ddagger.tv) \\
& + (1 - \lambda_2) \cdot \mathrm{sim}(c_i^\dagger.vv, c_j^\ddagger.tv)
\end{aligned}
$$

where parameters λ_1 and λ_2 both balance the weights of textual and visual features (set as 0.5 in this study). In this way, we make candidates understand each other on a semantic level, and that is in response to the third requisite of modeling the *inter-media* view.

3.2.3 Factor Fusion

We have modeled three factors that influence the confidence degree respectively, and now we would like to fuse them into the recommending functions. Similar to the relevance measurements, two situations are considered. For the

[1] http://www.webkit.org

situation that the referrer $c_i^\dagger$ and the recommended candidate $c_j^\ddagger$ are the same media, we can formally represent their recommending function f_α as follows.

$$
\mathrm{f}_\alpha(c_i^\dagger, c_j^\ddagger) = \begin{cases} c_i^\dagger.auth \cdot \Gamma(c_i^\dagger, c_j^\ddagger) \cdot \mathrm{rel}_\alpha(c_i^\dagger, c_j^\ddagger), & \mathrm{rel}_\alpha(c_i^\dagger, c_j^\ddagger) \geq \theta \\ 0, & otherwise \end{cases}
$$

Here θ is an empirical parameter that reduces the noise of the recommendations from other irrelevant candidates. In the same way, when $M(c_i^\dagger) \neq M(c_j^\ddagger)$ (inter-media), we can represent another recommending function f_β for cross-media learning.

$$
\mathrm{f}_\beta(c_i^\dagger, c_j^\ddagger) = \begin{cases} c_i^\dagger.auth \cdot \Gamma(c_i^\dagger, c_j^\ddagger) \cdot \mathrm{rel}_\beta(c_i^\dagger, c_j^\ddagger), & \mathrm{rel}_\beta(c_i^\dagger, c_j^\ddagger) \geq \theta \\ 0, & otherwise \end{cases}
$$

So far, we manage to finish the definition of the recommending function set $F = \{f_\alpha, f_\beta\}$, and therefore complete the mapping model $R : C \times C \times F \to \texttt{float}$. Thus given a referrer and a recommended candidate, and with a suitable recommending function chosen, we can decide the confidence degree r of this potential recommendation. Further, we eliminate recommending actions with the confidence degree of 0, and at the same time maintain actions which have positive r values in the action set A.

3.3 Unifying the Framework

The previous two sections indicate that on one hand, a candidate's authority relies on the recommendations from others, on the other hand, its authority influences the confidence degree of its recommendation to others. Therefore, we propose a unified cross-media framework based on iterative recommendation (**cmFIR**), and then dual-estimate the confidence degree and authority at the same time.

After we obtaining the entire action set A and quantifying its every details, we can continue to estimate authority of every candidate by Eq. 1. Since this is a cross-media task, we would like to study on the leverage of different media's recommendation. The equation is reorganized and split by views of *intra-media* and *inter-media* as follows:

$$
\begin{aligned}
c_i.auth = \ & \mu \cdot \sum_{a \in A_{c_i}^\dagger} \left\{ \frac{r}{|A_{c_j}^\dagger|} \ \middle|\ a = \langle c_j^\dagger, c_i^\ddagger, r \rangle, \mathrm{M}(c_j^\dagger) = \mathrm{M}(c_j^\ddagger) \right\} \\
& + \nu \cdot \sum_{a \in A_{c_i}^\ddagger} \left\{ \frac{r}{|A_{c_j}^\dagger|} \ \middle|\ a = \langle c_j^\dagger, c_i^\ddagger, r \rangle, \mathrm{M}(c_j^\dagger) \neq \mathrm{M}(c_j^\dagger) \right\}
\end{aligned}
$$

where μ and ν specify the relative contributions to the authority for intra-media and inter-media recommendations. Note that $\mu + \nu = 1$. No matter which media c_i is in, it means we only take the intra-media recommendations if $\nu = 0$, or we only consider inter-media when μ is 0. The leverage of this parameter pair will be further discussed later.

Once we have estimated every candidate's authority in a single round, with the new authority we need to update their confidence degrees of recommending actions in their referrer-action subsets. To realize this thought, we propose an iterative recommendation based dual-estimation algorithm, whose outline is shown in Algorithm 1.

Usually the convergence of the iterative algorithm is achieved when total difference between the authority computed at two successive iterations for any candidate falls below a given threshold (0.0001 in this study). Benefiting from the normalization in the authority estimation, the convergence can be guaranteed.

Algorithm 1 Dual-estimation Algorithm

Input: Dataset C of size N, recommending action set A
Output: Authority $\overrightarrow{q} = (c_1.auth, c_2.auth, \ldots, c_N.auth)$

1: Initialize $\overrightarrow{q}$ as $(1, 1, \ldots, 1)$;
2: For each action $a = \langle c_i^\dagger, c_j^\ddagger, r \rangle \in A$:
   i. Estimate the value of r with the mapping model R;
   *ii.*Update $A_{c_i}^\dagger$ and $A_{c_j}^\ddagger$ if $r = 0$;
3: For each action $c_i \in C$:
   Re-estimate its authority based on $A_{c_i}^\ddagger$ with Eq.2;
4: Repeat Step 2 and 3 if $change(\overrightarrow{q}) \geq threshold$;

At last, let's briefly analyze the complexity of this algorithm. The two relevance functions are static, thus we only have to calculate once before we begin to iterate. In a single iteration, we first estimate all recommending confidence degrees with the mapping model R. Obviously the complexity is proportional to the size of the action set, denoted as $O(|A|)$. And then we need to update every authority by observing all actions in the corresponding recommended-action subset. Note that $\bigcup_{c \in C} A_c^\ddagger = A$. So the estimation work also takes the complexity of $O(|A|)$. Suppose that there are k iterations, the complexity of the whole algorithm becomes $O(k * |A|)$. Particularly, since the authority estimation of each candidate is independent, we can run the estimation step in complete parallel. And it is the same with the degree updating step. The algorithm is expected to get the linear speedup and obtain the final complexity of $O(\frac{k*|A|}{m})$ with m processes, which is quite acceptable in practice.

4. EXPERIMENTS

4.1 Dataset

We randomly choose 8 news topics with special coverage and handcrafted timelines by editors from 5 selected news websites: *New York Times*, *BBC*, *CNN*, *Reuters* and *Yahoo! News*. We query each event confining to these sites and crawl webpages' html docs. Timestamps, text contents, images and their contexts are then extracted. Besides news documents, these 5 sites consist of manual text timelines as our reference standards to evaluate proposed systems with textual bias. Table 1 shows the details.

4.2 Evaluation Metrics

4.2.1 ROUGE

ROUGE is a standard of automatic evaluation of text summaries. In ROUGE evaluation, the summarization quality is measured by counting the number of overlapping units, such as N-gram, word sequences, and word pairs between the candidate timelines and the reference timelines. According to [13], among all sub-metrics, unigram-based ROUGE has been shown to agree with human judgment most bigram-based ROUGE fits summarization well. The official package (version 1.55) offers precision-based and recall-based indicators. To evaluate the quality of timelines with textual bias, we take F-score performance R_F-1 and R_F-2 in terms of unigram-based and bigram-based ROUGE in later experiments. Note that the higher the they scores, the more similar two timelines are.

Table 1: Statistics of Datasets.

Event (Query)	Document	$|C_S|$	$|C_I|$	Time Span
Japan Earthquake	314	16275	255	Mar 9-Apr 10, 2011
Steve Jobs & iPhone	287	10766	220	Aug 25-Oct 25, 2011
Kim Jong Il's Death	174	8262	148	Dec 17, 2011-Jan 12, 2012
Occupy Wall Street	369	19459	343	Sept 17-Dec 10, 2011
NBA Lockout	332	20377	307	July 1-Dec 28, 2011
Murdock's Eavesdropping	149	9148	145	June 21-Aug 31, 2011
Euro 2012 Qualifiers	173	8986	160	Oct 7-Nov 16, 2011
Russia's Election	177	7063	152	Dec 3, 2011-Mar 10, 2012

* We use their abbreviations (JE, SJI, KJI, OWS, NBA, ME, EQ and RE) to denote above datasets for a more concise show.

4.2.2 QUALITY *and* SATISFACTION

We build an evaluation system which includes two golden indexes, $NQDCG$ and $NSDCG$, since there is golden criterion to evaluate cross-media timelines.

On explicit level, an image may either has an appropriate topic focus and significantly enriches the text content, or appears redundantly. We employ five volunteers as the news readers to rate the quality of images showed to them in timelines with three levels, judging if the images fit the text well. The levels range from 1 to 3 where level 3 denotes the best. To evaluate the whole timeline with ratings, we estimate *average normalized quality discounted cumulative gain (NQDCG)* scores as follows:

$$NQDCG = \frac{1}{T} \sum_{t \in T} \frac{\sum_{i=1}^{K_t} \frac{2^{\text{rate}^Q(i|t)} - 1}{\log_2(1+i)}}{\text{ideal}^Q(t)}$$

where $rate^Q(i|t)$ denotes the rating level of the ith image in date t's timeline. In order to avoid the impact of summaries sizes, we use the ideal total quality gain of date t $ideal^Q(t)$ for normalization. And specifically,

$$\text{ideal}^Q(t) = \sum_{i=1}^{K_t} \frac{2^{\max(rate^Q)} - 1}{\log_2(1 + i)}$$

The main idea about the usage of logarithm is that more important sentences pick more important images. In this way images and sentences can be well organized to help to read. Besides the quality, the attitude of readers to the images in holistic view also concerns us. So the judges quantize how the images influence their reading experience with three grades (-1, 0 ,1) at the same time. An image may get high grade if it does well in harmoniously complementing the information as well as increasing reading enjoyment. We also estimate *average normalized satisfaction discounted cumulative gain (NSDCG)* as follows:

$$NSDCG = \frac{1}{T} \sum_{t \in T} \frac{\sum_{i=1}^{K_t} \frac{2^{\text{rate}^S(i|t)} - 1}{\log_2(1+i)}}{\text{ideal}^S(t)}$$

$$\text{ideal}^S(t) = \sum_{i=1}^{K_t} \frac{2^{\max(rate^S)} - 1}{\log_2(1 + i)}$$

4.3 System Setup and Baselines

We manage to implement several baselines which can tackle the same task in some ways. In order to setup the systems, we tentatively set $\mu = \nu = 0.5$, $\sigma = 10$ and tune them later.

First, we ignore images and only compare our method with three existing text summarization algorithms with textual-bias. Centroid [18] uses MEAD algorithm to extract sentences and images according to centroid value and positional value. The graph-based GMDS by Wan et al. [21] constructs a sentence connectivity graph and selects important sentences based on the concept of eigenvector centrality. Yan et al. propose an evolutionary trans-temporal method ETTS [24] to generate text timelines.

We also implement three more baselines that can joint two type of media in some ways. But note that we provide our high quality text timeline as their knowledge base. Their work is to assert some of the images in data collection to construct the final timeline.

The Random method randomly picks the images to assign. The second is Comity [1] which is used for mining images from web. Concretely, it forms bi-gram and tri-gram search queries based on the text summaries and then uses an optimal algorithm to assign the returning images. Third, CCA semantically models text and image by *LDA* and then uses *canonical correlation analysis* to reveal cross-modal correlations [19]. It also helps to assign images to the given text timeline. All these methods study on neither the mutually influence between different media nor the temporal impact.

4.4 Results

4.4.1 Improvement of Text Timeline

We compare four systems that generate text timelines on all 8 datasets, by taking R_F-1 and R_F-2 performance with textual bias. The details are shown in Table 2.

The GMDS system outperforms centroid-based summarization methods. This is due to the fact that its graph-based framework ranks each sentence using eigenvector centrality which implicitly accounts for information subsumption among all sentences. ETTS gets good performance, indicating that the temporal property it uses for timeline generation makes difference. As expected, our cmFIR method outperforms the others, highlighting the contribution of cross-media mutually understanding. Thus the "opinions" from images can practically improve the quality of textual media.

More specifically, we have an interesting finding that our method is markedly superior to *ETTS* on the five datasets, *OWS*, *NBA*, *ME*, *EQ* and *RE*. Unlike the other three bursting events, they are developing gently and need information supplements from inter-date and inter-media. Our framework meets these demands well.

4.4.2 Overall Comparison of Image-text Timeline

We compare our approach with three visual-media-focused methods by analyzing the results shown in Figure 3. The randomly assignment has the worst performance as expected. The QUALITY of Comity looks not bad but it gets poor scores of SATISFACTION due to that it picks many discordant images when taking no contextual influence into account.

It's worth noting that CCA system gets a pretty better result than the previous two and we can verify the superiority of cross-modal learning on semantic level. Be aware of that it uses the text timelines we provide. However, cmFIR also defeats CCA by a significant upgrade with SATISFACTION. It indicates the effectiveness of our framework which considers individuality and global coherence simultaneously. And further, like the ROUGE results, when other methods are playing especially poorly on the last five datasets, our method is still maintaining high quality.

Table 2: ROUGE performance of text timelines

(a) R_F-1 Score ($\sigma = 10, \mu = 0.5$)

System	JE	SJI	KJI	OWS
Centroid	0.358	0.320	0.351	0.302
GMDS	0.262	0.341	0.368	0.314
ETTS	0.389	0.359	0.399	0.331
cmFIR	**0.398**	**0.362**	**0.405**	**0.375**

System	NBA	ME	EQ	RE
Centroid	0.289	0.286	0.277	0.298
GMDS	0.289	0.289	0.290	0.305
ETTS	0.308	0.332	0.317	0.327
cmFIR	**0.359**	**0.351**	**0.341**	**0.368**

(b) R_F-2 Score ($\sigma = 10, \mu = 0.5$)

System	JE	SJI	KJI	OWS
Centroid	0.0922	0.0841	0.0996	0.0723
GMDS	0.0937	0.0856	0.1078	0.0748
ETTS	0.1156	0.0961	0.1247	0.0845
cmFIR	**0.1182**	**0.0981**	**0.1269**	**0.0986**

System	NBA	ME	EQ	RE
Centroid	0.0703	0.0589	0.0599	0.0714
GMDS	0.0708	0.0634	0.0612	0.0755
ETTS	0.0794	0.0716	0.0689	0.0853
cmFIR	**0.0883**	**0.0795**	**0.0772**	**0.0934**

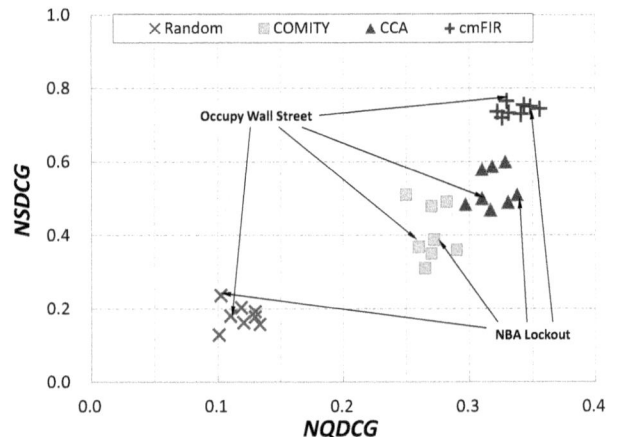

Figure 3: Cross-media evaluation: QUALITY and SATISFACTION of images ($\sigma = 10, \mu = 0.5$)

4.4.3 Tuning Parameters

Each time we tune one parameter with the other fixed and obtain the score of R_F-1. To identify leverage of intra- and inter-media, we provide experiments on the performance of varying μ/ν in Figure 4. The performance get worse when taking intra-media or inter-media bias in isolation, i.e. when $\mu = 0$ or $\nu = 0$. Thus a balance of the cross-media learning is essential for the task of image-text timeline generation.

Another key parameter σ measures the temporal influence from inter-date candidates to intra-date candidates and hence the size of neighbors. We can also learn the similar conclusion about the data sensitivity from Figure 5. The events with high burstiness prefer a smaller value to dominate the influence from neighbors, and vice versa. Develop-

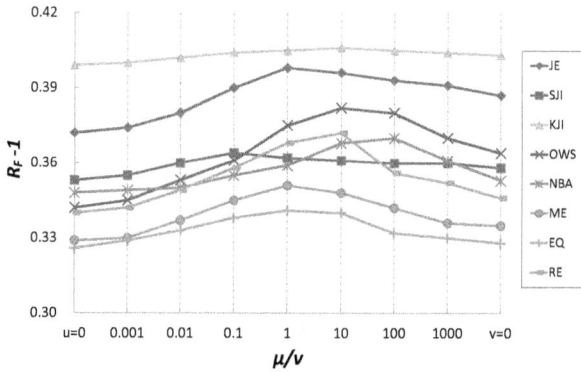

Figure 4: μ/ν: intra- and inter-media leverage

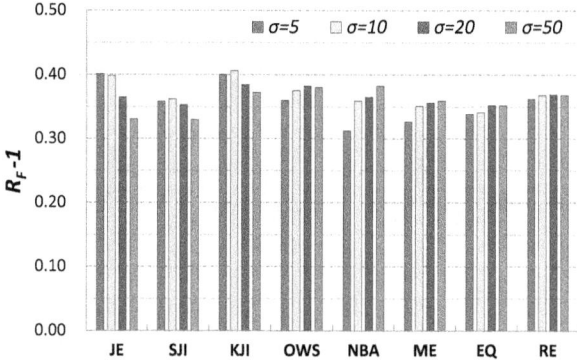

Figure 5: Impact of changing value of σ

Table 3: Average runtime on different datasets

Dataset	JE	SJI	KJI	OWS	NBA	ME	EQ	RE
$|A|$ ($\times 10^6$)	23.5	19.3	11.3	30.7	31.8	14.2	14.5	12.1
Iterations	8.5	8.3	6.4	9.7	11.3	7.7	7.0	8.5
Runtime (s)	115	104	73	137	155	103	97	85

ing a parameter automatic adapting framework can be one of the future work.

4.4.4 Runtime Analysis

At last, we also analyze the time performance of our multi processes algorithm on a PC server (16G RAM, 2.67GHz 4-processors CPU). The average iterations and runtime (of all 12 runs when tuning parameters) are shown in Table 3.

4.5 Sample Output and Analysis

Table 4 shows parts of our generated timelines. We notice that each component summary's content can represent the right day's important occurrences well, so that readers can catch the complete context of the story when browsing the whole timeline. This merit can be indicated from the part timeline of event JE. The focused topics of the presented three summaries are changing from tsunami to nuclear crisis, and from emergency reaction to post-disaster news (i.e. rescue and reconstruction). Instead of picking contiguous parts, we pick three discontinuous but typical dates as another sample output for event OWS. Three summaries highlight the activities of "corporate zombies", "government response" and "worldwide follows" respectively, and at the same time keep good information diversity in each.

5. CONCLUSIONS

In this paper, we study the challenging problem of automatically generating cross-media timelines and present a novel solution. Our method follows a recommendation-based idea. Specifically, to pursue the requisites that an ideal timeline should have, we model the authority, temporal gap and semantic relevance respectively. A unified framework is proposed to fuse factors, and make data improve each other iteratively. The temporal and semantic gaps are bridged. We also build new self-contained metrics for evaluation. The experimental results show our solution can provide satisfying image-text timelines with limited cost.

As a future work, we plan to adapt parameters automatically on the basis of different types of dataset. Improving the timeline quality by concerning the interactivity of different media (i.e. images order) is also significative. Furthermore, our framework is universal, so that the media other than text and image can be adopted as well.

Acknowledgment

We gratefully acknowledge the valuable comments from all anonymous reviewers. Special thanks to Huan Wang. This work is supported by NSFC with Grant No. 61073081.

6. REFERENCES

[1] R. Agrawal, S. Gollapudi, A. Kannan, and K. Kenthapadi. Enriching textbooks with images. In *Proceedings of the 20th ACM CIKM*, pages 1847–1856, 2011.

[2] R. Aliguliyev. A new sentence similarity measure and sentence based extractive technique for automatic text summarization. *Expert Systems with Applications*, pages 7764–7772, 2009.

[3] D. Cai, S. Yu, J. Wen, and W. Ma. Vips: a visionbased page segmentation algorithm. Technical report, Microsoft Technical Report, MSR-TR-2003-79, 2003.

[4] M. Chandra, V. Gupta, and S. Paul. A statistical approach for automatic text summarization by extraction. In *Communication Systems and Network Technologies (CSNT)*, pages 268–271, 2011.

[5] X. Chen, Y. Mu, S. Yan, and T. Chua. Efficient large-scale image annotation by probabilistic collaborative multi-label propagation. In *Proceedings of the 18th ACM MM*, pages 35–44, 2010.

[6] Y. Chen, O. Jin, G.-R. Xue, J. Chen, and Q. Yang. Visual contextual advertising: Bringing textual advertisements to images. In *Proceedings of the 24th AAAI Conference, AAAI*, 2010.

[7] K. R. M. R. B. David, E. V. Hatzivassiloglou, J. L. K. A. N. Carl, and S. B. S. S. Sigelman. Tracking and summarizing news on a daily basis with columbia's newsblaster. In *Proceedings of HLT 2002*, page 280, 2002.

[8] M. Fattah and F. Ren. Ga, mr, ffnn, pnn and gmm based models for automatic text summarization. *Computer Speech & Language*, pages 126–144, 2009.

[9] Y. Feng and M. Lapata. Topic models for image annotation and text illustration. In *Human Language Technologies: The 2010 Annual Conference of the NAACL*, pages 831–839, 2010.

Table 4: Parts of timelines

(a) Japan Earthquake (contiguous)

March 11, 2011	March 12, 2011	March 13, 2011
– Japan's most powerful earthquake since records began has struck the north-east coast, triggering a massive tsunami. – In one of the worst-hit residential areas, people buried under rubble could be heard calling out "help" and "hen are we going to be rescued." – At least 350 people are dead and hundreds missing after a tsunami caused by a huge 8.9-magnitude quake devastated north-east Japan. – The northeastern Japanese city of Kesennuma, with a population of 74,000, was hit by widespread fires and one-third of the city was under water. – 8.9 magnitude earthquake hits Japan, 30-foot tsunami triggered.	– The one of the buildings surrounding a nuclear reactor at the Fukushima Dai-ichi nuclear power plant collapsed, causing an explosion. – An explosion happened late Monday morning at the Fukushima Daiichi's No. 3 nuclear reactor building. – Earlier, Japan warned of a meltdown at the nuclear reactor damaged after the quake, but said the risk of radiation contamination was small. – A powerful explosion has hit a nuclear power station in north-eastern Japan which was damaged in Friday's devastating earthquake and tsunami. – A series of earthquakes rattled Tokyo and northeastern Japan on Wednesday evening but caused no apparent damage.	– An official says that a third reactor at a troubled nuclear facility has failed. – Japanese authorities warned against the yen's rise as the currency rallied broadly early in Asia on Monday. – A Japanese rescue team member walks through the completely leveled village of Saito, in northeastern Japan. – West Sussex firefighters were mobilised as part of the UK response to the rescue effort following the 8.9-magnitude earthquake. – The troubles at an earthquake-damaged nuclear plant in northern Japan will raise fresh questions about the country's ambitious plans to develop...

(b) Occupy Wall Street (discontinuous)

Oct 3, 2011	Oct 6, 2011	Oct 15, 2011
– More than 700 protesters were arrested on Saturday on Brooklyn Bridge. – Protesters dressed as "corporate zombies", in full zombie regalia and clutching fake cash, parade down Wall Street. – A spirited and leaderless protest in the Wall Street section of New York has entered its third week, helping to inspire a growing number of demonstrations united in their passion if not necessarily their reasons for hitting the streets. – They may not be in the "other" 99 percent, but wealthy stars are still lending support to the Wall Street protests. – A large rally is planned for Wednesday in New...	– Some have compared the protesters to a left-leaning version of the Tea Party movement or perhaps an American response to the 'Arab Spring'. – Now, almost three weeks later, the once-haphazard movement is growing much larger and more coordinated. – President Obama says the protesters are expressing the frustration Americans feel. – For more than three weeks hundreds, at times thousands, of people have gathered in New York as part of the Occupy Wall Street movement. – About 4,000 protesters march in Portland, Ore. More demonstrations unfold in Houston, Austin, Tampa, and San Francisco.	– The "Occupy Wall Street" movement went global Saturday, crossing the Atlantic to many European cities, where protesters turned out by the thousands for largely peaceful demonstrations. – Thousands took to the streets in front of the European Central Bank in Frankfurt as well as in other major cities, including the country's capital Berlin, where protesters marched to the Office of the Chancellor. – Around 250 protesters set up camp outside St Paul's Cathedral in the heart of London on Sunday. – A crowd of about 3,000 people joined for Occupy Denmark on Saturday. – Rome protest against cuts descends into violence...

[10] T. Jiang and A. Tan. Discovering image-text associations for cross-media web information fusion. *Knowledge Discovery in Databases: PKDD 2006*, pages 561–568, 2006.

[11] E. Kuiper, M. Volman, and J. Terwel. The web as an information resource in k–12 education: Strategies for supporting students in searching and processing information. *Review of Educational Research*, pages 285–328, 2005.

[12] X. Li, E. Gavves, C. Snoek, M. Worring, and A. Smeulders. Personalizing automated image annotation using cross-entropy. In *Proceedings of the 19th ACM MM*, pages 233–242, 2011.

[13] C. Lin and E. Hovy. Automatic evaluation of summaries using n-gram co-occurrence statistics. In *Proceedings of NAACL-HLT 2003*, pages 71–78, 2003.

[14] D. Lowe. Object recognition from local scale-invariant features. In *Proceedings of the 7th IEEE ICCV*, pages 1150–1157, 1999.

[15] T. Mandl. Vague transformations in information retrieval. *ISI*, pages 312–325, 1998.

[16] R. Mihalcea and P. Tarau. A language independent algorithm for single and multiple document summarization. In *Proceedings of IJCNLP*, 2005.

[17] S. Panjwani, L. Micallef, K. Fenech, K. Toyama, et al. Effects of integrating digital visual materials with textbook scans in the classroom. *International Journal of Education and Development using ICT*, 2009.

[18] D. Radev, H. Jing, M. Stys, and D. Tam. Centroid-based summarization of multiple documents. *Information Processing and Management*, pages 919–938, 2004.

[19] N. Rasiwasia, J. Costa Pereira, E. Coviello, G. Doyle, G. R. Lanckriet, R. Levy, and N. Vasconcelos. A new approach to cross-modal multimedia retrieval. In *Proceedings of the 18th ACM MM*, pages 251–260, 2010.

[20] L. Tan, Y. Song, S. Liu, and L. Xie. Imagehive: Interactive content-aware image summarization. *Computer Graphics and Applications, IEEE*, pages 46–55, 2012.

[21] X. Wan and J. Yang. Multi-document summarization using cluster-based link analysis. In *Proceedings of the 31st international ACM SIGIR*, pages 299–306, 2008.

[22] J. Wang, L. Jia, and X. Hua. Interactive browsing via diversified visual summarization for image search results. *Multimedia Systems*, pages 379–391, 2011.

[23] Y. Wu, E. Y. Chang, K. C.-C. Chang, and J. R. Smith. Optimal multimodal fusion for multimedia data analysis. In *Proceedings of the 12th ACM MM*, pages 572–579, 2004.

[24] R. Yan, L. Kong, C. Huang, X. Wan, X. Li, and Y. Zhang. Timeline generation through evolutionary trans-temporal summarization. In *Proceedings of the Conference on EMNLP*, pages 433–443, 2011.

[25] R. Yan, X. Wan, M. Lapata, X. Zhao, P. Cheng, and X. Li. Visualizing timelines: Evolutionary summarization via iterative reinforcement between text and image streams. In *Proceedings of the 21st ACM CIKM*, pages 275–284, 2012.

Geo-visual Ranking for Location Prediction of Social Images

Xinchao Li, Martha Larson, Alan Hanjalic
Multimedia Information Retrieval Lab, Delft University of Technology
Delft, The Netherlands
{x.li-3,m.a.larson,a.hanjalic}@tudelft.nl

ABSTRACT

Predicting geographic location using exclusively the visual content of images holds the promise of greatly benefiting users' access to media collections. In this paper, we present a visual-content-based approach that predicts where in the world a social image was taken. We employ a ranking method that assigns a query photo the geo-location of its most likely geo-visual neighbor in the social image collection. The novelty of the approach is that ranking makes use not only of the photos themselves, but also their geo-visual neighbors. In contrast to other approaches, we do not restrict the locations we predict to landmarks or specific cities. The approach is evaluated on a set of 3 million geo-tagged photos from Flickr, released by MediaEval 2012. Experiments show that the proposed system delivers a substantive performance improvement compared with previously proposed, related visual content-based approaches. The discussion illustrates how photo densities, geo-visual redundancy and uploader patterns characteristic of social image collections impacts the performance.

Categories and Subject Descriptors

H.3 [**Information Storage and Retrieval**]: Content

Keywords

Multimedia geo-coordinate prediction; Vision-based image location prediction; Geo-visual ranking

1. INTRODUCTION

With the rapid development of photo capturing devices, including cameras, phones and most recently tablets, we are witnessing an explosion of social image data. We understand social images to be photos that were taken by users in the course of their daily lives for sharing with other users or for personal reasons such as preserving memories. The location at which the photos are taken is an important piece of information that can support users in searching, browsing and

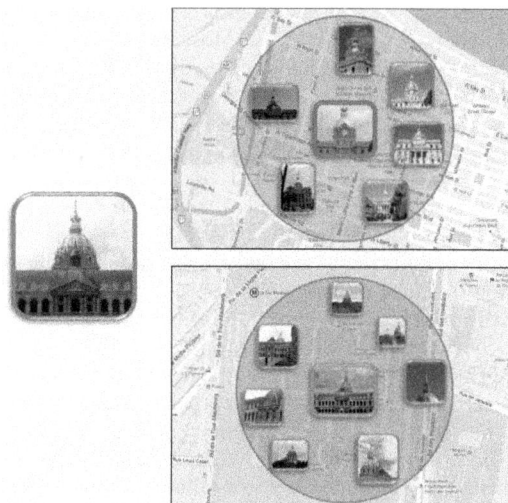

Figure 1: **Illustration of the principle exploited by geo-visual ranking (GVR): A query photo (left) matches two candidate photos well. The incorrect (red) match is disambiguated from the correct (green) match by using the geo-visual neighbors of each candidate photo.**

organizing their photo collections as well as images shared on social photo-sharing websites such as Flickr. Today's mobile devices now have the ability to automatically assign geo-coordinates to images. The task of automatic location prediction is motivated, however, by the fact that despite GPS technology most social images remain untagged [20].

Recently, increased research attention has been devoted to techniques that can automatically estimate the geographic location of media (also referred to as *geo-coordinate prediction* or *geo-tagging*) [3, 4, 6, 7, 12, 17, 20]. Geo-location information supports an array of applications that make use of social image collections, such as finding popular objects and events in one particular area [19], generating representative and diverse views of the popular landmarks [10], as well as recommending virtual tours by presenting information mined from user-generated travelogues and photos [5].

A variety of information sources have been exploited for predicting geo-location. User-contributed text annotations have been used as a basis of a large range of successful geo-coordinate predication algorithms [20, 23]. This work exploits the natural link between text annotation and location (e.g., tags often include place names and other location-specific vocabulary) in order to predict at which location around the globe an photo was taken. The drawback of textual annotations (i.e., metadata) is that it needs to be manually created the user, a time consuming task. As a result, a large percentage of images are not associated with any tags and cannot be geo-located with text based approaches.

An appealing alternative to text-based approaches to geocoordinate prediction are visual-content-based approaches. Such approaches have the potential to make location prediction possible for social images with no tags, and to enhance the location prediction in cases that tags are present. However, as can be seen from previous work, exploiting visual information is challenging, and the performance of visual-content-based approaches falls short of the performance of text-based approaches in predicting the location of a photo around the globe [3, 4]. Most visual-content-based approaches narrow the domain of prediction and tackle the task of location prediction within a geographically constrained area [25, 26] or reduce this to specific landmark recognition [2, 11, 13, 24]. A survey of recent work, including the overview given in [15], reveals that visual-content-based geo-location prediction of photos at a world-wide (i.e., global) scale, has yet to be thoroughly investigated.

In this paper, we tackle the task of visual-only global-scale prediction of social images. The approach that we propose specifically addresses the shortcomings of the limited previous approaches that have been proposed in this area. Previous work takes one of two approaches to the task. First, a first nearest neighbor (1-NN) approach is used, which retrieves the geo-tagged image within a collection that is closest to the query image (i.e., the image for which we are attempting to predict the geo-coordinates). Once this image has been identified, the 1-NN approach propagates the geo-coordinates from the 1-NN to the query image. This approach has the weakness that it fails in cases where the visually most similar image in the collection was taken at another location. Second, a clustering approach is used, which attempts to discover geo-areas that are characterized by multiple visually similar images. The query image is then assigned the geo-location associated with the most likely cluster. This approach works less well in practice than 1-NN, but has sound motivation: a combination of multiple images potentially produces a more stable and reliable visual representation of a location. The weakness of this approach is that the clustering step occurs independently of the geo-location prediction step, and it is possible that information in the photo collection is not fully exploited during geo-location prediction.

Our approach, designated Geo-Visual Ranking (GVR), has been formulated to address the weaknesses of these two approaches. Instead of relying on a 1-NN photo, or on precalculated clusters, it identifies a set of candidate photos that are visually close to the query photo and models each candidate photos using a *geo-visual expansion set* of photos that are geographical neighbors of the candidate. The candidate photos are ranked according to the visual similarity of their geo-visual expansion sets and the query photo. Geo-coordinate prediction occurs by propagating the geo-coordinates of the top ranked candidate to the query photo.

The insight exploited by the GVR approach is illustrated in Fig. 1. Here, the query image is shown to be visually similar to two candidate photos located in radically different geo-locations, which would make it hard to correctly estimate its geo-location using the visual 1-NN approach. It can be seen that taking the geo-visual neighbors of the two candidate photos makes it possible to visually disambiguate the two locations. The fact that we are matching photos and not clusters means that we propagate a very precise geo-location, rather than a cluster centroid. Because, as mentioned above, clustering is not guaranteed to be optimal for geo-location prediction, the cluster-based prediction could possibly be very remote from the best possible prediction given the data collection.

The remainder of this paper is organized as follows. The related work on vision-based location prediction is reviewed in Section 2. In Section 3, the geo-visual ranking (GVR) approach for location estimation is introduced. Section 4 details the experimental framework, and Section 5 presents the results of experiments confirming the performance of GVR. In Section 6, a closer analysis of experimental result is conducted with respect to characteristics of social images. Finally, Section 7 provides a conclusion and outlook.

2. RELATED WORK

The task of predicting the location at which a photo was taken on the basis of its visual content has drawn much research attention from the computer vision community. Given a database of photos for which the geo-location is known, the task involves predicting the geo-location for query photos whose location is unknown. Work addressing this task falls into two categories: *local level* prediction, where the possible locations at which a query photo can occur are highly constrained and *global level* prediction, which involves prediction where around the globe the query photo was taken.

2.1 Geo-prediction at the local level

In the "where am I" computer vision contest in ICCV 2005, participants focus on the street level location prediction. Zhang and Kosecka [26] use a wide-baseline matching technique based on SIFT features [14] to select the closest views, and generate the estimated location by performing position triangulation on top two best reference views selected by the camera motion estimation. As photos are densely sampled along the street, the system can achieve a very precise prediction—all the estimation errors are less than 16m.

Steinhoff et al. [22] apply fast nearest neighbor search within a collection of photos represented by local image features to achieve realtime location estimation on mobile devices. Experiment are conducted in an urban environment covering an area of a few city blocks; the reported accuracy is comparable to that of a GPS. Chen et al. [2], investigate the problem of city-scale landmark recognition for cell phone images. They collected 150k panoramic images of San Francisco using surveying vehicles, which are further converted into 1.7 million perspective images. A vocabulary-tree-based retrieval scheme using DoG key points and SIFT descriptors [14] is built to approach this task. Our approach is similar to these approaches in that it exploits local image features, but it goes far beyond them in that it predicts the geo-location of photos at a global level.

2.2 Geo-prediction at the global level

There is relatively less related work dedicated to the problem of visual-content-based geo-prediction at the global level. As pointed out in [3], for specific landmarks, in particular, landmarks for which visual features are highly discriminative, the performance is even comparable with tag-based system. However, for social images that have been taken at a large number of locations around the world, visual variability is extremely high and the ability of visual features to discriminate between locations is quite weak, falling far short of the discriminative power of textual descriptions. As a result, visual-content-based prediction of geo-location at a global level is a challenging problem.

A major contribution to the area has been made by Hays and Efros [7]. In order to predict the location of social images at the global scale, they first retrieve visually similar photos and form clusters using geo-clustering. The geo-centroid of cluster containing the most photos is used for location prediction. Because [7] is the related work that is closest to our own, we choose this method, which we designate *IM2GPS*, as an experimental condition against which to evaluate our approach. In [7], encouraging performance was achieved by *IM2GPS*, but the performance does not match that of a simple visual 1-NN approach. Since our goal is to combine the strengths of clustering and of 1-NN, we also use 1-NN, designated as *VisNN*, as a baseline in our experiments. Further [7] mentions that geo-clustering is unfavorable in the case of queries for which relatively fewer visually similar images exist in the collection. The averaged performance is even worse than simply 1-NN approach, especially for localization accuracy within $200km$. In order to examine the ability of our approach to compensate for this issue, we carry out a detailed analysis of the results of the experiments with respect to different query types corresponding to queries with relatively more or less geo-neighbors or visual-neighbors.

Other work that has been carried out on visual-content-based geo-prediction at the global level has developed algorithms to address a version global geo-location prediction problem that is not comparable with our own because it is in some way simplified. Li et al. [13] propose an approach to automatically mine the popular landmarks from large scale Flickr dataset and perform object recognition with a multi-class support vector machine for top 500 discovered landmarks. The landmarks are located all over the globe, but this work does not address the global problem since it limits the prediction possibilities to a finite set of locations. Kalantidis et al. [24] also mine from the geo-tagged photos from 22 European cities to find representative scenes and apply a scene matching-based approach to location estimation by matching photos with these representative scenes. This approach addresses a relatively less-limited global prediction problem. However, by addressing cities the authors are focusing only on locations that are represented by a large number of photos in the collection and leaving locations that are represented by a relatively small number of photos out of consideration.

3. GEO-VISUAL RANKING (GVR)

The problem of predicting the geo-location of an image can be seen as the problem of finding the geo-coordinates of the location of the camera when the photo was taken. This problem can be formulated as finding a location $\tilde{g}$ with the highest probability of being the location g where the query photo q was taken. Under this formulation, geo-location involves finding the g that maximizes the conditional probability $P(g|q)$. This conditional probability can be formulated

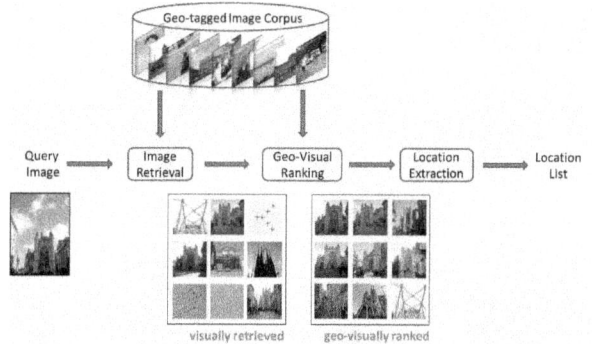

Figure 2: Geo-visual ranking system overview

as Apply Bayes Law, we arrive at the expression,

$$P(g|q) \propto P(g)P(q|g) \qquad (1)$$

where $P(g)$ represents the prior likelihood of a photo having been taken at a location. Assuming that this prior is uniform, the estimated location can be formulated as,

$$\tilde{g} = \arg\max_{g \in G} P(q|g) \qquad (2)$$

where G is the set of all possible locations around the world.

Under this formulation, the critical step in prediction of geo-location is the estimation of $P(q|g)$, which represents the correlation between visual image content and the location where the photo was taken. Making the best possible estimate of the model also requires making the right choice concerning how to define a location. The advantage of defining a location to be a single geographical point, is that the resulting prediction of geo-location can be very precise. The advantage of modeling a location as an area larger than a single point is that more images are available in the collection in order to contribute to the model. In the remainder of this section, we present these two methods of modeling a location and then go on to introduce our GVR approach which seeks to combine the advantages of both.

3.1 Modeling location with a single photo

First, a location can be modeled as a single photo. Under this assumption, it is clear that there is a very precise connection between the visual content of the photo and a geo-location. The visual first-nearest-neighbor approach, used as a baseline in [7], adopts the assumption that there exists one best candidate photo in the collection that can propagate its geo-tag to the query photo. A location is thus defined as any point at which a photo in the dataset was taken, and is modeled with only the visual content of that photo. The similarity between the query photo and a photo geo-tagged with geo-location g is used as an estimate for $P(q|g)$.

3.2 Modeling location with a set of photos

The main disadvantage of modeling a location as a single point represented by a single photo is that one photo can only cover limited visual aspects of a single location, and the collection might lack exactly the right match between the query photo and a photo at the correct geo-coordinates. In order to address this problem, location can be modeled as an area a rather than geo-coordinates g, as depicted in the example, Fig. 1. In choosing to model the location as an area rather than a point, we are leveraging the assumption that photos taken in the same area are visual similar because they contain similar visual content i.e., depict the same buildings, objects, scenes, landscapes and events. When we make a choice to model the location, we estimate $P(q|a)$, rather than $P(q|g)$.

The challenge that arises now is how to determine a, which in turn determines which photos contribute to $P(q|a)$. If our model assigns a high value to $P(q|a)$, we still have to map from a to the exact geo-coordinates g. If we would like a highly precise prediction, we are motivated to keep a as small as possible, since without further evidence we must simply make some reasonable prediction of g, such as the centroid of a. However, if a is too small then we end up predicting using only a single photo, and we have arrived back to the original problem. We note that clustering approaches applied independently of the geo-prediction step do not guarantee an optimal a.

The solution that we propose in this paper, is not to leave the choice of a to a clustering algorithm that is not optimized for a predicting geo-location, but rather to keep a always centered on individual candidate photos, for which we know a very precise geo-location and can for this reason use to predict a precise geo-location for the query photo.

3.3 Geo-visual expansion of candidate photos

Our approach consists of three steps, as depicted in the system overview, Fig. 2. In the first step, "Image Retrieval", we create a set of candidate photos by retrieving all visually similar images from the database up to a visual similarity threshold, k. In the second step, "Geo-Visual Ranking" we perform geo-visual expansion of each candidate photo, a, to create a geo-visual expansion set E_a. Note that E_a contains photos that are not only the geo-graphical neighbors of photo a, but also visual neighbors of the query photo, as illustrated in Fig. 3. Formally, expressed for each candidate photo, E_a is formed according to,

$$E_a = E_{vis@k} \cap E_{geo} \qquad (3)$$

where $E_{vis@k}$ is the set of top k visual-neighbors of the query, and E_{geo} is the set of geo-neighbors of photo a within a radius r_{geo}.

These photos in this expansion set E_a each make a contribution to $P(q|a)$ that reflects the closeness of their similarity to the query photo q. Formally, $P(q|a)$ is expressed as,

$$P(q|a) \propto \sum_{e \in E_a} Sim_{vis}(e, q) \qquad (4)$$

where E_a is the set of geographically nearby photos of photo a with high visual similarities to query q.

The photos are ranked by $P(q|a)$. Then, in the third step, "Location extraction", the geo-location of the top ranked photo is propagated to the query photo. The rationale underlying the GVR approach is that having multiple images in the area a that are both visually similar to the candidate image a and also visually similar to the query image q raises the confidence that the location g, represented by a, is tightly correlated with the specific visual content of the query image.

In Eq. (3), the radius of the geo-visual expansion set r_{geo} controls the scale at which the approach exploits the correlation between image content and location. Unlike a cluster,

Figure 3: Illustration of geo-visual neighbors

which represents an entire geo-area, the images in the geo-visual expansion set are intended to model a single set of geo-coordinates, those of the candidate photo. In the experiments, we will discuss the performance of our approach, including the parameters k and r_{geo} and also the relationship between the choice of r_{geo} and the precision of the resulting geo-location predictions.

4. EXPERIMENTAL FRAMEWORK

4.1 Dataset

To verify the performance of the GVR approach, we carry out our experiments on a set of photos released by the MediaEval 2012 Placing Task [18]. The set contains $3,185,258$ geo-tagged Flickr (http://www.flickr.com/) photos randomly sampled with a method that attempts to maintain coverage of the globe. Since the release includes only the metadata and not the images themselves, we re-crawled the images using the links in the metadata. Because some photos were removed after the dataset was collected, the final collection contains $3,001,071$ photos. We randomly select $100,000$ photos which we use as a test set for our experiments.

4.2 Calculating visual similarity

Our GVR approach to geo-location prediction exploits visual similarity between photos. To calculate this similarity, we implemented a content-based image search engine that represents the state of the art and is able to efficiently visual similarity between millions of photos. We made our choice of image features based on the assumption that what we need to match in the photos is their conceptual content, i.e., depicted objects and scenes. The match must be close enough to distinguish similar photos taken at different locations. To ensure a reliable retrieval, we use local invariant descriptors as our image features. We chose SURF [1, 16], since it has been reported to be faster and more compact than SIFT [9].

To index the features, we adopt the bag-of-visual-words method, which can provide good scalability for a large scale dataset [21]. To further speed up the retrieval time and accuracy, we also adopt the state-of-the-art technique proposed in [8], that represents subregions of the feature space with signatures. In the experiments, we use the software BoofCV to extract SURF descriptors with default parameters, and use Mahout k-means to cluster these descriptors into $20,000$ visual words on a Hadoop-based distributed server. During retrieval, the Hamming threshold used in [8] is set to 12 to guarantee a reliable and fast search.

4.3 Experimental comparison

We compare our GVR approach to two other approaches that represent the state-of-the-art in visual-content based approaches for predicting the geo-location of social images in a setting without constraints (e.g., not tested for specific regions or landmarks). In total, the experiments compare three algorithms: $VisNN$: Visual 1-NN approach, which uses a single photo as one location and uses the visual similarity between photo and query as the rank score. $IM2GPS$: Method used in [7], which performs mean-shift clustering on the geo-locations of the top N photos that are visually similar to the query photo. A cluster's centroid is used to represent the geo-location of that cluster. The geo-locations are further ranked by cluster size. In the experiments, the parameter N is set to 130 and bandwidth $scale$ used in mean-shift clustering is set to 0.00001 to gain the best performance. GVR: The proposed geo-visual ranking approach, which uses a set of geo-visual neighbors as one location and uses the sum of visual similarity between neighbors and the query as the rank score. As mentioned in Section 2, these approaches allow us to compare our GVR approach with the strengths of both a 1-NN ($VisNN$) approach and a clustering approach ($IM2GPS$).

4.4 Evaluation procedure

To evaluate the performance of the proposed system, we use a standard procedure from the literature. First we define an evaluation radius r_{eval}. This radius controls the precision of the evaluation. A photo is considered to be correctly predicted, if its predicted geo-coordinates falls within r_{eval} of the ground truth location. Formally, expressed, the correctness of a photo with respect to an evaluation radius r_{eval} is calculated by the evaluation function $f_{r_{eval}}$,

$$f_{r_{eval}}(g, \tilde{g}) = \begin{cases} right , \ geoDist(g, \tilde{g}) \leq r_{eval} \\ wrong , \ otherwise \end{cases} \quad (5)$$

where $geoDist(g, \tilde{g})$ is the geographical distance between g and $\tilde{g}$.

The evaluation metric we use is the Hit Rate at top K (HR@K): given a query, the system finally returns a ranked list of possible locations. HR@K measures the proportion of queries that are correctly located in the top K listed locations. As, in this paper, we focus on the ability of the system to output a single accurate prediction, we adopt HR@1 to evaluate the system.

5. EXPERIMENTAL RESULTS

In this section, we investigate the performance of our approach with respect to the parameters k and r_{geo} in Eq. (5), and also discuss the relationship between the choice of r_{geo} and the evaluation radius r_{eval} in Eq. (3).

5.1 Geo-neighbour radiuses

In the proposed system, to identify the geo-neighbors of a candidate photo, we need to set the geo-neighbor radius (r_{geo}), which controls the scale of the correlation between image content and location. We first investigate the interaction of r_{geo} with different levels of precision of evaluation. Fig. 4 illustrates the system performance within different evaluation radiuses (r_{eval}) for different geo-neighbor radiuses, ranging from $100m$ to$10km$. The number of candidate locations here is set to $k = 500$. As shown in Fig. 4, the hit rate is quite stable when the geo-neighbor radius less than $1km$, but as it increases to$10km$, the performance drops sharply. This is due to the fact that a larger geo-neighbor

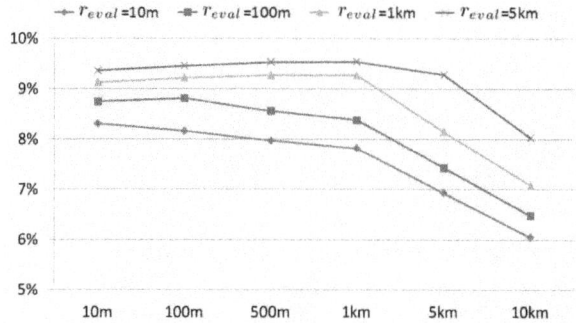

Figure 4: HR@1 with respect to different evaluation radiuses (r_{eval}) for different geo-neighbor scales (r_{geo}), shown on the x-axes.

radius will include more photos as neighbors. Photos near to the query photo's location, but lying outside the evaluation radius, receive a high rank but do not contribute to performance. This phenomenon is also confirmed by hit rate in other evaluation radiuses ($r_{eval} = 10m$, $r_{eval} = 100m$). We conclude that it is wise to set the geo-neighbor radius r_{geo} to be less than evaluation radius r_{eval}.

For evaluation radius 1km, the hit rate for geo-neighbor radiuses from $10m$ to $1km$ are stable. This is due to the fact that photos share the same content are very close to each other. A large geo-neighbor radius is not necessary because two photos located in places separated by a large distance, e.g., $1km$, are less likely to share the same content, and the visual similarity between them photo can be expected in general to be low low. To make a balance between computing complexity and robustness, in what follows, the geo-neighbor radius is set to be equal to evaluation radius r_{eval} if $r_{eval} < 1km$, otherwise uniformly set to $1km$.

5.2 Number of candidate photos

Next we turn to the issue of k, the number of candidate photos in the initial, visually retrieved candidate set. Fig. 5 illustrates the system performance with various numbers of candidate photos, ranging from 10 to$10,000$.

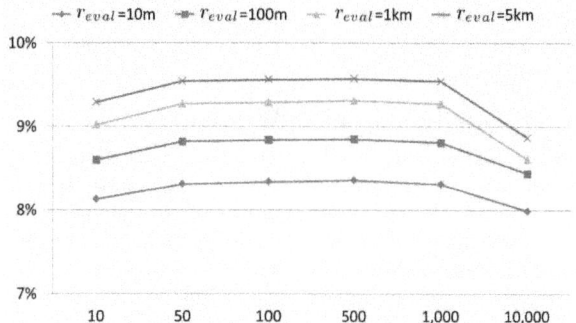

Figure 5: HR@1 with different evaluation radiuses for different number of location candidates.

In general, as more candidate photos are used, there are more possibilities to find the right location, and thus, the hit rate grows steadily. However, as the number of location candidates is increased to $10,000$, the hit rate drops for all evaluation radiuses. This drop can be attributed additional candidate photos also introducing, more "noise" locations, which will especially affect query images with few visual neighbors in their geo-neighborhoods. On another hand, as more candidate photos are used, the corresponding computational complexity also increases. In what follows, the number of location candidates is set to a sensible level, namely $k = 500$.

5.3 General performance evaluation

Fig. 6 illustrates the performance for different schemes within different evaluation radiuses. This figure reveals that GVR consistently outperforms both $VisNN$ and $IM2GPS$ across the board with respect to different evaluation radiuses. The average gain in performance is 6% over $VisNN$ and 150% over $IM2GPS$. In the next section, we turn to an analysis that will give us an understanding of the source of the gains achieved by GVR.

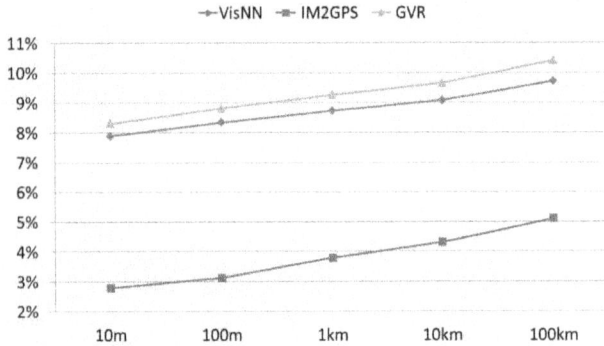

Figure 6: **HR@1 with different evaluation radiuses for** $VisNN$, $IM2GPS$ **and** GVR.

6. EXPERIMENTAL ANALYSIS

In this section, we carry out a closer analysis of our experimental results. We consider our GVR approach to be a social image collections approach, because there are certain properties that are characteristic of social image collection and GVR is able to function robustly in light of these properties. We examine three characteristics in more detail: photo density distribution, geo-visual redundancy and uploader patterns.

6.1 Photo density distribution

Social images can be taken anywhere in the world, but they are far from evenly distributed over the globe. Instead, they are more densely distributed in some regions, due to factors such as the presence of a large local population of people who own digital photo devices or of landmarks that get frequently photographed. Fig. 7 illustrates the system performance for query photos located in regions with different degrees of photo density. We define density degree to be the number of geo-neighbors with in 1km radius of the true location of the query photo. The bins in Fig. 7 are formed such that each bin contains approximately the same number of query photos.

It can be seen that GVR and $VisNN$ perform similarly at relatively low densities. As densities get very high, however, GVR outperforms $VisNN$. This difference indicates that

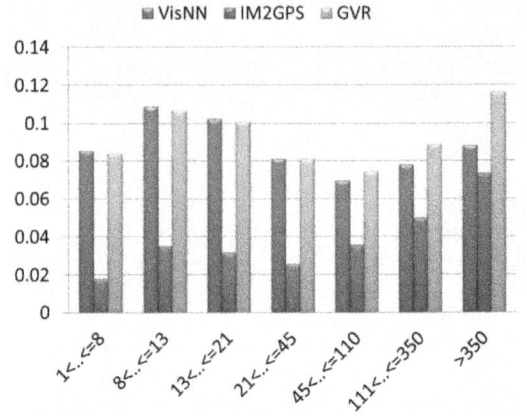

Figure 7: **HR@1 with** $r_{eval} = 1km$ **for queries with different density degree for** $VisNN$, $IM2GPS$ **and** GVR.

GVR is better able to take advantage of a large number of photos taken at one place than $VisNN$. It can also been seen that GVR outperforms $IM2GPS$ across the board. Recall that $IM2GPS$ exploits an effectively limited number of photos that are very visually similar to the query, but that GVR is able to exploit a greater number of photos, including ones that are less visually similar. We take this trend to be evidence of the benefit of using geo-visual expansion rather than clustering.

Interestingly, Fig. 7 reveals that for all three approaches the performance increases as the number of photos within 1km of the query photo goes from 1–8 to 8–13, but decreases as the number of photos goes from 8–13 to 13–21. This decrease can be attributed to a change in the uploader patterns. For photos from 8–13, there is still a relatively higher chance that all photos from a given region will be uploaded by a single person. This means, that although less photos are available in a region, their visual similarity is likely to be higher, improving geo-location predication performance. We return to examine uploader patterns in an additional experiment at the end of this section.

6.2 Geo-visual redundancy

With visual-content based approaches, it is not only the density of photos for a given region that is important, but also the visual similarity of these photos. Recall from Section 2 that the authors of $IM2GPS$ [7] point out that their approach suffers for queries with relatively few visually similar images in the collection. In order to delve deeper into the impact of visually similar photos in the regions of the query photos, we now turn to analyze our results in terms of *geo-visual redundancy*. For the purpose of our investigation, we define geo-visual redundancy for a given photo as the size of that photo's geo-visual expansion set (cf. Eq. 3) calculated using a large number of visual neighbors ($k = 10,000$) and a standard geo-radius ($r_{geo} = 1km$). Of the set of query photos (total $100,000$ queries), the geo-visual redundancy ranges from 0 to 413. The distribution of the query photos over this range is illustrated in Fig. 8.

Over half of the queries do not have visual similar photos within their geo-neighborhood, which suggests that in these cases there is not another photo in the dataset that depicts the same scene or object at the query location. This ob-

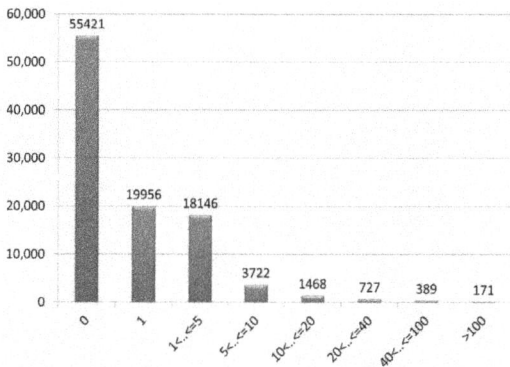

Figure 8: Distribution of queries over different levels of geo-visual redundancy calculated over the social image collection.

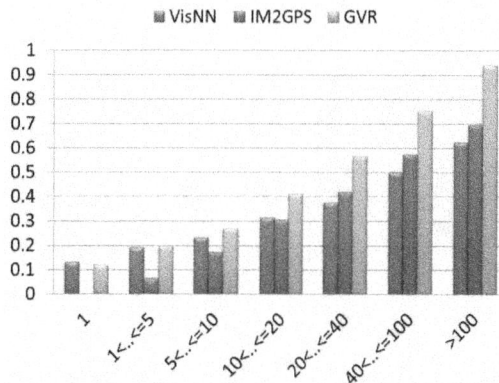

Figure 9: HR@1 with $r_{eval} = 10m$ for queries with different levels of geo-visual redundancy for $VisNN$, $IM2GPS$ and GVR.

servation demonstrates how challenging it is to predict the geo-location of a social image purely from its visual content.

Fig. 9 breaks down the geo-location prediction performance measured in our experiments over different levels of geo-visual redundancy for two typical levels of evaluation precision. For query images with very low visual redundancy our proposed GVR approach matches the ability of $VisNN$ to outperform $IM2GPS$. The strength of GVR in cases of low visual redundancy is due to the following effect. The clusters used by $IM2GPS$ are not optimized for geo-prediction. Photos visually similar to the query photo are limited in number in the collection and the risk is high that they were taken at diverse or geographically widespread geo-locations. Choosing the cluster to which the majority of visually similar photos belong, the approach applied by $IM2GPS$, can easily lead to a inaccurate geo-location prediction. This is especially unfavorable for the user scenario that most query photos have low geo-visual redundancy (cf. Fig. 8), the average performance over all queries will be heavily determined by this kind of queries. This effect accounts for the fact that $IM2GPS$ is outperformed by $VisNN$ and GVR on average, as shown in Fig. 6.

GVR on the other hand, focuses on exploiting visual similarity within a geo-constrained region. Visual similarity to the query photo is not enough to allow a photo to contribute to predicting the geo-location. Instead, a photo must belong to a geo-visual set and the whole set must together support the prediction.

For queries with a geo-visual redundancy level greater than 20, both $IM2GPS$ and GVR outperform $VisNN$. This strength is due to the fact that both $IM2GPS$ and GVR use multiple photos to model an individual location. In this case, even if the top-1 visually similar photo is not located at the query's location, there are many photos within the query's top-k visual neighbors are located in the right location. This information is especially beneficial to the queries with many visual neighbors located in the same location of the query. In this case, $VisNN$, which only use a single photo as one location, may yield the wrong prediction because it makes the decision on the basis of a single match with a visual outlier.

For queries with a redundancy level greater than 3, GVR outperforms both $VisNN$ and $IM2GPS$. The gain is substantial, e.g., for query photos for which the geo-visual re-

dundancy is larger than 100, the gain achieved by GVR is 52% compared with $VisNN$. In short, Fig. 9 provides evidence that GVR has achieved its goal of addressing the weaknesses of both 1-NN neighbor and of clustering-based approaches. These results substantiate the conclusion that by incorporating the geo-relation between photos that are visually similar to the query, GVR can better model the correlation between the image content and the location where the image was taken. GVR not only shows a strong ability to predict geo-location for query photos with high geo-visual redundancy in the collection, it also maintains reliable performance for queries with low geo-visual redundancy.

6.3 Uploader patterns

In social image collections, one uploader may upload many images. These images are often taken in the same place, at around the same time and with the same camera, e.g., a large set of photos taken at a particular New Year's Eve party. Photos of one uploader have a high chance of being visually similar to each other. For this reason, visual-content-based approaches to geo-location often leverage one photo uploaded by a user to predict the locations of other photos uploaded by that same user. Although we wish our system to leverage patterns in the social image collection, we consider it important that the system can make a reliable prediction of the geo-location of a photo, without requiring that another photo taken by the same user is in the collection.

To investigate the impact of uploader patterns, we perform a further experiment that, for each query, removes other photos from the same uploader as the query photo from the collection. We then calculate the proportion of the original correctly predicted photos that can no longer be correctly predicted. The results of this experiment, depicted in Fig. 10, reveal that $VisNN$ has a strong dependence on the presence of photos in the collection that were taken by the same uploader.

In contrast, GVR is able to make more correct predictions without relying on same-uploader photos being present in the collection, especially for queries with high level of geo-visual redundancy in the collection. Such redundancy provides a rich geo-visual neighbor information which can be effectively exploited by GVR even in the absence of photos from the same uploader as the query photo.

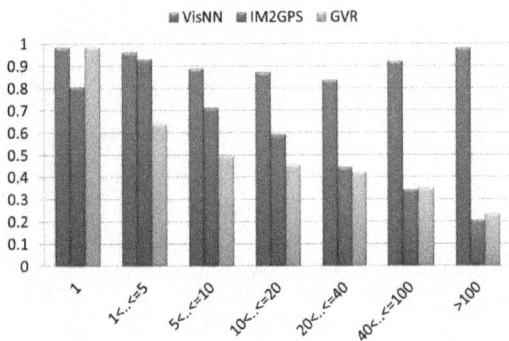

Figure 10: Proportion of queries with different levels of geo-visual redundancy that can no longer be correctly predicted when same-uploader photos are removed from the collection with $r_{eval} = 1km$.

7. CONCLUSION

We have presented a geo-visual ranking approach to the task of predicting the geo-location, over the entire globe, of social images. Our approach addresses the challenging task of predicting geo-location using only the visual content of images. The main contribution of the approach is that it improves over two previous approaches, addressing the disadvantages of both 1-NN and clustering. We also carry out an evaluation that is unconstrained, in that we sample 100,000 images randomly from the collection to use as queries and do not put special focus on frequently photographed areas or on a limited set of locations or landmarks. The GVR approach achieves sound performance for geo-location prediction, especially for photos with high geo-visual redundancy, i.e., many geo-visual neighbors in the collection. Crucially, the GVR approach also retains reliable performance for queries with low geo-visual redundancy, which are highly problematic for the state-of-the-art $IM2GPS$ approach. In terms of user upload patterns, the GVR approach is able to predict the geo-location of a photo when another photo from the same uploader is present in the collection, but also yields sound performance when it is not. Future work will include investigation of the prior probability of image location. Initial exploratory experiments did not succeed in deriving additional gains from the prior. We conjecture that this may be due to the fact that high prior locations are already have an advantage under our approach (cf. Fig. 7). We would like to explore the issue in more depth and arrive at insight or an alternate method for estimating the prior.

8. REFERENCES

[1] H. Bay, A. Ess, T. Tuytelaars, and L. Van Gool. Speeded-up robust features (SURF). *Computer vision and image understanding*, 110(3):346–359, 2008.

[2] D. Chen et al. City-scale landmark identification on mobile devices. In *Proc. CVPR '11*, 2011.

[3] D. J. Crandall, L. Backstrom, D. Huttenlocher, and J. Kleinberg. Mapping the world's photos. In *Proc. WWW '09*, 2009.

[4] G. Friedland, J. Choi, H. Lei, and A. Janin. Multimodal location estimation on Flickr videos. In *Proc. WSM '11*, 2011.

[5] Q. Hao et al. Travelscope: standing on the shoulders of dedicated travelers. In *Proc. MM '09*, 2009.

[6] C. Hauff and G. Houben. Placing images on the world map: a microblog-based enrichment approach. In *Proc. SIGIR '12*, 2012.

[7] J. Hays and A. Efros. IM2GPS: estimating geographic information from a single image. In *Proc. CVPR '08*, 2008.

[8] H. Jégou, M. Douze, and C. Schmid. Improving bag-of-features for large scale image search. *International Journal of Computer Vision*, 87(3):316–336, 2010.

[9] L. Juan and O. Gwun. A comparison of SIFT, PCA-SIFT and SURF. *International Journal of Image Processing (IJIP)*, 3(4):143–152, 2009.

[10] L. S. Kennedy and M. Naaman. Generating diverse and representative image search results for landmarks. In *Proc. WWW '08*, 2008.

[11] H. Kretzschmar, C. Stachniss, C. Plagemann, and W. Burgard. Estimating landmark locations from geo-referenced photographs. In *Proc. IROS '08*, 2008.

[12] M. Larson et al. Automatic tagging and geotagging in video collections and communities. In *Proc. ICMR '11*, 2011.

[13] Y. Li, D. Crandall, and D. Huttenlocher. Landmark classification in large-scale image collections. In *Proc. ICCV '09*, 2009.

[14] D. Lowe. Distinctive image features from scale-invariant keypoints. *International journal of computer vision*, 60(2):91–110, 2004.

[15] J. Luo, D. Joshi, J. Yu, and A. Gallagher. Geotagging in multimedia and computer vision–a survey. *Multimedia Tools Appl.*, 51(1):187–211, 2011.

[16] K. Mikolajczyk and C. Schmid. Scale & affine invariant interest point detectors. *International journal of computer vision*, 60(1):63–86, 2004.

[17] O. A. B. Penatti, L. T. Li, J. Almeida, and R. da S. Torres. A visual approach for video geocoding using bag-of-scenes. In *Proc. ICMR '12*, 2012.

[18] A. Rae and P. Kelm. Working notes for the Placing Task at MediaEval 2012. In *MediaEval 2012 Workshop*, 2012.

[19] T. Rattenbury, N. Good, and M. Naaman. Towards automatic extraction of event and place semantics from Flickr tags. In *Proc. SIGIR '07*, 2007.

[20] P. Serdyukov, V. Murdock, and R. van Zwol. Placing Flickr photos on a map. In *Proc. SIGIR '09*, 2009.

[21] J. Sivic and A. Zisserman. Video Google: a text retrieval approach to object matching in videos. In *Proc. ICCV '03*, 2003.

[22] U. Steinhoff et al. How computer vision can help in outdoor positioning. In *Proc. AmI '07*, 2007.

[23] O. Van Laere, S. Schockaert, and B. Dhoedt. Finding locations of Flickr resources using language models and similarity search. In *Proc. ICMR '11*, 2011.

[24] K. Yannis et al. VIRaL: Visual image retrieval and localization. *Multimedia Tools and Applications*, 51:555–592, 2011.

[25] A. R. Zamir and M. Shah. Accurate image localization based on Google Maps street view. In *Proc. ECCV '10*, 2010.

[26] W. Zhang and J. Kosecka. Image based localization in urban environments. In *Proc. 3DPVT '06*, 2006.

Recommendations for Video Event Recognition using Concept Vocabularies

Amirhossein Habibian, Koen E. A. van de Sande, and Cees G. M. Snoek
ISLA, Informatics Institute, University of Amsterdam
Science Park 904, 1098 XH, Amsterdam, The Netherlands
{a.habibian, ksande, cgmsnoek}@uva.nl

ABSTRACT

Representing videos using vocabularies composed of concept detectors appears promising for event recognition. While many have recently shown the benefits of concept vocabularies for recognition, the important question what concepts to include in the vocabulary is ignored. In this paper, we study how to create an effective vocabulary for arbitrary-event recognition in web video. We consider four research questions related to the number, the type, the specificity and the quality of the detectors in concept vocabularies. A rigorous experimental protocol using a pool of 1,346 concept detectors trained on publicly available annotations, a dataset containing 13,274 web videos from the Multimedia Event Detection benchmark, 25 event groundtruth definitions, and a state-of-the-art event recognition pipeline allow us to analyze the performance of various concept vocabulary definitions. From the analysis we arrive at the recommendation that for effective event recognition the concept vocabulary should *i)* contain more than 200 concepts, *ii)* be diverse by covering *object, action, scene, people, animal* and *attribute* concepts, *iii)* include both general and specific concepts, and *iv)* increase the number of concepts rather than improve the quality of the individual detectors. We consider the recommendations for video event recognition using concept vocabularies the most important contribution of the paper, as they provide guidelines for future work.

Categories and Subject Descriptors

I.2.10 [**Artificial Intelligence**]: Vision and Scene Understanding—*Video analysis*

General Terms

Algorithms, Experimentation, Measurement

Keywords

Event recognition, Concept representation

1. INTRODUCTION

We consider the problem of event recognition in arbitrary web video. Among the many challenges involved, resulting from the uncontrolled recording condition of web videos and the large variations in the visual appearances of events, probably one of the most fundamental questions in event recognition is what defines an event in video? The Oxford English dictionary defines an event as "anything that happens". With such a broad definition it is not surprising that the topic has been addressed in the multimedia retrieval community by many researchers from diverse angles [2, 26, 19, 3, 11].

In this paper, we study event representations that contribute to defining events for automatic recognition. We are inspired by findings from cognition, where research has repeatedly shown that humans remember events by their actors, actions, objects, and locations [20]. Studying event representation based on such high-level concepts is now within reach because of the continued progress in supervised concept detection [22] and the availability of labeled training collections like the ones developed in benchmarks like TRECVID [21], ImageNet [5] and several other venues [13, 7]. In this paper, we name the set of available concept detectors as the *vocabulary* and we study its ideal composition for effective recognition of events in arbitrary web video.

1.1 Representing Events in Video

The state-of-the-art in event recognition represents a video in terms of low-level audiovisual features [15, 23, 14, 9]. In general, these methods first extract from the video various types of static and/or dynamic features, *e.g.*, color SIFT variations [25], MFCC [9], and Dense Trajectories [15]. Second, the descriptors are quantized and aggregated [15]. The robustness and efficiency of various low-level features for recognizing events are evaluated in [23, 9]. Despite their good recognition performance, especially when combined together [14, 9, 15], low-level features are incapable of providing understanding of the semantic structure present in an event. Hence, it is not easy to derive how these event definitions arrive at their recognition. Therefore, essentially different representations are needed for events. We focus on high-level representations for event recognition.

Inspired by the previous works in object recognition [24, 10], scene recognition [10, 17] and activity recognition [18], others have also explored high-level representations for recognition of events [12, 1, 27, 8]. In all these works, the video is represented as the output of numerous pre-trained concept detector scores. In [12], for example, Merler *et al.*

Table 1: Examples of videos and human-added textual descriptions, from which we study how humans describe events.

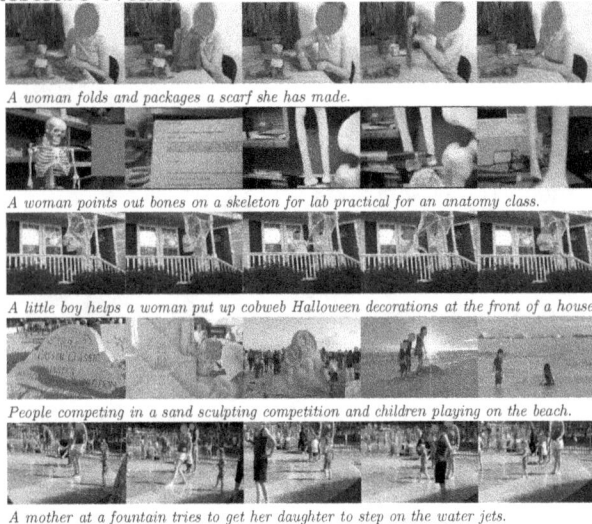

A woman folds and packages a scarf she has made.

A woman points out bones on a skeleton for lab practical for an anatomy class.

A little boy helps a woman put up cobweb Halloween decorations at the front of a house.

People competing in a sand sculpting competition and children playing on the beach.

A mother at a fountain tries to get her daughter to step on the water jets.

arrive at a robust high-level representation of events using 280 concept detectors, which outperforms a low-level audiovisual representations using a state-of-the-art recognition pipeline following three consecutive steps. First, frame extraction, where the videos are decoded and a subset of frames are extracted. Second, concept detection, where a set of pre-trained concept detectors are applied on the extracted frames. Each frame is then represented as a concept vector obtained by concatenating all the detector outputs. Finally, video pooling, where the frame representations are averaged and aggregated into the video level representation. However, in the paper by Merler *et al.*, as well as all the others [1, 27, 8], the question what concepts to include in the vocabulary to represent events is ignored. In this paper, we adopt the event recognition pipeline of [12], but we place special emphasis on what concepts to insert in the vocabulary for effective event recognition.

1.2 What Concepts?

Our study is inspired by the pioneering work of Hauptmann *et al.* [6] who focus on concept vocabularies for broadcast news video. They examined how big the concept vocabulary should be and what concepts should be part of the vocabulary for effective shot retrieval. In their work, the presence and absence of 320 human-annotated concepts was used as the main source for the investigations. By inserting the same amount of noise into each of the human annotations they were able to study news video retrieval accuracy under varying levels of concept quality, arriving at the prediction that 5,000 detectors with modest quality would be sufficient for general-purpose broadcast news video retrieval. However, it is not clear whether their conclusion generalizes to *event* recognition on the challenging domain of unconstrained web video. Regarding the important question what concepts to include in the vocabulary, Hauptmann *et al.* [6] conclude that frequent concepts contribute more to overall news video retrieval performance than rare concepts, but they do not make a distinction with respect to concept type.

In this paper, we start from the analysis by Hauptmann

et al. [6]. We adopt three of their research questions, as well as their idea to insert (additional) noise into the concepts. However, our work is different with respect to the following five aspects. First, we focus exclusively on events, whereas [6] also considers news use cases like *Find shots of U.S. Maps depicting the electoral vote distribution (blue vs. red state)* and *Find shots of Refugee Camps with women and children visible*. Second, our domain of study is unconstrained web video, rather than the highly structured broadcast television domain. Third, we place special emphasis on the importance of various concept types in the vocabulary (e.g., objects, scenes, actions etc.), rather than considering all concepts equally important. Fourth, in our analysis we do not rely on human concept annotations directly, but instead we use real detector predictions with varying levels of accuracy per concept. Finally, we evaluate retrieval accuracy on video-level rather than shot-level. Because of all these differences, we feel a new study on concept vocabularies is justified.

1.3 Research Questions

Our study on the effectiveness of concept vocabularies for video event recognition, is directed by the following four research questions:

RQ1 *How many concepts to include in the vocabulary?*

RQ2 *What concept types to include in the vocabulary?*

RQ3 *Which concepts to include in the vocabulary?*

RQ4 *How accurate should the concept detectors be?*

As humans remember events by the high level concepts they contain, *viz.*, actors, actions, objects, and locations [20], studying the characteristics of the concepts that humans use to describe events could be inspirational for automated event recognition. Therefore, before describing our experimental protocol to address the research questions, we first study the vocabulary that human uses to describe events in videos.

2. HUMAN EVENT DESCRIPTION

To analyze the vocabulary that humans use to describe events, we utilize a set of textual descriptions written by humans to describe web videos containing events. We process textual descriptions for 13,265 videos, as provided by the TRECVID 2012 Multimedia Event Detection task corpus [21]. For each web video in this corpus a textual description is provided that summarizes the event happening in the video by highlighting its dominant concepts. Table 1 illustrates some videos and their corresponding textual descriptions.

After removing stop words and stemming, we end up with 5,433 distinct terms from the 13,265 descriptions making up a human vocabulary for describing events. Naturally, the frequency of these terms varies, as also observed by [6]. Most of the terms seldom occur in event descriptions. Whereas, only a few terms have high term frequencies. To be precise, 50% of the terms occur once in the descriptions and only 2% occurs more than five times. Terms like `man` , `girl`, `perform` and `street` appear most frequent, while `bluefish`, `conductor`, `Mississippi` and `Bulgarian` are instances of less frequent terms.

Looking into the vocabulary, we observe that the terms used in human description can be mapped to five distinct

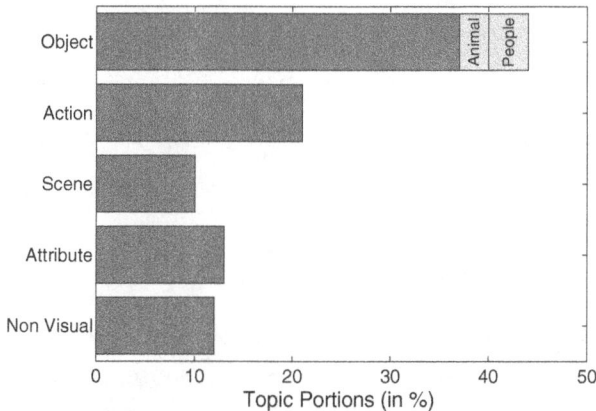

Figure 1: We divide the human vocabulary for describing events into concept types containing objects, actions, scenes, attributes and non-visual concepts. Our analysis reveals that objects and actions constitute 65% of the human vocabulary when describing events.

Table 2: Number of videos in the dataset used for our experiments split per event. Partitioning available from *http://www.mediamill.nl/datasets*.

	Train Set		Test Set	
Event	Positives	Negatives	Positives	Negatives
Attempting board trick	98	8742	49	4376
Feeding animal	75	8745	48	4377
Landing fish	71	8769	36	4389
Wedding ceremony	69	8771	35	4390
Working wood working project	79	8761	40	4385
Birthday party	121	8719	61	4364
Changing vehicle tire	75	8765	37	4388
Flash mob gathering	115	8725	58	4367
Getting vehicle unstuck	85	8755	43	4382
Grooming animal	91	8749	46	4379
Making sandwich	83	8757	42	4383
Parade	105	8735	50	4375
Parkour	75	8765	38	4387
Repairing appliance	85	8755	43	4382
Working sewing project	86	8754	43	4382
Attempting bike trick	43	8797	22	4403
Cleaning appliance	43	8797	22	4403
Dog show	43	8797	22	4403
Giving directions location	43	8797	22	4403
Marriage proposal	43	8797	22	4403
Renovating home	43	8797	22	4403
Rock climbing	43	8797	22	4403
Town hall meeting	43	8797	22	4403
Winning race without vehicle	43	8797	22	4403
Working metal crafts project	43	8797	22	4403

concept types as typically used in the multimedia and computer vision literature: *objects, actions, scenes, visual attributes* and *non visual concepts*. We manually assign each vocabulary term into one of these five types. After this exercise we observe that 44% of the terms refer to *objects*. Moreover, we note that a considerable number of objects are dedicated to various types of *animals* and *people*; *i.e.*, `lion`, and `teen`. About 21% of the terms depict *actions*, like `walking`. Approximately 10% of the concept types are about *scenes*, such as `kitchen`. *Visual attributes* cover about 13% of the terms; *i.e.*, `white`, `flat`, and `dirty`. The remaining 12% of the terms belong to concepts, which are *not visually depictable*; *i.e.*, `poem`, `problem`, and `language`. We summarize the statistics of our human event descriptions in Figure 1.

We observe that when describing video events, humans use terms with varying generalizations. Some terms are very specialized so refer to specific objects; like, `salmon`, `cheesecake` and `sand castle`. While other terms are more general, so refer to broader set of concepts; like `human`, `vegetation` and `outdoor`. We analyze the generalization of the vocabulary terms using their depth in the WordNet hierarchy. In this hierarchy, the terms are structured based on their hypernym/hyponym relations, so the more specialized terms are placed at the deeper levels. Our study shows that the 5,433 vocabulary terms have an average depth of 9.07±5.29. The high variance in term depths indicates that the human vocabulary to describe events is composed of both specific and general terms.

To summarize, we observe that the vocabulary that humans use to describe events is composed of a few thousand words, derived from five distinct concept types: *objects, actions, scenes, visual attributes* and *non visual concepts*. Moreover, we observe that the vocabulary contains both specific and general concepts. Strengthened by these observations about the human vocabulary for describing events, we design four experiments to answer our research questions on the ideal composition for recognizing events in arbitrary web video.

3. EXPERIMENTAL SETUP

To answer the research questions raised in the introduction of the paper, we create a rigorous empirical setting. First, we introduce the video dataset used to evaluate the event recognition experiments. Then we explain the pool of concept detectors, which we employ to create vocabularies. Finally, the pipeline used for event recognition using concept vocabularies is presented.

3.1 Video Dataset

For the event recognition experiments, we rely on the video corpus from the TRECVID 2012 Multimedia Event Detection task [21]. To the best of our knowledge this is the largest publicly available video corpus in the literature for event recognition. The corpus consists of over 1,500 hours of user-generated video with a large variation in quality, length and content. Moreover, it comes with ground truth annotations at video level for 25 real-world events, including life events, instructional events, sport events, etc.. We extract two partitions consisting of 8,840 and 4,434 videos from the development set of the corpus. Development set is the annotated part of the corpus, which is suitable to develop and validate the methods. In this paper we use the larger partition as the training set, on which we train our event recognizers, and we report all results on the smaller partition. We summarize the training and test set statistics of the video dataset per event in Table 2.

3.2 Implementation Details

Concept Vocabulary To create the vocabularies, we need a comprehensive pool of concept detectors. We build this pool of detectors using the human annotated training data from two publicly available resources: the TRECVID 2012 Semantic Indexing task [21] and the ImageNet Large-Scale Visual Recognition Challenge 2011 [4]. The former has annotations for 346 semantic concepts on 400,000 keyframes from web videos. The latter has annotations for 1,000 semantic concepts on 1,300,000 photos. The categories are

Figure 2: Random examples of the 1,346 concept detectors included in the overall vocabulary used in our experiments, grouped by the concept type.

quite diverse and include concepts from various types; *i.e.*, *object*, *scene* and *action*.

Leveraging the annotated data available in these datasets, we train 1,346 concept detectors in total. We follow the state-of-the-art for our implementation of the concept detectors. We use densely sampled SIFT, OpponentSIFT and C-SIFT descriptors [25] with Fisher vector coding [16]. The visual vocabulary used has a size of 256 words. As a spatial pyramid we use the full image and three horizontal bars. The feature vectors representing the training images form the input for a fast linear Support Vector Machine.

As summarized in Figure 1, the concepts that humans use to describe events are derived from *object*, *action*, *scene*, *attributes* and *non visual* concept types. The *non visual* concepts cannot be detected by their visual features, so we exclude them from our study. Regarding to the importance of the actors in depicting events [20], as well as their high frequency in human descriptions, we consider *people* and *animal* as extra concept types in our experiments. Inspired by this composition, we divide our concept pool by manually assigning them to one of these types. Consequently, we end up with the following concept types: *object* containing 706 concepts, *action* containing 36 concepts, *scene* containing 135 concepts, *people* containing 83 concepts, *animal* containing 338 concepts and *attribute* containing 48 concepts. Figure 2 gives an overview of the concept types and example instances.

Event Recognition In the event recognition experiments, we follow the pipeline proposed in [12]. We decode the videos by uniformly extracting one frame every two seconds. Then all the concept detectors are applied on the extracted frames. Concatenating the detector outputs, each frame is represented by a concept vector. Finally the frame represen-

tations are aggregated into a video level representation by averaging and normalization. On top of this concept vocabulary representation per video, we use again a linear SVM classifier to train the event recognizers.

4. EXPERIMENTS

We perform four experiments to address our research questions. Each concept vocabulary used in the experiments is evaluated based on its performance in recognizing events using the pipeline and evaluation protocol described in section 3. Moreover, the vocabularies are all derived from the concept pool introduced in section 3.2.

- **Experiment 1: How many concepts to include in the vocabulary?** To study this question, we create several vocabularies with varying sizes and evaluate their performance for recognizing events. Each vocabulary is made of a random subset of the concept detectors from the concept pool. To compensate for possible random effects, all experiments are repeated 50 times and the results are averaged.

- **Experiment 2: What concept types to include in the vocabulary?** We look into this question by comparing two types of vocabularies: *(i) single type* vocabularies, where all concepts are derived from one type and *(ii) joint type* vocabularies, where concepts are derived from all available concept types. We perform this experiment for six kinds of single type vocabularies: *object*, *action*, *scene*, *people*, *animal* and *attribute* types respectively.

  To make the single type and joint type vocabularies more comparable, we force the vocabularies to be of equal size. We do so by randomly selecting the same number of concepts from the concept pool. All the experiments are repeated 500 times to balance possible random effects.

- **Experiment 3: Which concepts to include in the vocabulary?** In this experiment, we investigate whether the concept vocabulary for event recognition should be made of general or specific concepts. We manually extract two sets of general and specific concepts from the concept pool. The former contains 149 general concepts, *i.e.*, `vegetation`, `human` and `man made thing`, and the latter contains 619 specific concepts, *i.e.*, `religious figure`, `emergency vehicle` and `pickup truck`. The rest of concepts, which are not clearly general or specific, are not involved in this experiment. Using these sets we compare three types of vocabularies: *(i)* *general* vocabulary in which all the concepts are general, *(ii)* *specific* vocabulary in which all the concepts are specific and *(iii)* *mixture* vocabulary in which the concepts are randomly selected from both general and specific concept sets. We repeated this experiment for different vocabulary sizes and found that the results remained stable. The reported results are obtained for a vocabulary size of 70, averaged over 500 repetitions.

- **Experiment 4: How accurate should the concept detectors be?** In this experiment, we decrease the detector accuracies by introducing noise into the concept prediction scores. We gradually increase the amount of noise and measure how the event recognition performance responds.

The output of each concept detector, as a SVM classifier, is a real value number which is supposed to be larger than +1 and smaller than -1 for respectively positive and negative samples. But in practice, SVM only assigns these values to the samples which are confidently classified, while other samples are assigned to the unconfident area in between -1 and 1. Looking into the concept detector predictions, we observe that most of them are agglomerated in the unconfident area. The less accurate a concept detector is, the more samples are assigned to the unconfident area. To simulate the detector accuracy changes, we randomly select predictions and shift them towards center of the unconfident area, which has the least decision confidence. We gradually increase the amount of noise and repeat the experiments 50 times to compensate for possible random factors.

Each experiment results in a ranking of the videos from the test set based on the probability that the video contains the event of interest. As the evaluation criterion for these ranked lists, we employ average precision (AP) which is in wide use for evaluating visual retrieval results [21]. We also report the average performance over all events as the mean average precision (MAP).

5. RESULTS

5.1 Experiment 1: How many?

As shown in Figure 3, adding more concept detectors to the vocabulary improves the event recognition performance.

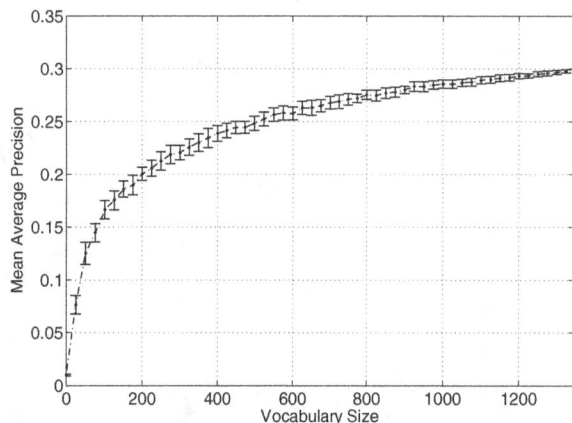

Figure 3: Experiment 1: Increasing the vocabulary size improves the event recognition performance. This improvement is especially prevalent for small vocabularies containing less than 200 concept detectors.

The improvement gain is particularly prevalent for small vocabularies. When increasing the vocabulary from 50 to 300, for example, the MAP increases from 0.125 to 0.221. The improvement is less prevalent when more than 1,000 detectors are part of the vocabulary. When increasing the vocabulary from 1,000 to 1,346 the absolute MAP improvement is only 0.012 on average.

The error bars plotted in Figure 3 indicate the variance in MAPs for various vocabularies. The variance demonstrates that with the same number of concept detectors, some vocabularies perform better than others. In the next two experiments, we study the characteristics of these optimal vocabularies.

Small vocabularies have poor performances in recognizing events. In addition, their efficiency could be rapidly increased by adding few more concepts to them. So, we recommend to include at least 200 concept detectors in the vocabulary.

5.2 Experiment 2: What concept types?

Table 3 compares single type and joint type vocabularies for recognizing events. Comparing the MAPs, we conclude that joint type vocabularies outperform single type vocabularies for all six concept types on average. It demonstrates that when creating the vocabulary, it is better to sample the concept detectors from diverse types. Hence, we need to detect the objects, people, actions and scenes occurring in the video *jointly* to recognize the event properly. In other words, all of the concept types contribute to the recognition of events.

When we analyze individual event recognition results, we observe a few cases exist where a single type vocabulary outperforms the joint type because of the tight connection between the event description and specific concepts. For example, using a single type vocabulary made of *animals* only, we achieve a higher average precision for *"feeding animal"*, *"grooming animal"* and *"dog show"* events in comparison to a joint type vocabulary. Similarly, *"flash mob gathering"*, *"rock climbing"* and *"town hall meeting"* are recognized better by the scene concepts than by the joint vocabulary. Never-

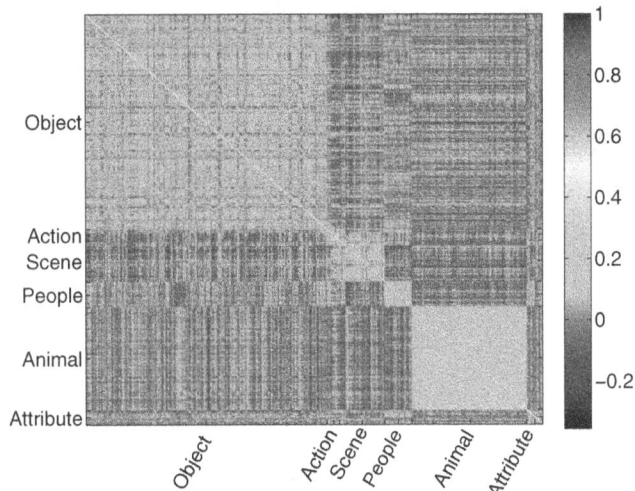

Figure 4: Experiment 2: Correlation between concept detector responses appears especially within a single concept type. Including too many concepts from the same type leads to decreased event recognition performance (matrix smoothed for better viewing).

Table 4: Experiment 3: Comparison of specific, general and mixture vocabularies. The results demonstrate that the general vocabulary outperforms the specific vocabulary on average. The best results are obtained when the vocabulary consists of both general and specific concepts.

Event	Specific	General	Mixture
Attempting board trick	0.090	0.108	**0.130**
Feeding animal	0.041	0.042	**0.045**
Landing fish	0.113	0.107	**0.139**
Wedding ceremony	0.071	0.140	**0.164**
Working wood working project	**0.083**	0.065	0.073
Birthday party	0.078	0.135	**0.138**
Changing vehicle tire	0.058	0.062	**0.071**
Flash mob gathering	0.301	0.284	**0.337**
Getting vehicle unstuck	0.195	0.246	**0.282**
Grooming animal	0.064	0.079	**0.081**
Making sandwich	0.059	0.089	**0.119**
Parade	0.073	**0.203**	0.161
Parkour	0.104	**0.226**	0.210
Repairing appliance	**0.111**	0.098	0.101
Working sewing project	0.076	0.075	**0.082**
Attempting bike trick	0.044	0.080	**0.090**
Cleaning appliance	**0.125**	0.092	0.123
Dog show	0.219	0.178	**0.230**
Giving directions location	0.028	0.019	**0.053**
Marriage proposal	0.013	0.017	**0.025**
Renovating home	0.023	0.074	**0.083**
Rock climbing	0.178	0.156	**0.194**
Town hall meeting	0.064	**0.226**	0.158
Winning race without vehicle	0.102	0.102	**0.117**
Working metal crafts project	**0.040**	0.021	0.036
Mean	0.094	0.117	**0.130**

theless, joint type vocabularies do better than single type vocabularies on average. Therefore, we consider joint type vocabularies more suited for general purpose event recognition.

The performance difference between the single type and joint type vocabularies varies per concept type. For some types, like *animal*, the difference is substantial (0.158 vs. 0.239), while for others, like *action*, it is almost negligible (0.067 vs. 0.076). We attribute the performance difference to at least two reasons. First, our concept detectors are trained on global image level, so they contain considerable amount of contextual information. Consequently, some single types may contain a wide sample of contextual information including 'semantic overlap' from other concept types. The *action*, for example, may contain action detectors in varying scenes using various objects. Second, when creating many concept detectors for a similar type, it is likely the detectors will be correlated to each other, especially for the less diverse types. To clarify this observation we plot the correlation between concept detectors within a concept type in Figure 4. As shown in this figure, the highly correlated concepts tend to belong to the same concept type. Therefore, including too many concepts from the same type in a vocabulary, especially from the less diverse concept types like *animal* and *people*, leads to correlated concepts and should be avoided.

We recommend to make the vocabulary diverse by including concepts from various concept types and to limit the number of concepts for the less diverse types.

5.3 Experiment 3: Which concepts?

Table 4 compares three types of vocabularies: specific, general and mixture. According to the MAPs, the general vocabulary performs better than the specific vocabulary, but the mixture vocabulary is the best overall performer.

We observe that for four events a specific vocabulary out-

performs the others: *"working wood working project"*, *"repairing appliance"*, *"cleaning appliance"* and *"working metal crafts project"*. For these events, there are some specific and discriminative concepts available in the vocabulary. For example, `lumber mill`, `crate` and `circular saw` concepts for *"working wood working project"* and `washing machine`, `refrigerator` and `microwave` concepts for *"repairing appliance"*. While the specific concepts may be distinctive for recognizing some events, the concepts typically occur in only few videos. Hence, they are absent in most videos and do not contribute much to event recognition. Therefore, if the vocabulary consists of specific concepts only, it will perform well in recognizing the events relevant to those concepts, but it will perform poor for other events. In contrast to the specific concepts, general concepts occur in a large numbers of videos. Although these concepts are not discriminative individually, taking several of them together into a vocabulary makes the event recognition better than using a specific vocabulary. Since it is able to simultaneously utilize distinctive specific concepts and general concepts, the best performance is obtained when the vocabulary contains a mixture of both specific and general concepts.

We recommend to insert both general and specific concepts into the event recognition vocabulary.

5.4 Experiment 4: How accurate?

As expected, the results in Figure 5 demonstrate event recognition performance degrades by adding more noise to the concept detector predictions in the vocabulary. When the noise amount is rather small, *i.e.*, up to 30%,, the event recognition remains relatively robust. For a vocabulary containing 1,346 concepts, the performance drops by only 3%

Table 3: Experiment 2: Comparison of single type and joint type vocabularies for event recognition. Each column pair compares a single and joint type vocabulary. To make the vocabularies more comparable within a concept type, we force them to be of equal size. Note that the number of concept detectors (in parenthesis) varies per concept type, so comparison across concept types should be avoided. The results demonstrate that for all the six concept types, joint type vocabularies outperform single type vocabularies on average.

| | Concept Type | | | | | | | | | | | |
| Event | Object(670) | | Action(34) | | Scene(128) | | People(78) | | Animal(321) | | Attribute(45) | |
	Single	Joint	Single	Joint	Single	Joint	Single	Joint	Single	Joint	Single	Joint
Attempting board trick	**0.368**	0.348	0.056	**0.073**	0.115	**0.169**	0.065	**0.119**	0.120	**0.271**	**0.082**	0.079
Feeding animal	0.035	**0.044**	0.029	**0.074**	0.024	**0.042**	0.040	**0.041**	**0.073**	0.045	**0.055**	0.037
Landing fish	0.337	**0.423**	0.055	**0.076**	0.157	**0.246**	0.074	**0.182**	0.323	**0.360**	0.054	**0.111**
Wedding ceremony	0.493	**0.520**	0.054	**0.073**	0.139	**0.193**	**0.141**	0.119	0.162	**0.388**	0.040	**0.070**
Working wood working project	0.194	**0.203**	0.029	**0.040**	0.074	**0.101**	**0.118**	0.072	0.116	**0.167**	0.032	**0.048**
Birthday party	0.264	**0.277**	0.098	**0.099**	0.115	**0.174**	**0.138**	0.131	0.139	**0.239**	0.058	**0.095**
Changing vehicle tire	0.171	**0.174**	0.034	**0.054**	0.073	**0.105**	0.036	**0.076**	0.054	**0.153**	0.043	**0.052**
Flash mob gathering	0.471	**0.494**	**0.257**	0.212	**0.349**	0.304	0.321	**0.337**	0.415	**0.475**	**0.273**	0.251
Getting vehicle unstuck	0.330	**0.362**	0.092	**0.138**	0.186	**0.268**	0.110	**0.217**	0.294	**0.338**	0.069	**0.154**
Grooming animal	0.126	**0.149**	0.033	**0.070**	0.129	**0.147**	0.075	**0.080**	**0.146**	0.127	**0.075**	0.068
Making sandwich	0.178	**0.197**	0.023	**0.061**	0.116	**0.127**	0.050	**0.098**	0.070	**0.176**	0.029	**0.066**
Parade	0.268	**0.304**	**0.169**	0.119	0.215	**0.219**	0.119	**0.182**	0.126	**0.275**	0.093	**0.141**
Parkour	0.398	**0.432**	0.023	**0.063**	0.150	**0.234**	0.034	**0.147**	0.089	**0.356**	0.031	**0.074**
Repairing appliance	0.244	**0.323**	0.063	**0.078**	0.192	**0.224**	0.086	**0.126**	0.104	**0.259**	**0.100**	0.083
Working sewing project	**0.295**	0.252	0.048	**0.075**	0.129	**0.163**	0.107	**0.123**	0.194	**0.238**	0.021	**0.082**
Attempting bike trick	0.480	**0.502**	**0.264**	0.076	**0.250**	0.245	0.037	**0.171**	0.129	**0.392**	0.031	**0.096**
Cleaning appliance	**0.079**	0.064	0.019	**0.039**	0.022	**0.049**	0.021	**0.045**	0.029	**0.058**	0.015	**0.035**
Dog show	0.500	**0.534**	0.093	**0.102**	0.423	**0.455**	0.114	**0.236**	**0.555**	0.512	0.116	**0.122**
Giving directions location	0.029	**0.031**	0.013	**0.027**	0.019	**0.025**	0.011	**0.021**	0.016	**0.029**	0.012	**0.021**
Marriage proposal	0.069	**0.075**	0.016	**0.024**	0.030	**0.033**	**0.027**	0.023	0.018	**0.050**	0.010	**0.016**
Renovating home	0.179	**0.232**	0.011	**0.049**	0.071	**0.120**	0.019	**0.078**	0.085	**0.192**	0.016	**0.053**
Rock climbing	0.347	**0.375**	0.027	**0.092**	**0.217**	0.176	0.101	**0.173**	0.309	**0.322**	0.063	**0.104**
Town hall meeting	0.424	**0.456**	0.059	**0.099**	**0.270**	0.244	0.116	**0.172**	0.266	**0.379**	**0.158**	0.115
Winning race without vehicle	0.139	**0.147**	**0.082**	0.061	0.075	**0.101**	0.069	**0.081**	0.088	**0.138**	**0.073**	0.060
Working metal crafts project	0.052	**0.054**	0.019	**0.032**	0.018	**0.033**	0.020	**0.029**	0.019	**0.038**	0.020	**0.024**
Mean	0.259	**0.279**	0.067	**0.076**	0.142	**0.168**	0.082	**0.123**	0.158	**0.239**	0.063	**0.082**

when the noise amount is 30%. When 50% noise is inserted into the concept detection results for the full vocabulary, the performance drops by 11%. It means that even if 50% of the detector predictions are distorted, the event recognition performance will be degraded by only 11%. Interestingly it implies that improving the current level of concept detector accuracy has at best a limited influence on event recognition performance.

What is more, improving the detector accuracies has the same effect on event recognition performance as adding more detectors to the vocabulary. If we insert 50% noise into the vocabulary made of 50 concept detectors, for example, the event recognition performance is 0.10 in terms of MAP. We may improve the accuracy by removing the noise again, or by adding 50 more (noisy) concept detectors to the vocabulary. In both cases the event recognition performance increases to 0.13 in terms of MAP. Considering the wide availability of large amounts of training data for concept detectors [7], adding more concept detectors seems to be more straightforward than improving the detector accuracies for event recognition vocabularies.

We recommend to increase the size of the concept vocabulary rather than improving the quality of the individual detectors.

6. RECOMMENDATIONS

In this paper we study what composition of detectors in a concept vocabulary leads to the most effective event recognition in arbitrary web video. We consider four research questions related to the number, the type, the specificity and the

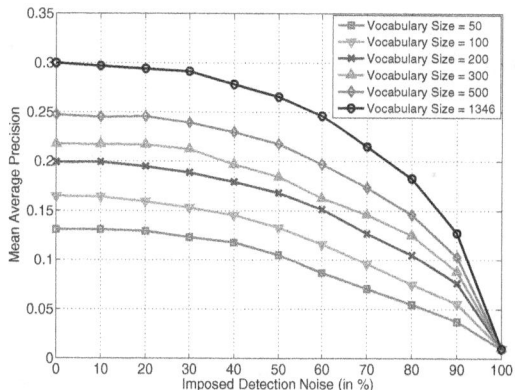

Figure 5: Experiment 4: Event recognition performance is robust when small amounts of noise are inserted into the concept detectors of the vocabulary. The more accurate the concept detectors in a vocabulary, the higher the event recognition performance. However, adding more detectors with the same noise levels may be a more straightforward way to increase event recognition performance.

quality of the detectors in concept vocabularies. From the analysis of our experiments using 1,346 concept detectors, a dataset containing 13,274 web videos, 25 event definitions, and a state-of-the-art event recognition pipeline, we arrive at the following four recommendations:

- **Recommendation 1:** Use vocabularies containing more than 200 concepts.

- **Recommendation 2:** Make the vocabulary diverse by including various concept types: *object*, *action*, *scene*, *people*, *animal* and *attributes*. However, selecting too many concepts from the same type, especially the less diverse concept types, leads to correlated concepts and should be avoided.

- **Recommendation 3:** Include both general and specific concepts into the vocabulary.

- **Recommendation 4:** Increase the size of the concept vocabulary rather than improve the quality of the individual detectors.

The recommendations may serve as guidelines to compose the appropriate concept vocabularies for future event recognition endeavors.

Acknowledgments This research is supported by the STW STORY project, the Dutch national program COMMIT, and by the Intelligence Advanced Research Projects Activity (IARPA) via Department of Interior National Business Center contract number D11PC20067. The U.S. Government is authorized to reproduce and distribute reprints for Governmental purposes notwithstanding any copyright annotation thereon. Disclaimer: The views and conclusions contained herein are those of the authors and should not be interpreted as necessarily representing the official policies or endorsements, either expressed or implied, of IARPA, DoI/NBC, or the U.S. Government.

7. REFERENCES

[1] T. Althoff, H. Song, and T. Darrell. Detection bank: An object detection based video representation for multimedia event recognition. In *ACM MM*, 2012.

[2] N. Babaguchi, Y. Kawai, and T. Kitahashi. Event based indexing of broadcasted sports video by intermodal collaboration. *IEEE TMM*, 4(1):68–75, 2002.

[3] L. Ballan, M. Bertini, A. Del Bimbo, L. Seidenari, and G. Serra. Event detection and recognition for semantic annotation of video. *MTAP*, 51:279–302, 2011.

[4] A. Berg, J. Deng, S. Satheesh, H. Su, and F.-F. Li. Imagenet large scale visual recognition challenge 2011.

[5] J. Deng, W. Dong, R. Socher, L. Li, K. Li, and L. Fei-Fei. Imagenet: A large-scale hierarchical image database. In *CVPR*, 2009.

[6] A. Hauptmann, R. Yan, W. Lin, M. Christel, and H. Wactlar. Can high-level concepts fill the semantic gap in video retrieval? a case study with broadcast news. *IEEE TMM*, 9(5):958–966, 2007.

[7] B. Huet, T. Chua, and A. Hauptmann. Large-scale multimedia data collections. *IEEE MM*, 19(3):12–14, 2012.

[8] L. Jiang, A. Hauptmann, and G. Xiang. Leveraging high-level and low-level features for multimedia event detection. In *ACM MM*, 2012.

[9] Y. Jiang. Super: towards real-time event recognition in internet videos. In *ACM ICMR*, 2012.

[10] L. Li, H. Su, E. Xing, and L. Fei-Fei. Object bank: A high-level image representation for scene classification and semantic feature sparsification. In *NIPS*, 2010.

[11] X. Liu, R. Troncy, and B. Huet. Finding media illustrating events. In *ACM ICMR*, 2011.

[12] M. Merler, B. Huang, L. Xie, G. Hua, and A. Natsev. Semantic model vectors for complex video event recognition. *IEEE TMM*, 14(1):88–101, 2012.

[13] M. Naphade, J. Smith, J. Tesic, S. Chang, W. Hsu, L. Kennedy, A. Hauptmann, and J. Curtis. Large-scale concept ontology for multimedia. *IEEE MM*, 13(3):86–91, 2006.

[14] P. Natarajan, S. Wu, S. Vitaladevuni, X. Zhuang, S. Tsakalidis, U. Park, and R. Prasad. Multimodal feature fusion for robust event detection in web videos. In *CVPR*, 2012.

[15] D. Oneata, M. Douze, J. Revaud, J. Schwenninger, D. Potapov, H. Wang, Z. Harchaoui, J. Verbeek, C. Schmid, R. Aly, K. Mcguiness, S. Chen, N. O'Connor, K. Chatfield, O. Parkhi, R. Arandjelovic, A. Zisserman, F. Basura, and T. Tuytelaars. Axes at trecvid 2012: Kis, ins, and med. In *TRECVID Workshop*, 2012.

[16] F. Perronnin and C. R. Dance. Fisher kernels on visual vocabularies for image categorization. In *CVPR*, 2007.

[17] N. Rasiwasia and N. Vasconcelos. Holistic context models for visual recognition. *IEEE PAMI*, 34(5):902–917, 2012.

[18] S. Sadanand and J. Corso. Action bank: A high-level representation of activity in video. In *CVPR*, 2012.

[19] A. Scherp, R. Jain, M. S. Kankanhalli, and V. Mezaris. Modeling, detecting, and processing events in multimedia. In *ACM MM*, 2010.

[20] J. M. Shipley and T. F. Zack, editors. *Understanding Events*. Oxford Series in Visual Cognition. Oxford University Press, 2008.

[21] A. Smeaton, P. Over, and W. Kraaij. Evaluation campaigns and trecvid. In *ACM MIR*, 2006.

[22] C. G. M. Snoek and A. W. M. Smeulders. Visual-concept search solved? *IEEE Computer*, 43(6):76–78, 2010.

[23] A. Tamrakar, S. Ali, Q. Yu, J. Liu, O. Javed, A. Divakaran, H. Cheng, and H. Sawhney. Evaluation of low-level features and their combinations for complex event detection in open source videos. In *CVPR*, 2012.

[24] L. Torresani, M. Szummer, and A. Fitzgibbon. Efficient object category recognition using classemes. In *ECCV*, 2010.

[25] K. E. A. van de Sande, T. Gevers, and C. G. M. Snoek. Empowering visual categorization with the GPU. *IEEE TMM*, 13(1):60–70, 2011.

[26] L. Xie, H. Sundaram, and M. Campbell. Event mining in multimedia streams. *Proc. IEEE*, 96(4):623–647, 2008.

[27] E. Younessian, T. Mitamura, and A. Hauptmann. Multimodal knowledge-based analysis in multimedia event detection. In *ACM ICMR*, 2012.

Fusing Matching and Biometric Similarity Measures for Face Diarization in Video

Elie Khoury*
*Idiap Research Institute
Rue Marconi 19
Martigny, Switzerland
elie.khoury@idiap.ch

Paul Gay*
†LIUM, University of Maine
Avenue Laennec
Le Mans, France
paul.gay@idiap.ch

Jean-Marc Odobez*
Idiap Research Institute
Rue Marconi 19
Martigny, Switzerland
odobez@idiap.ch

ABSTRACT

This paper addresses face diarization in videos, that is, deciding which face appears and when in the video. To achieve this face-track clustering task, we propose a hierarchical approach combining the strength of two complementary measures: (i) a pairwise matching similarity relying on local interest points allowing the accurate clustering of faces tracks captured in similar conditions, a situation typically found in temporally close shots of broadcast videos or in talk-shows; (ii) a biometric cross-likelihood ratio similarity measure relying on Gaussian Mixture Models (GMMs) modeling the distribution of densely sampled local features (Discrete Cosine Transform (DCT) coefficients), that better handle appearance variability. Experiments carried out on a public video dataset and on the data from the French REPERE challenge demonstrate the effectiveness of our approach in comparison with state-of-the-art methods.

Categories and Subject Descriptors

I.4.9 [**Image Processing and Computer Vision**]: Applications

Keywords

Face diarization; clustering; similarity measures

1. INTRODUCTION

We address the problem of face diarization within videos. That is, we aim to automatically answer the question "who (whose face) appears in the video, and when?", as illustrated in Fig. 1. This task has direct applications in the structuring and indexing of video programs (and beyond, of personal photo or video collections) through the generation of metadata. It is useful as a preprocessing step for browsing or fast annotation of the person identities or form the basis, with audio diarization, for further analysis of people behaviors and of their interaction or relationships [12].

The face diarization process usually consists of four main steps as shown in Fig. 2: (i) shot boundary detection, that aims to split the video stream into homogenous video clips; (ii) face detection, generally consisting in detecting frontal and profile faces within each shot; (iii) face tracking, that temporally extends the face detections within each shot, and finally (iv) a face clustering step that groups all face tracks which belong to the same person. In this paper, we focus on the later step that is the most important and challenging due to potentially large within person variabilities (pose variation, lighting conditions, occlusion, make-up or accessories like glasses) as compared to between person variabilities.

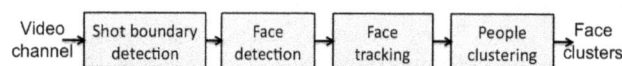

Figure 2: Face diarization process.

Most of the previous work on video face diarization have addressed the problem using matching-based face pairwise similarity measures [3, 20, 7, 10]. That is, they compare two clusters by directly computing the similarity between their corresponding face samples represented by a set of local descriptors like SIFT or Gabor filter outputs that are computed around detected interest points or landmarks. Such approaches are more appropriate for matching and comparing faces acquired within the same conditions. This often corresponds to faces appearing within a TV show episode, or during talk-shows or debates. However, when the face appearance variability increases due to pose, hair cut or illumination changes, the discrimination power of such matching similarity measures drops as the within person measure comparisons become closer to between-person ones. In short, such measures usually lack generalization capabilities.

To address this generalization issue, we propose to rely on biometric model-based approaches [4, 13, 21, 17], whose goals are specifically to handle face variations across conditions and time. In contrast to the matching case, their aim is to represent each face-cluster with a statistical model of the distribution of densely sampled local features (thus reducing alignment issues) whose parameter training leverages on statistics learned *a priori* from thousands of faces thanks to the use of Maximum a Posteriori (MAP) adap-

*This work was supported by the French Research Agency (ANR) under the Project SODA. The authors gratefully thank the ANR for their financial support. More information about ANR-SODA is available from the project web site http://anr-soda.univ-lemans.fr

†This work was done during the stay of the first two authors as visiting researchers at Idiap.

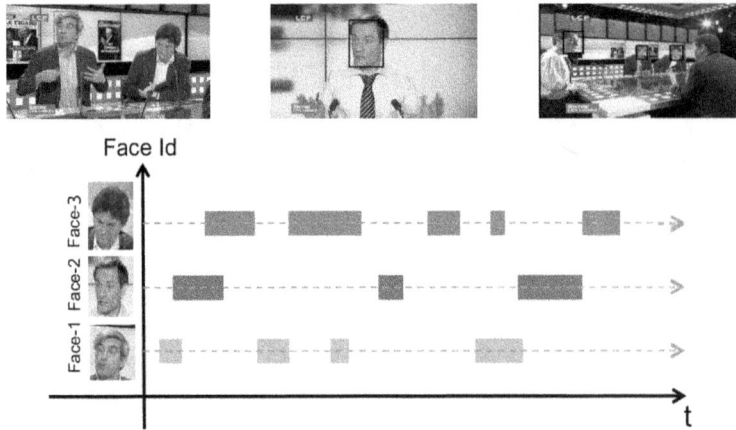

Figure 1: Face diarization task. Top row: Sample frames of a TV debate illustrating variability in face size, pose, background, number of people, etc. Bottom row: example of face diarization output. The system automatically retrieves 4 different faces that appear in the video. It provides all sequences of frames in which each face appears.

tation learning. The similarity between two face-clusters is then estimated by comparing indirectly their statistical models through their evaluation on the corresponding cluster data. Although the statistical modeling leads to less powerful plain matching capabilities, variabilities are better handled.

In this paper, we propose a novel hierarchical bottom-up clustering method that appropriately combines and takes advantage of a feature-based matching similarity measure and a model-based similarity measure. To the best of our knowledge, we are the first to investigate the model-based approach for face clustering, and hence also its combination with matching based methods. Indeed, a key assumption made by our bottom-up clustering method is that the optimal face representation and similarity comparison for clustering depends on the amount of data available and on the degree of face variability that are found in the data. On the one hand the feature-based matching similarity is optimal with relative small variabilities, i.e. when it is possible to perform direct comparison with high confidence, and is thus particularly robust for clustering faces acquired in similar conditions (close moment in time, same scene). In addition, as it has the advantage of being able to perfectly work with small-duration face tracks, it is more appropriate at an early stage of the clustering process. On the other hand the model-based method is optimal when more data is available in initial clusters and when more variabilities are present due to its robustness to several factors. Its exploitation is thus more appropriate at later stages of the clustering.

Experimental validations were conducted on two benchmarks datasets: the public dataset from the TV series "Buffy" provided by [6] exhibiting face variability across episodes, and 38 TV programs from the "REPERE" challenge [9] containing talks shows, news, and debates. They illustrate the behavior of the algorithm and the benefit of our approach, and demonstrate its state-of-the-art performance.

The remainder of this paper is organized as follows: in section 2, we review face clustering related work. Section 3 details the proposed matching-based and model-based measures as well as the hierarchical clustering proposed to combine them. Section 4 describes the datasets, metrics, and experimental results. Section 5 concludes the paper.

2. RELATED WORK

Face clustering requires the design of face representations and comparison approaches robust to intra-person variability (pose, lighting, partial occlusion,...). Below we first review methods that were specifically designed for face clustering, and then discuss biometric methods developed for the different but related face verification or recognition tasks.

In the work of [3, 5, 6, 7], researchers use local descriptors at facial landmarks as face representation. The first one [7] uses pixel-based descriptors while the others rely on points-of-interest descriptors like SIFT or SURF. If the data quality is not sufficient for reliable facial landmark detection, one alternative is to exploit those descriptors computed around automatically detected points-of-interest [3, 10, 19]. In this case, most of the time the spatial information is lost, although [19] keeps it by adding a spatial term depending on key-point positions to compare descriptors between two face images. In the paper, we will refer to these methods as relying on feature-based or matching similarity measures. They usually enable to perform pairwise comparison between images when small face variation are observed.

When clustering faces from videos, a useful preprocessing step can be done by tracking faces on consecutive frames within a shot. This produces face tracks, i.e. the images of a single character across multiple frames within a video shot. Comparing two face tracks offers the possibility to be more robust to pose variations, and this was used in most works cited above, e.g. by using as face-track distance the average of all face distances [10, 11].

Face representations have also been developed in the context of biometric tasks like face verification [4, 14, 17], and in the paper we will refer to them as model-based (or biometric) methods. Indeed, state of the art methods in this domain achieve high robustness by explicitly training a biometric model for each person they want to identify. The model is usually characterized by the parameters of the distribution (often a Gaussian Mixture Model, GMM) of densely sampled features. A first interesting property of these approaches is the use of a Universal Background Model (UBM) which is trained from a large number of subjects and aims at represent all the population. The UBM can be used as prior during fitting, preventing from over-fitting and allowing to handle small amount of data. In addition, the availability of the UBM model allows to compute a likelihood ratio of the test sample between the biometric model and the UBM. In other words, the ratio normalizes the likelihood of a test sample, allowing to detect for instance if a low likelihood of the sample for a biometric model is due to the inappropriateness of the biometric model or due to (potentially noisy) data itself. It is important to note that the UBM methodology has also been used with success for other modalities like in speaker diarization [21]. A second interest of these methods is the use of densely sampled features. For instance, a GMM (adapted from a UBM) representing the distribution of 2D DCT coefficients [14] of spatially neighboring blocks was shown in [4] to be more robust to alignment error than when using local descriptors, and the miss detection problem encountered with facial landmarks is also avoided. However, this is at the cost of the loss of the spatial information.

Despite their interesting properties, up to our knowledge these model-based techniques have never been used for a face clustering task. In our work, we aim at combining the feature-based method and the model-based method by making the following assumption. We state that when the clustering is performed over similar faces with little amount of data, the features-based method is more confident because the GMMs adapted from the UBM are too general to handle those little variations. On the other hand, when there is a high variability and relatively large amount of data, the model-based method becomes the optimal one. Indeed, it is more robust and there is enough data to learn it efficiently. We verified experimentally this assumption in section 4.

It should be noted that additional information can help the face diarization. To better compare people, [7] includes clothes information with a color histogram. [16] exploits uniqueness constraint of a face in a image and the fact that conversations in TV series induces a particular shot structure. Although promising, the inclusion of this additional information is beyond the scope of this paper.

3. PROPOSED FACE CLUSTERING

In this Section, we assume that a video has been first processed, using the different steps described in Fig. 2. At the end of this process, we end up with a set of face tracks $\{FT_i, i \in 1...N^{ft}\}$ that we would like to merge into clusters that contain only tracks of the same person.

Clustering overview. There is a large number of clustering methods. In the speaker diarization [21] and face clustering literature [20, 8], hierarchical bottom-up clustering approaches are dominantly used by state-of-the-art systems. Those approaches start with an over-segmentation of the data with high purity clusters (i.e. containing data of a single person) and then merge the more similar segments. If required, cluster representation is then updated and improved through model fitting as more and more data segments are included into each cluster. Hierarchical methods have no a priori knowledge about the desired number of clusters (the real number of persons), and leave the model selection issue to the choice of a threshold on a fitting criteria or distance. This threshold is often learned using a validation dataset.

In this paper, we follow this approach. Each face-track is initially considered as a cluster. Then, the cluster pairs that are most similar according to a similarity measure D_C are merged until a stopping criterion is verified.

In the following sections, we first describe our face representation, then the two cluster similarities involved in our algorithm, and finally the different clustering strategies we propose to appropriately combine them.

3.1 Face and face track representations

A face contains many discriminative features, like its shape, the eyes, the hair or the skin color. All those features can in principle be used jointly in order to recognize people. However, due to variations in illumination, scale, pose, or due to partial occlusions or un-aligned detections, representing faces (and more generally people) in an invariant yet discriminant fashion is difficult. In this paper, we adopted two types of features that contain complementary information regarding the clustering process.

SURF features. SIFT and SURF [2] features computed on regions around automatically detected points-of-interest are known to be robust to scale, rotation, and illumination variations. While initially developed for wide-baseline matching or image retrieval, they have also shown their interest in face clustering as well [20] due to their ability to provide a good matching measure of faces captured within a given context. For a given face F, the first face representation that we use is given by the set of associated SURF features: $\text{Surf}(F) = \{f_i^{surf}, i = 1, ..., N_F^{surf}\}$.

Discrete Cosine Transform (DCT) features. Detecting interest points is interesting for matching. Unfortunately the point locations do not carry any semantic information, which makes it difficult to build a single model from multiple faces of the same person. One alternative is to detect facial landmarks, and to rely on features extracted around them. However, detecting landmarks is not always trivial, and extracted features may be dependent on the precision of the localization. A solution is to extract features on a dense grid sampling of the face. Indeed, dense sampling has proven to be superior to interest points for many tasks of computer vision, including object, scene, and action recognition. In face biometry, dense feature sampling in combination with statistical models has also proved to be very competitive, even if the localization information is discarded, as shown for instance in [17].

We thus propose to adopt a similar strategy to extract the features of our second face representation: $\text{Dct}(F) = \{f_i^{dct}, i = 1, ..., N^{dct}\}$. More precisely, given the face image, we first estimate the eye locations and use them to register and normalize the image size. This results in an image of 80×64 pixels which is then pre-processed using the Tan and Triggs illumination normalization [15]. Then, the 2D DCT is applied on 8×8 densely sampled overlapping blocks (with a step of 1 pixel between block location), and only the subset of $D_{dim}^{dct} = 28$ low-frequency components of the DCT are kept using zig-zag pattern.

Face track representation. To avoid processing all images of a face track, we decided to only work with a limited number of images per track. More precisely, $N^{kf} = 9$ key-faces are selected from each face-track by dividing the track in equal intervals.

3.2 Matching cluster similarity

To define the cluster similarity, we first have to define the similarity between individual faces.

Face feature similarity. As feature similarity between two faces F_1 and F_2, we use the "Average N-Minimal Pair Distance" (ANMPD) $d_s(F_1, F_2)$ between the two sets of SURF features that was proposed in [10]. As its name suggests, the ANMPD measure returns the average of the N (we used $N = 6$ in this work) smallest distances between the SURF feature vectors that match between the two faces. The measure d_s is thus small when the face similarity is high.

Matching cluster similarity. Considering two face-clusters C_i and C_j with their associated set of keyfaces $\{F_a^i, a = 1, \ldots, N_i\}$ and $\{F_a^j, a = 1, \ldots, N_j\}$, we compared them using the following cluster similarity:

$$D_f(C_i, C_j) = \frac{1}{N_i N_j} \sum_{a=1}^{N_i} \sum_{b=1}^{N_j} d_s(F_a^i, F_b^j) \qquad (1)$$

By definition, this measure favors the creation of compact clusters where all faces are compared to each other. In practice, we have found this to work as effectively as other approaches which for instance only seeks for the best subset of most similar faces between the two image sets. Note that after merging C_i and C_j, the similaritys between the new cluster $C_{i'}$ and any other cluster C_k can be computed recursively as:

$$D_f(C_{i'}, C_k) = \frac{N_i \times D_f(C_i, C_k) + N_j \times D_f(C_j, C_k)}{N_i + N_j} \qquad (2)$$

3.3 Model-based similarity

As motivated in the introduction, statistical models for representing the distribution of local descriptors are powerful tools to handle face variabilities while keeping information about the distinctive features. In this work, we use Gaussian Mixture Models (GMM) which have proved to be robust in this context, and allow the exploitation of reliable Maximum A Posteriori (MAP) parameter estimation schemes. Below, we describe the model, how to learn it, and then define the inter-cluster similarity measure that we use.

Model and parameter learning. We model the likelihood of any DCT feature vector f^{dct} within a face image as:

$$p(f^{dct}|\Lambda) = \sum_{i=1}^{N_g} \omega_i \mathcal{N}(f^{dct}; \mu_i, \Sigma_i) \qquad (3)$$

where $\Lambda = \{\omega_i, \mu_i, \Sigma_i, i = 1\ldots N_g\}$ represent the GMM model parameters (we used $N_g = 200$ gaussians which is a good trade-off between effectiveness and efficiency). Thus, for a cluster C_i containing the faces $F_{ij}, j = 1, \ldots, N_i$, the set of local features is defined as the union of features over all faces: $\mathrm{Dct}(C_i) = \bigcup_j \mathrm{Dct}(F_{ij})$. Its log-likelihood L for a given model Λ is then given as:

$$L(\mathrm{Dct}(C_i)|\Lambda) = \prod_{f^{dct} \in \mathrm{Dct}(C_i)} p(f^{dct}|\Lambda) \qquad (4)$$

In practice, rather than using Maximum Likelihood, the GMM model parameters Λ_i of cluster i are learned through mean-only MAP adaptation from a prior universal background model (Λ_{ubm}) trained on an independent large dataset of images. This avoids the over-fitting problems that can occur given the large amount of parameters and the potentially low number of training faces.

Cross-likelihood ratio. To compare two face-clusters C_i and C_j with their corresponding model parameters, we rely on the Cross Likelihood Ratio (CLR) defined as:

$$CLR(C_i, C_j) = log \frac{L(\mathrm{Dct}(C_i)|\Lambda_j)}{L(\mathrm{Dct}(C_i)|\Lambda_{ubm})} + log \frac{L(\mathrm{Dct}(C_j)|\Lambda_i)}{L(\mathrm{Dct}(C_j)|\Lambda_{ubm})} \qquad (5)$$

The CLR is a symmetric similarity measure, which is positive when the clusters are similar, and negative in the other case. It captures how well the features from one cluster are likely according to the model of the other cluster, as compared to the likelihood given by the UBM model, and vice-versa. The UBM model thus serves as a reference. It allows to distinguish for instance whether a low data likelihood is due to an inadequacy with the tested model, or to the data itself.

Model-based similarity measure. The similarity measure that we used is defined as follows. Given an initial set of clusters $\{C_1, \ldots, C_{N_{init}}\}$, a model is trained for each cluster, and the CLR similarity between these clusters, denoted as $S_m(C_i, C_j) = CLR(C_i, C_j)$, is computed. Then, after each merge, we have a new cluster $C_{i'} = C_i \cup C_j$ with its size $N_{i'} = N_i + N_j$. We then define the new similarity of this cluster with any other cluster k as:

$$S_m(C_{i'}, C_k) = \frac{N_i \times S_m(C_i, C_k) + N_j \times S_m(C_j, C_k)}{N_i + N_j} \qquad (6)$$

Qualitatively, this means that rather than learning a single face model from all data belonging to a cluster -that could be corrupted in case of wrong merging of faces from different people- and exploiting it for likelihood evaluation, we prefer to rely on the original face models learned on purer clusters to evaluate the likelihood of a cluster k data, and defined this later one as a weighted average of its likelihood with respect to the models of all initial cluster belonging to the cluster i'.

3.4 Fusing matching-based and model-based methods

The matching similarity D_f and model-based similarity measure S_m satisfy different purposes. The first one is adequate to directly find matches between face tracks acquired in very similar conditions, while the second one, that may require to have sufficient data to adapt the GMM model, can better handle appearance variability at the cost of loosing some face representation accuracy. From a bottom-up clustering perspective, this means that the first one is more adapted at the beginning of the clustering process, whereas the second one can be applied later on. We therefore have adopted the following strategy:

- first, apply the clustering using only the feature-based similarity, ie define D_C as D_f;

- once a threshold is reached, i.e. $D_f(C_i, C_j) \geq T_f$ for any two cluster, use the current clusters as base cluster to learn GMM models (see previous section), and continue the clustering using a combination of the measures as cluster dissimilarity:

$$D_C(C_i, C_j) = D_f(C_i, C_j) - \alpha S_m(C_i, C_j) \qquad (7)$$

where $\alpha \geq 0$ denotes the contribution of the model-based similarity to the overall merging criterion.

Figure 3: Detected face samples for the character "Joyce" in Buffy: first three samples extracted from Episode 1, last three from Episode 3. Notice the higher appearance variability between the inter episode samples than the intra episode ones.

4. EXPERIMENTAL EVALUATION

We first describe the datasets used in our experiments before presenting the evaluation metrics in section 4.2. Further evaluation protocols and results are detailed in section 4.3.

4.1 Datasets Description

Two datasets are used in order to evaluate the different contributions of our work.

Buffy dataset. The first dataset was used in [8, 6]. It contains 327 face-tracks selected from episodes 9, 21 and 45 of the TV series "Buffy the vampire slayer", where each episode belongs to a different season of the series to provide face variabilities. Face tracks were obtained using an automatic system, and false positive tracks and face-tracks that did not belong to the 8 main actors were manually discarded. This dataset shows generally a higher appearance variability between inter episode tracks with respect to intra episode ones tracks, as illustrated in Fig 3.

REPERE dataset. The second dataset contains 38 video files from the french evaluation challenge REPERE [9]. The videos feature news, debates and talk-shows recorded from two french information TV channels (LCP and BFM). The videos were manually but partially annotated by ELDA[1]. The total duration of the recordings is 21.5 hours, with 3 hours manually annotated. There are 1076 face tracks (initial clusters) that belong to 264 people. This dataset is challenging due to the large number of clusters, very unbalanced cluster sizes (ranging from one when a person appears in a single shot, to several tenth for anchor men or invited people) and view point changes. As with the first dataset, an automatic face track extraction algorithm was applied to the videos, that lead to different types of error, ans we similarly filtered out false-positive erroneous tracks to allow evaluation of the clustering task only.

For experimental and hyper-parameter setting purposes and following the REPERE experimental protocol, the dataset was further divided into a development set (DEV), and a test set (TEST) of 28, and 10 videos, respectively.

4.2 Evaluation metric

Buffy dataset. To allow comparison on this dataset, we used the clustering metric proposed in [8] and also used in [6]. It computes the number of clicks that would be needed to manually correct the automatic output and obtain the ideal result. More precisely, in this scheme, it is assumed that one click is needed to associate the correct name to a cluster (even containing wrong face-tracks), and that one click is needed to provide the correct name of a face-track whose identity is different than that assigned to the cluster it belongs to.

REPERE dataset. In this case, we primarily evaluated the methods in term of Diarization error rate (DER) that was previously proposed for speaker diarization in the NIST RT [2] competitions, and provided as well the results in terms of clicks for comparison with the Buffy dataset. The DER is computed from the ratio of three error rates divided by the total duration of the video: a miss detection error rate, that counts the number of times a face that exists in the ground truth is not detected by the automatic system; a false alarm error rate, that counts the number of times a face is detected by the system while no corresponding face is available in the ground truth[3]; and the confusion error rate, that counts the number of times for a given face, the ground truth identity associated with the cluster label automatically provided by system does not match the one in the ground truth for that face. In this dataset, methods are applied separately to each of the videos, and the final performance is obtained by measuring the DER from the aggregated error rates.

Compared methods. We compared three methods with our system. The two first ones rely on the individual (dis) similarity measure: D_f corresponds to using only the feature-based matching dissimilarity measure. The clustering is conducted until a threshold T_f is reached. S_m corresponds to using only the model-based distance (until a threshold T_m is reached). Finally, D_C denotes the combined method, as described in section 3.4. Note that all involved thresholds are learned on the development set for the REPERE data.

4.3 Experimental Results

Results on the Buffy dataset. Fig. 4 and Table 1 present the results obtained with the different clustering methods. In addition, it also shows the results from [8, 6] and reported in [6]. All three methods perform bottom-up clustering and rely on a face represented using a fixed set of descriptors computed around facial landmarks, but differs on the metric used to compare two faces: L2 uses a Euclidian distance; LFW uses a metric learned from the Labeled-Face-in-the-Wild dataset; and UML uses a metric learned in a discriminative and unsupervised fashion using faces within tracks as positive samples, and faces from different tracks in a given shot as negative samples.

Fig. 4 shows the evolution of the performance metric in function of the number of cluster (in logarithmic scale), where for clarity we have split the results into two figures. From the top one, we can see that (i) both our feature-based D_f and model-based S_m approaches outperforms the landmark-based method relying on L2 and LFW metrics; (ii) the feature-based D_f outperforms S_m, probably due to the lack of training data at initialization for the model-based approach S_m; (iii) the feature-based D_f outperforms the UML approach [6] for a number of clusters higher than 60, but then perform worse as the number of clusters is reduced. This might be explained by the ability of our feature-based method to better match similar face images, and its higher difficulty when more variability is present.

The bottom plot of Fig. 4 further shows the result using our combined approach D_C (for $\alpha = 0.5$). As can be seen, it outperforms both the single measure based clustering D_f

---

[2]http://nist.gov/itl/iad/mig/rt.cfm
[3]Note that as we removed these false alarms after the tracking process, this rate will be 0 in reported experiments.

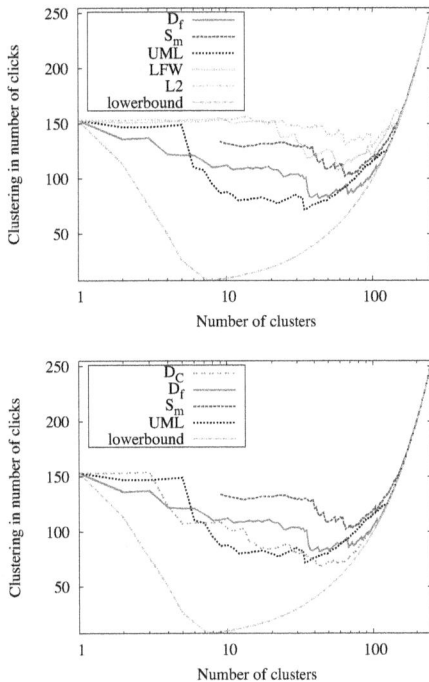

Figure 4: Results on the Buffy dataset. Number of clicks with regards to the number of clusters. Top: comparison between the proposed D_f and S_m measures and the L2, LFW and UML metrics [6]. Bottom: comparison of our proposed combination approach D_C with D_f, S_m and UML.

Table 1: Minimum number of clicks needed to correct the automatic on the Buffy dataset.

Method	Minimum Number of Clicks	Number of Clusters
L2	129	98
LFW	106	58
UML	72	34
D_f	82	43
S_m	102	65
D_C	**68**	44

and S_m, and is better than or equivalent to UML at the beginning of the clustering process (number of clusters higher than 38) and then is worse or better depending on the number of clusters. Table 1 details the values of the minimum number of clicks and its corresponding number of clusters for each of the methods. It shows that our combined approach D_C provides the best result with 68 clicks, showing its ability to achieve state-of-the-art results. In this case, 60 clicks come from the clustering errors, and the remaining 8 clicks come from annotating the clusters with their real names which makes the percentage of clicks due to the clustering errors equal to 23.3%.

In order to highlight the different behavior of the D_f and S_m measures, we computed their intra- and inter-episode values for the main character (Joyce) of the dataset. Fig. 5 plots the resulting corresponding cumulative histograms. Qualitatively, we can see from the top figure that D_f is suitable at comparing similar faces with high accuracy, as illustrated by the fact that 26% of intra-episode measures are lower

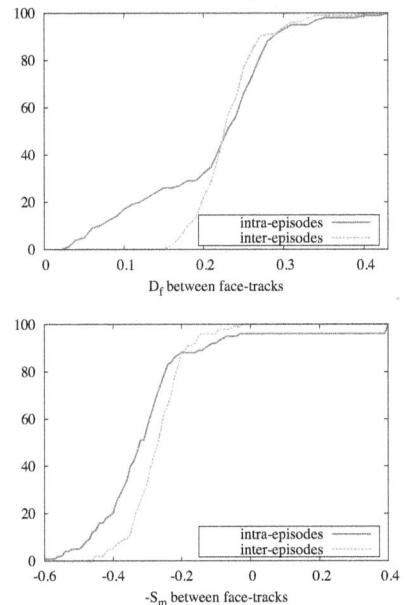

Figure 5: Cumulative percentage of tracks pairs from the character Joyce whose pairwise (dis)similarity measures are below a given threshold for the D_f (top) and $(-S_m)$ (bottom) measures when considering track pairs within an episode or between an episode.

than any inter-episode measure. As a comparison, for S_m, only 12% of intra-episodes have higher similarity than any inter-episode similarity.

Results on the REPERE dataset. For this dataset, as we deal with multiple videos, we need to set the parameters involved in the different algorithms: for the D_f and $(-S_m)$ approaches, this mainly corresponds to the thresholds T_f and T_m respectively to be used to stop the clustering process. For the combined approach[4], there are the coefficient α controlling the contribution of the model-based measure to the overall dissimilarity measure (cf Eq. 7), and the stopping threshold T_C. These parameters are tuned to provide the best result for a given approach on the development set (DEV), and then further used on the TEST set. Results are presented in Table 2, where the minimum DER obtained by optimizing the parameters is reported as **min-DER**. Note that we also report on the DEV set the DER (denoted **cross-DER**) obtained through cross-validation: for each video, the parameters are tuned using the remaining files and used to the DER on that file. This is repeated for all files, and finally their average DER is computed. The cross-DER reduces the impact of files that have relatively long duration and provide an idea of the performance variance due to parameter setting.

According to the results in Table 2, we can see that the combined approach outperforms both the D_f and S_m methods on the DEV and TEST sets: we obtain at least 14% relative gain (in terms of cross-DER) on the DEV set and around 35% of relative gain on the TEST set. Interestingly, we can notice that the S_m approach provides the more stable results with respect to the stopping criterion, as there

---

[4]For this combined approach, the threshold T_f for which only the feature-based measure is used in the initial clustering stage was set to 0.09, see Section 3.4.

the cross-validation on the DEV provides the same results than when doing a direct optimization of the results, and the TEST results are closer to the DEV ones. This is probably due to the use of the UBM model and the inherent data normalization that it provides in the cross-likelihood ratio.

Fig. 7 illustrates qualitatively the output of the 3 clustering methods for 2 different persons, and where each row corresponds to an automatic output cluster. For person 1, the S_m based clustering suffers not only from sub-clustering, but also from confusion (mixing up 2 different persons in the same cluster). On the other hand, the D_f based clustering suffers from sub-clustering. However, the clustering output for that person is perfect for the combined measure. Similar observation is found for person 2.

Impact of different α values. Fig. 6 shows the results obtained by varying the contribution of the model-based measure to the overall cluster dissimilarity measure. The behavior is quite similar on the two datasets, with optimal values found in the 0.3 to 0.5 range. It is also worthy to notice that the clustering error rate of the combination measure D_C in this range is lower than the error rates obtained by D_f and S_m alone (the curve keeps increasing beyond 0.7).

Difficulty of the databases. We also evaluated the clustering on REPERE database using the metric used on Buffy database. In this case, the percentage of clicks due to the clustering errors on both DEV and TEST sets are equal to 7.6% and 4.5%, respectively less than the one obtained on Buffy (23.3%). This shows that, the clustering task is more challenging on series and movies than on news and debates. Note however that in this domain, there is some discrepancies between programs, where lively talk-shows actually generate more errors than political debates.

5. CONCLUSIONS

We proposed a face diarization method which combines a feature-based and a model-based (dis)similarity measures. We show that each measure is the most efficient in different cases depending on the variability of the faces and the sizes of the clusters. The two approaches are combined appropriately, and this results in a decrease of the diarization error rate. As a future work, the automatic extraction of head pose [1] could be used to generate pose dependent face models and improve comparison between faces, while additional person detector [18] would allow a better tracking of people. We also plan to extend our work to a person diarization method, by integrating more visual features derived from clothes [16], and integrate audio information. The similarity between our face diarization method and the models from speaker diarization [21] should facilitate this integration.

6. REFERENCES

[1] S. O. Ba and J. M. Odobez. A rao-blackwellized mixed state particle filter for head pose tracking. In *ACM-ICMI Worksh. on Multi-modal Multi-party Meeting Processing(MMMP)*, pages 9–16, 2005.

[2] H. Bay, T. Tuytelaars, and L. V. Gool. Surf: Speeded up robust features. *ECCV*, pages 404–417, 2006.

[3] M. Bicego, A. Lagorio, E. Grosso, and M. Tistarelli. On the use of sift features for face authentication. In *CVPRW*, pages 35–35. IEEE, 2006.

[4] F. Cardinaux, C. Sanderson, and S. Bengio. User authentication via adapted statistical models of face

images. *IEEE Trans. on Signal Processing*, pages 361–373, 2006.

[5] W. Chu, Y. Lee, and J. Yu. Visual language model for face clustering in consumer photos. In *ACM Int. Conf. on Multimedia*, pages 625–628, 2009.

[6] R. Cinbis, J. Verbeek, and C. Schmid. Unsupervised metric learning for face identification in tv video. In *IEEE ICCV*, pages 1559–1566, 2011.

[7] M. Everingham, J. Sivic, and A. Zisserman. Taking the bite out of automated naming of characters in tv video. *Image and Vision Computing*, pages 545–559, 2009.

[8] M. Guillaumin, J. Verbeek, and C. Schmid. Is that you? metric learning approaches for face identification. In *IEEE ICCV*, pages 498–505, 2009.

[9] J. Kahn, O. Galibert, M. Carré, A. Giraudel, P. Joly, and L. Quintard. The repere challenge: Finding people in a multimodal context. In *Odyssey The Speaker and Language Recognition Workshop*, 2012.

[10] E. Khoury, C. Senac, and P. Joly. Face-and-clothing based people clustering in video content. In *ACM MIR*, pages 295–304, 2010.

[11] E. Khoury, C. Senac, and P. Joly. Audiovisual diarization of people in video content. *Multimedia Tools and Applications*, 2012.

[12] S. Kim, F. Valente, and A. Vinciarelli. Automatic detection of conflicts in spoken conversations: Ratings and analysis of broadcast political debates. In *IEEE ICASSP*, 2012.

[13] S. Lucey and T. Chen. A gmm parts based face representation for improved verification through relevance adaptation. In *CVPR*, pages II–855, 2004.

[14] C. Sanderson and K. Paliwal. Fast features for face authentication under illumination direction changes. *Pattern Recognition Letters*, (14):2409–2419, 2003.

[15] X. Tan and B. Triggs. Enhanced local texture feature sets for face recognition under difficult lighting conditions. *IEEE Transactions on Image Processing*, (6):1635–1650, 2010.

[16] M. Tapaswi, M. Bauml, and R. Stiefelhagen. "knock! knock! who is it?" probabilistic person identification in tv-series. In *IEEE CVPR*, pages 2658–2665, 2012.

[17] R. Wallace, M. McLaren, C. McCool, and S. Marcel. Cross-pollination of normalization techniques from speaker to face authentication using gaussian mixture models. *IEEE Transactions on Information Forensics and Security*, 7(2):553–562, 2012.

[18] J. Yao and J.-M. Odobez. Fast human detection from joint appearance and foreground feature subset covariances. *Computer Vision and Image Understanding (CVIU)*, 115(10):1414–1426, 2011.

[19] S. Zhao, F. Precioso, and M. Cord. Spatio-temporal tube kernel for actor retrieval. In *IEEE ICIP*, pages 1885–1888, 2009.

[20] S. Zhao, F. Precioso, M. Cord, and S. Philipp-Foliguet. Actor retrieval system based on kernels on bags of bags. In *EUSIPCO*, pages 234–778, 2008.

[21] X. Zhu, C. Barras, S. Meignier, and J. Gauvain. Combining speaker identification and bic for speaker diarization. In *Europ. Conf. on Speech Communication and Technology*, pages 2441–2444, 2005.

Table 2: REPERE dataset. Diarization error rate (DER) on the DEV and TEST sets. The hyper-parameters tuned on the DEV set (corresponding to the min-DER results) were: $T_f = 0.15$ for D_f; $T_m = 0.15$ for S_m measure; and $(\alpha, T_C) = (0.3, 0.13)$ for the combined approach. These parameters were used on the TEST set. Cross-DER are the results obtained through parameter cross-validation on the DEV set.

Method	cross-DER (DEV)	min-DER (DEV)	DER (TEST)
D_f	6.41%	5.13%	8.33%
S_m	6.68%	6.68%	8.21%
D_C	**5.49%**	**4.37%**	**5.28%**

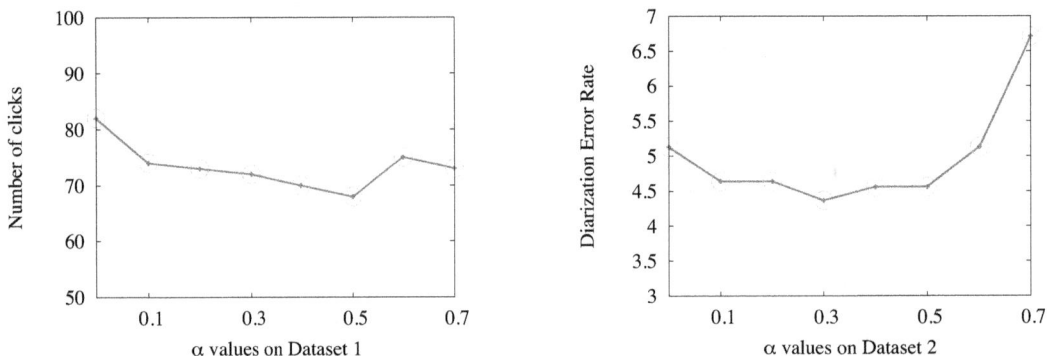

Figure 6: Impact of α on the performance on the two datasets. For the Buffy dataset the minimum number of clicks is used as measure. For the second dataset, we report the min-DER on the DEV set.

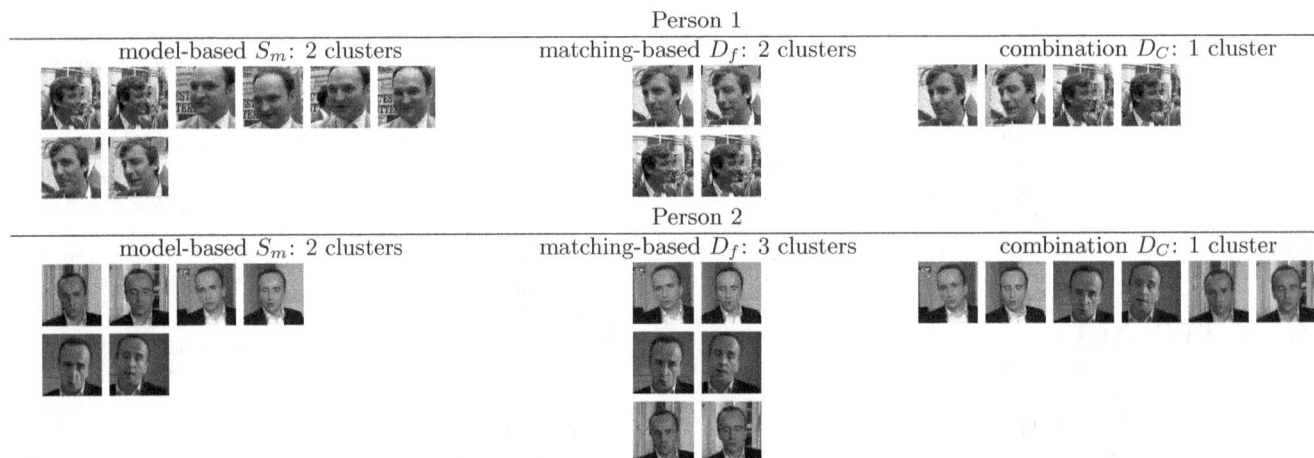

Figure 7: Illustration of the clustering results for the 3 methods discussed here. For each person and each method, all the clusters containing that person are represented by 2 images per face track. Each row corresponds to an automatic output cluster.

Getting the Look: Clothing Recognition and Segmentation for Automatic Product Suggestions in Everyday Photos

Yannis Kalantidis[1,2]
ykalant@image.ntua.gr

Lyndon Kennedy[1]
lyndonk@yahoo-inc.com

Li-Jia Li[1]
lijiali@yahoo-inc.com

[1]Yahoo! Research
[2]National Technical University of Athens

ABSTRACT

We present a scalable approach to automatically suggest relevant clothing products, given a single image without metadata. We formulate the problem as *cross-scenario retrieval*: the query is a real-world image, while the products from online shopping catalogs are usually presented in a clean environment. We divide our approach into two main stages: a) Starting from articulated pose estimation, we segment the person area and cluster promising image regions in order to detect the clothing classes present in the query image. b) We use image retrieval techniques to retrieve visually similar products from each of the detected classes. We achieve clothing detection performance comparable to the state-of-the-art on a very recent annotated dataset, while being more than 50 times faster. Finally, we present a large scale clothing suggestion scenario, where the product database contains over one million products.

Categories and Subject Descriptors

H.3.3 [**Information Storage and Retrieval**]: Information Search and Retrieval—*search process, retrieval models*; I.4.10 [**Image Processing and Computer Vision**]: Image Representation

Keywords

Clothing suggestion, clothing detection, large-scale clothing retrieval, clothing segmentation, automatic product recommendation

1. INTRODUCTION

Many hours are spent every day in front of celebrity and non-celebrity photographs, either captured by professionals in fashion magazines or by friends on Facebook and Flickr. With online clothing shopping revenue increasing, it is apparent that suggesting related clothing products to the viewer can have substantial impact to the market. As

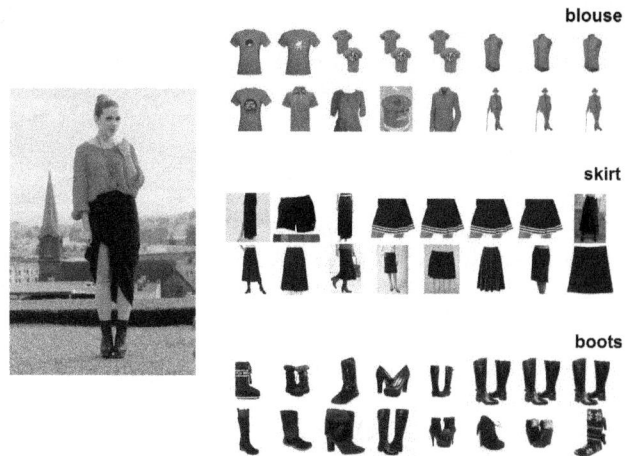

Figure 1: Left: The query image, which is a real world image depicting the person whose clothing style we want to 'copy'. Right: Clothing product suggestions, based on the detected classes and the visual appearance of the corresponding regions.

only a very small percentage of such images has metadata related to its clothing content, suggestions through automatic *visual* analysis can be a very appealing alternative to costly manual annotation.

We formulate automatic suggestion of products from online shopping catalogs as a *cross-scenario retrieval* problem[8], since the query is a real-world image, while the related products are usually presented in a clean and isolated environment. As we want our approach to be able to handle product database sizes containing millions of items, we need to apply large scale image retrieval methods that use indexes of sub-linear complexity. However, the difference in context between the query and results does not allow traditional image retrieval techniques to be directly used.

The example seen in Figure 1 depicts the main use case for the desired application. The query image on the left is a real-world photo with a stylish woman in a prominent position. Product photos from online shopping databases are like the ones shown on the right, *i.e.* clean photos of clothing parts that are either worn by models or are just presented on a white background. Product photos are usually accompanied by category level annotation.

We divide our approach in two main stages: a) Detect the clothing classes present in the query image by classification of promising image regions and b) use image retrieval techniques to retrieve visually similar products belonging to each class found present.

The contribution of our work is threefold: We present a novel framework for a fully automated cross-scenario clothing suggestion application that can suggest clothing classes for a query image in the order of a few seconds. We propose a simple and effective segment refinement method, in which we first limit segmentation only on image regions that are found to have a high probability of containing clothing, over-segment and then cluster the over-segmented parts by appearance. Finally, we present a novel region representation via a binary spatial appearance mask normalized on a pose estimation referenced frame that facilitates rapid classification without requiring an actual learning step. The presented framework is fast and scalable, allowing our clothing classification and similar product search to trivially scale to hundreds of product classes and millions of product images respectively. To our knowledge, this is the first time that clothing suggestion together with fine-grained clothing detection and segmentation is performed at this scale and speed.

The rest of the work is organized as follows: Section 2 discusses the related work. Section 3 presents our clothing class detection approach and Section 4 describes the large scale retrieval experiments. Section 5 presents the experimental evaluation of the approach and finally Section 6 concludes the paper and summarizes the work.

2. RELATED WORK

There has been a great deal of work in the last few years on the subject of clothing recognition. However, many works focus on special clothing classes and applications [3, 15, 14, 5, 2] and it is only recently that generic clothing recognition has been directly tackled [16]. The vast majority of the related work, as well as the approach presented here, is based on person detection and pose estimation.

In [5], Gallagher and Chen attempt to jointly solve identity recognition and clothing segmentation. They limit their approach on the torso region, which they segment using graph cuts based on a clothing model learned from one or multiple images believed to be the same person wearing the same clothing. The clothing model of each person utilizes a automatically extracted clothing mask for the torso region. In this work, we extract a *global* clothing prior probability map for the whole body, that is in our case inferred from all training images and clothing classes.

Chen *et al.* [2] focus on attribute learning, *i.e.* learning semantic attributes to describe clothing. They model clothing style rules by a conditional random field on top of the classification predictions from individual attribute classifiers and propose a new application that predicts the dressing style of a person or an event by analyzing a group of photos. Song *et al.* [14] advocate the prediction of human occupations via their clothing. They represent image patches with semantic-level patterns such as clothes and haircut styles and use methods based on sparse coding. As in [5], both the approaches of [2] and [14] focus only on the torso region and therefore cannot be used for generic clothing parsing.

Wang and Ai [15] are interested in images with a large number of people present and propose a novel multi-person clothing segmentation algorithm for highly occluded images. Cushen and Nixon [3] focus on the semantic segmentation of

primarily monochromatic clothing and printed/stitched textures. Once again, as in the works described above, only the torso/upper human body part is analyzed and represented in both works.

Recently, Liu *et al.* [8] first introduced the notion of cross-scenario clothing retrieval. In their approach, they use an intermediate annotated auxiliary set to derive sparse reconstructions of the aligned query image human parts and learn a similarity transfer matrix from the auxiliary set to the online shopping set to derive cross-scenario similarities. Their approach is fast, it works however on the more general upper- and lower-part clothing matching and similarity between two pieces of clothing is measured by the number of common attributes. In another very recent work, Liu *et al.*[7] also presented the 'magic closet system' for clothing recommendations. They treat the clothing attributes as latent variables in a latent Support Vector Machine based recommendation model, to provide occasion-oriented clothing recommendation. Both these approaches cannot be applied to finer clothing detection, where a more accurate segmentation of the clothing is needed.

A recent work closely related to ours is the work by Yamaguchi *et al.* [16]. The authors start from superpixels and articulated pose estimation in order to predict and detect the clothing classes present in a real-world image. They also proceed by using the clothing estimates to improve pose estimation and introduce the *Fashionista* dataset that we also use in this work. Since this approach tackles the generic clothing classification problem it is the work that we compare against in the experiments section.

As in [16], an accurate pose estimation provides a good starting point for our algorithm. Bad pose estimations are one of the main reasons behind failure cases (see Figure 2 (right) and Section 5).

3. CLOTHING CLASSIFICATION

In this section, we describe our novel approach for detecting and classifying clothing regions in the query image. For the query image, we start from a successful pose estimation, and present a novel approach to isolate the most promising parts of the image in terms of clothing. We then use segmentation to segment them into visually coherent regions and proceed by clustering the segments to allow spatially distant ones to merge into a single non-connected region (*e.g.* the two sides of an open jacket). To describe the region's location and shape relative to the detected human pose we present a novel binary representation, the *spatial appearance mask*, with which we classify all query regions by proximity to a set of annotated samples from training images. There is no actual learning involved, the training set regions are represented by spatial appearance masks and indexed in an LSH index.

3.1 Articulated Pose Estimation

A popular choice when it comes to clothing recognition is to start from human *pose estimation*. Specifically, as in [16] and [8], we base our approach on the articulated pose estimation algorithm of Yang and Ramanan [17]. Given an image I where a person is successfully detected, we are provided with a set of $N_p = 26$ *body parts*, denoted as $P = \{p_1, \ldots, p_{N_p}\}$, where each p_i represents a square region in the image space. The parts from all detections are ordered in the same way, e.g. the first two parts p_1, p_2 always refer to the person's

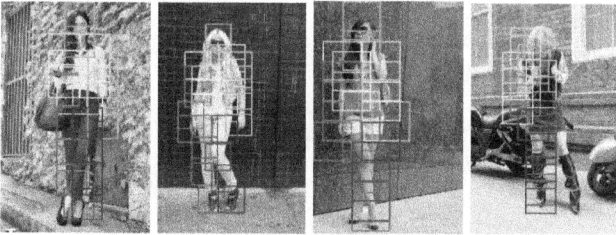

Figure 2: Example results of pose estimation. In many cases, the results are good (as in the first three images); however, there are also some failure cases (as in right-most image).

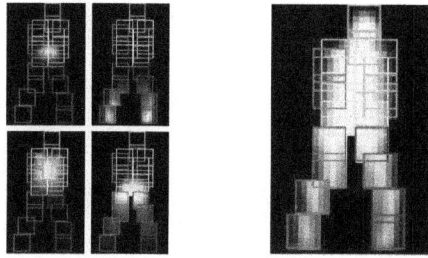

Figure 3: Prior probability maps, quantized and normalized on pose estimation body parts. They are presented here on an arbitrary pose. Left: Probability maps for belt, boots, blouse and skirt (from left to right and top to bottom). Right: The global *clothing prior probability map* $\mathcal{P}$.

head area. Figure 2 depicts such pose estimations, with the body parts depicted as colored boxes.

To speed up computations we choose to spatially quantize the body part regions. This quantization step also adds robustness to our representation against small translations, deformations and noise. After scaling all body parts to a fixed width of $w = 78$ pixels, we split each region in a $N \times N$ non-overlapping grid, where each cell is of size $N_c = w/N$. We denote a set of quantized body parts, *i.e.* a set of N_p, $N \times N$ matrices, as $\tilde{P} = \{\tilde{p}_1, \dots, \tilde{p}_{N_p}\}$. We also define the simple indicator function $I_i(\mathbf{x})$, as a function that is equal to 1 if the region of part p_i contains pixel $\mathbf{x} = (x, y)$.

Since body parts are overlapping, each location can appear in more than one of the parts. The set of parts that $\mathbf{x}$ belongs to is defined as $B(\mathbf{x}) = \{i : I_i(\mathbf{x}) = 1, i = 1, \dots, 26\}$. Each pixel $\mathbf{x}$ is mapped by a linear function $T_i(\mathbf{x}) : \mathbb{N}^2 \rightarrow \{1, \dots, N\} \times \{1, \dots, N\}$ onto one of the cells of the quantized part $\tilde{p}_i$, for each of the quantized body parts of $B(\mathbf{x})$ it belongs to.

The complete quantized pose estimation $\tilde{P}$ can be also expressed as a single $N_p \times N^2$-dimensional vector $\bar{P}$, by first unwrapping each quantized body part $\tilde{p}_i$ as a N^2-dimensional vector and then concatenating all N_p parts. In the rest of this paper we will always use a bar over the corresponding notation to refer to vectorized versions of matrices or sets of matrices. For the rest of this paper, we choose N to be equal to 6 and therefore end up with 936-dimensional vectors after concatenating all quantized body part vectors.

3.1.1 The Global Clothing Prior Probability Map

We want to focus all subsequent steps on image regions that are more likely to contain clothing. We therefore propose to calculate a prior probability map of clothing appearance, normalized on the detected pose estimation regions. As a training set, we need an image collection annotated with clothing segmentation. In the present work we use the Fashionista dataset [16], but any other dataset annotated with clothing may be used. Given a set C of classes $c \in C$, we first create a prior probability map for each clothing class and then accumulate all classes' maps together, normalize them and create a global *clothing prior probability map*, that we denote as $\mathcal{P}$. We will subsequently use this prior map as a binary mask in order to segment only probable human regions for clothing (see Section 3.2). The global clothing prior probability map we calculate is depicted in Figure 3 (right).

To create the map for a given class c, each image pixel $\mathbf{x}_c$, *i.e.* a pixel at location $\mathbf{x}$ annotated with label class c,

casts a vote for this class at every cell $T_i(\mathbf{x}_c)$, for $i \in B(\mathbf{x}_c)$. Accumulating the votes of all pixels annotated with label class c across all images of the training dataset and then normalizing the total sum of each non-empty body part to 1, we end up with a prior probability map $\mathcal{P}_c$ for clothing class c.

The global clothing prior probability map $\mathcal{P}$ is defined as the *union* of all $\mathcal{P}_c, c \in C$. Thresholding $\mathcal{P}$ at a certain probability level π_t we get the binary clothing mask:

$$\mathcal{P}_b = \begin{cases} 0 & \text{where } \mathcal{P} < \pi_t \\ 1 & \text{where } \mathcal{P} \geq \pi_t \end{cases} \quad (1)$$

As any other pose estimation, the quantized maps $\mathcal{P}_c, \mathcal{P}$ and $\mathcal{P}_b$ can also be expressed as a $N_p \times N^2$-dimensional vectors, denoted $\bar{\mathcal{P}}_c, \bar{\mathcal{P}}$ and $\bar{\mathcal{P}}_b$ respectively. A simple approach is to set π_t to 0.5, and therefore $\mathcal{P}_b$ is 1 when the quantized cell is more probable to contain clothing.

Figure 3 (left) shows examples of class probability maps, all presented on an arbitrary pose estimation outline. Without loss of generality, we limit our approach to a single person detection per image in our experiments, keeping the most confident detection returned by [17].

3.2 Segmentation and Clustering

Given a query image I with a successful pose estimation P, we start by applying the binary clothing mask $\bar{\mathcal{P}}_b$ on the detected body parts, and therefore produce an image I_s that is nonzero only in the regions that are more likely to contain clothing:

$$I_s(\mathbf{x}) = I(\mathbf{x}) \times \mathcal{P}_b(T_i(\mathbf{x})) \quad (2)$$

Example of such an image is shown in Figure 4 (left).

We proceed by segmenting the resulting image, using the popular segmentation of Felzenszwalb and Huttenlocher [4]. It is a fast graph-based approach, and the depth of segmentation can be parameterized. After running the algorithm on image I_s, we get an initial segmentation S_{init}, *i.e.* a set of arbitrary shaped segments. Segmentation results are shown in Figure 4 (middle).

It is noticeable that, no matter how lenient the segmentation thresholds are, there are some clothing segments that we need to combine, but are however spatially distant from each other. For example, the segments belonging to the left and right parts of an open jacket (see Figure 4 (left)) could never be merged, although they share the same visual appearance, since the blouse segments appear between them.

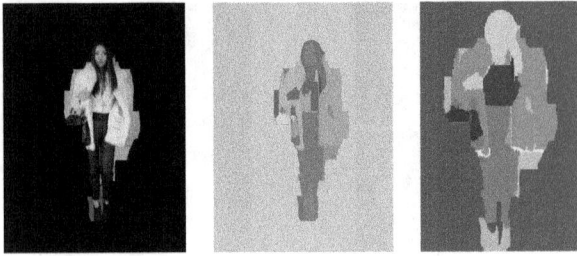

Figure 4: Segmentation and clustering steps

To rectify this, we need to somehow further merge the segmentation results, allowing such non-neighboring segments with the same visual appearance to merge. We therefore choose to perform a rapid clustering step on the extracted segments, in the visual feature space. To make the clustering process more meaningful, we set the initial segmentation thresholds low, thus *over-segmenting* the image.

For the clustering process we adopt the recent approach of Avrithis and Kalantidis [1]. *Approximate Gaussian Mixture (AGM)* clustering is chosen because it satisfies our two major requirements: it automatically estimates the number of segment clusters K needed on the fly and is very fast. The AGM algorithm is a variant of Gaussian Mixture Models and therefore produces a set of cluster centers μ_k, where $k = 1 \ldots K$. Since we do not really need the generalization capabilities of this expressive model, we choose to simply assign each segment s to the centroids with the highest *responsibility* [1].

Clustering needs to be performed on a visual feature space, we therefore extract visual features for each segment s of the initial over-segmentation S_{init} and calculate the corresponding feature vector $f(s)$. The visual features used are discussed in Section 4.1. Features from all segments are given as input to the AGM algorithm and we get *clusters of segments* as output. We then merge all segments that are clustered together, ending up with a set S_K of K segments, where $K < |S_{init}|$. These segments are the tentative clothing regions that we need to classify and determine whether they correspond to an actual clothing piece. Segmentation results after clustering and merging the initial segments are shown in Figure 4 (right).

3.3 Classification

Having robust segments, we now want to detect whether some of them might correspond to a clothing class. Since speed is an issue, we represent the segments as binary vectors and use a multi-probe locality-sensitive hashing (LSH) index to get promising matches sublinearly [6]. Then we proceed with measuring similarity between the query and the results in the top-ranked list and calculate class probabilities by summing overlap similarities. This approach requires no actual learning, just building approximate nearest neighbor structures and is extremely efficient in terms of query time.

3.3.1 Representing the Segments

The approach we follow to represent and classify the segments, derives from the following intuitions: 1) a clothing class is always found at a consistent spatial region both in the query and the training images, when referring to a common normalized pose estimation frame; 2) clothing classes

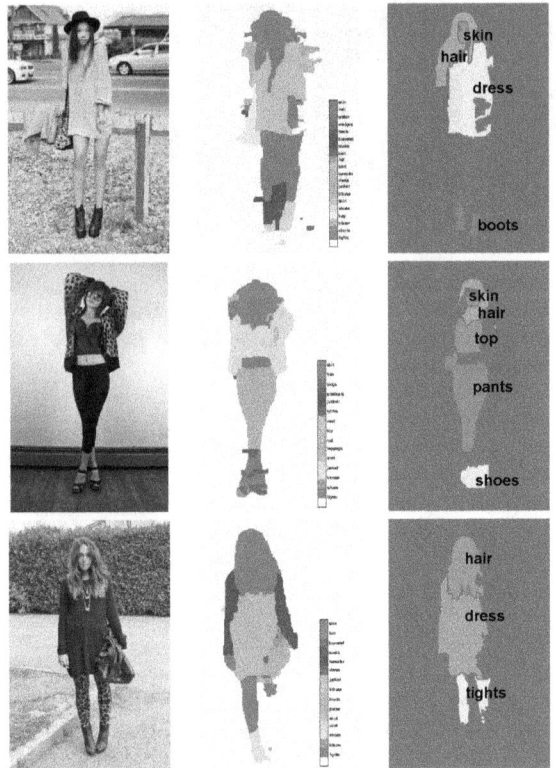

Figure 5: Sample clothing classification results. Left: Original image. Middle: result by [16]. Right: Our result.

cannot be distinguished by color or texture visual features (you can have blue suede shoes, a blue suede skirt and a blue suede hat); 3) basing our approach on shape alone would fail, since clothing classes' boundaries are highly non-consistent among different human poses and viewpoints; 4) we need to choose some representations that facilitate rapid classification for a dataset with up to 10^2 classes.

We therefore propose to use as segment representation a binary spatial appearance mask, projected on the common (normalized) space of the N_p quantized body parts. This will once again result in a $N_p \times N^2$-dimensional vector $\bar{M}_b$ and we are able to represent the segment positions on a normalized frame, without using visual appearance, while at the same time having a flexible binary representation. The segment's shape and size properties are also implicitly captured, as the resulting binary mask is not length normalized.

More precisely, given a pixel at location $\mathbf{x_s}$ belonging to the set of pixels $\mathbf{X}_s$ of a candidate segment s, we can use the functions $T_i(\mathbf{x}_s)$ for $i \in B(\mathbf{x}_s)$ to cast votes at every relevant bin on a—initially empty—quantized body parts set $\tilde{M} = \{\tilde{p}_1, \ldots, \tilde{p}_{N_p}\}$. Thresholding $\tilde{M}$ at a certain value γ we get the binary set:

$$\tilde{M}_b = \begin{cases} 0 & \text{where } \mathcal{P} < \gamma \\ 1 & \text{where } \mathcal{P} \geq \gamma \end{cases} \quad (3)$$

We set $\gamma = N_c^2/2$, where N_c is the quantization cell side, *i.e.* the cell will be deemed as active for the mask when at least half of the underlying pixels belong to the segment. The vector corresponding to $\tilde{M}_b$ is noted as $\bar{M}_b$.

3.3.2 Classification Using a Multi-Probe LSH Index

Following the process described in the previous subsections, we have extracted a binary vector $\bar{M}_b$ for every segment that we want to classify. For the training set images the exact clothing segment regions are given, together with their class label. Therefore segmentation and clustering is unnecessary and we only need to follow the process of Section 3.3.1 and extract the normalized binary mask for each segment.

We choose the *Jaccard similarity coefficient* as a similarity measure between the binary vectors. The Jaccard coefficient of sets $\bar{M}_b^1$ and $\bar{M}_b^2$ is denoted $J(\bar{M}_b^1, \bar{M}_b^2)$ and defined as the size of the intersection divided by the size of the union of the sample sets, or in our case binary vectors. Since we need to get reliable matches, *i.e.* matches with significant overlap, we therefore choose to use instead of J the thresholded function $\mathcal{J}^\tau(a,b) = J(a,b)$ iff $J(a,b) \geq \tau$ and 0 otherwise.

Matching each query vector with all training vectors sequentially is a very poor choice in terms of scalability. We therefore choose to first use a sublinear algorithm to get promising candidates and then match the query vector only on the top-ranked list. Therefore, after extracting binary vectors from each clothing segment of the training set, we add the binary vectors of all segments of all classes in a multi-probe LSH index [6], together with their corresponding labels. Since the vectors are binary, *Hamming distance* is set as the dissimilarity measure. Given a query vector $\bar{M}_b^Q$, the LSH index returns the set of the n nearest neighbors of the query from the database, in terms of Hamming distance. The neighbors form a set $\mathcal{N} = \{\bar{M}_b^1, \ldots, \bar{M}_b^n\}$, along with the corresponding class set $\mathcal{C} = \{c_1, \ldots, c_n\}$, where c_1 is the clothing class associated with database vector $\bar{M}_b^1$. We can now define the probability that the segment described by $\bar{M}_b^1$ belongs to class c as

$$P(c|\bar{M}_b^Q) = \frac{\sum_{i=1}^n b_c(i) * \mathcal{J}^\tau(\bar{M}_b^Q, \bar{M}_b^i)}{\sum_{i=1}^n \mathcal{J}^\tau(\bar{M}_b^Q, \bar{M}_b^i)} \quad (4)$$

where $b_c(i) = 1$ iff $c_i = c$ and 0 otherwise. We classify the query vector to class c^*, where

$$c^* = \begin{cases} \arg\max_c P(c|\bar{M}_b^Q), & P(c|\bar{M}_b^Q) \geq \tau_{class} \\ NULL, & P(c|\bar{M}_b^Q) < \tau_{class} \end{cases} \quad (5)$$

Where $NULL$ refers to 'no clothing' or 'background' class. Therefore, c^* is the class with the highest probability if this probability is over a threshold, otherwise we mark the segment as *null* or background. It makes sense to use $\tau_{class} = 0.5$ and assign the class if the probability of the class given the region is more than half. For multi-probe LSH, we use the FLANN [10] library implementation. Some classification results are shown in Figure 5.

4. SIMILAR CLOTHING SUGGESTION

Given the clothing classes present in an image, the second step is to retrieve visually similar products from a large product database. As mentioned before, the vast majority of product images are not everyday photographs, but clean photos with the clothing parts in a prominent position and almost always on a white background. We therefore follow a different methodology for product images to accurately grab the actual product region and subsequently describe its visual characteristics. In this section, we first discuss the visual features used to describe a region, either coming from a product or a tentative query image segment. We then present our product image parsing methodology and finally the indexing system used for retrieval.

4.1 Visual Features

We describe the visual attributes of a region by capturing *color* and *texture* characteristics. For product images, feature extraction can be done offline and thus extraction speed is not a big issue. However, at query time we need to extract visual features for many segments, *i.e.* for every one of the initial segmentation S_{init}, and require visual features that can be rapidly extracted. We therefore stick to simple descriptors rather than using more sophisticated ones, *e.g.* like SIFT [9].

To describe color we quantized the RGB values of each pixel to a uniform color dictionary of 29 elements. For texture we used *Local binary patterns* (LBPs) [11] and specifically just calculate the 9-dimensional histogram of *uniform patterns*. As argued in [11], uniform patterns are in fact the vast majority, sometimes over 90 percent, of the 3×3 texture patterns in surface textures.

We l_1-normalize color and texture features independently and then concatenate them to get the final 39-dimensional descriptor.

We also experimented with including a skin detector in the feature set. We tried to concatenate some skin pixel statistics as extra dimensions in the feature vector and this did not improve performance, therefore skin information was not included as a feature. A possible reason for this is that skin-like color clothing parts are no so infrequent in the datasets. We used skin detection when parsing product images, however, since cases of product image with visible body parts of a human model are frequent (see Section 4.2).

4.2 Describing Product Images

To accurately segment the region of the product in the product database images, we use the *grabcut* algorithm [12]. We initialize the algorithm using the whole image as bounding box and run for a few iterations. In most cases we are actually able to get the product's region without keeping background information. To avoid extracting noisy features from the pixels on the boundary, we also filter the binary region area with a small morphological erosion filter of size 3×3. Product images and the segments kept after grabcut are depicted in Figure 6.

The grabcut algorithm extracts the prominent foreground object, so in cases where the clothing product is worn by a person, it will include the model's region too. To avoid keeping person pixels as product pixels, we use skin as a mask and keep only non-skin pixels as the product's region. Since in most cases only a part of the model-person is shown in the product image, *e.g.* only legs are visible in skirt images or torso in blouse images, we cannot use full pose estimation.

For all pixels that remain active after eroding and applying the binary skin mask, we extract color and texture features, as described in Section 4.1. This way, each product is represented by a feature vector comparable to the one extracted by a query image region.

Figure 6: Sample pairs of product images (left) and the regions kept for feature extraction after grabcut (right— background depicted with black color).

4.3 Indexing and Retrieval

After having one feature vector per image for the whole product collection, we need to be able to quickly retrieve such vectors that are similar to a query region vector. Since feature vectors are not sparse, inverted indexes are not efficient in our case. We instead choose to use a fast approximate k-nearest neighbor index, using a forest of *randomized kd-trees* [13]. Once again we used the FLANN library [10] as the ANN implementation.

As the query feature vectors are also classified, we only need to search for similar product *within* that class. We therefore create and store in memory indexes *per class* and at query time only query the corresponding index for each clothing region. For each search, we get the k most similar products and then threshold the distance to actually display only the results that are visually very close to the query. In cases where no products are below the distance threshold, that specific query region is discarded.

The aforementioned approach can easily scale to millions of products on a singe machine. Indexes for 1 million product images can fit in around 450MB of memory. Retrieval speed is determined by the number of leaves checked by the ANN structure and query time per region in our experiments was in the order of a few milliseconds.

5. EXPERIMENTAL EVALUATION

We use two datasets for evaluating the proposed approach. For experiments on clothing class detection we use the publicly available annotated part of the *Fashionista* dataset[1] presented in [16]. It consists of 685 photos real-world photos with a human model in a cluttered but prominent position. The ground truth of this dataset contain 53 different clothing labels, plus the labels *hair*, *skin*, and *null*. For the large scale clothing suggestion scenario, we have crawled a product database of approximately 1.2 million products from Yahoo Shopping[2]. The products we crawled are all related to the clothing classes that we detect.

For the clothing class detection experiment, we follow the protocol of [16]; we measure *pixel accuracy* per image and then compute the mean across all query images. Standard deviation is also reported in the cases where 10-fold cross validation is used. As baseline we set the pixel accuracy

[1]http://www.cs.sunysb.edu/~kyamagu/research/clothing_parsing/
[2]http://shopping.yahoo.com/

k_init	$\lambda_{AGM} = 0.20$	$\lambda_{AGM} = 0.22$	$\lambda_{AGM} = 0.23$
200	36.3(22.9)	36.3(20.4)	36.3(14.2)
400	29.9(21.6)	29.9(19.1)	29.9(13.9)
500	27.2(20.3)	27.2(18.8)	27.2(13.7)
700	20.8(16.5)	20.8(14.9)	20.8(13.2)

Table 1: Average number of initial(final) segments for different parameter combinations

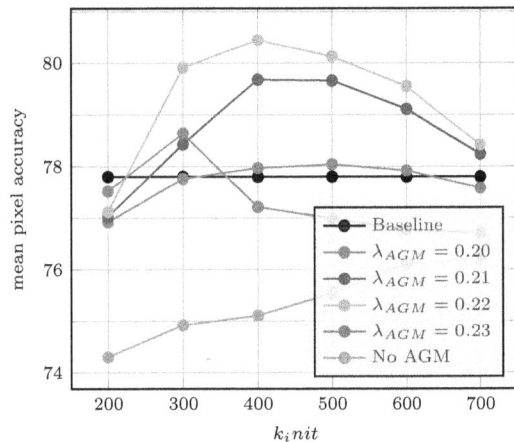

Figure 7: Mean pixel accuracy for different values k_{init} of the threshold function for the initial segmentation [4] and different expansion factor λ_{AGM} values for the subsequent segment clustering [1].

under the naive assumption of predicting all regions to be background, again as in [16].

5.1 Parameter Tuning

For parameter tuning, we use a small random sample of 50 images as validation set and leave the rest as training.

The first parameter to tune is the threshold for the initial segmentation [4]. We present results when varying the value k_{init} of the threshold function. Smaller value yields more segments. The rest of the initial segmentation parameters are $\sigma = 0.5$ for smoothing and $k_{min} = 300$ as the minimum component size. The Approximate Gaussian Mixture (AGM) clustering algorithm [1] has two parameters: the expansion factor λ_{AGM} and the merging threshold τ_{AGM}. We set $\tau_{AGM} = 0.55$ as suggested and vary the expansion factor λ_{AGM} to get various clustering results. The smaller λ_{AGM} is, the more final segments will be kept. We run AGM for a fixed number of 10 iterations.

The time needed, after pose estimation, for the extraction of the final segments is on average 700msec, of which 261msec is on average the time needed for the initial segmentation, 30.4msec for the AGM clustering algorithm and the rest for visual feature extraction. Figure 7 plots mean pixel accuracy for different values of k_{init} and the expansion factor. The average number of initial and final segments for different parameter combinations is shown in Table 1.

The best combination of values from this tuning experiment are $k_{init} = 400$ and $\lambda_{AGM} = 0.23$. The first one favors over-segmentation and is slightly smaller than the values suggested by [4].

Method	mean pixel accuracy	average time
[16]	80.7	334 sec
Ours	80.2 ± 0.9	5.8 sec
Baseline	77.6 ± 0.6	—

Table 2: Cross-validated results on the Fashionista dataset. Performance in terms of mean pixel accuracy and timings in terms of average detection time per image are presented.

Figure 8: Sample failure cases. Left: Stripes distort the segmentation. Right: Common misclassifications, *e.g.* skin for leggings or shorts for skirt.

5.2 Clothing Class Detection

As mentioned above, we evaluate the performance of the proposed approach following the protocol of the Yamaguchi et al.[16], using a 10-fold cross-validation on the Fashionista dataset. Performance and time results, averaged over all folds are presented in Table 2 for the proposed approach, for the baseline and for [16]. The proposed approach provide results comparable to [16] and does so in *only a small fraction of the time that [16] needs*. Their approach requires over 5 minutes to parse a photo[3] in the unconstrained case, *i.e.* the general case where there is no prior knowledge of the clothing present in the query image, while ours requires only 5-6 seconds. Moreover, since the application we care about is clothing suggestion, we are far more interested in *precision* of the detections than recall. [16] focuses a lot on recall of the garments and usually yields many of false positives in the unconstrained case. This is visible in Figure 5, where the number of garments that the [16] detects is far greater than the true number.

Failure cases of the proposed approach usually start from an erroneous pose estimation. Also, clothes with periodic color changes (*e.g.* stripes) pose a big challenge for our approach due to the initial color segmentation, and are usually cases that clustering cannot rectify. Finally, the misclassification for highly overlapping classes (*e.g.* pants and jeans or blouse and tops) is another main source for failure cases. Figure 8 depicts some failure cases.

5.3 Large Scale Clothing Suggestion

Our motivation behind clothing detection has been the automatic suggestion of clothing. To experiment and evaluate this scenario in a large scale environment, we developed a web-based application. Given a real-world image as query, the application detects the clothing classes present and returns related clothing products for each class to the user.

Our 1.2 million product image database is a subset of Yahoo! Shopping and is loosely annotated by clothing *category*.

---

[3]Time is measured when running the code provided by the authors of [16].

Clothing category	Proposed (%)	Random (%)
Dress	68	10
Skirt	59	2
Blouse	37	4
Top	55	6
Jackets & coats	43	3
Pants & Jeans	69	12
Boots	66	14
All	**54**	8

Table 3: User evaluation results for our suggestions and random suggestions. We present average precision at 10 results, for some sample clothing categories and for all categories.

pose	segmentation	classification	retrieval	total
1.7sec	0.7sec	3.2sec	0.3sec	5.8sec

Table 4: Time analysis for our clothing suggestion approach.

Since the categorization of the shopping catalog is different from the one we used for clothing detection, some of the initial classes had to be merged together (*e.g.* jackets and coats both belong to a single product category). Figures 1 and 9 depict results of our clothing suggestion application. The query image is shown on the left, and the suggested relevant clothing is on the right.

Given that there is no annotated clothing product database available we are unable to evaluate clothing suggestions directly and perform a user evaluation instead. We modified our online interface and presented each user both clothing suggestions from our algorithm and random products from the detected clothing catagories, mixed in random order. We then asked them to say whether each suggested product is visually relevant or not to the clothes worn in the image. We collect 178 image annotations from 11 users. Results in terms of precision are presented in Table 3. Users noted on average more than half of the suggested items as relevant while for the random products typically less than 10% were relevant.

Table 4 presents the time analysis for the different stages of the proposed clothing suggestion approach. We run all our experiments on a single quad-core machine and the code is implemented in MATLAB and C++. Since many computationally heavy parts of the approach are performed independently on different regions in the image (*e.g.* visual feature extraction, region classification and retrieval) the total query time can be further decreased by parallelization.

6. DISCUSSION

In this paper we present a fully automated clothing suggestion approach that can trivially scale to hundreds of product classes and millions of product images. We achieve clothing detection performance comparable to the state-of-the-art on a very recent annotated dataset, while being more than 50 times faster. Moreover, we present a clothing suggestion application, where the product database contains over one million products. The resulting suggestions might be used as-is, or they could be incorporated in a semi automatic annotation environment, assisting human annotators and significantly speeding up this costly process.

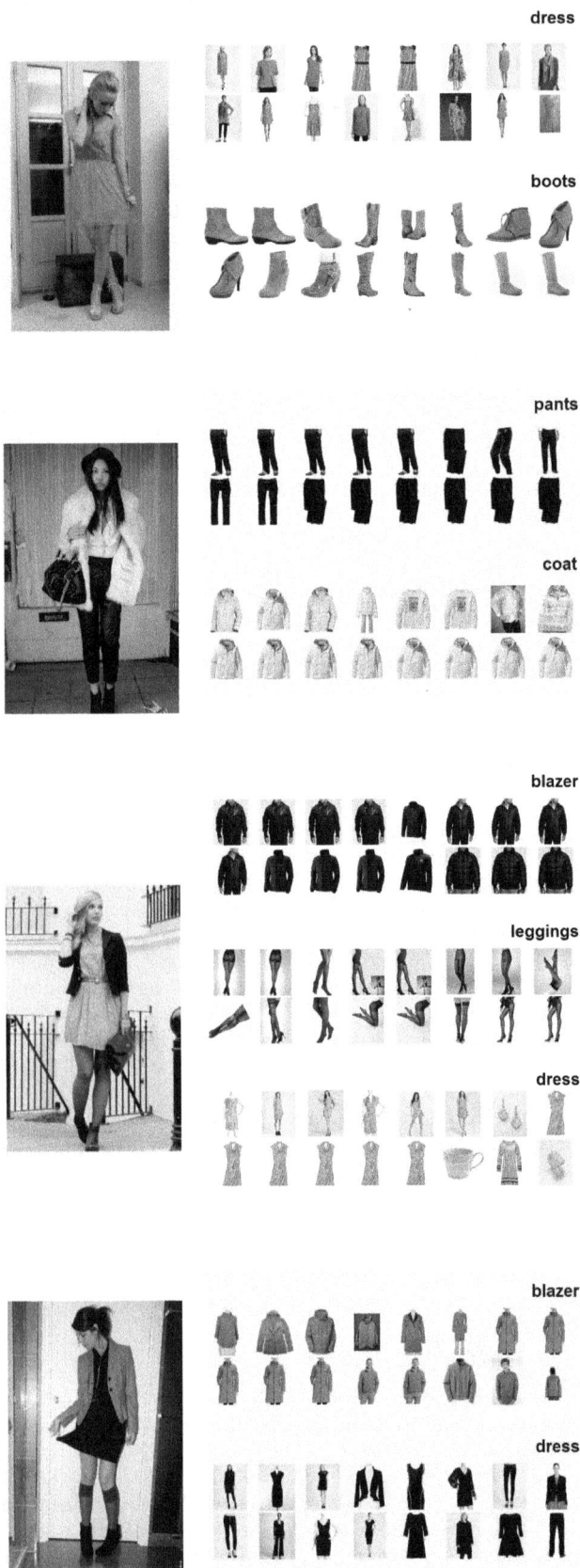

Figure 9: Clothing suggestion results.

As future work, a finer model that takes into account clothing class *co-occurrences* in the training set can boost detection performance, while also help mis-classifications. For distinguishing intra-class variations and styles (*e.g.* long to short sleeve blouses) attributes can be a good solution [2]. Gender classification on the detected people can also boost performance. By generalizing our model, we can include both attributes and gender information for the clothing class detection and suggestion stages of our approach.

7. REFERENCES

[1] Y. Avrithis and Y. Kalantidis. Approximate gaussian mixtures for large scale vocabularies. In *ECCV*, 2012.

[2] H. Chen, A. Gallagher, and B. Girod. Describing clothing by semantic attributes. In *ECCV*, 2012.

[3] G. Cushen and M.S. Nixon. Real-time semantic clothing segmentation. In *ISVC*, 2012.

[4] P.F. Felzenszwalb and D.P. Huttenlocher. Efficient graph-based image segmentation. *IJCV*, 59(2):167–181, 2004.

[5] A.C. Gallagher and T. Chen. Clothing cosegmentation for recognizing people. In *CVPR*, 2008.

[6] A. Gionis, P. Indyk, R. Motwani, et al. Similarity search in high dimensions via hashing. In *VLDB*, 1999.

[7] S. Liu, J. Feng, Z. Song, T. Zhang, H. Lu, C. Xu, and S. Yan. Hi, magic closet, tell me what to wear! In *ACM Multimedia*, 2012.

[8] S. Liu, Z. Song, G. Liu, C. Xu, H. Lu, and S. Yan. Street-to-shop: Cross-scenario clothing retrieval via parts alignment and auxiliary set. In *CVPR*, 2012.

[9] D.G. Lowe. Distinctive image features from scale-invariant keypoints. *IJCV*, 60(2):91–110, 2004.

[10] Muja M. and Lowe D.G. Fast approximate nearest neighbors with automatic algorithm configuration. In *VISSAPP'09*, 2009.

[11] T. Ojala, M. Pietikainen, and T. Maenpaa. Multiresolution gray-scale and rotation invariant texture classification with local binary patterns. *PAMI*, 24(7):971–987, 2002.

[12] C. Rother, V. Kolmogorov, and A. Blake. Grabcut: Interactive foreground extraction using iterated graph cuts. In *TOG*, volume 23, pages 309–314, 2004.

[13] C. Silpa-Anan and R. Hartley. Optimised kd-trees for fast image descriptor matching. In *CVPR*, pages 1–8. IEEE, 2008.

[14] Z. Song, M. Wang, X. Hua, and S. Yan. Predicting occupation via human clothing and contexts. In *ICCV*, 2011.

[15] N. Wang and H. Ai. Who blocks who: Simultaneous clothing segmentation for grouping images. In *ICCV*, 2011.

[16] K. Yamaguchi, M.H. Kiapour, L.E. Ortiz, and T.L. Berg. Parsing clothing in fashion photographs. In *CVPR*, 2012.

[17] Y. Yang and D. Ramanan. Articulated pose estimation with flexible mixtures-of-parts. In *CVPR*, 2011.

Bundle Min-Hashing for Logo Recognition

Stefan Romberg
Multimedia Computing and Computer Vision Lab
Augsburg University
Augsburg, Germany
romberg@informatik.uni-augsburg.de

Rainer Lienhart
Multimedia Computing and Computer Vision Lab
Augsburg University
Augsburg, Germany
lienhart@informatik.uni-augsburg.de

ABSTRACT

We present a scalable logo recognition technique based on feature bundling. Individual local features are aggregated with features from their spatial neighborhood into bundles. These bundles carry more information about the image content than single visual words. The recognition of logos in novel images is then performed by querying a database of reference images. We further propose a novel WGC-constrained RANSAC and a technique that boosts recall for object retrieval by synthesizing images from original query or reference images. We demonstrate the benefits of these techniques for both small object retrieval and logo recognition. Our logo recognition system clearly outperforms the current state-of-the-art with a recall of 83% at a precision of 99%.

Categories and Subject Descriptors

H.3.3 [**Information Storage and Retrieval**]: Information Search and Retrieval; I.5.4 [**Pattern Recognition**]: Computer Vision

General Terms

Algorithms, Experimentation

1. INTRODUCTION

In computer vision, the bag-of-visual words approach has been very popular in the last decade. It describes an image by multiple local features; their high-dimensional descriptor vectors are clustered and quantized into individual integer numbers - called visual words. An image is then modeled as an unordered collection of word occurrences, commonly known as bag-of-words. This description provides an enormous data reduction compared to the original descriptors. Its benefits are a fixed-size image description, robustness to occlusion and viewpoint changes, and eventually simplicity, i.e. a small computational complexity.

It has been observed that the retrieval performance of bag-of-words based methods improves much more by reduc-

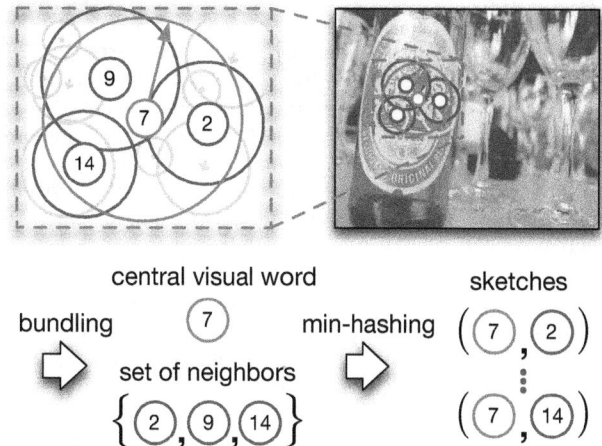

Figure 1: **Bundle Min-Hashing**: The neighborhood around a local feature, the *central feature* (red), is described by a feature bundle. Features that are too far away or on scales too different from that of the central feature are ignored during the bundling (yellow). The features included in such a bundle (blue) are represented as a set of visual word occurrences and indexed by min-hashing (see Section 3.2).

ing the number of mismatching visual words than by reducing quantization artifacts. Inspired by this observation we exploit a feature bundling technique that builds on visual words, but aggregates spatial neighboring visual words into feature bundles. An efficient search technique for such bundles based on min-hashing allows for similarity search without requiring exact matches.

Compared to individual visual words such bundles carry more information, i.e. fewer false positives are retrieved. Thus the returned result set is much smaller and cleaner. Our logo recognition framework exploits a bundle representation that retrieves approximately 100 times fewer images than bag-of-words while having equal recall performance. The core components of our logo recognition system are:

- We adopt the retrieval technique of [15] based on feature bundles to the problem of logo recognition and show that such a system significantly outperforms the current state-of-the-art.

- A *1*P-WGC-RANSAC variant for fast (real-time) spatial re-ranking is proposed that yields superior results compared to existing approaches by exploiting a weak-geometric constraint to speed up the computation

- We demonstrate that recall of a system targeting high precision for small object retrieval can be increased by exploiting synthetically generated images both for query expansion as well as database augmentation.

2. RELATED WORK

We present related work suited to image and object retrieval. As our approach is based on min-hashing, we also briefly highlight the related work relevant in the context of min-hashing.

Visual Words and Bundling. An early approach to feature bundling was used as a simple post-retrieval verification step where the number of matching neighboring features was exploited to discriminate true feature matches from random matches [17]. Later it was proposed to bundle multiple SIFT features that lie in the same MSER region into a single description [18]. The authors then defined a weak geometric similarity criterion. However, this work used single visual words for lookups in the inverted index, the bundles and the weak geometric similarity are used for post-retrieval verification only. In [3] the most informative projections that map the visual words from the 2-D space into feature histograms (termed "spatial bag-of-words") are learned. An approach, which is similar yet more unbiased to certain image layouts, splits the original feature histograms by random projections into multiple smaller "mini bag-of-features" [8]. Separate lookups and an aggregating scoring are used to find the most similar images in an image database. Another approach bundles triples of visual words including their spatial layout into visual signatures that are then subsequently indexed by a cascaded index making testing of images for the presence of pairs and triples possible and efficient [16].

Min-hashing (mH). Min-Hashing is a locality-sensitive hashing technique that is suitable for approximate similarity search of sparse sets. Originally developed for detection of duplicate text documents, it was adopted for near-duplicate image detection and extended to the approximation of weighted set overlap as well as histogram intersection [5]. Here, an image is modeled as a sparse set of visual word occurrences. Min-hashing then allows to perform a nearest-neighbor search among all such sparse sets within an image database. This approach is described in Section 3.1.

Geometric min-hashing (GmH). A conceptually similar approach to ours is geometric min-hashing [4]. However, its statistical preconditions for the hashing of sparse sets are totally different to our setting. There are two major differences: (1) GmH samples several central features by min-hash functions from all over the image. Thus, neither all nor even most features are guaranteed to be included in the image description. (2) Given a central feature (randomly drawn by a hash function) the local neighborhood of such feature is described by a single sketch. This makes GmH very memory efficient, but not suitable for generic image retrieval because of low recall. Consequently, the authors use it to quickly retrieve images from a large database in order to build initial clusters of highly similar images [4]. These clusters are then used as "seeds"; each of the contained

image is used as query for a traditional image search to find more cluster members that could not be retrieved by GmH.

Partition min-hashing (PmH). In [10] a scheme is introduced that divides the image into partitions. Unlike for normal min-hashing, min-hashes and sketches are computed for each partition independently. The search then proceeds by determining the sketch collisions for each of the partitions. This scheme is conceptually similar to a sliding window search as partitions may overlap and are processed step by step. The authors show that PmH is significantly faster than mH and has identical collision probabilities for sketches as mH in the worst case, but theoretically better recall and precision if the duplicate image region only covers a small area. However, in [15] we observed that PmH performs worse than mH on the logo dataset.

3. BUNDLE MIN-HASHING

We build our bundling technique on min-hashing mainly for two reasons: (1) Feature bundles can be naturally represented as sparse sets and (2) min-hashing does not imply a strict ordering or a hard matching criterion. This requirement is not met by local feature bundles. Due to image noise, viewpoint and lighting changes, the individual local features, their detection, and their quantization are unstable and vary across images. Even among two very similar images, it is extremely unlikely that they share identical bundles. We therefore utilize the min-hashing scheme as a robust description of local feature bundles because it allows to search for similar (not identical) bundles.

The proposed bundling technique is an efficient search method for similar images with higher memory requirements than pure near-duplicate search methods, but similar to that of bag-of-words. Its performance is close to bag-of-words, but at a much lower response ratio, i.e. higher precision.

3.1 Min-hashing (mH)

Min-Hashing is a locality-sensitive hashing technique that allows for approximate similarity search of sparse sets. It models an image as a sparse set of visual word occurrences. As the average number of visual words per image is much smaller than the vocabulary size for large vocabularies, the resulting feature histograms are sparse and are converted to binary histograms (i.e. sets representing whether a visual word is present at least once).

If one were able to do a linear search over all sets in a database, he might define a threshold on the overlap $ovr(I_1, I_2)$ between two such sets I_1 and I_2. This is equivalent to a threshold on the Jaccard similarity and determines whether these two sets are considered "identical" or matching. However, as the linear search over a database is infeasible in practice the min-hashing scheme provides an efficient way to index these sets based on this overlap criterion.

Given a set of l visual words of an image $I = \{v_0, ..., v_{l-1}\}$, the min-hash function is defined as

$$mh(I) = \operatorname*{argmin}_{v_i \in I} h(v_i) \qquad (1)$$

where h is a hash function that maps each visual word v_i *deterministically* to a random value from a uniform distribution. Thus, the min-hash mh itself is a visual word, namely that word that yields the minimum hash value (hence the name min-hash). The probability that a min-hash function

mh will have the same value for two different sets I_1 and I_2 is equal to the set overlap:

$$P(mh(I_1) = mh(I_2)) = ovr(I_1, I_2) = \frac{|I_1 \cap I_2|}{|I_1 \cup I_2|} \quad (2)$$

Note that an individual min-hash value not only represents a randomly drawn word that is part of the set, but each min-hash also implicitly "describes" the words that are *not* present and would have generated a smaller hash - because otherwise it would have been a different min-hash value.

The approximate search for similar sets is then performed by finding sets that share min-hashes. As single min-hashes alone yield true matches as well as many false positives or random collisions, multiple min-hashes are grouped into k-tuples, called *sketches*. This aggregation increases precision drastically. To improve recall, this process is repeated n times and independently drawn min-hashes are grouped into n tuples of length k. The probability that two different sets have at least one of these n sketches in common is then given by

$$P(collision) = 1 - (1 - ovr(I_1, I_2)^k)^n \quad (3)$$

This probability depends on the set overlap. In practice the overlap between non-near-duplicate images that still show the same object is small. In fact, the average overlap for a large number of partial near-duplicate images was reported to be 0.019 in [10]. This clearly shows that for applications which target the retrieval of partial-near-duplicates e.g. visually similar objects rather than full-near-duplicates, the most important part of that probability function is the behavior close to 0.

The indexing of sets and the approximate search are performed as follows: To index sets their corresponding sketches are inserted into hash-tables (by hashing the sketches itself into hash keys), which turn the (exact) search for a part of the set (the sketch) into simple lookups. To retrieve the sets similar to a query set, one simply computes the corresponding sketches and searches for the sets in the database that have one or more sketches in common with the query. A lookup of each query sketch determines whether this sketch is present in the hash table, which we denote as "collision" in the following. The lookups can be done efficiently in constant time as hash table offer access in amortized $\mathcal{O}(1)$. If there is a query sketch of size k that collides with a sketch in the hash table, then the similarity of their originating sets is surely > 0, because at least k of the min-hash functions agreed. To avoid collisions resulting from unrelated min-hash functions, the sketches are put into separate hash tables: the k-th sketch is inserted into the k-th hash table.

3.2 Bundle Min-Hashing

The idea of our bundling technique is simple: We describe the neighborhoods around local features by bundles which simply aggregate the visual word labels of the corresponding visual features. The bundling starts by selecting *central features*, i.e. all features in an image with a sufficient number of local features in their neighborhood. Analogous to the feature histogram of a full image, the small neighborhood surrounding each central feature represents a "micro-bag-of-words". Such a bag-of-words vector will be extremely sparse because only a fraction of all features in the image is present in that particular neighborhood. Since the features of a bundle are spatially close to each other, they are likely to describe the same object or a region of interest.

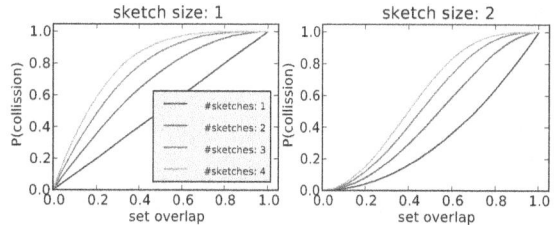

Figure 2: Collision probabilities given the set overlap between bundles. Left: Single min-hash (as used by Bundle Min-Hashing). Right: Sketches of size 2.

More specifically, given a feature $\mathbf{x}_i$ its corresponding feature bundle $b(\mathbf{x}_i)$ is defined as the set of spatially close features for a given feature $\mathbf{x}_i$:

$$b(\mathbf{x_i}) = \{\mathbf{x}_j | \mathbf{x}_j \in N(\mathbf{x}_i)\} \quad (4)$$

where $N(\mathbf{x}_i)$ is the *neighborhood* of feature $\mathbf{x}_i$ which is described at the end of this section. We further assume that for all features $\mathbf{x}_i$ in an image the descriptor vectors have been quantized to the corresponding visual words $v_i = q(\mathbf{x}_i)$.

The bundle $b(\mathbf{x}_i)$ is then represented by the corresponding set of visual words of all features included in that bundle:

$$W_i(b(\mathbf{x_i})) = \{ q(\mathbf{x}_j) \mid \mathbf{x}_j \in b(\mathbf{x}_i) \} \quad (5)$$

The resulting set W_i is then subsequently indexed by regular min-hashing

In extensive experiments we observed the following: First, sketches of size 2 perform best compared to sketches of size 3. Second, we found that the performance increases drastically if the first sketch element is not determined by min-hashing but rather set to the visual word of the central feature itself. That is, for each bundle the n-th sketch is given as 2-tuple

$$(v_i, \ mh_n(W_i(b(\mathbf{x}_i))) \ ) \quad (6)$$

where v_i denotes the visual word label of the central feature and mh_n denotes the min-hash returned by the n-th min-hash function from the set of all visual words W_i present in bundle $b(\mathbf{x_i})$. The full process is illustrated in Figure 1.

The major advantage can be seen when comparing the collision probabilities of a single min-hash and sketches of size 2 (see Figure 2). With our approach two bundles (the central feature plus a single min-hash) with an overlap of only 0.2 have a 50% chance that one of 4 sketches collide. This means, while there are multiple feature bundles that need to be described, each with several sketches, only very few sketches are needed per bundle to achieve a high probability to retrieve similar sets. This keeps the memory requirements for the indexing low. Further redundancy is added as images contain multiple bundles that may overlap. If some bundles do not match (collide) across images, there is the chance that other bundles in the same images collide.

Bundling Strategy. The bundling strategy $N(\mathbf{x}_i)$ we use is based on the intuition that features which are spatially close to each other are likely to describe the same object. That is, given a central feature we bundle it with its direct spatial neighbors. We require that at least two other features are present in its neighborhood and that these must be on a similar scale. This is in line with the observation that true feature correspondences are often at the same scale [6]. It also rules out features without good neighbors and decreases the number of bundles even below the number of local features in an image. Thus, each feature that is closer to a given central feature $\mathbf{x}_i$ than a given cut-off radius r_{max} is included in the respective bundle $b(\mathbf{x}_i)$: The radius r_{max} is chosen relative to the scale (patch size) of the central feature s_i. The minimum and maximum scales s_{min} and s_{max} control the scale band considered for determining the neighbors relative to the scale of the central feature. Figure 1 shows the bundling criterion for $s_{min} = 0.5$, $s_{max} = 2.0$ and $r_{max} = 1.0$ (red circle = radius of the central feature itself).

Implementation. The features within a certain distance to a central feature are efficiently determined by orthogonal range search techniques like kd-trees or range trees which allow sub-linear search once all coordinates are indexed.

Also, we use randomizing hash functions instead of precomputed permutation tables to compute the hashes. These hash functions return a uniformly drawn random value deterministically determined by the given visual word and a seed that is kept fixed. This implementation is both substantially more memory efficient and faster than lookup tables.

Adjustable Search. The representation of bundles by multiple sketches has an advantageous side-effect: it facilitates a search tunable from high precision to high recall *without* post-retrieval steps or redundant indexing. Once bundles have been indexed with k sketches per bundle, the strictness of the search may be changed by varying the number of sketches *at query time* from $1...k$. As the sketch collision probability is proportional to the set overlap, sets (=bundles) that have a high overlap with the query will be retrieved earlier than bundles with smaller overlap. Thus, by varying the number of query sketches one can adjust the strictness of the search (see Table 1: mean precision mP and mean recall mR change with varying #sketches). As the i-th sketch was inserted into the i-th hash table, querying sketches from $1...i$ will yield only bundles were the corresponding sketches and hash functions in tables $1...i$ agreed at least once.

3.3 Ranking and Filtering

Once the images which share similar bundles with the query are determined, they may be ranked by their similarity to the query. One possibility is to compute a similarity based on the number of matching bundles between these images.

However, a ranking based on the cosine similarity between the full bag-of-words histogram of the query image and the retrieved images performs significantly better than a ranking based on the sketch collision counts, as it is difficult to derive a good measure for image similarity based on a few collisions only. Thus, in our experiments we rank all retrieval results by the cosine similarity between the bag-of-words histograms describing the full images.

In other words, the retrieval by feature bundles is effectively a filtering step: The bundles are used to quickly fetch a small set of images that are very likely relevant. These images are then ranked by the cosine similarity between bag-of-words histograms [17] obtained with a vocabulary of 1M words (see Section 3.4.3). We also address the problem of visual word burstiness by taking the square root of each tf-idf histogram entry as proposed in [7]. This is important for logo recognition as logos often consist of text and text-like

elements which are known to be prone to yield repeated visual words ("visual words bursts"). The small response ratio of the retrieval with bundles is a major benefit: Small result sets of high precision can be processed quickly even with sophisticated re-ranking methods.

3.4 Experiments

3.4.1 Dataset

The dataset we chose to evaluate our logo retrieval approach is FlickrLogos-32. It consists of 32 classes of brand logos [16]. Compared to other well-known datasets suited for image retrieval, e.g. Oxford buildings, images of a similar class in FlickrLogos-32 share much smaller visually similar regions. For instance, the average object size of the 55 query images (annotated in the ground truth) of the Oxford dataset is 38% of the total area of the image (median: 28%) while the average object size in the test set of the FlickrLogos dataset is only 9% (median: 5%) of the whole image. As the retrieval of the Oxford buildings is sometimes coined "object retrieval", the retrieval task on the FlickrLogos dataset can be considered as "small object retrieval".

The dataset is split into three disjunct subsets. For each logo class, we have 10 train images, 30 validation images, and 30 test images - each containing at least one instance of the respective logo. For both validation and test set the dataset also provides a set of 3000 negative (logo-free) images.

This logo dataset is interesting for the evaluation of small object retrieval and classification since it features logos that can be considered as rigid 2-D objects with an approximately planar surface. The difficulty arises from the great variance of object sizes, from tiny logos in the background to image-filling views. Other challenges are perspective tilt and for classification eventually the task of multi-class recognition.

Our evaluation protocol is as follows: All images in the training and validation set, including those that do not contain any logo are indexed by the respective method (In total: 4280 images). The 960 images in the test set which do show a logo (given by the ground truth) are then used as queries to determine the most similar images from the training and validation set. The respective retrieval results are then ranked by the cosine similarity (see Section 3.3).

3.4.2 Visual Features

For all of our experiments we used SIFT descriptors computed from interest points found by the Difference-of-Gaussian detector. To quantize the descriptor vectors to visual words we use approximate k-means which employs the same k-means iterations as standard k-means but replaces the exact distance computations by approximated ones. We use a forest of 8 randomized kd-trees to index the visual word centers [12]. This kd-forest then allows to perform approximate nearest neighbor search to find the nearest cluster for a descriptor vector both during clustering as well as when quantizing descriptor vectors to single visual words. The vocabulary and IDF weights have been computed with data from the training and validation set of FlickrLogos-32 only.

3.4.3 Evaluation

As a retrieval system should have both high precision and high recall, we measure the retrieval performance by mean average precision (mAP) which describes the area under the precision-recall curve. A system will only gain high mAP

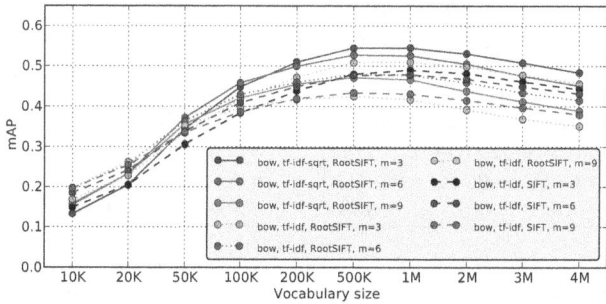

Figure 3: Retrieval score (mAP) for several bag-of-words variants on the FlickrLogos-32 dataset.

scores if both precision and recall are high. Here, the AP is computed as $AP = \sum_{i=1}^{N} \frac{1}{2}(P_i + P_{i-1}) \cdot (R_i - R_{i-1})$ with $R_0 = 0, P_0 = 1$ where P_i, R_i denote precision/recall at the i-th position in the retrieved list.

The response ratio (RR) measures the retrieval efficiency. It describes the number of retrieved images in relation to the database size. The higher the response ratio the more images are in the result list, which is usually post-processed or verified by computationally expensive methods. A low response ratio will thus increase the overall efficiency of the search.

The precision among the top-ranked images is measured by the average top 4 score (Top4) defined as average number of correctly retrieved images among the top 4 results.

Bag-of-words. As baseline on this particular dataset we show the performance of approaches based purely on the cosine similarity between bag-of-words. Thus, we evaluate the retrieval performance of a plain bag-of-words search with varying vocabularies and varying patch sizes of the descriptors. We are especially interested in the impact of extremely large visual vocabularies on the performance. Thus, we vary the vocabularies from 10,000 (10K) to 4,000,000 (4M) words.

The results are shown in Figure 3. In [15] we have already shown that IDF-weighting is always beneficial in the bag-of-words framework, even for large vocabularies greater than 1 million words. Thus tf-idf weighting was used in all cases. As found in prior works, large vocabulary show significantly better performance. The peak is consistently at 500K/1M words. The patch size that is described by a SIFT descriptor depends on the scale but is also controlled by a magnification factor m. We further test how this magnifier changes the performance. The best performance is obtained with descriptors computed with a magnifier of $m = 3$ as in Lowe's work. In addition we compare the performance of bag-of-words based on standard SIFT with that of the relatively new RootSIFT variant [2]. Clearly, the bag-of-words based on RootSIFT outperforms the SIFT-based bag-of-words. Finally, the burstiness measure proposed in [7] where the square root is taken for each element of the tf-idf weighted histogram further improves the retrieval performance (denoted as "tf-idf-sqrt"in Figure 3) as it down-weights repeating and thus less informative visual words ("bursts").

For further experiments we therefore use visual words computed from RootSIFT descriptors and re-rank the results retrieved by feature bundles by the cosine similarity

between bag-of-words histograms with square-rooted tf-idf weights. For re-ranking the best-performing vocabulary of 1M words is used, disregarding which vocabulary was used when building the feature bundles.

Feature Bundles. In order to find the best bundle configurations we have performed extensive evaluations on the parameters of the bundle configuration. Due to limited space, we cannot show a detailed evaluation for each of these parameters. Instead, we report the best-performing bundle configuration (with respect to mAP) in Table 1. Similar to bag-of-words the bundles profit from large vocabularies, but the peak is at $200K$-$500K$ words. More importantly, the bundles are on par with bag-of-words, but have an order of magnitude lower response ratio (RR) as shown in Table 1.

Note that we re-rank the result lists determined by bundle min-hashing by the cosine similarity as given by the bag-of-words model. As the bundling is by definition only able to find correspondences between images that share visual words, the result set of the retrieval by feature bundles is a subset of the result set obtained with bag-of-words retrieval. This clearly demonstrates the discriminative power of feature bundles for efficient filtering before more expensive post-retrieval steps are applied to the result set.

4. FAST RE-RANKING: 1P-WGC-RANSAC

In order to ensure that the top retrieved images correctly show the query object we employ a spatial verification step on the list of retrieved images. The gold standard for this purpose is RANSAC. Our approach is based on a variant that uses single feature correspondences to estimate a transformation between two images [13]. The associated scale and dominant orientation of the two local features of each correspondence is used to estimate a similarity transform (4 degrees-of-freedom with translation, rotation and uniform scaling). The major benefit is that a single correspondence generates a hypothesis. Evaluating all these correspondences makes this procedure deterministic, fast and robust to small inlier ratios. The top 10 hypothesis with the highest score (determined by the symmetric transfer error and truncated quadratic cost function as in [9]) are kept for further refinement. If the top hypothesis have more than 15 inliers these are then refined by a local optimization (LO) step that estimates a fully projective transformation between images via least-median-of-squares.

While RANSAC is in general considered as slow and costly this is not entirely true. In fact we found that most of the time was spent for the projective re-estimation. Moreover, while this refinement improves the visual quality of the estimated transformation it has little effect on the induced ranking. Thus, we propose a new variant 1P-WGC-RANSAC *without* subsequent LO step that is faster than a non-WGC-constrained RANSAC and much faster than a variant estimating a fully projective transformation between images.

For 1P-WGC-RANSAC, a weak geometric consistency constraint (WGC) is imposed. Only correspondences from features with orientations and scales that are consistent with the estimated transformation may be scored as inliers. We found that this constraint has little impact on the quality of the re-ranking. However, it acts as filtering that can be employed *before* the inliers are determined. If a feature correspondence violates the WGC constraint it is directly treated as outlier. Thus, the error function within

#sketches	s_{min}	s_{max}	r_{max}	Voc.	mAP	AvgTop4	mP	mR	RR	∅#bundles	rel. storage
bag-of-words, tf-idf-sqrt weighting				200K	0.510	2.88	0.010	**0.952**	0.912	2468.1 words	1.0
bag-of-words, tf-idf-sqrt weighting				500K	0.545	3.06	0.011	0.932	0.845	2468.1 words	1.0
bag-of-words, tf-idf-sqrt weighting				1M	0.545	**3.16**	0.012	0.911	0.763	2468.1 words	1.0
4	0.5	2.0	1.0	200K	**0.554**	3.14	0.317	0.639	0.025	1640.9	2.66
3	0.5	2.0	1.0	200K	0.545	3.13	0.338	0.623	0.022	1640.9	1.99
2	0.5	2.0	1.0	200K	0.527	3.09	0.367	0.592	0.018	1640.9	1.33
1	0.5	2.0	1.0	200K	0.479	3.04	**0.423**	0.520	**0.012**	1640.9	**0.66**

Table 1: Comparison of bag-of-words retrieval with Bundle Min-Hashing: The upper part shows three different bag-of-words retrieval runs with corresponding scores. The lower part contains the bundle configuration that resulted in the highest mAP for 1, 2, 3 and 4 sketches per bundle. The columns s_{min}, s_{max}, r_{max} and $Voc.$ denote the bundling parameters (as described in Section 3.2) and the vocabulary size. The scores follow in the order of mean Average Precision, average top 4 score, mean precision, mean recall and response ratio. The column ∅#bundles denotes the average number of bundles stored in the hash table per image. The last column shows the number of hash table entries (sketches) relative to the number of visual words per image.

the RANSAC framework is speeded up as there is no need to compute the perspective mapping for these false correspondences. Here, we use the following constraint: scale change must be in $[0.5, 2.0]$ and angles must differ less than $30°$.

We compare our approach to that of Philbin et al. [13] and Arandjelovic et al. [2] on the Oxford5K dataset [13] following the common test protocol: The top 1000 retrieval results per query are re-ranked with an early stop if 20 images in a row could not be verified successfully. Images are scored by the sum of the IDF weights of all inlier words and verified images are placed above unverified images in the result list. The results are shown in Table 2. Here, "SP" and "RANSAC" denote that spatial re-ranking was performed.

One can see that our implementation (using DoG-SIFT) yields slightly higher (1M words) or even significantly higher scores (100K words) than that of Philbin et al. [13] (using Hessian-affine SIFT). Quite surprisingly, the performance after re-ranking with the smaller vocabulary of 100K words is close to the one with 1M words. This demonstrates that the proposed scheme is able to deal with a small vocabulary, its less discriminative correspondences and small inlier ratios.

Similar on the FlickrLogos-32 dataset (see Table 3): The spatial verification of the top 200 images further improves the result as well. For both datasets the projective re-estimation does not improve the performance. It further refines the homography but is not able to discard additional false positives. Most likely a simple 4-dof geometric constraint for re-ranking is sufficient to filter out false positives. This underlines that re-ranking does not require to estimate fully affine/projective homographies.

To measure the time we performed all experiments on the same machine using 1 thread for execution of our C++ program and measured the wall time as median over 10 runs. In summary the WGC-constrained 1-point RANSAC without LO is about 30% faster than without the WGC constraint, has slightly better performance for small vocabularies and is much faster than with LO refinement. Its throughput is extremely high (e.g. see ★ in Table 2: reranked 5813 images ≈ 440 images/s ≈ 2.3 ms per image, single-threaded, including I/O) making it suitable for real-time applications.

5. WARPING

While current local features are by design scale invariant and also somewhat robust to changes in lighting and image noise, it is well known that local features such as SIFT

Method	Voc	mAP	Time
Philbin et al.[13], bow	100K	0.535	—
Philbin et al.[13], bow+SP	100K	0.597	—
bow, tf-idf, SIFT	100K	0.571	—
1P-RANSAC, incl. LO	100K	0.678	$160s$
1P-RANSAC, no LO	100K	0.680	$72s$
1P-WGC-RANSAC, incl. LO	100K	0.693	$115s$
1P-WGC-RANSAC, no LO	100K	0.692	$53s$
Philbin et al.[13], bow	1M	0.618	—
Philbin et al.[13], bow+SP	1M	0.645	—
Arandjelovic et al.[2] SIFT, bow	1M	0.636	—
Arandjelovic et al.[2] SIFT, bow+SP	1M	0.672	—
bow, tf-idf, SIFT	1M	0.647	—
1P-RANSAC, incl. LO	1M	0.712	$54s$
1P-RANSAC, no LO	1M	0.711	$15s$
1P-WGC-RANSAC, incl. LO	1M	0.704	$50s$
1P-WGC-RANSAC, no LO	1M	0.703	$12s$
Arandjelovic et al.[2] RootSIFT, bow	1M	0.683	—
Arandjelovic et al.[2] RootSIFT, bow+SP	1M	0.720	—
bow, tf-idf, RootSIFT	1M	0.675	—
1P-RANSAC, incl. LO	1M	0.728	$92s$
1P-RANSAC, no LO	1M	0.729	$17s$
1P-WGC-RANSAC, incl. LO	1M	0.723	$55s$
1P-WGC-RANSAC, no LO ★	1M	0.723	$13s$

Table 2: Comparison of spatial re-ranking results for the Oxford5K dataset following the protocol in [13].

Method	Voc.	mAP	Time
bow, tf-idf-sqrt	100K	0.448	—
1P-RANSAC, incl. LO	100K	0.513	$953s$
1P-RANSAC, no LO	100K	0.513	$387s$
1P-WGC-RANSAC, incl. LO	100K	0.510	$731s$
1P-WGC-RANSAC, no LO	100K	0.510	$325s$
bow, tf-idf-sqrt	1M	0.545	—
1P-RANSAC, incl. LO	1M	0.565	$510s$
1P-RANSAC, no LO	1M	0.565	$153s$
1P-WGC-RANSAC, incl. LO	1M	0.568	$447s$
1P-WGC-RANSAC, no LO	1M	0.568	$111s$

Table 3: FlickrLogos-32: Spatial re-ranking results.

are particularly susceptible to changes in perspective. With increasing vocabulary size this effect gets more severe: descriptors computed from image patches that are actually

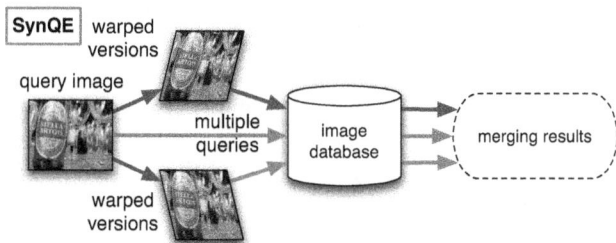

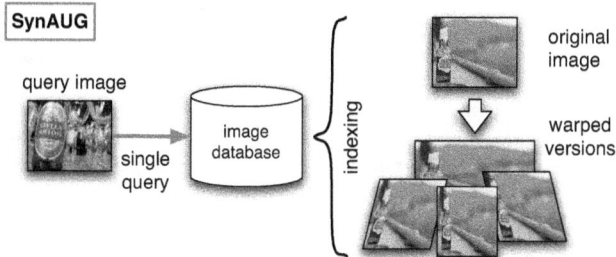

Figure 4: Top: Synthetic query expansion. Bottom: Synthetic database augmentation.

Figure 5: FlickrLogos-32: Impact of synthetic query expansion and database augmentation on bag-of-word retrieval performance.

identical but seen from a different perspective are quantized to different - and therefore unrelated - visual words.

There exist several partial solutions to this problem. The most popular is query expansion (QE) where the top-ranked retrieved images are exploited to augment the original query. The augmented query is then re-issued in order to retrieve images that have not been found in the first round. Consequently, query expansion fails - and causes the results to be worse than without - if the top-retrieved images are false positives. This may happen if the query is actually challenging or only few true positives are contained in the database.

We propose a different method to overcome this problem, especially suited for small objects where it is crucial to find the few true matching visual words. It is a purely data-driven approach that synthesizes new images from existing images by applying transformations to the image itself, a process often called "warping". There are different ways to exploit image warping:

1. *Synthetic Query Expansion (SynQE)*:
   Multiple versions of the query image may be synthesized simulating the query as it may be seen under different conditions and perspectives. Each image is then treated as an individual query; their corresponding result lists are then merged into a single list. This method is illustrated in the upper half of Figure 4.

2. *Synthetic Database Augmentation (SynAUG)*:
   The database is augmented by adding new generated images synthesized from each original database image. This is especially useful if it is desired that a query containing certain predefined objects - such as logos - should find the true results with high probability from a limited set of manually managed reference images. This method is illustrated in the lower half of Figure 4.

3. *SynQE + SynAUG*: The combination of (1) and (2). This can be seen as counterpart to ASIFT [11] working with discrete visual words and an inverted index or another database instead of comparing raw descriptors between two images.

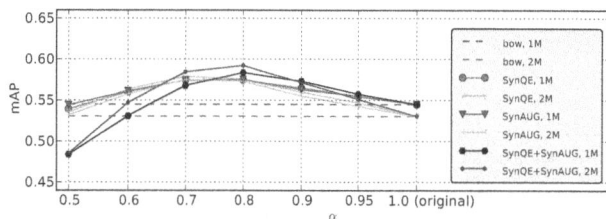

We choose the following simple transformations to synthesize new images: $S_x(\alpha)$, $S_y(\alpha)$, $S_x(\alpha)R(45°)S_x(\alpha)$ and $S_x(\alpha)R(-45°)S_x(\alpha)$. $S_x(\alpha)$ denotes the matrix for scaling by factor α in x-direction, $S_y(\alpha)$ analog in y-direction and $R(45°)$ denotes the matrix for rotation by 45°. The last two transformations are opposed shearings along x direction.[1] The inverse transformations of the former four are added as well, resulting in a total of eight transformations.

For SynQE multiple queries are issued to the index yielding multiple separate result lists. These are merged subsequently: images contained in multiple result lists get the maximum of each individual cosine similarity score as proposed in [1]. Similar for SynAUG: once a synthetic image is found it votes with its score for the original image and the maximum of all votes is taken as final similarity measure.

We test these techniques with a bag-of-words retrieval as described in Section 3.4.3 (RootSIFT, tf-idf-sqrt) and a vocabulary of 1M and 2M words. The scaling parameter α is varied from 0.95 to 0.5 to test which group of transformations works best for simulating the perspective change in practice. The corresponding results are shown in Figure 5.

Both SynQE and SynAUG improve the retrieval performance with a maximum at $\alpha = 0.7/0.8$. The combination of both, i.e. SynQE+SynAUG slightly increases the performance further. An even larger visual vocabulary of 2M words increases the performance dramatically over its baseline (11.6%) but somewhat surprisingly only slightly above those of the vocabulary with 1M words.

To summarize, the obtained results underline that discrete visual descriptions benefit from synthetic image generation. In the following we refer to the transformation group with $\alpha = 0.7$ when referring to SynQE and SynAUG.

6. LOGO RECOGNITION

Now that we have discussed visual features, vocabularies, feature bundling, re-ranking and synthetic query expansion we present our final logo recognition system:

Indexing. The logo classes that our system should be able to detect are described by a set of images showing these logos in various poses. We refer to this set as *reference set* and use the images within the training and validation set of the FlickrLogos-32 dataset for this purpose. Feature bundles are computed for each image in the reference set and inserted into the hash table associated with the information to which class a reference image belongs. Optionally, SynAUG is applied: Artificially generated transformed versions of the original images are used to augment to the reference set.

---

[1]These are equivalent to the two shearings along y-direction.

Method	Precision	Recall
Romberg et al. [16]	0.98	0.61
Revaud et al. [14]	≥ 0.98	0.73
bag-of-words, 100K	0.988	0.674
bag-of-words, 1M	0.991	0.784
bag-of-words, 1M, SP	0.996	0.813
bag-of-words, 1M, SP+SynQE	0.994	0.826
bag-of-words, 1M, SP+SynAUG	0.996	0.825
BmH, 200K, collision count	0.688	0.411
BmH, 200K, CosSim	0.987	0.791
BmH, 1M, collision count	0.888	0.627
BmH, 1M, CosSim	0.991	0.803
BmH, 1M, CosSim+SP	0.996	0.818
BmH, 1M, SP only	0.996	0.809
BmH, 1M, CosSim+SP+SynQE	**0.999**	**0.832**
BmH, 1M, CosSim+SP+SynAUG	0.996	0.829

Table 4: FlickrLogos-32: Logo recognition results.

Testing. An image is being tested for the presence of any of the logo classes by computing feature bundles and performing lookups in the hash table to determine the reference images that share the same bundles. The retrieved list of images is then re-ranked as described in Section 3.3. Optionally, SynQE and SynAUG may be applied: Multiple transformed versions of the original query image are used to query the database multiple times or the database is augmented with synthetic images as described in Section 5. Afterwards the fast spatial re-ranking with 1P-WGC-RANSAC without projective refinement (see Section 4) is applied to the retrieved list. Finally a logo instance is classified by a k-nn classifier: A logo of the class c is considered to be present if the majority of the top k retrieved images is of class c. In our experiments we chose $k = 5$.

Experimental Setup. The evaluation protocol is identical to that in [16]: The training and validation set including non-logo images are indexed by the respective method. The whole test set including logo and logo-free images (3960 images) is then used to compute the classification scores.

Results. Table 4 shows the obtained results for various approaches. Revaud et al. use a bag-of-words-based approach coupled with learned weights that down-weight visual words that appear across different classes [14]. It can be seen that a bag-of-words-based search as described in Section 3.4.3 followed by 5-nn majority classification already outperforms this more elaborate approach significantly. In fact, our approach using bag-of-words to retrieve the logos and performing a majority vote among the top 5 retrieved images already outperforms the best results in the literature so far.

Bundle Min-Hashing also outperforms the former scores *out of the box.* The difference between a ranking based on sketch collision counts ("collision count) and a ranking based on cosine similarity ("CosSim") makes clear that the result lists obtained by BmH must be re-ranked to ensure that the top-most images are indeed the most similar ones. We compared BmH with 200K words (highest mAP for BmH only, see Table 1) with a larger vocabulary of 1M words (slightly lower mAP). The preferable vocabulary of 1M words slightly improves the results but also reduces the complexity of the system as it eliminates the need for two different vocabularies for bundling and re-ranking. Moreover, the response

ratio of this system is 100 times smaller ($RR = 0.0096$ for BmH with 1M words) than that of bag-of-words.

Finally, it can be seen that both SynQE and SynAUG consistently improve the classification performance for both bag-of-words and Bundle Min-Hashing. As there is actually little difference SynAUG is the preferred method as the database augmentation can be performed off-line.

7. CONCLUSION

In this work we introduced a robust logo recognition technique based on finding local feature bundles in a database of reference images. This approach in combination with the new 1P-WGC-RANSAC variant for extremely fast re-ranking as well as synthetic query expansion and synthetic database augmentation significantly outperforms existing approaches.

8. REFERENCES

[1] R. Arandjelovic and A. Zisserman. Multiple queries for large scale specific object retrieval. In *BMVC*, 2012.

[2] R. Arandjelovic and A. Zisserman. Three things everyone should know to improve object retrieval. In *CVPR*, 2012.

[3] Y. Cao, C. Wang, Z. Li, and L. Zhang. Spatial-bag-of-features. In *CVPR*, 2010.

[4] O. Chum, M. Perdoch, and J. Matas. Geometric min-Hashing: Finding a (thick) needle in a haystack. In *CVPR*, 2009.

[5] O. Chum, J. Philbin, and A. Zisserman. Near duplicate image detection: min-hash and tf-idf weighting. In *BMVC*, 2008.

[6] H. Jégou, M. Douze, and C. Schmid. Improving Bag -of-Features for Large Scale Image Search. *IJCV*, 2009.

[7] H. Jegou, M. Douze, and C. Schmid. On the burstiness of visual elements. In *CVPR*, 2009.

[8] H. Jegou, M. Douze, and C. Schmid. Packing bag-of-features. In *ICCV*, 2009.

[9] K. Lebeda, J. Matas, and O. Chum. Fixing the Locally Optimized RANSAC. In *BMVC*, 2012.

[10] D. Lee, Q. Ke, and M. Isard. Partition Min-Hash for Partial Duplicate Image Discovery. *ECCV*, 2010.

[11] J. Morel and G. Yu. ASIFT: A New Framework for Fully Affine Invariant Image Comparison. *SIAM*, 2009.

[12] M. Muja and D. Lowe. Fast approximate nearest neighbors with automatic algorithm configuration. In *VISAPP*, 2009.

[13] J. Philbin, O. Chum, M. Isard, J. Sivic, and A. Zisserman. Object retrieval with large vocabularies and fast spatial matching. In *CVPR*, 2007.

[14] J. Revaud, C. Schmid, M. Douze, and C. Schmid. Correlation-Based Burstiness for Logo Retrieval. In *ACM MM*, 2012.

[15] S. Romberg, M. August, C. X. Ries, and R. Lienhart. Robust Feature Bundling. In *LNCS*, 2012.

[16] S. Romberg, L. Garcia Pueyo, R. Lienhart, and R. van Zwol. Scalable Logo Recognition in Real-World Images. In *ICMR*, 2011.

[17] J. Sivic and A. Zisserman. Video Google: a text retrieval approach to object matching in videos. *ICCV*, 2003.

[18] Z. Wu, Q. Ke, M. Isard, and J. Sun. Bundling features for large scale partial-duplicate web image search. In *CVPR*, 2009.

Fast Nonrigid 3D Retrieval Using Modal Space Transform

Jianbo Ye
The University of Hong Kong
bobye@hku.hk

Zhicheng Yan
University of Illinois at
Urbana-Champaign
zyan3@illinois.edu

Yizhou Yu
The University of Hong Kong
yizhouy@acm.org

ABSTRACT

Nonrigid or deformable 3D objects are common in many application domains. Retrieval of such objects in large databases based on shape similarity is still a challenging problem. In this paper, we first analyze the advantages of functional operators, and further propose a framework to design novel shape signatures for encoding nonrigid object structures. Our approach constructs a context-aware integral kernel operator on a manifold, then applies modal analysis to map this operator into a low-frequency functional representation, called *fast functional transform*, and finally computes its spectrum as the shape signature. Our method is fast, isometry-invariant, discriminative, and numerically stable with respect to multiple types of perturbations.

Categories and Subject Descriptors

H.3.3 [**Information Storage and Retrieval**]: Information Search and Retrieval—*Retrieval models*; H.4 [**Information Systems Applications**]: Miscellaneous; I.3.5 [**Computer Graphics**]: Computational Geometry and Object Modeling—*Geometric algorithms, languages, and systems*

Keywords

Content-Based Object Retrieval, Shape Retrieval, Biharmonic Distance, Functional Map, Shape Signature

1. INTRODUCTION

Content-based 3D object retrieval facilitates the search for desired objects within a large 3D object repository. It has become increasingly popular due to the rapid development of 3D scanning technologies and the emergence of large 3D object databases. Content-based object retrieval is useful in many application domains, including CAD/CAM, medicine, molecular biology, 3D computer games and virtual worlds.

Since many 3D object models, such as avatars, creatures and biomedical objects, can take various types of deformations, it is much desired for an object retrieval technique to be able to recognize deformed versions of an object. Nonetheless, nonrigid object

retrieval is a very challenging task because a deformed object may not be visually similar to the original one any more. Important criteria for measuring the performance of nonrigid object retrieval techniques include *isometry invariance*, *discrimination power*, *efficiency* and *stability*. In addition, there exist other considerations, including *extensibility*, *applicability* and *complexity of implementation*.

In this paper, we first analyse functional operators over modal space and further introduce spectrum-based shape signatures to encode the structure of a nonrigid shape. The basic idea underlying our shape signature is to compute the spectrum of the newly proposed functional operator, which is constructed from an intrinsic, context-aware integral kernel operator by projecting it to the linear space spanned by low-frequency modes defined over an object surface, while the integral kernel operator is itself based on a modal based pairwise distance. The resulting transformation matrix can be analytically written in a succinct form. Our method is isometry-invariant and stable with respect to noise, holes and nonisometric deformations. The implementation of our shape signature is based on linear FEM. The signature itself can be efficiently computed for meshes in a wide range of resolutions and topologies. To further boost retrieval performance, we incorporate a pseudo-relevance feedback mechanism to iteratively improve similarity ranking among retrieved object instances.

Our experiments demonstrate that our new shape signature for nonrigid objects can outperform all non-hybrid methods participating in the nonrigid track of the SHREC'11 contest [9] on a representative mixed dataset combining the dataset from the nonrigid track of SHREC'11 and another custom built dataset. In particular, our method achieves obviously higher precision than other methods when recall is above 50%.

The rest of the paper is organized as follows. Related work will be discussed in Section 1.1. In Section 2, we discuss the fundamental mathematics behind our signature design. In Section 3, we briefly sketch our numerical implementation. In Section 4, we present experimental results to validate our shape signature. Section 5 concludes our paper.

1.1 Related Work

Among extensive work on 3D object retrieval, most techniques are devoted to rigid objects and are based on extrinsic geometry such as Euclidean distance, curvatures and snapshots of 3D canonical views. Nevertheless, nonrigid models have gained increasing popularity. Their extrinsic geometry often varies under nonrigid deformations. Isometric shape deformation was initially addressed in [8], where researchers began to consider bending invariant or insensitive 3D shape recognition.

In our knowledge, two major classes of approaches are proposed for nonrigid shape retrieval during the last decade. The first class includes all local feature based approaches. Inspired by the success of the SIFT feature descriptor in image retrieval, researchers proposed analogous descriptors based on extrinsic curvatures and tangential fields, such as meshSIFT [12] and MeshHOG [25], for representing local features on mesh surfaces. ShapeGoogle [14, 4] emphasizes the robustness of association and classification, especially for objects with missing parts and topological noises. It integrates the local Heat Kernel Signature (HKS) [22, 6] with the bag-of-word framework. By extracting isometrically invariant dense point descriptors and quantizing them into binary codes, shapes are registered for efficient indexing, comparison and association.

The second class emphasizes coarser-scale or global structures of a 3D nonrigid shape. The skeleton-based method in [23] encodes the geometric and topological information in the form of a skeleton graph and uses graph matching to retrieve similar skeletons. Another method based on Gromov-Hausdorff distance has been proposed in [5] for matching nonrigid shapes. Statistical techniques, such as histograms and D2 distributions [18], are also popular in designing descriptors in respect of coarse-scale structures.

Among those methods concerning global shapes, spectrum-based techniques became popular in recent years. Shape-DNA [17] proposes to use the spectrum of the Laplace-Beltrami operator as an isometry-invariant shape descriptor. Another similar method, SD-GDM [20] proposes to compute a singular value decomposition (spectra) for the geodesic distance matrix, which seems to outperform shape-DNA [9]. However, compared to shape-DNA, matrix assembly in SD-GDM requires all-pairs geodesic distances, which are computationally prohibitive to obtain even with the latest developments in fast geodesic distance computation [24, 15], and a uniform mesh decimation is typically employed in practice to speed up this process.

Local features, such as SIFT [11] and its variants, have been successfully adopted in image retrieval. However, in the context of 3D nonrigid shape retrieval, local feature based methods have been outperformed by shape descriptors emphasizing coarser-scale structures. We provide the following explanations for this phenomenon. First, pixel values captured by a camera are related to photometric properties of real scenes and objects. Photometric properties tend to have higher frequencies than pure geometry. For example, there could be high-frequency texture patterns over a geometrically flat surface. Given such high-frequency photometric properties, it is possible for a local feature descriptor to encode sufficiently discriminative visual information for recognition or retrieval tasks. Second, 3D scanning techniques are not as mature as digital photography. Even when a 3D surface does have high-frequency details, such as pores and wrinkles on skin, it is unlikely for them to be accurately captured by a 3D scanner. Very often, such high-frequency details are buried in noises. Therefore, high-frequency geometry over a 3D surface tend to be inaccurate and unreliable, thus unsuitable for retrieval tasks.

2. OUR APPROACH

2.1 Laplace-Beltrami Operator

Shape-DNA [17] exploits eigenvalues to achieve an impressive shape retrieval performance, while there are a number of other methods, such as [18, 22], utilizing eigenvectors. All these methods compute the spectrum of the Laplace-Beltrami operator Δ_M, where M is the underlying manifold embedded in the 3D Euclidean space as a surface, by solving the following eigenvalue problem,

$$-\Delta_M u = \lambda u. \qquad (1)$$

The Laplace-Beltrami operator is a generalized operator for func-

tions defined on Riemannian manifolds. By solving the above equation, we obtain a complete set of modal bases $\{\phi_i\}_{i=0}^\infty$ over a manifold, where each ϕ_i corresponds to a normalized eigenvector with eigenvalue λ_i in an ascending order.

2.2 Functional Operator

The eigenvectors of Laplace-Beltrami operator intrinsically span a low-frequency functional space Φ which is useful in modal analysis. For example, in [13], the authors construct intrinsic flexible maps between two shapes by solving for a linear transform matrix between their modal spaces $\Phi_1 \mapsto \Phi_2$ subject to certain constraints.

We instead focus on intrinsic functional transforms i.e. maps between Φ and itself. Of course, Laplace-Beltrami operator is itself a functional transform that map $\phi_i \mapsto -\lambda_i \phi_i$, which is isometry-invariant. We in this section introduce a new set of functional transforms which are experimentally shown to be more robust in presence of their spectrums than Laplace-Beltrami operator.

Given a symmetric function, $k(\cdot, \cdot)$, let us consider the following integral kernel operator,

$$\mathcal{K}f(y) = \int_M k(x,y)f(x)\mathrm{d}x. \qquad (2)$$

If $k(\cdot, \cdot)$ is isometry-invariant, the spectrum of $\mathcal{K}$ is also isometry-invariant. For example, in the non-rigid track of the 2011 3D shape retrieval contest (SHREC'11) [9], the retrieval performance of SD-GDM [20], a method based on geodesic distance matrices (GDM), is ranked first. It outperforms shapeDNA. GDMs are in fact a class of integral kernel operators. If we set $k(x,y)$ as the geodesic distance between x and y, the spectrum of $\mathcal{K}$ is the mathematically precise form of SD-GDM and is provable isometry-invariant.

The major important contribution of our approach is instead naively computing transforms matrix in complexity of geometry (i.e. pairwise values $k(x_i, x_j)$ for all $x_i, x_j \in M$), we restrict the kernel to modal space Φ (i.e. applying the kernel to functions in Φ, the space spanned by the lower eigenvectors and then projecting the solution back onto Φ). We can write the transform matrix by

$$\widetilde{K} = \Phi^T \mathcal{K} \Phi, \qquad (3)$$

where $\Phi = [\phi_0, \phi_1, \ldots, \phi_m, \ldots]$.

It is worth noting that this restriction is not a simple efficient approximation, the functional transforms before and after restriction are different in both theory and numerics. Precisely speaking, the original functional space before restriction is generally a Banach space (and is numerically approximated in a Sobolev space, i.e. $W_{q,p}(M) = \{f \in L^p(M) : D^\alpha f \in L^p(M), \forall \alpha \le q\}^1$); while the functional space Φ in restriction is an infinite dimensional Hilbert space or inner product space (and is numerically approximated by truncating lower eigenvectors, converges in a weak sense). Hence the spectrums of $\mathcal{K}$ in these two functional spaces can be different (although they are identical for Laplace-Beltrami operator).

In our experiments (see comparison of track BiHDM and R-BiHDM in section 4.2), it is indicated spectrum computed by modal space restriction can better tolerate manifold deformations, and outperforms the spectrum of a pairwise kernel in retrieval tasks.

2.3 Distance Map Based on Modals

---
[1]Here, the notation $D^\alpha f = \frac{\partial^{|\alpha|} f}{\partial x_1^{\alpha_1} \ldots \partial x_i^{\alpha_i}}$, for $\alpha = (\alpha_1, \alpha_2, \ldots, \alpha_i)$

Computing the geodesic distance matrix is very computationally expensive for large meshes. We choose to compute (squared) biharmonic distance [10] instead because it exhibits multiple nice properties while being more efficient to compute, and can be restricted in modal space analytically in a succinct way.

In the continuous case, the (squared) biharmonic distance is defined as follows,

$$d^2(x,y) = \sum_{i=1}^{\infty} \frac{(\phi_i(x) - \phi_i(y))^2}{\lambda_i^2}, \qquad (4)$$

where ϕ_i and λ_i are the eigenfunctions and eigenvalues (resp.) of the semi-positive definite Laplace-Beltrami operator, $-\Delta\phi_i(x) = \lambda_i\phi_i(x)$, where $0 = \lambda_0 < \lambda_1 \leq \lambda_2 \leq \ldots$ and $\int_M |\phi_i|^2 = 1$. The distance is a metric, and is smooth, locally isotropic, globally "shape aware", isometry invariant, insensitive to noise and small topology changes, parameter-free, and practical to compute on a discrete mesh. In [10] these two types of distances have been extensively compared in detail. Biharmonic distance provides a nice trade-off between being nearly geodesic for small distances and global shape-awareness for large distances.

Additionally note that we can have different weight choices instead of $1/\lambda_i^2$, e.g. $\lambda_i \exp(-\lambda_i t)$. It is of course interesting to justify specific choices. But in our experiments, we in "hard-code" choose biharmonic weights to achieve favorable results. See section **??** for a more extensive discussion.

2.4 Functional Biharmonic Distance Map

Combining previous two section together, i.e. let $k(x,y) = d^2(x,y)$, we fomulate $\widetilde{K}$ explicitly as follows.

$$\begin{aligned} \mathcal{K}\phi_0(y) &= \sum_{i=1}^{\infty} \int_M \frac{(\phi_i(x) - \phi_i(y))^2}{\lambda_i^2} \phi_0(x)\mathrm{d}x \\ &= \frac{1}{\sqrt{A}} \sum_{i=1}^{\infty} \frac{1}{\lambda_i^2} + \sqrt{A} \sum_{i=1}^{\infty} \frac{\phi_i^2(y)}{\lambda_i^2} \end{aligned}$$

where A is the total area of M, and note $\phi_0 = 1/\sqrt{A}$. Let $\langle \cdot, \cdot \rangle$ be the standard inner product of L^2 functions, we have

$$\begin{aligned} a_0 &= \langle \phi_0, \mathcal{K}\phi_0 \rangle = \sum_{i=1}^{\infty} \frac{2}{\lambda_i^2}, \\ a_j &= \langle \phi_j, \mathcal{K}\phi_0 \rangle = \sqrt{A} \int_M \sum_{i=1}^{\infty} \frac{\phi_i^2}{\lambda_i^2}\phi_j \quad j > 0. \end{aligned} \qquad (5)$$

We also have

$$\begin{aligned} \mathcal{K}\phi_j(y) &= \sum_{i=1}^{\infty} \int_M \frac{(\phi_i(x) - \phi_i(y))^2}{\lambda_i^2} \phi_j(x)\mathrm{d}x \\ &= \int_M \sum_{i=1}^{\infty} \frac{\phi_i^2}{\lambda_i^2}\phi_j - \frac{2\phi_j(y)}{\lambda_j^2} \end{aligned} \quad j > 0,$$

where $\langle \phi_0, \mathcal{K}\phi_j \rangle = a_j$ and $\langle \phi_i, \mathcal{K}\phi_j \rangle = -\frac{2}{\lambda_j^2}\delta_{ij}$. Thus we have obtained the projected matrix $\widetilde{K}$, called reduced biharmonic distance matrix(R-BiHDM),

$$\widetilde{K} = \begin{bmatrix} a_0 & a_1 & a_2 & \ldots \\ a_1 & -2/\lambda_1^2 & & \\ a_2 & & -2/\lambda_2^2 & \\ \vdots & & & \ddots \end{bmatrix}. \qquad (6)$$

The above matrix is infinite. Let $\widetilde{K}_m$ be an $(m+1) \times (m+1)$ square matrix formed by the following two steps: i) take the first $m+1$ rows and first $m+1$ columns of $\widetilde{K}$; ii) when calculating each a_j in this truncated matrix, every infinite summation in (5) is

approximated by the first m terms. As $m \to \infty$, the largest tens of eigenvalues of $\widetilde{K}_m$ enjoy quick convergence rate. Figure 1 shows the maximum error of the first 30 eigenvalues versus m, the number of eigenpairs of the Laplace-Beltrami operator. It is observed that the asymptotic eigenvalues converge linearly.

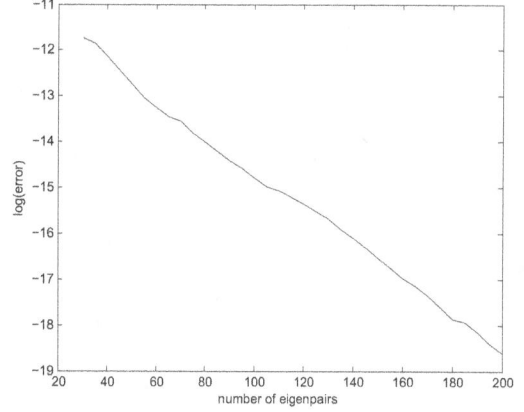

Figure 1: Convergence of the first 30 eigenvalues of an R-BiHDM.

Note that $\mathrm{tr}(\widetilde{K}) = 0$. We denote all eigenvalues of $\widetilde{K}$ in a magnitude descending order as $\{\mu_j\}_{j=0}^{L}$. We have observed that $\mu_0 > 0$ and $\mu_j < 0 \quad \forall j > 0$. (Such matrix has a single positive eigenvalue, and the rest are negative. See [1] and references therein) Hence a scale invariant spectrum can be defined as

$$\bar{\mu}_j = \left| \frac{\mu_j}{\mu_0} \right|. \qquad (7)$$

Our shape signature is defined as a vector $S = [\bar{\mu}_1, \bar{\mu}_2, \ldots, \bar{\mu}_L]^T$, which in theory is also isometric invariant. In practice, we select L ranging from $10 \sim 30$, and $m > \max\{60, 2L\}$.

To compare two shape signatures, S^p and S^q, one can reference the dissimilarity measures in [20]. In particular, let us mention two useful ones here, mean normalized Manhattan distance,

$$D_1 = \sum_{j=1}^{L} \left| \frac{S_j^p - S_j^q}{S_j^p + S_j^q} \right|,$$

which is used in SD-GDM, and normalized Euclidean distance

$$D_2^2 = \sum_{j=1}^{L} \frac{(S_j^p - S_j^q)^2}{S_j^p S_j^q}, \qquad (8)$$

which performs better for our approach by experiments.

3. IMPLEMENTATION

Computing eigenspace of the Laplace-Beltrami operator on a manifold is well studied in the literature. It involves space discretization and a sparse eigensolver. In experiments, we use the finite element method [26] (also adopted in [17, 16]) to discretize manifolds. It can handle meshes with a wide range of simplicial degrees and topologies, including non-manifolds. We found a linear FEM enough for our approach. Although solving PDEs with FEM is sampling invariant, mesh quality during discretization is an important factor affecting numerical accuracy. Fortunately, there is already considerable amount of work [7, 3] in mesh generation, repairing and quality improvement. Our method only assumes that the mesh is properly refined to at least a few thousand triangles and has no (near) degenerate faces.

Once the stiff and mass matrices have been assembled, the rest is to solve a sparse symmetric generalized eigenvalue problem that has efficient solvers, such as IRAM [2] and Krylov-Schur [21].

4. EXPERIMENTAL RESULTS

4.1 Efficiency

Efficiency is usually important for shape retrieval techniques to be practical on large datasets. Very few works in 3D shape retrieval reports their timings. Most existing techniques in shape analysis and higher-level geometry processing are computationally expensive. Computational intensity is a major limitation for methods based on optimization, geodesic computation, per-node based quantization. In contrast, our approach can always compute shape signatures in an efficient manner. Because our approach is directly based on computing lower eigenvalues/eigenvectors of Laplace-Beltrami operator and requires very little extra cost of assembly R-BiHDM (see eq. (6)) and solving for its eigenvalues. The eigensolver of Laplace-Beltrami operator contain a sparse direct preconditioner in complexity $O(n^2)$ and a dimensional free iterative eigensolver in complexity $O(n)$.

On an Intel Core2 Duo CPU E8400@3.00GHz, running times required for the methods used in the subsequent section 4.2 are reported in Table 1. Such running times are based on our implementation of R-BiHDM and SD-GDM [20][2], and the original authors' implementation of meshSIFT [12][3].

Model	#vert.	Time	Model	#vert.	Time
R-BiHDM: linear FEM			SD-GDM		
gmm_prisms	969	0.5s	gmm_prisms	969	14.8s
abstract	4096	1.7s	ant_dec	2502	2m28s
nonrigid ant	9501	4s	abstract	4096	12m13s
human meta	13336	5.8s	meshSIFT		
helicopter	22664	9.8s	ant_dec	2502	1m31s
bimba_cvd	74764	41s	abstract	4096	2m5s
desktop	106961	1m20s	nonrigid ant	9501	13m5s

Table 1: Timings for constructing shape signatures or descriptors. Our shape signature can be computed much more efficiently than most successful methods in the literature. For a mesh with 10k vertices, we can compute its signature within seconds.

It is seen from the timing table that, computations of SD-GDM and meshSIFT are expensive even for a mesh with only thousands vertices and grow super linearly, while our method is much faster at the same resolutions (see timing of model "abstract").

4.2 Signature Based Retrieval

We have tested the nonrigid shape retrieval performance of our method on a representative large dataset, which mixes the dataset from the nonrigid track of SHREC'11 with another dataset custom

[2]Geodesic distance is computed using the fast marching Matlab toolbox, http://www.mathworks.com/matlabcentral/fileexchange/6110

[3]This code can be downloaded at https://mirc.uzleuven.be/MedicalImageComputing/downloads/meshSIFT.php

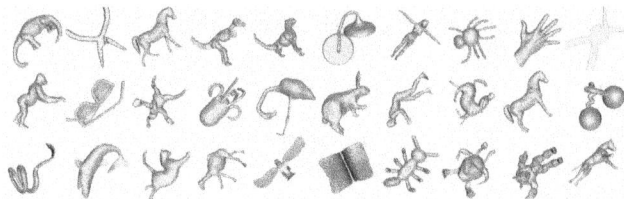

Figure 2: 30 classes of nonrigid models in the nonrigid track of SHREC'11

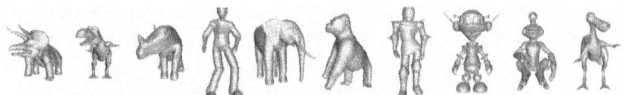

(a) Representative query meshes, including 4 bipeds, 3 dinosaurs and 3 quadrupeds

(b) Ambiguous meshes, including 13 bipeds, 13 dinosaurs and 14 quadrupeds

Figure 3: Examples from our custom built dataset

built by ourselves. The SHREC'11 nonrigid track dataset serves as a background dataset. It has 600 watertight triangle meshes that were derived from 30 original models. The custom built dataset contains 200 deformed meshes derived from 4 biped models, 3 dinosaur models and 3 quadruped models (Figure 3(a)) as well as 40 background meshes (other biped, dinosaur and quadruped models, see Figure 3 (b)). This mixed dataset was designed to be more challenging and practical than the SHREC'11 nonrigid track dataset because it contains multiple similar meshes from each category of models, such as bipeds, dinosaurs and quadrupeds. Distinguishing similar models from the same category requires a retrieval technique to be more discriminative and stable. We have performed retrieval tests on the 200 deformed meshes in the mixed dataset with a total of 840 (200+40+600) meshes.

We applied the same evaluation methodology of the SHREC'11 contest to evaluate our method. It is based on the Precision-Recall curve and five quantitative measures: Nearest Neighbor (NN), First Tier (FT), Second Tier (ST), E-measure (E), and Discounted Cumulative Gain (DCG). We refer to [19] for detailed definitions. In our method, we use Normalized Euclidean distance to measure similarity among R-BiHDM signatures (see eq. (7)).

We have compared the retrieval performance of our method with that of Shape-DNA (OrigM-n12-norm1) [17], meshSIFT [12], and SD-GDM [20]. These are the best performing non-hybrid methods in the nonrigid track of the SHREC'11 contest[4]. The parameters in these methods were set empirically to produce best performance. We have also compared our method, i.e. R-BiHDM, with pairwise

[4]A hybrid technique combining SD-GDM and meshSIFT in SHREC'11 did achieve a better performance, but it falls out of scope in our state-of-art evaluation.

METHOD	NN	FT	ST	E	DCG
shape-DNA	0.985	0.841	0.906	0.666	0.954
MeshSIFT	0.995	0.790	0.890	0.650	0.950
SD-GDM	1.000	0.929	0.986	0.731	0.991
BiHDM-n25	1.000	0.930	0.983	0.722	0.990
R-BiHDM-n30	1.000	0.970	0.996	0.739	0.997
R-BiHDM-n25	1.000	0.975	0.997	0.742	0.998
R-BiHDM-n23	**1.000**	**0.976**	**0.997**	**0.742**	**0.998**
R-BiHDM-n20	1.000	0.975	0.997	0.742	0.998
R-BiHDM-n15	1.000	0.970	0.994	0.739	0.997

Table 2: Retrieval performance evaluated using five standard measures on the mixed dataset.

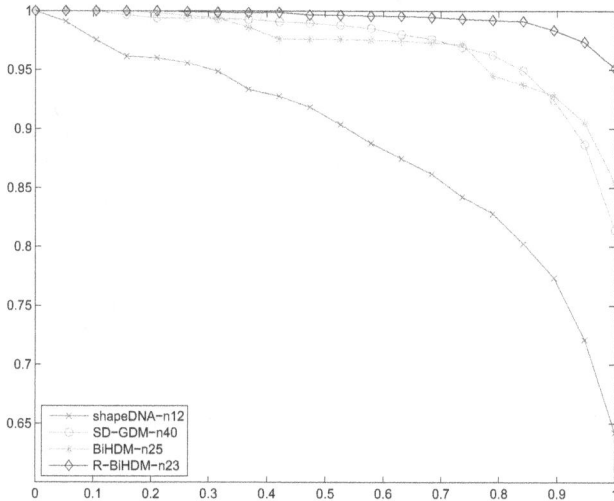

Figure 4: Precision-recall curves of R-BiHDM, SD-GDM and shapeDNA on the mixed dataset.

biharmonic distance matrix (BiHDM). Detailed comparison results on the mixed dataset are shown in Table 2 and Figure 4.

According to the statistics, our method achieves better performance than all of these methods. In particular, our method has obvious improvements in the 1-Tier precision. And according to the PR curves, our method achieves higher precision when recall is above 50%. Furthermore, the retrieval performance is stable when the number of chosen eigenvalues ranges from 15 to 30. The primary goal of shapeGoogle [14] is to achieve a high level of robustness in the presence of partial shapes and topological noises. However, it does not address the identical problem as ours. In our experiments (based on implementation provided by authors), its retrieval performance is not comparable to the other methods we compared with. The results indicate that our method exhibits strong discriminative power on datasets with very similar shape instances.

5. CONCLUSIONS

In this paper, we have first given a brief introduction to existing methods for nonrigid 3D shape retrieval, and paid special attention to global structure coding. We have further proposed a novel method for building shape signatures. Our method uses biharmonic

distance to construct a context-aware integral kernel operator on a manifold, then applies modal restriction to project this operator into a low-frequency representation, and finally computes its spectrum. Our method is isometry-invariant, discriminative, and numerically stable with respect to multiple types of perturbations. Our current implementation is based on FEM. We have evaluated our newly proposed method on representative datasets. Evaluation results indicate our method is surprisingly promising as a structural descriptor.

Our method has a few limitations that need further investigation. Although it has strength in identifying global non-rigid structures, how to enhance our method for retrieving meaningful partial shapes still remains unknown. Furthermore, it assumes the surface, which is a 2D manifold, is connected. It is unclear how to extend our method for matching and retrieving complicated models with many disconnected parts.

Acknowledgments

The authors would like to thank anonymous reviewers for their comments and suggestions. This work was partially supported by Hong Kong Research Grants Council under General Research Funds (HKU718712).

6. REFERENCES

[1] A.Y. Alfakih. On the eigenvalues of euclidean distance matrices. *Computational and Applied Mathematics*, 27(3):237–250, 2008.

[2] W.E. Arnoldi. The principle of minimized iterations in the solution of the matrix eigenvalue problem. *Quart. Appl. Math*, 9(1):17–29, 1951.

[3] M. Attene and B. Falcidieno. Remesh: An interactive environment to edit and repair triangle meshes. In *Shape Modeling and Applications, 2006. SMI 2006. IEEE International Conference on*, pages 41–41. IEEE, 2006.

[4] A.M. Bronstein, M.M. Bronstein, L.J. Guibas, and M. Ovsjanikov. Shape google: geometric words and expressions for invariant shape retrieval. *ACM Transactions on Graphics (TOG)*, 30(1):1, 2011.

[5] A.M. Bronstein, M.M. Bronstein, R. Kimmel, M. Mahmoudi, and G. Sapiro. A gromov-hausdorff framework with diffusion geometry for topologically-robust non-rigid shape matching. *International Journal of Computer Vision*, 89(2):266–286, 2010.

[6] Michael Bronstein and Iasonas Kokkinos. Scale-invariance in local heat kernel descriptors without scale selection and normalization, 2009.

[7] P. Cignoni, M. Corsini, and G. Ranzuglia. Meshlab: an open-source 3d mesh processing system. *ERCIM News*, 73:45–46, 2008.

[8] A. Elad and R. Kimmel. Bending invariant representations for surfaces. In *Computer Vision and Pattern Recognition, 2001. CVPR 2001. Proceedings of the 2001 IEEE Computer Society Conference on*, volume 1, pages I–168. IEEE, 2001.

[9] Z. Lian, A. Godil, B. Bustos, M. Daoudi, J. Hermans, S. Kawamura, Y. Kurita, G. Lavoué, H. V. Nguyen, R. Ohbuchi, Y. Ohkita, Y. Ohishi, F. Porikli, M. Reuter, I. Sipiran, D. Smeets, P. Suetens, H. Tabia, and D. Vandermeulen. SHREC '11 Track: Shape Retrieval on Non-rigid 3D Watertight Meshes. pages 79–88.

[10] Y. Lipman, R. M. Rustamov, and T. A. Funkhouser. Biharmonic distance. *ACM Transactions on Graphics, ACM 0730-0301//10-ART*, 2007.

[11] D.G. Lowe. Distinctive image features from scale-invariant keypoints. *International journal of computer vision*, 60(2):91–110, 2004.

[12] C. Maes, T. Fabry, J. Keustermans, D. Smeets, P. Suetens, and D. Vandermeulen. Feature detection on 3d face surfaces for pose normalisation and recognition. In *Biometrics: Theory Applications and Systems (BTAS), 2010 Fourth IEEE International Conference on*, pages 1–6. IEEE, 2010.

[13] M. Ovsjanikov, M. Ben-Chen, J. Solomon, A. Butscher, and L. Guibas. Functional maps: A flexible representation of maps between shapes. *ACM Transactions on Graphics (TOG)*, 31(4):30, 2012.

[14] M. Ovsjanikov, A.M. Bronstein, M.M. Bronstein, and L.J. Guibas. Shape google: a computer vision approach to isometry invariant shape retrieval. In *Computer Vision Workshops (ICCV Workshops), 2009 IEEE 12th International Conference on*, pages 320–327. IEEE, 2009.

[15] Gabriel Peyré and Laurent D. Cohen. Heuristically driven front propagation for fast geodesic extraction. *Intl. Journal for Computational Vision and Biomechanics 1(1)*, pages 55–67, 2009.

[16] Martin Reuter. Hierarchical shape segmentation and registration via topological features of laplace-beltrami eigenfunctions. *International Journal of Computer Vision*, 89(2):287–308, 2010.

[17] Martin Reuter, Franz-Erich Wolter, and Niklas Peinecke. Laplace-beltrami spectra as 'shape-DNA' of surfaces and solids. *Computer-Aided Design*, 38(4):342–366, 2006.

[18] R.M. Rustamov. Laplace-beltrami eigenfunctions for deformation invariant shape representation. In *Proceedings of the fifth Eurographics symposium on Geometry processing*, pages 225–233. Eurographics Association, 2007.

[19] Philip Shilane, Patrick Min, Michael M. Kazhdan, and Thomas A. Funkhouser. The princeton shape benchmark. In *Shape Modeling International*, pages 167–178. IEEE Computer Society, 2004.

[20] Dirk Smeets, Thomas Fabry, Jeroen Hermans, Dirk Vandermeulen, and Paul Suetens. Isometric deformation modelling for object recognition. *CAIP 2009, LNCS 5702*, pages 757–765, 2009.

[21] G. W. Stewart. A Krylov–Schur algorithm for large eigenproblems. *SIAM Journal on Matrix Analysis and Applications*, 23(3):601–614, 2001.

[22] Jian Sun, Maks Ovsjanikov, and Leonidas J. Guibas. A concise and provably informative multi-scale signature based on heat diffusion. *Comput. Graph. Forum*, 28(5):1383–1392, 2009.

[23] H. Sundar, D. Silver, N. Gagvani, and S. Dickinson. Skeleton based shape matching and retrieval. In *Shape Modeling International, 2003*, pages 130–139. IEEE, 2003.

[24] Vitaly Surazhsky, Tatiana Surazhsky, Danil Kirsanov, Steven J. Gortler, and Hugues Hoppe. Fast exact and approximate geodesics on meshes. *ACM Transactions on Graphics*, 24(3):553–560, July 2005.

[25] A. Zaharescu, E. Boyer, K. Varanasi, and R. Horaud. Surface feature detection and description with applications to mesh matching. In *Computer Vision and Pattern Recognition, 2009. CVPR 2009. IEEE Conference on*, pages 373–380. Ieee, 2009.

[26] OC Zienkiewicz, RL Taylor, and JZ Zhu. *The Finite Element Method–Its Basis and Fundamentals, volume 1*. Elsevier Butterworth-Heinemann, Amsterdam, London,, 2005.

A Shape-based Approach for Leaf Classification using Multiscale Triangular Representation

Sofiene Mouine
Inria Paris-Rocquencourt
78153 Le Chesnay, France
sofiene.mouine@inria.fr

Itheri Yahiaoui
Inria Paris-Rocquencourt
78153 Le Chesnay, France
CReSTIC Université de
Reims, FRANCE
itheri.yahiaoui@inria.fr
itheri.yahiaoui@univ-reims.fr

Anne Verroust-Blondet
Inria Paris-Rocquencourt
78153 Le Chesnay, France
anne.verroust@inria.fr

ABSTRACT

In this paper we introduce a new multiscale shape-based approach for leaf image retrieval. The leaf is represented by local descriptors associated with margin sample points. Within this local description, we study four multiscale triangle representations: the well known triangle area representation (TAR), the triangle side lengths representation (TSL) and two new representations that we denote triangle oriented angles (TOA) and triangle side lengths and angle representation (TSLA). Unlike existing TAR approaches, where a global matching is performed, the similarity measure is based on a locality sensitive hashing of local descriptors. The proposed approach is invariant under translation, rotation and scale and robust under partial occlusion. Evaluations made on four public leaf datasets show that our shape-based approach achieves a high retrieval accuracy w.r.t. state-of-art methods.

Categories and Subject Descriptors

H.3.3 [**Information Storage and Retrieval**]: Information Search and Retrieval

Keywords

shape descriptor, leaf image retrieval, plant identification, multiscale triangle representation, local description

1. INTRODUCTION

The large number of existing plant species in the world makes human identification of them tedious and time consuming, particularly for non-expert stakeholders such as land managers, foresters, agronomists, amateur gardeners, etc. Hence, an automatic plant identification tool should speed up the plant species identification task. This identification tool may be useful even for experienced botanists.

Plant identification is based on the observation of its organs, i.e. buds, leaves, fruits, stems, etc.. An interesting review of existing approaches developed for plant species identification can be found in [11]. A large amount of information about the taxonomic identity of a plant is contained in its leaves. This is due to the fact that leaves are present on the plants for at least several months, which is not generally the case for other organs such as fruits or flowers. Therefore, most plant identification tools based on Content-Based Image Retrieval techniques [3, 5, 7, 8, 9, 10, 20, 27] work on leaf image databases. Leaves can be characterized by their shape, color and texture. Leaf color may vary with the seasons and geographical locations. In addition, different plant species can have almost the same color leaves. Thus, color is not sufficiently discriminant to be used alone in a plant identification task. In this paper, we focus on the shape of the leaf and on shape-based approaches for leaf recognition. To describe the shape of a leaf, one can develop a specific approach or adapt a generic shape retrieval method to the particular case of leaves.

Specific approaches [8, 13] are based on the botanical characterization of leaf shapes. They extract morphological characters such as: Aspect Ratio, Rectangularity, Convex Area Ratio, Convex Perimeter Ratio, Sphericity, Circularity, Eccentricity and Form Factor.

Shape feature extraction techniques (cf. [26] for a survey) can be subdivided into two families: global approaches, where the shape is represented by one feature descriptor, and local approaches, where a set of local descriptors are computed at some interesting points of the shape. When global features are extracted, a global measure is used to compute the similarity of the shapes. The Curvature Scale Space approach [28] has been tested on leaves in [8, 28]. Fourier-based descriptors have also been used [30, 32, 41]. Multiscale approaches [2, 12, 20, 23, 28] have been introduced to enrich the shape description and render it more robust to noise and contour deformations.

Local approaches compute local features of landmark points of the object. Landmark points can be boundary points [6, 25] or salient points [29] of the shape. Then, a feature-to-feature matching is performed to retrieve the most similar pairs of points of two different shapes. A 2D histogram derived from the shape context [6] computing inner distances and angles between sample points of the leaf margin has been proposed in [5, 25]. Local approaches obtained good

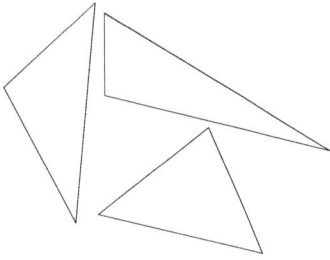

Figure 1: Three triangles having the same area

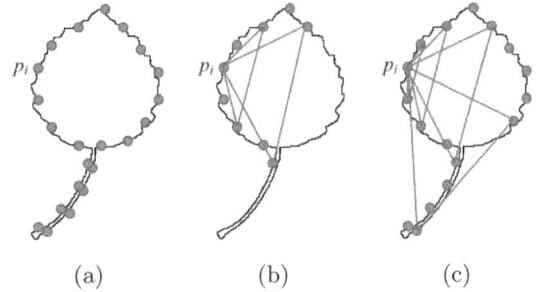

Figure 2: Multiscale triangular representation. (a) N boundary points of the leaf. Here $N = 22$. (b) N_s boundary points are selected on each side of p_i. p_i is represented by two triangles ($N_s = 2$ with $d(1) = 2$ and $d(2) = 4$) (c) p_i is represented by four triangles and logarithmic distance between triangle points ($N_s = 4$ with $d(1) = 1$, $d(2) = 2$, $d(3) = 4$ and $d(4) = 8$)

results on the Swedish leaf dataset [25] and on the Image-CLEF2011 plant identification task [29].

We want to benefit here from the advantages of both the multiscale approaches and the local ones. For this purpose, we associate a multiscale local description of the shape based on triangles to a sample of the shape contour points. Before describing our approach, let us study the possible triangle representations.

Several authors have proposed representations based on triangles built from feature points [18, 19, 36]. Tao an Grosky [36] describe the shape by a Delaunay triangulation and estimate the density of triangles discrete angles by a global histogram. In [18, 19], the authors use the angles given by the medians of the triangles joining the labelled feature points to encode their spatial relationships.

Multiscale schemes based on triangles have been introduced to describe the contour of a shape [2, 14, 21, 33, 34]. All of them represent the triangles by their areas at each scale. Shen et al. [21] showed that the triangle area representation (TAR) is affine-invariant and proposed a fast error minimization algorithm for computing correspondence matching. El Rube et al. [14] suggested computing TAR at multiscale wavelet levels (MTAR) to reduce the noise effect on the shape boundary. More recently, Alajlan et al. [1, 2] made the triangle normalization locally for each scale and used a dynamic space warping matching to compute the optimal correspondence between two shapes.

Although TAR is affine-invariant and robust to noise and deformation, it has a high computational cost since all the boundary points are used. Moreover, TAR has two major limitations:

- The area is not informative about the type of the triangle (isosceles, equilateral, etc.) considered, which may be crucial for a local description of the boundary.

- The area is not accurate enough to represent the shape of a triangle. Figure 1 shows three triangles that are equal in area but which have different shapes.

In fact, the triangles in Figure 1 are not similar triangles. They do not fulfill any of the following three properties:

(i) All three pairs of corresponding side lengths are in the same proportion.

(ii) All three pairs of corresponding angles are the same.

(iii) Two pairs of side lengths have the same proportion and the included angle is equal.

To our knowledge, the Triangle Area Representation has not been really compared to other triangle representations (using side lengths, angles, etc.). We want here to take into account the similarity property in our triangle representation. Thus, in Section 2, we present three other triangle descriptions (TSL, TSLA and TOA), based on the triangles

side lengths, their angles, or both, and integrate these representations in a multiscale based approach. Experiments made on four public leaf datasets are presented in Section 3.

2. MULTISCALE TRIANGLE REPRESENTATION

The shape boundary is represented by a sequence of N sample points $p_1, ... p_N$ uniformly distributed over the contour and numbered in a clockwise order. Then, each contour point p_i is represented by N_s triangles computed at different scales (see Figure 2). N_s is then the number of triangles and the number of scales. Unlike other multiscale triangular representations, we introduce $d(k)$ the distance between the triangle points at scale k, expressed in the number of boundary points, with $1 \leq k \leq N_s$ and d being an increasing function such that $d(N_s) \leq N/2$. In addition, to describe p_i, we do not systematically use all the remaining boundary points. We select only two sets of N_s points on both sides of p_i. The choice of N_s depends on whether we are seeking to capture local or global information. The distance $d(k)$ may be either uniform or logarithmic (cf. Figure 2). In what follows, each boundary point p_i is associated with N_s triangles $T_i^1, ..., T_i^{N_s}$, T_i^k being the triangle defined by the contour points $p_{i-d(k)}$, p_i and $p_{i+d(k)}$, $1 \leq k \leq N_s$.

Four triangle representations associated to each p_i are introduced:

$\text{TAR}(p_i) = (\text{TAR}(T_i^1), ..., \text{TAR}(T_i^{N_s}))$,
$\text{TSL}(p_i) = (\text{TSL}(T_i^1), ..., \text{TSL}(T_i^{N_s}))$,
$\text{TSLA}(p_i) = (\text{TSLA}(T_i^1), ..., \text{TSLA}(T_i^{N_s}))$ and
$\text{TOA}(p_i) = (\text{TOA}(T_i^1), ..., \text{TOA}(T_i^{N_s}))$.

The shape is then described by N feature vectors $\mathcal{T}(p_i); 1 \leq i \leq N$, $\mathcal{T}$ being either TAR, TSL, TSLA or TOA triangle representation. We will show that all these triangle representations are invariant to translation and rotation of the shape. By normalizing the description locally, we also obtain a scale invariant description of the shape.

2.1 Triangle area representation(TAR)

Here, for each triangle T, $\text{TAR}(T) = \mathcal{A}(T)$, where $\mathcal{A}(T)$ is the signed area of T. TAR is affine-invariant, robust to noise

128

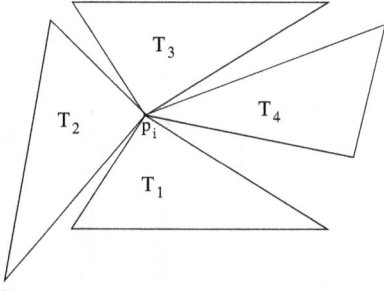

Figure 3: Triangles having the same TSL representation

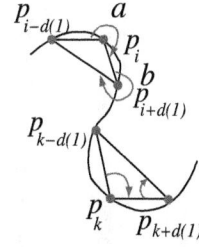

Figure 4: TOA representation

and provides information about local concavities or convexities at a given boundary point as the signed area is computed. Let $(x_{i-d(k)}, y_{i-d(k)}), (x_i, y_i)$ and $(x_{i+d(k)}, y_{i+d(k)})$ be the respective coordinates of the points $p_{i-d(k)}$, p_i and $p_{i+d(k)}$. The signed area of the triangle formed by this triplet is given by:

$$\mathcal{A}(T_i^k) = \frac{1}{2} \begin{vmatrix} x_{i-d(k)} & y_{i-d(k)} & 1 \\ x_i & y_i & 1 \\ x_{i+d(k)} & y_{i+d(k)} & 1 \end{vmatrix}$$

A normalization is made locally with respect to the maximum area in each scale as in [2]. However, the TAR used in this paper is quite different from the original TAR.
- We consider here a subset of points on the contour, unlike the original TAR where all boundary points are used.
- We define the number of scales as a parameter (N_s). In [2], $\frac{N}{2} - 1$ scales are systematically used where N is the number of points on the contour.
- The matching process is different. A dynamic space wrapping is used in [2] to compare global signatures of the shapes at each scale. Here, the feature associated to a contour point takes into account all the selected scales and then a similarity measure based on a locality sensitive hashing is used to find similar points.

2.2 Triangle side lengths representation (TSL)

TSL uses only the side lengths to represent a triangle.
Let L_{1k}, L_{2k} and L_{3k} be the three side lengths sorted in ascending order ($L_{1k} \leq L_{2k} \leq L_{3k}$) of triangle T_i^k formed by the points $p_{i-d(k)}$, p_i and $p_{i+d(k)}$, $k \in \{1, ..., N_s\}$ of the shape contour. Let $M_k = L_{1k}/L_{3k}$ and $N_k = L_{2k}/L_{3k}$.
Then $\text{TSL}(T_i^k) = (M_k, N_k)$.
The three side lengths of T_i^k are proportional to M_k, N_k and 1; this is also the case for any triangle similar to T_i^k. Thus similar triangles have an equal TSL representation and TSL is invariant under scale, translation, rotation and reflection around the contour points.
Figure 3 shows an example of four triangles having the same TSL representation. T_2 is a result of a rotation of T_1 around p_i while T_3 is the mirror image of T_1 w.r.t. a horizontal line. Note that the vertex angle p_i of T_4 is different from the vertex angle p_i of the other triangles. However, the TSL representation is the same since the triangle side lengths are sorted.

2.3 Triangle represented by two side lengths and an angle (TSLA)

Let θ be the absolute value of the vertex angle at point p_i of triangle T_i^k. TSLA representation of T_i^k is the triplet (M_k, N_k, θ), where $(M_k, N_k) = \text{TSL}(T_i^k)$. TSLA is more accurate than TSL. For example, the similar triangles T_1 and T_4 in Figure 3 have different TSLA representations because the respective angles at p_i are distinct. On the other hand, $\text{TSLA}(T_1)$ and $\text{TSLA}(T_3)$ are equal. Like TSL, the TSLA representation is invariant under scale and reflection around the contour points.

2.4 Triangle represented by two oriented angles (TOA)

TOA uses only angle values to represent a triangle.
Let $a_k = \angle p_{i-d(k)} p_i p_{i+d(k)}$ and $b_k = \angle p_i p_{i+d(k)} p_{i-d(k)}$ two successive oriented angles of triangle T_i^k.
Then $\text{TOA}(T_i^k) = (a_k, b_k)$.
The angle orientation provides information about local concavities and convexities (cf. Figure 4). In fact, an obtuse angle means convex, an acute angle means concave. TOA is not invariant under reflection around the contour point: here, only similar triangles having equal angles at p_i will have equal TOA values.

2.5 Matching Method

TSL, TSLA and TOA represent local descriptions of contour points. In fact, a feature vector F_i is associated to each contour point p_i $i \in \{1, .., N\}$. The size of the signature using TSL, TSLA and TOA depends on the number of scales N_s.
$\text{Size}[(TSL(p_i))] = \text{Size}[(TOA(p_i))] = 2 \times N_s$.
$\text{Size}[(TSLA(p_i))] = 3 \times N_s$
$\text{Size}[(TAR(p_i))] = N_s$
When a small number of scales is used, we obtain a compact representation of each contour point. The matching process is a feature-to-feature comparison. It is the same for all the triangle descriptors presented above. The features matching is done by an approximate similarity search technique based on a Locality Sensitive Hashing (LSH) method [31]. We use the Multi Probe Locality Sensitive Hashing technique [22] and the distance L_2 to compute the similarity between two feature vectors. The principle of this algorithm is to project all the features in an L-dimensional space and to use hash functions to reduce the search and the cost time. At query time, the features $F_1, F_2, ..., F_n$ of the query image are mapped onto the hash tables and the k-nearest neighbors ($k - nn$) of each feature F_i are searched for in the buckets associated to F_i. These n lists of candidate feature matches

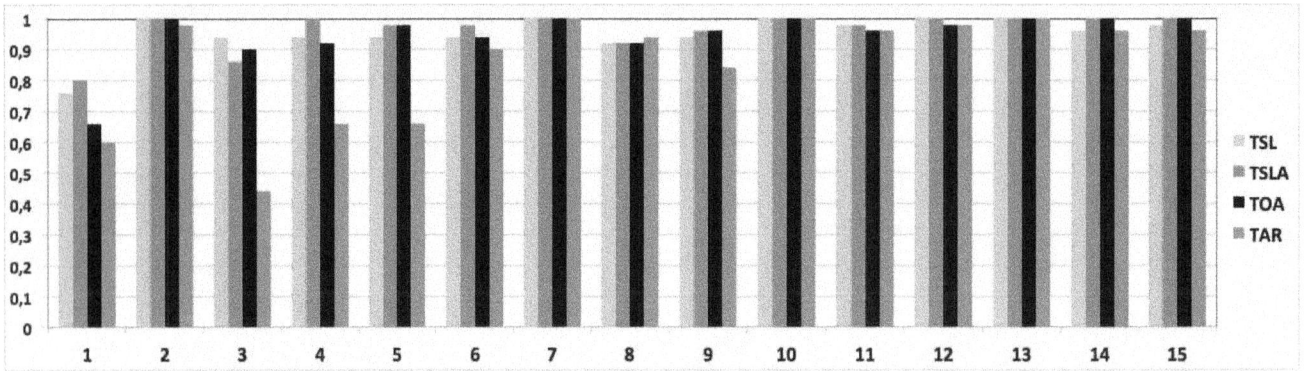

Figure 5: Results per class on the Swedish leaf dataset

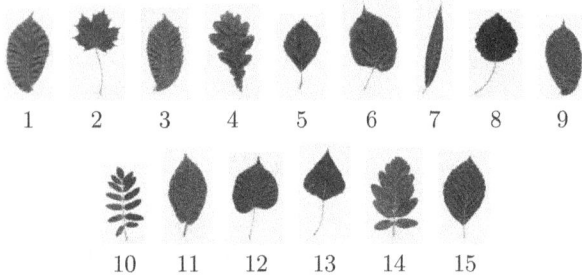

Figure 6: Overview of the Swedish leaf dataset. One image per species is kept.

Method	Classification rate
TSLA	**96.53%**
TSL	**95.73%**
TOA	95.20%
TAR	90.40%
Shape Tree [15]	**96.28%**
SPTC+DP[1]	95.33%
MDS+SC+DP[1]	95.33%
IDSC + DP[1]	94.13%
IDSC + learned distance [4]	93.80%
sPACT (on contour) [37]	90.77%
Fourier[1]	89.60%
SC + DP[1]	88.12%
Söderkvist [35]	82.40%

Table 1: classification rates on the Swedish leaf dataset.

are used as input for a voting system to rank images according to the number of matched features.

3. EXPERIMENTAL RESULTS ON LEAVES

Our descriptors have been tested on four leaf datasets: the Swedish leaf dataset[35], the Flavia dataset [38], the ImageCLEF dataset in 2011 [16] and in 2012 [17]. In all the experiments, a leaf image contains a single leaf on an uniform background. A preprocessing step is required to isolate the leaf area. First, we apply the Otsu threshold method to remove the background and keep only the mask corresponding to the leaf. A closed contour is then extracted from the leaf mask. Note that the input of all the representations described above is a sequence of N boundary points regardless of other leaf features like texture, color and venation.

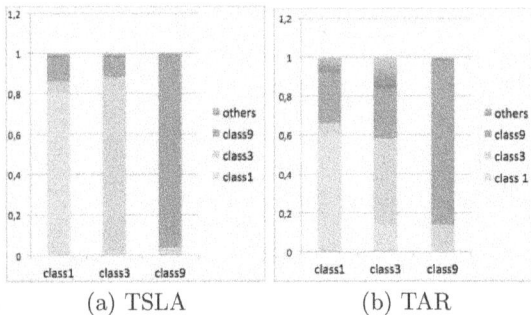

(a) TSLA   (b) TAR

Figure 7: classification results of the first, the third and the From Flaviaes

3.1 The Swedish leaf dataset

The Swedish leaf dataset [35] contains 1125 images of leaves uniformly distributed in 15 species. Figure 6 shows sample leaves. The Swedish leaf dataset is very challenging because of its high inter-species similarity. One can notice the similarity of shapes of the first, third, and ninth species. To compare our approach with existing ones, we adopted the evaluation protocol used in [25, 37, 35, 4]. We randomly split each class into two sets: a training set containing 25 images and a testing set consisting of the remaining 50 images; we computed the classification rate given by the nearest neighbor (1-NN).

Table 1 shows the classification rate of the different representations compared to shape-based methods found in the literature. The number of boundary points is the same for all the proposed descriptors ($N = 400$). We are positioned first using the TSLA representation with 6 scales ($N_s = 6$) and a logarithmic periodicity between scales ($d(k) = 2^k$). TSLA outperforms all state-of-art methods while the TSL representation obtains the third best score with 95.73% using 7 scales ($N_s = 7$) and a logarithmic distance between triangles at different scales. The parameters that give the best results for the TOA and the TAR descriptors are respectively $N_s = 64$, $d(k) = 2 \times k$ and $N_s = 4$, $d(k) = 2^k$.

---

[1]methods tested in [25]

130

Figure 8: Sample leaves from the Flavia dataset. One image per species is shown.

To compare the triangular representations, we use the same parameters that give the best classification rate (96.53%) with TSLA and we apply them on TSL, TOA and TAR. The performance of the descriptors for each class is shown in Figure 5. Examining the results per class on the Swedish leaf dataset, we notice that:
- The lowest classification rates are obtained on the first class for TSL, TSLA and TOA. However, the TSLA descriptor performs better than all the other representations. This is due to the leaf shape similarity between the first, the third and the ninth classes.
Figure 7 shows that classification errors are due to the confusion between these classes.
- The TSLA descriptor performs either as well as or better than the TSL descriptor on 14 out of 15 classes. This confirms our initial assumption: by adding an angle to the TSL representation, we obtain a more accurate description of the contour.
- The TSL, TSLA, TOA descriptors give higher classification rates than the TAR descriptor on 14 out of 15 classes. The difference is significant in the third, fourth and fifth class. This confirms that the triangle side lengths and angles are more informative than area about the shape of the triangle.

3.2 The Flavia dataset

The Flavia dataset is composed of 1907 scans of leaves belonging to 32 species (see Figure 8). Several methods were tested in [24] on Flavia. To compare our approach with these methods, we used the same evaluation metrics as those in [24]: the Mean Average Precision (MAP) and the recall/precision curves. The precision P and the recall R values are given by:

$$P = \frac{\#\text{relevant images}}{\#\text{retrieved images}}, \; R = \frac{\#\text{retrieved relevant images}}{\#\text{relevant images}}$$

The MAP value is measured on a set of queries Q and is defined as follows:

$$MAP = \frac{\sum\limits_{q \in Q} AP(q)}{|Q|}$$

where the average precision score $AP(q)$ is computed for each query q:

$$AP(q) = \frac{\sum\limits_{k=1}^{n} (P(k) \times f(k))}{\#\text{retrieved relevant images for q}}$$

Methods in [24]	D2	MSDM	GEDT	REM
MAP	42.82	47.91	48.01	57.21
Ours	TAR	TSL	TOA	TSLA
MAP	50.81	**65.94**	**68.37**	**69.93**

Table 2: Mean Average Precision on the Flavia dataset

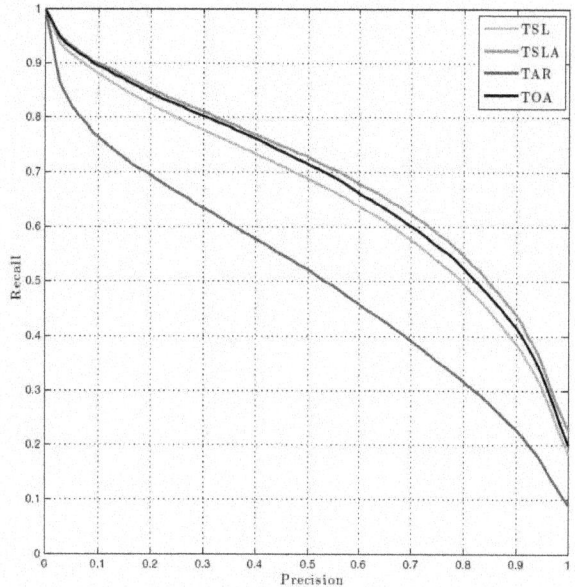

Figure 9: Recall/Precision curves on the Flavia dataset

$P(k)$ is the precision at cut-off k in the list of retrieved images and $f(k)$ is equal to 1 when the image at rank k is relevant and 0 otherwise. The results are reported in Table 2. The TSL, TOA, and TSLA descriptors significantly outperform other methods. In this experiment, we used the same parameters for all the representations: 400 boundary points and 10 scales ($N = 400$, $N_s = 10$). Despite the high similarity of the shapes of different species, our approach shows a high capability to discriminate between species.

The recall/precision curves in Figure 9 show the performance of our descriptors on the Flavia dataset. We observe that TSL, TOA, TSLA perform in a similar way. The TAR representation gives the lowest performance. The recall/precision curves also prove that the angular information (TSLA, TOA) enhances the retrieval performance.

3.3 Comparison with ImageCLEF2011 results

Let us now introduce the context of the plant identification task of ImageCLEF 2011[16]. The ImageCLEF2011 dataset contains three categories of images:
- scans of leaves acquired using a flat-bed scanner
- scan-like leaf images acquired using a digital camera
- free natural photos
For each category, the images are divided into two sets: a training set and a test set. The goal of the task is to find the correct tree species of each test image. The identification score is quite different from the classic measures such as the MAP value and recall-precision curves. Two assumptions guided the identification score S definition:

- The leaves from the same tree may be more similar than leaves from different trees (the classification rate on each individual plant is averaged).

- Photos taken by the same person will have nearly the same acquisition protocol (S measures the mean of the average classification rate per user).

Then, S is defined as follows in ImageCLEF 2011:

$$S = \frac{1}{U} \sum_{u=1}^{U} \frac{1}{P_u} \sum_{p=1}^{P_u} \frac{1}{N_{u,p}} \sum_{p=1}^{N_{u,p}} s_{u,p,n}$$

U: number of users (who have at least one image in the test data).

P_u: number of individual plants observed by the uth user.

$N_{u,p}$: number of pictures taken of the pth plant observed by the uth user.

$s_{u,p,n}$: classification score (1 or 0) for the nth picture taken of the pth plant observed by the uth user.

We focus on scans and scan-like images. The first category contains 2349 images for training and 721 test images. For the scan-like category, 717 images are used for training and 180 images for testing. Table 4 shows the identification scores of our descriptors compared to other submitted runs of ImageCLEF2011. Our identification scores are higher than all the scores of the other methods on scans as well as scan-like images. If we average the score between the two categories, the TOA representation is slightly better. Note also that the identification score using TOA is nearly the same on scans and scan-like images, although the noise that may exist in scan-like images (shadows, cluttered background, etc.). This demonstrates that a shape-based approach is suitable for a plant identification task.

run_id	Scans	Scan-like
IFSC_USP_run2	**0.562**	0.402
inria_imedia_plantnet_run1	**0.685**	0.464
IFSC_USP_run1	0.411	0.430
LIRIS_run3	0.546	0.513
LIRIS_run1	0.539	**0.543**
Sabanci-okan-run1	**0.682**	0.476
LIRIS_run2	0.530	0.508
LIRIS_run4	0.537	**0.538**
inria_imedia_plantnet_run2	0.477	**0.554**
IFSC_USP_run3	0.356	0.187
DFH+GP [39]	**0.778**	**0.725**
TSL	**0.802**	**0.757**
TOA	**0.794**	**0.780**
TSLA	**0.796**	**0.779**
TAR	**0.721**	**0.636**

Table 3: Normalized classification scores of the scan and scan-like images on the ImageCLEF2011 dataset using the evaluation metric of [16]

3.4 Comparison with ImageCLEF2012 results

The formula used to rank the runs in the ImageCLEF2012 plant identification task [17] is nearly the same as in 2011 (see [17] for details). The scan dataset contains 4870 images for training and 1760 test images. The scan-like category contains 1819 images for training and 907 images for testing. We obtain the second best results for all the triangle descriptors on the scan images and the three descriptors TSL,

	Scans	Scan-like
Top 3 Scores	**0.58**	**0.59**
	0.49	**0.55**
	0.47	**0.54**
TSL	**0,52**	**0.61**
TOA	**0.54**	**0.63**
TSLA	**0.53**	**0.63**
TAR	**0.52**	**0.51**

Table 4: Normalized classification scores of the scan and scan-like images using the evaluation metric of [17] (ImageCLEF2012)

TSLA and TOA outperform the ImageCLEF2012 runs for the scan-like images. Note that the method that achieved the best score on scans (0.58) used a set of 27 features describing the shape, the texture and the color of the leaf [40]. In our case, we used only one shape descriptor.

3.5 Robustness to partial occlusion

In this experiment, we evaluate the performance of the proposed shape representation under partial occlusion. Partial occlusion may be due to uneven lighting conditions or overlapping objects. We picked five leaf images from the Flavia dataset and we applied three different types of occlusion: lobe occlusion, half leaf occlusion and multi occlusions. This eliminates from 20% up to 50% of the contour points. (cf. Figure 11). Taking into account that some boundary points are more sensitive to occlusion than others, we simultaneously applied multi occlusions of different parts of the leaf for the image I_5 in Figure 11.

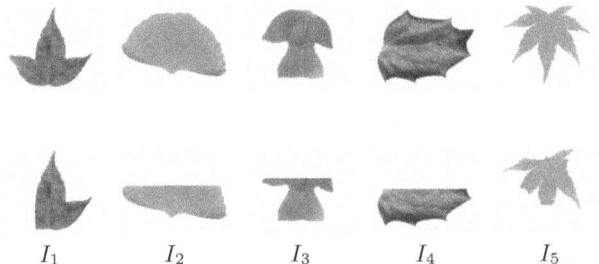

Figure 10: Partial occlusions on Flavia leaf images. First row: original images. Second row: occluded leaves

	I_1	I_2	I_3	I_4	I_5	Average	Lost
TSL	100	86.6	93.3	100	93.3	94.4	5.4
TSLA	100	100	93.3	100	60	90.6	9.4
TOA	100	100	100	100	80	96	4
TAR	93.3	86.6	80	100	73.3	86.6	13.4

Table 5: Classification rates of occluded images.

In fact, the robustness of the descriptor depends on the choice of the number of triangles N_s. Here, the descriptor parameters are the same as those used previously on the Flavia dataset. Five retrieval tests were carried out using the occluded leaf images as queries. The results are presented in Table 5. We compare the obtained results to the scores of classification when original images are used as queries (100%

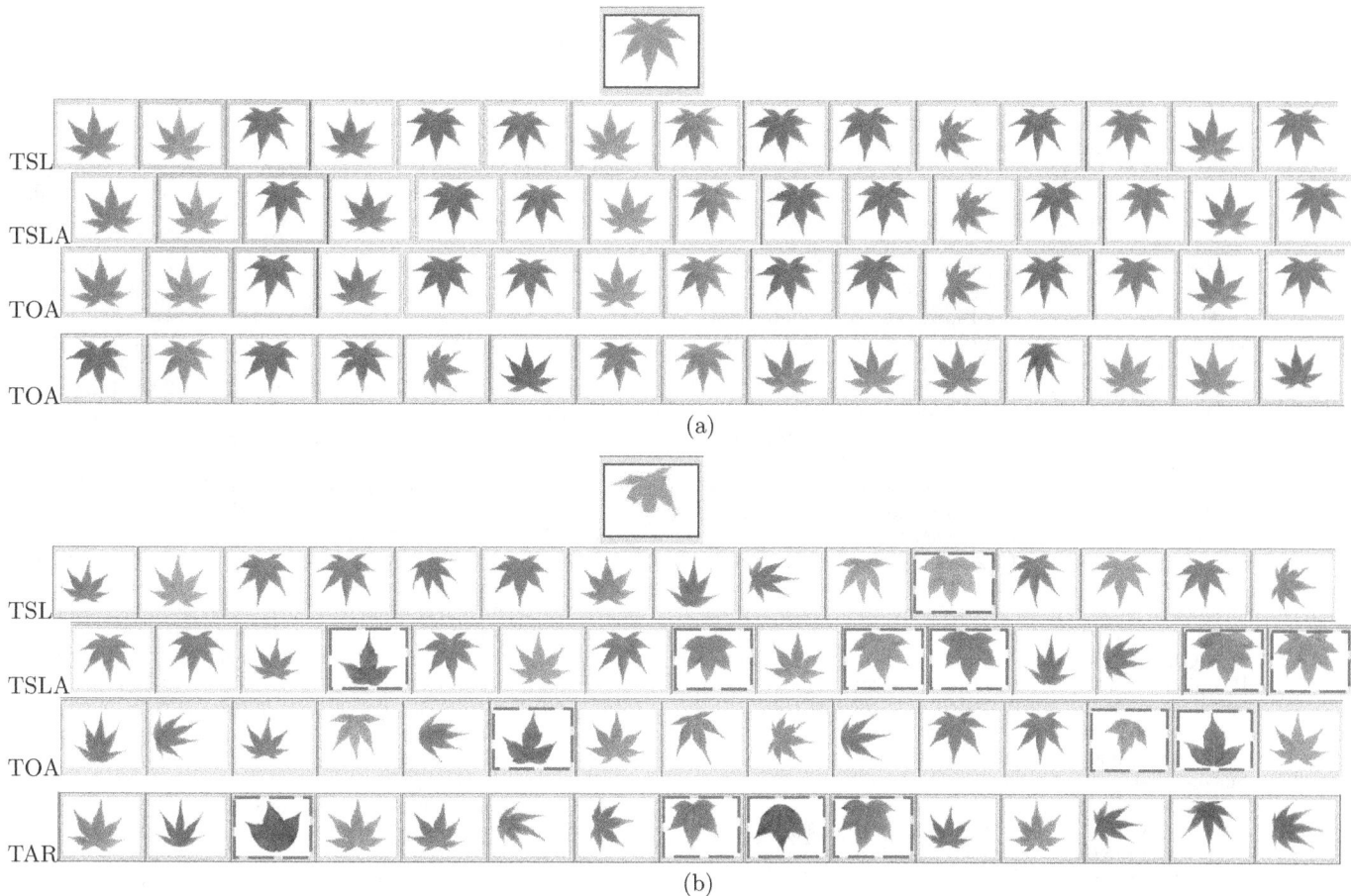

Figure 11: Examples of retrieval queries. The query image is framed by a solid blue line. False positives are framed by a dashed red line (a) the original image is used as a query image (b) the occluded image (I_5) is used as a query image

for all the descriptors with $knn = 15$).

The percentage of lost information is less than 10% for TSL, TSLA and TOA. The TOA descriptor obtained the best average score of classification (96%) over the five occluded images. The TSL description is the the best in term of robustness against multi occlusions applied on the image I_5. Retrieval queries using I_5 can be seen in Figure 10.

4. CONCLUSION

In this paper, we have presented a multiscale shape-based approach for leaf classification. We have compared four triangle representations based either on area (TAR) or side lengths and angles. We have introduced two triangle representations: TSLA and TOA. The experiments carried out on four leaf datasets show that using angles and side lengths, is more appropriate than the area for triangle description. However, to compare our descriptors to the original TAR, a matching method based on dynamic programming should be developed. Moreover, the angular information provides a more precise description when it is jointly used with the triangle side lengths. Our approach is invariant to translation, rotation and scale. We have also shown that the different local descriptors are robust under partial occlusion.

In our future work, we want to include other leaf features such as venation points to increase the accuracy of the leaf species identification.

5. ACKNOWLEDGEMENTS

This research has been conducted with the support of the Agropolis Foundation through the Pl@ntNet project. We would like also to thank Vera Bakić for her help to accomplish this work and Richard James for revising the English of this paper.

6. REFERENCES

[1] N. Alajlan, M. Kamel, and G. Freeman. Geometry-based image retrieval in binary image databases. *Pattern Analysis and Machine Intelligence, IEEE Transactions on*, 30(6):1003 –1013, June 2008.

[2] N. Alajlan, I. E. Rube, M. S. Kamel, and G. Freeman. Shape retrieval using triangle-area representation and dynamic space warping. *Pattern Recognition*, 40(7):1911 – 1920, 2007.

[3] A. R. Backes, D. Casanova, and O. M. Bruno. A complex network-based approach for boundary shape analysis. *Pattern Recognition*, 42(1):54–67, 2009.

[4] X. Bai, X. Yang, L. Latecki, W. Liu, and Z. Tu. Learning context-sensitive shape similarity by graph transduction.

Pattern Analysis and Machine Intelligence, IEEE Transactions on, 32(5):861 –874, May 2010.

[5] P. Belhumeur, D. Chen, S. Feiner, D. Jacobs, W. Kress, H. Ling, I. Lopez, R. Ramamoorthi, S. Sheorey, S. White, and L. Zhang. Searching the world's herbaria: A system for visual identification of plant species. In *European Conference on Computer Vision (ECCV)*, pages 116–129, 2008.

[6] S. Belongie, J. Malik, and J. Puzicha. Shape matching and object recognition using shape contexts. *IEEE Transactions on Pattern Analysis and Machine Intelligence*, 24(4):509 –522, Apr. 2002.

[7] O. M. Bruno, R. de Oliveira Plotze, M. Falvo, and M. de Castro. Fractal dimension applied to plant identification. *Information Sciences*, 178(12):2722 – 2733, 2008.

[8] C. Caballero and M. C. Aranda. Plant species identification using leaf image retrieval. In *ACM International Conference on Image and Video Retrieval (CIVR)*, pages 327–334, 2010.

[9] D. Casanova, J. B. Florindo, and O. M. Bruno. IFSC/USP at ImageCLEF 2011: Plant identication task. In *CLEF (Notebook Papers/Labs/Workshop)*, 2011.

[10] G. Cerutti, L. Tougne, A. Vacavant, and D. Coquin. A parametric active polygon for leaf segmentation and shape estimation. In *International Symposium on Visual Computing (ISVC)*, pages 202–213, 2011.

[11] J. S. Cope, D. Corney, J. Y. Clark, P. Remagnino, and P. Wilkin. Plant species identification using digital morphometrics: A review. *Expert Systems with Applications*, 39(8):7562 – 7573, 2012.

[12] C. Direkoğlu and M. S. Nixon. Shape classification via image-based multiscale description. *Pattern Recogn.*, 44(9):2134–2146, Sept. 2011.

[13] J.-X. Du, X.-F. Wang, and G.-J. Zhang. Leaf shape based plant species recognition. *Applied Mathematics and Computation*, 185(2):883 – 893, 2007.

[14] I. El Rube, N. Alajlan, M. Kamel, M. Ahmed, and G. Freeman. Robust multiscale triangle-area representation for 2D shapes. In *Image Processing, 2005. ICIP 2005. IEEE International Conference on*, volume 1, pages I –545–8, Sept. 2005.

[15] P. F. Felzenszwalb and J. D. Schwartz. Hierarchical matching of deformable shapes. In *Computer Vision and Pattern Recognition, 2007. CVPR '07. IEEE Conference on*, pages 1–8, 2007.

[16] H. Goëau, P. Bonnet, A. Joly, N. Boujemaa, D. Barthelemy, J.-F. Molino, P. Birnbaum, E. Mouysset, and M. Picard. The CLEF 2011 plant images classification task. In *CLEF (Notebook Papers/Labs/Workshop)*, 2011.

[17] H. Goëau, P. Bonnet, A. Joly, I. Yahiaoui, D. Barthélémy, N. Boujemaa, and J.-F. Molino. The ImageCLEF 2012 Plant identification Task. In *CLEF 2012*, Rome, Italy, Sept. 2012.

[18] D. Guru and P. Nagabhushan. Triangular spatial relationship: a new approach for spatial knowledge representation. *Pattern Recognition Letters*, 22(9):999 – 1006, 2001.

[19] N. Hoàng, V. Gouet-Brunet, M. Rukoz, and M. Manouvrier. Embedding spatial information into image content description for scene retrieval. *Pattern Recognition*, 43(9):3013 – 3024, 2010.

[20] C. Im, H. Nishida, and T. L. Kunii. A hierarchical method of recognizing plant species by leaf shapes. In *IAPR Workshop on Machine Vision Applications (MVA)*, pages 158–161, Nov. 1998.

[21] H. H. Ip and D. Shen. An affine-invariant active contour model (ai-snake) for model-based segmentation. *Image and Vision Computing*, 16(2):135 – 146, 1998.

[22] A. Joly and O. Buisson. A posteriori multi-probe locality hashing. In *16th ACM international conference on Multimedia*, pages 209–218, 2008.

[23] N. Kumar, P. N. Belhumeur, A. Biswas, D. W. Jacobs, W. J. Kress, I. C. Lopez, and J. V. B. Soares. Leafsnap: A computer vision system for automatic plant species identification. In *12th European Conference on Computer Vision (ECCV 2012)*, pages 502–516, Florence, Italy, Oct. 2012.

[24] H. Laga, S. Kurtek, A. Srivastava, M. Golzarian, and S. Miklavcic. A riemannian elastic metric for shape-based plant leaf classification. In *Digital Image Computing: Techniques and Applications*, 2012.

[25] H. Ling and D. Jacobs. Shape classification using the inner-distance. *IEEE Transactions on Pattern Analysis and Machine Intelligence*, 29(2):286 –299, Feb. 2007.

[26] Y. Mingqiang, K. Kidiyo, and R. Joseph. A survey of shape feature extraction techniques. *Pattern Recognition Techniques, Technology and Applications*, 2008. ISBN: 978-953-7619-24-4, InTech.

[27] F. Mokhtarian and S. Abbasi. Matching shapes with self-intersections: application to leaf classification. *IEEE Transactions on Image Processing*, 13(5):653 –661, May 2004.

[28] F. Mokhtarian, S. Abbasi, and J. Kittler. Robust and efficient shape indexing through curvature scale space. In *British Machine Vision Conference (BMVC)*, 1996.

[29] S. Mouine, I. Yahiaoui, and A. Verroust-Blondet. Advanced shape context for plant species identification using leaf image retrieval. In *2nd ACM International Conference on Multimedia Retrieval*, pages 49:1–49:8, 2012.

[30] J. C. Neto, G. E. Meyer, D. D. Jones, and A. K. Samal. Plant species identification using elliptic Fourier leaf shape analysis. *Computers and Electronics in Agriculture*, 50(2):121 – 134, 2006.

[31] L. Paulevé, H. Jégou, and L. Amsaleg. Locality sensitive hashing: A comparison of hash function types and querying mechanisms. *Pattern Recognition Letters*, 31(11):1348–1358, 2010.

[32] E. Persoon and K.-S. Fu. Shape discrimination using fourier descriptors. *IEEE Transactions on Pattern Analysis and Machine Intelligence*, 8:388–397, 1986.

[33] D. Shen, H. H. Ip, and E. K. Teoh. Affine invariant detection of perceptually parallel 3d planar curves. *Pattern Recognition*, 33(11):1909 – 1918, 2000.

[34] D. Shen, W. Wong, and H. Ip. Affine-invariant image retrieval by correspondence matching of shapes. *Image and Vision Computing*, 17(7):489–499, May 1999.

[35] O. J. O. Söderkvist. Computer vision classification of leaves from swedish trees. Master's thesis, Linköping University, SE-581 83 Linköping, Sweden, Sept. 2001.

[36] Y. Tao and W. I. Grosky. Image indexing and retrieval using object-based point feature maps. *J. Vis. Lang. Comput.*, 11(3):323–343, 2000.

[37] J. Wu and J. Rehg. Where am I: Place instance and category recognition using spatial pact. In *Computer Vision and Pattern Recognition, 2008. CVPR 2008. IEEE Conference on*, pages 1 –8, June 2008.

[38] S. Wu, F. Bao, E. Xu, Y.-X. Wang, Y.-F. Chang, and Q.-L. Xiang. A leaf recognition algorithm for plant classification using probabilistic neural network. In *Signal Processing and Information Technology, 2007 IEEE International Symposium on*, pages 11 –16, Dec. 2007.

[39] I. Yahiaoui, O. Mzoughi, and N. Boujemaa. Leaf shape descriptor for tree species identification. In *IEEE International Conference on Multimedia and Expo, ICME 2012*, pages 254–259, 2012.

[40] B. Yanikoglu, E. Aptoula, and C. Tirkaz. Sabanci-Okan system at ImageClef 2012: Combining features and classifiers for plant identification. In *CLEF (Online Working Notes/Labs/Workshop)*, 2012.

[41] C. T. Zahn and R. Z. Roskies. Fourier descriptors for plane closed curves. *IEEE Trans. Comput.*, 21(3):269–281, Mar. 1972.

Social Event Detection with Robust High-Order Co-Clustering

Bing-Kun Bao[12], Weiqing Min[12], Ke Lu[3], and Changsheng Xu[12]

[1] National Laboratory of Pattern Recognition Institute of Automation, Chinese Academy of Science, China

[2] China-Singapore Institute of Digital Media, Singapore

[3] University of Chinese Academy of Sciences, China

bkbao@nlpr.ia.ac.cn, wqmin@nlpr.ia.ac.cn, luk@ucas.ac.cn, csxu@nlpr.ia.ac.cn

ABSTRACT

This paper is devoted to detecting social, real-world events from the sharing images/videos on social media sites like Flickr and YouTube. The fast growing contents make the social media sites become gold mines for social event detection, but we still need to overcome the challenge of processing the associated heterogeneous metadata, such as time-stamp, location, visual content and textual content. Different from the traditional early or late fusion with different types of metadata, we represent them into a star-structured K-partite graph, that is, social media itself is regarded as the central vertices set and different types of metadata are treated as the auxiliary vertices sets which are pairwise independent with each other but correlated with the central one. Based on this graph, Social Event Detection with Robust High-Order Co-Clustering (SED-RHOCC) algorithm is proposed and it includes two steps: 1) coarse event detection, 2) clusters and samples refinement. In the first step, by revealing the inter-relationship on the constructed star-structured K-partite graph and the intra-relationship within some metadata sets such as time-stamp, we co-cluster social media and the associated metadata separately and iteratively to avoid information loss in early/late fusion. After that, a post process is utilized to refine the clusters and social media samples in the second step. MediaEval Social Event Detection Dataset [1] and its subset are selected to demonstrate the effectiveness of our proposed approach in handling the datasets with and without non-event samples.

Categories and Subject Descriptors

I.5.3 [**Pattern Recognition**]: Clustering

General Terms

Theory, Algorithms, Experimentation

Keywords

Social media, Social event detection, Co-clustering, High-order co-clustering

1. INTRODUCTION

With the explosive growth of social media sharing websites, such as Flickr and YouTube, there are billions of images and videos shared in the Internet. It was reported by Flickr that about 7,000 images were uploaded to the site every minute. Such massive collections of images and videos provide us an informative source to capture various social, real-world events. Motivated by this observation, the social topic detection from those public social media sharing websites has emerged as a hot research topic and received a lot of attention. For example, MediaEval[1], a benchmarking initiative, holds a challenge of social event detection every year. Although a lot of efforts have been made, the results can still be further improved.

Different from the traditional topic detection problems, which generally involve a single modality such as document, social media includes unstructured and heterogeneous metadata in multiple modalities. Therefore, a new issue arising for social event detection is the integration/fusion of multiple heterogeneous metadata, such as time-stamp, location, visual content and textual content [2] [3] [4] [5] [6] [7]. Some work focuses on utilizing a known clustering in the currently examined domain to supervise the multi-modal fusion. Becker *et al.* exploited a number of metadata including time-stamp, location and textual information, then trained a classifier to learn the similarity metric between social media pairs, and clustered those social media into different event groups [3]. Petkos *et al.* trained a classifier to predict the "same cluster" relationship by using the set of pairwise similarities for all modalities, and the predicted relationship set was used to obtain the final multimodal clustering [2]. However, this kind of methods heavily rely upon the existing knowledge of social event set. Another portion of social event detection methods work on sequentially processing those heterogenous metadata. Wang *et al.* performed two clustering phases, in which one is based on time, the other one is based on location, tag and text [8]. Papadopoulos *et al.* divided social event detection into three steps, that is, photo filtering by city-level and finer-grained classifiers, event partitioning by temporal information, and event expansion with other associated metadata [9].

---

[1]http://www.multimediaeval.org/

This paper casts the social event detection as a clustering problem and attempts to co-cluster the social media as well as multiple types of heterogeneous metadata. Ideally, each cluster of social media corresponds to one social event. Two steps, coarse event detection and clusters and samples refinement, are utilized to achieve our co-clustering result. In the first step, we first model the inter-relationship on K-partite graph which is constructed with social media set and the associated $K-1$ types of metadata, then the intra-relationship on some metadata sets is revealed by global regularization, at last, we formulate the overall objective function by integrating the inter- and intra- relationship models to iteratively co-cluster all the involved K sets at the same time. Specifically, in our work, star-structured K-partite graph is constructed by regarding social media set as the central vertices set and four types metadata (time-stamp, location, visual content and textural content) as the auxiliary vertices sets which are pairwise independent with each other but correlated with the central one. Also, we investigate the intra-relationship on time space, since the event usually lasts a specific time period. In the step of clusters and samples refinement, a post-process is utilized to 1) filter and merge clusters, and 2) prune and replenish social media samples. Based on the above two steps, we propose Social Event Detection with Robust High-Order Co-Clustering, referred to SED-RHOCC, which not only simultaneously co-clusters multiple heterogeneous metadata together to coarsely detect social events, but also has the ability to prune away the non-event clusters as well as the non-topic social media samples.

The rest of this paper is organized as follows: in Section 2, we briefly review the related work. Section 3 introduces our SED-RHOCC method in detail. The algorithm and its complexity analysis are described in Section 4. The experimental results on MediaEval Social Event Detection Dataset and its subset are reported in Section 5, followed by the conclusions in Section 6.

2. RELATED WORK

Since our work involves social event detection and co-clustering, we review related work in these two areas.

2.1 Social Event Detection

Event detection on social media websites has received considerable attention. Papadopoulos et al. proposed a framework to detect landmark and event to improve the user browsing and retrieval experience [9]. Chen et al. discovered social event from Flickr photos by using both user tags and other metadata including time and location (latitude and longintude) [4]. Firan et al. collected the event categories and exploited the social information produced by users in form of tags, titles and photo descriptions for classifying pictures into different event categories and [10]. Moreover, MediaEval, a benchmarking initiative, held a challenge of social event detection every year [1] [11]. Many effective methods are proposed to tackle this challenge. In 2011 challenge, Brenner et al. combined various information from tagged photos with external data sources to train a classification model [12]. Liu et al. solved the event detection problem in three steps. First all the event instances were queried by given some conditions. Then, the relationship between events and photos was measured by an event identification model. At last, they employed visual pruning and

owner refining heuristics to improve the results [13]. In 2012 challenge, Schinas et al. proposed an approach based on the use of a "same class" model, which is trained using data from SED 2011 challenge and predicts whether two images belong to the same event [14]. Brenner et al. combined data of various modalities from annotated photos as well as from external data sources within a framework that has a classification model at its core [15].

Clustering is a widely accepted method to detect event not only in document set but also in social media set. Some work utilizes deterministic clustering to group samples into different topics, e.g. K-means clustering, Single-Link and Single-Pass clustering [16]. Since social media involves heterogeneous metadata from multiple modalities, the most challenging part of social event detection is how to appropriately integrate the associated metadata together. Quack et al. proposed a method to mine events and objects from community photo collections. The photos are clustered into potentially interesting entities through a processing pipeline of several modalities, including visual, textual and spatial proximity. The obtained clusters are analyzed and automatically classified into objects and events [17]. In [18], Makkonen et al. extracted meaningful semantic features including name, time and location, and learned a similarity function that combines these metrics into a single clustering solution. Petkos et al. utilized the similarities on multiple modalities to train a classifier to predict the "same cluster" relationship, then clustered the test samples with the predicted "same cluster" relationships [2]. Similarly, Becker et al. learned similarity metrics by a classifier which is trained by clustered social media data with heterogenous metadata, and proposed a single-pass incremental clustering algorithm with a tunable threshold parameter to handle the new-coming samples [3]. However, this kind of methods needs a known clustering in the currently examined domain, which is usually not available. Some other work solves the problem on heterogenous metadata by sequentially processing those metadata in different steps. In [19], the data based on the most reliable information (time-stamp and geotags) were first clustered to obtain robust event candidates, and then the additional contextual information (e.g. user-defined tags, titles, visual content) is employed to filtering and refining the event candidates. Wang et al. performed two clustering phases, in which one was based on time, the other one is based on location, tag and text [8]. Papadopoulos et al. divided social event detection into three steps, that is, photo filtering by city-level and finer-grained classifiers, event partitioning by temporal information, and event expansion with other associated metadata [9].

In our work, we construct star-structured K-partite graph to integrate the heterogeneous metadata, and co-cluster the social media set and the associated metadata sets to solve the above issues in traditional fusion methods.

2.2 Co-clustering

Co-clustering has recently received a lot of attention as it is a good method to simultaneously cluster heterogeneous yet correlated modalities. Different from the traditional one-way document clustering methods, co-clustering regards the correlations between different metadata as joint probability distribution to simultaneously cluster all the involved sets. Dhillon et al. proposed a spectral co-clustering algorithm by finding minimum cut vertex partitions in a bipartite graph between two heterogeneous types of domains [20]. However, the limitation of this method is that each datum of one source needs to be associated with at least of one datum from another source. To overcome this limitation, Dhillon *et al.* proposed information-theoretic co-clustering approach by finding a pair of maps from rows to rows clusters and from columns to column clusters with minimum mutual information loss on two heterogeneous types of two domains [21]. Later, Banerjee *et al.* suggested a generalization maximum entropy co-clustering approach by appealing to Bregman information principle [22]. In addition to these pair-wise co-clustering approaches, Gao *et al.* dedicated on multiple types of heterogeneous data by using the proposed consistent information theoretic co-clustering method on star structure, in which there is a central domain that connects any other domains to form a star structure of the inter-relationship [23]. To handle the noisy data in real world datasets, Deodhar *et al.* proposed Robust Overlapping Co-Clustering(ROCC) on two sources [24].

Considering that the cluster numbers of different metadata sets are not the same, our work inspires the idea of consistent information theoretic co-clustering [23] to coarsely detect the social event. The difference from this work is that we take intra-relationship within time space into consideration.

3. SOCIAL EVENT DETECTION WITH HIGH-ORDER CO-CLUSTERING

Our work considers the social media with four types of heterogenous metadata, that is, time-stamp, location, visual content and textural content. As defined in [25], an event refers to a specific thing that happens at a specific period and place. So, we need to take intra-relationship among time-stamp into the consideration. In this section, we first introduce the notation involved in our work, then we coarsely detect social event based on the modeling of inter-relationship on star-structured K-partite graph and that of intra-relationship on time space, at last, we prune and refine the obtained clusters and their corresponding social media samples to achieve a good clustering result.

3.1 Notation

Before delving in, we give a brief introduction about the notation: Sets such as $\mathcal{X}$ are denoted by upper case letters in Euler script. Matrices are denoted using upper case bold letters, for example, $\mathbf{G}$. Vectors are denoted by low case bold letters, for example, $\mathbf{h} = [h_1, h_2, \cdots, h_n]^T$. Upper case letters like X are used to denote random variables.

Suppose that we have a collection of n images downloaded from the social media networks, e.g. Flickr, $\mathcal{X} = \{x_1, x_2, \cdots, x_n\}$. There are four types of metadata associated with x, that is, time-stamp, location, visual content and textual content. Considering that time-stamp and location are continuous values, we segregate time-stamp by a predefined time interval and group location by cities. By this way, we get the time set $\mathcal{T} = \{t_1, t_2, \cdots, t_{|t|}\}$, and location set $\mathcal{L} = \{l_1, l_2, \cdots, l_{|l|}\}$, where t_i indicates the i-th time interval and l_i indicates the i-th city. For visual and textual content, let visual word set be $\mathcal{V} = \{v_1, v_2, \cdots, v_{|v|}\}$, and keyword set be $\mathcal{W} = \{w_1, w_2, \cdots, w_{|w|}\}$. We aim to partition $\mathcal{X}$ by co-clustering $\mathcal{T}$, $\mathcal{L}$ $\mathcal{V}$, $\mathcal{W}$ and $\mathcal{X}$ into $|\hat{t}|$, $|\hat{l}|$, $|\hat{v}|$, $|\hat{w}|$ and $|\hat{n}|$ clusters simultaneously. Let the clus-

tered social media sets be $\hat{\mathcal{X}} = \{\hat{\mathcal{X}}_1, \hat{\mathcal{X}}_2, \cdots, \hat{\mathcal{X}}_{|\hat{n}|}\}$, time clusters be $\hat{\mathcal{T}} = \{\hat{\mathcal{T}}_1, \hat{\mathcal{T}}_2, \cdots, \hat{\mathcal{T}}_{|\hat{t}|}\}$, location clusters be $\hat{\mathcal{L}} = \{\hat{\mathcal{L}}_1, \hat{\mathcal{L}}_2, \cdots, \hat{\mathcal{L}}_{|\hat{l}|}\}$, visual word clusters be $\hat{\mathcal{V}} = \{\hat{\mathcal{V}}_1, \hat{\mathcal{V}}_2, \cdots, \hat{\mathcal{V}}_{|\hat{v}|}\}$ and keyword clusters be $\hat{\mathcal{W}} = \{\hat{\mathcal{W}}_1, \hat{\mathcal{W}}_2, \cdots, \hat{\mathcal{W}}_{|\hat{w}|}\}$. Let column vectors $\mathbf{h}^x = \{h_1^x, \cdots, h_{|n|}^x\}$, $\mathbf{h}^t = \{h_1^t, \cdots, c_{|t|}^t\}$, $\mathbf{h}^l = \{h_1^l, \cdots, c_{|l|}^l\}$, $\mathbf{h}^v = \{h_1^v, \cdots, c_{|v|}^v\}$ and $\mathbf{h}^w = \{h_1^w, \cdots, c_{|w|}^w\}$ be the assigned cluster indexes for the elements in $\mathcal{X}$, $\mathcal{T}$, $\mathcal{L}$, $\mathcal{V}$ and $\mathcal{W}$ respectively.

Define X, T, L, V and W as discrete random variables which take values in sets $\mathcal{X}$, $\mathcal{T}$, $\mathcal{L}$, $\mathcal{V}$ and $\mathcal{W}$ respectively, the probability of $X = x$, $T = t$, $L = l$, $V = v$ and $W = w$ be $p(x)$, $p(t)$, $p(l)$, $p(v)$ and $p(w)$. The joint probabilities of $(X, T) = (x, t)$, $(X, L) = (x, l)$, $(X, V) = (x, v)$, $(X, W) = (x, w)$ are defined as $p(x, t)$, $p(x, l)$, $p(x, v)$ and $p(x, w)$ respectively. So as the discrete random variables $\hat{X}$, $\hat{T}$, $\hat{L}$, $\hat{V}$ and $\hat{W}$. Similarly, we have $p(\hat{\mathcal{X}})$, $p(\hat{\mathcal{T}})$, $p(\hat{\mathcal{L}})$, $p(\hat{\mathcal{V}})$, and the joint probabilities $p(\hat{\mathcal{X}}, \hat{\mathcal{T}})$, $p(\hat{\mathcal{X}}, \hat{\mathcal{L}})$, $p(\hat{\mathcal{X}}, \hat{\mathcal{V}})$, $p(\hat{\mathcal{X}}, \hat{\mathcal{W}})$.

3.2 Coarse Event Detection

As discussed before, we regard the social event detection as a co-clustering problem, which groups the social media set and all of four metadata sets into several subgroups to describe the various aspects of certain event. Considering that the number of clusters for five involved sets ($\mathcal{X}$, $\mathcal{T}$, $\mathcal{L}$, $\mathcal{V}$, $\mathcal{W}$) are not the same, spectral graph partition [20] [26] is not suitable for our problem. Thus, we adopt information-theoretic co-clustering [21] to coarsely detect the social event as it has less restriction and meets our needs. The method of event detection is inspired by the recent work on consistent information theoretic co-clustering [23] with the difference that we take the intra-relationship on time space into consideration. In this subsection, we first construct star-structured K-partite graph with the social media set and its associated metadata sets, then respectively present the model of inter-relationship on the constructed graph and that of the intra-relationship on time space. At last, an overall objective function is formulated to achieve the coarse event detection.

3.2.1 Star-structured K-partite Graph

A K-partite graph is a graph that the vertices in graph can be partitioned into K disjoint sets and edges exist between any two disjoint sets [27]. The star-structured K-partite graph is a specific case of K-partite graph where there is a central vertice set that connects the other sets so as to form a star structure of the inter-relationships [28]. In our problem, social media itself is regarded as the central vertice set and four types of metadata are treated as the auxiliary vertice sets which are pairwise independent with each other but correlated with the central one.

As shown in Figure 1, we define star-structured K-partite graph as $(\mathcal{X}, \mathcal{T}, \mathcal{L}, \mathcal{V}, \mathcal{W}, \mathbf{E}_T, \mathbf{E}_L, \mathbf{E}_V, \mathbf{E}_W)$, where $K = 5$, $\mathbf{E}_T(i, j) = e(x_i, t_j)$ denotes the co-occur times between the i-th social media sample and the j-th time interval, $\mathbf{E}_L(i, j) = e(x_i, l_j)$ denotes that between the i-th social media sample and the j-th location, $\mathbf{E}_V(i, j) = e(x, v)$ denotes that between the i-th social media sample and the j-th visual word, and $\mathbf{E}_W(i, j) = e(x, w)$ denotes that between the i-th social media sample and the j-th keyword. The joint probabilities $p(x, t)$, $p(x, l)$, $p(x, v)$ and $p(x, w)$ can be calculated by normalizing the corresponding co-occur times. For example, $p(x,t) = \frac{e(x,t)}{\mathbf{1}^T \mathbf{E}_T \mathbf{1}}$.

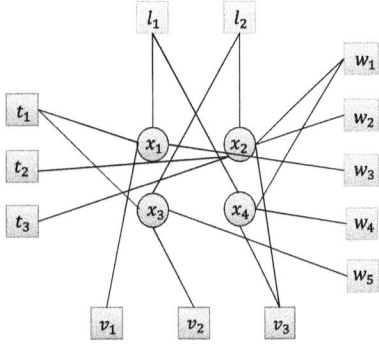

Figure 1: Star-structured K-partite Graph.

3.2.2 Modeling of Inter-relationship in K-partite Graph

In our work, the modeling of inter-relationship in star-structured K-partite graph is followed by consistent information theoretic co-clustering (CIT) [23], which divides the original high-order co-clustering problem into several sub-problems: $\mathcal{X} - \mathcal{T}$, $\mathcal{X} - \mathcal{L}$, $\mathcal{X} - \mathcal{V}$ and $\mathcal{X} - \mathcal{W}$ co-clusterings, with the constraints that their clustering results on the central set $\mathcal{X}$ are exactly the same and the overall partitioning is optimal under a certain objective function. Compared with another solution of co-clustering on inter-relationship, i.e., consistent bipartite graph partitioning (CBGC) [26], C-IT has no restriction that each social media item needs to be associated with a certain time interval, location, visual word and keyword clusters.

According to CIT, the objective is to minimize the linear combination of mutual information losses on K-partite graph, that is,

$$J_{inter} = a[I(X;T) - I(\hat{X};\hat{T})] + b[I(X;L) - I(\hat{X};\hat{L})]$$
$$+ c[I(X;V) - I(\hat{X};\hat{V})] + d[I(X;W) - I(\hat{X};\hat{W})] \quad (1)$$

where parameters a, b, c, d $(a+b+c+d = 1)$ are the weighting factors determining which part of partite graph we trust more. $I(X;T)$ is the mutual information between X and T, which is defined as

$$I(X;T) = \sum_x \sum_t p(x)p(t|x)log\frac{p(t|x)}{p(t)} \quad (2)$$

So as $I(\hat{X};\hat{T})$, $I(X;L)$, $I(\hat{X};\hat{L})$, $I(X;V)$, $I(\hat{X};\hat{V})$, $I(X;W)$ and $I(\hat{X};\hat{W})$. The first term in Eqn. (1) indicates the subproblem of $X - T$ co-clustering, the second one stands for that of $X - L$ co-clustering, the third one corresponds to that of $X - V$ co-clustering, and the fourth one expresses that of $X - W$ co-clustering.

After deduction, the loss in mutual information can be expressed as 1) a weighted sum of the relative entropies between row distributions and row prototype distributions, referred to Eqn. (3) (5) (7) (9), or as 2) a weighted sum of the relative entropies between column distributions and column prototype distributions, referred to Eqn. (4) (6) (8) (10),

$$I(X;T) - I(\hat{X};\hat{T}) = \sum_{\hat{\mathcal{X}}} \sum_{x \in \hat{\mathcal{X}}} p(x)D(p(T|x)\|q(T|\hat{\mathcal{X}})) \quad (3)$$

$$I(X;T) - I(\hat{X};\hat{T}) = \sum_{\hat{\mathcal{T}}} \sum_{t \in \hat{\mathcal{T}}} p(t)D(p(X|t)\|q(X|\hat{\mathcal{T}})) \quad (4)$$

$$I(X;L) - I(\hat{X};\hat{L}) = \sum_{\hat{\mathcal{X}}} \sum_{x \in \hat{\mathcal{X}}} p(x)D(p(L|x)\|q(L|\hat{\mathcal{X}})) \quad (5)$$

$$I(X;L) - I(\hat{X};\hat{L}) = \sum_{\hat{\mathcal{L}}} \sum_{l \in \hat{\mathcal{L}}} p(l)D(p(X|l)\|q(X|\hat{\mathcal{L}})) \quad (6)$$

$$I(X;T) - I(\hat{X};\hat{V}) = \sum_{\hat{\mathcal{X}}} \sum_{x \in \hat{\mathcal{X}}} p(x)D(p(V|x)\|q(V|\hat{\mathcal{X}})) \quad (7)$$

$$I(X;T) - I(\hat{X};\hat{V}) = \sum_{\hat{\mathcal{V}}} \sum_{v \in \hat{\mathcal{V}}} p(v)D(p(X|v)\|q(X|\hat{\mathcal{V}})) \quad (8)$$

$$I(X;T) - I(\hat{X};\hat{W}) = \sum_{\hat{\mathcal{X}}} \sum_{x \in \hat{\mathcal{X}}} p(x)D(p(W|x)\|q(W|\hat{\mathcal{X}})) \quad (9)$$

$$I(X;T) - I(\hat{X};\hat{W}) = \sum_{\hat{\mathcal{W}}} \sum_{w \in \hat{\mathcal{W}}} p(w)D(p(X|w)\|q(X|\hat{\mathcal{W}})) \quad (10)$$

where $q(t|\hat{\mathcal{X}}) = p(t|\hat{\mathcal{T}})p(\hat{\mathcal{T}}|\hat{\mathcal{X}})$, similarly as $q(x|\hat{\mathcal{T}})$, $q(l|\hat{\mathcal{X}})$, $q(x|\hat{\mathcal{L}})$, $q(v|\hat{\mathcal{X}})$, $q(x|\hat{\mathcal{V}})$, $q(w|\hat{\mathcal{X}})$ and $q(w|\hat{\mathcal{W}})$. $D(\cdot\|\cdot)$ denotes relative entropy, also known as Kullback-Leibler (KL) divergence.

To solve the overall consistent co-clustering problem, we first optimize each sub-problem, and then determine the clustering result for the central set $\mathcal{X}$ by minimizing Eqn. (1), based on the foregoing clustering results of $\mathcal{T}, \mathcal{L}, \mathcal{V}, \mathcal{W}$.

3.2.3 Modeling of Intra-relationship on Time Space

Besides the inter-relationship in K-partite graph, we also require that cluster assignment should be smooth over $\mathcal{T}$. Therefore, the global regularization on $\mathcal{T}$ should be considered in our co-clustering task. Let $\mathbf{S} \in \Re^{|t| \times |t|}$ be the sysmmetric weight matrices respectively. Each element of $\mathbf{S}(i,j)$ measures the similarity between the i-th and the j-th time intervals, and is assumed to be nonnegative. In our problem, we represent time value as the days elapsed since the beginning of Unix epoch. If two times are more than a week apart, their similarity is 0. Otherwise, the similarity between two time-stamps t_i and t_j is computed as

$$\mathbf{S}(i,j) = 1 - \frac{|t_i - t_j|}{\tau}, \quad (11)$$

where $\tau = 7$, which is equal to the number of days in a week. Recall that column vector $\mathbf{h}^t$ is the assigned cluster index for the elements in $\mathcal{T}$. Similarly to [29], we have the following objective function for time space.

$$J_{intra} = \sum_{i \neq j} (h_i^t - h_j^t)^2 \mathbf{S}(i,j) \quad (12)$$

Intuitively, if t_i and t_j are more similar, that is $\mathbf{S}(i,j)$ is larger, $|h_i^t - h_j^t|$ should be smaller.

Define the Laplacian matrix $\mathbf{G}$ and its corresponding diagonal matrices $\mathbf{D}$ as

$$\mathbf{G} = \mathbf{D} - \mathbf{S} \quad (13)$$

where $\mathbf{D}_{ii} = \sum_{i \neq j} \mathbf{S}(i,j)$ for $\forall i$. Then J_{intra} can be deducted to

$$J_{intra} = (\mathbf{h}^t)^T \mathbf{G} \mathbf{h}^t \qquad (14)$$

3.2.4 Unified Problem Formulation for Coarse Event Detection

By integrating all the above two folds, that is, inter-relationship on K-partite graph and intra-relationship on $\mathcal{T}$, we have the loss function of our problem as follows,

$$J = \alpha J_{inter} + (1 - \alpha) J_{intra}, \qquad (15)$$

the parameter α in Eqn. (15) is the weight to balance these two folds. Then our objective becomes to solve the following optimization problem,

$$\min_{\mathbf{h}^x, \mathbf{h}^t, \mathbf{h}^l, \mathbf{h}^v, \mathbf{h}^w} J$$
$$= \min_{\mathbf{h}^x, \mathbf{h}^t, \mathbf{h}^l, \mathbf{h}^v, \mathbf{h}^w} \alpha \Big\{ a[I(X;T) - I(\hat{X};\hat{T})] + b[I(X;L) - I(\hat{X};\hat{L})]$$
$$+ c[I(X;V) - I(\hat{X};\hat{V})] + d[I(X;W) - I(\hat{X};\hat{W})] \Big\}$$
$$+ (1 - \alpha)(\mathbf{h}^t)^T \mathbf{G} \mathbf{h}^t \qquad (16)$$

3.3 Clusters and Samples Refinement

At last, we provide a heuristic to prune and refine the obtained clusters and their corresponding social media samples. The process includes two steps: 1) filter and merge clusters; 2) prune and replenish social media samples.

For clusters, since we have no idea of the final number of clusters, some clusters with error values larger than a predefined "error cut-off value" will be filed out. And a "closest" pair of clusters, between which the distance is small, will be merged together into a new cluster in this step.

For social media samples, we need to prune the noisy ones and replenish the wrongly discarded ones. We assume that social media samples which are assigned to the same event should be similar in the given four types metadata. We define the overall distance for x to its cluster center $\hat{\mathcal{X}}$ be

$$dis = a|t - t_c| + b\sigma(l - l_c) + c\|\mathbf{v} - \mathbf{v}_c\|_2^2 + d\|\mathbf{w} - \mathbf{w}_c\|_2^2, \quad (17)$$

where $\sigma(l - l_c) = 0$, if $l = l_c$, otherwise 1. $\|\cdot\|_2$ is the ℓ_2-norm of a vector. $t_c = \sum_{j:x_j \in \hat{X}} t_j$, l_c is set to the most associated city (place) in $\hat{\mathcal{X}}$, $\mathbf{v}_c = \sum_{j:x_j \in \hat{X}} \mathbf{v}_j$, and $\mathbf{w}_c = \sum_{j:x_j \in \hat{X}} \mathbf{w}_j$. We prune the samples whose distance is larger than a predefined threshold.

Also, similar to [13], we assume that a person can not attend more than one event simultaneously. Therefore, all the photos that have been taken by the same owner during the event duration should be assigned to the same cluster.

4. SED-RHOCC ALGORITHM

The objective function (15) can be optimized by an iterative procedure. If we fix cluster assignments $\mathbf{h}^t$, $\mathbf{h}^l$, $\mathbf{h}^v$ and $\mathbf{h}^w$, the best assignment $(h_i^x)^\star$ of x_i can be obtained by using Eqn. (18),

$$(h_i^x)^\star = \arg \min_{h_i^x} aD(p(T|x_i)\|q(T|\hat{X})) + bD(p(L|x_i)\|q(L|\hat{X}))$$
$$+ cD(p(V|x_i)\|q(V|\hat{X})) + dD(p(W|x_i)\|q(W|\hat{X})) \qquad (18)$$

Similarly, $(h_i^t)^\star$, $(h_i^l)^\star$, $(h_i^v)^\star$ and $(h_i^w)^\star$ can be optimized by

---

Algorithm 1 Social Event Detection with Robust High-order Co-clustering (SED-RHOCC) Algorithm

Input:
  Co-occur times matrices $\mathbf{E}_T, \mathbf{E}_L, \mathbf{E}_V, \mathbf{E}_W$
  Number of clusters: $|\hat{n}|, |\hat{t}|, |\hat{l}|, |\hat{v}|, |\hat{w}|$
  weighting factors: a, b, c, d
  Objective function parameter: α
Output:
  Cluster assignments $\mathbf{h}^x$, $\mathbf{h}^t$, $\mathbf{h}^l$, $\mathbf{h}^v$ and $\mathbf{h}^w$
1: **Initialization:**
  Set $p(x,t) = \frac{\mathbf{E}_T}{1^T \mathbf{E}_T 1}$, $p(x,l) = \frac{\mathbf{E}_L}{1^T \mathbf{E}_L 1}$,
    $p(x,v) = \frac{\mathbf{E}_V}{1^T \mathbf{E}_V 1}$, $p(x,w) = \frac{\mathbf{E}_W}{1^T \mathbf{E}_W 1}$;
  Initialize cluster sets $\mathbf{h}^x(0)$, $\mathbf{h}^t(0)$, $\mathbf{h}^l(0)$, $\mathbf{h}^v(0)$ and $\mathbf{h}^w(0)$;
  Compute $q^{(0)}(\hat{\mathcal{X}}, \hat{\mathcal{T}})$, $q^{(0)}(X|\hat{\mathcal{X}})$, $q^{(0)}(T|\hat{\mathcal{T}})$, $q^{(0)}(T|\hat{\mathcal{X}})$, $q^{(0)}(\hat{\mathcal{X}}, \hat{\mathcal{L}})$, $q^{(0)}(L|\hat{\mathcal{L}})$, $q^{(0)}(L|\hat{\mathcal{X}})$, $q^{(0)}(\hat{\mathcal{X}}, \hat{\mathcal{V}})$, $q^{(0)}(V|\hat{\mathcal{V}})$, $q^{(0)}(V|\hat{\mathcal{X}})$, $q^{(0)}(\hat{\mathcal{X}}, \hat{\mathcal{W}})$, $q^{(0)}(W|\hat{\mathcal{W}})$, $q^{(0)}(W|\hat{\mathcal{X}})$
2: **Coarse Event Detection**

  - 2.1: Cluster assignment on $\mathcal{X}$ by using Eqn. (18), and compute distributions
  - 2.2: Cluster assignment on $\mathcal{T}$ by using Eqn. (19), and compute distributions
  - 2.3: Cluster assignment on $\mathcal{L}$ by using Eqn. (20), and compute distributions
  - 2.4: Cluster assignment on $\mathcal{V}$ by using Eqn. (21), and compute distributions
  - 2.5: Cluster assignment on $\mathcal{W}$ by using Eqn. (22), and compute distributions
  - 2.6: Compute objective function value using (15), and compute the change in objective function ΔJ. If $\Delta J >= 10^{-3}$, go to step 2.1.

3: **Clusters and Samples Refinement**

  - 3.1: Filter clusters with large errors
  - 3.2: Merge similar clusters
  - 3.3: Prune social media samples with far distance to the cluster center
  - 3.4: Replenish the wrongly discarded social media samples

4: **Return:** Identified clusters.

---

using Eqn. (19) (20) (21) and (22),

$$(h_i^t)^\star = \arg \min_{h_i^t} \alpha a D(p(X|t_i)\|q(X|\hat{\mathcal{T}})) + (1 - \alpha)(\mathbf{h}^t)^T \mathbf{G} \mathbf{h}^t \qquad (19)$$

$$(h_i^l)^\star = \arg \min_{h_i^l} bD(p(X|l_i)\|q(X|\hat{\mathcal{L}})) \qquad (20)$$

$$(h_i^v)^\star = \arg \min_{h_i^v} bD(p(X|v_i)\|q(X|\hat{\mathcal{V}})) \qquad (21)$$

$$(h_i^w)^\star = \arg \min_{h_i^w} bD(p(X|w_i)\|q(X|\hat{\mathcal{W}})) \qquad (22)$$

The pseudo-code for Social Event Detection with Robust

High-order Co-clustering (SED-RHOCC) algorithm is shown in Algorithm 1. Specifically, the algorithm starts with an initial co-clustering $(\mathbf{h}^x)^{(0)}$, $(\mathbf{h}^t)^{(0)}$, $(\mathbf{h}^l)^{(0)}$, $(\mathbf{h}^v)^{(0)}$ and $(\mathbf{h}^v)^{(0)}$ (see step 1). Then we coarsely detect social event in step 2. In step 2.1, we fix $\mathbf{h}^t$, $\mathbf{h}^l$, $\mathbf{h}^v$ and $\mathbf{h}^v$ to minimize the function in Eqn. 18, and compute the required marginals of $q(\cdot)$. The following $\mathcal{T}$, $\mathcal{L}$, $\mathcal{V}$ and $\mathcal{W}$ clusterings are equal to minimize Eqn. (19) (20) (21) and (22) (see step 2.2-2.5). This iterative process stops when the objective function no longer decreases (see step 2.6). In step 3, we do a post process to filter and merge clusters, as well as the social media samples.

5. EXPERIMENTS

We evaluate the performance of the proposed methods using MediaEval SED Dataset[2] with attached multi-modality descriptions.

5.1 Dataset

5.1.1 MediaEval SED Dataset

MediaEval SED Dataset, which was released in 2012, consists of 167,332 photos collected from Flickr. The collected photos were captured between the beginning of 2009 and the end of 2011 by 4,422 unique Flickr users. Accompanying metadata (Flickr ID, capture date and time, username, title, description, keywords and in about one fifth of the cases, geographic coordinate) were provided in a seperate XML file. MediaEval social event detection 2012 challenge consisted of 3 tasks. The first challenge relates the technical events that took place in Germany, the second one is to find all soccer events taking place in Hamburg (Germany) and Madrid (Spain), and the third one is to find demonstration and protest events of the Indignados movement occuring in plublic places in Madrid. For these three challenges, the dataset provided the ground truth which implicitly classified 2,234 samples into 18 events for the first challenge, 1,684 samples into 79 events for the second one, and 3,992 samples into 52 events for the third one. Figure 3 shows some exemplary photos of different soccer events.

In our experiment, we focus on the second task, that is, soccer event detection. We construct two datasets to evaluate for different purposes. For the first one, we select all the ground truth of soccer event to build a soccer event subset. This dataset does not include any non-event samples, and will be used to demonstrate the effectiveness of the coarse event detection. For the second one, we choose the whole MediaEval SED dataset to evaluate our proposed SED-RHOCC algorithm.

5.1.2 Pre-process

Note that the provided textual metadata (title, description and tags) include non-English terms, we utilize Google Translate API to translate them into English. Then textual metadata are cleaned by removing the stopwords, html tags and camera related words such as "Cannon", "35mm". Next, we prune spelling errors and non-words based on the Word-Net [30]. Following, we group the photos by their capture date. At last, the associated geo-tags are segregated into cities.

---

[2] http://mklab.iti.gr/project/sed2012

5.2 Evaluation Metrics and Features

It is a non-trivial task to validate the clustering and co-clustering results. In the evaluation, we choose normalized mutual information (NMI) to measure the clustering performance.

The NMI is widely used to determine the quality of clusters. For two random variables X and Y, it is defined as [31]:

$$NMI = \frac{I(X,Y)}{H(X)H(Y)} \quad (23)$$

where $I(X,Y)$ is the mutual information between X and Y, and $H(X)$ and $H(Y)$ are the entropies of X and Y respectively. Given a clustering results, the NMI in (23) is estimated as [31]:

$$NMI = \frac{\sum_{i=1}^{\hat{m}} \sum_{j=1}^{\hat{m}} \hat{m}_{ij} \log\left(\frac{m\hat{m}_{ij}}{\hat{m}_i(\hat{m}^\star)_j}\right)}{\sqrt{\left(\sum_{i=1}^{\hat{m}} \hat{m}_i \log \frac{\hat{m}_i}{m}\right)\left(\sum_{j=1}^{\hat{m}} (\hat{m}^\star)_j \log \frac{(\hat{m}^\star)_j}{m}\right)}} \quad (24)$$

where $\hat{m}_i$ is the number of data contained in the i-th obtained cluster, $(\hat{m}^\star)_j$ is the number of data in the j-th groundtruth class, and $\hat{m}_{ij}$ denotes the number of data that are in the intersection between the i-th obtained cluster and the j-th groundtruth class. Obviously, the large this value, the better the performance of clustering.

The features we used to represent time-stamp, location, visual content and textual content are listed as follow:

- Time-stamp: we represent time value as days elapsed since the beginning of Unix epoch.

- Location: we assign the nearest city to the goe-tagged samples. For non-goe-tagged samples, we set the location as 0;

- Visual content: Each image is represented as a vector of Bag-of-Word (BOW) features. The generation of visual words comprises three steps: 1) we apply the Difference-of-Gaussian filter on the grayscale image to detect a set of salient points; 2) we then compute the Scale-Invariant-Feature-Transform (SIFT) [32] features over the local areas defined by the detected salient points; and 3) we perform the vector quantization on SIFT region descriptors to construct the visual vocabulary by K-means clustering approach. In this work, we generate 1024 clusters, and thus the dimension of BOW image representation vector is $r = 1024$.

- Texture content: term frequency - inverse document frequency (TF-IDF) weights are computed for textual metadata, including title, description and tags.

5.3 Experimental Results

5.3.1 Soccer Event Subset

This subset is composed of all the soccer event samples, and does not include any non-event ones, i.e. the ground truth set. We use this subset to demonstrate the effectiveness of our first step: coarse event detection. Considering that some events in ground truth includes a very small amount of samples, which is very challenging to detect, we only focus on the event which includes more than 10 samples. After reduction, we have a ground truth of 30 events with 1456 samples in this subset.

Figure 2: Exemplary photos of different soccer events.

Two kinds of baselines are selected in this experiment. The first one is Normalized cut (N-cut) [33], in which the overall similarities between sample pairs are calculated by linear combination of the similarities on different metadata. The second one is consistent information theoretic co-clustering (CIT) [23], which integrates multiple metadata into K-partite graph but does not consider the intra-relationship within the time space.

In N-cut, the similarity between two time-stamps is computed by using Eqn. (11). The similarity between two locations is set as 1 when two samples are associated with the same city, otherwise, 0. We use cosine similarity to calculate the similarities between texture features, and that between visual features are calculated based on Euclidean distance. The fusion parameters are set as $a = 0.1, b = 0.1, c = 0.1$, and $d = 0.7$, with which we achieve the best performance. In CIT, weighting parameters are set as $a = 0.5, b = 0.1, c = 0.3$ and $d = 0.1$. In SED-RHOCC, the weighting parameters are set equal to those in CIT, and α is set to 0.9.

Table 1 illustrates the NMI values of two baselines and our proposed approach. We can see that co-clustering methods, i.e. CIT and SED-RHOCC, outperform the single clustering method, i.e. N-cut. Moreover, with considering intra-relationship on time space, the performance increases about 0.02. Please note that NMI is much higher than the reported results in the second task of MediaEval 2012 challenge, since we only focus on the clusters whose elements is more than 10.

Figure 3 shows the NMI value comparison under different α. When α is set to 0.9, the result achieves best.

Table 1: NMI of different approaches on soccer event subset.

N-cut	CIT	SED-RHOCC
0.7457	0.9363	**0.9575**

5.3.2 MediaEval SED dataset

In this experiment, we consider all the 79 soccer events in the dataset, which is more than that in Section 5.3.1. Considering that MediaEval SED dataset is mixed with a lot of non-event and non-soccer event samples which are not relevant to soccer matches. We need to classify them into soccer event and non-soccer event classes at first. To this end, we identify multiple soccer stadiums for each given cities, and extract all the dates and times of soccer matches in these two cities between the beginning of 2009 and the end of 2011 from *playerhistory.com*. More details of this step

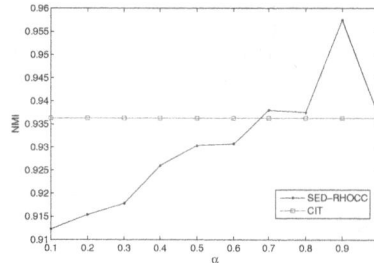

Figure 3: Performance comparison with varying α.

are introduced in [34]. Then, we select the positive samples which are exactly associated with those credible times and locations, and the non-relevant samples which are not taken in given times are chosen as negative samples. Next, a linear SVM is trained to classify each sample into soccer event class or non-soccer event one. Finally, we substantially reduce the number of samples to 2152.

Table 2 shows NMI of different approaches on the whole MediaEval SED dataset. Before step of clusters and samples refinement, the first step of our approach achieves 0.6834 in NMI. After the second step, the value increases to 0.7076.

Table 2: NMI of different approaches on the whole MediaEval SED dataset.

N-cut	Coarse Event Detection	SED-RHOCC
0.3930	0.6834	**0.7076**

6. CONCLUSIONS

In this paper, we have proposed a novel social event detection approach, called SDE-RHOCC, to detect social and real-world events from photos posed on social media sites including Flickr. The merits of the proposed SDE-RHOCC approach are that 1) it constructs star-structured K-partite graph to integrate the heterogeneous metadata during the co-clustering process, which avoids the information loss in early and late fusion; 2) the intra-relationship within time space is considered to improve the clustering performance; 3) the information-theoretic co-clustering framework is adopted with no limitation on the cluster numbers of each metadata set. The experiments on MediaEval Social Event Detection Dataset and its subset demonstrated the effectiveness of our proposed approach in the social media dataset including and excluding non-event data.

Acknowledgement

This work was supported by National Program on Key Basic Research Project (973 Program, Project No. 2012CB316304), the Natural Science Foundation of China (Grant No. 61201374, 61225009), China Postdoctoral Science Foundation (Grant No. 2011M500430). This research is supported by the Singapore National Research Foundation under its International Research Centre @ Singapore Funding Initiative and administered by the IDM Programme Office.

7. REFERENCES

[1] S. Papadopoulos, E. Schinas, V. Mezaris, R. Troncy, and I. Kompatsiaris, "Social event detection at MediaEval 2012: Challenges, dataset and evaluation," in *Proceedings of the MediaEval 2012 Workshop*, Pisa, ITALY, 2012.

[2] G. Petkos, S. Papadopoulos, and Y. Kompatsiaris, "Social event detection using multimodal clustering and integrating supervisory signals," in *Proceedings of the 2nd ACM International Conference on Multimedia Retrieval*, Hong Kong, CHINA, 2012.

[3] H. Becker, M. Naaman, and L. Gravano, "Learning similarity metrics for event identification in social media," in *Proceedings of the 3rd ACM International Conference on Web Search and Data Mining*, 2010, pp. 291–300.

[4] L. Chen and A. Roy, "Event detection from flickr data through wavelet-based spatial analysis," in *Proceedings of the 18th ACM conference on Information and Knowledge Management*, 2009.

[5] J. Zhuang, T. Mei, S. C. Hoi, X.-S. Hua, and S. Li, "Modeling social strength in social media community via kernel-based learning," in *Proceedings of the ACM international conference on Multimedia*, 2011, pp. 113–122.

[6] T. Yao, T. Mei, and C.-W. Ngo, "Co-reranking by mutual reinforcement for image search," in *Proceedings of the ACM International Conference on Image and Video Retrieval*, 2010, pp. 34–41.

[7] M. Wang, K. Yang, X.-S. Hua, and H.-J. Zhang, "Towards a relevant and diverse search of social images," *IEEE Transactions on Multimedia*, vol. 12, no. 8, pp. 829–842, 2010.

[8] Y. Wang, L. Xie, and H. Sundaram, "Social event detection with clustering and filtering," in *Proceedings of the MediaEval 2011 Workshop*, Pisa, ITALY, 2011.

[9] S. Papadopoulos, C. Zigkolis, Y. Kompatsiaris, and A. Vakali, "Cluster-based landmark and event detection on tagged photo collections," *IEEE Multimedia*, pp. 52–62, 2010.

[10] C. Firan, M. Georgescu, W. Nejdl, and R. Paiu, "Bringing order to your photos: event-driven classification of flickr images based on social knowledge," in *Proceedings of the 19th ACM International Conference on Information and Knowledge Management*, 2010, pp. 189–198.

[11] S. Papadopoulos, R. Troncy, V. Mezaris, B. Huet, and I. Kompatsiaris, "Social event detection at MediaEval 2011: Challenges, dataset and evaluation," in *Proceedings of the MediaEval 2012 Workshop*, Pisa, ITALY, 2011.

[12] M. Brenner and E. Izquierdo, "MediaEval benchmark: Social event detection in collaborative photo collections," in *Proceedings of the MediaEval 2011 Workshop*, Pisa, ITALY, 2011.

[13] X. Liu, B. Huet, and R. Troncy, "Eurecom@ MediaEval 2011 social event detection task," *Proceedings of the MediaEval 2011 Workshop*, 2011.

[14] E. Schinas, G. Petkos, S. Papadopoulos, and Y. Kompatsiaris, "CERTH@ MediaEval 2012 social event detection task," in *Proceedings of the MediaEval 2012 Workshop*, 2012.

[15] M. Brenner and E. Izquierdo, "QMUL@ MediaEval 2012: Social event detection in collaborative photo collections," in *Proceedings of the MediaEval 2012 Workshop*, 2012.

[16] J. Allan, *Topic detection and tracking: event-based information organization*. Springer, 2002, vol. 12.

[17] T. Quack, B. Leibe, and L. Van Gool, "World-scale mining of objects and events from community photo collections," in *Proceedings of the International Conference on Content-based Image and Video Retrieval*, 2008, pp. 47–56.

[18] J. Makkonen, H. Ahonen-Myka, and M. Salmenkivi, "Simple semantics in topic detection and tracking," *Information Retrieval*, vol. 7, no. 3, pp. 347–368, 2004.

[19] M. Zeppelzauer, M. Zaharieva, and C. Breiteneder, "A generic approach for social event detection in large photo collections," in *Proceedings of the MediaEval 2012 Workshop*, 2012.

[20] I. S. Dhillon, "Co-clustering documents and words using bipartite spectral graph partitioning," in *Proceedings of the International Conference on Knowledge Discovery and Data Mining*, San Francisco, California, USA, 2001, pp. 269–274.

[21] I. S. Dhillon, S. Mallela, and D. S. Modha, "Information-theoretic co-clustering," in *Proceedings of the International Conference on Knowledge Discovery and Data Mining*, Washington, USA, 2003.

[22] A. Banerjee, I. Dhillon, J. Ghosh, S. Merugu, and D. Modha, "A generalized maximum entropy approach to bregman co-clustering and matrix approximation," *Journal of Machine Learning Research*, vol. 8, pp. 1919–1986, 2007.

[23] B. Gao, T. Y. Liu, and W. Y. Ma, "Star-structured high-order heterogeneous data co-clustering based on consistent information theory," in *Proceedings of the International Conference on Data Mining*, 2006, pp. 880–884.

[24] M. Deodhar, G. Gupta, J. Ghosh, H. Cho, and I. Dhillon, "A scalable framework for discovering coherent co-clusters in noisy data," in *Proceedings of the 26th International Conference on Machine Learning*, 2009, pp. 241–248.

[25] J. Allan, J. Carbonell, G. Doddington, and J. Yamron, "Topic detection and tracking pilot study final report," in *DARPA Broadcast News Transcription and Understanding Workshop*, 1998.

[26] B. Gao, T. Liu, X. Zheng, Q. Cheng, and W. Ma, "Consistent bipartite graph co-partitioning for star-structured high-order heterogeneous data co-clustering," in *Proceedings of the 8th International Conference on Knowledge Discovery in Data Mining*, 2005.

[27] B. Long, X. Wu, Z. Zhang, and P. Yu, "Unsupervised learning on k-partite graphs," in *Proceedings of the 12th International Conference on Knowledge Discovery and Data Mining*, 2006, pp. 317–326.

[28] J. Shao, W. Yin, S. Ma, and Y. Zhuang, "Topic discovery of web video using star-structured k-partite graph," in *Proceedings of the International Conference on Multimedia*, 2010, pp. 915–918.

[29] M. Belkin and P. Niyogi, "Laplacian eigenmaps for dimensionality reduction and data representation," *Neural Computation*, vol. 15, no. 6, pp. 1373–1396, 2003.

[30] G. Miller and C. Fellbaum, "Wordnet: An electronic lexical database," 1998.

[31] A. Strehl and J. Ghosh, "Cluster ensembles – a knowledge reuse framework for combining multiple partitions," *The Journal of Machine Learning Research*, vol. 3, pp. 583–617, 2003.

[32] D. Lowe, "Distinctive image features from scale-invariant keypoints," *International Journal of Computer Vision*, vol. 60, no. 2, pp. 91–110, 2004.

[33] J. Shi and J. Malik, "Normalized cuts and image segmentation," *IEEE Transactions on Pattern Analysis and Machine Intelligence*, vol. 22, no. 8, pp. 888–905, 2000.

[34] M. Brenner and E. Izquierdo, "Social event detection and retrieval in collaborative photo collections," in *Proceedings of the 2nd ACM International Conference on Multimedia Retrieval*, 2012.

Social Events and Social Ties

Javier Paniagua, Ivan Tankoyeu, Julian Stöttinger, Fausto Giunchiglia
DISI, University of Trento
via Sommarive 14
38123 Povo, Trento, Italy
[paniagua | tankoyeu | julian | fausto]@disi.unitn.it

ABSTRACT

This paper is based upon an approach for automatic detection of personal events in on-line personal photo collections and proposes a powerful exploitation of these events: We compose social events out of personal events and then automatically reveal interpersonal ties. Trying to tame the stream of big data in social networks we solely rely on image meta-data of time and space. We validate our assumptions *in the wild* using 1.8 million public images of more than 4100 users. The proposed approach has three main steps: (i) personal event detection using individual, unsorted photo collections, in which we make use of the spatio-temporal context embedded in digital photos to detect event boundaries within the collection; (ii) social event detection for which we use a tailored similarity measurement between personal events of different users; and (iii) an analysis of event co-participation to propagate social connections. Experiments validate that the fully automated approach is able to accurately detect 78.76% of social events and reconstruct the interpersonal ties of a user with a verified true positive rate of 45%. This rate is probably much higher: Since most interpersonal ties are undefined in the universe of social networks, our experimental ground-truth of course remains fragmentary.

Categories and Subject Descriptors

J.4 [**Computer Applications**]: Social and behavioral sciences; J.7 [**Computer Applications**]: Computers in other systems

General Terms

Algorithms

Keywords

Media Indexing, Social Events, Event Detection, Social Networks Discovery

1. INTRODUCTION

Multimedia data, being heterogeneous and unstructured by its nature, requires a non-trivial approach to index it. Recent research

has shown considerable attention towards event-centred media indexing techniques [1], [18]. This tendency is a result of events being natural aggregators of contextual information. Events can be used to represent context in a semantically meaningful way that follows how we humans process our experiences.

Some of the on-line social media platforms (e.g. Flickr[1], Facebook[2]) allow users to organize their media items according to social events. Web services such as Flickr offer the use of machine tags for this purpose. Still, even if social events can be represented in this way, the absence of automated solutions hampers the use of this feature, and is the reason why contextual information which can be used to facilitate media indexing and information enrichment is still relatively unexploited.

In this paper we approach the problem of **social events** detection through the layer of **personal events**. These personal events are detected by performing an analysis of contextual information in each personal photo collection, using spatial-temporal metadata to find the boundaries between personal events. The algorithm that does this contextual analysis (described in detail in [11]) uses spatial and temporal metadata in photos to find the home location or locations of the user and then depending on this information selects slightly different parameters to find routine events and special events.

Once personal events are detected, the next step consists on finding the intersections between these personal events coming from different users. These intersections are found by calculating the proximity measurement of personal events in the spatial and temporal dimensions. At this stage we make the following assumption: if two or more personal events from users intersect, then they are assumed to be *different personal accounts of the same social event*. The number of intersections can possibly indicate the scale of the detected social event.

Further analysis of social events and their impact on information enrichment leads to the novel and efficient approach of discovery **social ties** through event co-participation. The key idea of this approach is that the link between the participation in events and the creation of interpersonal ties can be exploited to recommend new user contacts or "friends" in cases where the number of events that a pair of users co-participate in is above significant threshold. The proposed approach has the following advantages: (i) it suggests new interpersonal connections independently from existing social links and (ii) it can establish new "friendship links" to users with similar interests (e.g., concerts, sport competitions). Additionally, we found a correlation between the degree of co-participation in events and social closeness.

We work with the following user scenario that allows us to understand the approach from the perspective of the user:

---

[1] www.flickr.com
[2] www.facebook.com

George is an aircraft fan and each year he visits some of the European air shows such as the ones held in Farnborough and Paris. Last time he attended MAKS in Moscow. Each time he takes a lot of photos, all of them automatically geo-tagged. Being a communicative person he gets to know a lot of people during these trips. Recently he has joined an on-line social network for the aircraft amateurs. He would like to find the users in the network he may know in real life and enrich his media collection by including photos from the other users. To do this he uploads all his media taken within air show events to the system. In order to help George we propose the following three detection steps:

- personal events
- social events
- social ties

While the approach to personal event detection has been recently presented in [11], the focus of this paper is on issues related to the detection of social events and social ties.

For experimental validation we collected and explored more than 4100 personal collections with a total of 1 892 200 photos publicly available on Flickr. Large-scale experiments on our dataset demonstrate that the proposed approach is able to correctly detect social events in 78.76% of the cases.

We also achieve promising results for the event-based approach to social tie propagation. It demonstrates that 2 participants of the same event are familiar with each other in 41.39% of the cases, seeing an increase of this value to above 76% when both users co-participate in 2 or more events.

The paper is organized as follows. In Section 2 state of the art techniques are presented. Section 3 introduces the notion of events, distinguishing between social and personal events. Section 4 is dedicated to the description of our social event detection approach. Section 5 presents the theory for our event-based approach to social tie propagation. The description of the data set and experimental results are given in Section 6. Finally, we present our conclusions in Section 7.

2. STATE OF THE ART

In this section we describe the state of the art approaches for social event detection task and related work on social ties detection.

2.1 Social Event Detection

Recently, numerous studies have been devoted to the social event detection problem. Authors in [3] and [4] use on-line sources of publicly available information (e.g., LinkedData, Freebase) to find additional information related to social events. This information is used as a hint to detect the relevance of photos to the given set of social events in the MediaEval benchmark [18]. For the same task, authors in [5] utilize mainly three kinds of features: temporal, spatial and textual. Moreover, they involve visual features for removing noisy pictures. The final step of their approach enriches the detected set with photos that lack textual features using metadata about the owner of the collection.

A multimodal clustering algorithm is proposed for social event detection in [6]. The essence of the approach lies in the classification of distance matrices. These matrices are created computing pairwise distances for each modality. Modalities are based on the following features: temporal, spatial, visual and textual. The authors in [7] exploit machine-learning techniques to identify events in social media streams. They apply support vector machines to classify the dataset of Flickr photos related to events and annotated

by machine tags from LastFM[3]. Becker et al. define the problem of event identification in social media [8]. They present an incremental clustering approach for assigning documents to event-related clusters. The similarity metric learning approach is utilized by the authors in order to increase the performance of their technique.

The methodology of [20] initially classifies the dataset according to the location of the media, and then relies on a set of topics that match the description of the event detection challenge and are likely to be found within textual metadata in the media analyzed. [21] employs "same class" model for organization of photos into a graph. A community detection algorithm is applied for the analysis of the graph to derive candidate clusters. The last processing step classifies on the relevance to the given challenges. Zeppelzauer et al. [19] approach the task using a spatio-temporal clustering technique to come up with the event candidates, and in further steps these candidates are filtered taking into account textual and visual information.

Some approaches rely on metadata coming from external sources. In [22] the authors detect events related to football matches relying on DBpedia and WordNet to establish if events are relevant to the challenge. Dao et al. [23] employ a watershed-based image segmentation technique for social event detection. In this approach "markers" are produced by using keywords and spatial features with involvement of external data sources.

In contrast with approaches that employ textual and visual cues, our approach is purely based on spatial and temporal features for the social event detection task.

2.2 Social Ties Detection

There are previous studies that infer social ties using knowledge about temporal and spatial proximity, i.e. co-occurrences in time and space. [12] predicts social ties based on mobile phone data. Temporal and spatial metadata from photos, as analyzed in [13], can be seen as another source to predict social ties. We argue that metadata from photos are an indirect evidence of *intersections* between users' lives and instead it is co-participation in the same events the underlying phenomena that points towards the existence of social ties.

Some of the potential sources of bias identified in [13] are related to users having potentially inaccurate GPS-enabled equipment or being overly active photographers. We can infer social ties avoiding these issues since our approach depends exclusively on the co-occurrence of event-related tags without regard to their frequency and independently of the availability of GPS information or even timestamps.

A wide variety of social ties recommendation techniques have been presented recently. They differ from each other mainly in the nature of the information being processed.

Friend-of-Friend (FoF) is one of the most popular and simple techniques. Here we consider the concept of "friend" as a single or bi-directional social link. FoF exploits an existing social network to find the "social proximity" number [14] of shared contacts between two users. The probability of friendship between the users depends on this number. Facebook[4] and LinkedIn[5] have social recommendation services (e.g., "People You May Know") that are based on this approach.

Authors in [14] recommend social connections based on similar interests between users. The approach does an analysis of the content generated by users. A similar approach is used in [15]. The

---

[3] http://www.last.fm
[4] http://www.facebook.com
[5] http://www.linkedin.com

proposed friendship-interest propagation framework combines random walk in social network analysis and a coupled latent factor model. A fusion of FoF and interest-based friendship propagation is presented in [14].

Mobile phone short-range technologies (e.g. Bluetooth) are used by Quercia et al. [16]. They exploit *duration* and *frequency* to infer social closeness between two persons. Duration is computed from the total time those persons spend co-located while the number of meetings per time unit between them indicates frequency.

3. PERSONAL VS SOCIAL EVENTS

Life can be seen as a chain of events that chronologically pace our everyday activities and index our memories. Different events such as a birthday, a business trip or a winter vacation are the lens through which we see and memorize our own personal experiences. According to [9], humans identify activity boundaries at points that correspond to a maxima in the number of changing physical features, thus aggregating memories around events. An autobiographical memory records a connected set of personal events and can be characterized by a high personal belief of accurateness, certain perceptual qualities, detailed accounts of the personal circumstances and highly vivid details [10].

Brown [2] showed that the retrieval time in our autobiographical memory is hardly affected from the time that passed since a personal event occurred. Therefore we argue that this is the best way to index media over a long period of time; autobiographical memory is the structure that can be retrieved in the most convenient way for the user. Details about a certain personal event may have vanished already, but in our memory the personal event itself is still very vivid and at hand [17] states that the brain operates in this way to cope with the increased "difficulty" brought by indexing new information when it is dissimilar from the "current moment" beyond a certain threshold.

Events are more than simple aggregators for our memories, being essential for collective experiences to take place. These collective experiences arise when two people exchange their individual views of the world and discover common interests and goals based on the roles they play in the events they co-participate in. Thus, we can say that events have a social impact in the shaping of interpersonal ties between individuals.

Personal events form a hierarchical narrative-like structure that is connected by causal, temporal, spatial and thematic relations [2]. Figure 1 shows a distinction of personal and social event with regard to the memory and experience. Personal events are put into context and are stored in our autobiographical memory. In this sense, we refer to our personal events as an *individual experience*. In the course of producing and collecting personal media, people try to represent the memorable events. Unfortunately, the *representations* are not able to provide the full context of these memories.

In contrast, a **social event** is a convergence of multiple personal events. A social event, being one of the nodes in the collective memory, builds the basis for the *collective experience*, our common denominator for social communication. Since personal media is shared between people who are either participating or interested in specific social events, social media collections are built. When these collections serve as personal media collections, a loss in context is observed: A media collection taken by multiple people is not necessarily a representation for one's personal memory, and therefore an automated approach to reason about such an index is to the greatest possible extent unfeasible.

Events provide the common framework inside which the local experience-driven contextual information can be not only codified

but also shared and reduced to a common denominator. Consider a simple example of a photo taken within an party that can be contextualized to a specific place, time or set of participants. We can say that the context accumulated by an event entity contains values for the *five Ws* (Who, What, When, Where and Why) to fill the complete story.

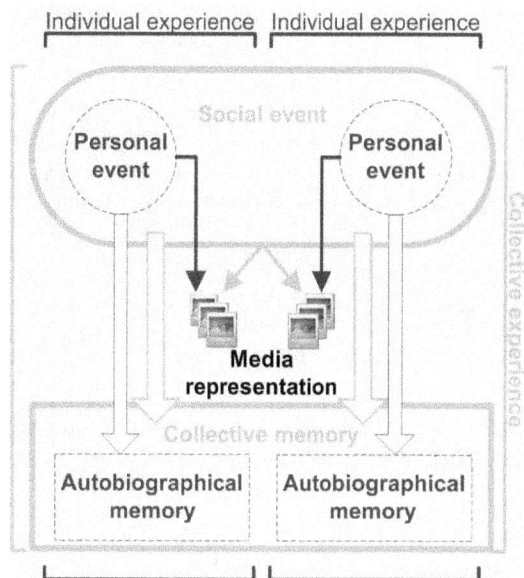

Figure 1: Distinction between personal events and social events.

Personal photos are visual representations of our personal memory; events are mental pivots which are used by humans to facilitate the extraction of their memories and to ease the explanation of the reality. Therefore we aim at organizing photo collections following this new paradigm and advocate the use of a personal focus for media indexing using personal events.

4. FROM PERSONAL TO SOCIAL EVENTS

In our approach, social events are detected by clustering personal events that are significantly similar. We compute a similarity score in order to match two events using a combination of metadata features. According to [17], of all these metadata features, time and space are the most important to segment our perception of reality in events.

Consider our driving example. For this step we assume George's photo collection of air show visits is already organized into personal events (this step is automated using the approach described in [11]). We can use these "personal" air show events to find other personal events belonging to other users. If we can match his personal events with personal events from other users we will end up with a richer set of photos that will better represent a given air show event, and not just the scenes that were subjectively interesting for George or for each of the other users.

We can group personal events into richer social events working with temporal and spatial proximity. Personal events happening at roughly the same time in the same places are likely different personal accounts of the same social event.

Accordingly, the similarity function used in our approach combines two separate functions that work with time and space. Consequently, we represent an event E as a pair of temporal and spatial information like this:

$$E = <t, P> \qquad (1)$$

where t is the time period at which the event occurs and P is a set of geographic points (such as the ones provided by embedded GPS metadata in photos).

The algorithm first determines if there is a time overlap between events. If two events E_A and E_B are defined as:

$$E_A = <t_A, P_A> \quad \text{and} \quad E_B = <t_B, P_B>$$

then time similarity is computed by taking into account how much of t_A overlaps with t_B. An example can be seen in Figure 2a.

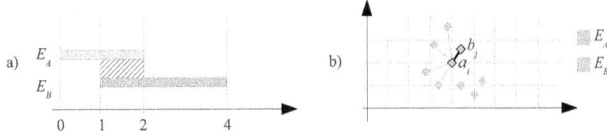

Figure 2: a) Time overlap of t_A and t_B and b) selecting the minimum spatial distance of all points p_{bj} of P_B to a particular point p_{ai} of P_A

We take the inverse of the time overlap function, called t_{sim}, to compare how similar two event instances are:

$$t_{sim}(t_A, t_B) = 1 - \begin{cases} \frac{t_A \cap t_B}{t_A \cup t_B}, & \text{if } t_A \cup t_B \neq \varnothing. \\ 0, & \text{otherwise.} \end{cases} \qquad (2)$$

Events that are completely temporally-similar will have $t_{sim} = 0$ while events that are not similar at all will have $t_{sim} = 1$.

For spatial analysis we use the Haversine distance [denoted $d(p, q)$ for two geographic points p and q] to build another function that selects the minimum distances from a spatial point p to the closest spatial point of a set P:

$$d_{min}(p, P) = \min_{i=1}^{n} d(p, p_i) \qquad (3)$$

where $P = \{p_1, p_2, ..., p_n\}$.

The spatial similarity s_{sim} between two sets of geographic points P_A and P_B is then given by:

$$s_{sim}(P_A, P_B) = \frac{\sum_{i=1}^{n} d_{min}(p_{ai}, P_B)}{n} \qquad (4)$$

where $P_A = \{p_{a1}, p_{a2}, ..., p_{an}\}$ and $P_B = \{p_{b1}, p_{b1}, ..., p_{bm}\}$.

Both t_{sim} and s_{sim} are *directed*, that is, $t_{sim}(t_A, t_B)$ is not the same as $t_{sim}(t_B, t_A)$. Non-directed versions of these function are:

$$nt_{sim}(t_A, t_B) = min(t_{sim}(t_A, t_B), t_{sim}(t_B, t_A))$$
$$\text{and} \quad ns_{sim}(P_A, P_B) = min(s_{sim}(P_A, P_B), s_{sim}(P_B, P_A))$$

Two events E_A and E_B are similar when:

$$nt_{sim}(t_A, t_B) < c_T \quad \text{and} \quad ns_{sim}(P_A, P_B) < c_S$$

where $c_T = 0.5$ and $c_S = 1.0$. These thresholds are learned experimentally as described in detailed in Section 6.2.

5. FROM SOCIAL EVENTS TO SOCIAL TIES

The last decade has shown an enormous growth in interest towards on-line social networking services[6]. The effectiveness of these services strongly depends on the ability to reconstruct existing social connections between their members acquainted off-line and on the usefulness for building new connections on-line.

The social function of events plays a significant role in the development of interpersonal ties. Events can be seen as compositions of semantically meaningful entities of which participants, their relationship and roles represent the social dimension of events. In this way we can work with events as a leverage to extract the social connections of an individual.

We found that events are useful for reconstructing already existing social ties and for aiding the user in enlarging his social network. To some extent, they encode the interests (e.g., sport events, concerts) of the users that participated in them. Moreover, it is through co-participation in events that one can find other people to share interests and, consequently, build and strengthen interpersonal ties.

Since the approach in this paper only relies on event co-participation to recommend interpersonal ties, it constitutes an alternative to other approaches based on the analysis of shared contacts.

In our example, George could use our approach to find other users that attended the same air shows. The higher the number of events that George shares with one particular user, the higher the probability that both can have shared interests. This makes them suitable candidates to establish a social tie.

According to our results in Section 6.3, people that attend 2 or more events establish a social tie in more than 76% of the cases. That is, when George uploads his photos of air shows, the system would only need spatial and temporal features to suggest present or future acquaintances, even if George did not have any contacts already registered on the social network.

To come up with the results in Section 6.3, we have to test if event co-participation is a good predictor of social ties. In order to achieve this we calculate the probability of one user having another user as a contact based on the number of events that they share. If there is at least 1 photo of user u tagged with the ID of an event E_i we say that u $participated - in$ E_i holds ($u \in E_i$). Co-participation of two users u_A and u_B in an event E_i is verified if both $u_A \in E_i$ and $u_B \in E_i$ hold.

The degree of co-participation represent the number of events that are shared between two users. That is, let $E_{part}(u_0)$ be the set of events in which user u_0 was a participant, and $E_{part}(u_1)$ the corresponding set for user u_1. We define:

$$N_c(u_0, u_1) = |E_{part}(u_0) \cap E_{part}(u_0)| \qquad (5)$$

as the *degree of co-participation* between users u_0 and u_1.

P_{st} of existence of a social tie between two users u_0 and u_1 follows the natural logarithm of the degree of co-participation N_c:

$$P_{st}(u_0, u_1)) = k \ln(N_c(u_0, u_1)) \qquad (6)$$

where k indicates proportionality.

---
[6] http://www.searchenginejournal.com/the-growth-of-social-media-an-infographic/32788/

6. EXPERIMENTAL SET-UP

In this section we present the experimental validation of the proposed approach. First, in Section 6.1 we discuss the data set collected for the experiments. In Section 6.2 we describe the experimental results of social event detection while in Section 6.3 we present the analysis of experimental results for social ties.

6.1 Data Set

To build our dataset we collected events from Yahoo! Upcoming[7], photo albums associated to them from Flickr[8] and their corresponding contact lists.

Our ground truth provides validation for social event detection based on metadata from photos that were annotated with *machine tags*[9] of the form 'upcoming:event=ev_{id}' where ev_{id} refers to an event instance in the Upcoming service. In this way an event from Upcoming can be linked to photos in Flickr that constitute the depiction of such event. In a first instance, photos of the same user that are grouped by the same machine tag are ground truth for that user's personal events. Moreover, personal events from different users that have the same machine tag indicate that these personal events are different accounts of an underlying social event.

Social ties are validated using information about Flickr contacts for each user. Two users that took photos and tagged them using the same machine tag provide evidence that they were co-participants in the same event identified by that tag. We exploit this fact to build participant lists from machine tags contained in photos from different users. To build our ground truth we extracted Flickr contact lists for all the users involved. By testing if two users have each other in their contact lists we can establish whether users that co-participate in a particular event are socially connected or not.

The dataset consists of more than 11 180 events with photos contributed by more than 4100 different users. Of these events, 1291 have photos owned by more than 1 user, a condition necessary if we are to analyze co-participation and its relation to acquaintance. The dataset includes metadata of photos uploaded in the years 2007 - 2012. For this study we only required the Flickr user ID of the owner of each photo, tags for Upcoming events and the list of Flickr contacts for each user. Nevertheless the crawler also retrieved timestamps and, when available, geo-tagging information. The average number of events per user in the part of the collection that we analyzed is 2.05. In the same manner, we computed the average number of participants per event which is 3.71, and the average number of contacts per user which is 213.52. This dataset is available on request.

6.2 Social Event Detection

To derive social events from personal photo streams we proceeded in two phases. First, we found personal events within the user's photo stream using the approach described in [11]. After all individual photo streams were processed and personal event instances detected, we analyzed each personal event against all others, using the spatial-temporal similarity function described in Section 4.

This similarity function works with two thresholds c_T and c_S above which we do not consider that two personal events are accounts of the same social event. To set these two thresholds we divided our dataset in two groups, using 50% of the detected personal event instances to tune these thresholds and the remaining

[7] http://upcoming.yahoo.com/
[8] http://www.flickr.com/
[9] http://tagaholic.me/2009/03/26/
what-are-machine-tags.html

c_T	c_S	U-joint	Correct	O-joint	Correct%
0.75	0.50	28	265	32	81.54
0.75	1.00	26	265	32	82.05
0.75	5.00	23	264	34	82.24
0.75	10.00	23	263	34	82.19
0.50	0.50	28	267	31	81.90
0.50	**1.00**	**26**	**267**	**31**	**82.40**
0.50	5.00	23	264	34	82.24
0.50	10.00	23	263	34	82.19
0.25	0.50	45	254	14	81.15
0.25	1.00	45	254	14	81.15
0.25	5.00	43	254	15	81.41
0.25	10.00	43	253	15	81.35

Table 1: Results for the parameter learning phase, comparing correctly detected social events against under-joint (U-Joint) and over-joint (O-joint) social events. Best results where achieved using $c_T = 0.50$ and $c_S = 1.00$.

50% to test. Pairs of personal events for which the similarity function produced results below the thresholds tested were considered to be part of a bigger social event. In this way we were able to combine several personal events into social event candidates.

To validate a detected social event, each one of them was automatically scanned looking for upcoming tags. If the detected social event had only one upcoming tag throughout its whole photo set then we considered this case as a true positive. It was not possible to do automatic evaluation on detected social events without Upcoming tags or with multiple Upcoming tags. Manual inspection was required in these cases, in order to see if photos coming from different users were still about the same event.

Table 1 shows the parameter learning process. We have selected $c_T = 0.50$ and $c_S = 1.00$ where the percentage (column "Correct%") of correct detections (column "Correct") is higher. A correct social event detection means that there is only one cluster corresponding to a particular social event in our ground truth. Incorrect detections happen due to under-joining (column "U-joint") and over-joining (column "O-joint") of social events. Under-joining is seen when there is more than one cluster related to the same social event in the ground truth. Over-joining happens when a cluster contains photos that relate to more than one social event in the ground truth. Naturally, personal events that have been aggregated into detected social events but are unrelated to events in the ground truth are left out of the analysis. Any attempt to include these would require at least manual inspection to see if they are correct or correspond instead to the U-joint or O-joint categories.

In the same Table 1 we can also see that there are small variations for temporal threshold c_T of 0.75 and 0.50, with $c_T = 0.50$ resulting in slightly less over-joining for the same values of c_S, while a value of 0.25 results in an increased number of partial social events (under-joining). Based on the set of experiments run, $c_T = 0.50$ and $c_S = 1.00$ produce the best results.

After submitting the testing subset to evaluation we found that the event similarity function produced correct results ("Correct") in 78.76% of the cases, partial social events ("U-joint") in 9.56% of the cases and social events with multiple tags ("O-joint") in 11.68% of the cases.

6.3 Social Ties Detection

A first rapid analysis reveals that of the 1291 events with more than 1 participant, 1039 (80.48%) have at least 1 pair of participants

Co-participation degree	1	2	3	4	5	6	7	8	9	11	12	13
Contacts	3649	534	166	49	27	21	7	7	2	3	2	1
Non-contacts	5167	166	18	5	3	1	0	0	0	0	0	0
Contacts (%)	41.39	76.29	90.22	90.74	90.0	95.45	100.0	100.0	100.0	100.0	100.0	100.0

Table 2: Experimental results for the degree of co-participation in events. The comparison is made counting occurrences of pairs of users participating in the same event. We establish two groups to clasify user pairs depending on whether these user pairs have each other as contacts (the "Contacts row") or not (the "Non-contacts" row). Additionally, we provide the results of the "Contacts" row as a percentage relative to the total number of user pairs (the "Contacts (%)" row)

that have each other as contacts. This is a good hint that further analysis can give an answer to our hypothesis.

Table 2 shows the complete analysis for all the degrees of co-participation that are present in the dataset. We compare occurrences for users that are contacts against occurrences for users that are not contacts. In Figure 3 we can see that for a co-participation degree of 1 only 41.39% of all analyzed pairs are of users that have each other as contacts. For a co-attendance of 2 the ratio increases to more than 76% and for degrees of 3 and greater the ratio consistently stays above 90%.

The coarse analysis of the derived data shows that the probability confirms our equation given in 6.

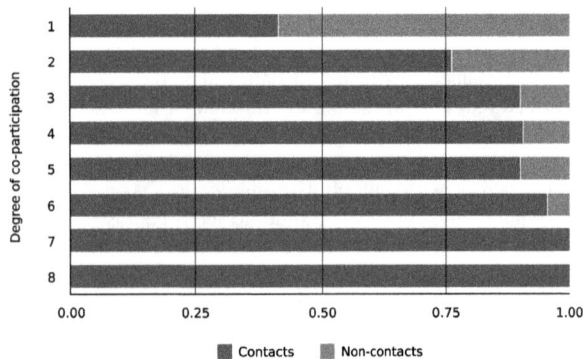

Figure 4: Shared contacts per degree of event co-participation. Included in parentheses are the number of occurrences for pairs of users with such characteristics.

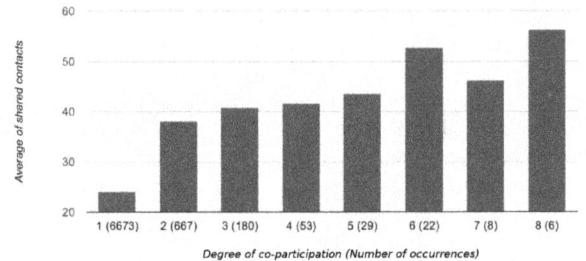

Figure 3: Ratio of users with social ties vs. users without social ties per degree of co-participation in the same events.

Additionally we can see a trend in Figure 4 showing that for increasing degrees of event co-participation there is a corresponding increase in the average of shared contacts. This supports the idea that events are suitable containers of social information. An increasing number of shared events indicates a growing degree of social closeness. This is sustained by the results we obtained taking the alternate approach of measuring the social closeness which is done by calculating the number of shared contacts.

7. CONCLUSION

This paper presents the novel and robust approach for social event detection task. It also demonstrates how social events can be used for discovery of interpersonal ties.

In the first part of our paper we focus on the social event detection task. We use 50% of our dataset to train our algorithm and select the correct parameters for temporal and spatial similarity. Afterwards we use the remaining 50% for evaluation, reaching a precision of 78.76% for full events. If we consider partial events as valid, our precision measurement rises to 88.32%.

In the second part of this paper we show how to automatically discover social connections via a semantically meaningful analysis of the layer of events. The approach presented in the paper is simple

and robust. The experimental results show that two users know each other in more than **76%** of the cases if they co-participated in at least **2** events.

We also show that the degree of event co-participation is an indicator of social closeness. This is sustained by the analysis performed on the dataset using the well-known FoF approach (see Figure 4).

People that co-participate in an event are likely to have similar interests, especially when we are talking about events such as sport competitions, concerts, festivals and others. Therefore, events can be used not only for reconstructing existing social ties but also for creating new connections based on similar interests. The approach can be applied easily by social networking services in order to enrich a user's interpersonal ties.

8. ACKNOWLEDGMENTS

This work was partially supported by the European Commission under contract FP7-287704 CUBRIK.

9. REFERENCES

[1] Mezaris, Vasileios and Scherp, Ansgar and Jain, Ramesh and Kankanhalli, Mohan and Zhou, Huiyu and Zhang, Jianguo and Wang, Liang and Zhang, Zhengyou Modeling and representing events in multimedia *Proceedings of the 19th ACM international conference on Multimedia, Scottsdale, Arizona, USA,* 2011.

[2] Norman R. Brown. On the prevalence of event clusters in autobiographical memory. *Social Cognition,* 2005.

[3] Timo Hintsa, Sari Vainikainen, and Magnus Melin. Leveraging linked data in Social Event Detection. *CEUR Proceedings of the MediaEval 2011 Workshop,* 2011.

[4] Markus Brenner and Ebroul Izquierdo. Mediaeval benchmark: Social event detection in collaborative photo collections. *CEUR Proceedings of the MediaEval 2011 Workshop,* 2011.

[5] Liu Xueliang, Benoit Huet, and Raphaël Troncy. Eurecom@ mediaeval 2011 social event detection task. *CEUR Proceedings of the MediaEval 2011 Workshop*, 2011.

[6] Georgios Petkos, Symeon Papadopoulos and Yiannis Kompatsiaris Social event detection using multimodal clustering and integrating supervisory signals. *Proceedings of the 2nd ACM International Conference on Multimedia Retrieval, ICMR'12*, 2012

[7] Timo Reuter and Philipp Cimiano Event-based classification of social media streams. *Proceedings of the 2nd ACM International Conference on Multimedia Retrieval, ICMR'12*, 2012

[8] H. Becker, M. Naaman, and L. Gravano. Learning similarity metrics for event identification in social media. In Proceedings of WSDM, pages 291-300, 2010

[9] Zacks, J M and Tversky, B, Event structure in perception and conception. *Psychological bulletin, 1 pp 3-21, 2001*

[10] *Marilyn C. Smith, Uri Bibi, and D. Erin Sheard. Evidence for the differential impact of time and emotion on personal and event memories for september 11, 2001.* Applied Cognitive Psychology, 17(9):1047–1055, 2003.

[11] *Ivan Tankoyeu, Javier Paniagua, Julian Stöttinger, and Fausto Giunchiglia. Event detection and scene attraction by very simple contextual cues. In* ACM MM workshop on modeling and representing events, *2011.*

[12] *Eagle, Nathan and Pentland, Alex (Sandy) and Lazer, David Inferring friendship network structure by using mobile phone data* Proceedings of the National Academy of Sciences, 36, vol. 106, 2009.

[13] *Crandall, David and Backstrom, Lars and Cosley, Dan and Suri, Siddharth and Huttenlocher, Daniel and Kleinberg, Jon Inferring social ties from geographic coincidences* Proceedings of the National Academy of Sciences, 52, vol. 107, 2010.

[14] *Chen, Jilin and Geyer, Werner and Dugan, Casey and Muller, Michael and Guy, Ido Make new friends, but keep the old: recommending people on social networking sites*

Proceedings of the 27th international conference on Human factors in computing systems CHI '09, *pp.201–210, 2009.*

[15] *Yang, Shuang-Hong and Long, Bo and Smola, Alex and Sadagopan, Narayanan and Zheng, Zhaohui and Zha, Hongyuan Like like alike: joint friendship and interest propagation in social networks* Proceedings of the 20th international conference on World wide web WWW '11, *pp.537-546, 2011.*

[16] *Quercia, Daniele and Capra, Licia FriendSensing: recommending friends using mobile phones* Proceedings of the third ACM conference on Recommender systems RecSys '09, *pp.273-276, 2009.*

[17] *Kurby, Christopher and Zacks, Jeffrey Segmentation in the perception and memory of events* Trends in cognitive sciences, *pp.72-79, 2008.*

[18] *S. Papadopoulos, E. Schinas, V. Mezaris, R. Troncy, I. Kompatsiaris, Social Event Detection at MediaEval 2012: Challenges, Dataset and Evaluation* Proceedings at MediaEval'12 Workshop, Pisa, Italy, *2012.*

[19] *M. Zeppelzauer, M. Zaharieva, C. Breiteneder A Generic Approach for Social Event Detection in Large Photo Collections* Proceedings at MediaEval'12 Workshop, Pisa, Italy, *2012.*

[20] *K. N. Vavliakis, F. A. Tzima, P. A. Mitkas Event Detection via LDA for the MediaEval2012 SED Task* Proceedings at MediaEval'12 Workshop, Pisa, Italy, *2012.*

[21] *E. Schinas, G. Petkos, S. Papadopoulos, Y. Kompatsiaris CERTH @ MediaEval 2012 Social Event Detection Task* Proceedings at MediaEval'12 Workshop, Pisa, Italy, *2012.*

[22] *M. Brener, E. Izquierdo QMUL @ MediaEval 2012: Social Event Detection in Collaborative Photo Collections* Proceedings at MediaEval'12 Workshop, Pisa, Italy, *2012.*

[23] *M.S. Dao, G. Boato, F.G.B. De Natale, T. T. Nguyen A Watershed-based Social Events Detection Method with Support of External Data Sources* Proceedings at MediaEval'12 Workshop, Pisa, Italy, *2012.*

Heterogeneous Features and Model Selection for Event-Based Media Classification

Xueliang Liu
EURECOM
Sophia-Antipolis, France
xueliang.liu@eurecom.fr

Benoit Huet
EURECOM
Sophia-Antipolis, France
benoit.huet@eurecom.fr

ABSTRACT

With the rapid development of social media sites, a lot of user generated content is being shared in the Web, leading to new challenges for traditional media retrieval techniques. An event describes the happening at a specific time and place in real-world, and it is one of the most important cues for people to recall past memories. The reminder value of an event makes it extremely helpful in organizing human life. Thus, organizing media by events has recently drawn much attention within the multimedia research community. In this paper, we focus on two fundamental problems related to event based social media analysis: the study of feature importance for modeling the relation between events and media, and how to deal with missing and erroneous metadata often present in social media data. These issues are studied within an event-based media classification framework. Different learning approaches are employed to train the event models on different features. We find, through experiments on a large set of events, that the best discriminant features are tags, spatial and temporal feature. We address the missing value problem by extending the feature with an extra attribute to indicate if the values are missing. Promising results are achieved demonstrating the effectiveness of the proposed method.

Categories and Subject Descriptors

H.3.3 [**Information Storage and Retrieval**]: Information Search and Retrieval; H.3.1 [**Content Analysis and Indexing**]: miscellaneous

Keywords

Events, social media, classification, missing value, feature importance

1. INTRODUCTION

Recent years have witnessed the rapid development of electronic capturing devices and social media web services,

which has made it easy for people to capture and share media data online. Nowadays, there is exponential growth of social media available online in the form of images and videos. The Web 2.0 provides users facilities to share and access data, while its advent demands effective data management and indexing technologies. How to search for media efficiently and effectively, how to leverage big data to solve the large scale problems in industry and research communities, are still open challenges.

An event describes a real world happening and is defined according to Who?, What?, When? and Where?. Recently, organizing media data by events has drawn much attention in the multimedia research community. Events can serve as powerful instruments to organize media, thanks to their intrinsically multi-faceted nature. Furthermore, it is the most natural way for human beings to store and recall their memories. Associating media to events and modeling events is an area that has started to receive considerable attention. For example, in [24], the authors proposed a method to retrieve media from the same events on given event record samples, and they formulate the similarity of events and media data with visual and time features. [10] and [22] studied how to categorize media data by event. In [10], a naive Bayes classifier is built for each event using text and temporal features, to categorize social media data by events. The authors of [22] focused on how to assign media data to events. They modeled the similarity of events and media data by multimodal features. From this fruitful research, it can be concluded that events are an effective way to organize the content and could help facilitate the search and retrieval of social media data.

However, there are still some fundamental questions which are not addressed by previous work. While work to model the similarity of social media on the basis of text/time, or the similarity between events and social media with respect to time, location or text features have been conducted, the importance and effectiveness of those features has not been studied in details until now. Since event and social media data is very sparse, weak representative features may degrade the performance of a proposed system. In addition, missing attributes are unavoidable in user generated data. As an example, location is very effective to measure the similarity of events and media data, but in Flickr, only about 20% of uploaded media is labeled with a geo tag. Due to limited availability, location information is often not taken into consideration [24] and in other works, the data with missing values is simply discarded from further analysis [10].

In this paper, we report the study of both the feature

selection and missing value handling in the scope of event based media categorization. In details, we address the problem of categorizing media data by events, while investigating how to select the representative features and to incorporate the missing attributes in the system. The contributions of this paper are three-folds:

- To identify the most representative features; We study the feature selection problems in event based media analysis. We learn the event model using multimodal features and find out that the most representative features are tags, location and time.

- To model the event accurately; We employ and compare different learning approaches to model the events. Our results highlight the effectiveness of the decision tree based approach on heterogeneous data.

- To deal with missing attributes for some samples; We use a method inspired from the one presented in [15] to represent the feature with missing value, that is to add an extended attribute to indicate if the value is missing or not. Our result shows the benefits of this missing attribute handling approach.

The rest of this paper is organized as follows; We review the related work in Section 2. The approaches and features used to model events are described in Section 3. Experimental results are presented in Section 4. Finally, the contributions and future work are summarized in Section 5.

2. RELATED WORK

In the work presented here, we define an event as a public happening taking place at a given location and time involving several people. Last.FM and eventful are event repositories designed to help users sharing their experiences and interests on the Web. These sites also host substantial amounts of user-contributed materials (e.g. photographs, videos, and textual content) for a wide variety of real-world events of different type and scale. How to mine the relation between events and social media data has gathered recent attention.

Events are important parts in our lives and as such many of the documents uploaded to social media sites are captured during events. Classifying social media documents with respect to the events they originate from is thus a promising approach to better manage and organize the huge amount of social media data. The problem of media categorization by event was studied by [10, 22]. In [10], the authors studied how to exploit the social textual information produced by users for classifying pictures into different event categories. They employed a naive Bayes classifier to model an event by text and time features. In [22] the authors focused on how to assign media data to events, they modeled the similarity of events and media data by multimodal features, and used a rule-based approach to detect new events. Other than mining the media metadata, visual content analysis is also involved to model events. In [24], a method was proposed to retrieve media from the same events on record samples. The authors formulate the similarity of events and media data with visual and time features, and the problem was solved using the Local Sensitive Hashing approach under the map-reduce framework. In [17], a demonstration was proposed to categorize photos by events/sub-events based on visual content analysis.

Since many media are captured during events, the problem of associating media data to its originating events is also addressed by the research community. In [1], the authors proposed approaches to exploit the rich "context" associated with social media content and applied clustering algorithms to identify events. [8] analyzed Twitter messages corresponding to large scale media events to improve event reasoning, visualization, and analytic. In [14], the authors proposed a system to present the media content from live music events, assuming a serial of concerts by the same artist such as a world tour. By synchronizing the music clips with audio fingerprint and other metadata, the system gives a novel interface to organize user-contributed content.

Other related research works focus on mining the events patterns from social media data. The Social Event Detection Task in the MediaEval workshop focuses on discovering events and detecting media items that are related to either a specific social event or an event-class of interest [18]. A solution to this problems is proposed in [26] which studies how to exploit the social interaction and other similarity between media data to detect events. [21] presented methods to mine events and object from community photo collections using clustering approaches. In their system, the photos are grouped according to several modalities (visual and textual features) and the clusters are classified as objects or events according to their duration and users, based on fact that events are usually characterized by a short duration. A very similar framework is proposed to classify the events and landmarks in [19]. Furthermore, event based research also studies the problem of discovering events directly from Twitter post [27, 23]. In [27], the authors studied how to employ a wavelet-based techniques to detect events from Twitter stream. A similar method can be found in [6] to detect events from Flickr time series data. In [23], the authors investigate how to filter the tweets to detect seismic activity as it happens. They considered each Twitter user as a sensor and applied Kalman filtering and particle filtering techniques to estimating the centers of earthquakes and the trajectories of typhoons.

It can be seen that previous event based social media analysis studied the problem in two aspects: associating media with events and discovering events from social media stream. In theses works, many multimodal features, such as tag, time, location and visual features are exploited, and as a result encouraging performance is achieved. The role events can play in organizing and managing media data is verified. However, there are still some fundamental questions which are not addressed by these works. For examples, the importance and effectiveness of individual multimodal features is not studied. In addition, missing attributes are unavoidable in user generated data. Modeling data with missing value is a common problem in data mining [11]. It is also a long-standing but not so well studied problem in the multimedia community. In [24, 10], the attributes with missing values are discarded since too hard to be modeled in the proposed approach. In [15], an additional indicator is concatenated to the feature vector to highlight missing data. As far as we know, no prior work addresses this issue in event based social media analysis. In this paper, we focus on feature selection and deal with missing values, by extending the framework of event based social media categorization, proposed by [10].

3. OUR PROPOSAL

Our study is set within an event based social media classification framework. For each event in the dataset, we train an event model using the photos originating from that event. To evaluate the effectiveness of different learning approaches and features for modeling events. We use KNN, SVM, Decision Tree and Random Forest to learn the models based on temporal (date and time), location (geo-coordinates), tag (annotations) and visual features for each event. Building models on an event basis allows adding new events without affecting previously learned models and reduces the impact of the increase of events in the dataset. The positive examples of an event are represented by the pictures originating from the event, while the negative ones are randomly selected from the pictures corresponding to the remaining events in the dataset. Now, we shall briefly review the classification algorithms under comparison, and then, detail the features to be evaluated.

3.1 Classification algorithm

To evaluate the performance of different learning approaches for modeling the events, we implement four approaches that are popularly employed in social media analysis, listed below, to train the event models.

- **K-Nearest Neighbor** The K-Nearest Neighbor algorithm (KNN) is among the simplest of all classification algorithms: KNN is a type of instance-based learning; it classifies objects based on the k closest training examples in the feature space. An object is classified by a majority vote over its neighbor's classes, with the object being assigned to the class most common amongst its k nearest neighbors. Despite its simplicity, KNN has been successful in a large number of classification and regression problems. It is often successful in classification situations where the decision boundary is very irregular.

- **Support Vector Machine** Support Vector Machine (SVM) [5] is one of the most effective supervised classification methods. Given a set of training examples, each marked as belonging to one of two categories, the SVM training algorithm builds a model that assigns new examples into one category or the other, based on the "margin maximization" strategy. An SVM model is a representation of the examples as points in space, mapped so that the examples of the separate categories are divided by a clear gap that is as wide as possible. Support Vector Machines are very effective in high dimensional spaces, and popularly used in practice due to its better performance compared with some other classifiers [4].

- **Decision Tree** Decision tree (DT) [3] uses tree structure to make a decision. A decision tree can be constructed top-down using the information gain, which measures each attribute's discrimination power. It begins at the root node with some ancestor nodes determined by the attribute with the highest information gain, then attaches all examples where the attribute values of the examples are identical to each node. All sub-trees are built using recursion. Decision trees are commonly used in operations research, specifically in decision analysis, to help identify a strategy most likely to reach a goal.

- **Random Forest** Random forest [2] is an ensemble classifier that consists of many decision trees and outputs the class that is the mode of the classes output by individual trees. Although it suffers from over-fitting with noisy dataset, it is one of the most accurate learning algorithms available which runs efficiently on large databases with thousands of input variables without variable deletion.

3.2 Feature with missing value

As an event is defined as "something happening at a given place and time" in this paper, several features can easily be mapped to metadata or content available in photos. The time can be represented by the photos taken time, while the place is represented by the GPS metadata. The topic of events can be mined from the content of media, in the form of visual or textual features. Here are the four features investigated in our experiments:

- **Temporal feature** Time is one of the most key components of an event. The temporal feature used in this paper is the photo taken time, which is represented as the number of past seconds from Unix epoch. The taken time is compulsory in photo metadata.

- **Location feature** Nowadays, geographical metadata is a common component in social media data [12]. We extract the GPS metadata, that is the latitude and longitude coordinates, as the location feature. GPS information is not required in photos metadata. To cope missing value, the method proposed in [15] is employed: the feature vector is filled with zero if the value is missing while we add binary flag to indicate availability or not. The binary flag indicates whether the feature value is missing or present. Experiments on KDD 2009 data show that this strategy improves the test performances considerably [15].

- **Tag Feature** In Web 2.0 web services, tags are manually labeled by Internet users and have become an effective way to organize, index and search media content. Since tags appear distinctly in the metadata, we employ the Boolean weighting schemes to measure the term's frequency of tags [16]. In detail, for each event we create a word vocabulary with the 200 most frequent tags and the tags in a photo are projected on the vocabulary, creating a vector. Each dimension in the vector corresponds to a separate term. If a term occurs in the document, its value in the vector is 1, or 0 otherwise. Tag metadata is also not compulsory and the same strategy as on location feature is used to handle missing values for the tag feature. Hence, the tag feature is a 201-D vector.

- **Visual Feature** Visual features are also representative for the photo content. In our work, we obtain multiple types of low level visual the features that has been popularly used in visual content analysis [7] such as: 64-D color histogram, 73-D edge histogram and 64 Gabor features. The three visual features are concatenated into 201-D and normalized during pre-processing. Visual features are dense and without missing values.

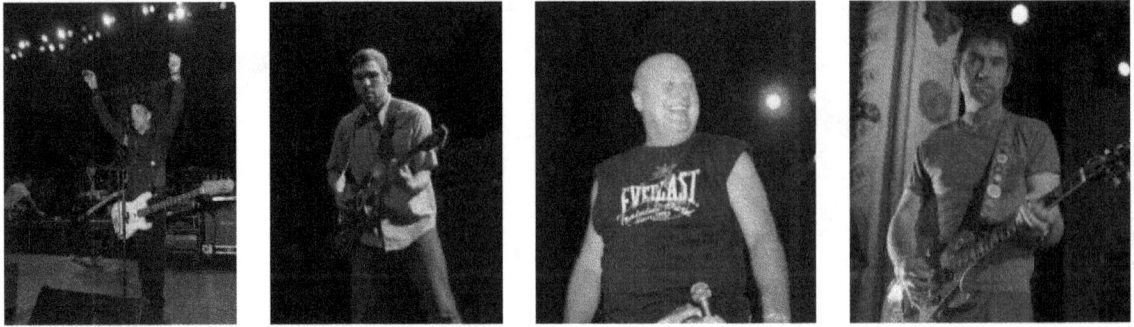

Figure 1: Some photo examples from the dataset

The various feature vectors representing each photo can either be used separately or concatenated together in order to learn the event model.

4. EXPERIMENTS

4.1 Dataset

We have developed a system to evaluate both the feature importance and the missing value processing approaches on the task of associating photos with events. The EventMedia dataset, created by Troncy et al [25] using the linking data techniques is employed. In EventMedia, the events originate from three large public event repositories (last.fm, eventful and upcoming) and media data connected by event machine tags were crawled from social media sharing platforms such as Flickr or twitter. There are about 100000 events in this corpus, illustrated with 1.7M photos. The data is saved in RDF format and can be queried through a SPARQL entry point[1]. Since we need sufficient exemplars for training and testing, we only choose the events with at least 40 photos labeled with location metadata. In EventMedia, there are 674 events which fit this condition and are hence used as our event collection[2], along with the associated 92K photos. Figure 2 reports of the number of photos associated to events while some photos exemplars from the dataset are shown in Figure 1.

4.2 Experiments setting

For each event in the dataset, we use the photos originating from the event as the positive samples, and randomly select 4 times more photos taken from other events as the negative samples. Both the positive and negative data are split into two equal parts randomly, one for training, the other for testing.

For each photo in the dataset, the features detailed in section 3.2 are computed. In our quest to identify the most representative features, we compare 4 features vectors to train our event models with 4 different learning approaches; The unidimensional temporal feature is concatenated with the location feature as a 4-D spatio-temporal feature vector, the 201-D tag feature vector alone, the 201-D visual features vector alone and finally, we also concatenate all of the features together into a single 406-D feature vector.

For the learning process the following parameters are employed. For the KNN approach, we set the parameter k to 10, experimentally. For the SVM approach, we choose the

[1]http://eventmedia.eurecom.fr/sparql

[2]http://www.eurecom.fr/~liux/ICMR13.html

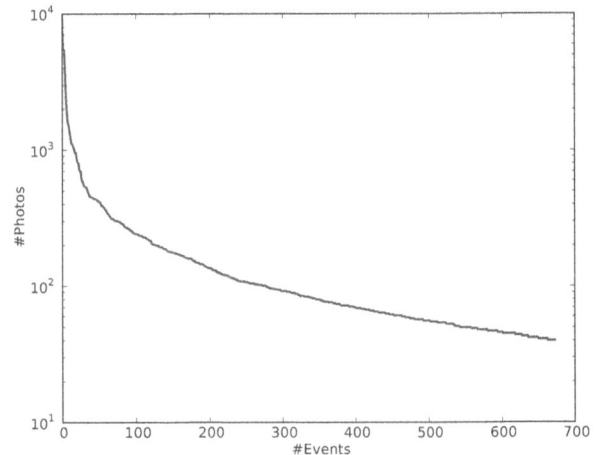

Figure 2: The statistics of number of photos per event, ranging from 40 to several thousand

RBF kernel and use grid search method to select the best parameters. For the Decision Tree approach, we set the depth of the tree as $\sqrt{N}$, where N is the length of feature. For examples, for the 201-D tag feature, the depth of the tree is $\sqrt{201} = 14$. We use the same depth parameter to train the Random Forest model, while the number of tree is set to 10 experimentally.

4.3 Evaluation criteria

Due to the very imbalanced nature of the dataset, we cannot use criteria like accuracy to evaluate the performance of the algorithms. Since the ratio of positive vs negative sample is 1:4, classifying all of the testing data as negative would lead to an accuracy of 80%. For such imbalanced dataset, the Receiver Operator Characteristic (ROC) curve and Precision-Recall (PR) curve measures are better suited [20].

The ROC curve is a graphical plot which illustrates the performance of a binary classifier system as its discrimination threshold varies. It is created by plotting the fraction of true positives out of the positives vs. the fraction of false positives out of the negatives, with varying threshold.

The ROC curve is an important tool to measure performance of a classification system with imbalanced testing data [13, 9]. The area under curve (AUC) measures the

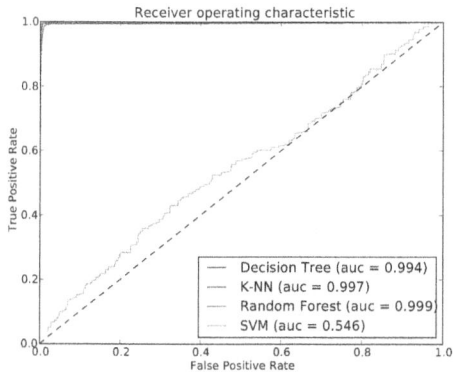

(a) ROC curve with spatial temporal feature

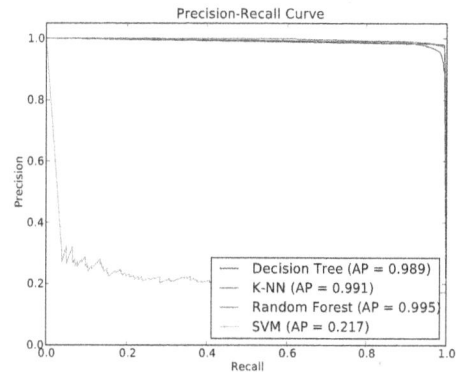

(b) PR curve with spatial temporal feature

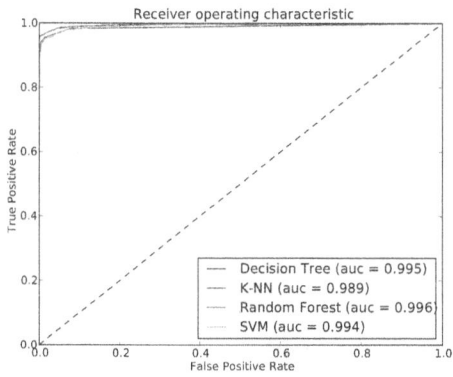

(c) ROC curve with tag feature

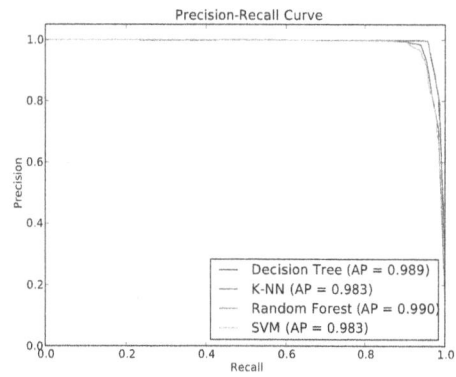

(d) PR curve with tag feature

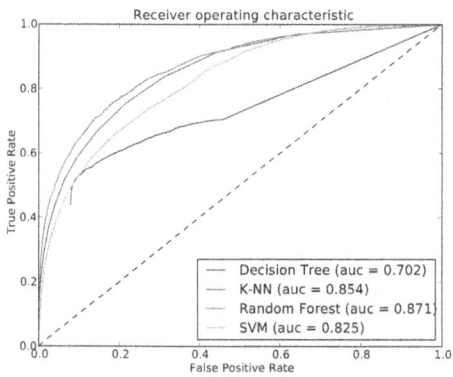

(e) ROC curve with visual feature

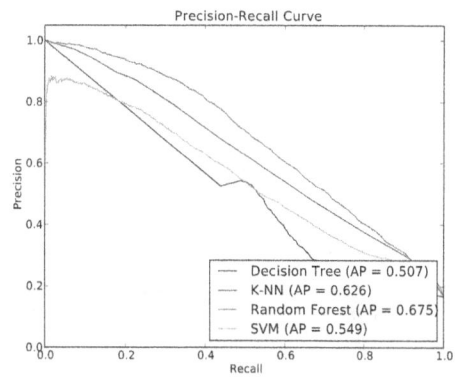

(f) PR curve with visual feature

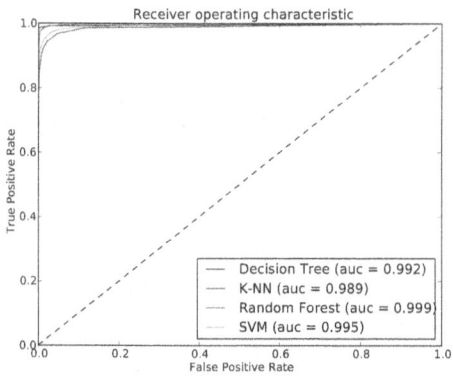

(g) ROC curve with all concatenated features

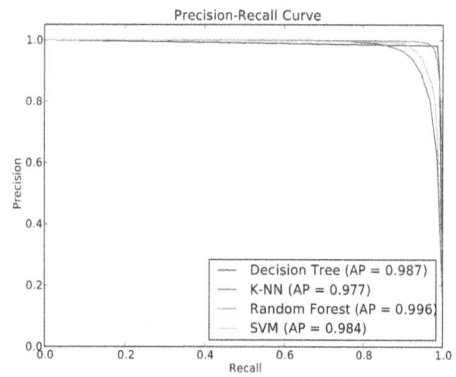

(h) PRC curve with all concatenated features

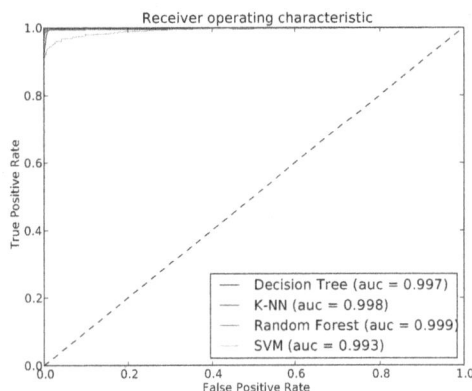

(i) ROC curve with ST+ tag feature   (j) PR curve with ST+ tag feature

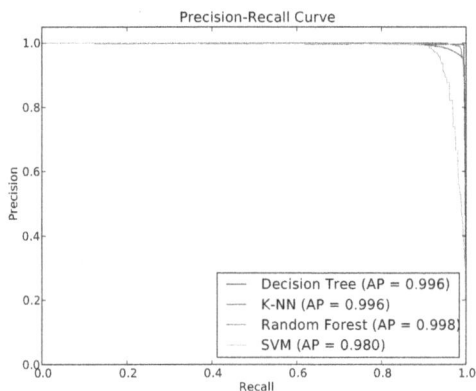

Figure 1: ROC and PR curves with different features

probability that a classifier will rank a randomly chosen positive instance higher than a randomly chosen negative one, which gives the credibility of trained models.

When dealing with highly skewed datasets, Precision-Recall (PR) curve is another informative measure of a system's performance. In pattern recognition, PR curve measures the relation between fraction of retrieved instances that are relevant (Precision), and the fraction of relevant instances that are retrieved (Recall). The PR curve only takes the positive samples into account and it is always used for scoring highly imbalanced systems. The area under curve is called as Average Precision (AP), which is one of the most popular criteria used for evaluating classification and information retrieval tasks.

4.4 Results

From the whole dataset, we randomly select 100 events to train the 1-vs-all classifiers with different learning approaches and features. The results are reported in Figure 1. Comparing the four classification approaches KNN, SVM, DT and RF, the Random Forest method offers the best performance regardless of the features employed for training. For examples, even with the 4D spatial and temporal feature, the AUC under ROC curve and average precision are 0.999 and 0.995 respectively, as shown in Figure 1(a) (b). Decision Tree and KNN models also offer competitive performance for modeling the data. Compared with Decision Tree, the KNN algorithm has better performance on spatio-temporal feature and visual feature, but fails to model the tag and concatenated features very well. SVM provides, as expected, good performance with the higher dimensional data, such as the tag, visual and the concatenated features. However, it is not well suited to model low dimensional data such as the 4-D spatio-temporal feature (AUC and AP value are 0.546 and 0.217, see the curve in Figure1(a) (b).

We also study the impacts of different features in modeling the events. We found that the most effective feature is the tag (Figure 1(c)(d)), which is also the most reliable feature independently of the learning approach employed. The spatio-temporal feature has a good performance with KNN, Decision Tree and Random Forest (see Figure 1(a)(b)). It is also the feature with the lowest dimension hence the models are learned effectively. Figure 1 also shows that the visual

feature is not very robust compared with the other two features, and the average AUC and AP values under the four methods is 0.813 and 0.589 respectively. The reason is that most of the events in EventMedia are concerts and therefore, the photos originating from any events share a similar visual atmosphere. As part of our extensive set of experiments, we also study the fusion of different features, which is to concatenate all of the features together to train the model. The result are reported in Figure 1(e)(f). The performance of those models trained on the concatenated feature does not improve when compared with the tag feature, due to the relatively low discriminative power of the visual feature within this class of event (live events/concerts). The best performance overall is actually achieved when model is trained with both the spatio-temporal feature and tag feature concatenated, as shown in Figure 1(i)(j).

From these figures, we can conclude that:

1. Tag is the most representative feature when modeling event, followed closely by the spatio-temporal feature. In addition, the combination of spatio-temporal and tag feature obtains the best performance overall.

2. On modeling the photos features which are very parse and with missing value, the Decision Tree and KNN methods obtain a better performance compared with SVM, while the previous approaches are designed to deal with problems with irregular decision boundary.

4.5 Evaluation of the impact of Missing Value

In the dataset, the location feature and tag feature are not necessarily available, which results in many missing values in the feature vectors. To handle the missing values, we propose to extend the features with an indicator to show if the feature values is missing or not. In the experiments, we evaluate and compare our approach with the common strategy for handling missing values: replacing the missing data by zero vectors.

We train the models using KNN, the approach which offers the best efficiency with the least computational burden, and Random Forest, which offers the best effectiveness overall on our dataset. The results of modeling events with both KNN and RF for the two feature types subject to missing values are reported in Figure 3.

In the dataset, only 39.7% of the photos have geo-location metadata available. Figure 3(a)(b) shows the performance of KNN and RF model trained using the location feature under the different missing values processing techniques. The evaluation criteria are the same as in the previous section: ROC and PR curves. It can be seen in the two figures that compared with the method that simply fills the missing values with zeros, the method used in this paper achieves better performance with the AUC increasing from 0.996 to 0.997 and AP increasing from 0.989 to 0.992 using KNN classification. The same conclusion could be obtained from the models trained with the Random Forest method, though two models have the same performance measure with the AUC criteria, but better performance measured with AP (from 0.994 to 0.995).

A similar phenomenon can be observed in Figure 3(c)(d), which show the results on tag features. 56.9% of the photos in the dataset have tags labels. When both learning approaches are trained with tag feature, the AUC increases from 0.986 to 0.989 in KNN model, and from 0.995 to 0.996 in Random Forest model (Figure 3(c)), while the AP increases from 0.982 to 0.985 in KNN model, and 0.988 to 0.989 in Random Forest model respectively.

From the four figures, it can be concluded that the proposed approach, extending the feature with an indicator of missing value, brings more information to the representation allowing to better model event media.

5. CONCLUSION

The exponential growth of social media data available online, witnessed over recent years, brings new challenges for managing and organizing media efficiently and effectively. Thanks to its multi-dimensional nature (Who, What, When, Where), events are a powerful instrument to organize media. Associating media to events and modeling events are activities which have started to receive considerable attention in research community.

In this paper, we focus on studying the feature and model selection, as well as handling the issue of potential missing value for the task of event based media categorization. These are fundamental questions, yet not addressed by previous work. We tackle these problems within an event-based photo classification framework, and compare various learning approaches (KNN, SVM, Decision Tree and Random Forest) to train the model with different features, such as spatio-temporal, tag, visual features. Our experiment results show that the best model is learned by Random Forest with the combination of spatio-temporal and tag features. To deal with the missing value issue, we propose to extend the feature with an indicator which specifies whether the value is missing or not. The performance obtained in our comparative study highlights the fact that of the common method consisting in simply filling the missing value with zeros is outperform by our missing value handling approach.

In the work presented here, the event models are learned using either individual or concatenation of feature. In future, we would like to study how to better fuse such features, how to fuse the classifying results and to make a more sophisticated decision. As a general conclusion, this paper will benefit the media based social event detection task by exploring multiple features and models in order to achieve the best possible classification performance.

6. REFERENCES

[1] H. Becker, M. Naaman, and L. Gravano. Event Identification in Social Media. In *12th International Workshop on the Web and Databases*, Providence, USA, 2009.

[2] L. Breiman. Random forests. *Machine Learning*, 45:5–32, 2001.

[3] L. Breiman, J. Friedman, R. Olshen, and C. Stone. *Classification and Regression Trees*. Wadsworth and Brooks, Monterey, CA, 1984. new edition [?]?

[4] R. Caruana and A. Niculescu-Mizil. An empirical comparison of supervised learning algorithms. In *Proceedings of the 23rd international conference on Machine learning*, pages 161–168, New York, USA, June 2006.

[5] C.-C. Chang and C.-J. Lin. LIBSVM: A library for support vector machines. *ACM Transactions on Intelligent Systems and Technology*, 2(3):27:1—-27:27, 2011.

[6] L. Chen and A. Roy. Event detection from flickr data through wavelet-based spatial analysis. In *ACM conference on CIKM*, 2009.

[7] T.-S. Chua, J. Tang, R. Hong, H. Li, Z. Luo, and Y.-T. Zheng. NUS-WIDE: A Real-World Web Image Database from National University of Singapore. In *Proc. of ACM Conf. on Image and Video Retrieval*, Santorini, Greece, 2009.

[8] N. Diakopoulos, M. Naaman, and F. Kivran-Swaine. Diamonds in the rough: Social media visual analytics for journalistic inquiry. In *2010 IEEE Symposium on Visual Analytics Science and Technology*, pages 115–122, Oct. 2010.

[9] T. Fawcett. An introduction to roc analysis. *Pattern Recogn. Lett.*, 27(8):861–874, June 2006.

[10] C. S. Firan, M. Georgescu, W. Nejdl, and R. Paiu. Bringing order to your photos: Event-Driven Classification of Flickr Images Based on Social Knowledge. In *Proceedings of the 19th ACM international conference on Information and knowledge management*, page 189, New York, USA, Oct. 2010.

[11] J. W. Grzymala-Busse and M. Hu. A comparison of several approaches to missing attribute values in data mining. In *Revised Papers from the Second International Conference on Rough Sets and Current Trends in Computing*, RSCTC '00, pages 378–385, London, UK, UK, 2001. Springer-Verlag.

[12] J. Hays and A. A. Efros. IM2GPS: estimating geographic information from a single image. In *IEEE Conference on Computer Vision and Pattern Recognition*, pages 1–8, 2008.

[13] H. He and E. A. Garcia. Learning from imbalanced data. *IEEE Transactions on Knowledge and Data Engineering*, 21(9):1263–1284, 2009.

[14] L. Kennedy and M. Naaman. Less talk, more rock: automated organization of community-contributed collections of concert videos. In *18th ACM International Conference on World Wide Web*, pages 311–320, Madrid, Spain, 2009.

[15] H.-Y. Lo, K.-W. Chang, S.-T. Chen, and et al. An ensemble of three classifiers for kdd cup 2009: Expanded linear model, heterogeneous boosting, and

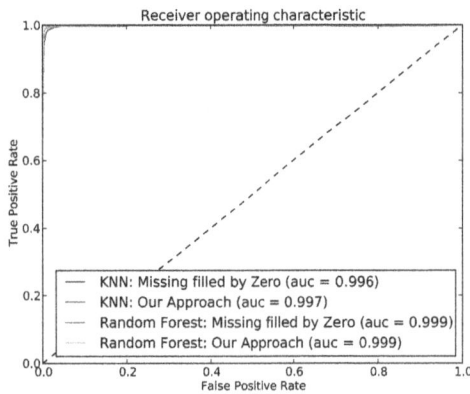

(a) ROC curve with spatial temporal feature

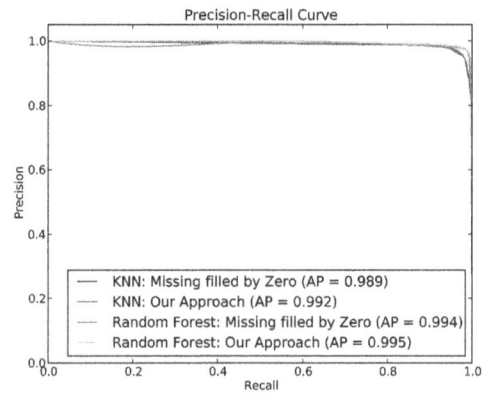

(b) PR curve with spatial temporal feature

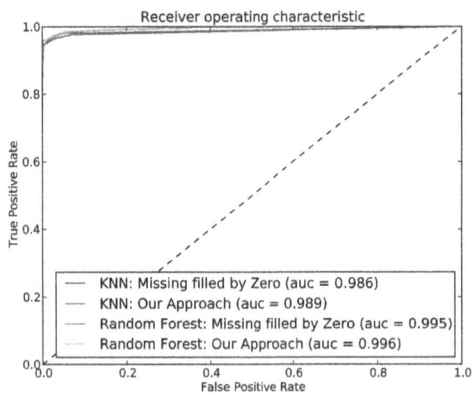

(c) ROC curve with tag feature

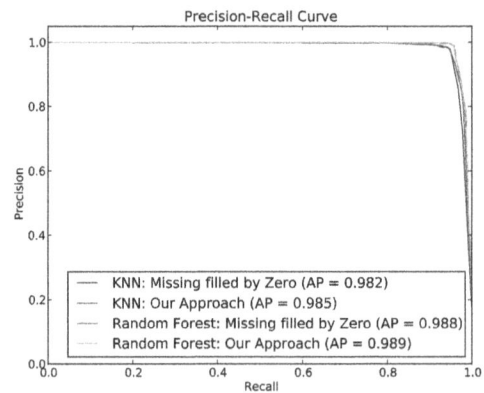

(d) PR curve with tag feature

Figure 3: Performance of KNN and Random Forest methods with missing value features

selective naive bayes. *Journal of Machine Learning Research - Proceedings Track*, 7:57–64, 2009.

[16] C. D. Manning, P. Raghavan, and H. Schütze. *Introduction to Information Retrieval*. 1 edition, July 2008.

[17] R. Mattivi, J. Uijlings, F. De Natale, and N. Sebe. Categorization of a collection of pictures into structured events. In *Proceedings of the 2nd ACM International Conference on Multimedia Retrieval*, page 1, New York, USA, June 2012.

[18] S. Papadopoulos, E. Schinas, V. Mezaris, R. Troncy, and I. Kompatsiaris. Social event detection at mediaeval 2012: Challenges, dataset and evaluation. In *MediaEval'12*, pages –1–1, 2012.

[19] S. Papadopoulos, C. Zigkolis, Y. Kompatsiaris, and A. Vakali. Cluster-Based Landmark and Event Detection for Tagged Photo Collections. *IEEE Multimedia*, 18(1):52–63, 2011.

[20] D. M. W. Powers. Evaluation: From Precision, Recall and F-Factor to ROC, Informedness, Markedness Correlation. Technical Report SIE-07-001, School of Informatics and Engineering, Flinders University, Adelaide, Australia, 2007.

[21] T. Quack, B. Leibe, and L. Van Gool. World-scale mining of objects and events from community photo collections. In *Proceedings of the 2008 international conference on Content-based image and video retrieval*, page 47, New York, USA, July 2008.

[22] T. Reuter and P. Cimiano. Event-based classification of social media streams. In *International conference on Multimedia Retrieval*, pages 22–22, 2012.

[23] T. Sakaki, M. Okazaki, and Y. Matsuo. Earthquake shakes Twitter users: real-time event detection by social sensors. In *International conference on WWW*, pages 851–860, Apr. 2010.

[24] M. R. Trad, A. Joly, and N. Boujemaa. Large scale visual-based event matching. In *Proceedings of the 1st ACM International Conference on Multimedia Retrieval*, pages 1–7, New York, USA, Apr. 2011.

[25] R. Troncy, B. Malocha, and A. Fialho. Linking Events with Media. In *6th International Conference on Semantic Systems*, Graz, Austria, 2010.

[26] Y. Wang, H. Sundaram, and L. Xie. Social event detection with interaction graph modeling. In *ACM conference on Multimedia*, 2012.

[27] J. Weng and B.-s. Lee. Event Detection in Twitter. In *Fifth International AAAI Conference on Weblogs and Social Media*, pages 401–408. HP Laboratories, 2011.

Jointly Exploiting Visual and Non-visual Information for Event-Related Social Media Retrieval

Minh-Son Dao, Giulia Boato,
Francesco G.B. De Natale
mmLAB - DISI - University of Trento
Via Sommarive 5, 38123 Povo (TN), Italy
{dao, boato,denatale}@disi.unitn.it

Truc-Vien T. Nguyen
CIMeC - University of Trento
Corso Bettini 31, 38068 Rovereto (TN), Italy
trucvien.nguyenthi@unitn.it

ABSTRACT

In this contribution, we propose a watershed-based method with support from external data sources and visual information to detect social events in web multimedia. The idea is based on two main observations: (1) people cannot be involved in more than one event at the same time, and (2) people tend to introduce similar annotations for all images associated to the same event. Based on these observations, the metadata is turned to an image so that each row contains all records belonging to one user; and these records are sorted by time. Thus, the social event detection is turned to watershed-based image segmentation, where Markers are generated by using (keyword, location, visual) features with support of external data sources, and the Flood progress is carried on by taking into account (tags set, time, visual) features. We test our algorithm on the MediaEval 2012 dataset both using only external data but also introducing visual information.

Categories and Subject Descriptors

H.3 [**Information Storage and Retrieval**]: Information Search and Retrieval

General Terms

Theory, Experimentation

Keywords

Social Event Detection, Watershed, Relatedness

1. INTRODUCTION

In the last decades there has been a lot of research both from academia and industry on multimedia data indexing and retrieval. In particular, a recent trend suggests to organize media collections following the concept of event [15][24], in order to facilitate their organization and management.

Indeed, it has been proven that users find it easier to navigate and search through photo galleries if the pictures are grouped into events [5]. This is due to the fact that for users there is a clear link between the contents and their own experiences (e.g., their wedding, the mountain trip of last summer, their mum's birthday) and this is the most natural way of indexing their data.

Social events, such as concerts or world sport championships or, on a smaller scale, a local festival or a soccer match, build collective experiences that allow us to share personal experiences. They can therefore be used as the primary means for organizing and indexing media (e.g., photos, videos, journal articles), but also to share them (e.g., through social networks). Effective approaches to manage large-scale multimedia data collections need to both allow event detection [9][23] and retrieve all corresponding media. This is very challenging due to the heterogeneity, multimodality and generally unstructured form of such content [21].

The literature in this topic is wide. Event detection in social media (e.g., Facebook and Twitter) is studied in both [3] and [27]. Personal photo collections are considered in [15] and [8] and organized via event clustering techniques. Collaborative photo collections are taken into account in [6] by detecting events exploiting user-supplied tags. Wider information is elaborated to analyze semantics in [22], by focusing on the domain of pictures and extracting event and place semantics from tags assigned to photos in Flickr, and also in [20], where a set of pictures is used to produce two image similarity graphs one using visual features and the other using textual features, and then combined in a single hybrid similarity graph. A number of features including time, location and textual information are exploited in [1], to face this issue as an unsupervised clustering problem. More recently the same authors in [2] designed a two-step method to first cluster the input Twitter stream and then perform event versus non-event classification on the clusters. An interesting concept of social interactions is defined and used in [26], where social affinity is computed via a random-walk on a social interaction graph to determine similarity between two pictures.

Recent approaches propose multimodal techniques: in [5] data of various modalities such as time, location, textual and visual features are combined within a framework that incorporates external information from datasets and online web services. In [11] the authors propose to use the social information produced by users in the form of tags, titles and photo descriptions for classifying photos in event categories.

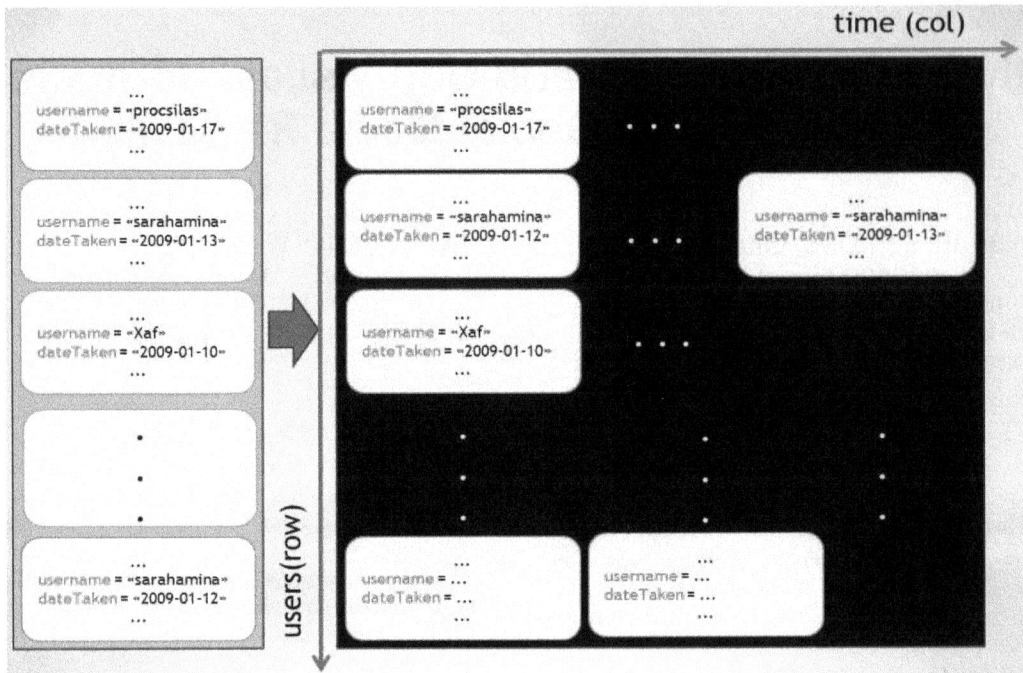

Figure 1: User-time Image (left: metadata, right: UT image layout)

In [13], the authors exploit geotagging information retrieved from online sources to determine the bounding box for a set of venues, while they use time information to determine the set of events that can be compared to the set of events occurred at the examined venue. Finally, [21] proposes a novel multimodal clustering approach, predicting the same cluster relationship exploiting pairwise similarities for all different modalities and achieving supervised fusion of the heterogeneous features.

The importance of this research challenge is not only demonstrated by the state of the art facing this issue but also by the international challenges that are proposed around the social event detection problem. In particular, within the MediaEval workshop both in 2011 [12] and 2012 [19] there has been a social event detection (SED) challenge on a collection of Flickr images. In this context social events are defined like events planned by people and attended by people, with media illustrating the event also captured by people [19].

Starting from this definition we present here a novel approach for SED that exploit relations among users and relations among events with support of external data sources. In particular, we rely on two crucial aspects: (1) people cannot be involved in more than one event at the same time, and (2) people tend to introduce similar annotations for all images associated to the same event. The whole picture metadata is organized in an image where each row contains all data corresponding to the same user. Such records are arranged exploiting the time information. A watershed-based image segmentation is then applied, where Markers are set on the basis of keywords and location features and external data sources, while Flood is set on the basis of tags and time features. Such a scheme results to be very flexible, allowing facing different challenges just by rearranging a few parameters. In order to discriminate different events organized in the same location we introduce here also visual information

that allows checking visual signature of the event. Moreover, this kind of information will also increase recall when annotation of a picture is very poor. Results on the MediaEval 2012 [1] dataset demonstrate the effectiveness of the proposed solution.

2. WATERSHED-BASED SOCIAL EVENT DETECTION

Following [4], the main difference between web pages and online social networks is that while the former are based on content, the latter are based on users. Moreover, this research also introduced five basic characteristics that differentiate a social network from a regular websites: *user-based, interactive, community-driven, relationships, and emotion over content*. In this research, we take into account the first, the third, and the fourth characteristics, and two crucial aspects mentioned in section 1 to introduce a user-centric method to analyze events on social networks, namely a watershed-based social event detection.

Let's imagine that there is one user get involved in a certain event; the basic progress how that event is populated on social networks could be as follows: (1) the user takes pictures or records videos at the time that event happens; (2) next, the user uploads, annotates, and shares his/her media into one social network; (3) then, his/her friends start commenting, tagging, sharing, and updating that event over the network. Thanks to the relationships and community-driven characteristics, information related to that event will be populated and evolved throughout the network dramatically. This leads to the fact that, if we start from any node of social networks and follow its tracks, we can gather a great quantity and variety of information related to an event.

Unfortunately, tracking information in social networks can

---

[1] www.multimediaeval.org/mediaeval2012/

be difficult due to its architecture which is usually protected by copyright or due to technological issues. Therefore, there is the need to create a new data structure for detecting events from data extracted from social networks that must allow: (1) user-account-based data storing; (2) time-based aligning. In this work we call such data structure *UT image* (user-time image).

2.1 User-Time Image

Since social networks are managed by user account, crawling all data belonging to one user account is a feasible task. Thus, we can consider data crawled from social networks as a metadata file (e.g., xml file) where each node contains all information related to one media item related to a certain event.

Starting from the assumptions reported above, we define the *UT image*, by turning the whole metadata crawled from social networks to an image, so that each row of the UT image contains all records (nodes) belonging to one user account and these records are sorted by time (i.e., $dateUT(i, j-1) \leq dateUT(i,j)$). In other words, pixel (i,j) of UT image (i.e., $UT(i,j)$) represents the jth time-ordered record taken by the ith user; and information such as description, tags, location, time written in j^{th} time-ordered record are considered as low-level features extracted from pixel $UT(i,j)$. Figure 1 and 2 illustrate one example of *UT image* and its entries created by XML file offered by MediaEval2012[2].

Figure 2: UT image and its pixels

2.2 Generic Algorithm

The significant characteristic of *UT image* is that if entry $UT(i,j)$ belongs to event e, the left- or right-neighbour entry of $UT(i,j)$ can either belong to the same event e or another event. That leads to the idea of using watershed transform with markers to detect events. The whole architecture is illustrated in Figure 3; the output of this process is a set of data related to a query event.

In other words, this algorithm can *segment* all data extracted from social networks into separated groups by inspiring the idea of watershed image segmentation approach. Algorithms 1, 2 and Figures 4, 5 explain and illustrate how the proposed method runs, respectively. Here, **markers** are generated by using (*keywords, location*) (is explained Algorithm 2) or (*keywords, location, visual*) (is described in Algorithm 4) features with support of *external data sources*, and

---

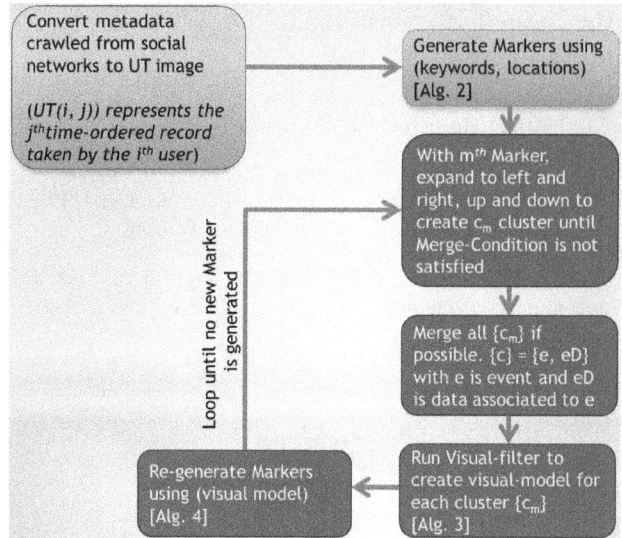

Figure 3: Overview Diagram

the **flooding** progress is carried on by taking into account (*tags set, time, visual*) features to build **Merge-Condition** (i.e., fill catchment basins). The **Merge-Condition** is built on the similarity of *tags set* (using Jaccard index[3]), *time* (using time-segmentation algorithm described in [14] to decide the time border of each event), and *visual similarity* described in section 2.6.

Algorithm 1 Watershed-based Social Events Detection

Input: UT image, Keywords, Locations
Output: Set of Events with Associated Images

1. Generate Set of Markers $\{m_i\}$ by calling **generateMarkers**(Keywords, Locations) function

2. FOR each Markers m_i MERGE left- and right-neighbours to the same Cluster c_i UNTIL **Merge-Condition** is not satisfied

3. FOR each Cluster c_i MERGE cluster c_j to c_i, $i \neq j$ IF it satisfies the **Merge-Condition**

4. Return set of remained clusters $\{c_i\}$, each cluster represents one event. NOTE: $\{c\} = \{e, eD\}$ where e is event, and eD is data associated to e.

2.3 Keywords and Locations Features

Keywords are considered as special "terms" that can model/represent the characteristics of events. In order to determine which pixels correspond to a set of *keywords* (e.g., "conference", "workshop"), we employ *tf-idf*, a statistical measure which reflects how important a word is to a document in a collection or corpus. It is often used as a weighting factor in information retrieval and text mining. The *tf-idf* weighting scheme assigns to term t a weight in document d given by

$$tf - idf_{t,d} = tf_{t,d} \times idf_t$$

Algorithm 2 generateMarkers

Input: UT image, Keywords, Locations
Output: Set of Markers

1. USING tf-idf technique applied on *Keywords* to DE-TECT and RANK UT(i, j).

2. APPLY threshold α to get the most related UT(i, j) to CREATE the CANDIDATE set $\{Can\}$

3. SELECT a subset $\{SCan\} \subset \{Can\}$ so that $SCan_k$ must contain *Locations*

4. Return $\{SCan\}$ as set of Markers

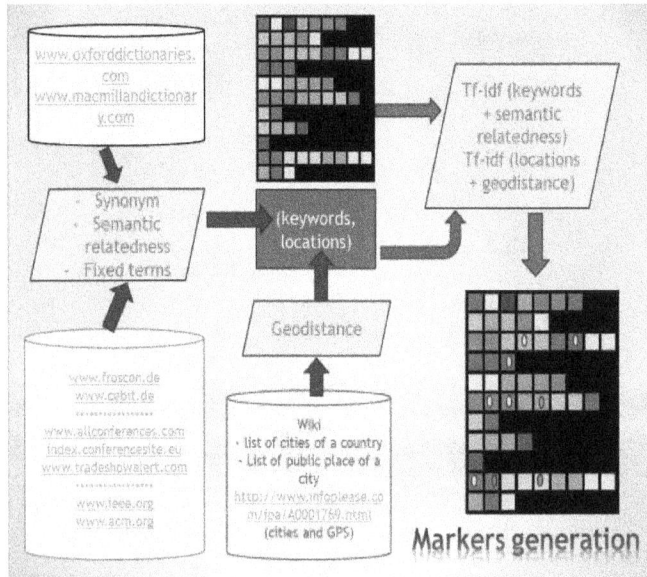

Figure 4: Markers Generation

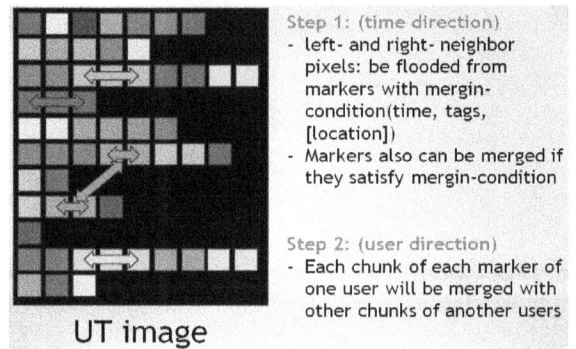

Figure 5: Flooding Progress

where tf stands for term frequency and idf stands for inverse document frequency. In this work, we apply $tf\text{-}idf$ with *keywords* as a set of terms. Thus, we retrieve set of entries $UT(i, j)$ that are considered as revevant to *keywords*.

It is important to notice that not all keywords may be considered equally important: some of them perfectly represent an event (e.g., a "conference" is for sure a "technical event", thus this keyword is crucial in the recognition of technical events), while some other may refer to different type of events (e.g., the term "meeting" can refer to "technical event" but also to other types of events). Therefore, we need to assign a special weight for each keyword to increase the precision. In order to do this, we use the "semantic relatedness" technique [16] to measure the similarity between two terms by exploiting Wikipedia, a semi-structured, collaborative web-based resource, thus taking advantage of human knowledge created through collective efforts of millions of contributors.

To measure the similarity between two terms, we consider each term as a representative Wikipedia article. For instance, the term *exhibition* is represented by the Wikipedia page[4]. We use the Normalized Google Distance [7], where

---
[4]http://en.wikipedia.org/wiki/Exhibition

the similarity judgement is based on term occurrence on web pages. The method was employed in [16] to compute relatedness between Wikipedia articles. In this method, pages that link to both terms suggest relatedness.

$$Relatedness(a,b) = \frac{log(max(|A|,|B|)) - log(|A \cap B|)}{log(|W|) - log(min(|A|,|B|))}$$

where a and b are the two articles of interest, A and B are the sets of all articles that link to a and b, respectively, and W is the entire Wikipedia.

Locations are used to determine where the event happened. It could be *city's names, venues, public places*, or even corresponding (*latitude, longitude*) coordinates. Specially, with locations recorded by (*latitude, longitude*) coordinates, we use *Haversin* formula to calculate the great-circle distance d between two locations:

$$d = 2r.arcsin\left(\sqrt{sin^2\left(\frac{\sigma_2 - \sigma_1}{2}\right) + cos(\sigma_1) cos(\sigma_2) sin^2\left(\frac{\lambda_2 - \lambda_1}{2}\right)}\right)$$

where σ_i and λ_i are the latitude and longitude of location i; r is the radius of the sphere.

By using this formula and defining the radius of a closed-circle around a location, we can determine the known place nearest to a given location exploiting names of cities, venues, or public places. Unfortunately, it is very difficult to define generic markers that can run on all situations. Therefore, we build **generateMarkers** function separately for each query type, with support of External Data Sources.

2.4 External Data Sources

Events can be seen as indices of people's mind to memorize their experience of the world. Generally, people consider their events as pairs of their conceptualization of the world, expressed by natural language, and experience of the world, represented by multimedia. Since people are individuals, they have their own ways to acknowledge events; even when they observe the same event. Interestingly, the research reported in [17] shows that perception and cognition people relied on to tag media of events (i.e., to explain event's conceptualization from media of events) are influenced by cultural differences. Therefore, we find diverse terms for annotating events in data crawled from social networks. This leads to the fact that we cannot use a *fixed keyword* for querying events. There must be a set of keywords that is able to cover the conceptualization of querying event.

In order to satisfy this requirement, external data source is a good solution, in our work. The role of external data sources is to increase the diversity of (keywords, locations) features in order to increase the precision/recall rate of markers.

Keywords: There are three steps to enrich set of keywords: (1) using synonym sources to find all synonymic keywords related to core keywords defined beforehand; (2) assigning weights to these keywords using semantic relatedness as described in section 2.3; (3) [optional] building a dataset of special *names*, *acronyms*, or *terms* that are very popular in certain communities by mining from website/social networks related to these communities. For example, with a conference event, an acronym of a conference name definitely can help to detect the event exactly regardless the lack of location and keywords information. In fact, a lot of people just annotate conference events they get involved in by the conference's acronym only.

Locations: We build a dataset that contains a tube of location information as *(nation, state/province, city, venue, (lat,long))* by extracting information from several geographic websites/API, namely *GeoNames*.

2.5 Time Aligning

The original *UT image* is not aligned by time direction (i.e. $UT(i,j)$ and $UT(i,r)$ do not have the same time information). In order to speed-up flooding progress, time aligning task is considered. We define the new *UaT image* (User-aligned-Time image) so that *UaT(i,j)* will contain time-ordered nodes created by i^{th} user at j^{th} day. In other words, we treat $UaT(i,j)$ as a blob whose content is a list of time-ordered nodes recorded in the same day by the same user.

2.6 Visual Similarity

Visual features are used as the last information exploited in the flooding step to increase precision rate (i.e., get rid of irrelevant images) and recall rate (i.e., look for more relevant images) because not all nodes contain necessary information for merging, such as keywords, locations, time. In this case, query by sample is used, where the sample is the set of all images that are already collected by Algorithm 1.

We reuse the algorithm introduced in [9] for getting an event descriptor, namely *common patterns*. These common patterns are built by using *gist*, *saliency*, and *perspective-invariant correspondences*. The first one is achieved through dominant color analysis; the second is derived from the analysis of dominant colors within the salient area; and the last is calculated using SURF features. The Algorithm 3 aims to increase recall rate of searching events.

The significant contribution of this algorithm is to introduce a new way to generate online detectors for detecting new images associated with detected event. Meanwhile traditional methods need to have pre-prepared dataset or predefined event/concept models for training, in this algorithm detectors evolve by being fed by images which are detected in previous cycles: the more images detectors detect, the more mature the detectors become (i.e., the accuracy increases).

In order to increase recall, we propose a new *re-generateMarkers with visual features* algorithm to create a new set of Markers with support of "common patterns". The idea of this algorithm is to detect UaT(i, j)s that have not been detected yet by the first generateMarkers due to the lack of time, location, or keywords information.

Then the Algorithm 1 is called again for the new cycle of

Algorithm 3 Visual Filter

Input: UaT image, a given event e with its associated information (e.g. Keywords, Locations, Time, Images)
Output: Set of Associated Nodes of e

1. Generate "common patterns" by using algorithm presented in [9]

2. FOR each row of UaT image DO

   (a) i = the left-most node of event e at the current row

   (b) j = the right-most node of event e at the current row

   (c) WHILE (image of UaT(i-1, current row) satisfies "common patterns") or (image of UaT(i-1, current row) ≈ image of UaT(i, current row)) DO

      i. IF satisfying time or/and location condition THEN
         - add UaT(i-1, current row) to e
         - i = i - 1;

   (d) WHILE (image of UaT(j+1, current row) satisfies "common patterns") or (image of UaT(j+1, current row) ≈ image of UaT(j, current row)) DO

      i. IF satisfying time or/and location condition THEN
         - add UaT(j+1, current row) to e
         - j = j + 1;

3. Return e with new associated data

---

searching. This cycle will stop when no more Markers are detected.

3. EXPERIMENTAL RESULTS

In order to have a thorough evaluation of the proposed method, we choose Social Event Detection (SED) task of MediaEval 2012[5] as de facto standard to compare with. As already mentioned in the state of the art, MediaEval is a benchmarking activity to examine how social events can be detected by automatically analyzing social multimedia content. The purpose of SED 2012 is to discover social events (i.e., the events are planned and/or attended by people, and that the media associated with the events are captured by people), and detect related media items.

SED 2012 requires participants *"finding a set of photo clusters, each cluster comprising only photos associated with a single event"*. SED 2012 contains:

- **Dataset**: A collection of 167.332 photos crawled from Flickr between the beginning of 2009 and the end of 2011. This collection was captured by 4.422 unique Flickr users, and all licensed under a Creative Commons license. All information associated with these photos (e.g., tags, geotags, time-stamps) and these photos themselves are packed into the XML photo metadata archive (i.e., each node of this XML contain all information related to one image). Moreover, 80%

---

[5]http://www.multimediaeval.org/

Algorithm 4 re-generateMarkers with visual features

Input: UaT image, event e with its associated data eD detected by previous runs of Alg. 1
Output: Set of new Markers nM

1. $nM = \phi$

2. FOR all UaT(i, j) $\notin eD$ DO

   (a) IF ((time of UaT(i, j) $\in$ time of eD) OR (location of UaT(i, j) $\in$ location of eD) OR (keywords of UaT(i, j) $\in$ keywords of eD)) AND (image of UaT(i, j) "common patterns") THEN

      • add UaT(i, j) to nM

3. Return nM

---

of geotags are removed randomly. The ground truth of each event is a text file where each line contains a list of photos belonging to that event.

- **Evaluation**: There are two evaluation measures used: (1) the macro version of Harmonic mean (F-score) of Precision and Recall for the retrieved images; (2) Normalized Mutual Information (NMI) for comparing two sets of photo clusters. The former measures only the goodness of the retrieved photos but not the number of retrieved events. Moreover, it does not evaluate how accurate the correspondence between retrieved images and events. The latter evaluates the goodness of the retrieved photos and their assignment to different events.

- **Challenges**: There are three challenges: *Challenge 1*: Find technical events that took place in Germany in the test collection; *Challenge 2*: Find all soccer events taking place in Hamburg (Germany) and Madrid (Spain) in the test collection; *Challenge 3*: Find demonstration and protest events of the Indignados movement occurring in public places in Madrid in the test collection.

- **Participants**: There is a number of participants joining in this task and submitting their results. Each participant can submit maximum five runs whose parameters are initialized differently. Notice that, the first run cannot exploit visual information. Moreover, not all of participants join all challenges. THESS-UNI [25] (using non-visual information); TUWIEN [28] (using both visual information and non-visual information); (3) CERTH [18] (using visual information) and; (4) mmLAB-UNITN [10] (using non-visual information) for comparison since they submitted for both challenge 1 and 3 as ours. It should be noted that method introduced in [10] is a part of the proposed method (without using visual information).

We select Challenges 1 and 3 for evaluation of the proposed work. Three runs are performed by the proposed method for each challenge in order to set off advantages of the proposed method: **run 1**: generic algorithm without using visual information (Algorithm 1); **run 2**: with support of *visual filter* algorithm (Algorithm 3); **run 3**: with *regenerateMarkers* (Algorithm 4) and *visual filter* (Algorithm 3) algorithms.

3.1 Challenge 1

This challenge required to find all technical events organized in Germany. The technical events, defined in SED 2012, are public events such as exhibitions and fairs (e.g., the annual CeBIT exhibition taking place in Hannover). The difficulty of this challenge is that the technical event could be expressed in diffirent ways depending on how people explain their acknowledgement about that event. Some use very clear keyword such as "technical event", "conference", "exhibition", anothers use acronym, others write their comments in free-style form (which somehow totally does not relate to technical event) to annotate the event they get involved in. In order to cope with this challenge we decide to build (keywords, locations) as follows:

Keywords: (1) define core keywords, such as "conference", "exhibition", and "workshop" and extend the set of keywords by collecting "synonym" defined by Oxford[6] and Macmillan dictionary[7]; (2) assign weights to keywords using semantic relatedness as described in Section 2.3; and (3) create the list of conferences (acronym, full name) by crawling data from some related websites[8]. We also consider some technical events only organized in Germany (e.g., FrosCon[9], CeBIT[10]); and extract *time* information from these specially technical events (i.e., start and end days). With this last group of keywords, the step 3 of Algorithm 2 is not applied.

Locations: Since the challenge requires to detect events taking place in Germany, we create a sub-dataset $Ger - GeoNames$ of $GeoNames$ contains only information related to Germany.

F-Score	CERTH	TU-WIEN	THESS-UNI	proposed method
run 1	18.37	0.61	31.10	70.15
run 2	16.34	**2.15**	26.26	78.13
run 3	**18.66**	0.0	25.31	**86.28**
run 4	N/A	0.56	**84.58**	N/A
run 5	N/A	0.55	56.50	N/A

Table 1: Challenge 1 Results: F-Score

NMI	CERTH	TU-WIEN	THESS-UNI	proposed method
run 1	0.1599	0.01	0.211	0.6011
run 2	0.1545	**0.02**	0.165	0.6921
run 3	**0.1877**	0.0	0.160	**0.7512**
run 4	N/A	0.01	**0.724**	N/A
run 5	N/A	0.01	0.578	N/A

Table 2: Challenge 1 Results: NMI

As we can observe from the results denoted in Tables 1 and 2, the proposed method works better than other methods both in the first run (i.e., not pruning parameters) and further runs (i.e., with pruning parameters exploiting visual

---

[6] www.oxforddictionaries.com
[7] www.macmillandictionary.com
[8] www.allconferences.com,   index.conferencesite.eu, www.tradeshowalerts.com,   www.conferencealerts.com, www.ieee.org, www.acm.org
[9] www.froscon.de
[10] www.cebit.de

features). As we mentioned above, since the term "technical event" is lack of expressiveness, enriching the set of keywords influences totally the final results. Thanks to the *generateMarkers* leveraged by external data source, we can initialize precise markers (i.e., $UaT(i,j)$ that definitely belonged to an event). Besides, the well-scheduled attribute of technical event (i.e., having fixed start and end days) guarantees the productivity of merge-condition step. All these things lead to a high precision rate of the first run. The significant improvement in F-score in following runs is gained by using visual information. As we mentioned above, some of users do not bother to put detail annotations in their comments, but only acronym of conferences or their own emotional expression. Moreover, not all users put the same tags for all images associated with one event (e.g., only a few images are tagged). Therefore, using "technical event common patterns" extracted from all images collected by the first run to predict new images belonging to the same event does create a significant improvement in results.

3.2 Challenge 3

This challenge required to find all Indignados movement events that took place in Madrid. The difficulty of this challenge is the unscheduled and unwell-organized attributes of events. They are, as described in SED 2012, *"to a large extent spontaneous events, with any organization efforts related to them being typically centered around social media channels"*. In order to cope with this challenge we decide to build (keywords, locations) as follow:

Keywords: (1) define core keywords, both in general concepts (e.g., "demonstration", "protest", "movement") and in special case (e.g., "indignados", "spanish revolution", "yeswecamp", "15m"); then extend the set of keywords by collecting "synonym" defined by Oxford and Macmillan dictionary; (2) assign weights to keywords using semantic relatedness, as above.

Locations: Create the list of public places of Madrid (name, lat-long coordinates)

The results reported in Tables 3 and 4 again demonstrates the significant productivity of the proposed method. Although the F-score of the first run is lower than other methods, the NMI is higher. This confirms the high goodness of the retrieved photos and their assignment to different events generated by the proposed method. One of the main things contributing to this success is the user-based data structure (*UaT image*) that helps to decrease the misclassification among images belonging to a single event by user-cluster orientation. The visual information contributes significantly in this challenge. Since "movement" images contains mostly scenes with crowds and banners, the set of "common patterns" extracted from images queried by the first runs is more precise than in Challenge 1. That leads to more related images that are picked out from the metadata in following runs.

In general, the effectiveness of the generic algorithm is better than other methods. Clearly, the markers generating progress plays a very important role in the proposed method, since it defines the F-score rate; and flooding progress influences the NMI rate, especially the *Merge-Condition*, since it decides how well we can detect images associated to the event detected by the markers generating progress. Finally, the visual information plays a very important role in the

F-Score	CERTH	TU-WIEN	THESS-UNI	proposed method
run 1	**66.87**	37.43	84.29	60.96
run 2	48.07	47.58	86.11	78.23
run 3	50.76	29.33	85.38	**90.12**
run 4	N/A	**36.83**	89.83	N/A
run 5	N/A	36.72	89.83	N/A

Table 3: Challenge 3 Results: F-Score

NMI	CERTH	TU-WIEN	THESS-UNI	proposed method
run 1	**0.4654**	0.26	0.376	0.6011
run 2	0.3984	**0.31**	0.315	0.7123
run 3	0.415	0.22	0.330	**0.8521**
run 4	N/A	0.26	**0.738**	N/A
run 5	N/A	0.25	0.347	N/A

Table 4: Challenge 3 Results: NMI

whole system. That helps to increase the number of image associating with a query event.

4. CONCLUSIONS

In this paper, we introduce an innovative method for querying social events. The idea is based on five basic characteristic of social networks: *user-based, interactive, community-driven, relationships, and emotion over content*; and two crucial aspects observed in real-world: (1) people cannot be involved in more than one event at the same time; (2) people tend to introduce similar annotations for all multimedia associated to the same event. Based on this idea the user-aligned-time image is created where $UaT(i,j)$ contains all information recorded by i^{th} user at j^th day. Each $UaT(i,j)$ is a list of nodes ordered by time-ascending. This image suits for applying watershed-based idea with two main algorithms *generateMarkers* and *Merge-Condition*. The productivity of the proposed method is leveraged by using: (1) external data sources with support of semantic relatedness algorithm and; (2) visual information. The former is to enrich the set of "keywords" expressing the concept of exploited event (i.e., terms are annotated by users with respect to the event they get involved in). The latter is to increase the recall rate and assert the precision rate of querying progress. A thorough evaluation with MediaEval2012 SED benchmark is carried on by several runs and compared to other methods working on the same topic and the same database. The results demonstrate the high performances of the proposed method in general case (i.e., without visual information) and after pruning (i.e., with visual information).

In the future, more natural language processing issues can be investigated to improve the generateMarkers, and more evaluation w.r.t dataset (e.g. MediaEval 2011) and methods/challenges (e.g. challenge 2 in MediaEval 2012) will be carried on, especially with event model created by tag sets and external data source. The set of *keywords* used in this paper is tuned to specific requirements of the challenge (i.e., "conference", "workshop", "exhibition"). Those *keywords* clearly can be expanded to include more scenarios, e.g. using Wikipedia categories to find other terms belonging to the same topic and in other languages. In such a way we could also improve the recall. The location information will be pruned better by defining geo-distance sphere for each location. Since each city have its own size, it is not fair to apply the same radius (e.g. 50 miles) for all. At the moment, the UaT image is very sparse, and that is a reason of consuming a lot of storage space and increasing the fee of searching. In the future, we will take into account this issue. The structure of UaT image is good for using cloud-computing platform. Let's imagine that each $UaT(i,j)$ becomes one node in cloud-computing platform, there will be a significant benefit to decrease both in storage and running cost. The computational complexity has not concerned enough in the current moment. We will investigate now to analyze the computational complexity in the future.

5. ACKNOWLEDGMENTS

This work has been partially supported by the EU EIT under the framework of the S-MAX project.

6. REFERENCES

[1] H. Becker, M. Naaman, and L. Gravano. Learning similarity metrics for event identification in social media. In *Proceedings of ACM WSDM 2010*, pages 291–300, 2010.

[2] H. Becker, M. Naaman, and L. Gravano. Beyond trending topics: real-world event identification on twitter. In *Proceedings of ICWSM 2011*, pages 438–441, 2011.

[3] E. Benson, A. Haghighi, and R. Barzilay. Event discovery in social media feeds. In *Proceedings of ACM HCL 2011*, pages 389–398, 2011.

[4] B. Biswanath, A. Mislove, M. Cha, and K. P. Gummadi. On the evolution of user interaction in facebook. In *Proceedings of ACM WOSN 2009*, pages 37–42, 2009.

[5] M. Brenner and E. Izquierdo. Social event detection and retrieval in collaborative photo collections. In *Proceedings of ACM ICMR 2012*, 2012.

[6] L. Chen and A. Roy. Event detection from flickr data through wavelet-based spatial analysis. In *Proceedings of ACM CIKM 2009*, pages 523–532, 2009.

[7] R. L. Cilibrasi and P. M. B. Vitanyi. The google similarity distance. *IEEE Transaction on Knowledge and Data Engineering*, 19(3):370–383, Mar. 2007.

[8] M. Cooper, J. Foote, A. Girgensohn, and L. Wilcox. Temporal event clustering for digital photo collections. *ACM TOMCCAP*, 1(3):269–288, 2005.

[9] M. Dao, G. Boato, and F. DeNatale. Discovering inherent event taxonomies from social media collections. In *Proceedings of ACM ICMR 2012*, 2012.

[10] M. Dao, G. Boato, F. DeNatale, and T.-V. Nguyen. A watershed-based social events detection method with support of external data sources. In *Proceedings of MediaEval Workshop 2012*. MediaEval, 2012.

[11] C. S. Firan, M. Georgescu, W. Nejdl, and R. Paiu. Bringing order to your photos: Event-driven clasification of flickr images based on social knowledge. In *Proceedings of ACM CIKM 2010*, pages 189–198, 2010.

[12] M. Larson, A. Rae, C.-H. Demarty, C. Kofler, F. Metze, R. Troncy, V. Mezaris, and G. Jones. Working notes proceedings of the mediaeval 2011 workshop. In *Proceedings of MediaEval 2011*, 2011.

[13] X. Liu, R. Troncy, and B. Huet. Finding media illustrating events. In *Proceedings of ACM ICMR 2011*, 2011.

[14] A. C. Loui and A. Savakis. Automated event clustering and quality screening of consumer pictures for digital albuming. *IEEE TMM*, 5(3):309–402, September 2003.

[15] R. Mattivi, G. Boato, and F. DeNatale. Event-based media organization and indexing. *Infocommunication Journal*, 2011(3), 2011.

[16] D. Milne and I. H. Witten. An effective,low-cost measure of semantic relatedness obtained from wikipedia links. In *Proceedings of the 22nd Conference on Artificial Intelligence*, 2008.

[17] R. Nisbett, K. Peng, I. Choi, and A. Norenzayan. Culture and systems of thought: Holistic versus analytic cognition. *Psychology Review*, 108(2):291–310, 2001.

[18] S. Papadopoulos, G. Petkos, M. Schinas, and Y. Kompoatisiaris. Certh@mediaeval2012 social event detection task. In *MediaEval 2012 Workshop*. MediaEval Benchmark, 2012.

[19] S. Papadopoulos, E. Schinas, V. Mezaris, R. Troncy, and I. Kompatsiaris. Social event detection at mediaeval 2012: challenges, dataset and evaluation. In *Proceedings of MediaEval 2012*, 2012.

[20] S. Papadopoulos, C. Zigkolis, Y. Kompatsiaris, and A. Vakali. Cluster-based landmark and event detection for tagged photo collections. *IEEE Multimedia*, 18(1):52–63, January 2011.

[21] G. Petkos, S. Papadopoulos, and Y. Kompatisiaris. Social event detection using multimodal clustering and integrating supervisory signals. In *Proceedings of ACM ICMR 2012*, 2012.

[22] T. Rattenbury, N. Good, and M. Naaman. Towards automatic extraction of event and place semantics from flickr tags. In *Proceedings of ACM SIGIR 2007*, pages 103–110, 2007.

[23] M. R. Trad, A. Joly, and N. Boujemaa. Large scale visual-based event matching. In *ACM ICMR 2011 Conference Proceedings*. ACM, 2011.

[24] R. Troncy, B. Malocha, and A. Fialho. Linking events with media. In *I-Semantics*, 2010.

[25] K. N. Vavliakis, F. A. Tzima, and P. A. Mitkas. Event detection via lda for the mediaeval2012 sed task. In *MediaEval 2012 Workshop*. MediaEval Benchmark, 2012.

[26] Y. Wang, H. Sundaram, and L. Xie. Social event detection with interaction graph modeling. In *Proceedings of MM 2012*, pages 865–868, 2012.

[27] K. Watanabe, M. Ochi, M. Okabe, and R. Onai. Jasmine: a real-time local-event detection system based on geo-location information propagated to microblogs. In *Proceedings of ACM CIKM 2011*, pages 2541–2544, 2011.

[28] M. Zeppelzauer, M. Zaharieva, and C. Breiteneder. A generic approach for social event detection in large photo collections. In *MediaEval 2012 Workshop*. MediaEval Benchmark, 2012.

Automated Social Event Detection in Large Photo Collections

Maia Zaharieva
University of Vienna,
Research Group
Multimedia Information
Systems
zaharieva@cs.univie.ac.at

Matthias Zeppelzauer
Vienna University of
Technology, Institute of
Software Technology and
Interactive Systems
mzz@ims.tuwien.ac.at

Christian Breiteneder
Vienna University of
Technology, Institute of
Software Technology and
Interactive Systems
cb@ifs.tuwien.ac.at

ABSTRACT

The detection of a specific social event requires for high semantic understanding in the interpretation of particular event characteristics such as its type and location. In many cases, photos capturing different events at the same (or highly similar) locations can hardly be distinguished by each other. Available metadata can provide assistance where there is no expert knowledge at hand. However, metadata often lack completeness and reliability. In this paper, we explore the feasibility of a fully automated approach for the detection of specific social events. In comparison to related approaches, we do not incorporate query-specific processing and we perform no manual adaptation of the input query. The resulting approach is applicable to arbitrary event types.

Categories and Subject Descriptors

H.3 [**Information Storage and Retrieval**]: Information Search and Retrieval

General Terms

Algorithms, Experimentation, Performance

Keywords

Event detection, Generic approach, MediaEval Benchmark, Event clustering

1. INTRODUCTION

Social events are defined as events that are "planned by people, attended by people, and captured by people" [16]. Today, image capturing becomes an easy and natural process supported by a vast number of everyday devices and online media sharing platforms are facing an immense growth of data. For example, Flickr[1] reports an upload of 1.42

---

[1]http://flickr.com

million images per day in average for 2012. Evidently, not all uploaded pictures capture social events. However, the prominent role in one's life requires for advanced ways of image retrieval.

Usually, all online sharing platforms allow for some media annotation by the uploading user. Both textual analysis of the available metadata and visual analysis of the images can be performed to provide efficient access to relevant photos. However, both metadata and visual content bear notable challenges for information retrieval. User-provided annotations are often contributed in an unstructured way without controlled vocabularies. Additionally, the quality of annotations varies significantly resulting in partly incomplete data and misleadingly or even falsely tagged images [6]. However, larger timescales prove to exhibit more reliable trends in contrast to short time ranges where more individualistic tags are presented [9]. Thus, the extraction of dictionary terms over multiple users can provide for more reliable tag selection and following image retrieval. From an image content point of view, challenges originate in the enormous diversity of the media data. Different photos of the same event expose different points of view and different levels of details. Hence, the problem of intra-class and inter-class similarity becomes very challenging. While there can be a broad visual range of relevant images for a single event (see Figure 1), different events can also appear highly similar (e.g. sharing the same location, general appearance or details). Crowds can participate in an event or people can accidentally come together at the same place and same time (e.g. at city landmarks). A sign can be informative or provide humorous information but it also can be a significant part of a demonstration.

Recent research on social event detection strongly relies on the use of external sources for semantic interpretation of both available metadata and input textual query. While a vast number of sources provide a valuable access to additional knowledge that can be applied to expand and interpret textual information, little research is done in the exploration of the possibilities and the reliability of already provided data.

In this paper, we propose a generic approach that intentionally does not make use of any external sources in order to evaluate the potential of media content and its metadata. Achieved results provide a baseline to measure the benefit of using additional sources for semantic interpretation and show that available data is in fact not to be underestimated. While achieved results show a high potential in the processing of textual information, the analysis of visual data in

Figure 1: Example images for an event (Primavera Sound 2009 in Barcelona, Spain).

the context of social events is still highly challenging and, currently, does not substantially improve the overall performance of the system. Finally, recent approaches present mostly highly tailored systems that account for specific input queries. In contrast, in this paper, we propose a generic approach that is applicable to arbitrary event types and that does not make any assumptions about the data or the existing event types. Furthermore, the proposed system does not require for any manual intervention in topic selection or query interpretation but operates fully automatically.

This paper is organized as follows. Section 2 outlines recent research in social event detection. Section 3 presents the proposed generic approach in detail. Section 4 discusses the performed experiments and achieved results. Finally, Section 5 concludes the paper and provides an outlook for future work.

2. RELATED WORK

Research on social event detection in image collections can be basically divided into two categories according to whether they use external online sources to interpret or expand given textual queries or not. In general, external resources such as DBpedia[2] or WordNet[3] provide an access to an enormous amount of additional (partially) structured information. Such information can be very valuable in the context of semantic understanding. In order to measure the benefit of using such external sources, first the potential of the media content and its metadata has to be evaluated. However, the quality and the possibilities of available image data has not be fully explored yet.

An example for an approach that does not make use of any external sources is the work of Chen and Roy [7]. The authors present a wavelet-based spatial analysis to cluster Flickr images into periodic and aperiodic events. The proposed approach strongly relies on existing geo-tags which are often not available for all images in existing data sets. Several works explore methods to distinguish between events and a second image class. Examples for such classes are places [17] or landmarks [19], both exhibiting highly distinguishable visual features. In contrast, social event detection

[2]http://dbpedia.org/
[3]http://wordnet.princeton.edu

aims at the identification of photo clusters corresponding to a single event type independently of the variety of image concepts in the data set or the high range of visual variance within a single photo cluster. Recently, Petkos et al. proposed a multimodal clustering approach for the detection of social events [18]. The authors use pairwise similarities over all modalities to predict a "same cluster" relationship (term frequency for the textual features and the Scale Invariant Feature Transform (SIFT) [13] for the visual ones). However, the adjustments of weights for the different modalities require for existing clustering from the same domain as the input query and, thus, cannot be performed fully automatically.

Recent works in the context of the Social Event Detection (SED) in the MediaEval Benchmark[4] rely strongly on external resources. However, most presented approaches build upon highly specialized processing steps or even upon separate methods for different queries. For example, Liu et al. extract information about different soccer clubs using FBLeague[5] and about known events from services such as Last.fm[6] and Upcoming[7] [12]. Several approaches perform topic expansion using manually generated topic-related terms [4, 5, 8, 23]. Although such approaches achieve notable performance, their applicability to an arbitrary query is limited since they require human interaction.

Schinas et al. present a more general way to use external sources in order to improve their term models [22]. For this purpose, the authors collect Flickr data of images that have geotags associated with the location of interest or are relevant to the event type. However, it is not clear how such event-relevant tags are determined. Reuter and Cimiano use Last.fm data to train event classifiers on an appropriate data set tailored to each query [20]. Therefore, the approach cannot be applied to different data sets and an arbitrary query.

Finally, there is little research on the use of visual features for social event detection. Schinas et al. apply GIST and SURF [1] features to detect events in a Flickr data set [22]. However, the performance of the proposed features is not evident since the authors do not provide any information on the results of textual and visual features separately. Similarly, Petkos et al. apply SIFT features but they provide no discussion of any improvements in the performance of their approach [18]. Brenner and Izquierdo apply MPEG-7 color and texture features for visual pruning [4]. The authors report slightly lower performance than using a text-based only approach.

In general, an approach for social event detection should be applicable to a wide range of queries and event types. It is not practical to employ a system adjusted to specific queries. Furthermore, although the use of external information sources is highly reasonable for gaining additional knowledge, such use should not be tailored to the needs of a specific query. The goal of the approach presented in this paper is to explore the feasibility of a generic approach that does not make any assumptions about the data set and event types, is not shaped for a specific query, and does not require for any manual intervention.

[4]http://www.mediaeval.org
[5]http://www.fbleague.com
[6]http://www.last.fm
[7]http://upcoming.yahoo.com

3. APPROACH

The approach we discuss in this paper is an extension of the methodology we successfully applied in [25]. The fundamental idea is to enable a completely generic way for social event search in image collections using a simple textual query. Since the approach is not based on any assumptions about the query or the image collection itself, it can be applied in arbitrary settings. Furthermore, the approach does not depend on or require for access to any query-specific online processing systems but relies only on the available metadata and the actual content of the photos.

In comparison to the original method presented in [25], we introduce different enhancements: First, the semantic interpretation of the textual query is now the result of a fully automated process. Following, no manual intervention is required. Second, the number of parameters are reduced in order to make the method more general and robust. Third, the visual matching builds upon independently generated visual models which improves their robustness and expressiveness.

Figure 2 provides an overview of the proposed approach. In a first step both, the textual query and the metadata of the image collection are preprocessed and semantically interpreted. Next, temporal clustering is performed by the capture date of the images. The resulting temporal clusters are more likely to represent images corresponding to the same event and form the basis for further processing. The temporal clusters are subsequently matched against different constraints specified in the query (temporal constraints, location, and keywords describing the type of events). We dynamically generate dictionaries for locations and the event type to make matching more robust. Additionally, visual dictionaries are generated for content-based matching. The results are clusters which represent individual events that well match the provided constraints of the query. The following sections provide details on the individual processing steps.

3.1 Text preprocessing

Text preprocessing consists of two steps, semantic interpretation and text filtering, which are subsequently applied to both, the textual query as provided by the user and the image metadata of the underlying photo collection.

Semantic interpretation tries to determine the type (noun, verb, or adjective) and the meaning of a word (e.g. person or location). We employ GATE (A General Architecture for Text Engineering)[8] to extract information such as dates, locations, person names, and nouns from the input textual query and the image collection metadata. Nouns are important since they may serve as useful keywords describing the query type. Terms that do not fall into one of these categories are stored separately. Additionally, image metadata occasionally contain geo coordinates. We process the coordinates with the GeoNames database[9] in order to obtain additional location information. The GeoNames database returns venue, country and alternative names for a given geolocation.

Temporal parameters of input queries are not trivial to interpret in the absence of a well-defined input format. Currently, we only perform a single date recognition that can

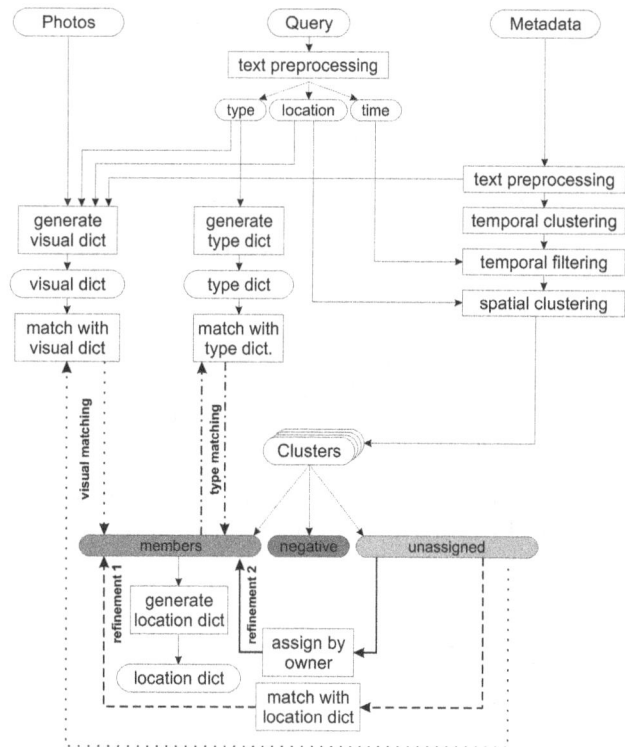

Figure 2: Approach overview.

be a year, a month, a fixed datum or a combination of a month and a year (e.g. January, 2013) as recognised by GATE which is then automatically transformed to a time range (e.g. from 2013-01-01 to 2013-01-31). More sophisticated temporal queries such as "mid summer photos", "images taken between 1st and 14th of September 2011 or 2012" are not automatically interpreted yet but can be manually specified if required.

The following *text filtering* aims at increasing the expressiveness of the data and at reducing potential ambiguities. It removes misleading words (e.g. photo, foto, location, iPhone) and such with low expressiveness (e.g. that, something, again) using a predefined stop word list. Words containing special characters or having a length of three or less characters are removed as well. In general, the removal of short words represents a tradeoff between broadness of applicability and robustness of detection. In our experiments we observe, that the robustness gained justifies this restriction. Finally, the textual description is transformed into a canonical form (stems) using the Porter stemming algorithm[10].

In contrast to recent approaches for event detection, the preprocessing presented is completely general and is not tailored to a specific textual query or makes any assumptions about the images in the collection. Additionally, we replace the manual interpretation of the queries by an automatic procedure.

3.2 Temporal clustering

The proposed approach starts processing the most reliable information available (time and location) and integrates less reliable data (user-defined tags, title, and visual content) at

---

[8]http://gate.ac.uk
[9]http://www.geonames.org

[10]http://snowball.tartarus.org

a later stage in the process. The most reliable information contained in provided metadata is the capture date of the photos which is available for all images.

Photos are clustered by their capture date to obtain initial event clusters. We perform a simple day-by-day segmentation of the images which yields clusters each representing one day. This clustering is simple, parameter-free, robust, and fast. A limitation of the approach is that it may over-segment events that last several days. However, this can be easily corrected after event clustering is finished by merging events which take place at consecutive days and that share similar description and location [23].

Alternatively, we investigate a more advanced segmentation technique based on [10] for temporal clustering. However, preliminary experiments yield suboptimal results. The technique tends to under-segmentation which is more disturbing for the further analysis than the over-segmentation obtained with the day-by-day segmentation. Furthermore, the method introduces additional parameters that require for specialized tuning for each collection.

Finally, all clusters that do not coincide with the temporal specifications of the input query are rejected.

3.3 Spatial clustering

The clusters constructed so far are temporally consistent but may represent different locations and event types. In the next step, we match the locations of the photos in the clusters with the desired location(s) specified in the query. For each photo we collect all available location information extracted in preprocessing (data derived from geo-coordinates and locations mined from the textual descriptions). Following, we match the location information against the query locations using the Jaccard index and assign a photo to the best matching location. This is different from the approach in [25] where we used a threshold for location matching. From experiments we learn that a hard threshold is suboptimal in this situation and taking the best match provides more robust solutions.

Based on the assignment of locations, the original clusters are split into subclusters with spatio-temporally consistent images. However, many photos cannot be assigned to any query location since no location information is available. Such photos are kept in a list of *unassigned* cluster members. We try to assign these unassigned photos in later processing steps by contextual and content-based visual information. Photos with a different location than specified in the query are kept in a *negative list* and are not investigated further.

3.4 Contextual refinement

We observe that many relevant photos for a given query reside in the unassigned list since they do not contain explicit location information. In a refinement step (refinement 1 in Figure 2) we try to assign such photos to a query location by contextual information.

In a first step we build a dictionary for each location. The dictionary contains the most frequent terms (occurrence frequency above 5%) contained in the metadata of the photos of a particular location. Next, we remove terms that are shared by several location dictionaries to make the dictionaries more discriminative. Finally, each image in the unassigned list is matched against the location-based dictionaries using the Jaccard index. The location of the best matching dictionary (maximum Jaccard index) is assigned to the pho-

tos. In case that no dictionary matches, the photo remains in the unassigned list.

3.5 Owner-based refinement

A basic assumption is that photos taken by the same user at the same time must stem from the same location. This is another clue to assign non-geotagged photos to a location. We collect the user names of photos which are already assigned to a spatio-temporal cluster and search for photos of the same users (from the same day) in the unassigned set (refinement 2 in Figure 2). If unassigned photos exist for a particular user name, they are assigned to the respective spatio-temporal cluster. While this refinement in most cases adds additional relevant photos to the clusters, we observe that in some cases photos from the same user, captured at the same time are assigned to different locations. Such cases occur when image descriptions contain references to several different locations independent from the location of photo capture.

3.6 Matching of query type

The clusters generated so far are spatio-temporally consistent but may represent photos of different types of events, such as soccer events or exhibition events. We build a dictionary for the event type of the current query from the metadata of all photos in the collection which share one or more terms with the query type. From the metadata of these photos a dictionary of terms is generated. We remove terms with an occurrence frequency below 10% in order to retain only the most representative terms for the query type. The dictionaries represent an extended (and more abstract) model since it contains synonyms and related terms to the query type. For soccer events for example, the dictionary contains terms such as "football", "futbol", "stadium", "Messi", etc.

We match the members of the spatio-temporal clusters against the dictionary and keep only those images with a Jaccard index above a certain threshold t_{type}. In our experiments a threshold of 2 provides a good tradeoff for the evaluated queries. Additionally, we add photos from the unassigned list to the clusters using the same matching criterion (*extended type match*).

3.7 Visual matching

The approach as discussed so far exploits textual information only. To explore the applicability of visual-based information we employ visual models which are subsequently used to assign an image to a cluster. Initial experiments investigate the construction of bag-of-visual-words models from images classified as relevant by the previous steps of the approach [25]. In other words, the output of the text-based approach (T) is used as a basis for the visual models in the combined (textual-visual, TV) approach. Achieved results indicate a notable drop in the performance of the algorithm of up to 25% in terms of F1-score (see Table 1 for details). The core reason for such decrease in the performance is the noisy input used to build visual models. Precision of $50 - 60\%$ of a cluster declared as relevant by the previous steps of the approach is not sufficient to build a reliable and discriminative visual model.

In order to improve the quality of the visual models, we select photos from the image collection whose location and type information coincide with the one of the input textual query. In this context, time information is neglected since events of the same type at the same location usually share high visual similarity although they might happen at different times. Analysis of the results shows that the precision of such an input image set can increase to up to 95% (details are discussed in Section 4).

Similar to [25] we apply PHOW features (dense SIFT descriptors) [2] to construct a bag-of-visual-words model from the selected image set. Additionally, we increase the number of visual words from 300 to 500 to further improve the robustness of the model for larger image collections. Performed experiments show an increase of F1-score of up to 4%. Finally, an image is assigned to a cluster if the Chi-square distance to its model is below a predefined threshold (set to 0.05 in the experiments discussed in the following section).

4. EXPERIMENTS

4.1 Data sets and challenge definition

For the experiments we employ data from the Social Event Detection (SED) task of the MediaEval Benchmark[11] from 2011 and 2012. Both datasets contain images collected from Flickr[12] and corresponding metadata such as date, title, description, tags, etc. in a XML format. Table 1 summarizes some details on the explored data. Each of the data sets specifies a corresponding set of challenges. The challenges are:

C1 *Find all soccer events taking place in Barcelona (Spain) and Rome (Italy) in the test collection.*

C2 *Find all events that took place in May 2009 in the venue named Paradiso (in Amsterdam, NL) and in the Parc del Forum (in Barcelona, Spain).*

C3 *Find technical events that took place in Germany in the test collection.*

C4 *Find all soccer events taking place in Hamburg (Germany) and Madrid (Spain) in the test collection.*

C5 *Find demonstration and protest events of the Indignados movement occurring in Madrid in the test collection.*

data set	SED 2011	SED 2012
number images	73.645	167.332
geotagged images	20%	20%
unique users	4171	4422
challenges	C1, C2	C3, C4, C5

Table 1: Key figures of the SED2011 and 2012 datasets.

Two evaluation measures are used for all experiments: 1) *Harmonic mean (F1-score)* of recall (R) and precision (P) for the retrieved images, and 2) *Normalized Mutual Information (NMI)* measuring the goodness of clustering of the retrieved events. Data sets and corresponding ground truth information are provided by the organizers of the SED task

and are available from the MediaEval Benchmark website[13]. Table 2 summarizes information about the distribution of images and events among the defined challenges.

Furthermore, we explore the distribution of term frequencies for all challenges (see Figure 3). We compute a dictionary of all photos which match the query type, e.g. "soccer". Results show that most terms (88% of terms) in the generated dictionaries have an occurrence frequency lower than 5%. Only terms with higher occurrence frequency can be considered to be reliable and representative for the query type. Analysis of queries and the corresponding dictionaries show that if the input query is specific enough, the dictionaries are highly expressive and contain mostly query-relevant terms. However, for very general query types such as "technical event" or "public event" the corresponding dictionaries lack expressiveness.

challenge	# events	# images	mean	σ
C1	11	434	39	86
C2	25	1640	66	232
C3	18	2186	121	134
C4	79	1612	20	27
C5	52	3981	77	159

Table 2: Ground truth distribution. *Mean* **shows the average number of images per event,** σ **the corresponding standard deviation.**

Since the provided data sets contain web links to the images (and not the images themselves), in the course of time some photos have been removed from Flickr. While this is not crucial for text-based analysis, visual-based approaches can experience a reduction of the overall performance. In the context of our experiments, this is the case with the explored data sets for SED 2011 where 3054 images were not available at the time of the download (corresponding to 10% and 2% of the true positives for C1 and C2 respectively).

4.2 Experimental Results

In a first experiment we compare our original approach with the performance of related work reported on the SED 2011 data set and challenges C1 and C2. Seven out of eight presented approaches rely strongly on external resources or apply specific runs tailored to the needs of the corresponding challenge (see Table 3 for a summary). For example, Brenner et al. extract soccer clubs and stadium names from web services for challenge C1 and music related venues, events, and artists for challenge C2 [3]. Presented approaches are highly specialized and are not generally applicable to arbitrary queries and event types. Although our approach does not depend on online information systems that provide query-specific information (e.g. a database of soccer clubs), it proves to be competitive with results in the top range of reported performances. While most of the related work presents text-based approaches only, Liu et al. show that a combination with visual features does not lead to any improvement of the results achieved. Experiments with our approach even lead to a remarkable decrease in the performance on the SED 2011 data set. This is mainly due to the missing images from the original set and the noisy input for the visual models as discussed in Section 3.7 and Section 4.1.

---

[11]http://www.multimediaeval.org
[12]http://www.flickr.com/

[13]http://multimediaeval.org

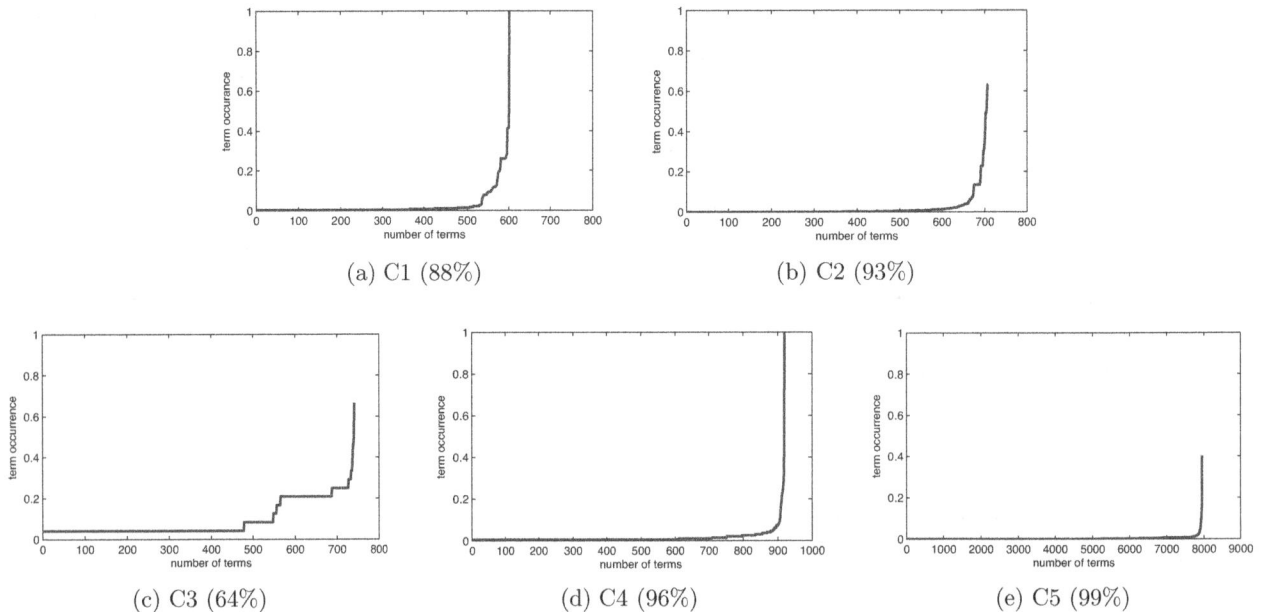

(a) C1 (88%) (b) C2 (93%)

(c) C3 (64%) (d) C4 (96%) (e) C5 (99%)

Figure 3: Distributions of the term frequencies for all challenges. In brackets the percentage of terms with occurrence frequency below 5% is given.

Experiments with the SED 2012 data set show notable decrease in the performance of the approach (see Table 4). The main reasons are the quality of the query keywords and the increased complexity of the data set due to its larger size. For example, the event type of challenge C3 is "technical" which completely lacks in expressiveness. Challenge C4 introduces ambiguity in the interpretation of keywords (e.g. Barcelona as location vs. Barcelona as soccer club name). The experiment demonstrates the complexity in the semantic interpretation of textual annotations and the subjectivity (query dependance) of reported results. A top performing system can easily fail to achieve good results using different data sets and different queries.

challenge	T/TV	R	P	F1	NMI
C3	T	00.36	02.01	00.61	0.01
	TV	00.36	01.20	00.55	0.01
C4	T	03.41	59.78	06.46	0.06
	TV	03.41	45.45	06.35	0.06
C5	T	26.80	62.00	37.43	0.26
	TV	27.93	53.59	36.72	0.25

Table 4: Experimental results for the SED 2012 data set without introduced enhancements (T: text-based approach, TV: text-visual approach).

The introduction of the enhancements discussed in Section 3.3 and Section 3.7 notably improves the achieved results (see Table 5). Challenge C3 still outlines the boundaries of a fully automated and generic system since it cannot be handled properly without additional knowledge. However, the performance for challenges C4 and C5 notably increases: F1-score for challenge C4 increases from 6% to 38% and for challenge C5 from 37% to 50%. Although, in general, the results are suboptimal, they are in a range reported by related work using either external resources or tailored

system calls. This is an indicator that the information represented in the metadata is not exploited to its full extend by existing approaches yet. While our approach outlines initial experiments only, it already demonstrates that there is a lot of usable information that we can get out of the data before consulting external sources. Furthermore, the achieved performance clearly outperforms results reported by a related work where the authors report results on social event detection without using query-specific external resources [14]. Finally, experiments with parameter optimization for single queries further increase the F1-scores to 80%, 53%, 46% and 53% for challenges C1, C2, C4 and C5 respectively. However, such tailored settings decrease the applicability of a system to both arbitrary data sets and event queries.

challenge	T/TV	R	P	F1	NMI
C3	T	03.14	06.04	04.13	0.03
	TV	03.05	06.04	04.06	0.03
C4	T	47.83	31.50	37.98	0.32
	TV	47.95	26.57	34.20	0.29
C5	T	52.65	47.25	49.80	0.33
	TV	55.74	35.44	43.33	0.28

Table 5: Experimental results for the SED 2012 data set (with introduced enhancements).

All performed experiments show low influence of the use of visual features to improve the overall performance of the approach. The selection of a basic image set to build visual models independently of the previous steps of the approach improves their robustness and the precision of the selected images (see Table 6). For example, the precision of the image set for challenge C5 increases from 53% to 90%. For challenge C4 precision decreases to 27% for location 2 (Madrid). However, this is a result from the word ambiguity (location vs. a soccer club name). Closer inspection of the selected

Approach	query-specific external information sources	T/TV	C1 F1	C1 NMI	C2 F1	C2 NMI
Brenner et al.[3]	DBpedia, Last.fm, WordNet, Google MAP	T	68.70	0.41	33.00	0.50
Hintsa et al.[11]	DBpedia, Last.fm, Upcoming , Freebase	T	-	-	68.67	0.68
Liu et al.[12]*	Last.fm, Upcoming, Eventful, FBLeague	T	59.13	0.25	68.95	0.62
		TV	-	-	68.72	0.61
Morchid et al.[14]	Web	T	10.13	0.03	12.44	-0.01
	-	T	-	-	03.53	0.03
Ruoco et al.[21] *	DBpedia, Last.fm	T	58.65	0.25	68.95	0.62
Papadopoulos et al.[15]*	Web	T	77.37	0.63	64.00	0.38
Wang et al.[24]*	Flickr, Last.fm	T/TV	64.90	0.24	50.44	0.45
Proposed approach	-	T	67.87	0.39	47.96	0.21
	-	TV	43.44	0.23	38.21	0.15

Table 3: Comparative results for the SED 2011 data set without introduced enhancements (T: text-based approach, TV: text-visual approach). The results show the best scores achieved by the corresponding authors, although they partially origin from different runs or different calls of the developed systems (marked by *).

images shows a majority of photos from soccer games from different locations such as Madrid but also false ones such as a game of Real Madrid F.C. in Barcelona (see Figure 4 for example images). Due to the high visual similarity such (actually) falsely assigned images do not impede the performance of the visual models. In general, the main reason for the low influence of visual models turns out to be the large diversity of images selected to build the models (see for example Figure 1). A possible solution for this issue is to build multiple models for each location spanning visually similar images.

challenge	location	# images	P
C1	1	39	82.02
	2	2	50.00
C2	1	57	94.74
	2	519	70.91
C3	1	5	00.00
C4	1	17	58.82
	2	22	27.27
C5	1	100	90.00

Table 6: Image selection based on type and location.

5. CONCLUSION

We present a generic approach for the detection and clustering of photos corresponding to the same social event that is applicable to arbitrary event types. In contrast to recent work on this topic the proposed approach does not perform query-specific processing. The approach exploits only the Flickr metadata of the images and employs no specific external data sources, pre-trained models, and challenge-specific processing. We evaluate the approach on all challenges specified in the SED2011 and SED2012 benchmarks using the provided data collections of Flickr images. Experiments show that we obtain comparable performance to other approaches evaluated in the SED benchmark, although related approaches perform challenge-specific processing to optimize their performance. We observe that the retrieval results highly depend on the amount of information provided in the query. Especially abstract and ambiguous event descriptions challenge generic approaches. Additionally, the

strong focus on the media content and corresponding metadata provides insights on the reliability and expressiveness of the data itself. The potential of the available data is not to be underestimated. There is still a lot of unexploited information in both media content and metadata that is valuable for social event detection. Future work will explore the qualitative assessment of available Flickr metadata. Furthermore, we will investigate the improvement of dictionaries for general query types and visual model enhancement to increase the overall performance of the approach.

6. ACKNOWLEDGMENTS

This work has been partly funded by the Vienna Science and Technology Fund (WWTF) through project ICT12-010.

7. REFERENCES

[1] H. Bay, A. Ess, T. Tuytelaars, and L. Van Gool. Speeded-up robust features (surf). *Journal of Computer Vision and Image Understanding*, 110(3):346–359, 2008.

[2] A. Bosch, A. Zisserman, and X. Muñoz. Image classification using random forests and ferns. In *IEEE International Conference on Computer Vision (ICCV'07)*, pages 1–8, 2007.

[3] M. Brenner and E. Izquierdo. Mediaeval benchmark social event detection in collaborative photo collections. In *MediaEval 2011 Workshop*, 2011.

[4] M. Brenner and E. Izquierdo. Qmul @ mediaeval 2012: Social event detection in collaborative photo collections. In *MediaEval 2012 Workshop*, 2012.

[5] M. Brenner and E. Izquierdo. Social event detection and retrieval in collaborative photo collections. In *ACM International Conference on Multimedia Retrieval (ICMR'12)*, pages 21:1–21:8, 2012.

[6] D. C. Bulterman. Is it time for a moratorium on metadata? *IEEE MultiMedia*, 11(4):10–17, 2004.

[7] L. Chen and A. Roy. Event detection from flickr data through wavelet-based spatial analysis. In *ACM Conference on Information and Knowledge Management (CIKM'09)*, pages 523–532, 2009.

[8] M.-S. Dao, G. Boato, F. G. D. Natale, and T.-V. T. NGuyen. A watershed-based social events detection

Figure 4: Example images corresponding to query location and event type as selected as an input for the visual models. First row: challenge C4, 4(a)-4(b) are true positives, 4(c)-4(d) are false positives. Second row: challenge C5, 4(e)-4(f) are true positives, 4(g)-4(h) - false positives.

method with support of external data sources. In *MediaEval 2012 Workshop*, 2012.

[9] M. Dubinko, R. Kumar, J. Magnani, J. Novak, P. Raghavan, and A. Tomkins. Visualizing tags over time. *ACM Transactions on the Web*, 1(2), 2007.

[10] J. Foote and M. Cooper. Media segmentation using self-similarity decomposition. In *Proc. SPIE 5021 Storage and Retrieval for Media Databases*, pages 167–175, 2003.

[11] T. Hintsa and S. V. M. Melin. Leveraging linked data in social event detection. In *MediaEval 2011 Workshop*, 2011.

[12] X. Liu, B. Huet, and R. Troncy. Eurecom @ mediaeval 2011 social event detection task. In *MediaEval 2011 Workshop*, 2011.

[13] D. G. Lowe. Distinctive image features from scale-invariant keypoints. *International Journal of Computer Vision*, 60(2):91–110, Nov. 2004.

[14] M. Morchid and G. Linares. Mediaeval benchmark: Social event detection using lda and external resources. In *MediaEval 2011 Workshop*, 2011.

[15] S. Papadopoulos, Y. Kompatsiaris, and A. Vakali. Certh @ mediaeval 2011 social event detection task. In *MediaEval 2011 Workshop*, 2011.

[16] S. Papadopoulos, E. Schinas, V. Mezaris, R. Troncy, and I. Kompatsiaris. Social event detection at mediaeval 2012: Challenges, dataset and evaluation. In *MediaEval 2012 Workshop*, 2012.

[17] S. Papadopoulos, C. Zigkolis, Y. Kompatsiaris, and A. Vakali. Cluster-based landmark and event detection for tagged photo collections. *IEEE MultiMedia*, 18(1):52–63, 2011.

[18] G. Petkos, S. Papadopoulos, and Y. Kompatsiaris. Social event detection using multimodal clustering and integrating supervisory signals. In *ACM International Conference on Multimedia Retrieval (ICMR'12)*, pages 23:1–23:8, 2012.

[19] T. Rattenbury, N. Good, and M. Naaman. Towards automatic extraction of event and place semantics from flickr tags. In *ACM SIGIR International Conference on Research and Development in Information Retrieval*, pages 103–110, 2007.

[20] T. Reuter and P. Cimiano. Event-based classification of social media streams. In *ACM International Conference on Multimedia Retrieval (ICMR'12)*, pages 22:1–22:8, 2012.

[21] M. Ruocco and H. Ramampiaro. Ntnu@mediaeval 2011 social event detection task (sed). In *MediaEval 2011 Workshop*, 2011.

[22] E. Schinas, G. Petkos, S. Papadopoulos, and Y. Kompatsiaris. Certh @ mediaeval 2012 social event detection task. In *MediaEval 2012 Workshop*, 2012.

[23] K. N. Vavliakis, F. A. Tzima, and P. A. Mitkas. Event detection via lda for the mediaeval2012 sed task. In *MediaEval 2012 Workshop*, 2012.

[24] Y. Wang, L. Xie, and H. Sunduram. Social event detection with clustering and filtering. In *MediaEval 2011 Workshop*, 2011.

[25] M. Zeppelzauer, M. Zaharieva, and C. Breiteneder. A generic approach for social event detection in large photo collections. In *MediaEval 2012 Workshop*, 2012.

A Semantic Model for Cross-Modal and Multi-Modal Retrieval

Liang Xie
whutxl@hotmail.com

Peng Pan*
panpeng@mail.hust.edu.cn

Yansheng Lu
lys@mail.hust.edu.cn

School of Computer Science and Technology, Huazhong University of Science and Technology
Wuhan, China, 430074

ABSTRACT

In this paper, a semantic model for cross-modal and multi-modal retrieval is studied. We assume that the semantic correlation of multimedia data from different modalities can be depicted in a probabilistic generation framework. Media data from different modalities can be generated by the same semantic concepts, and the generation process of each media data is conditional independent under the semantic concepts. The semantic generation model (SGM) for cross-modal and multi-modal analysis is proposed based on this assumption. We study two types of methods: direct method Gaussian distribution and indirect method random forest, to estimate the semantic conditional distribution of SGM. Then methods for cross-modal and multi-modal retrieval are derived from SGM. Experimental results show that SGM based methods for cross-modal retrieval improve the accuracy over the state-of-the-art cross-modal method, but don't increase the time consuming, and the SGM multimodal retrieval methods also outperform traditional methods in image retrieval. Moreover, indirect SGM based method outperforms direct SGM method in the two types of retrieval, which proves that indirect SGM can better describe the semantic distribution.

Categories and Subject Descriptors

H.3.3 [**INFORMATION STORAGE AND RETRIEVAL**]: Information Search and Retrieval – *Retrieval models*; I.2.6 [**ARTIFICIAL INTELLIGENCE**]: Learning – *Concept learning, Parameter learning*

General Terms

Theory, Experimentation

Keywords

Cross-modal retrieval, Multi-modal retrieval, Semantic model

---

* Corresponding author

1. INTRODUCTION

With the rapid development of modern computer science and information technology, unstructured multimedia data such as text, image, video and audio, have been widely used on the web. In recent years, due to the popularization of the internet and the increase in network bandwidth and storage capacity, multimedia data is becoming more and more important on the web. In order to facilitate the management of a variety of multimedia content, we need effective multimedia retrieval methods.

Most of the traditional multimedia retrieval methods for text retrieval, image retrieval, video retrieval and audio retrieval, are mainly focused on unimodal data. They are limited to retrieve the unimodal data and cannot adapt to the cross-modal and multi-modal retrieval problems. With the development of multimedia technology, the cross-modal and multi-modal retrieval are increasingly demanded. In reality, users may want to use a query image to retrieve texts or other different modalities, or they may want to combine a image and text to retrieve images with complementary texts.

Unlike traditional unimodal retrieval methods, in cross-modal retrieval, the modality of retrieved results is different from the query examples. For example, the user can use an image to retrieve texts, videos and audios. The key point of cross-modal retrieval is to model the correlation of different media modalities, and the difficulty of the cross-modal problem is bridging the semantic gap. However, when the documents for retrieval are multimodal, current cross-modal methods can't be directly applied to multi-modal retrieval.

Multi-modal retrieval methods can handle media content with multiple modalities [11, 12, 13], in multi-modal retrieval all the queries and documents to be retrieved may contain more than one modality. Multi-modal retrieval methods can be used to improve the performance of unimodal retrieval. The main difference between multi-modal retrieval and cross-modal retrieval is that in multi-modal retrieval both queries and documents to be retrieved must share at least one identical modality. Multi-modal methods always fuse different modalities for retrieval rather than correlate these modalities. For example, in many works for multimodal image retrieval, the query image may be associated with text words, and the image documents to be retrieved also contain surrounding texts. In the case that queries do not share the same modality with documents to be retrieved, which is the problem dealt by cross-modal methods, traditional multi-modal methods cannot work.

In this paper, we propose the semantic generation model (SGM) to obtain the joint probability of multiple modalities, which is used to describe the documents with different modalities, as well as the semantic correlation of different modalities. According to the joint probability, we get effective similarity measurement for cross-modal and multi-modal retrieval. We first adopt Gaussian for the semantic conditional distribution, and estimate it directly. Then we introduce a discriminative approach to estimate the semantic conditional probability distribution indirectly, which can obtain more accuracy results. Our model's in-depth analysis of the semantic correlation of multimedia data can bridge the semantic gap effectively.

2. Related Work

Generation models have been widely applied to a typical cross-modal problem: image annotation [2, 3]. When annotating images, it needs to get the correlation between images and annotations, and the correlation is generally based on latent variables. The advantage of these generation models is that they can depict the correlation in a probabilistic framework. Cross-media relevance model (CMRM) use images as latent variables, based on these latent variables it learns the joint distribution of image features and annotation words [2]. Correspondence LDA (Corr-LDA) use topics as latent variables, it is derived from latent Direchlet allocation, a topic model which is widely used in text analysis [3]. The difference between Corr-LDA and the traditional LDA is that Corr-LDA jointly models images and words. Image features and words are generated by topics simultaneously, and they correlate according to these topics. According to the correlation, images can be annotated by the associated words.

Recently the problem of cross-modal retrieval has obtained some research [4, 5, 6, 7, 9]. Most cross-modal retrieval methods focus on the content correlation of multimedia data. Canonical correlation analysis (CCA) is a data correlation analysis method which is also used for dimensionality reduction. CCA can jointly model heterogeneous data and is shown effective in cross-modal retrieval [9]. In [6], relative importance of object is leveraged to construct tag features, and kernel CCA is used for cross-modal retrieval. Zhuang et al. [4, 5, 7] propose a variety of cross-modal retrieve methods. These models use the co-occurrence of the heterogeneous media data in the same multimedia documents, and then establish the association of cross-media data. The semantic correlation of multimedia data has also been studied for cross-modal retrieval. Rasiwasia et al. [9] propose a cross-modal method called semantic correlation match (SCM). Image and text features are first mapped into the CCA space respectively, and then image and text are represented as semantic vectors. The elements in semantic vectors are the posterior probabilities with respect to pre-defined semantic classes. Images and text are finally mapped into the same semantic space, and the cross-modal retrieval can be implemented in this space. SCM is also applied to image retrieval, and it performs better than unimodal image retrieval methods.

Many efforts have been devoted to multi-modal analysis and retrieval [10, 11]. Most of them are based on the fusion of multi-modal data. There are two fusion strategies: early fusion and late fusion. The fusion methods do not consider the correlation of different modalities. Thus they often have limited improvement over unimodal methods. Many generation models have also been used for multi-modal retrieval and they can model the correlation of multiple modalities. mm-PLSA proposed in [12] derives the traditional PLSA model to a multilayer model. It performs better than unimodal retrieval systems. PLSA is also used for multi-modal retrieval in [13], which has been shown better than LSI methods as well as other unimodal and multi-modal methods.

However, these models lack the analysis of semantic correlation, which may be benefit to the multi-modal retrieval.

3. Semantic generation model

The core idea of semantic generation model (SGM) is that if multimedia data from different modalities share the same semantic concept, then they can be generated by this concept, and they should be generated independently. This means given a semantic concept, the generation processes of different data are conditional independent. These generation processes are analogous to the generation of media data in the real world. For example, given the conception of tiger, using the camera to get an image of tiger, are independently with recording the sounds of the tiger to get an audio. Although the generation processes of the two media data are independent, they both describe the conception of tiger, which makes them correlated. SGM has a good description for the real correlation of media data. In addition, the conditional independent property of the generation processes makes the model concise and easy to be solved.

In this paper, we will only concentrate on multimedia documents with two modalities: text and image, which are most widely used on the web. However, our model is also suitable for other modalities. Let $\mathbf{S}$ represents the semantic concept, we use the 1-of-K scheme that $\mathbf{S}$ is a K-dimensional vector $[S_1,...,S_K]$, one of the elements in the vector equals 1, and all remaining elements equal 0. K is the total number of semantic concepts, $S_k(k=1,...,K)$ denotes whether $\mathbf{S}$ represents the kth semantic concepts. $\mathbf{S}$ follows the multinomial distribution with parameter $\boldsymbol{\mu}$, which is a K-dimensional vector $[\mu_1,...,\mu_K]$. We denote the visual feature extracted from the image as $\mathbf{I}$, which follows the semantic conditional distribution $p(\mathbf{I}|\mathbf{S},\theta_I)$ with parameter θ_I, and denote the textual feature extract from the text as $\mathbf{T}$, which follows the semantic conditional distribution $p(\mathbf{T}|\mathbf{S},\theta_T)$ with parameter θ_T.

SGM assumes the following generative process from which a multimedia document d consists of image and text are generated:

(1) Choose a semantic concept $\mathbf{S} \sim Multi(\boldsymbol{\mu})$

(2) Choose an image $\mathbf{I} \sim p(\mathbf{I}|\mathbf{S},\theta_I)$

(3) Choose a text $\mathbf{T} \sim p(\mathbf{T}|\mathbf{S},\theta_T)$

For document with multiple images and texts, step (2) and (3) can be repeated multiple times. The graphical illustration of the generative process is shown in Figure 1. The document in Figure 1 only contains a text-image pair.

From the generative process above we obtain the joint distribution of the document and a semantic concept:

$$p(\mathbf{I},\mathbf{T},\mathbf{S}) = p(\mathbf{I}|\mathbf{S},\theta_I)p(\mathbf{T}|\mathbf{S},\theta_T)p(\mathbf{S}|\boldsymbol{\mu}) \qquad (1)$$

Marginalizing over $\mathbf{S}$, then we get the joint distribution of image and text features, which also describes the probability of the multimedia document:

$$p(d) = p(\mathbf{I},\mathbf{T}) = \sum_{\mathbf{S}} p(\mathbf{I}|\mathbf{S},\theta_I)p(\mathbf{T}|\mathbf{S},\theta_T)p(\mathbf{S}|\boldsymbol{\mu}) \qquad (2)$$

If the document consists of multiple images and texts, then the probability of document $p(d) = p(\mathbf{I}_1,...,\mathbf{I}_m,\mathbf{T}_1,...,\mathbf{T}_n)$, where m, n is the number of images and texts respectively. The joint

176

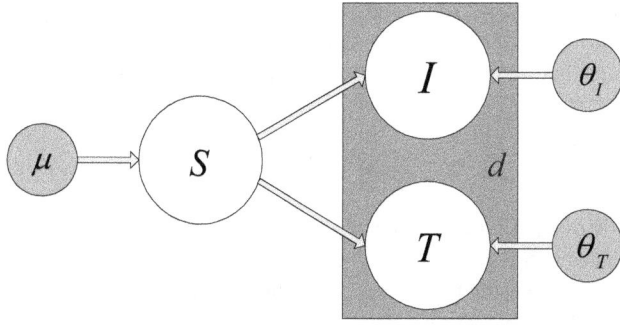

Figure1. The graphical illustration of the SGM

probability of multiple images and texts is similar to the equation (2), it also contains conditional semantic probabilities for these images and texts.

Images and texts are correlated according to their generation from semantic concepts, then the semantic correlation of them can be described by the joint probability. If images and texts are seman-

tically correlated, then they are likely to be generated by the samesemantic concept, and the joint probability of them is larger.There are two advantages of the model. One is that images and texts are correlated in the high level semantics which make the cross-modal and multi-modal retrieval become more effective. The other is the conditional independence enables images and text to be modeled separately, which makes the model easy to be solved and our model more easily extended to the semantic model with more than two modalities.

4. Estimation for SGM

In order to estimate the joint probability distribution of our model, we need to estimate the prior parameter μ, as well as the semantic conditional probability distribution parameters θ_I and θ_T. In this section we only consider documents consist of a text-image pair for training. Let the number of the text-image pairs $(\mathbf{I}_n, \mathbf{T}_n)$ in the training set are N. Using maximum likelihood estimation, the log-likelihood function of the training data can be expressed as:

$$\max_{\mu,\theta_I,\theta_T} \sum_{n=1}^{N} (\log p(\mathbf{I}_n | \mathbf{S}_n, \theta_I) + \log p(\mathbf{T}_n | \mathbf{S}_n, \theta_T) + \log p(\mathbf{S}_n | \mu)) \quad (3)$$

Then we can write (3) in the summation of three parts:

$$\max_{\mu,\theta_I,\theta_T} \sum_{n=1}^{N} \log p(\mathbf{I}_n | \mathbf{S}_n, \theta_I) + \sum_{n=1}^{N} \log p(\mathbf{T}_n | \mathbf{S}_n, \theta_T) + \sum_{n=1}^{N} \log p(\mathbf{S}_n | \mu) \quad (4)$$

From (4), it can be seen that the semantic conditional probability of image feature I_n, text feature T_n, and the multinomial of semantic concept S_n, are independent of each other. Thus we can maximize the three terms separately, which will maximize the entire expression (3). In the following subsections, we will estimate the three parts respectively.

4.1 Estimation of prior

Maximizing the third term of (4), we can get the optimal estimation function of parameter μ:

$$\arg\max_{\mu} \sum_{n=1}^{N} \log p(\mathbf{S}_n | \mu) \quad (5)$$

According to the properties of multinomial distribution we can get the constraint $\sum_{k=1}^{K} \mu_k = 1$. Then using the method of Lagrange multipliers we obtain the estimation:

$$\mu_k = \frac{N_k}{N} \quad k = 1, \ldots, K \quad (6)$$

where N_k is the number of training data with the kth semantic concept S_k.

The prior probabilities of semantic concepts are:

$$P(\mathbf{S} | \mu) = \prod_{m=1}^{K} \mu_k^{s_k} \quad (7)$$

where s_k is the kth element of vector $\mathbf{S}$.

4.2 Direct estimation of semantic conditional distributions

Similar to the estimation of multinomial parameter, the estimations of semantic conditional distribution of images and text are also independent. Without loss of generality, we use $\mathbf{X}$ to represent image as well as text features, and we assume that the image and textual features are generated by the same type of distribution. Then the semantic conditional distribution of a media data $\mathbf{X}$ can be expressed as $p(\mathbf{X} | \mathbf{S}, \theta_X)$, the optimal function is:

$$\arg\max_{\theta_X} \sum_{n=1}^{N} \log p(\mathbf{X}_n | \mathbf{S}_n, \theta_X) \quad (8)$$

The traditional method is to directly estimate the conditional distribution $p(\mathbf{X} | \mathbf{S}, \theta_X)$, that is to define it as a parametric distribution, e.g. Gaussian distribution. In this case θ_X can be seen as the parameter of the distribution which generates data $\mathbf{X}$.

We choose Gaussian distribution here to solve the problem. Assume that each semantic concept S_k ($k = 1, \ldots, K$) corresponds to a Gaussian distribution with mean μ_k, and all the Gaussians share the same covariance matrix Σ, which makes the model easy to be estimated and more effective. Thus each media data $\mathbf{X}$ (an image or a text) follows the Gaussian distribution $N(S_k, m_k, \Sigma)$ ($k = 1, \ldots, K$). Using the maximum likelihood estimation, the estimations of means and covariance matrix are:

$$m_k = \frac{\sum_{n=1}^{N} M_{nk} X_n}{\sum_{n=1}^{N} M_{nk}} \quad k = 1, \ldots, K \quad (9)$$

$$\Sigma = \frac{\sum_{n=1}^{N} \sum_{k=1}^{K} M_{nk} (X_n - \mu_k)(X_n - \mu_k)^T}{N} \quad (10)$$

Where M_{nk} indicates whether the training data $\mathbf{X}_n$ is correspond to the kth semantic concept S_k, if $\mathbf{X}_n$ belongs to S_k then $M_{nk} = 1$, otherwise $M_{nk} = 0$.

The model based on direct method which uses Gaussian distribution to predict the conditional probabilities is denoted as SGM_Gaussian. The disadvantage of the direct estimation is that the true distribution of media data is always too complex to be depicted by general parameter distributions such as Gaussian. Mixture models such as Gaussian mixtures may be used as the conditional distribution. However, solving mixture models usually need expectation-maximization (EM) algorithm, which needs some iteration and may converge to a local maximum of the likelihood function. Therefore it is need to consider other indirect methods rather than using the parameter distribution directly.

4.3 Indirect estimation of semantic conditional distributions

In this section we consider the discriminative methods which can be utilized to estimate semantic conditional distributions indirectly. Unlike traditional generative methods which directly model semantic conditional distributions, discriminative methods estimate the posterior probability distributions of semantic concepts. If we have estimated a posterior distribution, then we can obtain the semantic conditional distribution by using the Bayes rule. Discriminative methods have the superiority that they avoid directly estimating the complex distribution of media data, and it can obtain a relative accurate estimation of the posterior distribution. Then it will lead to accurate estimation of semantic conditional distribution. When the posterior has been estimated, we can use the equation below to obtain the semantic conditional distribution:

$$p(\mathbf{X} \mid S, \theta_X) = \frac{p(S \mid \mathbf{X}, \theta_X) p(\mathbf{X})}{p(S \mid \boldsymbol{\mu})} \tag{11}$$

where $p(\mathbf{X})$ is the prior of media data $\mathbf{X}$. In general, we can assume that all the priors of the media data are the same. $p(S \mid \mathbf{X}, \theta_X)$ can be obtained by using equation (7). In this case, θ_X is no longer the parameter of the semantic conditional probability distribution, it is now the discriminative model parameter which is used to predict the posteriors over $\mathbf{X}$. Then the estimation of semantic conditional distribution is converted to estimation of the posterior of the semantic concept.

From equation (11) we can know if the posterior is accurate, then the semantic conditional probability calculated by posterior is also accurate. Many discriminative methods can obtain the posterior of semantic concepts, such as logistic regression, probability svm, and ensemble learning methods, etc. A representative ensemble learning method: Bagging, is able to provide smooth and precise prediction of posterior probabilities. We adopt random forest which is a special Bagging method. Random forest is the ensemble of decision trees, Bagging and random feature selection are used when learning the random forest [1]. At first bootstrap is used to get new training set from original training set, and then random feature selection is applied to learn a decision tree on the new training set. The next decision tree is also learned using the same procedure. At the prediction stage, given a new media data, each decision tree will output a result. The final result can be obtained by averaging all the output of the trees in random forest.

Traditional decision trees can only output class labels (or semantic concepts in this paper). However, we need the decision trees to output posterior probabilities, so it is necessary to extend the decision trees. Posteriors of each decision tree are computed by:

$$p(S_k \mid \mathbf{X}, T) = \frac{N_k}{N} \quad k = 1, \dots, K \tag{12}$$

where N is the number of training data in the leaf node which data X will be lead to in the prediction. N_k is the number of

training data from the kth semantic concept. Suppose that there are M decision trees in the random forest, and then the posterior outputted by random forest is the average of posteriors of the M trees:

$$p(S \mid X, \theta_X) = \frac{1}{M} \sum_{m=1}^{M} p(S \mid X, T_m) \quad m = 1, \dots, M \tag{13}$$

where T_m denotes the mth decision tree in the random forest. The model using random forest to predict the posteriors, which are used to compute the semantic conditional probabilities indirectly, is denoted as SGM_RF.

5. CROSS-MODAL AND MULTI-MODAL RETRIEVAL

In this section we will use SGM on two types of retrieval for multiple modalities: cross-modal retrieval and multi-modal retrieval. In contrast to traditional models, the adaptability of our model ensures that both cross-modal and multi-modal retrieval methods based on SGM can be easily derived.

5.1 Cross-modal retrieval based on SGM

In cross-modal retrieval, each text or image can be seen as an individual document. SGM establishes the semantic correlation between images and texts, which is used to measure the semantic similarity between images and texts. We consider two types of cross-modal retrieval: image query, where an image query example is used to retrieve texts; and text query, where a text query example is used to retrieve images.

In image query, suppose the query image is $\mathbf{I}_q$, for each text $\mathbf{T}_n$ ($n = 1, \dots, N_T$, where N_T is the number of texts in the database), the similarity of the query image $\mathbf{I}_q$ and text $\mathbf{T}_n$ can be expressed by the conditional probabilities of texts on the image:

$$Sim(\mathbf{I}_q, \mathbf{T}_n) = p(\mathbf{I}_q \mid \mathbf{T}_n) = \frac{p(\mathbf{I}_q, \mathbf{T}_n)}{p(\mathbf{T}_n)} \tag{14}$$

The joint probability $p(\mathbf{I}_q, \mathbf{T}_n)$ describes the possibility of whether $\mathbf{I}_q$ and $\mathbf{T}_n$ are in the same document. Thus we can use the joint probability of SGM and substitute it into (14), and then the similarity can be expressed as:

$$Sim(\mathbf{I}_q, \mathbf{T}_n) = \sum_{k=1}^{K} \frac{p(\mathbf{I}_q \mid S_k, \theta_I) p(\mathbf{T}_n \mid S_k, \theta_T) p(S_k)}{p(\mathbf{T}_n)} \tag{15}$$

If the semantic conditional probabilities of the image and text in (15) are predicted by SGM_Gaussian, then the retrieval method is called as Cross-Modal SGM_Gaussian.

If we use random forest to predict the posteriors of semantic concepts, and use equation (11) to substitute $p(\mathbf{I}_q \mid S_k, \theta_I)$ and $p(\mathbf{T}_n \mid S_k, \theta_T)$ in (15), then (15) is transformed to the equation expressed by posteriors:

$$Sim(\mathbf{I}_q, \mathbf{T}_n) = \sum_{k=1}^{K} \frac{p(S_k \mid \mathbf{I}_q, \theta_I) P(S_k \mid \mathbf{T}_n, \theta_T) p(\mathbf{I}_q)}{p(S_k)} \tag{16}$$

This retrieval method is called as Cross-Modal SGM_RF.

In text query, the similarity of query text $\mathbf{T}_q$ and each image $\mathbf{I}_n$ ($n = 1, \dots, N_I$, where N_I is the number of images in retrieval set) is also a conditional probability which is slight different to the similarity in image query:

$$Sim(\mathbf{T}_q, \mathbf{I}_n) = p(\mathbf{T}_q \mid \mathbf{I}_n) \tag{17}$$

There are also two methods to compute the conditional probability in (17) which is similar to image query.

Given a query $\mathbf{X}$ (it may be an image or a text) to retrieve data $\{\mathbf{Y}_1, \ldots, \mathbf{Y}_N\}$ which is different modality from $\mathbf{X}$, the steps of cross-modal retrieval based on SGM are:

1. Compute the semantic conditional probabilities $p(\mathbf{X} \mid S_k, \theta_X)$ for $\mathbf{X}$ on all the semantic concepts $S_k, k = 1, \ldots, K$;

2. For each data $\mathbf{Y}_n (n = 1, \ldots, N)$ to be retrieved, compute all the semantic conditional probabilities $p(\mathbf{Y}_n \mid S_k, \theta_X)$;

3. If $\mathbf{X}$ is an image, $\mathbf{Y}_n (n = 1, \ldots, N)$ is a text, then use (13) to compute the similarity between $\mathbf{X}$ and each $\mathbf{Y}_n$, otherwise use (14) to compute the similarity.

4. Sort all the similarity $Sim(\mathbf{X}, \mathbf{Y}_n)(n = 1, \ldots, N)$ in descend order, and then return the data most similar to the query $\mathbf{X}$ in semantic.

The probabilities $p(\mathbf{Y}_n \mid S_k, \theta_X)$ in the algorithm can be precomputed to reduce the computation cost. Conditional semantic probabilities of images and texts can be either computed by direct method Gaussian or indirect method random forest.

5.2 Multi-Modal retrieval

In multi-modal retrieval, both the queries and the data to be retrieved are multi-modal, this means they may be the combination of texts and images. In this section we consider the multi-modal image retrieval, where each document in the retrieval is a text-image pair. The text in a document is seen as the complementary information for the image in the document, using the text may get higher accuracy than using the image alone in the retrieval. Similar to the cross-modal retrieval, in multi-modal retrieval the semantic correlation between two documents can be also based on the SGM. Suppose the query example is $\mathbf{d}_q = (\mathbf{I}_q, \mathbf{T}_q)$, for each document $\mathbf{d}_n = (\mathbf{I}_n, \mathbf{T}_n)$ ($n = 1, \ldots, N$), where N is the number of documents which are text-image pairs in the database), the similarity between $\mathbf{d}_q$ and $\mathbf{d}_n$ can be described by the conditional probability:

$$Sim(\mathbf{d}_q, \mathbf{d}_n) = p(\mathbf{d}_q \mid \mathbf{d}_n) = \frac{p(\mathbf{I}_q, \mathbf{T}_q, \mathbf{I}_n, \mathbf{T}_n)}{p(\mathbf{I}_n, \mathbf{T}_n)} \tag{18}$$

$p(\mathbf{I}_q, \mathbf{T}_q, \mathbf{I}_n, \mathbf{T}_n)$ describes the possibility of whether $\mathbf{d}_q$ and $\mathbf{d}_n$ is the same document, thus we can use SGM to describe the joint probability:

$$p(\mathbf{I}_q, \mathbf{T}_q, \mathbf{I}_n, \mathbf{T}_n)$$
$$= \sum_{k=1}^{K} p(\mathbf{I}_q \mid S_k, \theta_I) p(\mathbf{T}_q \mid S_k, \theta_T) p(\mathbf{I}_n \mid S_k, \theta_I) p(\mathbf{T}_n \mid S_k, \theta_T) p(S_k) \tag{19}$$

$p(\mathbf{I}_n, \mathbf{T}_n)$ is the probability of $\mathbf{d}_n$ which is also the joint probability based on SGM. We finally compute the similarity by the semantic conditional probabilities:

$$Sim(\mathbf{d}_q, \mathbf{d}_n)$$
$$= \frac{\sum_{k=1}^{K} p(\mathbf{I}_q \mid S_k, \theta_I) p(\mathbf{T}_q \mid S_k, \theta_T) p(\mathbf{I}_n \mid S_k, \theta_I) p(\mathbf{T}_n \mid S_k, \theta_T) p(S_k)}{\sum_{k=1}^{K} p(\mathbf{I}_n \mid S_k, \theta_I) p(\mathbf{T}_n \mid S_k, \theta_T) p(S_k)} \tag{20}$$

The semantic conditional probabilities of texts and images can be estimated by using Gaussian distribution in section 4.2. In this case the multi-modal retrieval method, which use (20) for similarity, is called as Multi-Modal SGM_Gaussian. If we use the posterior to predict the semantic conditional probabilities indirectly, using the equation (11), the similarity can be written as:

$$Sim(\mathbf{d}_q, \mathbf{d}_n)$$
$$= \frac{p(\mathbf{I}_q)p(\mathbf{T}_q)\sum_{k=1}^{K} p(S_k \mid \mathbf{I}_q, \theta_I) p(S_k \mid \mathbf{T}_q, \theta_T) p(S_k \mid \mathbf{I}_n, \theta_I) p(S_k \mid \mathbf{T}_n, \theta_T) / p(S_k)^3}{\sum_{k=1}^{K} p(S_k \mid \mathbf{I}_n, \theta_I) p(S_k \mid \mathbf{T}_n, \theta_T) / p(S_k)}$$
$$\tag{21}$$

The posterior probabilities of semantic concepts can be estimated by the random forest in section 4.3. This multi-modal retrieval method, which use (21) for similarity, is called as Multi-Modal SGM_RF.

6. Experiments
6.1 Dataset

In our experiment we use the "feature articles" of Wikipedia in Rasiwasia et al. [9]. This dataset contains 2866 documents, each document is composed of a pair of image and text together with the semantic category of the document. The semantic categories are treated as the semantic concepts in this paper, and there are totally 10 categories in the dataset. The dataset is split into two parts, of which 2173 documents are in training set, and the rest 693 documents are in test set. The representation of text is derived from a latent Dirichlet allocation (LDA) model of 10 topics, where texts are represented by their topic assignment probability distributions. Image representation is based on scale invariant feature transformation (SIFT), where images are represented by the SIFT descriptor histograms quantized with a codebook of 128 codewords.

The training set is used to estimate our two models: SGM_Gaussian and SGM_RF. In SGM_RF the number of decision trees in random forest is 500. Then we test our cross-modal and multi-modal retrieval methods derived from these two models on the test set.

6.2 Evaluation of Cross-Modal retrieval

We evaluate our models on two types of cross-modal retrieval: text retrieval using an image query, and image retrieval using a text query. In the first case each image in the test set is used as a query, producing a ranking of all texts in the test set. In the second case the roles of images and texts are reversed. In all cases performance is measured by mean average precision (MAP) and precision-recall (PR) curves [9]. Average precision is the average of precision values at the ranks where relevant items occur, which is further averaged over all queries to given mean average precision. MAP is widely used in the information retrieval.

We compare the retrieval performance of two kinds of SGM, and SCM proposed in [9]. Table 1 shows the MAP scores obtained from the three cross-modal methods. As can be seen from this table, both two types of SGM methods perform better than SCM on MAP score. This means that SGM models the semantic correlation of heterogeneous modalities better than SCM. In addition, Cross-Modal SGM_RF has a significant improvement over Cross-Modal SGM_Gaussian on MAP score. This accord with our argument in section 4, that Gaussian distribution can't depict the true probability distribution of media data on semantic concepts well. As discriminative method, random forest can get precise posteriors of semantic concepts which will lead to more precise semantic conditional probabilities than Gaussian. SCM also predict the posteriors of semantic concepts on images and texts, and use posteriors to correlate images and texts, but it lacks the further analysis of semantic correlation in a probabilistic framework. SGM_RF use posteriors of semantic concepts in a probabilistic framework to model the semantic correlation.

Table 1. MAP scores of cross-modal retrieval

Models	Image query	Text query	Average
SCM [9]	0.277	0.226	0.252
Cross-Modal SGM_Gaussian	0.308	0.221	0.264
Cross-Modal SGM_RF	0.358	0.278	0.318

Figure 2 and Figure 3 show the PR curves of the three methods, from Figure 2 and Figure 3 we can see that Cross-Modal SGM_RF performs better than the other two methods. And Cross-Modal SGM_Gaussian performs slightly better than SCM. Performances of the three methods on PR curves are consistent with MAP scores above.

We next analyze the time complexity of our cross-modal retrieval methods. The cross-medal retrieval based on SGM has significantly improvement over SCM without increasing time complexity. Suppose there are N media data to be retrieved. The retrieval time of SGM is $N \cdot T_{SGM} + T_{rank}$, where T_{SGM} is the time of using SGM to compute the similarity, and T_{rank} is the time cost of ranking the similarities. The retrieval time of SCM is $N \cdot T_{SCM} + T_{rank}$, where T_{SCM} is the time of using the SCM to compute the similarity. The time complexity of SGM is similar to SCM, the only difference is the time consuming of computation of similarities. SCM use normalized correlation (NC) to measure the similarity, which need to compute the inner product of posterior vectors, so the time consuming of this computation is similar to the computation of conditional probabilities in SGM. Table 2 shows the retrieval time of two methods: SCM and Cross-Modal SGM_RF, and all the 693 test data are used as query in this retrieval. Since Cross-Modal SGM_Gaussian is the same as Cross-Modal SGM_RF in time consuming, we do not show it in this comparison. The experiment environment is: CPU Core i7 2.76Hz, memory 4GB, OS windows7, development environment matlab2012. The result of table 2 shows that both SGM and SCM have acceptable response time in retrieval (a little more than 7s for 693 queries). And the result approves that the time complexity of the two models are roughly the same.

Table 2. Response time of retrieval for 693 queries

Model	Image query	Text query	Average
SCM	7.35s	7.41s	7.38s
Cross-Modal SGM_RF	7.22s	7.36s	7.29s

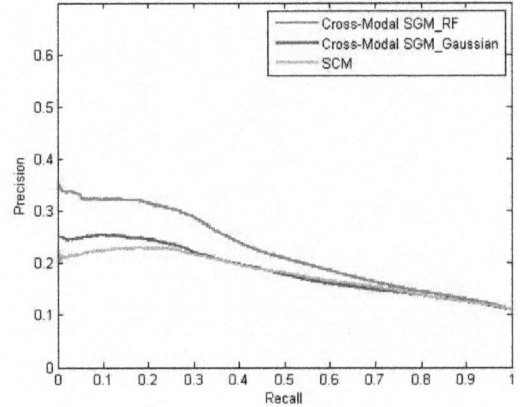

Figure 2. PR curves of image query

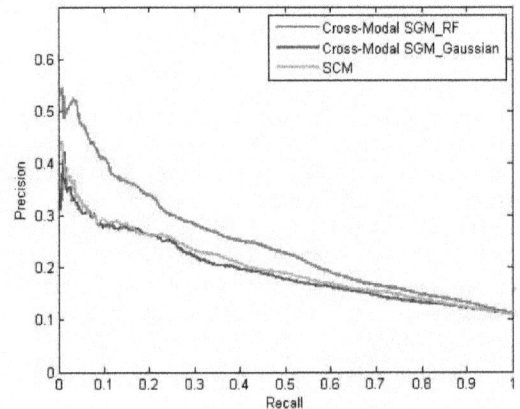

Figure 3. PR curves of text query

6.3 Evaluation of Multi-Modal image retrieval

We compare our two types of multi-modal image retrieval method based on SGM: Multi-Modal SGM_RF and Multi-Modal SGM_Gaussian, with several state-of-the-art unimodal image retrieval methods, as well as the cross-modal retrieval methods SCM, which can also be used for the image retrieval. [9] propose two proxy methods to use SCM for image retrieval. In the first, a query image is complemented with a text and the latter is used to rank the images in the retrieval set. The image in the query is not used, and the text in the query serves as its proxy. In the second, images in the retrieval set are complemented by texts, which are ranked by similarity to the query image. In this case, the images in the retrieval set are not used, and the texts are served as a proxy for them. However, both the two proxy cross-modal retrieval methods don't fully utilize the complementary information of text.

Name: Kakapo
Category: biology

The Kakapo is the only species of flightless parrot in the world, and the only flightless bird that has a lek breeding system. "Collins Field Guide to New Zealand Wildlife", Terrence Lindsey and Rod Morris, Harper Collins Publishers (New Zealand) limited, 2000 Males loosely gather in an arena and compete with each other to attract females. Females watch the males display, or "lek".Merton, D.V. (1976). Conservation of the kakapo: a progress report. In ''Proc. Science in Nat. Parks.''. National Parks Authority, Wellington, N.Z. National Parks Series No. 6: 139–48. They choose a mate based on the quality of his display; they are not pursued by the males in any overt way. No pair bond is formed; males and females meet only to mate.

During the courting season, males leave their home ranges for hilltops and ridges where they establish their own mating courts. These leks can be up to 7 kilometres (4 mi) from a Kakapo's usual territory and are an average of 50 metres (160 ft) apart within the lek arena. Males remain in the region of their court throughout the courting season. At the start of the breeding season, males will fight to try to secure the best courts. They confront each other with raised feathers, spread wings, open beaks, raised claws and loud screeching and growling. Fighting may leave birds with injuries or even kill them. Each court consists of one or more saucer-shaped depressions or "bowls" dug in the ground by the male, up to 10 centimetres (4 in) deep and long enough to fit the half-metre length of the bird. Kakapo are one of only a handful of birds in the world which actually construct their leks. Bowls are often created next to rock faces, banks, or tree trunks to help reflect sound – the bowls themselves function as amplifiers to enhance the projection of the males booming mating calls. Each male bowls are connected by a network of trails or tracks which may extend 50 metres (160 ft) along a ridge or 20 metres (60 ft) in diameter around a hilltop. Males meticulously clear their bowls and tracks of debris. One way researchers check whether bowls are visited at night is to place a few twigs in the bowl; if the male visits overnight, he will pick them up in his beak and toss them away.

To attract females, males make loud, low-frequency (below 100 Hz) booming calls from their bowls by inflating a thoracic sac. They start with low grunts, which increase in volume as the sac inflates. After a sequence of about 20 loud booms, the volume drops off. The male Kakapo then stands up for a short while before again lowering his head, inflating his chest and starting another sequence of booms. The booms can be heard at least one kilometre (0.6 mi) away on a still night; wind can carry the sound at least five kilometres (3 mi). Males boom for an average of eight hours a night; each male may produce thousands of booms in this time. This may continue every night for three or four months during which time the male may lose half his body weight. Each male moves around the bowls in his court so that the booms are sent out in different directions. These booms are also notorious for attracting predators, due to the long range at which they can be heard.

Name: Nuthatch
Category: biology

Name: Kakapo
Category: biology

Name: Splendid Fairywren
Category: biology

Name: Black Vulture
Category: biology

Name: Velociraptor
Category: biology

Figure 4. Example of text query and the top images retrieved by Cross-Modal SGM_RF

SCM cannot combine images and texts, which will clearly improve the performance of retrieval. Multi-modal image retrieval based on SGM can combine images and texts and use them for the query and retrieval set. In order to prove the combination can improve the retrieval, we also compare our methods to the text proxy retrieval for all images in query and retrieval set. For text proxy retrieval we use the normalized correlation (NC) to measure the similarity of text features (LDA in our experiment).

Table 3 shows MAP scores of each image retrieval methods. It should be noted that computation of MAP scores is slightly different from the previous section about cross-modal retrieval, as the retrieval set no longer includes the query image itself and the corresponding text article. The MAP scores of two unimodal image retrieval methods: SMN and SIFT features, are 0.161 and 0.140 respectively, which is lower than other methods. Two SCM proxy methods get higher MAP scores than unimodal methods, but perform worse than using proxy text for query and ranking. This means that there is improvement in approaching the image retrieval problem from a cross-modal point of view, but the improvement is partly attributed to the semantic information of texts. Baseline method is a simple combination of text LDA features and image SIFT features, the MAP score of Baseline Method is slightly lower than using LDA alone, this means that a simple combination two modal features is not beneficial for retrieval. The MAP Scores of Multi-Modal SGM_RF and Multi-Modal SGM_Gaussian are 0.641 and 0.581 respectively, which are higher than all the other methods. This proves that combine texts and images can be benefit for retrieval, and SGM can be well adapted to multi-modal retrieval. And Table 3 also shows that Multi-Modal SGM_RF outperforms Multi-Modal SGM_Gaussian, which indicates that SGM_RF obtained by indirect estimation is better than SGM_Gaussian obtained by direct estimation.

Since the multi-modal SGM methods has the same time complexity with the cross-modal SGM methods, and SCM proxy methods are also similar to SCM in cross-modal retrieval, we do not repeat compare the time consuming of the multi-modal retrieval methods.

Table 3. MAP scores of image retrieval

Methods	MAP Score
Multi-Modal SGM_RF	0.641
Multi-Modal SGM_Gaussian	0.581
Baseline (Text LDA features + Image SIFT features and Ranking by NC)	0.545
Text LDA features (Proxy Text Query and Ranking by NC)	0.553
SCM [9] (Proxy Text Ranking)	0.277
SCM [9] (Proxy Text Query)	0.226
Image SMN (Gaussian Mixture) [8]	0.161
Image SIFT Features (Histogram)	0.140

6.4 Illustrative Examples

This section shows some illustrative examples of the cross-modal retrieval and multi-modal retrieval based on SGM. Figure 4 shows an example of text query cross-modal retrieval. The text query is on the top-left of Figure 4, and associated image of the text in on the top-right of Figure. The top five images retrieved by the Cross-Modal SGM are at the bottom of Figure 4. We can see from Figure 4 that our cross-modal retrieval method can find the media data which is semantic correlated to the queries, but has a different modality. The top relevant results obtained by the retrieval are in the same semantic class with the queries (both biology in the two types of retrieval). However, in cross-modal retrieval, our model can only obtain good performance in highlevel of semantic concepts such as biology. For the specific semantic concepts such as bird, our model cannot effectively distinguish it with other biology concepts. Figure 5 shows the example of Cross-Modal SGM_RF for image retrieval. The image in the far-left of Figure 5 is the query example, and images on the right of the query image

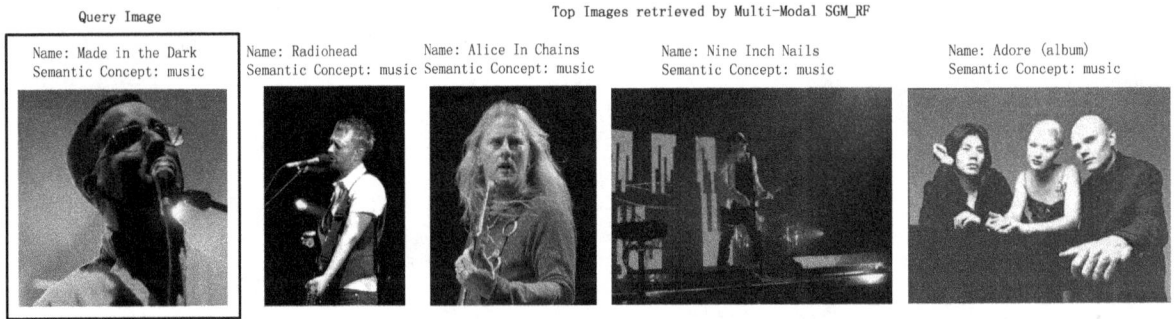

Figure 5. Example of multi-modal image retrieval

are the corresponding top retrieved results. These images are used to depict the retrieval result more concretely. We can see that the query image and retrieved images are semantic correlated, they are all about music. More concretely, they are all about the music people.

7. CONCLUSION

In this paper, we propose the semantic generation model (SGM) which has a good description for the semantic correlation of multiple modalities. The SGM_Gaussian, which directly use Gaussian as the semantic conditional distribution, and the SGM_RF, which use random forest to indirectly estimate the semantic conditional distribution, are studied. Then the two types of SGM are applied to cross-modal and multi-modal retrieval tasks. The experimental results show that the SGM based methods outperform the state-of-art cross-modal retrieval method. SGM is also shown to be suitable for multi-modal retrieval, while other cross-modal methods can't perform well in multi-modal retrieval, and multi-modal methods can't analyze the cross-modal correlation. Moreover, SGM_RF based methods have significant improvement over SGM_Gaussian based methods in both cross-modal and multi-modal retrieval, due to the more accuracy prediction of SGM_RF than SGM_Gaussian.

Our model can be improved in two aspects. One is to further improve estimation of the semantic conditional probability in our model. Variety of direct or indirect methods can be considered, such as nonparametric methods, probability svm, boosting, etc. And the other is to improve the model for the semantic correlation. It includes introducing a more complex topic model such as LDA, PLSA, and enriching semantic knowledge for the model.

8. REFERENCES

[1] Breiman, Leo (2001). Random Forests. Machine Learning 45 (1): 5-32. DOI: 10.1023/A:1010933404324.

[2] Jeon, J., Lavrenko, V.,Manmatha, R. Automatic image annotation and retrieval using cross-media relevance models. In Proc. ACM SIGIR Conf. Research and Development in Informaion Retrieval, New York, NY, USA (2003) 119–126

[3] D. Blei, Michael, and M. I. Jordan. Modeling annotated data. In the Proceedings of the 26th annual international ACM SIGIR conference.

[4] Y. Yang, Y. Zhuang, F. Wu and Y. Pan. Harmonizing hierarchical manifolds for multimedia document semantics understanding and cross-media retrieval. IEEE Transactions on Multimedia, 10(3):437–446, 2008.

[5] Yang, Y., Xu, D., Nie, F., Luo, J., Zhuang, Y. Ranking with local regression and global alignment for cross media retrieval. In ACM Multimedia, pp. 175-184(2009).

[6] Learning the Relative Importance of Objects from Tagged Images for Retrieval and Cross-Modal Search. S. J. Hwang and K. Grauman. International Journal of Computer Vision (IJCV), Vol. 100, Issue 2, pp. 134-153, November 2012.

[7] Y. Zhuang, Y. Yang, and F. Wu. Mining semantic correlation of heterogeneous multimedia data for cross-media retrieval. IEEE Transactions on Multimedia, 10(2):221–229, 2008.

[8] N. Rasiwasia, P. Moreno, and N. Vasconcelos. Bridging the gap: Query by semantic example. IEEE Transactions on Multimedia, 9(5):923–938, 2007.

[9] N. Rasiwasia, J. Costa Pereira, E. Coviello, G. Doyle, G. R. Lanckriet, R. Levy, and N. Vasconcelos. A new approach to cross-modal multimedia retrieval. In Proceedings of the international conference on Multimedia, MM '10, pages 251–260, New York, NY, USA, 2010. ACM.

[10] P. K. Atrey, M. A. Hossain, A. E. Saddik, and M. S. Kankanhalli. Multimodal fusion for multimedia analysis: A survey. MMSJ, 2010.

[11] T. Pham, N. Maillot, J. Lim, and J. Chevallet. Latent semantic fusion model for image retrieval and annotation. In Proceedings of the sixteenth ACM conference on Conference on information and knowledge management, pp 439–444. ACM, 2007.

[12] R. Lienhart, S. Romberg, and E. H¨orster. Multilayer plsa for multimodal image retrieval. In ACM International Conference on Image and Video Retrieval (CIVR), 2009.

[13] C. Pulla, C.V. Jawahar, Multi modal semantic indexing for image retrieval. In Conference on Image and Video Retrieval, 2010, pp. 342–349

Direct Modeling of Image Keypoints Distribution through Copula-based Image Signatures

Miriam Redi
EURECOM, Sophia Antipolis
2229 route des crêtes
Sophia-Antipolis
redi@eurecom.fr

Bernard Merialdo
EURECOM, Sophia Antipolis
2229 route des crêtes
Sophia-Antipolis
merialdo@eurecom.fr

ABSTRACT

Local Image Descriptors (LID) aggregation models such as Bag of Words and Fisher Vectors represent an image based on the distribution of its LIDs *given* a global model, e.g. a visual codebook or a Gaussian Mixture.

Inspired by Copula theory, in this paper we propose a LID-based feature that represents *directly* the behavior of the image LID distribution, without requiring to compute a global model. Following the definition of Copula, we represent the distribution of the image LIDs by describing, on one side, its marginals, and on the other side, a Copula function. The Copula defines the dependencies between the marginals and their mapping to a multivariate probability distribution function. We test the resulting feature for scene recognition and video retrieval (Trecvid data), showing that our approach outperforms, in both tasks, the Bag of Words and the Fisher Vectors Model.

Categories and Subject Descriptors

I.4.7 [**Image Processing and Computer Vision**]: Feature Extraction

Keywords

Scene Recognition, Feature Extraction, CBIR, Gaussian Copulae

1. INTRODUCTION

Content-based image recognition and retrieval (CBIR) techniques are of crucial importance for the management of large collections of multimedia data. CBIR systems build models of the image space by learning image signatures with kernel machines. One of the key elements for the development of effective CBIR systems is the discriminative power of the image signature.

Due to their high discriminative power, signatures based on the *aggregation of local image descriptors* (LIDs) received a lot of attention in the recent years. Among those, the Bag

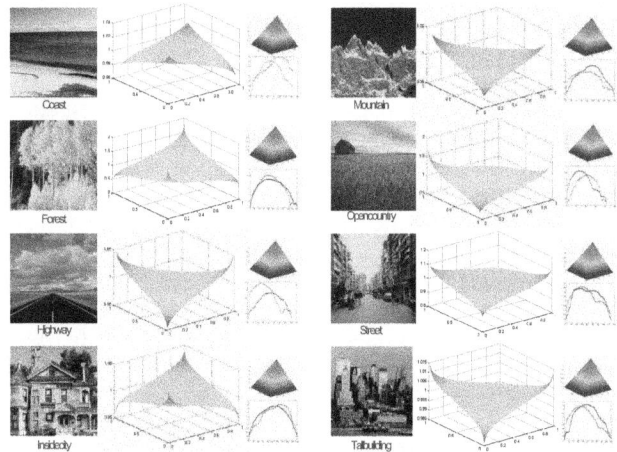

Figure 1: The shape, for different classes, of Gaussian Copula PDF (big plot), CDF and marginals (small plot) arising from the first two dimensions, , i.e. the most informative, of the set of image PCA-SIFT [9].

of Words (BoW) model [1] is probably the most widely used method for LID-based analysis. According to this model, k-dimensional LIDs are first extracted from the surrounding of interest [5] or dense [4] points in a set of training images, and then clustered into a visual codebook. Such codebook is then used to map each new image into a fixed length signature, approximating the *multivariate* probability density function (PDF) of the image LIDs given the global codebook. Similarly, Fisher Vectors [8] approximate the distribution of the image LIDs by analyzing, with Fisher Kernels, the similarity between the PDF of the image LIDs and the global PDF of all the LIDs in a training set. Both approaches *represent the joint probability of the image LIDs indirectly*: they describe the behavior of the LIDs in an image *given* a model of the global LIDs space, obtained through operations (generally very expensive) in the k-dimensional space, such as clustering or mixture modeling. Despite its proved accuracy, this type of representation leads to a lack of discriminative power for complex classification tasks, and to high computational complexity in the training phase.

The MEDA [18] signature is an alternative algorithm for LIDs aggregation that partially addresses these problems. In MEDA, each dimension of the LID is quantized into n uni-dimensional bins. The MEDA feature vector is then built to represent the collection of the k approximated *monovariate* marginal functions. Despite its efficiency, one of the major issues regarding MEDA is that the one-dimensional quantization *breaks the correlation between the LIDs components*, losing a lot of precious information arising from the intra-dimension relations and the multivariate LID modeling.

Our idea is to build a LID-based feature vector that can compensate this loss of information. Copula theory [22] tells us that marginals can actually play an important role in multivariate modeling. According to this theory, the PDF of a k-dimensional vector X can be decomposed into k marginal distributions and one Copula function. While the marginals describe the probability of each variable of the random vector, the Copula function represents the dependencies between the marginals, and defines the probability of the vector by mapping the marginal PDF of the variables to their joint PDF. Such mapping is either pre-defined or calculated based on the marginal values, without therefore involving computationally expensive multidimensional searches. For this reason, Copulae are employed as efficient tools for multivariate modeling, and widely adopted in financial and medical data analysis. Here, we apply Copulae to CBIR and LID-based analysis. The main intuition is that, for an image I, we can fit a Copula with the marginals of the LIDs in I, and then describe I according to the resulting PDF shape. Following Copula Theory, in order to build such representation, we should study separately the LIDs marginals and their dependencies.

Given these observations, in this paper we present COMS (COpula and Marginals Signature): a Copula-inspired extension of MEDA that, by using Copulae, allows for *efficient multivariate analysis of image LIDs using pure marginal information*. COMS combines the MEDA vector with its complementary feature, that we name CoMEDA - Copula over MEDA. While MEDA models the pure monovariate information of the marginal *distributions*, CoMEDA represents the Copula structure: the marginal *dependencies*, namely the mapping between the LIDs marginal values and the LIDs joint density. The resulting COMS feature (MEDA + CoMEDA) reflects directly the PDF of the LIDs in an image, without involving the estimation of a global LID model such as visual codebooks. COMS is therefore much more discriminative and much faster in the training phase compared to both Fisher Vectors and BoW.

How do we model such feature? In our approach, we focus on a particular type of Copula, the Gaussian Copula. This function describes the CDF (Cumulative Distribution Function[1]) of a random vector through the shape of a multivariate normal CDF with the following properties: (1) its variables are the normal inverse of the marginals of the vector, (2) its covariance matrix is the correlation matrix between the marginal inverses and (3) its mean is zero. The Gaussian Copula function depends on one parameter only, namely its covariance/correlation matrix, corresponding to the dependencies between the marginals. We therefore store in the CoMEDA vector the values of the correlation coefficients of the marginal inverses. By doing so, we represent in a single feature the marginal dependencies determining the Copula structure. We then match the CoMEDA features using traditional kernel machines such as Support Vector Machines.

Despite the accuracy of CoMEDA as a stand-alone descriptor for CBIR, we know from Copula Theory that we can achieve a complete representation of the image PDF

---

[1] As we will see later, the Copula-based PDF is easily inferable from the equation of a Copula CDF

only when we combine marginals and Copula together. We therefore concatenate MEDA and CoMEDA in a single, very discriminative, Copula-inspired image descriptor, COMS, which we then use as input for the learning system.

We test the effectiveness of our approach by comparing it with existing methods in two challenging tasks, namely scene recognition (for small-scale indoor/outdoor scenes [17, 16], and large scale scene recognition on sun database [25]), and video retrieval (TRECVID data [23]). We show that the Copula-based model outperforms traditional BoW-based and Fisher Vectors-based classification.

The remainder of this paper is organized as follows: in Sec.2 we outline the related work in the field. We then explain the statistical differences between our proposed approach and the existing methods in Sec.3, and in Sec.4 we give some highlights on Copula Theory. Sec.5 explains in details our approach and finally Sec.6 validates our theory with experimental results.

2. RELATED WORK

In this section we outline the research works that directly link with our approach. Since the CoMEDA feature is based on local image descriptor aggregation, and inspired by Copulae, we will here first summarize the relevant work concerning LID-based image representation, and then highlight the related work from Copula Theory.

Features based on LID aggregation can be divided into two groups, based on the type of LID probability distribution they are trying to approximate: *multivariate* and *monovariate* approaches.

Multivariate LIDs Aggregators. As mentioned in the previous section, the BoW model is probably the most popular framework for image representation based on locally extracted descriptors. It aims at describing the image based on the LIDs global density, by vector quantizing the LIDs space into a set of visual codewords. The BoW was first introduced by Csurka et al. in [1], applying k-means clustering on a training set of LIDs and then using the centroids of the resulting clusters as visual words. Various techniques have been proposed later on to vector quantize the LID space and improve the construction of the visual codebooks. For example, in [11] mean-shift clustering is used, [15] hierarchically quantizes LIDs in a vocabulary tree and [13] uses Extremely Randomized Clustering Forests to build efficient visual codebooks. Another way to define visual codebooks is proposed in [24], where the codebook is composed of the hypercubes resulting from the quantization of each dimension of the LID into a fixed lattice. While generally the visual word assignment is performed by counting the number of occurrences of each visual word in a given image, Jegou et al in [7] improve this approach by computing, for each point, the element-by-element distance with the closest visual word, and store in the VLAD vector the resulting values. Similar to this approach, Perronnin et al. in [8] first estimate the global LIDs density using Gaussian Mixtures over a LID training set, and then use Fisher Kernels over image keypoints to generate the Fisher Vector signatures, that reflects the way in which the parameters of the image LIDs distribution should be changed to fit the global Gaussian Mixture. Fisher Vectors are proved to be one of the most effective solutions for LID-based image analysis. Despite its computational cost, the multivariate analysis performed by the mentioned approaches leads to quite accurate features for CBIR.

Monovariate LIDs Aggregators. In order to overcome some of the computational issues, and to highlight the discriminative power of the LIDs marginals, a 1-dimensional search approach was proposed in [18]. The MEDA descriptor in [18] concatenates the marginal approximation by counting the occurrences of the LIDs component on a predefined set of one-dimensional bins. This approach is very efficient, and it provides a new source of information in the LID analysis, because it exploits the marginal information. However, such monovariate analysis breaks the relations between the LID components, losing precious information for image discrimination. The MultiMEDA kernel presented in [19] is a first attempt to improve the MEDA analysis by adding some multivariate information: assuming component independence, MultiMEDA multiplies the LID marginal values, generating a multidimensional probability out of the MEDA marginal approximations.

Even if MultiMEDA improves the MEDA discriminative power, it is still based on the assumption that the LIDs components are independent and that their marginals are uncorrelated. However, LID vectors arise from the analysis of an entire image region, and each element in a LID is crucial to define the surroundings of an interest point. It is therefore important to analyze the real multivariate information that characterizes those vectors. Given these observations, our idea is to use Copulae to build a complete multivariate analysis of the LID space and generate a feature vector out of such analysis. Why Copulae? Copulae are statistical tools for linking the marginals of the variables in a random vector with their multivariate joint distribution, modeling separately marginal distributions and their dependence structure. We can therefore use them to analyze the LIDs multivariate density by using marginal distributions only, in an efficient and statistically meaningful way.

Copulae first appeared in [22] in the field of probabilistic metric spaces, and they were then widely adopted in finance and actuarial sciences. In particular, Gaussian Copulae are very popular in civil engineering and medical computations, due to their efficiency for multivariate modeling. They allow estimating the joint probability of a vector in a quadratic time, overcoming many computational problems of multivariate modeling. Copulae have indeed been employed in literature for clustering on simulated data [3], and on scientific data [2]. In the image processing domain, Copulae have been used for vector quantization in image coding [6] and for dual polarization synthetic aperture radar image analysis [10]. The only work that applies Copulae to CBIR is, to our knowledge, the work in [20] for the construction of efficient visual codebooks . COMS is, as far as we know, one of the first attempts to build a LID-based feature vector for CBIR using Copulae over the image LIDs.

Overall, our approach is different from all the mentioned approaches because we are not analyzing the independent marginal behavior (such as [18] and [19]), but we are instead trying to estimate the multivariate density of the image LIDs through Copulae. However, we do not compute any global model through clustering [1, 15, 11], Gaussian mixture modeling [8], or other operation in the k-dimensional space [24]. We directly estimate the PDF of the image LIDs and then store in COMS the parameters of such distribution. COMS is therefore statistically different from the space determined

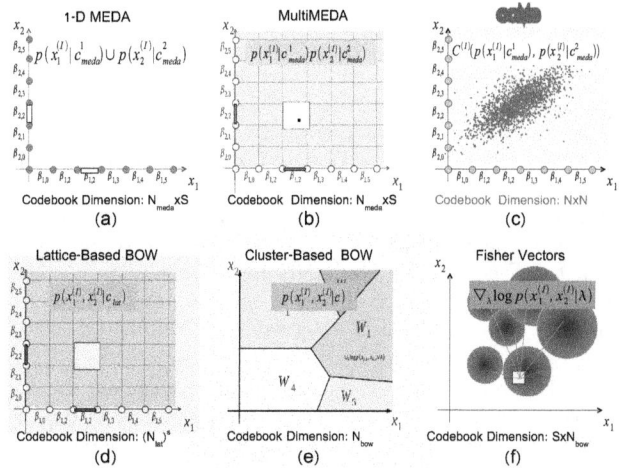

Figure 2: Comparison between the existing LID aggregators and our Copula-Based approach, based on the probabilistic analysis they perform on the image LIDs.

by BoW, MEDA and Fisher Vectors. We will see in the next section a detailed analysis of those differences.

3. WHAT ARE WE MODELING?

In this section, we will show the novelty introduced by the COMS with respect to existing approaches, and show that it represents a new source of information about the LIDs space. Assume for an image I we have a set of m k-dimensional LIDs $x^{(I)} = \{x_j^i\}_{j=1,\dots,k}^{i=1,\dots,m}$: in the following, we will outline the type of probabilistic analysis performed on the LIDs x by the most popular methods for LID-based image analysis.

Multivariate modeling approaches. In the **BoW-like models** [1, 15, 11] a codebook c of N_{bow} k-dimensional vectors is obtained through the clustering of the LID of a training set. An approximation of the joint probability of the LIDs $p_{bow}(x^{(I)}) = p(x^{(I)}|c)$ is then obtained by counting the occurrences of the visual words in an image, see Fig. 2 (e). Similarly (Fig. 2 (d)) **Lattice- based BoW** models like [24], build a vocabulary of hypercubes generated through the quantization of each dimension of the LID in a fixed number of N_{lat} bins, and then reduce such vocabulary c_{lat} according to the informativeness of the resulting codewords. **Fisher Vectors** [8] approximate the LIDs joint distribution by first estimating a universal Gaussian Mixture Model (GMM) on a training set, as shown in Fig. 2 (f). They then compute the log likelihood of the image LIDs with respect to the parameters λ of the GMM. Finally, they store in a feature vector the concatenation of the resulting partial derivatives, namely $p_{fv}(x^{(I)}) = \nabla_\lambda \log p(x^{(I)}|\lambda)$.

Monovariate modeling approaches. Opposite to the other approaches, the **MEDA** [18] model generates a codebook c_{meda}^j of $1 - d$ letters through one-dimensional marginal quantization, see Fig. 2 (a). The resulting MEDA vector represents the approximation of the marginals: $p_{meda}(x^{(I)}) = \cup_{j=1}^k p_j(x_j^{(I)}|c_{meda}^j)$. An extension of MEDA that allows for multidimensional probability estimation given marginals is **Multi-MEDA** [19] (Fig. 2 (b)), that performs a kernelized Cartesian product of the marginal approximations in MEDA, assuming independence between LIDs components, giving $p_{Mmeda}(x^{(I)}) = \prod_{j=1}^k p_j(x_j^{(I)}|c_{meda}^j)$.

Our Approach. Our approach, **COMS**, depicted in Fig. 2 (c), is different from all the other approaches, and lies in an intermediate point between the marginal and the multivariate analysis. We estimate the joint distribution of the image through a Gaussian Copula $C_\Sigma(p_1, \ldots, p_k)$ over the MEDA-based approximated marginal distributions. This leads to a reliable representation of the multivariate LIDs distribution given the image monovariate marginal approximations. The peculiarity of the Copula-based distribution is that it depends on one parameter only, namely the correlation Σ between the inverse of the image marginals. We therefore first store in CoMEDA the values of Σ directly, giving $p_{CoMeda}(x^{(I)}) = corr(p_1^{-1}(x_1^{(I)}|c_{meda}^1), \ldots, p_k^{-1}(x_k^{(I)}|c_{meda}^k))$. CoMEDA represents the multivariate complement of the monovariate MEDA vector, since it represents the dependencies between the marginal distributions. Therefore in COMS, MEDA+CoMEDA, namely the union of the two fundamental element of the LIDs density according to Copula theory, we model a complete Copula-based distribution, $p_{COMS}(x^{(I)}) = C_\Sigma(p_1(x_1^{(I)}|c_{meda}^1), \ldots, p_k(x_k^{(I)}|c_{meda}^k))$.

The Copula modeling that we perform is therefore different ($p_{COMS} \neq p_{meda}, p_{Mmeda}$) from the marginal modeling approaches, because, despite the underlying marginal analysis, it does not assume independence between the LID components, but it models instead a real joint PDF based on the marginal dependencies. On the other hand, we can also say that $p_{COMS} \neq p_{bow}, p_{fv}$ because, first of all, the shape of Copula-Based joint probability described by COMS is different from the shape of the Mixture Model estimated by BoW and Fisher Vectors. This suggests that, by introducing COMS in the LIDs-based analysis, we add some new, complementary information regarding the LIDs distribution. Moreover, due to the simplicity of the Copula algorithm, we can build one Copula per image representing its joint PDF: we can then discriminate between different images using the distribution information given by the specific shape of the image Copula. While BoW approximates the joint LIDs distribution through Vector Quantization given a global codebook, and while Fisher Vectors store the results of parameter adaptation for GMM fitting, COMS directly stores the parameter of the image joint PDF, leading to a more informative image feature. Since both MEDA and CoMEDA arise from the analysis of the image LIDs marginals, COMS does not require an unsupervised search on a training set in the k-dimensional space such as GMM, k-means or hypercube exploration to define the global LID density, saving a lot of computational time on training.

4. COPULA THEORY

Copulae [22] are structures that allow linking the marginal distributions of the variables in a random vector with their joint density function. While traditional multivariate analysis combines the study of marginal and joint densities, Copula Theory provides statistical models to study separately the marginal distributions and their dependencies. The main idea is that the joint distribution of the variables in a random vector X of length k can be decomposed into k marginal distributions and a Copula function C. C represents the link between the marginals: their dependency structure, their mapping to a multivariate cumulative distribution function (CDF).

Such mapping is either given explicitly or, as in our case,

inferred through the analysis of the marginal behavior, without recurring to complex multivariate modeling. The advantage of using Copulae for multivariate modeling is therefore that they can estimate the multidimensional distribution of a random vector very efficiently, given just the values of its marginals. In this section, we give some highlights on the Copula theory, and in particular on Gaussian Copulae, that we will then apply for CBIR purposes. It is outside of the scope of this paper to cover all the aspects of Copulae, therefore we will introduce only the basic tools to understand our COMS feature. For ease of understanding, we will outline the theory through the bivariate case analysis ($k = 2$), that is easily extendable to the multivariate scenario.

4.1 Copulae: Linking Marginals with Joint Distributions

Given a 2-dimensional random vector $x = \{x_1, x_2\}$, we define $u = F_1(x_1) = [P(x_1 \leq X_1)]$, $v = F_2(x_2) = [P(x_2 \leq X_2)]$ as the marginal cumulative distribution functions (CDFs) of X_1 and X_2 respectively, and $F(x_1, x_2) = P[x_1 \leq X_1, x_2 \leq X_2]$ as the vector cumulative joint distribution.

As said, a Copula C, is defined as a unique mapping[2] that assigns the joint CDF of X given each ordered pair of values of its marginals, namely:

$$F(x_1, x_2) = C(F_1(x_1), F_2(x_2)) = C(u, v),$$

and, following Sklar's theorem and assuming that F_1, F_2 are continuous:

$$C(u, v) = F(x_1, x_2) = F(F_1^{-1}(u), F_2^{-1}(v)), \quad (1)$$

which allows to construct a Copula from a given multivariate distribution function F.

The Copula function by itself describes the vector CDF. However, we might want to represent the vector in terms of probability density function (PDF), i.e. $f(x_1, x_2) = P[x_1 = X_1, x_2 = X_2]$. In order to obtain $f(x_1, x_2)$ we have to compute *copula density*, namely the CDF derivative, i.e., following Eq. (1) :

$$f(x_1, x_2) = \frac{\delta^2 C(u, v)}{\delta u, \delta v} = \frac{f(F^{-1}(u), F^{-1}(v))}{f(F^{-1}(u)), f(F^{-1}(v))},$$

where f is the PDF corresponding to F.

The copula describes therefore the dependence between the components of a random vector, no matter the function describing their marginal distributions: if we know the mapping C, the joint distribution $f(x_1, x_2)$ can be inferred from the marginal CDFs u and v.

4.2 Gaussian Copulae

A particular type of Copulae is the Gaussian Copula, which belongs to the class of Elliptical Copulae (i.e. Copulae following Elliptical distributions such as Laplacian, T-Student, etc..). The Gaussian Copula structure is a multivariate normal distribution: in this model, F corresponds to the multivariate Gaussian CDF, while F^{-1} corresponds to the inverse of the univariate normal CDF.

---

[2]In order to be defined as a two-dimensional Copula, C needs to fulfill the following requirements (see [14]):
- It is defined over the interval [0, 1]
- $\forall t \in [0, 1]$, then $C(t, 0) = C(0, t) = 0$ and $C(t, 1) = C(1, t) = 1$
- $\forall u_1, u_2, v_1, v_2 \in [0, 1]$, with $u_1 \leq u_2$ and $v_1 \leq v_2$, $C(u_2, v_2) - C(u_1, v_2) - C(u_2, v_1) + C(u_1, v_1) \geq 0$

A Gaussian Copula C_Σ is then defined for the 2-dimensional random vector x as (following Eq. (1)):

$$C_\Sigma(u,v) = \phi_\Sigma(\Phi^{-1}(u), \Phi^{-1}(v)), \qquad (2)$$

being $\Phi^{-1}(\cdot)$ the inverse of the univariate normal CDF, and ϕ_Σ the bivariate (or multivariate, when $k > 2$) standard with mean zero and covariance Σ, , giving

$$C_\Sigma = \frac{1}{\sqrt{det(\Sigma)}} exp\left(-\frac{1}{2} \cdot \begin{pmatrix} \Phi^{-1}(u) \\ \Phi^{-1}(v) \end{pmatrix}^T \Sigma^{-1} \mathbf{I} \begin{pmatrix} \Phi^{-1}(u) \\ \Phi^{-1}(v) \end{pmatrix} \right), \qquad (3)$$

How to find the covariance matrix Σ? When dealing with normal distributions, the correlation values between two variables fully define their dependencies. In Gaussian Copulae, Σ corresponds therefore to the correlation matrix between the inverse standard univariate normal CDF

$$\Sigma(\Phi^{-1}(u), \Phi^{-1}(v)) = \frac{cov(\Phi^{-1}(u), \Phi^{-1}(v))}{\sigma(\Phi^{-1}(u))\sigma(\Phi^{-1}(v))} \qquad (4)$$

4.3 Why Gaussian Copulae?

As said, the Gaussian Copula function arises from pure marginal analysis: both the variables (inverse normal of marginal CDFs) and the parameter (correlation between the inverse marginal CDFs in Eq. (4) are constructed by manipulating the marginal distributions with simple operations ($O(k)$ for $\Phi^{-1}(\cdot)$, and $O(k^2)$ for Σ). Gaussian Copulae represent therefore an efficient way to estimate the joint PDF of vectors that (I) have a small dimensionality, namely a low value of k and (II) have marginals that can be easily modeled. In fact, local image descriptors satisfy conditions (I) and (II). The dimensionality of LIDs is generally $k \leq 128$. Moreover, it exists a descriptor for LID marginal approximation, MEDA, which have been proved to effectively model the univariate distributions of the LID components. Gaussian Copulae can be therefore very efficient tools to estimate the joint PDF of LIDs.

Moreover, a Gaussian Copula C_Σ depends on one parameter only, namely the covariance-correlation matrix Σ, whose computational time that is quadratic with k, making it easy to characterize an image through its Copula shape. Furthermore, various fast implementations are available to easily and fastly treat with multivariate normal densities, due to their popularity, making the computation of this Copula very easy. This motivates us to use Gaussian Copulae to efficiently and effectively approximate the distributions of the LIDs in an image and generate an image signature out of it.

5. COMS: MULTIVARIATE LID ANALYSIS FROM MARGINAL VALUES

In this section, we show how to exploit Copulae Theory to aggregate LIDs and build effective and efficient compact image signatures based on local descriptors.

In order to perform LID-based analysis, for each image I, we first extract m salient points and describe them using a k-dimensional normalized SIFT [12] descriptor $x^{(I)} = (x_1^i, \ldots, x_k^i)$, $i = 1, \ldots, m$. For an image I, we define $p_j(x_j^{(I)})$ and $P_j(x_j^{(I)})$ $j = 1, \ldots, k$, as the marginal probability distribution and cumulative distribution of the j_{th} component of the image LIDs, and $p(x^{(I)})$ as their joint density.

The main idea is that, similar to Copula Theory, we can approximate $p(x^{(I)})$ for an image I by extracting (A) its set of marginals $p_j(x_j^{(I)})$ and (B) a Gaussian Copula Function, and use it as a discriminative image signature for CBIR purposes. While (A) it already exists a feature (i.e. MEDA) approximating the marginals, we are missing (B) a feature to represent the Copula structure. We therefore design CoMEDA for this purpose (See Fig. 3 for a visual explanation of our approach).

Therefore, we first (A) extract from image I the MEDA vector $v^{(I)}$ containing the LIDs marginals approximations. We then (B) use them, as shown in Sec.5.2, to estimate the marginal CDFs and fit an image-specific Gaussian Copula $C_\Sigma^{(I)}$, that defines an approximation of the joint distribution of the image LIDs. We characterize the image I with the Copula structure of its LIDs by storing in the CoMEDA feature the values of the image-specific covariance matrix $\Sigma^{(I)}$, namely the unique parameter of the resulting Copula-based PDF. Finally, we achieve a complete model of the LID density by combining the CoMEDA feature of an image I with its marginal counterpart, i.e. the MEDA vector for image I, into a final image signature, namely COMS.

5.1 MEDA: Modeling Marginal Distributions of Local Features

In order to build a complete Copula-based representation of the Image I, we first perform marginal analysis through the MEDA descriptor. The MEDA descriptors [18] were designed to highlight the discriminative power of the LIDs marginals. The MEDA signature represents the concatenations of the approximations of the k marginals of the image LIDs.

First, it quantizes each component j of the LIDs in an image I, in a set of n discrete bins $\beta_{j,b}$, $b = 1, \ldots, n$. The MEDA vector is then produced by collecting the frequencies of such bins over the set of x_i extracted from an image I. By doing so, MEDA describes the univariate behavior of the image LIDs, and stores in a single descriptors the set of k approximated marginals distributions $\tilde{p}_j(x_j^{(I)})$. As a matter of fact, the final image signature $v^{(I)}$ is a $k \times n$ histogram, obtained by counting how many LIDs at a given dimension j fall into a given bin b

$$v^{(I)}(j,b) = p(x_j|\beta_{j,b}) = \#\{x^i : x_j^i \in \beta_{j,b}\}.$$

5.2 Fitting a Copula with the Image LIDs

Once we have extracted the marginal information from the Image LIDs, we should calculate the corresponding Gaussian Copula. This will allow us to characterize each image with the distribution of its LIDs (using the parameters of the Copula-based density as signature).

First, for each dimension of the LID, for each of the k marginals $\tilde{p}_j(x_j^{(I)})$ that we obtain with the MEDA histogramming[3], we compute the corresponding k univariate CDFs $u^{(I)}(1) = P_1(x_1^{(I)}), \ldots, u^{(I)}(k) = P_k(x_k^{(I)})$, normalized in the interval $[0,1]$. According to the Gaussian Copula theory, we then compute normal inverse CDF over the resulting LIDs Cumulative Distribution Functions, namely

$$\Phi^{-1}(u^{(I)}(1)), \ldots, \Phi^{-1}(u^{(I)}(k)). \qquad (5)$$

---

[3]In practice, we will use for our experiments a more refined way to estimate the marginal distribution shape, namely a kernel density estimator [21]

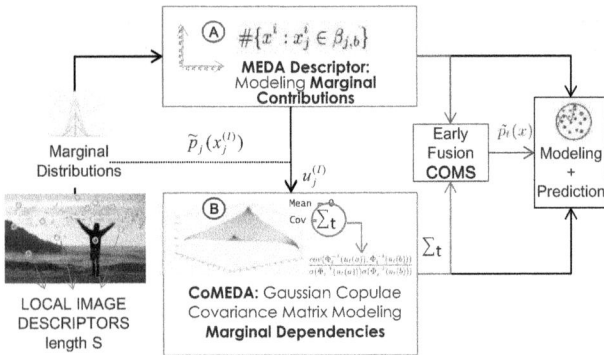

Figure 3: Our Copula-based LID aggregator.

If we now want to define a Gaussian Copula $C_\Sigma^{(I)}$ representing the CDF of the LIDs for image I, we should extend the multivariate Gaussian in Eq. (2), for SIFT vector analysis with $k \gg 2$, giving, for image I,

$$C_\Sigma^{(I)}(u^{(I)}(1), \ldots, u^{(I)}(k)) = \phi_\Sigma^{(I)}(\Phi^{-1}(u^{(I)}(1)), \ldots, \Phi^{-1}(u^{(I)}(k))). \quad (6)$$

and from the Copula theory, we know that $\Sigma^{(I)}$ can be computed as the correlation matrix between the inverse of the LID marginals, namely:

$$\Sigma^{(I)}(a, b) = \frac{cov(\Phi^{-1}(u^{(I)}(a)), \Phi^{-1}(u^{(I)}(b)))}{\sigma(\Phi^{-1}(u^{(I)}(a)))\sigma(\Phi^{-1}(u^{(I)}(b)))} \quad (7)$$

where $a, b = 1, \ldots, j$, $cov(\cdot, *)$ corresponds to the covariance between $(\cdot)$ and $(*)$, and $\sigma(\cdot)$ is the standard deviation of variable $(\cdot)$.

5.3 The CoMEDA vector

How can we capture the behavior of the Copula structure we just described, and store it into a single effective feature? As we can observe, Eq. (6), has only one parameter, the covariance matrix $\Sigma^{(I)}$. Such covariance matrix describes the dependencies structure between the LIDs marginals and determines the equation of the multivariate distribution.

We therefore fill the CoMEDA vector $\mu^{(I)}$ for an Image I with the values corresponding to $\Sigma^{(I)}$, namely the correlation coefficients of the inverse marginal approximations of the LIDs in the image. The complexity of CoMEDA is quadratic with the number of dimensions of the LIDs, and its dimensionality is $\frac{k \times k}{2}$, being $\Sigma^{(I)}$ typically a symmetric matrix. CoMEDA does not imply therefore exponential computation or multidimensional vector quantization for multivariate LID representation. This low dimensional feature (we will select $k = 36$) can be easily then used as input for discriminative classifiers, that will learn a model of the LIDs space based on the CoMEDA feature representation.

5.4 COMS: MEDA + CoMEDA

CoMEDA gathers the main element of the Copula structure: it stores the LIDs multidimensional information arising from the dependencies between marginal distributions.

However, we can observe that the shape of Eq. (2) is determined both by $\Sigma^{(I)}$ and by the behavior of the LIDs marginal distributions, specific of the image I. Recall that, as a matter of fact, Copula theory states that the joint distribution of a random vector can be represented by its marginal distributions and a multivariate Copula structure. This suggests us that, in order to have a complete representation of

the LID space, we should combine the CoMEDA feature of image I with a descriptor approximating the marginal behavior of I, e.g. MEDA. Therefore, for each image, we concatenate these two types of information regarding the LID distribution, MEDA and CoMEDA, both very discriminative features, into a single image descriptor COMS $h^{(I)} = \{v^{(I)}, \mu^{(I)}\}$. By doing so, we enrich the representation of the LID space, and determine a good approximation of the complete LID joint distribution.

6. EXPERIMENTS

In this section we will show the performances of our Copula-based approach, comparing it with the most effective LID aggregators available in literature. We test the effectiveness of our approach for two, challenging tasks, namely video retrieval and scene recognition.

Since all the descriptors work over the same input, namely local image descriptors, the first step of our experiments is to compute the image LIDs. Since we want to keep the dimensionality low, from all the images/keyframes in our datasets we compute PCA-Sift [9] ($k = 36$) around interest points extracted with the Hessian detector. We then aggregate them using the following approaches for comparison:
(1) *Bow*, the Bag of Words Model computed, as in [1], through a codebook built with k-means clustering
(2) *Meda*, the marginal-based descriptor in [18]
(3) *Fisher*, the Fisher Vectors approach, computed using and adapting the implementation in [8]
(4) *CoMeda*, our Copula-based descriptor, i.e. the values of the correlation coefficients of the inverse of the marginals
(5) *COMS*, the early combination of MEDA and CoMEDA

Moreover, in order to prove the reasonableness of our Copulae-based LID processing, we compute another feature, that we call MVN (Multivariate Normal), that stores the values of the mean and covariance matrix of the image LIDs vectors (different from CoMEDA, that treats LIDs marginals). The difference of effectiveness between COMS (or other multivariate approaches) and MVN will show the discriminative value added by treating the LIDs with models more complex than a simple multivariate Gaussian PDF.

Then, we use the computed descriptors as input to Support Vector Machines (SVM) with chi-square or Radial Basis Function kernels to build models able to predict the image category, or the presence of a given concept (in the case of Video Retrieval). Finally, in order to further prove the effectiveness of the combination of MEDA and CoMEDA, we combine and weigh the predictions coming from the MEDA-only model and the CoMEDA-only model, and we name this class of experiments *Posterior*.

We show that our approach outperforms the other methods in all the databases considered for scene recognition and for video retrieval. Overall, we can say that posterior fusion of MEDA and CoMEDA is slightly more effective than *COMS*, because we add one parameter to weigh the contribution of the two descriptors. We can also observe that the simple MVN descriptor has a weaker discriminative power compared to all the other descriptors, suggesting that adding complexity in the LID modeling actually is useful for CBIR performances improvement. Regarding computational costs, as we can see from Fig. 4 (c), the time to compute CoMEDA, for the training set, has the same order of magnitude as the MEDA feature, because it does not require to estimate a universal model such as the BoW codebook.

Average Precision on the Test Set, Video Retrieval

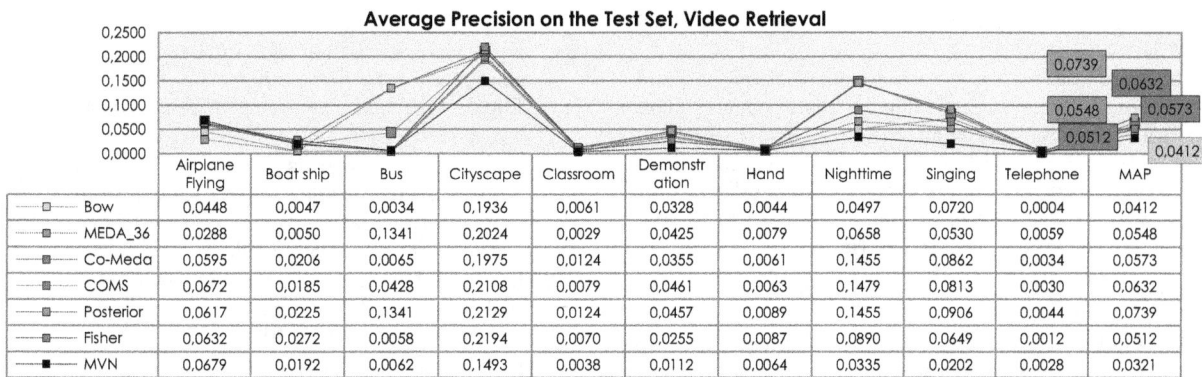

	Airplane Flying	Boat ship	Bus	Cityscape	Classroom	Demonstration	Hand	Nighttime	Singing	Telephone	MAP
Bow	0,0448	0,0047	0,0034	0,1936	0,0061	0,0328	0,0044	0,0497	0,0720	0,0004	0,0412
MEDA_36	0,0288	0,0050	0,1341	0,2024	0,0029	0,0425	0,0079	0,0658	0,0530	0,0059	0,0548
Co-Meda	0,0595	0,0206	0,0065	0,1975	0,0124	0,0355	0,0061	0,1455	0,0862	0,0034	0,0573
COMS	0,0672	0,0185	0,0428	0,2108	0,0079	0,0461	0,0063	0,1479	0,0813	0,0030	0,0632
Posterior	0,0617	0,0225	0,1341	0,2129	0,0124	0,0457	0,0089	0,1455	0,0906	0,0044	0,0739
Fisher	0,0632	0,0272	0,0058	0,2194	0,0070	0,0255	0,0087	0,0890	0,0649	0,0012	0,0512
MVN	0,0679	0,0192	0,0062	0,1493	0,0038	0,0112	0,0064	0,0335	0,0202	0,0028	0,0321

(a)

Accuracy on the Test Set, Scene Recognition

	Bow	Meda	CoMeda	COMS	Posterior	Fisher	MVN
Outdoor	71,4892	71,6471	71,6244	74,951	76,2299	74,0665	69,6271
Indoor	22,8536	22,9252	24,2833	26,585	27,3495	25,5934	22,245
SUN	8,0554	8,5945	10,0302	11,234	11,4408	11,1285	8,5340

(b)

Training Set Processing Time (seconds)

	Bow	Fisher	CoMeda	Meda
Outdoor	14429	7031	1023	401
Indoor	86685	38294	9428	87

(c)

Figure 4: Experimental Results for Scene Recognition and Video Retrieval.

6.1 Scene Recognition

In this section we present the results of our experiments for small scale (indoor/outdoor) and large scale scene recognition. The goal for this task is to build a model able to classify test images with the correct class, selected out of a set of pre-defined mutually exclusive categories. We achieve this goal by learning our features with a one-vs.-all multi-class SVM, and assigning the image category according to the classifier that outputs the highest score. The typical evaluation measure for this task is the average accuracy on the test set. In the following we will see the experimental setup and results for the various datasets considered. A visual representation of the results can be found in Fig. 4(b).

6.1.1 Small Scale Scene Recognition

Outdoor Scenes: The Outdoor Scenes Dataset [16] contains 2600 color images from 8 categories of natural outdoor scenes. As in [16], we retain 100 images per class for training and the rest for testing. The LID aggregators that we compare are the following: *bow* with 720 visual words; *Meda* with percentile quantization, as proposed in [18], with 10 bins per dimension (it is therefore 360-dimensional), *Fisher* with 64 Gaussians in the mixture (final dimension is 2304), then *CoMeda* (dimensionality 1296), and *COMS*, with 1656 components, and finally *MVN* with 36*36(covariance)+36(mean)=1332 dimensions.

Our results show that, even if *CoMeda* by itself does not outperform *Meda*, when they are combined together with early (*COMS*) and *Posterior* fusion, namely when we follow the Copula Theory approach, the resulting model is much more efficient than both Bag of Words and Fisher Vectors.

Indoor Scenes: The Indoor Scenes Dataset [16] contains around 15000 color images from 67 categories of diverse indoor scenes. Following the approach in [17], we retain 20 images per class for testing and we train our models with the remaining images. The details of the features that we compare follow: *bow* with 1300 visual words; *Meda* with percentile quantization, as proposed in [18], with 10 bins per dimension (resulting in a feature with 288 components), *Fisher* with 32 Gaussians in the mixture (final dimension is 1152), then *CoMeda* (dimensionality 1296), and *COMS*,

with 1656 components, and finally *MVN* with 36*36(covariance)+36(mean)=1332 dimensions.

Results for indoor scenes show a similar trend as the experiments on the outdoor scenes datasets. The CoMEDA feature used as a stand-alone descriptor is actually more performing (+6%) than BoW, and it is improved by its combination with the MEDA descriptor (+ 16% of *COMS* and +20% of *Posterior* over *bow*), with a great improvement, 6% over the Fisher Vectors-based classification.

6.1.2 Large Scale Scene Recognition

The sun database [25] contains around 899 categories for more than 130, 000 images. As in [25], we select a subset of images spanning 397 scenes consisting in 10 folds that contains, for each category, 50 images for test and 50 for training. The LIDs aggregators that we compute for this database are as follows: *bow* with 500 visual words; *Meda* with uniform quantization, as proposed in [18], with 10 bins per dimension (resulting in a feature with 360 components), *Fisher* with 32 Gaussians in the mixture (final dimension is 1152), then *CoMeda* (dimensionality 1296), and *COMS*, with 1584 components, and finally *MVN* with 36*36(covariance)+36(mean)=1332 dimensions.

In the results for this dataset, we can see a homogeneous accuracy score obtained the COMS/*Posterior*/*Fisher* descriptor, all outperforming by around 40% the simpler approaches such as MEDA and BoW.

6.2 Video Retrieval

For this task, we focus on the challenging TRECVID 2010 [23] light Semantic Indexing Task, where 10 concepts have to be detected in a video corpus of around 400 hours. We use around 60000 shots for training and an equal number for testing. Once we have created the model using SVMs, the test videos are ranked according to their prediction concept score, and results are compared in terms of Mean Average Precision (MAP). Here, we compute MEDA with fixed quantization (with a number of bins tuned, as in [18], for each concept), *bow* with 500 visual words, *Fisher* with 32 Gaussians in the mixture (final dimension is 2304), then *CoMeda* (dimensionality 1296), and *COMS*, with 1584 components, and finally *MVN* with 36*36(covariance)+36(mean)=1332 dimensions.

As shown in Fig. 4 (a), the effectiveness of our method is even more clear for this challenging task: while *COMS* outperforms *bow* by more than 50% and *Fisher* by 23%, the posterior fusion of MEDA and CoMEDA is further improving the performances of our proposed method for video retrieval, with an increase of around 78 % over BoW and 44% over the Fisher Vector-based retrieval.

7. CONCLUSIONS

We presented a new method for LIDs aggregation. We are inspired from the Copula theory: we exploit the MEDA marginal approximations to feed a Gaussian Copula and build an image signature representing the multivariate PDF of the image LIDs that we name COMS. The resulting image representation is shown to be more discriminative than BoW and Fisher Vectors for image and video retrieval.

The work in this paper can be extended by finding more effective kernels for Copula-based signature matching, such as kernels based on Bhattacharyya distance or Kullback-Leibler divergence. Moreover, we could use different Copula structures, such as Clayton or T-student Copulae and build more discriminative features out of them.

8. REFERENCES

[1] G. Csurka, C. Dance, L. Fan, J. Willamowski, and C. Bray. Visual categorization with bags of keypoints. In *Workshop on statistical learning in computer vision, ECCV*, volume 1, page 22. Citeseer, 2004.

[2] E. Cuvelier and M. Noirhomme-Fraiture. Clayton copula and mixture decomposition. *ASMDA 2005*, pages 699–708, 2005.

[3] F. Di Lascio and S. Giannerini. A new copula–based clustering algorithm.

[4] L. Fei-Fei and P. Perona. A bayesian hierarchical model for learning natural scene categories. In *Computer Vision and Pattern Recognition, 2005. CVPR 2005. IEEE Computer Society Conference on*, volume 2, pages 524–531. Ieee, 2005.

[5] R. Fergus, P. Perona, and A. Zisserman. Object class recognition by unsupervised scale-invariant learning. In *Computer Vision and Pattern Recognition, 2003. Proceedings. 2003 IEEE Computer Society Conference on*, volume 2, pages II–264. IEEE, 2003.

[6] X. Guo, L. Wang, J. Zeng, and X. Zhang. Vq codebook design algorithm based on copula estimation of distribution algorithm. In *2011 First International Conference on Robot, Vision and Signal Processing*, pages 178–181. IEEE, 2011.

[7] H. Jegou, M. Douze, C. Schmid, and P. Perez. Aggregating local descriptors into a compact image representation. In *Computer Vision and Pattern Recognition (CVPR), 2010 IEEE Conference on*, pages 3304–3311. IEEE, 2010.

[8] H. Jégou, F. Perronnin, M. Douze, J. Sánchez, P. Pérez, and C. Schmid. Aggregating local image descriptors into compact codes. *IEEE Transactions on Pattern Analysis and Machine Intelligence*, 2011.

[9] Y. Ke and R. Sukthankar. PCA-SIFT: A more distinctive representation for local image descriptors. 2004.

[10] V. Krylov, G. Moser, S. Serpico, and J. Zerubia. Supervised high-resolution dual-polarization sar image classification by finite mixtures and copulas. *Selected Topics in Signal Processing, IEEE Journal of*, 5(3):554–566, 2011.

[11] B. Leibe, A. Leonardis, and B. Schiele. Robust object detection with interleaved categorization and segmentation. *International Journal of Computer Vision*, 77(1):259–289, 2008.

[12] D. Lowe. Distinctive image features from scale-invariant keypoints. *International journal of computer vision*, 60(2):91–110, 2004.

[13] F. Moosmann, B. Triggs, F. Jurie, et al. Fast discriminative visual codebooks using randomized clustering forests. *Advances in Neural Information Processing Systems 19*, pages 985–992, 2007.

[14] R. Nelsen. *An introduction to copulas*. Springer Verlag, 2006.

[15] D. Nister and H. Stewenius. Scalable recognition with a vocabulary tree. In *Computer Vision and Pattern Recognition, 2006 IEEE Computer Society Conference on*, volume 2, pages 2161–2168. Ieee, 2006.

[16] A. Oliva and A. Torralba. Modeling the shape of the scene: A holistic representation of the spatial envelope. *International Journal of Computer Vision*, 42(3):145–175, 2001.

[17] A. Quattoni and A. Torralba. Recognizing indoor scenes. In *Computer Vision and Pattern Recognition, IEEE Conference on*. IEEE, 2009.

[18] M. Redi and B. Merialdo. Marginal-based visual alphabets for local image descriptors aggregation. In *Proceedings of the 19th ACM international conference on Multimedia*, pages 1429–1432. ACM, 2011.

[19] M. Redi and B. Merialdo. Exploring two spaces with one feature: kernelized multidimensional modeling of visual alphabets. In *Proceedings of the 2nd ACM International Conference on Multimedia Retrieval*, page 20. ACM, 2012.

[20] M. Redi and B. Merialdo. Fitting gaussian copulae for efficient visual codebooks generation. In *Content-Based Multimedia Indexing (CBMI), 2012 10th International Workshop on*, pages 1–6. IEEE, 2012.

[21] B. Silverman. *Density estimation for statistics and data analysis*, volume 26. Chapman & Hall/CRC, 1986.

[22] A. Sklar. Fonctions de répartition à n dimensions et leurs marges. *Publ. Inst. Statist. Univ. Paris*, 8(1):11, 1959.

[23] A. F. Smeaton, P. Over, and W. Kraaij. Evaluation campaigns and trecvid. In *MIR '06*, New York, NY, USA, 2006. ACM Press.

[24] T. Tuytelaars and C. Schmid. Vector quantizing feature space with a regular lattice. In *11th IEEE International Conference on Computer Vision (ICCV '07)*, pages 1–8, Rio de Janeiro, Brazil, 2007. IEEE Computer Society.

[25] J. Xiao, J. Hays, K. Ehinger, A. Oliva, and A. Torralba. Sun database: Large-scale scene recognition from abbey to zoo. In *Computer vision and pattern recognition (CVPR), 2010 IEEE conference on*, pages 3485–3492, 2010.

Identification of Plants from Multiple Images and Botanical IdKeys

Asma Rejeb Sfar
INRIA Saclay
Palaiseau, France
asma.rejeb_sfar@inria.fr

Nozha Boujemaa
INRIA Saclay
Palaiseau, France
nozha.boujemaa@inria.fr

Donald Geman
Johns Hopkins University
Baltimore, MD, USA
geman@jhu.edu

ABSTRACT

Automatic retrieval tools are becoming increasingly important in botany and agriculture due to the growing interest in biodiversity and the ongoing shortage of skilled taxonomists. Our work is motivated by a botanical field scenario where the basic unit of observation is a plant. We describe a novel, image-based retrieval system for both educational and decision-making purposes. Given multiple leaf images of the same plant, the algorithm displays a ranked list of the most relevant species, along with a varied set of representative images from each estimated species. We focus on leaves but the strategy is generic, based on a hierarchical representation of latent variables called *identification keys* (IdKeys) which embody domain knowledge about taxonomy and landmarks. For each query image, keys are estimated sequentially, proceeding from landmarks to the genus and finally to an estimated set of species. The results over multiple queries are then collated into a single ranked list of species. Experiments demonstrate that the proposed approach achieves excellent performance on several databases of uncluttered leaf images as well as providing an instructive interface for measuring diversity and identifying new species.

Categories and Subject Descriptors

H.3 [**Information Storage and Retrieval**]: Information Search and Retrieval

General Terms

Algorithms, Experimentation, Performance

Keywords

Plant identification, multiple queries, botanical IdKeys, hierarchical search

1. INTRODUCTION

Taxonomic identification usually refers the *species* organism. Taxonomists often present organized written descriptions of the characteristics of similar species so that other biologists can identify unknown specimens. In botany, this task implies comparisons among stored and observed characteristics and then assigning a particular plant to a known taxonomic group, ultimately arriving at a species [8]. However, due to the large variation of patterns among fundamental features and the very large number of biologically relevant plant categories (more than $200,000$ [23]), identifying botanical species can be an onerous and time-consuming task even for experts. Finding a species quickly often requires knowing in advance the name of the family or the genus involved, and an expert on one genus or family may be unfamiliar with another. The difficulty is further increased by the ongoing shortage of skilled taxonomists (known as the *taxonomic impediment* [4]).

The goal of this work is to present an effective educational and decision-support system largely driven by a botanical field scenario where the basic unit of observation is a plant. Our algorithm incorporates botanical knowledge to identify the plant species and could be used by both experts and non-experts. Given multiple samples of a plant organ, e.g., a leaf, the algorithm displays a ranked list of the most relevant species, along with a varied set of representative images from each species on the list. Consequently, the problem entails dealing with multiple image queries as well as the retrieval of the most similar species to the unknown plant, which could aid botanists (or even non-expert users) and dramatically accelerate recognition. In addition, by providing the user with additional images that illustrate the visual variation and diversity of each species, our algorithm also serves an educational purpose.

Due to the visual complexity and diversity of botanical objects, one sample alone will usually not capture sufficient information for an effective similarity search or an accurate identification. In particular, standard object recognition systems based on a single image are often not capable of achieving very high accuracy. For example, due to the large intra-class variability and inter-class similarity of leaves, using a single leaf sample for an accurate identification purpose could be extremely difficult. Taxonomic categories (e.g., genus or species) are often determined by subtle differences in leaf characteristics and there is frequently less variation in appearance between leaf images of different categories than within a single category, as shown in Figure 1. Moreover, leaves may exhibit different appearances due to local context, such as location and climatic conditions. They may also vary continuously or discretely even along a single stem as they develop (known as *leaf heteroblasty*). Figure 2 illustrates the large visual variation of some leaves from the same plant. The identification task is further complicated by erosion effects and self-folding as shown in Figure 3.

Figure 1: Intra-species diversity versus inter-species similarity of leaves: (a) is *Ilex aquifolium* while both (b) and (c) are *Quercus ilex*.

Figure 2: Large visual variation within the same plant from *Broussonetia papyrifera* (top row) and *Gleditsia triacanthos* (bottom row).

Figure 3: Visual feature disruption due to erosion and self-folding.

With these considerations in mind, we view the process as interactive with a user in the loop, playing an important role at both the beginning and the end of the process, with the algorithm in between. Initially, the user provides multiple images of the same plant; again, we are imagining a field scenario in which the user has the plant in sight if not "in hand." Then the system provides a ranked list of estimated species along with a varied set of representative images, after which the user analyses the provided information to refine the system estimates and possibly conjecture a new species. Furthermore, we propose to compute such a list using domain-specific information rather than solely relying on generic computer vision techniques. Then, the contributions of this work can be summarized as follows.

- Exploit domain-specific knowledge, namely hierarchical representation of botanical *identification keys* (Id-Keys), and mimic the *process* of identification described

by botanists in order to capture subtle characteristics and structure the search.

- Use multiple image queries to capitalize on access to the plant itself and thereby benefit from complementary examples of appearance. Process each single image individually and then collate the results into a single ranked list of the most likely species.

- Display each estimated species together with both the most similar and the most different training image on average to the query, thereby illustrating the intra-species variability and the inter-species similarity and serving an educational role.

We apply the strategy to leaves, but it could be adapted to other botanical organs such as flowers or fruits and even more general biological entities given an appropriate taxonomy and well-defined IdKeys. Note that all organisms present a hierarchical taxonomy (family-genus-species) as well as natural well-defined and named key points. Different organ images might be also considered to represent a single query.

The rest of the paper is organized as follows: After describing the most related work in §2, the system architecture is presented in §3, including IdKey estimation, where a hierarchical representation is introduced, feature extraction, the classification framework used and the retrieval procedure based on multiple image queries. The experimental results are reported in §4, conducted on several leaf databases, and we draw some conclusions in §5.

2. RELATED WORK

In computational vision, work on plant identification is relatively recent, largely confined to leaves and in a few other cases to flowers [20, 6]. More specifically, most state-of-the-art methods are based on a single leaf analysis, including leaf shape, texture, venation and morphological characteristic analyses. Many of these methods were recently reviewed in [5].

Several shape-based approaches, including leaf boundary analysis, have been adapted or introduced to solve the plant retrieval problem. Wang et al. [26] combined different features based on a centroid-contour distance curve for leaf image retrieval. Ling and Jacobs [16] introduced shape descriptions based on the *Inner Distance* (IDSC), which they combined with shape contexts (Belongie et al. [3]) to outperform many other approaches on two different leaf datasets. Felzenszwalb and Schwartz [9] proposed a hierarchical shape matching algorithm (Shape-Tree) that performed even better on a publicly available leaf dataset (15 Swedish species [25]). The authors of [2] made use of the IDSC to classify larger leaf datasets (more than 150 species) collected in the context of the Smithsonian project (Electronic Field Guide, 2008). Yahiaoui et al. [28] presented a leaf-boundary based approach that attempts to outline foliar properties and achieved the best results using the ImageCLEF2011[1] plant identification framework. More recently, Kumar et al. [15] proposed computing curvature histograms along the contour of the leaf at multiple scales to classify 184 tree species in the Northeastern U.S (not yet publicly available)

---

[1]http://www.imageclef.org/2011/Plants

while introducing the first mobile app (Leafsnap) for identifying plant species. However it should be emphasized that the performance of boundary-based approaches is often sensitive to the quality of the contour resulting from a segmentation process, which naturally complicates distinguishing between species with very similar shapes.

To account for such distinctions, some work combines shape with venation features [22, 19] or more standard texture information [17]. Other work makes use of morphological leaf information. Du et al. [7] extracted properties of the leaf boundary, including aspect ratio, rectangularity, area ratio of convexity, perimeter ratio of convexity, sphericity, circularity and form factor, in order to classify 20 species of plant leaves. The authors of [1] obtained good results in the ImageCLEF2012 Plant Identification Task [2] by addressing simple and compound leaves separately using many morphological features and a single leaflet analysis for compound leaves. Also, several approaches have exploited specific landmarks and some measurements for leaf retrieval and plant identification. In [14], landmarks were manually captured and linear and angular measures were derived from the landmark configuration in order to examine relationships between three species of *Acer* genus. One difficulty in such approaches is the automatic extraction of the landmarks. Recently, Mzoughi et al. [18] introduced an automatic method for detecting different leaf parts for identification purposes.

Our work is somewhat similar to these morphological approaches in that we propose to automatically detect botanical IdKeys; we go a step further by using a hierarchical representation of such keys and multiple uncluttered images of leaves as a query. In fact, to the best of our knowledge, there has been no previous work on plant identification which makes use of multiple leaf images from the same plant to identify the species. One similar work is the interactive system recently introduced in [12] which supports five different organs and views of plants to aid botanists in the identification task using standard local features and a large-scale matching on collaborative photos. Such a system also provides the user with additional information about the species involved, namely all pictures of the training set through a specific browsing window. However, we propose to summarize each estimate using two informative illustrations.

3. PROPOSED APPROACH

Figure 4 provides an overview of our method. Given a multiple-image query, we first estimate botanical IdKeys as well as species for each single image *individually*. To this end, we use a hierarchical representation derived from domain knowledge and multiple key-based local features within a likelihood ratio framework. Then, the results are collated into a single ranked list in order to suggest the most relevant species along with additional representative images.

3.1 IdKey estimation

Botanists generally select one or several leaves (or even other organs such as fruits or flowers when they are available) from a single plant and use *identification keys* (IdKeys) [8] which are examined sequentially and adaptively to identify the unknown species. In essence, one is posing and answering a series of questions about plant attributes (e.g,

---

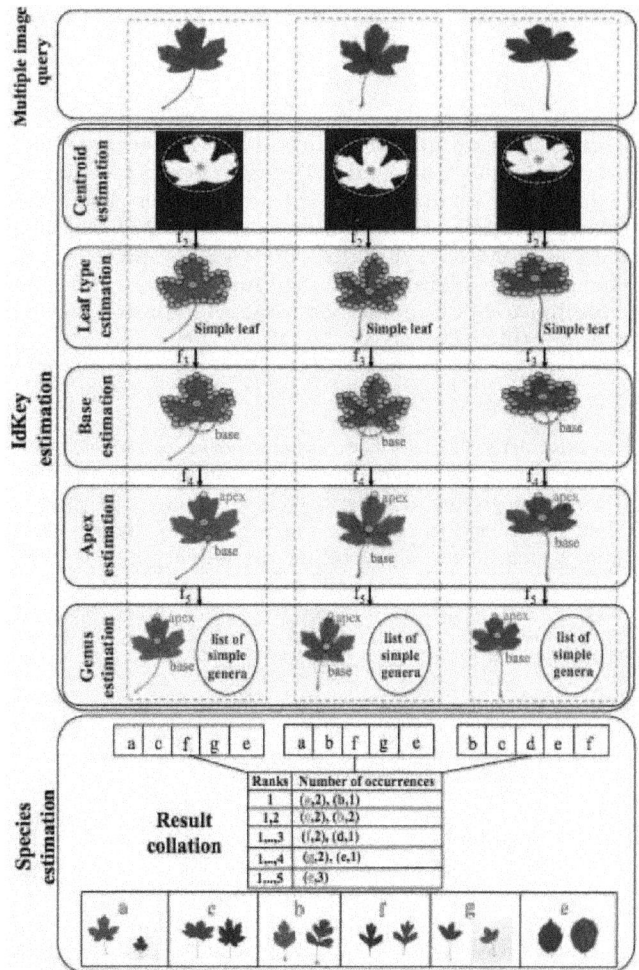

Figure 4: Method Overview: Species identification using botanical IdKeys and multiple image queries.

shape, color, distinguishing landmarks, internal structure) with the aim of focusing on the most discriminating features and narrowing down the set of possible species, much like a game of *twenty questions*. Here, we investigate an algorithm of this nature, focusing on determining botanical species from a set of uncluttered leaf images using a hierarchical representation of botanical IdKeys for each single image.

3.1.1 Hierarchical representation of IdKeys

Hierarchy is a powerful organizing principle for both representation and search [24]. The variation here is based on IdKeys, but the principle is quite general: the original problem is decomposed into more tractable sub-problems sharing more homogenous properties and one monolithic classifier is replaced by a hierarchy of classifiers which gather increasingly detailed information about the object under investigation. There is then a steady progression from coarse queries to those dedicated to very specific subsets of hypotheses.

In our setting, a leaf is represented by an ordered set of attributes corresponding to IdKeys. In particular, these keys must encode invariable characteristics, i.e., be independent of the context, such as geography, climatic conditions, sea-

---

[2] http://www.imageclef.org/2012/plant

193

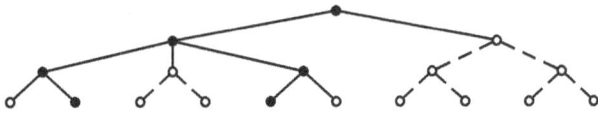

Figure 5: Example of a three-level hierarchy using three IdKeys. Only one of the two possible values of the first key is kept, denoted by a full circle, then two possible values are kept for the second key and two for the third key. Finally only two complete paths through the hierarchy are retained and only these combinations of key values would be considered for the identification task.

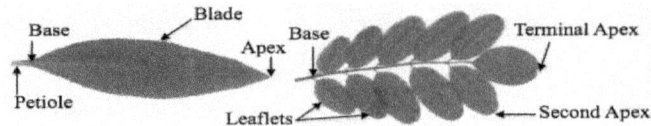

Figure 6: The main features of a typical simple leaf (on the left) and compound leaf (on the right).

son and instantiation. They could refer to geometric properties not directly observable, such as landmarks, or to predetermined groups of species, such as families and genera. More formally, they can be seen as auxiliary hidden variables which facilitate estimating the primary hidden variable, namely the species itself.

Let $\mathcal{K} = \{\mathcal{K}_1, \cdots, \mathcal{K}_N\}$ denote the set of IdKeys with $\mathcal{K}_i$ assuming values in Θ_i, and hence $\mathcal{K} \in \Theta = \prod_{i=1}^{N} \Theta_i$, where N is the number of IdKeys used. Let $\mathcal{Q} = \{\mathcal{Q}_1, \cdots, \mathcal{Q}_K\}$ denote a multiple-image query, where K is the number of images in $\mathcal{Q}$. We assume every instance $\mathcal{Q}_j$ (a single image from $\mathcal{Q}$) has a well-defined set of IdKeys $\mathcal{K}(\mathcal{Q}_j)$, and that determining the class $Y(\mathcal{Q}_j)$ (the botanical species) of $\mathcal{Q}_j$ is facilitated by knowing these keys. The IdKeys are the attributes we query before making a final guess about $Y(\mathcal{Q}_j)$ for each single image. In fact, estimating the IdKeys at full resolution may not be feasible and even narrowing down the possible values of $\mathcal{K}_i$ to a subset of Θ_i still simplifies estimating $Y(\mathcal{Q}_j)$.

The search strategy is breadth-first, coarse-to-fine: starting from the root, classifiers are executed sequentially and adaptively, and any node classifier is applied if and only if all ancestor classifiers have been performed and are positive. Figure 5 illustrates the search based on three IdKeys. At the end of the search, only two paths, i.e., two elements of the full key space, are considered for the species identification task.

In our case, depending on the leaf type Θ_2 (i.e., simple or compound), we consider five or six IdKeys to simplify the species identification of each $\mathcal{Q}_j$. Three landmarks are considered for simple leaves, centroid, base and apex; and four landmarks for compound leaves, centroid, base, terminal apex and second apex (see Figure 6). These landmarks are combined with both the leaf type and the leaf genus to construct the IdKey hierarchy. The full tree then has six (resp. seven) levels, five (resp. six) corresponding to the five (resp. six) keys and the sixth (resp. seventh) to the species. For $\Theta_i, i = 3, \ldots, N$, the possible values are discretized; e.g., the landmark locations have a resolution of 5×5 and are restricted to the boundary points. The number of leaf types is actually two (simple and compound) and the number of genera, $|\Theta_N|$, depends on the dataset.

Let $\mathcal{C} = \prod_{l=1}^{N} \Theta_l \times \mathcal{Y}$, which is the complete set of possible leaf hypotheses or descriptions $(\theta_1, ..., \theta_N, y)$, namely IdKey instantiation and species. Let T denote the full tree graph. Associated with every $t \in T$ we have:

- C_t: The set of interpretations (or hypotheses) $C_t \subset \mathcal{C}$ entertained at node t, ranging from very coarse cells near the root (e.g., restricting only the centroid) to fine cells at the terminal nodes (fully specified descriptions).

- H_t: The hypothesis $I \in C_t$, where I is an image to be classified. The alternative is $H_{(t)} : I \in \mathcal{C} \setminus C_t$.

- F_t: An SVM used as a test statistic.

- f_t: The final classifier mapping images to $\{0, 1\}$, where $f_t(I) = 1$ (respectively, $f_t(I) = 0$) indicates acceptance (resp., rejection) of H_t, and where the decision is based on thresholding the ratio of likelihoods of F_t under the two hypotheses.

Each of these ingredients will be explained in more detail in the remainder of this section and those ensuing. Level one corresponds to the centroid of the blade (resp. of the leaflets in the case of a compound leaf), which can be directly calculated from the raw image data once the leaf petiole is removed using the Otsu segmentation algorithm [21] and straightforward post-processing; see Figure 4. It should be noted here that we are not concerned by imperfect contours or incomplete petiole removal since our method is robust to such problems. Each C_t at level one is a singleton representing the computed centroid and no test is required. In contrast, the leaf type (level two), the base (level three) and the apex(es) (level four or four and five depending of the results of level two) are all estimated using learned classifiers (see §3.1.3). Each landmark detected reduces the number of candidate points for the next detection by excluding its neighborhood from the list of candidates (the dashed blue circles in Figure 4 illustrate the excluded neighborhoods for the apex estimation after detecting the leaf base). Due to the use of pose-indexed features (see §3.1.2), only one classifier f_t (and thus one SVM) needs to be learned for the $(N-1)$ first levels. In our experiments, we maintain one path through the hierarchy through level $(N-1)$, i.e., we only entertain a single candidate for leaf type and landmarks. For each genus (level N), we learn a dedicated classifier conditioned on the accumulated information. The features are computed in multiple local coordinate systems (see §3.1.2). Several candidate genera are kept in estimating the species, for which we again utilize the same coordinate systems as those used for the genera.

3.1.2 Feature extraction

As indicated above, the features provided to the learning algorithm are defined in one or more local coordinate systems. We do not use the same frames (i.e., coordinate systems) to estimate the different IdKeys. The motivation is to *focus attention* around each landmark (which is the strategy reported by botanists) and directly extract local features

Figure 7: Local coordinate systems used for respectively (from left to right) leaf type, base and apex estimations.

which are invariant to pose, orientation and scale variations, thereby avoiding any need for global image transforms, e.g., geometric normalization. For the leaf type, the frame is determined by the estimated centroid and the axes are parallel to the image borders. For the base and the apex(es), we use a reference frame with the estimated width of the leaf (radius of the excircle) and the x-axis is directed towards the centroid of the leaf without the petiole (i.e., centroid of the blade or the leaflets, depending on the leaf type); see Figure 7. However, for both the genera and the species, multiple frames are used: two frames for simple leaves, one centered on the apex and the other on the base, and three frames for compound leaves, one centered on the terminal apex, another on the second apex and the last one on the base.

Focusing of this nature is enabled by "pose-indexed" (or "frame-indexed") features X, introduced in [11] for detecting cats. Although we have many categories of deformable objects, the class of features we use is essentially the same and we refer to [11] for details. Basically, given a frame consisting of two distinguished points and a distinguished scale, there is a candidate feature $X = X(w, j)$ for each (local) window w and for each local image property j: the feature X is just the property histogram in w. We use only shape and texture as properties; specifically, we used Hough, EOH and Fourier histograms as base features (more details of these global features can be found in [10]).

3.1.3 Node classifier

Recall that $f_t = f_t(I)$ is designed to separate images in C_t from images in the complement of C_t. For $l = 1, ..., (N-1)$, the leaf type and landmark levels, all the nodes t at level l share the same classifier f_l. However, for the genera and species, the classifier is in fact node-dependent. The framework is largely classifier-independent in that any learning algorithm could be chosen to induce f_t from the training data at node t. We have chosen to use SVM scores for test statistics and a likelihood framework. The SVM F_t is trained using the feature sets defined in the previous section with, at each level, different positive and negative images; for example, to detect landmarks, the positive images are annotated by the apex(es) or base accordingly and the negative images are randomly annotated, whereas for each distinct taxonomic category (resp. the leaf type), images belonging to that category (resp. to simple leaves) are positive and all others negative. The corresponding classifier f_t is then based on the likelihood ratio:

$$L_t(I) = \frac{P(F_t = F_t(I)|I \in C_t)}{P(F_t = F_t(I)|I \notin C_t)}$$

For the leaf type and landmark levels only a single estimate is retained, namely the one corresponding to the node t at which the likelihood ratio L_t is maximized. In contrast, *all* the detected genera ($f_g(I) = 1$) are considered for species

identification. If C_t corresponds to a genus, let

$$f_t(I) = \begin{cases} 1 & \text{if } \log(L_t(I)) > \rho \\ 0 & \text{else} \end{cases}$$

Here, ρ is a threshold used to control the false negative genus rate, that is to allow only a very small number of instances in which $I \in C_t$ but $f_t(I) = 0$ (missed detections). This can be accomplished at the expense of (temporary) low specificity (i.e., a high false positive rate), but this is a favorable tradeoff in our context.

The hierarchy is processed breadth-first coarse-to-fine: at each level, all the children of a *positive* node t (i.e., one for which $f_t(I) = 1$) are retained and tested at the next level. Whereas false positives can be successively pruned, if the true hypothesis is rejected at a node containing it then it cannot be recovered. Hence only the classifiers for species which belong to the retained genera are performed. Finally, those species for which $f_t(I) = 1$ (where t is the node for the genus of the species) are then sorted according to their likelihood ratios. The advantage of mapping the SVM score to a likelihood ratio is that it takes into account the distribution under both hypotheses. In particular, this mapping is *not* monotone, i.e, does not preserve the ordering of SVM scores across a level, which might naturally occur on different scales.

3.2 Species retrieval using a multiple image query

Using multiple-image queries rather than a single image improves the identification accuracy by taking advantage of the complementaries of different leaf appearances, as illustrated in Figure 8. First, the hierarchical representation of and search for IdKeys ensures both quick and effective species estimation for each image query Q_j. Then, the individual ranked estimates are collated into a single set of estimated species for Q. More specifically, they are combined by scoring each species by the number of its occurrences at the first r ranks.

Let $\widehat{Y}_r$ denote the combined set of estimates at rank r for all the images of Q. The rth species returned for Q, denoted $\hat{y}_r$, is then defined recursively as the most frequent species in the union of $\{\widehat{Y}_1, ..., \widehat{Y}_r\}$ other than $\hat{y}_1, ..., \hat{y}_{r-1}$. An illustrative example is shown in Figure 4. This aggregation of results improves the identification accuracy, as confirmed on several leaf datasets as described in §4.3. It is also independent of the process used to estimate the species of each query image. The same framework could then be used on other applications such as using multiple organ queries.

Each estimated species could also be illustrated by a varied set of representative images in order to provide useful information about the unknown plant (represented by Q) and its most closely related species. In our setting, we illustrate each returned species with both the most similar and the most different training leaf on average to the query. These additional images illustrate both the intra-class variability and inter-class similarity (e.g., see the two first estimated species for the first query, i.e., plant ID = 212, in Figure 8) and consequently could be useful in studying similar species, for instance helping botanists discover new relations or distinctions between or within different taxonomic groups.

Let $\mathcal{M}_Q$ denote the feature vector obtained by averaging the individual feature vectors over all Q_j, so $\mathcal{M}_Q$ represents the compound query Q. For each rank r, let X_{I_T} denote the feature vector of the training image I_T from the same species as $\hat{y}_r$; X_{I_T} is the feature vector used at the last level of the hierarchy, namely for genus and species identification using multiple local coordinate systems as explained in §3.1.2. Let $d_{Q,I_T} = ||\mathcal{M}_Q - X_{I_T}||$ be the difference in $L2$ norm between Q and I_T. Then, the most similar and the most different training images to Q consist of those which respectively minimize and maximize d_{Q,I_T}. Some examples are illustrated in Figure 8.

4. EXPERIMENTS

In this section we describe the datasets we have used to evaluate the proposed approach and compare our results with those previously obtained.

4.1 Datasets

We considered three challenging leaf datasets from different geographical areas. Each image represents a single leaf on a white background.

Smithsonian: This standard database has 6717 leaf images containing 202 different species from the Northeastern U.S area. The number of exemplars per species varies from 2 to 63. These images were provided by the Smithsonian botanical institution within the framework of the US National Herbarium. One particularity of this data is that the images present various poses and orientations of leaves as well as different structures of basal and apical parts as shown in Figure 9. Thus, good performance on such a dataset suggests robust and effective IdKey estimation.

Swedish: This has 1125 leaf images containing 75 images from each of 15 different Swedish plant species. This dataset was the first publicly available leaf data, introduced by the authors of [25] for research. Although it contains relatively few varieties of species (e.g., only two compound species), we chose it in order to be able to compare our performance (especially when using a single image query) with various methods since it was used to evaluate several previous studies.

ImageCLEF2011: Used in the ImageCLEF2011 plant identification task[1], this dataset has 3070 scanned leaves of 71 species from the French Mediterranean and was constructed through a citizen sciences initiative conducted by Telabotanica[3], a French social network of amateur and expert botanists (more details can be found in [13]). The main interest of this data is that, unlike the others, it contains useful additional information, including the plant identifier, the author and the location of each leaf. This provides an opportunity to evaluate the multiple-image query approach in the conditions of a real-world application, namely a botanical field scenario in which the basic unit of observation is a plant, which is the main goal of this work. Thus each query will contain different leaf images of the same plant (and not just of the same species). In particular, the dataset contains 55 plants.

We organized each dataset into its proper taxonomic hierarchy (genus, species) and annotated it with the different botanical points. These annotations, together with taxonomic labels will be made publicly available to other researchers.

[3] http://www.tela-botanica.org/site:accueil?langue=en

Table 1: Rates of well estimated IdKeys

IdKeys	Leaf types	Botanical points
Smithsonian leaves	98.4%	90.4%
Swedish leaves	99.2%	95%
ImagClef2011 leaves	95.8%	92.4%

4.2 Evaluation of the IdKey estimation

First, we present the results of the IdKey estimation for all the data introduced in the previous section in Table 1. We achieve over 95% accuracy for leaf type estimation and over 90% for botanical point detection, and thereby confirm efficient discrimination between simple and compound leaves as well as reasonable invariance to shape and structure. Figure 9 shows botanical point (i.e., base, apex(es)) detection results for different kinds of leaves (e.g., toothed, lobed, concave, convex, symmetric, asymmetric).

Figure 9: Random sample of image queries with the estimated botanical points from Smithsonian leaves. False detections are framed with a red box. Note that the entire detection process is considered erroneous if any point is not accurately detected.

4.3 Evaluation of the species identification

To evaluate the performance of species identification, we provide the rate on the holdout test data at which the true species coincides with our top estimate ("top-1") and appears among our top five estimates ("top-5") using both single and multiple-image queries. For both the Smithsonian and Swedish subsets, a multiple-image query represents random images from the same species since there is no information about the plants used in these datasets. However, for ImageCLEF2011, we re-organized the testing data to extract the different testing plants and to be able to evaluate the efficiency of our approach in the conditions of a real-world application. Note that there is no plant used in both the testing and training sets. Rather than using all the test images, we consider only random images of different plants, i.e., we compute the recognition rate for the 55 plants of this dataset. Each query represents a single or multiple image(s) of the same plant. We used cross-validation on the training images in order to fix the threshold $\rho = -4$; the negative value promotes a low missed detection rate.

Smithsonian Data: We used 4435 images for training and 2282 images for testing. Table 2 reports the recognition rates for both the top-1 and the top-5 responses while considering different numbers of images per query. The correct

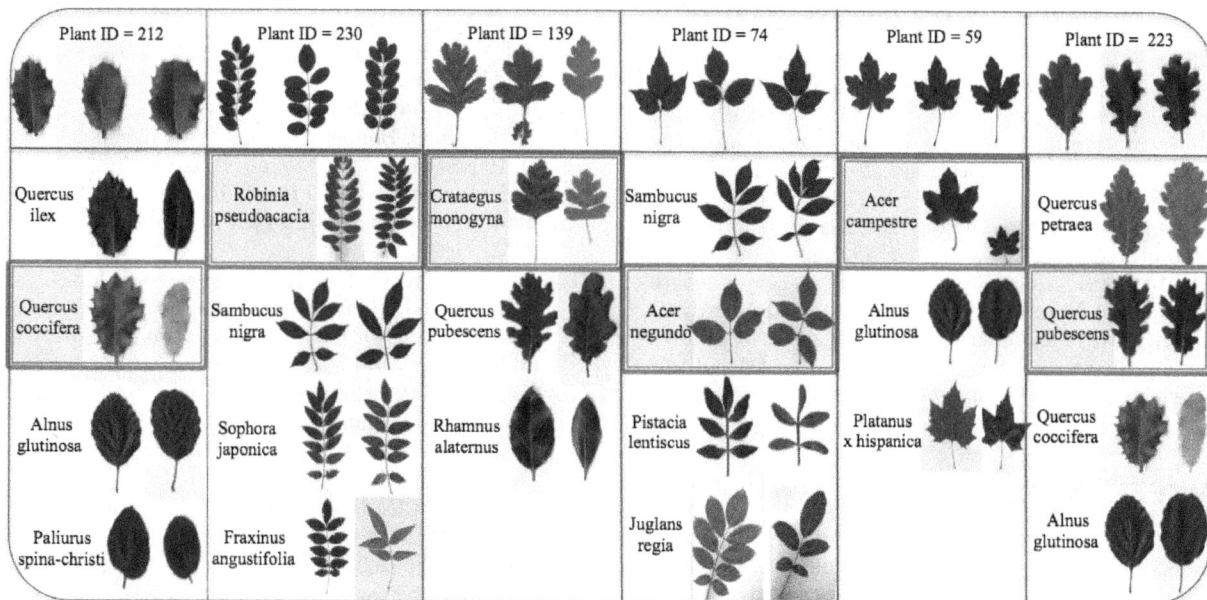

Figure 8: Examples of plant identification evaluation on ImageClef2011 data. Each column shows one example. For each example the top row shows the query plant which is represented by three images, while rows 2-5 show the top four species returned (when they exist). Each species returned is displayed with both the most similar (on the left) and the most different (on the right) training image on average to the query and which belong to that species. Correct species are framed with a green box.

Table 2: Performance of IdKeys on the Smithsonian data

Nb images/Query	1	3	5	10
Perf. (top-1)	78.5%	85.3%	89.1%	**90.6%**
Perf. (top-5)	88.4%	95.3%	**96.7%**	95.1%

Table 3: Different results on the Swedish data

Methods	Perf. (top-1)
IdKeys+5 images/Query	**100%**
IdKeys+3 images/Query	99%
IdKeys	**98.4%**
sPACT [27]	97.92%
Shape-Tree [9]	96.28%
SPTC+DP [16]	95.33%
IDSC+DP [16]	94.13%
SC+DP [16]	88.12%
Söderkvist [25]	82.40%

Table 4: Performance of IdKeys on the Image-Clef2011 data

Nb images/Query	1	3	5	10
Perf. (top-1)	61.8%	65.5%	74.5%	**78.2%**
Perf. (top-5)	83.6%	**98.2%**	96.4%	96.4%

species appears in the top-5 over 95% of the time considering multiple-image queries. In particular, we achieve 78.5% accuracy for the top-ranked species using a single image per query and over 90% using 10 images. In [2], the IDSC was used with the nearest neighbor classifier to identify botanical species within two subsets of the Smithsonian database, achieving a recognition rate of 60% − 70% for the top-1 matching species. We did not process those subsets since we were not able to know the species considered. However, we were able to compare our method with the IDSC approach on the Swedish data, as described below.

Swedish Data: Following the work in [16] and [25], we randomly select 25 training images from each species and test the remaining images in order to evaluate our performance. We also compare our results with the state-of-the-art results on this dataset, including those of the IDSC [16], the Shape-Tree [9] and sPACT [27] methods which all use single image queries. We achieve the best performances using the IdKeys approach (also using single image queries) with over 98% accuracy for the top-1 estimate (see Table 3). Using multiple image queries improves the recognition rates, achieving 100% accuracy with using 5 images per query, as shown in Table 3.

ImageCLEF2011 Data: Finally, we apply our approach in a real-world context using a set of leaf images from the same plant for each query thanks to the additional infor-

mation provided with this dataset. Table 4 shows our performance when considering different numbers of images per query for both the top-1 and the top-5 responses. In particular, using multiple-image queries improves the identification performance, reaching over 95% accuracy for the top-5 estimates. The results on a random sample of test plants is shown in Figure 8. Of particular note is first the high similarity between leaves of some species and the variation in appearance of leaves within others; for example, note the visual difference between the leaf images of the first plant (i.e., plant ID=212) and those from the training set. This is essentially due to the use of different plants and conditions to collect training and test data.

5. CONCLUSION AND FUTURE WORK

We have introduced a generic retrieval-based approach for both plant identification and educational purposes using multiple image queries as well as a hierarchical search and representation derived from domain knowledge in the form of IdKeys. We have achieved excellent recognition rates on several databases of uncluttered leaf images, including a large-scale subset with more than 200 species; the correct species appeared among the top five estimates over 95% of the time by considering only 3 images per query. Future work is aimed at including cluttered images and investigating efficient IdKeys for other botanical organs such as flowers, thereby allowing us to apply our framework on multiple queries which could represent either single or multiple plant organ(s).

6. REFERENCES

[1] A. Arora, A. Gupta, N. Bagmar, S. Mishra, and A. Bhattacharya. A plant identification system using shape and morphological features on segmented leaflets: Team iitk, clef 2012. In *CLEF (Online Working Notes/Labs/Workshop)*, 2012.

[2] P. Belhumeur, D. Chen, S. Feiner, D. Jacobs, W. Kress, H. Ling, I. Lopez, R. Ramamoorthi, S. Sheorey, S. White, and L. Zhang. Searching the world's herbaria: A system for visual identification of plant species. In *ECCV*, pages 116–129, 2008.

[3] S. Belongie, J. Malik, and J. Puzicha. Shape matching and object recognition using shape contexts. *Pattern Analysis and Machine Intelligence, IEEE Transactions on*, 24(4):509–522, 2002.

[4] M. Carvalho, F. Bockmann, D. Amorim, C. BrandŃo, M. de Vivo, J. Figueiredo, and al. Taxonomic impediment or impediment to taxonomy? a commentary on systematics and the cybertaxonomic-automation paradigm. *Evolutionary Biology*, 34:140–143, 2007. 10.1007/s11692-007-9011-6.

[5] J. S. Cope, D. Corney, J. Y. Clark, P. Remagnino, and P. Wilkin. Plant species identification using digital morphometrics: A review. *Expert Systems with Applications*, 39(8):7562 – 7573, 2012.

[6] M. Das, R. Manmatha, and E. Riseman. Indexing flower patent images using domain knowledge. *IEEE Intelligent Systems*, 14:24–33, 1999.

[7] J.-X. Du, X. Wang, and G.-J. Zhang. Leaf shape based plant species recognition. *Applied Mathematics and Computation*, 185(2):883–893, 2007.

[8] T. Elpel. *Botany in a Day: The Patterns Method of Plant Identification*. Thomas J. Elpel's herbal field guide to plant families of North America. Hops Press, 2004.

[9] P. Felzenszwalb and J. Schwartz. Hierarchical matching of deformable shapes. In *CVPR*, pages 1–8, june 2007.

[10] M. Ferecatu. *Image retrieval with active relevance feedback using both visual and keyword-based descriptors*. PhD thesis, Université de Versailles SaintQuentin-en-Yvelines, 2005.

[11] F. Fleuret and D. Geman. Stationary features and cat detection. *Journal of Machine Learning Research (JMLR)*, 9:2549–2578, 2008.

[12] H. Goëau, P. Bonnet, J. Barbe, V. Baric, A. Joly, and J.-F. Molino. Multi-Organ Plant Identification. In *ACM International Workshop on Multimedia Analysis for Ecological Data*, 2012.

[13] H. Goëau, P. Bonnet, A. Joly, N. Boujemaa, D. Barthélémy, J.-F. Molino, P. Birnbaum, E. Mouysset, and M. Picard. The ImageCLEF 2011 plant images classication task. In *ImageCLEF 2011*, 2011.

[14] R. Jensen, K. Ciofani, and L. Miramont. Lines, outlines, and landmarks: Morphometric analyses of leaves of acer rubrum, acer saccharinum (aceraceae) and their hybrid. *Taxon*, 2002.

[15] N. Kumar, P. Belhumeur, A. Biswas, D. Jacobs, W. J. Kress, I. Lopez, and J. B. Soares. Leafsnap: A computer vision system for automatic plant species identification. In *ECCV*, 2012.

[16] H. Ling and D. Jacobs. Shape classification using the inner-distance. *IEEE Trans. Pattern Anal. Mach. Intell*, 29:286–299, 2007.

[17] S. Mouine, I. Yahiaoui, and A. Verroust-Blondet. Advanced shape context for plant species identification using leaf image retrieval. In *Proceedings of the 2nd ACM International Conference on Multimedia Retrieval*, ICMR, pages 49:1–49:8, New York, NY, USA, 2012. ACM.

[18] O. Mzoughi, I. Yahiaoui, and N. Boujemaa. Extraction of leaf parts by image analysis. In *Proceedings of the 9th international conference on Image Analysis and Recognition - Volume Part I*, ICIAR, 2012.

[19] Y. Nam, E. Hwang, and D. Kim. A similarity-based leaf image retrieval scheme: Joining shape and venation features. *Computer Vision and Image Understanding*, 110(2):245 – 259, 2008.

[20] M.-E. Nilsback and A. Zisserman. A visual vocabulary for flower classification. In *CVPR*, 2006.

[21] N. Otsu. A Threshold Selection Method from Gray-level Histograms. *IEEE Transactions on Systems, Man and Cybernetics*, 1979.

[22] J. Park, E. Hwang, and Y. Nam. Utilizing venation features for efficient leaf image retrieval. *Journal of Systems and Software*, 81(1):71 – 82, 2008.

[23] R. Scotland and A. Wortley. How many species of seed plants are there? *Taxon*, 2003.

[24] C. N. Silla, Jr. and A. A. Freitas. A survey of hierarchical classification across different application domains. *Data Min. Knowl. Discov.*, 2011.

[25] O. Söderkvist. Computer vision classification of leaves from swedish trees. Master's thesis, 2001.

[26] Z. Wang, Z. Chi, and D. Feng. Shape based leaf image retrieval. *Vision, Image and Signal Processing, IEE Proceedings*, 2003.

[27] J. Wu and J. Rehg. Where am i: Place instance and category recognition using spatial pact. In *CVPR*, 2008.

[28] I. Yahiaoui, O. Mzoughi, and N. Boujemaa. Leaf shape descriptor for tree species identification. In *ICME*, pages 254–259. IEEE, 2012.

HSOG: A Novel Local Descriptor based on Histograms of Second Order Gradients for Object Categorization

Di Huang*
IRIP Lab, SCSE
Beihang University
100191, Beijing, China
dhuang@buaa.edu.cn

Chao Zhu*
LIRIS, MI Department
Ecole Centrale de Lyon
69134, Lyon, France
chao.zhu@ec-lyon.fr

Charles-Edmond Bichot
LIRIS, MI Department
Ecole Centrale de Lyon
69134, Lyon, France
charles-edmond.bichot@ec-lyon.fr

Yunhong Wang
IRIP Lab, SCSE
Beihang University
100191, Beijing, China
yhwang@buaa.edu.cn

Liming Chen
LIRIS, MI Department
Ecole Centrale de Lyon
69134, Lyon, France
liming.chen@ec-lyon.fr

ABSTRACT

This paper presents a novel local image descriptor for object categorization that extracts the Histograms of the Second Order Gradients and is thereby named as HSOG. The HSOG descriptor is in contrast to the widely used ones in the literature, e.g. SIFT, DAISY, HOG, LBP, etc., which are based on the first order gradient information. The contributions of this work can be summarized as: (1) the design of HSOG; (2) the prove of its discriminative power and its complementation to the first order gradient based descriptors; (3) the analysis of performance variation caused by different parameter settings; and (4) the multi-scale extension which further improves the categorization accuracy. The experimental results achieved on the Caltech 101 and Caltech 256 databases clearly highlight the effectiveness of the proposed approach.

Categories and Subject Descriptors

I.4.7 [**Image Processing and Computer Vision**]: Feature Measurement—*Feature representation*; I.4.8 [**Image Processing and Computer Vision**]: Scene Analysis—*Object Recognition*

General Terms

Algorithms, Experimentation, Performance

Keywords

Local Descriptor, Feature Extraction, Object Categorization

*denotes that these authors equally contribute to this work.

1. INTRODUCTION

Machine-based visual object categorization has attracted increasing attention in pattern recognition and computer vision because of its application potentials and scientific challenges, and visual content representation is treated as a quite important issue within this field. Recently, local image descriptors [15, 21, 29, 8, 13, 2, 24, 16, 6] calculated based on interest regions have proven competent compared with the global ones, and these local features are highly distinctive to identify specific objects, partially invariant to illumination variations, robust to external occlusions, and insensitive to local image distortions. There also exist some studies on the discussions of their performance comparison [18, 19, 20, 22].

For some time, it has been admitted that visual processing of human beings should not be explained only by first order mechanisms which capture spatio-temporal variations in luminance, and the second order based ones extract complementary information, i.e. difference of texture and spatial frequency as well [23]. Despite the great variety in design principle and specific implementation, the overwhelming majority of existing local descriptors share one common ground that they make use of the information of the first order gradients, e.g. locations, orientations, and magnitudes. In contrast, quite limited efforts have been made on the utilization of second order gradients. Brown et al. [5] proposed an unified framework for local descriptor design, and pointed out that high order gradients (2nd and 4th) are helpful in the application of multi-view stereo matching. However, to the best of our knowledge, local image descriptors that introduce the second order gradients are seldom investigated in the literature for the purpose of object recognition. Intuitively, the second order gradient information should not only possess certain discriminative power to distinguish different object classes, but also be complementary to the information provided by first order gradients. This intuition could be characterized by an analogy of object motion that it requires both the velocity and acceleration for a comprehensive motion process description. According to this analogy, within a pre-defined distance between two pixels of an image, the first order gradients imitate the velocity of the gray

Figure 1: An illustration of intra-class changes. Examples are from the speed boat class of the Caltech 256 dataset, but possess very different appearances.

Figure 2: An example of inter-class similarities. Images in the upper row are from the bike class while the ones in the bottom row are from the motorbike class of the Caltech 256 dataset; they are very similar in appearance.

value variation while the second order based ones simulate the corresponding acceleration. As a result, in order to address the confusion caused by intra-class variations as well as inter-class similarities (see Figure 1 and 2 for two examples) and ameliorate the quality of visual content representation, first and second order gradients are both necessary.

In this paper, we propose a novel and powerful local image descriptor, named Histograms of the Second Order Gradients (HSOG), for the issue of object categorization. Just as its name implies, HSOG encodes the second order gradient information to represent local image variations. To better describe the diversity of object appearances, unlike the way for the second order gradient calculation using steerable filters as in [5], we design a map based approach. Specifically, for a certain image region, HSOG begins with computing its first order Oriented Gradient Maps (OGMs), each of which is for a quantized direction, and the histograms of second order gradients are then extracted from the OGMs. The histograms are further concatenated, and after dimensionality reduction, a compacted local image representation is finally constructed. Additionally, we embed spatial information by adopting the multi-scale strategy to improve categorization performance. Experiments are carried out on the standard Caltech 101 and Caltech 256 datasets, and the results clearly illustrate the effectiveness of the proposed descriptor and its complementation to the first order gradient based ones.

The remainder of this paper is organized as follows. Section 2 presents a brief overview of related work. Section 3

introduces HSOG in detail. Section 4 discusses and analyzes the experimental results. Section 5 concludes the paper.

2. RELATED WORK

In the last decade, a number of effective local descriptors have been proposed and exploited in object recognition and other related categorization tasks.

A typical representative of local image descriptors is Scale Invariant Feature Transform (SIFT), proposed by Lowe [15], which has been widely investigated and has played a dominant role in object recognition. Its descriptor is represented by a 3D histogram of the gradient locations and orientations whose contributions are weighted by their gradient magnitudes. The quantization of gradient locations as well as orientations makes the SIFT descriptor robust to small geometric distortions and small errors in the previous step of region detection. Some efforts to improve the SIFT descriptor were later reported in the literature.

Ke and Sukthankar [12] proposed PCA-SIFT descriptor, which applies Principal Component Analysis (PCA) on the normalized gradient patches to enhance the distinctiveness and reduce the dimensionality of the SIFT features.

Mikolajczyk and Schmid [18] extended SIFT to the Gradient Location and Orientation Histogram (GLOH) descriptor to increase its robustness and distinctiveness. It replaces the rectangular location grid used in SIFT with a log-polar one, and applies PCA to reduce the size of the descriptor.

Van de Sande et al. [25] extracted the SIFT features in different color spaces and compared their performance, including HSV-SIFT [4], HueSIFT [27], OpponentSIFT, C-SIFT, rgSIFT, RGB-SIFT, and Transformed color SIFT, showing that combining SIFT with color clues is a promising way to improve the accuracy in object recognition.

Belongie et al. [3] proposed a SIFT-like descriptor named Shape Context represented by a 2D histogram of edge point locations, where the log-polar location grid is used. It aims to describe the distribution of edge points on a shape with respect to the reference point.

Inspired by SIFT, Bay et al. [2] introduced the Speeded-Up Robust Features (SURF) descriptor. Instead of the gradient information used in the SIFT descriptor, SURF computes the Haar wavelet responses, and exploits integral images for computational efficiency. As a result, it runs times faster than SIFT.

Dalal and Triggs [8] presented the Histogram of Oriented Gradient (HOG) descriptor. It combines the properties from both the SIFT and GLOH, because it is also represented by a 3D histogram of gradient locations as well as orientations, and employs both rectangular and log-polar location grids. The main difference between HOG and SIFT is that HOG is computed on a dense grid of uniformly spaced cells, with overlapping local contrast normalization.

Ojala et al. [21] proposed Local Binary Patterns (LBP) for texture classification, and such a descriptor encodes the sign information between the central pixel and its surrounding ones within a given neighborhood. It was soon successfully applied to face recognition [1].

Heikkila et al. [10] combined both the strengths of SIFT and LBP to build the Center-Symmetric LBP (CS-LBP). It adopts the SIFT-like approach for descriptor construction, but replaces its gradient information with CS-LBP features. Instead of comparing each pixel with the central one, CS-

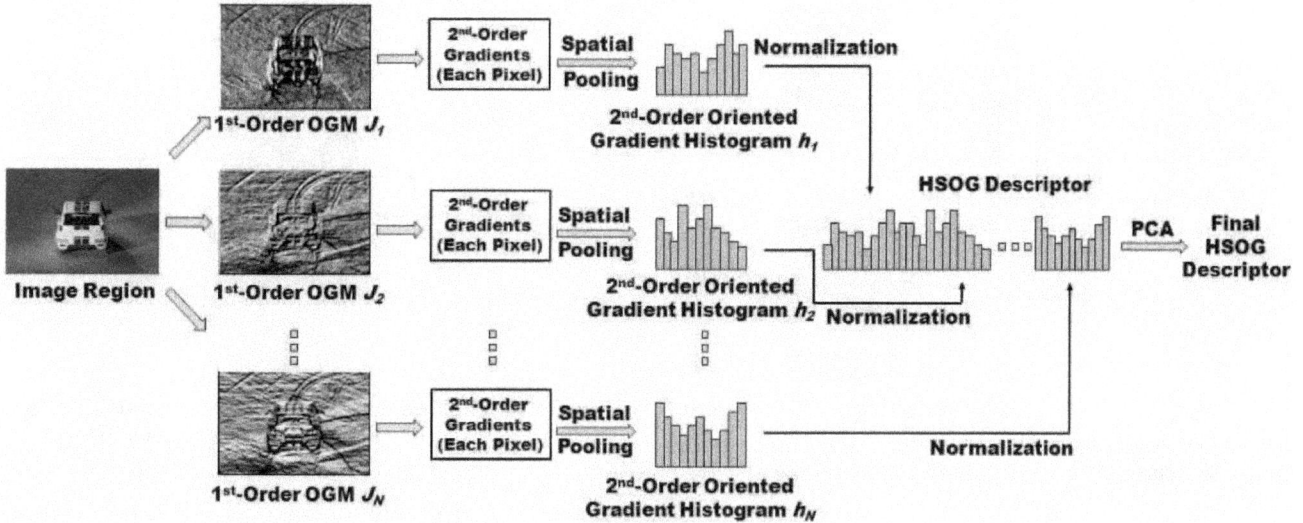

Figure 3: Construction process of the proposed HSOG descriptor.

LBP only compares center-symmetric pairs of pixels, which reduces the size of the LBP histogram.

In order to improve the efficiency of local descriptors, Tola et al. [24] replaced the weighted sum rule employed in SIFT by the sum of convolutions. More recently, Zhu et al. [31] introduced DAISY into the domain of object recognition, and proved that when displaying a similar recognition accuracy to SIFT, DAISY can operate 12 times faster.

3. HSOG DESCRIPTOR CONSTRUCTION

In this section, we present the Histograms of the Second Order Gradient (HSOG) descriptor in detail. Its construction is composed of four main steps: (1) computation of the first order Oriented Gradient Maps (OGMs); (2) computation of the second order gradients based on these computed OGMs; (3) spatial pooling; and (4) dimensionality reduction. The entire process is illustrated in Figure 3.

3.1 First Order Oriented Gradient Maps

The input of the proposed HSOG descriptor is an image region around the keypoint, which is either detected by interest point detectors, e.g. Harris-Laplace, or located on a dense sampling grid. To calculate the first order gradients, we introduce OGMs, a biological vision based representation method originally proposed for 3D face recognition [11]. It achieved the state of the art performance and proved insensitive to affine illumination and geometrical transformations.

Specifically, for each pixel (x, y) within the given region I, a certain number of gradient maps $G_1, G_2,..., G_N$, one for each quantized direction o, are first computed. They are formally defined as:

$$G_o = \left(\frac{\partial I}{\partial o}\right)^+; \quad o = 1, 2, ..., N. \tag{1}$$

where '+' indicates that only positive values are kept to preserve the polarity of the intensity changes, while the negative ones are set to zero.

Each gradient map describes gradient norms of the input image region in a direction o at every pixel location. We then convolve its gradient maps with a Gaussian kernel G. The standard deviation of the Gaussian kernel G is proportional to the radius of the given neighborhood, R, as in (2).

$$\rho_o^R = G_R * G_o \tag{2}$$

The purpose of the convolution with Gaussian kernels is to allow the gradients to shift within a neighborhood without abrupt changes.

At a given pixel location (x, y), we collect all the values of these convolved gradient maps at that location and build the vector $\rho^R(x, y)$.

$$\rho^R(x, y) = \left[\rho_1^R(x, y), \cdots, \rho_N^R(x, y)\right]^T \tag{3}$$

This vector, $\rho^R(x, y)$, is further normalized to unit norm vector, which is called in the subsequent entire orientation vector and denoted by $\underline{\rho}^R$, and the image region can be thus represented by entire orientation vectors. Specifically, given an image region I, we generate an Oriented Gradient Map (OGM) J_o for each orientation o defined as:

$$J_o(x, y) = \underline{\rho}_o^R(x, y) \tag{4}$$

Fig. 4 illustrates such a process. Thanks to the computation of gradient maps as well as the following normalization step, OGMs possess the property of being invariant to affine lighting transformations, which can be inherited by the whole HSOG descriptor.

3.2 Second Order Gradient Computation

Once the first order OGMs of all quantized directions are generated, they are used as the input for computing the second order gradients in the same image region. Precisely, for each first order OGM, $J_o(x, y)$, $o = 1, 2, ..., N$, we consider

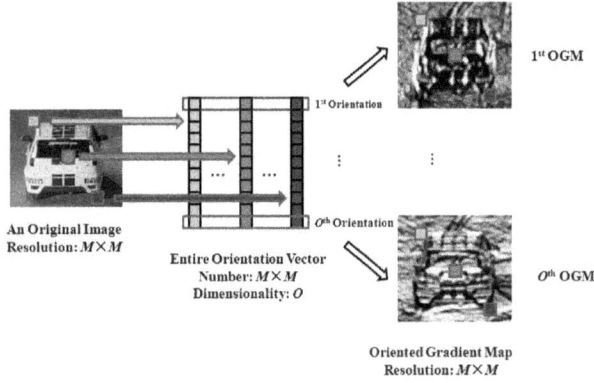

Figure 4: A demonstration of the oriented gradient maps for each of the quantized orientations o.

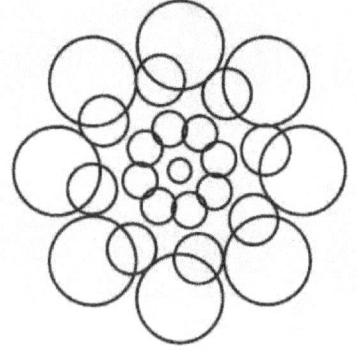

Figure 5: The Spatial pooling arrangement (DAISY-style in [5]) of the proposed HSOG descriptor.

it as a regular image, and calculate the gradient magnitude mag_o and orientation θ_o at every pixel as (5) and (6).

$$mag_o(x,y) = \sqrt{\left(\frac{\partial J_o(x,y)}{\partial x}\right)^2 + \left(\frac{\partial J_o(x,y)}{\partial y}\right)^2} \quad (5)$$

$$\theta_o(x,y) = \arctan\left(\frac{\partial J_o(x,y)}{\partial y} \Big/ \frac{\partial J_o(x,y)}{\partial x}\right) \quad (6)$$

where $o = 1, 2, ..., N$;

$$\frac{\partial J_o(x,y)}{\partial x} = J_o(x+1,y) - J_o(x-1,y) \quad (7)$$

$$\frac{\partial J_o(x,y)}{\partial y} = J_o(x,y+1) - J_o(x,y-1) \quad (8)$$

Then, each orientation θ_o is mapped from $[-\pi/2, \pi/2]$ to $[0, 2\pi]$, and quantized into N dominant orientations, keeping consistent with the number of the first order OGMs. After quantization, the entry n_o of each direction θ_o is calculated as (9).

$$n_o(x,y) = \mod\left(\left\lfloor\frac{\theta_o(x,y)}{2\pi/N} + \frac{1}{2}\right\rfloor, N\right), o = 1, 2, ..., N \quad (9)$$

3.3 Spatial Pooling

Spatial pooling is an effective way for local descriptors to encode coarse spatial information of image pixels. It divides the input image region into sub-regions and accumulates a histogram of certain property (gradients, edge points, binary patterns, etc.) within each sub-region. All these histograms are then concatenated to construct the final descriptor. Brown et al. analyzed different spatial pooling schemes and compared their performance in the work [5], indicating that the best performance was achieved by the DAISY-style arrangement, as illustrated in Figure 5. Therefore, we follow this way for spatial pooling of the HSOG descriptor.

The input image region is divided into circles of different size located on a series of concentric rings, and the radius of each circle is proportional to its distance from the central pixel. As a result, there are four parameters that determine

the spatial arrangement of the HSOG descriptor: the radius of the region area (R); the number of quantized orientations (N); the number of concentric rings (CR); the number of circles on each ring (C). The influence of different parameters will be discussed experimentally in section 4.

The total number of the divided circles can be calculated as $T = CR \times C + 1$. Within each circle CIR_j, $j = 1, 2, , T$, and for each first order OGM J_o, $o = 1, 2, ..., N$, a second order oriented gradient histogram, h_{oj}, is built as (10) by accumulating the gradient magnitudes mag_o of all the pixels with the same quantized orientation entry n_o.

$$h_{oj}(i) = \sum_{(x,y) \in CIR_j} f(n_o(x,y) == i) * mag_o(x,y) \quad (10)$$

where $i = 0, 1, ..., N-1$; $o = 1, 2, ..., N$, $j = 1, 2, ..., T$,

$$f(x) = \begin{cases} 1, \text{if } x \text{ is true} \\ 0, \text{otherwise} \end{cases} \quad (11)$$

Then, for each first order OGM J_o, its second order oriented gradient histogram h_o is generated by concatenating all the histograms from T circles:

$$h_o = [h_{o1}, h_{o2}, h_{o3}, \cdots, h_{oT}]^T \quad (12)$$

where $o = 1, 2, ..., N$. The HSOG descriptor is obtained by concatenating all N histograms of the second order oriented gradient as (13). Each histogram h_o is normalized to an unit norm vector $\hat{h}_o$ before the concatenation.

$$\text{HSOG} = [\hat{h}_1, \hat{h}_2, \hat{h}_3, \cdots, \hat{h}_N]^T \quad (13)$$

3.4 Dimensionality Reduction

The dimension of the achieved HSOG descriptor is $T \times N^2$, which is relatively high (from hundreds up to more than one thousand) for the following steps. To remove redundant information and reduce dimensionality, we further employ the well known Principal Component Analysis (PCA) technique, because it has been successfully applied in the PCA-SIFT and GLOH cases for the same objective.

In order to build the eigenspace, we located 76,000 local image patches by applying the Harris-Laplace interest point detector [17] on a diverse collection of images which is out

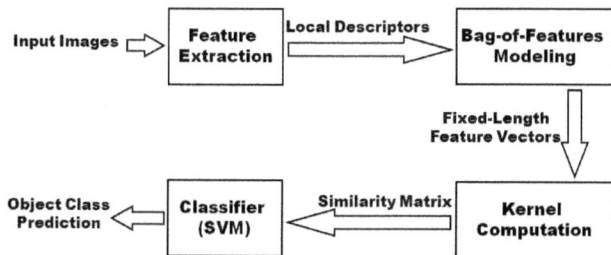

Figure 6: Flowchart of our approach for visual object categorization.

of the set for validation. Each of these patches was adopted to compute its HSOG descriptor, and PCA was applied on the covariance matrix of these descriptors. The matrix consisting of the top n eigenvectors was stored and utilized as the projection matrix.

For a certain image region, its HSOG descriptor is first computed and then projected into a low-dimensional feature space by multiplying the pre-trained projection matrix. The dimension of the final HSOG descriptor is hence reduced to n. We experimentally test good values for n, and set $n = 128$ in the following experiments.

4. EXPERIMENTAL EVALUATION

We evaluate the proposed HSOG descriptor in the context of visual object categorization on two standard datasets: i.e. Caltech 101 [14] and Caltech 256 [9]. Caltech 101 contains a total number of 9146 images split into 101 different classes including chairs, faces, airplanes, animals, vehicles, flowers, etc. and an additional background category. The number of images in each class varies from 31 to 800, and most categories have about 50 images. As an extension of Caltech 101, Caltech 256 is made up of 30607 images from 256 categories as well as an additional clutter category. Each category contains at least 80 images. Compared to Caltech 101, Caltech 256 is more challenging because it contains more categories and presents much higher inter-class similarities and intra-class variations in object scale, location, pose, etc.

4.1 Experimental Setup

We follow the approach whose flowchart is illustrated in Fig. 6 for object categorization.

For each image in both databases, the Harris-Laplace detector is first adopted to detect interest points, and a local region around each interest point is then selected to extract the HSOG descriptor. For the purpose of comparison, several state-of-the-art descriptors are also extracted from these regions, including SIFT, DAISY, CS-LBP and T3-S4 (steerable filters with the DAISY-style spatial pooling in [5]) from interest regions, as well as HOG from the entire image. We implement the CS-LBP and T3-S4 descriptors according to [10] and [5] and with the help of the source code available online for computing SIFT [1], DAISY [2], and HOG [3].

In this paper, we use the popular Bag-of-Features (BoF) framework [7] due to its great success in object recognition tasks. The main idea of BoF is to represent an image as

an orderless collection of local image descriptors. More precisely, a visual vocabulary is constructed at first by exploiting a clustering algorithm on training data, and each cluster center is considered as a visual word in the vocabulary. All the descriptors extracted from an image are then quantized to their closest visual word in an appropriate metric space. The number of the descriptors assigned to each visual word is accounted into a histogram as the final BoF based representation. In our case, a vocabulary of 4000 visual words is constructed for each kind of local descriptors respectively by applying the k-means clustering algorithm on a subset of descriptors randomly selected from training data as [26].

The Support Vector Machine (SVM) algorithm is applied to classification. When all local image descriptors are transformed to fixed length feature vectors by the BoF modeling, the χ^2 distance is computed as (14) to measure the similarity between each pair of the feature vectors F and F' (n is the size of both feature vectors).

$$dist_{\chi^2}(F, F') = \sum_{i=1}^{n} \frac{(F_i - F_i')^2}{F_i + F_i'} \qquad (14)$$

The kernel function based on the distance as defined in (15) is adopted for the SVM training and prediction.

$$K_{\chi^2}(F, F') = e^{-\frac{1}{D} dist_{\chi^2}(F, F')} \qquad (15)$$

where D is the parameter for normalizing distances, and we set it to the average value of the distance between each pair of images in the training set. Finally, each image for test is classified into object class with the maximum SVM output decision value. We tune the parameters of the classifier on the training set via cross-validation, and obtain the recognition accuracy on the test set.

To carry out the experiments on Caltech 101 and Caltech 256, we follow the common training and testing settings as in [30, 28, 9]. In Caltech 101, 30 images are randomly selected from each category, while 15 are for training and the rest 15 for testing. In Caltech 256, 30 images are randomly selected as training samples and the other 25 images are randomly chosen as testing ones respectively from each category. We report the recognition accuracy on all 102 classes of Caltech 101 averaged over three splits, and on 256 classes of Caltech 256 (excluding the clutter category) for a single split.

4.2 Parameter Selection

Recall that the HSOG descriptor has four parameters: the radius of the region area (R); the number of quantized orientations (N); the number of concentric rings (CR); as well as the number of circles on each ring (C). To evaluate their impacts on the performance of the descriptor, we draw a series of line graphs of the recognition accuracy on Caltech 101 for different R by alternately changing one parameter while fixing the others for N, CR and C. The results are shown in Figure 7.

It can be observed from Figure 7 (a) that the descriptors with 8 orientations perform clearly better than that with 4 and 6; while the one with 10 orientations shows no superiority to that with 8, indicating that 8 orientations are sufficient to describe local image variations. From Figure 7 (b), we can see that the performance keeps improving when the number of concentric rings increases, showing that the

---
[1]Code for SIFT: http://www.vlfeat.org/
[2]Code for DAISY: http://cvlab.epfl.ch/ tola/daisy.html
[3]http://www.robots.ox.ac.uk/~vgg/research/caltech/phog.html

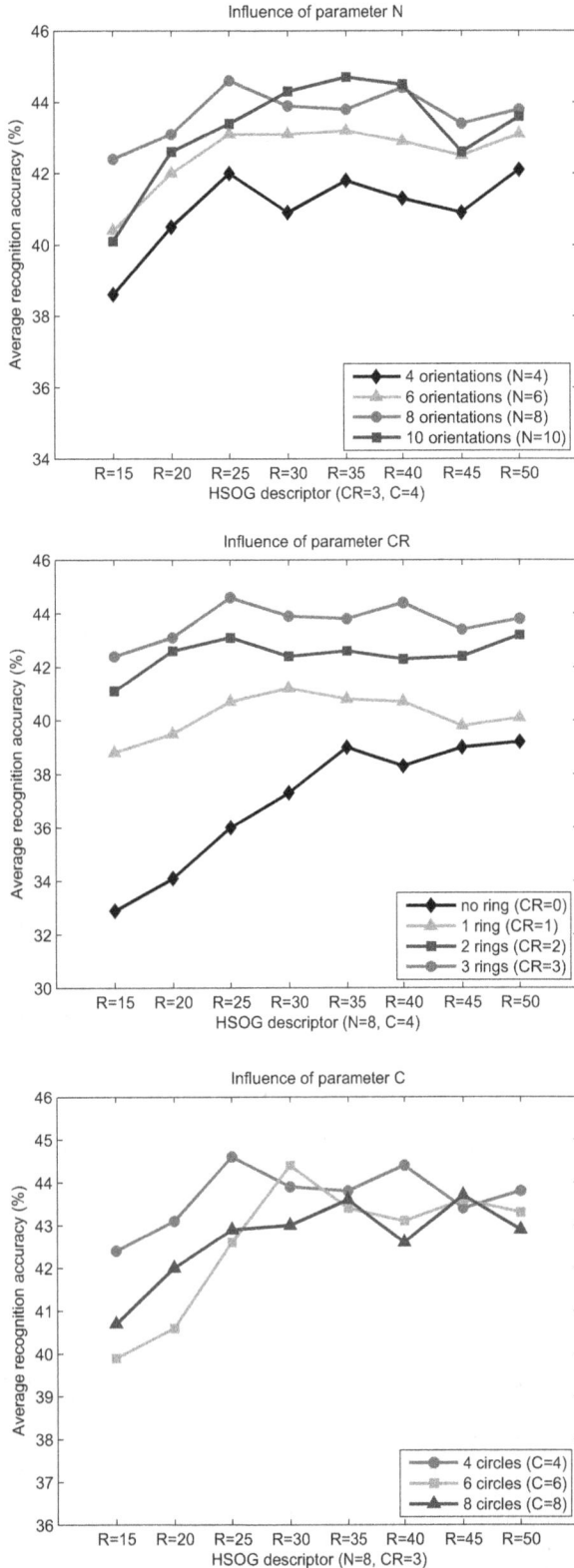

descriptor based on more rings is better, because more neighboring information is included. Fig. 7 (c) shows that raising the number of the circles on each ring does not improve performance, implying that large number of circles on each ring is unnecessary, due to overlapping of adjacent regions.

Another phenomenon from these three figures is that the performance rises continuously with the size of region area R when it is small. After R reaches a certain point (about 25 pixels), the performance improvement is not obvious if R continues increasing. Therefore, we choose the best parameter setting for the proposed HSOG descriptor as follows: $R = 25$, $N = 8$, $CR = 3$, $C = 4$.

4.3 Multi-Scale Extension

To compute the proposed HSOG feature, a local region around keypoints should be fixed. The optimal size of such regions is often decided based on the scale of keypoints given by detectors or chosen manually. In Sec. 4.2, we experimentally evaluated the impacts of different region sizes, and selected a good one. However, a single size of local region is probably not sufficient to characterize the neighborhood of a keypoint. More spatial information can be embedded if the regions of multiple sizes are considered. Therefore, we adopt the multi-scale scheme to further improve the discriminative power of the HSOG descriptor.

We use the late fusion manner to combine different HSOG descriptors from multi-scale regions, since this strategy does not increase the dimensionality of the features, and the similarity scores based on different parameters can be calculated individually, leading to a realistic implementation of parallel computing, e.g. GPU programming, without increasing the time cost. Specifically, for each keypoint p, we choose a certain number of concentric regions around p with increasing sizes. The HSOG descriptor is then extracted in each image region and applied for object categorization independently by the method described in Sec. 4.1. The kernel matrices of different descriptors are combined using the Multiple Kernel Learning (MKL) algorithm [32] to achieve final results.

From the results shown in Table 1, we can see that the performance of HSOG is significantly improved from 44.64% (the best single scale) to 52.55% (4-region fusion) and 54.25% (8-region fusion). This approximate 10% improvement clearly proves the effectiveness of the multi-scale fusion. Furthermore, 8-region fusion performs better than 4-region fusion, indicating that performance could benefit from more regions.

Table 1: Performance comparison of HSOG (multiscale vs. single scale) using different parameter settings on the Caltech 101 dataset.

Type	Performance (%)			
Single-scale	$R = 15$	42.35	$R = 20$	43.07
	$R = 25$	44.64	$R = 30$	43.92
	$R = 35$	43.79	$R = 40$	44.44
	$R = 45$	43.40	$R = 50$	43.79
Multi-scale	$R = 25$ to 40	52.55		
	$R = 15$ to 50	54.25		

Figure 7: Impact of different parameters in HSOG. (a) number of quantized orientations N; (b) number of concentric rings CR; (c) number of circles on each ring C.

4.4 Performance Evaluation and Comparison

We evaluate HSOG with the best parameter setting both on the Caltech 101 and Caltech 256 datasets: $N = 8$; $CR =$

3; $C = 4$, with the dimension of 128. As stated in Sec. 4.1, we compare HSOG with several state-of-the-art ones such as SIFT, DAISY, HOG, CS-LBP, and T3-S4. SIFT adopts the standard configuration of 128-dimension as in [15]. DAISY uses the same parameter setting as HSOG, and its dimension is 104. HOG considers the gradient orientations of 0°-180° into 20 bins with 3 levels of spatial pyramid, resulting in 420-dimension. The parameters of CS-LBP are set according to [10], the 4×4 grid with CS-LBP$_{2,8,0.01}$, resulting in 256-dimension. T3-S4 utilizes second order steerable filters with 8 orientations, and the same parameter setting as HSOG for spatial pooling, resulting in 104-dimension (named T3i-S4-13 in [5]).

Table 2: Performance and consumed time comparison between HSOG and the state-of-the-art descriptors on Caltech 101.

Descriptor	Results (%)	Time (s)
SIFT	40.92	0.316
HOG	37.84	0.253
DAISY	42.48	0.108
CS-LBP	35.62	0.087
T3i-S4-13	39.54	0.279
HSOG (Ss)	**44.64**	0.985
HSOG (Ms)	**52.55** /46.54	-
HSOG (Ss) + SIFT	52.81 /49.54	-
HSOG (Ss) + HOG	**53.86** /51.37	-
HSOG (Ss) + DAISY	51.70 /49.48	-
HSOG (Ss) + CS-LBP	50.92 /48.10	-
HSOG (Ms) + SIFT	56.01 /52.68	-
HSOG (Ms) + HOG	**56.34** /52.48	-
HSOG (Ms) + DAISY	54.58 /51.18	-
HSOG (Ms) + CS-LBP	54.64 /51.50	-

Table 3: Performance comparison between HSOG and the state-of-the-art descriptors on Caltech 256.

Descriptor	Results (%)
SIFT	20.68
HOG	19.55
DAISY	21.61
CS-LBP	20.39
T3i-S4-13	20.28
HSOG (Ss)	**22.36**
HSOG (Ms)	**27.92** /25.52
HSOG (Ss) + SIFT	**30.45** /28.21
HSOG (Ss) + HOG	28.70 /26.39
HSOG (Ss) + DAISY	28.83 /26.61
HSOG (Ss) + CS-LBP	29.67 /27.55
HSOG (Ms) + SIFT	**32.47** /29.68
HSOG (Ms) + HOG	30.52 /28.05
HSOG (Ms) + DAISY	30.33 /27.83
HSOG (Ms) + CS-LBP	32.05 /29.33

* The numbers on the right side of the slash sign are achieved by the combination of T3i-S4-13 and corresponding first order based descriptors.

We can see from Table 2 and 3 that:
• The single-scale HSOG descriptor outperforms existing popular ones on first order gradients, i.e. HOG, CS-LBP, DAISY, and SIFT, and the performance achieved by multi-scale HSOG which combines the ones of four different regions

is significantly increased by over 10%, clearly demonstrating the effectiveness of the HSOG descriptor.
• The HSOG descriptor obviously surpasses T3i-S4-13 using both the single-scale and multi-scale schemes, proving that the proposed map based manner is a better way than steerable filters to encode the 2nd order gradients for object recognition, which is further confirmed by the comparison of their fusion with the first order based descriptors. The classification accuracies of HSOG are on the left side of the slash '/'; while the ones of T3i-S4-13 are on its right side.
• The combination of single scale (Ss) HSOG or multi-scale (Ms) HSOG with SIFT, HOG, DAISY or CS-LBP improves the result again, indicating that HSOG provides complementary information to that given by the existent local image descriptors, and their joint use is a promising way for visual content representation.

At the same time, we calculated the average computation time required on Caltech 101 for each input image (about size of 300×250) by different local descriptors using an Intel Core 2 Duo CPU @ 3.16 GHz with 3GB RAM, and it can be seen that the current version of HSOG is 3 times slower than SIFT. Nevertheless, it should be noted that since each first order OGM and its second order gradients can be computed individually, the current implementation of HSOG can be accelerated by GPU programming as we mentioned in section 4.3, which makes HSOG run approximately N times faster (N is the number of OGMs, e.g. 8 in our case), leading to a consumed time comparable to the existing ones.

5. CONCLUSION

This paper presented a novel local image descriptor for object categorization, making use of the histograms of second order gradients. The accuracies achieved on the Caltech 101 and Caltech 256 datasets clearly demonstrated that the proposed HSOG descriptor possesses a good discriminative power to distinguish different object categories, particularly as embedded with more spatial information provided by the multi-scale strategy. Furthermore, the information given by HSOG proves complementary to that based on the existing ones, such as SIFT, DAISY, HOG, CS-LBP etc. which use the first order gradient information.

Evaluating the proposed HSOG descriptor in the application of local image matching as in [5] would be an interesting perspective for future work.

6. ACKNOWLEDGMENTS

This work is in part supported by the National Basic Research Program of China (No. 2010CB327902), the National Natural Science Foundation of China (NSFC) under Grant No. 61202237, the French research agency ANR through the VideoSense project under the grant 2009 CORD 026 02, and the Fundamental Research Funds for the Central Universities.

7. REFERENCES

[1] T. Ahonen, A. Hadid, and M. Pietikainen. Face recognition with local binary patterns. In *Proc. European Conference on Computer Vision*, 2004.

[2] H. Bay, T. Tuytelaars, and L. van Gool. Surf: speeded up robust features. In *Proc. European Conference on Computer Vision*, 2006.

[3] S. Belongie, J. Malik, and J. Puzicha. Shape matching and object recognition using shape contexts. *IEEE Transactions on Pattern Analysis and Machine Intelligence*, 24(4):509–522, 2002.

[4] A. Bosch, A. Zisserman, and X. Muoz. Scene classification using a hybrid generative/discriminative approach. *IEEE Transactions on Pattern Analysis and Machine Intelligence*, 30(4):712–727, 2008.

[5] M. Brown, H. Gang, and S. Winder. Discriminative learning of local image descriptors. *IEEE Transactions on Pattern Analysis and Machine Intelligence*, 33(1):43–57, 2011.

[6] J. Chen, S. Shan, C. He, G. Zhao, M. Pietikainen, X. Chen, and W. Gao. Wld: A robust local image descriptor. *IEEE Transactions on Pattern Analysis and Machine Intelligence*, 32(9):1705–1720, 2010.

[7] G. Csurka, C. R. Dance, L. Fan, J. Willamowski, and C. Bray. Visual categorization with bags of keypoints. In *Proc. European Conference on Computer Vision Workshop*, 2004.

[8] N. Dalal and B. Triggs. Histograms of oriented gradients for human detection. In *Proc. IEEE Computer Society Conference on Computer Vision and Pattern Recognition*, 2005.

[9] G. Griffin, A. Holub, and P. Perona. Caltech-256 object category dataset. Technical report, California Institute of Technology, 2007.

[10] M. Heikkila, M. Pietikainen, and C. Schmid. Description of interest regions with local binary patterns. *Pattern Recognition*, 42(3):425–436, 2009.

[11] D. Huang, W. Ben Soltana, M. Ardabilian, Y. Wang, and L. Chen. Textured 3d face recognition using biological vision-based facial representation and optimized weighted sum fusion. In *Proc. IEEE Computer Society Conference on Computer Vision and Pattern Recognition Workshops*, pages 1–8, 2011.

[12] Y. Ke and R. Sukthankar. Pca-sift: a more distinctive representation for local image descriptors. In *Proc. IEEE Computer Society Conference on Computer Vision and Pattern Recognition*, 2004.

[13] S. Lazebnik, C. Schmid, and J. Ponce. A sparse texture representation using local affine regions. *IEEE Transactions on Pattern Analysis and Machine Intelligence*, 27(8):1265–1278, 2005.

[14] F.-F. Li, R. Fergus, and P. Perona. Learning generative visual models from few training examples: an incremental bayesian approach tested on 101 object categories. In *Proc. IEEE Computer Society Conference on Computer Vision and Pattern Recognition Workshop*, 2004.

[15] D. Lowe. Distinctive image features from scale invariant key points. *International Journal of Computer Vision*, 60(2):91–110, 2004.

[16] B. Manjunath and W. Ma. Texture features for browsing and retrieval of image data. *IEEE Transactions on Pattern Analysis and Machine Intelligence*, 18(8):837–842, 1996.

[17] K. Mikolajczyk and C. Schmid. Scale and affine invariant interest point detectors. *International Journal of Computer Vision*, 60(1):63–86, 2004.

[18] K. Mikolajczyk and C. Schmid. A performance evaluation of local descriptors. *IEEE Transactions on Pattern Analysis and Machine Intelligence*, 27(10):1615–1630, 2005.

[19] P. Moreels and P. Perona. Evaluation of features detectors and descriptors based on 3d objects. *International Journal of Computer Vision*, 73(3):263–284, 2007.

[20] T. Ojala, M. Pietikainen, and D. Harwood. A comparative study of texture measures with classification based on feature distributions. *Pattern Recognition*, 29(1):51–59, 1996.

[21] T. Ojala, M. Pietikainen, and T. Maenpaa. Multiresolution gray scale and rotation invariant texture analysis with local binary patterns. *IEEE Transactions on Pattern Analysis and Machine Intelligence*, 24(7):971–987, 2002.

[22] T. Randen and J. H. Husoy. Filtering for texture classification: a comparative study. *IEEE Transactions on Pattern Analysis and Machine Intelligence*, 21(4):291–310, 1999.

[23] A. T. Smith and N. E. Scott-Samuel. First-order and second-order signals combine to improve perceptual accuracy. *Journal of the Optical Society of America*, 18(9):2267–2272, 2001.

[24] E. Tola, V. Lepetit, and P. Fua. A fast local descriptor for dense matching. In *Proc. IEEE Computer Society Conference on Computer Vision and Pattern Recognition*, 2008.

[25] K. E. A. van de Sande, T. Gevers, and C. G. M. Snoek. Evaluating color descriptors for object and scene recognition. In *Proc. IEEE Computer Society Conference on Computer Vision and Pattern Recognition*, 2008.

[26] K. E. A. van de Sande, T. Gevers, and C. G. M. Snoek. Evaluating color descriptors for object and scene recognition. *IEEE Transactions on Pattern Analysis and Machine Intelligence*, 32(9):1582–1596, 2010.

[27] J. van de Weijer, T. Gevers, and A. D. Bagdanov. Boosting color saliency in image feature detection. *IEEE Transactions on Pattern Analysis and Machine Intelligence*, 28(1):150–156, 2006.

[28] M. Varma and D. Ray. Learning the discriminative power-invariance trade-off. In *Proc. IEEE International Conference on Computer Vision*, 2007.

[29] P. Viola and M. Jones. Rapid object detection using a boosted cascade of simple features. In *Proc. IEEE Computer Society Conference on Computer Vision and Pattern Recognition*, 2001.

[30] H. Zhang, A. C. Berg, M. Maire, and J. Malik. Svm-knn: discriminative nearest neighbor classification for visual category recognition. In *Proc. IEEE Computer Society Conference on Computer Vision and Pattern Recognition*, 2006.

[31] C. Zhu, C.-E. Bichot, and L. Chen. Visual object recognition using daisy descriptor. In *Proc. IEEE International Conference on Multimedia and Expo*, 2011.

[32] A. Zien and C. S. Ong. Multiclass multiple kernel learning. In *Proc. International Conference on Machine Learning*, 2007.

Towards Automatic Object Annotations from Global Image Labels

Christian X. Ries
Augsburg University
Universitätsstr. 6a
86150 Augsburg
ries@informatik.uni-augsburg.de

Fabian Richter
Augsburg University
Universitätsstr. 6a
86150 Augsburg
richter@informatik.uni-augsburg.de

Rainer Lienhart
Augsburg University
Universitätsstr. 6a
86150 Augsburg
lienhart@informatik.uni-augsburg.de

ABSTRACT

We present an approach for automatically devising object annotations in images. Thus, given a set of images which are known to contain a common object, our goal is to find a bounding box for each image which tightly encloses the object. In contrast to regular object detection, we do not assume any previous manual annotations except for binary global image labels. We first use a discriminative color model for initializing our algorithm by very coarse bounding box estimations. We then narrow down these boxes using visual words computed from HOG features. Finally, we apply an iterative algorithm which trains a SVM model based on bag-of-visual-words histograms. During each iteration, the model is used to find better bounding boxes which can be done efficiently by branch and bound. The new bounding boxes are then used to retrain the model. We evaluate our approach for several different classes of publicly available datasets and show that we obtain promising results.

Categories and Subject Descriptors

H.3.3 [**Information Storage and Retrieval**]: Information Search and Retrieval

Keywords

automatic annotation; visual features; color model; object detection

1. INTRODUCTION

Object detection is an important step towards automatic image understanding. Almost all current object detection frameworks require a training and validation set with object annotations. The most common form of object annotations are labeled rectangular regions. However, in many cases manual object annotations are not (sufficiently) available for training, especially in real world datasets. Labeling

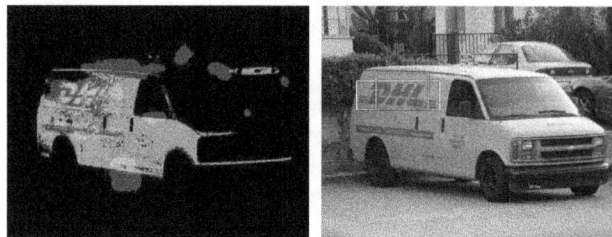

Figure 1: A sample result for an image from the FlickrLogos-32 dataset: The left image shows the result of applying a mined color model (dark green area), a HOG model (dark blue area), and the combination of both (cyan area). The right image shows the final result of our algorithm (green box, white box is the ground truth annotation).

them manually is very tedious. In some cases it is even inacceptable due to the nature of the positive class, e.g. for adult images which are needed for training a filtering algorithm. Contrary to these difficulties, it is relatively easy today to collect positive images for many object classes via the Internet. Our goal is to determine object annotations automatically from such positive image sets.

Therefore, we present an approach to automatically determine object annotations by finding regularities among images in a set of positive images (images showing instances of the desired object class), which are not present in a set of negative images (images without instances of the desired object class). We only assume a single global binary label per image. Our motivation is to provide a preprocessing step for common object detection frameworks, which require object annotations in the form of rectangular bounding boxes.

We use a two-stage algorithm for initializing and then narrowing down bounding boxes within a set of positive images. The initializing step of our algorithm finds regions of interest (ROI) based on a discriminative color model and discriminative visual words computed from gradient features. The second step builds bag-of-visual-words histograms from the initial ROIs and trains a SVM model which is then re-applied to the training set in order to improve the bounding boxes.

Figure 1 shows an example result in order to illustrate our goal and the two stages of our algorithm. In the left image, the initialization of our algorithm by a coarse color model and a gradient feature-based model is shown. The right image shows the improved bounding box found by our algorithm.

Since we do not use manual annotations, we require all instances of the wanted object to have visual features in common, namely color and gradient features. Also, the negative dataset must be a representative background dataset, e.g. randomly downloaded images from the Internet.

We conduct experiments on six classes of the FlickrLogos-32 [10] dataset for which these assumptions hold. Also, we evaluate our approach on the Oxford 17 Flowers dataset [8].

2. RELATED WORK

As mentioned in the introduction, our algorithm consists of two main stages. The first stage is an initialization step which includes building a color model from binary image labels. The color model itself is a color histogram which corresponds to the model suggested by Jones and Rehg [6]. However, since Jones and Rehg construct their histogram from pixel-wise annotations which we do not have, we follow the approach by Ries and Lienhart [9] which only requires weakly labeled data (i.e. binary image labels).

The second stage of our algorithm utilizes bag-of-visual-words histograms as for instance proposed in [3]. These histograms are built from clustered histograms of oriented gradients (HOG) which are recently among the most popular local features. HOG features were first introduced in [1].

Since our algorithm requires rapid exhaustive maximum search within our training images based on visual-word histograms, we propose using the efficient sub window search algorithm (ESS) by Lampert [7]. The ESS algorithm is based on linear support vector machines (SVM) which we implement using SVMLight by Joachims [5].

Our algorithm was inspired by the recent state-of-the art object detection algorithm by Felzenszwalb et al. [4]. Felzenszwalb et al. also try to improve the regions of interest within the positive training images iteratively. However, they aim for correcting inaccuracies among the readily provided manual annotations while we try to find regions of interest from scratch.

3. PROBLEM AND APPROACH

Given a representative set P of images with instances and a set N of images without instances of a given object class, we aim to find a bounding box for each image of the positive dataset P which describes the position of the instance of the object class all images in P have in common. We do not assume any further annotations. However, a few assumptions about the object instances must hold: (1) The objects must have common visual features across the positive images, which cannot be found in the negative set. (2) In the positive images the background must be visually more diverse than the object instances.

For our approach these features are color and image gradients. Thus the objects must have a distinct color scheme and some visual structures in common, which we can catch with gradient-based features. Our negative images may be random images from an image repository as a few noisy images will not affect our approach.

Our goal is to estimate a rectangular bounding box $\hat{r}_i$ for each image i in the positive image set. A bounding box $r_i = (x_i, y_i, w_i, h_i)$ is a rectangle with upper left corner $(x_i, y_i)^T$, width w_i, and height h_i, specified in image coordinates. For

simplicity we only search for the single best rectangle $\hat{r}_i$ in each image i, even if the image shows multiple instances of the wanted object. However, all of the methods we use can be extended to multiple instances per image.

Let r_i be the optimal (i.e. the ground truth) rectangle in image i from set P. Then, our goal is to find an rectangle $\hat{r}_i$ which maximizes the overlap $o(\hat{r}_i, r_i)$ between $\hat{r}_i$ and r_i for all images:

$$o(\hat{r}_i, r_i) = \frac{\hat{r}_i \cap r_i}{\hat{r}_i \cup r_i} \qquad (1)$$

This overlap definition is a common quality measure for bounding boxes and is for instance used in the Pascal VOC challenge [2]. If an image shows multiple object instances, r_i is considered to be the one instance with which our estimation produces the best overlap. Remember that the ground truth r_i is only used for evaluation.

Our approach to this problem consists of two major stages. We first find initial bounding boxes based on color and gradient features. We thus estimate a color model for the wanted object class from image set P and then use it to create a coarse region of interest (ROI) for each image in P. Based on these ROIs, we determine local gradient features which are likely to describe the wanted object the same way we determined positive colors. The bounding boxes are then narrowed down by combining the responses of both models.

Afterwards, we train a linear SVM model on Bag-of-Visual-Words histograms for these bounding boxes. This model is used to further improve the ROIs within our images. For this purpose, we iteratively re-apply the trained SVM to the training data in order to get better training examples from improved bounding boxes for the following iteration. The following sections describe each individual step in detail.

4. INITIALIZATION

The first step of our algorithm is finding initial bounding boxes for each positive training image. We first apply a color model for a coarse first estimation and then use HOG features to improve these estimations.

4.1 Color models from global image labels

We first initialize our regions of interest based on a color model. Thus, we first need to build a model which discriminates positive colors (object colors) from negative colors (background colors). In other words, we need a binary decision function $h_c(\mathbf{p_j}) \in [0, 1]$ which determines for each pixel $\mathbf{p}_j$, if its color c_j belongs to the wanted object.

Usually, such color models are either parametric functions on some color space or histograms of color occurrence frequencies [6] which are then thresholded. We chose the latter variant (with 32^3 bins in YCbCr color space), since color histograms provide a detailed partitioning of the color space at the expense of requiring more storage space. In [9], Ries and Lienhart describe a method for creating a color histogram-based model from global image labels only. Thus, we do not have to violate our assumption about not having manual annotations of regions of interest.

The main idea of [9] is to statistically determine which colors appear regularly in positive images and less regularly in negative images. Let $f_N(c)$ and $f_P(c)$ be the relative numbers of negative images and positive images in which color c occurs. The underlying assumption is that the relative occurrence frequency $f_N(c)$ of a color c in a set of random negative images is representative for any given set of images which do not feature any particular common object. Thus, the occurrence of the respective color in any random background image is assumed to be normally distributed around the relative occurrence $f_N(c)$ observed in the negative images. If a color not only appears as a background color in a set of positive images, it will occur significantly more often as expected and therefore can be considered a positive color.

Thus, if $f_P(c) < f_N(c)$, color c is considered a negative color. Otherwise, the probability $P(f_P(c)|\neg object)$ of c being a negative color if it is observed in $f_P(c)$ of the positive images is compared against a threshold θ_c. The probability $P(f_P(c)|\neg object)$ is a normal distribution over $f_P(c)$ with $\mu = f_N(c)$ and $\sigma^2 = f_N(c)(1 - f_N(c))$. Thus, the larger the difference between $f_N(c)$ and $f_P(c)$ the smaller $P(f_P(c)|\neg object)$.

As suggested in [9], we use the 0.97 quantile for θ_c, i.e. we adaptively select the top colors for each class. This threshold is relatively strict, however, a flood fill algorithm (seeded at pixels where $h(c) = 1$) is used on the positive images in order to extend the color model to chromatically and spatially related colors. Finally, we can use our model to determine for a given pixel $\mathbf{p}_j = (x_j, y_j)^T$ with color c_j within an image if it is a positive pixel:

$$h_c(\mathbf{p}_j) = \begin{cases} 1 & \text{if } P(f_P(c_j)|\neg object) < \theta_c \\ 0 & \text{otherwise} \end{cases} \quad (2)$$

Note that for simplicity, we re-wrote the respective decision function h from [9] by aggregating all constants into θ_c and by making it a function on a pixel $\mathbf{p}_j$.

Now we have a set $X_i = \{\mathbf{p}_j | h_c(\mathbf{p}_j) = 1\}$ of color-based positive pixel locations in a given image i. Based on this set we compute an initial bounding box as described in the following section.

4.2 Finding Bounding Boxes based on positive pixels

After creating an initial model which assigns a binary value to each pixel within an image, we can use the positive pixels to form a bounding box. We assume that the majority of positive pixels is located on the wanted object and thus close to its center while only a few are at a large distance of the object. Therefore, we expect the distribution which generated the positive pixels to be a normal distribution centered at the wanted object's centroid. We thus fit a normal distribution into the two-dimensional distribution of positive pixels as follows.

We first compute the center pixel $\mu_i = (\mu_{i,x}, \mu_{i,y})^T$ of the object as the mean value of all positive pixels X_i and the corresponding standard deviations $\sigma = (\sigma_{i,x}, \sigma_{i,y})^T$. Our bounding box coordinates $\hat{r}_i = (x_i, y_i, w_i, h_i)$ are then

$$\begin{aligned} x_i &= \mu_{i,x} - \sigma_{i,x}(1 + \beta) \\ y_i &= \mu_{i,y} - \sigma_{i,y}(1 + \beta) \\ w_i &= 2\sigma_{i,x}(1 + \beta) \\ h_i &= 2\sigma_{i,y}(1 + \beta) \end{aligned} \quad (3)$$

The factor β is used to enlarge the bounding box. According to an exhaustive parameter sweep, $\beta = 0.6$ is a good choice which we use for all experiments.

If the color model fails and does not find any positive pixels, we use the full image for the following step, since we know the object is present at some location in the image.

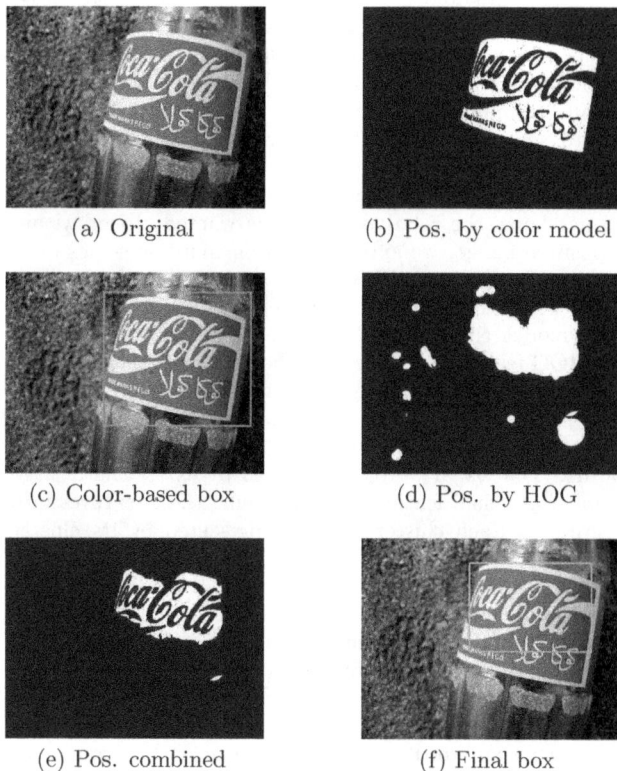

(a) Original

(b) Pos. by color model

(c) Color-based box

(d) Pos. by HOG

(e) Pos. combined

(f) Final box

Figure 2: Example for the initial bounding boxes. (a) shows the original image, (b) the positive pixels found by the color model as white pixels, (c) the resulting bounding box based on color model, (d) the positive pixels determined by HOG features, (e) the combined model (i.e. "AND" between (b) and (d)), (f) final bounding box based on combined model.

Also note that we could use the same method for creating multiple bounding boxes, by fitting a Gaussian mixture with multiple peaks into the two-dimensional distribution of positive pixels using an EM algorithm. In this paper however, we only examine the single-object problem.

While the color model described in the previous section overall correctly identifies most positive pixels and a large portion of negative pixels, it does not yield very accurate regions of interest for multiple reasons. First, positive colors naturally also appear in the background. Second, for some classes (e.g. brand logos) the actual wanted object may be surrounded by a background area of the same color. Also, there are obviously always a few noisy colors, i.e. false positive and false negative colors. Thus, if we use the color model to find a ROI as described in the following section, we usually "overdetect" the object.

In figure 2, an example for the abovementioned problem is shown. The wanted object (the brand logo) is detected together with a larger background area due to false positive detections (see figures 2b and 2c) which are difficult to avoid by a color model. We therefore utilize a second feature which is based on gradients in order to improve our initialization.

4.3 HOG-based models

Since the color model often produces false positive regions, we add another feature to our initialization process. Histograms of oriented gradients (HOG) [1] model edge-based information and are thus complementary to our color model. We use an implementation of HOG which is analogous to the implementation described in [4]. The HOG descriptor is usually computed on a dense grid of cells. We set the cell size to 8 pixels and concatenate groups of four neighboring cells into a single feature vector in order to increase the expressiveness of a single feature as suggested in [1]. Since we do not know the relative size of the wanted object within a positive image, we extract HOG on multiple scales on a scale space pyramid with scaling factor $(2^{-0.5})^{-0.5}$.

We now use the HOG features in the same way as the color model, thus we need to limit the infinite set of potential HOG features to a finite number of identifiable features. This can be done by a Bag-of-Visual-Words (BOW) model.

A BOW model requires a Visual Dictionary which is a finite set of prototypical visual features, the so-called visual words. The visual words are created by extracting a large number of visual features and clustering these features into k groups. Each cluster is then represented by its cluster id, thus the number of different local features is reduced to k. For our experiments, we cluster the HOG features into $k = 1,000$ visual words.

Since we now have a limited number of different features, we can apply the same strategy we use for the initial color-based bounding boxes. We simply count the relative numbers $f_P(w)$ and $f_N(w)$ of positive and negative images with a given visual word w. However, since we are confident, that the color model is very likely to return a region which includes the actual object, we only count images for $f_P(w)$ where w is found inside the color-based bounding box.

We then compute probability $P(f_P(w)|\neg object)$ analogous to $P(f_P(c)|\neg object)$ in section 4.1 and use an equation which is analogous to equation 2 in order to determine if a HOG grid point $\mathbf{p}_l$ is a positive pixel:

$$h'_w(\mathbf{p}_l) = \begin{cases} 1 & \text{if } P(f_P(w_l)|\neg object) < \theta_w \\ 0 & \text{otherwise} \end{cases} \quad (4)$$

where w_l is the visual word observed at grid point $\mathbf{p}_l$. Since from h'_w we do not obtain a decision at every possible pixel location j, we define

$$h_w(\mathbf{p}_j) = \begin{cases} 1 & \text{if } \exists l : h_w(\mathbf{p}_l) = 1 \wedge \parallel \mathbf{p}_l - \mathbf{p}_j \parallel^2 < w_{hog} \\ 0 & \text{otherwise} \end{cases} \quad (5)$$

where w_{hog} is the width of one HOG cell and $\mathbf{p}_l$ is a HOG grid point for which $h_w(\mathbf{p}_l)$ can be determined as described above. This provides us with a binary map of positive and negative pixels analogous to the color model.

In contrast to the color model, however, we must choose a less strict threshold θ_w since we cannot use an additional flood fill algorithm on the HOG features. Besides, the number of different HOG features is far smaller than the number of different colors. Thus, we use an adaptive threshold which depends on the lowest value p_{best} of $P(f_P(w)|\neg object)$ found for any word w. Empirically, we define $\theta_w = 20 \cdot p_{best}$, i.e. we use all visual words within a certain interval defined by the best word with regards to their probability. Note that this strategy ensures that if the visual words are not very characteristic for a given class (i.e. if p_{best} is large) we will select a large number of visual words. Thus, a "bad" set of visual words results in large areas of positive pixels which

are neutral for the combined model explained below and do not produce false negative pixels.

4.4 Combined Initialization

As mentioned above, our assumption is that the wanted objects are characterized by both, distinct colors and distinct gradient features. Therefore, we expect to find positive colors as well as positive visual words on the wanted object. We thus now determine locations, where both are present by applying a decision function which combines color and gradient evidence at each pixel $\mathbf{p}_j$ by

$$h(\mathbf{p}_j) = \begin{cases} 1 & \text{if } h_c(\mathbf{p}_j) \wedge h_w(\mathbf{p}_j) \\ 0 & \text{otherwise} \end{cases} \quad (6)$$

We now use updated pixel sets $X'_i = \{\mathbf{p}_j|h(\mathbf{p}_j) = 1\}$ to create new bounding boxes as described in section 4.2.

In figure 2, all stages of the initialization process are shown. Figures 2b and 2c show the positive pixels determined by color model h_c and the resulting bounding box. Figures 2d and 2e show the positive pixels determined by the hog feature model h_w and the combined model h. Finally, figure 2f shows the bounding box based on the positive pixels of the combined model. Another example for the three components of the initial model is shown in figure 1 (left).

The combined model stil tends to detect false positive regions. We thus try to further improve our bounding boxes with an iterative algorithm explained in the next section.

5. ITERATIVE ALGORITHM

In the previous sections we have explained how we create an initial bounding box for each of our positive images based on occurrence statistics of colors and HOG features. We now want to show that we can use these initial bounding boxes for a discriminative, iterative algorithm in order to further improve the bounding boxes.

5.1 Representation of examples by BOW histograms

At first glance, the nature of the classes we use for our experiments (e.g. brand logos) indicates the usage of rigid templates which are applied (enhanced by deformable geometric layouts) by state-of-the-art object detection algorithms, for instance [4, 11]. Such templates basically consist of given aspect ratios of horizontal and vertical cells.

However, we do not use manual annotations for regions of interest and our initial bounding boxes which are created by the initial models are often highly noisy. Thus, no meaningful single aspect ratio can be selected because we cannot expect to find similar HOG cells at similar relative grid locations. Since the initial bounding boxes often deviate significantly from the actual object position, we also cannot expect to learn a meaningful part representation.

These problems can be sidestepped to some extent (at the expense of a much less specific model) by using BOW histograms. A BOW histogram is an occurrence histogram over the k clusters of our visual dictionary within a ROI. We L1-normalize all BOW histograms in order to obtain relative occurrence frequencies.

Therefore, bounding box $\hat{r}_i$ of image i is represented by a k-dimensional relative word occurrence histogram vector $\mathbf{x}_i$. Thus, it is guaranteed that each bounding box is represented by a vector of the same dimensionality k which is independent of the actual number of cells within the bounding box.

However, we still limit the set of aspect ratios we use to model examples to a reasonable set. At the same time, we only want to have training examples with approximately the same number of HOG cells for comparability. We therefore use a template set T consisting of templates for which we define a constant minimum width and height $c \in \mathbb{Z}$ and a maximum width and height $1.5c$:

$$T = \{(w,h)|w,h \in [c,1.5c] \wedge w \cdot h \approx c \cdot 1.5c\} \quad (7)$$

As a default value, we choose $c = 8$. If we assume that additional information about the absolute size of the images or the usual relative sizes of the wanted objects is available, we can adjust c accordingly. For instance, for a dataset which only consists of images with relatively large objects (e.g. Oxford 17 Flowers) it is reasonable to increase c.

Note that vector $\mathbf{x}_i$ can only be created for a template rectangle which lives on the multi-scale HOG grid. The initial rectangle $\hat{r}_{i,h}$ created by our initial model h on the original image scale, however, lives in image coordinates which usually do not match the HOG grid. Thus, for representing an arbitrary bounding box $\hat{r}_{i,h}$ by a bounding box $\hat{r}_i$ on the multi-scale HOG grid, we find the template rectangle $\hat{r}_i$ in scale space which best matches $\hat{r}_{i,h}$ with regards to overlap. Histogram vector $\mathbf{x}_i$ is then computed from $\hat{r}_i$.

For our negative examples, we randomly sample valid bounding boxes (i.e. rectangles which fit one of our templates on a random scale) from a set of m negative images.

Due to the inaccurate initial bounding boxes, all positive examples include a number of noisy (negative) visual words. We thus use a linear SVM classifier which is to some extent robust to noisy input data. We expect our SVM classifier to learn which visual words are found in most positive examples, while the remaining (non-object) words appear more at random since they originate from background areas.

Another advantage of BOW models and linear SVMs is that they allow applying an efficient algorithm for multiscale subwindow search. We propose using the Efficient Subwindow Search (ESS) algorithm introduced by Lampert et al. [7] which is explained in the following section.

5.2 Training and Detection

In this section we explain the classification method we use and how we efficiently search for the best rectangles within the positive images during each iteration. In the first iteration of our algorithm, we perform SVM training on the bounding boxes found by the initial model. For the remaining iterations, we train our current new model on the best detections found by the previous model.

The iterative algorithm terminates after a given number of iterations or if the bounding boxes do not change anymore between subsequent iterations. For our experiments, we only use two iterations since our linear classifier does not improve beyond a few iterations. The reason for applying the iterative algorithm, however, is mainly to show that our initial models deliver bounding boxes which can be used to train a discriminative classifier in an iterative fashion to further improve the bounding boxes.

5.2.1 Training and Efficient Classification

We have a set of n positive BOW histograms $\mathbf{x}_i, i \in \{0,...,n\}$ and m negative histograms $\mathbf{x}_j, j \in \{0,...,m\}$. We

now need to devise a decision function $f(\mathbf{x}_l)$ which returns a score value for an unknown example $\mathbf{x}_l$ (i.e. the BOW representation of an arbitrary rectangle r_l of image l) indicating either positive or negative classification. Since we need to perform an exhaustive search for the best rectangle in an image, we propose using an efficient search algorithm analogous to the approach by Lampert et al. [7] which requires a linear decision function. Thus, for $f(\mathbf{x}_l)$ we use a linear SVM model which is defined as

$$f(\mathbf{x}_l) = \beta + \sum_k \alpha_k \langle \mathbf{x_1}, \mathbf{x}_k \rangle \quad (8)$$

where $\mathbf{x}_k$ denotes the k-th training example (including positive and negative examples), $\langle \cdot, \cdot \rangle$ is the scalar product, and α_k and β are constant weights and bias which have to be learned. We use the SVM implementation by Joachims [5] for learning the optimal α-weights. Note that for some training examples $\alpha_k = 0$ since they are not selected as support vectors during training. The bias β may be neglected since it does not influence the maximum search explained below.

Each visual word v then obtains an individual weight w_v:

$$w_v = \sum_k y_k \alpha_k x_{k,v} \quad (9)$$

where $x_{k,v}$ is the v-th entry of BOW histogram $\mathbf{x}_k$ (thus the frequency of visual word v in the $k-th$ training example), and $y_k \in \{1,-1\}$ is the respective image's label.

Following Lampert et al., we now re-write the linear SVM function 8 as a function on the respective rectangle r_l, from which $\mathbf{x}_l$ was extracted, as follows

$$f(r_l) = \beta + \sum_{\mathbf{p} \in P_{r_l}} w_{v,\mathbf{p}} \quad (10)$$

Where $\mathbf{p}$ denotes a two-dimensional point on the HOG grid of image l and P_{r_l} is the set of all points enclosed by rectangle r_l. Note that the function $f(r_l)$ is a function which computes the sum over values within a given rectangle and can thus be computed very rapidly for arbitrary rectangles by using integral images.

5.2.2 Branch And Bound

Using integral images on visual word weights as described above, we can evaluate the classification score of an arbitrary rectangle with only four look-ups. Still, we have to evaluate many possible rectangles, since we perform multi-scale search with multiple templates. In order to further speed up the search, we suggest utilizing a branch and bound search strategy, also proposed by Lampert et al. [7]. The main idea is computing a maximum quality (i.e. an upper bound) for a set of potential rectangles in order to be able to dismiss a large number of rectangles at a time instead of evaluating each rectangle individually. Since we use a linear SVM, we can compute the upper bound based on per-point contributions and thus by using integral images as described above.

We first require a bounding function $\hat{f}(R)$ which is defined on a set of rectangles R and has to fulfill two conditions. First, $\hat{f}(R)$ must be an upper bound of $f(r)$. Function $\hat{f}(R)$ is an upper bound if its value is at least as large as the SVM score of the best individual rectangle within R. Second, $\hat{f}(R)$ must converge to $\hat{f}(R) = f(r)$ if R only contains r as a single element. A valid bounding function, for which both conditions hold is

$$\hat{f}(R) = f^+(\cup r) + f^-(\cap r) \quad (11)$$

where $f^+(\cup r)$ are the positive summands of f on the union $\cup r$ of all rectangles in R and $f^-(\cap r)$ are the negative summands of the intersection $\cap r$ of all rectangles in R. It is relatively straightforward to show that $\hat{f}(R)$ is at least as large as the SVM score of the best $r \in R$ and thus that the function is a valid bound. For further details refer to [7].

Now we can efficiently search by branch and bound. Thus, we first split the set of all possible rectangles into two disjoint subsets and compute the bound of both sets. According to their bounding function values, both sets are added to a priority queue (where the set with the highest bound value is on top). Then, we iteratively repeat this process for the current top set of rectangles of the queue. When the top set of rectangles in the priority queue only consists of one single rectangle, we have found the globally optimal rectangle.

5.2.3 Using a predefined aspect ratio

Due to our scaling pyramid, we have much more small candidate rectangles than large ones. Hence our approach tends to prefer small boxes over large ones, since the training algorithm is more likely to select histograms from larger scales as positive examples. Also, squared boxes which only cover a principal part of the object are often preferred, since our algorithm does not explicitly prohibit finding a common partial object instead of the full wanted object.

If we however assume that we roughly know the actual aspect ratio of the wanted object, we can use this information in order to find better fitting bounding boxes based on the ones we found. Thus, we apply an heuristic which only requires defining the object as being "horizontal", "vertical", or "squared" for each class. Based on this information, we first enlarge the bounding box found by our SVM by 10% at each edge and then transform the box into a horizontal or vertical bounding box while preserving the area of the box. For horizontal and vertical boxes we simply use an aspect ratio of $\frac{2}{1}$ or $\frac{1}{2}$, respectively. For the "squared" case we assign a squared bounding box with roughly the same area as the original rectangle.

6. EVALUATION

As mentioned in section 3, our goal is to find an optimal bounding box with regards to overlap as defined in the problem statement in equation 1. Thus, for evaluation we use rectangular ground truth annotations r_i for each positive image i. Given this annotation, we can compute an overlap value for our estimated bounding box $\hat{r}_i$ for each image. This enables us to plot an overlap-recall (OR) curve which shows the relative number of images (the recall) in which the overlap of our estimation surpasses a given value. Since we only aim to find a single best bounding box for each image, only the best overlapping ground truth rectangle is counted for our evaluation.

Each plot shows the result after applying our color model (labeled as "init color"). The results for the combined initial model of color and HOG (equation 6) are shown as "init color AND hog". If we do not find a bounding box within an image, we count overlap 0 for the respective model and image. Note that in a detection scenario, one could simply use the full image as a bounding box in this case in order not to miss the object (given the fact that we already know the image is positive). However, the overlap is then completely independent from the quality of the model and depends from the size of the object only.

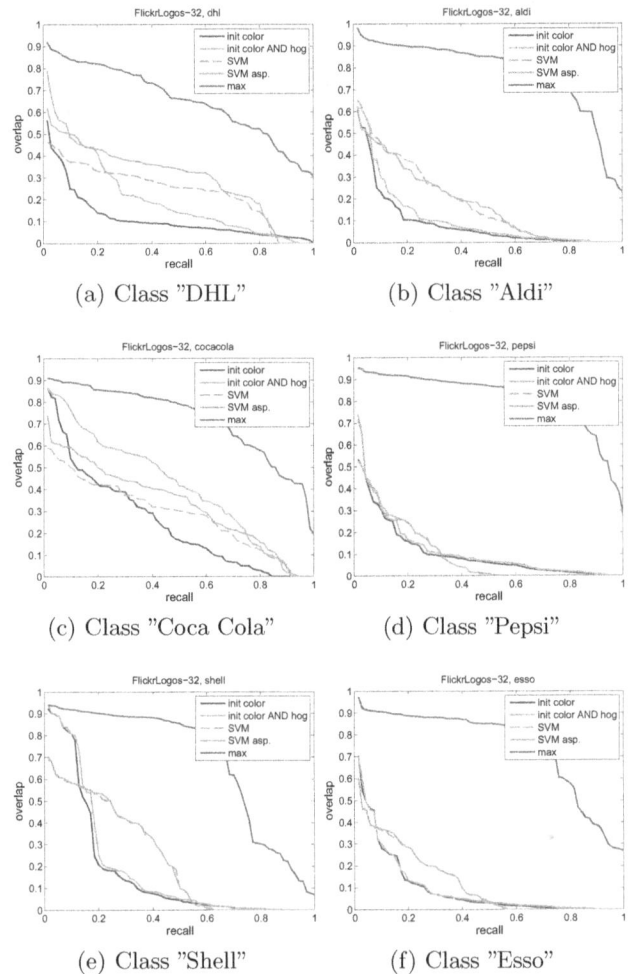

(a) Class "DHL" (b) Class "Aldi"

(c) Class "Coca Cola" (d) Class "Pepsi"

(e) Class "Shell" (f) Class "Esso"

Figure 3: Overlap-recall curves for all six logo classes.

For clarity, we only show the result after the final iteration of our iterative algorithm in our OR curves, labeled as "SVM". Each plot also provides the final result we obtain if we apply our aspect ratio heuristic (see 5.2.3) after each iteration (labeled "SVM asp").

For each class, we also plot the best possible result labeled as "max". This curve shows the best overlap recall curve we could reach if we always found the best overlapping rectangle for each image in the search space. Note that a perfect overlap score of 1.0 is very unlikely to be obtainable since the annotations do not live on the HOG cell grid and also the number of our templates (i.e. the different aspect ratios we use for searching) is limited. Also note that the initial models are not affected by these limitations.

6.1 FlickrLogos-32

We first test our approach on the same six classes from FlickrLogos-32 [10] used in [9]: "DHL", "Aldi", "Shell", "Esso", "Coca Cola", and "Pepsi". These classes are selected in [9] since they all have a distinct color scheme. Each class consists of 70 positive images and FlickrLogos-32 also provides a negative set with 6,000 images which we all use for creating the initial model. For SVM training, we sample 5 random bounding boxes (based on our set of templates) as negative

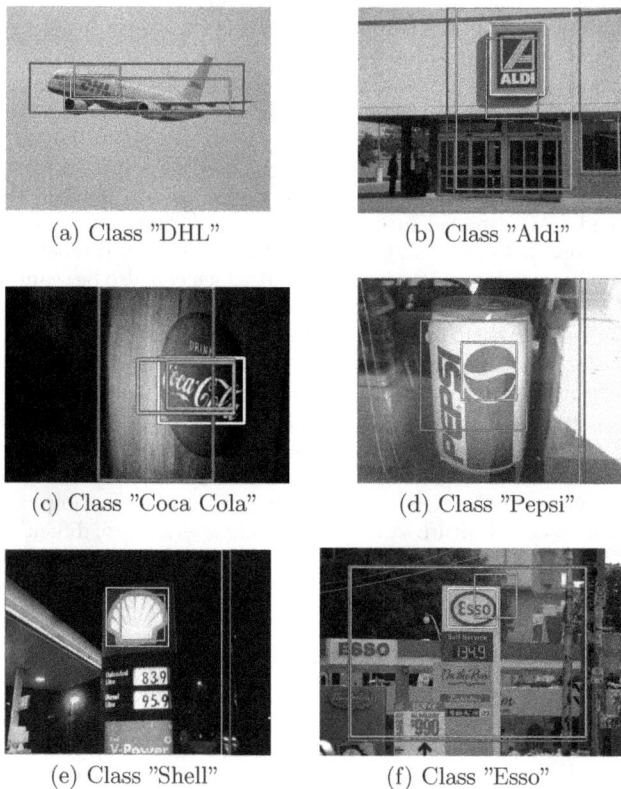

(a) Class "DHL"

(b) Class "Aldi"

(c) Class "Coca Cola"

(d) Class "Pepsi"

(e) Class "Shell"

(f) Class "Esso"

Figure 4: One example result for each logo class. The dark green rectangle indicates the bounding box found by the color model, cyan shows the initial combined model, and light green is the final result of our algorithm. The white rectangle is the respective ground truth annotation which is used to compute the overlap for our OR curves.

examples from each negative image. Since we hence have a very unbalanced dataset, we weight the training examples proportionally by factor m/n for the SVM training where m is the number of negative examples and n is the number of positive examples. In figure 3, we show our resulting OR curves. A few qualitative examples are shown in figure 4.

The combined initial model outperforms the individual color model for classes "DHL", "Aldi", and "Coca Cola". For the remaining classes, the combined model is identical to the color model, thus the initial HOG model is relatively poor and does not contribute to reducing background areas.

Also, our iterative algorithm further improves the rectangles significantly in comparison to the initial bounding box for all logo classes except "Pepsi" and "Coca Cola". Interestingly, for "Coca Cola" our combined initial model performs even better than the iterative algorithm, since the visual words describing the Coca Cola logo are very specific and the initial models are not bound to the HOG grid. The aspect ratio heuristic slightly improves the results for all classes, which are not defined as "squared" ("DHL", "Coca Cola", and "Aldi" are "horizontal" or "vertical").

For the class "Pepsi" our approach fails to improve the overlap beyond the initial models. The Pepsi logo is visually not as characteristic as the other logos with regards to HOG features. It consists of two plain uniformly-colored ar-

eas with relatively soft, curved edges. Therefore the edges (and thus gradients) do not provide much more information than the colors. Also the Pepsi logo comes in two different variants and is often small and rotated in the training data.

Obviously, our results are not even close to perfect detection. However, note that the overlap score we use quickly diminishes with slight deviations from the ground truth rectangle. For instance, the example shown in figure 4b has an overlap of only 0.49 although it is subjectively a reasonable detection. Only examples 4a and 4e slightly surpass an overlap of 0.5, and only 4c (scarcely) reaches 0.8. For this reason, the widely acknowledged Pascal VOC challenge [2] (from which we adopted the overlap criterion) defines an overlap of 0.5 or higher as a correct detection.

Also note that a small overlap indicates that at least the general position of the object may have been found. This observation is confirmed by the fact that estimating the correct aspect ratio improves the results for some classes. Similarly, small overlap values are also produced by strong overdetection, however it is unlikely for our SVM results due to the limited sizes of our templates.

Given the fact that we do not utilize any manual annotations or additional information except for binary image labels and one general aspect ratio, we think that our results are promising and that the approach is worth further research.

6.2 Oxford Flowers

For our second experiment (also analogous to [9]), we use the Oxford 17 Flowers [8] dataset. This dataset provides 17 different flower classes, each of which consists of 80 positive images. Since no negative set is provided, we adopt the strategy of [9] and simply use all 16 remaining classes as negative images for a given positive class.

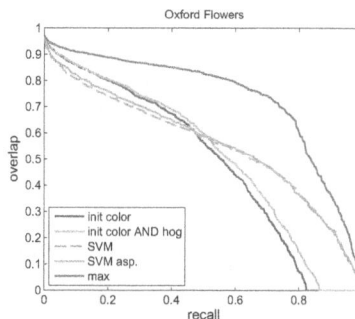

Figure 5: Overlap-recall curve over all (annotated) images from Oxford Flowers dataset.

The Flowers dataset comes with pixel annotations. Since for our evaluation we need ground truth bounding boxes, we use a blob detector on the pixel annotations and fit a rectangle around each blob we find. Note that if two instances of an object overlap in an image, we will hence only obtain one single bounding box surrounding both instances. Also note that the number of annotations per class strongly varies (one class even has none).

Our experiment is conducted analogously to the experiment on FlickrLogos-32. Since the flower images are smaller than the logo images, however, we consider less scales for our multi scale search. Also, the negative set is much smaller, so we double the number of random instances per image.

213

Figure 6: A few example results for the Oxford Flowers dataset. Rectangle colors are analogous to figure 4.

Since we have a large number of classes, we do not plot each class separately but combine them all into one single plot which is shown in figure 5. The results show that we increase the overlap with the ground truth in comparison to the initial model, but there is still room for improvement. Again, the HOG model does not contribute much to the combined model since the positive HOG features on the flower images are naturally less different from the background than for brand logos. Also, for most flower classes color is a stronger feature than gradients.

The results also show that our iterative algorithm is slightly worse than the combined initial model for the top overlaps (on the left of the plot) which is due to the fact that the initial model is not bound to the rigid HOG grid. However, applying the algorithm still improves the overall performance clearly since many objects are detected which are missed by the initial model as the right half of the plot indicates.

Again, we also show a few qualitative results in figure 6. In 6a and 6b our algorithm improves the detection in comparison to the initial models. Figures 6c and 6d show examples where our algorithm fails to improve the bounding box beyond the color model. For 6c, one can see that there are structures in the background which closely resemble the actual respective object. Thus, the HOG model cannot distinguish the background from the foreground while the color model is not affected by this type of noise.

7. CONCLUSION AND FUTURE WORK

In this paper we have suggested an approach to automatically creating rectangular annotations for a given set of images which feature a common object. We only use binary image labels, i.e. we are only given positive and negative sets of images. Our approach then aims to find regions of interest for all positive images.

We propose an algorithm which starts with coarse initial bounding box estimations and iteratively improves these boxes based on a bag-of-visual-words model. During each iteration, the algorithm performs an exhaustive search for the current best bounding box which can be done efficiently by

using a linear SVM model and branch and bound. Based on the bounding boxes found, the model is then re-trained.

Our results are promising given the fact that we do not utilize any previous knowledge except binary image labels (and a coarse estimation of the aspect ratio). Yet there is still much room for improvement which is also shown by our evaluation. Thus, there are many options for future work.

For instance, we think that our initial models can be refined and extended in order to produce better initial estimations. Also, we can enrich our BOW model by geometric information by using a spatial layout which can also be seamlessly integrated into our search algorithm as shown by Lampert et al. [7]. Besides, our detection algorithm is still very basic. Adopting more ideas from state-of-the-art object detection algorithms, such as latent models, may also improve our approach if adjusted to accept noisy initial bounding boxes as an input instead of manual annotations.

Also, our test classes are relatively easy, since the wanted objects are homogenous and mostly rigid, so another important aspect of future work will be dealing with more difficult classes and detecting multiple objects per image.

8. REFERENCES

[1] N. Dalal and B. Triggs. Histograms of oriented gradients for human detection. In *IEEE CVPR05*, volume 1, pages 886–893 vol. 1, Jun. 2005.

[2] M. Everingham, L. Van Gool, C. K. I. Williams, J. Winn, and A. Zisserman. The pascal visual object classes challenge. *IJCV*, 88(2):303–338, Jun. 2010.

[3] L. Fei-Fei and P. Perona. A bayesian hierarchical model for learning natural scene categories. In *IEEE CVPR05.*, volume 2, pages 524–531 vol. 2, Jun. 2005.

[4] P. Felzenszwalb, R. Girshick, D. McAllester, and D. Ramanan. Object detection with discriminatively trained part-based models. *IEEE PAMI*, 32(9):1627–1645, Sep. 2010.

[5] T. Joachims. Advances in kernel methods. chapter Making large-scale support vector machine learning practical, pages 169–184. MIT Press, Cambridge, MA, USA, 1999.

[6] M. J. Jones and J. M. Rehg. Statistical color models with application to skin detection. *IJCV*, 46(1):81–96, Jan. 2002.

[7] C. Lampert, M. Blaschko, and T. Hofmann. Efficient subwindow search: A branch and bound framework for object localization. *IEEE PAMI*, 31(12):2129–2142, Dec. 2009.

[8] M.-E. Nilsback and A. Zisserman. A visual vocabulary for flower classification. In *IEEE CVPR06*, volume 2, pages 1447–1454, 2006.

[9] C. X. Ries and R. Lienhart. Deriving a discriminative color model for a given object class from weakly labeled training data. In *ACM ICMR12*, pages 44:1–44:8, New York, NY, USA, 2012. ACM.

[10] S. Romberg, L. G. Pueyo, R. Lienhart, and R. van Zwol. Scalable logo recognition in real-world images. In *ACM ICMR11*, pages 25:1–25:8, New York, NY, USA, 2011. ACM.

[11] L. Zhu, Y. Chen, A. L. Yuille, and W. T. Freeman. Latent hierarchical structural learning for object detection. In *IEEE CVPR 2010*, pages 1062–1069, 2010.

A Naïve Mid-level Concept-based Fusion Approach to Violence Detection in Hollywood Movies

Bogdan Ionescu
LAPI, University Politehnica of
Bucharest
061071 Bucharest, Romania.
bionescu@imag.pub.ro

Jan Schlüter
Austrian Research Institute for
Artificial Intelligence
A-1010 Vienna, Austria.
jan.schlueter@ofai.at

Ionuţ Mironică
LAPI, University Politehnica of
Bucharest
061071 Bucharest, Romania.
imironica@imag.pub.ro

Markus Schedl
Department of Computational
Perception, JKU
A-4040 Linz, Austria.
markus.schedl@jku.at

ABSTRACT

In this paper we approach the issue of violence detection in typical Hollywood productions. Given the high variability in appearance of violent scenes in movies, training a classifier to predict violent frames directly from visual or/and auditory features seems rather difficult. Instead, we propose a different perspective that relies on fusing mid-level concept predictions that are inferred from low-level features. This is achieved by employing a bank of multi-layer perceptron classifiers featuring a dropout training scheme. Experimental validation conducted in the context of the Violent Scenes Detection task of the MediaEval 2012 Multimedia Benchmark Evaluation show the potential of this approach that ranked first among 34 other submissions in terms of precision and F_1-score.

Categories and Subject Descriptors

I.2.10 [**Artificial Intelligence**]: Vision and Scene Understanding; I.5.3 [**Pattern Recognition**]: Classification—*violence detection*.

Keywords

violence detection, multimodal video description, multi-layer perceptron, Hollywood movies.

1. INTRODUCTION

Video broadcasting footage (e.g., YouTube, Dailymotion) is now the largest broadband traffic category on the Internet, comprising more than a quarter of total traffic (source CISCO systems, http://www.cisco.com). In this context, one of the emerging research areas is the automatic filtering of video contents. The objective is to select appropriate

content for different user profiles or audiences. A particular case is the filtering of affect content related to violence, for instance for banning children from accessing it or for automatic video content rating.

Defining the term "violence" is not an easy task, as this notion remains subjective and thus dependent on people [1]. Definitions range from literal ones such as "actions or words which are intended to hurt people"[1] or "physical violence or accident resulting in human injury or pain" [2] to more technical film-making related where this notion is defined by specific visual-auditory indicators, e.g., high-speed movements or fast-paced music [3].

In this paper we address the problem of violence detection in the context of typical Hollywood movies. Our approach relies on fusing mid-level concept predictions made using multi-layer perceptron classifiers. The final goal is to automatically localize the occurrence of violence within a video.

The remainder of the article is organized as follows: Section 2 presents a detailed overview of the current state-of-the-art of the research in violent scene detection. Section 3 introduces the proposed approach, while Section 4 details the classification scheme involved. Experimental validation is presented in Section 5. Section 6 concludes the paper.

2. PREVIOUS WORK

. Due to the complexity of the research problem, starting with the formulation of the task (i.e., defining violence) to the inference of highly semantic concepts out of low-level information, the problem of violence detection in videos has been marginally studied in the literature. Some of the most representative approaches are reviewed in the sequel.

A related domain is the *detection of affective content* in videos, which refers to the intensity (i.e., arousal) and type (i.e., valence) of emotion that are expected to arise in the user while watching a certain video [4]. Existing methods attempt to map low-level features (e.g., low-level audio-visual features, users' physiological signals) to high-level emotions [5]; or to mid-level features as in the approach in [6] that studies the interrelationship of violent game events and the underlying neurophysiologic basis (brain activity) of a player.

---

[1]Source: Cambridge dictionary,
http://dictionary.cambridge.org

If we refer to violence as an expected emotion in videos, affect-related features may be applicable to represent the violence concept [7].

Another related domain is *action recognition*, which focuses on detecting *human violence in real-world scenarios*. An example is the method in [8] that proposes an in-depth hierarchical approach for detecting distinct violent events involving two people, e.g., fist fighting, hitting with objects, kicking. The information used consists of computing the motion trajectory of image structures (acceleration measure vector and its jerk). The framework is preliminarily validated on 15 short-time sequences including around 40 violent scenes. Another example is the approach in [9] that aims to detect instances of aggressive human behavior in public environments. The authors use a Dynamic Bayesian Network (DBN) as a fusion mechanism to aggregate aggression scene indicators, e.g., "scream", "passing train" or "articulation energy". Evaluation is carried out using 13 clips featuring various scenarios, such as "aggression toward a vends machine" or "supporters harassing a passenger". The method reports an accuracy score close to 80%.

The use of Bag-of-Visual-Words (BoVW) statistical models has also been exploited. For instance, [10] addresses fight detection using BoVW along with Space-Time Interest Points (STIP) and Motion Scale-Invariant Feature Transform (MoSIFT) features. In addition, for the purpose of evaluation and to foster research on violence detection, the authors attempt to introduce a standard testing data set consisting of 1,000 clips of action scenes from hockey games. Ground truth is provided at frame level (as "fight" or "nonfight" labeling). Highest reported detection accuracy is near 90%. A similar experiment is the one in [11] that uses BoVW with local spatio-temporal features. Experimental tests show that for this scenario motion patterns tend to provide better performance than spatio-visual descriptors. Tests are conducted on sports and surveillance videos.

A broader category of approaches focus on a more general framework, such as detecting *video shots/segments with violent content* that may be considered disturbing for different categories of viewers. These methods are typically addressing video TV broadcasting materials, such as Hollywood entertainment movies. One of the early approaches in this direction is the one in [12], where the violent events are located using multiple audio-visual signatures, e.g., description of motion activity, blood and flame detection, violence/nonviolence classification of the soundtrack and characterization of sound effects. Only qualitative validation is reported. Other examples include the following: [3] exploits shot length, motion activity, loudness, speech, light, and music. Features are combined using a modified semi-supervised learning scheme that uses Semi-Supervised Cross Feature Learning (SCFL). The method is preliminarily evaluated using 4 Hollywood movies, yielding a top F_1-score of 85%; [13] combines audio-visual features (e.g., shot length, speech, music ratios, motion intensity) to select representative shots in typical action movies with the objective of producing automatic video trailers. Content classification is performed with Support Vector Machines (SVMs); [14] uses various audio features (e.g., spectrogram, chroma, energy entropy, Mel-Frequency Cepstral Coefficients (MFCC)) and visual descriptors (e.g., average motion, motion orientation variance, measure of the motion of people or faces in the scene). Modalities are combined by employing a meta-classification

architecture that classifies mid-term video segments as "violent" or "non-violent". Experimental validation is performed on 10 movies and highest F_1-score is up to 58%; [15] proposes a violent shot detector that uses a modified probabilistic Latent Semantic Analysis (pLSA) to detect violence from the auditory content while the visual information is exploited via motion, flame, explosion and blood analysis. Final integration is achieved using a co-training scheme (typically used when dealing with small amounts of training data and large amounts of unlabeled data). Experimental validation is conducted on 5 movies showing an average F_1-score of 88% (however there is no information on the ground truth used). More recently, approaches also consider the benefits of temporal integration of features and late fusion integration schemes, e.g., [16].

Although most of the approaches are multimodal, there are some attempts to exploit the benefits of single modalities, e.g., [18] uses Gaussian Mixture Models (GMM) and Hidden Markov Models (HMM) for modeling audio events over time series. For experimentation, authors model the presence of gunplay and car racing scenes with audio events such as "gunshot", "explosion", "engine", "helicopter flying", "car braking", and "cheers". Validation is performed on a very restrained data set (excerpts of 5 minutes extracted from 5 movies) leading to average F_1-scores of up to 90%; [19] uses face, blood, and motion information to determine whether an action scene has violent content or not. The specificity of the approach is in addressing more semantics-bearing scene structure of video rather than simple shots.

In general, most of the existing approaches focus more or less on engineering content descriptors that may be able to highlight the specificity of violent contents or on the detection of concepts associated with it. Unfortunately, there is a lack of a unified evaluation framework. Almost all of the existing approaches are tested either on very limited data sets (just a few excerpts), on "closed" data or on specific domains (e.g., only sports). Another problem lies in the violence related ground truth that reflects different understandings of the concept. It tends to vary dramatically from method to method and to be adapted to each of the data set (proof is the high disparity of reported results and also the very high accuracy in some cases). This hinders reproducibility of the results and renders impossible performance comparison.

In the context of movie violence - which is the subject of this work - there is a sustained effort made by the community of the Violent Scenes Detection task of the MediaEval Multimedia Benchmark Evaluation [2] to constitute a reference evaluation framework for validating violence detection methods. It proposes a standardized data set together with a detailed annotation ground truth of several audio-visual concepts related to violence [2] (see Section 5).

In this paper we propose a different perspective that exploits the use of mid-level concepts in a multiple neural network fusing scheme. The proposed approach goes beyond the current state-of-the-art along these dimensions:

• by addressing a highly complex scenario where violence is considered to be any scene involving human injury or pain;

• thanks to the fusion of mid-level concept predictions, the method is feature-independent in the sense that it does not require the design of adapted features;

• violence is predicted at frame level which facilitates de-

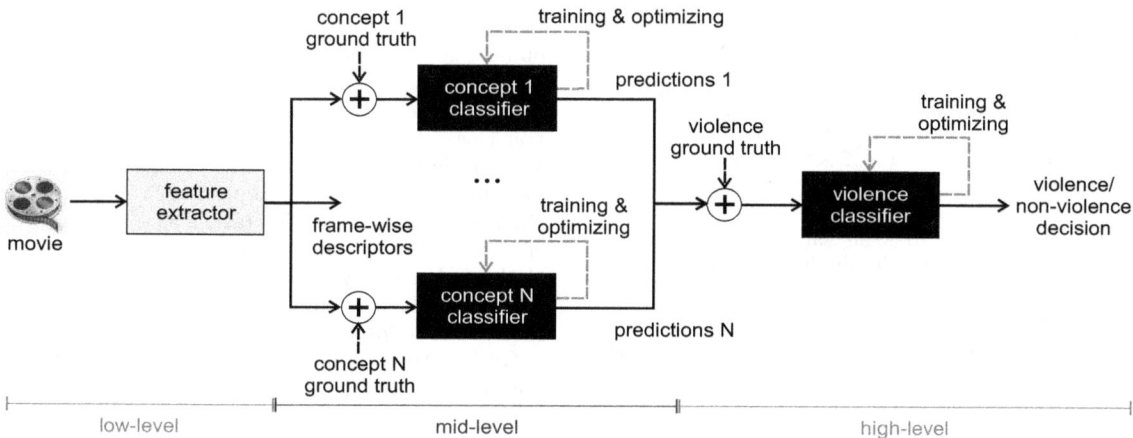

Figure 1: Method diagram (semantic level increases from left to right).

tecting segments of arbitrary length, not only fixed length (e.g., shots);

• evaluation is carried out on a standard data set [2] making the results both relevant and reproducible.

3. PROPOSED APPROACH

Instead of focusing on engineering a best content description approach suitable for this task, as most of the existing approaches do, we propose a novel perspective. Given the high variability in appearance of violent scenes in movies and the low amount of training data that is usually available, training a classifier to predict violent frames directly from visual and auditory features seems rather ineffective.

We propose instead to use high-level concept ground-truth obtained from manual annotation to infer mid-level concepts as a stepping stone towards the final goal. Predicting mid-level concepts from low-level features should be more feasible than directly predicting all forms of violence (highly semantic). Also, predicting violence from mid-level concepts should be easier than using directly the low-level content features.

A diagram of the proposed method is shown in Figure 1. First, we perform feature extraction. Features are extracted at frame level (see Section 5.2). The resulting data is then fed into a multi-classifier framework that operates in two steps. The first step consists of *training* the system using ground truth data. Once we captured data characteristics we may *classify* unseen video frames into one of the two categories: "violence" and "non-violence". Consecutively, violence frames are aggregated to segments. Each of the two steps is presented in the sequel.

3.1 Concept and violence training

To train the system we use ground truth data at two levels: ground truth related to concepts that are usually present in the violence scenes, such as presence of "fire", presence of "gunshots", or "gory" scenes (more information is presented in Section 5) and ground truth related to the actual violence segments. We used the data set provided in [2].

The mid-level concept detection consists of a bank of classifiers that are trained to respond to each of the target violence-related concepts. At this level, the response of

the classifier is optimized for best performance. Tests are repeated for different parameter setups until the classifier yields the highest accuracy. Each classifier state is then saved. With this step, initial features are therefore transformed into concept predictions (real valued between $[0;1]$).

The high-level concept detection is ensured by a final classifier that is fed with the previous concept predictions and acts as a final fusion scheme. The output of the classifier is thresholded to achieve the labeling of each frame as "violent" or "non-violent" (yes/no decision). As in the previous case, we use the violence ground truth to tune the classifier to its optimal results (e.g., setting the best threshold). The classifier state is again conserved.

3.2 Violence classification

Equipped with a violence frame predictor, we may proceed to label new unseen video sequences. Based on the previous classifier states, new frames are now labeled as "violent" or "non-violent". Depending on the final usage, aggregation into segments can be performed at two levels: arbitrary length segments and video shot segments. The *segment-level* tagging forms segments of consecutive frames our predictor tagged as violent or non-violent and the *shot-level* tagging uses preliminary shot boundary detection [20].

For both approaches, each segment (whether obtained at the level of frames or shots) is assigned a violence score corresponding to the highest predictor output for any frame within the segment. The segments are then tagged as "violent" or "non-violent" depending on whether their violence score exceeds the optimal threshold found previously in the training of the violence classifier.

4. NEURAL NETWORK CLASSIFIER

To choose the right classification scheme for this particular fusion task, we conducted several preliminary experimental tests using a broad variety of classifiers, from functional-based (e.g., Support Vector Machines), decision trees to neural networks. Most of the classifiers failed in providing relevant results when coping with high amount of input data, i.e., labeling of individual frames rather than video segments (e.g., a movie has around 160,000 frames and the training data consist of million frames). The inherent parallel architecture of neural networks fitted well these requirements, in

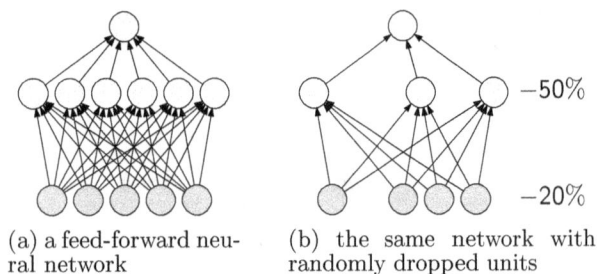

(a) a feed-forward neu-   (b) the same network with
ral network   randomly dropped units

Figure 2: Illustrating random dropouts of network units: 2a shows the full classifier, 2b is one of the possible versions trained on a single example.

particular the use of multi-layer perceptrons. Therefore, for the concept and violence classifiers (see Figure 1) we employ a multi-layer perceptron with a single hidden layer of 512 logistic sigmoid units and as many output units as required for the respective concept. Some of the concepts from [2] consist of independent tags, for instance "fights" encompasses the five tags "1vs1", "default", "distant attack", "large" and "small" (in which case we use five independent output units).

Networks are trained by gradient descent on the cross-entropy error with backpropagation [26], using a recent idea by Hinton et al. [25] to improve generalization: For each presented training case, a fraction of input and hidden units is omitted from the network and the remaining weights are scaled up to compensate. Figure 2 visualizes this for a small network, with 20% of input units and 50% of hidden units "dropped out". The set of dropped units is chosen at random for each presentation of a training case, such that many different combinations of units will be trained during an epoch.

This helps generalization in the following way: By randomly omitting units from the network, a higher-level unit cannot rely on all lower-level units being present and thus cannot adapt to very specific combinations of a few parent units only. Instead, it is driven to find activation patterns of a larger group of correlated units, such that dropping a fraction of them does not hinder recognizing the pattern. For example, when recognizing written digits, a network trained without dropouts may find that three particular pixels are enough to tell apart ones and sevens on the training data. A network trained with input dropouts is forced to take into account several correlated pixels per hidden unit and will learn more robust features resembling strokes.

Hinton et al. [25] showed that features learned with dropouts generalize better, improving test set performance on three very different machine learning tasks. This encouraged us to try their idea for our data as well, and indeed we observed an improvement of up to 5%-points F_1-score in all our experiments. As an additional benefit, a network trained with dropouts does not severely overfit to the training data, eliminating the need for early stopping on a validation set to regularize training.

5. EXPERIMENTAL RESULTS

The experimental validation of our approach was carried out in the context of the 2012 MediaEval Benchmarking Initiative for Multimedia Evaluation, Affect task: Violent Scenes Detection [2]. It proposes a corpus of 18 Hollywood movies of different genres, from extremely violent movies to

movies without violence. Movies are divided into a development set, consisting of 15 movies: "Armageddon", "Billy Elliot", "Eragon", "Harry Potter 5", "I am Legend", "Leon", "Midnight Express", "Pirates of the Caribbean 1", "Reservoir Dogs", "Saving Private Ryan", "The Sixth Sense", "The Wicker Man", "Kill Bill 1", "The Bourne Identity", and "The Wizard of Oz" (total duration of 27h 58min, 26,108 video shots and violence duration ratio 9.39%); and a test set consisting of 3 movies - "Dead Poets Society", "Fight Club", and "Independence Day" (total duration 6h 44min, 6,570 video shots and violence duration ratio 4.92%). Overall the entire data set contains 1,819 violence segments [2].

Ground truth is provided at two levels. Frames are annotated according to 10 violence related high-level concepts, namely: "presence of blood", "fights", "presence of fire", "presence of guns", "presence of cold weapons", "car chases" and "gory scenes" (for the video modality); "presence of screams", "gunshots" and "explosions" (for the audio modality) [1]; and frame segments are labeled as "violent" or "non-violent". Ground truth was created by 9 human assessors.

For evaluation, we use classic precision and recall:

$$precision = \frac{TP}{TP+FP}, \quad recall = \frac{TP}{TP+FN} \quad (1)$$

where TP stands for true positives (good detections), FP are the false positives (false detections) and FN the false negatives (the misdetections). To have a global measure of performance, we also report F_1-scores:

$$F_1\text{-}score = 2 \cdot \frac{precision \cdot recall}{precision + recall} \quad (2)$$

Values are averaged over all experiments.

5.1 Parameter tuning and preproceesing

The proposed approach involves the choice of several parameters and preprocessing steps.

In what concerns the multi-layer perceptron, we follow the dropout scheme in [25, Sec. A.1] with minor modifications: Weights are initialized to all zeroes, mini-batches are 900 samples, the learning rate starts at 1.0, momentum is increased from 0.45 to 0.9 between epochs 10 and 20, and we train for 100 epochs only. We use a single hidden layer of 512 units. These settings worked well in preliminary experiments on 5 movies.

To avoid multiple scale values for the various content features, the input data of the concept predictors is normalized by subtracting the mean and dividing by the standard deviation of each input dimension. Also, as the concept predictors are highly likely to yield noisy outputs, we employ a sliding median filter for temporal smoothing of the predictions. Trying a selection of filter lengths, we end up smoothing over 125 frames, i.e. 5 seconds.

5.2 Video descriptors

We experimented with several video description approaches that proved to perform well in various video and audio classification scenarios [17, 22, 23, 27]. Given the specificity of the task, we derive *audio*, *color*, *feature description* and *temporal structure* information. Descriptors are extracted at frame level as follows:

- **audio** (196 dimensions): we use a general-purpose set of audio descriptors: *Linear Predictive Coefficients*

(LPCs), *Line Spectral Pairs* (LSPs), *MFCCs, Zero-Crossing Rate* (ZCR), and *spectral centroid, flux, rolloff,* and *kurtosis*, augmented with the variance of each feature over a window of 0.8 s centered at the current frame [24, 27];

- **color** (11 dimensions): to describe global color contents, we use the Color Naming Histogram proposed in [22]. It maps colors to 11 universal color names: "black", "blue", "brown", "grey", "green", "orange", "pink", "purple", "red", "white", and "yellow";

- **features** (81 values): we use a 81-dimensional Histogram of Oriented Gradients (HoG) [23].

- **temporal structure** (single dimension): to account for temporal information we use a measure of visual activity. We use the cut detector in [21] that measures visual discontinuity by means of difference between color histograms of consecutive frames. To account for a broader range of significant visual changes, but still rejecting small variations, we lower the threshold used for cut detection. Then, for each frame we determine the number of detections in a certain time window centered at the current frame (e.g., for violence detection good performance is obtained with 2 s windows). High values of this measure will account for important visual changes that are typically related to action.

5.3 Cross-validation training results

In this experiment we aim to train and evaluate the performance of the neural network classifiers according to concept and violence ground truth. We used the development set of 15 movies. Training and evaluation are performed using a leave-one-movie-out cross-validation approach.

5.3.1 Concept prediction

First, we train 10 multi-layer perceptrons to predict each of the violence-related high-level concepts. The results of the cross-validation are presented in Table 1. For each concept, we list the input features (visual, auditory, or both) and average precision, recall and F_1-score at the binarization threshold giving the best F_1-score (real valued outputs of the perceptrons are thresholded to achieve yes/no decisions).

Results show that the highest precision and recall are up to 24% and 100%, respectively, while the highest F_1-score is of 26%. Detection of fire performs best, presumably because it is always accompanied by prominent yellow tones captured well by the visual features. The purely visual concepts (first four rows) obtain high F_1-score only because they are so rare that setting a low threshold gives a high recall without hurting precision. Manually inspecting some concept predictions shows that *fire* and *explosions* are accurately detected, *screams* and *gunshots* are mostly correct (although singing is frequently mistaken for screaming, and accentuated fist hits in fights are often mistaken for gunshots).

5.3.2 Violence prediction

Given the previous set of concept predictors of different qualities, we proceed to train the frame-wise violence predictor. Using the concept ground truth as a substitute for concept predictions will likely yield poor results - the system would learn, for example, to associate blood with violence,

Table 1: Evaluation of concept predictions.

concept	visual	audio	precision	recall	F_1-score
blood	✓		7%	100%	12%
coldarms	✓		11%	100%	19%
firearms	✓		17%	45%	24%
gore	✓		5%	33%	9%
gunshots		✓	10%	14%	12%
screams		✓	8%	19%	12%
carchase	✓	✓	1%	8%	1%
explosions	✓	✓	8%	17%	11%
fights	✓	✓	14%	29%	19%
fire	✓	✓	24%	30%	26%

then provide inaccurate violence predictions on the test set where we only have highly inaccurate blood predictions. Instead, we train on the real-valued concept predictor outputs obtained during the cross-validation described in Section 5.3.1. This allows the system to learn which predictions to trust and which to ignore.

The violence predictor achieves precision and recall values of 28.29% and 37.64%, respectively and an F_1-score of 32.3% (results are obtained for the optimal binarization threshold). The results are very promising considering the difficulty of the task and the diversity of movies. The fact that we obtain better performance compared to the detection of individual concepts may be due to the fact that violent scenes often involve the occurrence of several concepts, not only one, which may compensate for some low concept detection performance. A comparison with other techniques is presented in the following section.

5.4 MediaEval 2012 results

In the final experiment we present a comparison of the performance of our violence predictor in the context of the 2012 MediaEval Benchmarking Initiative for Multimedia Evaluation, Affect task: Violent Scenes Detection [2].

In this task, participants were provided with the development data set (15 movies) for training their approaches while the official evaluation was carried out on 3 test movies: "Dead Poets Society" (34 violent scenes), "Fight Club" (310 violent scenes) and "Independence Day" (371 violence scenes) - a total of 715 violence scenes (ground truth for the test set was released after the competition). A total number of 8 teams participated providing 36 runs. Evaluation was conducted both at video shot and segment level (arbitrary length). The results are discussed in the sequel.

5.4.1 Shot-level results

In this experiment, video shots (shot segmentation was provided by organizers [2, 1]) are tagged as being "violent" or "non-violent". Frame-to-shot aggregation is carried out as presented in Section 3.2. Performance assessment is conducted on a per-shot basis. To highlight the contribution of the concepts, our approach is assessed with different feature combinations (see Table 3). A summary of the best team runs is presented in Table 2 (results are presented in decreasing order of F_1-score values).

The use of mid-level concept predictions and multi-layer perceptron (see ARF-(c)) ranked first and achieved the highest F_1-score of 49.94%, that is an improvement of more than 6 percentage points over the other teams' best runs, i.e.,

Table 2: Violence shot-level detection results at MediaEval 2012 [2].

team	descriptors	modality	method	precision	recall	F_1-score
ARF-(c)	concepts	audio-visual	**proposed**	46.14%	54.40%	49.94%
ARF-(a)	audio	audio	**proposed**	46.97%	45.59%	46.27%
ARF-(av)	audio, color, HoG, temporal	audio-visual	**proposed**	32.81%	67.69%	44.58%
ShanghaiHongkong [30]	trajectory, SIFT, STIP, MFCC	audio-visual	temp. smoothing + SVM with χ^2 kernel	41.43%	46.29%	43.73%
ARF-(avc) [34]	audio, color, HoG, temporal & concepts	audio-visual	**proposed**	31.24%	66.15%	42.44%
TEC [33]	TF-IDF B-o-AW [16], audio, color	audio-visual	fusion SVM with HIK and χ^2 kernel & Bayes Net. & Naive Bayes	31.46%	55.52%	40.16%
TUM [29]	energy & spectral audio	audio	SVM linear kernel	40.39%	32.00%	35.73%
ARF-(v)	color, HoG, temporal	visual	**proposed**	25.04%	61.95%	35.67%
LIG [31]	color, texture, SIFT, B-o-AW of MFCC	audio-visual	hierarch. fusion of SVMs & k-NNs with conceptual feedback	26.31%	42.09%	32.38%
TUB [7]	audio, B-o-AW MFCC, motion	audio-visual	SVM with RBF kernel	19.00%	62.65%	29.71%
DYNI [32]	MS-LBP texture [35]	visual	SVM with linear kernel	15.55%	63.07%	24.95%
NII [28]	concept learned from texture & color	visual	SVM with RBF kernel	11.40%	89.93%	20.24%

Notations: SIFT - Scale Invariant Features Transform, STIP - Spatial-Temporal Interest Points, MFCC - Mel-Frequency Cepstral Coefficients, SVM - Support Vector Machines, TF-IDF - Term Frequency-Inverse Document Frequency, B-o-AW - Bag-of-Audio-Words, HIK - Histogram Intersection Kernel, k-NN - k Nearest Neighbors, RBF - Radial Basis Function, MS-LBP - Multi-Scale Local Binary Pattern.

Table 3: Feature combinations.

run	description
ARF-(c)	use of only mid-level concept predictions;
ARF-(a)	use of only audio descriptors (the violence classifier is trained directly on the audio features);
ARF-(v)	use of only visual features;
ARF-(ac)	use of only audio-visual features;
ARF-(avc)	use of all concept and audio-visual features (the violence classifier is trained using the fusion of concept predictions and features).

team ShanghaiHongkong [30], F_1-score of 43.73%. For our approach, the lowest discriminative power is provided by using only the visual descriptors (see ARF-(v)), where the F_1-score is only 35.65%. Compared to visual features, audio features seem to show better descriptive power, providing the second best F_1-score of 46.27%. The combination of descriptors (early fusion) tends to reduce their efficiency and yields lower performance than the use of concepts alone, e.g., audio-visual (see ARF-(av)) yields an F_1-score of 44.58%, while audio-visual-concepts (see ARF-(avc)) 42.44%.

Another observation is that, despite the use of general purpose descriptors (see Section 5.2), the representation of feature information via mid-level concepts allows better performance than other, more elaborate content description approaches or classification, such as the use of SIFTs, B-o-AW of MFCC or motion information.

Figure 3 details the precision-recall curves for our approach. One may observe that the use of concepts alone (red line) provides significantly higher recall than the sole use of audio-visual features or the combination of all for a precision of 25% and above.

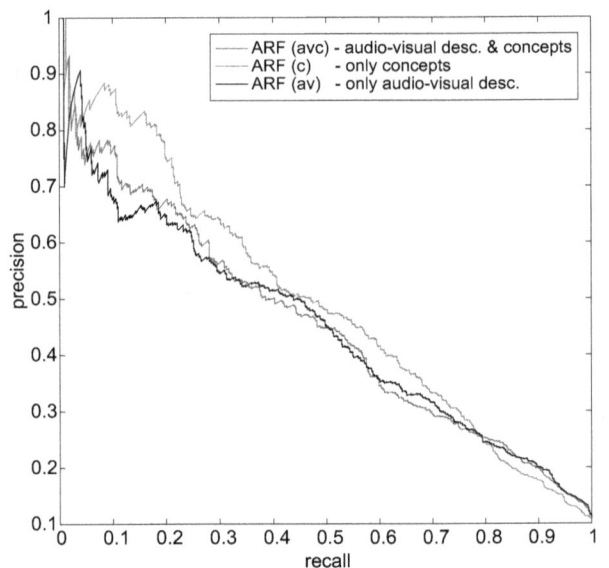

Figure 3: Precision-recall curves for the proposed approach.

5.4.2 Arbitrary segment-level results

The final experiment is conducted at segment level. Video segments of arbitrary length are tagged as "violent" or "non-violent". Frame-to-segment integration is carried out as presented in Section 3.2. The performance assessment in this case is conducted on a per-unit-of-time basis.

Using the mid-level concepts, we achieve average precision and recall values of 42.21% and 40.38%, respectively, while the F_1-score amounts to 41.27%. This yields a miss rate

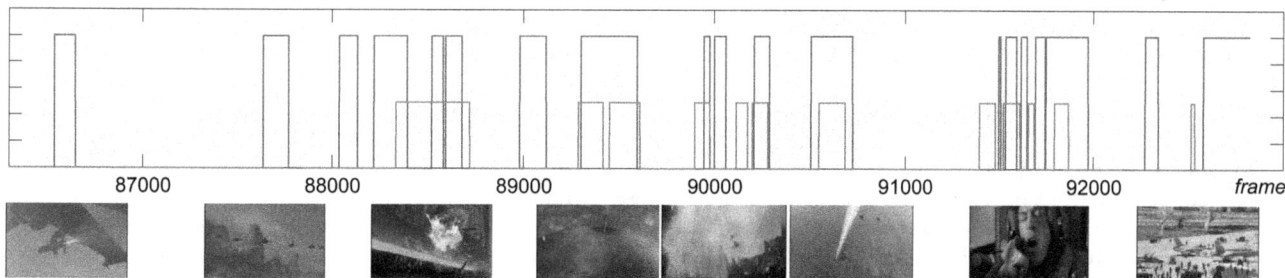

Figure 4: Examples of violent segment detection in movie "Independence Day" (the oX axis is the time axis, the values on oY axis are arbitrary, ground truth is depicted in red while the detected segments in blue).

(at time level) of 50.69% and a very low false alarm rate of only 6%. These results are also very promising considering the difficulty of detecting precisely the exact time interval of violent scenes, but also the subjectivity of the human assessment (reflected in the ground truth). Comparison with other approaches was not possible in this case as all other teams provided only shot-level detection.

5.4.3 Violence detection examples

Figure 4 illustrates an example of violent segments detected by our approach in the movie "Independence Day". For visualization purposes, some of the segments are depicted with a small vignette of a representative frame.

In general, the method performed very well on the movie segments related to action (e.g., involving explosions, firearms, fire, screams) and tends to be less efficient for segments where violence is encoded in the meaning of human actions (e.g., fist fights or car chases). Examples of false detections are due to visual effects that share similar audiovisual signatures with the violence-related concepts. Common examples include accentuated fist hits, loud sounds or the presence of fire not related to violence (e.g., see the rocket launch or the fighter flight formation in Figure 4, first two images). Misdetection is in general caused by limited accuracy of the concept predictors (see last image in Figure 4, where some local explosions filmed from a distance have been missed).

6. CONCLUSIONS

We presented a naive approach to the issue of violence detection in Hollywood movies. Instead of using content descriptors to learn directly how to predict violence, as most of the existing approaches do, the proposed approach relies on an intermediate step consisting of predicting mid-level violence concepts. Predicting mid-level concepts from low-level features seems to be more feasible than directly predicting all forms of violence. Predicting violence from mid-level concepts proves to be much easier than using directly the low-level content features. Content classification is performed with a multi-layer perceptron whose parallel architecture fits well the target of labeling individual video frames. The approach is naive in the sense of its simplicity. Nevertheless, its efficiency in predicting arbitrary length violence segments is remarkable. The proposed approach ranked first in the context of the 2012 Affect Task: Violent Scenes Detection at MediaEval Multimedia Benchmark (out of 36 total submissions). However, the main limitation

of the method is its dependence on a detailed annotation of violent concepts, inheriting at some level its human subjectivity. Future improvements will include exploring the use of other information sources, such as text (e.g., subtitles that are usually provided with movie DVDs).

7. ACKNOWLEDGMENTS

This work was supported by the Austrian Science Fund (FWF): Z159 and P22856-N23, and by the research grant EXCEL POSDRU/89/1.5/S/62557. We acknowledge the 2012 Affect Task: Violent Scenes Detection of the MediaEval Multimedia Benchmark http://www.multimediaeval.org for providing the test data set that has been supported, in part, by the Quaero Program http://www.quaero.org. We also acknowledge the violence annotations, shot detections and key frames made available by Technicolor [1].

8. REFERENCES

[1] Technicolor, http://www.technicolor.com.
[2] C.-H. Demarty, C. Penet, G. Gravier, M. Soleymani, "The MediaEval 2012 Affect Task: Violent Scenes Detection in Hollywood Movies", Working Notes Proc. of the MediaEval 2012 Workshop [17], http://ceur-ws.org/Vol-927/mediaeval2012_submission_3.pdf.
[3] Y. Gong, W. Wang, S. Jiang, Q. Huang, W. Gao, "Detecting Violent Scenes in Movies by Auditory and Visual Cues", 9th Pacific Rim Conf. on Multimedia: Advances in Multimedia Information Processing, pp. 317-326. Springer-Verlag, 2008.
[4] A. Hanjalic, L. Xu, "Affective Video Content Representation and Modeling", IEEE Trans. on Multimedia, pp. 143-154, 2005.
[5] M. Soleymani, G. Chanel, J. J. Kierkels, T. Pun. "Affective Characterization of Movie Scenes based on Multimedia Content Analysis and User's Physiological Emotional Responses", IEEE Int. Symp. on Multimedia, Berkeley, California, USA, 2008.
[6] M. Mühling, R. Ewerth, T. Stadelmann, B. Freisleben, R. Weber, K. Mathiak, "Semantic Video Analysis for Psychological Research on Violence in Computer Games", 6th ACM Int. Conf. on Image and Video Retrieval, pp. 611–618, Netherlands, 2007.
[7] E. Açar, S. Albayrak, "DAI Lab at MediaEval 2012 Affect Task: The Detection of Violent Scenes using Affective Features", Working Notes Proc. of the

MediaEval 2012 Workshop [17], http://ceur-ws.org/Vol-927/mediaeval2012_submission_33.pdf.

[8] A. Datta, M. Shah, N. Da Vitoria Lobo, "Person-on-Person Violence Detection in Video Data", Int. Conf. on Pattern Recognition, 1, p. 10433, Washington, DC, USA, 2002.

[9] W. Zajdel, J. Krijnders, T. Andringa, D. Gavrila, "CASSANDRA: Audio-Video Sensor Fusion for Aggression Detection", IEEE Conf. on Advanced Video and Signal Based Surveillance, pp. 200-205, London, UK, 2007.

[10] E. Bermejo, O. Deniz, G. Bueno, and R. Sukthankar, "Violence Detection in Video using Computer Vision Techniques", Int. Conf. on Computer Analysis of Images and Patterns, LNCS 6855, pp. 332-339, 2011.

[11] Fillipe D. M. de Souza, Guillermo C. Chávezy, Eduardo A. do Valle Jr., Arnaldo de A. Araújo, "Violence Detection in Video Using Spatio-Temporal Features", 23rd SIBGRAPI Conf. on Graphics, Patterns and Images, pp. 224-230, 2010.

[12] J. Nam, M. Alghoniemy, A.H. Tewfik, "Audio-Visual Content-Based Violent Scene Characterization", IEEE Int. Conf. on Image Processing, 1, pp. 353 - 357, 1998.

[13] A.F. Smeaton, B. Lehane, N.E. O'Connor, C. Brady, G. Craig, "Automatically Selecting Shots for Action Movie Trailers", 8th ACM Int. Workshop on Multimedia Information Retrieval, pp. 231Ű-238, 2006.

[14] T. Giannakopoulos, A. Makris, D. Kosmopoulos, S. Perantonis, S. Theodoridis, "Audio-Visual Fusion for Detecting Violent Scenes in Videos", Artificial Intelligence: Theories, Models and Applications, LNCS 6040, pp 91-100, 2010.

[15] J. Lin, W. Wang, "Weakly-Supervised Violence Detection in Movies with Audio and Video based Co-training", 10th Pacific Rim Conf. on Multimedia: Advances in Multimedia Information Processing, pp. 930-935, Springer-Verlag, 2009.

[16] C. Penet, C.-H. Demarty, G. Gravier, P. Gros, "Multimodal Information Fusion and Temporal Integration for Violence Detection in Movies", IEEE Int. Conf. on Acoustics, Speech, and Signal Processing, Kyoto, 2012.

[17] MediaEval Benchmarking Initiative for Multimedia Evaluation, http://www.multimediaeval.org/.

[18] W.-H. Cheng, W.-T. Chu, J.-L. Wu, "Semantic Context Detection based on Hierarchical Audio Models", ACM Int. Workshop on Multimedia Information Retrieval, pp. 109 - 115, 2003.

[19] L.-H. Chen, H.-W. Hsu, L.-Y. Wang, C.-W. Su, "Violence Detection in Movies", 8th Int. Conf. Computer Graphics, Imaging and Visualization, pp.119-124, 2011.

[20] A. Hanjalic, "Shot-Boundary Detection: Unraveled and Resolved?", IEEE Trans. on Circuits and Systems for Video Technology, 12(2), pp. 90 - 105, 2002.

[21] B. Ionescu, V. Buzuloiu, P. Lambert, D. Coquin, "Improved Cut Detection for the Segmentation of Animation Movies", IEEE Int. Conf. on Acoustics, Speech, and Signal Processing, France, 2006.

[22] J. Van de Weijer, C. Schmid, J. Verbeek, D. Larlus, "Learning color names for real-world applications",

IEEE Trans. on Image Processing, 18(7), pp. 1512-1523, 2009.

[23] O. Ludwig, D. Delgado, V. Goncalves, U. Nunes, "Trainable Classifier-Fusion Schemes: An Application To Pedestrian Detection", IEEE Int. Conf. On Intelligent Transportation Systems, 1, pp. 432-437, St. Louis, 2009.

[24] Yaafe core features, http://yaafe.sourceforge.net/.

[25] G. Hinton, N. Srivastava, A. Krizhevsky, I. Sutskever, R. Salakhutdinov, "Improving Neural Networks by Preventing Co-Adaptation of Feature Detectors", arXiv.org, http://arxiv.org/abs/1207.0580, 2012.

[26] D. E. Rumelhart, G. E. Hinton, R. J. Williams, "Learning Representations by Back-Propagating Errors", Nature, 323, pp. 533–536, 1986.

[27] C. Liu, L. Xie, H. Meng, "Classification of Music and Speech in Mandarin News Broadcasts", Int. Conf. on Man-Machine Speech Communication, China, 2007.

[28] V. Lam, D.-D. Le, S.-P. Le, Shin'ichi Satoh, D.A. Duong, "NII Japan at MediaEval 2012 Violent Scenes Detection Affect Task", Working Notes Proc. of the MediaEval 2012 Workshop [17], http://ceur-ws.org/Vol-927/mediaeval2012_submission_21.pdf.

[29] F. Eyben, F. Weninger, N. Lehment, G. Rigoll, B. Schuller, "Violent Scenes Detection with Large, Brute-forced Acoustic and Visual Feature Sets", Working Notes Proc. of the MediaEval 2012 Workshop [17], http://ceur-ws.org/Vol-927/mediaeval2012_submission_25.pdf.

[30] Y.-G. Jiang, Q. Dai, C.C. Tan, X. Xue, C.-W. Ngo, "The Shanghai-Hongkong Team at MediaEval2012: Violent Scene Detection Using Trajectory-based Features", Working Notes Proc. of the MediaEval 2012 Workshop [17], http://ceur-ws.org/Vol-927/mediaeval2012_submission_28.pdf.

[31] N. Derbas, F. Thollard, B. Safadi, G. Quénot, "LIG at MediaEval 2012 Affect Task: use of a Generic Method", Working Notes Proc. of the MediaEval 2012 Workshop [17], http://ceur-ws.org/Vol-927/mediaeval2012_submission_39.pdf.

[32] V. Martin, H. Glotin, S. Paris, X. Halkias, J.-M. Prevot, "Violence Detection in Video by Large Scale Multi-Scale Local Binary Pattern Dynamics", Working Notes Proc. of the MediaEval 2012 Workshop [17], http://ceur-ws.org/Vol-927/mediaeval2012_submission_43.pdf.

[33] C. Penet, C.-H. Demarty, M. Soleymani, G. Gravier, P. Gros , "Technicolor/INRIA/Imperial College London at the MediaEval 2012 Violent Scene Detection Task", Working Notes Proc. of the MediaEval 2012 Workshop [17], http://ceur-ws.org/Vol-927/mediaeval2012_submission_26.pdf.

[34] J. Schlüter, B. Ionescu, I. Mironică, M. Schedl , "ARF @ MediaEval 2012: An Uninformed Approach to Violence Detection in Hollywood Movies", Working Notes Proc. of the MediaEval 2012 Workshop [17], http://ceur-ws.org/Vol-927/mediaeval2012_submission_36.pdf.

[35] S. Paris, H. Glotin, "Pyramidal Multi-level Features for the Robot Vision @ICPR 2010 Challenge", 20th Int. Conf. on Pattern Recognition, pp. 2949 - 2952, Marseille, France, 2010.

An Information Retrieval Approach to Identifying Infrequent Events in Surveillance Video

Suzanne Little[*]
Iveel Jargalsaikhan
Cem Direkoglu
Noel E. O'Connor
Alan F. Smeaton
CLARITY, Centre for Sensor
Web Technologies
Dublin City University, Ireland

Kathy Clawson
Hao Li
Jun Liu
Bryan Scotney
Hui Wang
, University of Ulster
Belfast, United Kingdom

Marcos Nieto
Vicomtech-IK4
San Sebastian, Spain

ABSTRACT

This paper presents work on integrating multiple computer vision-based approaches to surveillance video analysis to support user retrieval of video segments showing human activities. Applied computer vision using real-world surveillance video data is an extremely challenging research problem, independently of any information retrieval (IR) issues. Here we describe the issues faced in developing both generic and specific analysis tools and how they were integrated for use in the new TRECVid interactive surveillance event detection task. We present an interaction paradigm and discuss the outcomes from face-to-face end user trials and the resulting feedback on the system from both professionals, who manage surveillance video, and computer vision or machine learning experts. We propose an information retrieval approach to finding events in surveillance video rather than solely relying on traditional annotation using specifically trained classifiers.

Categories and Subject Descriptors

H.1.1 [**Systems and Information Theory**]: Information Theory; I.2.10 [**Vision and Scene Understanding**]: Video analysis

Keywords

surveillance event detection, video analysis

1. VIDEO SURVEILLANCE EVENT DETECTION

Efficiently and reliably finding complex events of interest in video surveillance footage presents several challenges. These include: the volume of data to be processed, especially in relation to the frequency of event occurrence; the low resolution and high noise of the video including activity occlusion and multiple co-occurring

---

[*]Contact author: suzanne.little@dcu.ie

events; the low inter-class variance between many events and, finally, users' misleading expectations of the computer's ability to accurately and confidently identify people, objects and activities. In this paper we present the outcomes from our experiences in applying multiple computer-vision based approaches to support interactive user retrieval of video segments from surveillance video with feedback from end users including professionals from major companies in transport and event stadium surveillance and security.

By surveillance video we are generally considering fixed CCTV cameras placed for security observation purposes where video archives will be accessed post-event for investigative or judicial reasons. Events of interest may include (but are not limited to): unauthorised access, accident, anti-social behaviour, abandoned luggage, unauthorised photography/filming, sabotage or equipment tampering, etc. Such complex events can be identified with varying but generally low levels of success using computer vision techniques. Simpler analysis tasks include person detection, gesture modelling and object detection that can then be used by semantic classifiers for the more complex events.

In our research we aim to develop a standards-based video archive search platform that allows authorised users to perform semantic queries over various remote and non-interoperable video archives of CCTV footage from geographically diverse locations. At the core of the semantic search interface is the output of algorithms for person/object detection and tracking, activity detection and scenario recognition. The project also includes research into interoperable standards for surveillance video, discussion of the legal, ethical and privacy issues and how to effectively leverage cloud computing infrastructures in these applications.

To facilitate these aims, we took part in the TRECVid Interactive Surveillance Event Detection task 2012 [16]. TRECVid is an annual benchmarking exercise sponsored by the US National Institute of Standards and Technology (NIST) with the aim of stimulating video information retrieval research and improving the performance of systems using large, challenging, realistic and noisy datasets for real world problems. Surveillance Event Detection using CCTV footage has been a TRECVid task for the previous five years but, due in part to the lack of significant improvements in detection rates, was changed this year to include an interactive element. Previously, a set of test (unannotated) videos would be processed by one or more event classifiers and the ordered list of possible matches would be evaluated to determine the system's performance. This year a human computer interface could be used to find matching video segments in the test set with a 25 minute search time limit per user per event class.

Our approach was to combine individual methods for video analysis and annotation and provide a dashboard style search interface that enabled the user to view results for various algorithms and filter them by factors such as confidence, level of motion, camera, number of people etc. The use of a search interface changes the problem from a pure annotation task, where the objective for each individual classifier is to maximise precision and recall for one or more events over all videos, to an information retrieval task, where fuzzy, difficult to predict factors such as user understanding and patience, interface aesthetics, minimising false alarms and optimising for high precision in the top ranked results have the greatest influence on the success of the system.

This paper describes the process of bringing our independent algorithms together, the analysis of the surveillance video characteristics and the discussions we held with professional end user partners to establish the challenges to be faced in developing systems to support usable, practical search systems in this field. The next section analyses the characteristics of the TRECVid dataset, describes user profiles from our interactive retrieval evaluations and discusses the implications of the specific characteristics of surveillance event detection, as listed in this section, on an information retrieval (IR) user model. Section 3 presents, at a high level, the main computer vision approaches that were applied to analyse and identify video segments to show to the user and some preliminary evaluation scores relating to their performance. Finally the conclusions and future work from our collaboration are presented.

2. TRECVID INTERACTIVE EVALUATIONS

2.1 Dataset characteristics

As listed in the first section, there are three main challenges associated with visual events in surveillance videos: low event frequency, noisy and low-resolution data and difficult to describe events. The video dataset used in the TRECVid task comprises 145 hours of footage, captured over a number of days from five fixed cameras in an airport, that has been previously annotated with ten events (PersonRuns, Pointing, CellToEar, ObjectPut, Embrace, People-Meet, PeopleSplitUp, ElevatorNoEntry, OpposingFlow, TakePicture) of which three (ElevatorNoEntry, OpposingFlow, TakePicture) are not currently used. 100 hours is used for training and 45 is reserved for testing of which 15 hours were used this year. The video is provided in MPEG-2 at 25 frames per second, 720×576 frame resolution. For our submissions we used two cameras (CAM1, CAM3) and focussed on three events – ObjectPut, PersonRuns and Pointing. These events were performed by a single person, had a reasonable number of training examples in the chosen videos and were gesture-based.

Table 1 summarises the frequency and duration of events in the training dataset (100 hours) calculated from the manual annotations provided in ViPeR format [7] by the TRECVid organisers. Median duration is given as there are a few very long segments in the provided annotations that we think are incorrect and therefore overly inflate the mean.

Many approaches to event detection that use motion information apply a sliding temporal window to segment the continuous CCTV footage [1, 17]. The size of this window is critical; note median ObjectPut duration is 10 frames compared with PersonRuns at 67 frames or PeopleSplitUp at 167 frames. The most common configuration is a sliding window size of 15 frames with steps of between 4 and 10 frames. Subsampling of the videos either by resizing the frames to a lower resolution or by only extracting features from a subset of frames (e.g., every second frame) is also often applied to reduce the computational effort. The cumulative effect of these de-

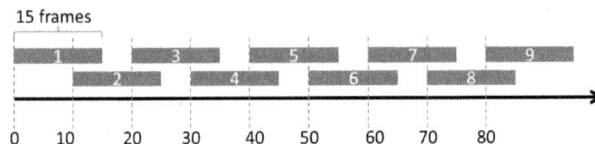

Figure 1: Illustration of temporal sliding window over continuous video footage

cisions sets the sampling density of the video. For example, Figure 1 illustrates a sliding temporal window of size 15 frames with a step size of 10 frames. If applied over 1 minute of video (at 25 fps) containing 1500 frames this would produce 120 video segments (15 frames in length) to be analysed.

60% of ObjectPut and 32% of Pointing events take place in less than 15 frames. PersonRuns events have much longer durations with less than half a percent (4 samples) under this threshold. In contrast, events with duration greater than that of the sliding window will be described by a sequence of partial events spanning multiple windows that need to be classified and fused to identify the event's start and end points. Smoothing the degree of varation across a sequence of windows by using a smaller step size would potentially improve the accuracy but would increase the computational load.

Subsampling of videos, by selecting every 2nd or 3rd frame, can also improve computational efficiency, especially where expensive descriptors are being calculated. However, if the duration of events is less than 3 frames (and Table 1 shows some are) important information is lost. Some of our approaches (described in section 3) used every 2nd frame for person tracking or to calculate motion trajectories for example as it improved responsiveness. Of the three events we investigated, over 4% of the ObjectPut events in the training set had a duration of 2 frames or less while for Pointing and PersonRuns it was just under 1%. This means that some relevant event segments will never be detected or shown to the user – reducing the maximum possible recall for the final system. Large window sizes are also likely to mute the important features for an event of very short duration.

The spatial location and relative size of the person involved in the event is also useful to consider. The region of interest (ROI) where the actual event activity takes place is not provided in the original annotations. We performed manual annotations on a subset of training videos from cameras 1 and 3 for ObjectPut and Pointing events on every second frame annotated with the event. Figure 2 shows four example heat maps indicating the normalised frequency of each frame pixel being part of the event. These graphics show clear hot spots for some events and differences in the location of events within the same camera area. Section 3.2 also discusses how this prior probability can be exploited to improve classifier confidence.

Figure 3 shows the pixel area of the event regions as a percentage of the total frame size (720×576) based on the approximate region of interest dimensions from our manual annotations. The area of the region of interest for these events is rarely more than 12% of the total frame. While there is certainly some connection to the camera configuration – note approximate similarity of ROI sizes between the different events on CAM1 but less so on CAM3 (a wider viewing area) – it's clear that these are difficult even for people to visually identify due to the typically short duration and the small activity area. The heat maps show that while there are some spots where the events most frequently occur, there's still variation

Table 1: Characteristics of the 7 main events in TRECVid Dev08/Eval08 training video dataset

Event	Frequency (#)			Duration (# frames (secs))			
	All	CAM1	CAM3	CAM1		CAM3	
				median	min/max	median	min/max
CellToEar	828	40	284	16.5 (0.66s)	5/429	17 (0.68s)	1/123
Embrace	940	27	629	66 (2.64s)	27/636	71 (2.84s)	1/2034
ObjectPut	**3177**	**706**	**903**	**11 (0.44s)**	**1/625**	**9 (0.36s)**	**1/419**
PeopleMeet	2719	813	906	65 (2.6s)	1/1176	106.5 (4.26s)	1/3236
PeopleSplitUp	1571	762	235	179 (7.16s)	1/7169	135 (5.4s)	1/4287
PersonRuns	**673**	**25**	**218**	**54 (2.16s)**	**14/268**	**67.5 (2.7s)**	**18/276**
Pointing	**4097**	**926**	**1106**	**24 (0.96s)**	**1/2717**	**21.5 (0.86s)**	**1/360**

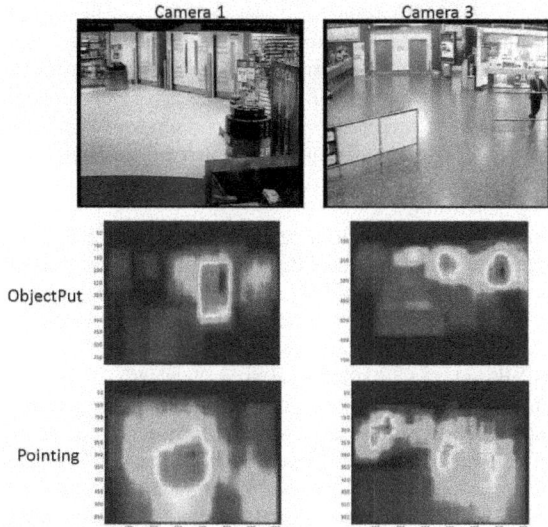

Figure 2: Heat maps showing frequency of pixel involvement in event

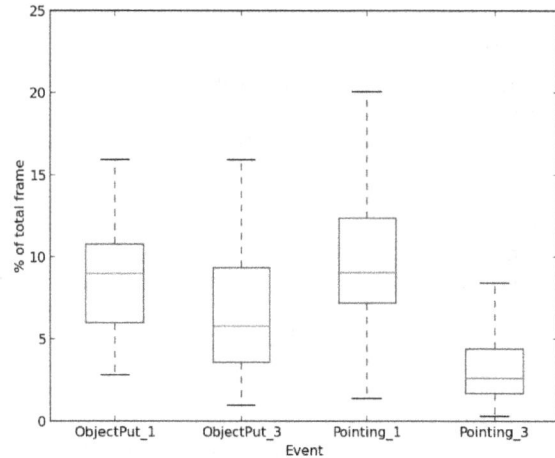

Figure 3: Event region size per camera as % of total viewing frame

both within and between events and cameras. The challenge is assisting the viewer to rapidly and accurately scan suggested matches. More analysis over all events and cameras is required to determine any significant trends.

Event frequency for the TRECVid dataset, a genuine sample collected from a real life situation, shows that the occurance of events ranges from just under 7 events per hour (PersonRuns) up to almost 41 events in an hour (ObjectPut). However, the events annotated for the TRECVid task are somewhat artificial – a point made by our users during the evaluations (see discussion in section 2.4) – and therefore frequency for true events of interest in the surveillance space is likely to be even less than that demonstrated here.

2.2 User profiles

Based on our visits to end users, we identified two main categories of user – *professionals* and *computer experts*. In this section we describe the characteristics of each user category. Eight users (four in each class) from four institutions completed the evaluation. All users were given an introduction to TRECVid and a demonstration of the search interface. They were given time to familiarise themselves with the interface and the three events using video loaded from the training dataset.

Professionals generally worked directly in managing surveillance video systems or archives in a major company in transport or stadium surveillance. These users had no previous experience of TREC-

Vid, evaluation workshops or of how research in information retrieval fields is evaluated. They view and search surveillance videos as part of their everyday tasks and therefore have high knowledge of surveillance video characteristics (resolution, view point etc.) and understood how difficult and time consuming current methods are for identifying events of interest. They gave minimal importance to completing the task and, in some cases, found the specific events used by TRECVid (e.g., Pointing) to be of little practical interest. The discussions held with these users during the evaluation was enlightening with respect to identifying their expectations of what multimedia information retreival systems were capable of and what events were likely to be useful for their work.

Our *computer experts* had experience in programming, often specifically in machine learning or computer vision. They understood the purpose of the evaluation exercise and treated it more competitively. At the conclusion of the time period spent on each task a notification dialogue would tell the user how many segments they had selected and the amount of search time they had spent. This was often ignored by the professionals but noted by the computer experts. Computer experts were generally more forgiving of obvious mis-classifications and displayed more willingness to try different settings, camera filters and looked at results from all of the different algorithms.

Table 2 shows the search time spent by each user type – quantifying the main difference between the two classes. Note that Person-Runs had fewer segments identified by the underlying classifiers. Our prediction was that computer experts with superior understanding of how computer vision and search systems worked would have

Table 2: Average search time (seconds) per event class for each class of user

	computer expert	professional	all
ObjectPut	1109	238	673
PersonRuns	187	95	141
Pointing	1020	184	602

an advantage in navigating and applying the various options and, having more patience with underperforming algorithms, would find more correct results.

2.3 Interaction paradigm

We've discussed the characteristics of the TRECVid surveillance video dataset and looked at the relative frequency, varying duration and area of the event's region. We've also described the two main classes of user we used for the TRECVid evaluation task. In putting together a system to support these users in finding as many instances as possible of events in the surveillance video test set, decisions and trade-offs need to be made to determine where in the interaction paradigm the processing burden for various tasks is best placed.

Option 1 is to optimise the underlying classification systems for recall and allow the user to act as a filter, removing false alarms. The system tries to reduce the amount of video the user needs to view while avoiding losing relevant segments. The motivation is that segments can't be selected by the user as matches if they have not been annotated by at least one of the underlying classification options. Providing low-level filtering options (amount of activity, number of people etc.) also contributes to this paradigm by giving the user more precise control. This is the option we chose to use for the TRECVid interface.

Maximising recall in an interactive system would seem to be an attractive option as conventional thinking among information retrieval developers is that recall is paramount in applications such as security, science, health etc. where consequences for missing information are higher. However, direct feedback from the professional users indicates that false alarms (incorrect suggestions) are highly detrimental, reducing user confidence in the system performance and limiting its practical utility. In discussion users commented that in many scenarios they were willing to miss some examples rather than having to deal with too many results. Further research is required here to establish the limits of this thinking and the specific conditions where recall can be sacrificed for higher user confidence and more satisfactory interactions.

Option 2 would be to optimise for precision on very specific objects, events, cameras and configurations so that each classifier is highly specialised but (hopefully) more reliable. The user would then act as a form of late fusion, choosing the different classifiers based on detecting component objects or events. The interface would need to be carefully designed to support the professional user by using familiar, consistent terminology and some training would be beneficial to ensure users understand the different options available to them.

The trade-off between precision and recall is influenced by the user characteristics and their requirements. The dataset characteristics also bring two complicating factors when considering the design of the interaction. The first relates to the event duration and small relative region size. For the TRECVid task we chose to display results ordered by classifier confidence in a grid using loop-

ing animated gifs downsampled to half-size and showing every 3rd frame to exploit the users' ability to quickly scan and identify correct results – particular the experienced professionals. As discussed in the section 2.1, some events have durations less than 2 frames and are very difficult to identify from a small, downsampled gif. In addition, the mean region of interest size shows that activities in the TRECVid dataset tended to occur in a small region and were much harder to spot than anticipated. This trade-off for 'human processing' is equivalent to the traditional one for computer vision classifiers between ensuring good coverage through dense feature sampling and reducing computational complexity.

The second complicating factor of the dataset was the question of how to consistently segment the videos. In using an information retrieval style interface that displays lists of order results, some method was required to define start and end times of the events. Each classifier used a different approach to determining the length of video segments including a temporal sliding window, fixed trajectory lengths, aggregating confidence values across frame-based sequences to produce segments and using person-based tracking. For TRECVid, it is very important that the start and end frame values are accurate as they are used automatically to assess the correctness of each result.

Overall, the effect of event duration and relative size of event area to frame size makes it hard for a user to easily spot events when shown an out-of-context video segment. Improvements are likely by using fast-browsing or summarisation (without frame-based downsampling) rather than requiring the user to filter video segments. Based on the dataset and user characteristics and our experiences with the professional users in TRECVid, we propose that an interactive user information retrieval approach supported by a structure of highly specialised semantic classifiers is likely to be better for surveillance video due to the infrequency of events, user dislike of false alarms and the general difficulty of automatically identifying events. The next section presents the evaluation results for both user classes from the interactive runs submitted to TRECVid using a simple, retrieval interface with classifiers optimising for recall.

2.4 Preliminary results and feedback

Table 3 shows the evaluation results for the interactive runs submitted to TRECVid. These comprised the set of all segments identified by users in either the computer expert or professional class ordered by the frequency of the segments selection and the normalised confidence score of the underlying classifier. #Sys is the number of video segments identified for the event by the system, #Cor is the number of these segments that are correct. RFA is the rate of false alarms defined as the number of incorrectly identified segments (#Sys-#Cor) per hour. PMiss is the number of missed detections over the total number of observed events for the target class (#Targ). DCR is Detection Cost Ratio which measures performance in terms of the cost per unit time and is calculated as the product of PMiss and RFA. Therefore a perfect system will receive a DCR of 0. The video segments in the results list, defined by start and end frame numbers, are matched with the ground truth annotations using the Hungarian Solution to the Bipartite Graph [13].

The most surprising feature of the interactive results was the high number of false alarms. Our prediction was that having a user act as a result filter would greatly reduce the incorrect annotations. One possibility is that the high RFA is due to the sensitivity of the event alignment method used in the evaluation. It is likely that the event segments found by the classifiers have a shorter duration or inexact overlap with the groundtruth event segments. This would be interesting to explore further, as for surveillance video retrieval tasks it

226

Table 3: summary of results for interactive runs

user, event	#Targ	#Sys	#Cor	RFA	PMiss	DCR
P ObjectPut	621	48	3	2.951	0.995	1.010
C ObjectPut	621	64	3	4.000	0.994	1.015
P PersonRuns	107	10	2	0.525	0.981	0.984
C PersonRuns	107	14	2	0.787	0.981	0.985
P Pointing	1063	25	12	0.853	0.989	0.993
C Pointing	1063	100	25	4.919	0.976	1.001

Figure 4: Examples of Person Tracking

is less critical to find the exact boundaries of the event but rather to identify that an event has occured, particularly if the task is interactive.

Our user evaluations provided us with the opportunity to meet with professional end users from major companies in the security and surveillance field and discuss their requirements for event retrieval. Many of the users we met with were unaware of TRECVid and information retrieval research in general. The particular activities annotated in the dataset were not of interest to our users who were often confused as to why we had annotated events such as Pointing.

We expected that the computer experts would produce better results due to a clearer understanding of the task and a willingness to spend more time searching for relevant segments. Contrary to our expectations the professionals results were slightly better. This is most likely due to the smaller number of correct results in the segments found by the underlying classifiers and available to the users while searching. The computer experts were also more likely to find more segments and hence have a higher false alarm rate.

The evaluation metric is based on how closely the start and end frames of the segment match with those identified by the humans who created the ground truth. The various methods for segmenting the video will have different levels of precision in determining the exact start and end point. It is not clear if the surprising number of false alarms, even in results chosen by our users, is due to overly stringent restrictions on the start/end numbers by the matching algorithm. For interactive retrieval of video for surveillance tasks this level of precision may not be necessary.

3. COMPUTER VISION TECHNIQUES FOR MULTIMEDIA IR

At the backend of our interface we applied a number of computer vision techniques to provide semantic annotations indicating which segments of the test videos were likely to contain an event. This section gives high-level descriptions of these components, including the evaluation results from processing the TRECVid dataset without the user intervention, and outlines some future directions.

3.1 Person tracking

All events in TRECVid and most of general interest in surveillance involve people and therefore person detection and tracking is a key component. We were interested in using this to identify regions of interest for other classifiers to analyse and to produce raw statistics about video scenes such as the number of people (crowded), the degree of activity or motion. In this section we describe how existing techniques were adapted to handle the type of footage available in the TRECVid dataset.

For detection, we used HOG descriptors [3] and a pre-trained person detector which yields a "sparse" set of detections in time, i.e. there are a lot of misdetections. False negatives can be solved

using tracking approaches, which are anyway needed to provide time coherence to detections, so that we can reconstruct the trajectory of objects.

For the tracking, we have implemented a Rao-Blackwellized Data Association Particle Filter (RBDAPF) [9]. This type of filter has been proven to provide good multiple object tracking results even in the presence of "sparse" detections as the ones we have in these sequences, and can be tuned to handle occlusions. The Rao-Blackwellization can be understood as splitting the problem into linear/Gaussian and non-linear/non-Gaussian parts. The linear part can be solved with Kalman Filters, while the non-linear one must be solved with approximation methods like particle filters. In our case, the linear part is the position and size of a bounding box that models the persons. The non-linear part refers to the data association that is the process of generating a matrix that links detections (the HOG ones, for instance), with objects or clutter. The association process can be strongly non-linear so that sampling approaches can be used. In our case we have implemented ancestral sampling [6].

The control of input/output of new persons is handled thanks to the use of the data association filter that classifies detections according to the existing objects, removes objects that remain undetected for a sufficiently long time, and creates new objects when detections not associated to previous objects appear repeatedly.

Preliminary results indicate that this approach is able to detect and track up to four or five simultaneous persons whose full body is clearly seen in the scene. With more than five persons we have found that in these types of images multiple occlusions happen and the full-body detector does not provide good detection results.

High-levels of occlusion and very crowded scenes remain a challenge. Figure 3 shows the pixel area of the event region relative to the total frame size is often only between 4 and 12% and for some configurations may be less than 5%. The relative size of people will be even smaller and the camera configuration means that often only the head/shoulders is consistently visable. Future plans are to apply this work to real data from project partners, to use research datasets such as CUHK occlusion[1] to improve the ability to track occluded persons and to examine applying fluid dynamics models (such as [8]) to recognise other crowd-based behaviour and events.

3.2 Region-based activity recognition (rb1)

The motivation behind region-based activity recognition was to use the output from person tracking to segment the frames and identify likely regions for further analysis. This was trialled on a subset of the training data and used as input for the manual region of interest annotation activities but due to difficulties with accurate tracking in crowded scenes it was found to be insufficient to apply unsupervised on the test videos at this stage. Therefore a frame-based approach employing a fixed grid was applied. Comparison systems were implemented that use prior-probability based on the region of interest data to improve overall detection scores. This section de-

---

[1] http://www.ee.cuhk.edu.hk/~xgwang/CUHK_pedestrian.html

scribes the two frame-based methodologies for event recognition: using Optical Flow features with a Hidden Markov Model (HMM) classifier (rb1c) compared with dense SIFT features processed with a Bag of Words (BoW) and applied with an SVM classifier (rb1a).

For the Optical Flow features we computed a normalised histogram of oriented optical flow (90 bins, equally spaced) where the magnitude of each bin corresponded to the sum of the magnitude of the optical flow. To describe these we used 2D Zernike Moments [24](p689) of Efros Descriptor Images [10] as follows. We calculate the optical flow vector field F for each frame and split F into two scalar fields, Fx and Fy, corresponding to the horizontal and vertical components of the flow. Then we half-wave rectify Fx and Fy into 4 non-negative channels: $Fx+$ $Fx-$ $Fy+$ and $Fy-$. Finally, we blur with a Gaussian to remove spurious motions. These channels, known as Efros descriptors [10] may be regarded as distinct images. As features, we calculate 2D Zernike moments of each of the new channels (16 features per channel, per frame), resulting in a 64×1 feature vector per frame. These features are concatenated into a single vector (154×1) and the feature space is reduced to 16×1 using principal components decomposition.

As a constrasting approach, we also extracted dense SIFT features [2] around spatial interest points and clustered these features to create a visual bag of words. For classification model learning and test set evaluation, histograms of visual words are used as input features to an SVM with radial basis function (RBF).

To generate classification models, we trained our HMM and SVM using ground truth events from the TRECVid training dataset. Specifically, we utilised the manually identified regions of interest within each frame as a unique event instance. To apply frame-based classification to the TRECVid test data, we adopt a grid based approach. Each frame is divided into 36 equally-sized regions and each region is evaluated separately. After classification using both methods, we threshold to retain only the top n video segments (ranked by confidence), and link these segments temporally to derive start and end times. The final confidence score is the mean confidence across the linked time period. We deliberately set n high to allow high false positive rates, in the hope that this will allow a higher proportion of true positives to be captured and therefore be available through the user interface.

Given that a fixed grid was used to segment the test video frames, we were also interested in using the prior probability information about the location of our events to improve the final confidence measure. We represented each heat map (shown in figure 2) as a pixel-level probability distribution whose sum is 1. Based on this the probability of an event occuring within a single grid region was calculated as the sum of probabilites from within that grid. The result of this is a 6×6 matrix containing update weights that we applied to adjust the final classification score (SVM classifier – rb1b; HMM classifier – rb1d).

The next steps for this approach are to incorporate the improvements in person tracking and exploiting the tracking to move from a frame-based, fixed-grid method to motion history images (MHI) [5]. The use of prior probability displays some promise (see section 3.4) so we are interested in completing more events and further testing its usefulness.

3.3 Motion trajectory (mt1)

Person-based activity recognition using motion trajectory is a common approach [21, 17, 1] based on identifying and describing patterns of movement. The types of events we were interested in identifying in the TRECVid dataset involved temporal actions by a single person, therefore classifiers using motion trajectory descriptions was a clear avenue of investigation.

To represent motion, we used salience point trajectory as a low-level feature and described it using four different descriptors. First, in order to extract the motion trajectory, we applied a background subtraction algorithm [12] to detect foreground regions. This processing helps to reduce computational complexity and increases the accuracy of point tracking by reducing the search area. Salience points [19] are located within the foreground regions by a Harris Corner Detector and are tracked over video sequences using the Kanade-Lucas-Tomasi (KLT) algorithm [15]. In the experiments, we have observed that longer salience point trajectories are likely to be erroneous. Thus we empirically set the maximum trajectory length to be 15 frames.

We adopted Heng et al.'s [20] approach to describe the trajectory features. For each trajectory, we calculated four descriptors to capture the different aspects of motion trajectory. Among the existing descriptors, HOGHOF [14] has shown to give excellent results on a variety of datasets [21]. Therefore we computed HOGHOF along our trajectories. HOG (histograms of oriented gradient) [3] captures the local appearance around the trajectories whereas HOF (histograms of optical flow) captures the local motion. Additionally, MBH (motion boundary histogram), proposed by Dalal et al. [4], and TD (trajectory descriptor) [20] are computed in order to represent the relative motion and trajectory shape.

In order to represent the video scene, we have built a Bag-of-Features (BoF) model based on our four descriptors. This requires the construction of a visual vocabulary. In our experiments, we cluster a subset of 250,000 descriptors sampled from the training videos with the k-means algorithm for each descriptor. The number of clusters is set to $k = 4000$, which has shown empirically to give good results in [14]. The BoF representation then assigns each descriptor to the closest vocabulary word in Euclidean distance and computes the co-occurrence histogram over the video sub-sequence.

For classification, we used a non-linear support vector machine (SVM) with a Radial Basis Function (RBF) kernel. Using the cross-validation technique, we empirically found the parameters of cost (32) and gamma (1×10^{-5}) of the kernel. In order to represent the video frame, we utilized a temporal sliding window approach. In the experiments, we set the window size to 25 frames and sliding step size to 8 frames.

Here we have implemented an action detection algorithm that is based on sparse motion trajectory. Since trajectory is suitable for representing gesture-like movements, we mainly focused on building a classifier for Pointing events using this method. Although we have not considered any spatial association between the extracted trajectories' descriptors, this approach performed reasonably well on the challenging TRECVid SED dataset. In the future, we would like to explore an alternative way to represent the video scene rather than the Bag-of-Features (BoF) approach that ignores the spatial information.

3.4 Evaluation

Table 4 shows the outcome of the automatic classification runs submitted to TRECVid 2012. Section 2.4 defines the metrics (RFA, PMiss, DCR).

The purpose of the different runs for the 'rb1' configuration was to evaluate and compare two frame-based supervised-learning techniques for event classification (HMM with optical flow features and SVM with BoW), considering whether or not a priori information could increase accuracy and reliability of event classification. Across the 'rb1' experiments, the SVM incorporating a priori information was slightly more successful.

One factor worth mentioning is the high RFA across all exper-

Table 4: Sumary of results for automatic runs

run, event	#Targ	#Sys	#CorDet	RFA	PMiss	DCR
mt1, ObjectPut	621	9	0	0.59027	1.000	1.0030
mt1, PersonRuns	107	20	3	1.11496	0.972	0.9775
mt1, Pointing	1063	136	16	7.87029	0.985	1.0243
rb1a, ObjectPut	621	457	11	29.25123	0.982	1.1285
rb1a, Pointing	1063	981	50	61.06030	0.953	1.2583
rb1b, ObjectPut	621	308	3	20.00364	0.995	1.0952
rb1b, Pointing	1063	950	57	58.56805	0.946	1.2392
rb1c, ObjectPut	621	730	24	46.30352	0.961	1.1929
rb1c, Pointing	1063	2174	96	136.28712	0.910	1.5911
rb1d, ObjectPut	621	876	22	56.0102	0.965	1.2246
rb1d, Pointing	1063	1286	56	80.67043	0.947	1.3507

iments. During temporal linking and thresholding, our threshold was set intentionally to overestimate event occurrence. Future objectives include the reduction of RFA, by modification of threshold values and generation of enhanced / improved event models for classification. It is envisaged that we calculate non motion-based descriptors for event classification, and combine these with our existing optical flow feature sets. The inclusion of the user gave a 1% improvement in the performance over the fully automatic classifiers. As discussed in section 2.4, this is considerably less than we expected given the generous thresholding and the ability of the user to determine an event match.

One consideration that we realised after submission was that the ObjectPut definition used by the manual annotators sets the start frame as when the person has released the object. We didn't take this into account when defining the training segment. Therefore assumptions about the ability to detect the motion of a person's downward gesture before releasing the object were incorrect. This illustrates the effect that decisions about temporal segmentation of the video can have on performance.

The retrieval of events in surveillance video is a very challenging task and the low absolute values for the DCR metric reflect this. Our numbers are reasonable for the TRECVid challenge where we ranked in the second quartile for almost all of our runs.

4. CONCLUSIONS AND FUTURE WORK

Future work will continue on improving the accuracy and responsiveness of the underlying computer vision systems and is likely to focus more on developing specific components to work in collusion with each other. We aim to complete the annotation of region of interest and analysis of dataset characteristics and have held discussions with fellow TRECVid participants to collaboratively perform manual annotations. The team from the City College of New York Media [23] have also developed an automatic method for generating heat maps similar to those we have produced. Comparison of techniques using these approaches would be very interesting.

Also of interest is using more formal early fusion techniques. Currently all output is presented equally to the user which caused some inconsistencies as different methods for calculating confidence values and different thresholds were used. We intend to apply fusion [22] and hierarchical modelling techniques [18, 11] to enable classification and tracking of both low-level (person/object) and more complex events as required by our users.

We began this work with the aim of bringing together disparate computer vision methods to support event retrieval in surveillance video, initially for the TRECVid 2012 challenge. Through the process of analysis the dataset characteristics, charting the decisions and tradeoffs during implementation and exploring our assumptions with professional users who manage CCTV collections in their daily work, we have established better understanding of how to manage the challenges presented by this type of data.

A surprising outcome was changing our expectations for a surveillance retrieval system based on feedback from professional users. They found it difficult to see the relevance in the events we were exploring even after explaining the purpose of TRECVid and that actions such as 'Pointing' were examples. It also changed our assumptions about the trade-off between precision and recall. Users have told us that false alarms (common when aiming to maximise system recall) are more irritating than we had expected.

An information retrieval approach for finding events in surveillance video will need to be responsive to users' needs in different scenarios and, given the data characteristics and the difficulty of confidently and accurately finding many of the events of interest, a hierarchical, tool-kit based approach is likely to be the most effective. This would combine a number of generic (e.g., person tracking) and highly specific (e.g., 'whole arm non-aggressive pointing') computer vision based classifiers to enable semi-customised services based on the needs of surveillance professionals. Our future work will be to build upon the feedback gathered from our professional users and develop collections of semantic classifiers to address their requirements for video retrieval in the surveillance domain.

Acknowledgements

The research leading to these results has received funding from the European Union Seventh Framework Programme (FP7/2007-2013) under grant agreement number 285621, project titled SAVASA.

5. REFERENCES

[1] J. Aggarwal and M. Ryoo. Human activity analysis: A review. *ACM Comput. Surv.*, 43(3), Apr. 2011.

[2] A. Bosch, A. Zisserman, and X. Munoz. Representing shape with a spatial pyramid kernel. In *Proceedings of the 6th ACM International Conference on Image and Video Retrieval*, pages 401–408, 2007.

[3] N. Dalal and B. Triggs. Histograms of oriented gradients for human detection. In *IEEE Computer Society Conference on Computer Vision and Pattern Recognition*, pages 886–893, 2005.

[4] N. Dalal, B. Triggs, and C. Schmid. Human detection using oriented histograms of flow and appearance. In *European*

Conference on Computer Vision (ECCV), pages 428–441, 2006.

[5] J. Davis. Hierarchical motion history images for recognizing human motion. In *Proceedings of the IEEE Workshop on Detection and Recognition of Events in Video*, pages 39–46, 2001.

[6] C. R. del Blanco, F. Jaureguizar, and N. Garcia. An advanced Bayesian model for the visual tracking of multiple interacting objects. *EURASIP Journal on Advances in Signal Processing*, 130, 2011.

[7] D. Doermann and D. Mihalcik. Tools and techniques for video performance evaluation. In *Proceedings of the 15th International Conference on Pattern Recognition*, volume 4, pages 167–170, 2000.

[8] C. Dogbe. On the modelling of crowd dynamics by generalized kinetic models. *Journal of Mathematical Analysis and Applications*, 2011.

[9] A. Doucet, N. Gordon, and V. Krishnamurthy. Particle filters for state estimation of jump markov linear systems. *IEEE Transactions on Signal Processing*, 49(3):613–624, 2001.

[10] A. Efros, A. Berg, G. Mori, and J. Malik. Recognizing action at a distance. In *Proceedings of the Ninth IEEE International Conference on Computer Vision*, pages 726–733, 2003.

[11] J. Ijsselmuiden and R. Stiefelhagen. Towards high-level human activity recognition through computer vision and temporal logic. In R. Dillmann, J. Beyerer, U. Hanebeck, and T. Schultz, editors, *KI 2010: Advances in Artificial Intelligence*, volume 6359 of *Lecture Notes in Computer Science*, pages 426–435. Springer Berlin Heidelberg, 2010.

[12] P. Kelly, C. Ó Conaire, C. Kim, and N. O'Connor. Automatic camera selection for activity monitoring in a multi-camera system for tennis. In *Third ACM/IEEE International Conference on Distributed Smart Cameras*, pages 1–8, 2009.

[13] H. W. Kuhn. The hungarian method for the assigment problem. *Naval Research Logistic Quarterly*, 2:83–97, 1955.

[14] I. Laptev, M. Marszalek, C. Schmid, and B. Rozenfeld. Learning realistic human actions from movies. In *IEEE Conference on Computer Vision and Pattern Recognition*, pages 1–8, 2008.

[15] B. Lucas and T. Kanade. An iterative image registration technique with an application to stereo vision. In *Proceedings of the 7th International Joint Conference on Artificial intelligence*, 1981.

[16] P. Over, G. Awad, M. Michel, J. Fiscus, G. Sanders, B. Shaw, W. Kraaij, A. F. Smeaton, and G. Quéenot. TRECVid 2012 – an overview of the goals, tasks, data, evaluation mechanisms and metrics. In *Proceedings of TRECVID 2012*. NIST, USA, 2012.

[17] R. Poppe. A survey on vision-based human action recognition. *Image and Vision Computing*, 28(6):976 – 990, 2010.

[18] M. Ryoo and J. Aggarwal. Semantic representation and recognition of continued and recursive human activities. *International journal of computer vision*, 82(1):1–24, 2009.

[19] C. Tomasi and J. Shi. Good features to track. *CVPR94*, pages 593–600, 1994.

[20] H. Wang, A. Klaser, C. Schmid, and C. Liu. Action recognition by dense trajectories. In *IEEE Conference on Computer Vision and Pattern Recognition (CVPR)*, pages 3169–3176, 2011.

[21] H. Wang, M. Ullah, A. Klaser, I. Laptev, and C. Schmid. Evaluation of local spatio-temporal features for action recognition. In *BMVC 2009-British Machine Vision Conference*, 2009.

[22] P. Wilkins, A. F. Smeaton, and P. Ferguson. Properties of optimally weighted data fusion in cbmir. In *Proceedings of the 33rd international ACM SIGIR conference on Research and development in information retrieval*, pages 643–650, 2010.

[23] X. Yang, Y. Tian, C. Yi, and L. Cao. MediaCCNY at TRECVID 2012: Surveillance event detection. In *TRECVid 2012 - TREC Video Retrieval Evaluation Workshop*, Gaithersburg, MD, 2012.

[24] F. Zernike. *Physica*, volume 1. 1934.

Exploiting Language Models to Recognize Unseen Actions

Dieu-Thu Le
DISI, University of Trento
dle@disi.unitn.it

Raffaella Bernardi
DISI, University of Trento
bernardi@disi.unitn.it

Jasper Uijlings
DISI, University of Trento
jrr@disi.unitn.it

ABSTRACT

This paper addresses the problem of human action recognition. Typically, visual action recognition systems need visual training examples for all actions that one wants to recognize. However, the total number of possible actions is staggering as not only are there many types of actions but also many possible objects for each action type. Normally, visual training examples are needed for all actions of this combinatorial explosion of possibilities. To address this problem, this paper is a first attempt to propose a general framework for *unseen* action recognition in still images by exploiting both visual and language models. Based on objects recognized in images by means of visual features, the system suggests the most plausible actions exploiting off-the-shelf language models. All components in the framework are trained on universal datasets, hence the system is general, flexible, and able to recognize actions for which no visual training example has been provided. This paper shows that our model yields good performance on unseen action recognition. It even outperforms a state-of-the-art Bag-of-Words model in a realistic scenario where few visual training examples are available.

Categories and Subject Descriptors

I.2.7 [**Artificial Intelligence**]: Natural Language Processing—*Language Models, Text Analysis*; I.4.8 [**Image Processing and Computer Vision**]: Scene analysis—*Object Recognition*

General Terms

Theory, Experimentation

Keywords

human action recognition, object recognition, language models

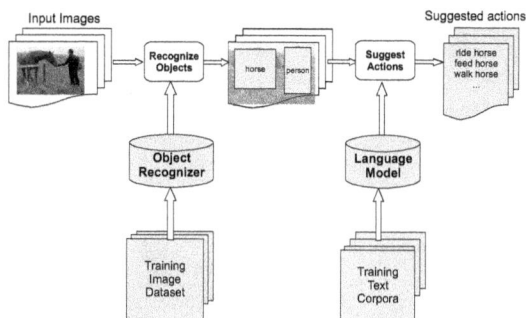

Figure 1: **Human action suggestion framework: Object recognizers and language models are learned from general datasets. Actions are suggested based on objects recognized in images.**

1. INTRODUCTION

The problem of action recognition has challenged the Computer Vision community for quite a long time. Currently, research on action recognition in still-images focuses on data sets of around 40 human actions defined by "verb-object" relations, like "playing violin" or "riding a bike", where each action has a good number of training examples. However, the combinatorial explosion of verb-object relations makes the task of learning human actions directly from their visual appearance computationally prohibitive and makes the collection of proper-sized image datasets infeasible. Furthermore, actions are a rather complex semantic concept, since an action is expressed by the combination of a verb with an agent and a patient, as well as other possible elements of what, in computational linguistics and artificial intelligence, is known as a "frame". We assume that one can know an action by knowing the frame it belongs to.

Therefore, we aim to develop an action recognizer that can recognize *unseen* actions based on their frames, where unseen means that no visual training examples with action labels are available. Having such a system enables us to handle much more actions than currently considered within the Computer Vision community and will guarantee the scalability and stability of results. To this end, we propose a framework in which the knowledge extracted from language models is learned from an open domain and very large text corpora.

Like other action recognition work, we consider only images that contain human actions. We focus on identifying these actions based on objects which are recognized in the images. In brief, this paper addresses the following research questions: (1) Can language models built from general text corpora suggest good actions given the objects in the image? (2) How can we integrate a language model with an object recognition model to recognize unseen actions? (3) How does our resulting framework compare to a state-of-the-art Bag-of-Words model on action recognition in a realistic scenario where only few examples are available for training?

2. RELATED WORK

Visual features.

Several researchers noted that actions are highly semantic and can therefore best be recognized through their components rather than global appearance. [6] proposes a model of person-object interaction features based on spatial co-occurrences of body parts and objects, expressing the position in terms of scale-space *coordinates*. [13, 26] shows the importance of exploiting human *poses* too, while [11] investigates the interaction with *spatial information*. Recently, [28] integrated recognized objects, scenes, and human poses into one model: An action is represented by a sparse, weighted sum of action bases, consisting of attributes (verbs related to the action) and parts (objects and poses). All these methods, while successful, need many visual training examples. Our work aims to reduce the reliance on visual training data; we exploit language models to provide probabilities on the relation between those entities for which good detectors exist.

Linguistic features.

Language models have been successfully used in computer vision. In [8], the meaning of images is represented through object-verb-scene triples. A triple works as an intermediate representation of images and descriptive sentences and is used to match the two. [24] also attempt to generate sentences for images by using an online learning method for multi-keyphrase estimation using a grammar model. Similarly, [27] take an image description to consist of a noun, a verb, a scene, and a preposition and aim to generate a never seen descriptive sentence for a given image. To this end, they combine object and scene detectors from computer vision with language models extracted from a dependency parsed corpus to compute the probability of the action and of the preposition to be associated with the image. In particular, they define their vocabulary to consist of verbs, nouns, locations, and prepositions. They select the most likely description by calculating probabilities from co-occurrence statistics from a subset of the Gigaword corpus [10]. Similarly to [27] we extract co-occurrence statistics from a text corpus and transform them into probability scores. Differently from them, we exploit language models which are not tailored to the specific action detection task but which are built independently. This might effect our system performance, but it makes our results more general and stable. Moreover, we perform action recognition rather than generating descriptive sentences.

Unseen action/event recognition.

Several other studies have been able to do unseen event or action recognition. Both [16] and [14] learn attributes of an image. Unseen events can be retrieved by a manual definition of such event in terms of attributes. [22] use a manually defined ontology of events in terms of objects to recognise previously unseen events. In contrast, we learn relations between objects and actions from language.

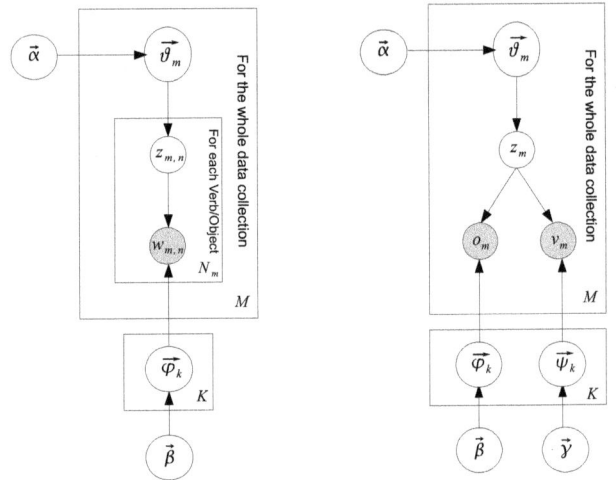

Figure 2: Generative graphical model of LDA (left) vs. ROOTH-LDA (right)

3. RECOGNIZING UNSEEN ACTIONS

We propose a framework (see Figure 1) able to recognize human actions in still images (e.g., "a person is riding a bike") without having previously seen their image representations; we do not rely on the standard visual learning paradigm where many training images are needed to learn a specific action. Instead, we only learn the visual appearance of *objects*. Then we exploit linguistic corpora to learn which verbs can relate a human actor with the visually detected objects. The object appearance models and language models are learned from unrelated datasets, which makes our system highly flexible and ensures stability and scalability.

Specifically, we first learn the appearance models for a set of objects O using standard object localisation systems [9, 25]. Then, given an image I, we use the localization systems to predict the probability of the presence of an object $o^i \in O$. From our previously built *universal* language model, harvested from general text corpora, we predict the probability that a verb v^j is associated with an object: $P(v^j|o^i)$. Hence the object recognizer suggests objects for the language model which in turn finds the most probable actions. We use a weighted linear combination to combine these two probability models for the prediction of the action $a^{ij} \equiv \{o^i, v^j\}$:

$$P(a^{ij}|I) = \alpha \times P(o^i|I) + (1 - \alpha) \times P(v^j|o^i, \phi). \quad (1)$$

3.1 Language Model

We exploit a language model to select plausible verbs for a recognized object in an image ($P(V|O)$). Computational linguists have already tackled an analogous task, known as "selectional preferences": compute the plausibility of a noun to be the object of a given verb. Such systems have obtained high correlation with human judgements. In this paper, we compare two language models: We take an off-the-shelf Distributional Semantics Model (DSM) called Type Distributional Memory (TypeDM) [1], and implement ROOTH-LDA [21] which is a variant on Latent Dirichlet Allocation.

TypeDM.

DSMs are based on the hypothesis that the meaning of a word is given by the contexts in which it occurs. Distributional Memory (DM) [1] is a DSM built as a multitask semantic model, viz. distributional information are extracted once and for all from the corpus in the form of a set of weighted $\langle word_1, link, word_2 \rangle$ tuples; the weights are assigned by Local Mutual Information (LMI); the links could be of different levels of lexicalization giving rise to different DM models. TypeDM has shown to perform best on different tasks. We have used TypeDM directly as a pre-computed semantic resource of weighted tuples: we extracted all tuples in which a verb is linked to a noun $\langle word\text{-}v, link, word\text{-}n \rangle$, where we ignored *link* for simplicity; we ranked all these tuples based on the noun (the object) and compute the probability of the verb given the object as follows:

$$P(v^j|o^i) = \frac{P(v^j, o^i)}{P(o^i)} = \frac{LMI_{ij}}{\sum_{j=1}^{L} LMI_{ij}} \qquad (2)$$

where L is the number of tuples with $w_2 = o^i$, and the LMI are the weights provided by the TypeDM tuples.

Since we took directly the weights of tuples from TypeDM, this model can only predict verb-object pairs that have occurred in the corpora.[1] Every association (V, O) that has not been seen in the corpora will be assigned 0 to its probability.

ROOTH-LDA.

A topic model (e.g., LDA [2]) is a generative model that discovers the abstract "topics" in a collection of documents. LDA was used successfully for preference selection [19, 21].

The most straightforward way of applying LDA (Figure 2, left) provides us with semantic clusters of verbs/objects, but does not jointly model both of them. Therefore it does not provide the conditional probability of a verb given an object. This joint probability is instead obtained by the ROOTH-LDA model (Figure 2, right) proposed in [21] inspired by [20]. We follow this method and adapt it to our goal.

A relation m is a pair of $< v_m, o_m >$, which is generated by picking up a distribution over topics $\vec{\vartheta}_m$ from a Dirichlet distribution $(Dir(\vec{\alpha}))$. Then the topic assignment z_m for both v_m and o_m is sampled from a multinomial distribution $Mult(\vec{\vartheta}_m)$. Finally, a particular verb v_m is generated by sampling from multinomial distribution $Mult(\vec{\psi}_{z_m})$ and a particular object o_m is generated from $Mult(\vec{\varphi}_{z_m})$ (Figure 2, right). In this way, we keep two different verb-topic and object-topic distributions that share the same topic indicators. We have estimated the model by Gibbs Sampling with relatively simple algorithms following the sampling method for LDA described in [12]. In particular, the topic z_i of a particular verb v_i and object o_i is sampled from the following multinomial distribution:

$$p(z_i = k| \vec{z}_{\neg i}, \vec{v}, \vec{o}) = \frac{n_{k,\neg i}^{(o)} + \beta}{\sum_{o=1}^{V_o} n_{k,\neg i}^{(o)} + V_o \times \beta}$$

$$\times \frac{n_{k,\neg i}^{(v)} + \gamma}{\sum_{v=1}^{V_v} n_{k,\neg i}^{(v)} + V_v \times \gamma} \times \frac{n_{m,\neg i}^{(k)} + \alpha}{\sum_{k=1}^{K} n_{m,\neg i}^{(k)} + K \times \alpha} \qquad (3)$$

where $\vec{v}$, $\vec{o}$ and $\vec{z}$ are the vectors of all verbs, objects and their topic assignment of the whole data collection; α, β, γ are Dirichlet parameters. $n_{k,\neg i}^{(o)}$, $n_{k,\neg i}^{(v)}$ is the number of

---

[1]TypeDM could also be used to compute the plausibility of verb-object pairs never occurred in the corpus.

times object o and verb v is assigned to topic k accept the current one. Let V_o and V_v be the number of objects and verbs in the dataset and K be the number of topics, the two verb-topic and object-topic distributions are computed as:

$$\varphi_{k,o} = \frac{n_k^{(o)} + \beta}{\sum_{o=1}^{V_o} n_k^{(o)} + \beta}; \qquad \psi_{k,v} = \frac{n_k^{(v)} + \gamma}{\sum_{v=1}^{V_v} n_k^{(v)} + \gamma} \qquad (4)$$

Finally, to get the conditional probability of a verb v^j given an object o^i, we calculated it through the topic indicator z by summing up over z all products of the conditional probability of the corresponding verb and object given the same topic.

$$P(v^j|o^i) = \frac{P(v^j, o^i)}{P(o^i)} \propto \frac{\sum_{k=1}^{K} P(v^j|z=k) \times P(o^i|z=k)}{\sum_{k=1}^{K} P(o^i, z=k)}$$

$$= \frac{\sum_{k=1}^{K} \psi_{v^j,k} \times \varphi_{o^i,k}}{\sum_{k=1}^{K} \varphi_{o^i,k}} \qquad (5)$$

As LDA-ROOTH is a generative model, it also predicts the probability of (V,O) pairs that did not occur in the corpus.

3.2 Object Localisation System

In this paper we use two different object localisation systems [25, 9]. We do not want to base our object recognition on a global image impression, such as the common image-based BoW representation, as an action is really between a human and an object and less dependent on its surroundings.

The two object localisation systems [25, 9] differ in visual features but share similarities in training: Both need training images where objects are annotated using bounding boxes. In both methods, negative examples are automatically obtained from the training data by finding so-called hard examples: image windows that yield high object probabilities but do not correspond to the object. Given an image, both systems predict the most likely bounding boxes where a specific object o^i is present, together with its probability $P(o^i|I)$.

The part-based method of Felzenszwalb et al. [9] is based on a sliding window approach and Histogram of Oriented Gradient (HOG) [5]. For each object class the method automatically determines several poses. For each pose HOG-templates are learned for the complete object and for object-parts, the latter which are automatically determined using a latent, linear SVM. During testing, the HOG-templates are applied to a dense, regular search grid within the image. Locations with the highest template response for both parts and the complete object yield a predicted location with corresponding probability. The framework is widely used and this paper uses their publicly available code (see [9]).

The method of [25] is based on the BoW paradigm [4]. In common BoW, SIFT-descriptors [17] or variants are extracted on a densely sampled grid. Using a previously learned visual vocabulary (e.g. created by kmeans) each SIFT desciptor is assigned to a specific visual word. The BoW representation is given by a histogram of visual word counts within the image, often using the Spatial Pyramid [15] which regularly divides the image to introduce a rough form of spatial consistency.

In [25], the authors propose to represent not a complete image but only the object using BoW. However, such representation is computationally too expensive for a sliding window approach which visits over 100,000 locations. Therefore the authors propose Selective Search which uses multiple hierarchical segmentations to generate around 1500 high-quality, class independent, object locations. The BoW representation for these 1500 locations can be generated within reasonable time. In this paper, we model the BoW based localisation method after [25], using the publicly available selective search code. The BoW implementation itself is modelled after the fast implementation proposed by [23]. In experiments we denote this BoW localisation method by BoWL.

The details of our implementation are as follows. First, we extract SIFT descriptors [17] and two colour variants, RGB-SIFT and Opponent SIFT [25] at every single pixel in the image (ultra-dense). We use a single scale of 16 by 16 pixels and a Gaussian derivative filter with sigma = 0.667. Principal Component Analysis is used on the descriptors to reduce their dimensionality by a factor 3. Then each descriptor is assigned to a visual word using a Random Forest based visual vocabulary [18, 23], which is as accurate as the usual k-means clustering yet is much more computationally efficient. Specifically, we use four trees of depth ten, resulting in 4096 visual words per SIFT variant. The trees are learned beforehand on a random subset of all descriptors in the training set using the global image labels. The visual words and their locations are stored to be able to quickly compute visual word histograms from subregions within an image.

4. DATASETS

In this section, we will describe all datasets that we use in our experiments: a new action dataset, which contains 89 actions annotated by us to evaluate the performance of the action suggestion system; the image datasets used for training our object recognizers and the corpora from which we have built our language models.

4.1 89 action dataset

Most available datasets used for evaluating action recognizers are restricted to specific domains (e.g., playing musical instruments, sport activities, etc.) or consider a limited number of actions (7 everyday action, Stanford 40 action dataset). Moreover, all these data sets contain many learning examples well distributed over all actions, but this distribution does not reflect the reality where many more possible actions exist for which few examples are available. To overcome these limitations, we have collected a new dataset from 11.5 thousand images of the PASCAL 2012 VOC trainval set [7] selecting all those images representing a human action, obtaining 2,038 images. In PASCAL 2012 VOC there are in total 20 objects. Figure 3 reports for each object the number of images in total and the number of images that contain human actions.

As the images in this dataset were not collected for any specific kind of actions, we believe it gives a general overview of the possible human actions, involving the PASCAL objects. Starting from the object label assigned to each image in the PASCAL data set, we manually annotated the 2,038 images with a verb to obtain the label of the human action (verb-object). The data sets is annotated with 19 objects and 36 verbs, that combine into 89 actions. Considering the training vs. validation split used in the PASCAL competition, our human action data set consists of 1,104 images in the training set and 934 images in the validation set[2].

In the data set, there are objects, such as aeroplane, bird, potted plant, which are associated with only few actions

---

[2]We made the dataset available at http://disi.unitn.it/ dle/pascalaction.php

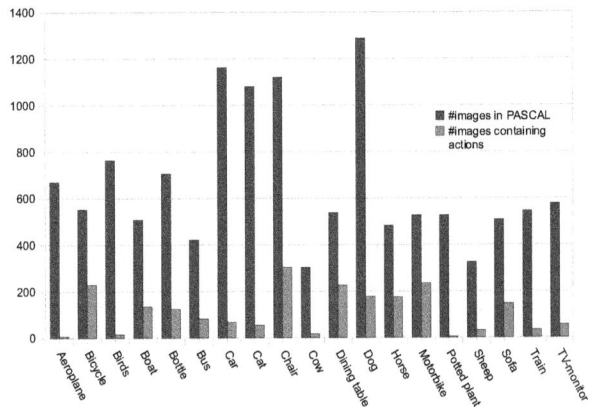

Figure 3: Images containing actions in the PASCAL VOC 2012 trainval dataset

(e.g., 8 images with actions related to aeroplanes, 15 images with birds). Objects that are involved in more actions are bicycle (ride, fix), chair (sit), motorbike (ride), bottle (drink). In many pictures, the action is simply a person touching or holding an object.

4.2 Language datasets

The language models are built from large open domain corpora. TypeDM [1], has been harvested from a concatenation of three corpora: Web-derived ukWac; a mid-2009 dump of the English Wikipedia; and the British National Corpus (BNC).[3] The model contains 2.83 billion tokens: 20,410 nouns and 5,026 verbs.

We have built the LDA-ROOTH model using our implementation (Section 3) estimating it on the BNC, which was PoS-tagged, and lemmatized with TreeTagger[4] and dependency parsed with MaltParser.[5] We have not estimated the LDA-ROOTH model on the whole corpus used to built the TypeDM, since building the LDA-ROOTH model is computationally expensive. The chosen number of topics is 200, the hyper-parameters α, β, γ were set to 0.5, 0.1 and 0.1 respectively and the number of iterations is set to 1,000.

Suggested verb-object combinations look quite interpretable and satisfactory as shown in Table 1. For example, verbs like "wear", "buy", "hang", "design", "dress" have a high weights in the cluster (Topic 46) in which the most probable object is "clothes" ; "spend", "take", "enjoy" are matching with nouns like "time", "day", "hour" (Topic 0); "carry", "conduct" with "research", "interview" (Topic 138) and so on. Totally, there are 33,258 objects and 8,888 verbs.

4.3 Object recognizer dataset

To train the object recognizer, [9, 25] used the trainval set of PASCAL VOC 2007 [7], which contains 20 objects: person, bird, cat, cow, dog, horse, sheep, aeroplane, bicycle, boat, bus, car, motorbike, train, bottle, chair, dining table, potted plant, sofa, TV/monitor. The training set consists of 5,011 images and 12,608 objects. Note that there is no overlap between this dataset and the 2012 VOC dataset from which we created our 89 action dataset.

---

[3]http://www.natcorp.ox.ac.uk/
[4]http://www.ims.uni-stuttgart.de/projekte/corplex/TreeTagger
[5]http://www.maltparser.org/

Topic 26:				Topic 46:				Topic 0:				Topic 88:			
Verb		Object		Verb		Object		Verb		Object		Verb		Object	
keep	0.56	pace	0.02	wear	0.48	clothes	0.04	spend	0.53	time	0.13	reduce	0.3	cost	0.06
maintain	0.04	record	0.02	remove	0.03	hat	0.03	take	0.02	day	0.06	increase	0.1	risk	0.04
gather	0.03	watch	0.01	buy	0.03	dress	0.02	enjoy	0.01	hour	0.06	cut	0.07	amount	0.02
check	0.02	secret	0.01	take	0.02	jacket	0.02	leave	0.01	year	0.05	incur	0.02	loss	0.01
stand	0.01	distance	0.01	pull	0.02	suit	0.02	last	0.01	night	0.03	control	0.02	emission	0.01
take	0.01	company	0.01	hang	0.01	shirt	0.01	work	0.01	lot	0.02	limit	0.02	number	0.01
mean	0.01	momentum	0.01	don	0.01	coat	0.01	devote	0.01	life	0.02	minimise	0.02	time	0.01
pick	0.01	control	0.01	sport	0.01	shoe	0.01	ask	0.01	evening	0.01	avoid	0.01	pollution	0.01
allow	0.01	child	0.01	put	0.01	uniform	0.01	use	0.01	month	0.01	eliminate	0.01	unemployment	0.01
force	0.01	peace	0.01	design	0.01	trouser	0.01	kill	0.01	week	0.01	involve	0.01	liability	0.01
remain	0.01	house	0.01	get	0.01	cap	0.01	talk	0.01	rest	0.01	reflect	0.01	intake	0.01
stay	0.01	diary	0.01	match	0.01	boot	0.01	visit	0.01	minute	0.01	impose	0.01	expenditure	0.01
steal	0	pressure	0.01	like	0.01	skirt	0.01	mean	0.01	deal	0.01	create	0.01	power	0.01
send	0	mind	0.01	knit	0.01	glass	0.01	read	0.01	part	0.01	assess	0.01	dependence	0.01
step	0	level	0.01	tear	0.01	jean	0.01	waste	0.01	weekend	0.01	curb	0.01	use	0.01

Table 1: Random ROOTH-LDA topics with their most probable verbs and objects

5. EXPERIMENTS

We test the performance of our framework in two settings: *categorization* and *retrieval*. In the *categorization* setting we test how well our framework can predict an action given a specific image and estimate the usefulness of the language model. For evaluation, for each image i we measure the position of the correct action p_i, and report both the average and median position (AvgPos, MedPos) over all N images, where: $AvgPos = \frac{\sum_{i=0}^{N} p_i}{N}$, and $MedPos$ is the median of the set $\{p_1, \cdots, p_n\}$. In the *retrieval* setting we test how good our system is in retrieving images for a particular action. We determine its performance in ranking the images for each action, and measure the Average Precision. We compare our system with a state-of-the-art BoW retrieval framework. Like in most work on human action recognition, we assume all images contain human actions.

5.1 Categorization experiments

We run three kinds of categorization experiments: first we evaluate the language model on its own – hence we take the correct object in the image as given by the gold standard; then we optimize our integration of the language model with an object recognizer. Finally, we evaluate our integrated framework on unseen action recognition.

5.1.1 Language model with object gold standard

In this experiment, we want to determine how well the respective language models can suggest the correct action in an image *given that we know the correct objects that appear in the image*. For the TypeDM, we extract all tuples associated with these objects. Totally, there are 14.2 thousand possible actions related to the 19 objects (viz., the PASCAL 20 objects without "person"). For the LDA-ROOTH model, we generate all possible combinations between these 19 objects and the 8.888 verbs in its vocabulary, obtaining 169 thousand combinations. We use the two models to suggest actions for each image given the correct objects. Remark: there are 5 actions in 36 images that do not occur in TypeDM: clean aeroplane, touch aeroplane, touch bus, touch motorbike, and touch sheep. As we cannot predict the correct action for these images using TypeDM, we cannot measure their position. Therefore we exclude these 36 images from our evaluation.

Figure 4 and Table 2 report the results. First of all, we observe that the average position is 28.8 for TypeDM model and only 73.6 for LDA-ROOTH. Furthermore, the boxplots in Figure 4 show that the average position is significantly affected by a few images for which the position number for

	TypeDM	LDA-ROOTH
Average Position	28.8	73.6
Median Position	1	45

Table 2: AvgPos and MedPos within 2,038 images of the 89 action dataset given object gold standard

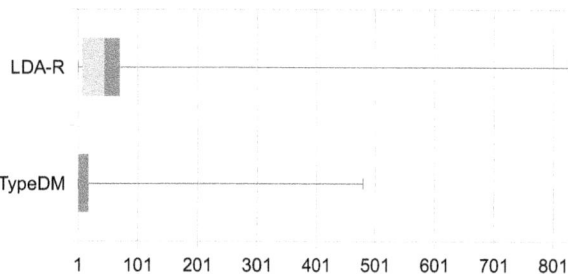

Figure 4: Correct action positions of 2,038 images in the 89 action dataset given the object gold standard. Boxplots show the smallest position, lower quartile, median, upper quartile and highest position

the correct action is high. For the median position, which is unaffected by outliers, we see a position of 1 for TypeDM and 45 for LDA-ROOTH. In fact, TypeDM puts the correct action at the first position in 65% of the images(!).

We conclude that TypeDM performs much better than LDA-ROOTH. There is one caveat: TypeDM was learned on more data. But this is made possible because TypeDM is computationally less expensive to learn. Hence, from a practical perspective, TypeDM is the model of choice. In the experiments below, we will evaluate the integration of the object recognizer considering only TypeDM.

5.1.2 Parameter optimization for the integration of the visual and language models

Our aim for this experiment is to find an optimal way to combine TypeDM with the object recognizer to suggest actions for images. We use a weighed linear combination as defined in Equation 1. We experiment with weight values α: $\{0.1, 0.2, ..., 0.9\}$. To avoid overfitting, we report results on three repetitions of two-fold cross-validation (Figure 5). The optimal values are: 0.4 for BoWL and 0.6 for the part-based method. We will use these alphas in the experiments below.

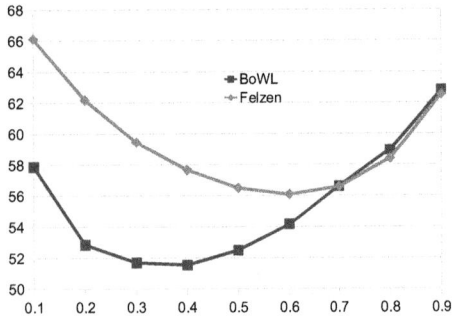

Figure 5: Alpha values and the corresponding average position over three runs

Model	BoWL		Felzen	
	AvgPos	MedPos	AvgPos	MedPos
General model	52.6	5	57.1	6
Tailored model	48.6	4	53.7	5
89 action model	10.3	3	12.3	4

Table 3: Average and median position obtained by two object recognizers integrated with TypeDM

5.1.3 Integrated visual and language models

In these experiments, we evaluate how a real system, consisting of a language model and an object recognizer, performs in three different scenarios.

Unbounded Action Prediction.

In this experiment, for each image the model assigns a ranked list of all 14.2 thousand actions in TypeDM, viz., the same scenario considered in the previous experiments. See Table 3 for the results achieved by integrating TypeDM with the BoWL and Felzen object recognizers.

First of all, one can see that the integration of TypeDM with BoWL performs better than the Felzenszwalb object recognizer (Felzen) in terms of AvgPos (52.6 and 57.1, respectively). Moreover, the median for both methods is pretty low: 5 for BoWL and 6 for the part-based object detector. This shows that our combination of TypeDM with the object recogniser yields an accurate action recognition system.

Tailored Action Prediction.

The verb and object co-occurrence frequency in texts may be different from the one in images. Therefore, in this experiment we want to adapt TypeDM to reflect the use of actions in the image dataset so to improve the model predictions.

To do this, we first define *general verbs* as those that go with many different objects. In images, the more objects a verb goes with, the more general it is (Figure 6). The top 5 general verbs based on this definition are: touch, sit, hold, feed, look. Similarly, general verbs in text are those whose probability distributions over objects do not vary much. That means, if a verb goes most of the time with a small number of objects, it is more specific; if a verb occurs with many different objects with similar probability, this verb is more general. Given this definition, we count within 90% of the probability distribution of a verb, how many objects a verb

is associated with (Figure 7). The top 5 most general verbs according to this definition are: use, take, get, see, stay.

We first make some qualitative observations: Most of the specific verbs in images are also quite specific in text ($\approx$70% verbs with 1 object in images have $\leq$ 8 objects in text). Most of the general verbs in images are also quite general in text ($\approx$80% verbs with more than 4 objects in images have $\geq$11 objects in text). However, there are some verbs (e.g., push, follow, stay, use) that are general in text but more specific in images. Some specific verbs in text (e.g., ride, feed) are general in the image dataset, this is due to the fact that our image dataset has several objects like sheep, horse, motorbike, bike that often go with these verbs.

To tailor the language model to further improve the performance of the system, we adjust the probability of each verb by exploiting the analysis of verbs in the image dataset. Our tailoring technique is rather soft, since we require to know only the number of the objects that go with each verb in the dataset. Theoretically, the specific objects used here do not need to coincide with the ones from the particular image dataset on which we do action prediction. Therefore, we could also obtain this information from another image dataset. In this paper, we do not, hence there is some bias.

The main idea is to lower down the probability of verbs general in text but specific in images and vice versa. We do this as follows. Let $NO(V)$ be the number of objects a verb V goes with in our image dataset, we tailor the probability as: $P_{\text{tailored}}(V, O) = P(V, O) \times NO(V)$.

The results in Table 3 show that this tailored model achieves better average position than the not-tailored one (from 52.6 to 48.6 and from 57.1 to 53.7 for BoWL and Felzen object recognizer, respectively). In Table 3, the median of BoWL is 4 and Felzen is 5, one position better than the general model. The results show the effectiveness of our tailoring method based on the generality of verbs.

Bounded Action Prediction.

In this last scenario, we assume that we want to predict the presence of an action out of the 89 actions in the image dataset. This setting corresponds to the standard scenario used in the action recognition literature, since most state-of-the-art methods are unable to recognise unseen actions.

As shown in Table 3 the AvgPos for BoWL is 10.3 and for Felzen is 12.3. The AvgPos improvement is mostly due to the fact that the lowest possible position in this evaluation scenario is only 89, it is mostly in the difficult images as it is highlighted by the median: 3 (BoWL) and 4 (Felzen), viz., only one position higher than the results we achieved for the tailored model and only two positions higher than the general model.

We conclude that our framework yields accurate action predictions, even in the more difficult and realistic scenario where the possible actions are not known beforehand.

Human Evaluation.

Finally, we briefly evaluate to which extent the results of the unbounded action scenario are underestimated because of an incomplete annotation. In particular, we randomly selected 100 images, where the gold standard is found within top 40 actions. A human annotator went through the ranked lists proposed by the tailored model using BoWL as object recognizer. Then the annotator manually marked the first correct action in the ranked list by looking at each image.

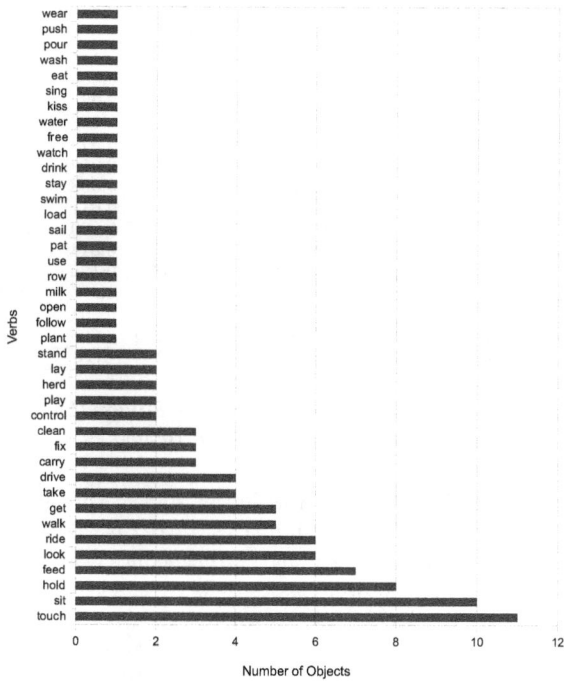

Figure 6: General verbs in images: based on verb-object associations (nr. of objects they go with)

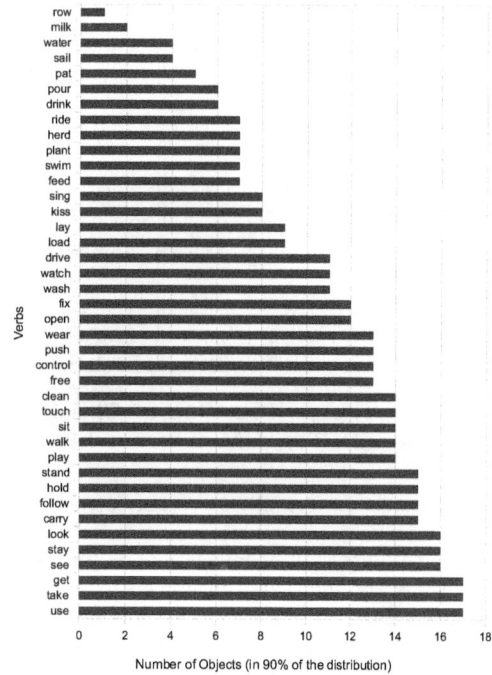

Figure 7: General verbs in text: based on verb-object associations (nr. of objects accounting for 90% of the probability distribution over the total objects of a given verb)

The AvgPos of these 100 images according to the gold standard is 17.2 and the AvgPos according to the human annotation is 5.6. This shows that the action performance of the system could be higher than that based on our current annotation. The reason is that there is usually more than one way of describing the same action in an image and that sometimes there are also different actions presented in the same image. This qualitative analysis suggests that our system for unseen action recognition works even better than is suggested by the experiments above.

5.2 Retrieval experiments

In this section we carry out an image retrieval experiment. We compare our system with a state-of-the-art BoW implementation. This BoW implementation uses the same features as BoWL (see Section 3.2), yet it represents the complete image using a Spatial Pyramid [15] of 1x1 and 1x3. Results on the Pascal VOC 2007 classification challenge are 60.4 MAP (mean average precision), sufficiently close to the 61.7 MAP reported by Chatfield et al. [3].

As the BoW method needs training examples, we split our action dataset into two by using the predefined Pascal 2012 training and validation split. To be able to optimize the parameters of the SVM using cross-validation we demand that an action has at least two training examples. For evaluation, an action should have at least one test example. These constraints results in a data set with 44 actions (whereas our model can retrieve all 84 actions found in the language model (89 minus the 5 not present in TypeDM).

Results on the action retrieval task for the BoW approach and our proposed model are reported in Table 4. Surprisingly, our model with BoWL object recognizer outperforms the

BoW approach: 0.22 vs. 0.19 MAP, respectively. The BoW method suffers, of course, from a lack of training examples. Yet our method has only seen the objects itself but never how an action looks like. Still, it gives results slightly better than the BoW system.

We conclude that our system is able to achieve good performance in image retrieval on unseen actions. In a real-world scenario, where training data is limited, our system even outperforms a state-of-the-art BoW implementation.

6. CONCLUSIONS

This paper has presented a framework for unseen action prediction in still images based on visual and language models. Particularly, we used a visual model to detect the appearance and locations of objects, and a language model for inferring the possible relations between these objects. We combine these to recognize unseen actions for which no visual training examples have been provided. All components of the system rely on general datasets and hence can be used to predict actions in any image dataset.

Empirical results on a real image dataset have shown that the system achieved good performance in predicting unseen actions: the median ranking of correct actions of a general model and of a model tailored to the image dataset is 5 and 4, respectively. In a realistic scenario where few training examples are available, our model outperforms with 0.22 MAP, a state-of-the-art Bag-of-Words approach that achieves 0.19 MAP.

In future work we want to investigate other visual information, such as relative positions between objects, scene recognition and exploit language models to find relations between them for a more accurate action prediction. For

Action	Classic BoW	Unseen Felzen	Unseen BoWL	Action	Classic BoW	Unseen Felzen	Unseen BoWL	Action	Classic BoW	Unseen Felzen	Unseen BoWL
drive bus (25)	0.717	0.816	0.814	pat dog (10)	0.083	0.050	0.220	watch TV (8)	0.032	0.114	0.243
sail boat (23)	0.822	0.444	0.657	hold bird (3)	0.015	0.013	0.207	feed bird (2)	0.009	0.005	0.068
sit table (111)	0.678	0.352	0.652	walk horse (8)	0.226	0.064	0.201	touch horse (8)	0.040	0.027	0.062
ride motorbike (85)	0.553	0.448	0.609	hold dog (35)	0.210	0.140	0.191	walk dog (16)	0.144	0.088	0.061
ride horse (75)	0.594	0.669	0.607	get bus (6)	0.118	0.122	0.183	take bus (2)	0.362	0.049	0.054
feed sheep (7)	0.040	0.096	0.540	row boat (24)	0.473	0.105	0.182	stay boat (8)	0.024	0.019	0.032
sit chair (148)	0.410	0.406	0.468	touch cat (7)	0.071	0.041	0.173	sit car (7)	0.354	0.068	0.028
sit sofa (59)	0.371	0.299	0.458	touch dog (6)	0.236	0.028	0.164	play dog (11)	0.020	0.011	0.021
hold cat (19)	0.123	0.060	0.395	lay sofa (11)	0.086	0.034	0.160	touch motorbike (14)	0.100	0.020	0.020
ride bike (84)	0.440	0.489	0.378	drive train (4)	0.074	0.417	0.130	drink bottle (15)	0.024	0.013	0.019
drive car (23)	0.204	0.612	0.367	hold bottle (40)	0.158	0.160	0.126	feed cat (4)	0.007	0.172	0.018
take train (8)	0.108	0.149	0.356	sit motorbike (18)	0.132	0.162	0.118	carry dog (2)	0.003	0.008	0.007
get train (3)	0.031	0.181	0.339	hold bike (10)	0.045	0.056	0.087	push chair (2)	0.009	0.001	0.006
walk bike (14)	0.127	0.192	0.280	herd sheep (2)	0.002	0.006	0.077	feed bottle (5)	0.033	0.008	0.004
milk cow (2)	0.006	0.003	0.003	touch sheep (5)	0.032	0.002	0.002	MAP	0.19	0.16	0.22

Table 4: (Mean) Average Precision of Classical BoW and our approach which integrates a Felzen/BoWL object recogniser with TypeDM. The number of training examples for Classical BoW are in brackets.

example, the positions between objects might correlate with prepositions used in language models (e.g., position "on" often goes with "ride horse") and some actions might appear more often in some specific scenes in images as well as in language models. Furthermore, we also want to consider the harder, rarely considered scenario where images may not contain any human action at all.

7. REFERENCES

[1] M. Baroni and A. Lenci. Distributional memory: A general framework for corpus-based semantics. *Computational Linguistics*, 36(4):673–721, 2010.

[2] D. M. Blei, A. Y. Ng, and M. I. Jordan. Latent dirichlet allocation. *JMLR*, 3:993–1022, 2003.

[3] K. Chatfield, V. Lempitsky, A. Vedaldi, and A. Zisserman. The devil is in the details: an evaluation of recent feature encoding methods. In *BMVC*, 2011.

[4] G. Csurka, C. R. Dance, L. Fan, J. Willamowski, and C. Bray. Visual Categorization with Bags of Keypoints. In *ECCV International Workshop on Statistical Learning in Computer Vision*, Prague, 2004.

[5] N. Dalal and B. Triggs. Histograms of oriented gradients for human detection. In *CVPR*, 2005.

[6] V. Delaitre, J. Sivic, and I. Laptev. Learning person-object interactions for action recognition in still images. In *NIPS*, 2011.

[7] M. Everingham, L. Van Gool, C. K. I. Williams, J. Winn, and A. Zisserman. The PASCAL Visual Object Classes (VOC) Challenge. IJCV, 2010.

[8] A. Farhadi, M. Hejrati, M. A. Sadeghi, P. Young, C. Rashtchian, J. Hockenmaier, and D. Forsyth. Every picture tells a story: generating sentences from images. In *ECCV*. Springer, 2010.

[9] P. F. Felzenszwalb, R. B. Girshick, D. McAllester, and D. Ramanan. Object detection with discriminatively trained part based models. *TPAMI*, 2010.

[10] D. Graff and C. Cieri. English gigaword. In *Linguistic Data Consortium*. 2003.

[11] A. Gupta, A. Kembhavi, and L. S. Davis. Observing human-object interactions: Using spatial and functional compatibility for recognition. In *TPAMI*, volume 31, pages 1775–1789, 2009.

[12] G. Heinrich. Parameter estimation for text analysis. Technical report, 2004.

[13] N. Ikizler, R. G. Cinbis, S. Pehlivan, and P. Duygulu. Recognizing actions in still images. In *ICPR*, 2008.

[14] C. Lampert, H. Nickisch, and S. Harmeling. Learning to detect unseen object classes by between-class attribute transfer. In *CVPR*, 2009.

[15] S. Lazebnik, C. Schmid, and J. Ponce. Beyond Bags of Features: Spatial Pyramid Matching for Recognizing Natural Scene Categories. In *CVPR*, New York, 2006.

[16] J. Liu, B. Kuipers, and S. Savarese. Recognizing human actions by attributes. In *CVPR*, 2011.

[17] D. G. Lowe. Distinctive Image Features from Scale-Invariant Keypoints. *IJCV*, 60:91–110, 2004.

[18] F. Moosmann, B. Triggs, and F. Jurie. Fast discriminative visual codebooks using randomized clustering forests. In *NIPS*, pages 985–992, 2006.

[19] A. Ritter, Mausam, and O. Eztioni. A latent dirichlet allocation method for selectional preferences. In *ACL*, 2010.

[20] M. Rooth, S. Riezler, D. Prescher, G. Carroll, and F. Beil. Inducing a semantically annotated lexicon via em-based clustering. In *ACL*, 1999.

[21] D. O. Séaghdha. Latent variable models of selection preference. In *ACL*, 2010.

[22] J. Stottinger, J. Uijlings, A. Pandey, N. Sebe, and F. Giunchiglia. (unseen) event recognition via semantic compositionality. In *CVPR*, 2012.

[23] J. R. R. Uijlings, A. W. M. Smeulders, and R. J. H. Scha. Real-time Visual Concept Classification. *IEEE Transactions on Multimedia*, 12, 2010.

[24] Y. Ushiku, T. Harada, and Y. Kuniyoshi. Efficient image annotation for automatic sentence generation. In *ACM MM*, 2012.

[25] K. E. A. van de Sande, J. Uijlings, T. Gevers, and A. Smeulders. Segmentation as Selective Search for Object Recognition. In *ICCV*, 2011.

[26] Y. Wang, H. Jiang, M. S. Drew, Z.-N. Li, and G. Mori. Unsupervised discovery of action classes. In *CVPR*, 2006.

[27] Y. Yang, C. L. Teo, H. Daumé, III, and Y. Aloimonos. Corpus-guided sentence generation of natural images. EMNLP, Stroudsburg, PA, USA, 2011.

[28] B. Yao, X. Jiang, A. Khosla, A. L. Lin, L. J. Guibas, and L. Fei-Fei. Action recognition by learning bases of action attributes and parts. In *ICCV*, 2011.

Large-Scale Visual Concept Detection
with Explicit Kernel Maps and Power Mean SVM

Mats Sjöberg, Markus Koskela, Satoru Ishikawa, and Jorma Laaksonen
Department of Information and Computer Science
Aalto University School of Science
P.O. Box 15400, FI-00076 Aalto, Finland
firstname.lastname@aalto.fi

ABSTRACT

Many emerging application areas in video and image processing require large-scale visual concept detection. Examples include content-based indexing of online user-generated videos and 24/7 archival of TV broadcasts. The current state of the art in concept detection uses bag-of-visual-words features with computationally heavy exponential kernel classifiers. We argue that this classifier approach is not feasible for large-scale real-time applications, and propose instead to use combinations of approximate additive kernel classifiers. By using explicit kernel maps and the power mean SVM, followed by fusion of classifiers trained on different features, we achieve high retrieval precision while retaining real-time performance for large sets of concepts. This paper presents a series of experiments with the large-scale TRECVID 2012 video database and the commonly used Fifteen Scene Categories image database. We show significantly improved retrieval performance over standard linear classifiers, and by late fusion over several visual features, the approximative additive kernels outperform any single exponential kernel in only a fraction of the detection time.

Categories and Subject Descriptors

H.3.1 [**Information Storage and Retrieval**]: Content Analysis and Indexing; H.3.3 [**Information Storage and Retrieval**]: Information Search and Retrieval; I.2.6 [**Artificial Intelligence**]: Learning—*Concept learning*

General Terms

Algorithms, Experimentation, Performance

Keywords

concept detection; linear classifiers; explicit kernel maps; homogeneous kernel maps; support vector machine; power mean SVM

1. INTRODUCTION

Visual concept detection facilitates high-level querying of audiovisual data by organizing the database in terms of mid-level concepts such as objects, persons or events [9]. The definition of a visual concept is intentionally broad in scope. The concepts in visual ontologies are assessed with criteria such as utility, observability by humans, and feasibility by automatic detection [14]. Examples of such *semantic concepts* include images containing "cats", videos depicting "people marching", or "explosions or fire". Statistical classifiers are trained on manually labelled data in order to predict the presence of such concepts in new images or video. This typically results in an estimate of the probability of a given concept being present in a given image or video shot.

Current state-of-the-art automatic concept detectors rely on local features such as SIFT [16] or SURF [1], bag-of-visual-words (BoV) histograms generated typically by k-means (or recently also with kernel k-means [38] or with GMMs), and computationally heavy kernel-based classifiers, such as non-linear SVMs, trained with general-purpose kernel SVM solvers such as the SMO algorithm [23]. This popular method has then been extended in numerous ways, such as with spatial pyramid matching [15] and soft cluster assignment [8], that further improve the detection accuracy.

However, there are many scenarios today that require extremely fast classification, preferably real-time or better for a typically large number of concepts. One such scenario is indexing of online video. For example in 2012, 72 hours of new video were uploaded to YouTube *every minute* [41]. Another example is broadcast television archival, in which at least the major TV channels are typically archived continuously. Media researchers and possibly also the general public are then given access to the archived material, but without advanced indexing methods it is difficult to retrieve relevant material from the archives. Manual annotation of such archives is clearly not feasible, so there has existed a growing interest in content-based retrieval methods in these kinds of application areas [11].

In such general domains, a large number of concepts is needed—at least in the order of hundreds—putting additional emphasis on fast detection methods. In fact, we argue that in such a setup, the critical efficiency criterion is the classifier evaluation cost, not training, even though most of the recent work on improving the efficiency of linear classification has concentrated on reducing the training complexity [13, 25, 10]. The classifiers need to be continuously evaluated for each new image or video keyframe that is processed and added to the database. With hundreds or thousands of concepts this becomes the computational bottleneck of the system, rather than the training stage, which has to be performed only intermittently. An example of recent work focusing on the cost of evaluation is [17].

There have been numerous approaches to reduce the computational complexity from the level of standard non-linear SVMs. Such approaches include using approximate SVM solvers [3, 37], reducing the number of support vectors [4, 6], and replacing the non-linear SVMs with linear classifiers [42]. It is also possible to speed up SVMs by using GPUs [29]. Using linear classifiers is particularly appealing, as both the training and classification time requirements can be several orders of magnitude smaller than with non-linear SVMs. Recent algorithms for training large-scale linear classifiers include the stochastic subgradient descent in Pegasos [25] and the dual coordinate descent algorithm in LIBLINEAR [10]. As a practical example, in our current implementation and the TRECVID data used in experiments reported in this paper, evaluating a linear classifier for a single image (excluding feature extraction) takes only a fraction of a millisecond whereas non-linear SVMs require 100–200 ms per image.

Linear classifiers have been shown to achieve competitive performance on very high-dimensional problems such as in document classification (e.g. [42]). However, they cannot typically match the performance of non-linear SVMs in vision problems, in which the dimensionalities are not as high (typically in the thousands). Recently there has been a lot of progress in improving the classification accuracy of linear classifiers, especially for multinomial distributions, e.g. histograms. One approach is to use linear approximations for additive non-linear kernels [17, 22, 33, 36], which has turned out to be a very promising approach as the approximations provide results very similar to the original non-linear kernels. Additive kernels typically achieve accuracies that lie between the linear classifiers and the state-of-the-art exponential kernels, and with recent algorithms their training and evaluating times are close to the state-of-the-art linear solvers. Other approaches include methods that modify the BoV representation to be better suitable for linear classifiers, such as sparse coding of local descriptors [39], the Efficient Match Kernel [2], supervector encoding [43] and the Fisher kernel [21].

With an eye on the aforementioned large-scale real-time classification scenario, we present in this paper a real-world study of speeding up visual concept detection while preserving the classification accuracy required. We experiment with two recently proposed methods to reach the performance of non-linear additive kernels with computational requirements on the level of linear classifiers: the homogeneous kernel maps proposed by Vedaldi and Zisserman [33, 34] and the power mean SVM recently proposed by Wu [37].

The experiments were carried out with the large-scale video database used in the *TRECVID 2012* evaluations [19] and with the image database Fifteen Scene Categories (*15 scenes*) [15]. The TRECVID database contains a very general and diverse set of videos from the Internet Archive. The videos have not been manually selected for ease of detection, as is the case in many other visual databases, and thus presents a very realistic video search scenario. The *15 scenes* dataset is considerably smaller and may even be regarded as toy data in this setting, but was used to further validate the experiment results and provide results that are comparable

to many previous publications (e.g. [15, 20], among numerous others).

The rest of the paper is organized as follows. Next, in Section 2, we review the class of additive non-linear kernels and the approximation methods employed. We then review the standard exponential kernels that are used as a benchmark in the experiments, in Section 3. Experiments using two datasets are reported in Section 4, and the paper is concluded in Section 5.

2. ADDITIVE KERNELS

Let us assume training data

$$\{(\mathbf{x}_1, y_1), (\mathbf{x}_2, y_2), \ldots, (\mathbf{x}_m, y_m)\}, \qquad (1)$$

where $\mathbf{x}_j \in \mathbb{R}_+^d$ and $y_j \in \{+1, -1\}$ are the (non-negative) feature vectors and the ground truth labels, respectively.

Non-linear kernel SVMs are computationally expensive for real-time applications, as the decision function is

$$d(\mathbf{x}) = \sum_{j=1}^{m'} \alpha_j K(\mathbf{x}_j, \mathbf{x}) + b \qquad (2)$$

i.e. the query feature vector $\mathbf{x}$ has to be compared to all support vectors of the model when classifying a new sample. This makes the complexity of evaluating a non-linear SVM to be $O(dm')$, where m' is the number of support vectors. On the other hand, the cost of evaluating a linear classifier is $O(d)$ as it only requires an inner product

$$d(\mathbf{x}) = \langle \mathbf{w}, \mathbf{x} \rangle + b \qquad (3)$$

with a weight vector $\mathbf{w}$, but linear classifiers typically cannot reach the accuracy of non-linear SVMs in the common tasks of computer vision.

The common non-linear kernels for multinomial distributions used in computer vision can be divided into two groups, additive and exponential kernels [32, 22]. A kernel is *additive* if it can be represented as a sum of feature-component-wise one-dimensional functions, i.e. if it can be written as

$$K(\mathbf{x}, \mathbf{z}) = \sum_{i=1}^{d} k_i(x_i, z_i) , \qquad (4)$$

where $\mathbf{x} = [x_1, \ldots, x_d]^T, \mathbf{z} = [z_1, \ldots, z_d]^T \in \mathbb{R}_+^d$.

Common additive kernels include the intersection kernel

$$k_{\text{int}}(x_i, z_i) = \min(x_i, z_i) , \qquad (5)$$

the χ^2 kernel

$$k_{\chi^2}(x_i, z_i) = -\frac{(x_i - z_i)^2}{x_i + z_i} , \qquad (6)$$

the Bhattacharyya kernel

$$k_{\text{bha}}(x_i, z_i) = \sqrt{x_i z_i} , \qquad (7)$$

and the Jensen-Shannon kernel

$$k_{\text{js}}(x_i, z_i) = \frac{x_i}{2} \log_2 \frac{(x_i + z_i)}{x_i} + \frac{z_i}{2} \log_2 \frac{(x_i + z_i)}{z_i} . \qquad (8)$$

In [37], the power mean kernel

$$k_{\text{pm}}(x_i, z_i; p) = \left(\frac{x_i^p + z_i^p}{2} \right)^{1/p} \qquad (9)$$

was proposed as a generalization of many additive kernels, such the ones in Eqs (5)–(7). The intersection, χ^2, and

Bhattacharyya kernels can be represented with the power mean kernel by setting $p = -\infty$, $p = -1$, and $p = 0$, respectively [37].

It has recently been shown that additive kernels can be approximated e.g. with piecewise linear approximations [17], mapping integer features to binary vectors [36], additive kernel PCA [22], or with homogeneous kernel maps [33, 34], often with negligible loss of accuracy compared to the original non-linear kernel [28, 34] Another type of approach was proposed in [37], in which the gradient calculation within the learning algorithm is approximated, instead of approximating the feature mapping.

2.1 Explicit kernel maps

The fast training and evaluating times of linear classifiers have raised interest in converting non-linear classifiers to linear ones. Non-linear kernel classifiers can be considered as linear classifiers in a feature space for which there exists a corresponding implicit feature map $\Psi : \mathbb{R}^d \to \mathbb{R}^D$. Therefore, one approach is to perform an explicit (either exact or approximate) feature mapping to convert the non-linear problem into a linear one and use a standard linear solver. With an exact feature map this is straightforward:

$$K(\mathbf{x}_i, \mathbf{x}_j) = \langle \Psi(\mathbf{x}_i), \Psi(\mathbf{x}_j) \rangle . \tag{10}$$

The exact mapping approach can work in certain cases, but, in general, the dimensionality D of the feature map Ψ can be high or even infinite, as is the case e.g. with the RBF kernel. Therefore, a more practical approach is to approximate the non-linear kernel. There are numerous methods for this purpose and a comprehensive review is outside the scope of this paper, but the most relevant approaches for this discussion are *kernel matrix approximation* and *feature mapping approximation*, as they lead to linear classifiers [42]. In kernel matrix approximation, the aim is to find a low-rank matrix $\hat{\Phi} \in \mathbb{R}^{r \times m}$ with $r \ll m$ so that

$$\hat{\Phi}^T \hat{\Phi} = \hat{\mathbf{K}} \approx \mathbf{K} , \tag{11}$$

where $\mathbf{K}$ is the kernel matrix. Assuming $\hat{\Phi} \equiv [\hat{\mathbf{x}}_1, \dots, \hat{\mathbf{x}}_m]$, we can then train a linear classifier on this new data. This kind of approximation does not, however, provide a straightforward way to evaluate the linear classifier.

The second approach is to try to find a mapping function $\hat{\Psi} : \mathbb{R}^d \to \mathbb{R}^r$ so that

$$\langle \hat{\Psi}(\mathbf{x}_i), \hat{\Psi}(\mathbf{x}_j) \rangle \approx K(\mathbf{x}_i, \mathbf{x}_j) . \tag{12}$$

Many such mappings have been proposed, such as random Fourier and binning features [24]. Again, a full review is outside the scope of this paper.

A useful mapping $\hat{\Psi}$ has to fulfill two requirements [34]: there has to be a way to compute the mapping efficiently, and it has to be sufficiently compact (low-dimensional or sparse). In the general case, finding such mappings is difficult, but it has turned out that with additive kernels this is possible. In [17], Maji et al proposed a sparse feature map for the intersection kernel, and subsequently Vedaldi and Zisserman proposed *homogeneous kernel maps* [33, 34] for any additive homogeneous kernel, such as the ones in Eqs (5)–(8). Such explicit kernel maps are convenient to use as they do not require any changes to the linear classification algorithm and are data independent. As a result, no learning is required and the kernel map can be computed on-the-fly using a look-up table.

The homogeneous kernel map of order n is a $(2n + 1)$-dimensional linear approximation of an additive kernel for a scalar feature, $\hat{\Psi}_n : \mathbb{R} \to \mathbb{R}^{2n+1}$. Due to the additivity property (Eq. (4)), one can then encode a d-dimensional feature vector as a $d(2n + 1)$-dimensional linear problem using the kernel map and use any standard linear solver with it to approximate the corresponding non-linear kernel. The complexity of evaluating the classifier is thus $O(d)$. In [33, 34], homogeneous kernel maps are provided for many common additive kernels used in computer vision.

For the Bhattacharyya kernel, the feature mapping is trivial and exact: $\Psi(x) = \sqrt{x}$, i.e. it can be obtained by taking a term-by-term square root of the feature vector.

2.2 Power mean SVM

The power mean SVM (PmSVM) was recently proposed by Wu [37] as an alternative method to approximate additive kernels by approximating the calculation of the gradient G, which is the computational bottleneck in the coordinate descent algorithm [10, 42], using second-order polynomial regression of scalar functions. PmSVM provides efficient training and classification with the power mean kernel of Eq. (9) for any $p < 0$, as well as with other additive kernels. In practice, PmSVM can be even faster to train than implementations of linear SVMs (e.g. LIBLINEAR) as it often requires less iterations to converge.

Consider the standard dual SVM problem for the power mean kernel

$$\min_{\boldsymbol{\alpha}} f(\boldsymbol{\alpha}) = \frac{1}{2} \sum_{i,j} \alpha_i \alpha_j y_i y_j K_{\mathrm{pm}}(\mathbf{x}_i, \mathbf{x}_j) - \sum_i \alpha_i$$
$$\text{s.t.} \quad 0 \leq \alpha_i \leq C \tag{13}$$

where $\boldsymbol{\alpha} = [\alpha_1, \dots, \alpha_m]^T$ are the Lagrange multipliers. The corresponding decision boundary is $\mathbf{w} = \sum_{j=1}^{m} \alpha_j y_j \Psi(\mathbf{x}_j)$.

The coordinate descent algorithm sequentially selects one variable i for update and fixes the others. The gradient G_i with respect to α_i is

$$\begin{aligned} G_i &= y_i \mathbf{w}^T \Psi(\mathbf{x}_i) - 1 \\ &= y_i \sum_{j=1}^{m} \alpha_j y_j K_{\mathrm{pm}}(\mathbf{x}_i, \mathbf{x}_j) - 1 \\ &= y_i g(\mathbf{x}_i) - 1 \\ &= y_i \sum_{k=1}^{d} g_k(x_{i,k}) - 1 , \end{aligned} \tag{14}$$

where

$$g_k(x) = \sum_{j=1}^{m} \alpha_j y_j k_{\mathrm{pm}}(x, x_{j,k}) \tag{15}$$

is a scalar function [37] (and $x_{i,k}$ is the kth component of the vector $\mathbf{x}_i$). Therefore, in order to approximate the gradient, it is sufficient to approximate the scalar functions $g_k(x)$. It turns out that $g_k(x)$ are smooth and monotone functions that can be approximated accurately using low-order polynomial regression. In [37], the approximation is done using a second-order polynomial

$$g_k(x) \approx \sum_{q=0}^{2} a_{k,q} (\ln(x + 0.05))^q , \tag{16}$$

where instead of x, $\ln(x + 0.05)$ is used in the approximation to get better results.

Classifying a new example $\mathbf{x}$ with PmSVM thus requires the evaluation of

$$d(\mathbf{x}) = \sum_{k=1}^{d} \sum_{q=0}^{2} a_{k,q} (\ln(x_k + 0.05))^q , \qquad (17)$$

so the classification complexity is $O(d)$.

3. EXPONENTIAL KERNELS

Exponential kernels are popular in many computer vision tasks and have often been reported to achieve better performance than additive kernels (e.g. [32, 22, 28]). In addition to the commonly-used RBF kernel, exponential kernels can be constructed from other kernels. Any kernel K can be exponentiated by $K' = \exp(\gamma K)$ with $\gamma > 0$ so that K' is also a valid kernel [26]. Such exponentiated kernels can also be considered as generalized RBF kernels, where the Euclidean distance has been replaced by another metric. A common family of exponential kernels is obtained by exponentiating additive kernels.

In this paper, we use the following exponential kernels as points of comparison to the approximation methods considered: the RBF kernel

$$K_{\mathrm{RBF}}(\mathbf{x}, \mathbf{z}) = \exp\left(-\gamma \|\mathbf{x} - \mathbf{z}\|_2^2\right) , \qquad (18)$$

the exponential intersection kernel (also known as the Laplacian kernel)

$$K_{\mathrm{int}}^{\exp}(\mathbf{x}, \mathbf{z}) = \exp\left(-\gamma \sum_{i=1}^{d} \min(x_i, z_i)\right) , \qquad (19)$$

and the exponential χ^2 kernel

$$K_{\chi^2}^{\exp}(\mathbf{x}, \mathbf{z}) = \exp\left(-\gamma \sum_{i=1}^{d} \frac{(x_i - z_i)^2}{x_i + z_i}\right) , \qquad (20)$$

where γ is the kernel width.

4. EXPERIMENTS

4.1 Databases

To measure the performance of linear and non-linear large-scale concept detection, we have performed experiments with two databases.

First, we use the videos from the *TRECVID 2012* semantic indexing evaluation [19], which in total contains about 28 000 short videos from the Internet Archive (approximately 600 hours or 150 GB, and about 1.8 million keyframes with our sampling method). Approximately 20 000 videos are used as training data, and the remaining 8000 for testing. The TRECVID ontology is based on LSCOM [14] and currently defines 500 concepts, although only 346 of them had four or more positive annotations in the year 2012 training data. Thus, detection results for 346 concept detectors was to be submitted for the evaluation, and 46 of them were evaluated for the official TRECVID results. As the performance measure, we use the current standard evaluation measure in TRECVID: mean extended inferred average precision (MX-IAP) [40] over the 46 evaluated concepts. It should be noted that the pooling technique used in the TRECVID evaluations can result in underestimation of the performance of new algorithms and new runs which were not part of the official evaluation, as all unique relevant shots retrieved by them will be missing from the ground truth. Some of the results presented in this paper are, however, very close to our submissions in the official evaluation [27].

We also present multi-class classification results on the widely used Fifteen Scene Categories (*15 scenes*) dataset [15]. The dataset contains 4485 greyscale images assigned to 15 categories, with 200 to 400 images belonging to each category. We used the experimental procedure described in [15], so there were 10 random splits into training and test sets with 100 images per class always used for training, and multi-class classification was done with one-versus-all SVMs.

4.2 Features

We extracted various BoV-based features from the images. We used the standard SIFT and color SIFT [30] with soft cluster assignment and different spatial pyramids, and with two different sampling strategies: the Harris-Laplace salient point detector (*SIFT* and *CSIFT*) and dense sampling (*SIFT^{ds}* and *CSIFT^{ds}*). For the color SIFT features we used the opponent color space. For the *15 scenes* dataset we exclude the color-based features, since it consists only of greyscale images.

We use three different spatial pyramids $\mathbf{\Lambda}_1$–$\mathbf{\Lambda}_3$, using the notation from [20], where the ith row λ_i of the spatial pyramid matrix $\mathbf{\Lambda}$ contains the region's relative heights s_i^y and widths s_i^x, shifts in y and x directions, d_i^y and d_i^x, and weights w_i:

$$\lambda_i = \left[\begin{array}{ccccc} s_i^y & s_i^x & d_i^y & d_i^x & w_i \end{array} \right] .$$

The spatial pyramids used in this paper are

$$\mathbf{\Lambda}_1 = \left[\begin{array}{ccccc} 1 & 1 & 1 & 1 & 1 \\ \frac{1}{2} & \frac{1}{2} & \frac{1}{2} & \frac{1}{2} & 1 \end{array} \right] ,$$

$$\mathbf{\Lambda}_2 = \left[\begin{array}{ccccc} 1 & 1 & 1 & 1 & 1 \\ \frac{1}{2} & \frac{1}{2} & \frac{1}{2} & \frac{1}{2} & 1 \\ \frac{1}{3} & 1 & \frac{1}{3} & 1 & 1 \end{array} \right] ,$$

and

$$\mathbf{\Lambda}_3 = \left[\begin{array}{ccccc} 1 & 1 & 1 & 1 & 1 \\ \frac{1}{2} & \frac{1}{2} & \frac{1}{2} & \frac{1}{2} & 1 \\ \frac{1}{4} & \frac{1}{4} & \frac{1}{4} & \frac{1}{4} & 1 \end{array} \right] .$$

The total numbers of regions in the spatial pyramids are $V_1 = 1 + 4 = 5$, $V_2 = 1 + 4 + 3 = 8$, and $V_3 = 1 + 4 + 16 = 21$, respectively. The BoV codebooks were generated using k-means with 1000 cluster centroids for $\mathbf{\Lambda}_1$ and $\mathbf{\Lambda}_2$ and with 200 centroids for $\mathbf{\Lambda}_3$.

It should be emphasized that while the computational requirements of feature extraction are also an important aspect in real-time applications, we do not consider speeding up feature extraction in this paper and the used features were not optimized for extraction time.

4.3 Classifiers

We use the homogeneous kernel map approximations of the intersection kernel (hkm$_{\mathrm{int}}$), the χ^2 kernel (hkm$_{\chi^2}$), and the Jensen-Shannon kernel (hkm$_{\mathrm{js}}$), as well as the exact kernel map for the Bhattacharyya kernel (ekm$_{\mathrm{bha}}$), obtained by taking a term-by-term square root of the feature vectors. The order of all homogeneous kernel maps was set to $n = 3$.

For the power mean SVM, we use two values of the p parameter: $p = -1$, corresponding to the χ^2 kernel, and

Table 1: MXIAP scores for the *TRECVID 2012* dataset for individual features and mean and fusion of all features. The highest scores among the non-exponential classifiers are highlighted.

	SIFT_{Λ_1}	$\text{SIFT}_{\Lambda_1}^{ds}$	CSIFT_{Λ_1}	$\text{CSIFT}_{\Lambda_1}^{ds}$	mean	fusion	(+%)
linear	0.083	0.060	0.085	0.076	0.076	0.132 }	+55%
ekm_{bha}	0.052	0.050	0.097	0.074	0.068	0.139	+43%
hkm_{js}	0.085	0.075	0.117	0.100	0.094	0.174	+49%
hkm_{χ^2}	0.116	0.087	0.129	0.110	0.111	0.182	+41%
hkm_{int}	**0.134**	**0.116**	0.137	**0.123**	**0.128**	0.191	+39%
pm_{χ^2}	0.128	0.111	0.137	0.114	0.123	**0.200**	+46%
pm_{int}	0.129	0.109	**0.139**	0.117	0.124	**0.200**	+44%
K_{RBF}	0.137	0.137	0.104	0.134	0.128	0.198	+45%
$K_{\chi^2}^{\text{exp}}$	0.166	0.148	0.159	0.151	0.156	0.217	+31%
$K_{\text{int}}^{\text{exp}}$	0.167	0.146	0.150	0.149	0.153	0.214	+28%

Table 2: Classification accuracies and standard deviations for the *15 scenes* dataset for four different features and mean and fusion of all features. The highest accuracies among the non-exponential classifiers are highlighted.

	SIFT_{Λ_1}	$\text{SIFT}_{\Lambda_1}^{ds}$	$\text{SIFT}_{\Lambda_2}^{ds}$	$\text{SIFT}_{\Lambda_3}^{ds}$	mean	fusion
linear	0.687 ± 0.006	0.706 ± 0.024	0.732 ± 0.009	0.711 ± 0.012	0.709 ± 0.013	0.765 ± 0.008
ekm_{bha}	0.698 ± 0.007	0.737 ± 0.011	0.758 ± 0.011	0.728 ± 0.013	0.730 ± 0.011	0.778 ± 0.011
hkm_{js}	0.727 ± 0.016	0.763 ± 0.013	0.788 ± 0.012	0.752 ± 0.008	0.758 ± 0.012	0.800 ± 0.008
hkm_{χ^2}	0.744 ± 0.005	0.769 ± 0.006	0.798 ± 0.011	0.760 ± 0.012	0.768 ± 0.009	0.807 ± 0.006
hkm_{int}	0.745 ± 0.005	$\textbf{0.773} \pm \textbf{0.011}$	0.798 ± 0.004	0.770 ± 0.013	$\textbf{0.771} \pm \textbf{0.008}$	0.811 ± 0.004
pm_{χ^2}	0.748 ± 0.005	0.736 ± 0.020	0.805 ± 0.006	0.770 ± 0.006	0.765 ± 0.009	0.814 ± 0.007
pm_{int}	$\textbf{0.750} \pm \textbf{0.003}$	0.738 ± 0.019	$\textbf{0.807} \pm \textbf{0.006}$	$\textbf{0.773} \pm \textbf{0.005}$	0.767 ± 0.008	$\textbf{0.815} \pm \textbf{0.007}$
K_{RBF}	0.728 ± 0.006	0.780 ± 0.004	0.798 ± 0.008	0.768 ± 0.007	0.768 ± 0.006	0.808 ± 0.006
$K_{\chi^2}^{\text{exp}}$	0.760 ± 0.007	0.789 ± 0.009	0.809 ± 0.005	0.780 ± 0.006	0.785 ± 0.007	0.821 ± 0.005
$K_{\text{int}}^{\text{exp}}$	0.761 ± 0.005	0.788 ± 0.008	0.804 ± 0.009	0.777 ± 0.005	0.782 ± 0.007	0.815 ± 0.009

$p = -8$, which is suggested in [37] to be a reasonable value in practice to simulate the intersection kernel ($p = -\infty$).

For comparison, we also use standard linear classifiers, as well as three exponential kernels, K_{RBF}, $K_{\text{int}}^{\text{exp}}$, and $K_{\chi^2}^{\text{exp}}$, Eqs (18)–(20). In our preliminary tests, we have observed that the homogeneous kernel maps and PmSVM reach the performance of the corresponding original additive kernels (Eqs (5), (6), and (8)), so we omit these kernels from these experiments.

To train the non-linear SVMs, we use the the C-SVC classifier of the LIBSVM software library [5] extended to support additional kernels. For linear classifiers we use the LIBLINEAR [7] library with the L_2-regularized logistic regression solver, and the implementation of homogeneous kernel maps for the intersection, χ^2, and Jensen-Shannon kernels available in the VLFeat library [31] . For the power mean SVM, we use the implementation available at [35].

The non-exponential classifiers contain only the penalty parameter C, while the exponential classifiers have two parameters, C and γ. We use cross-validation to select parameters for all cases except for PmSVM, which according to

[37] is not sensitive to the parameter C. We therefore use the default value $C = 0.01$ for PmSVM. For single parameter selection we use an approximate 10-fold cross-validation search that consists of a uniform sampling of the parameter space followed by another more detailed sampling in the best region. The two parameters for exponential kernels are selected similarly, but starting with a heuristic line search to identify a promising parameter region, followed by a grid search in that region.

In addition to using single features, we show the results with late fusion of multiple features, as it is a standard method to improve the results of visual concept detection. In the fusion experiments, we use arithmetic mean to fuse the feature-wise classifiers, since this has produced good results in previous experiments with TRECVID data [27].

4.4 Results

The results for *TRECVID 2012* and *15 scenes* datasets are shown in Tables 1 and 2. In Table 1, the TRECVID 2012 MXIAP scores are shown for different classifiers and four different features. To reduce the effect of the choice

Table 3: Average evaluation times for the _TRECVID 2012_ dataset for one concept and all 346 concepts.

	1 concept (ms)	346 concepts (s)
linear	0.019	0.0064
ekm$_{bha}$	0.019	0.0064
hkm$_{js}$	0.12	0.041
hkm$_{\chi^2}$	0.12	0.041
hkm$_{int}$	0.12	0.042
pm$_{\chi^2}$	0.15	0.051
pm$_{int}$	0.15	0.052
K_{RBF}	180	63
$K_{\chi^2}^{exp}$	210	74
K_{int}^{exp}	100	36

of features, the mean results over the feature-wise scores are also considered. On the right, the results of fusion over the four individual features are shown. As the TRECVID results are obtained from single runs, we analyzed the statistical significance of the differences in the MXIAP fusion results in Table 1 using paired t-test with $p = 0.01$ based on the 46 concept-wise results evaluated. Table 2 shows the multi-class classification results with the _15 scenes_ dataset. All results include the mean and standard deviation over 10 random splits to training and test sets. Similarly as in Table 1, the results for four individual features, as well as their mean and fusion results are included.

First of all, with both datasets, we can observe the high accuracy of the exponential kernels. This was to be expected, as exponential kernels have been found to be superior in many previous studies [32, 22, 28]. Furthermore, again unsurprisingly, the highest accuracies are obtained with exponential intersection and χ^2 kernels, which have been found to perform better than the RBF kernel for histogram features.

Both the homogeneous kernel map approximations and the power mean SVM clearly bring a notable performance increase over the standard linear classifiers, and are generally reaching the performance of the RBF kernel. Overall, the intersection kernel performs somewhat better than the χ^2 kernel, especially with the homogeneous kernel maps. The Jensen-Shannon kernel hkm$_{js}$, however, fails to reach the performance level of the intersection and χ^2 kernels. Also, using the exact kernel map for the Bhattacharyya kernel ekm$_{bha}$ does not result in a similar increase in performance as with the homogeneous kernel maps and the improvement over the linear classifiers is rather modest. This is somewhat in contrast to [22], where ekm$_{bha}$ was reported to lead to large improvements.

The computational efficiency of the classifiers varies considerably. Table 3 shows average evaluation times per image, with the TRECVID 2012 data, for a single concept and for all 346 concepts submitted to the 2012 evaluation. The homogeneous kernel map and power mean SVM variants are roughly 10 times slower than a linear classifier. In contrast, the evaluation times with the exponential kernels are on the order of 10,000 times longer. The evaluation times were measured on Intel Core 2 2.83 GHz processors.

The performance of all classifiers can be improved by us-

ing late fusion of multiple features. The rightmost column in Tables 1 and 2 show the results obtained by fusing classifier outputs of all features used in the corresponding experiments. The feature-wise results are fused by using arithmetic mean. The statistical significance analysis in Table 1 shows that the obtained differences in the fusion results between different classifiers are statistically significant except for three groups, within which the mutual differences were not significant. These groups are indicated with brackets in Table 1: (1) the linear classifier and ekm$_{bha}$, (2) hkm$_{int}$, pm$_{\chi^2}$, pm$_{int}$, and K_{RBF}, and (3) $K_{\chi^2}^{exp}$ and K_{int}^{exp}.

The relative improvement of fusion over the best individual features is clear, especially in the TRECVID concept detection (improvements shown as percentages in Table 1). The improvement is greatest for the linear classifiers. For the standard linear classifiers, the fusion result with all features is 55% over the best individual feature. For the homogeneous kernel maps and PmSVM, the improvement is about 40–50%, whereas for the best-performing exponential intersection and χ^2 kernels it is about 30%. Feature fusion thus seems to partially compensate for the performance differences of different classifiers in concept detection. In classification with the _15 scenes_ database (Table 2), the relative improvement of fusion over the single features is also consistent but less substantial. Interestingly, the fusion performance of PmSVM is consistently higher than with the homogeneous kernel maps, and even reaching the performance of the exponential intersection kernel with the _15 scenes_ database.

Another way of analyzing the results in Tables 1 and 2 is to compare the fusion results of the approximative additive kernels to the single feature results with the exponential kernels. In TRECVID concept detection (Table 1), the fusion results of intersection and χ^2 kernels are clearly higher than any of the individual features even with exponential kernels. Therefore, assuming that the number of concepts to detect is high enough, the feature extraction time required by multiple features is insignificant compared to the classifier evaluation time, it is possible to reach and even exceed the performance of single-feature exponential kernels with approximative additive kernels and fusion of multiple features, with several orders of magnitude shorter processing times.

5. CONCLUSIONS

Visual concept detection has attracted a lot of research attention in recent years as a method to facilitate semantic indexing and concept-based retrieval of multimedia content. Indeed, in recent studies it has been observed that, despite their limited accuracy, semantic concept detectors can be highly useful in supporting high-level indexing and querying on multimedia data [9]. This is mainly because such detectors can be trained off-line with computationally more demanding supervised learning algorithms and with considerably more positive and negative training examples than what are typically available at query time. Real-world multimedia retrieval requires, however, large concept ontologies to support a sufficient variety of queries. For example, the ImageNet Large Scale Visual Recognition Challenge 2012 (ILSVRC 2012) [12] contains 1000 object categories, and the Large-Scale Concept Ontology for Multimedia (LSCOM) [18] has 834 concepts defined. In TRECVID 2012, a total of 346 visual concepts were to be submitted to the semantic indexing full task.

The SIFT-based BoV features with exponential kernel SVMs can arguably be considered as the current standard technique for visual concept detection. To achieve top results in evaluations such as TRECVID, ILSVRC or PASCAL VOC, they have to be further extended and fine-tuned (recent successful extensions include e.g. sparse coding with max pooling [39] and the Fisher kernel [21]), and combined with other types of features, but these sophisticated methods are typically computationally extremely intensive and therefore unsuitable for real-time large-scale applications. This also means that the TRECVID results presented in this paper do not reach the top submitted results [19], partly as the set of features used is rather limited, and also as we use only the standard BoV framework here.

The central issue in this paper has been to enable real-time large-scale concept detection for large amounts of image or video material. In this setting, the time required for evaluating the classifiers is critical. Linear classifiers are therefore very appealing, and our results show that by using approximate additive kernels (either intersection or χ^2) and late fusion over several visual features one can achieve a higher detection accuracy with linear classifiers than with any single feature with exponential kernels in only a fraction of the evaluation time. The usefulness of fusion is emphasized by the fact that the improvement was obtained even by using a very simple fusion method and with features that were quite similar to each other.

The power mean SVM algorithm is equally recommendable: it achieved a performance very similar to the homogeneous kernel maps with fast training and comparable evaluation times, albeit with a very different approach. In fact, the experiment setting was slightly unbalanced against PmSVM, as we followed the suggestion in [37] that the algorithm is not sensitive to the value of the parameter C and skipped the cross-validation step. PmSVM achieved also rather similar values with the two values of p used in the experiments ($p = -1$, $p = -8$). In [37], it is stated that smaller values of p result in more accurate classifiers, but are slower. In our experiments, however, the difference in accuracy was not statistically significant and the difference in evaluation times is only about 2%.

As the average time for classifier evaluation in our setup with the TRECVID dataset for both the homogeneous kernel maps and the power mean SVM is around 0.1–0.2 ms, a single CPU core can evaluate about 5,000–10,000 classifiers per second. Assuming that a reasonable rate of analysis in a real-time video processing application could be one frame per second, we can see that this rate can be achieved by a single core with both the homogeneous kernel maps and PmSVM for several hundred concepts even when using fusion of multiple features while maintaining competitive detection accuracy. With exponential kernels this would require a large computing cluster.

It should be noted that the feature extraction methods used in these experiments were not optimized for speed and especially our current features that use the Harris-Laplace salient point detector are slow, taking on average 1–2 seconds per image. Further speed-up can undoubtedly be obtained by reconsidering the feature extraction components. Competitive results have been obtained e.g. with LBP-based features that are extremely fast to extract [38, 20]. Also, BoV feature extraction using GPUs has been shown to be very efficient [29].

6. ACKNOWLEDGMENTS

This work has been funded by the grants 255745 and 251170 of the Academy of Finland, TFMC 11863 of EIT ICT Labs, and *Next Media* and *D2I* SHOK projects. The calculations were performed using computer resources within the Aalto University School of Science "Science-IT" project.

7. REFERENCES

[1] H. Bay, T. Tuytelaars, and L. V. Gool. SURF: Speeded up robust features. In *Proc. ECCV 2006*, May 2006.

[2] L. Bo and C. Sminchisescu. Efficient match kernels between sets of features for visual recognition. In *Advances in Neural Information Processing Systems (NIPS)*, December 2009.

[3] A. Bordes, S. Ertekin, J. Weston, and L. Bottou. Fast kernel classifiers with online and active learning. *Journal of Machine Learning Research*, 6:1579–1619, September 2005.

[4] C. J. C. Burges and B. Schölkopf. Improving the accuracy and speed of support vector learning machines. In *Proc. NIPS*, 1997.

[5] C.-C. Chang and C.-J. Lin. LIBSVM: A library for support vector machines. *ACM Transactions on Intelligent Systems and Technology*, 2:27:1–27:27, 2011.

[6] T. Downs, K. E. Gates, and A. Masters. Exact simplification of support vector solutions. *Journal of Machine Learning Research*, 2:293–297, 2002.

[7] R. Fan, K. Chang, C. Hsieh, X. Wang, and C. Lin. LIBLINEAR: A library for large linear classification. *Journal of Machine Learning Research*, 9:1871–1874, 2008.

[8] J. C. Gemert, J.-M. Geusebroek, C. J. Veenman, and A. W. M. Smeulders. Kernel codebooks for scene categorization. In *Proceedings of European Conference on Computer Vision (ECCV 2008)*, 2008.

[9] A. G. Hauptmann, M. G. Christel, and R. Yan. Video retrieval based on semantic concepts. *Proceedings of the IEEE*, 96(4):602–622, April 2008.

[10] C.-J. Hsieh, K.-W. Chang, C.-J. Lin, S. S. Keerthi, and S. Sundararajan. A dual coordinate descent method for large-scale linear SVM. In *Proceedings of 25th International Conference on Machine Learning (ICML 2008)*, Helsinki, Finland, July 2008.

[11] B. Huurnink, C. G. M. Snoek, M. de Rijke, and A. W. M. Smeulders. Today's and tomorrow's retrieval practice in the audiovisual archive. In *Proceedings of the ACM International Conference on Image and Video Retrieval*, CIVR '10, pages 18–25, New York, NY, USA, 2010. ACM.

[12] ImageNet. ImageNet Large Scale Visual Recognition Challenge 2012 (ILSVRC 2012). *http://www.image-net.org/challenges/LSVRC/2012/*.

[13] T. Joachims. Training linear SVMs in linear time. In *Proceedings of the 12th ACM SIGKDD international conference on Knowledge discovery and data mining*, KDD '06, pages 217–226, New York, NY, USA, 2006. ACM.

[14] L. Kennedy and A. Hauptmann. LSCOM lexicon definitions and annotations version 1.0. Technical

Report #217-2006-3, Columbia University, March 2006. DTO Challenge Workshop on Large Scale Concept Ontology for Multimedia.

[15] S. Lazebnik, C. Schmid, and J. Ponce. Beyond bags of features: Spatial pyramid matching for recognizing natural scene categories. In *Proceedings of the IEEE Conference on Computer Vision and Pattern Recognition (CVPR 2006)*, 2006.

[16] D. G. Lowe. Distinctive image features from scale-invariant keypoints. *International Journal of Computer Vision*, 60(2):91–110, November 2004.

[17] S. Maji, A. Berg, and J. Malik. Classification using intersection kernel support vector machines is efficient. In *Proceedings of IEEE Conf. on Computer Vision and Pattern Recognition (CVPR 2008)*, pages 1–8, june 2008.

[18] M. Naphade, J. R. Smith, J. Tešić, S.-F. Chang, W. Hsu, L. Kennedy, A. Hauptmann, and J. Curtis. Large-scale concept ontology for multimedia. *IEEE MultiMedia*, 13(3):86–91, 2006.

[19] P. Over, G. Awad, M. Michel, J. Fiscus, G. Sanders, B. Shaw, W. Kraaij, A. F. Smeaton, and G. Queenot. Trecvid 2012 – an overview of the goals, tasks, data, evaluation mechani sms and metrics. In *Proceedings of TRECVID 2012*. NIST, USA, 2012.

[20] S. Paris, X. Halkias, and H. Glotin. Sparse coding for histograms of local binary patterns applied for image categorization: Toward a bag-of-scenes analysis. In *Proceedings of 21th International Conference on Pattern Recognition (ICPR 2012)*, Tsukuba, Japan, November 2012.

[21] F. Perronnin and C. Dance. Fisher kernels on visual vocabularies for image categorization. In *Computer Vision and Pattern Recognition, 2007. CVPR '07. IEEE Conference on*, pages 1 –8, June 2007.

[22] F. Perronnin, J. Sánchez, and Y. Liu. Large-scale image categorization with explicit data embedding. In *Computer Vision and Pattern Recognition (CVPR), 2010 IEEE Conference on*, pages 2297 –2304, June 2010.

[23] J. C. Platt. *Advances in Kernel Methods: Support Vector Learning*, chapter Fast Training of Support Vector Machines Using Sequential Minimal Optimization. The MIT Press, 1998.

[24] A. Rahimi and B. Recht. Random features for large-scale kernel machines. In *Advances in Neural Information Processing Systems (NIPS)*, 2007.

[25] S. Shalev-Shwartz, Y. Singer, and N. Srebro. Pegasos: Primal estimated sub-gradient solver for SVM. In *Proceedings of the 24th international conference on Machine learning*, ICML '07, pages 807–814, New York, NY, USA, 2007. ACM.

[26] J. Shawe-Taylor and N. Christiani. *Kernel Methods for Pattern Analysis*. Cambridge University Press, 2004.

[27] M. Sjöberg, S. Ishikawa, M. Koskela, J. Laaksonen, and E. Oja. PicSOM experiments in TRECVID 2012. In *Proceedings of the TRECVID 2012 Workshop*, Gaithersburg, MD, USA, November 2012.

[28] M. Sjöberg, M. Koskela, S. Ishikawa, and J. Laaksonen. Real-time large-scale visual concept detection with linear classifiers. In *Proceedings of 21st International Conference on Pattern Recognition*, Tsukuba, Japan, November 2012.

[29] K. van de Sande, T. Gevers, and C. Snoek. Empowering visual categorization with the GPU. *Multimedia, IEEE Transactions on*, 13(1):60–70, February 2011.

[30] K. E. A. van de Sande, T. Gevers, and C. G. M. Snoek. Evaluating color descriptors for object and scene recognition. *IEEE Transactions on Pattern Analysis and Machine Intelligence*, 32(9):1582–1596, 2010.

[31] A. Vedaldi and B. Fulkerson. VLFeat: A library of computer vision algorithms. *http://www.vlfeat.org/*.

[32] A. Vedaldi, V. Gulshan, M. Varma, and A. Zisserman. Multiple kernels for object detection. In *Computer Vision, 2009 IEEE 12th International Conference on*, pages 606 –613, oct 2009.

[33] A. Vedaldi and A. Zisserman. Efficient additive kernels via explicit feature maps. In *Proceedings of the IEEE Conf. on Computer Vision and Pattern Recognition (CVPR 2010)*, 2010.

[34] A. Vedaldi and A. Zisserman. Efficient additive kernels via explicit feature maps. *Pattern Analysis and Machine Intelligence, IEEE Transactions on*, 34(3):480 –492, march 2012.

[35] J. Wu. PmSVM: Power Mean SVM. *https://sites.google.com/site/wujx2001/home/power-mean-svm*.

[36] J. Wu. A fast dual method for HIK SVM learning. In *Proceedings of European Conference on Computer Vision (ECCV 2010)*, 2010.

[37] J. Wu. Power mean SVM for large scale visual classification. In *Proceedings of The IEEE Int'l Conference on Computer Vision and Pattern Recognition (CVPR 2012)*, Providence, USA, June 2012.

[38] J. Wu and J. Rehg. Beyond the Euclidean distance: Creating effective visual codebooks using the Histogram Intersection Kernel. In *Proceedings of IEEE 12th International Conference on Computer Vision (ICCV 2009)*, October 2009.

[39] J. Yang, K. Yu, Y. Gong, and T. Huang. Linear spatial pyramid matching using sparse coding for image classification. In *Computer Vision and Pattern Recognition, 2009. CVPR 2009. IEEE Conference on*, pages 1794 –1801, June 2009.

[40] E. Yilmaz, E. Kanoulas, and J. A. Aslam. A simple and efficient sampling method for estimating AP and NDCG. In *Proceedings of the 31st annual international ACM SIGIR conference on Research and development in information retrieval (SIGIR '08)*, pages 603–610, 2008.

[41] YouTube statistics. *http://www.youtube.com/t/press_statistics*.

[42] G.-X. Yuan, C.-H. Ho, and C.-J. Lin. Recent advances of large-scale linear classification. *Proceedings of the IEEE*, 100(9):2584 –2603, 2012.

[43] X. Zhou, K. Yu, T. Zhang, and T. Huang. Image classification using super-vector coding of local image descriptors. In *Proceedings of European Conference on Computer Vision (ECCV 2010)*, 2010.

A General Framework of Video Segmentation to Logical Unit based on Conditional Random Fields *

Su Xu
Interactive Digital Media
Technology Research Center
Institute of Automation
Chinese Academy of
Sciences, Beijing, China
su.xu@ia.ac.cn

Bailan Feng
Interactive Digital Media
Technology Research Center
Institute of Automation
Chinese Academy of
Sciences, Beijing, China
bailan.feng@ia.ac.cn

Zhineng Chen
Interactive Digital Media
Technology Research Center
Institute of Automation
Chinese Academy of
Sciences, Beijing, China
zn_chen@126.com

Bo Xu
Interactive Digital Media
Technology Research Center
Institute of Automation
Chinese Academy of
Sciences, Beijing, China
xubo@ia.ac.cn

ABSTRACT

Segmenting video into logical units like scenes in movies and topic units in News videos is an essential prerequisite for a wide range of video related applications. In this paper, a novel approach for logical unit segmentation based on conditional random fields (CRFs) is presented. In comparison with previous approaches that handle scenes and topic units separately, the proposed approach deals with them in a general framework. Specifically, four types of shots are defined and represented by four middle-level features, i.e., shot difference, scene transition, shot theme and audio type. Then, the problem of logical unit segmentation is novelly formulated as a problem of identifying the type of shot based on the extracted features, by leveraging the CRFs model. The proposed framework effectively integrate visual, audio and contextual features, and it is able to produce ideal result for both scene and topic unit segmentation. The effectiveness of the proposed approach is verified on seven mainstream types of videos, from which average F-measures of 88% and 86% on scenes and topic units are reported respectively, illustrating that the proposed method can accurately segment logical units in different genres of videos.

Categories and Subject Descriptors

I.5.4 [**Computer vision**]: Video Segmentation—Logical Unit Segmentation

*The work was supported by "The National Key Technology R&D Program", grant No. 61202326.

Keywords

Scene segmentation, Topic unit segmentation, Conditional random field

1. INTRODUCTION

Automatic segmentation of video is an essential prerequisite for a wide range of video related applications, such as content indexing, non-linear browsing, classification and summarization etc [12]. The task of automatic video segmentation is to divide video into different hierarchical units according to semantic or structural criteria, as shown in Figure 1. The basic units in the video are frames, and moreover the smallest physical unit on them is the shot that is defined as an unbroken sequence of frames recorded from the same camera [12]. Logical unit is a middle-layer segment consisting of the shots, which can be classified into scene and topic unit according to the type of videos. A scene is regarded as a series of shots for which the three properties, event or dramatic incident, setting and time, are consistent [12]. This term is mostly used with fictional narrative-driven video content, such as movie, TV-series, cartoon and sitcom. Topic unit is also consisted of a series of shots in which a subject matter is discussed [12]. TV-news, documentaries and educational videos are usually organized by it. A scene or topic unit contains a subtopic that may be a conversation between the actors in TV-series or a news item covering an intact story in TV-news, so they are parallel units in semantic level, as shown in Figure 1.

Video segmentation has been intensively studied in past decades. Most researchers design the algorithms only against a certain type of logical unit, for instance segmenting the movie, TV-series, sitcom and cartoon into scenes. In an early stage, graph-based approaches have received significant attention for recognizing scene pattern. In [18], Yeung et al. use pair-wise color histogram similarities between key-frames and time-constrained clustering for building scene transition graphs (STG) to represent the scenes. A similar approach is presented in [4], where Ngo et al. improve

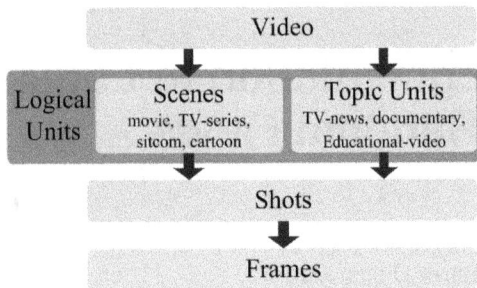

Figure 1: Hierarchical structure of video.

the performance of shots clustering by used normalized cut algorithm [6] to construct the STG. In [13], Rasheed et al. construct a weighted undirected graph in which the weights are color and motion similarities between scenes. This graph is iteratively segmented into scene sub-graphs using normalized cuts. The graph-based methods are very likely to break a scene into a few segments leading to poor precision in scene segmentation. To address this problem, Yun et al. [20] present a statistical approach, based on selecting an initial set of arbitrary scene boundaries and updating them by a Markov chain Monte Carlo (MCMC) technique. In [3], Chasanis et al. conduct shot grouping by spectral clustering, and then a sequence alignment algorithm is applied to the clustered outcome sequences instead of graph model for identifying the scenes. In [14], Sakarya et al. use graph partition to construct a one-dimensional signal that is obtained from the similarity matrix in a temporal interval. After filtering the signal, an unsupervised clustering is employed to find video scene boundaries.

Topic unit segmentation is usually used to partition TV-news into short stories that contain a single subject matter. Some methods of topic unit segmentation are based on a set of production rules of how TV-news should be composed. In [17], Gao et al. assume that news stories begin with the anchorperson shots, so they propose an unsupervised method that groups these shots using minimum spanning tree (MST) clustering to segment the news. In [1], Wang Ce et al. add silence and caption information to design heuristic rule for news story segmentation. However, these methods are only applicable to particular TV-news program. Besides heuristic rules, some authors exploit supervised methods for topic unit segmentation. In [2], Chaisorn et al. employ decision trees technique to classify the shots into one of 13 predefined categories and then perform the Hidden Markov Models (HMM) analysis to locate the boundaries of topic unit. In [10], Xie et al. propose a method of topic unit segmentation based on the robustness speech recognition technique. According to Chinese speech transcripts, the authors propose a multi-scale text-tiling approach that integrates both the specificity of words and the robustness of sub-words in lexical similarity measure to segment the units. In [16], Wang et al. employ a SVM-based method to identify program boundaries using a variety of low-level multi-modal features. In [5], Feng et al. firstly use an SVM-detector to segment news story, and then they employ dynamic programming (DP) scheme to refine the results, which can effectively increase precision of the results.

A common deficiency of the reviewed techniques is that they only design for particular type of logical unit. Although scene and topic unit are two kinds of logical unit, they have similar structure for which a general framework can be applied on both of them. Another deficiency is that they ignore the context information of neighboring shots to segment logical units. Due to semantic connectivity in logical units, the features of neighboring shots provide important context information to judge logical unit boundaries, which can effectively decrease miss or falseness of segmentation.

In this paper we propose a novel approach for logical unit segmentation. One novelty of our approach is that we exploit a general framework to segment scene and topic unit by transforming these problem into label identification. Such a framework is easily applicable to different genres of TV-program. Another novelty of our method is that the proposed approach employs Conditional Random Fields (CRFs) technique to predict labels. Because this technique adequately utilizes the context information of neighboring shot, it delivers significantly more accurate results than previous methods.

The rest of the paper is organized as follows: Section 2 describes the proposed framework in details; Section 3 shows experiments results and analysis; Section 4 concludes our work.

2. LOGICAL UNIT SEGMENTATION ALGORITHM

2.1 Analysis of proposed framework

According to the observations on a large number of videos, positional property of shots in the logical units can be classified into four categories: begin shot (BS) is a start point of the new logical unit; end shot (ES) indicates that a scene ends in this shot; middle shot (MS) is the internal shot between BS and ES; single shot (SS) is a kind of independent shot that contains completely semantic information. Such structures are given in Figure 2 (a) in which BS {1, 8}, MS {2, 3, 4, 5, 9, 10}, ES {6, 11} and SS {7} construct three typical logical units in two video sequences. In the scene sequence, repeating shot pattern of one person, a group of persons or the same setting can help identify the types of shots. BS is only similar with following shots, while the similar shots of ES only exist in the preceding ones; see shot 8 and shot 6 of scene sequence in Figure 2 (a) (similar shots are connected with arrows). MS connects with not only following shots but also preceding shots by visual similarity; see shot 4 of scene sequence in Figure 2. SS is contrary to MS, so there is not any similar shot in its neighbors; see shot 7 of scene sequence in Figure 2 (a). In topic unit sequence, the production rule of news, documentaries or other programs can help to identify the types of shots. Taking TV-news for instance, some news programs are produced by following rules: 1) a new topic begins with an anchorperson shot or a silence segment; 2) one topic has a headline caption to abstract its content. Therefore, anchorperson or silence feature indicates that a shot probably belong to BS; see shot 1 and shot 8 of topic unit sequence in Figure 2 (a). The ES does not have distinguishing features to indentify it, but it can be judged by the features of neighboring shots. For example, if the following shot has anchorperson or silence segment, the last one may be the ES; see shot 6 of topic unit sequence in Figure 2 (a). MS can be identified by headline caption; see

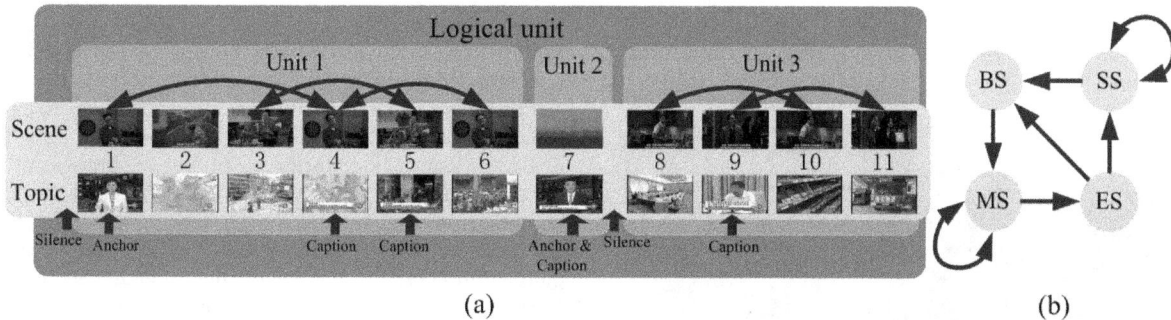

Figure 2: (a)The structure of shots in scene and topic unit sequence; (b)Sate transition graph of different types of shots in the logical units.

shot 5 of topic unit sequence in Figure 2 (a). SS commonly contains a complete subject matter in a single shot that can extract both anchorperson and headline caption from it; see shot 7 of topic unit sequence in Figure 2 (a). Stated thus, every shot in a logical unit has its positional property, so logical unit segmentation can be transformed into label identifiction problem. If we correctly identify all labels, we can obtain the logical unit boundaries between ES and BS, ES and SS or SS and SS.

To accurately identify the types of shots in a logical unit, the proposed framework employs CRFs technique that is an effective algorithm to predict multiple variables depending on each other. CRFs technique has several advantages on logical unit segmentation. Firstly, based on the idea of supervised learning, CRFs technique can train a reasonable model that reveals the production rules of logical unit. As stated above, the shot types can be identified by production rules that are quite different between scene and topic unit. Even in scenes, the shots are generally short in sitcoms, and their motion content is high. Conversely, the shots are long and the visual appearance is smooth in films. It is difficult to enumerate all the production rules of the different programs, but these rules can be simulated by a CRFs model according to training data. Secondly, CRFs model estimates the state transition probabilities, when the states transform between different types of label. State transition relationship is given in Figure 2 (b), where direction of arrows indicates the way of state transition and state transition probabilities can be calculated by training data. These transition directions and probabilities simulate the retaliation of different labels in the shot sequence conducting reasonable results of label estimation. Thirdly, CRFs technique counts all priori probabilities of the four states, which promote the accuracy of label estimation. For example, if there are not effective features to identify the type of a shot, it will count the most likely label from training data as the outputting label. Finally, comparing with HMM or other models, features of neighboring shots are taken into account when predict the current label. In scene sequence in Figure 2 (a), shot 4 is similar with shot 1 and shot 6, so the features of these shots provide context information to judge it as a MS. In topic unit sequence of Figure 2 (a), shot 3 does not have helpful features to identify its type, but due between anchorperson in shot 1 and headline caption in shot 4 this shot should express the detail of the report in one topic unit. For this reason, it probably belongs to MS. CRFs model integrates

the above advantages, so it can accurately predict label of shots for logical unit segmentation.

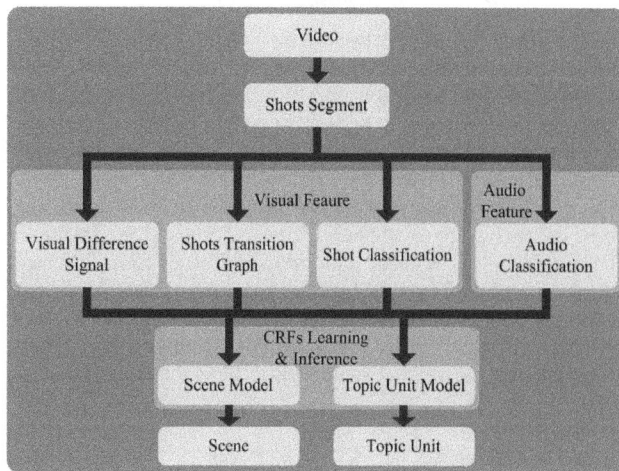

Figure 3: Flow chart of our algorithm.

In Figure 3, we summarize the main steps of our approach. The video is divided into shots using algorithm in [7]. Next, visual and audio features are extracted based on shot units, and then those features are discretized to train a CRFs model and predict the labels. In learning process, we build a list of feature vectors that map answer tags to train two different models against scene segmentation and topic unit segmentation. In the predicting process, we use the two models to predict labels in different genres of program respectively.

2.2 Features

Visual features are directly extracted from key-frames in shot units. To reduce computational complexity, we employ a common sampling strategy to select key-frames. Assuming a sampling step is n_t, and n_s is the number of frames in one shot. When $n_s > 3n_t$ key-frames are sampled by step n_t, otherwise the first, middle and last frame are selected as the key-frames. Using this strategy, no less than three key-frames would be selected to represent each shot, which is enough to compute features.

We choose four middle-level features: shot difference signal (SDS), scene transition graph (STG), shot theme (ST) and audio type (AT). SDS, STG and AT are used in scene segmentation, and all the features are used in topic unit segmentation.

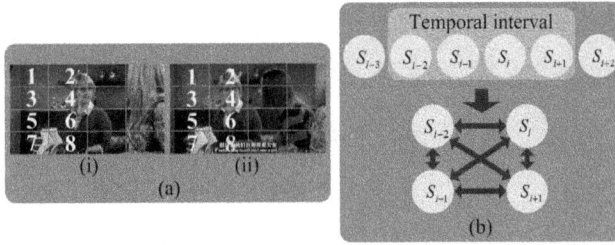

Figure 4: (a) Eight regions of the two key frames with similar RGB histograms; (b) A typical graph-based representation of a temporal interval.

2.2.1 Shot difference signal (SDS) feature

The first kind of feature in our algorithm is SDS that depicts visual dissimilarity of logical unit, and this signal is calculated by the graph partition model. Unlike distance between low-level features, SDS considers visual information of neighboring shots in a temporal interval, so it produces a signal with local invariance. Before calculating SDS, visual distance between each two shots must be defined according to RGB histogram of the key-frames. To be robust to noise, the metric in [17] is used. The two key-frames from different shots are divided into 16 blocks of the same size, as shown in Figure 4 (a). A 48-bin RGB normalized color histogram of each region with 16 bins in each color space is extracted. Distance between corresponding blocks is calculated as follows:

$$d = 1 - \sum_{i=1}^{48} \min(H_m^i, H_n^i) \quad (1)$$

Eight regions with the largest d are discarded to reduce the effects of object motion and noise; the metric D_k between two key frames is defined as the mean of the distances of the remaining regions, as shown in Figure 4 (a). Visual distance of shot D_s equals to the minimum D_k between two groups of key frames. The graph partition model of computing shot difference signal is explained as min-max cut [14]. All shots V in the temporal interval are partitioned into two disjoint subsets A and B, $A \cup B = V$ and $A \cap B = \phi$. Min-max cut criterion is defined as follow:

$$Mcut(A, B) = \frac{cut(A, B)}{assoc(A)} + \frac{cut(A, B)}{assoc(B)} \quad (2)$$

where $cut(A, B)$ and $assoc(A)$ are defined as follows:

$$cut(A, B) = \sum_{i \in A, j \in B} D_s(i, j) \quad (3)$$

$$assoc(A) = \sum_{i, j \in A} D_s(i, j) \quad (4)$$

If $2l$ shot sequence is considered, the signal of min-max cut is calculated as follows:

$$score(i) = Mcut(A, B) = \\ Mcut\{\{S_{i-l}, \ldots, S_{i-1}\}\{S_i, \ldots, S_{i+l-1}\}\} \quad (5)$$

where integer i is an index of shot that between $[i - l, i + l - 1]$. Figure 4 (b) illustrates a typical graph partition representation of a temporal interval when $l = 2$.

The SDS must be discretized in order to input CRF++ tools [9] that are open source tools for CRF application. Since the logical boundaries are probably obtained at its local maximum and this value should be larger than median or mean, discrete feature must reflect these characteristic. On one hand, range of the signal is divided into thirteen equal subintervals to map each value in signal sequence. On the other hand, each value is also labeled by three attribute: above or below median, above or below mean and local maximum or not. Therefore, SDS is transformed into 4 dimensional discrete features to input into CRFs model.

2.2.2 Scene transition graph (STG) feature

In contrast to SDS depicting visual dissimilarity, STG [18] clusters similar shots for purpose of constructing a connecting graph that depicts repeating shot pattern in a logical unit. The cut-edges of this graph are candidates of logical unit boundaries. To calculate this feature, shot difference D_s in SDS is employed. In clustering step, we choose a minimum spanning tree (MST) clustering in which time-constraint is easily added in clustering process. For the MST clustering, the distance matrix $A_{N \times N}$ and element $a(i, j)$ in the matrix are expressed as follow:

$$a(i, j) = \begin{cases} D_s(i, j) & if \ |i - j| < \sigma \\ 1 & if \ |i - j| \geqslant \sigma \end{cases} \quad (6)$$

If temporal distance between shots i and j is larger than threshold σ, they must belong to different logical units $a(i, j) = 1$, which is time-constraint in MST clustering. Object clusters are grouped through the following steps:

1. Calculate the minimum spanning tree (MST) of matrix $A_{N \times N}$.
2. Cut the edges whose weights exceed a threshold γ in the MST forming a forest.
3. Find all the trees contained in the forest and consider each tree as a potential cluster.

STG is constructed by backward searching in the same cluster as [18]. According to the result of STG analysis, each shot is classified into two categories: boundary of STG and interior node of STG, which are discrete STG feature.

2.2.3 Shot theme (ST) feature

Figure 5: Examples of the predefined theme shots: anchorperson (a) and (b), headline caption (c) and (d), highlight (e).

ST is an important feature in topic unit segmentation. In this article, shots are classified into four types of theme: anchorperson, headline caption, highlight and footage, as shown in Figure 5. Anchorperson and headline caption are effective features to depict TV news pattern in topic unit [9, 10], as shown in Figure 5 (a), (b), (c) and (d). Highlight shot is an important landmark in some documentaries, when the topic moves to the next subject, as shown in Figure 5 (e). If a shot cannot be classified into the above categories, it will be labeled as footage shot. Because this feature is extracted according to the priori knowledge of the certain programs, it is only used in topic unit segmentation.

The key-frames are divided into 16 blocks of the same size, and then 16-bin HSV normalized color histograms and discrete cosine transform (DCT) coefficients [19] are extracted from each block. Three parallel support vector machine (SVM) models are trained for anchorperson, headline caption and highlight to calculate final probability of ST according to following formula:

$$P_{theme} = \max\{PA_k, PC_k, PH_k\}, \ k \in S_i \qquad (7)$$

where PA_k, PC_k and PH_k are discriminative probability of anchorperson, headline caption and highlight respectively; k is index of key-frame of shot S_i. When $P_{theme} \geqslant 0.5$ shot theme is classified to the corresponding type, otherwise shot theme is labeled by footage shot.

2.2.4 Audio type (AT) feature

A change between logical units in the TV-program commonly accompanies a certain audio type. Therefore, AT is an effective clue that indicates a starting point of new logical unit. For example, there may be a silence or music appearing between different logical units. A helpful audio classification algorithm in [11] is used to classify sound types. Features are extracted from audio data across two shots during half second in each one. Then, all sounds are classified into silence, speech, music and noise by two cascaded SVMs, as shown in Figure 6.

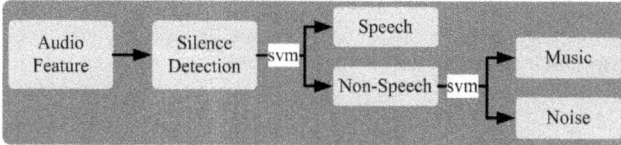

Figure 6: Flow chart of audio classify.

2.3 Logical unit model based on CRFs

There are many articles to introduce principle of CRFs, such as [15, 8], and due to the limited space, we will not go into these details of CRFs in this paper. To implement our algorithm, we use CRF++ tools to train the model and predict labels. In scene segmentation, we use 6 dimensional features in which components of SDS, STG and AT are 4, 1 and 1 respectively. In topic unit segmentation, 1 dimensional ST is added into above feature vector. To train a CRFs model, each feature vector must map a tag to indicate the type of shot. In predicting process, we only input a feature vector list to obtain boundaries of logical unit between ES and BS, ES and SS or SS and SS.

Let $S = \{s_i, \ i \in n\}$ represents n labels of shot sequence, and $X = \{X_i, \ i \in n\}$ is corresponding feature vector sequence. Each X_i in X represents a group of audio and visual features that are extracted from shot i. The goal of logical unit segmentation is to maximize the number of labels s_i that are correctly classified, which need to learn an independent per-position classier that maps $X = \{X_i\} \rightarrow S = \{s_i\}$ for

each shot i. The solution of CRFs to this problem is to model the conditional distribution $p(S|X)$. The probability assigned to a label sequence for a particular sequence of shots by a linear-chain CRFs is given by the equation below:

$$p(S|X) = \frac{1}{Z(X)} \exp\left(\sum_{i=1}^{n} \sum_{k=1}^{m} \lambda_k f_k(s_{i-1}, s_i, x_i) \right) \qquad (8)$$

where $Z(X)$ is a normalization function:

$$Z(X) = \sum_{s_i \in S} \exp\left(\sum_{i=1}^{n} \sum_{k=1}^{m} \lambda_k f_k(s_{i-1}, s_i, x_i) \right) \qquad (9)$$

function $f_k(\cdot) \in \{0, \ 1\}$ represents empirical function that depends on input variable. In theory, current label s_i can depends on the feature vector of all shots, but the feature vectors of neighboring shots are only considered in practice. In formula, k donates range of neighboring feature vectors to predict s_i. CRF++ tools use a template to control the value of k, and the detail can refer to [9]. Using $\lambda = \{\lambda_k, \ k \in m\}$ that is estimated in learning process, the maximum probability of the label sequence $S = \{s_i, \ i \in n\}$ in the condition $X = \{X_i, \ i \in n\}$ can be calculated, which $S = \{s_i, \ i \in n\}$ is desired of label sequence.

3. EXPERIMENT RESULTS

Table 1: The information of testing data set and training data set.

Testing data					
	genre	segment	time(min)	shots	scene
Scene	cartoon	3	56	783	30
	feature-film	3	90	735	40
	action-film	3	91	1859	52
	sitcom	5	106	1873	51
	TV-series	3	90	1987	61
Topic unit	news	6	167	2234	138
	documentary	6	160	1839	63
	total	29	760	11104	435

We choose about 12 hours data and cross-validation strategy to evaluate the performance of our method. In cross-validation, the half data set that is used to train model are not overlaps with testing data. The data sets that contain seven genres of TV-program can verify the effectiveness of our method in logical unit segmentation. Table 1 summarizes the information of training and testing data set. As shown in the Table 1, feature film contains a lot of conversation; action film contains some car chases and gun fights; sitcom is situation comedy; TV-series is a series of long television play. For each video, ground-truths of the logical unit boundaries are obtained by a human observer in accordance with definition in work [12]. Recall, precision, and F-measure are selected following the work [12] to evaluate the performance. In addition to use CRF++ tools, we also implement our method and comparative methods by C++ language and Opencv tools. Two CRFs model are respectively trained against scene segmentation and topic unit segmentation.

3.1 Impact of template ranges on performance

As mentioned in section 2.3, the template is employed to control the range of neighboring features used to predict

Table 2: Comparative results with other methods in scene segmentation using precision, recall and F-measure.

	Our method			Method in [14]			Method in [18]		
	Precision	Recall	F-measure	Precision	Recall	F-measure	Precision	Recall	F-measure
cartoon01	100%	90%	95%	62%	80%	70%	62%	80%	70%
cartoon02	100%	89%	94%	73%	89%	87%	73%	89%	80%
cartoon03	96%	88%	91%	77%	85%	80%	70%	88%	77%
feature-film01	83%	91%	87%	71%	91%	80%	75%	82%	78%
feature-film02	100%	87%	93%	92%	80%	86%	79%	73%	76%
feature-film03	95%	90%	92%	85%	87%	85%	73%	80%	75%
action-film01	61%	65%	63%	78%	82%	80%	74%	82%	78%
action-film02	79%	65%	71%	65%	65%	65%	80%	71%	75%
action-film03	75%	70%	72%	63%	73%	66%	77%	85%	81%
sitcom01	100%	88%	93%	70%	88%	78%	64%	88%	74%
sitcom02	100%	100%	100%	45%	83%	59%	56%	83%	67%
sitcom03	100%	85%	92%	65%	85%	73%	42%	62%	50%
sitcom04	100%	83%	91%	71%	83%	77%	69%	75%	72%
sitcom05	100%	90%	95%	75%	89%	80%	58%	70%	62%
TV-series01	90%	86%	88%	72%	86%	78%	79%	90%	84%
TV-series02	100%	90%	95%	83%	90%	86%	68%	81%	74%
TV-series03	96%	92%	94%	67%	82%	73%	70%	80%	74%
average	93%	85%	88%	71%	83%	76%	68%	80%	73%

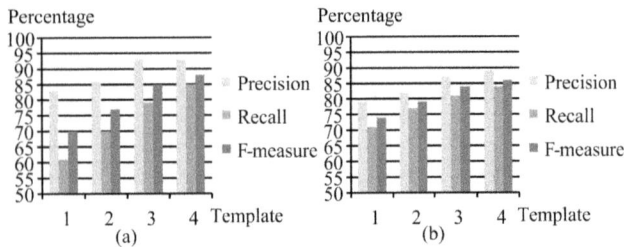

Figure 7: Result of scene (a) and topic unit (b) segmentation using different templates in CRFs model.

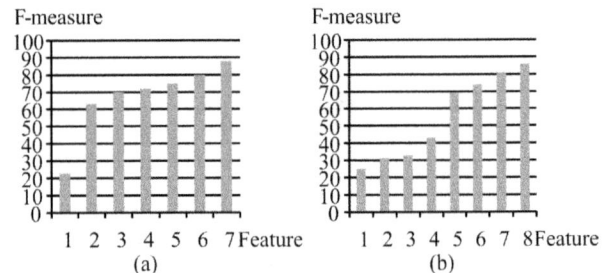

Figure 8: Result of scene (a) and topic unit (b) segmentation using different features.

current label in CRF++ tools. In the first experiment, we compare the results using different templates on logical unit segmentation. In Figure 7 (a) and (b), the performance of our algorithm on scene segmentation and topic unit segmentation are respectively presented by varying the template from 1 to 4. It can be observed that the algorithm yields better results with template range increasing. The probable reason for this phenomenon is that large template provides more context information on predicting labels than small one. Because repeating shots are usually separated by other shots, so large template can jump irrelevant shots to catch these repeating shots in the same scene, such as shot 4 of scene sequence in Figure 2 (a). In topic unit segmentation, taking shot 3 of topic sequence in Figure 2 (a) for example, when the template equal to 1, only the features from shot 2 and shot 4 can be used to predict this label. However, if the template increase to 2, the features of shot 1 and shot 5 containing anchorperson and caption information are also employed to predict its label. Therefore, the large template is more possible to contain important clues to identify shot types.

3.2 Impact of features on performance

Having examined the performance of different templates, we then compare the impact of different features on scene segmentation and logical unit segmentation respectively. Per-

formance of different features in scene segmentation is given in Figure 8 (a): 1-AT, 2-STG, 3-SDS, 4-STG and AT, 5-SDS and AT, 6-STG and SDS, 7-STG, SDS and AT. Performance of different features in topic unit segmentation is given in Figure 8 (a): 1- STG, 2- SDS, 3-AT, 4-STG, SDS and AT, 5-ST, 6-STG, SDS and ST, 7-AT and ST, 8-STG, SDS, AT and ST. From Figure 8 (a) and (b), we can learn that STG and SDS are more effective than AT in scene segmentation, but the results are contrary in topic unit segmentation. Furthermore, the most effective feature in topic unit segmentation is ST. Reasons of the this phenomenon are following: STG and SDS depict repeating shot pattern that is the production rule of the scene. On the contrary, repeating shot is not the major pattern in the News or documentaries, so STG and SDS lose their ability in topic unit segmentation. A new topic unit usually begins with silence and music, and thus AT is more useful than STG and SDS in topic unit segmentation. Since ST indicates the key point in the structure of topic unit, it is the most effective feature in topic unit segmentation.

3.3 Comparison with other methods on scene segmentation

To prove the effectiveness of our approach in scene segmentation, we also compare with two other methods [14] and [18], as shown in Table 2. Algorithm [18] is a classical method that is compared with many works, such as [3], [13], [4] et al, so it can be seen as a baseline. This method groups the shots by time-constrained clustering and uses the grouping results for building a STG. Algorithm [14] uses graph partition model to construct a one-dimensional signal and recognizes scene boundaries by clustering on this signal, which represents the state-of-the-art technique of scene segmentation. In comparative methods, we get a compromise between precisions and recalls listing best F-measures in Table 2. The averages of recall in three methods, 85%, 83% and 80% respectively, are very close. By manually browsing the results in the video, we found that most right scenes are same. A possible explanation is that the features in three methods can depict similar scene patterns. However, precisions of our method have obvious improvement. For CRFs model, if the pattern of a shot does not appear in training data or cannot be described by features, it tends to predict the label as the most likely type that is counted according to training data, so CRFs model can effectively control false detections and provide better precisions than other methods.

Results of action-film in our method are below the average. Weak efficacy of the features to depict scene patterns in action-film is responsible for this phenomenon. For example, few repeating shots cause the invalidation of SDS and STG. It is concluded that performance of CRFs model depends on the effectiveness of features. The ideal performance on action-film can be obtained by adding other effective features. Fortunately, CRFs model has ability to accept a large number of input features for prediction.

3.4 Comparison with HMM model on topic unit segmentation

Table 3: Comparative result with HMM model on topic unit segmentation using precision, recall and F-measure.

	CRF			HMM		
	Precision	Recall	F-measure	Precision	Recall	F-measure
news01	100%	89%	**94%**	88%	79%	83%
news02	100%	**100%**	**100%**	82%	75%	78%
news03	**96%**	**93%**	**95%**	85%	79%	82%
news04	100%	**94%**	**97%**	77%	72%	74%
news05	100%	**96%**	**98%**	88%	85%	86%
news06	100%	**100%**	**100%**	83%	77%	79%
documentary01	100%	100%	100%	100%	100%	100%
documentary02	100%	100%	100%	100%	100%	100%
documentary03	67%	60%	63%	55%	47%	50%
documentary04	71%	57%	63%	43%	50%	46%
documentary05	69%	55%	61%	45%	49%	47%
documentary06	66%	58%	62%	46%	46%	46%
average	89%	84%	86%	74%	72%	73%

In this section, we discuss the segmentation results on topic unit that include two kinds of data: news and documentary. Because there is not a publicly available dataset in topic unit segmentation and features in our method are quite different with other methods, we only compare results with HMM model based on same features. As shown in Table 3, performance of CRFs model on news has an obviously improvement. CRFs model predicting labels uses more context information than HMM model that only use last state

and the current features to predict the label according to Markov assumption.

Testing set of documentaries are two programs that contain six video segment. The first two video come from one program, while the last four come from another. In the first program, there is highlight shot in ST features between different topic units, as shown in Figure 3 (e). Such a program has excellent results on both CRFs model and HMM model, as shown in Table 3. In contrast, highlight shot does not exist in the second program. Although the performance of CRFs model is also superior to HMM model, it has obviously decline in comparison with the first program. This phenomenon further prove CRFs model depending feature efficiency on label production.

3.5 Accuracy of logical unit boundaries

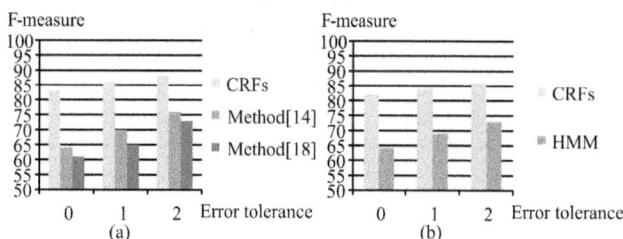

Figure 9: Comparative results (using F-measure) with different error tolerance in scene segmentation (a) and unit topic segmentation (b).

In the last experiment, we compare accuracy with different methods. In logical unit segmentation, a reasonable boundary error tolerance is no more than two shots. Average length of the shots near two seconds, so average of boundary error is no more than five seconds, which is acceptable according to audience experience. However, if a method can provide more accurate results, the feeling of audience in browsing video will be better. In the experiment, we find that CRFs model tends to miss the boundaries, but accuracy of right labels is better than other methods, as shown in figure 9 (a) and (b). When error tolerance becomes more rigorous, there is a slight F-measure decline using CRFs model in both scene segmentation and topic unit segmentation. The reason of this phenomenon is that CRFs model chooses the global optimum solution during inference.

4. CONCLUSIONS

In this paper a novel logical unit segmentation method, making use of CRFs technique, is presented. As one contribution of this method, the algorithm is developed for scene segmentation and topic unit segmentation in a general framework by transforming segmentation into label identifying problem, which can easily extend to different genres of TV-program. Another contribution of this method is that CRFs modal is exploited to identify label sequence by four kinds of middle-level features that depict the properties of the labels. Since the context information of neighboring shots is taken into account, CRFs model delivers accurate results on logical unit segmentation. In experiment, our method is successfully validated on various types of video and the encouraging experimental results demonstrate its effectiveness to logical unit segmentation.

5. REFERENCES

[1] W. Ce, W. Yun, L. Hua-Yong, and H. Yan-Xiang. Automatic story segmentation of news video based on audio-visual features and text information. In *Machine Learning and Cybernetics, 2003 International Conference on*, volume 5, pages 3008–3011 Vol.5, 2003.

[2] L. Chaisorn, T.-S. Chua, and C.-H. Lee. A multi-modal approach to story segmentation for news video. *World Wide Web*, 6(2):187–208, 2003.

[3] V. T. Chasanis, A. C. Likas, and N. P. Galatsanos. Scene detection in videos using shot clustering and sequence alignment. *Multimedia, IEEE Transactions on*, 11(1):89–100, 2009.

[4] N. Chong-Wah, M. Yu-Fei, and Z. Hong-Jiang. Video summarization and scene detection by graph modeling. *Circuits and Systems for Video Technology, IEEE Transactions on*, 15(2):296–305, 2005.

[5] B. Feng, P. Ding, J. Chen, J. Bai, S. Xu, and B. Xu. Multi-modal information fusion for news story segmentation in broadcast video. In *Acoustics, Speech and Signal Processing (ICASSP), 2012 IEEE International Conference on*, pages 1417 –1420, 2012.

[6] S. Jianbo and J. Malik. Normalized cuts and image segmentation. *Pattern Analysis and Machine Intelligence, IEEE Transactions on*, 22(8):888–905, 2000.

[7] Y. Jinhui, W. Huiyi, X. Lan, Z. Wujie, L. Jianmin, L. Fuzong, and Z. Bo. A formal study of shot boundary detection. *Circuits and Systems for Video Technology, IEEE Transactions on*, 17(2):168–186, 2007.

[8] R. Klinger, K. Tomanek, and R. Klinger. Classical probabilistic models and conditional random fields, 2007.

[9] T. Kudo. Crf++: Yet another crf toolkit, 2005.

[10] H. Lee, J. Yu, Y. Im, J.-M. Gil, and D. Park. A unified scheme of shot boundary detection and anchor shot detection in news video story parsing. *Multimedia Tools and Applications*, 51(3):1127–1145, 2011.

[11] Y. Li and C. Dorai. Svm-based audio classification for instructional video analysis. In *Acoustics, Speech, and Signal Processing, 2004. Proceedings. (ICASSP '04). IEEE International Conference on*, volume 5, pages 897–900, 2004.

[12] C. Petersohn. Logical unit and scene detection: a comparative survey. In *Multimedia Content Access: Algorithms and Systems II*, volume 6820, pages 02–17, 2008.

[13] Z. Rasheed and M. Shah. Detection and representation of scenes in videos. *Multimedia, IEEE Transactions on*, 7(6):1097–1105, 2005.

[14] U. Sakarya and Z. Telatar. Video scene detection using graph-based representations. *Signal Processing: Image Communication*, 25(10):774–783, 2010.

[15] C. Sutton and A. McCallum. An Introduction to Conditional Random Fields. *ArXiv e-prints*, 2010.

[16] J. Wang, L. Duan, Q. Liu, H. Lu, and J. Jin. A multimodal scheme for program segmentation and representation in broadcast video streams. *Multimedia, IEEE Transactions on*, 10(3):393 –408, 2008.

[17] G. Xinbo and T. Xiaoou. Unsupervised video-shot segmentation and model-free anchorperson detection for news video story parsing. *Circuits and Systems for Video Technology, IEEE Transactions on*, 12(9):765–776, 2002.

[18] M. Yeung, B.-L. Yeo, and B. Liu. Segmentation of video by clustering and graph analysis. *Computer Vision and Image Understanding*, 71(1):94–109, 1998.

[19] Z. Yu, Z. Hongjiang, and A. K. Jain. Automatic caption localization in compressed video. *Pattern Analysis and Machine Intelligence, IEEE Transactions on*, 22(4):385–392, 2000.

[20] Z. Yun and M. Shah. Video scene segmentation using markov chain monte carlo. *Multimedia, IEEE Transactions on*, 8(4):686–697, 2006.

Searching Informative Concept Banks for Video Event Detection

Masoud Mazloom, Efstratios Gavves, Koen E.A. van de Sande and Cees G.M. Snoek

ISLA, Informatics Institute, University of Amsterdam
Science Park 904, 1098 XH, Amsterdam, The Netherlands
{m.mazloom, egavves, ksande, cgmsnoek}@uva.nl

ABSTRACT

An emerging trend in video event detection is to learn an event from a bank of concept detector scores. Different from existing work, which simply relies on a bank containing all available detectors, we propose in this paper an algorithm that learns from examples what concepts in a bank are most informative per event. We model finding this bank of informative concepts out of a large set of concept detectors as a rare event search. Our proposed approximate solution finds the optimal concept bank using a cross-entropy optimization. We study the behavior of video event detection based on a bank of informative concepts by performing three experiments on more than 1,000 hours of arbitrary internet video from the TRECVID multimedia event detection task. Starting from a concept bank of 1,346 detectors we show that *1.)* some concept banks are more informative than others for specific events, *2.)* event detection using an automatically obtained informative concept bank is more robust than using all available concepts, *3.)* even for small amounts of training examples an informative concept bank outperforms a full bank and a bag-of-word event representation, and *4.)* we show qualitatively that the informative concept banks make sense for the events of interest, without being programmed to do so. We conclude that for concept banks it pays to be informative.

Categories and Subject Descriptors

1.2.10 [**Artificial Intelligence**]: Vision and Scene Understanding—*Video Analysis*

General Terms

Algorithms, Experimentation, Measurement

Keywords

Event recognition, concept detection, cross-entropy optimization

1. INTRODUCTION

Automated understanding of events in unconstrained video has been a challenging problem in the multimedia community for decades [16]. This comes without surprise as providing access to events has great potential for many innovative applications [4,33]. Traditional event detectors represent an event by a carefully constructed explicit model [9,13]. In [9], for example, Haering *et al.* propose a three-layer inference process to model events in wildlife video. In each layer event-specific knowledge is incorporated ranging from object-level motion, to domain-specific knowledge of wildlife hunting behavior. While effective for detecting hunting events, such a knowledge-intensive approach is unlikely to generalize to other problem domains. Hence, event representations based on explicit models are well suited for constrained domains like wildlife and railroad monitoring, but they are unable, nor intended, to generalize to a broad class of events in unconstrained video like the ones in Figure 1.

Recently, other solutions have started to emerge. We group related works based on the type of representation used: bag-of-words and bank-of-concepts.

1.1 Event as bag-of-words

Inspired by the success of bag-of-word representations for object and scene recognition [14,31], there are several papers in the literature that exploit this low-level representation for event detection. In [15] the team of Columbia University, showed that state-of-art event detection performance is feasible by combining bag-of-words derived from SIFT descriptors, with bag-of-words derived from both MFCC audio features and space-time interest points. Their idea of combining multi-modal bag-of-words was further extended by Natarajan *et al.* [23] and Tamrakar *et al.* [29], who adhere to a more is better approach to event detection by exhaustively combining various visual descriptors, quantization methods, and word pooling strategies. In [12] Inoue *et al.* stress the importance of Principal Component Analysis to reduce the dimensionality of the growing amount of visual descriptors. Their event detection results are benchmarked with state-of-the-art results also, but it requires less computation than [23, 29]. In benchmarks like TRECVID's multimedia event detection task [30] the bag-of-words representation has proven it's merit with respect to robustness and generalization, but from the sheer number of highly correlated descriptors and vector quantized words, it is not easy to derive how these detectors arrive at their event classification. Moreover, events are often characterized by similarity in semantics rather than appearance. Our goal is to find an

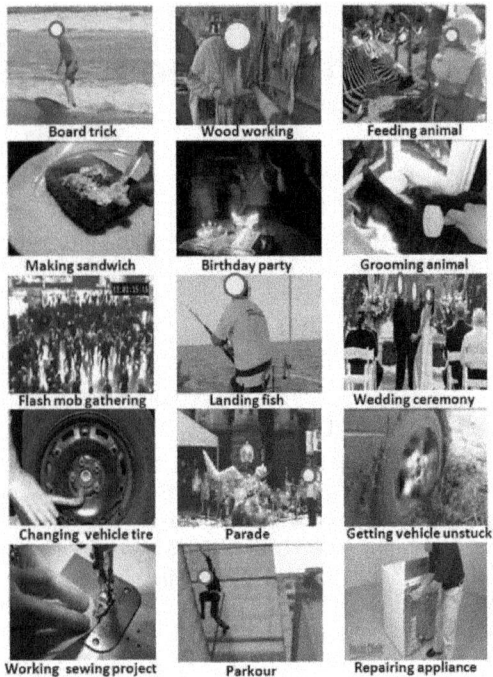

Figure 1: Eexample of fifteen arbitrary events in internet video content.

informative representation able to recognize, and ultimately describe, events in arbitrary video content. We argue that to reach that long-term goal a more semantic representation is urged for.

1.2 Event as bank-of-concepts

Inspired by the success of semantic concepts for improving video retrieval [10, 28], several papers in the literature exploit a bank of semantic concepts as the representation for learning event detectors. Ebadollahi *et al.*, for the first time, explored the use of semantic concepts for learning events [7]. For creating their bank-of-concepts, they employed the 39 detectors from the Large Scale Concept Ontology [22]. Each frame in their broadcast news video collection is then represented as a vector describing the likelihood of the 39 concept detectors. To arrive at an event classification score they employ a Hidden Markov Model. Due to the availability of large lexicons of concept annotations [5, 22], several others have recently also explored the utility of bank-of-concept representations [1, 8, 17, 21, 25]. In [21] Merler *et al.* argue to use all available concept detectors for event representation. Based on a keyframe representation containing 280 concept detector scores, and a support vector machine for learning, the authors show that competitive event detection results can be obtained. In [8] Gkalelis *et al.* propose to reduce, with the help of Mixture Subclass Discriminant Analysis, a bank-of-concepts consisting of 231 detector scores to a subspace best describing an event. Because for both [21] and [8] the resulting event detector operates on all concepts simultaneously, the precise explanation of an event cannot be provided. We are inspired by the concept bank approach to event representation [1, 7, 8, 21]. Our goal is to arrive at a more precise concept bank, while improving event detection accuracy. To that end we investigate whether we can

learn for a given event what concepts are most informative to include in its concept bank.

1.3 Contribution

We make three contributions in this paper. First, we model finding the bank of informative concepts out of a large set of concept detectors as a rare event search. Second, we propose an approximate solution that finds the near optimal concept bank using a cross-entropy optimization [18]. Third, we show qualitatively that the found concept bank makes sense for the events of interest, without being programmed to do so.

To the best of our knowledge no method currently exists in the literature able to determine the most informative concept bank for learning to detect an event. Note especially the algorithmic difference with concept selection for video retrieval [11,32]. In the retrieval scenario the selected detector score is exploited directly for search. In our approach, the bank of automatically found informative detectors is optimized for *learning* to recognize an event. We study the behavior of our informative concept banks by performing several experiments on more than 1,000 hours of arbitrary internet video from the TRECVID 2011 multimedia event detection task. But before we report our experimental validation, we first introduce our algorithm which learns from video examples the informative concept bank for video event detection.

2. INFORMATIVE CONCEPT BANKS

Our goal is to arrive at an event representation containing informative concept detectors only. However, we need to first define what is informative. For example, one can reasonably expect that for the event "feeding an animal", concepts such as "food", "animal" or "person" should be more important, and thus informative.

We start from a large bank of concept detectors for representing events. Given a set of exemplar keyframes of an event category, the aim is to find a smaller bank of informative concepts that accurately describe this event. Suppose that the cardinality of the bank of all available concepts is S. Then the number of concept subsets within this set is 2^S. When S increases, the process of finding the best subset, i.e., the informative concept bank, will be very hard. In fact the problem of finding the best concepts from a large lexicon is an NP-complete problem for which approximation methods are the only viable solution.

We consider the problem of finding the best subset of informative concepts as a rare event in the concepts space. Hence, searching for the bank of informative concepts becomes a rare event search that is properly modeled by a rare event simulation. For solving rare event search problems, in general, the cross-entropy optimization [24] is a well known and frequently used solution [18]. As the cross entropy requires only a small number of parameters, chances of overfitting are minimized. Moreover, convergence is relatively fast and a near-optimum solution is guaranteed. We first describe briefly the theory behind cross-entropy, and then present our learning algorithm based on cross-entropy optimization for finding the informative concept banks for event detection.

2.1 Cross-Entropy

We want to maximize the contribution of the individual

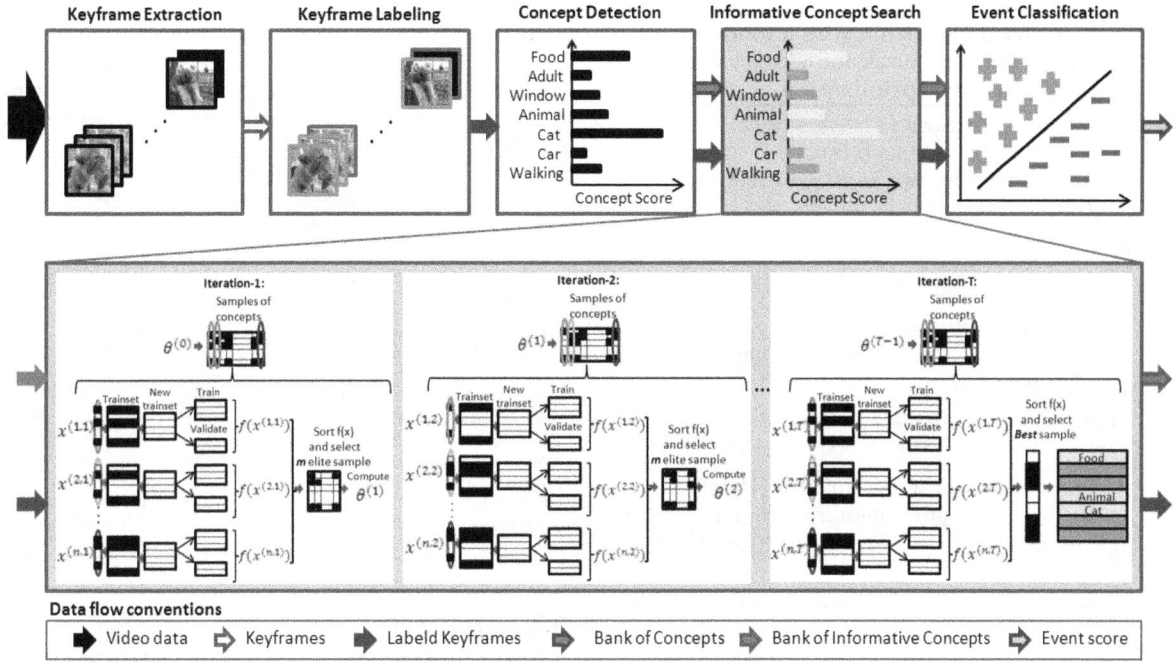

Figure 2: Flow chart for video event detection using an informative concept bank. We extract keyframes, label them based on event presence, and classify individual keyframes with a large number of concept detectors. We determine the informative concepts using the algorithm in Table 1. It selects random banks of concepts and determines their informativeness with the aid of an objective function (e.g., average precision) and cross-validation. After each iteration we update importance sampling parameter Θ^q. For the event *feeding an animal* the selection algorithm finds the concepts 'animal', 'cat', and 'food' to be the most informative. We represent each keyframe of the videos by this informative concept bank and use a classifier to infer a final event score.

concept detectors to the final classification of a video to one or the other event categories. We adopt the standard for the event detection benchmarks, mean average precision metric to measure the accuracy of our representation. Hence our objective function, $f(:)$, is the average precision.

We want to maximize the objective function $f(x)$ with respect to x, where x is a subset of the concept detectors that we have in our object bank. We thus want to identify the configuration x^* of concept detectors, which will return the maximum score $f(x^*)$.

The cross-entropy optimization [24] models the random variable x with the distribution $p(x; \Theta)$, where Θ is a variable that represents the distribution parameters. Since $x = \{x_i\}, i = 1, ..., S$ stands for the all S concept detectors, Θ_i is the variable that controls the participation of each of these concepts x_i to the final score $f(x)$. The cross entropy optimization estimates the optimal solution x^* for maximizing $f(x)$ as the expected value of $p(x; \Theta)$. Obviously, Θ plays an important role for x^*. We determine the optimal value for Θ by solving the following problem:

$$\Theta^* = \arg\max_{\Theta} \int_x I(f(x) \geqslant \alpha) p(x; \Theta) dx, \qquad (1)$$

where in this equation I is an indicator function, and α is a threshold that determines the minimum accuracy that a possible solution x should exhibit. Eq. 1 cannot be solved analytically, hence we need to derive an iterative approximation to Θ via the following three steps:

(1) Use $p(x; \Theta)$ to randomly generate n samples, that is:

$$x^1, ..., x^n \sim p(x; \Theta) \qquad (2)$$

(2) Evaluate each of x^j using $f(x)$. Then, sort the n samples descending order and select the top m samples $\{\hat{x^1}, ..., \hat{x^m}\}$, the *elite samples*.

(3) Finally, use the m elite samples to re-estimate Θ as the maximum likelihood estimators for maximizing $f(x)$.

The parameter Θ is updated in step 3 using the information from the m elite samples. Based on eq. 1 the solution vector Θ^q at iteration q minimizes the cross entropy distance between our current best model $p(x; \Theta^q)$ and the optimal $p(x; \Theta^*)$ one. From eq. 1, we observe that having more accurate elite samples generates solutions closer to the optimal Θ^*. Through the progression of iterations subsequent elite samples will exhibit higher and higher accuracy, leading to a better and better estimation of Θ_i^q. Repeating this update rule iteratively leads x to convergence towards x^* [24]. The stopping criterion for the algorithm may either be the accuracy standstill over the last iterations or reaching a maximum number of iterations.

2.2 Searching the informative concept bank

Now we present our algorithm for searching the informative concept bank for each event category. Since each concept is either selected, or not, we model function $p(x; \Theta)$ as

Table 1: The proposed algorithm which models finding an informative concept bank for video event detection as a cross-entropy optimization.

INPUT: Number of iterations (T), samples (n), elite samples (m), index of events (*event*)
OUTPUT: Informative concept bank per event (x^*)
1. for each *event*

2.   Initialize $\Theta^{(0)}$

3.   for $q = 1, \ldots, T$

4.   **Concepts sampling**: Generate n samples $\{x^{(1,q)}, \ldots, x^{(n,q)}\}$ by using current parameter $\Theta^{(q-1)}$.

5.   **Samples selection**: Find the m samples that perform best given the objective function $f(x)$.

6.   **Update parameter vector $\Theta^{(q)}$**: Based on the best concept samples from step 5, update parameter set $\Theta^{(q)}$ by using Eq. 4

7. $x^* \leftarrow \Theta^{(T)}$

Table 2: Our experiments are evaluated on the TRECVID 2011 Multimedia event detection corpus. The training set is based on the provided event kits only. Number of video and extracted keyframes per event detailed.

	Training set				Test set			
	Positive		Negative		Positive		Negative	
Name of event	Video	Frame	Video	Frame	Video	Frame	Video	Frame
Board trick	161	1,592	555	11,673	114	2,334	4,177	36,758
Feeding animal	162	1,332	554	12,220	114	401	4,177	38,691
Landing fish	122	996	594	12,261	85	1,291	4,206	37,801
Wedding ceremony	128	1,595	588	11,147	89	2,766	4,202	36,326
Wood working	143	1,304	573	12,191	100	945	4,191	38,147
Birthday party	173	1,216	1,175	24,628	172	2,032	31,863	251,699
Changing a vehicle tire	111	1,124	1,237	24,716	113	1,244	31,922	252,487
Flash mob gartering	172	1,893	1,176	23,942	135	1,933	31,900	251,798
Getting a vehicle unstuck	132	1,269	1,216	24,581	83	504	31,952	253,227
Grooming an animal	138	1,411	1,210	24,424	81	521	31,954	253,210
Making a sandwich	126	1,504	1,222	24,350	137	1,885	31,898	251,846
Parade	138	1,491	1,210	24,340	187	1,556	31,848	252,175
Parkour	112	1,873	1,236	23,978	102	2,943	31,933	250,788
Repairing an appliance	123	1,518	1,225	24,296	88	1,366	31,947	252,365
Working on sewing project	120	1,171	1,228	24,687	82	1,046	31,953	252,685

an one-trial binomial distribution, that is

$$x_i = Binomial(1, \Theta_i), for \quad i = 1, \ldots, S. \qquad (3)$$

Each concept x_i follows a distribution $p(x_i; \Theta_i)$, and $\Theta = \{\Theta_i\}$ $i = 1, \ldots, S$. Given Θ we generate at the q-th iteration n samples $x^{(1,q)}, \ldots, x^{(n,q)}$ for all concepts $i = 1, \ldots, S$. Each of these samples $x^{(j,q)}$ in reality is a binary vector, with $x_i^{(j,q)} = 1$ when a concept i is part of the solution for this concept and 0 otherwise. The parameters Θ_i^q of our binomial distributions directly measure the impact of concept i in the process of event detection for each event. Larger Θ_i^q makes the presence of concept i in the optimal solution more likely. In the end, the majority of concepts should not participate in finding an event category, so that their binomial parameter Θ_i^q is equal to 0.

For the purpose of event detection, the objective function typically needs labeled training data to quantify the accuracy of various banks. To do so, we separate the training data into a training and validation set. An event classifier is learned from the selected concepts in the training set and validated on the validation set. We use average precision to reflect the accuracy on the validation set. After each iteration we update Θ_i^q by maximum likelihood estimation on the m elite samples. For a Binomial distribution, this accounts to averaging over the elite samples:

$$\Theta_i^{(q)} = \frac{1}{m} \sum_{j=1}^{m} x_i^{(j,q)}. \qquad (4)$$

We visualize the overall flow chart for searching informative concept banks for video event detection in Figure 2. Our learning algorithm for obtaining the bank of informative concepts is summarized in Table 1.

3. EXPERIMENTAL SETUP

We investigate the effectiveness of informative concept banks for video event detection by performing a series of experiments on a large corpus of challenging real-world web video.

3.1 Data set

TRECVID Multimedia Event Detection For our experiments we adopt the large-scale publicly available video data set from TRECVID's 2011 multimedia event detection corpus [30]. This corpus contains a collection of 38,387 internet video clips, totaling 1,229 hours. The MPEG-4 formatted video data consist of user-generated content posted to various Internet video hosting sites. TRECVID divided the data set into three collections, an event kit containing a textual description of the events together with labeled training video. A development collection[1] containing test video for the events *Board trick, Feeding animal, Landing fish, Wedding ceremony*, and *Wood working*, and an opaque collection containing test video for the events *Birthday party, Changing vehicle tire, Flash mob gathering, Getting a vehicle unstuck, Grooming animal, Making sandwich, Parade, Parkour, Repairing appliance*, and *Working on sewing project*. Since the groundtruth annotations are defined on different partitions of the data, we group the fifteen events into two groups. The first five events defined on the development collection are in *group 1* and the ten remaining events are in *group 2*. For a visual impression of characteristic event examples we refer to Figure 1.

Training set In our experiments we adopt the event kit as our training set, which corresponds to 2,061 video clips with an approximate duration of 92 hours. We report our results for events in group 1 on the development collection which contains 4,291 video clips corresponding to 146 hours. For events in group 2 we report our result on the test collection that contains 32,035 video clips with an approximate duration of 991 hours. We shot segment the video and designate the middle frame as as keyframe. To assure sufficient training data, especially from single-shot video, we require at least 10 frames per video from the event kit. As an arbitrary internet video may contain several non-relevant frames like black frames, over-exposed frames and extreme close-ups, we manually verify all the extracted keyframes from the positively labeled videos in the event kit. We label a keyframe

---

[1]To be precise, we use part 1 of the development collection and ignore part 2 which contains background video clips only.

(a)   (b)

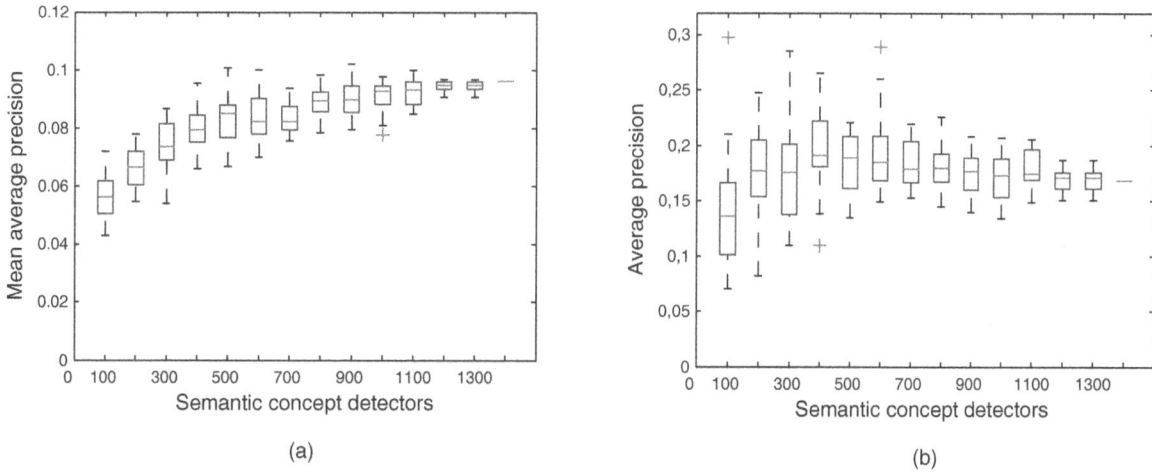

Figure 3: Experiment 1. (a) *Influence of concept bank size*: Event detection accuracy increases with the number of concepts in the bank, but the variance suggests that some concept banks are more informative than others. (b) *Influence of concept bank size for "Landing fish"*: For the event *Landing fish* a small bank of 100 (random) concepts clearly outperforms the bank using all 1,346 concepts. Indicating that much is to be expected from a priori search for the most informative concept bank for an event.

as positive if the context of the event is observable, if not we label it as negative. All the keyframes of negatively labeled videos are simply considered as additional negatives also.

Test set Similar to the training data we shot segment the videos in the development and opaque collection. To reduce computation we extract a fixed number of six frames per shot. Table 2 summarizes the number of labeled videos and keyframes available for each event in both our training and test sets.

3.2 Implementation details

Concept Bank We classify each keyframe in our data set with a bank of 1,346 concept detectors. The detectors are trained using annotations for 346 concepts from the TRECVID 2011 Semantic Indexing Task [2] and 1,000 concepts from the ImageNet Large Scale Visual Recognition Challenge 2011 [5]. We implement them using a bag-of-words with SIFT [19], OpponentSIFT and RGB-SIFT descriptors extracted at Harris-Laplace keypoints and dense sampled points, at every 6 pixels for two scales, using the Color Descriptor software from [31]. The codebook size is 4,096 and we employ a 1x3 spatial pyramid subdivision. As classifier we employ a Support Vector Machine with a fast approximate histogram intersection kernel [20].

Event detection As we focus on obtaining an informative concept bank for video event detection in this paper, we are for the moment less interested in the accuracy optimizations that may be obtained from various kernel settings [3, 6, 34]. Hence, we train for each event a one-versus-all linear support vector machine [26] and fix the value of its regularization parameter C to 100. We train and test the linear support vector machine on keyframe level. To arrive at a decision at video level, we employ max pooling over the classification scores per keyframe.

Cross entropy parameters After initial testing on small partitions of the data, we set the parameters of our cross-entropy learning algorithm to find the informative concept banks for each event as follows: number of iterations 20,

number of concept samples in each iteration 1,000, and number of elite samples in each iteration 200. Inside the objective function we use 5-fold cross-validation.

Evaluation criteria For both objective function $f(x)$ in our learning algorithm, as well as the final event detection performance we consider as evaluation criterion the average precision (AP), which is a well known and popular measure in the video retrieval literature [27]. We also report the average performance over all fifteen events as the mean average precision (MAP).

3.3 Experiments

In order to establish the effectiveness of informative concept banks for video event detection, we perform three experiments.

Experiment 1: Influence of concept bank size To assess the effect of a growing number of concepts in a bank on video event detection performance, we randomly sample a bank

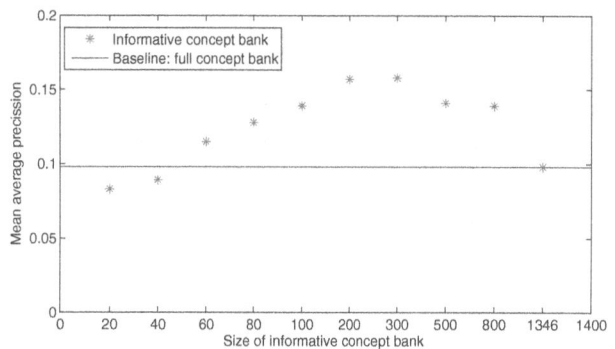

Figure 4: Experiment 2. The result of using different size of informative concept bank. The result shows that there is an informative concept bank composed of 300 concept detectors that reach 0.158 MAP in video event detection.

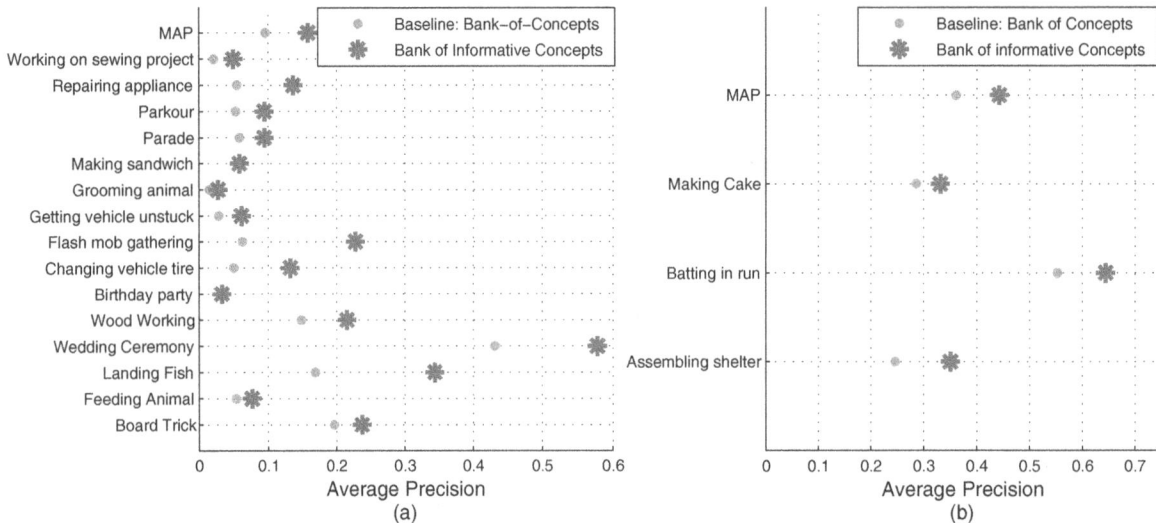

Figure 5: Experiment 2. (*a*) **An informative concept bank always outperforms a bank containing all available concept detectors for video event detection. On average the relative improvement is 65%.** (*b*) **Repeating experiment 2 on the dataset provided by [21] confirms the conclusion of (a).**

of concepts from our 1,346 concept-lexicon with a step size of 100. Each keyframe in our dataset is then represented in terms of the detector scores from the concepts in this random bank. We repeat this procedure 20 times for each bank size.

*Experiment 2: **All concepts versus informative concepts*** In this experiment we compare a bank based on all available concept detectors to a bank containing informative concepts. As the baseline, we represent each keyframe in our data set as a 1,346D vector of detector scores (see section 3.2). For finding the informative concept bank per event, we apply the cross-entropy optimization as described in section 2.2 on the training set only. We train an event detector on the most informative concept bank and report its performance on the (unseen) test set. Since we can fix the sample size inside our algorithm, we evaluate the following bank sizes: 20, 40, 60, 80, 100, 200, 300, 500, 800 to find the most appropriate setting for our dataset based on the MAP.

*Experiment 3: **Influence of event training examples*** To investigate the stability of informative concept banks for video event detection under limited number of training examples, we compare it with a bank containing all available concepts and an appearance-based bag-of-words using densely sampled SIFT descriptors, which are vector quantized into a 4K codebook. In all cases we employ a linear Support Vector Machine for event classification. We vary the number of positive training examples from 1 to 900 keyframes. The positive event training examples are randomly sampled from our pool of positively labeled keyframes, the negative examples are fixed per event (see Table 2). For each (random) set of positive examples we measure event detection performance on the test set and repeat this process 20 times.

4. RESULTS

4.1 Influence of concept bank size

We plot the results of experiment 1 in Figure 3(a). As expected the event detection accuracy increases when more and more concept detectors are part of the bank. Up to approximately 500 (random) concept detectors the increase in event detection accuracy is close to linear, afterwards it saturates to the end value of 0.096 MAP when using all 1,346 available concept detectors. Interestingly, the box plot reveals that there exist a bank, containing only 500 concepts, which performs better than using all concepts (compare the top of the whisker at 500 concepts, with an MAP of 0.102 with the maximum MAP of 0.096 when using all concepts). This result shows that some banks of concepts are more informative than others for video event detection.

When we zoom in on individual events the connection between concept banks and event definitions can be studied. We inspect the box plot of Figure 3(a) also for the 15 individual events (data not shown). The plots reveal several positive outliers using just a small number of concepts in the bank. Noticeable examples are obtained for the events *Landing fish, Wedding ceremony, Flash mob gathering*, and *Parkour*. Figure 3(b) details the box plot for *Landing fish*. For this event we observe an outlier bank with an AP of 0.292 containing only 100 randomly selected concepts (compare to the maximum of 0.170 when using all concepts). The results of experiment 1 show that, in general, the event detection accuracy increases with the number of semantic concepts in the bank. However, it also shows that some banks of concepts are more informative than others for specific events, and this may result in improved event detection accuracy.

4.2 All concepts versus informative concepts

We plot the result of experiment 2 in Figure 4 and Figure 5. The result in Figure 4 shows that by using the concept bank with size less than 40 concepts, the performance of event detection is below the baseline of 0.098. When we increase the size of concept bank from 60 to 300 concepts, the event detection accuracy also increases from 0.118 to 0.158. However, more is not better, as further increasing the size from 300 to 800 results in a decrease in MAP again from

(a)

(b)

Figure 6: Experiment 2. Informative concept banks for the events (a) *Flash mob gathering* and (b) *Batting in run*. Font size correlates with automatically estimated informativeness. Note that the algorithm found concepts that make sense without being programmed to do so.

0.158 to 0.133. The result in Figure 4 show that by selecting an informative concept bank with size 300 we can reach to the 0.158 MAP. We plot the result of using the informative concept bank of size 300 in the Figure 5(a). We observe that on average, the bank of informative concepts relatively improve the normal bank-of-concepts method 65% (0.158 vs 0.096 MAP). We can see that in all event categories, our representation based on the informative concept bank is better than using a representation using all concepts of bank. When we focus on the result of Figure 5(a) we find a considerable improvement for events such as *Landing fish*, *Wedding ceremony* and *Flash mob gathering*, where the improvements are 88%, 59%, and 175% respectively. Recall that we reach this result by using an informative concept bank containing only 23% of the concept detectors available. When relevant concepts are unavailable in the concept bank, the results will not improve, as can be seen for the event *Making sandwich*. Figure 6(a) highlights the informative concept bank for the event *Flash mob gathering*.

For sake of comparison with the state-of-the-art we also repeat experiment 2 for TRECVID's 2010 multimedia event detection corpus. This data set consists of three events: *Assembling a shelter, Batting in run, and Making cake*. Here we adopt the 280 concept bank provided by Merler *et al.* [21]. Again, we employ our cross-entropy algorithm for finding the most informative concept bank per event. The results

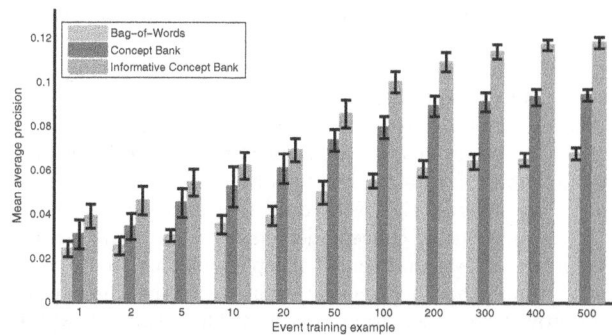

Figure 7: Experiment 3. An informative concept bank outperforms a full concept bank and bag-of-words, even for small amounts of training examples.

in Figure 5(b) confirm the results of experiment 2. Again the informative concept bank outperforms the baseline for all three events (0.443 vs 0.360 MAP) and uses only 36% of the available concepts (100 vs 280). Figure 6(b) shows the automatically selected concepts for the event *Batting in run*.

The results of experiment 2, and the same experiment on the dataset provided by [21], show that event detection using an automatically found bank of informative concepts outperforms a bank using all concepts, and always contains significantly less semantic concepts.

4.3 Influence of event training examples

We plot the results of experiment 3 in Figure 7. As expected the event detection accuracy increases when more and more positive event example are used for training the classifier. Independent of the number of training examples used, the accuracy of the informative concept bank outperforms both the concept bank using all available detectors and the bag-of-words. Moreover, the difference in accuracy between the three methods is increasing when the number of event training examples grows. For example, when we use only 1 positive event training example the difference between informative concept banks is small with 0.01 compared to a full concept bank and 0.015 compared to bag-of-words. When using 500 event keyframe examples the differences increases to 0.028 compared to bank of concepts and 0.058 compared to bag-of-words.

The result of experiment 3 shows an increasing video event detection accuracy when increasing the number of positive training examples. More surprising, concept banks outperform bag-of-words for small amounts of training examples. Moreover, we observe that independent of the number of positive training example used, the accuracy of the informative concept bank tends to be better than both the full concept bank and bag-of-words. We conclude that, compared to competing approaches, an informative concept bank is most robust under a limited number of training examples.

5. CONCLUSION

We study event detection based on banks of concept detectors. Different from existing work, which simply includes in the bank all available detectors, we propose a cross-entropy inspired algorithm that learns to find from examples the bank of most informative concepts. We study the behavior of informative concept banks by performing three experiments on the unconstrained web video collection from the TRECVID 2011 multimedia event detection task using a total of 1,346 concept detectors.

The result of experiment 1 gives an indication that large banks of concept detectors are important for covering a variety of complex events, as they may appear in unconstrained video. In general, the event detection accuracy increases with the number of concept detectors in the bank. However, it also shows that some concept banks are more informative than others for specific events, and this may result in improved event detection accuracy. The results of experiment 2, and the same experiment on the dataset provided by Merler *et al.* [21], show that event detection using an informative concept bank outperform banks using all concepts, and always contains significantly less detectors. Finally, experiment 3 reveals that our informative concept bank outperforms both a bank using all concepts and a bag-of-words for small amounts of training examples. What is more the concepts in the informative concept bank appear to have a semantic relation with the events they model. We conclude that for video event detection using concept banks it pays to be informative.

Acknowledgments This research is supported by the STW STORY project, the BeeldCanon project, the Dutch national program COMMIT, and by the Intelligence Advanced Research Projects Activity (IARPA) via Department of Interior National Business Center contract number D11PC20067. The U.S. Government is authorized to reproduce and distribute reprints for Governmental purposes notwithstanding any copyright annotation thereon. Disclaimer: The views and conclusions contained herein are those of the authors and should not be interpreted as necessarily representing the official policies or endorsements, either expressed or implied, of IARPA, DoI/NBC, or the U.S. Government.

6. REFERENCES

[1] T. Althoff, H. O. Song, and T. Darrell. Detection bank: An object detection based video representation for multimedia event recognition. In *ACM Multimedia*, 2012.

[2] S. Ayache and G. Quénot. Video corpus annotation using active learning. In *ECIR*, 2008.

[3] L. Ballan, M. Bertini, A. D. Bimbo, and G. Serra. Video event classification using string kernels. *MTAP*, 48(1), 2010.

[4] L. Ballan, M. Bertini, A. Del Bimbo, L. Seidenari, and G. Serra. Event detection and recognition for semantic annotation of video. *MTAP*, 51, 2011.

[5] J. Deng, W. Dong, R. Socher, L.-J. Li, K. Li, and L. Fei-Fei. ImageNet: A large-scale hierarchical image database. In *CVPR*, 2009.

[6] L. Duan, D. Xu, I. W.-H. Tsang, and J. Luo. Visual event recognition in videos by learning from web data. *TPAMI*, 34(9), 2012.

[7] S. Ebadollahi, L. Xie, S.-F. Chang, and J. R. Smith. Visual event detection using multi-dimensional concept dynamics. In *ICME*, 2006.

[8] N. Gkalelis, V. Mezaris, and I. Kompatsiaris. High-level event detection in video exploiting discriminant concepts. In *CBMI*, 2011.

[9] N. Haering, R. Qian, and I. Sezan. A semantic event-detection approach and its application to detecting hunts in wildlife video. *TCSVT*, 2000.

[10] A. G. Hauptmann, M. G. Christel, and R. Yan. Video retrieval based on semantic concepts. *Proceedings of the IEEE*, 2008.

[11] B. Huurnink, K. Hofmann, and M. de Rijke. Assessing concept selection for video retrieval. In *ACM MIR*, 2008.

[12] N. Inoue et al. TokyoTech+Canon at TRECVID 2011. In *NIST TRECVID Workshop*, 2011.

[13] Y. A. Ivanov and A. F. Bobick. Recognition of visual activities and interactions by stochastic parsing. *TPAMI*, 22(8), 2000.

[14] Y.-G. Jiang, J. Yang, C.-W. Ngo, and A. Hauptmann. Representations of keypoint-based semantic concept detection: A comprehensive study. *TMM*, 12(1), 2010.

[15] Y.-G. Jiang, X. Zeng, G. Ye, S. Bhattacharya, D. Ellis, M. Shah, and S.-F. Chang. Columbia-ucf trecvid2010 multimedia event detection: Combining multiple modalities, contextual concepts, and temporal matching. In *NIST TRECVID Workshop*, 2010.

[16] G. Lavee, E. Rivlin, and M. Rudzsky. Understanding video events: A survey of methods for automatic interpretation of semantic occurrences in videos. *TSMC*, 39(5), 2009.

[17] L.-J. Li, H. Su, E. P. Xing, and L. Fei-Fei. Object bank: A high-level image representation for scene classification & semantic feature sparsification. In *NIPS*, 2010.

[18] X. Li, E. Gavves, C. G. M. Snoek, M. Worring, and A. W. M. Smeulders. Personalizing automated image annotation using cross-entropy. In *ACM Multimedia*, 2011.

[19] D. G. Lowe. Distinctive image features from scale-invariant keypoints. *IJCV*, 60, 2004.

[20] S. Maji, A. C. Berg, and J. Malik. Classification using intersection kernel support vector machines is efficient. In *CVPR*, 2008.

[21] M. Merler, B. Huang, L. Xie, G. Hua, and A. Natsev. Semantic model vectors for complex video event recognition. *IEEE Trans. Multimedia*, 14(1), 2012.

[22] M. R. Naphade, J. R. Smith, J. Tešić, S.-F. Chang, W. Hsu, L. S. Kennedy, A. G. Hauptmann, and J. Curtis. Large-scale concept ontology for multimedia. *IEEE MultiMedia*, 13(3), 2006.

[23] P. Natarajan, S. Wu, S. N. P. Vitaladevuni, X. Zhuang, S. Tsakalidis, U. Park, R. Prasad, and P. Natarajan. Multimodal feature fusion for robust event detection in web videos. In *CVPR*, 2012.

[24] R. Y. Rubinstein and D. P. Kroese. *The Cross-Entropy Method: A Unified Approach to Combinatorial Optimization, Monte-Carlo Simulation and Machine Learning*. Springer, 2004.

[25] S. Sadanand and J. J. Corso. Action bank: A high-level representation of activity in video. In *CVPR*, 2012.

[26] S. Shalev-Shwartz, Y. Singer, N. Srebro, and A. Cotter. Pegasos: primal estimated sub-gradient solver for svm. *Math. Program.*, 127(1), 2011.

[27] A. F. Smeaton, P. Over, and W. Kraaij. Evaluation campaigns and TRECVid. In *ACM MIR*, 2006.

[28] C. G. M. Snoek and M. Worring. Concept-based video retrieval. *FnTIR*, 2(4), 2009.

[29] A. Tamrakar, S. Ali, Q. Yu, J. Liu, O. Javed, A. Divakaran, H. Cheng, and H. S. Sawhney. Evaluation of low-level features and their combinations for complex event detection in open source videos. In *CVPR*, 2012.

[30] TRECVID Multimedia Event Detection Evaluation Track, 2011. http://www.nist.gov/itl/iad/mig/med.cfm.

[31] K. E. A. van de Sande, T. Gevers, and C. G. M. Snoek. Evaluating color descriptors for object and scene recognition. *TPAMI*, 32(9), 2010.

[32] X.-Y. Wei, C.-W. Ngo, and Y.-G. Jiang. Selection of concept detectors for video search by ontology-enriched semantic spaces. *TMM*, 10(6), 2008.

[33] L. Xie, H. Sundaram, and M. Campbell. Event mining in multimedia streams. *Proceedings of the IEEE, 96*, 2008.

[34] D. Xu and S.-F. Chang. Video event recognition using kernel methods with multilevel temporal alignment. *TPAMI*, 30(11), 2008.

Tagging Human Activities in Video by Crowdsourcing

Long-Van Nguyen-Dinh
Wearable Computing Lab
ETH Zurich
Zurich, Switzerland
longvan@ife.ee.ethz.ch

Cédric Waldburger
Wearable Computing Lab
ETH Zurich
Zurich, Switzerland
wcedric@ee.ethz.ch

Daniel Roggen
Wearable Computing Lab
ETH Zurich
Zurich, Switzerland
daniel.roggen@ieee.org

Gerhard Tröster
Wearable Computing Lab
ETH Zurich
Zurich, Switzerland
troester@ife.ee.ethz.ch

ABSTRACT

Activity annotation in videos is necessary to create a training dataset for most of activity recognition systems. This is a very time consuming and repetitive task. Crowdsourcing gains popularity to distribute annotation tasks to a large pool of taggers. We present for the first time an approach to achieve good quality for activity annotation in videos through crowdsourcing on the Amazon Mechanical Turk platform (AMT). Taggers must annotate the start, end boundaries and the label of all occurrences of activities in videos. Two strategies to detect non-serious taggers according to temporal annotated results are presented. Individual filtering checks the consistency in the answers of each tagger with the characteristic of dataset to identify and remove non-serious taggers. Collaborative filtering checks the agreement in annotations among taggers. The filtering techniques detect and remove non-serious taggers and finally, the majority voting applied to AMT temporal tags to generate one final AMT activity annotation set. We conduct the experiments to get activity annotation from AMT on a subset of two rich datasets frequently used in activity recognition. The results show that our proposed filtering strategies can increase the accuracy by up to 40%. The final annotation set is of comparable quality of the annotation of experts with high accuracy (76% to 92%).

Categories and Subject Descriptors

D.2.8 [**Software Engineering**]: Metrics—*complexity measures, performance measures*; H.3.4 [**Information Storage and Retrieval**]: Systems and Software—*Performance evaluation (efficiency and effectiveness), Question-answering (fact retrieval) systems*; I.2.10 [**Computing Methodologies**]: Artificial IntelligenceVision and Scene Understanding[Video analysis]

General Terms

Experimentation, Human Factors, Performance, Measurement

Keywords

Amazon Mechanical Turk, Activity recognition, Crowdsourcing, Video annotation, Human Computation

1. INTRODUCTION

Activity recognition is useful in many applications such as ambient assisted living, human-computer interaction, video surveillance, or activity life logging. Human activity can be extracted and recognized from video footage, or data streams from on-body sensors, such as inertial measurement units. Regardless of the modality used to recognize activities, a labeled training dataset is required for supervised learning [3, 2, 4]. The training dataset must comprise the start and end time of the activities of interest. This is usually obtained by manual inspection of a video footage of an experimental recording where users demonstrate the activities of interest. Even when using on-body sensors for recognition, a video footage is shot for the purpose of labeling. Video labeling is extremely time-consuming and tedious: it may take 7-10 hours to annotate fine-grained activities in a 30-min video [14]. It is also costly to hire experts to do labeling.

In order to reduce cost and time of data labeling, crowdsourcing platforms (e.g., Amazon Mechanical Turk (AMT), Crowdflower) has become a new trend. Crowdsourcing platforms allow a large number of non-experts from all over the world and without any specific background to solve large-scale tasks for a small financial incentive. Therefore, crowdsourcing is generally employed for tasks that are easy for humans, but hard for computers. Since human activity in a video can be easily recognized by non-experts, we are interested in answering the following question: "Is crowdsourcing an alternative reliable way to get activity labeling from video footage?".

In this work, we investigate the ability of AMT workers and their behavior in annotating temporal boundaries and labels of activities occurring in videos. An approach to achieve good quality for activity annotation in videos through AMT and to handle temporal results from AMT is presented for the first time. Two filtering strategies to detect and remove non-serious taggers according to temporal annotated results are proposed and evaluated. Individual filtering checks the consistency in the answers of each tagger with the characteristic of dataset to identify and remove non-serious taggers. Collaborative filtering checks the agreement in annotations among taggers to detect non-serious taggers. After filtering, the majority voting applied to AMT temporal tags to generate one final AMT activity annotation set. We conduct the experiments to get activity annotation from AMT on a subset of two rich datasets frequently used in activity recognition (CMU and Opportunity [14, 1]). The final AMT annotation set is then compared with the ground truth annotated by experts to evaluate the quality of annotation from crowdsourcing.

2. RELATED WORK

Crowdsourcing services (e.g., Amazon Mechanical Turk (AMT), crowdflower[1], clickworkers[2]) has emerged recently as a new cheap labor pool for simple large-scale tasks. Crowdsourcing tasks can typically be accomplished easily and quickly by large number of workers. Crowdsourcing has been characterized in the annotation of datasets in natural language processing [17, 7, 21], speech recognition [11, 12], multimedia tagging [10, 22, 20, 19]. It has also been proposed in query processing [6] to answer queries that can not be answered by database or search engines. Data acquired from crowdsourcing is generated by low-commitment workers, thus it is commonly unreliable and noisy. Therefore, the same task is often redundantly performed by multiple workers and majority voting is a popular decision making method used to identify the correct answers [16, 7]. Moreover, in crowdsourcing, malicious workers often take advantage of the verification difficulty (the ground truth is unknown) and submit low-quality answers. Hence, it is necessary to include strategies to estimate the quality of workers in order to reject low-performing and malicious workers. The acceptance rate of a worker based on their work history is usually specified as a threshold to allow that worker to participate in the task. Verifiable questions or pilot tasks for which the requester knows the correct answers is a common empirical strategy to screen workers from crowdsourcing [9, 18, 11, 12]. Dawid and Skene [5] proposed a method that used the redundancy in acquiring answers to measure the labeling quality of the workers based on an expectation maximization algorithm. Bayesian versions of worker quality inference were recently proposed by Raykar et al. [13]. Ipeirotis et al. [8] improved the method by separating spammers who provide low-quality answers intentionally and biased workers who are careful but biased. The biased answers can then be recovered and yields much higher quality of results.

Amazon Mechanical Turk: Amazon Mechanical Turk is by far the most popular crowdsourcing platform with almost half a million turkers (i.e., workers) and about 50,000 - 100,000 HITs [3] available to the turkers at any time [15]. Therefore, in our work, AMT is chosen to evaluate activity annotations in videos from crowdsourcing. In AMT, turk-

ers can choose available HITs to complete and submit their results to AMT. The requester of the HIT retrieves all results from AMT after the HIT is accomplished. According to the quality of turkers' answers, the requester approves or rejects their work. A requester design a HIT template to describe the task they would like to distribute. AMT supports a number of template HITs, command line tools and developer APIs. The requester can define how many assignments (i.e., workers) per HIT are needed, duration for each HIT and cost per HIT. A worker is allowed to work only one assignment per HIT. To assure quality of works from turkers, *turker approval rate* which is provided by AMT according to turker's work history can be used as a threshold for eligibility to work. Specifically, turker approval rate is the percentage of turker's works accepted by requesters.

According to the best of our knowledge, there is no previous work that investigates the use of crowdsourcing in activity annotation in videos in which workers provide the starting and ending time of occurrences of activities. In the work by Zhao et al. [22], they extracted individual still images/video frames from the CMU video of activities [1] and then acquired labeling for the activity occurring in the image from crowdsourcing. However, using one video frame to ask for activity may have the limitations of ambiguation. It is more likely for users to recognize the activities by watching the continuous sequence of frames (e.g., it is hard to distinguish Open Door and Close Door activities with just only one frame of activity). It is more natural to ask Amazon Mechanical Turkers to watch a video and annotate activities occurring on the video.

3. CROWDSOURCING METHODOLOGY

To get activity labeling from turkers, a HIT interface is needed. Video footages for activity recognition are usually recorded at several perspectives in order to capture all activities. Therefore, the HIT interface should show different video perspectives synchronously. Turkers can navigate through videos and indicate the start, end times and labels of all activity instances occurring in the videos. In this section, we describe our HIT interface, technical details to run our HIT in AMT, and a data processing pipeline to evaluate answers from turkers and fuse their answers to get a final activity annotation.

3.1 HIT Interface Design

Figure 1 shows our HIT interface to collect activity annotation from different synchronized video perspectives. The interface consists of 4 different parts indicated with a color bar on the left which does not appear in the real interface. **Task Description (blue):** At the top, we describe the task that the turkers have to solve in order to get their answers accepted. Turkers have to answer correctly questions in the red section and specify start/end/tag triples for all occurrences of activities performed in the video in the yellow section. We estimate the minimum number of tags (N) labeled from the videos according to the approximation of activity duration. We let turkers know about this number N so that turkers can work carefully on our tasks in order to get all activities. Since we do not know the exact number of activities in each video, therefore, we use this N to verify the quality of turkers. It will be explained in Section 3.3. **Video Player (green):** This part allows to play all videos synchronously and to pause or restart all of them (turk-

---

[1] http://crowdflower.com
[2] http://clickworkers.com
[3] HIT = Human Intelligence Task represents a small task assigned to turkers with an allocated price and completion time

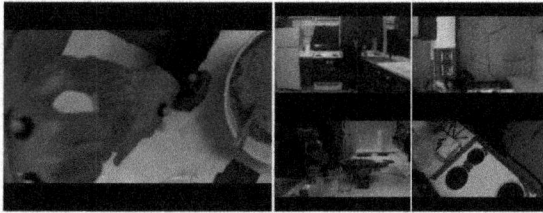

Figure 1: The HIT interface to collect activity annotation from different synchronized video perspectives.

ers can play videos again to check their answers). It also shows the current time in seconds. Moreover, turkers are able to transverse through all videos synchronously. To support turkers to find the exact starting and ending time of an activity, we also support buttons to go forward and backward in videos frame by frame.

Section 1 - Qualification test (red): As there are low-commitment turkers on AMT, we have to check whether an answer could be taken seriously or if it is just a random submission or spam. We use verifiable questions to screen workers as in [9, 18, 11, 12]. We ask for the starting time of 2 activities in the given video sequence and one boolean question about whether an activity occurs in the video. It does not take much time for requesters to prepare answers for those verification questions but it can ensure that turkers must watch the whole short video to answer correctly this section 1. Different HITs have different verification questions since they contain different videos. The questions also prepare for turkers what they will expect to do in the next section.

Section 2 - Tag Section (yellow): This is where turkers are asked to supply triples of start/end/label of all occurrences of activities in the videos. Possible activities are given in a list. The right-hand side lists all previously given triples for turkers to check and allows them to submit all tags at the end of the task.

We do not receive any negative feedback about our interface during the experiments which assures us that the interface works fine.

3.2 Running HIT in AMT

AMT supports a number of template HITs, but unfortunately does not offer a template to show videos synchronously, which is needed in our work to show different video perspectives at the same time. However, AMT can load custom tasks from an external server. External tasks can consist of HTML/Javascript to design a HIT Interface. To ensure that every turker has the same experience when working on our video tagging tasks, the interface should work correctly and look the same in every major browser. To meet this requirement, we use HTML5 and webm and h264 mp4 formats for videos. We test our interface with all major browsers including Chrome, Safari, Firefox, Opera and Internet Explorer. HTML5-Video implementation instead of Flash is also compatible with mobile browsers.

3.3 AMT Annotation Post-processing

In this section, we introduce a data processing pipeline to evaluate the quality of answers from turkers and fuse the answers to get a final activity annotation. The quality of answers decides whether we reject or approve an assignment of a HIT. Basically, assignments must fulfill all requirements specified in the HIT in order to get approved. In our work, we have two requirements: 1. Correctly answer three verifiable questions in the section 1 in the interface, and 2. Specify all occurrences of activities in videos. However, since we do not know the exact number of activity instances in each video, we check whether turkers provide at least N activity tags performed by a subject in the video. We propose two kinds of filtering techniques to improve the quality of the final activity annotation: individual filtering and collaborative filtering. Individual filtering examines answers in each assignment to decide whether it should be accepted or not. Collaborative filtering examines answers from all assignments to a HIT to detect and remove spammers, thus reject or accept the work.

Figure 2 shows different components of the data processing pipeline. The individual filtering can contains three components: Qualification Check, Overlapping Boundaries Removal, and Activity Count Check. The collaborative filtering contains a component: Spammer Removal. We describe each components as follows.

1. Qualification check: Assignments must answer correctly at least M verifiable questions over three to get into other steps. M = 1,2, or 3. Otherwise, they get rejected. Different turkers may have different decision when an activity starts (e.g., drink gesture can start from the time user picks up a cup or when user starts drinking). Therefore, we allow that the starting time answers can be different from the true answers within 2 seconds.

2. Overlapping Boundaries Removal: Activities of interest are performed and recorded in sequence, and thus non-overlapping. However, we observe that spammers tend not watch the videos and provide randomly overlapping starting and ending times of activities. To increase the quality of the final activity annotation, we remove activities tagged by a turker which are boundary overlapping.

3. Activity Count Check: The number of activities provided in the section 2 must be at least N. Otherwise, it is rejected.

4. Spammer Removal: We define spamming/outlier to be assignments which disagree with the majority most of

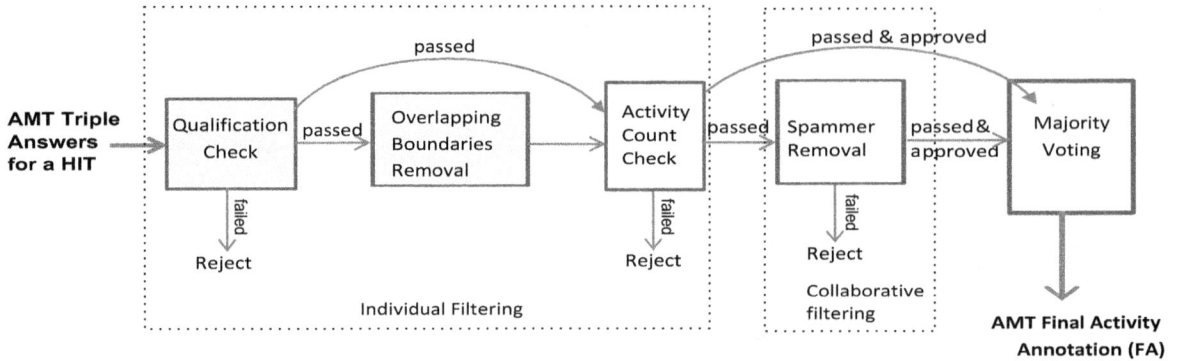

Figure 2: A data processing chain taking raw AMT output from turkers and producing a final activity annotation by majority voting. The output from turkers is evaluated with different components enabled or not.

the time. Specifically, the assignment which have a disagreement score d,

$d = \frac{\text{Tagging times disagree with majority}}{\text{Total tagging times}} > threshold$ is a spam. Score d is computed as follows.

- Step 1: We extract starting and ending times of all tagged activities from assignments of a HIT and put into a sorted list.

- Step 2: We scan through each temporal segment S (i.e., two consequence elements) in the sorted list, and the label of S is the majority voting among all activities containing this segment.

- Step 3: For each assignment having tags for S which disagree with the majority, the score d are accumulated by the length of S. At the end, d is compared with the threshold and spammers are detected and removed.

5. Majority Voting: At the end, the majority voting among qualified assignments is performed to generate a final list (FA) of good annotated activities. The list is then compared with the ground truth annotated by the experts for evaluation. The algorithm to get majority voting includes step 1 and 2 in the Spammer Removal section above. Table 1 shows an example to get majority among temporal segments of activity annotation.

Table 1: An Example of Majority Voting

start	end	tags (label:count)	majority vote
t1	t2	open Drawer: 5, take Scissors:2	open Drawer
t2	t3	open Drawer: 5, take Scissor:1, take Egg:1	open Drawer

4. EVALUATION

4.1 Datasets

The experiments are conducted on video footages from two public datasets for activity recognition: the Carnegie Mellon University (CMU) Kitchen dataset [1] and the Opportunity Dataset [14].

CMU Kitchen Dataset [1]
The CMU Kitchen dataset consists of videos and signals from other modalities (e.g. IMU, eWatch) recorded from different subjects performing different recipes in a kitchen. There are 5 video streams at different locations in the kitchen capturing all activities performed by the subjects. The ground truth labels which are annotated by the authors of the dataset are available for 10 subjects who baked the "brownie recipe". To compare our experiments with the ground truth provided by experts, we use one set of brownie-recipe videos of one subject which is labeled by CMU people to ask for activity annotation from turkers. Activities for a Brownie recipe in CMU datasets are listed in Table 3. The video duration is 6 minutes long. We segment the video into 3 short videos of about two minutes. We approximate about 8-14 activities instances occurred in each 2-min video. It is reasonable to ask turkers working on the short videos that contains a small number of activity instances. Five synchronized segments from 5 videos are shown in a HIT for annotation. The HIT interface for the CMU dataset is shown in 1.

Opportunity Dataset [14]
The Opportunity Dataset is a rich multi-modal dataset collected in a naturalistic environment akin to an apartment, where users execute daily gestures. There are 3 video streams captured from 3 different positions in the room synchronized with body-worn sensor signals. In our work, we use the videos of one subject performing 20 repetitions of 15 gesture classes as shown in Table 2. The video duration is 25 minutes long. We segment the videos into 30 short videos of 50 seconds. We estimate about 8-14 activity instances occurred in each video segment. We publish 30 HITs for the annotation for the Opportunity dataset. Note that in this dataset, there are three drawers at different heights and two different doors. The HIT interface for the Opportunity dataset is similar to 1, however we place a map of the kitchen in the task description part to show turkers where the door 1,2 or drawers 1,2,3 are.

Table 4 shows an overview of the experiments we conduct. We publish 3 HITs from the CMU dataset and 30 HITS from the Opportunity dataset. Each HIT has 10 assignments.

Table 2: Gestures in Opportunity dataset

drink Cup (D)	clean Table (CT)	open Drawer1 (ODr1)
close Drawer1 (CDr1)	open Drawer2 (ODr2)	close Drawer2 (CDr2)
open Drawer3 (ODr3)	close Drawer3 (CDr3)	open Door (OD)
close Door (CD)	open Fridge (OF)	close Fridge (CF)
open Dishwasher (ODi)	close Dishwasher (CDi)	

Table 3: Brownie-recipe Activities in CMU dataset

walk to Fridge	pour Water into Big Bowl
close Fridge	open Fridge
open Brownie Bag	open Brownie Box
crack Egg	open Cupboard Top Left
open Drawer	pour Big Bowl into Baking Pan
stir Big Bowl	pour Brownie Bag into Big Bowl
stir Egg	pour Oil into Small Measuring Cup
switch oven on	pour Water into Big Measuring Cup
take Fork	put Baking Pan into Oven
read Brownie Box	put Scissors into Drawer
take Oil	put Oil into Cupboard Bottom Right
take Big Bowl	take Brownie Box
take Egg	take Big Measuring Cup
take Baking Pan	take Small Measuring Cup
take Scissors	twist off Cap
twist on Cap	walk to Counter

Each assignment is annotated by a turker who must have at least 90% approval rate on their work history and different assignments of a HIT are completed by different turkers. We pay 30 cents for each assignment.

Table 4: AMT Experiment Summary

	# HITs	Assignments per HIT	Length(s)	Price per HIT (USD cent)	Turker Approval Rate
CMU	3	10	120	30	90
Opportunity	30	10	50	30	90

4.2 Evaluation on AMT Final Activity Annotation

To evaluate the quality of the AMT final activity annotation (FA) for a HIT, we compare the FA with the ground truth (GT) using an accuracy metric. The FA and GT are sets of <start,end,tag> triples. Each set contains non-overlapping activities. In our HIT, we do not ask turkers to annotate Null activities, we default the temporal segment without any tag as Null. The accuracy is defined as follows.

$$\text{Accuracy} = \frac{\text{Total match length between FA and GT}}{\text{Total annotation length}}$$

The total annotation length is the length of the HIT's video sequence. The total match length (ML) between the FA and the GT is the total length of temporal segments where both FA and GT agree on the activity tag. The algorithm to compute ML is discussed briefly. We extract start and end times of all triples in both FA and GT and put into a sorted list. We scan through each temporal segment S (i.e.,two consequence elements in the sorted list), if FA and GT agree on the activity tag for this segment, ML is increased by the length of S.

5. RESULTS AND DISCUSSION

5.1 Duration of task completion

Table 5 shows the average time that the CMU and Opportunity HITs need to be completed. **HIT Time** measures

the time from the moment when a turker starts a HIT until he submits his results. **Completion Time** measures how long it takes to get all assignments on a HIT completed.

Table 5: Time Requirement Overview

	HIT length (seconds)	Average HIT Time (mins)	Average Completion Time (hours)
CMU	120	14	62
Opportunity	50	12	71

The Opportunity and CMU HITs takes in average about 2-3 days to complete. Average HIT Time (12 mins for a 50-sec video) is comparable to works done by experts (7-10 hours for a 30-min video), thus turkers annotate data at a similar speed as the experts. The approximate price we pay for 30-min length video is 30 (cents) * 30 (mins) * 5 (accepted assignments for a HIT) ≈ 50$, which is significantly less than what we spend for an expert per day to annotate videos.

5.2 Turkers Statistics

We recruit totally 136 turkers working on our 33 HITs (118 turkers for the Opportunity HITs and 18 turkers for the CMU HITs). Figure 3 shows the histogram of accepted assignments for turkers working on our HITs. There are 38 turkers working on only one HIT and doing well. However, 26 turkers finish more than one HIT correctly. It is interesting that there are 4 dedicated turkers working successfully on more than 10 different HITs. It seems like they find our tasks pleasant.

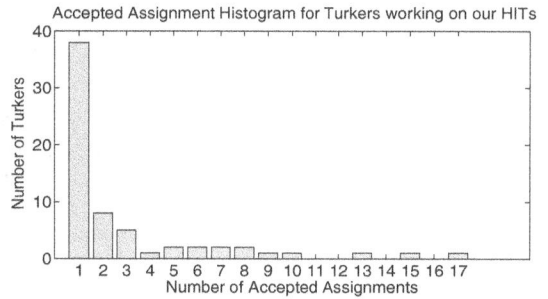

Figure 3: The histogram of accepted assignments for turkers working on our HITs

Figure 4 shows the histogram of rejected assignments for turkers working on our HITs. There are 70 turkers getting one assignment rejected (70/136 ≈ 51%). Only four workers failed the HITs 4-6 times. Figure 5 shows the histogram of turker accepted rate evaluated from the work on our HITs. There are two peaks at 0% accepted rate and 100% accepted rate. Together with Figure 3 and 4, the results show that there are many turkers work on our HIT once and fail. It could be that either they are spammers or they find our HIT difficult. However, many turkers succesfully work on our HITs multiple times.

5.3 Accuracy

To understand the quality of annotation from AMT for our HITs, we define six types of post-processing from the raw AMT results to get the FA by combining different com-

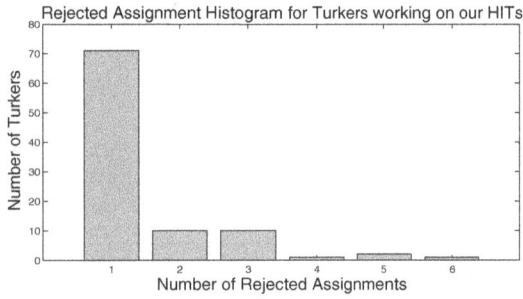

Figure 4: The histogram of rejected assignments for turkers working on our HITs

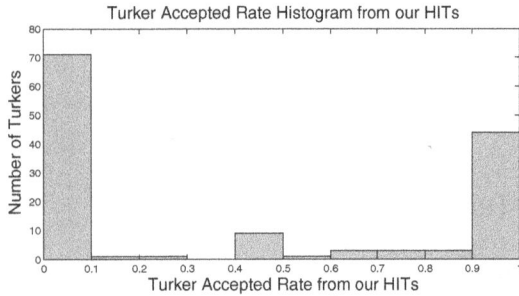

Figure 5: The histogram of turker accepted rate evaluated from the work on our HITs

ponents in Figure 2.

- Type 1 (No Check): In this type, all the answers from all assignments for a HIT are considered in majority voting step to get the FA.

- Type 2 (Qualification Check): In this type, all assignments that pass the qualification check will come to the majority voting step to get the FA.

- Type 3 (Qualification Check + Activity Count Check): Parameter N = 8 for the HITs

- Type 4 (Qualification Check + Overlapping Boundaries Removal + Activity Count Check): Even serious turkers may make a mistake, hence, we accept at most 2 overlapping tags and after overlapping boundaries removal, we decrease the required number of activities by 2. Thus, in this type, parameter N = 6 for the HITs.

- Type 5 (Qualification Check + Activity Count Check + Spammer Removal): Parameter N = 8 for our HITs.

- Type 6 (Check All): All checks are performed. Parameter N = 6 for our HITs.

In both Opportunity and CMU videos, the number of activity instances occurring in a segmented video is about 8-14. Thus, in our evaluation, we choose parameter N = 8 for Activity Count Check.

We find out that even dedicated workers who provided good tags for activities occurring in videos but still made mistakes in answering verifiable questions. Hence we relax the qualification check to remove out only the assignments

with at most one question answered correctly (i.e., parameter M = 2). In Spammer Removal, we choose a threshold = 0.3, it means if the disagreement score d >= 0.3 (i.e., less than 70% of annotation of the assignment agrees with the majority), the assignment is a spam and removed. For each HIT, we also compute the accepted rate(i.e., number of accepted assignments/total assignments per HIT) for type 6 only. It shows the real rejected and accepted rate we respond to turkers for each HIT.

Table 6 shows the accuracy, the average number of activities provided from accepted assignments for different types of evaluation of CMU HITs and the accepted rates.

Table 6: Results for 3 HITs in CMU dataset

	Accuracy					
	Type 1	Type 2	Type 3	Type 4	Type 5	Type 6
CMU HIT 1	0.71	0.72	0.72	0.77	0.76	0.77
CMU HIT 2	0.78	0.82	0.82	0.82	0.82	0.82
CMU HIT 3	0.81	0.82	0.82	0.82	0.82	0.82

	Average Number of Activities						Accepted Rate (%)
	Type 1	Type 2	Type 3	Type 4	Type 5	Type 6	
CMU HIT 1	7.2	11	10.14	10.14	10.67	10.14	50
CMU HIT 2	6.9	10.2	10.2	10.2	10.2	10.2	50
CMU HIT 3	7.36	10.14	10.14	10.14	10.14	10.14	60

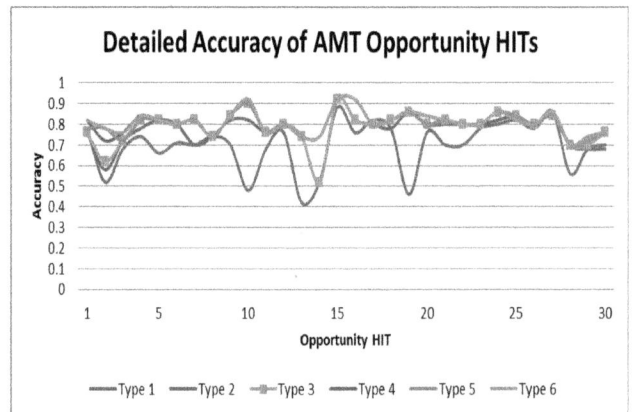

Figure 6: Detailed Accuracy of 30 AMT Opportunity HITs

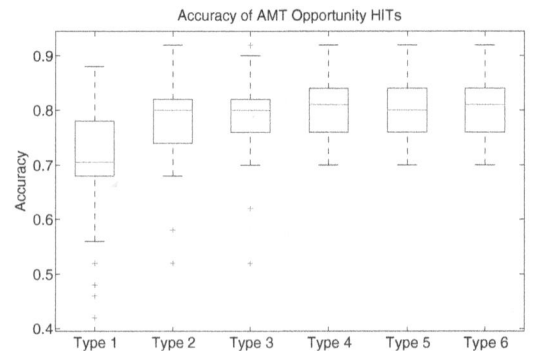

Figure 7: Box Plot of Accuracy of AMT Opportunity HITs

Figure 6 shows the detailed accuracy for 30 HITs in the Opportunity dataset. We summarize it in Figure 7. Figure

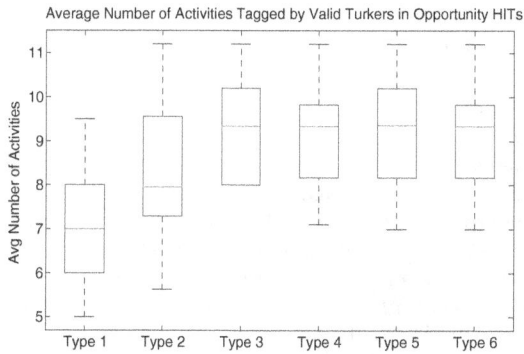

Figure 8: Box Plot of Average Number of Activities Tagged by Valid Turkers in Opportunity HITs

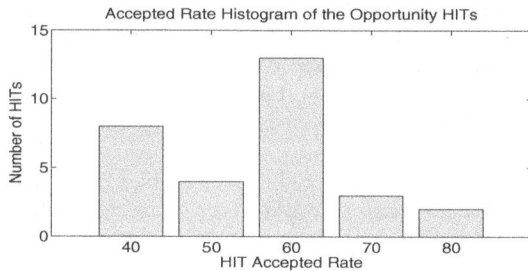

Figure 9: Accepted Rate in Opportunity HITs

8 summarizes the average number of activities provided by qualified assignments in each type in the Opportunity HITs.

Without any checking in Type 1, many Opportunity HITs get very low accuracy, thus even we recruit turkers with the approval rate at least 90%, there are still many non-serious turkers in AMT working in our tasks. It can be explained since every workers who just sign up into AMT system get 100% approval rate, some of them certainly are spammers. With Type 2, the accuracy is generally improved, there is still some HITs get bad accuracy and low average number of activities, it means some turkers may guess section 1 in the interface is qualification test and they tried to get good answers for section 1, but not for section 2. With Type 3, the accuracy is slightly better, however with Type 4, after we remove bad tags with the overlapping boundaries, we get very good and stable accuracies. The improvement from Type 3 to Type 4 can be intepreted that some spammers just tried to get a good result for section 1 that they think they can get their work approved and for section 2, they give non-sense or repeated activities which are overlapping many times. Type 4 and Type 5 have similar results. Therefore, the individual check with overlapping boundaries removal and the collaborative check to remove outliers are both good to detect and remove spammers. Type 6 is just a combination of Type 4 and Type 5. For Type 4, 5, 6, the accuracy is achieved from 76% to 92%. Most of the HITs are greater than 80% accuracy. The accuracy is increased by up to 40% compared to Type 1. For HITs that have the accuracy lower than 80%, we check the videos and turkers' answers and see that in the Opportunity videos, the door 2 position can not be seen clearly, so most of turkers can not tag open/close door 2 correctly. The toggle switch activity is

very short and there is a lot of disagreement between turkers and experts the starting and ending time of the toggle switch activities. This disagreement is also unavoidable since there is usually no standard definition when the start and end of an activity should be (e.g., drink gesture can start from the time user picks up a cup or when user starts drinking).

The CMU HITs have similar results of accuracy. Type 4, 5, 6 improve the accuracy compared to Type 1. In the CMU dataset, we see that the disagreement between turkers and experts on the boundaries of "crack Egg" activities usually occurs.

Figure 9 shows the accepted rate in the Opportunity HITs. Only five Opportunity HITs have the accepted rate between 70%-80%. The rest (25 Opportunity HITs) have high rejected rate betwen 40-60%. In CMU HITs (see Table 6), the accepted rate is about 50-60% which is similar to that shown in the Opportunity HITs. Thus, there are about 40% non-serious turkers with 90% approval rate working in our Opportunity and CMU HITs.

Notably, our first strategy was to publish tasks with qualification test (section 1 in the interface) only. After getting the results from those experiments, we selected the good turkers who answered the test correctly and invited them to a second round where we asked them to work on the actual video annotation (section 2 in the interface). We tried with three HITs of the CMU dataset for this strategy, however, we realized that turkers will not come back to the site soon enough or that they do not want to work our round 2 tasks. Hence, we decided to include the qualification tests into each experiment. However, the results show that many turkers did section 1 very well but did not provide any good tags for section 2 which we need the most. Thus, it does not guarantee that turkers who do well the qualification test will work well on real tasks. Requesters should always have strategies to validate the answers from turkers.

It is interesting that in both Opportunity HITs and CMU HITs, serious turkers usually provide all occurrences of activities in the video even we just ask them to provide at least N tags to get accepted.

6. CONCLUSION AND FUTURE WORK

In this paper, we conduct experiments to get activity annotation in videos from AMT in which turkers specify the temporal boundary and the label of all occurrences of activities in the videos. We introduce for the first time a methodology to use AMT to annotate activities occurring in video stream, with a data postprocessing stages to improve the annotation quality. The results show that even the HITs are distributed to high quality turkers in AMT (turkers' approval rate is at least 90%), quality of tagging still needs to be controled carefully. The results also show that using verifiable questions (qualification checking) is not enough to detect good turkers since many non-serious turkers can try to work well only for the qualification checking part. In our work, we propose two filtering strategies to detect non-serious turkers. Both strategies work efficiently in our experiments and increase the accuracy by up to 40%. It takes a similar amount of time for turkers and experts to annotate activities in the videos. The results show that the annotation from AMT has comparable quality to the annotation by experts (76%-92%).

In conclusion, this work shows the feasibility to use crowdsourcing to annotate human activity in videos. However, this work also shows several future research directions:

- We would like to investigate the ability of AMT turkers to annotate activities in the video without the prior knowledge of what kind of activities can occur in the video. This allows for richer description of the activities, but requires more sophisticated filtering and combination strategies taking into account semantic ambiguities.

- Future work must investigate whether the quality of annotation obtained through crowdsourcing is sufficient for the purpose of training activity recognition systems.

- We would like to investigate strategies to stop experiments when we get enough answers from good turkers or extend it otherwise. Thus, the amount of money to pay turkers can be reduced

- Finally we would like to characterize the joint influence on the annotation quality of, e.g. the influence of the user interface, the complexity of the activities in videos, the quality of the videos, the level of details in the requested annotations (primitive activities (e.g. take a cup) or high level activities (e.g. have breakfast) with/without object labeling). This requires comparative evaluations on more datasets of longer duration.

7. ACKNOWLEDGMENTS

We would like to thank Zack Zhu (ETH Zurich), and Alberto Calatroni (ETH Zurich) for their assistance and providing the Opportunity videos. This work has been supported by the Swiss Hasler Foundation project Smart-DAYS.

8. REFERENCES

[1] http://kitchen.cs.cmu.edu/.

[2] J. Aggarwal and M. Ryoo. Human activity analysis: A review. *ACM Comput. Surv.*, 43(3):16:1–16:43, Apr. 2011.

[3] L. Bao and S. S. Intille. Activity recognition from user-annotated acceleration data. In *Pervasive Computing: Proc. of the 2nd Int'l Conference*, 2004.

[4] L. Chen, J. Hoey, C. D. Nugent, D. J. Cook, and Z. Yu. Sensor-based activity recognition. In *IEEE Transactions on Systems, Man and Cybernetics*, 2012.

[5] A. P. Dawid and A. M. Skene. Maximum likelihood estimation of observer error-rates using the em algorithm. *Applied Statistics*, 28(1):20–28, 1979.

[6] M. J. Franklin, D. Kossmann, T. Kraska, S. Ramesh, and R. Xin. Crowddb: answering queries with crowdsourcing. In *Proceedings of the 2011 ACM SIGMOD International Conference on Management of data*, SIGMOD '11, pages 61–72, 2011.

[7] P.-Y. Hsueh, P. Melville, and V. Sindhwani. Data quality from crowdsourcing: a study of annotation selection criteria. In *Proceedings of the NAACL HLT 2009 Workshop on Active Learning for Natural Language Processing*, HLT '09, pages 27–35, 2009.

[8] P. G. Ipeirotis, F. Provost, and J. Wang. Quality management on amazon mechanical turk. In *Proceedings of the ACM SIGKDD Workshop on Human Computation*, HCOMP '10, 2010.

[9] A. Kittur, E. H. Chi, and B. Suh. Crowdsourcing user studies with mechanical turk. In *Proceedings of the SIGCHI conference on Human factors in computing systems*, CHI '08, pages 453–456, 2008.

[10] S. Nowak and S. Rüger. How reliable are annotations via crowdsourcing: a study about inter-annotator agreement for multi-label image annotation. In *Proceedings of the international conference on Multimedia information retrieval*, MIR '10, pages 557–566. ACM, 2010.

[11] G. Parent and M. Eskenazi. Toward better crowdsourced transcription: Transcription of a year of the let's go bus information system data. In *SLT*, pages 312–317, 2010.

[12] G. Parent and M. Eskenazi. Speaking to the crowd: Looking at past achievements in using crowdsourcing for speech and predicting future challenges. In *INTERSPEECH*, pages 3037–3040, 2011.

[13] V. C. Raykar and et. al. Learning from crowds. *Journal of Machine Learning Research*, 11:1297–1322, 2010.

[14] D. Roggen and et. al. Collecting complex activity data sets in highly rich networked sensor environments. In *7th Int. Conf. on Networked Sensing Systems*. IEEE Press, 2010.

[15] J. Ross and et. al. Who are the crowdworkers?: shifting demographics in mechanical turk. In *Extended Abstracts on Human Factors in Computing Systems*, CHI EA '10, pages 2863–2872, 2010.

[16] V. S. Sheng, F. Provost, and P. G. Ipeirotis. Get another label? improving data quality and data mining using multiple, noisy labelers. In *Proceedings of the 14th ACM SIGKDD international conference on Knowledge discovery and data mining*, KDD '08, pages 614–622, 2008.

[17] R. Snow, B. O'Connor, D. Jurafsky, and A. Y. Ng. Cheap and fast—but is it good?: evaluating non-expert annotations for natural language tasks. In *Proceedings of the Conference on Empirical Methods in Natural Language Processing*, EMNLP '08, pages 254–263, 2008.

[18] M. Soleymani and M. Larson. Crowdsourcing for affective annotation of video: development of a viewer-reported boredom corpus. In *33th ACM SIGIR, Workshop on Crowdsourcing for Search Evaluation*, 2010.

[19] C. Vondrick, D. Patterson, and D. Ramanan. Efficiently scaling up crowdsourced video annotation. *International Journal of Computer Vision*, pages 1–21, 2012.

[20] C. Vondrick and D. Ramanan. Video annotation and tracking with active learning. In *NIPS*, pages 28–36, 2011.

[21] A. Wang, C. D. V. Hoang, and M.-Y. Kan. Perspectives on crowdsourcing annotations for natural language processing, 2010.

[22] L. Zhao, G. Sukthankar, and R. Sukthankar. Incremental relabeling for active learning with noisy crowdsourced annotations. In *SocialCom/PASSAT*, pages 728–733, 2011.

Who Produced This Video, Amateur or Professional?

Jinlin Guo, Cathal Gurrin
CLARITY and Computing
School, Dublin City University
Glasnevin, Dublin 9, Dublin,
Ireland
{jinlin.guo, cgurrin}@computing.dcu.ie

Songyang Lao
School of Information System
and Management
NUDT, Changsha, Hunan,
China
laosongyang@vip.sina.com

ABSTRACT

As the increasing affordability for capturing and storing video and the proliferation of Web 2.0 applications, video content is no longer necessarily created and supplied by a limited number of professional producers; any amateur can produce and publish his/her video quickly. Therefore, the amount of both professional-produced as well as amateur-produced video on the web is ever increasing. In this work, we propose a question; whether we can automatically classify an Internet video clip as being either professional-produced or amateur-produced? Hence, we investigate features and classification methods to answer this question. Based on the differences in the production processes of these two video categories, four features including camera motion, structure, audio feature and combined feature are adopted and studied along with with four popular classifiers KNN, SVM GMM and C4.5. Extensive experiments over carefully-constructed, representative datasets, evaluate these features and classifiers under different settings and compare to existing techniques. Experimental results demonstrate that SVMs with multimodal features from multi-sources are more effective at classifying video type. Finally, for answering the proposed question, results also show that automatically classifying a clip as professional-produced video or amateur-produced video can be achieved with good accuracy.

Categories and Subject Descriptors

I.4 [**Image Processing and Computer Vision**]: Miscellaneous; I.5.4 [**Pattern Recognition**]: Computer Vision—*Applications*

General Terms

Experimentation, Performance

Keywords

Amateur-produced Video, Professional-produced Video, Camera Motion, Video genre Classification

1. INTRODUCTION

Video content has been historically created and supplied by a limited number of production companies, TV networks, and cable networks. They are produced by professionals and consumed by general public. The video quality was in general guaranteed since it was recorded by professional capturing device and subject to careful post-produced according to certain cinematic principles.

Nowadays, the increasing affordability for capturing and storing video has resulted in a massive amount of personal video content, and the proliferation of Web 2.0 applications is re-shaping the video consumption model. Especially, the rise of some easy-to-use social networking websites such as YouTube [1], makes it easy for users uploading, managing, sharing video. Therefore, the users on the Internet are no longer only video consumers, but also participators and producers, just as the slogan of Tudou [2], one of the most popular video sharing websites, "Everyone is the director of life". Now, hundreds of millions of Internet users are self-publishing consumers. This results in an explosive increase in the quantity of Internet video. Recent statistics show that, on the the primary video sharing website YouTube, 48 hours of video are uploaded every minute by users, resulting in nearly 8 years of content uploaded every day, and more video is uploaded to YouTube in one month than the 3 major US networks created in 60 years [3]. The video on the Internet, we call them user-uploaded video, may be either produced by amateur or professional based on its original producer (the user uploaded the video may be the authors of the video or not). Hence, the user-uploaded video can be categorized into amateur-produced video (APV) and professional-produced video (PPV) based on the author type.

We define an APV clip as being recorded by an amateur without much knowledge in producing video and generally using personal video capture devices, then uploaded to websites by the user (it may be the amateur or not) with little post-production. By contrast, the PPV is captured by professional devices and edited based on certain cinematic principles, such as news, sports and movies. Note that, a number of Internet video clips are made by extracting/ripping content from PPV such as TV programs, DVD movies, and then uploaded (sometimes even with some captions and background music added). In this work, we still consider them

---

[1] http://www.youtube.com
[2] http://www.tudou.com/
[3] http://www.youtube.com/t/press_statistics

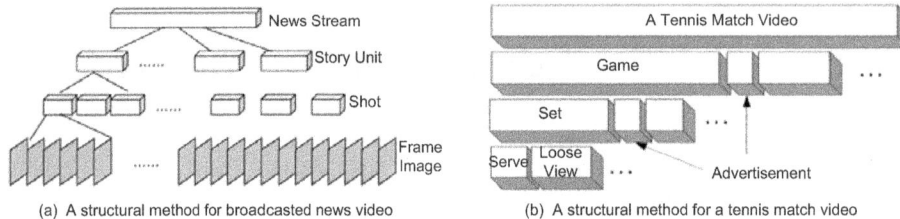

(a) A structural method for broadcasted news video (b) A structural method for a tennis match video

Figure 1: Two structural methods for broadcasted news video and tennis match video respectively

as PPV. Therefore, compared with PPV, the APV has the following characteristics [7].

- A great number of APV clips can be found on the Web. Since APV requires less production efforts, anyone can readily make short video clips by using a camcoder or even a smartphone. Easy of production creates a massive amount of APV content.

- Due to the uncontrolled capturing conditions and accompanied personal capture devices, APV is most of the time of lower quality than PPV.

- The APV is usually less structured: APV is not as well structured as PPV. The PPV clips are consumed by general public. They are produced following certain cinematic principles. The structure is understood such as the structures of news video and tennis video shown in Fig. 1. However, APV is usually captured by different amateurs, who generally do not follow professional guidelines and best practice when producing video. In most cases, there is no post-production before uploading to the video sharing websites. Therefore, there is less structure information existing in the APV.

The question raised here is whether we can automatically determine that a video clip was created by an amateur or professional? That is, can we classify an Internet video clip into PPV and APV automatically? This is helpful, for example, when generating ranked lists in response to a user query or when categorizing results. For example, a user searches for a concert video clip and prefers the clips published by official producer, rather than by the audience in the scene. In this work, we investigate features and techniques for answering this question. Our approach is based on the differences that are inherent in the production processes of these two video categories. Multimodal features including camera motion, structure information, audio feature and combined feature together with four popular classifiers are adopted and also evaluated within different experiment settings. Furthermore, with the goal of comparitive evaluation, two representative state-of-the-art frameworks are also implemented to classify APV and PPV.

The paper is structured as follows. In section 2, we briefly review the related work. In section 3, we detail the multimodal features and algorithms for classifying a user-uploaded video clip into PPV or APV. The experiment and results are presented and summarized in section 4. Finally, Section 5 concludes this work and outlines the future work.

2. RELATED WORK

Most relevant work in our context focuses on video genre classification. Some researchers have focused on classifying segments of video, such as identifying violent [10] or scary [18] scenes in a movie. However, most of the video classification work attempts to classify an entire video clip into one of several genres, such as *sports*, *news*, *cartoon*, *music*. In general, the previous methods can be categorized into four types: text-based approaches [1, 23], audio feature based approaches [5, 15, 17], visual feature based approaches [4, 20, 22], and those that used some combination of text, audio and visual features[3, 4, 8]. In fact, most authors incorporated audio and visual features into their approaches (we call it content-based approaches), and these approaches achieved good performance. Here we will give a brief review about the content-based approaches. Extensive surveys of these techniques can be referred in [2, 12].

The combination of audio and visual low-level features attempts to incorporate the audio and visual aspects that these features represent and complement each other. Audio features can be derived from either the time domain or the frequency domain. Time domain features such as the root mean square of signal energy (RMS), Zero-Crossing Rate (ZCR) and frequency domain feature MFCC are commonly used in previous work [3, 12].

Visual features in general include motion features [11], keyframe image features such as Scale Invariant Feature Transform (SIFT) [22] and color or texture [3, 4, 8], structure features, such as average shot length, gradual transition and cut shot ratios [8, 12, 21], identification of some simple objects [20], with research focussed on how to combine these features.

Ways of using these features investigated in existed work include many of the standard classifiers because of their ubiquitous nature, such as KNN [8, 22], Linear Discriminant Analysis (LDA) [8], SVM [3, 4, 5, 8, 16, 21], C4.5 decision tree [4, 9], GMM [11, 12, 17, 20]. Moreover, some more complicated methods such as HMM [4, 19, 20] and neural networks [12] were also introduced to video genre classification.

It should be noted that two evaluations strongly promoted the research on Internet video genre classification. The first one is set out by Google as an *ACM Multimedia Grand Challenge task* in 2009 (also in 2010) [4]. Followed that was the *Genre Tagging Task* in MediaEval 2011 [5], which focused on genre classification of Internet video.

The Internet video can be categorized into a number of

---

[4]http://www.sigmm.org/archive/MM/mm09/MMGC.aspx.htm

[5]http://www.multimediaeval.org/mediaeval2011/

genres. For instance, the genre classification defined in Google Video consists of 38 genres, such as *business, music, news, sports* and so on [6]. However, in this work, we focus on determining if a video clip is APV or PPV, namely if it is produced by amateur or professional.

Our approaches are based on the features including background or camera motion, structure, audio and combined feature that can discriminate the APV and PPV. Compared with previous work, our contributions in this work are that 1) we propose the question of recognizing the APV and PPV; 2) four commonly used classifiers with four features especially background or camera motion are evaluated with extensive experiments over carefully selected datasets, moreover, we compare and evaluate our approaches with two representative techniques in previous work to address this problem.

3. CLASSIFYING AMATEUR AND PROFESSIONAL PRODUCED VIDEO

In this section, we will describe the features and classifiers used for classifying APV and PPV in this work. Firstly, in section 3.1 the background or camera motion features are described. Structure information and audio features are described in section 3.2 and section 3.3 respectively. In section 3.4, the classification algorithms adopted are introduced.

3.1 Camera Motion Feature

As stated, the APV is generally recorded by person without much knowledge about cinematic principles using personal devices under uncontrolled capturing conditions, then uploaded to the sharing websites with less post-production (such as stabilization). Therefore, APV is apt to suffer from more irregular camera motion than PPV. The camera motion feature is likely to be a good potential discriminator between APV and PPV.

The visual quality of video is highly relevant to three properties of camera motion (CM) [6], that is, *speed, direction* and *acceleration*. These properties affect video quality in different ways. If the speed of CM is high, the captured frames will be blurred. When the speed is normal, but the direction of CM changes frequently, namely, the camera moves back and forth repeatedly, the captured video is regarded as shaky. When speed is normal and direction is consistent, but the accelerations of CM in consecutive frames are uneven, that is, the variance of acceleration is large, the captured video is inconsistent. The normal CM with few direction changes and steady accelerations lead to stable video.

Specifically, we adopt the block-match based optical flow approach in [6] to detect the background or camera motion features, since it is computational efficient. For a video clip c, by the method in [6], a set of motion vectors is obtained, set as $V = \{v_{k-1,k}\}_n$, where, $v_{k-1,k}$ is the CM vector extracted from the consecutive frame $k-1$ and k, n is the number of motion vectors extracted in c. Based on V, a set of acceleration vectors can be calculated, set as $A = \{a_{k-1,k+1}\}_{n-1}$, here,

$$a_{k-1,k+1} = (v_{k-1,k} - v_{k,k+1})/\Delta t \doteq v_{k-1,k} - v_{k,k+1} \quad (1)$$

where Δt is time interval between two consecutive-extracted frames. Since we sample the frames uniformly (five frames

per second), that is, Δt is a constant. Meanwhile, a set of direction changes is obtained, set as $\theta = \{\theta_{k-1,k,k+1}\}_{n-1}$ where $\theta_{k-1,k,k+1}$ is the direction change, namely the angle between $v_{k-1,k}$ and $v_{k,k+1}$, calculated by:

$$\theta_{k-1,k,k+1} = arccos\left(\frac{v_{k-1,k} \cdot v_{k,k+1}}{\|v_{k-1,k}\| \|v_{k,k+1}\|}\right) \quad (2)$$

We choose the mean, second order central moment (or variance), third order central moment and fourth order central moment of V, A and θ as the camera motion feature since these statistics represent the change and distribution properties of CM in clip c. Specifically, for V, the mean is computed as:

$$\bar{v} = \frac{\sum v_{i-1,i}}{n} \quad (3)$$

The t_{th} order central moment is calculated as:

$$m_t = \frac{\sum (v_{i-1,i} - \bar{v})^t}{n} \quad (4)$$

where $t \in \{2, 3, 4\}$.

For A and θ, the same statistics are calculated, but with the number of $n-1$. Finally, a 20 (by concatenating the mean, second order central moment, third order central moment and fourth order central moment of CM vector, acceleration vector and direction change value, namely, $4 * 2 + 4 * 2 + 4$) dimensional feature vector is obtained to represent the video clip c.

3.2 Structure Information

As stated in the Introduction, APV is not usually as well structured as PPV. Structure or temporal information is strongly related to PPV genre, e.g. *business* and *music* clips tend to have a high visual tempo, *business* uses a lot of gradual transitions etc. Therefore, structure information from the shot may help discriminate APV and PPV.

We extract structure information including *shot number, average shot length, cut shot ratio*. Here, we apply the shot boundary detector in [14], which finds two types of shot boundaries, i.e. cut and gradual transition. The average shot length is computed by averaging all the shot lengths in a video. Additionally, we calculate the ratio of cut shot to the overall shot boundaries.

3.3 Audio Feature

Audio information has the potential to be an important cue discriminating different video genres. Most of the common video genres have very specific audio signatures, e.g. in news there are a lot of monologues/dialogues, sports have a mixture of commentator speaking, applause and clapping, and movie contains a mixture of soundtrack and dialogues, etc.. However, because of the open and sharing of the video websites and the diversity of amateurs, APV can be about anything in any scene, and anyone can be a star, from lip-synching amateurs to skateboarding dogs. Therefore, the accompanied audio content in APV may be more complex and diversified. Audio features such as RMS, ZCR and MFCC are commonly used for video genre classification in previous work, especially the MFCC. In previous work, MFCC features directly or their statistics such as mean and standard deviation were used for video classification [3, 15]. In this work, we will use MFCC together with the bag-of-audio-word (BoAW) representation following the method in [5].

[6]http://video.google.com/genre.html

The BoAW is derived from the popular bag of word in text-document classification.

The process is as follows. Firstly, the signal is sampled at 16kHz, then MFCC features are calculated over 25ms windows/frames every 10ms. The "null" MFCC, which is proportional to the total energy in the frame, is also included. Furthermore, delta coefficients and acceleration coefficients, which estimate the first and second order derivation of MFCCs respectively and exhibits the dynamic characteristic of the audio content, are also adopted. In total, the extraction of MFCCs results in a 39-dimensional feature vector for each frame. Then, each video's accompanied audio is represented as a set of $d = 39$ dimensional MFCC feature vectors, where the total number of frames from an entire video depends on its duration.

In order to create the BoAW representation, a vocabulary with 2,000 audio words is created by K-means clustering on a randomly sample 500,000 MFCC feature vectors. Finally, all features of a video's soundtrack are assigned to their closest (using Euclidean distance) audio words. This produces histograms of audio word occurrences for each video clip, and are then used as feature input for classifying the APV and PPV.

3.4 Classification Algorithms

Some complicated methods such as HMM and neural networks were employed in previous work. However, they need much more time and computational effort to train classification models. In the context of this work, determining a video clip as APV or PPV is typically a binary classification question. Therefore, in this work, four popular and relative easy-to-perform classification approaches are selected for our evaluation experiments, namely, K-Nearest Neighbors (KNN), Support Vector Machines (SVM), Gaussian Mixture Model (GMM), and C4.5 decision tree.

KNN classifier generates clusters representing the classes of feature points and assigns a feature instance to the cluster that has k instances closest to it. In our work, cosine distance is adopted for KNN method and k is set as 1. SVMs map an input space into a high dimensional feature space through a kernel function and then constructs the optimal separating hyperplane in the high dimensional feature space. With respect to the SVM kernel, the Gaussian Radius Basis Function (RBF) kernel is used since it is widely used and always achieves good performance across different applications. When using the GMM method, one model is trained for one class of video. The Expectation-Maximization (EM) algorithm is adopted to estimate the parameters of a GMM. When testing, a sample is predicted to the class whose model outputs larger confidence. In this work, 9 mixture components are used in GMM. The C4.5 decision tree recursively subdivides a set of data by using the concept of entropy from information theory. The feature which provides the most information gain, as defined by the difference in entropy, at each recursion is used to form a decision based on the values of the feature. The result is a tree where each node has a feature and a decision depending on its value.

4. EXPERIMENTS AND RESULTS

4.1 Experimental Dataset

To evaluate the efficiency of the features and methods used in the work, we select about 150 hours', 2,000 video clips,

each of which either belongs to APV or PPV. The duration of each video clip is less than 10 mins.

In the 2,000 video clips, 500 are annotated as APV, while the others are labeled as PPV. The APV clips are from the NIST TRECVID 2011 Multimedia Event Detection (MED) task [13]. The MED dataset consists of publicly available video content posted to Internet video hosting sites. The annotation work is carefully conducted. Each video clip is viewed by three annotators. One clip is deemed as APV only when all three annotators consider it as APV. The annotations mostly rely on the semantics of video content, such as the scenes, dialogues in video. The annotations show that the annotators easily obtain consistency in most cases. The PPV clips were crawled from YouTube, including three video genres, news, sports, and movies. We checked the collected PPV clips carefully. Finally, 1,500 clips were selected, 500 clips for each genre. We determine a video as news or sports video only based on the TV channel logo, such as RTE NEWS, BBC, CCTV-4. The movie clips are fragments from multiple movies.

The experiments focus on the performance among features, video genres and classification methods. Besides the three single features namely camera motion feature (CMF), structure feature (SF) and audio feature (AF), we also evaluate the combined feature (CF) that are from the concatenation of the three single features and are normalized before input as features for classifiers. Firstly, we investigate the performance when only considering to classify a specific PPV genre and APV. Then experiment for discriminating any genre of PPV clip and an APV clip is implemented. Hence, we identify four experiments:

- News *vs.* APV.

- Sports *vs.* APV.

- Movies *vs.* APV.

- Mixture *vs.* APV.

The following experiments are conducted using five-fold cross validation. The mean accuracy and standard deviation over five-fold cross-validation are reported.

4.2 News *vs.* APV

The first experiment evaluates the performance of the four features with different classification methods when assuming the PPV is only news video. Experiments are conducted over the datasets including the 500 news clips and the 500 APV clips. In Table 1, we show the results. It should be noted that, the mean accuracies reported by SVM classifiers are based on the best parameters trained on the entire 1,000 video clips using five-fold cross validation.

Table 1 illustrates that in the three single features, CMF reports the best performance for all four methods. Especially compared with the structural feature (SF), the CMF achieves much better performance. Moreover, CMF also attains comparable accuracies with the combined feature (CF). When using GMM and C4.5, the CMF even outperforms the CF by a minor value. In the two cases where CMF is outperformed by CF when using KNN and SVM classifiers, the performance difference is marginal. The excellence of CMF for discriminating the news video and the PPV is in line with the differences between the two video categories. News video are usually recorded by experienced photographers. When capturing a news clip, the camera

Table 1: Accuracy(%) comparison on four features with four classification methods when the PPV only contains news video

	KNN	SVM	GMM	C4.5
CMF	91.4 ± 3.13	92.0 ± 2.33	88.3 ± 2.23	89.5 ± 2.21
SF	78.8 ± 1.68	82.3 ± 3.02	81.2 ± 2.91	85.8 ± 2.89
AF	90.3 ± 2.89	91.3 ± 1.92	82.3 ± 2.71	78.3 ± 1.99
CF	94.3 ± 2.20	92.4 ± 2.22	87.7 ± 2.20	88.4 ± 2.11

Table 2: Accuracy(%) comparison on four features with four classification methods when the PPV only contains sports video

	KNN	SVM	GMM	C4.5
CMF	78.3 ± 2.20	81.3 ± 1.63	82.1 ± 1.73	78.7 ± 2.63
SF	71.8 ± 2.18	72.6 ± 2.19	68.6 ± 2.67	77.2 ± 2.54
AF	87.4 ± 1.79	85.7 ± 2.31	83.3 ± 2.02	78.9 ± 2.27
CF	89.4 ± 2.49	87.2 ± 1.82	82.8 ± 1.70	83.2 ± 2.73

Table 3: Accuracy(%) comparison on four features with four classification methods when the PPV is only movie video

	KNN	SVM	GMM	C4.5
CMF	70.1 ± 3.73	78.1 ± 4.11	77.2 ± 2.73	76.1 ± 3.84
SF	77.6 ± 3.18	75.9 ± 2.89	78.3 ± 3.27	74.1 ± 4.54
SF	71.2 ± 2.92	76.2 ± 3.31	73.2 ± 3.02	73.6 ± 3.27
CF	81.5 ± 3.19	85.8 ± 3.34	82.6 ± 2.91	82.3 ± 2.96

is kept moving uniformly in most cases, that is, the camera moves toward a certain direction with relative uniform speed. However, camera motions in APV clips are more irregular since the APV clips are typically captured by personal easy-shaking small-size devices such as smartphones. Furthermore, post-processings such as stabilization may be performed on news video before broadcasting [7].

Audio feature (AF) also attains high accuracies with KNN and SVM algorithms. This may be attributed the audio content accompanied in news video is mainly from persons, such as the anchorpersons, interviewees or dialogs. In contrast, the audio content in APV can be anything, such as person voice, dog barking, music and so on. AF reports much reduced performance when using GMM and C4.5 methods compared with KNN and SVM. We consider that this because the GMM and C4.5 learns less discrimination information when using much higher dimensional audio features with BoAV representation (2,000 dimensions). Furthermore, KNN and SVM classifiers attain best performance overall.

4.3 Sports vs. APV

As a second experiment, we focus on discriminating the sports video and the APV. Results are shown in Table 2. It is worth noting that the sports video clips we collected from YouTube are mainly soccer, rugby and tennis matches. This table shows that the adopted features are less powerful for discriminating sports and APV than discriminating news and APV. Moreover, the table also shows a clear advantage of using audio feature (AF) over the other two single features. For all the classifiers, AF attains the best performance of the three single features. We speculate that in the sports video (especially in soccer, rugby and tennis matches), accompanied audio categories mainly include commentator speaking, applause and clapping from the audiences in live. However, the audio in APV is more diversified.

CMF report accuracies around 80 for all classifiers. The best is 82.1 ± 1.73 with GMM, whereas 78.3 ± 2.20 with KNN is the worst. Compared with APV, camera motions are also very strong in sports video, especially in field sports such as soccer matches. Several camera motion modes such as *zoom in/out*, *pan* and *tilt* are commonly existed in sports video, which makes the CMF is less discriminative for sports and APV.

Structure information is not sufficient to distinguish the sports video and APV. We attribute this most to the fact that complex camera motions in sports video result in poor

performance in shot boundary detection. Nevertheless, the combined feature (CF) achieves the best performance nearly for all classifiers, except when using GMM classifier. This proves that the three features are complementary and boost the classification accuracies.

4.4 Movies vs. APV

In an attempt to evaluate the power of the four features as well as four classifiers for discriminating movies and APV, we conduct the third experiment, in which, the PPV clips are all fragments from films. The movies collected for this experiments include clips from romance films, action films, horror films and thrillers.

The performance of the PPV only movies is listed in Table 3. Results show that the three single features report close performance with the four classification algorithms. For CMF, the best accuracy is 78.1 ± 4.11 with SVM classifier. With respect to structure information, accuracy attains the best of 78.3 ± 3.27 when using GMM method. Whereas, top accuracy is 76.2 ± 3.31 when adopting AF with SVM. Overall, the accuracies are around 75 but less than 80 when using single features. Another observation is that classifying movies and APV results in much more significant standard deviations. The intra-class differences in these selected movies are apparent. We only take audio features as example, in romance films, music and dialogs may be the main audio types. However, in horror films, synthetic horror sound is one of the most important "actors". Therefore, huge intraclass differences in these selected films results in significant performance variance.

Furthermore, performance of structure feature (SF) proves competitive to the other two single features. When using KNN and GMM methods, the SF yields higher performance than CMF and AF. We credit this to the structure information being strongly related to movie genre, e.g. action film clips tend to have a high visual tempo, romance movies use a lot of gradual transitions,etc.

Finally, when combining these simple features into composite features, accuracies are boosted significantly. Again, we deem this performance gain comes at the enhancement of discriminative power of the combined features (CF).

---

[7] For YouTube, the users are required to stabilize the video using the stabilizer tool in the YouTube Video Editor before uploaded it. However, firstly, the effectiveness of this tool on APV needs further evaluation. Secondly, the APV clips used in this work are not necessarily from YouTube

Table 4: Accuracy(%) comparison on four features with four classification methods when the PPV is mixture of multiple PPV genres

	KNN	SVM	GMM	C4.5
CMF	72.2 ± 3.03	80.7 ± 2.97	73.7 ± 3.13	72.4 ± 3.72
SF	75.1 ± 3.27	77.2 ± 3.39	78.6 ± 3.25	69.8 ± 3.64
AF	77.4 ± 2.89	78.7 ± 3.42	75.1 ± 2.92	70.9 ± 2.73
CF	82.6 ± 3.17	85.3 ± 2.88	80.8 ± 2.79	79.1 ± 3.23

4.5 Mixture *vs.* APV

With the goal of answering the question as stated in the Introduction, the fourth experiment is performed under the condition of the PPV clips are a mixture of clips from different PPV genres. In real scenario, there are much more PPV genres, such as those 38 genres defined in Google Video. In this work, we consider that the PPV consists of uniform mixtures of news, sports and movies. However, considering more PPV genres and random mixtures of PPV clips can be inspired by the experiment here and would be an obvious future research task.

In order to perform these experiments on balanced datasets, we divide 1,500 PPV clips into three uniform parts randomly. In practice, 500 clips for each PPV genre are divided into three uniform parts (167+167+166) randomly. Then three groups of 500 video clips are obtained by mixing three parts from each genre respectively. Experiments are performed on each group of 500 PPV clips versus the 500 APV clips with cross validation. Means accuracy and standard deviation are calculated over the performance from the cross validations.

Results are shown in Table 4. Similar observations as in section 4.4 can be found. When using the single features, the performance differences are marginal and most of the accuracies are between 70 to 80. This may be attributed the fact that none of these single features are sufficient to discriminate each PPV genre and APV. Because of the diversity in the collected PPV clips, significant standard deviations are also reported. Moreover, when combining these simple features into composite features, accuracies are boosted significantly.

When comparing four adopted classification algorithms, we find SVM classifiers outperform other methods when using three of four features. The lower two accuracies are reported by C4.5 decision trees with structure feature (SF) and audio feature (AF), namely 69.8 ± 3.64 and 70.9 ± 2.73 respectively, which are much worse than those obtained by the other three methods when using the same features. However, when using the combined feature (CF) as input for C4.5, the performance is significantly improved.

4.6 Summary of Experimental Results

In order to compare performance of the features and classification algorithms adopted, we aggregate the accuracies of the four features and four algorithms in the four experiments above, as shown in Table 1~4 . Table 5 compares the discrimination of these four features, in which, each value is the average of the four mean accuracies of corresponding feature in relevant experiments. Table 6 compares the performance of these four classifiers, in which, each value is the average of the four mean accuracies of corresponding classifier in relevant experiments.

Table 5: Averages of the evaluated four features on discriminating different PPV genres with APV.

	News vs.	Sports vs.	Movie vs.	Mixture vs.
CMF	90.3	80.1	75.4	74.5
SF	82.0	72.6	76.5	75.2
AF	85.6	83.8	73.6	75.5
CF	90.7	85.7	83.1	82.0

Table 6: Averages of the evaluated four classification algorithms on discriminating different PPV genres with APV.

	News vs.	Sports vs.	Movie vs.	Composite vs.
KNN	88.7	81.7	75.1	76.8
SVM	89.5	81.7	79.0	80.5
GMM	84.9	79.2	77.9	77.1
C4.5	85.5	79.5	76.5	73.1

Our first observation is that none of these single features are sufficient to discriminate each specific PPV genre and APV. When comparing these single features, we find CMF is better for distinguishing the APV with the PPV genres whose structure is clear and camera motion is simple and regular, such as news video. AF may yield better performance when it is used for discriminating APV with PPV genres which contain less audio types, such as news and sports video. Whereas, temporal SF may improves the performance when classifying APV with PPV genres in which, temporal structure is related with tempo or effect, such as movies. On the whole, CMF and AF prove to be more efficient at discriminating PPV and APV, leading to better classification accuracies.

A notable observation we can make is that combination of multimodal features boosts the classification performance significantly nearly for all algorithms in the four experiments. This means that information from multi-sources should be considered when classifying PPV and APV, especially when PPV contains more video genres. This is also in line with the conclusions in previous work [3, 8]. Therefore, adoption of multimodal features appears to be the road map for future work in discriminating PPV and APV.

With respect to specific PPV genres, news video is easier to be distinguished with APV, which may be attributed to the fact that many similar cinematic principles are complied with by different news video producers when producing news video, such as they are generally structure-clear. Therefore, even temporal structure feature yields good performance when classifying news video and APV.

The four classification algorithms show different performance when used with different features and for classifying different PPV genres and APV. KNN and SVM yield the best performance in discriminating news and APV, using camera motion and audio features. They are also good at distinguishing sports and APV when using audio features. Whereas, when using single features, GMM also yields good performance in classifying movie and APV. Another point worth noting is that for each algorithm, the overall performance decreases as the PPV contains more sub-genres of PPV. We illustrate this by Fig. 2

Globally, SVM and KNN yield excellent performance in each experiment with different features. GMM has the ad-

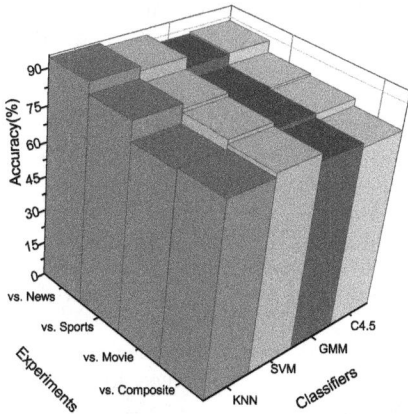

Figure 2: Accuracies of combined features with four classification algorithms in four experiments. It shows that the performance decreases as PPV contains more video genres.

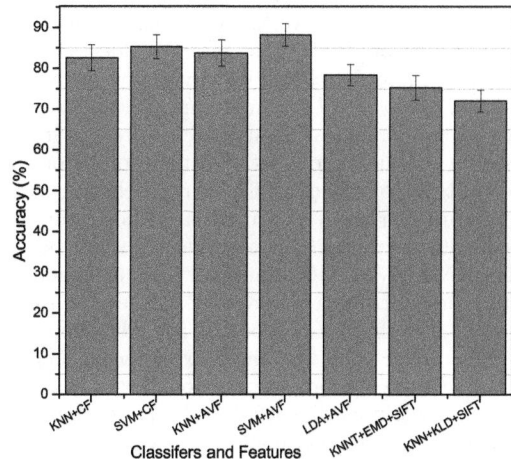

Figure 3: Performance comparison

vantage of training efficiently. The number of Gaussian components may affect the performance, and for different features, the number may be different. However, in our previous experiments, we set the number as a fixed value 9 for all features and all experiments, which may hinder its performance. The performance of C4.5 relies on the information contained in some discriminative features. Furthermore, when using high dimensional features, such as BoAW representation for audio features, poor accuracies are reported and training is time consuming.

4.7 Extended Experiments

In this section, we apply two state-of-the-art frameworks to the classification of APV and PPV in our context, and also compare our methods with them. One is the framework using audio-visual features (AVF) in [8], the other is the framework with SIFT features in [22]. These two frameworks are representative and originally used for common video genre classification. In [8] tens of audio-visual features, including audio, temporal structure, color, and contour, are combined to classify different video genres such as *news*, *sports*, *music*, *movies* and so on. Three classifiers were used, namely SVM, KNN and LDA. More, recently, there is a trend of using local image features which are scale-, affine- or other-property invariant in the retrieval of imagery and video data, and in [22], Zhang et al. introduced the most popular SIFT feature for video genre classification. With the goals of evaluating these two frameworks in our classification task of APV and PPV, and comparing them with our methods, we perform this extended experiment over the 2,000 clips collected in this work.

Experiments are performed in the same way as in section 4.5. Here, related parameter settings are the same as in [8, 22]. In [8], results from SVM, KNN and LDA with AVF are reported (i.e. SVM+AVF, KNN+AVF, LDA+AVF). In [22], results from KNN with earth mover's distance (EMD) and KullbackLeibler divergence (KLD), histogram representation of 1600-size codebook are also reported (i.e. KNN+ EMD+SIFT, KNN+KLD+SIFT).

Experimental results are shown in Fig. 3. Here, we also list our best performance from SVM and KNN, with the combined features in section 4.5 (i.e. SVM+CF, KNN+CF). It can be seen that, with the task of classifying APV and PPV, combination of multimodal features yields better performance. SVM with audio-visual feature (SVM+AVF) in [8] produces the best accuracy. We deem that the audio-visual feature captures more discriminative information. However, the combined feature (CF) in this work also achieves competitive performance. This may be attributed to the camera motion feature we adopted in this work. In [8], an action feature is also used, however, it is only calculated by assuming that a long shot represents high-action content, whereas short shots mean low-action content. In [8], the audio-visual feature reports much higher accuracies for classifying video genre than the accuracies here, since in that work, the experiments are performed as *one-vs.-all* style. In general, discriminating one specific video genre from a mixture (all) of multi-genres video is easier than classifying two mixtures. This can be validated in our previous experiments that, experiment 1, 2, 3, produce better performance than experiment 4 when using combined features.

From Fig. 3, we can also see that the popularly used SIFT feature reports much worse performance in classifying APV and PPV. In the original work [22], these methods achieve high accuracies, even 100. However, similar to [8], their experiments are also conducted to classify much more specific video genres, e.g. surveillance video captured by 5 different cameras are treated as 5 individual genres respectively, or one specific sports, such as *boxing*, represents one video genre. In our context, PPV includes multiple different video genres, and APV can be about anything. Furthermore, currently successful approaches to video genre classification seems to rely on the application of domain knowledge existing in video genres. Therefore, in our context, this domain-knowledge independent SIFT feature is not capable of discriminating the PPV and APV well.

5. CONCLUSIONS

A large volume of video content is poised to inundate the Internet. In this work, we propose a question of determining the producer of an Internet video as professional or amateur, namely, classifying a video clip as professional-produced video (PPV) or amateur-produced video (APV). Features and classification approaches are also investigated. Based on the differences between the production process of the two types of video, four features including camera motion feature, structure information, audio feature and combined features are adopted together with four popular classifiers KNN, SVM, GMM and C4.5. Four experiments are firstly performed over a carefully selected datasets including 1,500 PPV from YouTube and 500 APV from TRECVid MED datasets. The first three experiments focus on classifying one specific video genre from APV. The fourth one performs discriminating APV and any genre of PPV clip. Furthermore, we further implement two representative techniques in previous work to the task in this work and compare them with our methods. Experimental results demonstrate that SVMs with multimodal features from multi-sources are more effective at classifying the two types of video. Finally, for answering the proposed question, results also show that automatically classifying an clip as professional-produced video or amateur-produced video can be achieved with good accuracy. The future work will focus on two aspects. Firstly, we will conduct this work using more video genres, rather than only news, sports and movies in this work. Moreover, we will also consider evaluating more features from multi-sources and classification methods over larger scale of datasets.

6. ACKNOWLEDGMENTS

Thanks to the Information Access Disruptions (iAD) project (Norwegian Research Council), Science Foundation Ireland under grant 07/CE/I1147 and the China Scholarship Council for funding.

7. REFERENCES

[1] D. Brezeale and D. J. Cook. Using closed captions and visual features to classify movies by genre. In *Proc. MDM/KDD*, 2006.

[2] D. Brezeale and D. J. Cook. Automatic video classification: A survey of the literature. *IEEE Transactions on Systems, Man, and Cybernetics, Part C*, 38(3):416–430, 2008.

[3] H. K. Ekenel, T. Semela, and R. Stiefelhagen. Content-based video genre classification using multiple cues. In *Proc. AIEMPro*, pages 21–26, 2010.

[4] R. Glasberg, S. Schmiedeke, M. Mocigemba, and T. Sikora. New real-time approaches for video-genre-classification using high-level descriptors and a set of classifiers. In *Proc. ICSC*, pages 120–127, 2008.

[5] J. Guo and C. Gurrin. Short user-generated videos classification using accompanied audio categories. In *Proc. AMVA*, pages 15–20, 2012.

[6] J. Guo, C. Gurrin, F. Hopfgartner, Z. Zhang, and S. Lao. Quality assessment of user-generated video using camera motion. In *Proc. MMM*, pages 479–489, 2013.

[7] J. Guo, D. Scott, F. Hopfgartner, and C. Gurrin. Detecting complex events in user-generated video using concept classifiers. In *Proc. CBMI*, pages 1–6, 2012.

[8] B. Ionescu, K. Seyerlehner, C. Rasche, C. Vertan, and P. Lambert. Content-based video description for automatic video genre categorization. In *Proc. MMM*, pages 51–62, 2012.

[9] L. Li, N. Zhang, L.-Y. Duan, Q. Huang, J. Du, and L. Guan. Automatic sports genre categorization and view-type classification over large-scale dataset. In *Proc. ACM MM*, pages 653–656, 2009.

[10] J. Lin, Y. Sun, and W. Wang. Violence detection in movies with auditory and visual cues. In *Proc. CIS*, pages 561–565, 2010.

[11] P. Martin-Granel, M. Roach, and J. S. Mason. Camera motion extraction using correlation for motion-based video classification. In *Proc. IWVF*, pages 552–562, 2001.

[12] M. Montagnuolo and A. Messina. Parallel neural networks for multimodal video genre classification. *Multimedia Tools Appl.*, 41(1):125–159, 2009.

[13] P. Over, G. Awad, J. Fiscus, B. Antonishek, M. Michel, A. F. Smeaton, W. Kraaij, G. Quénot, et al. TRECVID 2011-An overview of the goals, tasks, data, evaluation mechanisms and metrics. In *Proc. NIST TRECVID Worshop*, 2011.

[14] M. J. Pickering, D. Heesch, R. O'Callaghan, S. Rüger, and D. Bull. Video retrieval using global features in keyframes. In *Proc. TREC Video Track*, 2002.

[15] M. Roach and J. Mason. Classification of video genre using audio. In *Proc. Eurospeech*, pages 2693–2696, 2001.

[16] M. Rouvier, G. Linarès, and D. Matrouf. Robust audio-based classification of video genre. In *Proc. INTERSPEECH*, pages 1159–1162, 2009.

[17] M. Rouvier, G. Linares, and D. Matrouf. On-the-fly video genre classification by combination of audio features. In *Proc. ICASSP*, pages 45–48, 2010.

[18] J. Wang, B. Li, W. Hu, and O. Wu. Horror movie scene recognition based on emotional perception. In *Proc. ICIP*, pages 1489–1492, 2010.

[19] J. Wang, C. Xu, and E. Chng. Automatic sports video genre classification using Pseudo-2D-HMM. In *Proc. ICPR*, pages 778–781, 2006.

[20] J. You, G. Liu, and A. Perkis. A semantic framework for video genre classification and event analysis. *Sig. Proc.: Image Communication*, 25(4):287–302, 2010.

[21] X. Yuan, W. Lai, T. Mei, X.-S. Hua, X. Wu, and S. Li. Automatic Video Genre Categorization using Hierarchical SVM. In *Proc. ICIP*, pages 2905–2908, 2006.

[22] N. Zhang and L. Guan. An efficient framework on large-scale video genre classification. In *Proc. MMSP*, pages 481–486, Saint Malo, France, 2010.

[23] W. Zhu, C. Toklu, and S.-P. Liou. Automatic news video segmentation and categorization based on closed-captioned text. In *Proc. ICME*, 2001.

Markov Random Fields for Sketch based Video Retrieval

Rui Hu   Stuart James   Tinghuai Wang   John Collomosse

Centre for Vision Speech and Signal Processing
University of Surrey
Guildford, UK
{r.hu, s.james, tinghuai.wang, j.collomosse}@surrey.ac.uk

ABSTRACT

We describe a new system for searching video databases using free-hand sketched queries. Our query sketches depict both object appearance and motion, and are annotated with keywords that indicate the semantic category of each object. We parse space-time volumes from video to form graph representation, which we match to sketches under a Markov Random Field (MRF) optimization. The MRF energy function is used to rank videos for relevance and contains unary, pairwise and higher-order potentials that reflect the colour, shape, motion and type of sketched objects. We evaluate performance over a dataset of 500 sports footage clips.

Categories and Subject Descriptors

H.3.1 [**Content Analysis and Indexing**]: Indexing Methods; H.3.3 [**Information Search and Retrieval**]: Retrieval models; Search process

Keywords

Sketch based Video Retrieval (SBVR), Markov Random Field (MRF), Storyboard Sketch, Semantic Labelling.

1. INTRODUCTION

Video repositories are typically searched by matching text queries to keywords that have been manually assigned to each clip. Although keywords are efficient *semantic* descriptors of content (e.g. "horse", "car") they are inefficient at describing the *appearance* or *motion* of those objects. Furthermore the level of annotation — at the level of the *clip*, rather than frames or even objects within frames — limits the spatial and temporal resolution at which video may be searched. Querying by *Visual* Example (QVE) offers a solution, yet many QVE systems require photorealistic queries (e.g. images [1], or video [2]) that may not be available to the user at query-time.

In this work we describe a novel system for searching video clips using *annotated free-hand sketches*. Our query sketches

depict the appearance and motion of objects, which are each annotated to indicate their semantic category. Rather than relying on keyword annotation at the level of the clip to match the latter, we harness a semantic segmentation algorithm to label video regions using a set of pre-determined object categories (e.g. grass, person, horse). In this respect, our system extends the "storyboard sketches" proposed by Collomosse *et al.* [3] for Sketch Based Video Retrieval (SBVR). Storyboard sketches are free-hand sketches drawn by the users depicting both the video content and dynamics (using arrows). Our system not only incorporates the annotation of objects in storyboard sketches with semantic tags, but also improves upon [3] through faster matching and the handling of non-linear object motion.

Our core contribution is a Markov Random Field (MRF) based framework capable of evaluating the support for a *query sketch* within a given *video*, and hence the likelihood of the two matching. We over-segment the video into a set of space-time sub-volumes, each of which forms a node in a graph with connectivity determined using space-time adjacency of sub-volumes. A graph-cut operation [4] identifies the sketched object under an MRF defined across the nodes in this graph, as well as determining a likelihood score for the purpose of inter-video comparison. The potentials on the MRF incorporate both semantic similarity, and appearance similarity as a function of colour, motion, and shape. In considering shape and motion, information from spatially 'higher order' segmentations of the video are also considered. We also correct for global camera motion in the scene present, caused by the camera tracking moving objects.

2. RELATED WORK

Sketch based QVE largely focuses on the image retrieval problem. Early sketch based image retrieval (SBIR) systems accepted queries comprising blobs of coloured texture, matched through region adjacency and topology [5, 6], shape [7], or spectral descriptors such as wavelets [8]. More recently, SBIR has been applied to large scale (>1 million record) retrieval by matching line-art query sketches to edge information within photographs [9, 10, 11, 12]. These systems have demonstrated the value of sketches as an effective tool for shape and appearance based SBIR.

Sketch has also been applied to motion retrieval within video using sketched object trajectories [13, 14]. However, the combined use of appearance and motion cues in SBVR has been sparsely researched. VideoQ [15] is one of the first SBVR systems that consider spatio-temporal attributes. However, VideoQ requires users draw exact motion curve and specify the object's speed (in pixels/second). More recent SBVR systems accept greater flexibility in the specification of both appearance and motion, making them more amenable to depictions of events recalled under the ambiguities of human episodic memory [3].

Our work is aligned with the latter approach of Collomosse *et al.*, which also seeks a maximum likelihood labelling of super-pixels to the objects depicted within a storyboard sketch. Given the ambiguity inherent in users' sketches, we also find it attractive to treat the sketch as a probabilistic model to be fitted to video under a constrained optimization. Nevertheless, there are a number of key differences between our contribution and this prior work [3].

First, we incorporate semantics within our optimization framework rather than relying on appearance and motion alone. This improves scalability over larger video datasets, as the ambiguity inherent in user sketches can result in numerous coincidental false positives (e.g. based on shape or colour) as the dataset grows. The presence of both semantic and appearance information in the sketch overcomes the in-principle limitation of matching based on appearance alone. Second, we formulate our optimization as an MRF which may be solved orders of magnitude faster than Collomosse *et al.*'s Linear Dynamic Systems (LDS) and to give a globally rather than locally optimal video labelling. These efficiencies are largely due to our video representation which employs space-time volumes as atomic units for labelling, rather than spatial (per-frame) super-pixels. Third, our representation of object motion admits non-linear trajectories which are unavailable to [3]. We further enhance the features matched by our system by incorporating a state of the art descriptor (GF-HOG) for sketch based shape matching [16].

Another trend of SBVR systems match query sketches with spatio-temporal sub-volumes segmented from video. Hu *et. al.* [17] track SIFT keypoints to form short trajectories which are clustered to form a set of space-time tokens. A Viterbi-like process matches the space-time graph of tokens to the colour and motion description of the query sketch. The approach is extended in [18] using a more robust motion clustering algorithm, where semantic information is also considered. However, as with early SBVR [15], retrieval performance is strongly dependent on the accuracy of the video segmentation.

In contrast to these approaches that pre-process video into segments offline, our contribution is to segment video at query-time using a Markov Random Field (MRF) optimization that simultaneously ranks clips for relevance and localises the sketched object. MRFs have been successfully used to find a globally optimal segmentation of images [4, 19] and videos [20, 21]. A restriction on their use is frequently cited to be high computational complexity, since individual pixels are used as the nodes in the graph (lattice). In this work we propose to represent each video by an irregular spatio-temporal graph, containing a few hundred nodes each of which is a spatio-temporal fragment within the video (analogous to a super-pixel within an image).

In MRFs commonly used for segmentation, an image or video is encoded as an undirected graph — representing anything from a regular lattice of pixels [4, 19, 21], to an irregular network of regions [20]. A Gibbs energy function is defined, often containing a unary data term and a pairwise term, the minimum of which is sought to divide (cut) the graph, and so yield a segmentation. Recent research has extend this function to include higher order constraints [22, 21] enforcing labelling consistency within a local neighbourhood. Our contribution is to apply this latter development to the SBVR problem; specifically to label spatio-temporal fragments to sketched objects. To the best of our knowledge, a graph cut solver has not been used in this way for SBVR — nor have the modalities of semantics, shape, motion and colour been previously combined within an SBVR system.

3. SYSTEM OVERVIEW

Our system accepts keyword annotated *storyboard sketches* [3] as queries to retrieve similar videos in a dataset. We formulate the video retrieval problem as a pixel labelling and matching problem which is solved by a graph cut optimization to simultaneously estimate the likelihood of the match, whilst also localising the sketch object in the video. Fig.2 shows two example sketch queries, their top returned results and the estimated foreground area. Given a video dataset, we pre-process each video in to a set of space-time subvolumes — analogous to the spatial concept of superpixels [23] — via a process described in section 4. The sub-volumes form nodes in an undirected graph with edges linking a pair of nodes when the respective sub-voumes are adjacent in space-time (section 5.1).

Upon accepting a query sketch, our retrieval system segments each video (i.e. label sub-volumes) into background and foreground regions; the latter being the sketched object of interest. The unary term in the graph cut measures the agreement between foreground nodes with a model built from the sketched query. Agreement is measured using a weighted combination of similarity scores expressing motion, colour, semantic and shape similarity. Similarly, a background model is also learnt offline from the video. Pairwise terms are computed between nodes using a similar set of appearance attributes. A graph cut solver generates an optimal labelling, with an associated normalised energy which is returned to the system as a (dis-)similarity measure to rank video clips with respect to the query.

3.1 Sketch Parsing and Description

The query sketch is a combination of strokes that coarsely depict object shape and colour, with the addition of 'motion strokes' that depict the movement of the object. Additionally, keywords are assigned to objects from a pre-determined set of categories, to specify its semantic class. Optionally, user may also depict the background color and semantics (e.g. green grass).

These attributes are extracted from the query using the following features:

Color distribution. A color histogram is computed from pixels within the sketch, indicating the frequency of occurrence for each of the 15 colours in the user's palette. The histogram encodes an area-weighted, non-spatial colour distribution of the desired object.

Shape. The GF-HOG framework of [9] is applied to compute a shape descriptor from the sketch. GF-HOG applies Laplacian constraints to smoothly extrapolate a dense field of edge orientations from sketched strokes. Histogram of Gradient (HOG) features are sampled along sketched strokes at varying spatial scales. A standard hard-assignment Bag of Visual Words (BoVW) pipeline converts these descriptors into a frequency histogram of codewords. We use a code-

Figure 1: Left: video frame. Middle: over segmented spatio-temporal supervoxel. Right: motion segmentation resulted subvolume.

book size of 1000 in our experiments. To enable comparison of this shape descriptor with videos at query-time, the common codebook generated during video ingest (section 4.3) is used to generate the BoVW histogram.

Motion direction. Strokes indicating the motion direction are drawn in a different ink which is used to depict the object. Simple arrow pictograms may be recognised in the sketch using [24] and the shaft of the arrow isolated. The shaft sampled at regular intervals to yield a sequence of vectors of constant length, which represent the motion of the according segment.

Semantics. Our interface provides keywords describing eleven semantic classes from which users can pick to annotate their sketched object. This information is encoded by a probability vector across those classess; each keyword on the object is weighted equally (e.g. 2 keywords produces a 50:50 distribution over two bins).

4. VIDEO PRE-PROCESSING

For each video within our dataset, we conduct the following pre-processing steps. Later, the representation parsed from the video in this pre-process is matched with the representation parsed from the sketch (section 3.1) at query-time, via the method outlined in section 5.

We begin by applying shot detection to temporally segment video into clips, each of which forms a candidate for retrieval within our video dataset. SIFT keypoints are detected on every frame of a clip, and correspondence robustly established between adjacent frames to compute inter-frame homographies which we take as approximating camera egomotion over time. We also compute the pixel-wise foreground probability for each frame. A background mosaic is constructed by warping and averaging temporally neighbouring frames under their homographies. The difference between the current frame and its temporally local background mosaic is used as the foreground probability map for that frame.

4.1 Spatio-temporal video over-segmentation

Many vision applications have benefit from representing an image as a collection of superpixels [22, 25, 20, 26]. Superpixels are spatially coherent groups of pixels that are similar in color and texture, so in turn tend to constitute a semantic object, or part thereof. This assumption leads to advantages of superpixel primitives over pixels, both in

terms of computational efficiency and improved local consistency in segmentation problems. In order to increase the chance that superpixels do not cross object boundaries, an oversegmentation is often preferred.

We oversegment our videos into a set of spatio-temporal sub-volumes, which we refer to as "supervoxels" by analogy with super-pixels. We adopt the video segmentation algorithm proposed in [23]. This algorithm can segment a video into a hierarchy scale of spatio-temporal supervoxels; here we use the volumes from the finest scale level. Fig.1 (middle) gives an example of an oversegmented video. Video clips in our dataset are typically segmented into around 2k supervoxels, ensuring compact graphs for the subsequent optimization process at query-time.

4.2 Motion segmentation

In addition to performing a supervoxel segmentation cued colour and texture, we run a coarser grain segmentation of the video sequence cued on motion. It is difficult to meaningfully describe motion at the fine scale of a supervoxel. Similarly, appearance attributes such as shape are better described over larger spatial areas.

We apply the motion segmentation algorithm proposed in [27], and implement their recommendation to post-process the resulting sparse point labelling to obtain a dense motion segmentation result. Example motion segmentation results are shown in Fig.1 (right).

The resulting coarse-scale supervoxels identified by the motion segmentation process are used later in the higher order term of our energy function (section 5.2) as a soft constraint to improve spatio-temporal labelling consistency. Shape features for each fine-scale supervoxel (obtained via 4.1) are later computed within the scope of the coarse scale supervoxel in which they predominantly reside. As we are not matching these coarse scale sub-volumes to the query sketch directly, we do not require each coarse supervoxel to exactly represent a single object.

4.3 Supervoxel feature extraction

Our retrieval process aggregates the fine-scale supervoxels obtained in section 4.1 to form objects represented by the query sketch. We therefore extract a set of features from each of these supervoxels, to encode similar cues to that parsed from the query sketch in section 3.1.

Foreground probability. Each supervoxel is assigned a probability of being in the foreground. This is obtained using the pixel-wise foreground score obtained using the mosaic background subtraction performed earlier. This score is averaged across the entire supervoxel.

Color distribution. As in section 3.1, a colour histogram is built to represent the color distribution of all the pixels the supervoxel contains. As pixels may deviate from the 15 colour user palette, the histogram bins are contributed to in proportion to the RGB distance between pixel colour and palette colour.

Motion direction. The footprint of the supervoxel is computed within each frame it spans, yielding a sequence of region masks from which we obtain a sequence of centroids. We average the vectors between these centroids to produce an indicative direction for each supervoxel. These vectors are later aggregated across supervoxels and matched to the sequence of motion vectors parsed from the sketched trajectory.

Shape. We apply the algorithm of Hu *et al.* [9] to compute a set of sparse GF-HOG descriptors across each video frame. Descriptors are quantised into visual words using a pre-computed codebook, obtained using k-means to cluster GF-HOG descriptors within video frames sampled at random across the dataset. In our experiments we constructed this codebook by sampling 10k random frames, and compute a codebook of size 1000. We aggregate descriptors within the local neighbourhood of the supervoxel into a frequency histogram, which is subsequently normalised. The neighbourhood is defined by the coarse supervoxel (obtained via the motion segmentation process of section 4.2) that predominantly contains the fine-scale supervoxel being processed.

Semantics. Pixelwise semantic labelling (also referred to as semantic segmentation) of images has started to gain attention in recent years. We apply the Semantic Texton Forests (STF)[28] classifier to label the pixels in each video frame as being in one of a pre-trained set of categories. In our experiments we train STF over eleven categories — corresponding to object classes within our video dataset, e.g. horse, grass, person, snow, et.al. In a one-off manual process, we hand-label around 250 frames from exemplar video clips in the dataset to serve as training data for STF. The pixel-wise labelling probabilities are accumulated within the supervoxel, and normalised to yield a probability distribution over the eleven semantic classes for each supervoxel.

5. GRAPH CUT BASED VIDEO RETRIEVAL

We propose a spatio-temporal graph representation of videos and formulate the video retrieval problem as a supervoxel-labelling and matching problem. Each supervoxel is assigned as either the user depicted foreground object (by query sketch) or the background. This is solved by graph cut as a global optimization problem. The normalised cost of the energy function (section 5.2) is used as the dissimilarity value of this video to the query sketch.

In the following, we explain in detail how we construct the graph model, formulate and optimize the energy function as well as how the retrieval system is built.

5.1 Spatio-temporal graph construction

For each video, we construct an undirected spatio-temporal graph $\mathcal{G} = \langle \mathcal{V}, \mathcal{A} \rangle$. The node set $\mathcal{V}$ contains the over-segmented spatio-temporal supervoxels (as introduced in section 4.1). Two terminal nodes indicating the foreground model (depicted by the user sketched query) and the background model learned from individual video or depicted by query sketch. The arc set $\mathcal{A}$ consists both the 'neighborhood links' (*n-links*) and the 'terminal links' (*t-links*). Each node (supervoxel) in the graph has two *t-links* connect this node to the two terminal nodes; and *n-links* indicate the connection to its adjacent supervoxels. Two supervoxels are considered as connected is they share boundary either spatially (intraframe) or temporally (inter-frame). Note that the segmented supervoxel could be of any shape and size both spatially and temporally. This makes our generated graph irregular unlike many pixel based models.

The arc between two nodes (*n-link*) indicates the similarity between these two adjacent supervoxels, which is precomputed offline, based on their color, motion, semantic and foreground probability similarity. Note that the shape feature is not considered when measuring the neighborhood similarity. The arc that connect each node to the terminal nodes (*t-link*) are defined as the cost of labelling the according supervoxel to foreground and background. In our case this is computed as their dissimilarity in the feature space to each model.

Note a similar concept of spatio-temporal graph is also used in [20] for video segmentation. The nodes in their graph are superpixels segmented from each frame by 2D image segmentation algorithm and the arcs are defined by inter and intra frame colour similarity within a neighborhood area. While in our work, the nodes in our graph are spatio-temporal coherent supervoxels. Our unary and pairwise term are built on appearance, motion and semantic features which brings more rich information to the graph optimization.

5.2 Definition of Energy Potentials

Given the graph $\mathcal{G}$, a finite set $\mathcal{L} = \{l_1, l_2, \ldots, l_L\}$ of labels. $\mathcal{L}^V$ represents all the possible labelling stragegies for the node set. $X \in \mathcal{L}^V$ is a map that assigns to each vertex v a label x_v in $\mathcal{L}$. An energy function E maps any labelling strategy X to a real number $E(X)$ denoted as its energy. Energy functions are defined as the cost of the according labelling strategy. Therefore, finding the optimum labelling strategy is equivalent to find the minimum cost of the energy function.

Similarly to [21], our energy function consists of unary, pairwise and higher order terms as:

$$
E(X) = \alpha \sum_{i \in \mathcal{V}} \psi_u(x_i) + \beta \sum_{i \in \mathcal{V}, j \in \mathcal{N}_i} \psi_p(x_i, x_j) + \gamma \sum_{i \in \mathcal{V}} \sum_{c \in \mathcal{S}} \psi_h(x_i) \quad (1)
$$

where $\alpha, \beta, \gamma, \in [0,1], (\alpha + \beta + \gamma = 1)$ are weights for the unary term ψ_u, pairwise term ψ_p, and the higher-order term ψ_h respectively. $\mathcal{V}$ corresponds to the set of all super-voxels in the video, $\mathcal{S}$ represents the set of sub-volumes segmented by motion segmentation, $\mathcal{N}_i$ indicates the neighbouring super-voxel set of the current super-voxel i. This energy function encourages the neighbouring consistency both spatially and temporally. Moreover, the higher-order potential term increase the label consistency inside the sub-volumes generated by motion segmentation. The detail of how each of the potentials are defined is described in the following.

5.2.1 Appearance and motion model

The unary term ψ_u exploits the fact that different appearance and motion homogeneous voxels tend to follow different labelling models. In our case, its a binary labelling problem. This term encourages each super-voxel been assigned to its most similar model. We use the cost of a label being assigned to super-voxel i as the unary potential, which is computed as a weighted sum of the dissimilarity of colour, shape, motion, semantics to the model as well as the the probability to be foreground or background. The unary term is computed as:

$$
\psi_u(x_i) = \theta_{cl}\psi_{cl}(x_i) + \theta_{sp}\psi_{sp}(x_i) \\
+ \theta_{mt}\psi_{mt}(x_i) + \theta_{sm}\psi_{sm}(x_i) + \theta_{fg}\psi_{fg}(x_i) \quad (2)
$$

where $\theta_{cl}, \theta_{sp}, \theta_{mt}, \theta_{sm}, \theta_{fg}, \in [0,1], (\theta_{cl} + \theta_{sp} + \theta_{mt} + \theta_{sm} + \theta_{fg}) = 1$, are weights of colour, $\psi_{cl}(x_i)$, shape $\psi_{sp}(x_i)$, motion $\psi_{mt}(x_i)$, semantics $\psi_{sm}(x_i)$, and foreground potentials $\psi_{fg}(x_i)$ respectively.

We now first explain how we build models for the foreground and background labels. In most graph cut based systems, labelling models are often pre-defined manually [21], or online learned [29]. In this paper we build the foreground model from the query sketch. The appearance, motion and semantic features extracted from the query sketch is used as the foreground object feature model. When the background is also defined in the query sketch, the model of which could be learnt similarly as we learn the foreground model. Otherwise, we assume the 1% supervoxels that has the lowest foreground probability as definite background. The background model is built as the area weighted average feature vectors of supervoxels from the definite background area.

For the colour shape and semantic features the distance between a node and the foreground/background node is computed using the cityblock measure. In the case of the motion the query motion stroke is quantised into same number of equal segments as the number of frames of the matching video. Nodes from the video are mapped onto the corresponding segments from the quantised query motion stroke. The angular distance is computed over each segment and averaged as the node motion dissimilarity term. The foreground probability of each supervoxel $f_i, (i \in \mathcal{V})$ is directly used as the unary potential to be labelled as the background model.

5.2.2 *Spatio-temporal Coherence model*

The pairwise term is often used to encourages spatial coherence in region labelling and discontinuities to occur at high contrast locations. Given the graph defined in our paper, each node is a spatio-temporal supervoxel. Appearance feature alone is not enough to define the voxel coherence. Therefore, we define the neighbouring coherence as a weighted fusion of the similarity values based on colour, motion and semantic features. Our pairwise term is defined as:

$$\psi_p(x_i, x_j) = \begin{cases} 0, & \text{if } x_i = x_j \\ e^{-d_{i,j}}, & \text{if } x_i \neq x_j \end{cases} \quad (3)$$

where $d_{i,j}$ is the weighted sum of distance between nodes i and j using different features. Given the feature representations of each supervoxel, the distance between which is computed similarly as we compute the distance to the foreground/background models (unary term). Note, that shape feature is not considered to measure the supervoxel similarity in the pairwise term.

5.2.3 *Motion segments Consistency Term*

In recent works, a higher-order term is often defined in the energy function to encourage the pixels belonging to a super-pixel to be assigned with the same label.

Similarly to [22, 21], we define a soft constraint to reflect the label consistency. However, different with their pixel-wise graph model where over-segmented superpixel is used in the higher order term to improve the labelling consistency, our model takes the supervoxels as nodes and the motion segmentation resulted sub volumes are used in the higher-order term to encourage spatio-temporal labelling consistency. We define this term as a weighted sum of unary potentials of all the supervoxels within the current subvolume

to be labelled the same as the current node i:

$$\psi_h(x_i) = \begin{cases} 0, & \text{if } i \notin m \\ \frac{1}{\sum_{j \in m} a_j} \sum_{j \in m} a_j \psi_j(x_i), & \text{if } i \in m, \end{cases} \quad (4)$$

where $m \in \mathcal{M}$ is one sub-volume of the motion segmentation sub-volume set $\mathcal{M}$, $j \in m$ represents each of the supervoxels that belongs to sub-volume m, $\sum_{j \in m} a_j \psi_j(x_i)$ is the weighted cost if all supervoxels constituting m are labelled as x_i (the current labelling for node i), weight a_j is the total number of pixels within supervoxel j, $\psi_j(x_i)$ is thus defined as the unary potential of supervoxels in m against label x_i. This function indicates that an optimal label assignment to node i should also fit all supervoxels within the same motion segmented subvolume. Since supervoxels within one motion segmented subvolume are represented by the same subvolume, it is not necessary to compute shape feature again in this higher-oder term.

5.3 Optimization

Similarly to [21], our 'higher order' term can also be effectively merged to unary term. So that the energy function Eq. 1 can be simplified to:

$$E(X) =$$
$$\sum_{i \in \mathcal{V}} (\alpha \psi_u(x_i) + \gamma \sum_{c \in \mathcal{S}} \psi_h(x_i)) + \beta \sum_{i \in \mathcal{V}, j \in \mathcal{N}_i} \psi_p(x_i, x_j) \quad (5)$$

The simplified energy function in Eq. 5 is of the form of Potts model. It can be minimised using the α-expansion and $\alpha\beta$-swap algorithm [4]. Each α-expansion iteration can be solved by performing a single graph-cut using the mincut/max-flow [30]. We also use the same technique in [31] to improve the optimization process.

5.4 Video retrieval

From Eq. 5, the energy of each optimization iteration defines the cost of the according labelling strategy. The optimized minimum energy indicates the cost of the best strategy to spatio-temporally cut the video clip into the query sketch depicted foreground object and the background. The more similar the sketch query depicted foreground object (and background if applicable) to the video, the smaller cost could spend to match them, i.e. given one video clip and several sketches each depicting a different object (and scene), the smaller the final energy cost to match the video clip to one of the sketches, the more similar the pair are. Therefore, the final optimized energy could be used as a dissimilarity between a video clip and a query sketch.

However, since the energy function defined in Eq. 5 is also related with the number of nodes (the unary and higher order term) and links (the pairwise term) within the graph, it can not be directly used to rank the similarity of a collection of videos to the query sketch. In our work we apply the normalised energy function in our video retrieval system. We normalise the energy as following:

$$E'(X) =$$
$$\frac{1}{|\mathcal{N}|} \sum_{i \in \mathcal{V}} (\alpha \psi_u(x_i) + \gamma \sum_{c \in \mathcal{S}} \psi_h(x_i)) + \beta \sum_{i \in \mathcal{V}} (\frac{1}{|\mathcal{N}_i|} \sum_{j \in \mathcal{N}_i} \psi_p(x_i, x_j))$$

where $|\mathcal{N}|$ is the total number of supervoxels in a video clip, $|\mathcal{N}_i|$ is the number of neighbours. and this normalised energy E' will be used as the dissimilarity score to rank videos in our retrieval system.

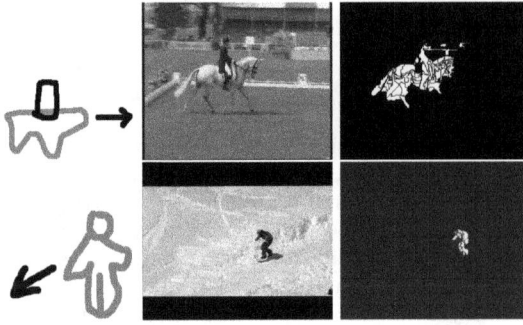

Figure 2: Left: The query sketch. Middle: top returned video frame. Right: The estimated foreground area that matches with the query sketch.

In our proposed video retrieval system, the off-line processing steps include: video pre-processing (section 4), computing the pair-wise potential and the unary potential to the background model built from the video itself. Upon accepting a query sketch, we first build the foreground model using the sketch and then match with the pre-computed features of supervoxels (the unary potential to the foreground), the higher order potential, and then the graph is optimized.

6. EXPERIMENTS

We evaluate our system over a sport footage composed of 500 video clips, among which there are 304 horse riding and 196 snow boarding/ski video clips. Objects/scene within these video clips contains: person, horse, grass, snow, stands, tree, sky, water. Camera motion happens in most of the clips. This dataset is comparable to the 'TSF dataset' used in [3] (which contains 298 clips); and the 200 similar clips used to evaluate VideoQ [15].

6.1 Parameter settings

In video preprocessing step, we use the default parameters for both the supervoxel and subvolume segmentation. We use the same parameters as in [9] to extract the GFHOG feature, for each point along sketch/edge we compute histogram distribution of eight orientations on a 3×3 grid with three window size (5, 10, 15).

In the graph cut model, there are two sets of weightings. One is the weights for the three energy terms, and the other is the weights of different features. Both weights can be freely adjusted by the users according to their preference. In our experiments, we use the same weighting parameters through all videos in our dataset. Weighting parameters for each term in the energy function are set by experience, we use $\alpha = 0.9$, $\beta = 0.05$, $\gamma = 0.05$. In the unary term we set $\theta_{cl} = 0.25$, $\theta_{sp} = 0.05$, $\theta_{mt} = 0.3$, $\theta_{sm} = 0.3$, $\theta_{fg} = 0.1$. Since shape feature is not considered in the pairwise and higher-order term, we set the feature weights for these two terms as: $\theta_{cl} = 0.3$, $\theta_{mt} = 0.3$, $\theta_{sm} = 0.3$, $\theta_{fg} = 0.1$.

6.2 Performance Evaluation

Our system takes into consideration spatio-temporal features to match video clips to sketch queries. In order to understand how each of these components works we first visualize some retrieval results of using color, motion, semantic keywords alone in Fig.4. Each of these features alone

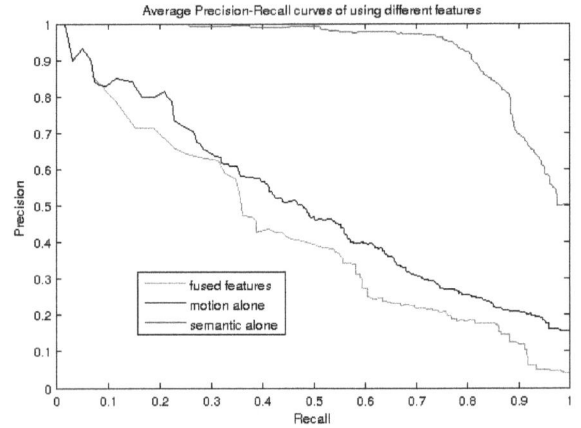

Figure 3: Average Precision-Recall curves of using motion stroke alone, semantic keywords alone to retrieve video clips and our annotated *storyboard sketches* that depicting the color, motion, shape and semantics of objects (and background if sketched).

is typically used in appearance, motion or keywords based video retrieval systems. This example shows that although each component alone is able to find the related clips by considering the particular feature, they are not sufficient to define the spatio-temporal aspect of a video clip. In comparision, *storyboard sketches* is a convenient yet powerful query mechanism for video retrieval to describe the spatio-temporal feature of the object/scene. In Fig.5 we show two typical query sketches used in our system, and the top 5 returned results. From this graph we can see that our system is able to return video clips that share spatio-temporal and semantic similarity.

The average Precision-Recall (P-R) curves are shown in Fig.3, this demonstrates 3 different PR curves the 'motion alone','semantic alone' and the 'fused features' results. For the motion PR curve five different motion strokes depicting unique directions of motions for the foreground objects are evaluated. The semantic performance is evaluated using 2 different semantic queries: 'horse' depicting the foreground object; and 'man' depicting the foreground together with 'snow' describe the background (the object class 'man' appears in all video clips, the background class 'snow' is used to discriminant from horse riding clips). We manually create groundtruth for each query by considering the related clips based on motion or semantics alone separately. We do not draw the precision recall curve of using shape and color feature alone, since without the support of motion, semantics or foreground probability; these features could easily match to background areas (Second row of Fig.4 – the red query retrieved the background).

The P-R curve 'fused features' in Fig.3 considers all 4 features combined as explained in section 5. In order to design reasonable set of queries to evaluate the proposed system, we use the groundtruth to select suitable candidates that have a combined direction, semantic class and colour of greater than 10 examples within the dataset. In total 7 free-hand sketch queries are used to evaluate our system. The 7 queries cover 4 motion directions, 7 colours and 2 semantic classes to demonstrate the range of the dataset. On average each

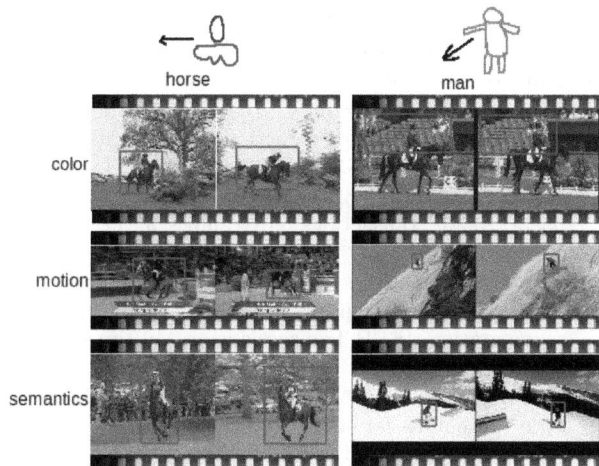

Figure 4: Example query sketches and their example results of using color, motion, semantics features alone individually. The blue bounding box indicate the area of interest that matched with the query sketch described by the according feature.

Figure 5: Example query sketches and the top 5 returned results, ranked from top to bottom. The red bounding box indicate the negative results, and the blue bounding box indicate the positive results.

query has 20 related video clips. A clip is considered relevant with the query sketch when it shares approximate shape, color, motion and semantics to the sketched foreground object (and background if sketched).The P-R curve for 'fused features' shows that our system achieves a comparable performance with that of the VideoQ [15] and [3]. Note that the performance of the curves in Fig. 3 are not comparable to each other, since the groundtruth of each are created by considering different aspects of the video.

Overall the dataset we obtain MAP=0.48 by considering all the features, the top 10 results have ∼=57% relevance. This performance is comparable to the performance achieved in VideoQ [15] and [3]. We also evaluate our system without using the shape component. The system achieves a MAP=0.45, and the top 10 results have ∼=53% relevance. This shows that although using shape feature alone is difficult to achieve satisfied retrieval result, our proposed method to incorporate the shape feature is efficient yet effective to improve the retrieval performance.

At run time, once the user submit a query sketch to the system, it takes on average around 53.42 seconds to rank the 500 video clips in the dataset. This improves the run time computational complexity in [3], which takes 2 minutes to ranks videos in a similar but smaller dataset.

7. CONCLUSION

We have presented a sketch based video retrieval (SBVR) system driven by free-hand sketches depicting object appearance and motion, and annotated with keywords to indicate semantics. To the best of our knowledge we are the first to combine shape, motion, colour and semantics within a single SBVR framework. Furthermore we have introduced the use of Markov Random Fields (MRFs), more commonly used for video segmentation, as a novel form of SBVR solution capable of both ranking clips for relevance, and localising sketched objects within retrieved clips. We have demonstrated good accuracy over a challenging dataset of 500 sports footage clips.

In adopting an MRF optimization over all videos, we follow recent SBVR approaches [3] that tackle ambiguity in sketch by phrasing the retrieval task as a model fitting problem. Here we extract a multi-modal representation of the object to be retrieved, and solve for the resulting MRF to compute the most likely supervoxel labelling given that model. Whilst this solution offers unique advantages in seeking a globally optimal labelling for a given sketch, it is open to two potential criticisms.

First, the run-time expense of performing an MRF solve for each video. We have addressed this by adopting a supervoxel representation that contains a relatively low (around 2k) number of nodes, and we show that it can be solved fairly efficiently. This is a significant reduction in complexity over [3] where set of per-frames superpixel (not per-clip supervoxels) are labelled at query time.

Second, the system might at first consideration be deemed unsatisfactory due to perceived sensitivity to the weights within our unary term that combine our various multi-modal features. In fact we regard this as a strength; users will frequently wish to express a preference between modalities. Consider a user sketching a red car in the absence of such a clip in the dataset. Would they prefer a set of results containing red objects, or car shaped objects, or red objects moving in the direction sketched? The balance between these modalities is user task specific, and in future an ideal candidate interactive specification through a relevance feedback interface. We believe this is the most promising future direction for our system.

8. REFERENCES

[1] Sivic, J., Zisserman, A.: Video Google: A text retrieval approach to object matching in videos. In: ICCV. Volume 2. (2003) 1470–1477

[2] Bertini, M., Del Bimbo, A., Nunziati, W.: Video clip matching using mpeg-7 descriptors and edit distance. In: CIVR. (2006) 133–142

[3] Collomosse, J., McNeill, G., Qian, Y.: Storyboard sketches for content based video retrieval. In: ICCV. (2009) 245–252

[4] Boykov, Y., Jolly, M.P.: Interactive graph cuts for optimal boundary and region segmentation of objects in n-d images. In: ICCV. (2001) 105–112

[5] Ashley, J., Flickner, M., Hafner, J.L., Lee, D., Niblack, W., Petkovic, D.: The query by image content (qbic) system. In: SIGMOD. (1995) 475

[6] Smith, J.R., Chang, S.F.: Visualseek: A fully automated content-based image query system. In: ACM Multimedia. (1996) 87–98

[7] Sciascio, E.D., Mingolla, G., Mongiello, M.: Content-based image retrieval over the web using query by sketch and relevance feedback. In: Proceedings of the Third International Conference on Visual Information and Information Systems. VISUAL (1999) 123–130

[8] Jacobs, C.E., Finkelstein, A., Salesin, D.: Fast multiresolution image querying. In: SIGGRAPH. (1995) 277–286

[9] Hu, R., Barnard, M., Collomosse, J.P.: Gradient field descriptor for sketch based retrieval and localization. In: ICIP. (2010) 1025–1028

[10] Hu, R., Wang, T., Collomosse, J.P.: A bag-of-regions approach to sketch-based image retrieval. In: ICIP. (2011) 3661–3664

[11] Eitz, M., Hildebrand, K., Boubekeur, T., Alexa, M.: Sketch-based image retrieval: Benchmark and bag-of-features descriptors. IEEE Transactions on Visualization and Computer Graphics 17 (2011) 1624–1636

[12] Cao, Y., Wang, C., Zhang, L., Zhang, L.: Edgel index for large-scale sketch-based image search. In: CVPR. (2011) 761–768

[13] Shim, C.B., Chang, J.W.: Efficient similar trajectory-based retrieval for moving objects in video databases. In: CIVR. (2003) 163–173

[14] Su, C.W., Liao, H.Y.M., Tyan, H.R., Lin, C.W., Chen, D.Y., Fan, K.C.: Motion flow-based video retrieval. IEEE Transactions on Multimedia 9 (2007) 1193–1201

[15] fu Chang, S., Chen, W., Meng, H.J., Sundaram, H., Zhong, D.: Videoq: An automated content based video search system using visual cues. In: Proceedings of ACM Multimedia. (1997) 313–324

[16] Hu, R., Barnard, M., Collomosse, J.: Gradient field descriptor for sketch based retrieval and localization. In: ICIP. (2010) 1025–1028

[17] Hu, R., Collomosse, J.P.: Motion-sketch based video retrieval using a trellis levenshtein distance. In: ICPR. (2010) 121–124

[18] Hu, R., James, S., Collomosse, J.P.: Annotated free-hand sketches for video retrieval using object semantics and motion. In: MMM. (2012) 473–484

[19] Rother, C., Kolmogorov, V., Blake, A.: "grabcut": interactive foreground extraction using iterated graph cuts. In: ACM SIGGRAPH. (2004) 309–314

[20] Li, Y., Sun, J., Shum, H.Y.: Video object cut and paste. ACM Transactions on Graphics 24 (2005) 595–600

[21] Wang, T., Collomosse, J.P.: Probabilistic motion diffusion of labeling priors for coherent video segmentation. IEEE Transactions on Multimedia 14 (2012) 389–400

[22] Kohli, P., Ladicky, L., Torr, P.H.S.: Robust higher order potentials for enforcing label consistency. International Journal of Computer Vision 82 (2009) 302–324

[23] Grundmann, M., Kwatra, V., Han, M., Essa, I.: Efficient hierarchical graph-based video segmentation. In: CVPR. (2010) 2141–2148

[24] Collomosse, J.P., McNeill, G., Watts, L.A.: Free-hand sketch grouping for video retrieval. In: ICPR. (2008) 1–4

[25] Csurka, G., Perronnin, F.: An efficient approach to semantic segmentation. International Journal of Computer Vision 95 (2011) 198–212

[26] Hu, R., Larlus, D., Csurka, G.: On the use of regions for semantic image segmentation. In: Indian Conference on Vision Graphics and Image Processing. (2012)

[27] Ochs, P., Brox, T.: Higher order motion models and spectral clustering. In: CVPR. (2012) 614–621

[28] Shotton, J., Johnson, M., Cipolla, R.: Semantic texton forests for image categorization and segmentation. In: CVPR. (2008) 1–8

[29] Yang, B., Nevatia, R.: An online learned crf model for multi-target tracking. In: CVPR. (2012) 2034–2041

[30] Boykov, Y., Kolmogorov, V.: An experimental comparison of min-cut/max-flow algorithms for energy minimization in vision. IEEE Transaction on Pattern Analysis and Machine Intelligence 26 (2004) 1124–1137

[31] Alahari, K., Kohli, P., Torr, P.H.S.: Reduce, reuse & recycle: Efficiently solving multi-label mrfs. In: CVPR. (2008)

Multimedia Information Seeking
through Search and Hyperlinking [*]

Maria Eskevich
Centre for Next Generation
Localisation
Dublin City University
Dublin 9, Ireland
meskevich@computing.dcu.ie

Gareth J. F. Jones
Centre for Next Generation
Localisation
Dublin City University
Dublin 9, Ireland
gjones@computing.dcu.ie

Robin Aly
University of Twente
P.O. Box 217
7500AE Enschede
The Netherlands
r.aly@ewi.utwente.nl

ABSTRACT

Searching for relevant webpages and following hyperlinks to related content is a widely accepted and effective approach to information seeking on the textual web. Existing work on multimedia information retrieval has focused on search for individual relevant items or on content linking without specific attention to search results. We describe our research exploring integrated multimodal search and hyperlinking for multimedia data. Our investigation is based on the MediaEval 2012 Search and Hyperlinking task. This includes a known-item search task using the Blip10000 internet video collection, where automatically created hyperlinks link each relevant item to related items within the collection. The search test queries and link assessment for this task was generated using the Amazon Mechanical Turk crowdsourcing platform. Our investigation examines a range of alternative methods which seek to address the challenges of search and hyperlinking using multimodal approaches. The results of our experiments are used to propose a research agenda for developing effective techniques for search and hyperlinking of multimedia content.

Categories and Subject Descriptors

H.3.1 [**Information Storage and Retrieval**]: Content Analysis and Indexing—*Indexing methods*

General Terms

Measurement, Performance

1. INTRODUCTION

From a digital library perspective, providing users with engaging ways to interact with audiovisual content, helping

---

[*]This paper was written collaboratively by organizers and participants of the MediaEval 2012 Search and Hyperlinking task. Please refer to the final section of the paper for a list of the names of the other authors.

them to discover, browse, navigate and search archives, is a prerequisite for opening up libraries in a way that increases their economic and/or cultural value. Users from a variety of backgrounds, such as professionals from the creative industry, journalists, students, researchers, and home users, can benefit from effective search and the interlinking of content.

Within audiovisual archives, the concept of hyper-video allows users to navigate between multimedia elements in a source content and related elements in the same content file or other multimedia sources. This can provide a means to explore additional (linked) information sources (detail-on-demand) while accessing content in a linear fashion (e.g., [12], [1],[23], [9]), or as an approach towards interactive non-linear access to video allowing users to generate narratives on-the-fly (e.g., [27], [28], [20]). In this paper, multimedia hyperlinking is addressed within an information seeking framework. This is enabled via an integrated approach that encompasses both the search process for relevant multimedia segments and the creation of links from these segments to other related multimedia segments in the archive.

To be able to investigate multimedia search and hyperlinking properly, it is crucial to develop test collections corpora and select metrics which evaluate information access in a meaningful way from the perspective of the user. Our investigation uses the test set developed for the multimedia Search and Hyperlinking using a task at MediaEval 2012 [4]. This approaches multimedia hyperlinking from an archival search scenario perspective in which a user searches for specific information within a collection of multimedia items in an audiovisual archive. The user seeks a single relevant known-item fragment of multimedia content where each content fragment in the result list is linked to other related multimedia fragments within the same collection. The tasks are based on the user-generated video collection Blip10000 for which search queries and relevance of automatically created links were created using the Amazon Mechanical Turk (AMT)[1] crowdsourcing platform. Unlike much existing work in audiovisual search this task is truly multimodal where relevance can be related to both visual and audio information streams. While our investigation builds on existing work in speech and video search, inter-item linking for multimedia collections is a much less well established, and our approaches to this task are thus more exploratory in nature. Our experimental search and hyperlinking methods explore use of audio and visual content, examining both search ef-

---

[1]https://www.mturk.com

fectiveness and the behaviour of linking when using different media streams [19].

In the remainder of this paper, Section 2 reviews the context of our evaluation approach based on related work in the field, Section 3 outlines the MediaEval 2012 Search and Hyperlinking task and dataset, Section 4 provides details of the different search and hyperlinking generation techniques used in our study, Section 5 presents the results of our experiments, and Section 6 summarizes our findings and discusses potential future research directions.

2. RELATED WORK

Realisation of an integrated multimedia search and hyperlinking system requires combination of multimedia search and methods for automated creation of inter-item hyperlinks for multimedia content. Research into the effectiveness of potential methods for undertaking these tasks requires the provision of suitable test collections. This section reviews existing work in multimedia search and hyperlinking, and in the development of experimental test collections.

Our investigation of multimedia focuses on both spoken content retrieval and video search. A range of previous investigations have explored effectiveness of these tasks. The spoken document retrieval (SDR) task at TREC [8] required participants to find relevant audio recordings based on textual queries. However, the temporal nature of audio content means that playback of single retrieved documents can make information access very inefficient, and a more direct pointer to the relevant content could be beneficial. Furthermore, when searching in videos it is desirable that users can also make use the visual modality to formulate their query. The search tasks in the TRECVid workshop envision a scenario where the user poses a multimodal query and systems return shots [30]. Here, shots are treated as isolated documents and systems that return a shot just before a relevant segment do not earn any evaluation scores. Methods for searching on multimedia content have to decide on a query representation, a document representation, and a function that ranks documents according to the query using these representations. In SDR, query terms are often considered as independent keywords and the audio documents are represented by the output hypotheses of an automatic speech recognition (ASR) system. Because of the semantic gap [31], recent approaches to visual search try to first recognize semantic concepts and then relate these to the user's query. Search based on spoken and visual content is mainly approached using pattern recognition, and therefore discards the semantics of words [35].

A previous task which went some way to combining spoken and visual search is the Rich Speech Retrieval task at the MediaEval 2011 [16], which required participants to return jump-in points to indicate the start, with corresponding end-points to indicate the end of the relevant content in videos for speech acts that are specified queries. The MediaEval 2012 Search and Hyperlinking task focuses on general queries rather than speech acts, although these were still collected using the same crowdsourcing strategy [5].

Research on hyperlinking in the literature has approached this from two distinct angles: link generation that dynamically defines links[2], and hypermedia modeling that describes user behaviour and data structures at a coarse level. Link

generation identifies anchors and links between both text and multimedia documents. Links are often created between text [22], or cross domain, e.g. between video collections and text [1]. In this paper, we generate links within a single video collection. The hypermedia modeling community focuses on developing models for hyperlinks in multimedia documents [10]. For example, whether links serve the purpose of creating sequential paths through a collection or provide details on the demand. The community excludes, however, the way links are defined. Our linking model focuses on topically linked video segments, rather than linking, for example, individual persons that appear in the video.

The notion of standardized tasks is not as strong in video linking research as in the search community. Research is therefore executed on individual data sets which limits repeatability. Our work is therefore among the first to carry out extensive analysis on a standardized hyperlinking task.

An important component in conducting research into multimedia search is the definition of a suitable evaluation framework. Most search evaluation tasks have utilized information needs developed by the task organizers or their associates, and with ground truth for search results created by professional annotators. This procedure has the potential disadvantage that it biases the types of investigated information needs to those imagined by the task organizers. Furthermore, the generation of ground truth in this way is expensive and may not reflect the relevance of the items to a more general population of users. By contrast, the MediaEval 2012 Search and Hyperlinking test collection was developed using crowdsourcing methods.

3. SEARCH AND HYPERLINKING TASK

The Search and Hyperlinking task at MediaEval 2012 [4] formed an initial experimental investigation of multimodal search and linking for video segments within a multimedia collection. The process was split into two intuitive sub-tasks focusing on search and hyperlinking activities. This allowed us to experiment with their combination in the task of first performing search and then forming inter-item links based on the search results. The overall task scenario is illustrated in Figure 1. User queries expressed in text, potentially enriched with visual information in multimodal queries, are entered into the search system to seek relevant segments. Since browsing through multimedia material is time-consuming, it is crucially important to start the playback of the video as close as possible to the beginning of the actual relevant segment, the so-called jump-in point. Further the user experience of browsing through the collection is enriched by the list of potential hyperlinks to the segment retrieved in the Search sub-task stage. In the following subsections we overview the description of the video dataset, and then continue with descriptions of the individual sub-tasks.

Blip10000 dataset The Blip10000 dataset created by the PetaMedia NoE [18] contains 14,838 Creative Commons videos from blip.tv, and corresponding user provided metadata. The data comprises a total of ca. 3,260 hours of data and is divided into development and test sets, of 5,288 and 9,550 videos respectively. Additionally, two transcripts were provided for all the videos in the collection, by LIMSI/Vocapia [15] and LIUM [26]. The full Blip10000 dataset used at MediaEval 2012 contains videos in different languages. How-

---

[2]Note that although the creation sometimes involves search, this is conceptually distinct from the first step in the search and hyperlink sub-tasks.

Search sub-task

Query: text, visual cues

Legend
known item
additional info.
→ link
⊢──⊣ segment

Hyperlinking sub-task

video 1
video 2
video 3

video 4
video 5
video 6

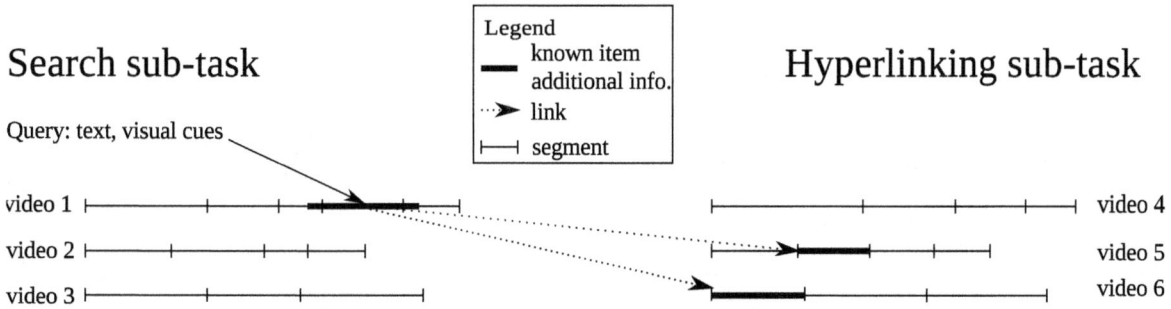

Figure 1: Overview of the search and hyperlinking task.

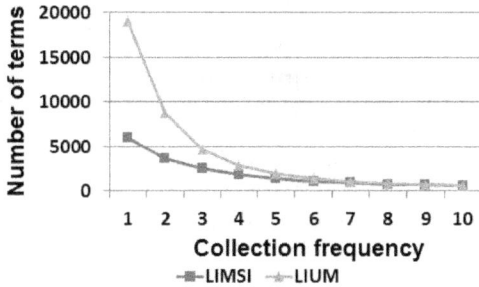

Figure 2: Number of terms with collection frequency equal to 1-10.

Table 1: Overview of the query set characteristics

query ID	WRR		OOV		query ID	WRR		OOV	
	limsi	lium	limsi	lium		limsi	lium	limsi	lium
1	0.90	0.70	0.13	0.13	16	0.92	0.77	-	-
2	0.76	0.71	-	-	17	0.71	0.59	-	-
3	0.83	0.70	-	-	18	0.67	0.67	-	-
4	0.84	0.74	-	-	19	0.70	0.74	-	-
5	0.86	0.72	0.13	0.13	20	0.50	0.48	-	-
6	0.44	0.33	-	-	21	0.53	0.67	0.22	0.22
7	0.67	0.63	0.14	0.14	22	0.86	0.89	-	-
8	0.88	0.74	0.15	0.10	23	0.47	0.40	-	-
9	0.69	0.62	-	-	24	0.72	0.56	-	-
10	0.77	0.68	-	-	25	0.38	0.08	-	-
11	0.65	0.74	0.07	0.13	26	0.52	0.48	0.25	0.25
12	0.42	0.09	-	-	27	0.65	0.57	-	-
13	0.59	0.64	-	-	28	0.73	0.50	0.14	0.14
14	0.75	0.60	0.17	0.17	29	0.54	0.42	-	-
15	0.83	0.72	0.09	0.09	30	0.71	0.71	-	-

ever, since the main focus of our current study is to define suitable techniques and evaluation methods for a complex search and hyperlinking user experience, we wished to work only with a monolingual English language dataset. To this end, we use a subset of the test set classified as English language by LIMSI/Vocapia, and transcribed by English language versions of both ASR systems. This resulted in a corpus to 4,890 video files. The transcripts generated by the ASR systems differ in various ways, especially in the number of terms with a total collection frequency equal to 1-10, see Figure 2.

In addition to spoken transcripts, the dataset was indexed with various visual information: shot boundaries of average shot length circa 30 seconds [14] with a single visual keyframe for each shot, concept-based descriptors based on a list of 589 concepts detected using the on-the-fly video detector Visor [2], and face detection results [3]. The concept list was created by taking the tags of the Tagging task set at MediaEval 2011 and calculating a score for each tag a representing its corporeality using the algorithm described in [17]. A threshold was chosen to cut the list off at a reasonable length.

MediaEval 2012 Test Query Set The MediaEval 2012 test query set consists of 30 textual queries. These include query statements both in a natural language sentence (NLS) and in the form of a search engine request (SER) style: e.g. Query 3: textual fields: NLS: "Curtis Baylor of Allstate gives a small piece of planning advice for small business using his basic three factors.", SER: "interviews with business professionals"; multimodal features: face: "yes", colours: "dark", video content: "Chair, Man, White Shirt". The NLS query set was used for all experiments reported in this paper.

The textual information for the search sub-task was collected via crowdsourcing on the AMT platform [4], while the multimodal features were created manually afterwards. The query set was created for a number of videos selected at random from the top 10 genre categories in the document collection. The average frequency of the query terms in the collection lexicon is relatively high (3015 and 2897 for LIMSI and LIUM respectively), although this was lower than those of the transcripts (6753 and 6342 for LIMSI and LIUM respectively). The level of out-of-vocabulary (OOV) terms is zero for 20 queries, and while for the remaining 10, it is not higher than 0.25, see Table 1. With these statistics in mind, the feature of the transcripts that has most potential to influence the retrieval performance is ASR errors. Table 1 shows the correct word recognition rate for words in relevant segments for the target segment (word recognition rate (WRR)) for each query.

Search sub-task evaluation We follow Search sub-task at MediaEval 2012, [4], in using three metrics in order to evaluate sub-task results: mean reciprocal rank (MRR), mean generalized average precision (mGAP) and mean average segment precision (MASP). Since browsing through multimedia recordings is time-consuming, we limit relevant results to a window of 60 seconds before and after the actual beginning of the relevant segment, so that retrieved segments outside of this window are considered non-relevant. Reciprocal Rank is calculated as the reciprocal value of the rank of the first correctly retrieved document [34]. mGAP [24] awards runs that not only find the relevant items earlier in the ranked output list, but also are closer to the jump-in point of the relevant content. MASP [7] takes into account the ranking of the results and the length of both relevant and irrelevant segments that need to be listened to before reaching the relevant item.

Hyperlinking sub-task evaluation Automated inter-item multimedia hyperlinking is an open research problem for which we currently lack complete understanding of the structure and basis of the linking. Thus we investigated link creation using different approaches to seek a better understanding of the different types of links that can be formed using different linking methods and query modalities. Similar to the creation of standard ad hoc search test collections [33], a posteriori evaluation strategy was used to carry out relevance assessment of proposed links. Since we had modifided the document set and carried out new runs, we were unable to use the MediaEval 2012 Search and Hyperlinking link relevance data, and thus repeated the assessment stage for our new runs. The top 10 ranked segments from the linking runs were evaluated using the AMT platform. The qrel set collected for each method ("run qrel") enables us to assess how effective it is for finding links that based the features used in this run (e.g. audio content, visual quality etc). The full set of all relevant segments gathered for all runs was formed into a single unified qrel file ("unified qrel"). Since the alternative approaches to hyperlink creation may use different segment definitions, these may result in overlap of the relevant links. In this case we combined these into a single relevant link after manual assessment. This unified list of manually assessed links was used to calculate mean average precision (MAP) across all the methods. Analyzing the results in this way enables us to examine the diversity of links proposed by each method.

As this approach to evaluation of the hyperlinking results is experimental, crowdsource workers were not given specific details (audio or visual features) to define videos relatedness. Within AMT the task and its setting is referred to as a 'Human Intelligence Task' or HIT. The following options were given in the HIT with a separate field for explanation of the choice and comments from the worker.

1. The video segments are totally unrelated to one another. The second video is something new and different from the first.
2. The video segments are related, they have the same topic or focus, though they give different information.
3. The video segments are related, but they give a different perspective or view on the same information.
4. The video segments are basically the same. If I saw one, I really wouldn't need to see the other.

If options 2, 3, or 4, or their combinations were selected, the passage being examined was considered relevant.

The questions requiring detailed answers were included to prevent low quality work being included in the relevance assessment results. Overall we approved 3165 HITs, and 1759 were rejected because the answers were not correct. With the price of the HIT equal to 0.09$, the overall cost of the evaluation was equal to 314$.

4. APPROACHES TO SEARCH AND HYPER-LINKING

In this section we introduce the different approaches to addressing the sub-tasks. Exact details of each run are given in Section 5.

Table 2: Overview of Search Sub-Task Types of Runs

Segmentation Method	Use of Metadata		Retrieval Model
	−	+	
Sentence	*S_bm25	*SM_bm25	BM25
Shot	Sh_tf-idf	ShM_tf-idf	TF-IDF
Speech Segment	*SpS_bm25	*SpSM_bm25	BM25
Time	TP_bm25		BM25
+	TP_lm		LM
Pause	TP_tf-idf		TF-IDF
Time	TOv_bm25	TOvM_bm25	BM25
+	TOv_lm	TOvM_lm	LM
Overlap	TOv_tf-idf	TOvM_tf-idf	TF-IDF

4.1 Search Sub-task

The main goal of the search sub-task is to find the exact topically coherent passage in the video collection relevant to the given query. Failure to achieve this task can negative impact on automatic hyperlinking performance and the overall user experience. According to the problem setup we have two types of queries: textual and multimodal (textual information is enriched with video content information). In this section we describe our approaches with respect to the following aspects: segmentation method, use of metadata, and use of different retrieval models. The overall list of the runs and naming convention is shown in Table 2. First we put the segmentation method with the first letters of the name, 'M' distinguishes runs that use the metadata, and then the retrieval model used is named (for example, Shot segmentation using Metadata and the TF-IDF IR model is named 'ShM_tf_idf'). Runs with labels starting with an asterix (*) use both textual and multimodal queries.

Video Segmentation Videos within the collection can vary in length and number of topics covered. Therefore they need to be segmented into shorter passages which can be handled as "documents" in the traditional retrieval setup. Segmentation can be based on audio and visual features: the former include time information (runs types 'TP', 'TOv') and various sub-structures found in the ASR transcript corresponding to the video (sentences (run type 'S') and speech segments (run type 'SpS'), pauses (run type 'TP')), the latter uses shot segmentation results (runs 'Sh').

Sentences and speech segments boundaries are taken from the ASR transcript. Time stamps in the ASR transcript allow addition of boundaries at pauses in the speech (a distance between two words of ≥ 0.5 seconds is considered to be a pause), segmentation into the range of different segment lengths with window overlap of different size. Another source for potential segment boundaries based on the video channel are the shot boundaries.

Retrieval models We experimented with three different retrieval models: BM25 [25], Hiemstra's Language Model [11] with default parameters, and TF-IDF. We used the Terrier[3] IR system for runs based on time segmentation (types 'T(M)', 'TOv(M)'), and the Lucene IR system for runs based on sentences and speech segments (types 'S(M)', 'SpS(M)') In all methods standard stop words removal and Porter stemming was carried out.

Metadata exploitation Since ASR transcripts contain

---
[3]www.terrier.org

errors, and may not contain all relevant information for the videos, any available metadata becomes potentially useful to compensate for this information loss. When available the metadata is used, though only provided at the video level rather than for a specific video segment.

4.2 Hyperlinking Methods

Since approaches to the hyperlinking sub-task are not as well established as those for the search sub-task, multiple approaches were implemented in order to get a broader perspective on potential solutions. We used all modalities of the provided dataset: metadata, information based on the audio (transcript words, transcript sentences and segmented speech units) and video (shots boundaries, visual concepts) processing. Additionally an enrichment tool (DBpedia Spotlight [21]) was used to identify named entities (NE) in the transcript and link these to Linked Data resources. Visual features were also enriched by clustering the information from SIFT descriptors into 500 clusters corresponding to visual words, as described in [29].

All approaches use the following main processing stages:

1. Retrieval of potential links to videos or video segments, when the retrieval units might be different from the target units (the whole video instead of the shot).

2. Re-ranking of the returned potential links.

3. Segment extraction. In cases where the retrieval units do not correspond to the target units.

The difference in implementation and ordering of these stages accounts for the differences in the results of the reported runs. Table 3, gives an overview of the representation of the data and retrieval techniques used for the runs. As in case of search sub-task, determining the boundaries of the target segment of a video link is important because they are shown to the user. When naming the runs we start with the first letters of the target segment (even though at retrieval stage those segments might be part of larger units), then after an underscore we add the types of the data used and conclude with adding the letter 'M' in case of use of metadata, for example the run that target to find the segments of shot size and uses speech transcript, visual words, and metadata is called 'Sh_TVWM'. In the next sections we describe run details of retrieval models, reranking strategies and segment extraction.

4.2.1 Retrieval Methods for Hyperlinking

Different retrieval techniques were used to identify and rank potential segments for hyperlinking. Videos and queries were represented as TF-IDF vectors with alternative compositions consisting of: transcript words only ('TrT_T'); transcript words and metadata ('TrT_TM' and 'Sh_TM',). Another approach was to have several TF-IDF vectors for each representation and to combine the ranking results later in the process, this approach is labeled run 'Sh_TVWM' and combines two vectors: transcript words and metadata, and visual words. In run 'Sh_TNE(M)', the TF-IDF vector uses Named Entities (NE) instead of words: a new weight called *TF-IS* (*term-frequency-inverse-support*) is used which depends on the number of URLs linking to this NE in an RDF graph of DBpedia Spotlight; and the metadata tags are ranked using the Jaccard similarity measure. The 'SpS_VCM' run uses speech segment boundaries (but not the transcript itself), and represents the videos by vectors of 508 visual concepts associated with their confidence scores provided with

the collection, with a utilizes Euclidean distance to rank the resulting hyperlinks.

4.2.2 Ranking Strategies

For each of the runs, except runs 'SpS_VCM' and 'Sh_TM', a post-processing step was performed to re-rank the result list obtained using the retrieval methods described in the previous section. Runs 'TrT_T(M)' used a re-ranking strategy in order to favour videos that were part of the same series of videos in the collection as that of the query. To do so, the scores of each such video were artificially increased to make them appear at the top of the list. The 10 videos associated with the highest scores were then extracted from this modified list at potential links. Run'Sh_TVWM' had two variations of re-ranking scheme: a score-based and a rank-based fusion that combined the similarity computations based on textual and visual information. In run 'Sh_TNE(M)', a short list of results was extracted for each comparison scheme (using words, NEs or tags) using a different threshold for each one. Scores of videos that appear in several of these short lists were added together and the final list of results obtained by selecting the 40 videos associated with the highest scores.

4.2.3 Segment Extraction Strategies

Our aim is to link the videos on the level of extracted segments, so users can be directed closer to the part of the video they are interested in. We experimented with two ways of retrieving segments: perform retrieval and re-rank directly on a set of segments, or run retrieval and re-rank on the entire video, and extract segments from the top results afterwards.

Segmentation relies on either audio or visual information. Runs 'TrT_T(M)' and 'SpS_VCM' use the transcript information. Run 'SpS_VCM' uses speech segment boundaries already available at the indexing stage. Run 'TrT_T(M)' extracts segments based on the topical relevance of the content of the complete video (if the video contained several topics[4]) subsequent to retrieval only for videos ranked in top positions. If segment extraction is not applied, a sliding window of 40 words is used to identify the segment in the transcript containing the largest number of content words in the query. Runs 'Sh_TM' and 'Sh_VWM' used visual segments extracted using visual analysis prior to retrieval and combination ranking using multimodal fusion, whereas run 'Sh_TNE(M)' segmented the retrieved video into shot segments only at the final stage.

5. EXPERIMENTS

In this section we give details of the exact runs and results of our experiments.

5.1 Search Sub-Task

Table 2 introduced in Section 4.1 shows the general types of the runs. Since the dataset provides two types of transcripts, some of the runs were carried out for both transcript types.

Sentence and speaker level segmentations output by the ASR system and visual shot boundaries were provided with

---

[4]To decide if a transcript contained several topics, a topic segmentation algorithm [32] parameterized to over-segment documents was applied. If the number of topic segments returned is small (less than 10), it was assumed that the transcript contained only one topic.

Table 3: Overview of Hyperlinking Types of Runs (BoW: bag of words, NE: Named entities, M - use of Metadata)

Run Type	Anchor Representation	Target Segment	Representation Metadata (BoW)	Speech	Visual	Ranking Function
TrT_T(M)	QueryBoW	Transcript Topics (TrT)	-	+	BoW	BM25
Sh_TM	QueryBoW	Shots (Sh)		+	BoW	TF-IDF
Sh_TVWM	QueryBoW Keyframe (Sh)	Shots		+	BoW Visual Words (VW)	TF-IDF
Sh_TNE(M)	QueryBoW+NE	Shots (Sh)	-	+	BoW+NE	TF-IDF
SpS_VCM	Keyframes concepts cores	Speech segment (SpS)			Visual Concepts (VC)	Euclid. Dist.

Table 4: MRR for segmentation using varying segment (60-180) and overlap (10-180) lengths

Segment Size (sec)	Overlap Size (sec)						
	10	30	60	90	120	150	180
LIMSI							
60	0.393	0.392	**0.408**	—	—	—	—
90	0.340	**0.429**	0.316	0.344	—	—	—
120	**0.337**	0.323	0.312	0.337	0.292	—	—
150	0.282	**0.305**	0.286	0.280	0.224	0.260	—
180	0.215	0.251	0.264	**0.269**	0.209	0.245	0.260
LIUM							
60	**0.358**	0.348	0.327	—	—	—	—
90	0.326	**0.349**	0.235	0.327	—	—	—
120	**0.322**	0.294	0.306	0.288	0.270	—	—
150	0.227	**0.281**	0.267	0.269	0.202	0.243	—
180	0.161	0.215	0.249	**0.276**	0.184	0.205	0.252

the dataset. Runs using fixed length time segmentation enabled us to vary the duration of segments in a controlled manner. Previous work on SDR has shown good performance for systems that retrieve segments with boundaries close to the actual relevant data. This can be assisted for fixed length segments by the incorporation of audio pauses (≥ 0.5 secs) as additional boundaries to divide speech segments, and a sliding window strategy with further filtering [6]. As a simple filtering technique to keep only the first segment after removing all overlapping segments further down the result list proved to be helpful to improve search retrieval results in [13]. We apply this filtering method to our time based segmentation runs. In order to choose the optimal values for time segmentation we carried out preliminary runs using different segment and segment overlap values. In these runs we use the Hiemstra language model (LM) with $\lambda = 0.15$, see Table 4 for MRR results. Using segment length equal to 90 seconds with an overlap of 30 seconds received the highest score amongst all runs based on LIMSI and LIUM transcripts, therefore we used these values for all time-based runs.

Table 5 shows results for all the runs. In general time based segmentation with overlapping windows shows the highest MRR values, meaning that these methods get the relevant content at the higher ranks. Amongst all runs 'TOvM_lm' achieves the highest score for both type of transcripts. mGAP values incorporating the distance to the beginning of the retrieved segment from the actual relevant jump-in point show less difference between the methods, meaning that some of the segments retrieved by time-based

segmentation at higher ranks start further from the jump-in point, than the shorter segments of the other runs being retrieved further down the list. The influence of segment length also affects MASP performance, where shorter segments ('S(M)_bm25') perform better than all other segmentation methods for both types of transcripts.

When we compare the results for the same methods using different types of transcripts, the segmentation methods that use shorter segments have better scores when LIUM transcript is used, whereas time-based segmentation performs better on the LIMSI transcript. Amongst methods that produce short segments ('S(M)', 'Sh(M)','SpS') and use LIMSI transcripts, the addition of metadata increases results in all cases expect for shot based segmentation. Addition of metadata increases the results for sentence and speech segment based runs for LIMSI transcripts (S_bm25 vs SM_bm25, SpS_bm25 vs SpSM_bm25). However for time based segmentation, it decreases results for runs using the TF-IDF retrieval model (10a vs 13a). TF-IDF and BM-25 perform better than LM when metadata is used, however when time segmentation is combined with pause information, LM outperforms BM25 and TF-IDF.

When we analyze run performance depending on query type, the difference between segmentation methods becomes more obvious. For queries with WRR equal or less than 0.55 (queries 6, 12, 23, 25, 26, 29) runs based on short segmentation units (sentences, shots, speech segments) get higher MRR values than time-based segmentation with overlapping windows (e.g., in the extreme cases it is equal to 1.0 vs 0.0 for queries 6, 25 for time segmentation and short units segmentation respectively). This is due to the fact that in longer segments the errors in ASR recognition cause this type of behaviour.

Queries containing terms that are not present in the collection lexicon (OOV terms) get better results for longer segments, and especially for runs that use metadata (e.g. only TOvM runs retrieve the relevant segment for queries 1, 8, 11; metadata increased the performance for all types of runs for queries 5, 7, 14, 15, 26, 28). This is due to the fact that metadata can contain the missing OOV words, and the longer segments contain more context that relates the segment to the terms appearing in the query that are present in the collection lexicon.

Addition of visual information in the multimodal queries decreases performance for both types of transcript, although more significantly for the runs based on LIUM transcripts. This may be caused by the fact that the queries are primarily expressed in terms of audio content, thus the video stream is less relevant for search.

Table 5: Evaluation metrics for Search sub-task.

Segmentation Type	LIMSI			LIUM		
	MRR	mGAP	MASP	MRR	mGAP	MASP
S_bm25	0.127	0.097	0.167	0.349	0.258	**0.213**
SM_bm25	0.277	0.206	**0.240**	0.349	0.258	**0.213**
Sh_tf-idf	0.187	0.120	0.066	0.275	0.158	0.032
ShM_tf-idf	0.158	0.096	0.055	0.269	0.154	0.029
SpS_bm25	0.235	0.188	0.140			
SpSM_bm25	0.363	0.264	0.220			
TP_bm25	0.212	0.150	0.082	0.164	0.128	0.128
TP_lm	0.336	0.236	0.097	0.318	0.237	0.181
TP_tf-idf	0.212	0.150	0.082	0.162	0.126	0.127
TOv_bm25	0.436	0.284	0.099	0.390	0.248	0.076
TOv_lm	0.364	0.241	0.078	0.355	0.232	0.066
TOv_tf-idf	0.414	0.276	0.085	0.405	0.260	0.078
TOvM_bm25	0.423	0.251	0.102	0.429	0.238	0.091
TOvM_lm	**0.470**	**0.290**	0.123	**0.449**	**0.250**	0.102
TOvM_tf-idf	0.428	0.256	0.103	0.418	0.239	0.087
*S_bm25	0.126	0.096	0.144	0.080	0.044	0.046
*SM_bm25	0.104	0.058	0.071			
*SpS_bm25	0.196	0.168	0.102			
*SpSM_bm25	0.121	0.072	0.070			

Table 6: MAP results for Hyperlinking sub-task.

Run Type	MAP using			
	run qrel		unified qrel	
	LIMSI	LIUM	LIMSI	LIUM
TrT_T	0.251	0.222	0.156	0.137
TrT_TM	0.334		**0.208**	
TrT_T_reranking1	0.346		0.206	
TrT_T_reranking2	0.315		0.192	
Sh_TM	0.254	0.312	0.099	0.134
Sh_TVWM_VisualReranking	0.194	0.245	0.076	0.105
Sh_TVWM_RankReranking	0.228	0.258	0.091	0.111
Sh_TNE	0.088	0.083	0.016	0.020
Sh_TNEM	0.088	0.083	0.016	0.020
SpS_VS	**0.404**		0.055	
*Sh_TNE	0.071	0.046	0.018	0.012
*Sh_TNEM	0.071	0.046	0.018	0.012
TOv_lm+Sh_TM			0.004	0.004
TOv_lm+ Sh_TVWM_RankReranking			0.003	0.002
TOvM_lm_+Sh_TM			0.015	0.019
TOvM_lm+ Sh_TVWM_RankReranking			0.014	0.018

5.2 Hyperlinking Sub-Task

As described in Section 3 the relevance assessment for the hypothesized hyperlinks was conducted after completing the runs. Table 6 shows the results of the runs using different transcript types, with MAP values for two types of qrels. The run using only visual features for retrieval (SpS_VS) has the highest MAP on its "run" qrel and the lowest on the "unified" qrel, this means that it is oriented to retrieve links based on video stream features, but cannot retrieve the other types of links. Use of visual words in combination with the transcript and metadata (runs 'Sh_TVWM_VisualReranking' and 'Sh_TVWM_RankReranking') decreases the result in comparison with the simple run based only on transcript and metadata ('Sh_TM'). We assume that visual features used are too low level to improve the results.

The results here cannot be considered definitive, further development of the evaluation set may change the results. For example it is notable that runs have very diverse qrel sets, so further runs may significantly change the unified qrels. Also we did not explicitly ask the assessors to pay attention to audio or visual features for each case, therefore it is hard to determine cases where visual or audio features have more importance.

5.3 Bridge between Search and Hyperlinking

Our target is to create links for the search output results, therefore in a real-life scenario we would have to use the segments extracted automatically as the link sources, and not the ones with the perfect boundaries. Therefore we created two additional types of runs: one using the same units in both search and hyperlinking sub-tasks (*Sh_TNE and Sh_TNEM), and the other using the two best results from the Search sub-task ('TOv' and 'TOvM'), and carry out hyperlink creation using the ASR transcripts in the source segment, rather than the manual ones used in the Hyperlinking task (runs TrT(M))). The second set of results clearly demonstrates that even a slight difference in Search sub-task

output effects hyperlink creation. This motivates further work on refinement of the output of the Search sub-task.

6. CONCLUSIONS AND FUTURE WORK

This paper has described our investigation into a scenario modeling multimodal search and automated hyperlinking of multimedia content, for a situation where a user wishes to search for a remembered specific item in a collection, but does not remember where it is located, and subsequently wants to follow hyperlinks to related videos in the collection that would enrich their browsing experience. We are among the first to work on both sub-tasks of multimedia search and hyperlinking creation using multimodal aspects of the collection with one scenario in mind, using a standard benchmark collection as the dataset.

We explored the space of possible approaches to the proposed search sub-task by varying segment length, use of metadata, and different retrieval models, in order to better understand and address the search sub-task for textual and multimodal queries. We investigated various use of audio and video features for the hyperlinking sub-task, and carried out several combination runs using search sub-task output and hyperlinking methods.

Use of visual features for the search sub-task impacted negatively on the results: multimodal queries received lower scores for the same methods, and shot segmentation did not outperform time or transcript based results.

Our proposed pooled strategy for evaluation of the hyperlinking sub-task did not include the distinction at the stage of relevance assessment whether the audio or the visual features were the basis for the decision. However, it did allow us to assess separately the performance of each individual method of hyperlink creation and compare this with a unified list of relevant data gathered from all runs. This showed that runs using visual features fail to hypothesize hyperlinks that are relevant because of the audio content. This other type of links can be found using methods based based on transcript and metadata processing. We tried to combine this method with low-level visual features. However this again resulted in a decrease in results. We can thus conclude that exploitation of visual features is a challenging issue for our future work.

The results of combination search and hyperlinking runs that reflect the full real-life scenario of search and link browsing showed the importance of appropriate search sub-task output.

7. ACKNOWLEDGMENTS

This work was supported by Science Foundation Ireland (Grant 08/RFP/CMS1677) Research Frontiers Programme 2008 and (Grant 07/CE/I1142) as part of the Centre for NExt Generation Localisation (CNGL) project at DCU; co-funded by European Commission's Seventh Framework Programme (FP7) as part of the AXES project (ICT-269980) and (FP7-269980); by the Dutch COMMIT program; by Ghent University, iMinds, the IWT Flanders, the FWO-Flanders, and the European Union, in the context of the iMinds project SMIF; by the Czech Science Foundation (grant no. P103/12/G084).

8. ADDITIONAL AUTHORS

Roeland J.F. Ordelman (University of Twente, The Netherlands, email: ordelman@ewi.utwente.nl), Shu Chen (Dublin City University, Ireland, email: shu.chen4@mail.dcu.ie), Danish Nadeem (University of Twente, The Netherlands, email: d.nadeem@utwente.nl), Camille Guinaudeau, Guillaume Gravier, Pascale Sébillot (IRISA/University of Rennes 1, IRISA/CNRS, IRISA/INSA, France, email: {cguinaud, ggravier, psebillo}@irisa.fr), Tom de Nies, Pedro Debevere, Rik Van de Walle (Ghent University, iMinds, MMLab, Belgium, email: {tom.denies, pedro.debevere, rik.vandewalle}@ugent.be), Petra Galuščáková, Pavel Pecina (Charles University in Prague, Czech Republic, email: {galus-cakova, pecina}@ufal.mff.cuni.cz), Martha Larson (Delft University of Technology, Delft, The Netherlands, email: m.a.larson@tudelft.nl)

9. REFERENCES

[1] M Bron, B Huurnink, and M de Rijke. Linking archives using document enrichment and term selection. In *Proceedings of TPDL 2011*, pages 2357–2360, 2011.

[2] K. Chatfield, V. Lempitsky, A. Vedaldi, and A. Zisserman. The devil is in the details: an evaluation of recent feature encoding method. In *Proceedings of BMVC 2011*, 2011.

[3] R.G. Cinbis, Jakob Verbeek, and Cordelia Schmid. Unsupervised Metric Learning for Face Identification in TV Video. In *Proceedings of ICCV 2011*, Barcelona, Spain, 2011.

[4] M. Eskevich, G.J. F. Jones, S. Chen, R. Aly, R.J.F. Ordelman, and M. Larson. Search and Hyperlinking Task at Mediaeval 2012. In *MediaEval*, volume 927 of *CEUR Workshop Proceedings*. CEUR-WS.org, 2012.

[5] M. Eskevich, G.J.F. Jones, M. Larson, and R.J.F. Ordelman. Creating a data collection for evaluating rich speech retrieval. In *Proceedings of LREC 2012*, Istanbul, Turkey, 2012.

[6] M. Eskevich, G.J.F. Jones, M. Larson, C. Wartena, R. Aly, T. Verschoor, and R.J.F. Ordelman. Comparing retrieval effectiveness of alternative content segmentation methods for internet video search. In *Proeedings of CBMI 2012*, 2012.

[7] M. Eskevich, W. Magdy, and G.J.F. Jones. New metrics for meaningful evaluation of informally structured speech retrieval. In *Proceedings of ECIR 2012*, pages 170–181, 2012.

[8] J.S. Garofolo, C.G.P. Auzanne, and E.M. Voorhees. The TREC spoken document retrieval track: A success story. In *Proceedings of RIAO 2000*, pages 1–8, 2000.

[9] A. Girgensohn, L. Wilcox, F. Shipman, and S. Bly. Designing affordances for the navigation of detail-on-demand hypervideo. In *Proceedings of AVI 2004*, pages 290–297. ACM, 2004.

[10] L. Hardman. *Modelling and authoring hypermedia documents*. PhD thesis, Universiteit Amsterdam, 1998.

[11] D. Hiemstra. *Using language models for information retrieval*. PhD thesis, University of Twente, 2001.

[12] P. Hoffmann, T. Kochems, and M. Herczeg. HyLive: Hypervideo-Authoring for Live Television. In *Changing Television Environments*, pages 51–60. Springer, 2008.

[13] T. Kaneko, T. Takigami, and T. Akiba. STD based on hough transform and SDR using STD results: Experiments at NTCIR-9 SpokenDoc. In *Proceedings of Ninth NTCIR Workshop Meeting*, 2011.

[14] P. Kelm, S. Schmiedeke, and T. Sikora. Feature-based Video Key Frame Extraction for low Quality Video Sequences. In *Proceedings of WIAMIS 2009*.

[15] Lori Lamel and Jean-Luc Gauvain. Speech processing for audio indexing. In *Advances in Natural Language Processing*, volume 5221 of *LNCS*, pages 4–15. 2008.

[16] M. Larson, M. Eskevich, R. Ordelman, C. Kofler, S. Schmiedeke, and G. J. F. Jones. Overview of MediaEval 2011 Rich Speech Retrieval Task and Genre Tagging Task. In *MediaEval 2011 Workshop*, Pisa, Italy, 2011.

[17] M. Larson, C. Kofler, and A. Hanjalic. Reading between the tags to predict real-world size-class for visually depicted objects in images. In *Proceedings of ACM MM*, 2011.

[18] M. Larson, M. Soleymani, M. Eskevich, P. Serdyukov, R.J.F. Ordelman, and G. J. F. Jones. The community and the crowd: Multimedia benchmark dataset development. *IEEE MultiMedia*, 19(3):15, 2012.

[19] M.A. Larson, S. Schmiedeke, P. Kelm, A. Rae, V. Mezaris, T. Piatrik, M. Soleymani, F. Metze, and G.J.F. Jones, editors. *Working Notes Proceedings of the MediaEval 2012 Workshop*, volume 927 of *CEUR Workshop Proceedings*. CEUR-WS.org, 2012.

[20] B. Meixner, K. Matusik, C. Grill, and H. Kosch. Towards an easy to use authoring tool for interactive non-linear video. *Multimedia Tools and Applications*, pages 1–26, 2012.

[21] P. N. Mendes, M. Jakob, A. García-Silva, and C. Bizer. DBpedia spotlight: Shedding light on the web of documents. In *Proceedings of the 7th International Conference on Semantic Systems (I-Semantics)*, 2011.

[22] D. Milne and I.H. Witten. Learning to link with wikipedia. In *Proceeding of CIKM 2008*, pages 509–518. ACM, 2008.

[23] J. Morang, R.J.F. Ordelman, F.M.G. de Jong, and A.J. van Hessen. InfoLink: analysis of Dutch broadcast news and cross-media browsing. In *Proceedings of ICME 2005*, Los Alamitos, 2005.

[24] P. Pecina, P. Hoffmannova, G. J. F. Jones, Y. Zhang, and D. W. Oard. Overview of the CLEF 2007 cross-language speech retrieval track. In *Proceedings of CLEF 2007*, pages 674–686, 2007.

[25] S. Robertson, H. Zaragoza, and M. Taylor. Simple BM25 extension to multiple weighted fields. In *Proceedings of ACM CIKM 2004*, 2004.

[26] A. Rousseau, F. Bougares, P. Deléglise, H. Schwenk, and Y. Estèv. Lium's systems for the iwslt 2011 speech translation tasks. In *Proceedings of IWSLT 2011*, 2011.

[27] I. Sawhney, N. and Balcom, D. and Smith. Authoring and navigating video in space and time. *MultiMedia, IEEE*, 4(4):30–39, 1997.

[28] F. Shipman, A. Girgensohn, and L. Wilcox. Authoring, viewing, and generating hypervideo: An overview of Hyper-Hitchcock. *ACM Trans. Multimedia Comput. Commun. Appl.*, (2):15:1—-15:19, 2008.

[29] J. Sivic and A. Zisserman. Video google: a text retrieval approach to object matching in videos. In *Proceedings of ICCV 2003*, pages 1470 –1477 vol.2, 2003.

[30] A. F. Smeaton, P. Over, and W. Kraaij. Evaluation campaigns and trecvid. In *Proceedings of MIR 2006*, Santa Barbara, California, USA, 2006.

[31] A. W. M. Smeulders, M. Worring, S. Santini, A. Gupta, and R. Jain. Content-based image retrieval at the end of the early years. *IEEE Trans. Pattern Anal. Mach. Intell.*, 22(12):1349–1380, 2000.

[32] M. Utiyama and H. Isahara. A statistical model for domain-independent text segmentation. In *Proceedings of ACL 2001*.

[33] E. Voorhees, D.K. Harman, National Institute of Standards, and Technology (US). *TREC: Experiment and evaluation in information retrieval*. MIT press USA, 2005.

[34] E.M. Voorhees. The TREC-8 Question Answering Track Report. In *Proceedings of TREC-8*, pages 77–82, 1999.

[35] R. Yan. *Probabilistic Models for Combining Diverse Knowledge Sources in Multimedia Retrieval*. PhD thesis, Carnegie Mellon University, 2006.

Explicit Diversification of Image Search

Jonathon S. Hare
jsh2@ecs.soton.ac.uk

Paul H. Lewis
phl@ecs.soton.ac.uk

Electronics and Computer Science, University of Southampton, United Kingdom

ABSTRACT

Search result diversification can increase user satisfaction in answering a particular information need. There are many ways of diversify search results. In some cases the user has a clear idea of how they would like to see their results diversified. This work presents a system that is capable of diversifying search results along specific user-specified axes of diversity.

Categories and Subject Descriptors

H.3.3 [**Information Storage and Retrieval**]: Information Search and Retrieval

Keywords

Image search; Diversity; Result diversification

1. INTRODUCTION

The information need of a user is often better satisfied by a retrieval system when the result set for a particular query shows many different aspects of that query. This is especially important when the query is poorly specified or ambiguous [4, 2]. By presenting a diverse range of results covering many possible representations of a query the probability of finding relevant images is increased. In terms of image search there are many ways of diversifying results; often these are implicit and involve removing near duplicates [3]. Sometimes, however, users have an explicit idea about how they would like their results to be diversified. The demonstration described in this work shows an image search engine with explicit result diversification.

Our linked-data diversity search tool uses semantic web technologies to perform web-based image searches along specific axes of diversity. The initial vision for this tool was described briefly in [5]. Unlike a normal search engine the application requires you to be a little more specific with your query - at a minimum it requires a "subject" of the search, and an "axis" along which you would like to see the results presented. For example, you could ask the engine to find images about "David Beckham", organised by the various clubs he has played for. The implementation builds on top of existing web and image search engines and semantic web

tools. Specifically, Microsoft's Bing Search API[1] is used as the basis for the image and web search, and DBpedia [1] is used as the semantic knowledge store that helps provide query diversification.

2. DEMO

A live version of the tool is deployed at `http://degas.ecs.soton.ac.uk/~jsh2/diversity`. Figure 1 illustrates a search for images of the objects manufactured by the Japanese car manufacturer Mazda. The subject of the search was "mazda", and the axis of diversity was "manufacturer". The performance of the tool is very heavily query dependent, and is affected by how well the query terms are modelled in DBpedia as well as the performance of the underlying search engine. However, in a number of practical queries that have been tested, the results are often quite good and they can be maximised through iterative querying by the user.

3. DESCRIPTION

An overview of the tool can be seen in Figure 2. The search engine itself works by consuming machine-readable data from DBpedia and combining it with links to image documents from Bing's search engine. A flowchart of the processes taken within the tool is shown in Figure 3.

The search process starts with the formation of the query by the user. The search specification consists of a mandatory subject and diversity axis. In addition, extra contextual search terms can be provided to narrow down the search. The user interface of the tool allows queries to be entered in two different ways; firstly, the user can enter the subject term(s), context term and a term describing the diversity axis in three separate free-text fields. Alternatively, there is a "wizard" interface in which the subject of the search can be entered, and on the following screen the user is able to select from a pull-down list of diversity axes directly relevant to that subject, in addition to entering additional context terms.

Once the query has been specified the following steps are taken within the search engine:

1. The Bing API is used to perform a web search, restricted to the Wikipedia domain, for the subject terms. The top-matching Wikipedia URL is returned.

2. The Wikipedia URL for the subject terms is transformed to a DBpedia URI that represents the subject.

---

[1]`https://datamarket.azure.com/dataset/bing/search`

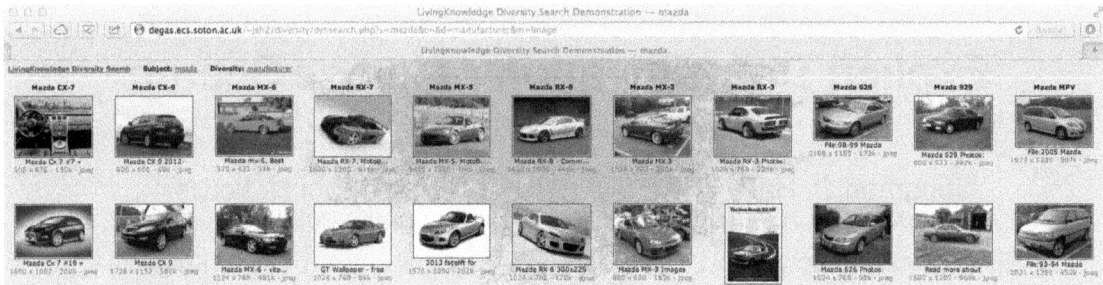

Figure 1: Search for images of objects *manufactured* by *Mazda*

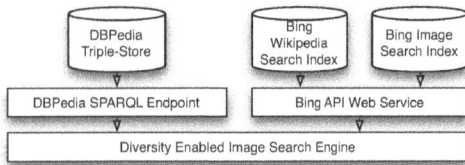

Figure 2: Overview of the diversity search tool.

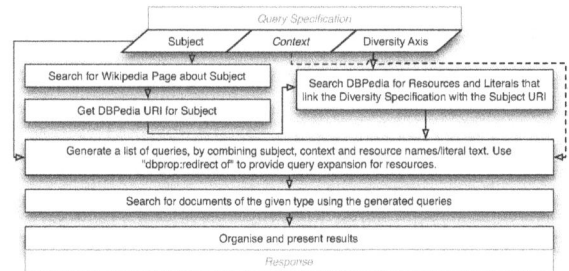

Figure 3: Flowchart illustrating the steps taken in producing diversified search results.

3. The diversity axis of a search is internally represented as a DBpedia URI. The URI is created as follows:

   (a) If the user entered a URI directly, then this is used by the engine.

   (b) If the user entered a free-text term for the axis, then the engine tries to guess the correct URI by performing a SPARQL query against DBpedia of the form `select distinct ?p where {<db_uri> ?p ?obj filter regex(?p, "axis_term")}`. If there are no results then the query is repeated with the `<db_uri>` and `?obj` swapped.

   (c) If the user used the wizard to select the diversity axis, then the search engine already has the correct URI. The axis choices presented to the user are determined by querying the DBpedia SPARQL interface with two queries: `select distinct ?x ?y where {<db_url> ?x ?y}` and `select distinct ?x ?y where {?y ?x <db_url>}`. The set of returned ?x's that are of URI type are used to form the list of possible diversity axes.

4. The search engine now proceeds to look for resources related to the *subject* along the *diversity axis* using the following query: `select distinct ?x where {<db_url> <div_axis> ?x}`. If the result set of this query is empty, then the reverse query is performed: `select distinct ?x where {?x <div_axis> <db_url>}`. Each ?x value is considered to be a point on the axis.

5. The search engine now iterates through the ?x objects returned by the previous step and builds queries which are sent to the Bing image search API. The query sent to the API has the following form: `+"subject" +"context" +"axis_term"`. The actual construction of the `axis_term` part of the query depends on the type of the ?x object in question; if the ?x object is literal, then it is used directly. If it is a URI, then a lookup step takes place to determine a list of potential

terms that describe the URI, and each of these is used in turn for the Bing query.

6. Finally, the tool performs a rendering step to display the results of the search, organised by each of the ?x points on the axis of diversity.

4. ACKNOWLEDGMENTS

The described work was funded by the European Union Seventh Framework Programme (FP7/2007-2013) under grant agreement 231126 (LivingKnowledge).

5. REFERENCES

[1] S. Auer, C. Bizer, G. Kobilarov, J. Lehmann, R. Cyganiak, and Z. Ives. DBpedia: A Nucleus for a Web of Open Data. *The Semantic Web*, pages 722–735, 2007.

[2] H. Chen and D. R. Karger. Less is more: probabilistic models for retrieving fewer relevant documents. In *ACM SIGIR'06*, pages 429–436, New York, NY, USA, 2006. ACM.

[3] M. Paramita, M. Sanderson, and P. Clough. Diversity in photo retrieval: overview of the ImageCLEFPhoto task 2009. In *CLEF working notes*, Corfu, Greece, 2009.

[4] K. Song, Y. Tian, W. Gao, and T. Huang. Diversifying the image retrieval results. In *ACM MM'06*, pages 707–710, New York, NY, USA, 2006. ACM.

[5] P. Zontone, G. Boato, F. G. B. D. Natale, A. D. Rosa, M. Barni, A. Piva, J. Hare, D. Dupplaw, and P. Lewis. Image diversity analysis: Context, opinion and bias. In *The First International Workshop on Living Web: Making Web Diversity a true asset*, volume 515. CEUR-WS, October 2009.

Twitter's Visual Pulse

Jonathon S. Hare
jsh2@ecs.soton.ac.uk

Sina Samangooei
ss@ecs.soton.ac.uk

David P. Dupplaw
dpd@ecs.soton.ac.uk

Paul H. Lewis
phl@ecs.soton.ac.uk

Electronics and Computer Science, University of Southampton, United Kingdom

ABSTRACT

Millions of images are tweeted every day, yet very little research has looked at the non-textual aspect of social media communication. In this work we have developed a system to analyse streams of image data. In particular we explore trends in similar, related, evolving or even duplicated visual artefacts in the mass of tweeted image data — in short, we explore the visual pulse of Twitter.

Categories and Subject Descriptors

H.4 [**Information Systems Applications**]: Miscellaneous

Keywords

Stream analysis; near-duplicate image detection; trend analysis; Twitter analysis

1. INTRODUCTION

There is currently a massive amount of research being performed by the natural-language understanding and data-mining communities on trying to understand and harness the mass of information being tweeted across the world. The aims of this research are diverse, from trying to understand opinions about current events, to detecting disasters as they happen, to predicting future stock prices.

Virtually all the current research looking at Twitter concentrates on the short textual messages that compose a Tweet and on the social network of Twitter users. Millions of images are tweeted every day. However, there has been very little research looking at non-textual aspects of social media communication. Recently, we've been exploring some different aspects of this mass of tweeted image data.

This paper describes a demonstration system we have built for investigating trends in streams of images in Twitter. Specifically, we've investigated and designed a system for detecting near-duplicates in live streams of images (where we *forget* after a period of time) and coupled this to the live Twitter sample stream. We detect duplicates using a graph-based approach in which Locality Sensitive Hashing is applied to local features to efficiently determine feature matches between images. The system also incorporates a modular approach to actually extracting images from Tweets. Currently we have modules for a number of the most common image hosting sites used by Twitter.

2. TECHNICAL DESCRIPTION

The system is built from three main components: 1) a tool called PicSlurper, that is responsible for reading the Tweets in the Twitter stream and parsing them to extract any images; 2) a component for detecting near duplicates within the most recent images; and 3) a visualisation, showing currently trending images as well as historical trends. The system is able to process the Twitter sample stream (>100,000 images per day) in real-time on a standard PC. The system built on top of OpenIMAJ [3] and is available as part of the OpenIMAJ codebase[1].

2.1 PicSlurper

Tweets do not themselves contain images; rather they contain links to images hosted by a variety of different providers. This means that to extract images from Tweets, we need to be able to extract the links from the Tweet and resolve the image content. Even this is not simple, as each image hosting provider uses a different technique for providing the image; usually the image is embedded in an html page.

PicSlurper is a tool we have developed to extract the images from a stream of Tweets (either read from a file, or in real-time from the live Tweet data provided by the Twitter API). Internally, PicSlurper has a set of consumer modules that deal with specific hosting sites. When PicSlurper extracts a URL from a Tweet, it asks each module if it is able to extract an image from the URL. If a module is able to extract the image, then the module is used to download the image, and the image and the respective Tweet metadata are emitted for further processing. If no module is able to deal with the link(s) in the Tweet (or if there are no links), then the Tweet is ignored and nothing is emitted. Currently, we have modules for a number of the most popular image hosting services used with Twitter: Facebook, imgur, Instagram, ow.ly, Tmblr, Twiple, TwitPic, yfrog, and of course Twitter's own image hosting service. Using PicSlurper with the Twitter sample stream[2] we are able to extract over 100,000 images per day; the actual number of tweets processed is far higher than this though (it varies a lot, but between 30 & 80 tweets per second is normal).

2.2 Streaming Duplicate Detection

Our streaming duplicate detection is heavily inspired by the techniques proposed in [2], however it does have a number of differences. Most notably, in our technique, we are

---

[1] http://www.openimaj.org
[2] https://dev.twitter.com/docs/api/1.1/get/statuses/sample

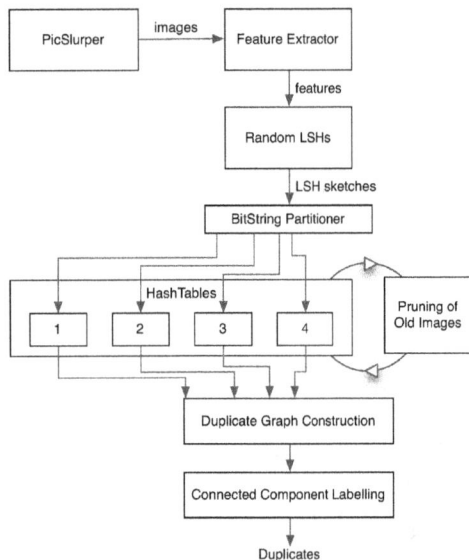

Figure 1: Flowchart illustrating the streaming duplicate detection algorithm.

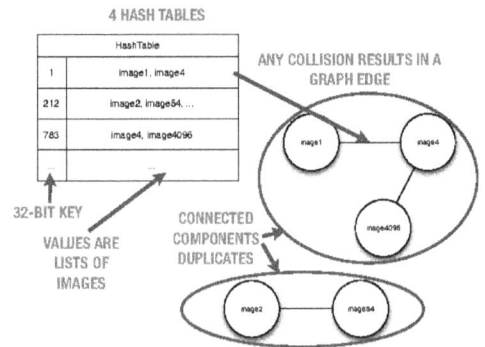

Figure 2: Illustration of the how the hash tables define the duplicates graph.

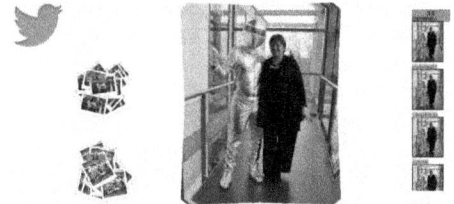

Figure 3: The trending image visualisation.

only interested in images within a time-window, so we have to continually remove old images as new ones arrive. In the approach, two images are defined as near-duplicates if they share a certain number of (local) features. To detect all near-duplicates we build an undirected weighted graph where the vertices are images and the edge weights represent the number of matching features between the images. Once the graph is constructed, edges with low-weight are pruned, and connected-component analysis is performed to extract all the sets of near-duplicates. The largest sets of duplicates are said to be trending and are emitted to the visualisation component of the system.

To efficiently assess whether features match, Locality Sensitive Hashing is used to create sketches (compact binary strings) from the features. The sketches are produced such that the Hamming distance between sketches approximates the Euclidean distance between the features [1]. As in [2], we choose our sketches to be 128 bits in length, and set the minimum Hamming distance for two sketches/features to be classed as matching at 3 bits. Rather than explicitly compute Hamming distances between all features, a more efficient (approximate) scheme is used: The 128-bit sketches are partitioned into 4 32-bit strings and represented as 32-bit integers. For a pair of matching sketches there could be at most 3 different bits, so at least one of the pairs of integers from the sketches must be the same. By using the four integers from each sketch as keys in four hash tables and storing the images containing the features as the values in the tables, the graph construction becomes trivial. As we are interested in temporal detection of duplicates, we regularly prune *old* images from the hash tables so that their respective contents only cover images from a fixed window into the past. The overall process we use is illustrated in Figure 1. Figure 2 illustrates the duplicate detection from the hash tables through construction of a graph.

The specifics of the image analysis and feature extraction up to the point of sketch construction are as follows: 1) images are resized to 150px on the longest side; 2) SIFT

features detected at peaks in a difference-of-Gaussian pyramid [4] are extracted; 3) Low-entropy features are removed [2]; and finally, 4) log-scaling is applied to make the feature values more uniform [2].

2.3 Visualisation

Currently we have the system set up so that the PicSlurper & duplicate detection modules produce information about the trending images (and the Tweets in which they occur) in a file in JSON format. A visualisation written in HTML and JavaScript continually polls this file and displays the currently trending images. The visualisation is depicted in Figure 3. A video describing the system and showing the visualisation is online at http://youtu.be/CBk5nDd6CLU.

3. ACKNOWLEDGMENTS

The described work was funded by the European Union Seventh Framework Programme (FP7/2007-2013) under grant agreements 270239 (ARCOMEM), and 287863 (TrendMiner).

4. REFERENCES

[1] W. Dong, M. Charikar, and K. Li. Asymmetric distance estimation with sketches for similarity search in high-dimensional spaces. In *SIGIR'08*, pages 123–130. ACM, 2008.

[2] W. Dong, Z. Wang, M. Charikar, and K. Li. High-confidence near-duplicate image detection. In *ACM ICMR'12*, pages 1:1–1:8. ACM, 2012.

[3] J. S. Hare, S. Samangooei, and D. P. Dupplaw. OpenIMAJ and ImageTerrier: Java libraries and tools for scalable multimedia analysis and indexing of images. In *Proceedings of ACM Multimedia 2011*, MM '11, pages 691–694. ACM, 2011.

[4] D. Lowe. Distinctive image features from scale-invariant keypoints. *IJCV*, 60(2):91–110, January 2004.

Mobile Video Browsing with a 3D Filmstrip

[Demo Paper]

Marco A. Hudelist
Institute of Information Technology
Alpen-Adria-University Klagenfurt
9020 Klagenfurt, Austria
marco@itec.aau.at

Klaus Schoeffmann
Institute of Information Technology
Alpen-Adria-University Klagenfurt
9020 Klagenfurt, Austria
ks@itec.aau.at

Laszlo Boeszoermenyi
Institute of Information Technology
Alpen-Adria-University Klagenfurt
9020 Klagenfurt, Austria
laszlo@itec.aau.at

ABSTRACT

As mobile devices become more and more pervasive, they are increasingly used to record and watch personal and professional videos. Common video browsers on smart phones and tablets, however, fail to provide users an efficient and engaging experience to browse through video content.

In this demo paper, we present an early prototype for browsing videos on tablets: browsing video with a 3D filmstrip. A video is split up into equidistant, uniformly sampled time segments. The segments are represented by key-frames shown on the surface of a filmstrip, allowing an immediate overview of great parts of the video. Further, a user can scroll through the filmstrip, start playback for any segment and refine the preview of segments by simple touch gestures.

Categories and Subject Descriptors

H.3.3 [**Information Storage and Retrieval**]: Information Search and Retrieval

General Terms

Algorithms, Design, Experimentation, Performance

Keywords

Video Browsing, Image Browsing, Mobile devices, Touchscreens

1. INTRODUCTION

Tablets and smart phones are increasingly becoming the preferred recording device, especially for non-professional users. Due to their mobile nature they are highly available and the provided quality of the recordings comes closer to the one of dedicated consumer cameras. With the increased volume of video files on such mobile devices, finding certain scenes inside a video (e.g., to show it to a friend) becomes difficult with the built-in default video tools. The navigation possibilities are limited and do not offer efficient features for browsing and searching. In most cases a user is limited to a set of control buttons (play/pause, fast-forward, fast-backward) and a seeker bar. Hence, getting a quick overview of the content of a video is a challenging and time consuming task. The need for improved (mobile) video browsing is acknowledged by earlier work (see for example [3], [4], [5] and [7]).

In this work we present an early prototype to improve video browsing on tablet PCs. Based on our work in mobile image browsing [1], we use a 3D interface in order to provide a good overview of the video content as well as a very intuitive touch-based interaction. We are currently preparing a user study in order to evaluate its efficiency in direct comparison to default video search tools on tablet PCs (i.e., video players).

2. RELATED WORK

A very prominent example for combining 3D-like arrangements with similarity based video browsing are the Fork-, Cross- and RotorBrowsers in [2]. Based on a user-chosen focal shot different similarity threads of shots are positioned around it (in a fork, star or cross formation), which can be used to navigate through the video grounded on different similarity analysis. In [6] a 3D ring is used to navigate a video hierarchically. Each new hierarchy level is represented by a new ring giving the user a better idea about where in the hierarchy she/he currently is. ProPane [3] focuses on better utilizing touchscreen interaction for video browsing and provides a very precise control on browsing speed. Browsing is even possible in a frame-by-frame manner, which can be especially useful for professional users. Navigation between key-frames of a video as well as navigating between correlated different videos is provided in [4]. The interaction is based on the usage of swipe gestures. The user can swipe left and right to jump between key-frames of the video and up and down to change videos. A combination of a storyboard-like arrangement of key-frames and hierarchy-browsing is proposed in [5]. A user starts with a set of thumbnails representing different time ranges of the video. To refine the search the user can choose one thumbnail and therefore descend one hierarchy level. The new set of thumbnails represent the chosen segment in finer detail.

3. 3D FILMSTRIP

Figure 1: Initial view of the 3D Filmstrip.

The idea of our interface is based on old filmstrips used with analog video cameras and movie projectors. Each image on the filmstrip represents a certain segment of the video (see Figure 1).

In our current version the equidistant segments are uniformly sampled from the video and represented by a key-frame (a later version may be based on shots). Manipulation of the filmstrip is possible by applying different gestures. To get a quick overview of the whole video a user can perform a swipe/drag gesture with a single finger on the area around the filmstrip. This creates a kind of fly-over experience, where the filmstrip seems to move towards or away from the user. The filmstrips angle is adjustable by applying the same swipe/drag gesture with two fingers (see Figure 2).

Figure 2: 3D Filmstrip after tilting and scrolling.

The filmstrip can be navigated by using single finger swipe/drag gestures. In this situation the key-frames scroll forward or backward (i.e., to the left or to the right) accordingly. It is also possible to start playback for a corresponding video segment by simply tapping on it. The playback directly starts in the filmstrip view and can be brought to full screen with a double-tap.

A user also has the possibility to change the sampling-granularity. To increase granularity (e.g., to go from 10 second segments to 5 second segments) a pinch-in/zoom-in gesture can be used. The application then creates the additional screenshots and the length of the filmstrip is increased accordingly. Similarly, to decrease the granularity the user can apply a pinch-out/zoom-out gesture. This feature can be used progressively to refine a search for a certain scene. For example, a user starts with low granularity, scrolls to a promising part of the filmstrip and increases granularity until the wanted scene appears.

4. FUTURE WORK

In future work we will experiment with different kind of content analysis in order to further improve the user experience of the filmstrip. One example would be the use of face recognition to allow users to quickly browse all scenes of a video that contain faces. Moreover, it would also be possible to let the user choose a certain face beforehand from a list and then populate the filmstrip with video segments where that particular face was recognized.

For evaluation we currently prepare to compare the filmstrip with the default video player of iOS in terms of search time. Similar to a Known-Item-Search (KIS) scenario, test candidates will have to watch a short clip of a longer video. Consequently, test candidates will have to search for the clip in the whole video by using either the filmstrip or the default video player.

Acknowledgments

This work was funded by the Federal Ministry for Transport, Innovation and Technology (bmvit) and the Austrian Science Fund (FWF): TRP 273-N15 and the European Regional Development Fund and the Carinthian Economic Promotion Fund (KWF), supported by Lakeside Labs GmbH, Klagenfurt, Austria.

5. REFERENCES

[1] Ahlström, D., Hudelist, M. A., Schoeffmann, K. and Schaefer, G. 2012. A user study on image browsing on touchscreens. In *Proc. of the 20th ACM international conference on Multimedia* (MM '12). ACM, New York, NY, USA, 925-928.

[2] de Rooij, O., Snoek, C. G. M. and Worring, M. 2008. Balancing thread based navigation for targeted video search. In *Proc. of the 2008 international conference on Content-based image and video retrieval (CIVR '08)*. ACM, New York, NY, USA, 485-494.

[3] Ganhör, R. 2012. ProPane: fast and precise video browsing on mobile phones. In *Proc. of the 11th International Conference on Mobile and Ubiquitous Multimedia (MUM '12)*. ACM, New York, NY, USA, Article 20, 8 pages.

[4] Huber, J., Steimle, J., Lissermann, R., Olberding, S. and Mühlhäuser, M. 2010. Wipe'n'Watch: spatial interaction techniques for interrelated video collections on mobile devices. In *Proc. of the 24th BCS Interaction Specialist Group Conference* (BCS '10). British Computer Society, Swinton, UK, UK, 423-427.

[5] Hürst, W. and Darzentas, D. 2012. HiStory: a hierarchical storyboard interface design for video browsing on mobile devices. In *Proc. of the 11th International Conference on Mobile and Ubiquitous Multimedia (MUM '12)*. ACM, New York, NY, USA, Article 17, 4 pages.

[6] Schoeffmann, K. and del Fabro, M. 2011. Hierarchical video browsing with a 3D carousel. In *Proc. of the 19th ACM international conference on Multimedia (MM '11)*. ACM, New York, NY, USA, 827-828.

[7] Schoeffmann, K., Hopfgartner, F., Marques, O., Boeszoermenyi, L. and Jose, J. M., "Video browsing interfaces and applications: a review", in SPIE Reviews, Vol. 1, No. 1, pp. 1-35 (018004), SPIE, Online, March 2010.

Interactive Surveillance Event Detection at TRECVid2012

Suzanne Little*
Iveel Jargalsaikhan
CLARITY, Centre for Sensor
Web Technologies
Dublin City University, Ireland

Kathy Clawson
Hao Li
University of Ulster
Belfast, United Kingdom

Marcos Nieto
Vicomtech-IK4
San Sebastian, Spain

ABSTRACT

This demonstration shows the integration of video analysis and search tools to facilitate the interactive retrieval of video segments depicting specific activities from surveillance footage. The implementation was developed by members of the SAVASA project for participation in the interactive surveillance event detection (SED) task of TRECVid 2012. This year, for the first time, the purpose of the interactive SED task was to evaluate systems' ability to support users in identifying video segments that depict a specific activity (event) in a large collection of surveillance video footage. Project partners worked together to analyse video and provide a query interface enabling users to search and identify matching video segments. The collaborative integration of components from multiple partners and the participation of end user partners in evaluating the system are the novel aspects of this work.

Categories and Subject Descriptors

I.2.10 [**Vision and Scene Understanding**]: Video analysis; H.5.2 [**User Interfaces**]: Benchmarking

Keywords

TRECVid, surveillance video, event detection

1. SEARCHING CCTV ARCHIVES

The increasing ubiquity of CCTV and surveillance video systems results in very large archives of footage captured and recorded in remote locations, at different levels of coverage and with different formats, available metadata or searchable indices. Authorised users face many challenges accessing specific footage or finding relevant segments based on semantic descriptions such as 'white car', 'person running'.

The SAVASA project (http://savasa.eu) aims to develop a standards-based video archive search platform that allows authorised users to query over various remote and non-interoperable video archives of CCTV footage from geographically diverse locations. At the core of the search interface is the application of algorithms for person/object detection and tracking, activity detection and scenario recognition. The project also includes research into interoperable standards for surveillance video, discussion of the legal, ethical and privacy issues and how to effectively leverage cloud computing infrastructures in these applications. Project

---
*Contact author: suzanne.little@dcu.ie

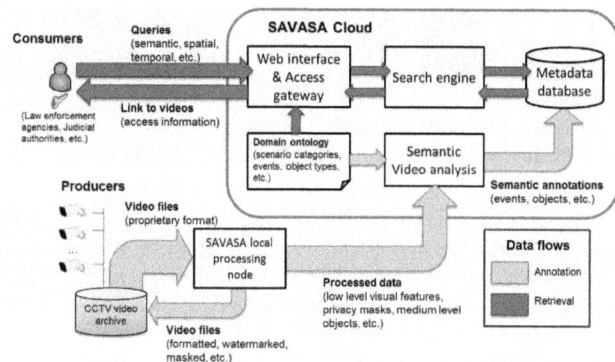

Figure 1: SAVASA framework (v1.0)

partners come from a number of different European countries and include technical and research institutions as well as end user, security and legal partners.

Figure 1 shows the current architecture of the SAVASA platform and illustrates how CCTV footage from "Producers" is analysed in a series of steps to produce a search index using terms from the domain ontology to facilitate advanced search by "Consumers" adhering to the legal and ethical access rights. The project is currently focusing on deploying components within the cloud infrastructure and ensuring security and access enforcement.

2. TRECVID SED INTEGRATION

To facilitate the aims of the SAVASA project, we took part in the TRECVid Interactive Surveillance Event Detection task 2012 [1]. TRECVid is an annual benchmarking exercise sponsored by the US National Institute of Standards and Technology (NIST) with the aim of stimulating video information retrieval research and improving the performance of systems using large, challenging, realistic and noisy datasets for real world problems. Surveillance Event Detection using CCTV footage has been a TRECVid task for the previous five years but, due in part to the lack of significant improvements in detection rates, was changed this year to include an interactive element. Previously, a set of test (unannotated) videos would be processed by one or more event classifiers and the ordered list of possible matches would be evaluated to determine the system's performance. This year a user interface could be used to identify video segments in the test set with a 25 minute search time limit per user per event class.

Our approach was to combine individual methods for video analysis and annotation and provide a dashboard style search interface (Figure 2) that enabled the user to view results for various algo-

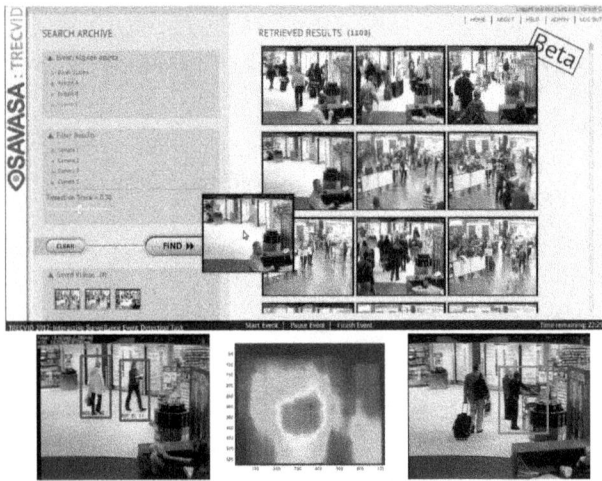

Figure 2: Screenshot of search interface (top) and Classifer examples: tracking, ROI heatmap, Pointing (bottom)

rithms and filter them by factors such as confidence, level of motion, camera, number of people etc. The interface was translated into Spanish to support user partners from Vicomtech-IK4, IKUSI, RENFE and HIB participating in the evaluations.

Two main methods were used to identify video segments showing one of three possible events – ObjectPut, PersonRuns, Pointing. The first classified events based on descriptors from motion trajectories. The trajectories were calculated using salient points identified by Harris Corner detectors and tracked using the Kanade-Lucas-Tomasi (KLT) algorithm. Trajectory length was empirically set to 15 frames and the trajectories described using HOG, HOF, MBH and TD descriptors. Descriptors were clustered using a Bag-of-Features approach to reduce the dimensionality before being classified via a trained SVM.

The second classifier looked at region-based identification and used two configurations to compare different approaches – Optical Flow features with a Hidden Markov Model classifier and dense SIFT features using Bag-of-Features and an SVM classifier. A method for person detection and tracking was implemented to provide input and to generate metrics about person density and activity to use in the interface. Persons were detected using HOG descriptors and tracked via a Rao-Blackwellized Data Association Particle Filter previously shown to produce good multiple object tracking results even with sparse detections. Due to the crowded nature of the scenes, the performance of the person detection was insufficient to be fully integrated in this stage and fixed regions were used instead.

The person tracking provided input for manual region of interest identification to determine *a priori* probability of an activity occurring in a region and confidence values of the region-based classifier were adjusted accordingly.

The challenges we faced in integrating difficult analysis and classification techniques included choosing suitable formats to exchange descriptors and upload resulting annotations, normalising the confidence values to merge results lists and choosing a fusion method to build the final list of results for submission from the list of segments found by all users. The results of our evaluation were competitive within the TRECVid framework but still show very low performance for any practical application purpose and provided us with interesting new directions to follow. The feedback given by the users regarding the interface, search options and their priori-

ties in surveillance video search was extremely valuable. Details regarding the classifiers and their evaluation performance can be found in [2].

3. PROPOSED DEMONSTRATION

This demonstration will show the evaluation interface used in the SED task by the end user partners from the SAVASA project. It illustrates how video analysis techniques from independent sources can be brought together to support interactive identification of surveillance events. Through the interface a specific event is chosen and by selecting different classifiers (systems) a ranked grid of animated GIFs shows the segments annotated with the event (Figure 2). The user can browse results and choose matching video segments to discover as many events as they can in the 25min time limit.

The TRECVid dataset, comprising CCTV footage from an airport, will be used to populate the demonstration prototype. This is a complex real-world dataset with difficult to identify activities, multiple cameras, a range of scales and significant variations in crowding and occlusions. A secondary contribution of this demonstration is the opportunity to explore and discuss the complexities of real-world activity recognition in surveillance video by choosing to apply different systems and confidence value filtering to change the results' list. A screen capture of the interface in action is available at http://youtu.be/ybJyHWRgJBc.

Acknowledgements

The research leading to these results has received funding from the European Union Seventh Framework Programme (FP7/2007-2013) under grant agreement number 285621, project titled SAVASA. Thanks to Kevin McGuinness for providing code for some interface components from the AXES project (http://www.axes-project eu) search interface.

4. ADDITIONAL AUTHORS

Cem Direkoglu (DCU, Ireland), Noel E. O'Connor (DCU, Ireland), Alan F. Smeaton (DCU, Ireland), Jun Liu (UU, UK), Bryan Scotney (UU, UK), Hui Wang (UU, UK), Seán Gaines (Vicomtech-IK4), Aitor Rodriguez (IKUSI, Spain), Pedro Sanchez (IKUSI, Spain), Ana Martínez Llorens (RENFE, Spain), Karina Villarroel Peniza (RENFE, Spain), Roberto Giménez (HIB, Spain), Raúl Santos de la Cámara (HIB, Spain), Anna Mereu (HIB, Spain), Celso Prados (INECO, Spain), Emmanouil Kafetzakis (NCSR "Demokritos", Greece)

5. REFERENCES

[1] P. Over, G. Awad, M. Michel, J. Fiscus, G. Sanders, B. Shaw, W. Kraaij, A. F. Smeaton, and G. Quéenot. TRECVid 2012 – An Overview of the Goals, Tasks, Data, Evaluation Mechanisms and Metrics. In *Proceedings of TRECVID 2012*. NIST, USA, 2012.

[2] S. Little, I. Jargalsaikhan, K. Clawson, M. Neito, H. Li, C. Direkoglu, N. E. O'Connor, A. F. Smeaton, A. Rodriguez, P. Sanchez, K. Villarroel Peniza, A. Martinez Llorens, R. Giménez, R. Santos de la Cámara, A. Mereu. SAVASA Project @ TRECVid 2012: Interactive surveillance event detection. In *TRECVid 2012 - TREC Video Retrieval Evaluation Workshop*, Gaithersburg, MD, 2012.

EventEnricher: A Novel Way to Collect Media Illustrating Events

Xueliang Liu
EURECOM
Sophia-Antipolis, France
xueliang.liu@eurecom.fr

Benoit Huet
EURECOM
Sophia-Antipolis, France
benoit.huet@eurecom.fr

ABSTRACT

Exploiting event context to organize social media draws lots of interest from the multimedia community. In this paper, we present our system, called EventEnricher, to infer the semantics behind events and explore social media to illustrate events. We extend the set of illustrating images for a particular event by querying social media with diverse multi-modal features and subsequently pruning the results using content based visual analysis. We integrate the solution into an intelligent interface that enables the user to browse the media collection illustrating events in an easy, effective and informative way.

Categories and Subject Descriptors

H.3.3 [**Information Storage and Retrieval**]: Information Search and Retrieval

Keywords

Events, Illustrating, Enricher, Social media

1. INTRODUCTION

The ever increasing amount of media available online, demands for intelligent ways to visualize and browse media collections. An event is the most natural way for humans to store and recall their memories. It can serve as a powerful instrument to organize media, thanks to its intrinsically multi-faceted nature. Hence, associating media to events has started to receive considerable attention [5, 1, 4, 3].

We propose a web service and interface called EventEnricher to help users infer the semantics behind the events and explore social media depicting events. There exist a special tag on the internet, called event machine tag to identify event in social media data. The machine tag is an additional metadata that is available from some events repositories (such as LastFM, Upcoming or Facebook) and media shared platform (such as Flickr and YouTube). When users take photos during the event, they are advised to upload them to media sharing websites with such a tag in order to explicitly associate the photos with the event. Hence, the machine tags provides explicit and accurate links between events and multimedia documents. However, the set of online media labeled with such a machine tag is generally a tiny subset of all media that are actually relevant for this

event. Our goal is to find as much as possible media resources that originate from events but have not been tagged with an event machine tag. We extend the set of illustrating images for a particular event by querying social media with diverse multi-modal features, and exploit content and context based analysis techniques to discard irrelevant media.

2. OUR PROPOSAL

We address this issue by analyzing the event multi-facets. Starting from an event description, three attributes can easily be mapped to metadata available in media shared platforms: the *what* dimension that represents the title, the *where* dimension which corresponds to the geo-coordinates attached to a media, and the *when* dimension that is matched with either the taken date or the upload date of a media. Querying Flickr or YouTube with just one of these dimensions returns far too many results: many events took place on the same date or at nearby locations and the title is often ambiguous. We also find that there are recurrent annual events with the same title and held in the same location, which makes the combination of "title" and "geo tag" inaccurate. In the following, we consider the two combinations "title" + "time" and "geotag" + "time" for performing search query and finding media that could be relevant for a given event. Thanks to the public REST API in most media sharing web sites, the query is easily performed.

However, it is well known that querying with metadata parameters does not achieve considerable accuracy. Therefore, a content based approach is employed to remove the irrelevant data. In details, we build a training dataset composed of the media labeled with the event machine tag. The photos resulting from query by title or location compose the testing dataset. The visual features used in our approach are 225D color moments in Lab space, 64D Gabor texture, and 73D Edge histogram. For each image pairs in the training data, the nearest neighbors algorithm using the *L1* distance measure in the training set is performed and the smallest distance is taken as threshold. The visual similarity between two images is computed as follows:

$$L_1(F_j, E_i) = \sum_k |F_j(k) - E_i(k)| \qquad (1)$$

where $F_j(k)$ and $E_i(k)$ are normalized concatenated low level feature vector of the images in the Testing and Training dataset respectively. F_j is added to the set of media illustrating the event when

$$\exists E_i \in E : L_1(F_j, E_i) < THD_i$$

where THD_i is the threshold which is also learned from the E data. As shown in Equation 2, we use a strict strategy to finalize the threshold, which is chosen as the minimal value of similarity of images pairs in training set. The threshold is also adaptive to different events due to the visual diversity within the training dataset.

$$THD_i = \min_{\{j\}\backslash i} \sum_k |E_j(k) - E_i(k)| \qquad (2)$$

It is clear that the strategy of deciding the threshold is rather conservative, many relevant media will also be pruned by our system. In order to bring visual diversity within the event illustration, the "owner" metadata is exploited. It is reasonable to assume that a person cannot attend more than one event at a time. Therefore, all the photos that have been taken by the same owner during the event duration should be assigned to the event. In effect, if the owner has shared additional photos during this period, they are automatically added as illustrative media for the event. For more details of our media collection approach please refer to [2].

3. BROWSING MEDIA WITH EVENTEN-RICHER

Based on our proposal, a web service is built to help user browse media data from events. Flickr is used as the basic media sharing platform, although EventEnricher can easily be extended to cater for other source such as YouTube, Google Picasa, etc... The users can interact with the system through 4 parts, as shown in Figure 1. Part (A) is the input parameter, while an event URL in last.fm, DailyMotion, Upcoming, or URI in EventMedia dataset [6] could be the input to query the event. When event information is retrieved, the abstract is presented in part (B), and the home page of the event is depicted in part (D). Then, the event's machine tag, title, geo location, time metadata are extracted and used to query the photos in Flickr, as described in [2]. The results from the query, as well as from the visual pruning and owner refinement process, can be accessed by the list in part (C). With a mouse click, the photos are presented in part (D), as shown in Figure 2.

Figure 2 also shows the effectiveness of our system on collecting event relevant photos. For last.fm event (id=1369317), only 10 photos are labeled with machine tag, and 285 and 48 photos are retrieved by the location and title based query. After the visual pruning and owner refinement process, a set of 262 photos illustrates the event.

4. CONCLUSION

In this paper, we present EventEnricher, a web interface to help users explore media collections taken during events. Thanks to the retrieval of many relevant media originating from events, we enrich the media from the query with time, location and title facets, and exploit the visual content and owner metadata to remove the noise data. Ultimately, we provide an environment for users to explore shared media taken during social events.

Acknowledgments

The research leading to this paper was partially supported by the project AAL-2009-2-049 "Adaptable Ambient Living Assistant" (ALIAS) co-funded by the European Commission and the French Research Agency (ANR) in the Ambient Assisted Living (AAL) programme.

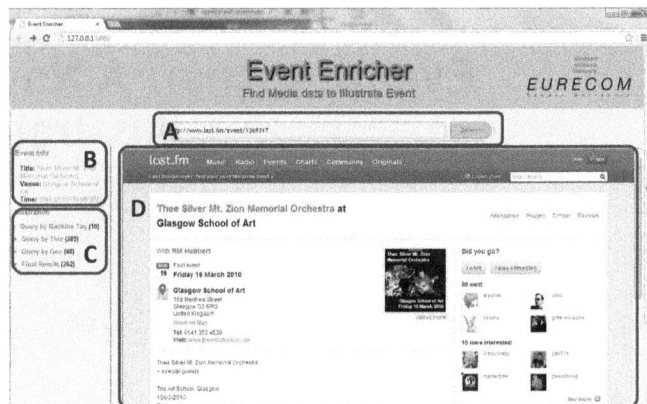

Figure 1: EventEnricher Interface, (A) Input URL; (B) Event Abstract; (C) Navigation of the Results; (D) Main-View: to show the event homepage and photos in the results

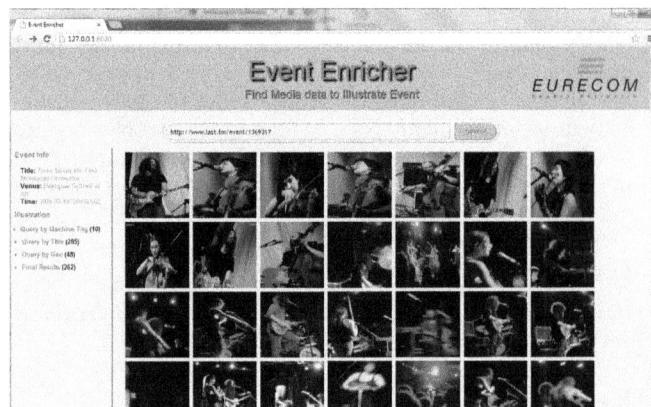

Figure 2: Results on Lastfm event:1369317

5. REFERENCES

[1] C. S. Firan, M. Georgescu, and et. al. Bringing order to your photos: Event-Driven Classification of Flickr Images Based on Social Knowledge. In *Proceedings of the 19th ACM ICDM*, New York, USA, Oct. 2010.

[2] X. Liu, R. Troncy, and B. Huet. Finding Media Illustrating Events. In *ACM International Conference on Multimedia Retrieval*, Trento, Italy, 2011.

[3] R. Mattivi, J. Uijlings, and et. al. Categorization of a collection of pictures into structured events. In *Proceedings of the 2nd ACM ICMR*, June 2012.

[4] T. Reuter and P. Cimiano. Event-based classification of social media streams. In *International conference on Multimedia Retrieval*, pages 22–22, 2012.

[5] M. R. Trad, A. Joly, and N. Boujemaa. Large scale visual-based event matching. In *Proceedings of the 1st ACM ICMR*, pages 1–7, Apr. 2011.

[6] R. Troncy, B. Malocha, and A. Fialho. Linking Events with Media. In *6th International Conference on Semantic Systems*, Graz, Austria, 2010.

Dynamic Multimedia Exploration Using SIFT Matching

Jakub Lokoč, Lukáš Navrátil, Jáchym Toušek and Tomáš Skopal
Charles University in Prague, Faculty of Mathematics and Physics,
Malostranské nám. 25, Prague, Czech Republic
www.siret.cz

ABSTRACT

In this demo paper, we focus on the dynamic multimedia exploration techniques which are an intuitive, effective and entertaining way to present a pre-selected subset of a multimedia database to the users. More specifically, we present an exploration schema employing a similarity model based on SIFT descriptors that can be used to explore image database according to regions in the images. We also provide a simple mechanism to reduce the number of nonrelevant SIFT descriptors in the query image. The reduction of SIFTs in the query image improves the speed and fluency of the exploration process as demonstrated in our demo application.

Categories and Subject Descriptors

H.2.4 [**Systems**]: Multimedia databases; H.3.3 [**Information Search and Retrieval**]: Retrieval Models, Search Process

General Terms

Theory, Experimentation

Keywords

Multimedia exploration, SIFT descriptors, SIFT matching

1. CONTENT-BASED EXPLORATION

Internet-scale multimedia management systems (google, bing, yahoo) usually provide basic filtering mechanisms employing keywords or simple low-level features to reduce huge volumes of managed multimedia data. However, the filtering process can still result into very large sets and thus other techniques, like the *content-based multimedia exploration* [1], are being designed. To provide the exploration facility, the multimedia data have to be transformed to an *exploration structure* employing the content of the data in the form of descriptors and a proper similarity function. The exploration structure is usually a graph with weighted edges where the nodes represent multimedia objects and the edge weights stand for similarity between them. Such a structure can be evaluated beforehand for huge multimedia collections or online in a meta-search systems combining the text-based retrieval with a content-based reranking/exploration functionality. The Smart Image Retrieval system (SIR) [3] is

an example of such online content-based meta-search exploration system. The SIR system first issues a keyword query to a text-based image retrieval system and immediately extracts descriptors (so-called feature signatures) for the resulting images. All pairs of the feature signatures are then compared by the signature quadratic form distance and finally the exploration graph is created and returned to a client. The client implements ZoomIn/ZoomOut operations and employs the particle physics model for visualization of the actually visible subset of the exploration graph. Since the utilized signature quadratic form distance is a global similarity measure, the exploration cannot reflect similarity of local regions. To overcome this limitation, we utilize the similarity model based on the SIFT descriptors for the multimedia exploration purposes. In the following section, we describe our exploration engine and discuss in detail the involved SIFT selection, matching and ranking techniques.

2. SIFT BASED EXPLORATION

The SIFT introduced by Lowe [4] describes an image by a set O of n-dimensional image feature vectors $o_i \in O \subset R^n$ which are invariant to image scale and rotation and can be used for robust matching of objects depicted in the image (often using L_2 distance). The SIFT-based matching of two images represented by SIFT sets O, P is achieved by mapping of $o_i \in O$ to the closest $p_j \in P$ if $L_2(o_i, p_j)/L_2(o_i, p_k) < \phi$, where $p_k \in P$ is the second closest SIFT descriptor to o_i and ϕ is a user defined threshold value. Our SIRSIFT meta-search exploration demo [5] is a client-server application, where the client utilizes the particle physics model for layout presentation [2] and issues exploration queries to the server web application. The web application is initialized by a keyword query, that starts the download and SIFT extraction process. To improve the performance of the service, the images and extracted SIFT descriptors are cached for a user-defined time period. The download process and the feature extraction run in the pipeline mode and so the overall time needed to get SIFT descriptors is decreased. In the following we describe the server-side processes in more detail.

2.1 Reducing Nonrelevant SIFTs In The Query

Whereas usual SIFT matching tasks try to match all SIFTs from all query images to all SIFTs in the database images, the exploration techniques provide mechanisms to simply put stress on the desired location in the query image. Usually, the exploration is navigated using the double click or mouse wheel operation over a user selected image. In our application, we determine the actual cursor location in the image and select only such SIFT descriptors from the image, which are close to the cursor. More specifically, we perform a kNN query in the picture coordinate system using the Euclidean distance and use only k closest SIFT descriptors (set of query descriptors Q) to the cursor location. Such simple specification of the query can significantly improve the matching quality, while the user is not bothered by a complex query region specification task.

2.2 SIFT Matching

In our SIFT-based exploration application we utilize a modification of the Lowe's matching algorithm. Instead of matching the query SIFTs $q_i \in Q$ to each image O separately, we match SIFT $q_i \in Q$ to union of all SIFTs from all images in the dataset. Hence, only such images are considered that contain the most similar SIFT descriptors to q_i, where only the k (≈ 40) most similar SIFT descriptors are detected. To further reduce the set of k candidates, we employ a similar technique as used in the original Lowe's matching algorithm. We evaluate the distance to the j-th closest descriptor (where $j = k * f$, f is approximately 10-20) and set the threshold for matching as $\theta = L_2(q_i, o_j)/L_2(q_i, o_k)$, where o_k (o_j) is the k-th (j-th) closest descriptor to q_i in the collection of all extracted descriptors D. The query descriptor $q_i \in Q$ is then mapped to candidate o_m in case o_m is the only descriptor from image O in the distance interval $(0, d(q_i, o_m) * \theta)$. The utilized SIFT matching technique has two advantages for meta-search exploration needs – first, an index can be employed for k-NN search in the set of all SIFTs, second, the distinctiveness of the matched SIFTs can be considered.

2.3 Similarity Modelling

As a result of the described SIFT matching technique, the set of mapped SIFT descriptors o_j is assigned to each query SIFT q_i. Reversely, all the mapped SIFT descriptors can be grouped according to the images they belong to, in other words, we can determine the set of all mappings $(q_i, o_j) \in M$ between the query image Q and a matched image O. The set of mappings between Q and O is then used to evaluate the similarity function. We have designed two similarity functions, where the first employs just distances between mapped SIFTs

$$sim_{dist}(Q, O) = \sum_{(q_i, o_j) \in M} \frac{1}{L_2(q_i, o_j)}$$

and the second uses also the distribution of mapped SIFT descriptors

$$sim_{center}(Q, O) = \sum_{(q_i, o_j) \in M} \frac{1}{L_2(q_i, o_j)} * \frac{1}{(max\{avgDist_j, m\})^{1/3}}$$

where $avgDist_j = avg_{(q_i, o_j) \in M} L_2(o_j, c)$ and c is the center of all the mapped descriptors in image O, m defines minimal value (if just one descriptor is mapped). The second similarity function considers also the layout of mapped descriptors which is motivated by the fact, that all query descriptors q_i are close to each other because of the technique described in section 2.1. Although the SIFT descriptors are scale invariant, making use of the layout information improves the ranking function significantly and so we used sim_{center} as the similarity function between query object Q and all mapped images O. So far, we have evaluated the

similarity between the query image Q and all images O the SIFT descriptors of which were mapped to query SIFT descriptors q_i. From this set of images, we select the k most similar images to Q and for each pair of the images O_i, O_j, we evaluate the similarity function sim_{dist}. To calculate $sim_{dist}(O_i, O_j)$ we determine the matching set M as $M_{ij} = \{(o_i, o_j) | \exists q \in Q : (q, o_i) \in M_i \land (q, o_j) \in M_j\}$, that is formed by tuples (o_i, o_j) of descriptors from images O_i and O_j, that were mapped to the same query descriptor q.

Having calculated all the similarities between all selected images, we can create a graph-based exploration structure, where the nodes represent the images and the edges are similarities of the connected images. To reduce the number of edges, we can eliminate those with low weights (low similarity). The reduced exploration graph is then sent to the client implementing particle physics model as in the Smart Image Retrieval engine (SIR) [3].

3. CONCLUSIONS AND FUTURE WORK

In this demo paper, we have demonstrated the dynamic multimedia exploration techniques employing a similarity model based on SIFT descriptors that can be used to explore multimedia data according to their local regions. We have also provided a simple mechanism to reduce the number of nonrelevant SIFT descriptors in the query image which improves the speed and fluency of the exploration as demonstrated in our demo application. In the future, we plan to optimize the exploration process by SIFT indexing techniques (native or bag of visual words based) and approximate search techniques. We would also like to combine the SIFT descriptors with other popular descriptors like feature signatures or MPEQ-7 descriptors.

Acknowledgments

This research has been supported in part by Czech Science Foundation projects P202/11/0968 and P202/12/P297.

4. REFERENCES

[1] C. Beecks, T. Skopal, K. Schöffmann, and T. Seidl. Towards large-scale multimedia exploration. In *Proc. 5th International Workshop on Ranking in Databases (DBRank 2011), Seattle, WA, USA*, pages 31–33, 2011.

[2] T. M. J. Fruchterman and E. M. Reingold. Graph drawing by force-directed placement. *Software: Practice and Experience*, 21(11):1129–1164, 1991.

[3] J. Lokoč, T. Grošup, and T. Skopal. Image exploration using online feature extraction and reranking. In *Proceedings of the 2nd ACM International Conference on Multimedia Retrieval*, ICMR '12, pages 66:1–66:2, New York, NY, USA, 2012. ACM.

[4] D. G. Lowe. Distinctive Image Features from Scale-Invariant Keypoints. *International Journal of Computer Vision*, 60(2):91–110, Nov. 2004.

[5] L. Navrátil, J. Toušek, and J. Lokoč. Smart Image Retrieval using SIFT descriptors (SIRSIFT), SIRET Research Group, http://www.siret.cz/sirsift, 2013.

The AXES PRO Video Search System

Kevin McGuinness,
Noel E. O'Connor
CLARITY: Centre for Sensor
Web Technologies
Dublin City University, Ireland

Robin Aly,
Franciska De Jong
University Twente,
Netherlands

Ken Chatfield,
Omkar M. Parkhi,
Relja Arandjelovic,
Andrew Zisserman
University of Oxford, UK

Matthijs Douze,
Cordelia Schmid
INRIA, France

ABSTRACT

We demonstrate a multimedia content information retrieval engine developed for audiovisual digital libraries targeted at media professionals. It is the first of three multimedia IR systems being developed by the AXES project. The system brings together traditional text IR and state-of-the-art content indexing and retrieval technologies to allow users to search and browse digital libraries in novel ways. Key features include: metadata and ASR search and filtering, on-the-fly visual concept classification (categories, faces, places, and logos), and similarity search (instances and faces).

Categories and Subject Descriptors

I.4.9 [**Computing Methodologies**]: Image Processing and Computer Vision—*Applications*; H.5.1 [**Information Interfaces and Presentation**]: Multimedia Information Systems—*Video*

General Terms

Design, Experimentation, Human Factor, Algorithms

Keywords

Multimedia IR, Computer Vision, Video

1. INTRODUCTION

AXES is an EU FP7 project aimed at developing tools that provide various types of users with new engaging ways to interact with audiovisual libraries, helping them discover, browse, navigate, search, and enrich archives. To achieve this goal, the project is developing a series of digital library search and navigation systems tailored for different user groups: professional users, researchers, and home users. The AXES PRO system that we will demonstrate targets the first of these groups: the professional user. The system brings together traditional text based IR techniques and state-of-the-art computer vision and content based multimedia search technologies, enabling the end user to leverage this combination of technologies in novel ways.

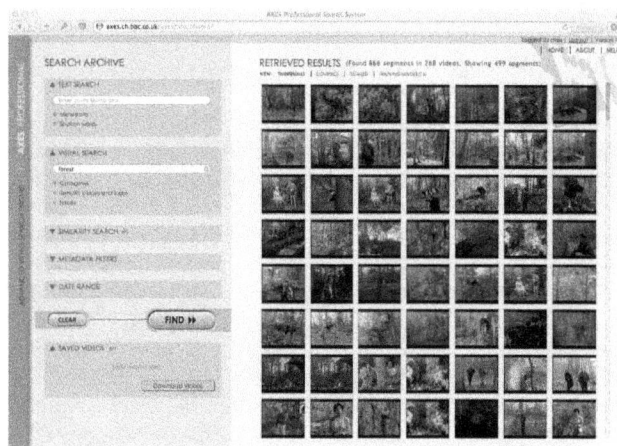

Figure 1: Screenshot of the AXES PRO system showing the thumbnail view of the search results.

2. SYSTEM OVERVIEW

User interface. AXES PRO has a browser-based UI composed of two panels: search archive and retrieved results. The search archive panel allows users to formulate queries using text and images. It supports visual search, metadata and ASR text search, metadata and date range filters, visual similarity search, and video saving and download. The results panel shows the query results in various ways.

The user interface includes three different result views: thumbnails, compact, and detailed. The thumbnails view (Figure 1) shows only thumbnails of the key frames associated with each result, allowing the user to visually browse through many results quickly. This view is most useful when the user is primarily interested in the visual appearance of results, as may be the case in a known-item or instance search scenario. The detailed view (Figure 2) shows more detailed information about each result, including the video title, language, creator/publisher, creation date, license, video description, clip duration, position of the clip in the video, and information about why the clip was retrieved (matched on text, or visual similarity, etc.). This view is most useful in scenarios where the user wishes to retrieve video segments by title or description. The extra detail, however, means that

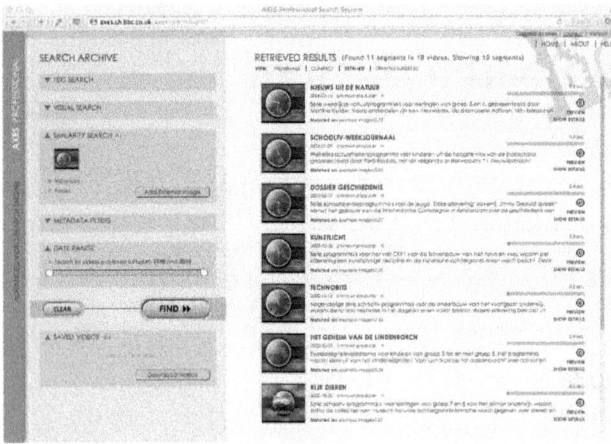

Figure 2: The detailed view of the search results.

fewer results can be shown simultaneously to the user. The compact view provides a middle ground between the detailed and thumbnail view, showing less information in a compact layout that allows more results to be shown simultaneously.

Text search. The system stores and indexes all metadata and spoken words available at index time. Spoken words are extracted from content using automatic speech recognition, but can also be provided in the form of transcripts. The user interface supports basic text-based search of these fields using a standard search and check box interface. This allows, for example, the user to search for videos by title, by description, or for videos containing specific spoken phrases. Queries may also use standard IR Boolean conjunctives, such as AND and OR. Users can also filter results on specific metadata fields and constrain the results by publication date.

Visual search. The user interface supports text-based queries that are used in conjunction with an external search engine to collect exemplars and train visual concept classifiers on-the-fly. The text query from the user is used to gather a representative sample of images from an external source. The current implementation uses Google Images to find the top-n images for the query. The system also retains a fixed collection of arbitrary images assumed to be non-relevant. Using this set of positive and negative examples, the system then trains a discriminative classifier (for example, a support vector machine) using image descriptors extracted from the examples. The trained classifier is applied to each image in the dataset in turn to produce a score, and the result list created by ranking the dataset by score.

The system supports three types of visual search: visual categories, faces, and specific places or logos. By allowing the user to specify the type of search, the system can use features and classifiers tuned to that particular class of visual search. For example, when the user chooses visual search by faces, the system detects faces, locates facial features using a pictorial structures based method, and extracts local descriptors at the detected facial landmarks. Technical details on the specific approaches and descriptors used can be found in [1, 2, 3, 4].

Similarity search. The system allows the user to drag and drop key frames from the retrieved results to be used for

similarity search. Visual queries can consist of a single image, or multiple examples. The user can also add images from their own computer or from an external URL. Region of interest selection is also supported.

Like visual search by text, the similarity search supports user selectable search types. The currently supported options are instance search and face search. Instance based similarity search uses the BigImbaz engine described in [5]. Face similarity search uses a system based on facial landmarks. A set of 9 facial landmark points are detected, located on the eyes, nose, and mouth. The face image is then warped using a similarity transform so that the landmark points are mapped as close as possible to a canonical configuration of a frontal pose. For each of the 9 landmarks, a histograms of oriented gradients (HOG) descriptor is extracted and these are concatenated to form the face signature. The high-dimensional face signature is then compressed into a lower dimensional signature by means of a linear projection. The projection matrix has been obtained by an off-line metric learning algorithm [6] so that the L2 distance between signatures after projection is small for face signatures of the same person and large for signatures of different people. The compressed face signature is then matched to face signatures in the database to find similar faces across other videos.

3. DEMONSTRATION

The demonstration will show the live system running on 400 hours of video content from the Dutch broadcaster NISV. We will demonstrate using various queries the available search modalities, including: on-the-fly visual search for categories, faces, specific places and logos; similarity search on instances and faces, text based search on ASR and metadata, and metadata filtering of results.

Acknowledgments. This work is supported by the EU Project FP7 AXES ICT-269980.

4. REFERENCES

[1] R. Arandjelovic and A. Zisserman. Multiple queries for large scale specific object retrieval. In *Proceedings of the British Machine Vision Conference*, 2012.

[2] K. Chatfield and A. Zisserman. VISOR: Towards on-the-fly large-scale object category retrieval. In *Proceedings of ACCV*, 2012.

[3] O. M. Parkhi, A. Vedaldi, and A. Zisserman. On-the-fly specific person retrieval. In *Proceedings of the International Workshop on Image Analysis for Multimedia Interactive Services*, 2012.

[4] R. Aly, K. McGuinness, S. Chen, N. E. O'Connor, K. Chatfield, O. M. Parkhi, R. Arandjelovic, A. Zisserman, UK B. Fernando, T. Tuytelaars, J. Schwenninger, D. Oneata, M. Douze, J. Revaud, D. Potapov, H. Wang, Z. Harchaoui, J. Verbeek, and C. Schmid. AXES at TRECVID 2012. In *Proceedings of the TRECVid Workshop*, 2012.

[5] Hervé Jégou, Matthijs Douze, and Cordelia Schmid. Improving bag-of-features for large scale image search. *International Journal of Computer Vision*, 87(3):316–336, 2010.

[6] M. Guillaumin, J. Verbeek, and C. Schmid. Is that you? metric learning approaches for face identification. In *Proceedings of ICCV*, 2009.

An Android Application for Leaf-based Plant Identification

Sofiene Mouine[†], Itheri Yahiaoui[†‡], Anne Verroust-Blondet[†], Laurent Joyeux[†],
Souheil Selmi[†], Hervé Goëau[†]

[†] Inria Paris-Rocquencourt 78153 Le Chesnay, France
[‡] CReSTIC Reims University, 51687 Reims, France

sofiene.mouine@inria.fr, itheri.yahiaoui@univ-reims.fr, anne.verroust@inria.fr,
laurent.joyeux@inria.fr, souheil.selmi@inria.fr, herve.goeau@inria.fr

ABSTRACT

This paper presents an Android application for plant identification. The system relies on the observation of leaf images. Unlike other mobile plant identification applications, the user may choose the leaf characters that will guide the identification process. For this purpose, two kinds of descriptors are proposed to the user: a shape descriptor based on a multiscale triangular representation of the leaf margin and a descriptor of the salient points of the leaf. The application achieves good identification accuracy and provides Android users a useful system for plant identification.

Categories and Subject Descriptors

H.5.1 [**Information Interfaces and Presentations**]: Multimedia Information Systems

General Terms

Algorithms, Experimentations

Keywords

Android application, plant identification, leaf descriptor, shape representation, local descriptor

1. INTRODUCTION AND MOTIVATION

Identifying plants is a challenging task considering the large number of existing species in the world. The inter-species similarity and the intra-species variability make the identification task particularly difficult and time consuming. We present here a practical plant identification tool based on the visual information provided by leaves. Our tool is an Android application which has been developed within the Pl@ntNet[1] project. The application is intended for mobile devices to allow a user to identify plants on the spot. It can also be used as an observation collector tool to enrich the knowledge database. Unlike similar applications where the identification is a black-box processing, our mobile system enables the user to choose a specific leaf descriptor (margin, venation points, both of them) that will be used as the basis of identification. Within this application, we focus on a

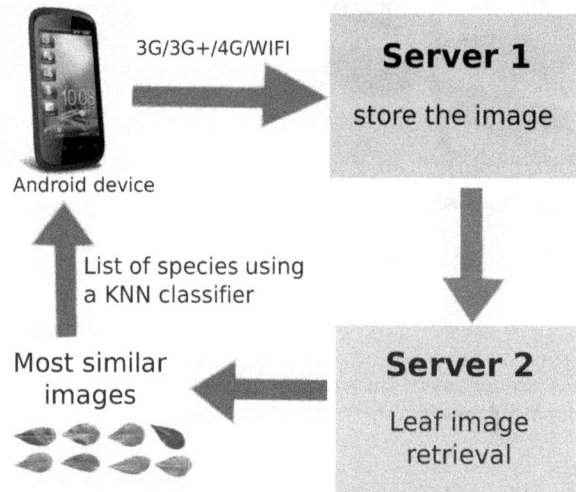

Figure 1: Plant identification process

set of leaf descriptors that have shown a noteworthy performance on several public leaf databases. In addition to leaf species identification, the user will also be able to compare the effectiveness of the descriptors for a given leaf image.

2. PLANT IDENTIFICATION PROCESS

The plant identification process is summarized in Figure 1. The user captures a leaf image with an Android device. Hypotheses made on the taken images are the same as those in [4]: the image contains a centred single leaf on a uniform background. Before launching the identification, the user has to select a leaf character that will be the basis of the identification (margin, venation points). Then, the leaf image is sent to a primary intermediate server with a degraded quality to save bandwidth. However, this step requires an adequate bandwidth. For this purpose, a 3G network or later networks are required. The role of the primary server is to store the image in order to broaden the knowledge about plant species. The identification step is performed on the second server using the descriptor previously selected by the user. The descriptors have been embedded in the IKONA content-based image retrieval system [1]. Finally, a

[1]http://www.plantnet-project.org/

ranked list of leaf species is returned and displayed on the Android device (cf. Figure 2). We use a knowledge database, which is off-line indexed using each of the descriptors suggested to the user. On the other hand, the signature of the image sent by the user is computed on-line and a large scale matching algorithm returns the most similar images [3]. A KNN Classifier is then used to build a list of species.

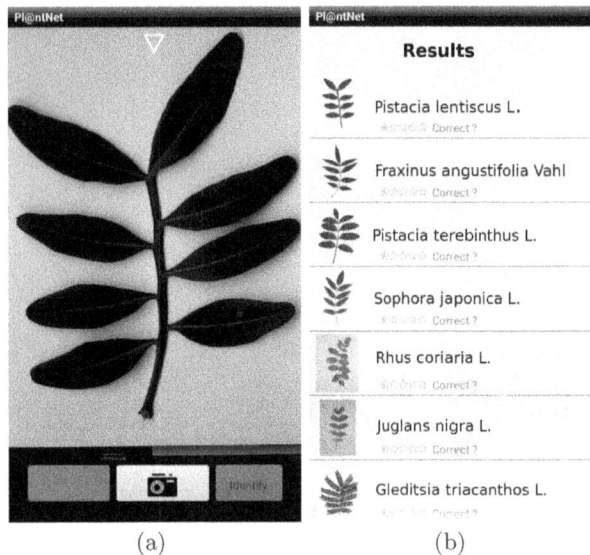

(a)   (b)

Figure 2: Screenshots of the Android application (a) Leaf image taken on a uniform background (b) Identification results. A ranked list of species is returned

2.1 Knowledge database

To identify the species of a leaf image, a retrieval technique is used. We need to have a knowledge database, i.e. a collection of annotated leaf images where a plant species is associated with each leaf image. This database will be used to find the most similar images to a query image. To do so, we use a subset of the training set of ImageCLEF 2012 plant identification task [2] freely available[2]: the training sets of scans and scan-like images are merged into one to form our knowledge database. It contains 6698 images belonging to 122 species. Thus, our Android application make it possible to identify leaves from 122 different species.

2.2 Architecture

The linkage between the GUI on the mobile device and the identification system on the second server is done by a RESTful java web service which offers an attractive scalable computing architecture. In our case, our RESTful identification web service can be either a server or a client. It plays the role of a server when it receives the leaf image taken by the user. It is a client when it interfaces the identification server using the selected descriptor. The data exchange between the web service and the identification server is ensured via sockets. Besides the abstraction of the architecture, the web service allows simple communication between the Android device and our identification system.

[2]http://imedia-ftp.inria.fr:8080/imageclef2012/ImageCLEF2012PlantIdentificationTaskFinalPackage.zip

2.3 Plant identification methods

Two kinds of methods are used within the Android application:
- A shape-based approach that describes the leaf margin using a multiscale triangular representation [6].
- A shape context based descriptor $SC2$ that represents the salient points of the leaf (essentially venation points) in the context defined by the leaf boundary [5].
- The combination of the methods mentioned above by a late fusion algorithm.

These techniques have shown their effectiveness for leaf image retrieval. The $SC2$ descriptor was tested on the ImageCLEF2011 leaf dataset. The shape-based approach using multiscale triangles has been evaluated on four public leaf datasets: Swedish, Flavia, ImageCLEF 2011 and 2012. It has also shown good robustness to partial occlusion. The identification results given by these descriptors can be found in [5, 6].

3. CONCLUSION

In this paper, an Android application for leaf species identification has been presented. It is based on a set of leaf descriptors that have given promising results on leaf datasets. The accuracy of the identification makes this application useful to amateur stakeholders as well as experts. Future work aims to expand the knowledge database by including leaf images from other species.

Acknowledgements

This research has been conducted with the support of the Agropolis Foundation through the Pl@ntNet project.

4. REFERENCES

[1] N. Boujemaa, J. Fauqueur, M. Ferecatu, F. Fleuret, V. Gouet, B. Lesaux, and H. Sahbi. Ikona: Interactive specific and generic image retrieval. In *International workshop on Multimedia Content-Based Indexing and Retrieval (MMCBIR)*, 2001.

[2] H. Goëau, P. Bonnet, A. Joly, I. Yahiaoui, D. Barthélémy, N. Boujemaa, and J.-F. Molino. The IMAGECLEF 2012 Plant identification Task. In *CLEF 2012*, Rome, Italy, Sept. 2012.

[3] A. Joly and O. Buisson. Random maximum margin hashing. In *CVPR*, pages 873–880, 2011.

[4] N. Kumar, P. N. Belhumeur, A. Biswas, D. W. Jacobs, W. J. Kress, I. C. Lopez, and J. V. B. Soares. Leafsnap: A computer vision system for automatic plant species identification. In *12th European Conference on Computer Vision (ECCV 2012)*, pages 502–516, Florence, Italy, Oct. 2012.

[5] S. Mouine, I. Yahiaoui, and A. Verroust-Blondet. Advanced shape context for plant species identification using leaf image retrieval. In *Proceedings of the 2nd ACM International Conference on Multimedia Retrieval*, pages 49:1–49:8, 2012.

[6] S. Mouine, I. Yahiaoui, and A. Verroust-Blondet. A shape-based approach for leaf classification using a multiscale triangular representation. In *Proceedings of the 3rd ACM International Conference on Multimedia Retrieval*, 2013.

Video2Book: Semi-Automatic Tool to Create Media Products from Videos on Smart Phones

Mohamad Rabbath
OFFIS - Institute for
Information Technology
Oldenburg
Germany
rabbath@offis.de

Volker Gollücke
University of Oldenburg
Oldenburg
Germany
golluecke@wi-ol.de

Susanne Boll
University of Oldenburg
Oldenburg
Germany
susanne.boll@uni-
oldenburg.de

ABSTRACT

Users nowadays increasingly use their smart phones to take photos and videos. Many of the users would like to create multimedia products such as physical photo books out of their photos or videos on the phone, however the screen of the phone is small for complicated editing and publishing process. In this demo paper we introduce an application that allows the user to automatically create a photo product out of his videos on the smart phone. The user can select one or several videos. The scenes of each video are detected using visual features, and for each scene a distinct good quality frame is selected. The videos are usually not very long and on average a video is 2 mins length in our dataset of users. We enrich the extracted representing frames with related photos from both the phone and from social networks like Facebook. We measure the similarity based on visual, metadata and social features. We apply a face recognition phase to enhance the accuracy of these features. At the end we compile the selected media content in an appealing photo product, that the user can edit later from any device. This process allows the user to make use of the phone videos to create appealing media products with little effort that suits the small screen.

Categories and Subject Descriptors

H.3.3 [**Information Search and Retrieval**]: Search process; H.3.3 [**Information Search and Retrieval**]: Selection process ; I.5.1 [**Models**]: Statistical

General Terms

Algorithms, Design, Human Factors

Keywords

smart phones, photo books, social media, social networks, multimedia retrieval

1. INTRODUCTION

With the rapidly growing market of smart phones users increasingly use their phones to take photos and videos and spend more time on photo and video applications. The report of [1] shows that on average the active smart phone user spent 231 minutes using photos and videos apps in March 2012 and this number is increasing. While most of these applications lie in the category of mul-

timedia sharing, till now very few help the user in creating tangible and virtual photo and video products directly from the mobile phone. Also the users may often share these photos or videos with friends in social networks such as Facebook, and recollecting them might be hard. In this demo paper we introduce an application that allows the user to easily create photo products such as photo books from the smart phone. The process copes well with the small screen of the mobile phone and requires minimal effort. The user can select one or more videos on the smart phone. The scenes inside each video are automatically detected using visual features. For each scene we calculate the sharpness of each frame within this scene and we select the frame with the highest sharpness as an indicator of the visual quality. Most of the videos on the mobile are short videos and need enrichment from related media content. We apply context-aware detection phase to automatically obtain media content related to the representative frames both on the phone and in social networks among user's contacts. At the end an aesthetic enriched photo book is created out of the video in an editable format.

2. DETECTING REPRESENTATIVE FRAMES

The user in this application is able to browse her videos and select those she wants on the smart phone. In order to cover all the important moments in the video we apply a scene detection approach such that introduced by [5]. This approach is computationally inexpensive and suitable to perform on the client, however the use of pixel difference between the frames makes it variant to the luminance and lighting conditions. Instead we calculate the distance between CEDD descriptors of the frames (colour edge directivity descriptor) [2]. However the CEDD is relatively expensive and therefore we do not calculate the distance between each consecutive frames but rather for each frames seperated by T window of time. If the distance D_{CEDD} is larger than a threshold $Th = 0.2$ then the process is repeated recursively with a smaller window of time $T/2$ till the boundary of the scene is detected. After detecting the boundaries between each two scenes one representative frame is selected for this scene. To efficiently detect a good representative frame for each scene we apply a fast wavelet-based algorithm introduced by [4]. The subbands of the DWT transform resulted from applying Low-High , High-Low and High-High pass filters are denoted as LH, HL, HH respectively. The energy of each subband in the logarithmic scale is calculated as descpribed in [4] for 3-levels of decomposition $n \in \{1, .., 3\}$. The overall energy in each level is defined as :

$$E_n = (1 - \alpha) \frac{E_{LH_n} + E_{HL_n}}{2} + \alpha E_{HH_n} \qquad (1)$$

Where E_{XY_n} is the energy of the respective subbands XY in level n. and the overall sharpness is defined as:

$$Sharpness = \sum_{n=1}^{3} 2^{3-n} E_n \qquad (2)$$

From each scene the frame with the highest sharpness is chosen.

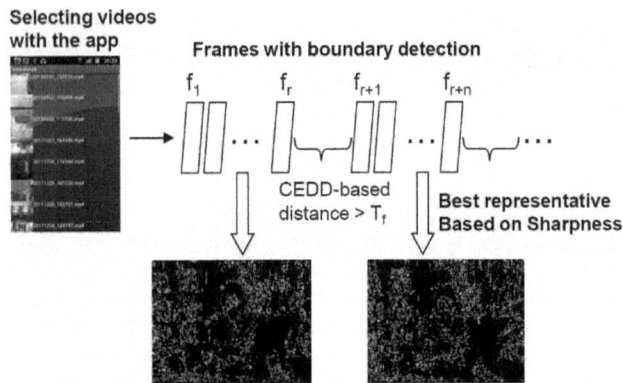

Figure 1: Detecting representative video frames on a smart phone.

We also offer an interactive refinement for each automatically extracted frame. The user is able to move from each representative frame in a step-wise way forward or backward to catch a specific important moments for the user.

3. ENRICHING WITH RELATED PHOTOS

The number of scenes in the phone videos are usually limited in number and need to be enriched with other media contents of the same event in order to create an appealing product. With the ever growing use of smart phones that are connected to the internet, people share their content directly or later in social networks like Facebook. It is a very challenging task to collect the related media content distributed in social networks. For this task we adopt the approach introduced in [3] where visual-based, tagged-based, friendship-based and structure-based features were exploited to connect the distributed content of events in Facebook. In our tool we automatically discover the related content in Facebook for each video frame. For this problem we first perform a face recognition approach on the mobile videos such that introduced by [6], however we use a social-aware approach which is a current research work of us. In this approach we estimate the likelihood of the presence of a person knowing the the pretense of others, and we exploit the currently existing Facebook tags of the user for this purpose. As visual features of the face we use the eigenface value with 32 dimensions after applying the PCA to obtain a relatively low dimensionality. The face recognition is performed as offline phase on the mobile when the user is not active.Using a probabilistic fusion approach by calculating the following probability:

$$p\left(event|f_{ij}\right) = \frac{p\left(F_{ij}|event\right)*p(event)}{p\left(F_{ij}|event\right)*p(event)+p\left(F_{ij}|\overline{event}\right)*p\left(\overline{event}\right)} \qquad (3)$$

Where $event$ denotes that two photos i, j belong to the same event, and $\overline{event}$ is its complement. F_{ij} is a set of visual-based, social-aware-based and structure-based features calculated between each two compared photos, and they are introduced in detail in [3] in addition to the facial features extracted from the face recognition approach. We retrieve the related photos of each previously extracted representative video frame, and allow the user to interactively select/deselect the retrieved photos as shown in Figure 2.

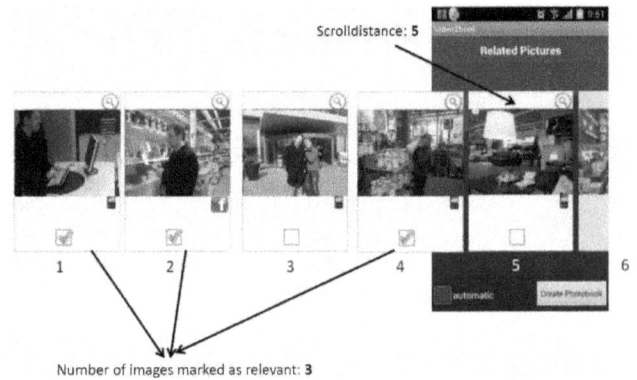

Figure 2: Detecting the related photos in Facebook of a video frame on the mobile. The user is able to deselect the undesired photos.

The enriched content allows the user at the end to obtain an appealing physical photo book with minimum authoring efforts, which can be as little as three clicks. A summarization of the whole process is shown in video [1].

4. CONCLUSION

In this demo paper we introduced a tool that enables the user to automatically create a product such as a physical photo book out of her videos on the smart phone with the minimum efforts. The representative video frames of each video are first detected. In the next step related photos of each frame are automatically retrieved from the shared photos of the user and her social contacts in Facebook, in order to collect enough suitable content to create an appealing photo product. In the detection step a face recognition approach is used as well as a mixture of features that are introduced in detail in other work of us. The user at the end can obtain a photo book out of her selected videos on the mobile.

5. REFERENCES

[1] photo-and-video-app-usage http://www.statista.com/statistics/232367/monthly-photo-and-video-app-usage-developmen

[2] S. A. Chatzichristofis and Y. S. Boutalis. Cedd: color and edge directivity descriptor: a compact descriptor for image indexing and retrieval. In *Proc. of the 6th Int. Conf. on Computer vision systems*, ICVS'08.

[3] M. Rabbath, P. Sandhaus, and S. Boll. Analysing facebook features to support event detection for photo-based facebook applications. In *ICMR'12*, pages 11–11, 2012.

[4] P. Vu and D. Chandler. A fast wavelet-based algorithm for global and local image sharpness estimation. *Signal Processing Letters, IEEE*, 19(7):423 –426, july 2012.

[5] X. Zeng, X. Xie, and K. Wang. Instant video summarization during shooting with mobile phone. In *Proc. of the 1st ACM Int. Conf. on Multimedia Retrieval*, ICMR '11.

[6] L. Zhang, L. Chen, M. Li, and H. Zhang. Automated annotation of human faces in family albums. In *Proc. of the eleventh ACM Int. Conf. on Multimedia*, MULTIMEDIA '03.

---

[1] http://www.youtube.com/watch?v=maG54MLPCVc&feature=youtu.b

Multimedia Interactive Therapy Environment for Children Having Physical Disabilities

Md. Abdur Rahman   Ahmad M. Qamar   Mohamed A. Ahmed

M. Ataur Rahman   Saleh Basalamah

Advanced Media Laboratory, Umm Al-Qura University

Makkah, Saudi Arabia

{marahman, amqamar, mamahmed, maataur, smbasalamah} @uqu.edu.sa

ABSTRACT

In this paper, we present an interactive multimedia environment that can be used to effectively complement the role of a therapist in the process of rehabilitation for disabled children. We use Microsoft Kinect 3D depth sensing camera with the online Second Life virtual world to record rehabilitation exercises performed by a physiotherapist or a disabled child. The exercise session can be played synchronously in Second Life. The physical activities of the users are synchronized with their virtual counterparts in the Second Life. The exercises can be recorded as well and made available for downloading to facilitate offline playback. A disabled child can follow the exercise at home in the absence of the therapist, since the system can provide visual guidance for performing the exercise in the right manner. Using the proposed system, parents at home can also assist the disabled child in performing therapy sessions in the absence of a therapist. Following the suggestions of therapists, the developed prototype can track several gestures of children who have mobility problems. Using a single Kinect device, we can capture high resolution joint movement of the body, without the need for any complicated hardware set up. The initial joint-based angular measurements show promising potential of our prototype to be deployed in real physiotherapy sessions.

Categories and Subject Descriptors

Computing Methodologies – Artificial Intelligence - Computer vision- Computer vision tasks- Biometrics

General Terms

Human Factors

Keywords

Kinect; Rehabilitation; Second Life.

1. INTRODUCTION

Recent advancements in several multidisciplinary areas such as 3D sensing, 3D virtual environment and ubiquitous multimedia environment have ushered in a new dimension of e-Health services for children with moderate physical disability. Using 3D sensors to measure improvement in patients with motor disabilities has many benefits as compared to doing so physically using conventional instruments that require physical contact with the subject. The technique is non-invasive and can hence be

applied seamlessly, repeatedly or incrementally without the intervention of a therapist or the awareness of the patient. Continuously generated sensory data can also inform the therapist about the speed of the joint movements which, to the best of our knowledge, is not possible to be measured with conventional non-invasive methods that require intervention from the therapist or technical staff. In [1] [4], the authors study the possibility of using Kinect for rehabilitation with young adults in an interactive environment. In [2], the authors devised a game to perform balance training exercises. In our research, we have built a multimodal multimedia game environment, which allows the user, either the therapist or the patient, to record a session with Kinect and tunnel the skeleton data to Second Life. The Second Life viewer uses user-skeleton data to render an avatar within the 3D game environment that imitates the movements of the user. The framework also contains an animation server to relay the skeleton data to another machine on the internet where a similar viewer can display the live user movements. The skeleton data can be saved to a file and played back later through the same viewer.

The remainder of the paper is organized as follows: Section 2 describes different modules of the developed prototype and their internals. Section 3 illustrates the implementation details. Section 4 outlines conclusive remarks and our future work.

2. DESCRIPTION OF THE SYSTEM

Figure 1 shows the salient components of the proposed multimedia therapy environment. We have leveraged the aforementioned advancements in a rehabilitation scenario for disabled children. In our proposed system we assume three types of *users*: disabled children, therapists and parents. As a *visualization interface*, we have used Second Life. An avatar is used to play the movements of the therapist. We assume that both the therapist and the disabled child use Kinect camera to either record or playback the therapy sessions. The session can be controlled by a menu driven interface as well as a speech-based interface. Details of the components of the system are as follows:

Sensory Data Manager processes the raw data stream coming from the Kinect device and extracts joint data from the input. The data set contains the locations of 20 body joints observed 30 times per second. ***Session Recorder*** records the exercise session which can then be saved to a user file through the session repository or forwarded to the media extractor for live-view in Second Life. The data can also be sent by the session recorder via network to an animation server that can play the session on a remote system running the Second Life viewer. ***Session Repository*** stores the session data to secondary storage so that it can be played back later in Second Life. ***User Profiles*** database is used to store detailed information about each disabled child such as family information, type of disability the child has, name of the therapist, types of therapy the child has to conduct, past history of therapy, etc. ***Animation Server*** facilitates the transmission of the session data over the network for remote viewing through the Second Life viewer. ***Media Extractor*** extracts session data, combines it with user preferences from the *User Profile* database and forwards it to the *Session Player*. The **Session Player** manages the movement of the avatar in the Second Life ***visualization interface***.

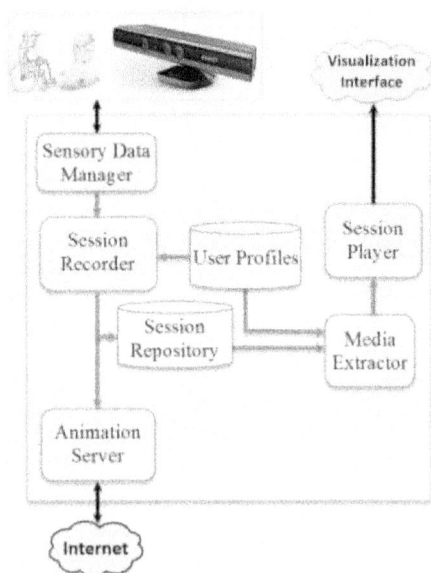

Figure 1. Block diagram of multimedia therapy environment.

The software environment is set up such that a therapist can record an exercise session. The session can then be transmitted live over the network or uploaded to a virtual rehabilitation center developed inside the Second Life virtual world. The virtual world center inside Second Life looks similar to the real center where the child goes for therapy. The child can log on to Second Life and visit the virtual center where the practice session is being played or has been made available for download. The child can then view the session being performed by an avatar on the screen. The system can record the child's session and send it to the therapist. Temporal data collected from a number of sessions over a long period can be used to monitor the effectiveness and progress of the rehabilitation process.

3. IMPLEMENTATION

The hardware used for our work consists of a PC running Windows 7 with 4GB of RAM. A Kinect for Windows device was attached to the system to capture joint data. The software platform used is RINIONS [3]. It can use both Microsoft and OpenNI [5] drivers to capture data from Kinect. Raw data captured from Kinect is processed to produce joint data. This data can follow three pathways. It can either be tunneled to the Singularity viewer application for Second Life or sent to an animation server over the network for remote viewing, e.g., by the parents. The remote viewing workstation should also have the Singularity viewer software running to display the session. The third option is to save the joint data to a repository. The same viewer can play back joint data from the repository over a network. Data played in the viewer appears in the form of an avatar performing inside Second Life.
As a sample exercise (see Figure 2), we have implemented a practice session that records the movement of the forearm from a

straight position to a folded position. In medical terminology, this movement is called "flexion-extension" of the elbow. The joint tracking facility records the co-ordinates of the wrist, elbow and shoulder joints that together form a triangle. The angle at the elbow is then calculated from this data. The measurements were comparable to those made by the therapist using a conventional device called a goniometer. This setup allows the therapist to record the angle of movement as well as the speed. Goniometers can only help a therapist record the angle in a static position by placing the device on the body of the subject. Our proposed technique is non-invasive and hence suits children who do not show enough patience with therapy sessions.

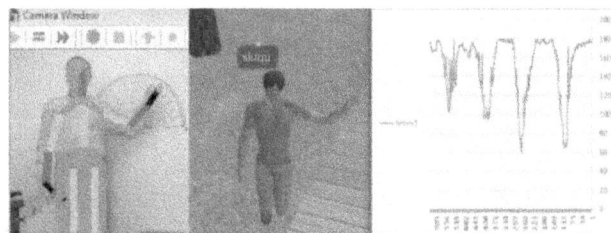

Figure 2. An instance of the Second Life virtual environment (center) mapped to physical environment (left) with the graph of the angle at the elbow formed by the moving arm (right).

4. CONCLUSION AND FUTURE WORK

Using off the shelf 3D sensor hardware with the Second Life virtual world, we have developed a multimedia environment where a trainee can view or download a physical training session performed by an avatar that was originally recorded by a trainer. It can also compare the two sessions to measure the level of conformity between them. With more data, statistical analysis can be done to measure the improvement in the subject's mobility. We have also implemented a forearm movement module to measure the mobility of the forearm in disabled children.

We envision further extension to the proposed demo. We are planning to add standard electronic medical record protocol for storing and sharing multimodal e-Health data. Our platform is extendable so that it can support additional natural user interfaces.

5. ACKNOWLEDGMENTS

This project was supported by the NSTIP strategic technologies program (11-INF1703-10) in the Kingdom of Saudi Arabia.

6. REFERENCES

[1] Chang, Y.-, Chen, S., and Huang, J. 2011. A Kinect-based system for physical rehabilitation: a pilot study for young adults with motor disabilities. *Research in developmental disabilities*, 32(6), 2566–2570.

[2] Lange, B. et al. 2012. Interactive game-based rehabilitation using the Microsoft Kinect. *2012 IEEE Virtual Reality*, 171–172.

[3] http://www.nsl.tuis.ac.jp/xoops/modules/xpwiki/?Rinions

[4] Harley, L. et al. 2011. The Design of an Interactive Stroke Rehabilitation Gaming System. *Proc. of the 14th Intl. Conf. Human-computer interaction: users and applications*, Orlando FL, 167-173.

[5] OpenNI, http://openni.org

Visualizing Progressive Discovery

Arjun Satish
University of California, Irvine
arjun@uci.edu

Ramesh Jain
University of California, Irvine
jain@ics.uci.edu

Amarnath Gupta
University of California, San
Diego
gupta@sdsc.edu

ABSTRACT

Computational problems are increasingly relying on context-aware approaches for tractable solutions. Usually, these approaches statically link additional sources of information to those already present in the problem space. We have been building CueNet, a context discovery framework, which will dynamically discover the most relevant context for a given application problem. In this demonstration, we will show how the identities of people in personal photos can be discovered through contextual information. We present Picatrix: an event based photo browsing web interface. Users can select a photo, and see a live visualization of how our context discovery algorithm, seeded with the initial information, discovers context from different data sources, and uses it to tag the faces in the given photo.

Categories and Subject Descriptors

H.5.1 [**Multimedia Information Systems**]

General Terms

Algorithms, Visualization

Keywords

CueNet, context, discovery, photo, tagging, visualization

1. INTRODUCTION

Some of the best advances in image retrieval have been due to disruptions in the image capture technology. For instance, statistical techniques have benefited with the advent of color images. The introduction of EXIF metadata in all digital cameras has given more variables to reason over the image content. In the last few years, smartphones have changed the way we looked at personal photographs. The interesting thing to note here is that the photos are exactly same as their counterparts from a few years ago, in the sense that they record the same kind of CCD sensor values in RGB format, with EXIF metadata containing approximate GPS locations. The disruption here is the smartphone itself, and the immersive sensor ecosystem it provides. We argue that photo capture is no longer an isolated activity, instead is a small part of a complex network of sensor data acquisition processes.

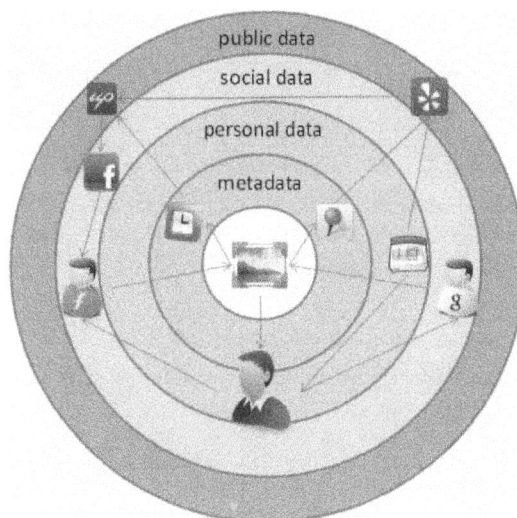

Figure 1: Navigation of the progressive discovery algorithm between various data sources.

The table below lists some sources of personal, social and public data whose acquisition can be conducted alongside the photo capture process.

PERSONAL	SOCIAL	PUBLIC
Emails	Friends Info	Places (yelp.com)
Calendar	Social Events	Events (upcoming.com)
Trip Planner	Tagged Photos	Conference Calendars

This situation is both a boon and a bane. A boon because this immersive sensor ecosystem provides a new window of opportunity; and a bane because now the contextual data related to a photo is non trivial to access, unlike the EXIF metadata, which is always part of the image file. This problem is amplified by the fact that there are thousands of potential data sources each containing terabytes of data. We have designed a context discovery algorithm which navigates between the different data sources to find the most relevant context for a given photo. In this demonstration, we will show how this algorithm finds the most relevant context to tag faces in a given personal photo.

2. PROGRESSIVE DISCOVERY

CueNet models an input photograph as a `photo-capture-event`[3] in an event graph[1]. This event graph containing the photo event, and its associated owner, is then used

(a) Picatrix - Our event based photo browsing interface.   (b) Algorithm discovering an event graph with five sources.

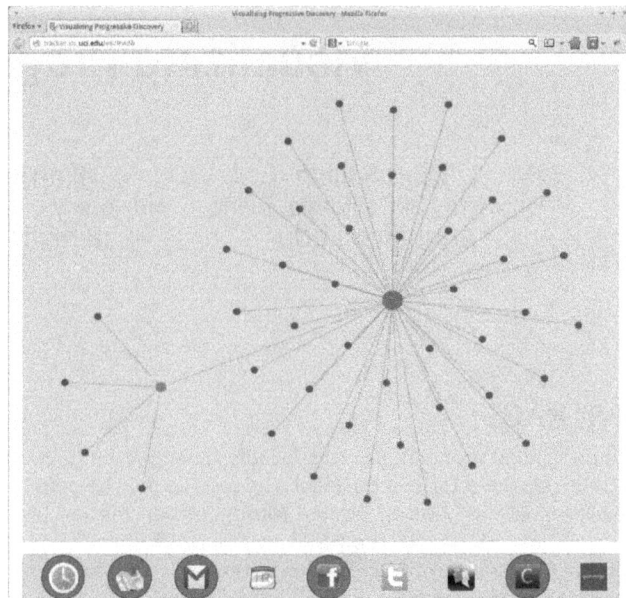

Figure 2: Demo Screenshots.

to construct queries to the different data sources discover events, and their associated properties. As data is brought in from different sources, they are merged into the graph.

Here is an **example** to illustrate CueNet's discovery process. Let's suppose that Joe takes a photo with a camera that records time and GPS in the photo's EXIF header. Additionally, Joe has two friends. One with whom he interacts on Google+, and the other using Facebook. The framework checks if either of them have any interesting event information pertaining to this time and location. We find that the friend on Google+ left a calendar entry describing an event (a title, time interval and name of the place). The entry also marks Joe as a participant. In order to determine the category of the place, the framework uses Yelp.com with the name and GPS location to find whether this was a restaurant, sports stadium or an apartment complex. If the location of the event was a sports stadium, it navigates to upcoming.com to find what event was occurring here at this time. If a football game or a music concert was taking place at the stadium, we can look at Facebook to see if the friend "Likes" the sports team or music band. By traversing the different data sources in this fashion, the number of people, who could potentially appear in Joe's photograph, was incrementally built up, rather than simply reverting to everyone on his social network or people who could be in the area where the photograph was taken. Finally, we can confirm who exactly was in the photograph by using face verification techniques[2], which will perform very well given that only two potential candidates exist. We refer to such navigation between different data sources to identify relevant contextual information as **progressive discovery**. Figure 1 shows this interaction.

3. DEMONSTRATION

During the demonstration, we will show how different photos obtain context from different sources depending on which

event(s) they were taken at. Specifically, We present the Picatrix web interface (figure 2(a) for a user to browse and navigate personal photos. As seen in the figure Picatrix provides a timeline to let users quickly sift through their different events. The user can select a photo, and the display shifts to a visualization of the available data sources, the extracted metadata from the photo, and an initial event graph containing the photo capture event, and the associated owner. When the user presses the `Play` button, the progressive discovery algorithm is initiated, and corresponding to its discoveries, graph nodes are generated on the event graph panel, and sources are highlighted on the source panel. The user can `Pause` the visualization and inspect the actual event/entity instances that were discovered; which source provided these instances; and how it was queried. Figure 2(b) shows a snapshot of the event graph and the state of the sources (similar to figure 1). By showing different discovery patterns for different photos, we will show the efficacy of the discovery algorithm.

A video of our demo can be seen here: http://www.ics.uci.edu/~arjun/cuenet/icmr-demo/.

4. REFERENCES

[1] A. Gupta and R. Jain. Managing event information: Modeling, retrieval, and applications. *Synthesis Lectures on Data Management*, 3(4), 2011.

[2] N. Kumar, A. C. Berg, P. N. Belhumeur, and S. K. Nayar. Describable visual attributes for face verification and image search. In *IEEE Transactions on Pattern Analysis and Machine Intelligence (PAMI)*, Oct 2011.

[3] U. Westermann and R. Jain. Toward a common event model for multimedia applications. *Multimedia, IEEE*, 14(1), 2007.

ObjectSense: A Scalable Multi-Objects Recognition System Based on Partial-Duplicate Image Retrieval

Shuang Wang[1], Yunfeng Xue[1], Lingyang Chu[1], Yuhao Jiang[2], Shuqiang Jiang[1]

Key Lab of Intelligent Information Processing, Institute of Computing Tech., CAS[1], Beijing, China

College of Information Science and Engineering, Shandong University of Science and Technology[2], Qingdao, China

{shuang.wang, yunfeng.xue, lingyang.chu, shuqiang.jiang}@vipl.ict.ac.cn[1]; yhjiang125@gmail.com[2]

ABSTRACT

In this demo, we present ObjectSense, a scalable object recognition system that recognizes multiple objects present in a static image or in the camera frames. Instead of applying learning based recognition framework, this system identifies objects through Partial-Duplicate Image Retrieval (PDIR) based method. First, objects are identified by measuring the similarity between an incoming image and reference image corpus that are labeled with the objects. To compute image similarities, we explore the Consistency Graph Model (CGM), which robustly rejects spatially inconsistent feature matches with the advantage of orientations and positions of local features. Then a kNN voting method is used to decide the object category based on the quantized image similarities. ObjectSense is scalable with promisingly high recall and accuracy, which fits well into recognition-guided shopping and human computer interaction. We built ObjectSense on two platforms, PC and Android.

Categories and Subject Descriptors

H.3.3 [**Information Search and Retrieval**]: Retrieval Models, Search Process; I.4.8 [**Scene Analysis**]: Object Recognition

Keywords

Multi-Objects Recognition, Partial-Duplicate Image Retrieval, kNN, Accuracy, Scalability.

1. INTRODUCTION

In recent years, computer-vision-based object recognition has seen its widespread application requirements across industries. However, state-of-the-art approaches are still challenged by problems of accuracy and speed.

The popular visual recognition works employ multi-class image classification-based framework, which usually proceed in two stages. First, the potentially emerged objects are represented by extracted visual features. Second, for each object label, a one-versus-all classifier is applied to reach a decision regarding the represented object. For this framework, the problems are: 1) Current classification methods still bring unsatisfactory accuracy rate. 2) Classification performance does not scale well with object classes. 3) Classification needs large training data to ensure its efficiency. 4) It does not work well when there are multiple objects in the view.

Our PDIR-based object recognition system has the following four advantages: 1) Scalable and stable. High accuracy rate is achieved for both small and large object corpus size. 2) High recall rate even when multiple objects appear. 3) No complex training or learning procedures are required. 4) Data corpus is incremental for new coming objects with few operations.

2. DATA CORPUS

For this demo, we generate a set of reference images for each object and take right the object as the ground-truth label for them. The reference images could be either downloaded from the Internet or taken with a camera of the real object. For each specified object, better performance will be achieved if reference images are under different imaging conditions (e.g. viewpoint, illumination, object distance). We consider such set of reference images to be an appropriate representation of corpus objects, some of which are displayed in Figure 1.

Figure 1: Objects from the data corpus

3. ALGORITHM

ObjectSense identifies objects by measuring the similarity between an incoming (or query) image and reference images of each known object in the data corpus and telling the most possible emerged objects based on the similarities.

We start with PDIR-based framework. In order to make this system robust to different imaging conditions such as viewpoint, illumination, occlusion and object distance(object size), the standard SIFT features [1] are extracted to represent the incoming image, which is expected to perform better for objects with rich texture information. Each SIFT will be quantized through a hierarchical vocabulary tree [2]. In this demo, we set the vocabulary size as 500,000. Two candidate SIFTs from query image and one corpus reference image are initially matched if they are assigned to the same visual word, known as a candidate match. However, because valid feature matches from the small duplicate object region, as a minority, may be overwhelmed by the rest noisy matches from large background region and thus weakening the relation between relevant images, we establish a mutual verification scheme between candidate matches through Consistency Graph Model (CGM), where each node corresponds to a candidate match and each edge weight corresponds to the mutual spatial consistency. We measure the mutual spatial consistency of two candidate matches in a coarse-to-fine manner through evenly sectored polar coordinate systems which softly quantize and combine the orientations and positions of the SIFTs. Consequently, spatially inconsistent matches will be removed by finding the most strongly connected subgraph within the CGM. After that, valid SIFT matches are held for the image similarity scoring pipeline together with the quantized mutual spatial consistency. The CGM greatly removes false recognition and brings high accuracy. Any feature match that passes the CGM could vote for its owner reference image, thus making the voting procedures for each object independent of each other. The independence of voting, together with the CGM, makes it possible to stably recognize every object in the incoming image, i.e. high recall. An inverted file [3] is used here to make the feature matching step very fast and to enable great scalability. New objects can be added to this system for recognition by simply collecting corresponding reference images and indexing them incrementally into the inverted file.

Now we have all corpus reference images scored based on their similarity to incoming image I_q. Next, we take kNN-like voting scheme to identify objects observed or labels for I_q. The jth corpus reference image labeled with the ith corpus object o_i is denoted by $I_j(o_i)$, $j \in [1, l_{o_i}]$. The final score of o_i will be calculated as follows:

$$s(o_i) = {}^1/_n \cdot \text{Top}(\text{SL}(o_i), n)$$

where

$$\text{SL}(o_i) = \{ \text{sim}(I_j(o_i), I_q) \mid j \in [1, l_{o_i}] \}$$

$\text{sim}(\cdot, \cdot)$ is the similarity score between two images, $\text{Top}(\cdot, n)$ takes the n largest elements. We consider o_i appears in I_q if $s(o_i) \geq t$, where t is a well-tuned threshold. Now let's assume that o_i is the ground truth label for I_q. If n is close to l_{o_i}, $s(o_i)$ will inevitably be small and false negative happens. If n is close to one, false positive rate rises. For this demo, we use n = 3.

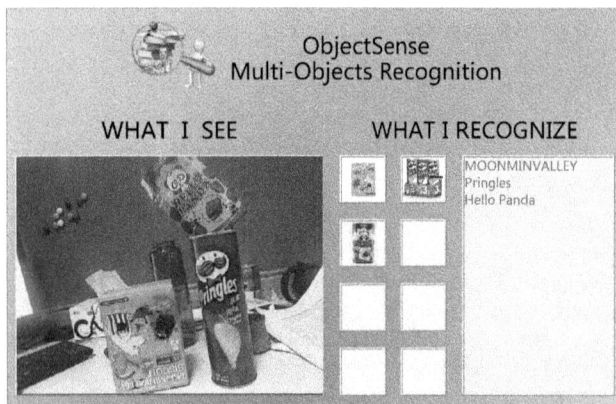

Figure 2: Screenshot of ObjectSense PC interface

4. INTERFACE

ObjectSense takes the current frame from the video sequence captured by a connected camera as the input and perform recognition algorithm on it. Real-time recognition is achieved by repeating the steps above. To present the outputs clearly and user friendly, ObjectSense displays each recognized object with both its name and its thumbnail as shown in Figure 2. We have also built a similar Android version for ObjectSense.

5. EVALUATION

To evaluate the performance of ObjectSense, we asked 20 users to test our system with 100 real objects, of which 70 are within the corpus while the rest are not. Each user conducted 200 recognition activities by interacting with ObjectSense holding one or several random objects in hand at a time. The average recognition precision rate is above 95% and the recall rate is higher than 90%.

Now, ObjectSense supports several hundred object categories and is feasible to scale to thousands with few expenses. Figure 3 shows the scalability of our system. The average time cost of recognition per frame stays relatively stable as corpus size (total number of corpus objects) increases to even 400. Moreover, SIFT extraction takes up a huge part of recognition in terms of time cost and our recognition framework is proved quite efficient.

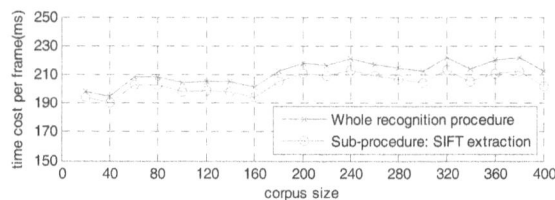

Figure 3: Speed test on different corpus sizes (total number of corpus objects)

6. CONCLUSION AND FUTURE WORK

In this demo, we have presented ObjectSense, a scalable multi-objects recognition system. We employ PDIR-based framework to score reference images in the data corpus and kNN-like scheme to vote for corpus objects based on the scores. ObjectSense works stably with high recall, accuracy and scalability.

In the future, we will experiment with some other image features to make ObjectSense more robust to objects with insufficient texture information. We will further bring ObjectSense closer to users' lives by making the best of the recognized objects such as e-shopping guide.

7. ACKNOWLEDGMENTS

This work was supported in part by National Basic Research Program of China (973 Program): 2012CB316400, in part by National Natural Science Foundation of China: 61070108, and 61035001, in part by the Key Technologies R&D Program of China under Grant no. 2012BAH18B02.

8. REFERENCE

[1] Lowe, D. G. (2004). Distinctive image features from scale-invariant keypoints. *International journal of computer vision, 60*(2), 91-110.

[2] Nister, D., & Stewenius, H. (2006). Scalable recognition with a vocabulary tree. In *Computer Vision and Pattern Recognition, 2006 IEEE Computer Society Conference on* (Vol. 2, pp. 2161-2168). IEEE.

[3] Sivic, J., & Zisserman, A. (2003, October). Video Google: A text retrieval approach to object matching in videos. In *Computer Vision, 2003. Proceedings. Ninth IEEE International Conference on* (pp. 1470-1477). IEEE.

Flexible Navigation in Smartphones and Tablets using Scalable Storyboards

Shuai Zheng[1,2,3], Luis Herranz[1,2], Shuqiang Jiang[1,2]

[1]Key Lab of Intelligent Information Processing, Chinese Academy of Sciences, Beijing 100190, China
[2]Institute of Computing Technology, Chinese Academy of Sciences, Beijing 100190, China
[3]School of Software Engineering, Beijing Jiaotong University, Beijing 100044, China
zs910504@yahoo.cn, luis.herranz@vipl.ict.ac.cn, sqjiang@ict.ac.cn

ABSTRACT

In this demo paper we present a multiscale browsing interface for handheld devices, in which the user can interactively change the scale of the storyboard to easily adjust the amount of information desired. Conventional and hierarchical storyboards provide one or very few possible lengths. In contrast, scalable storyboards allow the number of images and the storyboard itself to be adapted to the device constraints (e.g. aspect ratio, resolution) and navigation state with much finer granularity. Several levels and modes, including segment of interest, are provided for more intuitive and convenient navigation.

Categories and Subject Descriptors

H.3.1 [**Information Storage and Retrieval**]: Abstracting methods

General Terms

Algorithms, Design

Keywords

storyboards, browsing, navigation, adaptation, scalable summaries

1. INTRODUCTION

In recent years, mobile devices have become the main tool to access multimedia content. Typically, users use their phones or tablets to browse through hundreds of videos from diverse sources, ranging from online digital libraries (e.g. YouTube) to local video collections stored in the device. Current smartphones and tablets have enough storage capacity for hundreds of videos. For those reasons, intuitive and effective browsing interfaces are critical. When exploring large lists of videos, users cannot spend too much time visualizing the actual video. Instead, a quick idea about the content is enough, so compact visual abstracts are often used in search and browsing applications. In the case of mobile devices, these abstracts are often limited to the title and one keyframe. However, longer abstracts (e.g. storyboards, video skims) can provide more details about each video at the cost of slower browsing time. Conventional video summarization techniques[2] generate summaries with a certain

length (e.g. number of keyframes in storyboards, duration in video skims). This length is fixed and cannot be adjusted on demand, which is not very suitable for flexible navigation and visualization in dynamic interfaces. In this demo we present a flexible browsing interface in which storyboards can be adapted to different screen sizes and to the specific navigation state, based on the idea of scalable storyboards[1]. Compared with the other family of multiscale summaries, i.e. hierarchical summaries[3], scalable storyboards adaptation is much more flexible. In hierarchical summaries, users just can browse images in fixed navigation levels such as chapters or scenes, and navigate within units with strict boundaries. In contrast, scalable storyboards enable a more flexible adaptation with finer granularity. Users can select an arbitrary segment (segment-of-interest) to explore in more detail, and then the system will provide a more detailed storyboard focusing on that particular segment.

Compared with text and image processing, video analysis requires much more computational effort. Due to limited resources in mobile devices, such as processing capabilities or battery life, it is not feasible to include too complex analysis or analysis requiring to process all the frames (e.g. shot detection). To address this problem, we first extract a set of keyframes by sampling the video at constant intervals, obtaining a long storyboard, but approximately covering most of the content. Then we perform content analysis over the keyframes to organize them with a scalable structure (i.e. scalable storyboard), stored in a scalable description. When a certain number of keyframes is required in the storyboard, the system just needs to check the scalable description to retrieve the list of keyframes to create that particular scale of the storyboard. This simple adaptation strategy is very fast and requires very little computational effort.

2. SCALABLE STORYBOARDS

In general, when a new storyboard with a different length is required, the summarization process needs to be executed again, with appropriate parameters. In contrast, with scalable storyboards the analysis algorithm is executed only once, and extracting summaries with different lengths on demand is very simple and fast. We use a scalable representation based on hierarchical clustering[1]. The keyframe rate is one keyframe per minute, which is often more than enough for explorative browsing, and also not too high to allow fast videos analysis (e.g. the tablet used in the tests can process one hour videos in just a few seconds). During the interaction, the system solves an adaptation problem, in which the number of images required is dynamically computed based

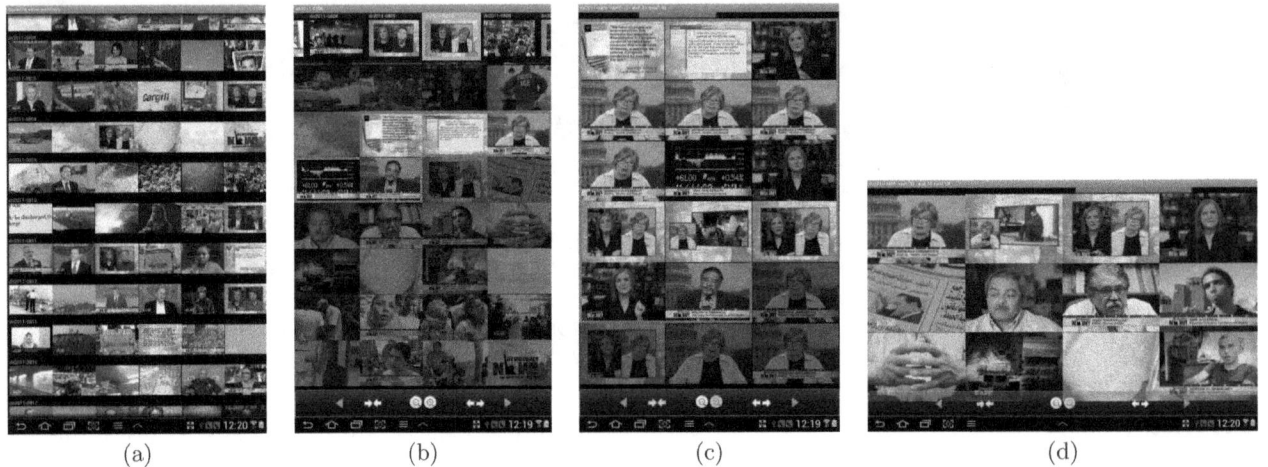

Figure 1: Navigation using scalable storyboards: a) collection browser, b) storyboard of the full video with a segment-of-interest highlighted, c) storyboard of the segment-of-interest conveniently scaled, d) landscape interface after rotation.

on device constraints (mainly display size/resolution) and the current navigation state (number of columns, temporal span, segment of interest boundaries). Then, the corresponding scale of the storyboard is displayed.

3. INTERACTION MODEL

The system provides navigation in three different levels (*collection*, *video* and *segment*), that can be dynamically changed by the user during the navigation process. Within each of these levels, the user can navigate through different adaptation dimensions:

- *Summarization detail*, related to the amount of information presented per time or area unit. Typically the user interface allows to adjust this scale indirectly by increasing or decreasing the number of columns of the storyboard.

- *Temporal span*, corresponding to the temporal interval presented in the display area.

- *Temporal position*, related with the position in the timeline of the temporal interval.

The user interface and an example of navigation is shown in Fig. 1. The control bar enables navigation by zooming in summarization detail, to different videos/segments and changing the temporal span. Pinch and flick gestures are also implemented to provide intuitive multitouch interaction. The collection browser (see Fig. 1a) displays a list of videos, in which each row represents the storyboard of a certain video item in the collection. Using the navigation controls, users can dynamically change the number of images in the storyboard to show fewer but larger images, or more result videos. When the user clicks on certain item, a full page storyboard is shown (video level, see Fig. 1b). In addition to summarization zooming, the user can change the temporal span and the temporal position of the segment, which provides navigation at segment level (see Fig. 1c and d). The duration and the temporal position of the segment is shown as a blue rectangle. A more flexible tool is the segment of interest navigation, which allows the user to select

several consecutive images and zoom to that particular segment (shown highlighted and with a red frame in Fig. 1b and c). Using scalable storyboards, the length of the storyboard is selected automatically to fit as many images as possible in the available display area with a very fine granularity of one image. The same mechanism also enables adaptation to different devices or adaptation to other orientation when the device is rotated (see Fig. 1d).

4. CONCLUSIONS

In this demo we have presented a browsing interface of video collections which allows users to have quick navigation at different levels, and providing functionality to dynamically change the detail scale. It also enables zooming to an arbitrary segment of interest to get more detailed information. The core of the interface is based on scalable storyboards, which enables displaying suitable storyboards regardless of the display area and navigation state.

Acknowledgments

This work was partly supported by the National Natural Science Foundation of China under Grants 61150110480 and 61070108, by the Chinese Academy of Sciences Fellowships for Young International Scientists under Grant 2011Y1GB05 and by the National Basic Research Program of China (973 Program): 2012CB316400.

5. REFERENCES

[1] Luis Herranz. Multiscale browsing through video collections in smartphones using scalable storyboards. In *ICME Workshops*, pages 278–283, 2012.

[2] Ba Tu Truong and Svetha Venkatesh. Video abstraction: A systematic review and classification. *ACM Trans. on Multimedia Computing, Communications and Applications*, 3(1):3, 2007.

[3] Xingquan Zhu, Jianping Fan, Ahmed K. Elmagarmid, and Xindong Wu. Hierarchical video content description and summarization using unified semantic and visual similarity. *Multimedia Systems*, 9(1):31–53, July 2003.

ZhiWo: Activity Tagging and Recognition System for Personal Lifelogs

Lijuan Marissa Zhou, Cathal Gurrin, Zhengwei Qiu
CLARITY, School of Computing, Dublin City University
Collins Avenue, Glasnevin, Dublin 9, Dublin, Ireland
{mzhou,cgurrin}@computing.dcu.ie, zhengwei.qiu2@mail.dcu.ie

ABSTRACT

With the increasing use of mobile devices as personal recording, communication and sensing tools, extracting the semantics of life activities through sensed data (photos, accelerometer, GPS etc.) is gaining widespread public awareness. A person who engages in long-term personal sensing is engaging in a process of lifelogging. Lifelogging typically involves using a range of (wearable) sensors to capture raw data, to segment into discrete activities, to annotate and subsequently to make accessible by search or browsing tools. In this paper, we present an intuitive lifelog activity recording and management system called ZhiWo. By using a supervised machine learning approach, sensed data collected by mobile devices are automatically classified into different types of daily human activities and these activities are interpreted as life activity retrieval units for personal archives.

Categories and Subject Descriptors

H.4 [**Information Systems Applications**]: Miscellaneous; D.2.8 [**Software Engineering**]: performance measures

Keywords

Lifelogging, Activity Recognition, Lifelog Retrieval

1. INTRODUCTION

Sensor technology has become prevalent in recent years as the cost of wireless communication and digital sensing devices decreases. Hence we have seen that more and more people start to use various of sensors for recording their lives, from photo capture to personal healthcare monitors and loggers. The output of such sensing activities is large amount of personal sensor data that, if semantically analysed, has significant potential to provide insights into a personal activity.

Lifelogs can be captured in many distinct ways with an abundance of types of sensors, both wearable and non-wearable. Wearable sensors include Fitbit, Bodymedia, GPS locator, Looxie, mobile phones, biomedical wearable textiles, Sensecams, wearable video glasses, etc. Such sensors can record aspects of live activity both individually and socially. An example is the SenseCam, a wearable camera integrated with Passive Infrared (PIR) sensor and accelerometer designed to record scenes we experience[1]. It is also possible to capture

data from non-wearable sensors, such as environmental sensors or software sensors to capture our interactions with information. While there are many sources of sensor data, the challenge is in extracting meaningful semantics and providing appropriate retrieval facilities over vast lifelog archives.

Within an Information Retrieval framework, a search engine, such as Google, is a step on the way, in that it allows text based searching of hyperlinked multimedia content, but this is only part of the solution as lifelogs pose major semantic gap challenges that can not rely on the presence of latent human annotations to index content. However, early systems that have been developed show potential of addressing the challenge. Zhou et. al. developed a lifelog events browsing system for group sharing[6]. Lee and Luštrek et. al. both proposed to use wearable sensors to recognize activities[4, 5, 2]. In this work, we develop a browsing interface through a timeline of semantic life activities, called ZhiWo. We propose that the semantic life activities can be automatically extracted from sensor sources present in a modern smartphone (photos, GPS, accelerometer etc.) and that we can automatically segment life activities into a sequence of activities and present in an easy way to browse daily timeline. This could have many potential uses, from healthcare monitoring, to new sources of contextual data for omnipresent information retrieval, to general quantified-self inspired lifelogging. The demonstration presented here is part of a larger project that addresses the creation of a cognitive science inspired, densely linked, hypermedia archive (the MemoryMesh) of life activities that can be browsed and searched in an omnipresent manner using both mobile and desktop devices.

2. THE ZHIWO SYSTEM

ZhiWo is a prototype human activity recognition system based on a concept of *"Knowing Me"*. The data source for ZhiWo is a raw sensor stream sampled from a smartphone worn on the body. ZhiWo semantically processes the sensor stream to identify distinct user activities (e.g. walking, resting, commuting, eating, shopping, etc.) based on a machine learning model trained by human annotation of activities on the mobile device. It provides browsing techniques based on an activity time-line view and can support locating specific activities of interest from within large lifelog archives.

2.1 Data Gathering with Mobile Phone

To achieve the greatest accessibility of data gathering for various users, we developed an application for smartphones (Android OS) for collecting lifelogs (see Figure 1). Users col-

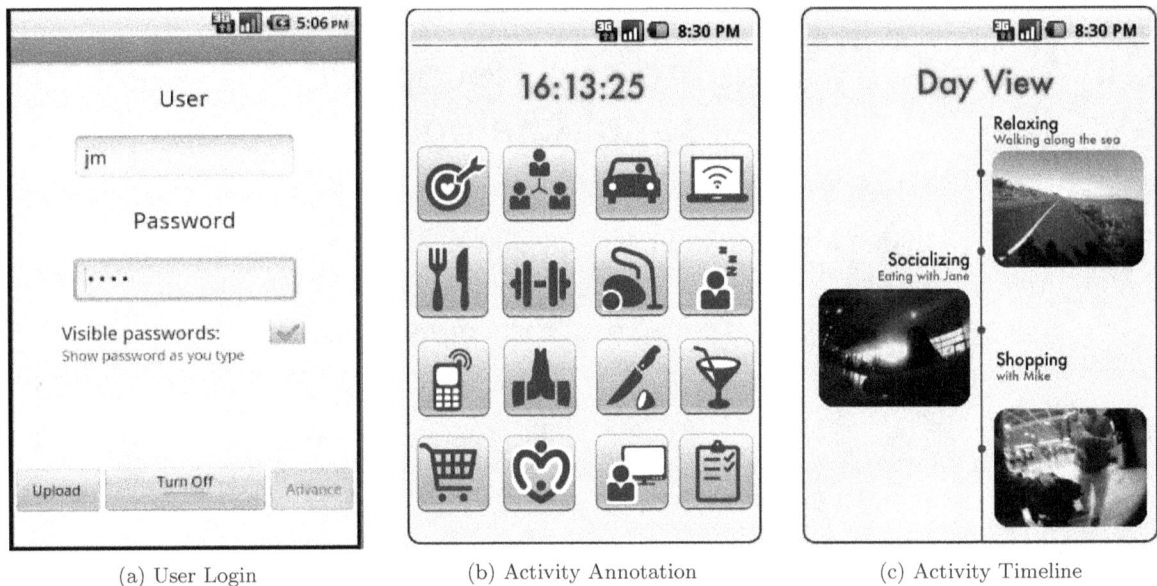

(a) User Login (b) Activity Annotation (c) Activity Timeline

Figure 1: Snapshots of the interfaces of ZhiWo personal daily activity tagging and recognition system

lect data by wearing the smartphone on a lanyard about the neck, or otherwise attached to the clothing in a manner so the smartphone camera is orientated towards the activities the user is engaged in. The data collected includes photos, tri-axial accelerometer readings, GPS, WIFI, bluetooth signals, and ambient environmental measurements such as temperature. This data can be either transferred to the server in real-time, uploaded on demand, or uploaded in bulk upon charging to save the battery power of the smartphone.

2.2 User Annotation of Personal Activities

Our experience shows that personal activity recognition models with supervised machine learning (ML) model outperform naive approaches of setting thresholds. Therefore, we applied a supervised ML method to identify different activities automatically (see Figure 1(b)). The ML technique we employed was an Support Vector Machine (SVM) with a linear kernel. We have identified a set of the sixteen most enjoyable life activities as defined in previous work of Kahneman et. al.[3] and our software automatically identifies appropriate activities, chosen from this sixteen. The source data for training the SVM is the sensor stream data, segmented into events, and the user annotation of life activities, which they can do by identifying their current activities through the interface of the smartphone application.

2.3 Activity Browsing and Retrieval

After training the activity recognition model, we obtain a predictive model to detect real-life human activities and to annotate them with the appropriate labels. The activity recognition output is a timeline of daily activities, segmented into days. Users can correct misclassified activities manually and this acts as an additional source for the activity detection model. As can be seen from Figure 1(c), users can view their past experiences as a sequence of activities across a timeline. Every activity is associated with a timeframe, an automatically selected keyframe image and a label, with a scale of days/months/years and can retrieve past activities according to a chronological or categorical query.

3. CONCLUSIONS

In this paper, we present a mobile platform for users to collect and manage their daily life activities based on lifelog sensor data. The system utilises SVMs to provide a predictive model to detect real-life human activities from sensor data collected from the mobile devices and to annotate them with appropriate labels. The aim of this research is to build a personal lifelog management and retrieval system based on activity recognition for personal life assistance.

4. ACKNOWLEDGEMENTS

This publication has emanated from research conducted with the financial support of Science Foundation Ireland under grant no. "SFI 11/RFP.l/CMS/3283".

5. REFERENCES

[1] S. Hodges, L. Williams, E. Berry, S. Izadi, J. Srinivasan, A. Butler, G. Smyth, N. Kapur, and K. R. Wood. Sensecam: A retrospective memory aid. In *Ubicomp*, pages 177–193, 2006.

[2] Y. Hong, I. Kim, S. Ahn, and H. Kim. Activity recognition using wearable sensors for elder care. In *Future Generation Communication and Networking, 2008. FGCN'08. Second International Conference on*, volume 2, pages 302–305. IEEE, 2008.

[3] D. Kahneman, A. Krueger, D. Schkade, N. Schwarz, and A. Stone. A survey method for characterizing daily life experience: The day reconstruction method. *Science*, 306(5702):1776–1780, 2004.

[4] S. Lee and K. Mase. Activity and location recognition using wearable sensors. *Pervasive Computing, IEEE*, 1(3):24–32, 2002.

[5] M. Luštrek and B. Kaluža. Fall detection and activity recognition with machine learning. *Informatica*, 33(2):197–204, 2009.

[6] L. M. Zhou, N. Caprani, C. Gurrin, and N. E. O'Connor. Shareday: A multi-modal lifelog system for group sharing. In *MMM*, 2013.

Connect Commercial Films with Realities

Cai-Zhi Zhu, Siriwat Kasamwattanarote, Xiaomeng Wu, Shin'ichi Satoh

National Institute of Informatics, 2-1-2 Hitotsubashi, Chiyoda-ku, Tokyo 101-8430, Japan

{cai-zhizhu, siriwat, wxmeng, satoh}@nii.ac.jp

ABSTRACT

Broadcast TV program is a quite informative media resource which records our daily life over the time. While for emphasizing real-time reporting, those out-of-date video archives once were elaborately created with high quality are always left without being fully used. In this paper, many known state-of-the-art retrieval technologies are integrated into a commercial film retrieval system, which manages to index a huge commercial dataset archived from five TV channels within recent three years. The final purpose is to connect images queried by users with our archived broadcast video dataset via searching relevant commercials and accessing their broadcast information, such as air time and replay frequency. This system also serves as one part of our ongoing broadcast TV program reusing project.

Categories and Subject Descriptors

H.3.3 [**Information Storage and Retrieval**]: Information Search and Retrieval – *clustering, retrieval models, search process.*

Keywords

Commercial Films; Broadcast Video Indexing; Video Search

1. INTRODUCTION

Although more and more media variants are available, as a traditional mass media, broadcast TV program still has a large amount of audiences for its high-quality and real-time advantages. Broadcast video can be regarded as a vivid diary which keeps recording what's going on around us in the world. On the other hand, those out-of-date TV programs are often undervalued for blindly pursuing real-time reporting. Therefore, leveraging multimedia computing techniques for reusing those archived TV video is undoubtedly meaningful. Taking advantage of most state-of-the-art image retrieval techniques, including RootSIFT [1], approximate k-means for training large vocabulary, LO-RANSAC [2] based spatial reranking, and average pooling of multiple images [3], in this demo we manage to connect TV commercials with query images provided by users. We have currently indexed TV commercials from five Japanese TV channels within recent three years, i.e. fifteen years' amounts in total. Given a query topic consisting of one or multiple images, our system is able to return relevant commercials, and allows users to play back videos or access their broadcast information, such as air time and replay frequency, by a click.

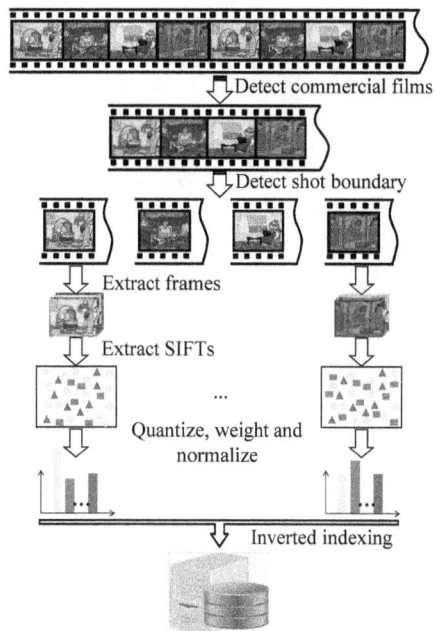

Figure 1. Offline indexing flowchart (better viewed in color).

2. FRAMEWORK

2.1 Database Preparation

We have currently archived three and a half years of full-day TV programs from seven Japanese TV channels. From which, we picked three-year (starting from Aug. 17th 2009 till Aug. 11th 2012) and five-channel (TBS, TV Tokyo, NET, FUJI and NTV) commercials into consideration. An effective and efficient dual-stage temporal recurrence hashing algorithm [4] is first applied to detect commercial films and cluster detected commercial reruns into groups. In our experiment only around 150 hours were needed to analyze all fifteen years' full-day TV programs and from which we get three years' duration commercials (Note in Japan commercials should last 15 or 30 seconds). In total we got around 4,500,000 commercials, and after clustering reruns we have 34,709 groups. We select a representative commercial from each group to form our database, around 250 hours in total.

2.2 Offline Indexing

The flowchart in Figure 1 illustrates how to index those representative commercial films. Basically we follow our pipeline [3] which was ranked first in TRECVID Instance Search 2011 challenge [5], but further optimize and expand some nodes in the pipeline with state-of-the-art retrieval techniques. Since each commercial film consists of multiple shots captured from different scenes, we first segment commercial films into shots and regard shots as units in the database (in total 356,019 shots). Then approximate k-means is applied to train a large vocabulary (up to one million) for quantization.

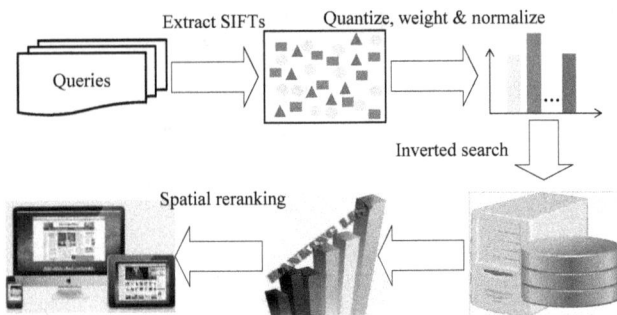

Figure 2. Online searching pipeline (better viewed in color).

Finally we build inverted indexing for all these commercial shots. The main novelty is that we take the average pooling of all images in each shot unit or query topic while computing similarity. More specifically, for each shot unit or query topic containing multiple images, average pooling is applied on multiple BoW vectors of those images and only one BoW vector will be output as its final representation. In this way the efficiency is ensured: (1) the database size equals to the number of shot units, and is irrelevant to the number of frames extracted from shot units; (2) The system will be queried only once even if multiple images contained in a query topic, and rank aggregation steps are completely avoided. The effectiveness of this method was proved in Instance Search 2011 challenge [3, 5].

2.3 Online Searching

The pipeline of online searching is shown in Figure 2. Note here a query topic may comprise one or multiple images, or even be a video segment. A similar process to the offline indexing will then be applied to get a BoW representation for the query. The initial ranking list will be ready after the inverted index search, and finally a LO-RANSAC [2] based spatial reranking will refine the ranking list. An example is shown in Figure 3.

2.4 Visualization of Broadcast Information

For each return commercial film, our demo system is able to visualize its replay frequency in different time granularities (hours,

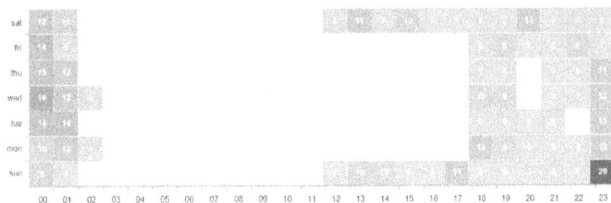

Figure 4. Replay frequency (shown in Arabic numbers) in hours of the commercial of Asahi beer returned in Figure 3.

days, weeks and months), and users can interact with the system from PC clients or iPad-like mobile devices. An interesting example is shown in Figure 4, which illustrates Japanese policy for the air time of beer commercials: beer commercials are not allowed to be broadcasted from 2:00 AM to 5:00 PM on weekdays and 2:00 AM to 11:00 AM on weekends. Note in Figure 4 slight noises exist in our grouping algorithm [3].

3. CONCLUSION

In this demo, we have shown a video searching system to connect commercial films with realities. With this system, users are able to access broadcast information of relevant commercials to their query images in hand thanks to our state-of-the-art video retrieval technique, which is super fast (searching time is less than a second) and accurate (leading in TRECVID2011 Instance Search).

4. REFERENCES

[1] R. Arandjelovic and A. Zisserman. Three things everyone should know to improve object retrieval. CVPR, 2012.

[2] O. Chum, J. Matas, and J. Kittler, Locally Optimized RANSAC. DAGM-Symposium. 2003.

[3] C.-Z. Zhu and S. Satoh. Large vocabulary quantization for searching instances from videos. ICMR, 2012.

[4] X. Wu and S. Satoh, Commercial mining based on temporal recurrence hashing algorithm and bag-of-fingerprints model. ICIP, 2011.

[5] D. Le, C.-Z. Zhu, S. Poullot, et al. National Institute of Informatics, Japan at TRECVID 2011. TRECVID, 2011.

Figure 3. Returned commercials by querying with a web image of "Asahi beer" (better viewed in color).

Expression Analysis In The Wild: From Individual To Groups

Abhinav Dhall
Research School of Computer Science
Australian National University, ACT 2601, Australia
abhinav.dhall@anu.edu.au

1. ABSTRACT

With the advances in the computer vision in the past few years, analysis of human facial expressions has gained attention. Facial expression analysis is now an active field of research for over two decades now. However, still there are a lot of questions unanswered. This project will explore and devise algorithms and techniques for facial expression analysis in practical environments. Methods will also be developed for inferring the emotion of a group of people. The central hypothesis of the project is that close to real-world data can be extracted from movies and facial expression analysis on movies is a stepping stone for moving to analysis in the real-world. For the analysis of groups of people various attributes effect the perception of mood. A system which can classify the mood of a group of people in videos will be developed and will be used to solve the problem of efficient image browsing and retrieval based on emotion.

Categories and Subject Descriptors

I.5 [**PATTERN RECOGNITION**]; I.4.8 [**IMAGE PROCESSING AND COMPUTER VISION**]: Scene Analysis; I.4.9 [**IMAGE PROCESSING AND COMPUTER VISION**]: Applications; H.5.1 [**INFORMATION INTERFACES AND PRESENTATION**]: Multimedia Information Systems

General Terms

Algorithms, Experimentation, Human Factors

Keywords

Group mood analysis, Expression analysis in the wild

2. OBJECTIVE

Automatic facial expression analysis deals with a computer based inference of a person's internal emotional state. It is an active field of research with applications in the field of human computer interaction, information retrieval and management, affective computing, medical diagnosis such as depression, stress, pain, lie detection and many others. With the growing popularity of data sharing and broadcasting web site such as YouTube, Flickr; everyday users are uploading millions of videos and images of social events. Generally, these video clips and images have been recorded in different conditions and may contain one or more subjects. From the perspective of automatic emotion analysis, these diverse scenarios are unaddressed. This PhD project aims at developing algorithms, techniques & applications for Facial Expression Recognition (FER) in practical environments.

3. MOTIVATION & BACKGROUND

Facial expression analysis has been a long studied problem [13], [3]. FER methods can be divided into static and temporal FER methods. Static methods generally deal with a frame only based FER [3]. Temporal FER methods deal with videos as human facial expressions are dynamic in nature and are a better representation for expression representation [1]. In this PhD project, both static and temporal facial expression methods are explored. Though temporal FER is preferred but in scenarios where only images are available, FER methods need to infer the expression using static information only. FER methods can also be classified on the basis of number of subjects in a sample: individual or group.

Broadly, FER systems can also be broadly divided into three categories based on the type of feature representation used: a) shape features based FER methods: where a geometric representation of the face is used [4] ; b) appearance feature based FER method: where texture information is used [3] [6] and c) hybrid FER methods which use both shape and appearance descriptors [12]. From designing a FER method which can work in real-world conditions, choosing the right descriptor is essential such that the facial dynamics are captured and the representation does not reach Bayes risk. Also, from an information retrieval perspective, affect is used as an attribute. For inferring affect, the systems generally need to be fast enough for efficient retrieval. This poses the problem of selecting robust features which can be computed efficiently.

Generally FER methods have been limited to lab-controlled data. This poses a complex problem of extending and porting the methods created for lab controlled data to real-world conditions. There has been little work on affect analysis in real-world scenarios. One of early work is by Zhang et al. [14] who analysed the affect of movies for efficient browsing

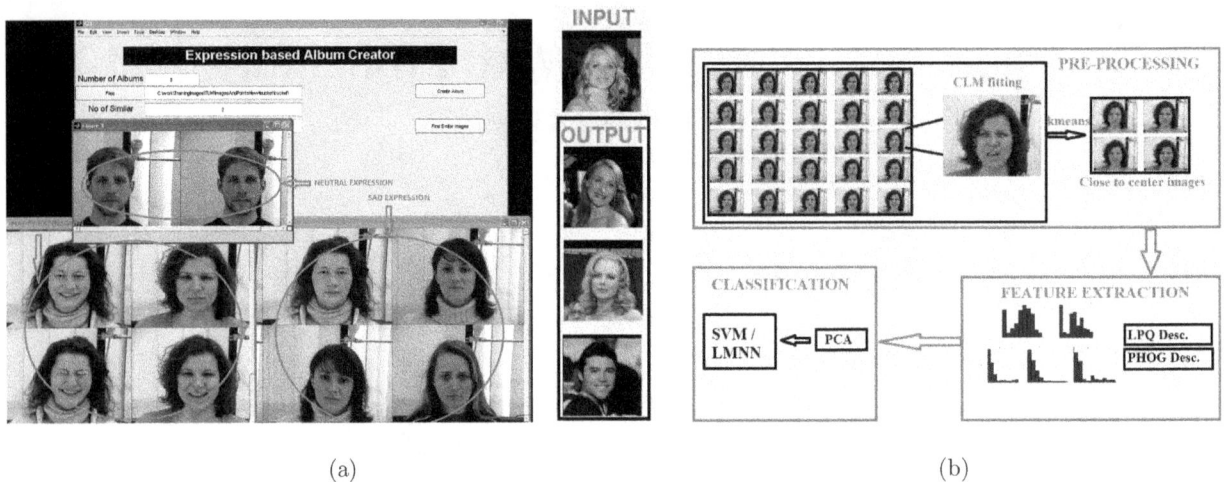

Figure 1: a) Expression based album creation and album by similar expression [4]. b) Key-frame based emotion detection [8].

of videos. However, this method does not take into consideration the facial expressions which are a strong cue. Neither this nor earlier affect analysis methods take into consideration the presence of multiple subjects. However, for moving to real-world scenarios, one needs to take these situations (multiple people in a scene) into consideration. This can be used for browsing and retrieving images and videos which contain subject(s) in tough conditions.

4. CHALLENGES

To transfer the current facial expression algorithms to work on data in the wild, there are several challenges. Consider an illustrative example of categorization i.e. assigning an emotion label to a video clip of a subject(s) protesting at the Tahir square in Egypt during the 2011 protests. In order to learn an automatic system which can infer the label representing the expression, we require labelled data containing video clips representing different expressions in diverse settings, along with a label which defines the emotional state. Traditionally, emotion recognition has been focussing on data collected in very controlled environments, such as research laboratories. Ideally, one would like to collect spontaneous data in real-world conditions. However, as anyone working in the emotion research community will testify, collecting spontaneous data in real-world conditions is a tedious task. As the subject in the example video clip generally moves his/her head, it poses another challenge of out-of-plane head movements. Head pose normalisation methods are required to capture the temporal dynamics of facial activity. With analyzing spontaneous expressions comes the problem of occlusion as subjects move their arms and hands as part of the non-verbal communication, this inter-occlusion needs to be handled for correct label inference.

The complexity of such video clips (like the one in the example above) is increased with the presence of multiple subjects. Research in this field has been focussing on recognition of a single subject's emotion i.e. given a video clip or image, only a single subject is present in it. However, data being uploaded on the web, specially revolving around so-

cial events such as the illustrated example contains groups of people. Group mood analysis finds it's application in opinion mining, image and video album creation, image visualisation and early violence prediction among others. There has been work in psychology on analysis of emotion of group of people, cues from this can be taken on creating models for handling group emotions. The **major challenges** for group mood analysis are: 1) labelled data representing various social scenarios; 2) robust face and fiducial points detector and 3) models which can take into consideration the affective compositional effects and the affective context. A simple solution to group mood analysis is emotion averaging. However, in real-world conditions averaging is not ideal. This motivates us to research for models which accommodate various attributes that effect the perception of group mood and their interaction.

5. PROPOSED METHODS

5.1 Facial Expression Based Album Creation

With the advancement in digital sensors, users captures a lot of images in scenarios like social events and trips. This leads to a complex task of efficiently retrieving and browsing through these huge collection of images. Generally people are the main focus of interest in social events. A structural similarity based method is proposed in [4]. Given an image with a face, fiducial points are computed using constrained local models. These fiducial points are used to compute a new geometric feature called Expression Image (EI). EI captures the shape of a face which is representation of an expression. Now given images in an album, EI is computed for each image and a structural similarity based clustering algorithm is applied. This creates clusters representing different emotions and such cluster representatives can be used as emotive thumbnails for browsing an album.

Further a 'browse by expression' extension is proposed, where given an input image with a subject showing a particular expression, the system retrieves images with similar expressions. Figure 1(a) defines the method output, the

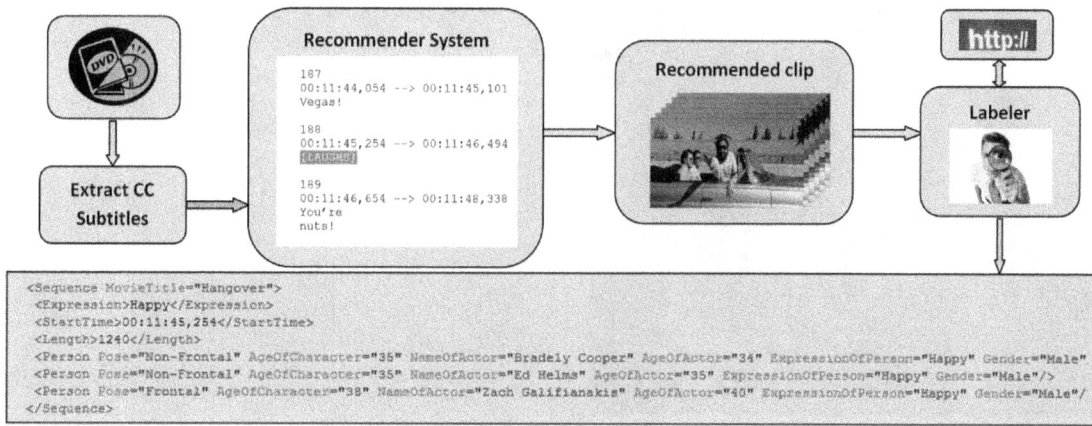

Figure 2: AFEW database creation pipeline

three sub groups in red circles are the cluster centres generated by similar expressions and the second illustration with a celebrity input image and the result images are similar expression images. Facial performance transfer [2] and similar expression [6] based classification have been explored as extension to this method.

5.2 Facial Expression Recognition Challenge

As part of the PhD project, an emotion detection method is proposed based on selecting key-frames [6]. Fiducial points are extracted using CLM and clustering is performed on the normalised shape points of all the frames of a video clip. The cluster centres are then chosen as the key-frames on which texture descriptors are computed. On analysing visually, the cluster centres corresponded to various stages of an expression i.e. onset-apex-offset. The method preformed well on the both task (subject independent and dependent) in the FERA 2011 challenge. Figure 1(b) describes the steps involved in the system.

5.3 Facial Expressions In The Wild

As discussed in the Section 4, data simulating 'in the wild' conditions is the first challenge for making FER methods work in real-world conditions. To over come this it is proposed to extract data from movies [9]. Even though movies are made in controlled conditions, they still resemble real-world conditions and clearly actors in good movies try to emulate natural expressions. It is very difficult to collect spontaneous expressions in challenging environments. A semi-

Figure 3: Group shot selection example. The first three columns show successively shot images and the fourth column is the recommended image based on highest mood score [10].

automatic recommender system based method is proposed for creating an expression dataset. The recommender system scans movie DVD's closed caption subtitles for emotion related keywords. Video clips containing these keywords are presented to an annotator, who then decides if the clip is useful. Meta-data information such as identity of actor, age, gender are stored for each video clip. This temporal dataset is called Acted Facial Expressions In The Wild database [9]. It contains 1426 short video clips and has been downloaded 50+ times in the past 14 months (http://cs.anu.edu.au/few).

A image only dataset, Static Facial Expressions In The Wild (SFEW) has been extracted from AFEW. Currently there are 700 images. Strict experimentation protocols have been defined for both AFEW and SFEW. The experiments on the databases show the short coming of current state-of-art FER methods which perform very well on lab-controlled data. Figure 2(a) defines the database construction process.

For progress in the field of FER, a grand challenge and workshop: Emotion Recognition In The Wild (EmotiW) is being organised as part of the ACM International Conference on MultiModal Interaction (ICMI 2013).

5.4 Group Mood Analysis

Images and videos uploaded on internet and in movies generally have multiple subjects. Emotion analysis of group of people is dependent on two main parts: the member's contribution and the scene context. As a pilot study, data is downloaded from Flickr based on keywords related to social events such as marriage, convocation, party etc. Face detector is applied on downloaded images and fast rejection is performed, if an image has less than three people. Then images are labelled for each person's happiness intensity, face clarity and pose. Also the mood of the group in an image is labelled. The database contains 8500 labelled faces and 4000 images.

A simple group analysis model is averaging of individual person's expression intensities. However, humans while perceiving the mood of group of people take into consideration various attributes. To understand these attributes, an online survey was conducted. In the survey, total of 150 individuals participated. The survey asked individuals to rank the happiness in set of two different images which contain group of people. To understand their perception behind making a

Figure 4: Attribute based group mood inference

decision various questions are asked such as: 'is your choice based on: large smiling faces; large number of people smiling; context and background; attractive subjects; age of a particular subject' and so on. After analysing this data various attributes are defined.

Attributes which effect group mood perception can be categorized into global and local attributes. Global attributes include but not limited to the location of a person in a group, a person's neighbor and the scene. Local attribute comprise of an individual person's mood, face clarity and so on. Figure 2(b) defines the attributes computed for members of a group [10]. These attributes are used as weights to each person's contribution towards the overall group's mood.

Group mood analysis is a weakly labelled problem. Even though a number of attributes are labelled in the training data, the survey conducted showed that there are factors such as age and gender too. To incorporate this information to the weighted group expression model, topic model is learnt. The attributes are augmented with a bag of words model which is learnt on low-level features extracted from faces. The augmented feature is then used to learn a graphical model. Experiments show that the performance of augmented feature based topic model is superior to that of weighted and average group expression models. Along with the quantitative analysis performed for comparing the proposed group expression models, various qualitative experiments are also conducted.

An interesting application of group expression analysis is group shot selection. Images are shot in succession/burst mode and mood is used as the deciding factor. Figure 3 describes the experiment, the fourth column displays the selected frame for each row of successive shots.

6. RESEARCH PROGRESS

First six months are thorough literature survey. Then similar expressions [4, 5] and FERA challenge [6] are explored. In the second year AFEW [9] and SFEW [8] databases are developed. Group expressions [10] [7] are explored in the third year. Research collaboration with graduate students at the HCC lab at the University of Canberra for depression detection [11].Thesis writing will be undertaken in the first half of the fourth year.

7. ACKNOWLEDGEMENT

My PhD research is sponsored by Ausaid's Australian Leadership Award scholarship. I am thankful to my supervisors: Dr. Roland Goecke, Prof. Tom Gedeon and other collaborators at the Australian National University, University of Canberra, Commonwealth Scientific and Industrial Research Organisation and the University of California San Diego.

8. REFERENCES

[1] Z. Ambadar, J. Schooler, and J. Cohn. Deciphering the enigmatic face: The importance of facial dynamics to interpreting subtle facial expressions. *Psychological Science*, pages 403–410, 2005.

[2] A. Asthana, M. de la Hunty, A. Dhall, and R. Goecke. Facial performance transfer via deformable models and parametric correspondence. *IEEE TVCG*, pages 1511–1519, 2012.

[3] M. Bartlett, G. Littlewort, C. Lainscsek, I. Fasel, and J. Movellan. Machine learning methods for fully automatic recognition of facial expressions and facial actions. In *IEEE SMC*, 2004.

[4] A. Dhall, A. Asthana, and R. Goecke. Facial expression based automatic album creation. In *ICONIP*, pages 485–492, 2010.

[5] A. Dhall, A. Asthana, and R. Goecke. A ssim-based approach for finding similar facial expressions. In *IEEE AFGR2011 workshop FERA*, pages 815–820, 2011.

[6] A. Dhall, A. Asthana, R. Goecke, and T. Gedeon. Emotion recognition using PHOG and LPQ features. In *IEEE AFGR2011 workshop FERA*, pages 878–883, 2011.

[7] A. Dhall and R. Goecke. Group expression intensity estimation in videos via gaussian processes. In *ICPR*, pages 3525–3528, 2012.

[8] A. Dhall, R. Goecke, S. Lucey, and T. Gedeon. Static Facial Expression Analysis In Tough Conditions: Data, Evaluation Protocol And Benchmark. In *ICCVW*, BEFIT'11, pages 2106–2112, 2011.

[9] A. Dhall, R. Goecke, S. Lucey, and T. Gedeon. A semi-automatic method for collecting richly labelled large facial expression databases from movies. *IEEE Multimedia*, 2012.

[10] A. Dhall, J. Joshi, I. Radwan, and R. Goecke. Finding happiest moments in a social context. In *ACCV*, 2012.

[11] J. Joshi, A. Dhall, R. Goecke, M. Breakspear, and G. Parker. Neural-net classification for spatio-temporal descriptor based depression analysis. In *ICPR*, pages 2634–2638, 2012.

[12] S. Lucey, I. Matthews, C. Hu, Z. Ambadar, F. de la Torre, and J. Cohn. AAM Derived Face Representations for Robust Facial Action Recognition. In *IEEE AFGR*, pages 155–162, 2006.

[13] Y. Yacoob and L. Davis. Computing spatio-temporal representations of human faces. In *In CVPR*, pages 70–75. IEEE Computer Society, 1994.

[14] S. Zhang, Q. Tian, Q. Huang, W. Gao, and S. Li. Utilizing affective analysis for efficient movie browsing. In *ICIP*, pages 1853–1856, 2009.

Towards Fusion of Collective Knowledge and Audio-Visual Content Features for Annotating Broadcast Video

Fréderic Godin
Multimedia Lab
Ghent University - iMinds
Ghent, Belgium
frederic.godin@ugent.be

Wesley De Neve
Multimedia Lab
Ghent Univ. - iMinds & KAIST
Ghent, Belgium
wesley.deneve@ugent.be

Rik Van de Walle
Multimedia Lab
Ghent University - iMinds
Ghent, Belgium
rik.vandewalle@ugent.be

ABSTRACT

Broadcasters produce vast collections of video content. However, the lack of fine-grained annotations makes it difficult to retrieve video fragments of interest from these vast collections. Indeed, manual annotation of video content is labour-intensive and time-consuming. Moreover, the applicability of algorithms for automatic annotation of video content is limited, given that too many prerequisites need to be fulfilled and that a lot of concepts are unidentifiable. At the same time, people are using social media to share their thoughts about the content they view on television. Therefore, in this Ph.D. research, we plan to investigate novel machine learning-based approaches towards the task of fine-grained annotation of broadcast video content, fusing the collective knowledge present in social media with the output of audio-visual content analysis algorithms.

Categories and Subject Descriptors

H.3.1 [**Information Storage and Retrieval**]: Content Analysis and Indexing; I.5.4 [**Pattern Recognition**]: Applications

General Terms

Algorithms, Design, Human factors

Keywords

Annotation; broadcast video; collective knowledge; content analysis; multi-modal fusion; signal processing; social media

1. INTRODUCTION

To facilitate keyword-based search in large collections of video content, retrieval algorithms make use of textual descriptions. These textual descriptions can be added manually or automatically. Manual annotation of video content is a time-consuming and labour-intensive task. Therefore, researchers have developed audio-visual content analysis algorithms that are able to annotate video sequences automatically. To that end, mappings have been defined between

low-level audio-visual content features and high-level semantic concepts. Despite promising results, two major problems can be identified:

- **Generalizability:** Visual concept detectors are often a combination of carefully engineered features and heuristic rules that are tailored on the training data. Therefore, as Yang and Hauptmann [10] prove, these approaches are not generalizable to similar content from other sources (or to other domains), and depend highly on the content prerequisites that need be fulfilled.

- **Concepts with limited audio-visual (AV) characteristics:** To be able to correctly detect a concept, that concept needs to exhibit discriminative AV characteristics. Otherwise detection becomes cumbersome. E.g., in soccer video sequences, when detecting yellow cards using AV features, a significant number of false positives are generated because of the lack of highly discriminative AV features [3].

In recent years, social media generated a substantial amount of collective knowledge [4], providing context for content. Therefore, we hypothesize that the solution to the problem of automatic annotation of video content lies in combining algorithms for collective knowledge analysis and algorithms for audio-visual content analysis. Indeed, the content prerequisites can be fulfilled by taking advantage of the collective knowledge available in social media. Moreover, previously undetectable concepts can be annotated, again using the collective knowledge available in social media. As such, the problem statement changes from how to detect semantic concepts to how to align content and context, namely multimedia objects and collective knowledge.

In this Ph.D. research, we aim at answering the following research question: how to make use of collective knowledge for the purpose of automatically annotating broadcast video at a fine-grained level, given that collective knowledge allows taking advantage of a rich concept vocabulary on the one hand, and that collective knowledge is often unstructured, multilingual, subjective, and noisy on the other hand?

This paper is structured as follows. In Section 2, we discuss related work in the field of fusion. We also briefly discuss the novelty of this Ph.D. research with respect to the related work. Next, in Section 3, we propose a novel method for fusing collective knowledge with AV features, with the overall aim of annotating broadcast video. In Section 4, we present initial experimental results. Finally, in Section 5, we provide conclusions and directions for future research.

2. RELATED WORK

Our initial experiments make use of Twitter (see Section 4). Therefore, our review of related work consists of a discussion of algorithms to analyze video content and unstructured textual data, and of techniques to fuse both. In Section 2.1, we discuss multi-modal fusion. In Section 2.2, we outline existing approaches for fusing video content and Twitter data. Finally, in Section 2.3, we detail the novelty of the proposed Ph.D. research.

2.1 Multi-modal fusion

In multi-modal fusion, complementary modalities are fused to increase the accuracy of the overall decision-making process [1]. Given that different streams of data can have different processing times, formats, or costs, most researchers opt for a late fusion approach that is layered in nature, first analysing the data streams independently and subsequently fusing the results obtained for the different streams.

Xie *et al.* [8] use a Hierarchical Hidden Markov Model (HHMM) in order to fuse audio and video streams. In addition, probabilistic Latent Semantic Analysis (pLSA) is used to cluster text transcript by topic. Both algorithms yield a mid-level semantic representation of their corresponding stream. Next, the mid-level representations are clustered, using a dynamic mixture model to group video fragments and their descriptions by topic. Similar techniques were applied in [9], with the aim of aligning webcast text and videos of sports games. In particular, pLSA is used for text-based clustering of events. Next, Conditional Random Fields (CRFs) are used to obtain event clusters that are aligned in time with segmented video sequences. The authors stress the importance of the use of sequential models because a lot of information is contained in previous and following states/topics/fragments.

2.2 Fusing Twitter and video streams

Given the scale and real-time nature of Twitter, event detection in Twitter is a highly popular research topic. A Twitter stream can be seen as a free stream of collective knowledge about events that happen in the world. When a broadcast video stream is available, microposts about certain fragments can be used to browse through the video and retrieve certain fragments.

Shamma and Churchill [5] use tweets to annotate broadcast videos of the inauguration of President Obama and the presidential debates of 2008. They apply the Term Frequency - Inverse Document Frequency (TF-IDF) principle in order to extract keywords that facilitate video browsing. In addition, they calculate Importance and Chatness scores to identify the most important events and the most discussed events in the video sequence, respectively. A similar idea is applied in [6], harnessing the *Wisdom of the Crowd* to detect the most important moments in live video streams for archiving purposes. The authors take into account the time between keyword occurrences, the cosine similarity between tweets, and the follow-followee relationships between Twitter users.

Highlight extraction from video sequences is also a very popular research topic. This holds particularly true for sports games. Lanagan and Smeaton [3] demonstrated that Twitter-driven detection of significant events in soccer and rugby games, combined with shot boundary detection, performs as good as event detection solely using audiovisual content analysis. For indexing and retrieval purposes, the authors make use of the bag-of-words model. This is done in a rough manner, using a timespan of at least one minute. To allow for more personalized and specialized event detection, the authors of [7] make use of spike detection and Support Vector Machines to detect and classify five types of soccer events and to discriminate between tweets from different teams, thus facilitating personalized, team-based video summarization.

2.3 Novel contributions

The big drawback of all previously described methods is that none of these methods uses video information to index the video content. All of these methods focus on extracting useful information of Twitter streams without taking into account the information contained within the video stream itself, despite the fact that researchers focused for more than a decade on video content analysis. The content and context are analysed separately. The rise of social media, however, makes it possible to take advantage of new information (context) about this content. Exploiting this content-context relationship gives several advantages, such as confidence-based algorithm selection using the context and exploiting the correlation between multiple streams.

To conclude, the novelty of the proposed Ph.D. research is as follows:

- Fusion and alignment of social media, especially Twitter, and video content, using multiple sources of information (see Section 3.2).

- Exploitation of the content-context relationship for algorithm selection using path planning (see Section 3.3).

- Provisioning of fine-grained non-expert annotations instead of coarse minute-by-minute descriptions.

3. PROPOSED METHOD

The goal of this Ph.D. research is to develop a collective knowledge-based framework for annotating broadcast video. The starting point is the Twitter data that are related to the broadcast video, and where the Twitter data form an unstructured, multilingual, noisy, and subjective but near-synchronous description of the broadcast video. Other sources of collective knowledge can be chosen too, or can be queried based on extracted information from the Twitter data. Think for instance about the retrieval of similar video clips from YouTube or the retrieval of similar images from Flickr or Facebook.

A schematic overview of the proposed framework is given in Figure 1. At the input side, we find the broadcast video (1). Based on what it knows about the broadcast video (e.g., the title of a show), the selection component will issue a number of queries (2) for initial information about the broadcast video (3). In our case, we will query Twitter in order to get a first timestamped description of the video. Next, an algorithm is selected that will fuse both the collective knowledge and the broadcast video, for instance making use of text processing techniques and computer vision algorithms to deduce new information (4). Based on this new information (5), we can again query sources of collective knowledge (2). An iterative process will take place until the selection component decides that a state of convergence has been reached. The output is an annotated broadcast video

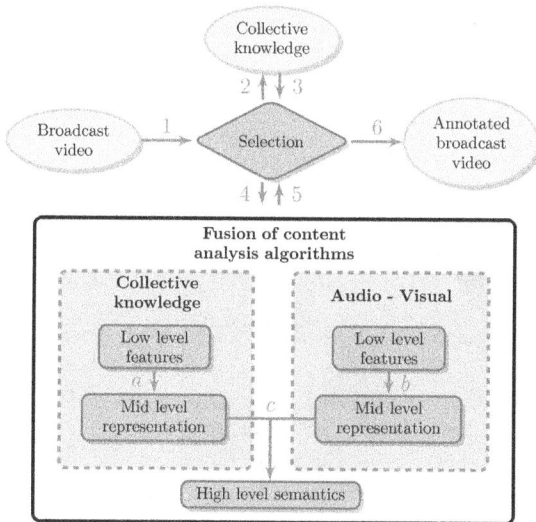

Figure 1: Schematic overview of the annotation framework.

of external text sources in a fusion approach to annotate sports video content can yield outstanding results [9].

In this Ph.D. research, we will apply a hybrid layered fusion approach. Different data streams will first be handled separately because of their different representation formats to yield a more uniform mid-level semantic representation (a and b). When two data streams are asynchronous, it should be clear that the fusion of these data streams will not be obvious. Therefore, at the highest level, the mid-level representations of several data streams can be fused using a sequential machine learning approach (c). To that end, Hidden Markov Models or Conditional Random Fields can be used, as well as a clustering approach based on Dynamic Mixture Models [8]. Collective knowledge fragments (events) and video fragments (shots) will be clustered based on the mid-level representations.

The mid-level representations are deduced from both the collective knowledge and the video sequence. There is no strict separation between them. For example, in order to be able to identify people in a video sequence by means of computer vision algorithms, we can infer an initial database of people from the Twitter data. Existing computer vision algorithms will be tailored to work with collective knowledge and new techniques will be developed to filter collective knowledge. To process vast streams of textual data, we can make use of topic models such as pLSA [8, 9] . The highest ranked keywords within a topic can be used to describe the content. Because collective knowledge is often subjective and opinionated, there is a need for sentiment analysis. This type of analysis has shown to be effective in selecting highlights during live broadcasts (see Section 4).

containing fragment-by-fragment descriptions that are able to facilitate more effective video retrieval (6).

3.1 Collective knowledge

Collective knowledge can be defined as unstructured knowledge, generated by users of social media who often do not have expert knowledge on the topic. This knowledge can take the form of text, images, and video sequences. Although the freely-available collective knowledge empowers us with massive amounts of new information, we can also identify a number of disadvantages. When collective knowledge takes the form of text (e.g., tags or micro posts), natural language or multiple languages can be used. In addition, the information may be opinionated, and even incorrect.

Therefore, we can identify the following tree major research challenges regarding the use of collective knowledge: (1) how to structure and filter the data?, (2) how to deal with noise?, and (3) how to deal with sentiment?

As mentioned before, our starting point will be the Twitter stream associated with the broadcast video. In other words, our starting point will be the observations, remarks, and opinions of the viewers of the broadcast video. It can be expected that these micro posts will contain a significant number of named entities, like persons, objects, organizations, and locations. The verification of the presence of these named entities in the broadcast video is one possibility to deal with the aforementioned research challenges.

3.2 Fusion of content analysis algorithms

One of the most interesting ways to verify the information in collective knowledge is to exploit the correlation between the collective knowledge and the broadcast video. If we have high confidence in the alignment and correctness of a part of the data, we can accept the non-verifiable data as correct too.

Currently, no fusion approach exists that aims at fusing a broadcast video and a corresponding Twitter stream, despite the fact that previous work has already shown that the use

3.3 Selection component

The selection component is responsible for guiding the annotation process. It is an iterative process, where, based on the available information, new information sources can be queried. These new sources of information may take the form of external sources of collective knowledge. However, these new sources of information may also take the form of internal sources, namely the output of algorithms.

This process can be described as the use of context to decide how to annotate best the content. Currently, researchers make use of if-else constructs to do this [1], an approach that is not scalable. It would be better to let the algorithms learn for themselves how to obtain good annotations by means of machine learning-based techniques, such as reinforcement learning or online learning. In the case of reinforcement learning, confidence measurements about the new annotations could be used to determine the best path. That way, the selection component will learn the best path itself, rather than using of a set of human-defined rules.

4. EXPERIMENTAL RESULTS

As a first experiment, we extracted highlights from soccer video sequences of the English Premier League 2011-2012 in real time, using the framework shown in Figure 2. We made use of a two-step algorithm to detect six important events (goal, penalty, foul, substitution, end of first half, end of second half) in the Twitter streams associated with the soccer games. First, a sliding window approach is applied in order to detect spikes (4). Next, tweets are classified within a spike using a Support Vector Machine (5). Because highlights are typically highly emotional moments, we made use

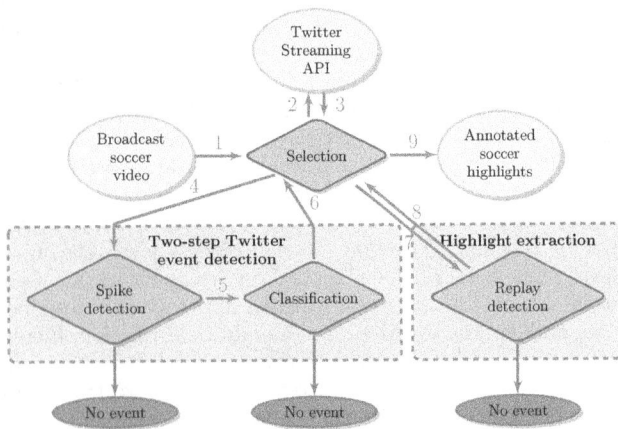

Figure 2: Instantiation of the proposed framework: highlight detection and extraction in soccer videos using Twitter

of features that resemble sentiment, such as the use of multiple exclamation marks or the capitalization of keywords and player names. The presence of keywords belonging to an event class were also added to be able to discriminate between events. Different from previous approaches [3, 2, 7], we made use of the video content to verify the correctness of the detected events. After the detection of an event on Twitter (6), the selection component decides to seek the corresponding fragment in the video sequence (7). Currently, replay detection is applied within a certain time span around the point of detection making use of logos. When found (8), an annotated replay fragment is delivered (9).

We evaluated our algorithm on detecting goals in 12 soccer games that contained 34 goals. Our algorithm obtained a precision and recall of 93.75% and 88.26%, respectively. This shows that video content analysis can benefit from external sources of collective knowledge. The time and type of the detected event allows us to define content prerequisites for applying video content analysis methods, making it possible to significantly reduce the amount of processing time needed. On top of that, we can easily extract other useful information from the collective knowledge such as the name of the player that scored the goal. This was previously a difficult task in video content analysis because of the lack of visually distinctive characteristics. Note that we did not only annotate the video content with objective concept information, but we also enriched the video content with subjective user information.

5. CONCLUSIONS AND FUTURE WORK

The lack of generalizability and the limited amount of detectable concepts are currently the main drawbacks of algorithms for automatic video annotation. In this Ph.D. proposal, we proposed a multi-modal fusion approach to overcome these limitations, making use of freely available collective knowledge in social media. To demonstrate the usefulness of the proposed approach, we successfully extracted goals and elaborate descriptions from broadcast soccer video sequences with limited effort.

In future research, we will further enhance the proposed annotation framework. One of our goals is to be able to annotate a full evening of broadcast video, with the broadcast video originating from several channels and containing several types of content. To that end, we will have to generalize the current annotation framework used. Further, compared to other external data sources, the power of collective knowledge lies in its user-generated nature. As such, in future research, we will design methods that are able to leverage collective knowledge for both the purpose of annotating content with a rich concept vocabulary and the purpose of enriching content with opinions and emotions.

6. ACKNOWLEDGMENTS

The research activities described in this paper were funded by Ghent University, iMinds, the Institute for the Promotion of Innovation by Science and Technology in Flanders (IWT), the Fund for Scientific Research-Flanders (FWO-Flanders), and the European Union.

7. REFERENCES

[1] P. K. Atrey, M. A. Hossain, A. El Saddik, and M. S. Kankanhalli. Multimodal fusion for multimedia analysis: A survey. *Multimedia Systems*, 2010.

[2] J. Hannon, K. McCarthy, J. Lynch, and B. Smyth. Personalized and automatic social summarization of events in video. In *Proc. of the 16th international conference on Intelligent user interfaces*, 2011.

[3] J. Lanagan and A. F. Smeaton. Using twitter to detect and tag important events in live sports. *Artificial Intelligence*, 2011.

[4] V. Robu, H. Halpin, and H. Shepherd. Emergence of consensus and shared vocabularies in collaborative tagging systems. *ACM Trans. Web*, 2009.

[5] D. Shamma, L. Kennedy, and E. Churchill. Tweetgeist: Can the twitter timeline reveal the structure of broadcast events? *Horizon, In CSCW 2010*, 2010.

[6] X. Shi, Z. Yang, M. Toyoda, and M. Kitsuregawa. Harnessing the wisdom of crowds: video event detection based on synchronous comments. In *Proc. of the 20th international conference companion on World wide web*, 2011.

[7] G. van Oorschot, M. van Erp, and C. Dijkshoorn. Automatic extraction of soccer game events from twitter. In *Proc. of the Workshop on Detection, Representation, and Exploitation of Events in the Semantic Web*, 2012.

[8] L. Xie, L. Kennedy, S. fu Chang, A. Divakaran, H. Sun, and C. yung Lin. Layered dynamic mixture model for pattern discovery in asynchronous multi-modal streams. In *International Conference on Acoustic, Speech and Signal Processing*, 2005.

[9] C. Xu, Y.-F. Zhang, G. Zhu, Y. Rui, H. Lu, and Q. Huang. Using webcast text for semantic event detection in broadcast sports video. *Multimedia, IEEE Transactions on*, 2008.

[10] J. Yang and A. G. Hauptmann. (un)reliability of video concept detection. In *Proc. of the int. conference on Content-based image and video retrieval*, 2008.

Next Generation Image and Video Browsing on Mobile Devices

Marco A. Hudelist

Institute of Information Technology
Alpen-Adria-University Klagenfurt
9020 Klagenfurt, Austria
marco@itec.aau.at
Advised by
Klaus Schoeffmann, Laszlo Böszörmenyi

ABSTRACT

Mobile multimedia devices, such as smart phones and tablet PCs, are gaining increased popularity for the purpose of image and video recording. For many users, these ubiquitous devices are a good replacement of traditional and usually heavyweight cameras. However, while content creation is very simple on such mobile devices, browsing and searching still lacks of appropriate interaction means that are specifically designed for multi-touch-based interaction on small displays. In this work, we present our initial concepts and ideas to improve image and video browsing on smart phones and tablet PCs with touchscreen interaction.

Categories and Subject Descriptors

H.3.3 [**Information Storage and Retrieval**]: Information Search and Retrieval

Keywords

Video Browsing, Image Browsing, Mobile devices, Touchscreens

1. INTRODUCTION

Due to their high availability, smart phones and tablet PCs are more and more used as a replacement for traditional and dedicated photo and video cameras. With the increased popularity of such devices and their ubiquitous use for recording purposes, the number of stored images and videos on mobile multimedia devices dramatically increases. However, as the volume of media files on such small devices increases, finding the proper image or video (e.g., to show it to a friend) becomes increasingly difficult. The reason for the problem is the fact that current mobile media browsing tools do not provide efficient features for searching and browsing. For example, the default image browsing app on an iPhone uses a fixed-size thumbnail list that can show only 24 images at a time, without any special features for search. The same app is used to browse videos, where videos are represented by a single key-frame. Efficient search within a video is another problem on such devices because most users are bound to video players with very limited navigation features.

In this work we present our initial concepts and ideas to improve exploratory image and video search on mobile multimedia devices. We focus not only on improved interaction models (e.g.,

multi-touch interaction) as well as advanced user interfaces (e.g., 3D visualizations), but also on the proper integration of available sensors (e.g., gyroscope and accelerometer). Moreover, we would like to investigate what kind of content analysis can be used on such devices for immediate content-based browsing right after content recording. Such a scenario is especially challenging because of the limited computing power, available on mobile devices.

2. RELATED WORK

Different approaches to improve image and video browsing on desktop PCs have been presented in the literature (see [16] for a recent review on video browsing). Many of these approaches use some kind of content analysis, similar to the approaches used in image and video retrieval [17]. In contrast to retrieval, in a typical browsing scenario the users doesn't formulate a concrete query for what they are looking for. Browsing is more an interactive search process where the user has a rough idea of what she/he is looking for and tries to interactively find it. Recent research results show that 3D visualizations and similarity-based arrangements can improve visual search on mobile devices [13].

Proposed interfaces cover a wide range of concepts with and without variants of content analysis. Some examples are a Fisheye-like view [2], a 3D ring [14], different 3D globe configurations [1] and a hexagonal lattice [12]. In our current research we are using color analysis in order to enhance image browsing combined in combination with 2D and 3D visualizations.

In the domain of video browsing many concepts for improved interfaces on desktop PCs have been proposed. One example is the extension of seeker-bars through abstract content visualizations. In [16], for example, the dominant colors of frames are shown in an enhanced seeker-bar, making it easier to quickly jump to scenes that are similar (e.g., moderation scenes with similar background or repeating shots of ski jumpers).

HiStory [7] proposes a hierarchical approach and presents the user a storyboard-like arrangement of thumbnails of the video. The user can refine the view by choosing one of the thumbnails, representing a specific time range in the video. The view is then recreated with a new set of thumbnails, representing the time range of the original thumbnail in finer granularity. In a similar storyboard arrangement Comp2Watch [9] tries to further apply summarization techniques to give users a quick meaningful overview of the contents of the video. Another example of hierarchical image browsing uses a 3D ring for visualization as in [15] where each new hierarchy level is represented as a new 3D ring giving a user a better understanding of where in the hierarchy she/he currently is browsing.

Extensions of mobile video browsing with the help of touchscreen gestures are shown in [5] and [6]. Through the usage of swipe-gestures it is possible to navigate inside a video and also between different interrelated videos. Further utilizing touchscreen gestures with focus on very precise video browsing is ProPane [4]. The interface gives the user precise control on browsing speed. It can even be performed on a frame-by-frame style, which was especially attractive for professional users, as shown in their user study.

Extending video browsing to the usage of multiple mobile devices the authors of [11] show usage scenarios enabled by using multiple physical objects to interact with videos. They derive their approach from working with documents in the real world.

Providing the user a view of different similarity characteristics on a given query the Fork-, Cross- and RotorBrowsers of [3] are a prominent example for similarity based video browsing. In the center of the screen a user-chosen focal shot is displayed. In different arrangements (fork formation, star formation or cross formation) similarity threads of shots are displayed around this focal shot. A user can use the different threads to navigate through the content.

An approach that relies heavily on object tracking is presented in [10]. A user has the ability to navigate in a video by selecting and manipulating objects of the video with her/his finger. On example is the navigation in a soccer game, where dragging the ball to a certain position jumps to the respective scene in the video. Unfortunately the system only works with a connection to a server since the algorithms used for the object tracking are too demanding for mobile devices.

Finally, in [18] video browsing is performed by using the built-in accelerometer exclusively, making it especially attractive for single-handed use.

3. ON-THE-FLY CONTENT ANALYSIS

On-the-fly content analysis enables new usage scenarios for mobile devices especially in domain of video browsing and video editing. Although tablet-PCs and smart phones already use multi-core CPUs and multi-core GPUs, deep content analysis (e.g., methods like Bag-of-Visual-Words) is typically not feasible on mobile devices due to the high memory requirements and limited battery power. This is especially true for the scenario of on-the-fly content analysis that will be the focus of our research. Since there isn't much prior work considering on-the-fly content analysis on mobile devices, we make first attempts in this field without claiming to provide optimal or final solutions. However, because of the current limitations of browsing tools on mobile devices, we expect that even rather simple content analysis methods can provide a significant improvement.

To better illustrate our first ideas, please consider the simple example of a mobile video browser that provides direct links to appearances of people to the user, based on face detection. Another example would be the usage by a small reporter team. In case of an unexpected but important event the team could use mobile devices instead of their currently unavailable professional equipment to record first footage of the event. After the footage is taken they could start filtering and editing the footage on-site with little to none delay, aided by an advanced browsing interface. The filtering process is enhanced by the usage of content analysis results that were already generated during the recording. In a short

amount of time the team could send a pre-edited reportage video to the headquarters of the TV station.

4. IMAGE BROWSING DESIGNS

In this section we present our first prototypes to improve image browsing on mobile devices by combining color sorting with 2D and 3D visualizations. As we could show in [1] that such representations can improve search performance on a tablet-PC, we now want to extend our investigation to smaller devices. In a current user study we are evaluating them for small mobile devices like smart phones. All interfaces use the same color sorting algorithm: images are sorted by their dominant hue level obtained through a 24-bins HSV histogram. Additionally, very bright images are placed at the beginning and very dark images are placed at the end.

Two interfaces of our previous user study [1] (an image grid and a 3D globe) are joined with two new prototypes: The ImagePane and an improved version of the 3D ring interface proposed in [13].

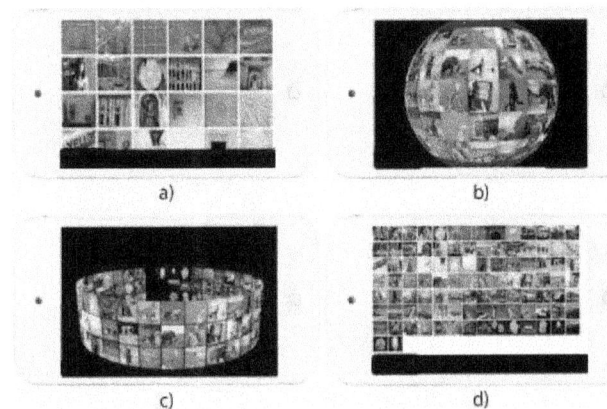

Figure 1: Image browsing on small touchscreen devices: a) Grid; b) 3D-Globe; c) 3D-Ring; d) ImagePane.

To evaluate the performance of the three novel interfaces a traditional grid arrangement is included in the user test as a baseline (see Figure 1a). It is designed in the same way as the photo browser on iOS and similar devices. We add color sorting for ensuring fairness in comparing this interface to the other ones. The user can scroll the list upwards and downwards by using swipe and drag gestures.

In the interface shown in Figure 1b, images are distributed on the surface of a 3D globe according to the earlier mentioned color sorting algorithm [1]. The surface is organized in a grid-like arrangement. The sequence of images is applied in a one by one fashion, going north to south and west to east. A user can rotate and tilt the globe by using swipe and drag gestures. Zooming the view is possible by using pinch gestures.

Figure 1c shows the third interface, which is an advanced version of the ring interface presented in [13]. Images are arranged on the surface of a 3D ring. The ring can be rotated by swiping and dragging gestures. Swiping up results in a zoomed view of the front part of the ring. Swiping down returns the user to the default view. Double tapping results in a zoomed view of the back part of the ring, as if the user is standing in the middle of it. Additionally the ring automatically rotates so that the tapped area is positioned in the center of the screen.

An extension of the traditional grid is the ImagePane interface (see Figure 1d). All images in the collection are displayed as small thumbnails in the default view. To perform a zoom operation the user can double-tap on an area of the pane. The view then zooms to this selected area of images. In this view the user also has the opportunity to scroll the pane in any direction by applying drag and swipe gestures. The user can leave this view again by performing another double-tap gesture.

5. VIDEO BROWSING DESIGNS

In this section we present our initial concepts for improved browsing and navigation within a single video. In future iterations we will integrate results of content analysis as well as extend our concepts for browsing many videos instead of a single video. These interfaces are currently targeted to be used on tablet-like devices.

Figure 2: Browsing a video using a 3D filmstrip.

Figure 2 shows an early version of our filmstrip interface. Each segment in the strip initially represents a 10 seconds segment of the video. To play the content of a certain segment a user has to tap the segment once. The video then starts playing back inside the region of the selected segment. The user can scroll the filmstrip in various ways. One way is a kind of fly-over view. For this, the user has to perform a drag gesture outside the filmstrip upwards or downwards on the screen. The filmstrip then moves towards or away from the user providing a quick overview of the contents of the whole video. It is also possible to change the tilting of the filmstrip. This is done by applying a drag gesture with two fingers up or down on the screen. Another possibility is the scrolling of the segments on the filmstrip. A drag gesture on the surface of the filmstrip to the left or to the right side results in a corresponding scroll action. The granularity of the segments can be adjusted by pinch-gestures. For example, to go from 10 second segments to 5 second segments the user has to perform a pinch-in gesture. On the other hand, a pinch-out gesture decreases granularity e.g. going from 10 second segments to 30 second segments. In a future iteration we will experiment with different segmentation methods (e.g., based on shot boundary detection).

Video browsing on tablets and smart phones is usually performed by holding the device in landscape orientation with both hands on the sides, to maximize usage of the available screen real-estate for the video content.

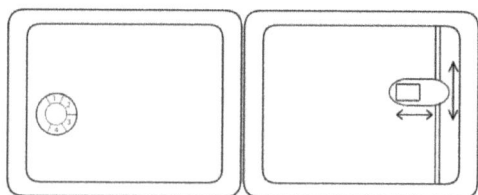

Figure 3: Sketch of the ThumbBrowser concept.

In such a configuration the thumbs become especially important. An intelligent video browser interface could consider this fact and optimize placement of browsing controls for the thumbs of the user. With traditional browsing interfaces the user has to release the comfortable two-handed holding position in order to be able to use the control buttons or the seeker-bar. A simple enhancement in this case would be the rearrangement of the controls to the sides (see Figure 3). Further, to reduce visual overhead, on-demand radial menus could be used to provide additional functions, e.g., for choosing between different content analysis result visualizations in contrast to buttons with fixed positions on the screen.

Bringing the idea of multiple windows of the same video to mobile devices is one of the ideas for the VideoPinch concept in Figure 4. A user starts with a single rectangle or frame resembling the whole video. By using a pinch gesture the user expands this single frame to multiple frames representing different time segments of the original video. She or he is therefore refining the search process, which can be repeated on all currently available frames. Although this concept isn't completely new on traditional desktop computers, combining it with the abilities of modern touchscreen technology could increase usefulness and usability radically. The frames could be freely dragged around the workspace. This enables e.g. lining up two segments of a video side by side for direct comparison purposes.

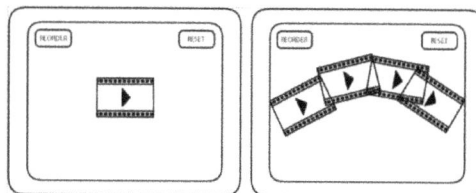

Figure 4: Sketch of the VideoPinch concept.

Further, two buttons help to restructure the content: a reset button and a reorder button. The reset button deletes all frames except one, which resembles again the whole video. It should therefore be used to start over again. On the other hand the reorder button will re-align the current frames in the order they would appear in the original video. To play/pause a video frame the user can use a single tap. Double tapping on a frame opens the corresponding video frame in a full screen view. Finally a triple tap resets the frames to the first frame of their corresponding segment of the original video.

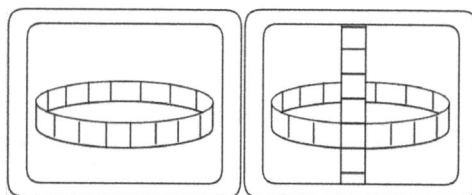

Figure 5: Sketch of the VideoRingX concept.

Extending the idea of the 3D ring image browser interface, the VideoRingX interface concept (Figure 5) displays screenshots of movie segments instead of images. The segments can be played/paused by single tap gestures. If users want to refine their browsing experience, they can tap and hold a segment. This will expand the segment in a horizontal filmstrip that can be scrolled up and down. Single tapping on the segments starts or pauses playback. Tapping and holding on a segment of the horizontal filmstrip further refines the search by expanding its time range into a new ring of segments.

6. RESEARCH METHOD

Due to the novel nature of the topic, an iterative research approach seems to be the best suited, where the phases Think/Design,

Realize/Implement and Evaluate are forming a circulatory. The Think/Design-Phase will be performed by doing literature surveys of compareable prior work. The results of ealier evaluation phases will also be incorporated in future stages. The Realize/Implementation-Phase will result in the creation of artifacts, which will in our case primarily be prototypes.

In order to evaluate our prototypes for image and video browsing, we will perform several user studies for different use scenarios. One such scenario will be Known-Item-Search (KIS), where a user has some knowledge of a specific segment of a video (or of an image) and wants to quickly find it, but doesn't know where or how to look for it. Further research on alternative, efficient, partly automatic evaluation techniques will also be part of our work. For example, we want to extend the common evaluation methods by doing justice to the mobile nature of the devices. Most of the time mobile device interfaces are evaluated in a fixed lab-like environment, although they truly are designed to be used on the go. We therefore plan to evaluate our future prototypes also in some more realistic scenarios (e.g., in a walking setting). Participants should be tested using the prototypes during the performance of common tasks like walking down a hallway, having to pay attention not only on using the device but also to avoid running into other people. The same evaluation could also be repeated outside a building where the lighting conditions are quite challenging for LCD screens. A further interesting setting is usage during participating in public transportation.

Acknowledgments

This work was funded by the Federal Ministry for Transport, Innovation and Technology (bmvit) and the Austrian Science Fund (FWF): TRP 273-N15 and the European Regional Development Fund and the Carinthian Economic Promotion Fund (KWF), supported by Lakeside Labs GmbH, Klagenfurt, Austria.

7. REFERENCES

[1] Ahlström, D., Hudelist, M. A., Schoeffmann, K. and Schaefer, G. 2012. A user study on image browsing on touchscreens. In *Proc. of the 20th ACM international conference on Multimedia* (MM '12). ACM, New York, NY, USA, 925-928.

[2] Chun, J., Han, S.H., Im, H., and Park, Y.S. 2011. A method for searching photos on a mobile phone by using the fisheye view technique. International Journal of Industrial Ergonomics, 41, 280-288.

[3] de Rooij, O., Snoek, C. G. M. and Worring, M. 2008. Balancing thread based navigation for targeted video search. In *Proc. of the 2008 international conference on Content-based image and video retrieval* (CIVR '08). ACM, New York, NY, USA, 485-494.

[4] Ganhör, R. 2012. ProPane: fast and precise video browsing on mobile phones. In *Proc. of the 11th International Conference on Mobile and Ubiquitous Multimedia* (MUM '12). ACM, New York, NY, USA, Article 20, 8 pages.

[5] Huber, J., Steimle, J., Lissermann, R., Olberding, S. and Mühlhäuser, M. 2010. Wipe'n'Watch: spatial interaction techniques for interrelated video collections on mobile devices. In *Proc. of the 24th BCS Interaction Specialist Group Conference* (BCS '10). British Computer Society, Swinton, UK, UK, 423-427.

[6] Huber, J., Steimle, J. and Mühlhäuser, M. 2010. Toward more efficient user interfaces for mobile video browsing: an in-depth exploration of the design space. In *Proc. of the international conference on Multimedia* (MM '10). ACM, New York, NY, USA, 341-350.

[7] Hürst, W. and Darzentas, D. 2012. HiStory: a hierarchical storyboard interface design for video browsing on mobile devices. In *Proc. of the 11th International Conference on Mobile and Ubiquitous Multimedia* (MUM '12). ACM, New York, NY, USA, Article 17, 4 pages.

[8] Hürst, W. and Meier, K. 2008. Interfaces for timeline-based mobile video browsing. In *Proc. of the 16th ACM international conference on Multimedia* (MM '08). ACM, New York, NY, USA, 469-478.

[9] Hsu, Y.-M., Tsai, M.-K., Lin, Y.-L. and Hsu, W. H. 2011. Comp2Watch: enhancing the mobile video browsing experience. In *Proc. of the 2011 international ACM workshop on Interactive multimedia on mobile and portable devices* (IMMPD '11). ACM, New York, NY, USA, 13-18.

[10] Karrer, T., Wittenhagen, M. and Borchers, J. 2009. PocketDRAGON: a direct manipulation video navigation interface for mobile devices. In *Proc. of the 11th International Conference on Human-Computer Interaction with Mobile Devices and Services* (MobileHCI '09). ACM, New York, NY, USA, Article 47, 3 pages.

[11] Lissermann, R., Olberding, S., Petry, B., Mühlhäuser, M. and Steimle, J. 2012. PaperVideo: interacting with videos on multiple paper-like displays. In *Proc. of the 20th ACM international conference on Multimedia* (MM '12). ACM, New York, NY, USA, 129-138.

[12] Schaefer, G., Tallyn, M., Felton, D., Edmundson, D. and Plant, W. (2012). Intuitive mobile image browsing on a hexagonal lattice. In Visual Communications and Image Processing (VCIP), 2012 IEEE (pp. 1-1). IEEE.

[13] Schoeffmann, K. and Ahlström, D. (2012). An evaluation of color sorting for image browsing. International Journal of Multimedia Data Engineering and Management (IJMDEM), 3(1), 49-62.

[14] Schoeffmann, K., Ahlström, D. and Beecks, C. 2011. 3D image browsing on mobile devices. In *Proc. of the IEEE International Symposium on Multimedia*, 335-336.

[15] Schoeffmann, K. and del Fabro, M. 2011. Hierarchical video browsing with a 3D carousel. In *Proc. of the 19th ACM international conference on Multimedia* (MM '11). ACM, New York, NY, USA, 827-828.

[16] Schoeffmann, K., Hopfgartner, F., Marques, O., Boeszoermenyi, L. and Jose, J. M., "Video browsing interfaces and applications: a review", in SPIE Reviews , Vol. 1, No. 1, pp. 1-35 (018004), SPIE, Online, March 2010.

[17] Smeulders, A.W.M., Worring, M., Santini, S., Gupta, A., Jain, R., "Content-based image retrieval at the end of the early years", in IEEE Transactions on Pattern Analysis and Machine Intelligence, vol.22, no.12, pp.1349-1380, Dec 2000.

[18] Wu, Y., Mei, T., Yu, N. and Li, S. 2012. Accelerometer-based single-handed video browsing on mobile devices: design and user studies. In *Proc. of the 4th International Conference on Internet Multimedia Computing and Service* (ICIMCS '12). ACM, New York, NY, USA, 157-160.

Semantic Indexing and Computational Aesthetics: Interactions, Bridges And Boundaries

Miriam Redi
EURECOM, Sophia Antipolis
2229 route des crêtes
Sophia-Antipolis
redi@eurecom.fr

ABSTRACT

Semantic Indexing and Computational Aesthetics are two closely related fields. For some aspects they are similar, complementary for others, and sometimes completely disjoint. Semantic Indexing is about automatically identifying content in natural images, namely recognizing objects and scenes. Computational Aesthetics provides a set of techniques to automatically assign a beauty degree to a given image. In our work, we enrich both types of visual analysis by exploring the synergy of those two fields. We investigate the role of Semantic Indexing techniques for Computational Aesthetics Frameworks, and, vice versa, the importance of Aesthetic features for Semantic Indexing prediction. We show the benefits and the limits of this synergy, and propose some improvements in this direction.

Categories and Subject Descriptors

I.4.7 [**Image Processing and Computer Vision**]: Feature Extraction

Keywords

Semantic Indexing, Computational Aesthetics, CBIR

General Terms

Algorithms

1. INTRODUCTION

With the increasing amount of visual content surrounding us, automatic image analysis systems become more and more important for the development of effective and efficient user centered visual applications. Research on Semantic Indexing (SI) [1, 8, 13] has already accomplished great advances in the field of automatic scene and object categorization. However, in the recent years, a new field for automatic image analysis has attracted the attention of multimedia researchers: Computational Aesthetics (CA), namely a set

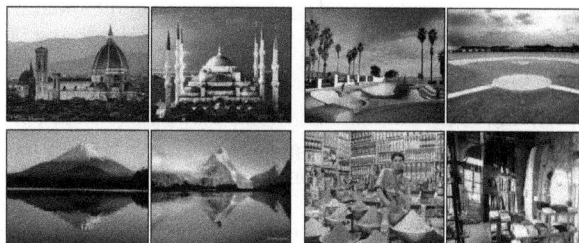

Figure 1: Similar images, similar aesthetics.

of techniques to automatically assess the image beauty and appeal. While SI systems predict the presence of given semantics in an image, Computational Aesthetics frameworks predict the aesthetic degree of its visual content.

Semantic Indexing techniques focus generally on the analysis of the *content* of the image: they learn models based on *semantic* features, namely low-dimensional description of the image content. Semantic features are extracted either locally [5], by studying the local shape of the edges, or by globally analyzing [8] the behavior of the image. On the other hand, Computational Aesthetic frameworks [2, 7] learn models able to predict image beauty based on *compositional* features, that describe how much an image is following given photographic rules [2], and what the general arrangement and layout of the image is. While SI features give information about the content, CA features collect the attributes related to the shooting process and the image composition.

Despite their different applications and underlying features, Semantic Indexing and Computational Aesthetics systems are closely related fields, as they both address image analysis issues. From a technical point of view, they share the same learning framework, adopted by CA systems from SI. In both cases, a model is learnt on annotated (with content or aesthetic degree) training data (namely semantic or compositional features) through machine learning techniques, and then used to label (with object/scenes categories or beauty degree) a test image. But analogies between SI and CA are not limited to their implementations. Content and Aesthetics are closely related in natural images also from a perceptive point of view. For example, as prove in [3] the type of object depicted in an image can influence the aesthetic judgment (e.g. people, animals, faces). Moreover, it is well known in photographic theory [4] that the image shooting process and its composition technique, as well as the emotion vehiculated and the degree of visual appeal, change according to the content to be depicted. Content is therefore important to determine the image composition, and, subsequently, its aesthetic degree. Similarly, given this relation, groups of semantically similar images must share the same compositional attributes, making compositional-aesthetic information an additional cue for SI.

These observations regarding the junctions between these two fields suggest us that the synergy between Semantic Indexing and Computational Aesthetics can help both image category and aesthetic degree prediction. We indeed investigate here the borders, boundaries and intersections between these two fields with the aim of improving the global effectiveness of CA and SI systems. Since the general frameworks for CA and SI have the same structure, it is practically straight forward to combine the knowledge of these two conjoint fields. Content and aesthetics are complementary source of information regarding the image depicted, and we can exploit their combination to enrich both the aesthetic and semantic learning.

In our work, we therefore address two questions: (1) How is Semantic Analysis influencing Aesthetic prediction? First, having a strong background on Semantic Indexing, we use for CA analysis the rules and features that we originally created for SI problems. We indeed explore the role of graded relevance learning systems and of our holistic semantic features [8] for image appeal prediction. (2) How is Computational aesthetics information affecting in Semantic prediction? To answer this issue, we look at the prediction improvements obtained by adding compositional features to classic SI frameworks for scene recognition. In both cases, we show that the combination of SI and CA information brings substantial improvements to both types of systems. We also observe that that there are some limits beyond which the interactions between this two fields is not bringing any new information, e.g. the quality of images that we consider.

2. THE SYNERGY OF AESTHETIC AND SEMANTIC ANALYSIS

In our work, we test the benefits that Semantic Indexing and Computational Aesthetic fields achieve through their interactions and we show the limits of this approach. We apply semantic indexing frameworks to aesthetic prediction and we borrow holistic features from both fields to improve the effectiveness of their prediction systems. In order to explore this combination, we perform two classes of experiments: (1) we show the role of holistic semantic features for image interestingness prediction through graded relevance-based learning, and (2) we build a scene recognition system that embeds several holistic aesthetic, affective and artistic features. In both cases, we show that the prediction (Aesthetic, for (1) and Semantic, for (2)) is improved through the combination of the two conjoint fields.

2.1 Retrieving Appealing Images by Learning Flickr-based Graded Judgments

Our first work that investigates the combination aesthetics-semantics is a learning framework that predicts the image "interestingness", typically related to the image "beauty" (see [11] for details). Our aim here is to build a system that, given an image (or a video sequence), can output a value corresponding to the appeal of its visual content.

We chose to model and predict the image interestingness

using a SI framework, based on learning techniques over discriminative visual (semantic and aesthetic) features.

We therefore first create a training/test database of Flickr images annotated with their corresponding Flickr "interestingness" degree (Non Interesting, Average Interesting, Very Interesting). We then compute a set of "compositional" features from emotion-based image recognition, computational aesthetics, and painting analysis[1]. We additionally create two new features for image appeal analysis, namely an edge-histogram[15] based measure of **Symmetry** and a **Uniqueness** feature based on spectral analysis representing how much a given image differs from the standard image behavior. We combine the resulting features in a 43-dimensional "compositional" feature vector (CV). Since the aesthetic appreciation and the image composition can change according to the image content, we also extract two *semantic* features, namely the MPEG7 **Edge Histogram Descriptor** (EHD) [15] and our **Saliency Moments Descriptor** (SMD) [8]. Why did we choose to embed such features into our aesthetic predictor? Both are semantic features related to aesthetics. EHD represents a holistic summarization of the image composition, which is typically very important to define the aesthetic degree of an image, and SMD summarizes the image content with visual saliency information, which has been proved [16] to be closely related to image aesthetics. We will combine the contributions of compositional and semantic features using posterior fusion.

We then model the feature space for interestingness prediction using a non-binary learning framework. We re-use our graded relevance learning framework for video retrieval [10], namely a semantic indexing system that can deal with multiple degrees of annotations. Such system can suit well the variety of the interestingness scores that we have in our training set. We therefore use training features with their corresponding very/average/non interesting annotations to train the graded relevance system. The resulting model will be able to predict the interestingness degree of a test image given the values of its semantic-compositional features.

In our experiments, we split the database into a train and a test subset, we learn a graded-relevance-based model for each type of feature (CV, EHD, SMD) and combine them with posterior fusion. We evaluate the results on the test subset using Mean Average Precision (MAP) over the list of the images that have been ranked in the top 10 %.

	SMD	EHD	CV	SMD+CV	ALL
Binary	0,16646	0,11358	0,17658	0,18918	0,18944
Graded	0,17648	0,12364	0,20284	0,21361	0,21484

In order to show the effectiveness of our approach, we also compare the results with a traditional binary-relevance system that uses the same setup. Results in Table 1 show the performances of the three features (CV, EHD, SMD) used as stand-alone descriptors and the prediction improvement after posterior fusion (+ 7% over CV-based classification only, which show the importance of semantic features in the interestingness-based retrieval) in the binary-relevance system. We can also observe the improvement (+ 6% for SMD-based retrieval, +8% for EHD-based retrieval, +15%

---

[1]The existing features we compute are: (a) Color names [6],(b) GLCM properties [6]. (c) HSV features [6]. (d) Level of detail [6]. (e) Rule of thirds [2]. (f) Low depth of field [2]. (g) Contrast [6]. (h) Image Order [12].

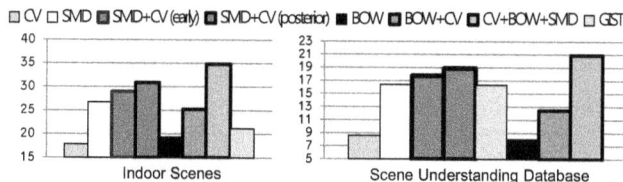

Figure 2: CA at the service of SI, results.

for CV-based retrieval, + 14% for all features) obtained using graded relevance retrieval.

2.2 Enhancing semantic features with compositional analysis for scene recognition

The second work we propose to investigate the relations between aesthetics and semantics focuses on the semantic scene categorization task, namely the automatic prediction of the image scene category (where was the image taken?) based on a pre-defined set of scene classes.

While traditional scene recognition systems are based on features that represent the image semantics, i.e. their content, here we go beyond the mere content representation, exploiting another cue for information: the image composition, which summarizes its aesthetic and affective properties, its layout and artistic traits. Why using this type of information for semantic analysis? It is well known in photography theory [4] that the photographic techniques and intent change according to the content, and it has been verified in [14] that groups of semantically similar images can share the same compositional attributes.

We therefore build a scene categorization system (see [9] for more details) that embeds and combine both aesthetic-compositional and semantic features. We extract from popular scene categorization datasets traditional semantic features such as the SMD [8] and the Bag of Words (BOW) [1]. Moreover, we analyze the image composition by storing the values of affective, aesthetic and artistic features in the compositional vector, computed as in Sec. 2.1.

We then use Support Vector Machines to model both sources of information (compositional and semantic), and predict the scene category. By doing so, we can use our compositional feature vector for scene classification and verify its discriminative power for scene categorization. We then combine the semantic and compositional information using different fusion methods (early, i.e. the feature combination, and posterior, i.e. the prediction combination).

We test the effectiveness of our approach for scene classification on a variety of challenging datasets for scene recognition, including the SUN [17] dataset, that contains around 400 categories of very diverse scenes. For each database, we first compute the classification accuracy given the model built using each feature (BOW, SMD, CV in Fig. 2). We then look at the classification performances resulting from using our CV as a stand-alone descriptor: in all databases, CV classification performances are much better than a random classifier, which tells us that CV (aesthetic information) carries some discriminative power for scene recognition. We then combine CV with SMD in a single early fused descriptor, showing that the early combination of semantic and aesthetic analysis brings substantial classification improvement (up to +8% compared to semantic analysis only). Finally, we combine the predictions of the semantic-only and

compositional-only models with posterior linear fusion. Due to the complementarity of compositional and semantic features, the categorization system benefits from this late fusion (+ 13-15% over semantic-only categorization).

2.3 The Boundaries: Where is The Limit?

Our experiments on the interactions between CA and SI pointed out not only the benefits of this synergy, but also the limitations and boundaries that this approach implies.

One first observation is that the boundary between semantic and aesthetic features is not always well established. For example, we can consider the EHD. The Edge Histogram [15] was originally built for image and video similarity assessment and concept detection, and it summarizes the local distribution of the relevant edges in the image. However, edge distribution can be seen as both semantic (it gives information about the shape of the objects) and compositional information (it can be seen as a general description of the image layout). Therefore, when we combine this type of semantic feature with the compositional analysis we perform with our compositional feature vector, we obtain a limited improvement (+0,57%) of the general MAP.

Another important deduction from our experiments is the limit of the effectiveness of compositional features for image categorization. The shooting process does not always follow compositional rules, and not always artistic and affective traits are defined. These attributes can be typically found in professional pictures, while there is a lack of attention regarding composition when dealing with user-generated or amateur pictures. For this reason, compositional features may not be clearly discriminative for the semantic classification in some type of datasets. As an example, we tried to use compositional features for the Semantic Indexing Task of the TrecVID [13] edition of 2010. The CV performances for retrieval were close to zero, and the weight assigned by the posterior fusion to the CV descriptor was null. The reason of this failure is the nature of the TrecVID videos: they are user-generated videos randomly taken by the internet. The frames therefore do not follow any particular photographic rule, and no particular attention is given on the artistic/affective factors.

3. RELATED WORK

We show here the novelty introduced by our work, one of the first attempt to improve Semantic Indexing and Computational Aesthetics through their interaction.

Semantic Indexing works generally by building frameworks for scene categorization using holistic features [8, 17], for object recognition using local features [1], or for concept detection for video retrieval [13]. Generally, such systems use local or global visual features that represent the pure image content, without considering all the information coming from the image composition, layout and shooting style. However, are compositional features useful for semantic analysis? In our work, we address this question by creating a scene categorization system that embeds some compositional features. To our knowledge, the closest work is the one presented by Van Gemert [14], that incorporates into the spatial pyramid descriptor some style attributes for object recognition. Our work differs from [14] first because of the final application (scene vs object recognition), and second because we directly apply the compositional features for semantic analysis rather than using composition to extend an existing algorithm.

On the other hand, existing aesthetic image analysis frameworks automatically define the beauty degree of an image, generally by using learning systems trained on compositional features. Datta et al. in their pioneer work [2] learn features that model photography rules, and Wong et Al improve it in [16] by adding saliency information in the prediction framework. Here, we go beyond the pure compositional analysis by extending the pool of features used for aesthetic prediction, and embedding semantic features in the CA framework. The use of semantic features for aesthetic prediction has been explored in [3], where semantic concepts such as animals, scenes, people, are detected and the probability of their presence is used as an attribute to predict image aesthetics. Our work differs from the one in [3] because we do not train any concept model (in order to avoid complexity and prediction noise generated by the low precision of semantic indexing systems), but we instead use the semantic features in an unsupervised way, and predict the aesthetics of an image given its semantic content without explicitly labeling it. Moreover, we also improve the CA learning framework by using a graded relevance semantic indexing system, previously used for video retrieval [10].

4. FUTURE WORK

Can we further investigate the synergy between those two fields? Two main tracks can be followed for our future work.

Improving CA with SI. As said, content plays an important role for aesthetic prediction, and different contents will generally show different compositional arrangements. We therefore aim to build a content-aware aesthetic framework with multiple aesthetic models, each one built according to the characteristics of a group of visually similar images. Some work has been done in this direction by Obrador et Al. [7], that build different aesthetic models for different image categories, using pre-defined manually labeled image categories. However, the relevance of an image to one category is not always binary, as shown in [10], thus changing the compositional rules and the aesthetic appreciation. Moreover, even if extended with automatic classification, such work would be strongly dependent on the classifier performances. Our idea is to perform an unsupervised pre-grouping of the training images, by automatically defining a set of appearance-based clusters based on semantic features. We could then infer an aesthetic model for each "semantic" cluster, and then predict the aesthetic degree of the image according to its group and to its aesthetic features.

Improving SI with CA. On the other hand, we can improve the scene categorization system by looking at the compositional features that are more useful to distinguish each class from the others. For example, symmetry might be more useful to identify a skyscraper scene, rather than contrast. For each classifier, we could design a set of category-specific compositional vector, which can be constructed based on the discriminative ability of each feature for the class.

5. REFERENCES

[1] G. Csurka, C. Dance, L. Fan, J. Willamowski, and C. Bray. Visual categorization with bags of keypoints. In *Workshop on statistical learning in computer vision, ECCV*, volume 1, page 22. Citeseer, 2004.

[2] R. Datta, D. Joshi, J. Li, and J. Wang. Studying aesthetics in photographic images using a computational approach. *Computer Vision–ECCV 2006*, pages 288–301, 2006.

[3] S. Dhar, V. Ordonez, and T. Berg. High level describable attributes for predicting aesthetics and interestingness. In *Computer Vision and Pattern Recognition (CVPR), 2011 IEEE Conference on*, pages 1657–1664. IEEE, 2011.

[4] B. Krages. *Photography: the art of composition*. Allworth Press, 2005.

[5] D. Lowe. Distinctive image features from scale-invariant keypoints. *International journal of computer vision*, 60(2):91–110, 2004.

[6] J. Machajdik and A. Hanbury. Affective image classification using features inspired by psychology and art theory. In *Proceedings of the international conference on Multimedia*, pages 83–92. ACM, 2010.

[7] P. Obrador, M. Saad, P. Suryanarayan, and N. Oliver. Towards category-based aesthetic models of photographs. *Advances in Multimedia Modeling*, pages 63–76, 2012.

[8] M. Redi and B. Merialdo. Saliency moments for image categorization. In *Proceedings of the 1st ACM International Conference on Multimedia Retrieval*, ICMR '11, 2011.

[9] M. Redi and B. Merialdo. Enhancing semantic features with compositional analysis for scene recognition. *Computer Vision–ECCV 2012. Workshops and Demonstrations*, pages 446–455, 2012.

[10] M. Redi and B. Merialdo. A multimedia retrieval framework based on automatic graded relevance judgments. *Advances in Multimedia Modeling*, pages 300–311, 2012.

[11] M. Redi and B. Merialdo. Where is the interestingness?: retrieving appealing videoscenes by learning flickr-based graded judgments. In *Proceedings of the 20th ACM international conference on Multimedia*, pages 1363–1364. ACM, 2012.

[12] J. Rigau, M. Feixas, and M. Sbert. Conceptualizing birkhoff's aesthetic measure using shannon entropy and kolmogorov complexity. *Computational Aesthetics in Graphics, Visualization, and Imaging*, 2007.

[13] A. F. Smeaton, P. Over, and W. Kraaij. Evaluation campaigns and trecvid. In *MIR '06*, New York, NY, USA, 2006. ACM Press.

[14] J. van Gemert. Exploiting photographic style for category-level image classification by generalizing the spatial pyramid. In *Proceedings of the 1st ACM International Conference on Multimedia Retrieval*, page 14. ACM, 2011.

[15] C. Won, D. Park, and S. Park. Efficient use of mpeg-7 edge histogram descriptor. *Etri Journal*, 2002.

[16] L. Wong and K. Low. Saliency-enhanced image aesthetics class prediction. In *Image Processing (ICIP), 2009 16th IEEE International Conference on*, pages 997–1000. Ieee, 2009.

[17] J. Xiao, J. Hays, K. Ehinger, A. Oliva, and A. Torralba. Sun database: Large-scale scene recognition from abbey to zoo. In *Computer vision and pattern recognition (CVPR), 2010 IEEE conference on*, pages 3485–3492. IEEE, 2010.

CueNet: A Context Discovery Framework to Tag Personal Photos

Arjun Satish
University of California, Irvine
arjun@uci.edu
SUPERVISED BY: Ramesh Jain (jain@ics.uci.edu) & Amarnath Gupta (gupta@sdsc.edu)

ABSTRACT

An image recognition problem is typically formulated as tagging a given set of images with labels from a predefined set. Context-aware approaches in problems like face recognition have utilized information about a user and the people she knows through different social networks. Traditionally, this context is *statically* linked to all of the available data. In this work, we propose a technique to dynamically *discover* which subset of all the available data is relevant context for the given recognition problem.

In this dissertation, we propose the CueNet framework, to discover candidate labels for the person identification problem in personal photos. We describe our context model, and how it allows heterogeneous data sources to contribute useful context for the identification problem. We design algorithms to extract contextual information from these sources to discover a subset of candidates who could potentially appear in personal photos. Our early experiments show that CueNet is capable of removing upto 99% of irrelevant candidates, and was able to correctly tag 80% of frontal faces.

Categories and Subject Descriptors

H.3.3 [**Information Search and Retrieval**]: Information Filtering; H.3.4 [**Systems and Software**]: Information Networks; H.5.1 [**Multimedia Information Systems**]

General Terms

Design, Algorithms, Experimentation

Keywords

CueNet, context, discovery, event, personal, photo, tagging

1. INTRODUCTION

With the popularity of global social networks and proliferation of mobile phones, personal photos have become a de facto standard of personal expression and communication.

Millions of photos are shared and recalled daily on websites like Facebook, Google+, Flickr and Instagram. However, almost all photos are annotated manually, necessitating an automatic tagging mechanism to make this process more frictionless. Prior research has shown that tags related to people and events are the most informative and popular[2]. In this work, we restrict our problem domain to tagging people in personal photos. In certain cases, events are also associated with photos.

Image based techniques like face recognition or verification have been used extensively to tag faces. When we take into account events like conferences where people often meet for the first time, the number of potential candidates becomes very large, which leads to more false positives. Face verification, on the other hand, requires matching the input face with every other face in the database. Again, with more people in the training set, the number of false positives can be very high. The interesting thing to note is that in both techniques, the idea is to match the given photo with **all** possible training sets, and therefore as the number of people in the training set increases, the quality of the final result reduces. We argue that these techniques do not *scale* with the increasing number of candidate labels.

Our motivation in building the CueNet framework is to provide a scalable approach to recognition problems by pruning the tag search space using event context. Various data sources provide contextual information in the form of instances of classes described in a given ontological event model. CueNet uses event based axioms and inference rules to algorithmically reason which co-occurring events are more relevant than others to the input event. The salient feature of CueNet is to be able to progressively discover these events, and their associated properties, from the different data sources and relate them to the photo capture event. We argue that given this structure and relations between the various events, CueNet can make assertions about the presence of a person in the photograph. By progressively discovering interesting properties, we restrict the number of potential candidates in the recognition problem. Because of this reduced number, traditional algorithms which use image features to identify relevant tags achieve a much higher accuracy than what they would otherwise do.

What is progressive discovery? We illustrate it with the following example. Let's suppose that Joe takes a photo with a camera that records time and GPS in the photo's EXIF header. Additionally, Joe has two friends. One with whom he interacts on Google+, and the other using Facebook. The framework checks if either of them have any

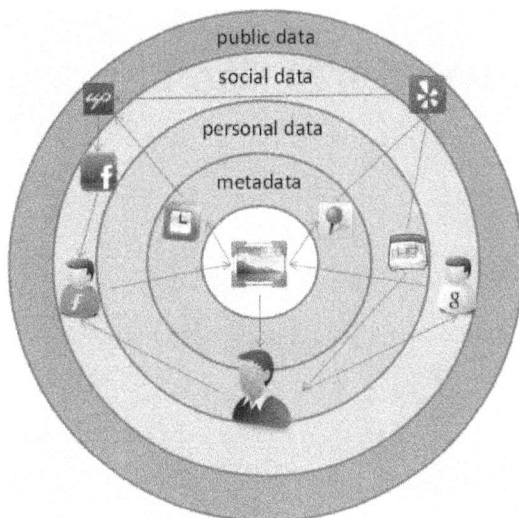

Figure 1: Navigation of a discovery algorithm between various data sources.

interesting event information pertaining to this time and location. We find that the friend on Google+ left a calendar entry describing an event (a title, time interval and name of the place). The entry also marks Joe as a participant. In order to determine the category of the place, the framework uses Yelp.com with the name and GPS location to find whether this was a restaurant, sports stadium or an apartment complex. If the location of the event was a sports stadium, it navigates to upcoming.com to find what event was occurring here at this time. If a football game or a music concert was taking place at the stadium, we can look at Facebook to see if the friend "Likes" the sports team or music band. By traversing the different data sources in this fashion, the number of people, who could potentially appear in Joe's photograph, was incrementally built up, rather than simply reverting to everyone on his social network or people who could be in the area where the photograph was taken. Finally, we can confirm who exactly was in the photograph by using face verification techniques [11], which will perform very well given that only two potential candidates exist. We refer to such navigation between different data sources to identify relevant contextual information as **progressive discovery**.

1.1 Related Work

The role of context in computing has been studied in [7]. The use of context in image retrieval is emphasized in [8, 10]. Barthelmess et al. extract semantic tags from noisy datasets containing discussions, speeches about a set of photos in question[3]. Naaman et al. have exploited GPS attributes to extract place and person information[13]. Rattenbury devised techniques to find tags which describe events or places by analyzing their spatiotemporal usage patterns[16]. The Computer Vision community has contributed extensive work in the area of detecting and recognizing faces [12]. Context information and image features are used in conjunction by [5, 6, 14] to identify tags. Systems like Picasa, iPhoto and [9] organize photos based on time, GPS coordinates and sometimes faces in the photo. These attributes do not capture event semantics[17].

1.1.1 Relative Significance

All these works either use no or fixed set of context sources. To the best of our knowledge, this is the first work to dynamically discover context for the person identification problem. Because of this change, we need to rethink/rebuild many parts of a face tagging pipeline. We focus mainly on three parts: discovering candidates for a single input photo; ranking these candidates for the photo; and finally extending these ideas to the scenario when multiple photos taken at the same event need to be tagged.

2. WHAT IS CONTEXT?

Our justification for the use of context begins with the statement: *For a given user, the correctness of face tags for a photograph containing people she has never met is undefined.* This observation prepares us to understand what context is, and how contextual reasoning assists in tagging photos. The description of any problem domain requires a set of abstract data types, and a model of how these types are related to each other. We **define** contextual types as those which are semantically different from these data types, but can be directly or indirectly related to them via an extended model which encapsulates the original one. For the person identification problem, the image, its features and the person label form the abstractions in the problem domain. The types used in the contextual domain, but not limited to, are **Events**, **Social Networks** and **Geographical Proximity** of people from the event. These contextual types, their axioms and the relationships they share with other contextual and data types forms the context model. At this point we will mention why context needs to be *discovered*. Given a stream of photos taken during a time interval, the source which contributed interesting context for a photo might not be equally useful for the one appearing next. This is because sources tend to focus on a specific set of event types or relationship types, and the two photos might be captured in different events or contains persons with whom the user maintains relations through different sources. For example, two photos taken at a conference might contain a user's friends in the first, but with advisers of these friends in the next. The friends might interact with the user through a social network, but their advisers might not. But by using a source like DBLP, the relations between the adviser and friends can be discovered. We say that the temporal relevance of these context sources is *low*. Therefore, we discover relevant context for every input photo. Photos taken at the same event might share some context, and we will exploit that similarity in this work.

3. PROBLEM STATEMENT

We assume that every input photograph contains EXIF metadata (specifically, timestamp and GPS coordinates) and an associated user. We are also given a database of people and images of their faces. At a high level, our problem is to associate a detected face in the input photo to a person in the database. Our approach consists of three steps: First, detect faces in the input photo. Second, using the contextual information from different sources, identify a subset of candidates who are most relevant to appearing in the photo. Third, we use face verification to validate the presence of these candidates. We use existing literature to address the first and third steps. The primary focus in this work will be on step two. We split this into three subproblems. First, we devise algorithms to find candidates for a single input photograph taken by a user. These candidates may or may not be sufficient to tag all detected faces. For a photo whose faces are not tagged by the discovery algorithm, we move onto subproblem two, which involves using ranking all the candidates given the contextual information extracted from various sources, the people already tagged in the photo, and characteristics of the events during which the photo was taken. Photos taken at the same event will consist of the same group of participants. Our final problem would constitute a procedure to re-use person tags available from other photos in same event to reduce the complexity of tagging each new photo, whose tags are in turn, used to tag the next photo. One advantage of this is the reduced number of queries to data sources for each new photo, as very similar information will be retrieved for most photos. Also, the distribution of face tags in other photos can be used for better ranking.

4. APPROACH

Figure 2 shows the different components of the CueNet framework. The Ontological **Event Models** specify various event and entity classes, and the different relations between them. These declared types are used to define the **Data Sources** which provides access to different types of contextual data. The **Person Verification Tools** consist of a database of people, their profile information and photos containing these people, and algorithms for face verification.

4.1 Context Discovery Algorithm

We have designed the context discovery algorithm, a tail recursive algorithm to discover candidates for a single input photo taken by a user. An event instance graph is created where each photo is modeled as a `photo-capture-event`. Each event and person is a node in the graph. All ontological relationship instances are edges in this graph. Each event is associated with time and space literals through data property edges, with people and other events through object property edges. The algorithm constructs queries to the different data sources based on the nodes and edges present in the graph. The responses from these sources are rendered as event graphs, and *merged* into the original graph. We find the new event participants and verify their presence in the photo. This process is repeated until all faces are tagged, or no new queries can be posed to the different sources.

4.2 Candidate Ranking

Many personal photos contain people whose participation in an event is not confirmed by any data source. Also, some events like conferences or parties might report hundreds of potential candidates for each photo. For these reasons, there arises a need to rank the candidates, based on who has already been tagged in the photo, the type of the event and its spatio-temporal descriptors. The intuition here is that people partition their connections based on the type of event being held. For example, people attend weddings and festivals with family and close friends, attend conferences with colleagues, and not often the other way around. Also, person co-occurrence in photos has been studied in literature recently [13, 18], and is found to be a reasonable measure to predict future co-occurrences in photos. Specifically, we rank the candidates as follows: we consider all the event

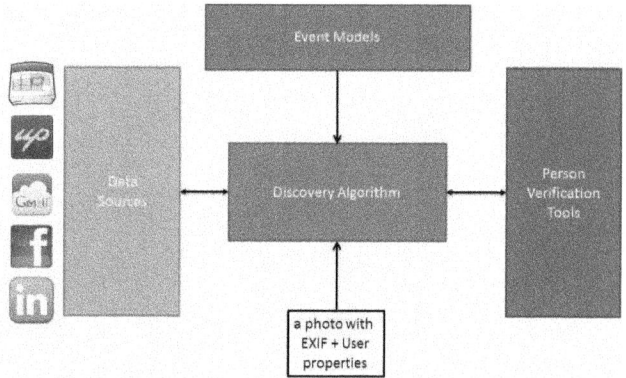

Figure 2: The Conceptual Architecture of CueNet.

graphs with more than one person. Initial scores are assigned to all the candidates. Those present in the event graph containing the current photo (to be tagged), are assigned a higher score than those who are not. Now, we use a rank propagation scheme [4] to propagate the scores within people. A person p_i transfers a score to p_j depending on three factors: the number of event paths between p_i and p_j, the type of this event, and the time difference between this event and the current one. For each path, we compute a score, which is expressed as the product of a ranking function F, a dampening factor α and the score of p_i.

$$s_\Delta = F \times \alpha \times s_i, \qquad (1)$$

$$s_j = s_j + \sum_p s_\Delta \qquad (2)$$

The function F, in turn, is proportional to the ontological distance, and inversely proportional to the time difference between the events in the path, and that of the input photo. We define ontological distance similar to the `isA` distance between two classes in an ontology [15]. Additionally, we also consider if any of the classes can be a subevent of the other or its parent or child subclass. s_Δ is calculated for each person, and added to their score s_j. The scores are propagated until convergence, and the candidates are sorted by their respective scores.

4.3 Source Selection

Uptil now, we were tagging a single photo at a time. For a set of photos taken at an event, the algorithm tags each one independent of the others. There are two problems with this. First, sources are queried multiple times for the same data. Second, people present in a photo can be very useful in ranking candidates for the next photo. We address this by adding to the ontological model, which specifies the known events and allowed subevents, the order of subevents occurring within an event. This is declaratively specified alongside the ontological model using a regular expression based event pattern language. An example of a pattern is the following:

Conference: (keynote+ $\rightarrow$ (session : (talk)$*^T$)$*^S$ $\rightarrow$ banquet)

The above expression denotes a simple conference event, which consists of one or more keynote events, followed by ($\rightarrow$) a succession of session events which happen in different places ($*^S$), each of which consists of different talks happening at different times, but at the same place ($*^T$), all of

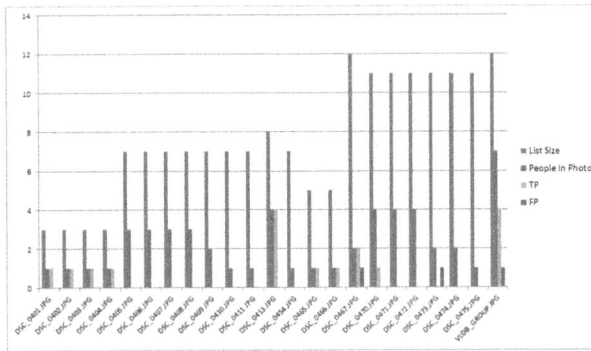

Figure 3: Evaluation using all sources of context.

which is finally followed by a banquet. We match the photo event stream with the available pattern, using a technique similar to [1]. A partially matched pattern suggests that the next photo belongs to the last matched event in the pattern, or one of the next events specified in the pattern. That way, instead of querying all data sources, we make more selective queries to discover context.

5. EXPERIMENTS

In order to evaluate the CueNet framework, we conducted experiments to tag photos taken at conference events by a user and photos taken at social events like parties, weddings, dinner meetings or family gatherings. Here we report an experiment studying the performance of CueNet while discovering candidates for a set of photos taken at a conference.

Setup: Users were asked to provide the Google Calendar, Facebook, Twitter profile and social graph information. Email information consisting of Date and People (CC, To, From fields) were extracted. Face verification was achieved with [11] and face.com. The ground truth was manually created. The complete candidate set contained 1894 different labels (total number of people referenced in various data sources). Conference information was semi-automatically collected from the proceedings.

Tagging using Event Context: The figure 3 shows various statistics for each photo, which includes the maximum size of the list which was generated by the discovery algorithm, the actual number of people in the photos, the number of true positives and false positives. As it can be seen, the size of the discovered candidate, never exceeded 12. This is 0.5% of the original candidate list. This list was used in tagging 80% of frontal faces correctly. We did not work on tagging faces with profile orientations or with obstructions (this is beyond the scope of this research).

Note: More experiments for the discovery algorithm including CPU efficiency, comparative study were reported in the full paper submitted to this conference. Evaluations for the ranking and source selection algorithms are being conducted, and will be reported in the dissertation.

6. REFERENCES

[1] J. Agrawal, Y. Diao, D. Gyllstrom, and N. Immerman. Efficient pattern matching over event streams. In *Proceedings of the 2008 ACM SIGMOD*. ACM, 2008.

[2] M. Ames and M. Naaman. Why we tag: motivations for annotation in mobile and online media. In *Proceedings of the SIGCHI conference on Human factors in computing systems*. ACM, 2007.

[3] P. Barthelmess, E. Kaiser, and D. McGee. Toward content-aware multimodal tagging of personal photo collections. In *Proceedings of the 9th international conference on Multimodal interfaces*. ACM, 2007.

[4] A. Borodin, G. Roberts, J. Rosenthal, and P. Tsaparas. Link analysis ranking: algorithms, theory, and experiments. *ACM Transactions on Internet Technology (TOIT)*, 2005.

[5] M. Boutell and J. Luo. Beyond pixels: Exploiting camera metadata for photo classification. *Pattern recognition*, 38(6), 2005.

[6] L. Cao, J. Luo, and T. Huang. Annotating photo collections by label propagation according to multiple similarity cues. In *Proceeding of the 16th ACM international conference on Multimedia*. ACM, 2008.

[7] G. Chen and D. Kotz. A survey of context-aware mobile computing research. 2000.

[8] R. Datta, D. Joshi, J. Li, and J. Wang. Image retrieval: Ideas, influences, and trends of the new age. *ACM Computing Surveys (CSUR)*, 40(2), 2008.

[9] A. Graham, H. Garcia-Molina, A. Paepcke, and T. Winograd. Time as essence for photo browsing through personal digital libraries. In *Proceedings of the 2nd ACM/IEEE-CS joint conference on Digital libraries*. ACM, 2002.

[10] R. Jain and P. Sinha. Content without context is meaningless. In *Proceedings of the international conference on Multimedia*. ACM, 2010.

[11] N. Kumar, A. C. Berg, P. N. Belhumeur, and S. K. Nayar. Describable visual attributes for face verification and image search. In *IEEE Transactions on Pattern Analysis and Machine Intelligence (PAMI)*, October 2011.

[12] S. Li and A. Jain. *Handbook of face recognition*. Springer, 2011.

[13] M. Naaman, R. Yeh, H. Garcia-Molina, and A. Paepcke. Leveraging context to resolve identity in photo albums. In *Digital Libraries, 2005. JCDL'05. Proceedings of the 5th ACM/IEEE-CS Joint Conference on*. IEEE, 2005.

[14] N. O'Hare and A. Smeaton. Context-aware person identification in personal photo collections. *Multimedia, IEEE Transactions on*, 11(2), 2009.

[15] S. Ranwez, V. Ranwez, J. Villerd, and M. Crampes. Ontological distance measures for information visualisation on conceptual maps. In *On the Move to Meaningful Internet Systems 2006: OTM 2006 Workshops*, pages 1050–1061. Springer, 2006.

[16] T. Rattenbury and M. Naaman. Methods for extracting place semantics from flickr tags. *ACM Transactions on the Web (TWEB)*, 3(1), 2009.

[17] N. Sawant, J. Li, and J. Wang. Automatic image semantic interpretation using social action and tagging data. *Multimedia Tools and Applications*, 2011.

[18] Z. Stone, T. Zickler, and T. Darrell. Autotagging facebook: Social network context improves photo annotation. In *Computer Vision and Pattern Recognition Workshops, CVPRW'08*. IEEE, 2008.

Toward Segmentation of Popular Music

Yun-Sheng Wang

Department of Computer Science, George Mason University

ywange@gmu.edu

ABSTRACT

This paper presents my dissertation framework to extract local keys, chords, and segment popular music from audio signals; all unsupervised. Music signals are denoised using wavelet transform to obtain a smoother approximation for chroma extraction. We extract a bag of local keys from the chromagram using an infinite Gaussian mixture and use the key information to extract a time series of chords. Using chords, we transform the bag of keys into a timed sequence of local keys. The two time series, local keys and chords, are used to construct multi-dimensioned "harmonic rhythm" as segmentation cues. We propose to calculate the strangeness of the cues from the perspective of keys, speed, and dependence as a basis for change detection in the framework of a martingale-based algorithm to find segmentation boundaries. Given the structural information, the chord sequence can be further improved in a refinement loop consisting of keys, chords, and segmentations.
abstract>

Categories and Subject Descriptors

H.5.5 [Sound and Music Computing]: Methodologies and techniques; modeling; signal analysis, synthesis, and processing.

General Terms

Algorithms

Keywords

Audio chord recognition, audio local key estimation, music segmentation and structural analysis, music information retrieval

1. INTRODUCTION

Music segmentation is the process of partitioning the target music signals into multiple sections so that each section is homogeneous within its boundary but distinct from its neighboring sections; in musicology, we call it form analysis. It usually serves as an intermediate step to solve a larger problem such as content-based information retrieval. In computer vision, an extracted image segment can be used as a query to retrieve the content of similar nature. For popular music, a short "catchy" melody or text, which typically resides in a verse or chorus section, can be used as a query to retrieve the popular song. However, there are a few notable exceptions due to the inherent differences in the format of audio and image data and what they represent. First, music signals are one dimensional time series so the boundaries of a segment can completely be represented by two time points. Second, for

Permission to make digital or hard copies of all or part of this work for personal or classroom use is granted without fee provided that copies are not made or distributed for profit or commercial advantage and that copies bear this notice and the full citation on the first page. To copy otherwise, or republish, to post on servers or to redistribute to lists, requires prior specific permission and/or a fee.
ICMR'13, April 16–20, 2013, Dallas, Texas, USA.
Copyright © 978-1-4503-2033-7/13/04...$15.00

western popular music, some segments are expected to repeat with certain order. Third, music is created to be pleasant to our ears so it follows certain "rules" to meet our expectations formed by previous listening experience. In traditional musical form analysis on common period music, cadence patterns and key schemes are often employed as cues, but their usages are not strictly followed in popular music. Therefore, four other cues are used in rock music to signal the beginning of a new segment: text, instrumentation, rhythm, and harmony, proposed in [18]. An example of text cue could be the arrival of the title line; the instrumentation cue could be the addition of guitar or background vocal. In our work, we propose to use keys and harmony (chords) to produce a multi-dimensional harmonic rhythm as the segmentation cue. Harmonic rhythm is delineated by [19] covering six dimensions: texture, phenomenal, bass pitch, root, density, and function. For our case, except bass pitch, the other five dimensions can be completely created from local keys and chords that correspond to the three rock cues (keys, rhythm, and harmony) described earlier. Our approach for segmentation is novel since, as described in the related work section, most existing work use the whole chromagram for music structure analysis while we extract and separate the harmonic content into five dimensions of harmonic rhythm as the segmentation cue.

Based on the above overview, we see that there are three types of information to be extracted from audio signals: local keys, chords, and segments. We have successfully extracted the two elements -- using undecimated wavelet transform on the audio signals, an infinite Gaussian mixture to extract a bag of local keys, and template-based chord recognition mechanism -- from the Beatles' 13 albums of 175 songs. We are currently combining the local keys and chords to create harmonic rhythm on a frame-by-frame basis to be used by the third component for music segmentation.

2. RELATED WORK

In this section, we review recent work that relates to the three proposed components that performs extraction of local keys and chords as well as segmentation, all from audio signals. For key and chord extraction, the most common technique for feature extraction is to transform sound waves into the frequency domain which is subsequently mapped into a chromagram to represent the energy level of the 12 pitch classes [5]. Since our approach to extract keys and chords is unsupervised, we provide detailed review on this line of work to contrast and highlight our contributions.

Most recent unsupervised local key estimation uses a probabilistic framework [2, 13, 16] which simultaneously estimate keys and chords by modeling the acoustic likelihood $p(X|K,C)$ and finding the best K and C by applying dynamic programming search technique [2] in 24 keys $\times$ 48 chords space. In [16], a key-chord model and state transition probabilities comprising three sub models (duration, key, and chord) were proposed using the same search space in [2]. Cosine similarity was computed between key template and observed data. The chord model determines the likelihood of observation given a chord being played. The best key-chord sequence is determined by search using the Viterbi algorithm which is similar to [13].

Most supervised chord extraction employs Hidden Markov Models (HMM), first proposed by [17]. This line of work typically requires labeled training data and is capable of incorporating other facet of musical elements such as beats or bass line information. Unsupervised approaches typically compare the energy levels of pitch classes within a chromagram, pioneered by [5], with pre-defined chord templates. The most recent work was proposed by [11] using a probabilistic framework where the overall chord probabilities are estimated directly from the music piece using the EM algorithm. The likelihood of each chroma frame given chord templates is modeled as a mixture where the estimated overall chord probabilities are the mixing proportion.

Methods employed for music segmentation can be categorized into repetition-, novelty-, and homogeneity-based [12]. A theme that connects these methods is a self-similarity matrix (SSM) which was first proposed by [4] for music visualization and subsequently used by many researchers for segmentation [8, 12]. In [8], timbre, chroma, and rhythm were used to produce SSMs and a shortest path algorithm was employed to find the segmentation points. Similarly in [12], using the three features, a probabilistic fitness function was introduced for. Most recently in [3], chroma and MFCCs and were used as features for clustering and results from the two-level clustering were combined to produce better segmentation results.

3. SYSTEM DESCRIPTION

Figure 1 depicts the high-level components and flow of our system. After performing a wavelet transform on the audio signals to extract a chromagram, we extract a bag of local keys and subsequently a time series of chords. Extracted chords are used to transform the bag of keys into a time series. Given the two time series, a multi-dimensional harmonic rhythm is formed to facilitate segmentation which is casted as a change detection problem. The last step is to use the segmentation information to refine chords. We describe each component in detail in the following subsections.

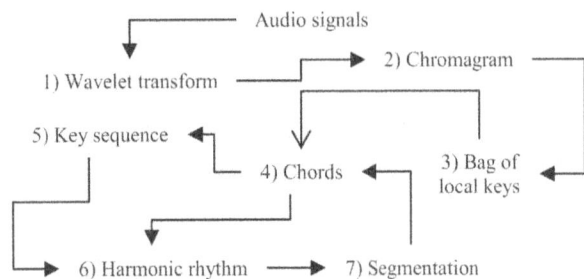

Figure 1. System components and flow

3.1. Audio Wavelet Transformation

We adopt undecimated wavelet transform (UWT) on the raw audio signals to reduce noise at the very beginning stage to obtain a smoother representation of raw signals before other audio processing tasks. Unlike a discrete wavelet transform (DWT), the UWT is shift-invariant which is a critical property for denoising

since the extraction and conversion of signals from audio CDs to WAV format can easily cause slight misalignment. Furthermore, the output at each level of UWT has the same sample length as that of the input which allows us to use existing tools for chroma extraction without further translation of the denoised signal. Daubechies (db) and Symlets (sym) are chosen as candidate base wavelets for UWT with different configuration parameters. To select the best configuration, two criteria are experimented in selecting the best configurations to represent denoised audio signals. The first criterion is entropy based where we choose the configuration that produces the wavelet approximation with the lowest Shannon entropy. For the second criterion, a correlation coefficient is used to measure the similarity between the original audio signals and wavelet approximation. The chosen denoised (smoothed) approximation of the original signal is used for chroma extraction. Figure 2 shows an example of UWT of 500 sampled audio signals and an example of its UWT approximation.

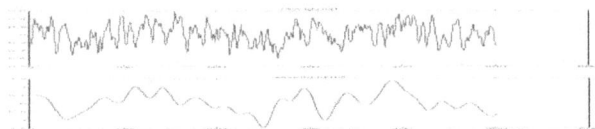

Figure 2. UWT example. Top plot: original audio signal with 500 samples. Bottom plot: UWT (sym8, level-4 approximation) transformed signal

3.2. Local Key Estimation

As discussed in the Introduction section, a key modulation point is one of the most obvious cues that signals the beginning of a new music segment. Therefore, our next step is to use the wavelet approximation to extract a chromagram using [10] and subsequently extract a bag of local keys from it.

Figure 3 depicts the infinite Gaussian mixture model (IGMM) for local key estimation. θ_i is a Gaussian component with mean (μ_i) and covariance ($\sum_i$). $\mathbf{c} = \{c_1, c_2, ..., c_n\}$ is an indicator variable establishing a mapping between each chroma vector in Y and θ. Hyper-parameter α is the prior for a discrete distribution for mixture proportions π_i where i = 1 ...k. A GMM would have a set value of k, but in the case of an IGMM, k is completely determined by the generative process which allows it to go into infinity. The mixing proportions (π) are modeled as a Dirichlet distribution which serves as a conjugate prior for multinomial component indicators (c). See [15] for details of an IGMM.

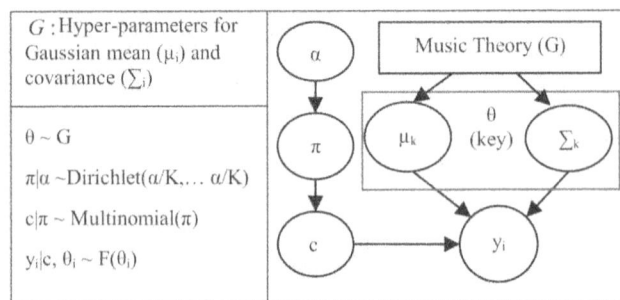

Figure 3. IGMM for keys generation

The most suitable evaluation method for this component is to use precision, recall, and F-measure which is a widely adopted metric for information retrieval task. We used musicologist Allan

Pollack's complete annotation of all the Beatles' recordings from the internet [14] as the ground truth to calculate the three measures. We strictly compared our results with Pollack's notes – i.e., related keys (fifth, relative or parallel major/minor) were not counted as correct recognition and no partial points are given. Table 1 depicts the findings of using the CUWT-4 denoised chromagram.

Table 1. Precision, recall, and F-measure for the IGMM bag-of-keys estimation

	# of songs	Precision	Recall	**F-Measure**
Single key	145	.698	.866	**.773**
2 ~ 4 key modulation	30	.650	.603	**.625**
Overall	175	**.690**	**.820**	**.750**

In Table 1, 69% of extracted keys are true keys and 82% of true keys are retrieved. The result is encouraging and indicates that a chromagram using level-4 approximation of UWT in conjunction with an IGMM generative process can be used to recognize global as well as local keys in a music piece. Since the overall precision is 13% lower than that of recall, we conclude that the algorithm generates a high number of false positives.

3.3. Chord Recognition

Given a bag of local keys for the chromagram, we recognize 5 chord classes (maj, min, aug, dim, sus) and 1 "N" label representing "no chord" or silent period on a frame-by-frame basis. The idea is that once we have local keys extracted, we only consider pitch energy of diatonic tones within the detected local keys and further adjust chroma energy using the Krumhansl & Kessler (KK) profiles [9] described in Figure 4.

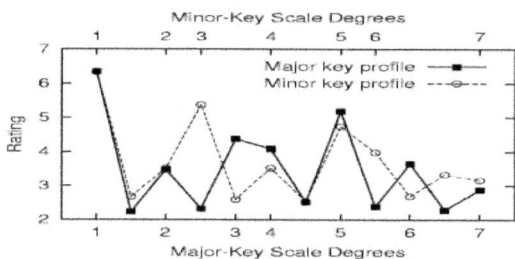

Figure 4. The Krumhansl & Kessler major- and minor-key profiles

Table 2. Average overlap score of chord recognition

Feature	Exact Match (no tolerance) (%)	+/- 1 Frame Tolerance (%)
CLP	64.5 (41.5)	68.3
CENS	51.9 (33.8)	54.8
CRP	56.2 (42.9)	59.3
CUWT-3	66.7 (43.5)	70.7
CUWT-4	**68.2 (42.9)**	**72.3**

We use the chord transcription prepared by [6] as the ground truth for the task. Table 2 depicts the average overlap (recognition) rate for the chord extraction task using the chromagram generated by the UWT (CUWT-3 & 4) approximations and features described in [10]. The number in the parenthesis represents the recognition rate without using the bag of local keys. We also see that the three

chroma features (CLP, CENS, and CRP) produced lower recognition rates which are consistent with the analysis described in [10] with the exception that the CLP outperforms CRP significantly. Furthermore, our UWT level-4 denoised chroma feature gives approximately 4% boost over CLP. Furthermore, if we can properly align our audio files with the ground truth, we estimate that our chord recognizer achieves an AOS of 72% on 5 classes of chords and 1 "N" (no chord) label without discarding any frames from the chromagram.

Up to this point, we have discussed components 1 through 4 as depicted in Figure 1. The chord recognition task enters the loop – consisting of components 4, 5, 6, and 7 – that iteratively improves the estimation of keys, chords, and segmentation. Given the time series of chords, we can transform the bag of local keys to a time series by calculating the maximum likelihood that leads to component 5. The key sequence refinement is only required when we have more than one key in the bag.

3.4. Segmentation

As described in the Introduction section, we propose to build a multi-dimensioned harmonic rhythm as the segmentation cue. Table 3 associates our wavelet-based chromagram, extracted local keys and chords to five dimensions of the harmonic rhythm. Suggested by [18], a key modulation (change of key) is the most obvious signal of a new segment and its cue, represented by the function dimension of the harmonic rhythm, is extracted by the local key estimator described in Section 3.2. The phenomenal and root dimensions are self-explanatory. The original definition of the texture dimension is the fastest rhythm played (such as violin or piano) in a music piece within a measure, but we use the chromagram extracted from wavelet approximations as the texture dimension. Since extracted keys and chords can never be 100% accurate, we use the density dimension to express the percentage of texture information represented by the phenomenal dimension that we extracted. Therefore, if the density is high, we are more confident about the cue within its time window.

Table 3. Segmentation cues

Dimension	Segmentation Cue
Texture	Wavelet-based chromagram
Phenomenal	Chords
Root/quality	Root progression
Density	% of energy in texture that articulates the phenomenal dimension
Function	The triad's position (roman numeral) in a key

In rock form analysis, [18] states that there is no need to wait for the complete unfolding of a harmonic pattern to see that it differs significantly from what has come before. It coincides with our listening experience of popular music, i.e., without formal music training, most listeners are capable of sensing a new "segment" that is coming up for a song that they listen to the first time. This is the main idea of our proposed segmentation process using machines, i.e., to mimic the human's perception of change based on the five cues from harmonic rhythm. Other than using the cue of local key changes, other dimensions will be inspected from the perspectives of speed and independency [19]; both are related to tension and resolution. Speed is one of the fundamental ways to create tension: the faster the motion, the greater the tension. As the tension builds up, listeners expect to hear a resolution which signifies a change; though such a change alone not necessarily warranties the beginning of a new segment. Specifically for the speed perspective, we will examine the speed of change on phenomenal and root dimensions of the harmonic rhythm to detect change. Independency among dimensions of harmonic rhythm also creates tension: the more divergent they are, the more tension they build; the resolution of such tension is the arrival of convergence. Since speed is the best indicator of (in)dependence among salient dimensions, we will detect the change points of divergence and convergence by examining the root, phenomenal, and density dimensions. Therefore, the task of music segmentation can be approached by detecting three changes – key, speed, and independence – from the harmonic rhythm.

The sequential probability ratio test (SPRT) and cumulative sum (CUSUM), originally developed for quality control purposes in manufacturing, are the first two approaches for change detection on sequential data; many methods were derived from them. See details in [1]. These methods are statistically parametric and require estimation of likelihood. However, it is impossible to assume any underlying distribution in harmonic rhythm, so a nonparametric method is in order. Recently, a non-parametric, martingale based change detection method was proposed in [7] by examining the strangeness of a newly arrived data point to see if the assumption of exchangeability is violated which signals a change in the data stream. For data points in the harmonic rhythm that fall inside a segment, we can safely assume that they are generated by the same latent variable and therefore exchangeable. Different from the online streaming data, we have the complete harmonic rhythm to help determine the appropriate strangeness measure for the speed and dependency cues of the target music. Based on the strangeness of the cues in sequence of the harmonic rhythm, we can detect the segmentation boundaries.

We have discussed all components and steps in Figure 1 except the processes from components 7 to 4, a part of an estimation refinement loop consisting of components 4, 5, 6, and 7. This last step uses the segmentation information to fine tune the time series of chords estimated in step 4.

4. EXPTECTED CONTRIBUTIONS AND DISCUSSIONS

The contributions and novelties of the dissertation can be categorized in two broad areas that are distinct from existing methods. First, at the high level, we employ a loop that iteratively improves previous estimations sequentially from keys, chords, and structure; all of them unsupervised and therefore training data is not required. Furthermore, all estimations use chromagrams extracted from approximation coefficients of undecimated wavelet transform of the audio signals. Second, at the low level, we extract a bag of local keys using an infinite Gaussian mixture so that the key information can be used to adjust the energy level in the chromagram to extract chords. Using the extracted keys and chords, we build a multi-dimensioned harmonic rhythm as segmentation cues for structure analysis which we cast as a change detection problem using strangeness-based martingale framework.

To date, components 1, 2, 3, and 4 are completed. We are currently working on building the harmonic rhythm from components 4 and 5 for segmentation which enables us to complete the loop as described in Figure 1. The remaining work can be summarized as the following: a) use chords to transform a bag of local keys into a time series, b) construct strangeness functions for the speed and dependency dimensions of the

segmentation cue for change detection, and c) use the structural information to refine chord sequence.

5. REFERENCES

[1] Basseville, M. and Nikiforov, I.V. 1993. *Detection of Abrupt Changes: Theory and Application.* Prentice Hall.

[2] Catteau, B., Martens, J., and Leman, M. 2007. A probabilistic framework for audio-based tonal key and chord recognition. *Adv. in Data Analysis—Proc. 30th Annu. Conf. Gesellschaft Für Klassifikation*, pp. 637–644.

[3] Chen, R and Li, M. 2011. Music structural segmentation by combining harmonic and timbral information. *Proc. Int. Conf. Music Inf. Retrieval (ISMIR)*

[4] Foote, J. 1999. Visualizing music and audio using self-similarity. *Proc. of ACM Multimedia*, pp. 77-80.

[5] Fujishima, T. 1999. Realtime chord recognition of musical sound: a system using Common Lisp Music. *Proc. of the International Computer Music Conference (ICMC)*, pp. 464-467.

[6] Harte, C., Sandler, M., Abdallah, S., and Gómez, E. 2005. Symbolic representation of musical chords: A proposed syntax for text annotations. *Proc. Int. Conf. Music Inf. Retrieval (ISMIR)*.

[7] Ho, S-.S. and Wechser, H. 2010. A martingale framework for detecting changes in data streams by testing exchangeability. *IEEE Trans. Pattern Analysis and Machine Intelligence*, vol. 32, no. 12.

[8] Jensen, K. 2007. Multiple scale music segmentatio nusing rhythm, timbre, and harmony. *EURASIP Journal on Advances in Signal Processing.* Article ID 73205.

[9] Krumhansl, C. 1990. *Cognitive Foundation of Musical Pitch.* Oxford University Press.

[10] Müller, M. and Ewert, S. 2011. Chroma Toolbox: MATLAB Implementations for Extracting Variants of Chroma-Based Audio Features. *Proc. Int. Conf. Music Inf. Retrieval (ISMIR)*.

[11] Oudre, L., Févotte, C., and Grenier, Y. 2011. Probabilistic template-based chord recognition. *IEEE Transactions on Audio, Speech and Language Processing*, 19(8):2249-2259.

[12] Paulus, J., Müller, M. and Klapuri, A. 2010. Audio-based music structure analysis. *Proc. Int. Conf. Music Inf. Retrieval (ISMIR)*.

[13] Pauwels, J., Martens, J.-P., and Leman, M. 2011. Improving the key extracting performance of a simultaneous local key and chord estimation system. *Proc. of the International Conference on Multimedia and Expo (ICME)*, IEEE, pp. 1-6.

[14] Pollack, A.W. Notes on … Series http://www.icce.rug.nl/~soundscapes/DATABASES/AWP/awp-alphabet.shtml. Retrieved on October 13, 2011.

[15] Rasmussen, C.E. 2000. The infinite Gaussian mixture model. *Advances in Neural Information Processing Systems*, pp. 554-560, MIT Press.

[16] Rocher, T., Robine, M., Hanna, P., and Oudre, L. 2010. Concurrent estimation of chords and keys from audio. *Proc. Int. Conf. Music Inf. Retrieval (ISMIR)*.

[17] Sheh, A. and Ellis, D. 2003. Chord segmentation and recognition using EM-trained hidden Markov models. In *Proc. Int. Conf. Music Inf. Retrieval (ISMIR)*.

[18] Stephenson, K. 2002. *What to Listen for in Rock: A Stylistic Analysis.* Yale University Press.

[19] Swain, J.P. 2002. *Harmonic Rhythm: Analysis and Interpretation.* Oxford University Press.

Author Index